ACCOUNTING FOR MANAGERS AND INVESTORS

Second Edition

Michael H. Granof

University of Texas

Philip W. Bell

University of Canterbury, Christchurch, New Zealand

Bruce Neumann

University of Colorado

 **PRENTICE HALL**
Englewood Cliffs, New Jersey 07632

Library of Congress Cataloging-in-Publication Data

Granof, Michael H.
    Accounting for managers and investors / Michael H. Granof, Philip
W. Bell, Bruce Neumann. -- 2nd ed.
        p.   cm.
    Includes index.
    ISBN 0-13-007923-5
    1. Accounting.   I. Bell, Philip W.   II. Neumann, Bruce R.
III. Title.
HF5635.G7718   1993
657--dc20
                                                    92-33042
                                                        CIP

Acquisition Editor   Joseph Heider
Production Editor   Maureen Wilson
Copy Editor   Patricia Daly
Cover Designer   Bruce Kenselaar
Prepress Buyer   Trudy Pisciotti
Manufacturing Buyer   Patrice Fraccio
Supplements Editor   Lisamarie Brassini
Editorial Assistant   Linda Albelli

© 1993 by Prentice-Hall, Inc.
A Simon & Schuster Company
Englewood Cliffs, New Jersey 07632

Printed in the United States of America
10 9 8 7 6 5 4 3 2

ISBN 0-13-007923-5

Prentice-Hall International (UK) Limited, *London*
Prentice-Hall of Australia Pty. Limited, *Sydney*
Prentice-Hall Canada Inc., *Toronto*
Prentice-Hall Hispanoamericana, S.A., *Mexico*
Prentice-Hall of India Private Limited, *New Delhi*
Prentice-Hall of Japan, Inc., *Tokyo*
Simon & Schuster Asia Pte. Ltd., *Singapore*
Editora Prentice-Hall do Brasil, Ltda., *Rio de Janeiro*

Contents

2

The Accounting Equation and the Three Fundamental Financial Statements 31

3

The Accounting Cycle   75

4

Accruing Revenues and Expenses   119

5   Measuring and Reporting Revenues   177

6   Valuation of Assets; Cash and Marketable Securities   217

7   Receivables and Payables   257

8 Inventories and Cost of Goods Sold   303

9 Long-Lived Assets and Depreciation   345

10 Liabilities and Related Expenses   395

11 Transactions Between a Firm and Its Owners   453

12
Special Problems of Measuring and Reporting Dividends and Earnings   491

13
Intercorporate Investments and Earnings   533

14
Statement of Cash Flows   581

15 Accounting for Changes in Prices   627

16 Financial Reporting and Analysis in Perspective   681

17 Focus on Costs   717

18 Establishing the Cost of a Product   759

19 Incremental Costs and Benefits: The Key to Management Decisions   803

20 Long-Run Planning, Investment Decisions, and Capital Budgeting   841

21

Budgeting for the Shorter Run   877

22

Reporting on and Controlling Performance   911

Preface

Accounting for Managers and Investors is intended to introduce students to the principles and practices of accounting in a way that captures the discipline's rigor, intellectual richness, and dynamism. Our aim is to provide readers with a solid grounding in accounting as it is carried out today. More importantly, we strive to insure that readers will understand the fundamental issues of measurement and reporting that confront economic entities. We hope that after studying this text, students will be able to both guide and adapt to the changes in accounting and business practices that are certain to occur in the course of their careers.

The text is entitled *Accounting for Managers and Investors* primarily because managers and investors are two large and easily identifiable groups which use accounting information. The text is decidedly oriented toward students who will eventually use, rather than prepare, accounting reports. Nevertheless, we believe that it is no less appropriate for students who are considering careers as professional accountants. After all, when professional accountants prepare financial statements, the needs of users must be paramount.

Accounting for Managers and Investors covers both financial and managerial accounting. The financial material has been drawn from *Financial Accounting: Principles and Issues* (by Granof and Bell). It has been cast so as to stress the managerial implications of financial reporting practices. For example, we make special efforts to point out how managerial actions may have an impact on reported earnings that is counter to the effect on the firm's true economic interest.

Accounting for Managers and Investors is directed mainly at graduate students in MBA or comparable programs and undergraduate students in business and liberal arts programs of high standards. For those who will continue to study accounting, we hope that it will instill an attitude of challenging the status quo, reacting creatively to changes in commercial practice, and anticipating the information requirements of the parties that will use their reports.

For students who will take no additional courses in accounting, we try to insure that they will acquire the requisite skills to interpret financial reports with sophistication. We want them to be able to derive the maximum amount of information from the statements. Equally important, however, we also would like them to be aware of the reports' limitations. We want them to know how the information in the reports was shaped and to be appropriately skeptical toward it. Further, we want them to be able to discuss financial reports with the accountants who prepared them, to elicit additional information by asking the proper questions, and to demand custom-tailored reports when it is within their authority to do so.

The most distinctive feature of our text relative to its competitors is its focus not only on the accounting principles that are currently accepted but also on the alternative possibilities as well. To be sure, the historical cost model and standards as established by the Financial Accounting Standards Board dominate our presentation. But we also elaborate upon, rather than give perfunctory mention to, other accounting models and means of accounting for specific types of transactions. Moreover, we intentionally seek to convey a sense of accounting's controversies. We see these debates as expressions of the profession's intellectual energy and challenges. To us, they are a positive feature of our profession, not one about which we should be embarrassed and from which students should be shielded. Even in the sections of the text pertaining to managerial accounting, we try to convey the message that some of today's accepted "principles" of product costing are likely to be relegated to courses in accounting history by the time current students are in the midpoints of their professional careers.

There is something to be said for restricting a first accounting course to current practices and the underlying theories. Many students have difficulty grasping even a single means of accounting for complex economic events. Why then confuse them with one or more options? Our response is that for many students—particularly those who are the more intellectually curious—the required extra effort is more than offset by the benefits. Among these are:

- Seeing present practices in a context of possible alternatives prevents simple mechanistic acceptance of them and deepens one's understanding of them. It also leads to a recognition of their inherent inadequacies.
- Financial statements intended to facilitate one type of decision may be inappropriate for others. Managers must be aware of the statements' shortcomings and be able to compensate accordingly.
- Knowledge of alternative accounting principles is essential to managers who engage in financial negotiations or other forms of advocacy proceedings. Managers must be able to present financial information in a way

that best serves their interests and, at the same time, challenges the data put forth by the opposition.

- Companies have considerable discretion over amounts reported in their financial statements. Analysts or other users of accounting information may have to adjust these statements to make the information comparable among firms.
- Current accounting conventions are only as immutable as the membership on present rule-making boards. Managers and investors need the skills to evaluate the impact of proposed changes in accounting principles.
- Manufacturing processes are undergoing major transformations—some as dramatic as those that occurred during the industrial revolution. It is certain that the managerial accounting systems of today will bear little resemblance to those of the future. Students need to develop an attitude of acceptance to change and the skills required to assess new systems and procedures as they are proposed.

The revised edition of this text bears the imprint of two additional authors, Philip Bell and Bruce Neumann. Both have contributed their years of teaching experience, technical expertise, and uncommon philosophical insights to the new version. Among the changes between this and the previous edition, for many of which they are responsible, are the following:

- Substantial revision to the early chapters in which we introduce the fundamental financial statements, transaction analysis, the accounting cycle, and the concept of accruals. We have tried to make the presentation more orderly and coherent.
- Increased emphasis on the significance of current cost and related price-level information and on the limitations of historical costs. Soon after the previous edition was published, the Financial Accounting Standards Board (FASB) diminished the status of current cost and related price-level disclosures from mandatory to voluntary. Now, however, there is again a movement toward more prominent reporting of market-based asset and liability values. Irrespective of the latest FASB pronouncements, we believe changes in current costs and the value of the monetary unit are relevant to most investment and management decisions. Therefore, students need to be aware of how to adjust historical-cost statements to take them into account.
- Completely rewritten chapters on the cash flow statement and greatly expanded coverage of pensions.
- Additional discussions of new financial trends and developments, such as leveraged buy-outs, junk bonds, and the savings and loan fiasco.
- Reordering of the chapters pertaining to managerial accounting so that the discussion flows in what we consider a more logical sequence.
- A shift in emphasis from manufacturing to service activities, to reflect changes taking place in the U.S. and other economically mature countries.
- New sections on recent innovations in management accounting, the most noteworthy of which is activity-based costing.
- Greater stress on practices in countries other than the U.S. It has been said that the true test of whether a text (or course) is "international"

is if it would be much different if targeted toward students in another country. Almost all of the material in this text has been used in university courses and executive development programs throughout the world.

- Many new problems and a glossary.

We are especially grateful to the numerous accounting instructors and students who have used the previous edition and have made helpful suggestions for improvement. We would especially like to thank Prof. James H. Sellers, The University of Texas at Tyler, and Prof. William T. Geary, The College of William and Mary, for their review of the manuscript.

MICHAEL H. GRANOF
PHILIP W. BELL
BRUCE R. NEUMANN

1

Accounting: A Dynamic Discipline

Accounting involves the collection, summarization, and reporting of financial data. It is a dynamic discipline, one in which new principles and procedures are constantly evolving. In our modern society, it is exceedingly difficult to carry out even routine activities without at least a rudimentary knowledge of accounting.

This text is directed primarily at current and future managers and investors who will use accounting in their professional or business endeavors. Its aim is to provide such readers with the knowledge and skills to take full advantage of accounting reports, to make them aware not only of the wealth of information that financial reports contain but also of the limitations. Perhaps, too, the managers and investors we address will be sufficiently stimulated by the issues discussed in this text to consider accountancy as a career.

WHAT IS ACCOUNTING?

Accounting is concerned with describing economic events, with measuring resources, and with determining periodic changes in those resources. Accounting measurements are almost always expressed in monetary units and pertain to economic organizations such as businesses, governments, or individuals. Accounting is a service function. It provides information that fulfills several broad objectives:

1. *Allocating the scarce resources of our society.* Under any form of economy, be it capitalism or socialism, decisions as to where capital should be invested are made on the basis of information contained in financial statements. In a free enterprise system, private investors make determinations as to the stock of companies they purchase largely on the basis of data contained in periodic financial reports. Bankers and other suppliers of funds study financial reports before making loan decisions. Government agencies use them in deciding whom to tax and whom to subsidize. The decisions of labor unions as to how much of a wage increase to seek are strongly influenced by reports of profit or loss.
2. *Managing and directing the resources within an organization.* Managers of profit and nonprofit entities alike rely upon accounting information to assure that they maintain effective control over both their human and material resources and that they allocate such resources to the products, subunits, or functions in which they can be most productive.
3. *Reporting on the custodianship of resources under the command of individuals or organizations.* Individuals, acting either as investors or merely as citizens, entrust resources to professional managers and governmental officials. They expect the managers and officials to provide them with periodic reports by which their performance can be evaluated.

Focus on Future

Accounting focuses on the *measurement* and *communication* of a wide range of financial data. Accountants provide the information required to make decisions as to where to allocate financial resources and how to control them effectively. Periodically, as the management process is being carried out, accountants "report the score"—they provide information by which the results of prior decisions can be evaluated.

Viewed from a slightly different perspective, accounting aims to enable managers, investors, creditors, and other users of financial statements to determine the future earning power of an enterprise. Decisions made today can affect only the future, not the past. Those who seek information from financial statements are primarily concerned with how well the enterprise will perform in the years to come rather than in years gone by. Will the enterprise be able to satisfy its obligation to those to whom it is indebted? Will it be able to meet the wage demands of its employees? Will it be able to provide adequate returns to its owners?

What will occur in the future, however, can best be predicted by what has taken place in the past. One of the best indicators of future earnings, for example, is past earnings. Accounting, in reporting on events of the past, facilitates decisions that will affect the future.

Financial versus Management Accounting

A distinction is commonly made between financial accounting and management accounting. *Financial accounting* focuses on providing information for parties external to the organization—actual and potential owners and lenders, creditors, labor unions, suppliers, financial analysts, economists, trade associations, and the public.

Management accounting is directed at insiders—directors, managers, and employees. It provides the information needed to establish the objectives of the organization, to develop the strategies and plans to fulfill those objectives, to administer and control the day-to-day activities of the organization, and to evaluate the success of the organization in fulfilling its objectives. When it issues reports to insiders, an organization need not satisfy externally imposed standards or adhere to specific accounting principles. The number, frequency, and content of reports can be determined at the discretion of management.

This text deals with both financial and managerial accounting. The first part is concerned mainly with financial accounting; the second with managerial accounting. The boundaries between the two are not, however, nearly as distinct as may be implied by the organization of the text. It is important for a manager to be as comfortable with financial accounting as with management accounting, since most transactions have both managerial and financial accounting ramifications. For example, the decision to replace an old machine with a new one is conventionally considered an issue of management accounting. How to report the event in the financial statements—an important factor to be considered in making the decision—is a topic of financial accounting.

GENERALLY ACCEPTED ACCOUNTING PRINCIPLES AND GENERAL-PURPOSE FINANCIAL REPORTS

The phrase *generally accepted accounting principles (GAAP)* refers both to accounting practices that are in widespread use because of convention and tradition and to those that are specifically mandated by recognized rule-making authorities.

Generally accepted accounting principles apply to general-purpose external financial reports. *General-purpose external financial reports* are intended primarily for investment decisions, although, of course, they may be appropriate for other kinds of decisions as well. They are designed for users who lack the authority to prescribe the specific information they need. They are not, therefore, directed to boards of directors, taxing authorities, banks, and regulatory agencies. In contrast to most investors, these groups have the power to stipulate the form and content of the reports they require.

General-purpose financial reports provide information about an enterprise's financial performance *during* a period as well as its financial condition *at the end* of the period. These reports address such specific questions as:

- How much better off is a firm at the end of a period than it was at the start? What were its revenues (inflows of resources) during the period?

What were its related expenses (outflows of resources)? What was its income (the difference between the two)?

- What are the firm's economic resources (assets) at the end of the period? What are the claims (liabilities and owners' equities) against those resources by lenders, suppliers, employers, and owners?
- What were the inflows and outflows of cash during the period? (In some respects, cash is accounted for no differently than other resources. Yet because cash is the medium of exchange in our society, it is the focus of considerably greater concern and attention.)

These questions are answered in three primary financial statements and in extensive notes and supplementary schedules. The three primary statements are

1. The *balance sheet,* which indicates, as of a specific date, the entity's financial resources as well as the claims against those resources both by outside parties and by owners
2. The *income statement,* which reports the *changes* in resources and claims during a specified period
3. The *statement of cash flows,* which reports on the receipts and disbursements of cash during a specified period

QUALITATIVE STANDARDS FOR ACCOUNTING

A central theme of this book is that there are few, if any, accounting principles or practices that are inherently correct. Nevertheless, there are several *standards* that accounting information should meet. In practice the standards are goals toward which accountants strive but can never fully achieve. Often, in fact, realization of one goal can be accomplished only at the expense of the realization of others.

Relevance

Above all, accounting information must be useful, It should have an effect in decision making. Unfortunately, what is relevant for one group of statement users may not be relevant for others. As a consequence, there is no such thing as "all-purpose" financial statements and no accounting principles that are preferable in all circumstances. The "general-purpose" financial statements included in a company's annual report facilitate only a small fraction of the many types of decisions that managers and investors must make.

Suppose, for example, that an equipment manufacturer compensates its sales force through commissions. The sales representatives receive a percentage of the dollar volume of sales that they make. Because the equipment must be custom-made, it is generally not delivered to the customer until six months after it is ordered. Generally accepted accounting principles dictate that, for purposes of public reporting, the firm record a sale in the period in which the equipment is *delivered* to the customer. Until then, the firm cannot know with assurance what the cost of manufacturing the equipment will be and has not yet exerted its primary productive efforts. For purposes of determining the compensation of the sales staff, however, it may make sense to record a sale as soon as a *noncancelable order is placed*. When the order is placed, the sales force has accomplished its mission and merits its reward. It would be perfectly appropriate to apply one principle of sales recognition in reports to stockholders and the general public and another in the statements from which sales commissions will be computed.

Reliability

Accounting information should be reliable. It should faithfully describe what it purports to describe. It should be *objective*; it should be *verifiable*. Qualified individuals, each working independently, should be able to examine the same data and derive similar measures or reach similar conclusions. Information contained in financial reports should not depend on the subjective judgments of the parties that prepare it.

Herein lies a conflict. Information that is most reliable may not be relevant to many decisions, and that which is most relevant may not be reliable. A few questions will illustrate the conflict.

1. Should a corporation report its land at *historical cost* or at *fair market value*? The most objective amount would be historical cost—that which the company paid for the land. This amount is readily verifiable. But of what relevance is it? The company may have bought the land decades ago, and the historical cost provides no indication of what it can be sold for today. Yet any amount other than historical cost (e.g., present market value) would likely involve estimates or appraisals and hence be less objective. *Conventional accounting reports are based on historical costs.* Increases in market values are *not,* as a rule, recognized. Some accountants maintain, however, that assets should be carried at the amounts for which they could be bought or later sold. Their position will be evaluated in later chapters.

2. Should a firm's statement of annual income reflect as earned revenue the potential selling price of goods that the company has produced but not yet sold? Or, alternatively, should the firm defer recognition of the revenue until it has actually sold the items, or even until it has actually collected the full selling price in cash? Income results from the entire process of production and sale, and since the firm is *usually* able to sell what it produces, financial statements in which income has been reported as soon as goods have been produced would be most relevant for most decisions. But the statements would be considerably less objective than those in which profit recognition is delayed until the goods have been formally sold—and hence a firm sales price has been established—or until cash has actually been collected and the full amount to be received is known with certainty.

3. Should a company's income statement include as current pension expenses only amounts actually paid to retired workers or amounts that will eventually have to be paid to present employees as well? A company provides its employees with retirement benefits. The liability for the pensions is incurred during the productive years of the employees.

The actual cash payment, however, does not have to be made until an employee retires, and the actual amount to be paid may depend on the number of years the employee survives after retirement. This amount cannot be determined with certainty until after the employee dies. Should the company report an estimate of the pension expense as the employee "earns" the right to the pension (the most relevant time), or should it wait until it actually disburses the cash (when the expense can be objectively determined)?

Many accounting issues are attributable to the conflict between the objectives of relevance and reliability. Accountants are continually faced with situations in which they must trade the realization of one goal for that of the other.

Financial Reports Are Not Precise

Reliability does not imply precision. Even if all amounts are shown to the nearest dollar (most major corporations now report in millions of dollars), financial statements can never be precise. Accounting statements are necessarily based on estimates.

Generally accepted accounting principles require that the cost of an asset be charged as an expense over its useful life. Assume a company purchases a car for $30,000. The car has an expected useful life of five years. The firm would charge an average of $6,000 as an expense during each of the five years the car is in service. Is it possible, however, to predict with precision how long an asset will last? Were the car estimated to last only four years, then the annual expense would be $7,500 per year ($30,000 divided by four years). This amount is 25 percent greater than the $6,000 derived from the estimate of five years—hardly a trivial difference!

Financial Reports Are Not Certain

Just as financial information cannot be precise, neither can it be certain. Financial reports imply predictions. Whatever other unique characteristics accountants have, they are not clairvoyant.

Financial statements must incorporate forecasts because the resources of a firm have value only insofar as they will provide benefits in the future. Equipment is an asset only because it will be used in productive activities of the future. Accounts or notes receivable are of value to the firm only if they will eventually be collected and transformed into cash. In assigning a value to equipment, the firm and its accountants must forecast its useful life. In measuring accounts or notes receivable, they must predict the likelihood of collection. Since these forecasts can never be completely certain, neither can the financial statements based on them.

Neutrality

General-purpose financial reports should be neutral. They should report economic activity as objectively as possible without influencing decisions or behavior in a particular direction.

Accounting information cannot, of course, fail to influence human behavior. Indeed, its very purpose is to affect financial decisions. The key is that it should not intentionally influence behavior *in a particular direction*.

Assume, for example, that proposed accounting rules pertaining to banks would reduce the value of reported assets and owners' equity. As a consequence, many banks would no longer be able to satisfy minimum statutory capital requirements and, counter to national economic interests, would be forced to cease operations. The standard of neutrality would dictate that rule-making authorities should not reject the proposals merely because they would be harmful to either the banks or to the national economy.

General-purpose accounting reports are comparable to automobile speedometers. They should reflect phenomena, either economic or physical, as faithfully as possible. It makes little sense to try to reduce highway speeds by intentionally miscalibrating speedometers. Drivers would eventually see through the ruse and adjust their actual speed accordingly. Correspondingly, it is equally foolhardy to attempt to control economic behavior by "miscalibrating" financial statements—the gauges of business activity.

Comparability

Financial statements should facilitate two types of comparisons: (1) comparisons among firms and (2) comparisons within a single firm over two or more periods of time. Comparability is generally enhanced when similar organizations base their financial reports on the same accounting principles and each adheres to consistent accounting policies over time.

Accounting reports of different organizations are not now as comparable as many financial specialists believe is desirable. The reasons are twofold. First, even today the accounting rule-making authorities allow individual companies a relatively free hand in selecting among alternative accounting practices. Second, the task of prescribing uniform accounting principles for the myriad transactions in which firms engage is enormously complex, time-consuming, and expensive. Accounting procedures that are appropriate for one transaction may be inappropriate for a transaction that is only slightly different.

In the last decade, the rule-making authorities have substantially increased the number of accounting standards and disclosure requirements. One adverse consequence of this has been a dramatic increase in the amount of society's resources directed to auditing and financial reporting.

ACCOUNTING PRINCIPLES AS FLEXIBLE RULES

Unlike principles of mathematics or physics, accounting "principles" are not basic truths or laws. They are rules and standards selected by rule-making authorities from among many possible rules and standards, some of which are equally defensible.

The example that follows is intended to demonstrate that there are numerous ways of describing economic events and of measuring economic values. The example contains technical terms that will be defined in subsequent chapters. For now, however, even a layperson will have sufficient understanding to appreciate its main points.

Example

Chemco, Inc., purchases a chemical solvent from a processor and resells it to its customers. The company was established on January 1, 1993. On that date the firm's owners contributed $18 million in cash, receiving in exchange 1,000 shares of common stock (certificates which indicate ownership). The following transactions and events took place during its first year of operations:

1. *Acquisition of long-lived assets.* The company acquired storage tanks, delivery trucks, and other equipment for $10 million (paid in cash). Management estimates that the useful lives of this equipment will be 10 years.
2. *Acquisition of goods intended for resale.* The company purchased solvent at two different prices during the year:

36 million gallons @ $.59/gal	$21,240,000
4 million gallons @ $.69/gal	2,760,000
40 million gallons	$24,000,000

The *weighted average* price of the 40 million gallons purchased was 60 cents per gallon (total cost of $24 million divided by 40 million gallons).

3. *Sales (i.e., deliveries) to customers*

36 million gallons @ an average price of $.70/gal	$25,200,000

4. *Cash collections from customers.* The company collected $20.8 million as follows:

On the $25.2 million of goods sold	$20,000,000
Customer deposits on goods to be shipped the following year (see item 5)	800,000
Total cash collections	$20,800,000

Since the company made sales of $25.2 million but collected only $20 million, at year end it had $5.2 million in accounts receivable (amounts owed by customers).

5. *Additional orders from customers*

1 million gallons @ $.80/gallon	$800,000

These orders were placed prior to year end and were accompanied by full payment.

6. *Operating costs for the year.* These costs included labor, selling and administrative costs, and advertising and amounted to $2 million. They were paid in cash.
7. *Year-end inventory.* Since the company purchased 40 million gallons

of solvent and sold only 36 million, it had 4 million gallons on hand at year end.

8. *Other information*
   a. Near the end of the year, the solvent producers announced a price increase from 69 cents to 75 cents per gallon. Correspondingly, Chemco raised its selling price from what was then 80 cents to 85 cents per gallon.
   b. At year end the replacement cost (new) of the tanks, trucks, and equipment had increased to $12 million.
   c. The company signed an employment contract with a top-notch sales executive. The new executive will considerably strengthen the firm's management team.

At year end the firm is required to prepare the three primary financial statements: a statement of income, a balance sheet, and a statement of changes in cash flow. The statements should answer the three basic questions: How much better off is the firm at the end of the year than at the beginning? What are the firm's year-end resources and what are the claims against these resources? What were the inflows and outflows of cash?

Statement of Cash Flows

The last question can be answered most easily and most objectively. The cash flows can be determined by summarizing the firm's checkbook or similar record of cash receipts and disbursements. Exhibit 1-1 presents the cash flows in a standard format.

Income Statement and Balance Sheet

The first two questions are more difficult. One possible set of answers is represented by the income statement and the balance sheet shown in Exhibits 1-2 and 1-3, respectively. The income statement reports on performance during

EXHIBIT 1-1
Statement of Cash Flows

Chemco, Inc.
Statement of Cash Flows
Year Ended December 31, 1993
(all amounts in millions)

Cash Flow from Operating Activities	
Collections from customers for goods delivered	$ 20.0
Collections from customers for goods ordered	.8
Payments to suppliers for solvent	(24.0)
Other operating costs	(2.0)
Net cash provided by operations	$(5.2)
Cash Flow from Investing Activities	
Purchases of tanks, trucks, and equipment	(10.0)
Cash Flow from Financing Activities	
Proceeds from issuance of stock	18.0
Net increase in cash	$ 2.8

the year, and the balance sheet on year-end financial position. The statements in Exhibits 1-2 and 1-3 have been prepared in accordance with "generally accepted accounting principles." The following subsidiary questions, however, suggest that other sets of answers, leading to dramatically different reported results, would be equally defensible:

1. *Which events should give rise to revenue? Revenue* is the inflow or other enhancement of assets from producing and delivering goods and rendering services. In calculating income, the primary measure of periodic performance, should "sales revenue" be recorded when the firm

   a. Receives a customer order?
   b. Delivers the goods to the customer?
   c. Collects the cash from the sale?

   Moreover, should the firm recognize revenue owing to

   a. Increases in the replacement cost of the goods on hand at year end?

EXHIBIT 1-2
Income Statement

Chemco, Inc.
Income Statement
Year Ended December 31, 1993
(all amounts in millions)

Sales revenue		$25.2
Less: expenses		
Cost of goods sold	$21.6	
Depreciation expense	1.0	
Other operating expenses	2.0	24.6
Net income		$ 0.6

EXHIBIT 1-3
Balance Sheet

Chemco, Inc.
Balance Sheet
As of December 31, 1993
(all amounts in millions)

Assets		
Cash		$ 2.8
Accounts receivable		5.2
Inventory		2.4
Tanks, trucks, and equipment	$10.0	
Less: accumulated depreciation	1.0	9.0
Total assets		$19.4
Liabilities and owners' equity		
Customer deposits (solvent to be delivered to customers)		0.8
Common stock (owners' initial contribution)		18.0
Retained earnings (income for year)		0.6
		$19.4

b. Anticipated changes in the selling price of goods on hand?

c. Improvements in the firm's executive team?

Undeniably, each of these events had a material impact on the firm's fiscal well-being. However, per today's accepted accounting principles, revenue would ordinarily be recognized only upon the *delivery* of goods to a customer. It would *not* be recognized as a consequence of customer orders (even if accompanied by cash), increases in replacement costs of goods on hand, anticipated changes in selling prices, or improvements in management. The reasons for these practices will be made clear throughout this text, as will the resultant limitations they impose on financial reports.

Under conventional accounting, therefore, the sales revenue to be reported on the income statement would be $25.2 million, the selling price of the solvent delivered. The difference of $5.2 million between the sales revenue of $25.2 million and the $20 million of cash actually collected would be recognized on the balance sheet as an asset: "Accounts receivable, $5.2 million."

2. *Which costs should be matched to revenues?* The company sold (delivered) 36 million gallons of solvent. As will be explained later in the text, to determine income the expenses incurred in earning revenues must be deducted from the revenues. The most significant expense in this example is the cost of the solvent sold.

During the year the company acquired 40 million gallons of solvent. Of this, 36 million was acquired at 59 cents per gallon and 4 million at 69 cents per gallon. Which solvent should be assumed to be sold first? That purchased first or that purchased last?

If we assume that the solvent purchased first was sold first, then the cost of the goods sold would be $21,240,000:

36 million gallons @ $.59	$21,240,000

If, by contrast, we assume that the solvent purchased last was sold first, then the cost of the goods sold would be $21,640,000:

4 million gallons @ $.69	$ 2,760,000
+ 32 million gallons @ $.59	18,880,000
Total	$21,640,000

Alternatively, if we assume that the solvent was mixed together, the cost assigned to the goods sold would be the *weighted average* of the two purchases. As indicated, the *weighted average* purchase price was 60 cents per gallon. Hence the cost of 36 million gallons would be $21,600,000:

36 million @ $.60	$21,600,000

Conventional practice would permit a firm to make any of these three assumptions as to flow of costs irrespective of which solvent was actually sold first. The income statement in Exhibit 1-2 reports cost of goods sold on the assumption that all solvent was sold at the weighted average of 60 cents per gallon.

3. *How should the cost of long-lived assets be allocated to the periods which they will benefit?* The firm acquired $10 million in tanks, trucks, and equipment. These assets have an estimated useful life of 10 years. Because they will benefit 10 years, accepted accounting principles require that their costs be spread over their estimated useful lives. In that way they will be matched to *all* the revenues that they help to generate not only those of the year of acquisition. The process of allocating an asset's cost over its useful life is known as *depreciation*.

   Must equal amounts ($1 million) be charged as depreciation expense each year or may the amounts vary? Although it is convenient to charge equal amounts each year, it is unlikely that the productivity of the assets will be the same. As the assets get older, for example, they will require greater maintenance and there will be more "down time" for repairs.

   The income statement in Exhibit 1-2 reports depreciation expense on a *straight-line* basis (i.e., it spreads the cost evenly among the 10 periods). Conventional practice, however, also permits the cost allocation to be made in any pattern that is systematic and rational. Under one pattern that is particularly popular, the depreciation charge would be $2 million rather than $1 million (a difference of 100 percent!). This seemingly minor change would transform the net income from a profit of $.6 million to a loss of $.4 million.

4. *What values should be assigned to assets?* Should assets be reported at the amount the firm paid for them (i.e., at their historical cost) or at their value in the marketplace (e.g., the amount that would have to be paid to replace them)?

   As indicated in the discussion under question 1, current accounting principles do not generally permit increases in the market prices of a firm's assets to be recognized in the financial statements. Thus the 4 million gallons of solvent that remain on hand at year end will be reported on the balance sheet at the average cost paid, 60 cents per gallon, rather than at the year-end replacement value of 75 cents per gallon. Were market values to be incorporated into the accounts, the inventory would be stated at $3 million rather than $2.4 million. Correspondingly, both revenues and income would be $.6 million greater.

   Similarly, were market values taken into account, the tanks, trucks, and equipment would be reported at the replacement value of $12 million rather than at the acquisition cost of $10 million. This increase, like that in the value of the solvent, would also be reflected in the computation of income, the measure of the change in resources that takes place during the period.

Some choices among alternative accounting principles have been made by the rule-making authorities of the profession and imposed upon all firms within their jurisdiction. Others are left up to individual firms. There are a multitude of possible combinations of principles, each producing a unique set of financial reports. Although this text highlights the principles that are generally accepted today, it also presents alternatives. A continuing message is that no single set of statements can capture the full range of economic events affecting a firm. Therefore the manager or investor must be willing to seek out supplementary data from other sources and to recast the statements to properly serve his or her own unique information requirements.

ECONOMIC CONSEQUENCES OF ACCOUNTING ALTERNATIVES

An Economic Event as Distinguished from the Description of That Event

As with any occurrence, the event itself must be distinguished from the description of it. The way in which a transaction is described will affect the *appearance* of an entity's fiscal performance or status but have no direct effect on its actual well-being. Yet because substantive economic decisions will be based on the description, the indirect economic consequences may be profound.

In the preceding example, the choices among the various ways of determining income would have no direct impact on the inherent financial worth of the enterprise or its first-year performance. The firm's year-end inventory has increased in market value irrespective of whether or not the change is incorporated into reported income. Similarly, the firm is better off for having received customer orders even if it doesn't recognize them as revenues. Obviously the firm will *appear* to be better off if it recognizes the increases in market value or takes account of the goods ordered. But the accounting description, by itself, will not affect the firm's financial condition.

Suppose, however, the company faces any one of the following circumstances. Here the indirect ramifications of accounting choices would be formidable.

- Federal, state, or local taxes are based on reported income.
- The firm is subject to financial restrictions imposed by a lender. The lender specifies that the borrower must maintain certain financial relationships (e.g., a stipulated ratio of debt to assets).
- The company ties the salary and bonuses of executives to reported earnings.
- The company's prices are established by a government regulatory authority. The authority sets prices so as to allow the firm a fair rate of return (i.e., income as a percentage of assets).
- The company and its labor union agree to submit a wage dispute to a mediator for resolution. The labor union asserts that the company can afford wage increases; the company contends that it cannot. The mediator will rely on the financial statements to determine which side is correct.

Under these circumstances, accounting choices will affect not only what is reported on the financial statements but substantive economic determinations as well. Indeed, the perception of financial condition will govern the reality.

As pointed out previously, neutrality is a widely accepted standard of general-purpose financial reporting. But changes in accounting principles will rarely, if ever, be "neutral" in their economic impact. Almost always, they will affect the distribution of resources in our society and thereby enrich some parties at the expense of others.

Accounting Principles and Advocacy Proceedings

Neutrality is a standard that applies to general-purpose reports, not necessarily to special-purpose reports. Therefore accountants, along with managers, attorneys, and other parties involved in advocacy proceedings, should be alert to opportunities to use accounting principles to their advantage. Whenever financial determinations are tied to accounting numbers, negotiators should do their best to assure that the underlying accounting principles produce the results that are the most favorable to their side. Accounting principles should be assessed and negotiated as carefully as any other contract terms. At the very least, negotiators should never yield control over accounting principles to the opposition.

Accounting Principles and the Stock Market

An overriding question faced by standard-setting boards is whether it really matters to investors whether they prescribe one accounting principle rather than another. Since investors wish to maximize their return on capital, the amount they will be willing to pay for a firm's common stock (which represents an ownership interest) depends on their expectations as to the firm's future performance. The greater the anticipated returns, the greater the amount investors will be willing to pay. Correspondingly, the brighter the future of the firm, the greater the ease with which it can attract investment capital.

As stated before, reported earnings of the past are widely accepted as the primary predictor of earnings of the future. Different accounting principles, however, result in different determinations of income. And one might hypothesize that the market price of the stock of a firm that *reports* higher earnings as a consequence of adopting more liberal accounting principles will be relatively higher than those of more conservative counterparts. If the hypothesis is correct, then the capital markets can be "fooled" by accounting information, and a measure of inefficiency is thereby introduced into the market system.

There is a substantial body of literature to suggest, however, that the capital markets are not so fooled—that, in fact, investors are aware of differences in earnings owing to differences in accounting principles and adjust accordingly. Assume, for example, that the common stock of firms in a specific industry were being traded, on average, at a price that was equal to 10 times annual earnings. If a company reported earnings of $5 per share, its common stock could be expected to sell for $50 per share. If it reported earnings of $4 per share, it could be expected to sell for $40 per share. But suppose that a company reported earnings of $5 per share because, relative to other firms in the industry, it adhered to more liberal accounting principles. Otherwise, it would have reported earnings of only $4 per share. Would its stock still be traded at $50 per share? Accounting researchers have conducted numerous statistical studies in which stock prices have been related to reported earnings. The evidence is persuasive that, in general, the market takes into account differences in accounting principles. Thus it is likely that the common stock would be traded at only $40 per share.

The market-oriented accounting studies suggest that the accounting profession need not be as concerned about mandating specific practices as was once generally believed. Regardless of the accounting alternatives that firms select, investors usually (the studies have shown apparent exceptions) make the adjustments necessary to make earnings of one company comparable with those of others. Obviously, however, investors can make the necessary adjustments only if they have the requisite information—the details of the underlying transactions—to do so. If, therefore, the studies imply that the accounting profession need not be especially concerned about specifying particular accounting practices, they also make clear that it should be very concerned with assuring that corporations disclose enough about their operations and financial position to enable investors to evaluate the results of transactions as they see fit.

The studies do *not* provide evidence that *individual* investors properly interpret financial statements. They deal exclusively with *investors as a group*. Moreover, they in no way imply that determinations other than investment decisions based on reported earnings will be unaffected by choices among accounting principles.

THE FINANCIAL ACCOUNTING STANDARDS BOARD

Since 1973, the *Financial Accounting Standards Board (FASB)* has been the designated standard-setting organization in the private sector. The board derives its authority from official recognition by the *Securities and Exchange Commission (SEC)* and the *American Institute of Certified Public Accountants (AICPA)* as well as from the general support of the corporate and investment communities.

The SEC has statutory authority, under the Securities and Exchange Act of 1934 and the Public Utility Holding Company Act of 1935, to control practices of financial reporting. Throughout its history, the SEC has generally relied upon the private sector to carry out the function of standard setting. At times, however, the SEC has exercised its authority and taken an activist role in promulgating accounting principles. In the mid-1970s, for example, in the face of charges that the private sector standard-setting bodies were insensitive to the interests of the public-at-large, the SEC not only issued pronouncements of its own but exerted pressure on the FASB to eliminate what it saw as accounting abuses. The pronouncements of the SEC are issued either as amendments to *Regulation S-X,* a document that prescribes the form and content of financial reports to be submitted to the SEC, or as *Accounting Series Releases,* statements that indicate the current positions of the agency on matters of financial reporting.

Prior to the formation of the FASB, the responsibility for developing accounting principles resided with the *Accounting Principles Board (APB)*. The APB was a committee of the AICPA, and its members were mostly practicing public accountants. During its life of 14 years (1959 to 1973), the APB issued 31 "opinions," which were binding upon CPAs. The board was dissolved and replaced by the FASB primarily as the result of criticism that it was too slow to react to reporting abuses; that its members, many of whom were partners in the biggest CPA firms, were overly influenced by their clients; and that its research capability was inadequate.

The FASB comprises seven members who serve full-time. The members are drawn from industry, the accounting profession, academia, and government. They are appointed by an independent board of trustees, the members of which are nominated by six sponsoring organizations having a direct interest in financial reporting.

Before the board issues a pronouncement, it allows for "due process." When the board identifies a problem, it appoints an advisory task force of specialists representing a broad spectrum of interested parties. The task force may include accountants, financial analysts, and industry executives. The board studies existing literature pertaining to the area and, if necessary, commissions special research studies. Based on the advice it receives from the task force and its own examination of the problem, the board publishes a "discussion memo" that addresses the key issues and sets forth possible ways to resolve them. It invites written comments from the public and holds public hearings. It then formulates a proposed statement and gives wide distribution to an "exposure draft" (a preliminary version) of the pronouncement. Taking into account public reaction to the exposure draft, it issues a final pronouncement. Through 1992 the board had issued over 110 such pronouncements (called *Statements of Financial Accounting Standards*) as well as numerous interpretations and technical bulletins.

In an effort to reduce controversy over each individual pronouncement, the board has embarked on a long-range project to develop a "conceptual framework" of financial reporting. The board believes that widespread agreement on the objectives of financial reporting, the bases of accounting measurement, the definitions of the key elements of financial statements, and similar issues that underlie virtually all accounting questions will facilitate the resolution of specific problems. To date, the board has issued six *Statements of Concepts*. Among their titles are "Objectives of Financial Reporting by Business Enterprises," "Qualitative Characteristics of Accounting Information," "Elements of Financial Statements of Business Organizations," and "Recognition and Measurement in Financial Statements of Business Enterprises."

Political Influence and the FASB

Because accounting principles have economic consequences, firms expend considerable resources trying to persuade the FASB to take positions that will serve their interests. As a result, standard setting is not carried out through detached theorizing alone. It is very much a political process, of which lobbying is an integral part.

Most commonly, firms oppose changes in accounting standards that will postpone recognition of income, reduce the reported value of assets, increase the reported value of liabilities, and accentuate year-to-year fluctuations of income. They fear that such changes will decrease a firm's attractiveness to investors and creditors or make it more difficult to meet financial requirements imposed by lenders or regulatory authorities. For example, firms with extensive foreign operations lobbied against proposed standards that would require earlier and more frequent recognition of gains or losses on changes in the values of foreign currencies. Small oil companies objected to a proposed standard that mandated that drilling costs, previously recognizable over a number of years, be shown as an expense as they were incurred (although large oil companies that already used that method favored the new standard).

But concern with accounting standards is not confined only to the firms to which they apply directly. Agencies of the federal government, for example, once fought proposals to reduce the reported value of banks and savings and loan associations. They presented evidence that the new rules would decrease the net worth of many financial institutions below the minimum required by regulatory authorities. They feared that forced liquidations of the institutions (or mergers with more financially sound entities) would further disrupt an already ailing industry and a depressed economy.

The FASB gives considerable weight to the views of its constituents. Nevertheless, it has not been sympathetic to appeals that a proposed standard be rejected or modified because of a potentially adverse impact on a particular industry. Instead, it has attempted to establish principles that most faithfully reflect the relevant economic events, irrespective of repercussions. It sees the mission of accounting as unbiased reporting and recognizes that once the profession waivers from this responsibility, even in the interest of a worthy cause, it will lose its credibility.

THE ACCOUNTING PROFESSION: A BRIEF BACKGROUND

Accountants serve in private industry, government, and nonprofit organizations. The title *accountant* is used to designate persons who provide a wide range of different services—from clerks who perform routine clerical functions to high-level executives who make major financial decisions. The cornerstone of the accounting profession, however, is the public accountant. *Public accountants* are those who make their services available to the public-at-large rather than to a single employer.

The public accountant who has satisfied various state-imposed education and experience requirements and has demonstrated technical competence on a nationally administered examination is recognized as a *certified public accountant (CPA)*. In most states a CPA must have earned a bachelor's degree; must have completed a specified number of courses in accounting and related disciplines such as business law, finance, and economics; and must have been employed as an independent auditor, under the supervision of another CPA, for at least one to three years.

Modern accounting can trace its roots to 1494, when an Italian monk named Luca Pacioli described a "double-entry" accounting procedure that forms the basis for accounting practice today. But public accounting as a profession is relatively new. The development of the profession was spurred primarily by new forms of economic activity associated with the Industrial Revolution. Many of the significant developments in the early stages of the profession's growth took place in Great Britain. By the latter half of the eighteenth century, small associations of professional accountants began to develop. In the early part of the twentieth century, the momentum for growth and innovation shifted to the United States. Since 1900 the number of public accountants in the United States has grown exponentially.

Certified public accountants are most commonly associated with income taxes. In truth, CPAs perform three primary functions: audits, management advisory services, and tax services. It is the audit function that is unique to, and most characteristic of, the public accounting profession.

Auditing and Financial Reporting

The purpose of the audit function is to enhance the credibility of financial reports. Report users want assurance that statements ''present fairly'' the results of the economic activities that they purport to describe.

Regulatory agencies such as the Securities and Exchange Commission and the New York Stock Exchange require that publicly held corporations under their jurisdiction have an *independent* party—a CPA—*attest to,* or vouch for, the fairness of the financial statements the companies issue to their stockholders. Similarly, banks, insurance companies, and other investors and lenders of funds also demand that financial statements on which they intend to rely be audited, or attested to, by CPAs.

Although the CPA firm is *not* assigned the responsibility of preparing external financial reports—*corporate management* is so charged—its influence over them is paramount. The CPA firm does not, of course, verify each of the transactions underlying the financial statements. In a large corporation the number of transactions in a year would make that an impossible task. Instead, the firm reviews the accounting systems used to accumulate and summarize the underlying data, tests a substantial number of transactions (especially those involving large dollar amounts), and, most importantly, makes certain that the financial statements have been prepared in conformity with generally accepted accounting principles. The end product of the independent CPA's examination is the *auditor's report,* an opinion on the financial statements. A typical report is shown in Exhibit 1-4. If auditors are unable to obtain sufficient evidential matter on which to base an opinion or if they take exception to the information as presented, they are required to disclaim an opinion, qualify their opinion, or express an ''adverse'' opinion (e.g., ''In our opinion the aforementioned consolidated financial statements do *not* fairly present the financial position. . . .'').

CPA firms range in size from those with a single practitioner to those with over 5,000 partners and tens of thousands in professional staff. Some have annual revenues of over $5 billion. Over 85 percent of the 2,600 companies that are listed on U.S. stock exchanges are audited by the six largest CPA firms (the *Big Six*). Owing to their size and the international scope of their operations, these six firms have had a predominant impact on the practice of accounting and the establishment of accounting principles throughout the world.

As professionals, CPAs are expected to adhere to the standards of their profession. The American Institute of Certified Public Accountants, the professional society of CPAs, has adopted a code of ethics to help assure that CPAs conduct themselves in a manner that is acceptable to their clients, their colleagues, and the public-at-large. The code is considerably more rigorous than that of any of the other major professions. In addition, the AICPA has promul-

EXHIBIT 1-4
Report of Independent Public Accountants

To the Board of Directors and Shareholders
of American Home Products Corporation:

We have audited the accompanying consolidated balance sheets of American Home Products Corporation (a Delaware corporation) and subsidiaries as of December 31, 1991 and 1990, and the related consolidated statements of income, retained earnings, additional paid-in capital and cash flows for each of the three years in the period ended December 31, 1991. These financial statements are the responsibility of the Company's management. Our responsibility is to express an opinion on these financial statements based on our audits.

We conducted our audits in accordance with generally accepted auditing standards. Those standards require that we plan and perform the audit to obtain reasonable assurance about whether the financial statements are free of material misstatement. An audit includes examining, on a test basis, evidence supporting the amounts and disclosures in the financial statements. An audit also includes assessing the accounting principles used and significant estimates made by management, as well as evaluating the overall financial statement presentation. We believe that our audits provide a reasonable basis for our opinion.

In our opinion, the financial statements referred to above present fairly, in all material respects, the financial position of American Home Products Corporation and subsidiaries as of December 31, 1991 and 1990 and the results of their operations and cash flows for each of the three years in the period ended December 31, 1991 in conformity with generally accepted accounting principles.

Arthur Andersen & Co.
New York, N.Y.
January 16, 1992

gated standards of auditing. *Standards of auditing* deal with the manner in which CPAs carry out independent examinations of financial statements. They differ from standards of accounting, which pertain to the preparation of the statements themselves.

Management Advisory Services

Most CPAs serve as financial advisors to their clients. Large CPA firms have separate management consulting divisions that provide a wide range of services to both industry and government. Although most consulting engagements are directly related to the accounting and reporting systems of their clients (a large number, for example, involve installation of data processing equipment), some are in such diverse fields as marketing, pensions, insurance, and production management. Smaller CPA firms often provide day-to-day business advice to their clients; some establish the accounting systems used by their clients and maintain a close watch over them to make certain that they are operating as planned.

In recent years the consulting activities of many firms, especially the larger ones, have come under fire for being incompatible with the primary function of CPAs, that of attesting to financial reports. Critics assert that CPAs who provide consulting services cannot be sufficiently independent of their clients to provide unbiased audit services. They question, for example, whether a CPA firm that has advised a client on means of increasing income, and has seen such advice followed unsuccessfully, could be sufficiently objective in auditing the financial reports that reflect the results of its own poor advice. CPAs respond that they have developed professional guidelines that minimize the possibility of bias and that the benefits of consulting services to their clients—and hence to society—far outweigh the risk of diminished independence.

Tax Services

For most U.S. corporations the effective tax rate, taking into account federal income taxes as well as all state and local taxes, is typically over 40 percent. For their foreign operations it may be considerably higher. It is critical therefore that managers assess the tax implications of proposed transactions *before* they enter into them, while they still have an opportunity to minimize the tax burden.

Accountants provide tax services both as members of internal tax staffs and as outside advisors. They do, of course, prepare tax returns for their companies or their clients, but their more important function is counseling managers or individuals *in advance* of a business undertaking.

Accountants in Industry

Accountants who are employed by business enterprises commonly serve in a staff capacity. They provide advice and service to virtually all units of the organization. The industrial accountants of today are likely to be responsible for maintaining financial records. In all probability, however, they will do much more. They will be key members of the management team, counseling on a wide range of corporate activities. The chief accountant of a company is often known as the *controller*. The following list is suggestive of the functions that are carried out by a controller's department:

Long-range and strategic financial planning
Data processing and information processing
Tax planning and administration
Budgeting
Reporting to stockholders and government agencies
Financial performance evaluation

The distinction between a *controller* and a *treasurer* varies from firm to firm, but in general the treasurer is concerned with relations between the company and its stockholders, bankers, and other creditors as well as with the administration of the firm's investments and insurance policies.

Many accountants in industry serve as *internal auditors*. Corporate internal audit departments have traditionally been responsible for verifying the accuracy and reliability of internal accounting reports and records. Today, they still perform that function. Their role has expanded, however, to include reviews of the efficiency and effectiveness of all corporate operating and management systems. In more progressive firms internal auditors function as a team of internal management consultants.

The *Institute of Management Accountants* is the leading professional association of industrial accountants. Through a related organization, the *Institute of Certified Management Accountants,* the association recognizes as *Certified Management Accountants (CMAs)* members of the profession who pass a rigorous examination and satisfy specified experience and educational requirements.

Accountants in Nonprofit Organizations

Government and other nonprofit (or, more properly, not-for-profit) organizations are unconcerned with the computation of net income; they are interested in public service, not profit. Yet financial budgets, accounting controls, and quantitative measures of performance are as necessary in nonprofit as in profit-making organizations. Unfortunately, many nonprofit organizations have been slow in realizing the importance of adequate accounting systems and reports. Today, however, they are attempting to make rapid reforms in the area of financial management, and as a result job opportunities in such organizations are abundant.

Nonprofit accounting is an especially challenging field. Administrators of nonprofit organizations require the same types of information as their counterparts in private industry to carry out effectively the functions of management. On a day-to-day basis, problems of planning, controlling, and evaluating performance in nonprofit organizations are remarkably similar to those in industry. Managing a government-owned electric utility is not very different from managing a comparable private utility. Controlling clerical costs in the tax-collection division of a municipality has much in common with controlling clerical costs in the billings office of a large insurance company.

The Governmental Accounting Standards Board (GASB) is in charge of establishing accounting and reporting standards for state and local governments. The GASB is the sister organization of the FASB and has comparable authority. The FASB is responsible for setting standards for nonprofit organizations that are not part of a government unit.

Litigation against Accountants

CPAs are continually the target of lawsuits charging them with negligence in carrying out their audits. Both statutory law and case precedent make it clear that accountants are expected to adhere to the standards of their profession. Should they deviate from these standards, and thereby fail to detect or report material errors in their clients' financial statements, they may be liable for the resultant losses suffered by statement users.

It has become increasingly common for both stockholders and creditors who have incurred losses as a consequence of a corporate collapse to look to the failed firm's auditors for recompense. In part, this is because CPA firms have "deep pockets." They are insured for losses and, in contrast to the failed company itself, can serve as a source of indemnification.

CPAs, it must be emphasized, are accountable only for *audit* failures, not *business* failures. An *audit failure* occurs when the auditor issues an inappropriate report on a client's financial statements. A *business failure,* by contrast, occurs when a firm is unable to meet its financial obligations. Auditors do not guarantee the fiscal health or even the survivability of their clients. They assure only that a firm's financial statements can be relied upon.

As painful as the proliferation of litigation has been to the accounting profession, it has provided the impetus for a quantum leap in the quality of audits. As a result of the judgments against it, the profession has assumed greater responsibility for the content of financial statements and has established standards that are both more specific and more rigorous than those of the past.

Although, as might be expected, the audit failures generate the headlines in the financial press, the number of failures in relation to total audits is remarkably small.

To the student considering accounting as a career, the possibility of litigation should be an incentive, not a deterrent, to entering the profession. It underscores the trust that society places in the accounting profession and the responsibility assumed by its individual members.

ACCOUNTING RESEARCH AND THEORY

Accounting is obviously a profession concerned primarily with practice, but it has an important research component as well.

Until the early 1970s, accounting researchers focused mainly on developing and prescribing "optimum" accounting principles. Typical of the questions accounting researchers addressed were those set forth in the example earlier in this chapter:

- Should changes in prices be recognized in the accounts? If so, when and how?
- How should the cost of long-lived assets be allocated over their useful lives?
- What assumptions as to flows of costs should be used in calculating both the cost of goods sold and year-end inventory?

In one mode of research, academicians attempted to answer these questions by identifying the decisions made by statement users and deducing the information that would be required to facilitate those decisions. In another, researchers sought to develop a "conceptual framework," maintaining that specific accounting issues could be resolved only after general principles were established. Akin to the models used in mathematical disciplines such as geometry, the frameworks of some researchers were built upon definitions, axioms, and postulates. This type of research was helpful in assuring a logical consistency to accounting principles. However, neither the resultant framework nor specific principles could be readily tested empirically for preferability and, therefore, the research did not yield definitive conclusions.

Starting in the 1970s, accounting research took a number of new directions. Some researchers, abandoning what they considered a futile search for optimum principles, focused instead on observing accounting practices and explaining their consequences. One ongoing line of research relates to the impact on stock prices of alternative accounting principles or of previously undisclosed news and information. Researchers might hypothesize, for example, that the stock market takes into account changes in the current market values of a firm's assets. Using exceedingly sophisticated statistical models, they then try to measure the extent to which current value information explains variations in stock prices that cannot be explained equally well by historical cost data. If the analysis supports the hypothesis, then the researcher has reason to believe that investors find the current value information useful; if the data do not support the hypothesis, then the utility of the current value information is seen as problematic.

In another line of study, researchers might attempt to explain why some firms opt for one accounting method while others opt for an alternative method. For example, researchers might hypothesize that because senior executives control reporting practices, firms in which executive compensation is tied to earnings will select more liberal (earning-enhancing) accounting principles than those in which it is not.

In a third line of research, researchers might employ the techniques of psychologists to investigate how decisions of individual users are affected by the amount of accounting data presented to them or by the style of presentation.

Although such research has been carried out for a relatively short period of time, the results have already provided considerable insight into why corporations select certain accounting practices over others and the consequences of the choices.

Summary

Accounting plays an essential role in our economy. It facilitates the allocation of resources both within and among organizations. It provides the information necessary to evaluate the performance of entities and the persons who manage them. Although accounting reports on what happened in the past, it is relied upon to make decisions that affect the future.

Accounting conveys information to a variety of users for a variety of purposes. There can be a number of ways in which to describe financial events. The most appropriate way depends on the requirements of the specific parties who will use the information. Above all else, accounting reports must be *relevant*; they must bear upon the decisions at hand. As a consequence, there is no single set of accounting principles that is inherently better than others.

Accounting information should be *reliable*. It should be objective and verifiable. But information that is most relevant for a particular decision may not always be the most reliable. Thus, in selecting among accounting principles, firms and their accountants must balance these two competing standards. Financial reports should also be *neutral*; they should not influence decisions in a particular direction. Moreover, they should be *comparable* with those of other firms and of the same firm in different periods.

A key objective of this chapter has been to emphasize that the study of accounting requires much more than becoming cognizant of generally accepted accounting principles. Generally accepted accounting principles are not universal truths. Many are rules selected by designated authorities from among other possibilities that are equally defensible. They are subject to change. They lead to financial reports that may be most appropriate for some purposes, but certainly not for all. It is essential therefore that persons who use financial reports in their personal or professional lives not only understand the reasons why financial reports are prepared as they are but are aware of their limitations. They must be able to distinguish the economic substance of events from the way in which the events are reported. They must be able to reformulate financial reports so that the reports most effectively serve their own unique information needs.

Questions for Review and Discussion

1. On January 15, the controller (the chief accounting officer) of the Highland Hills Corp. reported to the president that company income for the previous year was $1.5 million. Two months later, after conducting an examination of the company's books and records, Scott and Co., Certified Public Accountants, determined that the company had earned only $900,000. Upon receiving the report of the CPAs, the president declared that she was going to get either a new controller or a new

CPA firm. "One of the two," she commented, "must be either dishonest or incompetent." Do you agree?

2. The financial vice-president of a corporation recently urged that all amounts in the firm's annual report to stockholders be rounded to the nearest thousand dollars. "It is misleading," he said, "to give stockholders a report in which all figures are carried out to the last penny." Explain what the financial vice-president most likely had in mind by his comment.

3. The Mid-Western Gas and Electric Co. recently submitted statements of income to stockholders, to the Internal Revenue Service, and to the Federal Power Commission. In no two of the reports was net income the same, even though the period covered by the reports was identical. Release of all three reports was approved by the firm's certified public accountants. How is it possible for all three reports to be "correct"?

4. In preparing a financial statement to accompany his loan application to a local bank, Glen Ellison was uncertain as to whether he should report his home as having a value of $50,000 or $180,000. Ellison purchased his house 25 years ago at a price of $50,000; similar homes in his neighborhood have recently been sold for between $160,000 and $200,000. Which amount do you think would be more useful to the bank? Which amount is more objective?

5. Accounting statements report on the past. Yet they incorporate predictions of the future. Why? Provide examples.

6. General-purpose financial reports should be *neutral*. What is meant by "neutral" as it applies to financial reports? Why is neutrality a characteristic of financial reports that accountants can only strive toward but never fully achieve?

7. Provide two examples of how managers can use financial reports to their advantage in advocacy proceedings.

8. What do recent studies regarding the effect of alternative accounting practices on stock market prices suggest about the ability of investors to distinguish between an economic event and the description of it? What are the implications of these studies for rule-making authorities?

9. In the early stages of the development of the accounting profession, independent auditors would "certify" to the "accuracy" of a company's financial statements. Today independent certified public accountants express an "opinion" that the company's financial statements "present fairly" the firm's financial position and results of its operations. Why do you suppose CPAs are reluctant to "certify" to the "accuracy" of a company's financial statements?

10. What role does the Financial Accounting Standards Board play in the development of accounting standards? What role does the Securities and Exchange Commission play?

11. What three primary services do CPA firms render to their clients? Why are such services sometimes thought to be in conflict with one another?

12. Wilbur Wood is concerned about his prospects for reelection as mayor of the town of Wippakinetta. Mayor Wood had promised the citizens of Wippakinetta that as long as he was in charge of fiscal affairs, the town would never run a deficit—that is, expenditures would never exceed revenues. Yet in 1992 the town did, in fact, report a deficit of $900,000. The deficit was attributable entirely to the fleet of nine buses purchased by the city. The city purchased and paid for the nine buses in November 1992. At the time the city ordered the buses, it had met all requirements for a federal transportation grant for the full cost of the vehicles, but as the result of a bureaucratic snarl, payment of the grant was delayed until the following year.

The city accounting system requires that revenues be recognized only upon actual receipt of cash and that expenses be recorded upon cash payment.

a. What deficiencies do you see in Wippakinetta's accounting system? What revisions would you suggest?

b. Suppose alternatively that the city did not receive a federal grant to pay for the buses. It is the policy of the city to pay cash (not to borrow) for transportation vehicles and equipment. The useful life of the buses is approximately five years. In those years in which new buses must be acquired, reported municipal expenditures are substantially greater than in those in which buses are not acquired. As a consequence, some citizens believe that the operating efficiency of the city is less in the years in which buses are replaced than in others. Do you believe that the city is really less efficient by virtue of its acquisition of new buses? How might the financial reporting practices of the city be changed so as to reduce the confusion on the part of some of its citizens?

13. Critics of traditional financial accounting have asserted that financial reports are biased in that they fail to account for certain "social" benefits and costs incurred. They recommend that corporations prepare and distribute a "socioeconomic operating statement." The statement might take the following form:

Social benefits		
Improvement in the environment	$xxxx	
Minority hiring program	xxxx	
Day-care center	xxxx	
Staff services donated to hospitals	xxxx	$xxxx
Social costs		
Damage to the environment	$xxxx	
Work-related injuries and illness	xxxx	
Failure to install recommended		
safety equipment	xxxx	xxxx
Social surplus (deficit) for		
the year		$xxxx

Comment on the proposed financial report in terms of the dual accounting goals of relevancy and reliability.

Problems

1. *Financial statements are based on estimates. The impact of the estimates on reported earnings may be substantial.*

TransAmerica Airlines owns and operates 10 passenger jet planes. Each plane had cost the airlines $6 million. The company's income statement for 1992 reported the following:

Revenue from passenger fares		$30,000,000
Operating expenses (including salaries, maintenance costs, terminal expenses, etc.)	$22,000,000	
Depreciation of planes	5,000,000	27,000,000
Income before taxes		$ 3,000,000

Each plane has an estimated useful life of 12 years. The $5 million depreciation charge was calculated by dividing the cost of each plane ($6 million) by its useful life (12 years). The result ($500,000) was multiplied by the number of planes owned (10).

a. Suppose that the useful life of each plane was 8 years rather than 12 years. Determine income before taxes for 1992. By what percent is income less than that just computed?

b. Suppose that the useful life of each plane was 15 years. Determine income before taxes for 1992. By what percent is income greater than that originally computed?

c. It is sometimes said that accountants must be concerned that financial statements are precise to the penny. Based on your computations, do you agree?

2. *It is not always obvious when a company is "better off" by virtue of its production and sales efforts.*

In January, its first month of operations, the Quick-Cut Lawn Mower Co. manufactured 200 lawn mowers at a cost of $180 each. Although it completed all 200 mowers by the end of the month, it had not yet sold any of them.

In February the company produced 300 mowers. It sold and delivered to customers both the 200 mowers manufactured in January and the 300 manufactured in February. Selling price of the mowers was $300 each.

a. Determine income for January and for February.

b. Assume instead that on January 2 the company signed a noncancelable contract to sell 500 mowers at $300 each to a major chain of department stores. The contract called for delivery in February. The company completed but did not deliver 200 of the mowers by January 31. It completed the remainder and delivered all 500 by February 28. Determine income for each of the two months.

3. *The most relevant information may not always be the most reliable.*

The president and sole owner of the Blue Mountain Brewery asked his CPA to audit (i.e., to express her opinion on the fairness of) the financial statements of his company. The audited financial statements had been requested by a local bank to facilitate review of the company's application for a loan.

The controller of the company, who had actually prepared the statements, included among the firm's assets "Land—$3,000,000." According to the controller, the land was reported at a value of $3 million since the company had recently received offers of approximately that amount from several potential buyers.

After reviewing the land account, the CPA told the president that she could not express the usual "unqualified" opinion on the financial statements as long as land was valued at $3 million. Instead, she would have to express an "adverse" opinion ("the financial statements do *not* fairly present. . . .") unless the land was valued at $150,000, the amount the company had actually paid for it.

The president was dumbfounded. The land, he told the CPA, was purchased in 1921 and was located in the downtown section of a major city.

a. At what amount do you think the land should be recorded? Explain. Which amount is likely to be the more relevant to the local banker? Which amount is the more objective?

b. Which amount should be reported if the statements are to be prepared in accord with "generally accepted accounting principles"?

4. *Sometimes it is easy to assign specific costs to specific items sold; sometimes it is more difficult. Choice of method used to determine cost affects the determination of reported income.*

The De Kalp Used Car Co. purchased four cars in the month of June and sold three cars. Purchase prices and sale prices are as follows:

	Purchase Price	Sale Price
Car 1	$3,000	$5,000
Car 2	3,500	5,500
Car 3	4,000	6,000
Car 4	4,500	—

The Natural Foods Grocery Store purchased 300 pounds of nutrient grain in the month of June and sold 200 pounds. The grain is not prepackaged. Instead, as it is purchased, it is added to a single barrel; as it is sold, it is scooped out and given to the customer in a paper bag. During June, 100 pounds of grain were purchased on each of three separate dates. Purchase prices, in sequence, were $3.00, $3.50, and $4.00 per pound. All sales were at $5.00 per pound.

Determine the income of the two merchants for the month of June. (Ignore other costs not indicated.)

Are there other assumptions that you might have made regarding the cost of goods actually sold? Would income remain the same?

5. *Accounting reports that are suitable for making a long-term investment decision may not be appropriate for deciding whether to discontinue a product line.*

John Williams sells greeting cards. Operating out of a garage that he rents for $2,000 per year, he purchases greeting cards from a wholesaler and distributes them door to door. In 1992 he sold 1,000 boxes of cards at $6 per box. The cost of the cards from the wholesaler was $2 per box.

In 1993 Williams decided to expand his product line to include candy. In that year he sold 300 boxes of candy for $10 per box. The candy cost him $8 per box. By making efficient use of his garage, he found that he was able to store his inventory of cards in one-half the garage; thus he could use the other half for his candy. His sales of cards neither benefited nor suffered as the result of the new product. Sales in 1993 were the same as in 1992.

At the conclusion of 1993 Williams had to decide whether to continue selling candy or to return to selling cards only. His friend Fulton, an occasional accountant, prepared the following report for him.

Sales of candy (300 boxes @ $10)		$3,000
Less costs		
Cost of candy sold (300 boxes @ $8)	$2,400	
Rent (.50 of $2,000)	1,000	3,400
Net loss on sale of candy		($ 400)

On the basis of the report Williams decided to abandon his line of candy.

a. Do you think he made the correct decision? Explain.

b. Prepare a report comparing the total earnings of Williams in 1993 with those in 1992. How do you reconcile the apparent contradiction between your report and that of Fulton?

6. *Higher reported earnings for a particular year can sometimes be achieved by actions that do not serve the long-run interests of the enterprise.*

Don Watson, president of a construction corporation, was concerned about the poor performance of his company in the first 11 months of the year. If the company continued at its present pace, reported profits for the year would be down substantially from those of the previous year. Thinking of ways to increase reported earnings, the president hit upon what he considered to be an ingenious scheme: Two years earlier the company had purchased a crane at a cost of $300,000. Since the crane was now two years old and had an estimated useful life of 10 years, it was currently reported on the company's books at eight-tenths of $300,000, or $240,000. Prices of cranes had increased substantially in the last two years, and the crane could be sold for $360,000. The president suggested that the company sell the crane for $360,000 and thereby realize a gain on the sale of $120,000 ($360,000 less the book value of $240,000). Of course, the company would have to buy a new crane—and new cranes were currently selling for $480,000—but the cost of the new crane could be spread out over its useful life of 10 years. In future years, the president realized, depreciation charges would increase from $30,000 on the old crane ($300,000 divided by 10) to $48,000 on the new ($480,000 divided by 10). In the current year, however, the company would report a gain on sale of $120,000 and thereby increase reported income by that amount.

a. The scheme of the president is, in fact, consistent with generally accepted accounting principles. Do you think, however, that the company would really be $120,000 better off if it sold the old crane and purchased a new one than if it held on to the old one? Comment.

b. Would the scheme of the president be in the best interest of the stockholders "in the long run"?

c. Assume that generally accepted accounting principles require that fixed assets, such as the crane, be reported on corporate books at the price at which they could currently be sold (i.e., $360,000). Would the scheme of the president accomplish its desired results? Why do you suppose generally accepted accounting principles do not permit such assets to be valued at the prices at which they can be sold?

7. *Choices among a few accounting principles may result in a great number of possible reported incomes.*

Custom Exteriors contracts with homeowners to provide a special protective coating for the outside walls of their homes. The company, however, is primarily a sales organization. It subcontracts the actual work to a painting company. Custom Exteriors charges customers $800 per home; it pays the painting company $600 per home. Per the contract, customers do not have to pay for the work until 30 days after the job is completed. Custom Exteriors, however, must pay the painting company part of the contract price at the start of work and part upon completion.

During a recent year Custom Exteriors signed contracts to provide service to 300 homes. Work was completed on 280 homes; collections were made for work done on 240 homes.

During the year Custom Exteriors made cash payments of $173,000 to the painting firm. Of this amount, $168,000 was for homes that were completed and $5,000 was for homes that were still being serviced.

Custom Exteriors is uncertain whether, in calculating income, it should report revenues as earned when it signs a contract, when the work on a house is completed, or when it collects cash from a customer. Similarly it is unsure whether it should report as an expense the total cash payments made to the paint company or only that portion of the payment representing homes completed. If it recognized only that portion representing homes completed, then any payments made on a home before work was completed would be accounted for as a "deposit" rather than an expense.

a. Indicate three possible amounts that the company could report as "revenue from contracts" for the year.

b. Indicate two possible amounts that the company could report as "expenses."

c. Based on your responses to parts (a) and (b), indicate six possible amounts that could be reported as "income" (revenues less expenses).

8. *Unless a contract specifies accounting principles, each side is free to argue for those that best serve its interest.*

Bantham joins with nine others to form a partnership that trades in wheat. The partnership agreement provides that in the event a partner wants to leave the firm, the remaining partners will purchase his or her interest at an amount equal to the partner's original contribution plus any undistributed earnings.

Each partner contributes $50,000 to the partnership. During its first year of operations, the partnership engages in the following transactions:

January 10: Buys 30,000 bushels of wheat at $4.00 per bushel.
August 11: Buys 70,000 bushels of wheat at $4.25 per bushel.
September 2: Sells 20,000 bushels of wheat at $4.50 per bushel.

On December 31 the price of wheat is $4.80 per bushel. On that date Bantham decides that he wants to leave the partnership. He requests that in accordance with the partnership agreement, the other partners should pay him $50,000 (his original contribution) plus 10 percent of the partnership's earnings for the year. He and the partners agree that revenue should be recognized only upon sale of the wheat. They disagree, however, on how cost of wheat sold should be determined.

a. Suppose that you represent Bantham in negotiations with the partnership. How much income would you assert that the partnership earned during the year? Explain and justify your response. Be sure to calculate income as revenue less the cost of the 20,000 bushels that were sold. Ignore income tax considerations.

b. Suppose instead that you represent the partnership. You wish to minimize the amount that the partnership has to pay Bantham. How much income would you say the partnership has earned? Explain and justify your response.

9. *Disputes over accounting principles can exacerbate domestic quarrels.*

Susan and Jeff agree to a divorce settlement in which the two will split their property equally. It is agreed that Susan will be granted all the assets. She will then make a cash payment to Jeff in the amount of one-half of the value of the total property.

Susan's accountant has prepared the following financial report of their common property as of December 31, 1992, the agreed-upon settlement date:

Cash	$250,000
Automobile	24,000
House	190,000
Stocks and bonds	80,000
Total	$544,000

A note to the financial statement indicates that the value of all assets, other than cash, represents the amounts paid to acquire them.

According to real estate specialists, the house has a market value of $250,000. The "blue book" of used-car prices indicates that the car could be sold (to a dealer) for $12,000; it could be purchased (from a dealer) for $15,000. The stocks and bonds had a market value on December 31, 1992, of $90,000. On that day, however, securities prices were at an unusually high level. On average during 1992 they had a market value of only $81,000. On the day the accountant prepared his report (February 15, 1993), the securities had a market value of $82,000.

a. Suppose that you were the accountant for Jeff. Prepare a statement of assets that would be in the best interests of Jeff.

b. What is the amount of the cash payment to which you would assert that Jeff is entitled?

2

The Accounting
Equation and the
Three Fundamental
Financial Statements

In this chapter we shall consider the basic equation that underlies all accounting practices and the three primary financial statements, which we touched on briefly in Chapter 1: the balance sheet, the income statement, and the statement of cash flows. We shall also look at two statements that can be used to supplement these primary statements: the statement of changes in retained earnings and the statement of changes in other owners' equity accounts.

THE FUNDAMENTAL ACCOUNTING EQUATION

A firm's *assets* (A) are the resources which it owns or controls. Its *liabilities* (L) are the resources owed to others. Its *owners' equity* (OE) is the residual difference between the two—the interest of the owners in the firm's resources. Thus

$$\text{Assets} - \text{Liabilities} = \text{Owners' equity}$$

or

$$A - L = OE$$

This equation is the fundamental equation of accounting. It lies at the heart of almost everything that is done in the discipline. It is a *tautology,* an expression that is true by definition. What an entity (an individual, business, or government) owns in the way of resources (for example, cash, inventory, plant, or equipment) minus what is owes to others (for example, accounts or notes payable) composes the entity's financial net worth.

In an alternative form, the liabilities are moved to the right-hand side of the equal sign. Thus

$$A = L + OE$$

The fundamental equation now shows the firm's existing resources on the left and tells how these resources have been financed on the right. Assets (A) must have been financed either by borrowed capital (L) or contributed capital (OE). Liabilities are often termed *creditor equities*. Thus total equities equal the sum of liabilities and owners' equity. In its alternative form, the equation says simply that *assets* equal *equities*.

THE BALANCE SHEET

In either form, the fundamental equation of accounting yields an expression of an individual's or firm's financial position at a *moment in time*. When the expression is expanded to list specific assets and equities, it is called a *statement of position* or, more commonly, a *balance sheet*. Exhibit 2-1 illustrates a simple balance sheet.

Assets, Liabilities, and Owners' Equity Defined

What gives a resource sufficient value to be accorded accounting recognition? Generally it is that the resource is expected to yield *future economic benefits*. These economic benefits, either directly or indirectly, are *cash flows*. For example, merchandise inventory (in a trading entity) is an economic resource because it is expected to be sold in the future for cash. Raw materials inventory (in a manufacturing concern) is an economic resource because it will be used in the production of goods that will be sold for cash. Plant and equipment have economic value because, like raw materials inventory, they will be used to provide goods or services that will generate cash. Cash itself is a resource because it can be used to purchase inventory, plant and equipment, and other

EXHIBIT 2-1

The Austin Company
Balance Sheet
As of June 30, 1993

Assets		Equities	
Cash	$ 270,000	Liabilities	
Accounts receivable	450,000	Accounts payable	$ 490,000
Merchandise inventory	360,000	Wages payable	25,000
Buildings	1,610,000	Bonds payable	2,045,000
Equipment	650,000	Total liabilities	$2,560,000
Patents and copyrights	800,000	Owners' equity	1,580,000
Total assets	$4,140,000	Total equities	$4,140,000

resources that can be expected to generate additional cash. Moreover, cash is the resource of ultimate concern to the owners of a business because it is the medium of exchange in our society.

Assets have been defined in many ways. Consider one particularly rigorous definition:

> *Resources or rights incontestably controlled by an entity at the accounting date that are expected to yield it future economic benefits[1]*

Similarly, *liabilities* are

> *Obligations of an entity at the accounting date to make future transfers of assets or services (sometimes uncertain as to timing and amount) to other entities*

Owners' equity, then, is the difference between the two:

> *The residual interest in the assets of an entity that remains after deducting its liabilities, that is the interests of the owners in a business enterprise*

Classification of Assets and Liabilities

Assets and liabilities may be categorized by several different characteristics:

- *Liquidity,* which can be current or noncurrent: A *current* asset can be sold or transformed into cash and a *current* liability can be satisfied within one year or within the normal operating cycle of the business. *Noncurrent* assets and liabilities are not so liquid.
- *Physical form,* which can be tangible or intangible: A *tangible* asset has physical existence (such as buildings and equipment), whereas an *intangible* asset is characterized by legal rights (such as notes receivable or patents).
- *Valuation,* which can be monetary or nonmonetary: A *monetary* asset or liability has a *fixed* exchange value in terms of cash; examples are accounts receivable or payable. A *nonmonetary* asset or liability has no fixed exchange value, the amount of cash to be received or paid being dependent upon economic conditions; examples are plant and equipment and inventory.

Because *liquidity,* the ability to transform assets into cash, is such an important factor in economic decisions, balance sheets conventionally employ the *current versus noncurrent* classification. Balance sheets do not typically reflect either the monetary/nonmonetary or the tangible/intangible distinctions. The monetary/nonmonetary distinction, however, is essential to an understanding of some key accounting issues (such as how to account for transactions in foreign currencies) to be addressed later in the text. The tangible/intangible distinction is one that is perhaps the easiest to make in that it is based on physical form. Yet it is the least significant in accounting. The principles of accounting for intangible assets are indistinguishable from those for tangible assets.

[1]David Solomons, ''Guidelines for Financial Reporting Standards,'' a paper prepared for the Research Board of the Institute of Chartered Accountants in England and Wales, 1989.

Current Assets

Current assets include cash and such other assets that will either be transformed into cash or will be sold or consumed within one year or within the *normal operating cycle* of the business if longer than one year. For most businesses the normal operating cycle is one year or less, but for some (such as those in the tobacco and distilling industries where the products must be stored for a period of several years) it may be longer. *Cash* includes not only currency but savings bank or commercial bank deposits as well. Disbursements of cash include payments by check, bank transfer, and currency.

Marketable securities are shares of stock, bonds, treasury bills, and commercial paper held by the firm as short-term investments. They are ordinarily stated on the balance sheet at original cost. If, however, the market value of the portfolio of securities held is less than original cost, then they are presented at the lower, more conservative value. Owing to the ease with which marketable securities can be sold and thereby transformed into cash, the market value of the securities must be reported either parenthetically or in supplementary notes.

Accounts receivable are the claims upon customers that can be expected to be collected within the normal operating cycle (those that cannot are included among noncurrent assets). Deducted from accounts receivable is an *allowance for doubtful accounts*—an estimate of the amounts owed to the company that will be uncollectible. Thus the net amount of accounts receivable is not the total amount owed to the firm but only the portion that the firm estimates is actually collectible.

Inventories include both items available for sale to customers and raw materials, parts, and supplies to be used in production. Inventories are ordinarily reported at the cost incurred to either purchase or produce them. But in the event that the cost of replacing such items has declined, then the inventories may be "written down" to reflect the decline in value. As with marketable securities, increases in value are not ordinarily recognized.

Prepaid expenses are services or rights to services purchased but not yet consumed. As they are consumed they will be "charged off" as actual expenses. A firm might, for example, purchase a one-year insurance policy for $1,200 ($100 per month). At the time of purchase it would record the policy as a current asset, "Prepaid insurance—$1,200." Each month it would reduce the asset by one-twelfth of the original amount ($100) and would charge insurance expense with the same amount. Thus, after eight months, the balance in the prepaid insurance account would be only $400 (four months remaining times $100 per month). Other common prepaid expense accounts are prepaid interest, prepaid advertising, and prepaid rent. Prepaid expenses are one type of *deferred charge*—outlays made in one period to benefit future periods.

Noncurrent Assets

Noncurrent assets are resources that *cannot* be expected to be sold or consumed within the normal operating cycle of the business. Noncurrent assets are usually considered to be *long-lived*. Plant assets in particular are often referred to as *fixed assets*.

Property, plant, and *equipment* are recorded on the balance sheet at original cost. Deducted from each of the assets, other than land, is *accumulated depreciation*—an allowance to reflect the "consumption" of the assets over time by wear and tear as well as by technological obsolescence.

Depreciation in traditional terminology is the process of allocating (spreading) the cost of an asset over its useful life. Depreciation on each individual asset or group of similar assets is computed separately, and the total amount accumulated is a function of the original cost, age, and expected useful life of the asset. No depreciation is provided for land since it is not consumed over time and seldom declines in utility.

Investments and *other assets* include amounts owed to the company by outsiders that are not due for at least one year and amounts that the company has invested in other companies. If, for example, a company owns 30 percent of another company, its interest would ordinarily be included among investments and other assets. An interest in another company, however, may be classified as either "Marketable securities," a current asset, or as "Investments in subsidiaries," a noncurrent asset. The decision as to how the investment should be classified depends to a large extent on the *intent* of the company's management. If it intends to maintain its interest for a relatively long period of time and views ownership as a long-term investment, then the amounts owned should be classified as a noncurrent asset. If, on the other hand, the company purchases the interest with the intention of selling it as soon as additional cash might be needed (for example, if it purchases a few hundred shares of General Motors stock as a temporary investment with no intention of exercising significant control over the company), then the amount owned should be classified as a current asset.

Deferred charges such as prepaid expenses may also be included among noncurrent assets. If, for example, a company purchased an insurance policy or a license that had more than a one-year life, then the percentage of original cost representing the unexpired portion of the insurance policy or license would be included among noncurrent assets.

Some deferred charges represent outlays that will benefit future accounting periods but for which both the number of such periods and the value of the benefits are exceedingly difficult to measure. Consider the costs incurred to organize a corporation: the legal fees required to draw up the documents of incorporation, the costs of printing the shares of stock to be issued, and the fees paid to the state upon filing for a corporate charter. These costs—like those of buildings and equipment—are incurred to benefit the business over a long period of time. Just as income of a single year of operations would be understated if the entire cost of a building were charged as an expense at the time it was purchased, income would also be distorted if the costs of organizing the corporation were charged off in a single year. As a result, organizational costs are frequently reported as assets of the company, and each year a portion of the costs are *amortized* (i.e., depreciated) and charged off as an expense.

Deferred charges representing benefits that will accrue to the firm over a long period of time in the future are often a source of confusion. Deferred charges, unlike most other assets, are intangible and frequently have no market value. Amounts spent as organizational costs, for example, cannot readily be transferred to any other business entity; they cannot be sold to outsiders. How, then, can they be considered assets?

The question must be answered in terms of the nature of all assets. Assets can be defined as future services to be received in money or benefits convertible into money. They can readily be viewed as "bundles of services" available for use or sale by a particular entity. The determination of service potential is made with respect to the business entity issuing the financial reports—not with respect to the world at large.

In accordance with currently employed practices of valuation (alternative practices will be discussed in subsequent chapters), assets are measured and recorded at the time they are acquired at the price paid for them. As their service potential declines over time (e.g., as the assets are consumed), the reported value is reduced *proportionately* through the process of depreciation or amortization. If one-third of the services has been consumed, then the asset is reported at two-thirds its original cost. As long as the asset is not intended for sale to outsiders, market value seldom enters into the determination of the amount at which an asset is reported. Indeed, an automobile owned by a business might be reported at an amount either greater or less than the price at which similar used cars are being traded.

The outlay for organizational costs will benefit many accounting periods. To the extent that it has "future service potential"—the corporation would not exist without it—the outlay can properly be considered an asset. Even though it may have no value to outsiders, it should be reported on the balance sheet at initial cost less that fraction of cost representing services already consumed.

Current Liabilities

Liabilities are also categorized as either current or noncurrent. *Current liabilities* are expected to be satisfied out of current assets (or through the creation of other current liabilities) within a relative short period of time, usually one year. Most common categories of current liabilities are amounts owed to employees for wages and salaries; to suppliers for services, supplies, and raw materials purchased (conventionally called trade accounts, or simply *accounts payable*); to the government for taxes (taxes payable); and to banks or other lenders for loans (notes payable) and for interest on the loans (interest payable) that is payable within one year.

Net current assets (current assets minus current liabilities) are referred to as *working capital*.

Noncurrent Liabilities

Noncurrent liabilities include all other amounts owed, such as long-term notes and bonds. Bonds are similar to long-term notes, but they differ in that the promise to pay is usually included in a more formal legal instrument and in that the term of the loan is often longer. The same bond or note may be classified as both a current and a noncurrent liability. The portion that is due within one year would be considered current; the portion due beyond one year would be noncurrent.

Amounts that a company pays in advance to receive goods or services in the future are considered to be assets of the company. In the same sense, amounts that others pay to the company for goods and services to be provided are considered to be liabilities. Suppose, for example, that an airline sells a ticket for a trip the traveler intends to take a month after purchase. At the time of sale the airline receives an asset (cash or accounts receivable) equal to the price of the ticket. At the time of sale it incurs an obligation to provide services (i.e., one airline trip) to the customer. To be sure, the obligation is not liability in the usual sense, in that the airline has no monetary debt outstanding to the customer. But it is an obligation nonetheless. These amounts are reported among the liabilities and may be labeled as appropriate: "Advances from customers," "Revenues received but not yet earned," or, less descriptively but more generally, *deferred credits*. They are classified as *current* if the obligation is likely to be satisfied within one year; otherwise they are classified as *noncurrent*.

"Nonassets and Nonliabilities"

Not all amounts that a firm will have to pay to others if it continues in business are recorded as liabilities, nor are all amounts that it can be expected to receive recorded as assets. If a firm signs a three-year contract with a new president, for example, and promises to pay him or her $300,000 per year, the firm may be legally liable for the full $900,000 as long as the new president is willing to provide the required services. The firm would not, however, record the full amount as a liability. Only as the president "earns" the salary—that is, performs his or her side of the bargain—would the firm record as a liability amounts earned but not paid. Similarly accounted for would be a transaction in which a firm borrows $1,000 from a bank at a 12 percent rate of interest and gives the bank a one-year note. At the end of the one-year period, the firm will owe the bank $1,120—the principal of $1,000 plus interest of $120. At the time the note is signed, however, the only liability that would be recorded is the $1,000 actually borrowed. Each month, as the company has use of the borrowed funds, an additional $10 interest for one month will be recorded as a liability. The bank, for its part, would record as an asset a note for $1,000. It, too, would recognize an asset, "interest receivable," only as it earns the interest revenue with the passage of time.

In general, assets and liabilities arising out of *executory contracts* (those contingent upon the mutual performance of the two sides to the contract) are recorded only to the extent that one of the parties has fulfilled its contractual obligations. The reason for such limited accounting recognition of assets and liabilities will become considerably clearer as the relationship between balance sheet and income statement accounts is discussed more fully in subsequent chapters.

Owners' Equity

The stockholders' equity section of the corporate balance sheet is typically divided into two main parts. The first indicates the *capital contributed by shareholders*—either at the time the corporation was formed or when additional shares of stock were issued in the course of the corporation's existence. Corporations may issue several different types of stock.

Common stock generally gives its owners the right to vote for members of the corporation's board of directors as well as on numerous other corporate matters and the right to share in corporate profits whenever dividends are declared by the board of directors.

Preferred stock, on the other hand, generally does *not* carry voting rights, but it does ordinarily guarantee the owner that he or she will receive dividends of at least a minimum amount each year. The dividend rate is fixed at the time the stock is issued.

Often shares of both common and preferred stock are arbitrarily assigned a *par* or *stated* value (e.g., $100 per share). These values have some legal, but little economic, significance, and shares are often issued for amounts above or below these arbitrarily assigned values. Amounts that the company receives above the par values of the shares are categorized as *additional paid-in capital,* or *capital in excess of par,* and those below (almost always for preferred stock) as a *discount* on the shares issued.

The second part of the stockholders' equity section of a corporate balance sheet, *retained earnings,* indicates the accumulated earnings of the business. Retained earnings will be commented on in greater detail later in this chapter.

If the firm is not a corporation, that is, if it is a *sole proprietorship* (a firm owned by a single individual) or a *partnership* (a firm owned by two or more parties), then the owners' equity section of the balance sheet may take a somewhat different form. Since such enterprises do not issue stock and are not bound by many of the legal restrictions that apply to firms that do, it is generally most useful to readers of the financial reports to indicate the entire equity of each of the owners in a single separate account. The owners' equity section of a company owned by two partners, W. King and F. Prince, might appear as follows:

Partners' capital	
W. King, capital	$ 9,525,347
F. Prince, capital	7,526,322
Total partners' capital	$17,051,669

Recognition of Assets and Liabilities

When does an entity recognize the existence of an asset or a liability? That is, when does it enter (or change) its value on the balance sheet? Almost all accounting issues center on this key question.

In most circumstances, the value of an asset is based upon an *arm's-length transaction that has taken place in the past.* An ''arm's-length'' transaction is one with a party that is independent of the reporting entity (e.g., with a party other than an affiliate, owner, or officer of the entity).

Sometimes, however, it is necessary to recognize changes in value resulting from *economic events* in addition to those from transactions to which the reporting entity has been a party. For example, when a firm purchases merchandise inventory, it will record the inventory at the acquisition cost—the amount based upon the arm's-length purchase transaction. Suppose, however, that subsequent to purchase, the market value of the inventory were to decline. The firm would be required to reduce the carrying value of the inventory to the new market value, even if it never acquired additional inventory at the new price. Correspondingly, information that a loan is likely uncollectible would lead the lender to reduce the recorded value of the note receivable even though the lender has engaged in no transactions with the borrower since making the loan.

For the most part, however, accountants have been reluctant to recognize *increases* in values that are not the result of past transactions. For example, whereas the decline in inventory would be recorded, a corresponding increase would not. Owing to the adverse consequences of overstating assets (or understating liabilities), the accounting profession has traditionally been conservative. It has established more rigorous standards of evidential reliability for asset increases than for decreases. In this respect the accounting profession in the United States has been more reluctant than many of its overseas counterparts to record increases in values even in the absence of arm's-length transactions. For example, British and Australian companies are sometimes permitted to assign values to trademarks, even though the values are attributable to customer loyalty rather than specific purchase transactions. Nevertheless, as shall be pointed out throughout this text, even U.S. standards require asset values to be enhanced in some situations.

TRANSACTIONS AFFECTING THE BALANCE SHEET

The balance sheet is, in essence, an expression of the fundamental accounting equation ($A = L + OE$). It is affected by *all* economic events that are given accounting recognition.

Ever since the early Renaissance, the *double-entry* system has been central to accounting practice and theory. The double-entry system is a manifestation of the accounting equation. Every transaction or event that increases (or decreases) the left side of the accounting equation (assets) must increase (or decrease) the right side of the equation (equities) by an identical amount. Thus an increase in assets must be matched by an increase in claims against the assets either by creditors (liabilities L) or by the owners (owners' equity OE). Some transactions or events may affect only one side of the equation. But these involve only an exchange of one asset for another asset or one equity for another equity. Every transaction therefore must be recorded at least twice. A change in one element of the accounting equation must be matched by a change in another. *The equation must be maintained in balance.*

Formation of a Business Entity

Suppose that in March 1993 the Schaefer family establishes the Schaefer Corporation to open and operate a bookstore. The company will commence ongoing operations in April 1993. A. Schaefer contributes $30,000 cash in exchange for 200 shares of common stock. B. Schaefer contributes land that is worth $50,000 and a building that is worth $100,000 in exchange for 1,000 shares. (These values are indicative of what the new company would have to pay for the land and building in the marketplace.)

The initial contribution of resources must be recorded on the books of the corporation to show both the new assets and the claims against the assets. In this example, the assets are financed entirely by the owners. Hence the transactions result in an increase in assets (cash, building, and land) and in owners' equity (common stock). The common stock is assigned a value of $180,000, which, of course, corresponds to the market value of the contributed assets. The changes on the right side of the equation must equal those on the left. (Change is represented by the **Δ**.) Thus

Increase

$$
\begin{array}{c}
\text{Land} \\
+\$50{,}000 \\
\uparrow \\
\end{array}
$$

Building	Common stock: B. Schaefer
+$100,000	+$150,000
↑	↑
Cash	Common stock: A. Schaefer
+$30,000	+$30,000
↑	↑
ΔA	ΔL + ΔOE (1)

$$\Delta A \quad = \quad \Delta L \quad + \quad \Delta OE \qquad (1)$$

Decrease

In this and subsequent transactions, increases in accounts will be shown above the accounting equation, decreases below.

Debits and Credits

The requirement for dual recognition of all transactions has led to a shorthand means of expressing the required entries to the accounts:

> *Entries which increase assets are referred to as debits.*
> *Those which decrease assets are known as credits.*
>
> *Entries which increase equities are referred to as credits.*
> *Those which decrease equities are known as debits.*

Thus

Increase

$$
\begin{array}{ccc}
Debit & & Credit \\
\uparrow & & \uparrow \\
\Delta A & = & \overline{\Delta L \;+\; \Delta OE} \\
\downarrow & & \downarrow \\
Credit & & Debit \\
\end{array}
$$

Decrease

For each transaction as well as for the accounting records in their entirety, debits must equal credits and assets must equal equities.

   Use of *debit* to signify an increase in an entity's assets and *credit* to indicate an increase in its liabilities seems odd at first. A *credit* generally mean one is *better off*, a *debit* that one is *worse off*. In Italian Renaissance accounting, where the terms originated, however, accounts were kept for those who contributed funds to the enterprise. The terms as they apply to changes in an *entity's equities* are consistent with common parlance when *viewed by the outside holder of the equities*. Thus, when one deposits funds in a bank, one is *credited* with this amount (which is then a liability of the bank). When one withdraws funds, one's account is *debited* (and the bank's liability disappears).

Payment of Utility Deposits

Let us return to the illustration. Schaefer Corporation pays $600 in cash to its electric company as a security deposit. The transaction causes a decrease in (credit to) cash and an increase in (debit to) an asset, "utility deposits." The utility deposits are comparable to accounts or notes receivable. Schaefer Corporation is owed the funds (albeit at no specified date) from the utility. Thus

Increase

$$
\begin{array}{c}
\text{Utility deposit} \\
+\$600 \\
\uparrow \\
\Delta A \qquad = \qquad \Delta L \quad + \quad \Delta OE \qquad \text{(2)} \\
\downarrow \\
\text{Cash} \\
-\$600
\end{array}
$$

Decrease

Prepaid Insurance

Schaefer Corporation purchases a one-year casualty insurance policy on its building and equipment, paying $3,600 cash. The policy is to go into effect on April 1, which is when the corporation expects to commence operations. The insurance policy is an asset, comparable to buildings and equipment. The company anticipates receiving economic benefits (insurance coverage) from it over the following 12 months.

Increase

$$
\begin{array}{c}
\text{Prepaid insurance} \\
+\$3,600 \\
\uparrow \\
\Delta A \qquad = \qquad \Delta L \quad + \quad \Delta OE \qquad \text{(3)} \\
\downarrow \\
\text{Cash} \\
-\$3,600
\end{array}
$$

Decrease

Purchase of Merchandise Inventory

The company acquires $40,000 of new books as inventory stock. All acquisitions are "on account" (the company will pay at a later date). The transaction results in an increase in an asset and a corresponding increase in a liability:

Increase

$$
\begin{array}{ccccc}
\text{Merchandise} & & \text{Accounts} & & \\
\text{inventory} & & \text{payable} & & \\
+\,\$40,000 & & +\,\$40,000 & & \\
\uparrow & & \uparrow & & \\
\Delta A & = & \Delta L & + & \Delta OE \quad\quad (4)
\end{array}
$$

Decrease

Acquisition of Equipment

The company purchases computer equipment for $28,000, an amount which includes delivery and installation. It pays $4,000 and gives a note of $24,000 for the balance. The note is to be repaid in 12 monthly installments beginning April 30. Interest is to be charged at a rate of 18 percent annually (1.5 percent per month) on the unpaid balance:

Increase

$$
\begin{array}{ccccc}
\text{Equipment} & & \text{Note payable} & & \\
+\,\$28,000 & & +\,\$24,000 & & \\
\uparrow & & \uparrow & & \\
\Delta A & = & \Delta L & + & \Delta OE \quad\quad (5) \\
\downarrow & & & & \\
\text{Cash} & & & & \\
-\,\$4,000 & & & &
\end{array}
$$

Decrease

The delivery and installation charges are included in the cost of the asset as long as they are necessary to bring the equipment to a serviceable condition.

The note payable is classified as a current liability since it is to be repaid within one year. The interest to be paid, although most definitely an obligation of the company, is not, at this time, given accounting recognition because the company has not yet had the use of the borrowed funds and has not yet benefited from them.

Improvements to Building

The company contracts with a construction company to remodel its building. The agreed-upon price is $20,000. The company pays the contractor $10,500 while the work is in process. When the project is completed, Schaefer Corporation receives the final bill, still unpaid at month's end, of $9,500.

Increase

$$
\begin{array}{ccccc}
\text{Building} & & \text{Accounts payable} & & \\
+\,\$20,000 & & +\,\$9,500 & & \\
\uparrow & & \uparrow & & \\
\Delta A & = & \Delta L & + & \Delta OE \quad\quad (6) \\
\downarrow & & & & \\
\text{Cash} & & & & \\
-\,\$10,500 & & & &
\end{array}
$$

Decrease

The improvements to the building are as much an asset as the building itself, since they have been undertaken to benefit future accounting periods.

Long-Term Borrowing

Recognizing that it will be required to make substantial cash payments once it begins operations, the company borrows $50,000 from a local bank and signs a five-year note. Interest is to be paid monthly at an annual rate of 12 percent—that is, $6,000 per year, or $500 per month. Interest for the first month will be recorded when paid (as discussed later in this chapter).

Increase

$$
\begin{array}{ccccc}
\text{Cash} & & \text{Note payable} & & \\
+\$50,000 & & +\$50,000 & & \\
\uparrow & & \uparrow & & \\
\Delta A & = & \Delta L & + & \Delta OE \quad (7)
\end{array}
$$

Decrease

Purchase of Marketable Securities

Rather than deposit in its checking account the entire $50,000 that it has borrowed from the bank, the company purchases $10,000 in U.S. government securities. By doing so, the company is able to earn interest on what would otherwise be idle cash:

Increase

$$
\begin{array}{ccccc}
\text{Marketable securities} & & & & \\
+\$10,000 & & & & \\
\uparrow & & & & \\
\Delta A & = & \Delta L & + & \Delta OE \quad (8) \\
\downarrow & & & & \\
\text{Cash} & & & & \\
-\$10,000 & & & &
\end{array}
$$

Decrease

Recognition of Organization Costs

Schaefer Corporation engages an attorney to file the necessary documents of incorporation and provide legal assistance on a number of matters relating to the establishment of the business. Total costs, which the company pays in cash, are $6,000.

These costs, like the improvements to the building, will benefit the company only when it begins operations (in April). Therefore the costs must be *capitalized*—that is, recorded as an asset:

Increase

$$
\begin{array}{c}
\text{Organization costs} \\
+\,\$6{,}000 \\
\uparrow \\
\Delta A \qquad\qquad = \qquad \Delta L \quad + \quad \Delta OE \qquad\qquad (9) \\
\downarrow \\
\text{Cash} \\
-\,\$6{,}000
\end{array}
$$

Decrease

Organization costs are an *intangible* asset. Unlike most other assets, both tangible and intangible, organization costs cannot be sold or traded; nevertheless, they are an asset because (according to the definition of an asset) they are expected to yield *future economic benefits*.

Preparing a Balance Sheet

To prepare a balance sheet it is necessary only to sum the debits and credits in each account and to list and classify the accounts and balances. Exhibit 2-2 presents the Schaefer Corporation balance sheet as of March 31, 1993. (Balance sheets as well as other financial statements are *always* prepared at year end, but they may also be prepared as of any other date.)

EXHIBIT 2-2

The Schaefer Corporation
Balance Sheet
As of March 31, 1993

Assets			Equities		
Current			Liabilities		
Cash		$ 45,300	Current		
Marketable securities		10,000	Accounts payable		$ 49,500
Merchandise inventory		40,000	Note payable		24,000
Prepaid insurance		3,600	Total current		$ 73,500
Total, current		$ 98,900	Noncurrent		
Noncurrent			Note payable		50,000
Utility deposit		600	Total liabilities		$123,500
Organization costs		6,000	Common stock outstanding		180,000
Land		50,000			
Buildings		120,000			
Equipment		28,000			
Total, noncurrent		$204,600			
Total assets		$303,500	Total equities		$303,500

THE INCOME STATEMENT

The accounting equation and the balance sheet indicate net assets (assets less liabilities) and the owners' claims against such net assets at a *point* in time. The income statement, on the other hand, indicates changes in owners' equity (and

EXHIBIT 2-3

The Austin Company
Income Statement
Year Ended June 30, 1993

Revenue from sales			$1,220,000
Cost of merchandise sold	$700,000		
Wages and salaries	150,000		
Advertising	30,000		
Rent	40,000	$920,000	
Taxes		120,000	1,040,000
Net income			$ 180,000

thus changes in net assets) over a *period* of time resulting from the operations of the business, *excluding* contributions or withdrawals on the part of the owners (which are indicated in the statement of changes in owners' equity). The income statement indicates the revenues of the period and the expenses incurred in earning the revenues; an income statement for the Austin Company (*not* for the Schaefer Corporation, since so far it has neither earned revenues nor incurred expenses), in condensed form, is shown in Exhibit 2-3. This income statement is consistent with the company's balance sheet, shown in Exhibit 2-1.

Revenues and Expenses

Revenues are the inflows of cash or other assets attributable to the goods or services provided by the enterprise. Most commonly, revenues are derived from the sale of the company's product or service, but they can also be realized (recognized) from interest on loans to outsiders, dividends received on shares of stock of other companies, royalties earned on patents or licenses, or rent earned from properties owned.

Expenses are the outflows of cash or other assets attributable to the profit-directed activities of an enterprise. Expenses are a measure of the effort exerted on the part of the enterprise in its attempt to realize revenues. More formally,

> *Revenues are inflows or other enhancements of assets of an entity or settlements of its liabilities (or a combination of both) from delivering or producing goods, rendering services, or other activities that constitute the entity's ongoing major or central operations.*

> *Expenses are outflows or other using up of assets or incurrences of liabilities (or a combination of both) from delivering or producing goods, rendering services, or carrying out other activities that constitute the entity's ongoing major or central operations.*[2]

Gains and Losses

Gains and losses are similar, but not identical, to revenues and expenses. *Gains* and *losses* are increases or decreases in net assets resulting from transactions that are not typical of a firm's day-to-day transactions. Suppose, for example, that

[2]"Elements of Financial Statements," paragraphs 78 and 80, Financial Accounting Standards Board *Statement of Financial Accounting Concepts No. 6,* 1985.

a retail store sells office equipment that it used in its own accounting department. The difference between the selling price and its book value at time of sale would be recorded as a gain or loss. By contrast, however, if the firm were to sell ordinary merchandise, then the amount for which it was sold would be recorded as revenue; the cost of the goods sold would be reported as an expense.

Gains and losses that are exceptional in nature and are unlikely to recur are classified as *extraordinary items*. Examples are losses from fires, natural disasters, and expropriations of corporate property by foreign governments. To make certain that such unusual events do not distort comparisons of performance in past years and predictions of earnings in the future, they are reported separately in the statement of income. And since these events are likely to have a significant impact on income taxes, the applicable tax effect is also broken out.

Stocks versus Flows

Contrast the manner in which the date appears on the income statement with the way it appears on the balance sheet. The income statement is *for the year ended* June 30, 1993—it describes what has happened over a one-year period. The balance sheet is *as of* June 30, 1993—it describes the business as of a particular moment in time.

The relationship between the balance sheet and the income statement can be explained by analogy to a household bathtub filled with water. The water in the bathtub is comparable to the owners' equity—or, alternatively, to the firm's net assets (assets less liabilities). In describing the level of water in the tub one could say that at a given moment the tub contains *x* gallons of water. Similarly, one could describe a firm as having a particular level of net assets. Indeed, the balance sheet of a firm does exactly that. It indicates, and describes, the level of assets, of liabilities, and of the difference between the two—owners' equity.

Suppose, however, that the water is entering the tub through the faucets at the same time it is leaving through the drain. It would still be possible—and indeed necessary if comprehensive information is to be presented—to describe the level of water in the tub. One could say, for example, that at 11:03 P.M. there were 10 gallons of water in the tub. But this information would hardly constitute a very complete description of activity in the tub. Also needed would be data as to the rate at which the water level is rising or falling. More complete information might be as follows: Water is entering the tub at the rate of 3 gallons per minute; it is leaving at the rate of 2 gallons per minute; hence it is rising at the rate of 1 gallon per minute.

So also with the firm. Information is required as to the *rate* at which the equity of the owners is increasing or decreasing. The water entering the tub might be compared to revenues; the water leaving, to expenses; and the difference between the two, to income. Thus it might be said that assets are entering the firm at the *rate* of $3 million per year (i.e., revenues for the year are $3 million), that assets are leaving the firm at the *rate* of $2 million per year (i.e., expenses for the year are $2 million), and that the change in net assets (owners' equity) for the year is $1 million (i.e., income for the year is $1 million).

If the amount of water in the bathtub at 11:03 P.M. is 10 gallons and it is increasing at the rate of 1 gallon per minute, then the amount at the end of the minute will be 11 gallons. The beginning amount plus the net amount added during the period equals the ending amount.

So too with the firm. If the owners' equity at January 1, 1993, is $10 million and income for the year is $1 million, then owners' equity at the end of the year will be $11 million.

The balance sheet indicates the equity that the owners have in the firm at any given *point* in time. Such a point of time is usually the end of a month or the end of a year. The balance sheet also indicates the assets and the liabilities that result in the particular level of owners' equity.

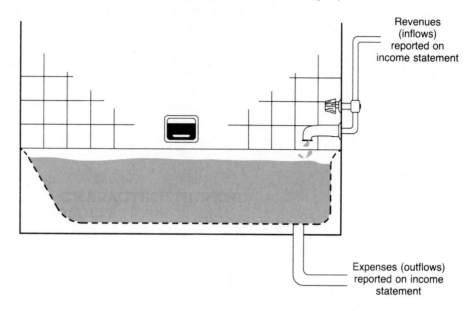

Revenues (inflows) reported on income statement

Expenses (outflows) reported on income statement

The income statement indicates the *rate* at which the equity of the owners is changing. It reveals the revenues, the expenses, and the resultant income for the period. Assuming that no assets or liabilities entered or left the firm from other sources (e.g., the owners neither contributed nor withdrew assets), then owners' equity at the beginning of the period per the balance sheet plus income for the period (per the income statement) must equal owners' equity at the end of the period (per the new balance sheet):

$$
\begin{array}{l}
\quad\ \text{Owners' equity, beginning of period} \\
+(-)\ \text{Income (or loss) for the period} \\
+(-)\ \text{Additional contributions (or withdrawals)} \\
\quad\quad \underline{\text{of owners during the period}} \\
=\ \text{Owners' equity, end of period}
\end{array}
$$

The owners' equity of the Austin Company as of June 30, 1993 (see Exhibit 2-1), was $1,580,000. If, during the following year ending June 30, 1994, the company had income of $250,000 and paid dividends of (that is, the owners withdrew) $190,000, then owners' equity as of June 30, 1994, would be $1,640,000:

Owners' equity 6/30/93		Income		Dividends		Owners' equity 6/30/94
$1,580,000	+	$250,000	−	$190,000	=	$1,640,000

Effect of Revenues and Expenses on the Accounting Equation

The key to understanding the relationship between the income statement and the balance sheet is in recognizing that revenues, by definition, are inflows or other enhancements of net assets $(A - L)$. Therefore they *must*, at the same time, be matched by an *increase* in owner's equity (OE). Correspondingly, expenses are outflows or reductions in net assets. They *must* be matched by a *decrease* in owners' equity.

The income statement explains the changes (excluding contributions to or withdrawals by the owners) in *retained earnings* that take place in an accounting period. Retained earnings, as indicated in the discussion of owners' equity, is one of the major divisions of owners' equity. It indicates the earnings of the business accumulated since its inception. The revenues are increases in retained earnings, the expenses decreases.

For example, with the exception of the initial contribution of capital (the issuance of the stock), the transactions in which the Schaefer Corporation engages in March do not affect owners' equity. The company has not yet begun operations. It has not yet earned any revenues nor incurred any expenses. All of its costs are intended to benefit future accounting periods, when the company carries out its planned activities. Therefore all of its costs are capitalized (recorded as assets). Indeed, after the firm receives its initial contribution of capital, the ''level'' of net assets (and therefore owners' equity) remains unchanged.

Consider now the transactions in which the Schaefer Company engages in April, after it has begun operations.

Purchase of Additional Merchandise

The company purchases additional merchandise on account for $110,000:

Increase

$$
\begin{array}{ccccc}
\text{Merchandise} & & \text{Accounts} & & \\
\text{inventory} & & \text{payable} & & \\
+\$110,000 & & +\$110,000 & & \\
\uparrow & & \uparrow & & \\
\Delta A & = & \Delta L & + & \Delta OE \qquad (10)
\end{array}
$$

Decrease

Payment of Amount Owed

The company pays the publishers $106,000 of what is owed for the books that it purchased:

Increase

$$
\begin{array}{ccccc}
\Delta A & = & \Delta L & + & \Delta OE \qquad (11) \\
\downarrow & & \downarrow & & \\
\text{Cash} & & \text{Accounts payable} & & \\
-\$106,000 & & -\$106,000 & &
\end{array}
$$

Decrease

These last two transactions are similar to those that took place in March. They result in changes in both assets and liabilities but do not affect net assets $(A - L)$. Therefore they do not affect owners' equity.

Sales Revenue and Cost of Goods Sold

During April the company sells books for $144,000. The books that are sold have cost the company $90,000. The customers pay cash of $32,000 and receive credit for the balance of $112,000.

As a result of these transactions, the net assets of the company increase by $54,000 ($144,000 less $90,000). The firm receives cash and claims to cash of $144,000. It surrenders assets of only $90,000. Because net assets have increased by $54,000, so also must owners' equity (more specifically, retained earnings).

The transaction may be recorded in two steps. The first will recognize the sale and the concurrent receipt of cash and creation of accounts receivable. The second will record the cost of the books sold and the associated reduction in merchandise inventory.

The increase in owners' equity ($144,000) attributable to the sale will be reported in parentheses as ''sales revenue.'' Sales revenue, as will be explained in greater detail in the next chapter, may be interpreted as a subaccount of retained earnings. It provides information on the reason for the change in retained earnings. This information is required for preparation of the income statement—the statement that explains the increase in owners' equity attributable to the operations of the enterprise.

The reduction in owners' equity ($90,000) associated with the reduction in merchandise inventory will be reported as ''cost of goods sold.'' Cost of goods sold, like sales revenue and all other revenues and expenses, may also be seen as a subaccount of retained earnings.

To record the sale, we have

Increase

$$
\begin{array}{ccccc}
\text{Cash} & & & & \\
+\$32,000 & & & & \\
\uparrow & & & \text{Retained earnings} & \\
\text{Accounts receivable} & & & \text{(sales revenue)} & \\
+\$112,000 & & & +\$144,000 & \\
\uparrow & & & \uparrow & \\
\Delta A & = & \Delta L & + \quad \Delta OE & \qquad (12)
\end{array}
$$

Decrease

To record the costs related to the sale, we have

Increase

$$
\begin{array}{ccccc}
\Delta A & = & \Delta L & + \quad \Delta OE & \qquad (13) \\
\downarrow & & & \downarrow & \\
\text{Merchandise inventory} & & & \text{Retained earnings} & \\
-\$90,000 & & & \text{(cost of goods sold)} & \\
& & & -\$90,000 &
\end{array}
$$

Decrease

Collection of Accounts Receivable

The Schaefer Corporation collects $68,000 that was owed to it by its customers. As a consequence, it exchanges one asset (accounts receivable) for another (cash). This transaction has no impact on the equity of the owners (O); the net assets ($A - L$) remained unchanged:

Increase

$$
\begin{array}{c}
\text{Cash} \\
+\$68,000 \\
\uparrow \\
\Delta A \qquad = \qquad \Delta L \quad + \quad \Delta OE \qquad\qquad (14) \\
\downarrow \\
\text{Accounts receivable} \\
-\$68,000
\end{array}
$$

Decrease

Wages and Salary Expense

During April the firm incurs $34,000 in wage and salary expenses. Of this amount, $30,000 is paid in cash. The balance is to be paid in early May.

The April wages and salaries reduce an asset (cash) by $30,000 and increase a liability (wages and salaries payable) by $4,000. Net assets ($A - L$) decrease by $34,000. Therefore owners' equity must also decrease by $34,000. Particularly notable about this transaction is that the wage and salary expense (the reduction in retained earnings) is determined by the wages and salaries *earned* by the employees—not by the amount of cash actually paid.

Increase

$$
\begin{array}{c}
\text{Wages and salaries} \\
\text{payable} \\
+\$4,000 \\
\uparrow \\
\Delta A \qquad = \qquad \Delta L \quad + \quad \Delta OE \qquad\qquad (15) \\
\downarrow \qquad\qquad\qquad\qquad\qquad \downarrow \\
\text{Cash} \qquad\qquad\qquad \text{Retained earnings} \\
-\$30,000 \qquad\quad \text{(wage and salary expense)} \\
-\$34,000
\end{array}
$$

Decrease

Insurance Expense

As previously noted, in March the Schaefer Corporation acquires a one-year (12-month) insurance policy at a cost of $3,600. The cost of the policy is recorded as "prepaid insurance," an asset. It is stated at $3,600 on the March 31 balance sheet. During April, one month of the insurance protection expires. Hence the asset, prepaid insurance, must be reduced by one-twelfth ($300) of its initial value. Correspondingly, owners' equity (insurance expense) must be reduced by the same amount:

Increase

$$\Delta A \quad = \quad \Delta L \quad + \quad \Delta OE \qquad (16)$$
$$\downarrow \qquad\qquad\qquad\qquad\qquad \downarrow$$

Prepaid insurance   Retained earnings
$-\$300$ (insurance expense)
$-\$300$

Decrease

Payment of Interest on Noncurrent Note

The company pays interest of $500 on its noncurrent note. The payment reduces cash and has no effect on any other asset or liability. It therefore reduces owners' equity:

Increase

$$\Delta A \quad = \quad \Delta L \quad + \quad \Delta OE \qquad (17)$$
$$\downarrow \qquad\qquad\qquad\qquad\qquad \downarrow$$

Cash   Retained earnings
$-\$500$ (interest expense)
$-\$500$

Decrease

Repayment of Current Note and Payment of Interest

As required by the short-term note issued to acquire computer equipment, the company repays $2,000 of the principal (the amount borrowed) and pays $360 in interest. The repayment of the principal reduces both cash and the note payable. It has no impact on either net assets or owners' equity. The payment of the interest, by contrast, reduces cash but does not reduce a corresponding liability. Therefore it reduces owners' equity:

Increase

$$\Delta A \quad = \quad \Delta L \quad + \quad \Delta OE \qquad (18)$$
$$\downarrow \qquad\qquad\quad \downarrow \qquad\qquad\quad \downarrow$$

Cash   Note payable, current   Retained earnings
$-\$2,360$ $-\$2,000$ (interest expense)
$-\$360$

Decrease

Sale of Marketable Securities and Recognition of Interest

The company redeems the $10,000 in marketable government securities that it acquired in March as a temporary investment. It receives $10,100, the additional $100 representing interest for the period.

Interest revenue has the same characteristics as sales revenue. It leads to an increase in net assets and a reciprocal increase in owners' equity:

Increase

$$
\begin{array}{cc}
\text{Cash} & \begin{array}{c}\text{Retained earnings}\\ \text{(interest revenue)}\end{array}\\
+\$10{,}100 & +\$100\\
\uparrow & \uparrow
\end{array}
$$

$$\Delta A \quad = \quad \Delta L \quad + \quad \Delta OE \qquad\qquad (19)$$

$$
\downarrow
$$

$$
\begin{array}{c}
\text{Marketable securities}\\
-\$10{,}000
\end{array}
$$

Decrease

Depreciation of Building and Equipment

The firm previously acquired and properly recorded a building at a total cost of $120,000 (including remodeling costs) and equipment at a cost of $28,000. The company estimates that the building will have an economic life of 20 years (240 months), after which it will have no value. Similarly it estimates that the equipment will have an economic life of five years (60 months), after which it too will have no value.

In effect, during April the firm "uses up" a portion of both the building and equipment—just as it consumes a share of the 12-month insurance policy. The costs of the building and equipment must therefore be spread over their useful lives. Thus, the stated value of the building and equipment must be reduced by 1/240 and 1/60, respectively. The reduction in the assets ($500 and $467) is offset by an equal reduction in owners' equity.

The process of allocating the cost of an asset to the accounting periods in which it provides its benefits is referred to as *depreciation*.

Increase

$$\Delta A \quad = \quad \Delta L \quad + \quad \Delta OE \qquad\qquad (20)$$

$$
\begin{array}{ccc}
\downarrow & & \downarrow\\
\begin{array}{c}\text{Building}\\ -\$500\end{array} & & \begin{array}{c}\text{Retained earnings}\\ \text{(depreciation expense)}\\ -\$967\end{array}\\
\downarrow & & \\
\begin{array}{c}\text{Equipment}\\ -\$467\end{array} & &
\end{array}
$$

Decrease

There is no need to record depreciation on land, since it does not ordinarily become less serviceable with time or use. Land, unlike most other assets, has an unlimited useful life.

Amortization of Organizational Costs

The number of years over which organizational costs benefit a corporation is not easily determined. But they must be allocated despite the difficulty of making the required estimates. The process of allocating organization costs, as well as other intangible assets, is referred to as *amortization,* which is identical in concept to depreciation.

Schaefer Corporation elects to *amortize* its $6,000 in organizational costs over a period of five years (60 months). Hence amortization expense is $100 per month:

Increase

$$\Delta A \quad = \quad \Delta L \quad + \quad \Delta OE \tag{21}$$

$$\downarrow \qquad\qquad\qquad\qquad \downarrow$$

Organization costs   Retained earnings
$-\$100$ (amortization expense)
                                $-\$100$

Decrease

APPLYING THE EQUATION: PREPARING THE BALANCE SHEET AND THE INCOME STATEMENT

Preparing the Balance Sheet

Exhibit 2-4 summarizes the changes that will take place in each of the Schaefer Corporation balance sheet accounts. The beginning balance in an account plus the increases, less the decreases, equals the ending balance. The column marked "Debits" includes the *increases to the asset accounts* as well as the *decreases to the equity accounts*. The column marked "Credits" includes the *decreases to the asset accounts* and the *increases to the equity accounts*.

The revenue and expense accounts are *not* reported on a balance sheet. They have been included in Exhibit 2-4 (which is a worksheet, not a balance sheet) to emphasize that revenues increase retained earnings and expenses decrease them. (The minus sign to the left of an expense in the exhibit indicates a decrease in retained earnings, not a decrease in the expense.)

A balance sheet as of April 30 can be prepared directly from the column in Exhibit 2-4 marked "Balance, April 30." Exhibit 2-5 presents such a balance sheet.

Preparing a Statement of Income

The statement of income indicates the changes in owners' equity attributable to the operations of the enterprise. It excludes contributions and withdrawals of the owners.

The statement of income may be prepared by summarizing the transactions that affect retained earnings (excluding any dividends). In our illustration, these transactions have been conveniently set forth in Exhibit 2-4. An income statement, such as that presented in Exhibit 2-6, can be prepared by recasting the entries to retained earnings. For most firms, a worksheet of the type in Exhibit 2-4 would be inadequate to accommodate all of the transactions of an accounting period. A more efficient means of keeping track of transactions is set forth in the following chapter.

EXHIBIT 2-4

The Schaefer Corporation
Changes in Accounts in April 1993

	Balance, March 31	Changes during Month Debits*		Changes during Month Credits*		Balance, April 30
Assets						
Cash	$ 45,300	+ $ 32,000	(12)	– $106,000	(11)	
		+ 68,000	(14)	– 30,000	(15)	$ 16,540
		+ 10,100	(19)	– 500	(17)	
				– 2,360	(18)	
Marketable securities	10,000			– 10,000	(19)	0
Accounts receivable		+ 112,000	(12)	– 68,000	(14)	44,000
Merchandise inventory	40,000	+ 110,000	(10)	– 90,000	(13)	60,000
Prepaid insurance	3,600			– 300	(16)	3,300
Utility deposit	600					600
Organization costs	6,000			– 100	(21)	5,900
Land	50,000					50,000
Buildings	120,000			– 500	(20)	119,500
Equipment	28,000			– 467	(20)	27,533
Total assets, and debits and credits involving assets	$303,500	$332,100		$308,227		$327,373
Equities						
Wages and salaries payable				+ $ 4,000	(15)	$ 4,000
Accounts payable	$ 49,500	– $106,000	(11)	+ 110,000	(10)	53,500
Note payable (current)	24,000	– 2,000	(18)			22,000
Note payable (noncurrent)	50,000					50,000
Common stock outstanding	180,000					180,000
Retained earnings†						
Sales revenue				+ 144,000	(12)	
Interest revenue				+ 100	(19)	
Cost of goods sold		– 90,000	(13)			
Wages and salary expense		– 34,000	(15)			
Insurance expense		– 300	(16)			17,873
Interest expense		– 500	(17)			
		– 360	(18)			
Depreciation expense		– 967	(20)			
Amortization expense		– 100	(21)			
Total equities, and debits and credits involving equities	$303,500	$234,227		$258,100		$327,373
Total debits and credits during April		$566,327‡		$566,327‡		

*Debits represent *increases to asset accounts* and *decreases to equity accounts*. Credits represent *decreases to asset accounts* and *increases to equity accounts*.
†The balance as of March 31 in retained earnings for the Schaefer Corporation is zero; the company has not yet begun operations and therefore does not yet have earnings.
‡The sum of the debits equals the sum of the credits, as it must if no error has been made.

THE STATEMENT OF CASH FLOWS

The third primary financial statement is the statement of cash flows. The statement of cash flows, as its title implies, reports on changes in the cash position during a period of time. It tells how a company acquired cash and what it did with it. It accounts for the difference between the cash on hand at the beginning of a period and that on hand at the end.

Cash is an asset that is of special concern in assessing a corporation's fiscal

EXHIBIT 2-5

The Schaefer Corporation
Balance Sheet
As of April 30, 1993

Assets		Equities	
Current		Liabilities	
Cash	$ 16,540	Current	
Accounts receivable	44,000	Accounts payable	$ 53,500
Merchandise inventory	60,000	Wages and salaries payable	4,000
Prepaid insurance	3,300	Note payable	22,000
Total, current	$123,840	Total current	$ 79,500
Noncurrent		Noncurrent	
Utility deposit	600	Note payable	50,000
Organization costs	5,900	Total liabilities	$129,500
Land	50,000	Owners' equity	
Buildings	119,500	Common stock outstanding	180,000
Equipment	27,533	Retained earnings	17,873
Total, noncurrent	$203,533	Total owners' equity	$197,873
Total assets	$327,373	Total equities	$327,373

EXHIBIT 2-6

The Schaefer Corporation
Income Statement
Month Ended April 30, 1993

Revenues	
Sales revenue	$144,000
Interest revenue	100
Total revenue	$144,100
Expenses	
Cost of goods sold	90,000
Wages and salaries	34,000
Insurance expense	300
Interest expense	860
Depreciation	967
Amortization of organization costs	100
Total expenses	$126,227
Net income	$ 17,873

health and performance. It is the objective of a corporation to generate cash. Owners contribute cash to an enterprise with the intention of eventually withdrawing more than they put in. Cash is the asset required to meet day-to-day operating costs, to pay interest and dividends, and to satisfy debts. Consequently, the Financial Accounting Standards Board has stipulated that *prediction* of cash flows is one of the primary purposes of financial accounting.

Distinction between Income and Cash Flow

As is evident from our illustration, the statement of income does not provide information on cash flows. As shown in Exhibit 2-6, the Schaefer Company would report income for April of $17,873. However, as shown in the schedule in Exhibit 2-4 the beginning-of-the-month cash balance was $45,300; the ending balance was $16,540. Cash *decreased* by $28,760.

The reasons for the difference between cash flow and income are apparent from an analysis of how different events affected each. Some events that affected owners' equity (and thus income) had no impact on cash. Other events affected cash but had no impact on income. To cite but a few examples:

- *Entry 11.* The company paid suppliers. This transaction reduced cash but did not affect owners' equity. Owners' equity was reduced only when the company sold the goods acquired (entry 13).
- *Entry 12.* The company sold merchandise. The sale increased owners' equity by the full amount of the sale, but cash was increased only as it was collected. In entry 14, the company collected a portion of its receivables from customers, but the increase in cash had no impact on owners' equity.
- *Entry 16.* The company recorded the expiration of a portion of its insurance policy. This decreased owners' equity, but the cash payment for the policy had been recorded the previous month.
- *Entry 20.* The company depreciated its building and equipment. The depreciation reduced owners' equity but not cash.

It is not uncommon for firms, especially new businesses, to experience severe cash crises, even while reporting substantial earnings. For example, a firm that has developed an innovative product may expand rapidly to meet expected demand. It may face significant cash outflows in acquiring plant, equipment, and inventory, in advertising, and in training. It may experience delays in collecting from its customers. Thus, even though its long-term prospects may be bright, it may be unable to meet its current obligations.

Preparing a Statement of Cash Flows

The statement of cash flows is conceptually simple. It is a summary of cash receipts and disbursements—all of the transactions that affect the cash account. The transactions are classified into three groups:

1. *Operating activities.* These include the firm's production, selling, and administrative activities.
2. *Investing activities.* These encompass the purchase and sale of marketable securities, plant and equipment, and the payment and collection of loans to others.
3. *Financing activities.* These incorporate the issuance and retirement of stocks and bonds and the payment of dividends.

The Schaefer Corporation's statement of cash flows for April is presented in Exhibit 2-7. As can be seen, the statement encompasses each of the entries to the cash account in the Exhibit 2-4 worksheet.

The statement of cash flows will be discussed further in Chapters 3 and 4, and in detail in Chapter 14 (when most readers can be expected to grasp more easily its technical aspects). But even here it may be useful, for our very simple Schaefer Corporation case, to *reconcile* Schaefer's cash flow from operations shown in Exhibit 2-7 (a *decline* in cash of $36,760) with its *positive* income of $17,873 (per Exhibit 2-6). The reconciliation helps to explain how

EXHIBIT 2-7

Schaefer Corporation
Statement of Cash Flows
Month Ended April 30, 1993

Cash Flow from Operating Activities	
Collections from customers	$ 100,000
Receipt of interest from marketable securities	100
Payments to suppliers	(106,000)
Payment of wages and salaries	(30,000)
Payment of interest	(860)
Net cash used for operating activities	$(36,760)
Cash Flow from Investing Activities	
Sale of marketable securities	$ 10,000
Cash Flow from Financing Activities	
Repayment of loan	$(2,000)
Net decrease in cash	$(28,760)

Schaefer's performance could appear so strong when measured by income, yet so weak when evaluated by cash flow.

Exhibit 2-8 reconciles income and cash flow from operations in the so-called indirect format. It is ''indirect'' because it accounts for the differences in terms of changes in *assets* and *liabilities*.

The reconciling items reinforce the point that every revenue and expense is associated with a change in an asset or liability. They can be explained as follows:

- Long-lived assets decreased because the company depreciated its buildings and equipment and amortized its organization costs. Depreciation and amortization were charged as expenses, but did not require an outlay of cash. They reduced net income (and, correspondingly, long-lived assets), but not cash.
- Accounts receivable increased because the company's sales to customers were greater than its collections from them. Therefore, revenue from sales (and hence income) was greater than cash flow.
- Prepayments decreased because the company consumed a portion of its prepaid insurance, for which it had paid in cash in a previous period. The consumption of the prepaid insurance is similar in concept to the consumption of long-lived assets in that it results in an expense, but not an outlay of cash.

EXHIBIT 2-8

Schaefer Corporation
Reconciliation of Net Income with Cash from Operations
Month Ended April 30, 1993

Net Income	$ 17,873
Add:	
(Increase) Decrease in long-lived assets	1,067
(Increase) Decrease in accounts receivable	(44,000)
(Increase) Decrease in prepayments	300
(Increase) Decrease in merchandise inventory	(20,000)
Increase (Decrease) in accounts payable	4,000
Increase (Decrease) in wages and salaries payable	4,000
Cash Flow from Operations	$(36,760)

- Merchandise inventory increased because the company purchased more inventory than it sold. The sale of the inventory was recorded as an expense (cost of goods sold), but the purchase of inventory resulted in an increase in accounts payable, not an expense (and hence not a decrease in income).
- Accounts payable increased because the company's payments to suppliers (for merchandise inventory) were less than its purchases. During the month the company purchased $110,000 in merchandise and paid for $106,000. In contrast, it sold merchandise with a cost of only $90,000. The difference between the expense (cost of goods sold) and cash paid was $16,000—the net of the $20,000 increase in merchandise inventory and the $4,000 increase in accounts payable.
- Wages and salaries payable increased because the company charged more as wage and salary expense than it actually paid its employees.

STATEMENTS OF CHANGES IN RETAINED EARNINGS AND OTHER OWNERS' EQUITY ACCOUNTS

If a firm has engaged in transactions with its owners, then neither the balance sheet nor the income statement may fully explain the changes in owners' equity accounts. Two other statements can be used to supplement the income statement and the balance sheet: *a statement of changes in retained earnings* and *a statement of changes in other owners' equity accounts*. Both provide a reconciliation of the beginning and ending balances in the accounts to which they pertain.

Statement of Changes in Retained Earnings

The statement of changes in retained earnings (Exhibit 2-9) is the link between the income statement and the balance sheet. The basic accounting equation can be expanded to show the two components of owners' equity:

Owner's equity

Assets – Liabilities = Capital contributed by owners + Retained earnings

Retained earnings are the sum of the earnings of the accounting periods that the company has been in existence less the amounts paid as dividends to stockholders. The retained earnings per the balance sheet at the beginning of the period (which, of course, must be identical to those at the end of the previous period), plus the income for that period per the income statement, less any dividends declared during the period, equal the retained earnings at the end of the period:

Retained earnings, balance at beginning of year + Income

– Dividends declared = Retained earnings, balance at end of year

Retained Earnings Contrasted to Assets

Retained earnings *do not* represent resources of the firm. Retained earnings per se cannot be distributed to stockholders. They cannot be used to purchase goods or services. Only cash or other assets are media of exchange. Retained earnings are nothing more than what remains after liabilities and other owners' equity accounts are subtracted from total assets. Retained earnings may be

EXHIBIT 2-9

Schaefer Corporation
Statement of Changes in
Retained Earnings
Month Ended April 30, 1993

Balance, April 1, 1993	$ 0
Net income for April 1993	17,873
	17,873
Less: Dividends declared	1,200
Balance, April 30, 1993	$16,673

interpreted as a residual claim against assets—what is left for the owners after all liabilities and claims represented by other owners' equity accounts have been satisfied. However, *there is no specific relationship between particular assets and particular claims*. The existence of retained earnings in no way implies the availability of cash for distributions to stockholders or for other corporate purposes. Moreover, the stated values of assets are not necessarily indicative of the amounts for which the assets could be sold if the business were dissolved. Hence retained earnings are unlikely to show the value of cash or other assets that may remain for stockholders.

Dividends

Dividends are distributions of the assets of the enterprise to its owners. The asset distributed most often is cash, but it could, in fact, be any asset of the firm. As the assets of the firm are reduced upon distribution to the owners, so also are the claims of the owners against such assets.

Statement of Changes in Other Owners' Equity Accounts

The statement of changes in other owners' equity accounts reports changes in a firm's capital structure. It indicates the increases or decreases in capital accounts that result when a firm issues or retires common stock or preferred stock. Firms may issue new stock to raise funds to expand the scale of operations, to compensate employees under stock option plans, and to acquire new businesses. They may retire stock to decrease the size of the company, to reduce the number of shareholders (e.g., to eliminate the interest of shareholders who are not members of a controlling group), and to alter their capital structures (e.g., to change proportions of common and preferred stock). The statement of changes in other owners' equity accounts reconciles the beginning and ending balances in the various accounts, other than retained earnings, that compose the owners' equity section of the balance sheet.

In practice, the statements of changes in retained earnings and in other owners' equity accounts take several forms. Often the two statements are combined into a single statement. Sometimes, particularly if there are no changes in accounts other than retained earnings, the reconciliation of retained earnings is included as part of the statement of income.

Suppose that during April, Schaefer Corporation declares dividends of $1 per share. Since there are 1,200 shares of stock outstanding, total dividends are $1,200. The dividends are paid in cash. The effect on the accounting equation is then

Increase

$$\Delta A \quad = \quad \Delta L \quad + \quad \Delta OE$$

$$\downarrow \qquad\qquad\qquad\qquad\qquad \downarrow$$

Cash	Retained earnings
$-\$1,200$	(dividends)
	$-\$1,200$

Decrease

The statement of changes in retained earnings would appear as presented in Exhibit 2-9.

If the dividend transaction were recorded in April, along with the other transactions of the month, then in the balance sheet presented in Exhibit 2-5 both cash and retained earnings would have been reduced by $1,200.

The amount shown as the ending balance in Exhibit 2-9 would be the balance in retained earnings on the April 30, 1993, balance sheet. The balance sheet presented in Exhibit 2-5 does not incorporate the dividend transaction; hence retained earnings (and, correspondingly, cash) are greater by $1,200, the amount of the dividend.

Exhibit 2-10 shows one form of the statement of changes in other owners' equity accounts. It assumes that the 1,200 shares of common stock issued in March have a par value of $150 and are issued "at par." It further assumes that in April the Schaefer Corporation issues an additional 500 shares of common stock, this time at a price of $160, which is $10 above par. Moreover, in April the company also issues 700 shares of preferred stock. The par value of the preferred stock is $100. It is issued at $102, for a total of $71,400.

EXHIBIT 2-10

Schaefer Corporation
Statement of Changes in Capital Stock
Month Ended April 30, 1993

	Preferred Stock	Common Stock	Additional Paid-in Capital
Balance, April 1, 1993	$ 0	$180,000	$ 0
Shares issued in April			
Common stock (500			
shares, par value, $150)		75,000	5,000
Preferred stock (700			
shares, par value, $100)	70,000		1,400
Balance, April 30, 1993	$70,000	$255,000	$6,400

Summary

In this chapter we have presented an overview of the three primary financial statements—the *balance sheet* (also called the statement of financial position), the *income statement,* and the *statement of cash flows.* We also considered two secondary statements, the *statement of changes in retained earnings* and the *statement of changes in other owners' equity accounts.* The chapter is intended to familiarize you with the purposes of each statement, with its basic format, and with the terminology conventionally employed.

The key to understanding both the balance sheet and the income statement is the accounting equation:

$$\text{Assets} = \text{Liabilities} + \text{Owners' equity}$$

The balance sheet is nothing more than an expression of the accounting equation. It lists the assets, the liabilities, and various classifications of owners' equity as of a particular date. A main theme of this chapter is that *all* accounting transactions have an impact on the accounting equation and thus on the balance sheet.

The income statement reports the changes in the retained earnings component of owners' equity, excluding dividends, during a period of time. It lists the revenues (increases in retained earnings) and the expenses (decreases in retained earnings). The difference between the revenues and expenses is the *income* for the period.

The statement of cash flows sets forth the changes in cash during a period. Cash, although accounted for and reported like other assets on the balance sheet, is of particular importance in evaluating the fiscal health of a corporation. It is the medium of exchange in our society. Indeed it is a primary objective of a corporation to generate cash.

The statement of changes in retained earnings accounts for the changes in retained earnings during the accounting period. It reconciles retained earnings at the beginning of the period with those at the end. As reflected in the statement, retained earnings are increased by net income and decreased by dividends.

The statement of changes in other owners' equity accounts reports on changes in a firm's capital structure. It indicates the increases or decreases in the capital stock accounts when a firm issues or retires its common or preferred stock.

Exercises for Review and Self-Testing

(The solutions to this exercise—and similar exercises in other chapters—will be found following the last problem in the chapter.)

1. A group of entrepreneurs forms a corporation. Together the owners contribute to the enterprise $100,000 cash. To provide evidence of their investment, the corporation issues to them 10,000 shares of common stock, assigning to each share a par value of $10.
   a. What are the total assets of the corporation immediately after it has been formed?
   b. What are the total equities of the corporation? That is, what are the total claims of the owners against these assets?
2. The corporation borrows $50,000 from a bank.
   a. What are the total assets of the corporation now?
   b. What are the total claims against these assets? Of these total claims (equities), how much are claims of outsiders (liabilities)? How much are the residual claims of the owners?
3. The company acquires an automobile for $10,000 cash.
   a. What are the total assets of the corporation?
   b. What are the corporation's liabilities? Its owners' equity?
4. The company acquires 300 units of inventory at a cost of $5 per unit. The purchase is made ''on account,'' with the firm promising to pay for the goods within 30 days.
   a. What are the total assets of the corporation now?
   b. What are the corporation's liabilities? Its owners' equity?

5. The firm sells 100 of the units of inventory for $7 per unit. The purchasers pay cash.
   a. What are the total assets of the corporation?
   b. What are the corporation's liabilities? Its owners' equity?
6. By how much has the equity of the owners increased since they made their initial contribution of cash? How much "better off" is the corporation (and thus its owners) since the owners made their contribution? What was the "income" of the corporation during the period in which the transactions took place?

Questions for Review and Discussion

1. Explain why the balance sheet of a firm might be dated "*as of* December 31, 1993," but the income statement is dated "*for the year ended* December 31, 1993."
2. What is meant by owners' equity? Why is owners' equity not necessarily indicative of the amount of cash that would be returned to the owners if the assets of a business were to be sold and the creditors paid the amounts owed to them?
3. A bookkeeper recently totaled up the recorded assets of a firm and found that they came to $1,398,576. The total liabilities came to $600,000 and the total owners' equity to $800,000. Are such totals possible in the context of the double-entry bookkeeping process if no error has been made? Suppose instead that assets were equal to liabilities plus owners' equity. Do such totals assure that no accounting errors have been made?
4. Which of the following events will be recognized on the books of United Electric Co.?
   a. The firm signs a three-year contract with its union.
   b. The firm issues 1,000 additional shares of common stock.
   c. An officer of United Electric sells on the open market 3,000 shares of company stock from her personal holdings.
   d. The passage of another year has reduced the remaining useful life of plant and equipment.
   e. The wholesale price of copper wire has *increased*. United Electric Co. has 100,000 feet of copper wire in inventory.
   f. The wholesale price of copper wire has *decreased*. United Electric Co. has 100,000 feet of copper wire in inventory.
5. Included among a firm's noncurrent assets are "unamortized corporate organizational costs, $25,000." What is meant by such an asset? Is it possible to sell such an asset? If not, why is it considered an asset?
6. The same firm has recorded among its current liabilities "advances from customers, $3,000." Why is such an amount a liability? What impact did receipt of the $3,000 have on the accounting equation?
7. A company reported substantial earnings for the last several years, yet it is about to file for bankruptcy. How is such a situation possible?
8. A firm recently received a check from a customer for $10,000, yet it did not record such amount as revenue. What are two possible reasons why cash received is not revenue?
9. A firm recently purchased equipment for $80,000 yet did not record an expense. Why not? Will the amount paid ever be reported as an expense? When?
10. What is meant by a *current asset*? How is it possible that shares of the common stock of XYZ Company owned by one company may be recorded as a current asset but those owned by another may be recorded as a noncurrent asset?
11. What is meant by *preferred stock*? What preferences do preferred stockholders have over common stockholders? What rights do common stockholders have that preferred stockholders generally do not have?

12. What are *extraordinary items*? Why are they reported on the income statement apart from ordinary operating revenues and expenses?
13. Is it possible for a firm to have a substantial balance in retained earnings and still be unable to declare a cash dividend? Why?

Problems

1. *Balance sheet accounts indicate the value assigned to resources or obligations as of a particular point in time. Income statement accounts provide information on inflows and outflows of resources during a particular period of time.*

   Some accounts are reported on the balance sheet; others are reported on the income statement. For each of the accounts indicated below, specify whether it would ordinarily be reported on the income statement or on the balance sheet.
   a. Sales revenue I
   b. Accounts receivable B
   c. Insurance expense I
   d. Prepaid insurance B
   e. Inventories B
   f. Cost of goods sold I
   g. Depreciation expense I
   h. Accumulated depreciation I ⟵ ?
   i. Interest expense I
   j. Notes payable B
   k. Retained earnings B
   l. Investment in subsidiary B ⟵ ?

2. *Account titles generally provide an indication of whether the account represents a "stock" (and is thereby reported on the balance sheet) or a "flow" (and is thereby reported on the income statement).*

   From the following account balances, taken from the books and records of the Julie Company as of December 31, 1993, prepare an income statement and a balance sheet. Title and date the statements as appropriate, and, insofar as the information permits, separate assets and liabilities into current and noncurrent classifications.

Cash	$18,000
A. Julie, capital	51,600
Sales	75,000
Cost of goods sold	52,000
Prepaid insurance	1,000
Advances from customers	3,000
Patents	8,000
Depreciation expense	2,500
Insurance expense	2,000
Interest revenue	500
Prepaid interest	200
Interest payable	600
Accounts receivable	10,000
Inventory	9,000
Rent expense	6,000
Advertising expense	5,000
Notes payable (due in three years)	8,000
Buildings and equipment	26,000
Notes receivable	10,000
Accounts payable	19,000

3. *All transactions increase or decrease the balances in some combination of asset, liability, and owners' equity accounts.*

For each of the following transactions, indicate whether assets (*A*), liabilities (*L*), or owners' equity (*OE*) would increase (+) or decrease (−). The first transaction is illustrated for you.

a. A corporation issues common stock in exchange for cash. (*A* +; *OE* +)

A + OE + b. It issues preferred stock in exchange for a building.

A + L + c. It purchases inventory, giving the seller a 30-day note for the amount of the merchandise.

A + L − d. It collects from a customer the amount the customer owed on goods purchased several months earlier.

?e. It exchanges shares of preferred stock for shares of common stock.

L − OE + f. It repays bondholders by issuing to them shares of common stock.

A − OE + g. It declares and pays a dividend to stockholders, thereby distributing assets of the company (cash) to the owners.

A − L + h. It returns to a manufacturer defective merchandise for credit on its account.

A − L − OE − i. It receives from a customer defective merchandise and reduces the balance owed by the customer. The merchandise had been sold at a profit. The goods returned have no value.

4. *Assets must equal liabilities plus owners' equity.*

The balances that follow were taken from the balance sheet of a corporation. Arrange a sheet of paper into three columns, each corresponding to a term in the accounting equation:

$$\text{Assets} = \text{Liabilities} + \text{Owners' equity}$$

Place each of the balances in the appropriate column. Total each of the columns to make certain that the equation is in balance.

Marketable securities	$ 20,000
Common stock	100,000
Buildings and equipment	300,000
Bonds payable	250,000
Accounts receivable	90,000
Prepaid rent	15,000
Preferred stock	50,000
Inventories	80,000
Taxes payable	25,000
Advances from customers	3,000
Accounts payable	17,000
Interest payable	8,000
Organization costs	12,000
Retained earnings	64,000

5. *Not all financial events give rise to assets or liabilities. Sometimes, assets or liabilities resulting from contractual arrangements are recognized only upon the performance of either of the parties to the contract.*

Indicate the nature (i.e., descriptive account title) of the assets and liabilities (if any) that would receive accounting recognition on the books of the Utica Company as a result of the following events or transactions:

a. The Utica Co. employs six men to perform routine maintenance work at a rate of $15 per hour. The men work a total of 200 hours. They have not yet been paid.

b. The Utica Co. signs a three-year contract with a security company, which will provide guard service for the company at a cost of $2,000 per month.

c. The security company performs one month's services as promised.

d. The Utica Co. orders machinery and equipment at a cost of $100,000.

e. The machinery and equipment previously ordered are received and installed as agreed upon by the manufacturer.

f. A customer orders 300 units of the company's product at a price of $20 per unit.

g. Utica Co. ships the merchandise previously ordered.

h. Utica Co. borrows $400,000 at an interest rate of 10 percent per year. The company gives the bank a four-year note.

i. One year elapses, and the Utica Co. has paid the bank neither principal nor interest on the note.

j. The Utica Co. guarantees to repair any defective products. During the year it sells 10,000 units of product. It estimates from previous experience that 5 percent of such units will be returned for repair work. It estimates also that the cost of such repairs will be $10 per unit.

6. *Retained earnings may be derived from other balance sheet accounts.*

From the following accounts, taken from the books and records of the Finch Company on December 31, 1993, prepare both an income statement and a balance sheet. Derive the amount of retained earnings.

Cash	$15,000
Accounts payable	12,000
Building and equipment	90,000
Cost of goods sold	60,000
Notes payable	5,000
Wages and salaries payable	3,000
Preferred stock	20,000
Common stock	50,000
Marketable securities	18,000
Inventory	22,000
Sales revenue	88,000
Tax expense	3,000
Taxes payable	1,000
Rent expense	4,000
Prepaid rent	1,000
Retained earnings	?

7. *In the absence of additional contributions by owners, owners' equity is increased by earnings and decreased by dividends and losses.*

The Gail Company was organized as a partnership on January 2, 1993. Each of its two owners contributed $100,000 in cash to start the business. After one year of operations the company had on hand the following assets: cash, $180,000; accounts receivable, $30,000; inventory available for sale, $100,000; furniture and fixtures, $250,000.

The company owed suppliers (i.e., accounts payable) $80,000 and had notes outstanding to a bank (due in 1997) of $160,000.

a. Prepare a balance sheet as of December 31, 1993.

b. Assuming that the owners neither made additional contributions of capital to the business nor made any withdrawals, compute income for 1993.

c. Assume instead that during the year the owners withdrew $40,000 from the business. Compute income for 1993.

8. *Owners' equity equals assets minus liabilities. Owners' equity is affected by income (or loss), capital contributions, and capital withdrawals (dividends).*

Fill in the missing amounts for a company in three *alternative* situations. Assume that there were no capital contributions by owners during 1993. (*Hint:* First compute owners' equity as of December 31, 1993.)

	(a)	(b)	(c)
Assets, December 31, 1993	$100,000	$50,000	?
Liabilities, December 31, 1993	25,000	10,000	$20,000
Owners' equity, January 1, 1993	60,000	?	80,000
Income, 1993	80,000	8,000	5,000
Dividends paid, 1993	?	4,000	10,000

9. *The balance sheet is closely related to the income statement.*

   The balance sheets and income statements of the Ames Corp. for the years ending December 31, 1993 through 1996, are shown in the table following. Also indicated are dividends paid during those years. Some critical figures, however, have been omitted. You are to provide the missing figures. The Ames Corp. began operations on January 1, 1993.

	1993	1994	1995	1996
	Balance Sheet			
Assets				
Cash	$100	$200	$?	$300
Accounts receivable	200	100	300	100
Inventory	350	?	100	100
Building and equipment	600	900	800	400
Liabilities and owners' equity				
Accounts payable	$200	$100	$200	$300
Notes payable	?	600	300	100
Common stock	200	200	200	300
Retained earnings	100	400	?	?
	Income Statement			
Sales	$?	$1,000	$?	$1,200
Cost of goods sold and other operating expenses	500	?	600	?
Net income	?	?	400	300
Dividends paid	$ 0	$ 150	$200	$?

10. *Retained earnings must not be associated with cash or any other specific assets.*

    As of December 31, 1993, the balance sheet of the Morgan Motors Co. appeared as follows (in thousands of dollars):

Cash	$ 85,000
Other current assets	75,000
Other assets, including buildings, land, and equipment	670,000
Total assets	$830,000
Liabilities	$220,000
Common stock (10,000,000 issued and outstanding)	10,000
Retained earnings	600,000
Total equities	$830,000

In 1994 the company had earnings of $40 million. Since there were 10 million shares of common stock outstanding (par value per share, $1.00), earnings per share were $4. In 1994 the company declared no dividends since the directors claimed funds were needed for expansion.

Shortly after the close of the year, the president of the company received a letter from a stockholder protesting the company's refusal to declare a dividend. The letter said in part,

When I studied accounting "retained earnings" were called "surplus." No amount of name changing can obscure the fact that the company has $600 million available for distribution to stockholders.

a. How would you respond to the angry stockholder? Does the company have $600 million available for distribution to stockholders?

b. Suppose the company did declare a dividend of $60 per share ($600 million). What effect would such a dividend most likely have on corporate operations?

c. Does the balance sheet provide assurance that the company could, in fact, declare a dividend of $60 per share even if it wanted to? Why?

d. Suppose that instead of earnings of $40 million the company had a loss of $10 million. The company nevertheless declared a dividend of $2.00 per share. A disgruntled stockholder questioned the decision and wrote to the president: "Dividends are supposed to be distributions of earnings. How is it possible to pay a dividend in a year in which there were no earnings?" How would you respond to his question?

11. *The balance sheet is nothing more than a detailed expression of the accounting equation.*

Arrange a sheet of paper into three columns, each corresponding to a term in the accounting equation:

$$\text{Assets} = \text{Liabilities} + \text{Owners' equity}$$

Indicate the impact that each of the following transactions would have on the accounting equation. Suggest titles for the specific accounts that would be affected.

a. Whitman and Farell form a corporation. The corporation issues 1,000 shares of common stock and sells 500 shares to each of the founders for $3 per share.

b. The corporation borrows $3,000 from a bank, giving the bank a one-year note.

c. The corporation purchases furniture and fixtures for $5,000. The company pays $1,000 cash and gives a six-month note for the balance.

d. The corporation rents a building. It pays, in advance, the first month's rent of $700.

e. The corporation purchases office supplies for $400 cash.

f. The corporation purchases inventory for future sale to customers for $1,200 cash.

Compute the balance in each of the accounts. Summarize the balances in the form of a balance sheet.

12. *Some transactions affect the composition of net assets (assets less liabilities) without affecting the level of net assets. Others increase or decrease the level of net assets—and thereby increase or decrease owners' equity.*

Arrange a sheet of paper into three columns, each corresponding to a term in the accounting equation. Indicate the impact that each of the following transactions would have on the accounting equation. Suggest titles for each of the specific accounts that would be affected.

a. Petrified Products, Inc., purchases furniture and fixtures for $30,000, giving a five-year note.

b. The company purchases "on account" merchandise inventory for $15,000.

c. The firm, realizing that it has purchased an excessive amount of furniture, sells a portion of it. It sells for $3,000 (cash) furniture that had initially cost $3,000.

d. The firm sells an additional amount of furniture. It sells for $5,000 (cash) furniture that had initially cost $2,000. (Has the "level" of net assets increased as the result of this transaction?)

e. The firm sells for $800 "on account" merchandise inventory that had been purchased for $600.

f. The firm purchases supplies for $300 on account.

g. The firm uses supplies that had originally cost $200.

h. The firm collects $600 of the amount owed to it by customers.

i. The firm pays one month's rent in advance, $400.

j. At the end of one month, the firm wishes to give accounting recognition to the fact that it has occupied the rented premises for the one month paid for in advance.

13. *The beginning balance in an account plus increases and minus decreases in that amount during a period equals the ending balance.*

The table following is a condensed balance sheet of the Withington Corporation as of December 31, 1992. On a sheet of paper, copy the account titles and the initial balances. Leave room for seven additional columns of figures. Label six of the columns Transaction 1, 2, 3, and so on, and the seventh column "Balance, 1/31/93."

Withington Corporation

	Balance 12/31/92	Transaction 1	2	3	4	5	6	Balance 1/31/93
Cash	$ 40,000							
Accounts receivable	25,000							
Inventory	57,000	+8,000						
Prepaid rent	2,000							
Equipment	85,000							
Building	200,000							
	$409,000							
Accounts payable	$ 19,000	+8,000						
Wages payable	4,000							
Notes payable	38,000							
Bonds payable	150,000							
Common stock	45,000							
Retained earnings	153,000							
	$409,000							

The following six transactions take place in January. Indicate the effect that each will have on the balance sheet. Summarize the effects of the six transactions on the December 31, 1992, balance by adding across the rows, and indicate the new balance in the column marked "Balance, 1/31/93."

a. The company purchases inventory on account, $8,000. (Transaction 1 is done for you.)

b. The company purchases equipment for $12,000, giving the seller a two-year note.

c. The company pays its employees the $4,000 owed.

d. The company declares and pays a dividend of $20,000.

e. The company reaches an agreement with its bondholders. In exchange for their bonds, they agree to accept shares of common stock that have a market value of $150,000.

f. The company collects $5,000 that was owed by its customers.

14. *Cash and retained earnings are the most significant assets and equities. The statement of cash flows accounts for changes in cash; the statement of income accounts for the changes (excluding dividends) in retained earnings.*

The accounting equation can be recast so as to emphasize the changes in cash and retained earnings. For each of the transactions described, indicate how it will affect the accounting equation as presented. The first transaction is done for you as an illustration.

a. The company purchases equipment for $70,000 cash.

b. It borrows $30,000 and issues a 60-day note.

c. It purchases inventory for $10,000 and promises to pay for it within 30 days.

d. It purchases inventory for $6,000 cash.

e. It purchases a building for $100,000 cash at the beginning of the year.

f. It records first-year depreciation on the building. The building has a 20-year life.

g. It sells for $5,000 goods that had been carried in inventory at $4,000. The customer agrees to pay within 30 days. (Analyze this transaction in two steps: the increase in the asset received and the decrease in the asset surrendered.)

h. It issues preferred stock for $100,000 cash.

i. It pays a utility bill (not previously recorded) of $1,000.

	Cash +	Other Assets =	Liabilities +	Retained Earnings* +	Other Owners' Equities
a.	− 70	Equipment +70			
b.	+30			+30	
c.		+10	+10		
d.	− 6	+ 6			
e.	−100	−100			
f.		− 5		− 5	
g.		AR +5/−4		+5/−4	
h.	+100				+100
i.	− 1				

15. *Underlying transactions can be reconstructed from a firm's statements of income and cash flow. Preparation of a balance sheet helps assure that all transactions have been accounted for.*

Nuth, Inc., began operations on January 1, 1993. Its statement of changes in cash flow and statement of income for the first year of operations are presented below.

a. Show the effect on the accounting equation of each receipt and disbursement of cash and each revenue and expense. Indicate the specific assets, liabilities, and owners' equities that would be increased or decreased.

Assume that all of the company's sales to customers were on credit (i.e., resulted in creation of accounts receivable). Assume also that the merchandise inventory, the insurance policy, and the buildings and equipment were acquired for cash. By contrast, the wages and salaries and the interest initially resulted in increases in liability accounts (i.e., "wages and salaries payable" and "interest payable"). These obligations were satisfied during the year to the extent indicated on the statement of cash flows.

b. Summarize in the form of a balance sheet the increases and decreases to each of the assets, liabilities, and owners' equities. Be sure that the retained earnings account is equal to reported income and that cash is equal to the net increase in cash.

Nuth, Inc.
Statement of Cash Flows
Year Ended December 31, 1993

Cash Flow from Operating Activities	
Collections from customers	$ 880,000
Payments to suppliers for merchandise inventory purchased	(500,000)
Payment of wages and salaries	(150,000)
Purchase of 2-year insurance policy	(16,000)
Payment of interest	(6,000)
Net from cash operating activities	$208,000
Cash Flow from Investing Activities	
Purchase of building and equipment	$(900,000)
Cash Flow from Financing Activities	
Issuance of stock	$ 600,000
Loan from bank	$ 100,000
Net cash from financing activities	$ 700,000
Net increase in cash	$ 8,000

Nuth, Inc.
Income Statement
Year Ended December 31, 1993

Sales revenues	$950,000
Expenses	
Cost of goods sold	420,000
Wages and salaries	154,000
Insurance expense	8,000
Interest expense	12,000
Depreciation	30,000
Total expenses	$624,000
Net income	$326,000

16. *Transactions that affect income do not necessarily affect cash; those that affect cash do not necessarily affect income.*

A company engaged in the transactions set forth in the schedule that follows. (All dollar amounts are in thousands.)

a. Complete the schedule so as to indicate the impact, if any, that each transaction would have upon (1) cash flow and (2) retained earning. The first two transactions are done for you as examples.

b. Compute the firm's *income* for the period. Compute its *net cash flow*.

	Cash Flow	Retained Earnings
1. The firm purchased merchandise, on account, for $800	$ 0	$ 0
2. It paid its suppliers $680 for the merchandise it purchased.	– 680	0
3. The firm made sales of $750, all of which were on account.		
4. The cost of the merchandise sold was $550.		
5. The firm received $600 from customers in payment on their account.		
6. It purchased a three-year insurance policy. Cost of the policy, paid for in cash, was $30.		
7. The firm gave recognition to the expiration of one-third of the policy.		
8. It borrowed $800 from a bank.		
9. It paid (in cash) $40 interest on the loan.		
10. It purchased plant and equipment for $200 (cash).		
11. It gave recognition to the expiration of one-fifth of the useful life of the equipment.		
12. The firm incurred $380 in wages and salary costs. Of this amount, it paid only $360, with the balance to be paid in the following accounting period.		
Net cash flow		
Net income (impact on retained earnings)		

17. *The three primary financial statements can be derived from transactions as they affect the accounting equation.*

A computer service corporation has just completed its first month of operations. The impact on the accounting equation of all the transactions in which the company engaged is summarized in the schedule that follows. From the information in the schedule prepare

a. An income statement

b. A statement of cash flows

c. A balance sheet

The schedule does not indicate the specific revenues and expenses that caused the increases and decreases in retained earnings. You should be able to determine them, however, from the asset or liability account with which the change in retained earnings is associated. (All dollar amounts are in thousands.)

Assets	=	Liabilities	+	Owners' Equity
1. Cash, +100				Common stock, +100
2. Customer accounts receivable, +90				Retained earnings, +90
3. Cash, +70				
Customer accounts receivable, −70				
4.		Salaries payable, +30		Retained earnings, −30
5. Cash, −25		Salaries payable, −25		
6. Prepaid rent, +15				
Cash, −15				
7. Prepaid rent, −12				Retained earnings, −12
8. Equipment, +80				
Cash, −80				
9. Equipment, −16				Retained earnings, −16

18. *Amounts reported on the statement of cash flows are also reflected on either or both the balance sheet and the income statement.*

The following statement of cash flows is in slightly different form than the one illustrated in the text (Exhibit 2-7). In the statement illustrated there, the specific cash flows associated with income were listed individually. In the statement below, these cash flows are combined into one amount, "net income." Net income is then adjusted for revenues or expenses that did not involve the receipt or disbursement of cash.

Statement of Cash Flows
Year Ended December 31, 1993
(in millions)

Cash Flow from Operating Activities		
Net income		$ 299
Add: Depreciation	$215	
Income taxes charged as an expense but		
not payable until the future	45	
Excess of collections from customers		
over sales	(30)	
Other adjustments to income	17	247
Net from cash operating activities		$ 546
Cash Flow from Investing Activities		
Purchase of buildings and equipment		$(869)
Investments in other companies		(105)
Sale of buildings and equipment (at a gain)		12
Sale of investments (at a loss)		11
Net cash from investing activities		$(951)
Cash Flow from Financing Activities		
Issuance of stock		$ 50
Loan from bank		782
Repayments of debt		(130)
Declaration and payment of dividends		(184)
Net cash from financing activities		$ 518
Net increase in cash		$ 113

For each item on the statement, indicate how it would be reflected on the income statement and the balance sheet. For example, depreciation would be reported as an expense on the income statement and would decrease fixed assets and retained earnings on the balance sheet.

19. *The distinction between income and cash flow is critical. The differences can be accounted for by focusing on the changes in the related balance sheet accounts.*

An income statement and comparative balance sheet for the Todd Company are presented below. The following additional information pertains to financial events that took place during 1993. (All dollar amounts are in thousands.)

- The company purchased equipment (for cash) at a cost of $35,000.
- It sold a parcel of land for $10,000 (cash), the same amount that it had paid for the land.
- It borrowed $15,000.
- It paid cash dividends of $12,000.

Todd Company
Statement of Income
Year Ended December 31, 1993

Sales revenue		$200,000
Expenses		
Cost of goods sold	$100,000	
Wages and salaries	32,000	
Depreciation	15,000	
Rent	10,000	
Interest	6,000	163,000
Net Income		$ 37,000

Todd Company
Statement of Position

	December 31, 1993	December 31, 1992
	(in thousands of dollars)	
Assets		
Current assets		
Cash	$ 20,000	$ 30,000
Accounts receivable	70,000	40,000
Inventory	44,000	39,000
Prepaid rent	5,000	5,000
	$139,000	$114,000
Noncurrent assets		
Land	$ 40,000	$ 50,000
Building	150,000	160,000
Equipment	45,000	15,000
	$235,000	$225,000
Total assets	$374,000	$339,000
Liabilities and owners' equity		
Current liabilities		
Accounts payable	$ 68,000	$ 71,000
Wages payable	4,000	5,000
Interest payable	2,000	3,000
	$ 74,000	$ 79,000
Noncurrent liabilities		
Notes payable	$ 75,000	$ 60,000
Owners' equity	225,000	200,000
Total liabilities and owners' equity	$374,000	$339,000

a. Did the sales of the company exceed its cash collections? By how much? (*Hint:* What balance sheet account would increase when customers increase their indebtedness to the company?)

b. Did the firm's purchases of inventory exceed the amount charged as cost of goods sold? By how much? (*Hint:* Which balance sheet account would be affected by purchases and sales of merchandise?)

c. Did the company's payments to suppliers exceed the amount of purchases? By how much? (*Hint:* In which balance sheet account would amounts owed to suppliers be recorded?)

d. Did the company pay more in wages than it recorded as wage and salary expense? By how much?

e. Did it pay more in interest than it recorded as interest expense?

f. The company reported a depreciation expense of $15,000. Was this expense associated with a decrease in cash? (*Hint:* Consider the impact of depreciation on the components of the accounting equation.)

g. What other transactions increased or decreased cash but had no impact on income?

h. Based on your responses above, complete the following schedule, which explains why the company's cash decreased by $10,000 in the face of $37,000 in reported income.

Net income	$ 37,000
Add: Depreciation (an expense not requiring the use of cash)	
Subtract	
Amount by which sales exceeded collections	
Amount by which purchases of inventory exceeded cost of goods sold	
Amount by which payments to suppliers exceeded purchases	
Amount by which wages paid exceeded wage expense	
Amount by which interest paid exceeded interest expense	
Add or subtract other transactions that affected cash but had no impact on income	
Net decrease in cash	$(10,000)

20. *Information about income, dividends, and new shares issued can be derived from the shareholders' investment section of the balance sheet.*

The following is taken from the owners' equity section of the balance sheet of a manufacturer of trucks and automobile parts and equipment:

	December 31, 1993	December 31, 1992
Common stock, par value $1.00 share		
Authorized 40,000,000 shares		
Issued 12,839,166 and 12,749,128 shares at		
December 31, 1993, and 1992, respectively	$ 12,839,166	$ 12,749,128
Additional paid-in capital	226,807,615	225,144,160
Earnings retained for use in the business	301,611,199	241,679,609
Cost of 630,883 shares of common stock held in		
treasury (deduction)	(15,678,303)	(15,678,303)
Total shareholders' investment	$525,579,677	$463,894,595

The firm's common stock is traded on the New York Stock Exchange. The company reported earnings in 1993 of $88,692,900.

a. What was the total amount of dividends that the company declared in 1993?

b. How many additional shares of common stock did the firm issue in 1993?

c. What was the average amount per share for which the additional shares were issued? (*Hint:* Consider changes in *both* the common stock and the additional paid-in capital accounts.)

d. How many shares of stock were issued *and* outstanding as of December 31, 1993? (Shares of stock that a company holds in its treasury are not considered to be outstanding.)

e. What was the approximate amount of earnings per share in 1993? Earnings per share is the earnings for the year per each share of common stock outstanding (i.e., earnings divided by number of common shares outstanding). Base the computation on number of shares outstanding on December 31, 1993.

Solutions to Exercise for Review and Self-Testing

1. a. Assets = $100,000
   b. Equities = $100,000
2. a. Assets = $150,000
   b. Total equities = $150,000; those of owners = $100,000; those of outsiders = $50,000
3. a. Assets = $150,000 (This transaction decreases ''cash'' and increases ''fixed assets''—i.e., the automobile.)
   b. Liabilities = $50,000; owners' equity = $100,000
4. a. Assets = $151,500
   b. Liabilities = $51,500; owners' equity = $100,000
5. a. Assets = $151,700 ($151,500 per above, plus $700 cash received upon sale, minus $500 of goods surrendered.)
   b. Liabilities = $51,500; owners' equity = $100,200 (The ''level'' of assets increased by $200 as a consequence of the sale of 100 units. Liabilities remained unchanged but the equity of the owners must have increased by $200.)
6. Owners' equity has increased by $200; the company is therefore $200 ''better off,'' and income, a measure of how much better off a company is at the end of a period than at the beginning, is also $200.

3

The Accounting Cycle

The accounting system is a model of logic and order. This chapter introduces the *accounting cycle* (as distinct from the *operating cycle*)—the procedures that lead from the initial recognition of a financial event to the preparation of financial statements. It explains the relationships among the various accounts that appear on the financial statements. In particular, it demonstrates the tie between the income statement and the balance sheet.

The accounting cycle is described in terms of conventional books and records. In firms in which the accounting system is computerized, the books and records may not take the physical forms suggested by the descriptions in this chapter. Data may be scattered throughout an electronic data bank rather than recorded in neat columns in a journal or ledger. Nevertheless, the underlying principles, the structure of accounts, and the final products (the financial statements) are virtually the same, irrespective of whether the system is maintained manually or electronically.

LEDGER ACCOUNTS

The basic accounting equation—assets = liabilities + owners' equity—or the slightly expanded equation—assets = liabilities + capital contributed by owners + retained earnings—serves as the basis for all accounting transactions. In theory, all accounting transactions that affect a business could be recorded in a single ledger (a book of accounts), derived from the basic equation. Changes in assets would be indicated on the left-hand side of the page; changes in liabilities or owners' equity would be indicated on the right.

Example

1. The CDE Company issues capital stock for $25,000 cash. (An asset, *cash*, is increased; owners' equity, *common stock*, is increased.)
2. The company purchases furniture and fixtures for $10,000 on account. (An asset, *furniture and fixtures*, is increased; a liability, *accounts payable*, is increased.)
3. The company purchases merchandise for $7,000 cash. (An asset, *merchandise*, is increased; an asset, *cash*, is decreased.)
4. The company pays $5,000 of the amount it owes on account. (An asset, *cash*, is decreased; a liability, *accounts payable*, is decreased.)

CDE Company
General Ledger

Assets		Liabilities and Owners' Equity	
1. Cash (asset +)	+ $25,000	**1.** Common stock (owners' equity +)	+ $25,000
2. Furniture and fixtures (asset +)	+ 10,000	**2.** Accounts payable (liability +)	+ 10,000
3. Merchandise (asset +)	+ 7,000		
Cash (asset −)	− 7,000		
4. Cash (asset −)	− 5,000	**4.** Accounts payable (liability −)	− 5,000
	$30,000		$30,000

The ledger indicates that after the fourth transaction, the firm has assets of $30,000 and liabilities and owners' equity of the same amount. The ledger reveals that the accounts are "in balance" (they would have to be unless an error was made), and it indicates the total assets and the total liabilities and owners' equity. But by itself it provides little information that is useful to either managers or owners. Since each side of the ledger page combines changes in more than one account, the balance in any particular account is not readily available. To find the amount of cash on hand, for example, one would have to search the entire page (or entire book if there were numerous transactions) for all entries affecting cash. How much more convenient it would be if a separate page were provided for each account. Thus

CDE Company
General Ledger

	Cash				Furniture and fixtures	
(1)	25,000	(3)	7,000	(2)	10,000	
		(4)	5,000			

	Merchandise				Accounts payable	
(3)	7,000			(4)	5,000	(2)	10,000

	Common stock	
	(1)	25,000

In the illustration each of the "T"'s represents a separate page in the general ledger, or book of accounts. There is a separate page or "T account" for cash, furniture and fixtures, accounts payable, etc.

An *increase* in an *asset* account is recorded on the *left* side of the ledger page or T account; a *decrease* in an asset account is recorded on the *right* side.

Conversely, an *increase* in a *liability* or *owners' equity* account is recorded on the *right* side of the ledger page or T account: a *decrease* in a *liability* or *owners' equity* account is recorded on the *left* side.

In other words entries to the *left* are the *debits,* those to the *right* are the *credits*. The balance in an account at any particular time can be determined by subtracting the amounts recorded on one side from those recorded on the other. The convention of recording increases in assets on the left side of the account and increases in liabilities and owners' equity on the right may be related directly to the accounting equation (assets = liabilities + owners' equity) in which assets appear to the left of the equal sign and liabilities and owners' equity to the right.

JOURNAL ENTRIES

Each T account represents a separate page in a book of accounts called the *general ledger*. Since transactions affect two or more accounts, each transaction must be recorded on two or more pages. No one page will contain a complete record of the transaction; at best it will indicate only one-half of the transaction. To maintain a comprehensive history of all transactions that affect the various accounts, firms maintain a *journal*—a book that serves as the source of many of the entries to the various accounts. *Journal entries* are ordinarily prepared from source documents, such as *invoices* (bills), *payment vouchers* (internal documents authorizing disbursements), *receiving* or *shipping reports, remittance advices* (documents indicating the receipt of cash), and *credit memoranda* (documents authorizing that a customer be given credit for merchandise damaged or returned or special allowances or discounts to which he or she may be entitled).

The use of journals and journal entries is easily illustrated. For instance, the purchase of merchandise for $7,000 necessitates that a debit entry be made to the merchandise account and a credit entry be made to the cash account. The journal is a convenient place to indicate both accounts affected by the transaction. At the time of purchase, the firm would record the following in the journal:

Debit: Merchandise	$7,000	
Credit: Cash	$7,000	

The words *debit* and *credit* are conventionally omitted from the entry and debits are distinguished from credits merely by the placement of the account titles and amounts. The account to be debited is placed along the left-hand margin, and that to be credited is indented slightly. Similarly, the amount to be debited is shown slightly to the left of that to be credited. A brief explanation is often indicated beneath the entry, and the entry is numbered or lettered to facilitate referencing. Thus

(1)

Merchandise $7,000
    Cash. $7,000
To record the purchase of merchandise

The amounts indicated in the journal would be posted to or recorded in the appropriate ledger accounts either at the time the transaction is recorded in the journal or, if more convenient, after a number of transactions have been recorded.

Some simple transactions can be used to illustrate the relationship between entries in the journal and those in the various ledger accounts. In this and in several subsequent examples the nature of the account (asset, liability, owners' equity) and whether it has increased (+) or decreased (−) may be indicated in parentheses next to each journal entry. This is done for pedagogical purposes. In practice, these explanatory notations are omitted.

Example

B. Heller, an electronics specialist, decides to establish a microcomputer repair service. He signs a lease on a store.

1. He takes $50,000 of his personal funds and deposits them in a checking account in the name of "Heller Computer Service."
2. He purchases tools and test equipment for $25,000. He gives a two-year note for the full amount.
3. He purchases parts for $15,000. He pays $10,000 cash and receives 30-days' credit for the balance.
4. He pays rent in advance for the first three months, $1,000 per month.

The *journal entries* that record these transactions include the following:

(1)

Cash in bank (asset +)...$50,000
    B. Heller, invested
        capital (owners' equity +) $50,000
To record the initial contribution of cash

(2)

Tools and equipment
    (asset +) $25,000
        Notes payable (liability +)......................................$25,000
To record the purchase of tools and equipment

(3)

Parts inventory (asset +)..$15,000
    Cash (asset −)...$10,000
    Accounts payable (liability +)...................................$ 5,000
To record the purchase of the parts

(Note that a journal entry can consist of more than one debit or credit.) The account "notes payable" is used to record a liability when a written note is given by the borrower. When short-term trade credit is accepted, the liability is recorded as an "account payable."

(4)

Prepaid rent (asset +) $3,000
    Cash (asset −)...$3,000
To record the rent paid in advance

"Prepaid rent" represents the right to use the store for three months. It is a current asset—one that will be "written off," or *amortized,* as it expires over the three-month period.

    The journal entries would be *posted* to the various ledger accounts:

Assets	Liabilities and Owners' Equity

Cash in bank		Accounts payable	B. Heller, invested capital
(1) 50,000	**(3)** 10,000 **(4)** 3,000	**(3)** 5,000	**(1)** 50,000

Tools and equipment	Notes payable
(2) 25,000	**(2)** 25,000

Parts inventory
(3) 15,000

Prepaid rent
(4) 3,000

If a balance sheet were to be prepared after the four transactions had been journalized and posted, then it would be necessary to determine and summarize the balances in each account. The balance in each account can be calculated by subtracting the total credits from the total debits. Thus the balance in the "Cash in bank" account is $50,000 minus the sum of $10,000 and $3,000, or $37,000.

A balance sheet for the business is presented in Exhibit 3-1.

EXHIBIT 3-1

Heller Computer Service
Balance Sheet
As of December 31, 1993

Assets			Liabilities and Owners' Equity		
Current assets			Current liabilities		
Cash in bank	$37,000		Accounts payable	$ 5,000	
Parts inventory	15,000		Noncurrent liabilities		
Prepaid rent	3,000	$55,000	Notes payable	25,000	$30,000
Noncurrent assets			Owners' equity		
Tools and			B. Heller,		
equipment		25,000	invested capital		50,000
			Total liabilities and		
Total assets		$80,000	owners' equity		$80,000

SPECIAL PROBLEMS OF ACCOUNTING FOR REVENUES AND EXPENSES

Transactions versus Economic Events

Revenues are the inflows of net assets from delivering or producing goods; expenses are the related outflows. Both revenues and expenses can result from transactions as well as from economic events *other than* transactions.

A *transaction* is an exchange of one item for another between the accounting entity and another party. Examples of transactions are purchases of inventory and equipment, sales of goods or services, collection of accounts receivable, issuance and repayment of debt. An *economic event* is any occurrence that affects a firm's financial well-being. Economic events include but are not limited to transactions. They *differ* from transactions because of *prepayments* and *accruals*. An earthquake that destroys a company's plant is an economic event but not a transaction. So too is the passage of time. Passage of time deteriorates a firm's assets, enables it to earn rent from a tenant, and causes it to owe interest on a loan.

The record-keeping process of accounting entities is quite naturally dominated by transactions. Transactions create financial documents such as checks and invoices, which trigger entries into journals. Other economic events, by contrast, may not be accompanied by comparable physical or electronic evidence. Often, as with depreciation, they are tied to transactions that may have taken place in the distant past (e.g., when an asset was acquired). They will not routinely be signaled by day-to-day business operations. Therefore they must be recognized by special entries, ones that are typically made either periodically (at the end of each month) or whenever financial statements are to be prepared.

The Issue of Recognition

Central to almost all issues of accounting are two intertwined questions:

1. What types of events should cause revenues and expenses to be recognized?
2. When should the revenues and expense be recognized?

As will be illustrated in this and subsequent chapters, the recognition of revenues and expense is *not* governed primarily by the receipt or disbursement of cash. If it were, income could easily be manipulated. Companies could postpone purchases of inventories and equipment or delay the payment of wages, interest, and rent. Instead, revenues and expenses are recognized when critical events take place. Examples of critical events that typically give rise to revenues and expenses are the *sale* of goods or services (not the collection of cash from customers), the *delivery* of merchandise to customers (not the acquisition of the merchandise or payment for it), the *performance* of services by employees (not the payment of wages), and the *use* of borrowed funds or rented premises (not the payment for them).

The recognition of a revenue or expense (and the related receivable or payable) as a result of an economic event other than a cash transaction involves a difference in *timing* between *revenue earned* and *cash received*, and/or *expense incurred* and *expenditure paid*. There may be an *initial prepayment*, and then a subsequent *earning* or *expensing* of that prepayment in another period. Or there may be an *initial accrual*, and then the *subsequent payment* in another period of what is owed. The modern accounting system is said, in a general sense, to be on an *accrual* basis, as distinguished from a *cash* basis.

Revenues and expenses are reported on the income statement but are, in essence, subaccounts of retained earnings. The next section will illustrate how common revenues and expenses are recorded. It will also demonstrate how, at the end of an accounting period, the balances in the revenue and expense accounts get transferred to retained earnings.

THE ACCOUNTING CYCLE

There are nine basic steps to the accounting cycle. We shall illustrate these using the Hawthorne Corporation as an example.

The Hawthorne Corporation was organized on June 1, 1993. The financial events described in this example take place during its first month of operation. The usual accounting cycle is one year, at the end of which a firm will prepare a complete set of financial statements. There is no conceptual reason, however, why the accounting cycle cannot be longer or shorter. To simplify our example, it will be assumed that the accounting cycle of the Hawthorne Corporation is one month.

Step 1: Journalizing the Transactions and Other Financial Events

A first set of financial events engaged in by the Hawthorne Corporation is described and journalized in Exhibit 3-2. These transactions are straightforward. Other than transaction 1, which records the issue of common stock, they have no effect on either the level of net assets or on owners' equity. They result in neither inflows nor outflows of net resources to the business and hence in neither revenues nor expenses.

A second set of transactions is more complex and warrants greater discussion, as we see next.

EXHIBIT 3-2
Hawthorne Corporation, Transactions

The company issues 10,000 shares of stock to its two cofounders for a price of $50 per share, which is received in cash.

(1)

Cash (asset +).....................$500,000
   Common stock (owners' equity +).....$500,000
To record the sale of common stock

The firm issues $100,000 of long-term bonds, payable on June 1, 2018.

(2)

Cash (asset +).....................$100,000
   Bonds payable (liability +)..........$100,000
To record the issue of long-term bonds

The company purchases a building for $300,000. It gives a down payment of $100,000 and a 10-year note for the balance.

(3)

Building (asset +)..................$300,000
   Cash (asset −).....................$100,000
   Notes payable (liability +)............200,000
To record the purchase of the building

The company purchases equipment for $100,000 and incurs installation and transportation costs of $20,000.

(4)

Equipment (asset +)................$120,000
   Cash (asset −).....................$120,000
To record the purchase of equipment

The installation and transportation costs are assumed to be necessary to bring the equipment to a *serviceable* condition; hence they are added to the cost of the equipment.

The firm rents out a portion of its building. It signs a five-year lease. Rent is to be $1,000 per month, and three months' rent is paid in advance. Occupancy is to begin July 1.

(5)

Cash (asset +).....................$3,000
   Rent received in advance (liability +)....$3,000
To record three months' rent received in advance

The company has received the cash. It is still obligated to provide services to the lessee. "Rent received in advance" can be viewed as "value of rental services yet to be furnished."

The company receives an invoice (a bill) from its attorneys—$5,000—for services performed in connection with drawing the corporate charter and issuing common stock.

(6)

Organization costs (asset +)...........$5,000
   Accounts payable (liability +)..........$5,000
To record the costs of organizing the corporation

The organization costs, like the cost of equipment and the prepaid rent, were incurred in order to benefit future accounting periods. Although they are "intangible"—they cannot be seen or felt—they are nevertheless *assets* of the company. Accounts payable, rather than cash, has been credited because the company has not yet paid the invoice.

EXHIBIT 3-2 Continued

The company hires J. Pringle as president. The two parties sign a two-year employment contract requiring the firm to compensate Pringle at a salary of $135,000 per year.

No entry is required.

Although the firm seemingly has incurred a liability of $270,000, the president has not yet performed any services for the company. As indicated previously, accountants generally record liabilities resulting from contracts only to the extent that services have been performed or cash has been paid. Thus, when Pringle has been employed for one month, the company will record a liability of one-twelfth of $135,000—$11,250.

The company purchases merchandise for $54,000.

(7)

Merchandise inventory (asset +) $54,000
     Accounts payable (liability +). $54,000
To record the purchase of merchandise

The firm purchases 100 shares of General Motors stock as a temporary investment. Cost per share is $61.

(8)

Marketable securities (asset +) $6,100
     Cash (asset −) $6,100
To record the purchase of 100 shares of General Motors stock

The company pays $5,000 of the amount it owes to its supplier.

(9)

Accounts payable (liability −) $5,000
     Cash (asset −) $5,000
To record the payment to the supplier

The company returns defective merchandise to the supplier. The merchandise cost $7,000. The supplier gives the company credit for the merchandise returned.

(10)

Accounts payable (liability −) $7,000
     Merchandise inventory (asset −) $7,000
To record the return of merchandise

The company learns through *The Wall Street Journal* that the market price of its General Motors stock has increased to $64 per share.

No entry is necessary.

Increases in the market value of assets generally are not recorded—mainly because of the accountant's preference toward conservative expressions of value.

The market price of the General Motors stock declines to $61 per share. The company sells 50 shares.

(11)

Cash (asset +) $3,050
     Marketable securities (asset −) $3,050
To record the sale of 50 shares of General Motors stock

(The stock was sold at original cost; hence there was no gain or loss on the sale.)

Sales Revenue

The Hawthorne Corporation sells merchandise for $83,000 (all sales are ''on account''):

(12)

Accounts receivable (asset +). $83,000
     Sales revenue (retained earnings +) $83,000
To record sales for the month

Sales revenue is typically recognized when merchandise is *delivered* to a customer (exceptions will be discussed in later chapters). Recognition of revenue increases net assets and correspondingly increases retained earnings. In this example, ''retained earnings'' will be parenthetically added to all revenues and expenses so as to emphasize that revenues and expenses are, in essence, increases or decreases in owners' equity.

Collection of Cash from Customers

The company collects $62,000 from its customers:

(13)

```
Cash (asset +) ..................................................$62,000
    Accounts receivable (asset -) ...................................$62,000
To record collection of cash from customers
```

The collection of cash does *not* create a revenue. One asset (cash) is exchanged for another (accounts receivable). Net assets, and hence owners' equity, remains unchanged.

Purchase of Merchandise

The company purchases additional merchandise inventory at a cost of $16,000 (on account):

(14)

```
Merchandise inventory (asset +) ................................$16,000
    Accounts payable (liability +) ..................................$16,000
To record the purchase of merchandise
```

Just as the collection of cash does not create a revenue, the acquisition of merchandise does not result in an expense. Instead, the company increases an asset (merchandise inventory) but at the same time increases a liability (accounts payable).

Cost of Goods Sold

The cost of the merchandise sold was $45,000:

(15)

```
Cost of goods sold (retained earnings -) ............................$45,000
    Merchandise inventory (asset -) ................................$45,000
To record the cost of goods sold as an expense
```

The cost of merchandise sold is ordinarily recognized as an expense in the same period as the revenue from the sale. Recognition of the expense results in a decrease in assets and a corresponding decrease in retained earnings.

Many companies do not keep track of the cost of particular items sold. Instead, they take advantage of a basic—and obvious—relationship between account balances and changes during a period:

Beginning balance + Additions – Reductions = Ending balance

As to inventory, the additions are the purchases during the period and the reductions are the goods sold. Thus

Beginning balance + Purchases – Cost of goods sold = Ending balance

And, by rearrangement,

Cost of goods sold = Beginning balance + Purchases – Ending balance

At period end, companies take an *inventory* (physical count) of goods on hand. By referring to invoices or comparable purchase documents, they determine the amount paid for those goods. Inasmuch as they also know the value of the goods on hand at the start of the period (from the financial statements of the previous period) and the amount that was purchased during the period (from purchase records), they can easily compute the cost of the goods that were sold during the period. Suppose that the Hawthorne Corporation's count of June 30 indicates merchandise inventory of $18,000. Beginning balance on June 1 was $0. Net purchases ($54,000 per entry 7 plus $16,000 per entry 14, less returns of $7,000 per entry 10) are $63,000. Therefore the $45,000 cost of goods sold was derived as follows:

Cost of goods sold = Beginning balance + Purchases − Ending balance

Cost of goods sold = $0 + $63,000 − $18,000

Cost of goods sold = $45,000

Payments to Suppliers
The company pays $38,000 of its debts to suppliers:

(16)

> Accounts payable (liability −) $38,000
>   Cash (asset −) $38,000
> **To record payments to suppliers**

This transaction decreases a liability and a corresponding asset. Of the three events associated with the merchandise (the purchase of the goods, the sale and delivery to the customer, and the payments to the suppliers), only the sale and delivery to customers leads to recognition of an expense. The others result in a reordering of the mix, but no change in the level, of net assets.

Purchase of Advertising Circulars
The company purchases $5,000 of advertising circulars:

(17)

> Advertising circulars (asset +) $5,000
>   Cash (asset −) $5,000
> **To record the acquisition of advertising circulars**

The advertising circulars are expected to benefit the future. Until consumed, they are an asset.

Advertising Expense
The company distributes $4,000 of the advertising circulars:

(18)

> Advertising expense (retained earnings −) $4,000
>   Advertising circulars (asset −) $4,000
> **To record consumption of advertising circulars**

The distribution of the circulars prompts the recognition of an expense. This transaction is another example of an expense that is driven by the consumption of, rather than the acquisition of or the payment for, an asset.

Wages and Salaries

The company pays wages and salaries of $13,000. The payment is made on the last day of the month and covers the wages and salaries of the entire period. Therefore the cash paid corresponds to the wage and salary expense.

(19)

```
Wage and salary expense (retained
  earnings  – ) ..................................................$13,000
      Cash (asset  – ) ...........................................$13,000
  To record wages and salaries
```

Had the payment been delayed until the next accounting period, the wage and salary expense would still have been the same. Wage and salary expense is determined by when the employees perform their services, not by when they are paid for them. Were the payment delayed, then the liability "wages and salaries payable," instead of "cash," would have been credited.

Step 2: Updating the Accounts: Recognizing Still Other Economic Events

At month end, the company is to prepare financial statements. Therefore it must bring its accounts up to date by recording the revenues and expenses that are attributable to events other than specific transactions.

Utilities Expense

The company estimates that it consumed $300 in electricity during the month:

(20)

```
Utility expense (retained earnings  – ).............................$300
    Accrued utilities expense
      (liability  + ) ................................................$300
  To record utility costs
```

The company must recognize an expense for the electricity used, even if it has not yet received a bill. The term *accrued* is commonly applied to an asset or liability that is not yet contractually receivable or payable, even though the related revenue or expense has been recognized.

Rent Revenue

In early June the company received $3,000 (three months') rent in advance (transaction 5). The amount was recorded as a liability—an obligation to provide services in the future. During the month the company provides one month of service, thereby earning revenue of $1,000:

(21)

```
Rent received in advance (liability  – ) ...........................$1,000
    Rent revenue (retained earnings  + ) .............................$1,000
  To record rent revenue for one month
```

Interest Expense

The company must record interest expense, which it calculates to be $3,000, attributable to outstanding bonds and notes (entries 2 and 3). It has had the use of the funds, and benefited from them, even if the interest is not yet due.

(22)

> Interest expense (retained earnings −) $3,000
> Accrued interest payable (liability +) $3,000
> **To record interest expense for one month**

Depreciation Expense

During the month the company purchased a building for $300,000 and equipment for $120,000 (entries 3 and 4). The building has a useful life of 25 years (300 months) and the equipment 5 years (60 months). At the end of June, the company must recognize the consumption of a proportionate share of the assets:

(23)

> Depreciation expense (retained earnings −) $3,000
> Building (asset −) $1,000
> Equipment (asset −) 2,000
> **To recognize depreciation for one month**

Amortization Expense

Upon its formation, the company paid $5,000 in attorneys' fees (entry 6). The fees were *capitalized* (recorded as an asset) as "organization costs" since, like outlays for buildings and equipment, they were incurred to benefit several accounting periods. They must therefore be amortized over a period of anticipated utility. Owing to the difficulties of defining, let alone measuring, the precise benefits provided by organization costs, companies have considerable latitude in determining the amortization period. Current standards allow for any number of years, up to a maximum of 40. The Hawthorne Corporation has elected to amortize the costs over four years (48 months).

(24)

> Amortization expense (retained earnings −) $104
> Organization costs (asset −) $104
> **To recognize amortization for one month**

Dividends

The company declared and paid cash dividends of 35 cents per share on its 10,000 shares of stock outstanding—a total of $3,500. Dividends are distributions of assets to the company's owners. Like expenses, they reduce the corporation's net assets and retained earnings.

(25)

> Dividends (retained earnings −) $3,500
> Cash (asset −) $3,500
> **To record the declaration and payment of dividends**

Step 3: Posting to Ledger Accounts and Computing Account Balances

The journal entries must be posted (recorded in) the ledger accounts. The ledger accounts as of June 30, in T account form, are presented in Exhibit 3-3. The two sides of all accounts other than revenues and expenses have been totaled and the resultant balances shown beneath the double rules.

EXHIBIT 3-3
Preclosing General Ledger Accounts

	Assets			Liabilities		Owners' Equity (Including Revenues, Expenses, and Dividends)

Cash

(1)	500,000	(3)	100,000
(2)	100,000	(4)	120,000
(5)	3,000	(8)	6,100
(11)	3,050	(9)	5,000
(13)	62,000	(16)	38,000
		(17)	5,000
		(19)	13,000
		(25)	3,500
377,450			

Accounts payable

(9)	5,000	(6)	5,000
(10)	7,000	(7)	54,000
(16)	38,000	(14)	16,000
		25,000	

Common stock

		(1)	500,000
			500,000

Marketable securities

(8)	6,100	(11)	3,050
3,050			

Rent received in advance

(21)	1,000	(5)	3,000
		2,000	

Retained earnings

Accounts receivable

(12)	83,000	(13)	62,000
21,000			

Accrued utility expense

		(20)	300
		300	

Sales revenue

		(12)	83,000

Advertising circulars

(17)	5,000	(18)	4,000
1,000			

Accrued interest expense

		(22)	3,000
		3,000	

Rent revenue

		(21)	1,000

Merchandise inventory

(7)	54,000	(10)	7,000
(14)	16,000	(15)	45,000
18,000			

Notes payable

		(3)	200,000
		200,000	

Cost of goods sold

(15)	45,000		

Equipment

(4)	120,000	(23)	2,000
118,000			

Bonds payable

		(2)	100,000
		100,000	

Wage and salary expense

(19)	13,000		

Building

(3)	300,000	(23)	1,000
299,000			

Advertising expense

(18)	4,000		

Organizational costs

(6)	5,000	(24)	104
4,896			

Utilities expense

(20)	300		

EXHIBIT 3-3 Continued

	Interest expense	
(22)	3,000	

	Depreciation expense	
(23)	3,000	

	Amortization expense	
(24)	104	

	Dividends	
(25)	3,500	

Step 4: Taking a Trial Balance

After the journal entries have been posted to the ledger accounts, a trial balance may be struck. A *trial balance* is a complete listing of the balances in each of the accounts. Naturally, the total debit balances must equal the total credit balances. If they do not, then either the accounts or the trial balance is in error.

Unfortunately, the equality of total debits and total credits is a necessary, but not a sufficient, condition for the accounts to be correct. Therefore, even if the debits equal the credits, the records may be in error. The company may have failed to record relevant financial events, recorded them in incorrect amounts, or debited or credited improper accounts.

A trial balance may be taken at any time. A trial balance struck before the end-of-period updating and correcting entries (correcting entries will be discussed in the next chapter) have been made is called an *unadjusted* trial balance. One prepared after the updating and correcting entries have been made is referred to as an *adjusted* trial balance.

A trial balance taken before the closing entries are made is called a *preclosing* trial balance; one taken after is known as a *postclosing* trial balance. Closing entries transfer the balances in revenue and expense accounts to retained earnings. Thus a *preclosing* trial balance will include revenue, expense, and dividend accounts. Retained earnings will not yet have been updated to incorporate income and dividends for the period. In the absence of unusual adjustments, the retained earnings will be those of the *start* of the period, not the end. The *postclosing* trial balance will *not* include revenue, expense, and dividend accounts, since the balances would have been transferred to retained earnings. Correspondingly, the retained earnings will be those of the end of the period, having been updated to include the balances transferred from the income and dividend accounts.

The *preclosing* trial balance of the Hawthorne Corporation is shown in Exhibit 3-4. The dotted line is included for illustration only. The accounts above the line are asset, liability, and owners' equity accounts. Those below are revenues, expenses, and dividends. The accounts above the line will appear unchanged on both the postclosing trial balance and the balance sheet, with the exception that retained earnings will be updated to incorporate the net sum of the accounts below the line.

The accounts below the line, except for dividends, will constitute the income statement. All of these accounts, including dividends, will be closed at period end and the balances transferred to retained earnings.

Step 5: Preparing the Income Statement

To prepare an income statement it is necessary only to extract the revenues and expenses from the *preclosing trial balance*. The income statement of the Hawthorne Corporation is presented in Exhibit 3-5.

EXHIBIT 3-4

Hawthorne Corporation
Preclosing Trial Balance
As of June 30, 1993

	Debit Balances	Credit Balances	
Cash	$377,450		
Marketable securities	3,050		
Accounts receivable	21,000		
Advertising circulars	1,000		
Merchandise inventory	18,000		
Equipment	118,000		
Building	299,000		
Organization costs	4,896		
Accounts payable		$ 25,000	Debits > Credits by $12,096
Rent received in advance		2,000	
Accrued utilities expense		300	
Accrued interest expense		3,000	
Notes payable		200,000	
Bonds payable		100,000	
Common stock		500,000	
Retained earnings (beginning)		0	
Sales revenue		83,000	
Rent revenue		1,000	
Cost of goods sold	45,000		
Wage and salary expense	13,000		
Advertising expense	4,000		
Interest expense	3,000		Credits > Debits by $12,096
Utilities expense	300		
Depreciation expense	3,000		
Amortization expense	104		
Dividends	3,500		
	$914,300	$914,300	

*This line is included for illustration only. Accounts above the line are assets, liabilities, and owners' equities; those below are revenues, expenses, and dividends.

EXHIBIT 3-5

Hawthorne Corporation
Income Statement
Month Ended June 30, 1993

Revenues		
Sales revenue	$83,000	
Rent revenue	1,000	$84,000
Expenses		
Cost of goods sold	45,000	
Wage and salary expense	13,000	
Advertising expense	4,000	
Interest expense	3,000	
Utilities expense	300	
Depreciation expense	3,000	
Amortization expense	104	68,404
Net income		$15,596

Step 6: Closing Revenues, Expenses, and Dividends

Revenues and expenses have two characteristics that differentiate them from balance sheet accounts. These two features dictate that they be "closed" at the end of an accounting period.

First, revenues and expenses are subaccounts of retained earnings. Revenues are increases in retained earnings; expenses, decreases. In fact, revenues and expenses could be debited or credited directly to retained earnings. Separate accounts are maintained primarily so that the information required for the income statement can easily be extracted and categorized. Once that is done, the balances in the revenue and expense accounts can be transferred to retained earnings.

Second, revenues and expenses measure flows of resources over a period of time. When that period is completed, the accounts must be "reset" to zero so that the measurement process can begin anew in the next period.

Closing entries therefore accomplish two objectives:

1. They transfer the balances in revenue and expense accounts to retained earnings.
2. They "zero out" the accounts so that those accounts are ready to "meter" the resource flows of the next accounting period.

The revenues and expenses may be closed directly to retained earnings. Many firms, however, close them to an intermediary account, "income summary." They then close "income summary" to retained earnings. "Income summary" is a temporary account. Its main purpose is to combine the revenues and expenses so that only a single entry for income need be made to retained earnings. Thus

(Closing entry 1)

Sales revenue	$83,000	
Rent revenue	1,000	
Income summary		$84,000

To close the revenue accounts

(Closing entry 2)

Income summary	$68,404	
Cost of goods sold		$45,000
Advertising expense		4,000
Wage and salary expense		13,000
Interest expense		3,000
Depreciation expense		3,000
Amortization expense		104
Utility expense		300

To close the expense accounts

(Closing entry 3)

Income summary	$15,596	
Retained earnings		$15,596

To close the income summary account and transfer its balance to retained earnings

The dividends account must also be closed. Dividends do *not* enter in the computation of income. They are a discretionary transfer of resources from the company to its owners. Dividends therefore are closed directly to retained earnings:

(Closing entry 4)

Retained earnings	$3,500	
Dividends		$3,500

To close the dividends account

Exhibit 3-6 shows the closing entries in diagram form.

The balances in the asset, liability, and common stock accounts need neither be transferred nor zeroed out. The balances at the end of one period will be those at the start of the next. For example, the cash balance of $377,450 at the close of business on June 30 will also be that at the start of July 1. To facilitate the summarization of the end-of-period balances, double lines have been drawn beneath the debits and credits. The differences between the sums are shown on the appropriate side of the T accounts.

Step 7: Taking a Postclosing Trial Balance

Exhibit 3-7 presents a *postclosing* trial balance. It includes only balance sheet accounts, since the income statement accounts as well as dividends have been closed to retained earnings. Whereas the preclosing trial balance shows the beginning-of-period retained earnings balance ($0), the postclosing trial balance reports the end-of-period balance ($12,096).

EXHIBIT 3-6
Closing Entries

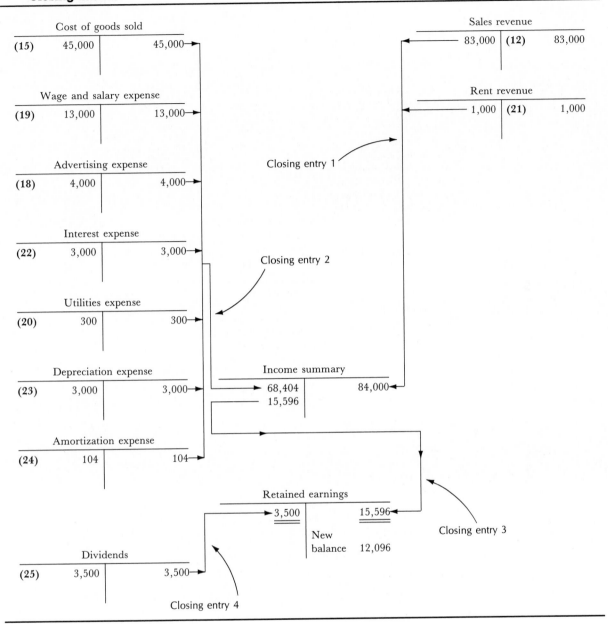

Step 8: Preparing a Balance Sheet

The balance sheet (also called a *statement of position*) is, in essence, a postclosing trial balance. As can be seen in Exhibit 3-8, the account balances are the same; they have merely been classified and reordered.

EXHIBIT 3-7

Hawthorne Corporation
Postclosing Trial Balance
As of June 30, 1993

Cash	$377,450	
Marketable securities	3,050	
Accounts receivable	21,000	
Advertising circulars	1,000	
Merchandise inventory	18,000	
Equipment	118,000	
Building	299,000	
Organization costs	4,896	
Accounts payable		$ 25,000
Rent received in advance		2,000
Accrued utilities expense		300
Accrued interest expense		3,000
Notes payable		200,000
Bonds payable		100,000
Common stock		500,000
Retained earnings		12,096
	$842,396	$842,396

EXHIBIT 3-8

Hawthorne Corporation
Balance Sheet
As of June 30, 1993
Assets

Current assets		
Cash	$377,450	
Marketable securities	3,050	
Accounts receivable	21,000	
Advertising circulars	1,000	
Merchandise inventory	18,000	$420,500
Noncurrent assets		
Equipment	118,000	
Building	299,000	
Organization costs	4,896	421,896
Total assets		$842,396

Liabilities and Owners' Equity

Current liabilities		
Accounts payable	$ 25,000	
Rent received in advance	2,000	
Accrued utilities expense	300	
Accrued interest expense	3,000	$ 30,300
Noncurrent liabilities		
Notes payable	200,000	
Bonds payable	100,000	300,000
Total liabilities		330,300
Owners' equity		
Common stock, 10,000 shares		
issued and outstanding	500,000	
Retained earnings	12,096	512,096
Total equities		$842,396

Step 9: Preparing a Statement of Cash Flows and Other Appropriate Statements

The third primary statement, the statement of cash flows, is conceptually straightforward. The statement summarizes and classifies each of the entries to the cash account. If there are a large number of transactions affecting cash, detailed analysis of the cash account can become mechanically complex. Means of simplifying the process will be explained in Chapter 14. Exhibit 3-9 presents a statement of cash flows, in this instance prepared directly from the entries to the cash account.

As was true with the Schaefer Corporation in Chapter 2 (see Exhibit 2-8), the difference between net income and cash from operations can be explained by changes in assets and liabilities. As shown in Exhibit 3-10,

- Depreciation and amortization (expenses not requiring an outflow of cash) caused long-lived assets to decline by $3,104.
- Sales were $21,000 greater than cash collections from customers.
- Inventory purchases were $63,000 (net of returns), but cost of sales was only $45,000. The $18,000 difference is reflected as an increase in merchandise inventory. Moreover, the company paid for only $43,000 of its $63,000 in purchases, the $20,000 difference being captured as an increase in accounts payable. This $20,000, plus the $5,000 in unpaid attorneys' fees (per transaction no. 6) accounts for the full $25,000 increase in accounts payable.
- Purchases of, and payments for, advertising circulars were $1,000 greater than the amount consumed and charged as an expense.
- Rent collections were $2,000 greater than rent earnings.
- Expenses for utilities and interest were $3,300 greater than related payments.

EXHIBIT 3-9

Hawthorne Corporation
Statement of Cash Flows
Month Ended June 30, 1993

Cash Flow from Operating Activities	
Collections from customers	$ 62,000
Payments to suppliers	(43,000)
Payment of wages and salaries	(13,000)
Collection of rent (in advance)	3,000
Purchase of advertising circulars	(5,000)
Net cash from operating activities	$ 4,000
Cash Flow from Investing Activities	
Purchase of building	$(100,000)
Purchase of equipment	(120,000)
Purchase of marketable securities	(6,100)
Sales of marketable securities	3,050
Net cash used for investing activities	$(223,050)
Cash Flow from Financing Activities	
Issue of common stock	$500,000
Issue of bonds	100,000
Payment of dividends	(3,500)
Net cash from financing activities	$596,500
Net increase in cash	$377,450

EXHIBIT 3-10

Schaefer Corporation
Reconciliation of Net Income with Cash from Operations
Month Ended April 10, 1993

Net income	*$15,596*
Add:	
(Increase) Decrease in buildings and equipment	3,000
(Increase) Decrease in accounts receivable, net	(21,000)
(Increase) Decrease in merchandise inventory	(18,000)
Increase (Decrease) in accounts payable	25,000
(Increase) Decrease in advertising circulars	(1,000)
Increase (Decrease) in rent received in advance	2,000
(Increase) Decrease in organizational costs (net of amortization)	(4,896)
Increase (Decrease) in accrued utilities expense and accrued interest expense	3,300
Cash flow from operations	*$ 4,000*

Exhibit 3-11 presents a statement of changes in owners' equity. The information was derived from the entries to the common stock and retained earnings accounts in Exhibit 3-3.

The accounting cycle is now complete, and a new accounting period can begin.

EXHIBIT 3-11

Hawthorne Corporation
Statement of Changes in Owner's Equity
Month Ended June 30, 1993

	Common Stock	Retained Earnings
Balance, June 1	$ 0	$ 0
Common stock issued	500,000	15,596
Dividends declared in June		(3,500)
Balance, June 30	$500,000	$ 12,096

CONTRA ACCOUNTS

Contra (meaning against or opposite) *accounts* are offset accounts. They are associated with specific asset or liability accounts, from which their balances are subtracted.

In the Hawthorne illustration, depreciation (entry **23**) was recorded with a debit to depreciation expense and a credit to building and to equipment. While the entry is correct, most firms would credit the contra accounts "building—accumulated depreciation" and "equipment—accumulated depreciation" rather than the asset accounts, "building" and "equipment." Whereas the building and the equipment accounts would have debit balances, the contra accounts would always have credit balances. The asset accounts would indicate the amounts paid for the buildings and equipment, the contra accounts the expired portion of the cost. The differences between the two would reflect the unexpired costs (i.e., the *book values* of the assets). The contra accounts would be reported beneath the related assets:

Equipment	$120,000	
Less: Accumulated depreciation	2,000	$118,000
Building	300,000	
Less: Accumulated depreciation	1,000	$299,000

The advantage of crediting the contra accounts rather than the asset accounts is that the balance sheet will show the original cost of the assets as well as the portion that has been depreciated. This additional information enables statement users to determine the percentage of asset costs that have already been depreciated (for example, 2/120, or 1.7 percent, of the equipment).

When an asset is sold or retired, both the accumulated depreciation and the asset cost must be removed from the accounts. Suppose, for example, that the equipment is sold for $125,000. The book value at the time of sale is $118,000. Hence there is a gain of $7,000. The following entry would be in order:

Cash	$125,000	
Accumulated depreciation	2,000	
Equipment		$120,000
Gain on sale of equipment		7,000
To record the sale of equipment		

The expression *allowance for depreciation* is sometimes used in place of *accumulated depreciation*.

BASIC BOOKS OF ACCOUNT

The basic accounting information-processing system is simple and straightforward. Relatively few books and records need be maintained or prepared—regardless of the size of the business enterprise and irrespective of whether the system will be manually or electronically maintained.

If the enterprise maintains a computerized accounting system, the journals or ledgers will not, of course, take the form to be illustrated. They would, however, serve the same function and be designed to accommodate the same information.

As we noted earlier in this chapter, the fundamental means of recording economic events and transactions is the *journal entry*. Journal entries are *posted* to the *general ledger,* a book in which all balance sheet and income statement accounts are maintained. General ledger accounts are represented in this text by T accounts. Posting involves nothing more than transcribing the entries from the journals to the appropriate accounts.

Special Journals

Although conceptually there is need for only a single, or *general,* journal in which to record transactions, in practice, most firms find that record keeping is facilitated by several supplementary, often called *special,* journals. Since a firm may enter into numerous transactions that affect identical accounts, it is relatively easy to combine the transactions into a single journal entry and periodically make but one entry to the account affected. Supplementary journals enable the firm to do just that. Most firms, for example, maintain a sales journal. The sales journal may be designed as follows:

Sales Journal

Date		Purchaser	Sales (Cr)	Cash (Dr)	Accounts Receivable (Dr)
Jan.	3	Burnet, Inc.	12 5 8 0 00	12 5 8 0 00	
	4	Silver Creek Co.	8 0 0 0 00		8 0 0 0 00
	4	Bertram Manufacturing	2 1 7 0 00		2 1 7 0 00
	5	Leander Processing	15 2 7 5 00		15 2 7 5 00

As each sale is made, the firm enters the name of the customer to whom the sale was made; the amount of the sale in the column "Sales (Credit)"; the amount of cash received, if any, in the column "Cash (Debit)"; and the difference between the amount of sale and the amount of cash received in the column "Accounts Receivable (Debit)." At the end of each month, the columns are totaled. Then either the following entry is made in the general journal or the amounts are posted directly to the appropriate general ledger accounts:

Cash	xxxx	
Accounts receivable	xxxx	
Sales		xxxx

Similarly, a firm might maintain a *cash receipts book* and a *cash disbursements book,* both of which are also supplementary journals. One column would indicate the amount of cash received or disbursed; other columns would be reserved for the accounts that are the most frequent corresponding elements of the journal entry. As with the sales journal, the columns are periodically totaled, and either a single summary entry is made in the general journal or the totals are posted directly to the general ledger accounts affected.

Subsidiary Ledgers

A firm almost always finds it necessary to keep records of each customer from whom it holds a receivable, each fixed asset owned, and each supplier to whom it is indebted. But it would obviously necessitate a general ledger of massive proportions if separate accounts were maintained for each customer, supplier, or fixed asset. Most firms maintain, in the general ledger, *control accounts* that summarize the numerous individual accounts. Control accounts are typically maintained for accounts receivable, accounts payable, and fixed assets. The individual accounts are maintained in *subsidiary ledgers*. The subsidiary ledger may be a book or electronic file, one page or record for each subsidiary account.

Obviously, the sum of the balances in a subsidiary ledger must equal the balance in the general ledger control account for which the subsidiary ledger provides support. Each time an entry is made to the general ledger control account, one or more entries of equal amount must be made to the subsidiary accounts.

Suppose, for example, that in the course of a month a firm makes sales, all on account, to a number of different customers. In the general ledger the firm would debit accounts receivable for the total amount of the sales. In the accounts receivable subsidiary ledger, the firm would debit the individual accounts of the various customers for the amount of each sale. As the customers pay the balances in their accounts, the firm would credit accounts receivable in the general ledger for the total amount collected within a period and credit the individual accounts for the amount of each remittance.

Summary

This chapter has emphasized that revenues and expenses are the inflows and outflows of resources from the production and delivery of goods and services. Recognition of revenues and expenses may be triggered by a specific transaction, such as the sale of goods, as well as by less specific economic events, such as the passage of time. Modern financial accounting is on an *accrual* rather than a cash basis. Therefore the recognition of revenues and expenses may not coincide with the receipt and disbursement of cash.

The chapter also described the fundamental *accounting cycle,* which consists of nine steps:

1. Transactions and other financial events are recorded in journals.

2. At the end of an accounting period, the accounts are updated to recognize financial events that have not been recorded in the normal course of operations.

3. The journal entries are posted to ledger accounts and the account balances computed.

4. The balances in the accounts are summarized in a *preclosing* trial balance. The sum of the debits must equal the sum of the credits. Otherwise the accounting equation would be out of balance, a condition indicative of an error.

5. On the basis of the balances in the revenue and expense accounts of the preclosing trial balance, an income statement is prepared.

6. The revenue, expense, and dividend accounts are "closed" by transferring the balances to retained earnings.

7. The balances in the remaining accounts are summarized in the form of a *postclosing* trial balance.

8. From the balances in the postclosing trial balance, a balance sheet is prepared.

9. The statements of cash flows and of changes in owners' equity accounts are prepared.

In addition, the chapter has provided an overview of the books and records maintained by business enterprises. The two basic books of account are the *general journal* and the *general ledger*. Transactions are recorded in the general journal and are then posted to the affected accounts, which are kept in the general ledger. To make it easier to process a multitude of diverse transactions, most firms also maintain specialized journals and ledgers, which support and supplement the general journals and ledgers.

The balance sheet of a company as of August 1 is as follows:

Assets		
Cash		$ 150,000
Accounts receivable		100,000
Inventory		250,000
Buildings and equipment	$800,000	
Less: Accumulated depreciation	280,000	520,000
		$1,020,000
Equities		
Accounts payable		$ 220,000
Contributed capital		200,000
Retained earnings		600,000
		$1,020,000

1. Prepare journal entries to record the following financial events that took place in August:
   a. The company purchased merchandise inventory for $320,000, on account.
   b. It made sales of $290,000, on account.
   c. The merchandise sold had originally cost $230,000.
   d. It collected $310,000 from customers.
   e. It paid suppliers $300,000.
   f. It recognized depreciation of $10,000.
   g. Employees earned wages and salaries of $20,000. They were paid only $15,000.
2. Post the entries to T accounts, each of which represents a ledger account. Determine the month-end balance in each account.
3. Prepare a preclosing trial balance.
4. Prepare an income statement for the month.
5. Prepare journal entries to close the revenue and expense accounts. Post them to the appropriate T accounts. Indicate postclosing balances in affected accounts.
6. Prepare a postclosing trial balance.
7. Prepare a balance sheet as of August 31.
8. Prepare a statement of cash flows.

Questions for Review and Discussion

1. "All accounting transactions can be recorded directly to balance sheet accounts. There is no reason to maintain income statement accounts." Do you agree? Explain.
2. What is the purpose of *closing entries*? Why must revenue and expense accounts have a zero balance at the start of each accounting period? Why aren't balance sheet accounts "closed" at the end of each accounting period?
3. If, prior to the end of an accounting period (before closing entries have been made), one were to take a trial balance of all *balance sheet* accounts (assets, liabilities, owners' equity), the debits would probably not equal the credits. Why not?
4. Virtually all transactions in which a firm engages trigger journal entries. But not all journal entries are triggered by specific transactions. Explain and give examples of journal entries that are not triggered by specific transactions.
5. What is meant by an *accrual*?

6. How does the accrual basis of accounting differ from the cash basis?
7. On January 1, a firm purchases a three-year insurance policy for $36,000. It pays in cash. What would be the impact of this transaction on each of the following December 31 financial statements?
   a. Income statement
   b. Balance sheet
   c. Statement of cash flows
8. The retained earnings account is generally one of the least active on the balance sheet. What types of transactions or financial events require an entry directly to the retained earnings account?
9. A company purchases merchandise listed in a catalog at a price of $50,000. It incurs shipping costs of $2,000, taxes and duties of $500, and insurance of $750. At what value should the goods be recorded on the company books? What general rule governs the values at which assets such as merchandise inventory and plant equipment should be initially recorded?
10. Do you agree with either or both of these statements? Explain.
    a. If at the end of an accounting period the trial balance is not in balance (the debits do not equal the credits), then an accounting error has been made.
    b. If at the end of an accounting period the trial balance is in balance, then an accounting error has not been made.
11. What accounting recognition would be given to each of the following financial events on the books of International Electric Co.?
    a. International Electric Co. owns 3,000 shares of Ford Motor Co. common stock. In the course of a year, the market price of the stock increases from $50 per share to $60.
    b. International Electric Co. has outstanding 20,000 shares of its own common stock. In the course of a year, the market price of the stock increases from $45 per share to $50 per share.
    c. William Barefield sells 100 shares of International Electric Co. to Jill Abelson for $45 per share.
12. What are *contra accounts*? Why are they used?
13. What is a *sales journal*? Why is it used?

Problems

1. *Financial accounting requires an understanding of only nine basic types of transactions.*
   An accounting transaction, when analyzed in terms of the basic accounting equation, can have only nine possible effects, summarized as follows:
   (1) Asset +; asset −
   (2) Asset +; liability +
   (3) Asset +; stockholders' equity +
   (4) Asset −; liability −
   (5) Asset −; stockholders' equity −
   (6) Liability +; liability −
   (7) Liability −; stockholders' equity +
   (8) Liability +; stockholders' equity −
   (9) Stockholders' equity +; stockholders' equity −
   Analyze each of the financial events listed below, and indicate which of the nine effects is best described. Make the assumption that each transaction is being entered directly into balance sheet accounts (i.e., the income statement is bypassed), but indicate which of the transactions would, in fact, ordinarily be reported on the income statement.
   a. Collection of an account receivable
   b. Purchase of merchandise on account

c. Sale of merchandise on account
d. Recognition of the cost of goods that have been sold
e. Declaration (but not payment) of a dividend
f. Payment of a dividend that had been previously declared
g. Recognition of one year's depreciation on a company-owned truck
h. Payment of one month's rent on a truck that the company leases from a "rent-a-truck" agency
i. Issuance of 1,000 shares of the company's own common stock in exchange for forgiveness on a $100,000 note payable
j. Exchange of 1,000 shares of common stock for 2,000 shares of preferred stock

2. *A familiarity with the "mechanics" of accounting facilitates an understanding of its underlying concepts, principles, and issues.*

Complete the following table by specifying whether each of the accounts would ordinarily be increased or decreased by a debit and a credit. The first one is done for you as an example.

	Would a *debit* increase/decrease the account?	Would a *credit* increase/decrease the account?
1. Cash	Increase	Decrease
2. Interest payable		
3. Interest receivable		
4. Interest revenue		
5. Interest expense		
6. Marketable securities		
7. Common stock		
8. Retained earnings		

3. *A preclosing trial balance summarizes the balances in all ledger accounts; only some of the accounts, however, are affected by year-end closing entries.*

Indicated in the table is the December 31 *preclosing* trial balance of the Boston Company (in thousands of dollars).
a. Prepare required year-end closing entries. What was the company's income for the year?
b. What will be the balance in retained earnings after closing entries have been made?

	Debits	Credits
Cash	$10,000	
Accounts receivable	12,000	
Inventory	5,000	
Supplies	1,000	
Prepaid rent	800	
Accounts payable		$ 3,000
Accrued interest payable		200
Notes payable		3,000
Retained earnings		23,600
Sales revenue		48,000
Cost of goods sold	35,000	
Supplies expense	4,000	
Rent expense	9,600	
Interest expense	400	
	$77,800	$77,800

4. *Not all of the economic events described in this problem require accounting recognition, but those that do affect only balance sheet accounts.*

Prepare journal entries (as necessary) to reflect the following economic events pertaining to the Edinburg Corporation in the month of June 1993.

a. The company issues $300,000 in long-term bonds. The bonds provide for the payment of interest twice each year at an annual rate of 8 percent. The bonds are payable 10 years from date of issue.

b. The company purchases a new typewriter. Suggested retail price of the type-writer is $400, but because the machine is on sale, the company pays only $320, in cash.

c. The company signs a contract with the Watchdog Security Service to receive guard service for the period July 1, 1993 to June 30, 1994. The contract calls for payment of $2,000 per month, payable 15 days after the close of the month in which the service is provided.

d. The firm receives a check for $5,000 from one of its customers for payment on merchandise that was delivered in January. The amount owed is included among the company's accounts receivable.

e. The firm purchases 100 shares of Exxon common stock for $84 per share as a short-term investment.

f. *The Wall Street Journal* reports that the price of Exxon stock has increased to $88 per share.

g. The company purchases manufacturing equipment for $86,000, pays $20,000 in cash and gives a three-year note for the balance In addition, the company incurs costs (paid in cash) of $2,000 to install the equipment.

h. The company issues 10,000 shares of its common stock for $12 per share. The common stock has a par value of $10 per share.

i. The company pays $600 rent on its office space. The rent is applicable to the month of May and had previously been recorded as a liability, "Accrued rent payable."

j. The company returns to the manufacturer raw materials that it deems defective. The company had been billed $900 for the materials and had recorded the amount as a liability.

5. *Revenues and expenses result in an increase or decrease in net assets (assets minus liabilities) as well as in owners' equity.*

If the basic accounting equation is expressed in the form, assets – liabilities = owners' equity, then which of the following transactions increase or decrease the right side (owners' equity) of the equation? Which transactions would represent revenues or expenses as opposed to only changes in asset and liability accounts?

a. A firm purchases fuel oil for cash.

b. It purchases fuel oil on account.

c. It uses the fuel oil previously purchased.

d. It pays for the fuel oil previously purchased on account.

e. It receives and pays the electric bill; no previous accounting recognition has been given to electric costs.

f. It provides services for a customer and bills him.

g. It collects the amount previously billed.

h. It borrows an amount from a bank.

i. It repays the amount borrowed.

j. It gives accounting recognition to interest on the amount borrowed and makes the interest payment.

6. *Transactions that affect only asset and liability accounts must be distinguished from those that involve revenue and expense accounts.*

Prepare journal entries to reflect the following transactions. Be certain to indicate the nature of each account affected.

a. A company purchases supplies for $500 cash.

b. The company uses $300 of the supplies.

c. The company purchases merchandise for $3,000 on account.

d. The company pays $1,500 of the $3,000 owed to suppliers.

e. The company sells for $4,000, on account, merchandise that had initially cost $3,000. (Two entries are required.)

f. The company collects $4,000 from its customers.

g. It borrows $10,000 at 6 percent annual interest.

h. The company pays one year's interest.

i. The company purchases for cash a machine for $6,000. The machine has an estimated useful life of three years.

j. The company gives accounting recognition to the use of the machine for one year.

7. *Balance sheet accounts for the end of one year can be derived from data pertaining to the following year.*

The following data pertain to Fowler, Inc. (in millions):

	1993	1992
Assets, December 31	$2,000	$?
Liabilities, December 31	900	?
Common stock outstanding, December 31	500	500
Retained earnings, December 31	600	?
Revenues	1,100	1,000
Expenses	800	700
Dividends	200	200

The expenses for 1993 include $300 million that has not yet been paid as of December 31. Other than this amount, there were no changes in liabilities during 1993.

a. Prepare in summary form the entries to close the revenues and expense accounts of 1993.

b. Determine the missing amounts for 1992.

8. *From the perspective of a bank, customer deposits are liabilities and mortgage loans are assets.*

The following balance sheet is from the semiannual financial statement of Farm & Home Savings Association of Nevada, Missouri (in thousands):

Consolidated Balance Sheet as of December 31

Assets	
Cash and securities	$ 130,810
First mortgage loans	1,981,427
Other loans	21,777
Stock in Federal Home Loan Bank of Des Moines	16,750
Accounts and notes receivable and other assets	37,858
Office buildings and equipment	36,653
Real estate purchases for development	32,910
Real estate	3,263
Total assets	$2,261,448
Liabilities and retained earnings	
Savings accounts	$1,834,271
Advances from Federal Home Loan Bank	240,468
Borrowers' tax and insurance reserve	11,909
Other liabilities	56,965
Deferred income	8,745
Retained earnings	109,090
Total liabilities and retained earnings	$2,261,448

Prepare journal entries to record the following transactions:
a. A depositor adds $500 to a savings account.
b. The bank makes a mortgage loan of $120,000 on a residential home.
c. A borrower makes a monthly mortgage payment of $620, comprising the following:

Interest	$450
Repayment of loan balance	30
Addition to tax and insurance reserve	140

d. The association borrows $250,000 from the Federal Home Loan Bank.
e. The association purchases $150,000 additional stock in the Federal Home Loan Bank.

9. *When a firm returns merchandise, it receives "credit" on its account.*
   Prepare journal entries to reflect the following events on the books of both Wholesale, Inc., and Retail, Inc.
   a. Wholesale, Inc., sells for $5,000 on account to Retail, Inc., merchandise that cost Wholesale, Inc., $4,000.
   b. Upon discovering that some of the merchandise does not meets its specifications, Retail, Inc., returns it to Wholesale, Inc. The returned merchandise had been sold to Retail for $1,000 and had cost Wholesale $800.
   c. Retail, Inc., pays the balance due on its account.

10. *The basic relationship, beginning balance + additions – reductions, can be used to derive a considerable amount of information.*
    The following data were drawn from a company's general ledger balance sheet accounts.

	Beginning Balance	Additions	Reductions	Ending Balance
Accounts receivable	$200	$1,900	$?	$300
Merchandise inventory	90	?	1,100	100
Wages payable	30	800	?	55
Interest payable	12	11	?	13
Rent receivable	24	?	190	26
Accounts payable (for purchases of merchandise)	60	?	?	50

By analyzing the data and giving recognition to the financial events that cause an account to increase and decrease, determine
a. Purchases of merchandise
b. Cost of goods sold
c. Sales revenue (All sales were initially "on account.")
d. Collections from customers
e. Rent revenue
f. Collections of rent
g. Wage expense
h. Wages paid
i. Interest expense
j. Interest paid
k. Payments to suppliers of merchandise

11. *The cash basis of accounting must be distinguished from the accrual basis.*

　　A firm engages in the following summary transactions in its first year of operations:

    a. It purchases furniture and fixtures at a cost of $80,000 (cash). Useful life of the assets is eight years.

    b. It acquires inventory for $300,000. It pays $280,000 and owes the remaining $20,000.

    c. It sells merchandise for $380,000. Cost of the goods sold is $290,000. It collects $330,000 and is owed the remaining $50,000.

    d. It leases its premises at a rate of $3,000 per month. During the year it makes 13 rent payments, including one payment for the first month of the following year.

Prepare two income statements for the year, one on a cash basis, the other on an accrual basis. Under the cash basis, revenues and expenses should be recognized only as cash is received or disbursed. Under the accrual basis, they should be recognized as significant economic events, including the passage of time, take place.

12. *A balance sheet prepared from a preclosing trial balance will not balance.*

　　The preclosing trial balance of Frost, Inc., as of December 31, 1993, is as follows:

	Debits	Credits
Cash	$ 3,000	
Accounts receivable	5,000	
Other assets	12,000	
Accounts payable		$ 5,000
Other liabilities		2,000
Capital contributed by stockholders		4,000
Retained earnings		6,000
Sales revenue		25,000
Cost of goods sold	18,000	
Other expenses	4,000	
	$42,000	$42,000

    a. If, from the trial balance, you were to prepare an income statement and a balance sheet, which accounts would have to be adjusted? Why?

    b. Prepare an income statement.

    c. Make the necessary closing entries.

    d. Prepare a balance sheet, taking into account the effect of the closing entries.

13. *The basic accounting equation can be expanded so as to highlight the relationship among the various balance sheet accounts and revenues, expenses, and dividends.*

　　Arrange a piece of paper in columns with the following headings, each of which corresponds to a term in the accounting equation:

Assets = Liabilities + Contributed capital + Retained earnings, 1/1 + Revenues − Expenses − Dividends

    a. Indicate the effect of each of the following events or other items of information on the accounting equation.

      (1) As of 1/1 a firm reported assets of $200,000, liabilities of $100,000, contributed capital of $10,000, and retained earnings of $90,000.

      (2) The firm purchased merchandise, on account, for $80,000.

      (3) It issued additional common stock for $40,000 cash.

      (4) It borrowed $10,000.

      (5) It made sales of $98,000, all of which were for cash.

(6) The cost of merchandise sold was $50,000.

(7) It incurred interest costs, which were paid in cash, of $7,000.

(8) Taxes assessed for the period, payable the following period, were $11,000.

(9) It declared and paid dividends of $4,000.

b. Determine, by summing the columns, the financial position of the firm at the end of the accounting period as well as the revenues, expenses, and dividends of the period.

c. Compute income for the period.

d. Determine the end-of-period balance in retained earnings after the balance of 1/1 is adjusted to reflect the revenues, expenses, and dividends of the period.

14. *Owners' equity increases whenever net assets (assets minus liabilities) increase, and decreases whenever net assets decrease.*

Indicate the effect (if any) that each of the several transactions described would have on owners' equity (after closing entries have been made):

a. The firm sold for $100 merchandise that had cost $80.

b. The firm purchased merchandise for $2,000.

c. The firm purchased a truck for $12,000 cash.

d. The firm purchased and used $300 of supplies.

e. The firm paid its advertising agency $600 for ads that had been run (and had been given accounting recognition) the previous month.

f. The firm received $750 in dividends on 1,000 shares of XYZ Co. stock that it owns.

g. The firm paid $45 interest on $1,000 that it had previously borrowed from a local bank.

15. *Because of the logical relationships inherent in an accounting system, lost data can be reconstructed.*

Given the following data about a company over a period of three years, determine the missing amounts.

	1993	1994	1995
Retained earnings, 1/1	$1,000	$5,000	$?
Revenues for the year	8,000	?	?
Expenses for the year	?	5,000	8,000
Income for the year	6,000	?	4,000
Dividends declared during the year	?	2,000	3,000
Retained earnings, 12/31	5,000	7,000	?

16. *Entries to revenue and expense accounts can be viewed as entries to retained earnings.*

Assume that a company maintains only four accounts: assets, liabilities, invested capital, and retained earnings. The following transactions occurred during its first month of operations:

(1) The owners of the company contributed a total of $100,000 to establish the business.

(2) The company issued bonds for $50,000; that is, it borrowed $50,000.

(3) The company purchased equipment for $60,000, giving the seller a note for the full amount.

(4) The company purchased merchandise for cash, $40,000.

(5) The company had sales of $30,000. Cash sales were $25,000, and those on account, $5,000.

(6) The company paid $2,000 rent for the current month.

(7) The company paid one month's interest on the bonds, $250.

(8) The company recognized one month's depreciation on the equipment purchased. The estimated useful life of the equipment is 60 months.

(9) The company paid insurance premiums for two months—the current month and the following month—$300 per month.

(10) The company collected $2,000 of the accounts receivable from customers.

(11) The company learned that $500 of the amount owed by customers would not be collectible owing to the bankruptcy of one customer.

(12) The company determined that of the merchandise purchased $22,000 remained on hand, unsold, at the end of the month.

a. Establish T accounts for each of the four accounts. Prepare a journal entry to record each of the transactions, and post the entries to the appropriate T accounts. Compute end-of-month balances in each account.

b. Determine income for the month.

c. Suppose that the company had paid a dividend of $2,000 to its owners. How would that affect the balance in the retained earnings account? How would it affect income for the month?

17. *Some errors affect only the income statement or the balance sheet; those that affect both are generally more serious.*

A bookkeeper made several errors as described below. For each, indicate whether, for the period in which they were made, they would cause a misstatement on the balance sheet only, on the income statement only, or on both the balance sheet and the income statement.

a. Failed to record a sale of $300, on account, to a customer.

b. Failed to record the collection of $200 owed by a customer for a purchase he had made several weeks earlier.

c. Incorrectly recorded the issuance of 1,000 shares of common stock at $2 per share; made the following journal entry:

Cash $2,000
    Marketable securities $2,000

d. Recorded the purchase of a new carburetor for a company-owned vehicle as an addition to fixed assets rather than as a repair.

e. Recorded funds given to a salesperson to entertain customers as a miscellaneous expense rather than a sales expense.

f. Failed to record the purchase of a new truck.

g. Failed to record depreciation on a company-owned car.

h. Incorrectly counted merchandise inventory on hand at year end.

i. Failed to record repayment of the company's loan from a bank.

j. Failed to record payment of interest on the same loan.

18. *At the conclusion of an accounting period, a firm must record financial events that did not automatically trigger journal entries during the period.*

The following events may not always be recognized during the accounting period. Hence they would be recorded at the end of the period. Prepare the necessary journal entries implied by the facts that follow. The firm's fiscal year ends December 31.

a. On August 1 a firm purchased as an investment $1 million in bonds that pay interest on January 31 and July 31. The annual rate of interest is 12 percent (6 percent per semiannual period). The purchase of the bonds was properly recorded, but no interest was recognized during the year.

b. The firm owns equipment that has a useful life of five years. The equipment was purchased three years earlier at a cost of $500,000. No depreciation has been recognized for the current year.

c. The company has not yet paid its rent for December. The rent is $4,500 per month.

d. The company has not yet recorded as an expense the cost of the goods which were sold during the year. At year end, a physical count indicates goods on hand that cost $8 million. Financial statements of the previous year indicated goods on hand at the end of that year of $6.4 million. During the current year the company purchased goods for $25 million. The purchases were added (debited) to inventory. (Thus the December 31 balance in the inventory account was $31.4 million.)

e. The company pays its employees once a month on the fifth day of the month following that in which the wages and salaries were earned. Wages and salaries earned during December totaled $38,000.

f. On January 15 of the new year, the company receives a phone bill of $545 for December service. The company does not close its books until mid-February to avoid having to estimate December charges prior to receipt of phone, utility, and similar bills.

19. *A balance sheet may not balance until a certain key account has been updated.*

Arrange a sheet of paper as indicated in the table below. Leave room for additional accounts that might be required. The first column indicates balances as of January 1.

a. Record the effect of the transactions described, all of which occurred in the month of January, in columns 2 and 3. Indicate the month-end balances in the accounts in columns 4 through 7 as appropriate. Record the total of each column.

(1) Sales for the month, all on credit, were $70,000.

(2) Collections from customers totaled $80,000.

(3) Purchases of merchandise intended for sale were $45,000. All purchases were "on account."

(4) Goods on hand at the month's end totaled $5,000.

(5) Other operating expenses were $15,000. They were paid in cash.

(6) Depreciation expense, in addition to other operating expenses, was based on an estimated useful life of five years (60 months) for all fixed assets. (Assume fixed assets were all purchased on 1/1.)

b. Why doesn't the balance sheet balance after all transactions have been posted?

c. Prepare a journal entry to close accounts as necessary.

Account	Balance 1/1	Transactions in January		Income Statement for January		Balance Sheet, 1/31	
		Dr.	Cr.	Dr.	Cr.	Dr.	Cr.
Cash	$20,000						
Accounts receivable	50,000						
Merchandise inventory	15,000						
Fixed assets	60,000						
Accounts payable	30,000						
Notes payable	25,000						
Common stock	2,000						
Retained earnings	88,000						

20. *Most firms close their books once a year. Financial statements, however, can be prepared at any time and for any time period. The balance sheet and the income statement may be derived from a preclosing rather than a postclosing trial balance. Retained earnings, however, must be adjusted for the income or loss of the period.*

Computer Rental Service, Inc., began operations on January 1, 1993. During its first month of operations, the following events took place:

(1) The company issued 2,000 shares of common stock at $100 per share.

(2) The company rented a store for $2,000 per month. It paid the first month's rent.

(3) The company purchased 20 computers at a price of $5,000 each. The company paid cash of $40,000 and promised to pay the balance within 60 days.

(4) The company purchased, on account, supplies for $5,000.

(5) The company rented out the computers. Total revenues for the month were $8,000. Of this amount $2,000 was collected in cash.

(6) The company paid $1,500 cash to cover other operating expenses.

(7) A count at month end indicated that $4,500 in supplies remained on hand.

(8) At month end the company gave accounting recognition to the depreciation of one month on its computers. The useful life of the computers is estimated at 36 months.

   a. Prepare journal entries to recognize these transactions.

   b. Post the journal entries to T accounts.

   c. Prepare a preclosing trial balance.

   d. Prepare an income statement and a statement of position (balance sheet).

21. *This example, based on an actual incident, stresses the need to distinguish between sales revenues and cash collections.*

     Boscoble Auto Parts began operations in December 1992. According to records maintained by the proprietor, sales for January, the first full month of operation, were $98,000. The company made sales both for cash and credit. At the end of each day, the proprietor recorded the day's ''sales'' in a book he called the ''sales journal.'' The single figure recorded each day was the sum of the sales for cash, the sales for credit, and the subsequent cash collections on previous sales for credit.

     Per supplementary records, which may be assumed to be correct, at the beginning of January the company had accounts receivable from customers of $8,000; at the end of January, accounts receivable had increased to $10,000. During the month, $22,000 had been collected from customers who had made purchases on credit.

     On January 31, a count of the parts on hand revealed that the company had an inventory of parts that cost $25,000. A count on January 1 had revealed an inventory of $15,000. During the month, the company had purchased from suppliers parts that cost a total of $65,000. Other cash operating expenses for January were $23,000.

     In an effort to assist the proprietor, the Small Business Administration has engaged you as a consultant to evaluate the firm's record-keeping system.

   a. What is the primary deficiency in the firm's accounting system? How can it be eliminated? What entry in a journal should the proprietor make each time (1) a cash sale is made, (2) a credit sale is made, (3) cash is collected on a previously recorded credit sale?

   b. Determine first total cash sales and then total credit sales. By how much were January sales overstated? The firm paid sales taxes to the state based on the amount recorded in the sales journal. The sales tax rate was 5 percent. How much of a refund from the state should the proprietor request?

   c. What was the cost of goods actually sold in January?

   d. What was the correct income (loss) for the month?

22. *This problem reviews the accounting cycle.*

     Upon receiving a gift of $4,000, J. Keats decides to enter the copy business. During the first month of operations, the following events take place:

   (1) Keats places the entire $4,000 in a bank account in the name of ''Fast-Copy Co.''

   (2) She signs a three-year lease on a store. Rent is to be at the rate of $400 per month. Keats pays three months' rent at the time she signs the lease, $400 for the current month and $800 in advance.

(3) She purchases furniture and fixtures for $1,500, paying $500 at the time of purchase and promising to pay the balance within 60 days.

(4) She signs a rental agreement with a manufacturer of copy equipment. The agreement stipulates that Keats will pay $200 per month plus 2 cents for each copy made.

(5) She places advertisements in the local newspapers. The cost of the ads is $600, payable in cash.

(6) She purchases paper and other supplies for $800 on account.

(7) She makes her first copies for customers. She sells 30,000 copies at 5 cents each. Customers pay cash for all copies.

(8) She takes an end-of-month inventory and finds $200 of supplies on hand.

(9) She withdraws $200 from the business to meet personal expenses.

(10) She pays the amount due the manufacturer of the copy equipment for the first month's operations.

(11) She gives accounting recognition to the use of the furniture and fixtures for one month. The furniture and fixtures have an estimated useful life of five years.

a. Prepare journal entries to record the transactions of the first month of operations.

b. Post them to T accounts.

c. Prepare an income statement for the month.

d. Prepare any closing entries that would be necessary if the books were to be closed at the end of the month. (Ordinarily books would be closed only at the end of a full accounting period, usually one year.)

e. Prepare a statement of position (a balance sheet).

23. *This problem not only reviews the accounting cycle but also highlights a key deficiency of income as a measure of financial strength.*

The stockholders of Regal Gifts, Inc., were extremely gratified to receive an income statement from management. It revealed that in its first year of operations, the company, which operates a gift shop, had earnings that far exceeded original expectations. Two months after receipt of the income statement, the company was forced to declare bankruptcy. The following information summarizes the major financial events of the company's first year of operations:

(1) Stockholders purchased 1,000 shares of common stock at a price of $100 per share.

(2) The company leased a store in a shopping center. Monthly rent was $1,000. During the year rent payments of $12,000 were made.

(3) The company purchased furniture and fixtures for the store at a cost of $30,000. The company paid cash of $20,000 and gave a one-year note for the balance. The estimated useful life of the furniture and fixtures is 10 years.

(4) In the course of the year, the company purchased at a cost of $240,000 merchandise intended for sale. The company paid $210,000 cash for the merchandise; as of year end, the balance was owed.

(5) The company had sales of $250,000. Sales were made for both cash and credit. As of year end, the company had outstanding receivables from customers of $40,000.

(6) The company paid salaries of $40,000.

(7) The company incurred and paid other operating costs of $15,000.

(8) As of year end, the company had $90,000 of merchandise still on hand.

a. Prepare journal entries to reflect the financial events of the company's first year of operations.

b. Prepare an income statement and a balance sheet.

c. Prepare a statement of cash flow.

d. Explain why the company may have been forced to declare bankruptcy.

24. *Transactions, in summary form, may be derived from the financial statements.*

Robertson, Inc., was organized on January 1, 1993. After one year of operations, the following balance sheet and income statement were prepared.

Robertson, Inc.
Balance Sheet as of December 31, 1993

Assets		
Cash		$ 199,000
Accounts receivable (from customers)		150,000
Inventory		180,000
Plant and equipment	$2,000,000	
Less: Accumulated depreciation	200,000	1,800,000
Total assets		$2,329,000
Liabilities and owners' equity		
Rent payable		$ 1,000
Notes payable (to bank)		900,000
Contributed capital		1,200,000
Retained earnings		228,000
Total liabilities and owners' equity		$2,329,000

Income Statement
Year Ended December 31, 1993

Sales revenue		$1,500,000
Less: Cost of goods sold	$1,000,000	
Depreciation expense	200,000	
Interest expense	60,000	
Rent expense	12,000	1,272,000
Income		$ 228,000

a. Prepare journal entries to reflect the economic events that occurred during the first year of operations. The entries may summarize a series of events. For example, in a single entry, you may record all sales for the year, including those for which cash has already been received as well as those for which the company still has a receivable.

b. Prepare a statement of cash flows.

25. *This problem, based on data from an annual report of Georgia-Pacific Corporation, is intended to demonstrate the relationship between the balance sheet and the statement of cash flows.*

The following are a firm's balance sheet as of December 31, 1993, and its statement of cash flows for 1994. The statement of cash flows is presented in *indirect form*. In contrast to the *direct form,* it shows net income as a source of cash from operating activities. Operating income is then adjusted to take into account revenues and expenses that were greater or less than the related cash flows. Based on the data in the two statements, prepare a balance sheet as of December 31, 1994.

Balance Sheet
December 31, 1993
(in thousands of dollars)

Assets

Current assets	
Cash	$ 32,000
Accounts receivable	535,000
Inventories	617,000
Refundable income taxes	—
Prepaid expenses	11,000
Total current assets	$1,195,000

Natural resources at cost less depletion	774,000
Property, plant, and equipment at cost less depreciation	2,500,000
Other assets	43,000
Total assets	$4,512,000

Liabilities and Shareholders' Equity

Current liabilities	
Commercial paper and other short-term notes	$ 275,000
Other short-term debt	44,000
Accounts payable	430,000
Current income taxes payable	38,000
Total current liabilities	$ 787,000
Long-term debt	1,656,000
Preferred stock	169,000
Common stock	972,000
Retained earnings	$ 928,000
Total liabilities and shareholders' equity	$4,512,000

Statement of Cash Flows
Year Ended December 31, 1994
(in thousands of dollars)

Cash from Operating Activities	
Net income	$ 160,000
Adjustments to net income for revenues and expenses not involving cash	
Amount by which customer collections exceed sales (decrease in accounts receivable)	32,000
Inventory and miscellaneous purchases not yet paid for (increase in accounts payable)	22,000
Inventory purchased but not yet charged as cost of goods sold (increase in inventory)	(100,000)
Tax refunds promised but not yet received (increase in refundable income taxes)	(50,000)
Taxes paid in excess of amounts charged as expenses (decrease in current income taxes payable)	(38,000)
Expenses prepaid (increase in prepaid expenses)	(12,000)
Depreciation of plant and equipment (decrease in property, plant, and equipment)	223,000
Depletion of natural resources (decrease in natural resources)	54,000
Total from operating activities	$ 291,000
Cash from and for Investing Activities	
Purchases of property, plant, and equipment	$(522,000)
Purchases of other assets	(10,000)
Purchases of natural resources	(162,000)
Total used for investing activities	$(694,000)
Cash from and for Financing Activities	
Common stock issued	$ 4,000
Preferred stock issued	28,000
New long-term borrowings	378,000
Repayment of commercial paper and other short-term notes payable	(125,000)
Other short-term borrowings	248,000
Cash dividends on common stock	(132,000)
Total from financing activities	$ 401,000
Net decrease in cash	$(2,000)

1.

(a)

Inventory $320,000
  Accounts payable $320,000
To record purchase of merchandise inventory

(b)

Accounts receivable $290,000
  Sales revenue $290,000
To record sales

(c)

Cost of goods sold $230,000
  Inventory $230,000
To record cost of sales

(d)

Cash $310,000
  Accounts receivable $310,000
To record collections

(e)

Accounts payable $300,000
  Cash $300,000
To record payments to suppliers

(f)

Depreciation expense . . . . $ 10,000
  Accumulated depreciation . . . . $ 10,000
To record depreciation

(g)

Wage and salary expense . . . . $ 20,000
  Wages and salaries payable . . . . $ 5,000
  Cash 15,000
To record wages and salaries

2. See Exhibit 3-12.

EXHIBIT 3-12

Cash			
Bal. 8/1	150,000	(e)	300,000
(d)	310,000	(g)	15,000
Bal. 9/1	145,000		

Accounts payable			
(e)	300,000	Bal. 8/1	220,000
		(a)	320,000
		Bal. 9/1	240,000

Accounts receivable			
Bal. 8/1	100,000	(d)	310,000
(b)	290,000		
Bal. 9/1	80,000		

Wages and salaries payable			
		(g)	5,000
		Bal. 9/1	

Contributed capital			
		Bal. 8/1	200,000
		Bal. 9/1	200,000

Inventory			
Bal. 8/1	250,000	(c)	230,000
(a)	320,000		
Bal. 9/1	340,000		

Retained earnings			
		Bal. 8/1	600,000

Buildings and equipment			
Bal. 8/1	800,000		
Bal. 9/1	800,000		

Sales revenue			
		(b)	290,000

Accumulated depreciation			
		Bal. 8/1	280,000
		(f)	10,000
		Bal. 9/1	290,000

Cost of goods sold			
(c)	230,000		

Wages and salary expense			
(g)	20,000		

Depreciation expense			
(f)	10,000		

3.

Preclosing Trial Balance

Cash	$ 145,000	
Accounts receivable	80,000	
Inventory	340,000	
Buildings and equipment	800,000	
Accumulated depreciation		$ 290,000
Accounts payable		240,000
Wages and salaries payable		5,000
Contributed capital		200,000
Retained earnings		600,000
Sales revenue		290,000
Cost of goods sold	230,000	
Wage and salary expense	20,000	
Depreciation expense	10,000	
	$1,625,000	$1,625,000

4.

Income Statement for August

Sales revenue		$290,000
Less: Expenses		
Cost of goods sold	$230,000	
Wage and salary expense	20,000	
Depreciation expense	10,000	260,000
Income		$ 30,000

5.

(cl 1)

Sales revenue..	$290,000	
Income summary		$290,000
To close revenue account		

(cl 2)

Income summary	$260,000	
Cost of goods sold		$230,000
Wage and salary expense		20,000
Depreciation expense		10,000
To close expense accounts		

(cl 3)

Income summary	$30,000	
Retained earnings..		$30,000
To close income summary account and transfer balance to retained earnings		

Sales revenue					Cost of goods sold			
(cl 1)	290,000	**(b)**	290,000		**(c)**	230,000	**(cl 2)**	230,000

Wage and salary expense					Depreciation expense			
(g)	20,000	**(cl 2)**	20,000		**(f)**	10,000	**(cl 2)**	10,000

Income summary					Retained earnings			
(cl 3)	30,000	**(cl 2)**	30,000				Bal. 8/1	600,000
							(cl 3)	30,000
							Bal. 9/1	630,000

6.

Postclosing Trial Balance

Cash	$ 145,000	
Accounts receivable	80,000	
Inventory	340,000	
Buildings and equipment	800,000	
Accumulated depreciation		$ 290,000
Accounts payable		240,000
Wages and salaries payable		5,000
Contributed capital		200,000
Retained earnings		630,000
	$1,365,000	$1,365,000

7.

Balance Sheet as of August 31

Assets
Cash		$ 145,000
Accounts receivable		80,000
Inventory		340,000
Buildings and equipment	$800,000	
Less: Accumulated depreciation	290,000	510,000
		$1,075,000

Equities
Accounts payable		$ 240,000
Wages and salaries payable		5,000
Contributed capital		200,000
Retained earnings		630,000
		$1,075,000

8.

Statement of Cash Flows for August

Cash Flow from Operating Activities

Collections from customers	$ 310,000
Payments to suppliers	(300,000)
Payments to employees	(15,000)
Net decrease in cash	$ 5,000

4

Accruing Revenues and Expenses

The primary purpose of this chapter is to examine in some depth the accrual basis of accounting and to explore its implications for both managers and investors. The *accrual basis* of accounting is the method whereby revenues and expenses are recognized at the time that they have their primary economic impact, *not necessarily when cash is received or disbursed*. Revenues are assigned to the accounting period in which a critical event, such as the rendering of services or the sale of goods, takes place. Costs are charged as expenses in the period in which the organization benefits from them. In commercial organizations, costs are incurred to generate revenues. Thus, to the extent practical, costs are matched to the revenues to which they are related.

The chapter first contrasts the accrual and cash bases of accounting. It then shows how all revenue and expenses are closely tied to assets and liabilities. These relationships between income statement and balance sheet accounts provide firms with considerable flexibility in how and when they record financial events. The chapter illustrates how a firm can employ any of several competing bookkeeping procedures as long as it updates and corrects its accounts at year end.

The chapter directs particular attention to cost of goods sold. Cost of goods sold is of special interest because it encompasses several subcategories of costs, all of which must be matched to revenues.

The chapter also introduces the general topic of financial analysis. It describes how the accounting structure allows an analyst to derive considerably more information about a company's performance than it may explicitly report. In addition, the chapter highlights several key ratios that are used by financial analysts.

DEFICIENCIES OF THE CASH BASIS

The superiority of the accrual method can be appreciated by comparing it with the cash method. With cash basis accounting, the critical economic event is the collection or disbursement of cash. Revenues attributable to the sale of goods or the provision of services are considered to be *realized* (and given accounting recognition) at the time that cash is collected from customers. Costs are charged as expenses only as actual payment is made for goods or services acquired.

The cash basis of accounting is deficient because it focuses on activities—the receipt or disbursement of cash—that by themselves have relatively little economic significance and that can be easily manipulated by management. When a firm acquires goods or services, the timing of payments is often discretionary. If a firm acquires goods near the end of one period, it can delay recording an expense simply by waiting until the start of the next period to write a check. The City of New York, for example, which had been on a cash basis of accounting, usually paid teachers their June salaries on June 30. One year, the city delayed payment until July, the start of a new fiscal year. By postponing the expenditure to the next fiscal year, it was able to give the appearance of having reduced its operating deficit.

The distorting effects of the cash basis are most pronounced when a cash disbursement is intended to benefit a large number of accounting periods. If a firm were to acquire equipment that was expected to be used for several years, then the entire expense would be reported in the year of payment. The revenues generated by the goods produced by the machine would be recognized, however, over the life of the machine.

ADVANTAGES OF THE ACCRUAL BASIS

Under the accrual concept, revenues are *recognized* when there is evidence that the firm is economically better off owing to its production and sales activities. The criteria for recognizing revenues will be discussed in the next chapter.

Costs are charged as expenses in the same period as the revenues to which they relate are recognized. If it is impractical to relate specific costs to specific revenues, then the costs are charged as expenses in the period in which the goods are consumed or the services provided. Costs which are intended to provide future benefits are *capitalized*—that is, recorded as assets (bundles of "prepaid" expenses)—until the benefits are actually realized. At the time office supplies are purchased, their cost is stored in an asset account, "supplies inventory." It is recorded as an expense only as the supplies are consumed. The supplies could be consumed either before or after they are actually paid for.

Similarly, the cost of services provided by an office staff is generally recorded as an expense during the period in which the firm benefits from their services even though their paychecks may be drawn in a subsequent (or for that matter a previous) accounting period.

Accrual accounting is as advantageous to managers as it is to investors. Both groups use financial reports to assess organizational performance of the past in order to predict and make plans for the future. Accrual accounting, inasmuch as it reports on inflows and outflows of all types of resources, not exclusively cash, generally provides a superior match of efforts to accomplishments.

THE RECORDING PROCESS IN PERSPECTIVE

In the previous chapter it was pointed out that routine journal entries are triggered by transactions, which often involve receipts and disbursements of cash. But revenues and expenses may be generated by economic events other than transactions. Indeed, accountants must identify the *critical event*—that which is central to the activity involved—in order to determine when to recognize a revenue or expense. For example, cash for rent may be received before, during, or after the period for which it is applicable. Rent revenue, however, must be recognized in the period earned irrespective of when the cash is received. Similarly, equipment may be purchased in one period but used over several. The use of the equipment, not the purchase, produces the expense.

Virtually all revenues and expenses are linked to specific assets and liabilities. Whenever a firm receives or dispenses resources but does not recognize a corresponding revenue or expense, it must add to, or subtract from, the related asset or liability.

Asset and liability accounts accommodate *timing* differences between cash flows and recognition of revenues and expenses. Under the cash basis of accounting, there is no need for assets and liabilities other than cash. Revenues coincide with cash receipts, expenses with cash disbursements. Neither resources other than cash nor obligations to provide goods or service are recognized as having value.

Four brief examples will illustrate the relationship, under accrual accounting, between income statement and balance sheet accounts.

Example 1: Resources Are Acquired before They Are Expensed

A company purchases a three-year insurance policy for $9,000, a transaction which, by itself, does not produce an expense. The cost must therefore be "stored" in an *asset account,* "prepaid insurance":

(a)

Prepaid insurance $9,000
   Accounts payable $9,000
To record the purchase of a three-year insurance policy

Over the course of the policy period an expense must be recognized and the prepaid insurance reduced:

(b)

Insurance expense		$3,000
Prepaid insurance		$3,000
To record the expiration of one year of the insurance policy		

When the policy is paid for (another transaction that does not result in an expense), an asset (cash) and a liability (accounts payable) will be reduced.

Example 2: Resources Are Disbursed after They Are Expensed

A firm maintains a loan balance of $100,000 for a year but pays the required interest of $12,000 in the following year. The use of the funds, not the payment of the interest, generates the interest expense. Therefore an expense of $12,000 must be charged and a corresponding amount reported in a *liability account,* "accrued interest payable":

(a)

Interest expense		$12,000
Accrued interest payable		$12,000
To record the interest for one year		

When the interest is paid, the liability is eliminated:

(b)

Accrued interest payable		$12,000
Cash		$12,000
To record the payment of interest		

Example 3: Resources Are Received before Revenue Is Recognized

A firm receives an advance of $25,000 for merchandise that it will sell (deliver) to a customer in a subsequent accounting period.

Revenue from sales is commonly recognized upon delivery of goods to the customer. Thus the cash received must be offset by a *liability,* "advances from customers":

(a)

Cash		$25,000
Advances from customers		$25,000
To record an advance payment from a customer for merchandise to be delivered in a subsequent period		

When the merchandise is delivered, revenue must be recognized and the liability eliminated:

(b)

> Advances from customers $25,000
> Sales revenues $25,000
> **To record a sale upon delivery of merchandise to the customer**

Example 4: Resources Are Received after Revenue Is Recognized

A consulting firm performs services for which it expects to bill a client $100,000 upon completion of the engagement. The critical financial event, that which generates the revenue, is the performance of the services. The revenue must be offset by an *asset*, ''accrued consulting revenues'':

(a)

> Accrued consulting revenues $100,000
> Consulting revenues $100,000
> **To record revenue from consulting**

When the firm bills the client, it will convert the accrued consulting revenues to an account receivable:

(b)

> Accounts receivable $100,000
> Accrued consulting revenues $100,000
> **To record the customer billing**

When it collects its cash, the firm will eliminate the receivable:

(c)

> Cash $100,000
> Accounts receivable $100,000
> **To record collection of cash**

THE RELATIONSHIP BETWEEN THE INCOME STATEMENT AND BALANCE SHEET ACCOUNTS

To expand upon the relationship between income statement and balance sheet accounts under accrual accounting, we note that when a firm acquires more supplies than it uses, the cost of supplies *used* will be charged as an expense; the cost of the remaining supplies must be added to supplies inventory. Conversely, if the firm uses more supplies than it acquires, the difference will be deducted from supplies inventory. Thus

$$\text{Supplies acquired} = \text{Supplies expense} + (-) \Delta \text{Supplies inventory}$$

In slightly modified form,

$$\text{Supplies expense} = \text{Supplies acquired} + \text{Supplies on hand beginning of period} - \text{Supplies on hand end of period}$$

Assume that a firm begins a period with a supplies inventory of $100. During the year it acquires supplies of $3,000. At end of year it has supplies on hand of $500. Therefore supplies expense (the amount consumed) must be $2,600:

Supplies acquired	$3,000	
+ Supplies on hand, beginning of period	100	$3,100
− Supplies on hand, end of period		500
= Supplies expense		$2,600

This basic relationship is equally applicable to all other accounts. Sales revenue, for example, would be the difference between cash collected from customers and the increase or decrease in accounts receivable or advances from customers:

$$\text{Sales revenue} = \text{Cash collections} + \Delta\text{Accounts receivable} - \Delta\text{Advances from customers}$$

Suppose, for example, that a firm begins a year with accounts receivable of $3 million. During the year it collects $40 million from customers. At year end it has no outstanding accounts receivable but $6 million in new advances from customers. Sales revenue would therefore be $31 million:

Cash collections	$40
+ ΔAccounts receivable, end of period	(3)
− ΔAdvances from customers, end of period	(6)
= Sales revenue	$31

As will be demonstrated later in the chapter, this association between balance sheet and income statement accounts is especially useful in deriving "missing" information. As long as three of the four elements of the equation are known, the fourth can easily be calculated.

ADJUSTING THE ACCOUNTS AT PERIOD END

Because each revenue and expense can be linked to an asset and liability, firms have considerable flexibility in maintaining their accounts. First, as illustrated in Chapter 3, firms can postpone recording financial events such as the passage of time until the end of a fiscal period. Then, when financial statements must be prepared, they can bring the accounts up to date with simple end-of-period adjustments.

Second, throughout the year firms can record transactions in ways that may be convenient but are conceptually in error. At year end, they can rectify their "mistakes" with correcting entries that are similar to the updating entries.

This section illustrates three methods of accounting for supplies. Only the first leads to balances in supplies expense and the related supplies inventory that are perpetually current. The other two permit the firm to make fewer journal entries during the year, but they result in accounts that are always out of date and need to be adjusted before financial statements can be prepared.

Suppose that at the beginning of an accounting period a company has on hand $1,000 in supplies. During the accounting period it purchases, for cash, $4,000 of supplies and consumes $2,000. The correct ending balance in the supplies account would be $3,000; supplies expense for the period would be $2,000 (the amount consumed):

Balance, supplies inventory, 1/1	$1,000	
Purchases 1/1–12/31	4,000	$5,000
Supplies used (expense), 1/1–12/31		2,000
Balance, supplies inventory, 12/31		$3,000

Perpetual Method: No Year-End Adjustment Required

The most direct and conceptually correct means of accounting for supplies would be to increase the supplies inventory account each time supplies were purchased and to decrease the account each time supplies were withdrawn and presumably used. Thus

(a) *Various Dates*

Supplies inventory $4,000
    Cash $4,000
To record the purchase of supplies

(If the $4,000 of supplies represents the sum of several purchases, then similar journal entries would be made for each purchase.)

(b) *Various Dates*

Supplies expense $2,000
    Supplies inventory $2,000
To record the use of $2,000 of supplies

At the end of the year, the accounts would appear as follows:

Supplies inventory					Supplies expense	
Bal. 1/1	1,000	(b) Var. dates	2,000		(b) Var. dates	2,000
(a) Var. dates	4,000					
	3,000					

Cash			
Bal. 1/1	xxx	(a) Var. dates	4,000

The accounts correctly reflect the ending inventory of $3,000 and supplies expense of $2,000. No adjusting entries are required. It is necessary only to "close" the supplies expense account. The problem with this method is that if supplies are withdrawn in small amounts at frequent intervals, record keeping in the course of the year becomes burdensome since a separate entry must be made for both each purchase and each withdrawal.

Periodic Method: Asset Account Overstated

As an alternative, a company can avoid making an accounting entry each time supplies are *withdrawn* from the storeroom. Instead of recording both the purchase and the use of supplies, it would record only the purchase. In the course of the year, the supplies inventory account would only be debited—never credited. At the end of the year, however, the firm would take a *physical inventory* (count) to determine the actual amount of supplies on hand. The company would assume that all supplies purchased plus those on hand at the beginning of the year must have been used during the year if they are not physically present at the conclusion of the year. It would adjust the accounts by crediting inventory with the amount required to reduce supplies inventory to reflect the inventory actually on hand and by debiting supplies expense with the same amount—the amount presumably used during the year. Thus

(a) Various Dates

```
Supplies inventory ..............................................$4,000
    Cash .......................................................$4,000
To record the purchase of supplies throughout the year
```

At the end of the year, prior to the physical inventory count, the accounts would show the following:

Supplies inventory	
Bal. 1/1	1,000
(a) Var. dates	4,000

Supplies expense			Cash	
			xxx	(a) Var. dates 4,000

Assume that a physical count at year end reveals supplies on hand of $3,000. Therefore $2,000 of supplies ($5,000 per the accounts less $3,000 on hand) must have been consumed. The appropriate adjusting journal entry would be

(b)

```
12/31 Supplies expense ......................................$2,000
      Supplies inventory ....................................$2,000
To adjust the accounts at year end to reflect the physical count of supplies
```

Supplies inventory				Supplies expense	
Bal. 1/1	1,000	(b) 12/31	2,000	(b) 12/31	2,000
(a) Var. dates	4,000				
	3,000				

Once the adjusting entries have been posted, the account balances would be identical to those derived from the procedure illustrated previously.[1] The former approach is often referred to as a *perpetual* method, since the inventory account is always reflective of the actual quantity on hand, and the latter approach as a *periodic* method, since periodic counts are necessary to bring the inventory account up to date.

Periodic Method: Expense Account Overstated

The same results could be obtained by a third procedure, which is also widely used. Instead of charging (debiting) all purchases of supplies to supplies inventory, a company could charge them to *supplies expense*.

At year end, the balance in the supplies account would still equal the beginning balance; no entries to the account would have been made during the year. The firm would then take a year-end count of supplies on hand. To adjust the inventory account to reflect the actual inventory on hand, it would debit (increase) or credit (decrease) the account to bring it up or down to the quantity indicated by the physical count. It would make the corresponding credit (or debit) to supplies expense. If more supplies were purchased than were actually used, then the firm would have to increase (debit) the supplies inventory account and decrease (credit) the supplies expense account. If more were used than purchased, then it would have to decrease (credit) the supplies inventory account and increase (debit) the supplies expense account.

(a) Various Dates

Supplies expense		$4,000
Cash		$4,000

To record the purchase of supplies

---

[1] Many firms use a modified version of this approach. Instead of initially debiting supplies inventory for purchases, they first debit an account called "purchases." At year end, they close the purchases account to supplies inventory. Then they adjust the new balance in the supplies inventory account to reflect the actual amount of goods on hand. Thus

(a) Various Dates

Purchases		$4,000
Cash		$4,000

To record the purchase of supplies throughout the year

(b) 12/31

Supplies inventory		$4,000
Purchases		$4,000

To transfer the balance in the purchases account to supplies inventory

(c) 12/31

Supplies expense		$2,000
Supplies inventory		$2,000

To adjust the accounts at year end to reflect the physical count of supplies

The advantage of this modification is that it provides, in the purchases account, direct information on total purchases during the year.

At the end of the year, before the adjusting entries were made, the accounts would appear as follows:

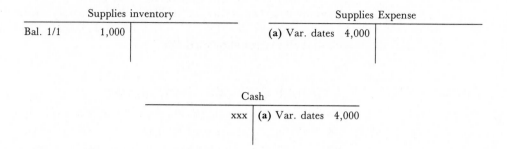

Supplies inventory

Bal. 1/1	1,000	

Supplies Expense

(a) Var. dates	4,000	

Cash

	xxx	(a) Var. dates	4,000

If, as before, the physical count at year end revealed that $3,000 of supplies were on hand, then supplies inventory would be understated by $2,000. Correspondingly, supplies expense would be overstated by that same amount. The required adjusting entry would therefore be

(b)

12/31 Supplies inventory $2,000
      Supplies expense $2,000
To adjust the inventory and expense accounts for the excess of the physical count over the balance in the inventory account

Supplies inventory

Bal. 1/1	1,000	
(b) 12/31	2,000	
	3,000	

Supplies expense

(a) Var. dates	4,000	(b) 12/31	2,000

The adjusted balances would, of course, be in accord with those derived by the other two methods.

A Warning

In making either updating or adjusting entries, accounting students are often unsure of the accounts to be adjusted. Although it may be obvious to them that one account must be corrected, they are unsure of the corresponding half of the entry. There is a temptation, in the face of uncertainty, to debit or credit either "Cash" or "Retained earnings." In fact, neither is likely to be affected by periodic adjustments. "Cash" needs to be debited or credited only upon the actual receipt or disbursement of cash. Indeed, unless the student can actually envision a transfer of cash—by check, in currency, or by notification of credits or charges by the bank—he or she can be reasonably certain that it is not "Cash" that should be debited or credited. Similarly, retained earnings in the ordinary course of business is affected directly by only two types of events:

the declaration of a dividend and the posting of year-end closing entries. Updating or adjusting entries affect either an asset or a liability account and its related revenue or expense account.

YEAR-END ADJUSTMENTS—AN EXAMPLE

Exhibit 4-1 indicates the December 31, 1993, trial balance of the Altoona Appliance Company, a retail store, before year-end adjustments have been made. The following additional information that requires accounting recognition is available to the accountant in charge of preparing annual financial statements.

Unexpired Insurance

The prepaid insurance ($40,000) indicated on the trial balance represents the unexpired portion of a three-year policy purchased in 1992. The required

EXHIBIT 4-1

Altoona Appliance Company
Trial Balance
December 31, 1993

	Debits	Credits
Cash	$ 105,000	
Accounts receivable	437,500	
Allowance for uncollectible accounts		$ 45,000
Merchandise inventory	652,000	
Prepaid insurance	40,000	
Supplies inventory	5,000	
Land	100,000	
Building	450,000	
Accumulated depreciation, building		110,000
Furniture and fixtures	47,000	
Accumulated depreciation, furniture and fixtures		14,100
Notes receivable	20,000	
Accounts payable		182,000
Sales taxes payable		2,000
Advances from customers		5,000
Common stock		250,000
Retained earnings		873,650
Sales revenue		3,302,000
Gain on sale of furniture and fixtures		12,000
Cost of goods sold	2,179,000	
Wages and salaries	567,000	
Delivery and shipping charges	33,500	
Depreciation expense	12,850	
Property taxes	1,800	
Supplies expense	9,400	
Other expenses	35,700	
Income taxes	100,000	
	$4,795,750	$4,795,750

insurance expense of $20,000 has not yet been charged for 1993. The following adjusts the accounts and brings them up to date:

(a)

Insurance expense $20,000
    Prepaid insurance $20,000
To record the expiration of one-third of a three-year policy

Depreciation

The company charges depreciation semiannually, June 30 and December 31. The building, which originally cost $450,000, is being depreciated over a 30-year period; furniture and fixtures, which originally cost $47,000, are being depreciated over a 10-year period. Thus depreciation charges for a full year are $15,000 and $4,700, respectively—for a half-year, $7,500 and $2,350.[2]

(b)

Depreciation expense $9,850
    Accumulated depreciation, building $7,500
    Accumulated depreciation, furniture and fixtures $2,350
To record depreciation for one-half year

Interest Earned

The note receivable, $20,000, is a one-year note and was received from a commercial customer on November 1, 1993. The note bears a rate of interest of 12 percent. Interest is payable at the expiration of the note. Interest earned in the two months in 1993 during which the company held the note must be recognized. Interest earned would be two-twelfths of 12 percent of $20,000, or $400.

(c)

Accrued interest receivable $400
    Interest revenue $400
To record the interest earned but not yet collected

Property Taxes

The company makes property tax payments once a year, on January 31. Total taxes payable on January 31, 1994, will be $22,800. Accounting recognition must be given to the portion—eleven-twelfths of $22,800—applicable to 1993. Additional tax expense for 1993, to be added to the expense of $1,800, which was recorded when the January 31, 1993, tax bill was paid, is therefore $20,900, and total tax expense for the year will be $22,700:

(d)

Property taxes (expense) $20,900
    Accrued property taxes payable $20,900
To record the portion of property taxes due in 1994 applicable to 1993.

---

[2]The amount to be charged for the second half of the year is less than that charged for the first ($12,850 per "depreciation expense" on the trial balance). As indicated by the account "gain on sale of furniture and fixtures," some fixed assets were sold during the year.

Supplies

A physical count indicated supplies on hand of $3,000. Supplies purchased during the year were charged entirely to supplies expense. The supplies inventory account must be credited by $2,000 to reflect the difference between the current balance in the account ($5,000 per the trial balance) and actual supplies in stock:

(e)

Supplies expense	$2,000	
Supplies inventory		$2,000

To adjust the accounts to reflect the physical count of supplies on hand

Wages and Salaries

The company pays its employees every two weeks. At year end, employees have worked four days for which they will not be paid until the first payday of the new year. Wages and salaries applicable to the four-day period total $10,900:

(f)

Wages and salaries (expense)	$10,900	
Accrued wages and salaries payable		$10,900

To record wages and salaries earned by employees but not yet paid

Inventory Shortage

The company maintains its merchandise inventory on a *perpetual* basis. Each time an item is sold, an entry is made in which merchandise inventory is reduced by the cost of the item sold, and cost of goods sold is charged for the same amount. Thus, at year end, the amount recorded in the accounts should be in agreement with that actually on hand. However, an actual count of merchandise on hand reveals an unexplained shortage of $6,000. The shortage, of course, must be accounted for:

(g)

Inventory shortage (expense)	$6,000	
Merchandise inventory		$6,000

To adjust the accounts to reflect the physical count of merchandise on hand

Income Taxes

Based on a preliminary computation, income taxes (both state and federal) for the year will total $155,000. To date, the company has made payments of $100,000 based on quarterly estimates of earnings. The company now forecasts that additional payments of $55,000 will be required. Although such payments need not be made until March 15, 1994, they represent an expense of the current year, 1993:

(h)

Income taxes (expense)	$55,000	
Accrued income taxes payable		$55,000

To record additional income tax expense based on a preliminary computation

EXHIBIT 4-2

Altoona Appliance Company
Worksheet
Year Ended December 31, 1993

	Unadjusted Trial Balance		Adjustments		Balance Sheet		Income Statement	
	Dr.	Cr.	Dr.	Cr.	Dr.	Cr.	Dr.	Cr.
Cash	105,000				105,000			
Accounts receivable	437,500				437,500			
Allowance for uncollectible accounts		45,000				45,000		
Merchandise inventory	652,000			6,000 (g)	646,000			
Prepaid insurance	40,000			20,000 (a)	20,000			
Supplies inventory	5,000			2,000 (e)	3,000			
Land	100,000				100,000			
Building	450,000				450,000			
Accumulated depreciation, building		110,000		7,500 (b)		117,500		
Furniture and fixtures	47,000				47,000			
Accumulated depreciation, furniture and fixtures		14,100		2,350 (b)		16,450		
Notes receivable	20,000				20,000			
Accounts payable		182,000				182,000		
Sales tax payable		2,000				2,000		
Advances from customers		5,000				5,000		
Common stock		250,000				250,000		
Retained earnings		873,650				873,650		
Sales revenue		3,302,000						3,302,000

Account	Unadjusted Dr	Unadjusted Cr	Adjustments Dr	Adjustments Cr	Income Statement Dr	Income Statement Cr	Balance Sheet Dr	Balance Sheet Cr
Gain on sale of furniture and fixtures		12,000				12,000		
Cost of goods sold	2,179,000				2,179,000			
Wages and salaries	567,000		10,900 (f)		577,900			
Delivery and shipping charges	33,500				33,500			
Depreciation expense	12,850		9,850 (b)		22,700			
Property tax expense	1,800		20,900 (d)		22,700			
Supplies expense	9,400		2,000 (e)		11,400			
Other expenses	35,700				35,700			
Income taxes	100,000		55,000 (h)		155,000			
Unadjusted totals	4,795,750	4,795,750						
Insurance expense			20,000 (a)		20,000			
Accrued interest receivable			400 (c)				400	
Interest revenue				400 (c)		400		
Accrued property taxes payable				20,900 (d)				20,900
Inventory shortage			6,000 (g)		6,000			
Accrued wages and salaries payable				10,900 (f)				10,900
Accrued income taxes payable				55,000 (h)				55,000
Totals			125,050	125,050	3,063,900	3,314,400	1,828,900	1,578,400
Net income					250,500			250,500
Adjusted totals					3,314,400	3,314,400	1,828,900	1,828,900

Capturing the Adjustments and Preparing the Statements

Exhibit 4-2 illustrates a worksheet that can be used to capture the adjustments and prepare the income statement and the balance sheet. The worksheet is a functional means of summarizing the adjustments and their impact upon the general ledger accounts. It eliminates the inconvenience of striking a new trial balance each time the need for an additional adjustment is uncovered. It does not, however, save the firm from having ultimately to post the adjustments to the actual general ledger accounts.

Note the following features of the worksheet:

- The first two columns (after the account titles) reflect the income statement and balance sheet amounts (per Exhibit 4-1) prior to the adjustments. The balances are obviously "preclosing" (if they were not, the amounts in the revenue and expense accounts would be zero). Therefore the balance in the retained earnings account does not yet incorporate income for the year.
- The second two columns summarize the year-end adjustments (journal entries **a** through **h**). Accounts that were affected by the adjusting entries, but which previously had zero balances and therefore were not included in the trial balance shown in Exhibit 4-1, are listed beneath the accounts which were included. The sums of the debits and credits in this column are equal. If they were not, then an error must have been made in either the entries themselves or in posting the entries to the worksheet.
- Columns 5 and 6 indicate the adjusted balance sheet accounts and columns 7 and 8 indicate the adjusted income statement accounts. The debit and credit columns of both the income statement and the balance sheet are "out of balance." The credit column of the income statement exceeds the debit column by the income for the year ($250,500). Correspondingly, the debit column of the balance sheet exceeds the credit column by the same amount. As pointed out in the illustration of the accounting cycle in the previous chapter, this imbalance exists because the retained earnings account has not yet been updated. When the revenue and expense accounts for the year are "closed" to retained earnings, the inequality will be eliminated.

Exhibit 4-3 depicts the affected accounts of the company after the foregoing transactions have been posted. Exhibit 4-4 illustrates another worksheet. In this worksheet, the first two columns are a preclosing trial balance after the adjustments have been posted. These amounts are identical to those in the income statement and balance sheet accounts in the right-hand columns of Exhibit 4-2. Therefore the worksheets of Exhibits 4-2 and 4-4 could easily have been combined.

The next two columns of Exhibit 4-4 include the closing entries (which are shown in Exhibit 4-5). The last two columns report the postclosing balances. The postclosing balances include only balance sheet accounts. The income statement balances have all been "zeroed out." Exhibit 4-6 presents the income statement and balance sheet, which incorporate the year-end adjustments.

EXHIBIT 4-3

General Ledger Accounts (Only Those Affected by Adjusting Entries)

Accrued interest receivable				Prepaid insurance		
(c)	400		Bal.	40,000	**(a)**	20,000
	400			20,000		

Supplies inventory				Merchandise inventory		
Bal.	5,000	**(e)**	2,000	Bal.	652,000	**(g)**	6,000
	3,000			646,000		

Accumulated depreciation, building			Accumulated depreciation, furniture and fixtures		
	Bal.	110,000		Bal.	14,100
	(b)	7,500		**(b)**	2,350
		117,500			16,450

Accrued wages and salaries payable			Accrued income taxes payable		
	(f)	10,900		**(h)**	55,000
		10,900			55,000

Accrued property taxes payable			Interest revenue		
	(d)	20,900		**(c)**	400
		20,900			400

Inventory shortage expense			Income taxes expense		
(g)	6,000		Bal.	100,000	
			(h)	55,000	
	6,000			155,000	

Insurance expense			Depreciation expense		
(a)	20,000		Bal.	12,850	
			(b)	9,850	
	20,000			22,700	

Property taxes expense			Supplies expense		
Bal.	1,800		Bal.	9,400	
(d)	20,900		**(e)**	2,000	
	22,700			11,400	

Wages and salaries expense		
Bal.	567,000	
(f)	10,900	
	577,900	

EXHIBIT 4-4

Altoona Appliance Company
Worksheet—Closing Entries
December 31, 1993

	Adjusted Trial Balance		Closing Entries		Postclosing Trial Balance	
	Dr.	Cr.	Dr.	Cr.	Dr.	Cr.
Cash	105,000				105,000	
Accounts receivable	437,500				437,500	
Allowance for un-collectible accounts		45,000				45,000
Accrued interest receivable	400				400	
Merchandise inventory	646,000				646,000	
Supplies inventory	3,000				3,000	
Prepaid insurance	20,000				20,000	
Land	100,000				100,000	
Building	450,000				450,000	
Accumulated deprecia-tion, building		117,500				117,500
Furniture and fixtures	47,000				47,000	
Accumulated deprecia-tion, furniture and fixtures		16,450				16,450
Notes receivable	20,000				20,000	
Accounts payable		182,000				182,000
Sales taxes payable		2,000				2,000
Advances from cus-tomers		5,000				5,000
Accrued property taxes payable		20,900				20,900
Accrued wages and salaries payable		10,900				10,900
Accrued income taxes payable		55,000				55,000
Common stock		250,000				250,000
Retained earnings		873,650		250,500 (c3)		1,124,150
Sales revenue		3,302,000	3,302,000 (c1)			0
Gain on sale of furni-ture and fixtures		12,000	12,000 (c1)			0
Interest revenue		400	400 (c1)			0
Cost of goods sold	2,179,000			2,179,000 (c2)	0	
Wages and salaries	577,900			577,900 (c2)	0	
Delivery and shipping charges	33,500			33,500 (c2)	0	
Depreciation expense	22,700			22,700 (c2)	0	
Property taxes	22,700			22,700 (c2)	0	
Supplies expense	11,400			11,400 (c2)	0	
Other expenses	35,700			35,700 (c2)	0	
Income taxes	155,000			155,000 (c2)	0	
Insurance expense	20,000			20,000 (c2)	0	
Inventory shortage	6,000			6,000 (c2)	0	
Income summary	0		3,063,900 (c2)	3,314,400 (c1)		
			250,500 (c3)			0
Totals	4,892,800	4,892,800	6,628,800	6,628,800	1,828,900	1,828,900

EXHIBIT 4-5

Closing Entries

(c1)

Sales revenue		$3,302,000
Gain on sale of furniture and fixtures		12,000
Interest revenue		400
Income summary		$3,314,400

To close the revenue accounts

(c2)

Income summary		$3,063,900
Cost of goods sold		$2,179,000
Wages and salaries		577,900
Delivery and shipping charges		33,500
Depreciation		22,700
Property taxes		22,700
Supplies expense		11,400
Other expenses		35,700
Income taxes		155,000
Inventory shortage		6,000
Insurance expense		20,000

To close the expense accounts

(c3)

Income summary		$250,500
Retained earnings		$250,500

To transfer income to retained earnings

ERRORS AND OMISSIONS

Organizations do, unfortunately, make errors. An examination of some common types of errors and their impact on financial reports provides additional insight into the accounting process.

Some errors are easily detectable. An entry to a journal may be made in which the debits do not equal the credits. Incorrect amounts may be posted to the ledger accounts. Then, when a trial balance is struck, the sum of the general ledger debits will not equal the sum of the credits.

Other errors, most particularly those related to updating or adjusting entries, are less easily detectable and are likely to affect both balance sheet and income statement accounts. Many such errors are, however, *self-correcting* over time. They will automatically be eliminated either upon the liquidation of the offending asset or liability or when other routine adjustments to the accounts are made. The errors may nonetheless be serious because the intervening financial statements will have been incorrect.

Consider a firm that maintains its inventory records on a periodic basis. The firm physically counts merchandise on hand at the end of each fiscal year. During the year it maintains accurate records of all purchases. In determining the cost of goods sold for the year, it computes goods available for sale (beginning inventory plus purchases during the year) and subtracts goods that remain

EXHIBIT 4-6

Altoona Appliance Company
Income Statement
Year Ended December 31, 1993

Revenues		
Sales	$3,302,000	
Interest	400	
Gain on sale of furniture and fixtures	12,000	
Total revenue		$3,314,400
Expenses		
Cost of goods sold	2,179,000	
Wages and salaries expense	577,900	
Delivery and shipping charges	33,500	
Depreciation expense	22,700	
Property tax expense	22,700	
Supplies expense	11,400	
Insurance expense	20,000	
Inventory shortage expense	6,000	
Other expenses	35,700	
Total expenses		2,908,900
Income before taxes		$ 405,500
Income taxes		155,000
Net income		$ 250,500

Altoona Appliance Company
Balance Sheet
December 31, 1993

Assets

Current assets		
Cash		$ 105,000
Accounts receivable	$437,500	
Less: Allowance for bad debts	45,000	392,500
Accrued interest receivable		400
Merchandise inventory		646,000
Supplies inventory		3,000
Prepaid insurance		20,000
Total current assets		$1,166,900
Noncurrent assets		
Land		$ 100,000
Building	$450,000	
Less: Accumulated depreciation	117,500	323,500
Furniture and fixtures	47,000	
Less: Accumulated depreciation	16,450	30,550
Notes receivable		20,000
Total noncurrent assets		$ 483,050
Total assets		$1,649,950

Liabilities and Stockholders' Equity

Current liabilities	
Accounts payable	$ 182,000
Sales tax payable	2,000
Advances from customer	5,000
Accrued property taxes payable	20,900
Accrued wages and salaries payable	10,900
Accrued income taxes payable	55,000
Total current liabilities	$ 275,800
Stockholders' equity	
Common stock	$ 250,000
Retained earnings	1,124,150
Total stockholders' equity	$1,374,150
Total liabilities and stockholders' equity	$1,649,950

unsold at the end of the year (ending inventory). If beginning inventory was $3 million, purchases were $30 million, and ending inventory was $6 million, then cost of goods sold during the year would be $27 million:

Beginning inventory	$ 3	
Purchases	30	$33
Ending inventory		(6)
Cost of goods sold		$27

If in the following year, purchases were $35 million and ending inventory was $2 million, then the cost of goods sold would be $39 million.

Beginning inventory (same as ending inventory of previous year)	$ 6	
Purchases	35	$41
Ending inventory		(2)
Cost of goods sold		$39

Suppose, however, that at the end of the first year the firm miscounted its inventory. Instead of $6 million, the firm counted goods on hand of $5 million. As a result of the miscount, cost of goods sold during the first year would have been reported as $28 million—*overstated* by $1 million. In the second year, the *beginning inventory* would have been understated by $1 million. Cost of goods sold for the second year (assuming a correct count at the end of the second year) would have been reported at $38 million—*understated* by $1 million (I = incorrect; C = correct):

	Year 1		Year 2	
Beginning inventory	$ 3 (C)		$ 5 (I)	
Purchases	30 (C)	$33	$35 (C)	$40 (I)
Ending inventory		(5) (I)		(2) (C)
Cost of goods sold		$28 (I)		$38 (I)

Cost of goods sold—and thus income—would be correctly stated for the two-year period combined but incorrectly stated for each of the two individual periods. Both current assets (inventory) and retained earnings would be in error after the first year, but correct after the second.

Consider also a firm that received a two-year, $1,000 note in June 1993. The note carried an interest rate of 14 percent. Interest was receivable annually each June; the principal, in its entirety, was due from the borrower at the expiration of the note in June 1995.

If the firm made proper adjusting entries, then revenue from the note would be $70 in 1993 (six months' interest), $140 in 1994 (one year's interest), and $70 in 1995 (six months' interest)—regardless of when cash payments were received. Suppose, however, that the firm neglected to "accrue" interest at the end of 1993 and instead recognized revenue only upon the receipt of cash. For the year ended 1993, revenues, current assets (accrued interest receivable), and

EXHIBIT 4-7
Impact of Failure to Accrue Interest Revenue

On June 30, 1993, a company receives a two-year note for $1,000 at 14 percent interest. Interest payments of $140 are due on June 30, 1994, and June 30, 1995.

	Company Correctly Accrues Interest at Year End	Company Recognizes Interest Revenues Only as Cash Is Received	Difference
Accrued interest receivable, 1/1/93	$ 0	$ 0	$ 0
Interest revenue, 1993	70	0	70
Interest (cash) received, 1993	(0)	(0)	(0)
Accrued interest receivable, 12/31/93	70	0	70
Interest revenue, 1994	140	140	0
Interest (cash) received, 1994	(140)	(140)	(0)
Accrued interest receivable, 12/31/94	70	0	70
Interest revenue, 1995	70	140	(70)
Interest (cash) received, 1995	(140)	(140)	(0)
Accrued interest receivable, 12/31/95	$ 0	$ 0	$ 0
Total interest (cash) received	$140	$140	$ 0
Total interest revenue recognized	$140	$140	$ 0

retained earnings each would be understated by $70. For the year ended 1994, revenues would be correctly stated, as the firm would have recorded $140 interest revenue upon the receipt of the cash interest payment. However, since the cash payment represented interest for the period June 1993 to June 1994, current assets, and thus retained earnings, would still be understated by $70—the interest for the period June 1994 to December 1994. For the year ended 1995, however, revenues would be *overstated* by $70, as the entire cash interest payment of $140 would be recorded as revenue. Current assets (accrued interest receivable would be zero), however, would now be correctly stated; so, too, would retained earnings. The differences are summarized in Exhibit 4-7.

Although in the *long run* many errors may be self-correcting, a primary purpose of accounting is to report changes in the welfare of an enterprise in the course of specific, relatively short periods of time. Firms are not permitted the luxury of allowing the passage of the years to compensate for their errors and omissions.

DERIVING MISSING INFORMATION

A complete set of financial statements, prepared in accordance with generally accepted accounting principles, contains an abundance of information as to a firm's operations and financial position. Sometimes, however, the data sought by an analyst are not available, perhaps because they are of a type not incorporated into one of the primary financial statements or perhaps because they got subsumed in the summary and aggregation of individual accounts. Moreover, managers and investors must sometime make do, especially in the case of companies not publicly traded, with financial reports that are missing one of the primary statements or contain other material omissions. The following two examples illustrate how the fundamental relationships between income statement and balance sheet accounts enable an analyst to derive missing data.

Example 1: Purchases of Inventory

An analyst needs to determine the amount of inventory *purchased* by a firm. The firm's comparative balance sheets report beginning-of-year and end-of-year inventory on hand of $5 million and $10 million, respectively. Its income statement discloses cost of goods sold of $50 million. Its statement of cash flow indicates payments to suppliers, but none of the three primary statements reveals purchases.

Using the relationship between inventory and cost of goods sold, the analyst can easily derive purchases. If

Beginning inventory + Purchases − Cost of goods sold = Ending inventory

then purchases equal cost of goods sold plus the increase in inventory:

Purchases = Cost of goods sold + Ending inventory − Beginning inventory

$$= \$50 + \$10 - \$5$$

$$= \$55$$

Thus, in summary:

Beginning inventory	$ 5
+ Purchases	55
= Goods available for sale	60
− Cost of goods sold	(50)
= Ending inventory	$10

Example 2: Sale of Equipment

As to equipment sold, an analyst needs to determine its initial cost, its accumulated depreciation, and the gain or loss on sale. This information may help the analyst confirm a suspicion that the firm is disposing of relatively new equipment which has decreased in value, perhaps because it is prematurely obsolete. The firm's financial statements reveal the following (in thousands):

	Balance Sheets		Income Statement	Statement of Cash Flows
	Beginning	Ending		
Equipment	$500	$720		
Less: Accumulated depreciation	(300)	(530)		
Net book value	$200	$190		
Acquisitions				$(480)
Cash received upon sale of equipment				125
Depreciation expense			$250	

A useful means of deriving missing data is to reconstruct the journal entry to record the relevant transaction. If all elements of the entry but one are known, the missing amount can easily be determined. In this case, the entry to record the sale of equipment, including the amount known from the information in the financial statements, would be

```
Cash..............................................................$125
Loss on sale of equipment .........................................      ?
Accumulated depreciation ..........................................      ?
        Equipment..................................................$  ?
  To record sale of equipment
```

In this situation, three of the four elements of the entry are unknown. The analyst must therefore pursue additional sources of information.

Accumulated depreciation is increased only by annual depreciation charges. It is decreased only by the sale or retirement of assets, when the accumulated depreciation applicable to the disposed-of asset is removed from the account (as in the entry just presented). Therefore, as to accumulated depreciation,

Beginning balance + Depreciation expense
        − Accumulated depreciation on retired assets = Ending balance

By rearrangement,

Accumulated depreciation on retired assets
        = Beginning balance − Ending balance + Depreciation expense

Based on the data in the financial statements,

Accumulated depreciation on retired assets = \$300 − \$530 + \$250

Accumulated depreciation on retired assets = \$20

Using similar logic, the analyst can deduce from the equipment account the initial cost of the equipment sold:

Beginning balance + Acquisitions − Retirements = Ending balance

By rearrangement,

Retirements = Beginning balance − Ending balance + Acquisitions

Based on data in the financial statements, the analyst can find

Retirements = \$500 − \$720 + \$480

= \$260

With information on three of the four components of the journal entry to record the sale of the equipment, the fourth, the loss on sale, can easily be calculated:

```
Cash..............................................................$125
Loss on sale of equipment .........................................      ?
Accumulated depreciation ..........................................     20
        Equipment .................................................$260
  To record sale of equipment
```

If the entry is to balance, the loss must have been \$115: \$260 − (\$125 + \$20).

Thus the analyst finds that during the year the company sold for \$125 equipment that had cost \$260. Since book value of the equipment (initial cost less depreciation) is $240, the sale has resulted in a loss of $115. The equipment was relatively new in that only $20 (7 percent of initial cost of $260) had been depreciated.

COST OF GOODS SOLD

It has been previously pointed out that, in accordance with the accrual concept, costs are *capitalized* as assets until the intended benefits are actually realized. In a business enterprise costs are incurred to generate revenues. Hence costs should be recognized as expenses at the same time that the benefits that they produce are recognized as revenues. In other words, costs should be *matched* with revenues.

In a retail sales operation the major cost incurred in the generation of revenue is that of the goods to be sold. As the goods to be sold are received, their cost is *stored* in an asset account, "Merchandise inventory." Only when they are actually sold, and when sales revenue is recognized, is the cost of the goods sold charged as an expense. In the period of sale, the following entry is made:

Cost of goods sold (expense) xxxx
       Merchandise inventory (asset) xxxx

It follows that in a manufacturing operation all costs of producing the goods intended for sale should also be stored as assets until the goods are actually sold. This means that not only should costs of raw materials be capitalized as assets, but so too should costs of labor, maintenance, machines used (i.e., depreciation), and all other costs that can be identified with the production process.

When raw materials are purchased, their cost is charged initially to an asset account, "raw materials." As they are placed in production, their cost is transferred to "work in process," another asset account, and when the goods are completed their cost is transferred to "finished goods," also an asset account.

This is also true of labor costs. Although labor, unlike raw materials, cannot be physically stored, the *cost* of labor, like the cost of raw materials, *can* be stored in an asset account. Labor costs are conventionally recorded initially in an asset account, "labor," and then transferred immediately (since labor cannot be physically stored) to "work in process." The labor account, although perhaps unnecessary since the costs are transferred immediately to work in process, is ordinarily maintained because it facilitates cost control by providing management with a record of labor costs incurred.

So also with other manufacturing costs. Even that portion of manufacturing equipment considered to be consumed in the accounting period must be capitalized as part of the cost of the goods produced. The equipment benefits the periods in which the goods that it has been used to produce are actually sold. Costs of using up the equipment (i.e., depreciation) must be added to work in process (an asset account) and thereby included in the cost of the finished goods. They will be charged as an expense (as part of cost of goods sold) when the finished goods are actually sold.

The published financial statements of many major corporations do not include as expenses either depreciation or wages and salaries. These costs are, of course, reflected in the income statement. However, along with other manufacturing costs they are initially incorporated into inventory and eventually reported as part of cost of goods sold.

The manufacturing cycle is depicted graphically in Exhibit 4-8. The key point that the exhibit illustrates is that cost of goods sold represents a conglomerate of several different types of costs. All such costs, even those of services that contribute to the value of the product but cannot be physically stored (labor and utility costs, for example), are accumulated and retained in asset accounts (such as factory labor, work in process, and finished goods) until the time of sale. Upon sale, when the goods are transferred to a customer, an asset account (finished goods) is reduced (credited) by the cost to manufacture the goods sold and an expense (cost of goods sold) is increased (debited).

The principles and issues relating to manufacturing costs are typically dealt with in courses in ''management'' and ''cost'' accounting.

EXHIBIT 4-8
Manufacturing Cycle

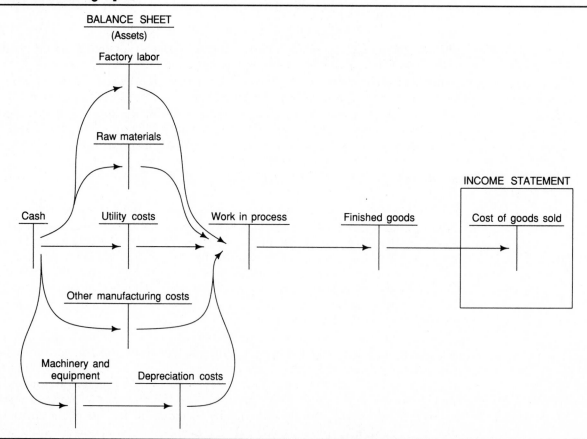

Principle of Matching

Central to modern accounting is the *principle of matching*. Insofar as practical, all costs should be associated with particular revenues. They should be recorded as expenses in the same periods in which the related revenues are recognized. Costs that are associated with revenues to be recognized in the future are to be maintained in asset accounts until such time as recognition is accorded the revenues and the costs can properly be charged as expenses.

Expenses can be defined as the goods or services consumed in the creation of revenues. Indeed, *all* expenses are incurred in the hope of generating revenues. If the objective of determining periodic income is to be best served, then all costs incurred by the firm should be capitalized as assets (i.e., charged initially to ''work in process'' or otherwise added to the cost of goods held in inventory) and recorded as expenses only as the goods are actually sold. Costs of borrowing necessary funds (interest), administering corporate headquarters, and advertising the products contribute as much to the generation of revenue as those of manufacturing products. Logically, such costs should also be added to the cost of goods to be sold.

In practice, however, many types of costs are not capitalized as assets. Instead they are charged as expenses in the period in which they are incurred, regardless of when the products are sold. The inconsistency of capitalizing some costs but not others has by no means been lost upon accountants. They have yielded to practical exigencies, however. It is simply too difficult to associate meaningfully—to match—certain expenses with specific revenues.

Consider, for example, costs of administration—the salaries of officers, secretaries, computer operators, and accountants; the fees paid to outside attorneys and auditors; the costs of renting office space and equipment. If a firm manufactured numerous types of products, it would be difficult, to say the least, to allocate such costs to specific products. Or consider sales costs. A salesperson might make numerous calls on customers before he or she receives an order. Is it possible, in any meaningful way, to associate costs of the unsuccessful calls with specific revenues to be generated in the future? Or consider interest costs. Funds borrowed benefit the entire company. Can the costs of borrowing be reasonably identified with sales of specific products?

Conventions

To reduce the need to make these troublesome allocations, accountants have adopted certain conventions as to which types of costs should be added to the cost of the product and which should be charged off as expenses in the period in which they are incurred. These conventions apply only to reports intended for external parties. They need not be applied to internal financial reports. Although there is no universal agreement on the conventions, as a general rule, *direct* manufacturing costs, such as factory labor and raw materials, are always charged to the product (i.e., included in ''work in process''). So are several types of *indirect* costs such as depreciation on manufacturing equipment, factory utility costs, rent on the factory building, and salaries of employees who are directly concerned with manufacturing operations. On the other hand, costs of selling, advertising and promotion, interest, employee health and recreational facilities, most taxes, and most other administrative costs are ordinarily considered to be *period* costs, which are charged as expenses as incurred.

The widely followed conventions do not, by any means, eliminate the need to allocate all common costs to specific products. *Factory overhead* costs (those which cannot readily be identified with specific products), such as supervision, utilities, maintenance, and rent, must still be allocated. And, as a consequence of the conventions, seemingly similar types of costs are sometimes accounted for differently. Depreciation on tables or chairs in a factory is considered to be a product cost; that on table or chairs in the corporate headquarters is considered to be a period cost; salaries of accountants who deal with factory costs are included among product costs; those of accountants who work with other types of costs are included as period costs.

Impact on Financial Statements

When a firm considers whether to include a specific cost as a product or a period cost, one relevant question must always be raised: What would be the impact of alternative classifications on both the income statement and the balance sheet?

If within an accounting period the enterprise sells the *same* number of goods that it produces (assuming no change in per unit costs from one period to the next), then it makes no difference whether a cost is classified as a product or a period cost. Suppose, for example, the salary of an accountant is $48,000 per year. During the year the firm produces and sells 48,000 units. If the salary is considered a period cost, then $48,000 will be reported as an expense among ''administrative'' expenses; if it is considered a product cost, then $48,000 will first be capitalized as ''work in process,'' then transferred to ''finished goods inventory,'' and finally reported in the same period as an expense, ''cost of goods sold.''

If the enterprise sells *fewer* goods than it produces, then reported expenses will be *greater* if the costs are categorized as period costs than if they are treated as product costs. Assume that the same firm produces 48,000 units but sells only 40,000 units. If the $48,000 salary of the accountant is classified as a period cost, then the full $48,000 will be charged off as an expense. If, however, it is classified as a product cost, then $1 ($48,000 divided by the number of units produced) will be added to the cost of each unit produced. Since 40,000 units are sold, only $40,000 will be included among cost of goods sold. The remaining $8,000 will be *stored* on the balance sheet, included in ''Finished goods inventory.'' Hence current assets, specifically inventory, will be $8,000 greater than if the salary were accounted for as a period cost.

If the enterprise sells more goods than it produces, then the reverse will be true. Reported expenses will be less if certain costs are treated as period rather than as product costs. Assume that in the following year the firm produces 48,000 units but sells 56,000 units, taking the additional 8,000 units from inventory. If the accountant's salary is treated as a period cost, then, as previously, the

EXHIBIT 4-9

Product versus Period Costs

	Year 1 Production = Sales	Year 2 Production > Sales	Year 3 Production < Sales
Number of units produced	48,000	48,000	48,000
Number of units sold	48,000	40,000	56,000
Manufacturing costs other than salary of accountant			
($40 per unit)	$480,000	$480,000	$480,000
Salary of accountant	48,000	48,000	48,000
I. Salary of accountant charged as a product cost			
Cost of goods manufactured	$528,000	$528,000	$528,000
Cost per unit of goods manufactured	11	11	11
Cost of goods sold (no. units sold × cost per unit)	528,000	440,000	616,000
Ending inventory	0	88,000	0
Period costs (salary of accountant)	0	0	0
II. Salary of accountant charged as a period cost			
Cost of goods manufactured	$480,000	$480,000	$480,000
Cost per unit of goods manufactured	10	10	10
Cost of goods sold (no. units sold × cost per unit)	480,000	400,000	560,000
Ending inventory	0	80,000	0
Period costs (salary of accountant)	48,000	48,000	48,000
Differences (I – II)			
Cost of goods sold	$48,000	$40,000	$56,000
Period costs (salary of accountant)	(48,000)	(48,000)	(48,000)
Net difference in costs	$ 0	($ 8,000)	$ 8,000

$48,000 will be reported as an expense. But if it is treated as a product cost, $56,000 of salary costs will be charged off as expense—$1 per unit produced and sold in the current period (48,000 units) plus $1 per unit of the goods sold in the current period but produced in the previous period (8,000 units).

Exhibit 4-9 contains an example to illustrate the differences.

MEASURES OF FINANCIAL PERFORMANCE AND HEALTH

The performance of a business over a *period* of time as well as its well-being at a *particular* time can never be evaluated by examining any single dollar amount that is reported in the firm's financial statements. Net income by itself, for example, tells nothing about how well a company has employed the resources within its command. A large company may have several times the earnings of a smaller company, yet relative to size, the performance of the smaller firm may be better.

Financial performance and fiscal health can best be described by ratios that relate one aspect of a firm's performance or status to another. Some of these ratios are, either by convention or requirement, reported in the body of the financial statements or in the accompanying supplementary data. Others must be calculated by the party engaged in the evaluation.

It is important that investors, creditors, managers, and accountants be familiar with the most widely used of the financial ratios. The ratios can be the basis for evaluating not only a business as a whole, but also its component units and the activities in which it engages. They can warn of fiscal stress. They can point to companies or components of companies to which (or away from which) resources should be directed. Moreover, it is essential that managers be aware of the criteria that outsiders will employ in evaluating their company in order that they can consider the impact on those criteria of any actions that they take. It is equally crucial that independent auditors be knowledgeable of the ratios because they may indicate fiscal stress and areas of high risk.

Ratios themselves, however, must never be evaluated in a vacuum. What are important are trends over time and comparisons with firms in the same or related industries. Should a key ratio or series of ratios increase or decrease from one year to the next, it may be a sign of either financial deterioration or improvement.

There are no fixed minimum or maximum values below which a ratio should not fall or above which it should not rise. But whenever the ratio of a particular firm is substantially out of line with those common in the industry, the analyst should be alert to either potential financial difficulty or unusual financial strength. Normal ranges for most ratios and percentages vary considerably from industry to industry. Some industries, electric utilities for example, require large amounts of invested capital to support their operations. Other industries, supermarkets for instance, require relatively small amounts of permanent capital. As a consequence, supermarkets can be expected to have a much higher ratio of sales to total fixed assets (fixed asset turnover) than would electric utilities. Supermarkets, on the other hand, tend to earn a relatively small profit on each dollar of sales since the *markup* on grocery products is relatively small. By contrast, once the physical facilities have been acquired, the cost of generating electricity is relatively low. Thus electric utilities would generally have a much higher ratio of net income to sales revenue (return on sales) than would supermarkets. Industry norms for a number of key indicators can be obtained from publications of industry trade associations or of financial service bureaus such as Dun and Bradstreet or Standard & Poor's.

The ratios that are to be described in this chapter are among the most fundamental of performance indicators. Other ratios will be discussed throughout the text in the sections pertaining to the accounts or activities on which the ratios focus.

The ratios are based on three primary groups of measures:

1. *Profitability and activity measures.* These indicate how well a firm is employing its assets. These measures may relate to specific assets, such as accounts receivable or inventory, or to all the resources within the firm's command.
2. *Liquidity ratios.* These show the ability of a firm to meet its obligations as they come due. They relate a firm's *liquid assets* (cash and assets that are most likely to be converted to cash) to its liabilities.
3. *Financing measures.* These reveal the proportion of assets financed by creditors as opposed to owners and indicate the ability of the firm to meet its fixed finance charges such as interest.

Profitability and Activity Measures

Earnings per Share

Earnings per share (EPS) is reported in the financial statements directly beneath net income. It is computed by dividing net income by the average number of common shares outstanding during the period (with adjustment for additional shares that the company may have to issue in the future.)[3] Earnings per share allows individual stockholders to determine their interests in total corporate earnings by multiplying EPS by number of shares owned. It facilitates comparisons of performance among years in which a greater or lesser number of shares may be outstanding.

To determine earnings per share, we look to an earlier example: Per its statement of income (Exhibit 4-6), Altoona Appliance Company had earnings of $250,500. Assume that there were 10,000 shares of stock outstanding. Earnings per share were therefore $25.05:

$$\text{Earnings per share} = \frac{\text{Net income}}{\text{Shares of common stock outstanding}}$$

$$= \frac{\$250,500}{10,000} = \$25.05$$

Return on Investment

The measure of corporate performance that is generally considered most relevant to both managers and investors is *return on investment.* Return on investment relates the earnings of the enterprise to the resources provided by its owners. The resources provided by the owners are measured by their equity—which, of course, is equivalent to net assets (i.e., assets less liabilities). Thus

$$\text{Return on investment (ROI)} = \frac{\text{Net income}}{\text{Owners' equity}^4}$$

The balance sheet of Altoona Appliance Company, Exhibit 4-6, indicates that the total investment of stockholders at the end of 1993 was $1,374,150. This amount includes the direct contributions of stockholders plus the resources that have been earned over the years and retained in the business (retained earnings). Income was $250,500. Hence return on investments is 18.2 percent:

$$\text{Return on investment} = \frac{\$\ 250,500}{\$1,374,150} = 18.2\%$$

Other means of computing return on investment, specifically tailored to managers or selected classes of stockholders, will be presented in Chapter 16.

---

[3]Owing in part to the required adjustment for the additional shares, the computation of earnings per share can be quite complex. The computation of EPS will be expanded upon and discussed in greater detail in Chapter 12.
[4]Preferably, owners' equity should be computed by calculating the average owners' equity during the year. This refinement is ignored for the sake of simplicity in this section of the text.

Profit Margins

Profit margins relate income to sales. *Gross profit* is defined as sales minus cost of goods sold. The *gross profit margin* is gross profit divided by sales. Returning to our earlier example, we see that Altoona's gross profit is

Sales	$3,302,000
Less: Cost of goods sold	2,179,000
Gross profit	$1,123,000

Its gross profit *margin* is 34 percent:

$$\text{Gross profit margin} = \frac{\$1,123,000}{\$3,302,000} = .34$$

The *net profit margin* relates net income to sales:

$$\text{Net profit margin} = \frac{\text{Net profit}}{\text{Sales}}$$

Altoona's net profit margin is 7.6 percent:

$$\text{Net profit margin} = \frac{\$\ 250,500}{\$3,302,000} = .076$$

Other performance and activity ratios compare individual revenues and expense with the assets or liabilities to which they relate (e.g., sales to accounts receivable, cost of goods sold to inventory, and interest to debt). These will be discussed in subsequent chapters.

Still other ratios are tied to stock market measures. Price/earnings (P/E) ratio, for example, compares earnings per share with the stock market price per share. The importance of the P/E ratio is indicated by its being incorporated in the daily stock market tables of *The Wall Street Journal* as well as many other financial periodicals.

Suppose that on December 31, 1993, the market price per share of Altoona was $320. Earnings per share, as just calculated, was $25.05. The price/earnings ratio would be approximately 12.8 to 1:

$$\text{Price/earnings ratio} = \frac{\text{Market price per share of common stock}}{\text{Earnings per share}}$$

$$= \frac{\$320.00}{\$25.05} = 12.8 \text{ to } 1$$

Liquidity Ratios

The most widely used measure of liquidity is the *current ratio,* which provides an insight into the ability of the enterprise to meet its short-term debts. As such it is especially meaningful to parties considering whether to extend credit to the firm. The current ratio compares current assets to current liabilities; that is, it relates cash and the assets that are most likely to be transformed into cash within a single business cycle to the debts that will fall due within that period:

$$\text{Current ratio} = \frac{\text{Current assets}}{\text{Current liabilities}}$$

The current ratio of Altoona is 4.2 to 1:

$$\text{Current ratio} = \frac{\$1,166,900}{\$\ 275,800} = 4.2 \text{ to } 1$$

A ratio of 1 to 1 or higher is generally considered acceptable.

Other, more stringent tests of liquidity include in current assets only cash and assets that are more easily transformed into cash. The numerator of the *quick ratio,* for example, comprises only cash, marketable securities, and accounts receivable.

Financing Ratios

Financing ratios assess the extent to which a firm is "leveraged"—that is, the extent to which it has financed its assets with debt rather than with the contributed or earned (reinvested) capital of owners. The debt-to-equity ratio, for example, compares total debt to total contributed capital:

$$\text{Debt-to-equity ratio} = \frac{\text{Total debt}}{\text{Total equity}}$$

Altoona's debt-to-equity ratio is 0.2 to 1:

$$\text{Debt-to-equity ratio} = \frac{\$\ 275,800}{\$1,374,150} = 0.2 \text{ to } 1$$

Importance of Comparisons

Financial statements provide an insight into a company's past operating performance and future earnings potential that is perhaps unmatched by any that can be obtained from other sources. But the picture presented has meaning only when viewed from the proper perspective. Managers, investors, and other users of the statements must be able to examine the financial data with reference to financial position and results of operations of both previous years and of other companies in the same or related industries. No set of dollar amounts, ratios, or other indicators of financial health have meaning in and of themselves. They are of significance only when compared with similar indicators of the same company in other years and of other companies in the same or related industries. Toward this end, corporate annual reports include complete financial statements for the year immediately prior to that being reported upon as well as summary information for a period of 5 to 10 years.

Financial statements are often "rounded" to the nearest thousand or even million dollars. The practice of rounding highlights the imprecision of financial statements; they are necessarily based on a number of estimates and judgmental determinations. Although such estimates and judgmental determinations unquestionably permit a degree of subjectivity to enter into the financial statements, and perhaps make them less comparable with those of other firms, they serve at the same time to make them more relevant for most decisions that they will be used to facilitate.

Summary

The primary purpose of this chapter has been to elaborate upon the accrual concept and to demonstrate some of its many ramifications for accounting practice. The *accrual concept* requires that transactions and other financial events be recognized at the time they have their primary economic impact, not necessarily when cash is received or disbursed. Revenues are assigned to the periods in which they are earned. Costs are matched to the revenues that they generate and are charged as expenses in the periods in which the revenues are recognized.

The economic benefits attributable to a cost may be both acquired and paid for in periods other than those in which the revenues to which they must be matched are recognized. The benefits attributable to supplies, for example, may be acquired (purchased) in one period, consumed in a second, and paid for in a third. The double-entry accounting system allows for costs that will benefit future periods to be *stored* in asset accounts and charged as expenses only as the revenues with which they are associated are recognized. Similarly, the obligation for the payment may be maintained in a liability account until such time as the required cash disbursement is actually made.

To reduce bookkeeping costs, accounting records are not always kept up to date. For instance, it is more convenient to record the use of supplies periodically rather than each time supplies are consumed. So too in the case of rent and interest revenue, where the benefits accrue over time; it would be impractical to update the books on an around-the-clock basis. As a consequence, firms must periodically bring the records to a current status by means of updating and adjusting entries.

The manner in which costs are accounted for in a manufacturing operation is another manifestation of the accrual concept and the related principle of matching. All manufacturing costs are maintained in asset accounts (e.g., raw materials, labor, work in process, finished goods) until the period in which they can properly be matched to revenues from the sale of the product and charged as expenses (cost of goods sold).

Not all costs are matched directly with specific revenues. The relationships between some costs and revenues are sufficiently indirect that accountants have surrendered to practical exigencies and make no attempt to match certain costs with particular revenues. These costs, often referred to as *period* costs,, are charged as expenses in the periods in which they are incurred, regardless of the amount of revenues recognized in that particular period.

A secondary objective of this chapter has been to introduce the general area of financial analysis. Financial statements typically reveal considerably more information about a firm's fiscal wherewithal than is readily apparent. Skilled financial analysts are able to take advantage of the relationships among income statement and balance sheet accounts to derive data that companies have not disclosed. They are also able to use financial ratios to compare the health and performance of a single company over several years and of two or more companies in the same year.

In the following chapter we shall expand still further upon the accrual concept by considering the criteria for recognition of revenue.

Exercise for Review and Self-Testing

Global Real Estate leases an office building to a corporate tenant for $300,000 per month. As of January 1, 1993, the tenant had paid two months' rent in advance. The firm included among its liabilities "Unearned rent, $600,000."

1. Assuming that the tenant occupied the apartment for 12 months in 1993, how much rent revenue should the firm recognize during the year? Does it matter how much cash the firm collected from the tenant?

2. Prepare a journal entry that the firm should make at the end of January, assuming that it received from the tenant no cash during the month.
3. Suppose instead that during 1993 Global Real Estate received a total of $2,400,000 from its tenant. Each time cash was collected, the firm made an entry in the following form:

Cash xxx
     Rent revenue xxx

It made no other entries with respect to rent.
   a. How much rent revenue should properly have been recognized during the year? By how much is rent revenue understated?
   b. At year end, what should be the balance in "Unearned rent"?
   c. What should be the balance in "Rent receivable"?
   d. Prepare a journal entry to adjust and update the accounts.
4. The firm contracted with a maintenance company to perform cleaning services at an annual cost of $120,000. At year end, what amounts should the firm report in its income statement account, "Cleaning expense," and its related balance sheet account, either "Cleaning costs payable" or "Prepaid cleaning costs," if it actually made cash payments of
   a. $80,000?
   b. $140,000?
   The maintenance company performed its services throughout the entire year.
5. What determines the amount reported as a revenue or expense for services received or provided? What determines the amount that is added to or subtracted from the related asset or liability account?

Questions for Review and Discussion

1. What is meant by the *accrual method* of accounting? How does it differ from the cash method?
2. Why does the accrual method provide greater insight into organizational performance than does the cash method?
3. What are *adjusting entries*? Why are they necessary?
4. What is a *periodic* method of inventory? How does it differ from a *perpetual* method?
5. A company charges all purchases of merchandise intended for sale to "Cost of goods sold." Is such practice acceptable? What year-end adjusting entry would be necessary to "correct" the accounts?
6. A bookkeeper incorrectly charges a prepayment of January 1993 made on December 28, 1992, to "Rent expense." What would be the impact of this error on the financial statements of the year ended December 1992 and that ended December 1993?
7. A manager of a manufacturing company noticed that the account "Labor cost" was included in the general ledger among the asset accounts. Since she was unable to visually inspect labor costs, she wondered how they could possibly be considered to be an asset. How would you answer her?
8. What is meant by the *matching principle*? If a company were to recognize revenue upon the collection of cash from the customer rather than upon the delivery of goods, when would you recommend that the cost of the goods sold be charged as an expense?
9. Distinguish between product costs and period costs. How would you defend the position of accountants who claim that depreciation should sometimes be accounted for as a product cost and sometimes as a period cost?

10. Suppose that in a particular accounting period a company sells the same number of goods that it produces. Would it make any difference insofar as net income is concerned if depreciation on office equipment used in the factory were considered a product or a period cost? What if the company sells only a portion of the goods that it produces?

11. What are the three primary groups of financial ratios? Give examples of each.

12. An accountant attempted to prepare both an income statement and a balance sheet from an adjusted trial balance. Closing entries had not yet been made. He was unable, however, to get his balance sheet to balance. Assets exceeded liabilities plus owners' equity by an amount exactly equal to income for the year. Which account was most likely in error? Why?

Problems

1. *Expenses must be recognized even if invoices have not yet been received.*

As you are getting ready to prepare year-end financial statements, you learn that your company has not yet received invoices (bills) for services it received in December. The company estimates that in January it will receive invoices as follows:

From the telephone company	$1,300
From the gas and electric company	3,270
From the outside maintenance service	1,000

a. Prepare any journal entries that you would consider necessary.

b. Suppose that you failed to make such journal entries. What effect would that have on income of the year, income of the following year, and current liabilities?

2. *All costs must be divided between the income statement and the balance sheet.*

A firm made the following payments during its first year of operation:

For rent	$12,000
For interest	8,000
For advertising	3,000
For manufacturing products	96,000

The firm's accountant has determined that the following amounts should properly be reported as expenses:

Rent expense	$10,000
Interest expense	7,000
Advertising expense	6,000
Cost of goods sold	80,000

Determine the amounts that should be reported in balance sheet accounts that correspond to each of the reported expenses.

3. *Costs may be accounted for in three ways.*

The December 31 balance sheet of a company reported accrued interest payable of $3,000 in connection with bonds outstanding of $100,000. Interest, at a rate of 12 percent, is payable semiannually on April 1 and October 1.

Prepare all required journal entries for the next year, including year-end adjusting entries, assuming that cash payments are made when due if, alternatively,

a. The company makes appropriate *accrual* entries every three months.

b. The company debits "interest expense" with the full amount of each cash payment.

c. The company debits "accrued interest payable" with the full amount of each cash payment.

4. *Alternative accounting practices can lead to the same results as long as proper end-of-year adjustments are made.*

Three companies each account for insurance costs differently. Each began the year with a balance of $400 in prepaid insurance costs, which represented two months of insurance remaining on a one-year policy. Upon the expiration of the policy, each renewed for another year, paying $3,600 in cash. The general ledgers of the three companies reported the following balances of year end, prior to adjustment:

	Company A	Company B	Company C
Prepaid insurance	$ 400	$4,000	$ 600
Insurance expense	3,600	0	3,400

a. Explain how each of the companies accounts for insurance costs.

b. Determine the "correct" amounts that should be reported as "Prepaid insurance" and "insurance expense."

c. Prepare the adjusting entries, if any, that should be made by each of the firms.

5. *Consider the relationship, if any, between revenue earned and cash collected.*

A company holds a note receivable of $100,000 from a customer. Interest is payable each month at a rate of 12 percent per year ($1,000 per month). For each of the following independent situations indicate the amounts that the firm should report on its December 31, 1993, financial statements for interest revenue, interest receivable, and unearned interest.

a. The balance in interest receivable as of January 1, 1993, was $2,000. The company collects $12,000 in interest payments.

b. The balance in interest receivable as of January 1, 1993, was $2,000. The company collects $14,000 in interest payments.

c. The balance in interest receivable as of January 1, 1993, was $2,000. The company collects $15,000 in interest payments.

d. The balance in unearned interest (interest paid by the borrower in advance) as of January 1, 1993, was $3,000. The company collects $9,000 in interest payments.

e. The balance in unearned interest as of January 1, 1993, was $3,000. The company collects $8,000 in interest payments.

6. *Costs must be matched with revenues.*

During the first three years of its existence, Bravo Company's manufacturing costs, end-of-year inventories, and sales were as follows:

Year	Manufacturing Costs	End-of-Year Inventories	Sales
1	$80,000	$ 80,000	None
2	90,000	130,000	$ 60,000
3	30,000	None	250,000

Ignoring all other costs and revenues, determine the income of Bravo Company for each of the three years.

7. *The significant economic (and therefore accounting) event is the declaration of a dividend, not the payment. Which event will reduce retained earnings?*

On December 13, 1993, the board of directors of a company declares a dividend of $0.75 per share of common stock. The dividend will be payable on January 18, 1994, to the "stockholders of record" (i.e., to those who owned the stock on a particular date) of January 10, 1994. The company has 100,000 shares of common stock outstanding.

a. Prepare an appropriate journal entry to record the declaration of the dividend.

b. Prepare an appropriate closing entry as of December 31, 1993.

c. Prepare an appropriate journal entry to record payment of the dividend.

8. *This exercise reviews the basic entries required to account for depreciable assets.*

Prepare journal entries to record the following events:

a. A company purchases two trucks, each for $15,000 cash. The estimated useful life of a truck is five years, after which it has negligible scrap or resale value.

b. The company records first-year depreciation on the trucks.

c. At the beginning of the second year, the company sells one of the trucks for $13,000 cash.

d. The company records second-year depreciation on the remaining truck.

e. At the beginning of the third year, the company sells the second truck for $8,000 cash.

9. *Should a dance studio recognize revenue when it signs a contract and collects cash or when it provides its services? Which is the more significant economic event?*

Foxtrot Dance Studio offers customers a "One-Year Learn-to-Dance Special." Customers pay $1,200 at the time they sign a contract and are entitled to four lessons per month for one year.

In November, 10 customers sign contracts and pay "tuition" for the series of lessons. In December, each of the customers takes four lessons.

a. Prepare a journal entry to record the sales of the contracts and the collection of the cash. Assume that revenue is to be recognized only as customers actually take their lessons.

b. Prepare any entries that will be appropriate when the customers take their first four lessons in December. (Ignore expenses incurred in connection with the lessons.)

c. Prepare any *closing* entries that might be necessary on December 31.

d. Suppose that the sales representatives of the firm are entitled to sales commissions based on the dollar amount of contracts signed. From the perspective of a sales manager, which is the more significant economic event—the signing of a contract, the collection of cash, or the providing of lessons? Comment on why different means of recognizing revenues or expenses are appropriate for financial statements that will be used for different purposes (e.g., evaluating the performance of salespeople as opposed to evaluating the performance of the organization as a whole).

10. *Firms do not have to give instantaneous accounting recognition to all economic events (including the passage of time), but prior to preparing financial statements they must bring the books up to date.*

In each of the following *independent* situations, prepare any necessary journal entries that would be required either to adjust a company's books or to bring them up to date in order to prepare year-end (December 31) financial statements. Assume that closing entries have not yet been made.

a. Property taxes, which amount to $15,000 annually, are payable on the last day of the city's fiscal year, which ends April 30. No property tax accruals have yet been made.

b. Employees are paid each Monday for wages earned during the previous week. December 31 falls on a Wednesday. Weekly payroll (for a five-day workweek) is $3,000.

c. As heating oil was purchased it was debited to "fuel expense." As of the end of the year, heating oil that had cost $300 was still on hand.

d. On March 1, the company purchased a one-year fire insurance policy at a cost of $3,600 paid in cash. The entire cost of the policy was charged to "insurance expense."

e. The company is on a periodic inventory basis. After taking year-end inventory and making appropriate adjustments to its accounts, it discovered that $400 of inventory was incorrectly omitted from the count.

f. The company is on a periodic inventory basis. After taking year-end inventory and making appropriate adjustments to its accounts, it discovered that goods that had cost $1,000 had just recently been purchased. No accounting recognition, however, had been given to either the purchase or the corresponding liability for payment. (Note that since the adjustment to the accounts resulting from the physical inventory count had already been made, the inventory account is *properly* stated.)

g. The company ran an advertisement in the December 30 edition of the local newspaper. The company has not yet received a bill for the advertisement or given it any other accounting recognition. The cost of the advertisement was $250.

h. The company is on a periodic inventory basis. After taking year-end inventory and making appropriate adjustments to its accounts, it discovered that a purchase of equipment was incorrectly debited to "inventory" rather than to "equipment." The cost of the equipment was $2,100. (The *physical* count was correctly taken; hence the inventory account is correctly stated.)

i. On June 1 the company borrowed $10,000 from a bank. It paid the entire interest for one year ($1,200) in advance at the time it signed the note. The advance payment of interest was properly recorded, but no entries pertaining to the interest have been made since the date of payment.

j. On November 1 customers placed orders for merchandise with a selling price of $15,900. The customers paid in advance, and their payment was properly recorded. The goods were delivered on December 29, but no accounting recognition has been given to the delivery. The company uses a periodic inventory method, and the goods were not included in the December 31 inventory count. (Hence both inventory and cost of goods sold are correctly stated.)

11. *Does choice of accounting method affect total reported earnings over the life of an enterprise?*
    Suppose that a company was organized on January 1, 1993. In each of the next 10 years it had sales of $100,000; the costs of the goods sold were $80,000 per year. In each year, the company collected in cash 75 percent of the sales of that year plus 25 percent of the sales of the previous year. Similarly, in each year the company paid in cash 75 percent of the costs incurred in that year plus 25 percent of the costs incurred in the previous year. The company ceased operations at the end of year 10. It remained in business in year 11 only to collect outstanding receivables and to liquidate remaining debts.

    a. Assuming that the company maintained its accounts on an *accrual* basis, compute total income for the 11-year period. Determine income for each of the 11 individual years.

    b. Assume instead that the company maintained its accounts on a *cash* basis (i.e., recognized revenues and expenses as cash was received or disbursed). Determine cash flow from operations for the 11-year period as well as for each of the 11 individual years.

12. *The impact of a change from cash to accrual accounting may affect earnings and financial ratios in a manner that is not obvious.*

In the years prior to 1993, Western Insurance Co. accounted for the commissions of its sales staff on a pay-as-you-go basis. Amounts paid to the sales staff as commissions were recorded as expenses in the period in which the cash disbursements were made.

In 1993, however, the company engaged a new firm of auditors. The new firm advised Western Insurance that to comply with generally accepted accounting principles, the company would have to report commissions as expenses in the year in which the salespersons had earned them. At the end of each year, the firm would have to show as a liability the amount of commissions earned in that year but not yet paid. The liability would ordinarily be liquidated in the following year when the commissions were actually paid.

As of both December 31, 1992, and December 31, 1993, the sales staff had earned $10 million in commissions that had not yet been paid. During both 1992 and 1993, the company *paid* salespersons a total of $80 million in commissions.

Western Insurance Co. has loans outstanding from banks and other lending institutions. Included in the debt agreements are two covenants relating to the firm's financial position and activities:

- The company shall not in any year pay dividends in an amount greater than reported earnings for the year.
- The company shall maintain a ratio of total debts to total owners' equity no greater than 1 to 1.

The firm calculated its earnings of 1993—*without* accruing the commissions as required by the new firm of auditors—to be $180 million. It paid dividends of $175 million.

As of December 31, 1993, the total liabilities of the company were $300 million; total stockholders' equity was $318 million. These amounts, like earnings, were computed without taking into account the accruals demanded by the new auditors.

The president of the firm has asked your opinion as to whether the accounting change (to be made retroactive to January 1, 1992) would place the firm in violation of either or both of the debt covenants.
a. What would be the effect of the change on each of the covenants? Explain and show computations.
b. Would the change have any effect on the economic well-being of the firm? Comment.

13. *This problem provides insight into how, in practice, accruals may be reported.*

Footnote 7 of the 1993 annual report of a textbook publisher reads as follows (all amounts in thousands):

Other Accrued Expenses		
	1993	1992
Payroll, commissions, etc.	$11,960	$11,092
Profit sharing	8,084	7,760
Future service costs on rental contracts receivable	8,001	7,865
Book manufacturing costs	6,237	4,488
Other taxes	2,098	2,222
Miscellaneous	2,795	3,385
Total	$39,175	$36,812

a. In which section of the balance sheet (assets, liabilities, owners' equity) should the accrued expenses be shown?

b. The firm's income statement contains only four lines relating to expenses: cost of goods sold; selling, general, and administrative expenses; interest; and income taxes. How are the accrued expenses most likely reflected in income?

c. There is no explanation in the annual report of the accrual, "Future service costs on rental contracts receivable." Indicate, in very general terms, the nature of this item. Show the entry, without using specific numbers, that the company must have made to record this accrual.

14. *An actual annual report highlights the relationships between accrued liabilities and both dividends and expenses.*

Note 6 of the 1990 financial statements of Champion International Corporation is as follows (all dollar amounts are in thousands):

Accounts Payable and Accrued Liabilities		
	December 31	
	1990	1989
Accounts payable	$289,449	$236,133
Dividends payable	23,861	19,072
Accrued liabilities:		
Payrolls and commissions	103,765	93,945
Employee benefits	48,035	52,165
Interest	31,214	32,283
Taxes, other than income taxes	37,915	31,249
Wood products restructuring	13,562	10,516
Other	77,409	102,250
	$311,900	$322,408
Total accrued liabilities	$625,210	$577,613

a. The statement of consolidated retained earnings reports that the company *declared* dividends of $90,593. How much did it actually *pay* in dividends?

b. Information derived from the income statement and another note reveals that interest expense was $174,889. How much interest did the firm *pay*?

c. Note 2, "Wood products restructuring program," reports that the company is in the process of selling or closing down certain wood products facilities. In 1990 it charged $20,900 in expenses and losses related to the sale or closing of wood products operations. How much did it *pay*?

15. *Many companies charge (debit) an account called "Purchases" for all acquisitions of merchandise inventory (instead of debiting "Merchandise Inventory"). This practice is acceptable but requires that an adjusting entry be made at year end to eliminate the balance in the purchases account.*

Examination of a company's general ledger as of the end of the year reveals the following account balances (both debit balances) pertaining to merchandise inventory:

Inventory	$100,000
Purchases	600,000

Upon inquiry, you learn that the balance in inventory represents that at the *beginning* of the year. No entries were made to that account during the year. All purchases during the year were debited to "Purchases." You also learn that a physical count at the end of the year revealed goods on hand of $60,000.

What adjusting entry would you propose, assuming that you want to eliminate the balance in the purchases account, to have the inventory account reflect the correct balance of goods on hand at year end, and to have a cost of goods sold account reveal the cost of merchandise sold during the year?

16. *A company can report a profit yet still experience a reduction in cash.*

Comparative balance sheets for House of Clothes, a chain of sportswear shops, for the years 1993 and 1994 are presented in the accompanying table. Also presented is an income statement for 1994. All sales were recorded initially as charge sales. All purchases of merchandise were made "on account."

a. Compute the amount of cash collections made in 1994 as a result of either current year or prior year sales. Be sure to relate sales to accounts receivable (that is, accounts receivable, 12/31/93 + sales − cash collections = accounts receivable, 12/31/94).

b. Compute the amount of cash disbursed in connection with each of the expenses. Be especially careful in computing cash expended, if any, in connection with purchases of inventory and with depreciation. (*Hint:* Compute first the amount of goods actually purchased.) Be sure to relate each expense to a corresponding asset or liability account (e.g., rent expense to prepaid rent; cost of goods sold to inventory.)

c. Does the difference between cash received and cash disbursed equal the difference between cash on hand at the beginning of 1994 and cash on hand at the end? (If not, review your computations.)

d. Comment on why net income cannot be used as a measure of cash received or disbursed.

House of Clothes
Balance Sheet
(in thousands)

		12/31/94		12/31/93
Cash		$ 3,800		$ 4,000
Accounts receivable		44,000		28,000
Prepaid rent		—		1,000
Inventory		14,000		17,000
Fixed assets	$20,000		$20,000	
Less: Accumulated depreciation	8,000	12,000	4,000	16,000
Total assets		$73,800		$66,000
Accounts payable		$ 4,000		$ 2,000
Accrued salaries payable		1,000		3,500
Accrued interest payable		100		200
Accrued rent payable		2,000		—
Notes payable		4,800		4,800
Common stock		10,000		10,000
Retained earnings		51,900		45,500
Total liabilities and owners' equity		$73,800		$66,000

Income Statement
Year Ended 12/31/94
(in thousands)

Sales		$220,000
Cost of goods sold		130,000
Gross margin		$ 90,000
Other expenses:		
Salaries	$67,000	
Interest	600	
Rent	12,000	
Depreciation	4,000	83,600
Net income		$ 6,400

17. *Incorrect journal entries can subsequently be corrected without having to first reverse the original entry.*

As management was about to prepare year-end financial statements, the journal entries indicated below, which were made by an inexperienced bookkeeper, came to its attention. You are to make the journal entries that would be required to correct the errors (*Hint:* First determine the entry that should have been made; then determine the most efficient means of eliminating the incorrect, and adding the correct, amounts.)

a. A customer made a payment to reduce the balance in his account.

Cash	$7,500	
Sales revenue		$7,500

b. The company sold for $3,000 a machine that had originally cost $4,000 when purchased three years earlier. Accumulated depreciation on the asset amounted to $2,000.

Cash	$3,000	
Sales revenue		$3,000

c. In January the company paid rent for the previous December. Before preparing the year-end financial statements as of December 31, the company had correctly accrued rent for December.

Rent expense	$5,000	
Cash		$5,000

d. The company charged depreciation of one year on equipment that had cost $6,000 and had a useful life of three years with no salvage value.

Allowance for depreciation	$2,000	
Depreciation expense		$2,000

e. The company paid a bill received from its advertising agency for an ad that it had run the previous year. The company had properly accounted for the ad at the time it was run.

Advertising expense	$6,750	
Cash		$6,750

f. The company paid $13,000 to Cooks Flight Service for repairs to its corporate jet. It had given no previous accounting recognition to the repair costs.

Fixed assets, airplane $13,000
Accounts receivable $13,000

18. *Ability to evaluate the effect of errors on the income statement and the balance sheet is persuasive evidence of an understanding of the double-entry bookkeeping system.*

On December 31, at the end of the 1993 annual accounting period, a firm made the errors listed below.

Under the assumption that none of the errors was explicitly discovered and corrected in 1994 but that some of the errors would automatically be corrected if normal accounting procedures were followed, indicate the effect of each error on the financial statements. In each case, indicate the amount of the overstatement or understatement the error would cause in the assets, liabilities, owners' equity, revenues, expenses, and net income. If the error would have no effect on an item, then so state. [The first error (part a) is posted for you as an example in the table below.]

a. It failed to record $9,000 of accrued salaries. The salaries were paid in 1994.

b. A portion of the company's warehouse was rented on December 1, 1993, at $15,000 per month to a tenant who paid the December, January, and February rents in advance. The firm did not make an adjustment for the unearned rent on December 31, which had been credited on receipt to the "rent revenue" account.

c. Through an oversight, the firm failed to record $214,500 of depreciation on store equipment. The equipment had a useful life of an additional five years. Depreciation was properly recorded in 1994 and no equipment was sold in 1994.

d. The firm failed to accrue one-half year's interest on a note receivable. The $1,000 note was received on July 1, 1992, and was due on June 30, 1994. Interest was at the rate of 6 percent per year, payable each year on June 30.

e. The firm made an error in adding the amounts on the year-end inventory sheets which caused a $7,500 understatement in the merchandise inventory. (Inventory on December 31, 1994, was properly stated.)

f. On January 2, 1993, the company purchased a two-year fire insurance policy for $8,000. It charged the entire amount to "insurance expense."

g. On December 31, 1993, the company declared a dividend of $600,000 payable on January 15, 1994. The bookkeeper failed to record the declaration.

h. The company owned 1,000 shares of General Motors common stock. On December 20, the company received notification from Gooder and Co., the firm's stockbroker, that General Motors had declared and paid a dividend of $1.20 per share. Since Gooder and Co. holds in its own name the shares owned by the company, it credited the company's account for $1,200. The bookkeeper first recorded the dividend in January 1994 when the cash was forwarded to the company.

	1993 Income Statement			December 31, 1993 Balance Sheet			1994 Income Statement			December 31, 1994 Balance Sheet		
Error	Revenues	Expense	Net income	Assets	Liabilities	Owners' equity	Revenues	Expense	Net income	Assets	Liabilities	Owners' equity
a.	None	Under $9,000	Over $9,000	None	Under $9,000	Over $9,000	None	Over $9,000	Under $9,000	None	None	None

19. *This problem provides a review of the accounting cycle from unadjusted trial balance to financial statements.*

The following table gives the unadjusted trial balance of the Coronet Company as of December 31, 1993. Other pertinent information is listed below the table.

The Coronet Company Unadjusted Trial Balance 12/31/93		
Cash	$ 3,000	
Accounts receivable	5,000	
Merchandise inventory	155,000	
Prepaid rent	1,500	
Furniture and fixtures	15,000	
Accumulated depreciation		$ 6,000
Accounts payable		9,000
Notes payable		6,000
Sales revenue		220,000
Selling expenses	55,000	
General expenses	18,000	
Interest expense	800	
Tax expense	3,500	
Capital received from stockholders		6,000
Retained earnings		9,800
	$256,800	$256,800

(1) Interest on the note, at a rate of 12 percent, is due semiannually, April 30 and October 31.
(2) Useful life of the furniture and fixtures is five years with no salvage value. Depreciation for the year has not yet been recorded.
(3) The company employs a periodic inventory system. A physical count at year end indicates merchandise on hand of $24,000.
(4) The company last paid its rent on December 1. Such payment was intended to cover the month of December. (Rent expense is included among "general expenses." The payment was properly recorded.)
(5) On December 31, the board of directors declared a cash dividend, payable January 12, of $4,000.
(6) Advertising costs of $700 were incorrectly charged to "general expenses" rather than "selling expenses."
(7) Estimated taxes for the year are $8,500. Of these only $3,500 have yet been paid.

a. Prepare all necessary updating and adjusting entries.
b. Post the entries to T accounts.
c. Prepare a year-end income statement, balance sheet, and statement of changes in retained earnings.

20. *This problem reviews the basic steps in the preparation of a worksheet.*

The end-of-year *unadjusted* trial balance of the Columbia Flying Service is presented on the following page. The accompanying additional information has come to your attention:

(1) Instructor salaries for the last week of the month have not yet been recorded. They will be payable the first week of the new year. Salaries for the one week are $13,500.

Columbia Flying Service
Unadjusted Trial Balance
December 31, 1993

Cash	$ 37,500	
Accounts receivable	45,000	
Supplies inventory	2,000	
Parts inventory	24,000	
Equipment	42,000	
Equipment, accumulated depreciation		$ 6,000
Planes	216,000	
Planes, accumulated depreciation		71,000
Prepaid insurance	15,000	
Accounts payable		8,000
Lessons paid for but not yet given		28,000
Notes payable		60,000
Common stock		10,000
Retained earnings		78,100
Revenues from lessons		895,000
Revenues from charters		156,000
Salaries	623,000	
Fuel expense	189,000	
Maintenance expense	51,000	
Supplies expense	6,000	
Insurance expense	34,000	
Advertising expense	13,000	
Rent expense	11,000	
Interest expense	2,400	
Licenses and fees	1,200	
	$1,312,100	$1,312,100

(2) In the course of the previous two weeks, lessons were given that had been paid for in advance. The amount charged for the lessons was $6,500.

(3) No depreciation has been recorded in 1993. The useful life of the planes is estimated at 10 years (no salvage value) and that of the equipment at 7 years (also no salvage value).

(4) Rent for December, $1,000, has not yet been paid.

(5) The company purchases a one-year insurance policy each year which takes effect on July 1. The entire cost of the current year's policy has been charged to "Insurance expense." The December 31, 1993, balance in "Prepaid insurance" was the same as that on January 1, 1993. No entries to the account have been made during the year.

(6) Interest on the $60,000 note outstanding is payable twice each year, April 1 and October 1. The annual rate of interest is 8 percent. The note was issued on April 1, 1993; the amount of interest expense represents the first interest payment, which was made on October 1.

(7) A physical count of parts on hand indicated an unexplained shortage of parts that had cost $2,000. An adjustment to inventory has not yet been made.

(8) All purchases of supplies are charged (debited) to "Supplies expense." The balance in "Supplies inventory" represents supplies on hand at the beginning of the year. A physical count on December 31, 1993, indicated supplies currently on hand of $4,000.

(9) On December 30, the company flew a charter for which it has not yet billed

the customer and which it has not yet recorded in the accounts. The customer will be charged $6,800.

    (10) Based on preliminary computations, the firm estimates that income taxes for the year will be $22,000.

a. Prepare all journal entries that would be necessary to adjust and bring the accounts up to date. (Add any additional account titles that you believe to be necessary.)

b. On a 10-column sheet of accounting paper (or on an electronic spreadsheet), copy the unadjusted trial balance given here. Leave an additional six or seven rows between the last account balance and the totals to accommodate accounts to be added by the adjusting entries. Use two columns for the account titles and two for the unadjusted account balances. Label the next two columns ''Adjustments'' (debits and credits), the next two ''Income statement'' (debits and credits), and the last two ''Balance sheet'' (debits and credits).

c. Instead of posting the journal entries to T accounts, post them to the appropriate accounts in the column ''Adjustments.'' When you have finished posting the entries, sum the two columns and make certain that the totals of debits and credits are equal.

d. Add (or subtract, as required) across the columns, and indicate the total of each account in the appropriate column under the income statement or balance sheet. Take care. Remember that credits have to be subtracted from debits. Make certain that amounts are transferred to the proper column; it is easy to make an error.

e. Add each of the four income statement and balance sheet columns. The difference between the debit and credit columns of the income statement should be the net income for the year. The difference between the debit and credit columns of the balance sheet should also be the income for the year. If the two differences are not equal, then an error has been made. Why shouldn't the balance sheet balance? That is, why shouldn't the debits of the balance sheet equal the credits? Look carefully at the balance indicated for retained earnings. Is the balance the before or after ''closing balance''? Does it include income of the current year?

f. From the worksheet, prepare in good form both an income statement and a balance sheet. Remember that retained earnings have to be adjusted to take into account income for the current year.

21. *An electronic spreadsheet helps to make clear the impact of adjusting entries on the income statement, the balance sheet, and key ratios.*

    The trial balance of the Silver Creek Sales Company as of December 31, 1993, is presented on p. 166. (All dollar amounts are in thousands.) The trial balance was made before the company took into account the following information, which will require the firm to make adjusting entries:

    (1) The company miscounted ending inventory. The correct ending inventory was $759 rather than $859.

    (2) A review of insurance policies indicated that prepaid insurance should have been $22, not $15. (Insurance expense, like other expenses for which there is no specific account, is included in ''other expenses.'')

    (3) The firm neglected to charge depreciation of $12 on certain items of furniture and fixtures.

    (4) The firm failed to record $17 of sales. The sales had been made ''on account.''

    (5) The firm pays December salaries of several employees in the first week in January and makes appropriate year-end accrual entries. It incorrectly omitted the wages of one employee, $2, from its accrual entry.

Silver Creek Sales Company
Trial Balance
December 31, 1993

	Dr.	Cr.
Cash	$ 230	
Accounts receivable	550	
Allowance for uncollectible accounts		$ 129
Accrued interest receivable	4	
Merchandise inventory	859	
Prepaid insurance	15	
Furniture and fixtures	368	
Accumulated depreciation, furniture and fixtures		90
Note receivable	236	
Accounts payable		190
Sales taxes payable		23
Advances from customers		12
Accrued wages and salaries payable		8
Common stock		500
Retained earnings		998
Sales revenue		3,500
Cost of goods sold	2,500	
Wages and salaries	288	
Other expenses	400	
Totals	$5,450	$5,450

(6) Several customers gave deposits totaling $13 on merchandise which was not in stock. It is the policy of the company to debit cash, and credit advances from customers, upon receiving customer deposits. The company inadvertently credited sales for the deposits.

a. Using an electronic spreadsheet such as Lotus, set up a worksheet comparable to that illustrated in Exhibit 4-2.

- Make certain that the amounts in the last four columns (for the income statement and the balance sheet) will be calculated automatically as the amounts per the trial balance, plus or minus the amounts in the appropriate adjustment columns.
- Include a row to indicate the sums of each of the columns.
- Do not include a row for "income summary." Instead, add a cell beneath the total of the expense column to indicate "income." This cell should be specified as the difference between the sum of the revenues and the sum of the expenses.
- Specify "retained earnings" in the adjusted balance sheet as the initial balance, plus or minus the adjustments, *plus* the income (per the income cell). In that way, retained earnings will automatically include income for the year and the balance sheet should always be "in balance."

b. Prepare adjusting entries to reflect the information presented above. Post the entries, one at a time, to the adjustment columns of the worksheet. After you post each of the entries, compute and/or note the following:

- Income
- Retained earnings
- The current ratio [Consider as current all assets and liabilities except for furniture and fixtures (net of depreciation) and notes receivable.]

- Return on investment (income as a percentage of the sum of common stock and end-of-year retained earnings)

Be sure to use the capabilities of the spreadsheet to compute automatically the current ratio and the return on investment.

22. *The following two problems highlight the relationships among the three basic statements. They demonstrate that, given two of the three statements, the third can be derived.*

Shown are the statements of income and cash flows of United General Corp. for 1993. Shown also is the firm's balance sheet as of December 31, 1992.

Based on the statements provided, prepare the firm's balance sheet as of December 31, 1993. Although there are many approaches that you might take to prepare the balance sheet, one that is recommended is to prepare journal entries that relate each of the elements of the statement of income to one on the statement of

---

United General Corp.
Statement of Income for 1993
(in thousands)

Sales	$1,234
Other revenues (from royalties)	40
Total revenues	1,274
Expenses	
Cost of goods sold	757
Selling and administrative expenses	166
Depreciation expense	70
Interest expense	13
Tax expense	126
Total expenses	1,132
Net income	$ 142

Statement of Cash Flows
Year Ended December 31, 1993
(in thousands)

Cash Flow from Operating Activities	
Collections from customers	$ 1,507
Collection of royalties	35
Payments of interest	(10)
Payment of selling and administrative costs	(150)
Payment of taxes	(120)
Payments on account (liquidation of accounts payable)	(810)
Net cash from operating activities	$ 452
Cash Flow from Investing Activities	
Purchase of equipment	(100)
Sale of land (at no gain or loss)	80
Net cash from investing activities	(20)
Cash Flow from Financing Activities	
Issuance of bonds	200
Payment of dividends	(50)
Net cash from financing activities	150
Net increase in cash	$ 582

Balance Sheet
As of December 31, 1992
(in thousands)

Assets		
Cash		$ 310
Accounts receivable		481
Merchandise inventory		227
Royalties receivable		3
Prepaid selling and administrative expense		46
Equipment	$450	
Less: Accumulated depreciation	130	320
Land		200
Total assets		$1,587
Equities		
Accounts payable (for merchandise inventory only)		$ 80
Interest payable		5
Taxes payable		9
Contributed capital		400
Retained earnings		1,093
Total equities		$1,587

cash flows. The offsetting debit or credit is likely to represent an addition to or subtraction from a balance sheet account (for example, debit cash, $1,507; credit sales revenue, $1,234; credit accounts receivable, $273).

Take note of the following additional item of information: During 1993 the firm *purchased* merchandise inventory at a cost of $800,000.

23. The following are a firm's statement of cash flows for a year and balance sheets for the beginning and end of that year. During the year, the firm purchased merchandise inventory at a cost of $2,400,000.

Statement of Cash Flows
Year Ended December 31, 1993
(in thousands)

Cash Flow from Operating Activities	
Collections from customers	$ 4,521
Collection of royalties	105
Payments of interest	(30)
Payment of selling and administrative costs	(450)
Payment of taxes	(360)
Payments on account (liquidation of accounts payable)	(2,430)
Net cash from operating activities	$ 1,356
Cash Flow from Investing Activities	
Purchase of equipment	(300)
Sale of land (at no gain or loss)	240
Net cash from investing activities	$(60)
Cash Flow from Financing Activities	
Issuance of bonds	600
Payment of dividends	(150)
Net cash from financing activities	$ 450
Net increase in cash	$ 1,746

Balance Sheet
December 31
(in thousands)

		1993		1992
Assets				
Cash		$2,676		$ 930
Accounts receivable		624		1,443
Merchandise inventory		810		681
Royalties receivable		24		9
Prepaid selling and administrative				
expenses		90		138
Equipment	$1,750		$1,450	
Less: Accumulated depreciation	600	1,150	390	1,060
Land		260		500
Total assets		$5,634		$4,761
Equities				
Accounts payable (for merchandise				
inventory only)		$ 210		$ 240
Interest payable		24		15
Taxes payable		45		27
Bonds payable		600		0
Contributed capital		1,200		1,200
Retained earnings		3,555		3,279
Total equities		$5,634		$4,761

a. Reconstruct, in summary form, the transactions that took place during the year and record them as journal entries. From the information provided in the statements and in the preceding paragraph pertaining to purchases, derive the revenues and expenditures for the year. For example, if you know the net change during the year in accounts receivable and the reductions in the account during the year (the collections from customers), it is possible to determine the additions (the sales). Be sure that your entries, taken together, reflect the net change in cash.

b. Prepare an income statement for the year.

24. *The accounting cycle in manufacturing firms is no different from that in other types of enterprises, but it is especially important that period costs be distinguished from product costs.*

　　The Highbridge Products Co. began operations on January 1, 1993. The following events took place in January:

(1) On January 2 the owners of the company contributed $250,000 in cash to start the business.

(2) The company borrowed $100,000 from a local bank. It agreed to make annual interest payments at a rate of 12 percent and to repay the loan in its entirety at the end of three years.

(3) The company rented manufacturing and office space. It paid three months' rent in advance. Rent is $4,000 per month.

(4) The company purchased manufacturing equipment at a cost of $36,000 and office furniture and equipment at a cost of $4,800. Both purchases were made on account.

(5) The firm purchased raw materials at a cost of $7,000 cash. Of these, raw materials that cost $6,000 were placed in production (added to "work in process").

(6) The firm hired and paid in cash factory workers, $6,000, and office workers, $1,500. The costs of the factory wages were added to "work in process"; the costs of the office workers were considered to be period costs and thereby charged directly to an expense account.

(7) Factory maintenance costs incurred during the month were $450; factory utility costs were $600. Neither costs have yet been paid. Both were added to work in process.

(8) The company recorded depreciation for the month: manufacturing equipment, $1,000; office equipment and furniture, $100. The depreciation costs on the manufacturing equipment were added to "work in process"; those on the office equipment and furniture were considered to be period costs and charged directly to an expense account.

(9) The company gave recognition to interest and rent costs for the month (see events 2 and 3 and determine the appropriate charge for one month). Seventy-five percent of the rent costs were allocated to the factory and added to "work in process." The remaining portion of the rent costs, as well as the entire amount of the interest costs, were considered period costs.

(10) The company completed, and transferred from "work in process" to "finished goods inventory," goods that had cost $14,000 to manufacture.

(11) The company sold for $20,000 (on account) goods that had cost $13,000 to manufacture.

(12) Selling and other administrative costs paid in cash were $1,000.

a. Prepare journal entries to reflect the events that took place in January.
b. Post the journal entries to T accounts.
c. Prepare a month-end income statement and balance sheet.

25. *Cost of goods sold combines all costs associated with the manufacture of a product. Convention often determines whether a particular type of cost is associated with the manufacture of a product or with the other activities engaged in by a firm:*

During March a company incurred the following costs, all of which were related directly to the manufacture of its product:

Raw materials	$100,000
Factory labor	200,000
Utility costs for factory	4,000
Depreciation on factory equipment	10,000
Rent on factory building	50,000

The company started and completed 10,000 units of product. There was no opening inventory.

a. How much cost should have been added during the month to "work in process"?
b. How much cost should have been transferred to "finished goods"?
c. Assume that the company sold 8,000 units. What amount should it report as "cost of goods sold"? What amount as "finished goods inventory"?
d. Assume that at the end of the month the company discovered that it had failed to record the wages of two secretaries. One was employed in the office of the factory, the other in the office of the marketing department. Each was paid $1,500. Comment on how the omission would affect cost of goods sold and finished goods inventory.

26. *The effects of classifying a cost as a product rather than a period cost will depend upon the relationship between number of units produced and number of units sold.*

   Management of a corporation is uncertain as to whether certain administrative, transportation, and depreciation costs should be classified as *product* or *period* costs. Such costs average approximately $120,000 per year. It asks your advice as to the significance over the next two years of its decision. Labor and material costs are estimated at $6 per unit. Selling price of the product is $10 per unit.

   a. Suppose that in both year 1 and year 2 the company expects to produce and sell 40,000 units per year. What would be the resultant differences in income, ending inventory, and retained earnings for (or after) each of the two years if the company classified the costs as period rather than product costs?
   b. Suppose instead that the company expected in year 1 to produce 40,000 units but sell only 30,000 units and in year 2 to produce 30,000 units and sell 40,000 units. What would be the resultant differences in income, ending inventory, and retained earnings for (or after) each of the two years if the company classified the costs as period rather than product costs?

27. *Under conventional accounting practices, the greater the number of units produced, the less the cost per unit—and the less the reported cost of goods sold.*

   The Prettyman Doll Co. requires $2 of raw materials and $4 of factory labor to produce each doll. In addition, the company estimates that depreciation costs on the factory building and equipment as well as other *fixed* factory costs total $40,000 per year. ("Fixed" factory costs, although considered product costs, do not vary with number of units produced. They would be the same regardless of whether the company produced 10,000 or 50,000 dolls per year.) Sales price per doll is $10.

   a. In both 1993 and 1994 the company produced 20,000 dolls and sold 20,000 dolls. Compute the manufacturing cost per doll. Determine also gross margin (sales less cost of goods sold) for each of the two periods.
   b. Assume instead that in 1993 the company produced 30,000 dolls but sold 20,000 dolls; in 1994 the company produced 10,000 dolls and sold 20,000 dolls. Determine the manufacturing cost per doll in each of the two years. Compute the amount that should be reported as "Finished goods inventory" at the end of 1993. Determine also the gross margin for each of the two years.
   c. Suppose that the company planned to issue additional capital stock in January 1994. The company controller thought it important that the firm impress potential purchasers with a significant growth in earnings. On the basis of this analysis, what steps might company management have taken in 1993 to give the *appearance* of improved performance?

28. *This is a challenging exercise that requires an understanding of the flow of costs in a manufacturing operation.*

   The following table gives information taken from the ledger accounts of the Wright Manufacturing Co. The figures reported are the total amounts debited or credited to the various accounts during a year. The figures do *not* represent ending balances and do *not* include beginning balances. Some amounts have been omitted. On the basis of your knowledge of the accounting flows in a manufacturing operation, you are to fill in the missing amounts. That is, you are to determine which accounts are normally associated with debits or credits to other accounts. (For example, by knowing the amount *credited* to accounts payable, you can determine the amount *debited* to raw materials inventory.) No closing entries have yet been made.

	Debits	Credits
Allowance for depreciation (factory)	$* 0	$ 17,000
Depreciation cost (factory)	?	?
Raw materials inventory	?	95,000
Factory labor cost	107,000	107,000
Work in process	?	?
Finished goods	212,000	?
Cost of goods sold	197,000	0
Factory wages payable	105,000	?
Accounts payable*	85,000	110,000

*Includes only amounts owed in connection with purchases of raw materials.

29. *Corporate performance may be evaluated by relating income to the investment of the owners, which may be expressed in terms of "book" or "market" values.*

Hoover Company, a manufacturer of vacuum cleaners, had, as of December 31, $491,091,068 in assets and $263,376,708 in liabilities. Net income for the year was $39,263,333. The common stock of the company, which is traded "over the counter," closed on December 31 at 12¾. There were 12,114,995 shares of common stock outstanding.
a. Compute the return on the stockholders' equity (ROI).
b. Compute the price/earnings ratio. Compute also the reciprocal of the price/earnings ratio (i.e., earnings/price) and express it as a percentage.

30. *Alternative borrowing arrangements have different effects upon the current ratio.*

The balance sheet of the First Corporation as of December 31, 1993, follows (in thousands).
a. Compute the current ratio as of December 31, 1993.
b. Suppose that the company were to borrow an additional $50,000 and give the bank a six-month note. How would that affect the current ratio?
c. Suppose instead that the company were to borrow $50,000 and give a note payable in full at the end of two years. How would that affect the current ratio?
d. Suppose instead that the company were to issue bonds for $200,000 and use the proceeds to purchase a new plant. How would that affect the current ratio?

First Corporation Balance Sheet
December 31, 1993

Assets		Liabilities and Owners' Equity	
Current assets		Current liabilities	
Cash	$ 10,000	Accounts payable	$ 30,000
Accounts receivable	20,000	Notes payable	20,000
Note receivable	50,000		
Marketable securities	15,000		$ 50,000
Inventories	5,000		
		Noncurrent liabilities	
	$100,000	Bonds payable	$100,000
Noncurrent assets		Owners' equity	
Plant and equipment	$120,000	Common stock	$200,000
Land	70,000	Retained earnings	20,000
Investment in			
subsidiaries	80,000		$220,000
	$270,000		
		Total liabilities and	
Total assets	$370,000	owners' equity	$370,000

31. *Alternative financing arrangements may have substantially different effects on the accounting equation as well as on earnings per share.*

The following information relates to the Emerson Corp.

Total assets, 12/31/93	$10,000,000
Total liabilities, 12/31/93	2,000,000
Total owners' equity, 12/31/93	8,000,000
Net income 1993	1,000,000
Number of shares of common stock outstanding	100,000

a. Determine earnings per share for 1993.

b. The Emerson Corp. is currently negotiating to purchase a new manufacturing facility. The present owners of the plant are asking $2,000,000 for the facility. Emerson Corp. estimates that the increased capacity of the new plant would add $300,000 annually to its income (prior to deducting financing costs). To purchase the plant, it would have to borrow the $2,000,000. It estimates that it could issue long-term bonds at an annual interest rate of 11 percent (i.e., $220,000 per year).

   (1) If the company were to purchase the plant and borrow the necessary funds, what effect would the purchase (excluding effects on earnings) have on "the accounting equation"?

   (2) What effect would it have on earnings per share (assuming that income would otherwise have been the same as in 1993)? Ignore income tax considerations.

c. Assume instead that Emerson is considering an alternative means of purchasing the new plant. Instead of offering the present owners of the plant $2,000,000 in cash, it would offer them common stock of the Emerson Corp. that has a present market value of $2,000,000. The common stock of the Emerson Corp. is currently being traded on a major stock exchange at $100 per share. The Emerson Corp. would issue 20,000 new shares of common stock. Obviously, the company would no longer have to issue the bonds.

   (1) What effect would the alternative purchase plan have on the accounting equation?

   (2) If you were a present stockholder of Emerson Corp. concerned primarily with earnings per share, would you prefer the original purchase plan or the alternative proposal? Why?

32. *The following three problems require a careful look at a set of financial statements.*

Summit Industries, Inc., is a diversified international manufacturer and marketer of major home appliances and industrial equipment and machinery. The income statement and balance sheet shown on p. 174 and on p. 175 appeared in the company's 1993 annual report.

a. Explain, as best you can from the information provided, the reason for the improvement in earnings in 1993 over 1992.

b. Did each major group of costs increase in proportion to the increase in sales revenue?

c. How do you account for the increase in income before extraordinary item by a greater percentage than net income *per common share* before extraordinary item?

d. What percentage of income (before extraordinary item) did the firm pay in taxes in 1993?

e. The extraordinary item represents a refund in income taxes owing to a settlement with the Internal Revenue Service. The amount in dispute resulted from a transaction that took place in 1988. What justification can there be for treating the refund as an "extraordinary item" as opposed to including it in "other income, net"?

Summit Industries, Inc.
Statement of Income

	Year Ended December 31	
	1993	1992
Net sales	$2,010,114,000	$1,655,979,000
Other income, net	9,588,000	9,309,000
	$2,019,702,000	$1,665,288,000
Costs and expenses		
Cost of products sold	1,657,748,000	1,363,339,000
Selling, general and administrative expenses	214,318,000	170,564,000
Interest	31,064,000	30,216,000
	$1,903,130,000	$1,564,119,000
Income before income taxes and extraordinary item	116,572,000	101,169,000
Income taxes	53,650,000	46,651,000
Income before extraordinary item	62,922,000	54,518,000
Extraordinary item	12,783,000	—
Net income	$ 75,705,000	$ 54,518,000
Net income per common share		
Based on average shares outstanding:		
Before extraordinary item	$4.87	$4.33
Extraordinary item	1.08	—
Net income	$5.95	$4.33

33. Refer to the financial statements of Summit Industries, Inc., as presented above and on page 175.
   a. Compare the ability of the company to meet its current obligations as they come due in 1993 with its ability in 1992. Why might the current ratio have declined between December 31, 1993, and 1992, even though reported income was substantially greater in 1993 than in 1992?
   b. Compare the return on the investment of stockholders in 1993 with that in 1992.
   c. Did the firm issue additional shares of common stock in 1993? How can you tell?
   d. Did the firm declare dividends in 1993? What was the probable amount? How can you tell?
   e. Suppose that the price at which the common stock of the firm was traded was $17 on December 31, 1993, and $24 on December 31, 1992. What were the price/earnings ratios (excluding the "extraordinary item") as of those dates? How would the increase in the market price of the shares be reflected in the financial reports of the firm?
   f. Based on number of shares of common stock outstanding and the market price per share ($24) on December 31, 1993, what was the total value of the shares outstanding? What was the total value of the equity of the common stockholders per the firm's balance sheet? Why are the two amounts not the same?
   g. Was the firm more highly "leveraged" in 1993 than in 1992?

Summit Industries, Inc.,
Balance Sheets

Assets	December 31, 1993	December 31, 1992
Current assets		
Cash	$ 18,242,000	$ 20,116,000
Income tax claim receivable	16,061,000	—
Trade receivables (less allowances of $7,615,000 in 1993 and $6,458,000 in 1992)	275,300,000	250,419,000
Inventories	484,386,000	395,149,000
Prepaid expenses and other current assets	3,551,000	3,935,000
Total current assets	$ 797,540,000	$669,619,000
Investments and other assets		
Investments in foreign companies and other assets	9,634,000	8,314,000
Excess of cost over purchased net assets	17,087,000	17,087,000
	$ 26,721,000	$ 25,401,000
Property, plant and equipment		
Land	11,147,000	11,294,000
Buildings	172,279,000	157,130,000
Machinery and equipment	361,918,000	328,614,000
	$ 545,344,000	$497,038,000
Less: Allowances for depreciation and amortization	208,500,000	196,918,000
	$ 336,844,000	$300,120,000
	$1,161,105,000	$995,140,000

Liabilities and equity	December 31, 1993	December 31, 1992
Current liabilities		
Trade accounts payable	$ 143,603,000	$ 92,922,000
Accrued payroll, payroll taxes, and amounts withheld from employees	38,438,000	31,009,000
Other payables and accruals	137,562,000	111,349,000
Accrued and deferred income taxes	3,941,000	1,555,000
Current maturities of long-term debt and redeemable preferred stock	14,339,000	11,131,000
Total current liabilities	$ 337,883,000	$247,966,000
Long-term debt	272,505,000	252,496,000
Convertible subordinated debentures	5,196,000	47,279,000
Deferred income taxes	20,673,000	18,650,000
Long-term warranties, pensions, and other liabilities	52,736,000	48,961,000
Redeemable preferred stock	67,059,000	72,168,000
Common stockholders' equity:		
Common stock, par value $1 a share: Authorized 50,000,000 shares; Issued 13,696,091 shares at December 31, 1993 and 11,850,660 shares at December 31, 1992	13,696,000	11,850,000
Other capital	139,994,000	99,379,000
Retained income	257,492,000	202,520,000
	$ 411,182,000	$313,749,000
Less: Cost of 436,500 shares of common stock in treasury	6,129,000	6,129,000
	$ 405,053,000	$307,620,000
	$1,161,105,000	$9

34. *The financial statements reveal more data than are reported.*

Review the financial statements of Summit Industries, Inc. Determine the following for 1993:

a. Purchases of inventories.

b. Collections from customers. Assume all sales were on account. Ignore the allowances pertaining to trade receivables.

c. Gain or loss on sale of equipment. The statement of changes in cash flow indicates the following:

Depreciation expense	$27,131,000
Proceeds from sale of property, plant, and equipment	6,746,000
Additions to property, plant, and equipment	67,101,000

d. Income taxes paid. The obligation for income taxes is reported as both a current and a noncurrent liability.

Solutions to Exercise for Review and Self-Testing

1. $3,600,000 (12 months × $300,000 per month), regardless of how much cash was actually collected.

2. Unearned rent $300,000
   Rent revenue $300,000
   To recognize rent revenue in January

3. a. $3,600,000 (12 months × $300,000 per month) should have been recognized in rent revenue. Rent revenue is understated by $1,200,000 ($3,600,000 minus the $2,400,000 of revenue actually recognized).

   b. The balance in ''Unearned rent'' should be zero: The tenant is no longer ''ahead'' in rent payments.

   c. The balance in ''Rent receivable'' should be $600,000. The firm began the year ''owing'' the tenant $600,000 in services; it earned $3,600,000 and was entitled to $3,000,000 from the tenant. It collected, however, only $2,400,000; it is owed the remaining $600,000.

   d. Unearned rent $600,000
      Rent 600,000
      Rent revenue $1,200,000
      To adjust the year-end rent accounts

4. $120,000 should be reported as ''Cleaning expense'' regardless of the amount of cash paid.

   a. $40,000 should be reported as a liability, ''Cleaning costs payable.''

   b. $20,000 should be reported as an asset, ''Prepaid cleaning costs.''

5. The reported revenue or expense depends upon the value of the services provided or received, regardless of the amount of cash received or paid. The difference between the value of the services provided or received and the amount of cash received would be added to or subtracted from a related asset or liability account.

5

Measuring and Reporting Revenues

The Earnings Process

In the previous chapters it was emphasized that revenues should be *recognized* (accorded accounting recognition and considered to result in an increase in net assets) when *earned*, not necessarily when the related cash is received. Omitted, however, was a discussion of when revenues should be considered to be "earned."

Recall the essence of the definition of revenues:

> *The inflow of assets into the firm as a result of production or delivery of goods or the rendering of services*

In the illustrations up to this point, revenues have been recognized either with the *passage of time* (when earned as rent or interest) or when goods or services have been *delivered*.

Recognition based on time or delivery is appropriate for most, but by no means all, types of revenues. The two sets of circumstances that follow illustrate the issue:

Company A produces ships under contract to the U.S. Navy. On January 2, 1993, the company signed a contract to produce one vessel at a sales price of $800 million. During 1993 and 1994 the company constructed the ship. In 1995 it delivered the vessel to the government. Cost of production was $600 million.

If the company were to report revenue at the time of sale (when the ship was delivered to the government), then it would report zero revenue in both 1993 and 1994, the years of construction prior to delivery. In 1995, when the ship was delivered, it would report $800 million in revenue. Costs of production would be *capitalized* and remain in asset accounts until charged as an expense in the period in which the revenue was recognized. Hence, ignoring certain *period* costs, the company would report expenses of zero in 1993 and 1994 and of $600 million in 1995. Income would be zero in 1993 and 1994 and $200 million in 1995.

There is nothing to suggest that the performance of the company was, in fact, $200 million better in 1995 than it was in either 1993 or 1994. The company exerted its main productive effort evenly through the three-year period. Were revenue to be recognized only at the time of sale, income in the first two years would be understated, while that in the third year would be overstated. The financial statements of neither the first two years nor the third year would serve adequately as a basis for predicting future annual cash flows. They would, therefore, be of diminished utility to investors and other groups of statement users.

Company B sells parcels of land in an undeveloped area. Sales representatives use high-pressure sales tactics. A customer is permitted to make a small down payment (10 percent of the purchase price) and pay the balance over 10 years. The company transfers title to land to the customer upon collection of the full sales price. Many customers have second thoughts about the wisdom of their acquisitions and fail to pay the balances on their obligations. When a customer defaults, the company retains title to the land as well as the amounts already paid. But it makes no effort to force further payment. The company has not been in existence sufficiently long to be able to make reliable estimates of the percentage of sales that will eventually be collected. In 1993 the company made "sales" of $50 million; on these sales, it collected only $12 million in cash. Cost of the land sold was $4 million. Other operating costs were $10 million.

If this company were to report revenues at the time of sale, then on the sales of 1993, it would report revenues of $50 million, cost of land sold of $4 million, and other operating expenses of $10. Reported income would be $36 million.

As indicated, however, collection of the $38 million balance on the sales is problematic. Hence the net worth of the company is most definitely not $36 million greater at the end of the period than at the beginning.

Prudence dictates that this company delay recognition of revenue until it actually has cash in hand. Recognition of the full amount of a sale at the time a contract is signed would clearly overstate the value of the assets to be received from the transaction. At the same time, there could be little justification for delaying recognition of revenue until the title to the land is delivered to the customer. Once the company has received cash, then it is unquestionably better off. It has no further fiscal obligation to the customer.

Need for Periodic Reports

The problem of determining when and how much revenue has been earned exists only because managers, investors, and other users of financial information insist on receiving *periodic* reports of income. If they were content to receive a single report of profit or loss *after* the enterprise had completed its operations and was ready to return to stockholders their original investment plus any accumulated earnings, then determination of income would be simple: Subtract from the total amount either available or already distributed to stockholders the amount of their total contributions to the firm. The difference would be income over the life of the enterprise. Indeed, in the sixteenth and seventeenth centuries, companies were frequently formed with an expected useful life of only a few years—perhaps to carry out a specific mission, such as the charter of a ship for a single voyage. Investors in these companies were satisfied to wait until the companies were liquidated to get reports of their earnings.

Most companies today have indeterminate lives, and both owners and managers demand periodic reports of economic progress. Since many transactions are not completed in the same accounting period in which they are started, accountants are forced to make determinations of when and how much revenue should be assigned to specific periods.

IMPACT UPON RELATED ACCOUNTS

Expenses

The issue of revenue realization does not, of course, have an impact solely upon revenue accounts. Directly affected also are expense accounts and, equally significantly, balance sheet accounts. As pointed out previously, the question of when to recognize *expenses* is inherently tied to that of when to recognize *revenues*.

Costs that *cannot* be associated directly with specific revenues are considered *period* costs. They are charged as expenses in the periods in which they are incurred.

Costs that *can* be associated directly with specific revenues are *matched* to them and are charged as expenses as the revenues are recognized. Most commonly, the costs are incurred prior to the point at which the revenues are recognized. In a previous chapter, for example, it was indicated that the costs of production in a manufacturing concern are typically incurred before the point of sale. At point of sale, revenues are recognized and the costs can properly be charged as expenses. Until they are charged as expenses, the costs are stored in asset accounts, such as "raw materials," "work in process," or "finished goods inventory."

Many situations also occur, however, in which costs should properly be reported as expenses in a period earlier than that in which they are incurred. Suppose that a company sells and delivers manufacturing equipment. The company guarantees to provide maintenance service on the machines for one year after sale. The cost of providing the maintenance service can be directly associated with the revenue generated by the sale of the equipment. It follows, therefore, that it should be *matched* with the sales revenue and charged as an expense (even if an estimate of the actual cost has to be made) in the same accounting period as that in which the related revenue is recognized. The journal entries required to implement this matching approach will be illustrated later in this chapter.

Discussion of the issues pertaining to expense recognition will be deferred to subsequent chapters when they are addressed in conjunction with the assets to which they relate.

Balance Sheet Accounts

The valuation of assets, liabilities, and owners' equity is also related to the recognition of revenue. Revenue has been defined as an inflow of cash or other assets attributable to the production or delivery of goods or services. When revenues are recognized, so also must the resultant increase in assets or decrease in liabilities. Indeed, recognition of revenues is equivalent to the recognition of an increase of owners' equity (i.e., in retained earnings). An increase of owners' equity must be accompanied by an increase in assets or a decrease in liabilities.

Exhibit 5-1 illustrates the operating cycle of a typical business. The enterprise starts with an asset, generally cash, and continuously transforms it into other assets—first to materials, equipment, and labor and then to work in process, finished goods, accounts receivable, and eventually back to cash. If the company

EXHIBIT 5-1
Operating Cycle of a Business

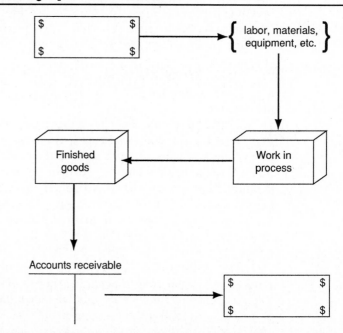

earns a profit, then ending cash is greater than beginning cash. The critical questions facing the firm are at which point (or points) in the production cycle should the increase in the "size" of the asset package be recognized; at which point is the enterprise "better off" than it was before; which are the *critical events* that trigger recognition of revenues?

Most commonly, especially in a manufacturing or retail operation, the firm recognizes the increase in the value of the assets at time of sale—when goods or services are delivered to customers. By selecting that point as the critical event, however, it is implicitly ignoring the value of the entire production cycle up to that point. It is asserting that all previous transactions involved nothing more than exchanges of assets and liabilities of equal magnitude—that the level of net assets remained unchanged. It is also implying that all subsequent transactions (e.g., collection of cash, fulfillment of warranty obligations) will also involve nothing more than exchanges of assets and liabilities of equal magnitude and that such exchanges will have no effect on the new level of net assets.

Time of sale is a *convenient* point to recognize revenues for *most* businesses; it is clearly not suitable for some businesses. It is inappropriate in situations in which delivery of goods provides little assurance that the amount owed by the customer will be collectible. It may be equally inappropriate where the enterprise has completed a significant portion of its economic activity and eventual collection of cash from a known customer is certain before the goods are actually delivered.

CRITERIA FOR REVENUE RECOGNITION

There are two widely accepted criteria as to when revenues should be recognized. Consistent with these guidelines, accounting standard-setting authorities have promulgated rules as to when revenues should be recognized in numerous specific situations. But they have addressed only a small fraction of all possible transactions. Hence individual companies and their accountants still must assume responsibility for interpreting and applying the general criteria.

Revenues should be recognized as soon as

1. The firm has exerted a substantial portion of its production and/or sales effort as measured by the proportion of costs already incurred to those expected to be incurred; the remaining costs can be estimated with reasonable reliability and precision.
2. The revenues can be objectively measured; eventual collection of a substantial portion of cash can reasonably be assured and an estimate can be made of amounts that will be uncollectible.

Rationale for the Criteria

The criteria reflect both the definition of "revenue" and the standards of reporting set forth in Chapter 1. Revenues, by definition, stem from the entire production and sales process in which a firm engages. Ideally, therefore, revenues should be recognized continuously throughout the production and sales process.

Each step in the production and sales process leaves the firm better off—closer to the ultimate realization of cash. Per the standards, however, accounting information must be reliable. Except in unusual situations, the benefit to the firm and its owners from the activities in which it engages cannot be determined with complete reliability until there has been an exchange transaction with outsiders. By virtue of an exchange with outsiders, the value of the consideration to be received by the firm is established. Without an exchange transaction, there can be no assurance that goods intended for sale will actually be sold—and if they can be sold, no assurance of the sales price. Because of their concern for reliability, accountants are exceedingly reluctant to acknowledge increments in asset value without the validation of a transaction with an independent party. Only in unusual circumstances are firms permitted to recognize changes in the values of assets until those assets have been sold.

To be sure, an exchange transaction in no way guarantees the eventual realization of anticipated cash. There are any number of reasons why customers will not pay the agreed-upon price for the goods or services purchased. And, at the same time, there are some situations (to be illustrated shortly) in which the consideration to be received can be reliably determined even in the absence of an exchange transaction. Hence the criteria are flexible. They provide that revenues can be recognized as soon as they can be measured objectively. Such time may be either prior or subsequent to the exchange transaction.

Correspondingly, the determination of income requires that costs be matched to revenues. If reported income is to be reliable, then estimates of costs must also be reliable. By requiring that a substantial portion of the costs be incurred before income is recognized at any point prior to the completion of a transaction, the guidelines enhance the probability that the amount will, in fact, ultimately be earned.

Ultimate reliability in the calculation of earnings cannot, of course, be obtained until *all* cash inflows and outflows associated with a transaction have occurred. That point may not be reached, however, until long after the main elements of the transaction have been completed. Were the financial statements not to recognize earnings until then, their relevance—their utility—to most groups of users would be severely diminished. Thus the criteria do not require certainty with respect to costs and revenues. Revenues can be recognized as soon as reliable *estimates* of costs and cash receipts can be made.

SELECTED POINTS OF REVENUE RECOGNITION

The two criteria for revenue recognition may be first satisfied when production begins, when all phases of the transaction are completed, or at any point in between. Four common points (or periods) of revenue recognition are

1. At the time of sale
2. In the course of production
3. At the completion of production
4. At some point after sale and/or delivery of goods, such as upon collection of cash

In the first part of this section, we shall provide an overview of these four points. In the second, we shall illustrate appropriate accounting entries.

Recognition at Time of Sale

For most manufacturing and retail concerns, the two criteria of revenue recognition are first satisfied at the point of sale, when the goods are *delivered* to the customer. At that time the firm has exerted a major portion of its economic activity, including its sales efforts. Most of the costs have been incurred, even though there might be additional costs, such as those pertaining to product warranties, guaranteed maintenance, and collection of receivables, that might be incurred in the future. A firm price has been established. Collection of cash can usually be reasonably assured, although the firm may have to estimate and make allowances for merchandise that will be returned and customers who will default on their accounts.

Recognition during Production

For some firms, especially those that provide goods or services under long-term contracts, the two criteria of revenue recognition are satisfied as production occurs—prior to point of sale. Recognition of revenue during the entire production process enables firms to avoid the erratic—and often misleading—pattern of income that may result from point of delivery revenue recognition (as was illustrated earlier in the shipbuilding example).

Percentage of Completion Method

A widely used means of recognizing revenue throughout the entire production process is known as the *percentage of completion method*. On any given contract, the proportion of total contract price to be recognized as revenue in each accounting period is the percentage of the total project completed during that period. Percentage completed is usually determined by dividing costs incurred to date by total anticipated costs. If 20 percent of the project is completed in a particular year, then 20 percent of the expected total revenues from the project would be recognized.

The percentage of completion or any other production-oriented means of revenue recognition is appropriate only when total costs of completing the project can be estimated with reasonable reliability and precision, the contract price is fixed and certain to be collected (as is often the case when the contract is with a government agency or major corporation), and there can be no question about the ability of the firm to complete the project and to have it accepted by the customer.

Another example of a situation in which revenues could be recognized in the course of production would be that in which a management consulting firm undertakes to advise a client on the installation of a new accounting system. Assuming that the consulting firm bills its clients on the basis of number of hours of service rendered, then the criteria would be reasonably satisfied as the consulting engagement progresses.

Recognition at Completion of Production

When a company is certain as to the price and quantity of its sales, it may recognize revenue at the completion of production.

Suppose, for example, that an electronics supplier contracted with a manufacturer to furnish a specified quantity of custom-designed components at an agreed-upon price. The customer, however, maintains a "just-in-time" manufacturing system. Instead of maintaining a costly inventory of raw materials, it requires its suppliers to deliver their components just in time to be used in the assembly process.

Upon completion of production, the supplier has satisfied the criteria for revenue recognition. It has exerted virtually all of its production and sales efforts; its revenues can be objectively measured and as long as the number of components returned is low and the customer is creditworthy, the eventual collection of cash is reasonably assured.

Recognition Subsequent to Sale

A number of circumstances may require that recognition of revenue be delayed until a time subsequent to sale. In some industries firms allow customers unlimited rights of return so that a sale is not final until long after merchandise has been delivered. A book publisher, for example, might permit a retailer to return all unsold copies of a particular title. In other situations, firms may have extensive warranty or other postsale obligations. A computer company, for example, may provide employee training and system-implementation assistance. In these situations, the criteria for revenue recognition may not be satisfied until cash has been collected and/or the postsale obligations fulfilled.

Installment Basis

In a previous illustration, a company sold parcels of land to customers who frequently elected not to fulfill their payment obligations. Hence the collection of cash could not be reasonably assured, and the revenue from sales could not be objectively measured until cash was actually in hand. Revenues could properly be recognized only as cash was collected—that is, using the installment basis of accounting.

The cash collection or *installment* basis of revenue recognition is *not* widely used today to account for routine merchandise sales—not even those in which the customer pays on "time" or on the "installment plan"—since it is generally possible to make reasonable estimates of credit losses. It is, however, used for real estate or other property transactions in which the collectibility of the receivable held by the seller is questionable. A builder, for example, might sell a recently constructed shopping center. The builder accepts from the purchaser a note for a portion of the selling price with the understanding that the purchaser will be able to make the required payments only if the stores in the shopping center are successfully leased. If there is uncertainty as to whether sufficient space in the shopping center can be rented to enable the purchaser to make payments on their note, the builder would delay recognition of the sales revenue until cash is actually in hand.

CONSERVATISM

The widely accepted practices of revenue and expense recognition, as well as the corresponding means of asset and liability valuation, are reflective of the accountant's bias toward *conservatism*. Because the concept of conservatism has such a wide-ranging effect on financial reporting, it is important that managers and investors be aware of how it should—and should not—be applied.

Conservatism is widely regarded as one of the pervasive attitudes which underlie financial reports. *Conservatism,* as it relates to accounting, means that it is generally preferable that any possible errors in measurement be in the direction of understatement rather than overstatement of net income and net assets. In matters of doubt, the recognition of favorable events should be delayed and that of unfavorable occurrences should be hastened.

Conservatism has its roots in the uncertainty that pervades all accounting measurements. It has been widely held that the interests of investors and creditors would be more adversely affected by overstatements of assets and profits than by understatements. More harm would accrue to them from an unforeseen or unreported loss than from an unanticipated gain. Moreover, it has sometimes been asserted that corporate managers are inherently optimistic. It is the role of the accountant to contain their optimism and to make certain that it does not spill over onto the company's financial statements.

The convention of conservatism must be applied judiciously. Insofar as accounting measurements are taken from a perspective of pessimism, they may easily be distorted. And to the extent that similar transactions (those which happen to result in gains rather than losses) are accounted for differently, the resultant financial statements may be internally inconsistent.

Moreover, understatement of earnings in one period may lead to overstatement in a subsequent period. It is not uncommon for newly appointed management teams to intentionally delay recognition of revenues to future periods and to charge costs of the future as current expenses. This practice, of course, reduces earnings in the year that the new management group takes over—a poor showing that can be blamed on the previous managers. But it also increases earnings of the future by adding revenues that should properly have been recognized in the past and eliminating expenses that should not have been previously charged. This type of manipulation—including early write-off of a substantial amount of costs previously treated as assets, sometimes referred to as "taking a big bath"—does as much to destroy the credibility of corporations and their accountants as the use of excessively liberal accounting methods.

ANALYSIS OF TRANSACTIONS

The impact of the alternative bases of revenue recognition on revenues and expenses as well as on assets and liabilities can readily be seen when transactions are analyzed in journal entry form. The journal entry is an expression of the principles previously set forth. The journal entry process may sometimes appear a bit tricky, but it can be simplified if a few guidelines are kept in mind.

1. In those periods in which revenues are recognized (and *only* in those periods), a revenue account must be credited. Since recognition of revenue implies an enhancement of net assets, a corresponding debit must be made to an asset or liability account.

2. In the periods in which revenues are recognized (and *only* in such periods), an expense account must be debited to give recognition to the related costs. The proportion of total expected costs that is charged as an expense in any particular period would be equal to the proportion of total anticipated revenues that is recognized in that period. Since recognition of expenses implies a reduction in net assets, a corresponding credit must be made to either an asset or a liability account. (This guideline gives effect to the *matching principle,* which holds that expenses must be matched with the revenues with which they can be associated.)

3. In all periods in which revenues are *not* recognized, transactions involve *only* exchanges of assets and liabilities; hence only asset and liability accounts should be debited or credited.

Some examples will illustrate these guidelines.

Example 1: Recognition of Revenues at Time of Sale—Warranty Obligation Outstanding

In 1993 the Orange Equipment Co. purchases equipment (intended for resale) for $50,000 cash. In 1994 it sells the equipment for $80,000 on account, giving the buyer a one-year warranty against defects. The company estimates that its cost of making repairs under the warranty will be $5,000. In 1995 the company collects the full sales price from the purchaser and incurs $5,000 in repair costs prior to the expiration of the warranty.

1993
(a)

Merchandise inventory (asset +)	$50,000
Cash (asset −)	$50,000
To record the purchase of the equipment	

One asset has been exchanged for another.

1994
(b)

Accounts receivable (asset +)	$80,000
Sales revenue (revenue +)	$80,000
To record the sale of the equipment	

Revenue is recognized at time of sale.

(c)

Cost of goods sold
  (expense +) $50,000
Warranty expense
  (expense +) 5,000
      Merchandise inventory (asset −) $50,000
      Estimated warranty costs
        (liability +) 5,000
To record the expenses associated with the revenue recognized

Every expense associated with the revenue must be recognized. The warranty expense charged and the estimated warranty costs credited represent an *estimate* of costs to be incurred in the future. Since these costs can be directly related to the sales revenue, they must be recorded in the same accounting period in which the revenue is recorded. The estimated warranty costs are reported as a liability. They are an obligation to provide future services.

1995
(d)

Cash (asset +) $80,000
    Accounts receivable
      (asset −) $80,000
To record customer payment

(e)

Estimated warranty costs
  (liability −) . . . .$ 5,000
    Cash (asset −) . . . .$ 5,000
To record costs incurred to fulfill the warranty obligations

The costs incurred to make repairs required under the warranty are *charged* (debited) against the liability that was established at the time the costs were charged as expenses. No additional revenues or expenses are recognized when repairs are actually made. The level of net assets remains the same. If the original estimate of warranty costs proves to be incorrect, then an adjustment can be made as soon as the error becomes known. Thus, if costs were greater than $5,000, the additional amount would be charged as an expense when incurred. If less, then at the expiration of the warranty, the estimated warranty costs account would be debited (decreased) and the warranty expense account credited (decreased) for the difference. (The credit to the warranty expense account will have the effect of reducing warranty expenses in a year subsequent to that in which the initial sale was made.)

Example 2: Recognition of Revenues at Completion of Production

In 1993 New York Instruments Co. receives an order from an electronics manufacturer to provide 10,000 units of a part. The purchaser agrees to pay $10 a unit, but under the terms of the contract the seller is to store and retain title to the goods until they are needed by the purchaser. Payment is to be made upon delivery of the goods. Cost of producing the part is $6 per unit. New York Instruments elects to recognize revenues upon completion of production.

The firm begins production of the parts in 1993 and completes and delivers them in 1994. Each of the following entries summarizes several individual entries that would be made as costs are incurred and the groups of units are completed and delivered.

During Production—1993, 1994
(a)

Work in process (asset +)..$60,000	
Cash (asset −) $60,000	
To record costs of production	

One asset is exchanged for another. (In practice, costs would be charged first to manufacturing accounts, such as labor and raw materials. They would then be transferred to work in process.)

At Completion of Production—1994
(b)

Finished goods at cost (asset +)..$60,000	
Work in process (asset −) $60,000	
To record completion of goods produced	

Costs are transferred from one asset account to another.

(c)

Finished goods at market value (asset +)..$100,000	
Manufacturing revenues (revenue +)...$100,000	
To recognize revenues upon completion of goods manufactured	

(d)

Cost of goods manufactured (expense +) $60,000	
Finished goods at cost (asset −)...$60,000	
To record the expense pertaining to the manufacture of the goods	

Revenues and expenses are recognized. As revenues are recognized, related expenses are also recognized. The realization of revenues is accompanied by an increase in the carrying value of the goods produced; that is, the recorded value of the finished goods increases from cost to market value, the amount of the increase being the income earned on the transaction.

At Time of Delivery—1994
(e)

Accounts receivable (asset +)..$100,000	
Finished goods at market value (asset −)..$100,000	
To record the delivery of goods	

The finished products, an asset, are exchanged for a receivable, also an asset.

As in the previous example, events in periods other than those in which revenues and expenses are recognized involve only exchanges among assets and liabilities.

Example 3: Recognition of Revenues during Production

The construction of the naval vessel described earlier can be used to illustrate the approach to recognizing revenues in which the amount of revenues recognized in any given period depends on the percentage of the entire project completed in that period. A company contracts to build a ship at a price of $800 million. It estimates that total construction costs will be $600 million. In 1993 it begins construction and incurs $120 million in costs; in 1994 it incurs $300 million, and in 1995 it incurs $180 million and completes the project. In 1995, the company collects the full contract price from the government.[1]

1993

(a)

Construction in progress at
    cost (asset +) $120,000,000
        Cash (asset −)..$120,000,000
To record costs incurred in construction of the vessel

This entry summarizes the effect of a number of entries, which would be made as construction progresses, involving various labor, material, and overhead accounts.

(b)

Construction in progress at contract
    value (asset +) $160,000,000
        Revenues from construction
            (revenue +) $160,000,000
To record revenues based on percentage of completion

(c)

Expenses relating to revenues
    from construction (expense +)..........................$120,000,000
    Construction in progress
        at cost (asset −)...................................$120,000,000
To record expenses pertaining to construction

The company has completed 20 percent of the project (percentage of completion assumed to be equal to the percentage of estimated total costs that have already been incurred). It is therefore appropriate to recognize 20 percent of *both* estimated revenues and expenses. The company will report revenues of $160 million, expenses of $120 million, and income of $40 million. The combined effect of entries (b) and (c) is to increase the

---

[1]The example is simplified for purposes of illustration. In practice, the government would make periodic cash payments to the contractor during construction of the vessel. The timing of the cash collections, however, would have no impact upon the timing of the revenue recognition.

value of the construction in progress (an asset) by the amount of the income recognized. An asset ("Construction in progress at contract value") is increased by the amount of revenues recognized. Another asset ("Construction in progress at cost") is reduced by the amount of expenses charged. As a consequence, construction in progress is now recorded at sales value, whereas, until entries (b) and (c) were made, it was recorded at cost.

At year end, both the revenue and the expense accounts are closed to retained earnings.[2]

(cl 1)

Revenues from construction............................$160,000,000
    Expenses relating to
      revenues from construction.............................$120,000,000
    Retained earnings.......................................40,000,000
To close revenue and expense accounts

The entries for 1994 are similar to those for 1993:

1994
(d)

Construction in progress
  at cost (asset +).......................................$300,000,000
    Cash (asset −)..$300,000,000
To record costs incurred in construction of the vessel

(e)

Construction in progress at contract
  value (asset +).......................................$400,000,000
    Revenues from construction
      (revenue +)..$400,000,000
To record revenues based on percentage of completion

(f)

Expenses relating to revenue
  from construction (expense +)..........................$300,000,000
    Construction in progress
      at cost (asset −)..................................$300,000,000
To record expenses pertaining to construction

In 1994 an additional 50 percent of construction is completed; hence it is necessary to recognize 50 percent of *both* total revenues and total estimated expenses. The company will report revenues of $400 million, expenses of $300 million, and income of $100 million.

As in 1993, it is necessary to close the revenue and expense accounts:

---

[2]In this example, the revenue and expense accounts are being closed directly to retained earnings. As explained in Chapter 3, revenues and expenses are often closed instead to income summary and the balance in income summary then transferred to retained earnings.

(cl 2)

Revenues from construction..............................	$400,000,000
Expenses relating to revenues	
from construction	$300,000,000
Retained earnings	100,000,000

To close revenue and expense accounts

By the conclusion of 1994, the firm will have reported income, for the two-year period combined, of $140 million: 70 percent of total expected income of $200 million. The work in progress will be stated at $560 million, which is $140 million more than its actual cost of $420 million. Retained earnings will correspondingly have increased by $140 million.

The entries for 1995 correspond to those of the preceding years; additional entries are required, however, to record the completion and delivery of the ship and the subsequent collection of cash.

1995
(g)

Construction in progress	
at cost (asset +)..	$180,000,000
Cash (asset −)..	$180,000,000

To record the costs incurred in the construction of the vessel

(h)

Construction in progress at contract	
value (asset +)..	$240,000,000
Revenues from construction	
(revenue +)	$240,000,000

To record revenues based on percentage of completion

(i)

Expenses relating to revenue	
from construction (expense +)...........................	$180,000,000
Construction in progress	
at cost (asset −).......................................	$180,000,000

To record expenses pertaining to construction

These entries are identical in form to those made in 1993 and 1994.

(j)

Completed ship at contract	
value (asset +).......................................	$800,000,000
Construction in progress	
at contract value (asset −)	$800,000,000

This entry simply reclassifies the asset from "work in progress" to "finished goods."

(k)

```
Accounts receivable
  (asset +) ........................................................$800,000,000
      Completed ship at contract
      value (asset −) ...................................................$800,000,000
  To record delivery of the ship
```

The completed ship is delivered. The purchaser is now indebted to the company for the contract price of the ship. From an accounting perspective, one asset is exchanged for another:

(l)

```
Cash (asset +)........................................................$800,000,000
      Accounts receivable
      (asset −) ...........................................................$800,000,000
  To record the collection of cash
```

The receivable is exchanged for cash; the manufacturing and collection cycle is now complete.

In 1995, the company will report revenues of $240 million, expenses of $180 million, and income of $60 million. When the revenue and expense accounts are closed, the accounting cycle will also be complete:

(cl 3)

```
Revenues from construction...............................$240,000,000
      Expenses relating to
        revenues from construction ...........................$180,000,000
      Retained earnings ......................................   60,000,000
  To close revenue and expense accounts
```

The entries for the entire period of three years are summarized in Exhibit 5-2. Upon completion of the ship, the company will have expended $600 million in cash to construct a ship which will be valued on its books at $800 million. Over the three-year period, it will have recognized revenues of $800 million, expenses of $600 million, and income of $200 million. Both assets (cash) and retained earnings will have increased by $200 million.

EXHIBIT 5-2
Recognition of Revenues during Production

	Cash			
Bal. 1/1/93	xxx	(a) 120,000,000		1993
(1) 1995	800,000,000	(d) 300,000,000		1994
		(g) 180,000,000		1995
Bal. 12/31/95	200,000,000			

EXHIBIT 5-2 Continued

Construction in progress at cost

(a) 1993	120,000,000	(c) 120,000,000		1993
(d) 1994	300,000,000	(f) 300,000,000		1994
(g) 1995	180,000,000	(i) 180,000,000		1995
Bal. 12/31/95	0			

Construction in progress at contract value

(b) 1993	160,000,000	(j) 800,000,000		1995
(e) 1994	400,000,000			
(h) 1995	240,000,000			
Bal. 12/31/95	0			

Completed ship at contract value

(j) 1995	800,000,000	(k) 800,000,000		1995
Bal. 12/31/95	0			

Accounts receivable

(k) 1995	800,000,000	(l) 800,000,000		1995
Bal. 12/31/95	0			

Retained earnings

	(cl 1)	40,000,000	1993
	(cl 2)	100,000,000	1994
	(cl 3)	60,000,000	1995
		200,000,000	Bal. 12/31/95

Revenues from construction*

1993 (cl 1)	160,000,000	(b) 160,000,000	1993
1994 (cl 2)	400,000,000	(e) 400,000,000	1994
1995 (cl 3)	240,000,000	(h) 240,000,000	1995

Expenses relating to revenues from construction*

(c) 1993	120,000,000	(cl 1) 120,000,000	1993
(f) 1994	300,000,000	(cl 2) 300,000,000	1994
(i) 1995	180,000,000	(cl 3) 180,000,000	1995

*Total revenues = $800,000,000
Total expenses = 600,000,000
Total income = $200,000,000

Example 4: Recognition of Revenues upon Collection of Cash (the Installment Basis)

In 1993 a real estate company sells a parcel of land to a developer for $2 million. The original cost of the land to the company was $1.5 million. Under the terms of the sales contract, the seller is to receive 5 percent of the selling price at the time of closing and transfer of title, 60 percent at the end of 1994, and the remaining 35 percent at the end of 1995. Because the ultimate collectibility of cash is highly uncertain, the company must recognize revenues only upon actual receipt of cash.[3]

The pattern of entries to be followed in this example is consistent with that established in the previous illustrations. A distinguishing feature of this example, however, is that the company physically surrenders the property sold *prior* to the time that it recognizes revenues and expenses. Inasmuch as expenses are associated with reductions in assets, the firm must retain an *accounting* interest in the property sold equal to the portion of the original cost of the land not yet charged as an expense (cost of land sold).

At Time of Sale and Collection of First Payment—1993
(a)

Accounting interest in land sold (asset +)	$1,500,000
Land (asset +)	$1,500,000

To record the sale of the land and transfer of title to purchaser

The purpose of this entry is simply to reclassify the property sold—to distinguish between land to which the company actually holds title and that in which it has merely an accounting interest.

(b)

Cash (asset +)	$100,000
Revenues from sale of land (revenue +)	$100,000

To record collection of 5 percent of the selling price and to recognize 5 percent of the revenues

(c)

Cost of land sold (expense +)	$75,000
Accounting interest in land sold (asset −)	$75,000

To record 5 percent of expenses applicable to the sale of land
(The original cost of the land to the company was $1.5 million; 5 percent of $1.5 million = $75,000.)

---

[3]In this example, recognition of revenues upon receipt of cash would be consistent with "Accounting for Sales of Real Estate," Financial Accounting Board *Statement of Financial Accounting Standards No. 66,* 1982.

The latter two entries recognize a portion of the total revenues to be realized on the sale and an identical portion of the related expenses.

At Time of Collection of Second Payment—1994

(d)

Cash (asset +)		$1,200,000
Revenue from sale of land		
(revenue +)		$1,200,000

To record collection of 60 percent of the selling price and to recognize 60 percent of the revenues

(e)

Cost of land sold		
(expense +)		$900,000
Accounting interest in land		
sold (asset −)		$900,000

To record 60 percent of the expenses applicable to the sale of the land

At Time of Collection of Third Payment—1995

(f)

Cash (asset +)		$700,000
Revenues from sale of land		
(revenue +)		$700,000

To record collection of 35 percent of the selling price and to recognize the remaining 35 percent of the revenues

(g)

Cost of land sold		
(expense +)		$525,000
Accounting interest in land		
sold (asset −)		$525,000

To record 35 percent of the expenses applicable to the sale of the land

By the time the final payment has been made, the company will have recorded revenues of $2 million, expenses of $1.5 million, and income of $500,000. It will report on the balance sheet an increase in cash of $2,000,000 and a decrease in land of $1.5 million.

The journal entries, as illustrated, though correct, point to an unavoidable conflict in the accounting process. A choice must sometimes be made between a more meaningful income statement and a more meaningful balance sheet. The set of entries are deficient in that the amount due from the customer—that is, an account receivable—is never incorporated into the accounts. This deficiency results because sales revenues are recorded only upon the receipt of cash. Hence the increase in assets associated with recognition of revenues can be reflected only upon the receipt of cash. As long as accountants insist that the income statement *articulate with* (be jointed to) the balance sheet, then the receivable cannot be recorded until the point of revenue recognition.[4] The conflict pervades accounting and arises in many other contexts.

REVENUE RECOGNITION—SELECTED INDUSTRY PROBLEMS

The criteria for revenue recognition cannot always be easily applied. The illustrations that follow are designed to demonstrate the difficulties of implementation. To a large extent, decisions as to the timing of revenue recognition are left to the good judgment of corporate managers and their accountants. As a consequence, companies in similar industries or even in the same industry have frequently drawn different conclusions as to the most appropriate basis of revenue recognition.

The rule-making bodies of the accounting profession, the Financial Accounting Standards Board and the American Institute of Certified Public Accountants, have issued a number of pronouncements and industry audit guides that have done much to narrow the alternatives available to companies in some industries. Nonetheless, differences in practice in other industries are still widespread and are likely to remain so in the foreseeable future.

Motion Picture Industry: Program Material for Television

When a motion picture studio produces feature films or other types of programs for television, it does not sell them outright. Instead, it licenses to the broadcasting companies the rights to exhibit the materials over a specified time period.

Over the years, motion picture studios have had diverse practices of revenue recognition on licenses of program materials. At least four points or periods of revenue recognition have been used and justified:

1. *Upon signing a license agreement with a broadcaster.* At that time, an exchange transaction has taken place, and the amount of revenue to be earned is generally known. If the program material has already been produced, the costs are also known; if not, they can generally be estimated.

2. *Upon completion of the program material* (assuming that a license agreement has already been signed). By now the revenues and costs are known and all significant production efforts have been exerted.

---

[4]The deficiency can be remedied, in part, by an artificial contrivance. Two related accounts—"Accounts receivable" and "Deferred revenue"—can be established. When a contract is first signed, the following entry can be made:

Accounts receivable (asset) $2,000,000
    Deferred revenue (liability) $2,000,000

Then, as each payment of cash is received, the entry can be "reversed":

Deferred revenue $100,000
    Accounts receivable $100,000

The balances in the two accounts, both of which are balance sheet accounts, will always *net* to zero. Thus they have minimal accounting significance. They do, however, provide information about the existence and magnitude of the receivable and provide a measure of control over amounts due from customers.

3. *At the start of the licensing period.* The material is transferred to the broadcaster and made available for its use. This point is comparable to the time when merchandise is delivered to the customer in the usual sales transaction.
4. *Over the period in which the licensee has the right to show the material.* The material is produced in order to be shown over a period of time. Recognizing revenues over the licensing period is comparable to recognizing rent over the rental period.

The Financial Accounting Standards Board has ruled in favor of option 3. Revenues should be recognized *at the start of the license period,* provided, however, that all the following conditions are met:

1. The license fee for each film is known.
2. The cost of each film is known or can be reasonably determined.
3. Collectibility of the full license fee is reasonably assured.
4. The film has been accepted by the licensee in accordance with conditions of the license agreement.
5. The film is available for its first showing.[5]

The board took a somewhat different position with respect to motion pictures that are to be shown in theaters rather than on television. The board stipulated that revenue from films shown in theaters should be recognized on the dates of exhibition rather than at the start of the license period. This applies to licenses in which the required payment is a percentage of box office receipts as well as a flat fee. The contractual arrangements between a motion picture producer and both broadcasters and theater owners obviously have much in common. But the board most likely considered the license fees to be generated by exhibitions in theaters rather than on television to be more difficult to estimate and less certain of ultimate collection.

Insurance Industry

A property insurance company typically insures property owners against losses from fire, theft, accident, and similar types of casualties. The policies that it writes are for a specified duration, often one to three years. Because the period of coverage is fixed, the company knows in advance how much revenue it will earn on each policy. It cannot, of course, determine the costs associated with a policy until the expiration of the policy and upon settlement of all claims. But based on its own experience, or those of other firms in the industry, it can usually make reliable estimates of the total losses that it will be required to cover.

A life insurance company, by contrast, may provide coverage for an indeterminate period (i.e., the life of the policyholder). It typically engages in a broader range of functions than the property company. Sales activities tend to be relatively more important, and many types of life policies require the company to provide savings and investment services in addition to insurance coverage. The period over which the policyholder pays premiums may not be known with certainty when the policy is written since it may be for his or her entire

---

[5]"Financial Reporting by Producers and Distributors of Motion Picture Films," Financial Accounting Standards Board *Statement of Financial Accounting Standards No. 53,* 1981.

life or such an extended period that there is considerable risk that the insured will either not survive for the full payment period or cancel the policy prior to dying. Moreover, the company may be obligated to provide both insurance coverage and related services for many years beyond the period during which the policyholder is liable for premiums. Nevertheless, both revenues and claims can be estimated on the basis of actuarial experience.

There are several bases for revenue recognition that can be justified and have, in fact, been used within the industry. Revenue may be recognized

1. Evenly throughout the known or estimated period of coverage. This basis is rooted in the assumption that the primary activity of the company is insurance coverage. The company provides the coverage uniformly over the life of a policy and therefore should recognize revenues over its life.
2. In part when the policy is written, in part evenly over the life of the policy. This basis gives recognition both to the service provided in the insurance coverage itself and to the substantial efforts incurred by a company in selling and writing a policy. These efforts may include sales and advertising, investigations, medical examinations, and initial clerical costs.
3. As premiums are due from policyholders. This basis takes into account the uncertainties involved in determining total revenues to be generated. For policies on which the premiums are paid throughout the policy period, the basis provides a reasonable match of revenues recognized and services provided.

In 1982, to reduce diversity of practice, the FASB ruled that revenue on *short-duration* policies, such as those for property coverage, should be recognized *evenly over the period for which the insurance protection is provided*. For *long-duration* policies, such as those for life insurance, revenue should be recognized *as the premiums are due from policyholders*. For both types of policies, estimates of costs, including anticipated claims, must be made and charged as expense in proportion to the revenues recognized.[6]

The different approaches taken by the FASB toward the two types of motion picture licenses and toward insurance coverage illustrate the difficulties of establishing specific rules of revenue recognition for firms in the same industry, let alone for all firms. Seemingly subtle differences in the types of products sold or services provided may justify significant differences in basis of revenue recognition.

Banks and Savings and Loans

When a bank or savings and loan association makes a loan, it often charges an *origination fee*. This fee is typically expressed in *points*. Each "point" is equal to 1 percent of the amount of the loan. For example, a fee of three points on a loan of $1 million would be 3 percent of $1 million, or $30,000. The fee is generally paid at the time the loan is made and is in addition to the usual interest that will be charged over the term of the loan.

[6]"Accounting and Reporting by Insurance Enterprises," Financial Accounting Standards Board *Statement of Financial Accounting Standards No. 60,* 1982.

To most lenders and borrowers the fee is a form of additional interest. It compensates the lender both for using its funds and for making and administering the loan. Banks and savings and loans charge points, rather than incorporating all compensation into the interest rate, for a number of reasons. One is that many borrowers like to be charged the *prime lending rate*—that charged to the most creditworthy customers—even though they may not qualify for it. By charging points, the bank can quote the prime rate but receive total compensation that reflects the borrower's actual credit status. Another is that the fee provides an immediate return to the bank, whereas ordinary interest is received only over the period of the loan.

The issue of revenue recognition that is controversial is whether points should be recorded as revenue when they are received or over the term of the loan. Prior to the applicable FASB pronouncement, most banks and savings and loans recognized the revenue when the points were paid—that is, "up front." The FASB, however, took the position that, in economic substance, loan origination fees are just another form of interest and should thereby be recognized as revenue over the term of the loan.[7]

Summary

Revenues should be realized when earned; costs should be charged as expenses at the time the revenues to which they are related are realized. This chapter has addressed the question of *when* revenues should be considered to be earned. We have not attempted to provide answers; indeed there are no definitive answers. Instead, we have explored the nature of the problems and set forth general guidelines for their resolution.

Revenues are commonly *recognized* (considered to result in an increase in net assets) at time of sale. They may also be recognized, however, during the process of production, at the completion of the process, or upon events subsequent to the sale. As a rule, revenues should be recognized as soon as

1. The firm has exerted a substantial portion of its production and/or sales effort as measured by the proportion of costs already incurred to those expected to be incurred; the remaining costs can be estimated with reasonable reliability and precision.
2. The revenues can be objectively measured; eventual collection of a substantial portion of cash can reasonably be assured and an estimate can be made of amounts that will be uncollectible.

We have tried to show some of the difficulties of applying these two criteria of revenue recognition by describing issues that have arisen in three specific industries. The issues are not of the type that can be resolved by methods that would be appropriate in the sciences. At best, a "resolution"—such as an edict by a rule-making authority—can represent a compromise among competing accounting standards and objectives or an arbitrary choice made in the interests of comparability among firms.

In illustrating the journal entries that would be required by the differing bases of revenue recognition, we have tried to demonstrate the relationships among revenue recognition, expense recognition, asset valuation, and liability valuation. Specific issues of asset and liability valuation (and, necessarily, expense recognition) will be addressed in Chapters 6 through 10.

---

[7]"Accounting for Nonrefundable Fees and Costs Associated with Originating or Acquiring Loans and Initial Direct Costs of Loans," Financial Accounting Standards Board *Statement of Financial Accounting Standards No. 91, 1987.*

Exercise for Review and Self-Testing

Surfside Construction Co. contracts with the city of Portland to construct five municipal swimming pools. Contract price is $1 million ($200,000 per pool); estimated total cost of construction is $800,000 ($160,000 per pool). The contract requires that the pools be turned over to the city when all five have been completed and that payment be made at that time.

Surfside elects to recognize revenues on the basis of number of units completed.

1. In 1993 Surfside incurs $500,000 in construction costs and completes two pools. The cost of each of the completed pools was as estimated, $160,000.
   a. Prepare a journal entry to record the costs incurred.
   b. Inasmuch as Surfside completes two pools, determine the percentage of total revenues that should be recognized. Determine the dollar amount of revenue that should be recognized.
   c. Based on the percentage of revenue recognized, determine the percentage and dollar amount of estimated costs that should be recognized as expenses.
   d. If revenues on the two completed pools have been recognized, then at what value (cost or contract) must the pools be carried on the books?
   e. If the costs of constructing the two pools are to be recognized as expenses, then what asset must be reduced (in an amount equal to the expenses)?
   f. Prepare two journal entries to recognize the revenues and the related expenses.
2. In 1994 Surfside incurs the $300,000 in estimated additional costs and completes the remaining three pools.
   a. Following the pattern established in the previous section, prepare journal entries to record the costs incurred and to give recognition to revenues and expenses. Do total revenues recognized over the two-year period equal the contract price? Do total expenses equal the estimated costs?
   b. In 1994 Surfside delivers the completed pools to the city and gives accounting recognition to the amount owed by the city. Prepare the appropriate journal entry.

Questions for Review and Discussion

1. It is sometimes pointed out that over the life of an enterprise, it matters little on what bases revenues and expenses are recognized; it is only because investors and others demand periodic reports of performance that problems of revenue and expense recognition arise. Do you agree? Explain.
2. "If financial statements are to be objective, then it is inappropriate to recognize revenues on a transaction until the seller has cash in hand; recognition of revenues at any point prior to collection of cash necessarily involves estimates of the amount of cash that will actually be collected." Do you agree?
3. What are the two criteria as to when revenues should be recognized? What is the rationale behind them?
4. The question of revenue and expense recognition is inherently intertwined with that of asset and liability valuation. Explain.
5. Accounting statements are said to be "conservative." What is meant by conservatism as the concept is applied to financial reports? How does the accountant justify being conservative? What problems might such conservatism create?

6. Why, when revenues are recognized on a percentage of completion basis, is it necessary to state construction in progress at contract value rather than at cost? Why, when revenues are recognized on a cash basis (i.e., subsequent to point of delivery), must there be an account "accounting interest in asset sold"?

7. The FASB has ruled that premiums from insurance policies of short duration, such as those on property, should be accounted for differently from premiums for policies of long-term duration, such as those on lives. What is the position of the FASB as to revenues from insurance premiums, and why should length of policy be a characteristic that justifies different bases of revenue recognition?

8. The Evergreen Forest Co. raises trees intended for sale as Christmas trees. Trees are sold approximately five years after they have been planted. What special problems of income determination does the company face if it is to prepare annual financial statements?

9. A greeting card company produces cards for the various holidays and commemorative occasions throughout the year. The cards are perishable; if they are not sold by the day for which they are intended, it is not feasible to save them until the next year. For cards to be sold to consumers, they must be displayed at retail outlets. Owing to the risk that they will not be sold, merchants are understandably reluctant to carry a large inventory of cards. To reduce merchants' risk, the greeting card company has agreed to repurchase all cards that remain unsold by the occasion for which they are intended at the full price paid by the merchant. The company estimates that 20 percent of all cards shipped to merchants will eventually be returned. On what basis do you think the company should recognize revenues? Would your response be different if 50 percent were to be returned?

10. A consumer finance company makes installment loans of small amounts (up to $10,000) to individuals. The loans are for a period of up to 36 months. The company faces intense competition from other firms in the industry and directs considerable resources to advertising and other sales efforts. When a customer applies for a loan, the company incurs substantial costs in conducting credit investigations and in completing the necessary clerical work to initiate the loan. Customers are charged interest on the outstanding balances of their loans. Although the rate of default on loans is low, many customers do not pay their installments on time. Collection costs are high. The company presently recognizes 20 percent of the expected interest revenue from a loan at the time it makes the loan. Thereafter it recognizes interest revenue on a cash collection basis. A portion of each payment made by the customer is considered to be for interest. Conventionally, interest revenue (or, correspondingly, interest expense) is recognized uniformly over the period of a loan in proportion to the loan balance outstanding. How can this company justify recognizing 20 percent of estimated total interest at the time it first makes a loan and the balance only as cash is collected?

11. The following statement of accounting policy was included in an annual report of Santa Fe Industries:

   Revenues from rail operations are recognized in income upon completion of service. Expenses relating to shipments for which service has not been completed are charged to income and not deferred.

   Why might such policy be considered objectionable? What "principle" does it violate? How do you suspect the controller of Santa Fe Industries would defend the policy?

Problems

1. *This exercise compares the effects of alternative bases of revenue recognition on earnings of a particular period as well as on earnings over the life of a project.*

The Anderson Construction Company agreed to construct six playgrounds for the city of Webster. Total contract price was $1.2 million. Total estimated costs were $960,000.

The following schedule indicates for the three-year period during which construction took place the number of units completed, the actual costs incurred, and the amounts of cash received from the City of Webster.

	Year		
	1	2	3
Units completed	1	2	3
Costs incurred	$480,000	$288,000	$192,000
Cash collected	240,000	360,000	600,000

a. Determine revenues, expenses, and income for each of the three years under each of the following alternatives:
   (1) Revenues recognized on the basis of the percentage of the project completed (Percentage of costs incurred indicates degree of completion.)
   (2) Revenues recognized as soon as each playground is completed
   (3) Revenues recognized upon the collection of cash
b. Are total earnings the same over the life of the project?

2. *When should the liability and expense associated with interest and loan origination fees be charged?*

   On December 31, 1993, a bank loans a customer $100,000. The term of the loan is two years and it cannot be prepaid. Interest, at a simple rate of 10 percent, is payable in full at the time the loan matures. Thus, at the end of two years, the customer will be required to pay $100,000 (the amount borrowed) plus $20,000 interest—a total of $120,000. The customer is a sound credit risk. There is little question about its ability to make the required payments.
   a. At what amount should the receivable be recorded on a balance sheet of the bank as of December 31, 1993? Justify your response in light of the bank's legally enforceable claim against the customer for $120,000.
   b. Suppose that the bank charges the company a loan origination fee of two points (2 percent of the amount loaned). The fee of $2,000 is paid by the customer on December 31, 1993. What is the amount of revenue on the origination fee that the bank should recognize in 1993? Justify your response, indicating specifically any assumptions that you might make as to the economic substance of the fee.

3. *Under the percentage of completion method, the percentage of total estimated costs recognized as expenses in each year must equal the percentage of total contract value recognized as revenues.*

   On January 3, 1993, Eastern Electric Co. contracted with United Power Company to produce generating equipment. Estimated cost of the equipment was $2.4 million; contract price was $2.8 million. Eastern Electric recognizes revenues on such contracts on a percentage of completion basis.
   In 1993 Eastern Electric incurred $1.8 million in costs on the project; in 1994 it incurred the remaining $600,000. In 1993 it received from United Power $800,000 in cash (which may be accounted for as an advance payment), and in 1994 it received the remaining $2 million.
   a. Prepare a journal entry to recognize the costs incurred (added to work in process) in 1993. Assume that they were paid in cash.
   b. Determine the percentage of revenues and expenses that should be recognized in 1993.

c. Prepare journal entries to recognize the revenues and expenses in 1993.

d. Prepare a journal entry to recognize the cash collected in 1993.

e. Prepare similar journal entries, plus any additional journal entries required to recognize completion of the equipment and delivery to customer in 1994.

4. *The journal entries associated with the percentage of completion method highlight the relationships among revenue recognition, expense recognition, and asset valuation.*

The Moshulu Construction Co. contracts with the Pelham Corporation to construct an office building. The contract price is $50 million. The Moshulu Co. estimates that the building will cost $40 million and will take three years to complete. The contract calls for the Pelham Corporation to make cash advances of $10 million during each of the first two years of construction and to make a final payment of $30 million upon completion of the building; these cash advances are to be accounted for on the books of Moshulu Co. as a liability until the project is completed.

The company elects to recognize revenues on the percentage of completion basis. Actual expenditures over the three-year period are as follows:

1993	$10,000,000
1994	25,000,000
1995	5,000,000

a. Prepare journal entries to account for the project over the three-year period. Assume that all costs are paid in cash as incurred.

b. Prepare an income statement and a balance sheet for each of the three years. Assume that at the start of the project the only asset of the company is cash of $20 million.

5. *It is sometimes necessary to recognize costs as expenses before they have actually been incurred.*

On December 31, 1993, the Valentine Roofing Co. reported among its liabilities the following balance:

Estimated costs to fulfill roof guarantees	$40,000

During 1994 Valentine constructed roofs for which it billed customers $3 million. It estimates that, on average, it incurs repair costs, under its two-year guarantee, of 2 percent of the initial contract price of its roofs. In 1994 the company actually incurred repair costs of $75,000, which were applicable to roofs constructed both in 1994 and in prior years.

a. Analyze both the liability and expense accounts pertaining to roof repairs in journal entry and T account forms for the year 1994.

b. How can a company justify charging repair expenses *before* they are actually incurred, based only on an *estimate* of what actual costs will be?

6. *Costs of fulfilling warranty obligations must be matched to the revenues with which they are associated.*

In 1992 the Gerard Company sold for cash 20 printing presses at a price of $100,000 each. The presses cost $80,000 to manufacture. The company guaranteed each press for a period of two years starting from the date of sale. The company estimated that the costs of making repairs as required by the guarantee would be approximately 2 percent of sales.

Actual expenditures for repairs of presses sold in 1992 were as follows: 1992, $14,000; 1993, $19,000; 1994, $12,000.

Prepare journal entries to record the sale of the presses and the subsequent repair costs.

7. *The differences between a* warranty *and a* service contract *may not be great, yet they may be sufficient to justify different bases of revenue and expense recognition.*

   a. Copco manufactures and sells office equipment. Its copy machine sells for $18,000. The selling price includes a three-year warranty. The company estimates that, on average, it will have to make one service call per month over the warranty period. A service call costs the company $50. The cost to manufacture the machine is $12,000.

      On June 30, the company sells one machine (for cash). On July 15 it makes its first service call on that machine. The cost of the call is paid in cash. During August Copco does not make a service call.

      Prepare the required journal entries for June, July, and August.

   b. Copco sells its mail machine for $18,000. The selling price also includes a three-year service contract. However, the company estimates that it will have to make *four* service calls per month at a cost of $50 each. The mail machine costs only $7,200 to manufacture. The company also sells both the mail machine and the service contract separate from each other. However, the price of the two together is slightly less than each independently.

      On June 30 Copco sells one machine for cash. During July the company makes four service calls on that machine. During August it is not required to make any service calls.

      Prepare the required journal entries for June, July, and August. State any assumptions that you might make. (Use your best judgment; several possible sets of entries would be equally defensible.)

   c. Justify your bases of revenue recognition and, if appropriate, explain any difference in the ways you accounted for the two Copco machines. Also explain how and why you allocated expenses as you did.

8. *Under the completion of production method, as with other methods, expenses are matched with revenues.*

   Lawncare, Inc., sells to Jaymart Stores lawnmowers that are specially manufactured for sale under a Jaymart brand name. A recent contract requires Lawncare to produce and deliver to Jaymart 1,000 mowers at a price of $300 per unit. Lawncare estimates that its manufacturing costs will be $200 per unit.

   a. Lawncare recognizes revenues and expenses on a completion of production basis inasmuch as sale and collection are assured when production is completed. Prepare journal entries to reflect the following events.

      (1) In a particular month Lawncare incurs $180,000 in production costs, all of which are added to work in process. All costs are paid in cash.

      (2) It completes 400 units and transfers them to finished goods inventory. The costs of the finished mowers were as estimated, $200 each. Lawncare gives accounting recognition to the associated revenues, expenses, and increase in the carrying value of the inventory.

      (3) It delivers to Jaymart 300 mowers and bills Jaymart for the items delivered.

   b. Lawncare also manufacturers lawn mowers under its own brand name for sale to department stores and lawn specialty shops. Sales to these stores are not made under any special contractual arrangements. Goods are shipped as ordered. Do you think that Lawncare should use the completion of production method to recognize revenues on these sales? Would the firm be consistent if it used another method?

9. *On what basis should a manufacturer of custom products recognize revenues?*

 The Harrison Co. manufactures video display monitors for sale to Save-More Discount Stores. Save-More sells the units under its own brand name. In 1993 Harrison Co. signed a contract to deliver Save-More 30,000 units at a price of $100 per unit over the next three years. By the end of 1993 Harrison had not yet delivered any units to Save-More but had 10,000 units 90 percent complete. In 1994 Harrison completed and delivered to Save-More 23,000 units—the 10,000 units started in the previous year plus 13,000 units started in 1994. In 1995 Harrison completed and delivered the remaining 7,000 units.

 Each unit cost Harrison $75 to manufacture. As agreed upon in the contract, Save-More made cash payment of $1 million to Harrison in each of the three years.
   a. Determine revenues, expenses, and income for each of the three years if revenue were to be recognized (1) in the course of production, (2) at time of delivery, (3) at time of cash collection. Are total revenues, expenses, and income the same under each of the three methods?
   b. Which basis of revenue recognition do you think results in the most reliable and relevant determination of corporate performance?

10. *The impact of alternative accounting practices on income as well as retained earnings (and thus on assets and liabilities) must be evaluated.*

 Waterloo Construction Co. begins operations in 1993. The company constructs bridges. Each bridge takes three years to complete, and construction is spread evenly over the three-year period. The contract price of each bridge is $3 million. In the period between 1993 and 1997 the firm begins construction of one bridge at the start of each year. Each bridge is started on January 1 and is completed after three years; for example, the bridge started on January 1, 1993, is completed on December 31, 1995.
   a. Assume that the firm recognizes revenues only upon the completion of a bridge. Determine annual revenues for the period 1995 to 1997.
   b. Assume that the firm recognizes revenue on a percentage of completion basis (one-third of the revenue on each bridge is recognized each year). Determine annual revenues for the period 1995 to 1997.
   c. Is there a difference in reported revenues?
   d. Determine the balance in retained earnings that the firm would report at the end of 1997 under each of the two methods. Be sure to take into account any revenues that would have been recognized in 1993 and 1994. Assume that no dividends have been declared; ignore expenses related to the revenues.
   e. Suppose that starting in 1998 the firm begins construction on two bridges each year. Determine annual revenues for the years 1998 to 2000.
   f. Under what circumstances does choice of accounting method have an impact upon reported revenues?

11. *The effect on income of using a convenient, but theoretically unacceptable, method of accounting may be immaterial; the effect on assets and retained earnings may be substantially greater.*

 Midstate Utility Company does not recognize revenues at the time it delivers electricity to customers. Instead, it recognizes revenues as it bills its customers for the electricity used. The company ordinarily bills customers on the fifteenth of each month for electricity that they used in the previous month.

 As of December 31, 1993, the company had delivered electricity for which it would bill customers on January 15, 1994, for $86 million. As of December 31, 1994, the company had delivered electricity for which it would bill customers, on January 15, 1995, for $90 million.

In response to a suggestion by its CPA firm that the company adjust its books at the end of each year to take into account the unbilled revenues, the company controller argued that the adjustments would have but an "immaterial" impact on the financial statements. In 1994 the company had revenues of $1.1 billion and income before taxes of $140 million. The company reported current assets of $170 million and retained earnings of $830 million.

Suppose that the company consistently followed the practice of recognizing revenues in the year in which electricity was delivered rather than that in which it was billed.

a. Compute the impact of the alternative procedure, in both absolute and percentage amounts, on revenues and profits of 1994 (ignore income taxes).
b. Compute the impact on current assets and retained earnings at the end of 1994.
c. Prepare any journal entries necessary to adjust the accounts on December 31, 1994, so that revenues are recognized at the time electricity is delivered rather than when it is billed.

12. *If revenues from the sale of an asset are to be associated with the collection of cash, so too must the cost of the asset sold.*

Land Developers, Inc., sells a parcel of land for $150,000. Terms of the contract require that the buyer make a down payment of $30,000 at the time the agreement is signed and pay the remaining balance in two installments at the end of each of the next two years. In addition, the contract requires the buyer to pay interest at a rate of 8 percent on the balance outstanding at the time of each of the two installment payments.

Land Developers, Inc., had purchased the land for $90,000.

Determine the revenues and expenses that the company should report upon each of the cash collections, assuming that it elects to recognize revenues on an installment (cash collection) basis.

13. *On what basis should revenues from membership fees be recognized?*

The Beautiful Person Health Club charges members an annual $240 membership fee. The fee, which is payable in advance, entitles the member to visit the club as many times as he or she wishes.

Selected membership data for the three-month period January to March 1993 are indicated in the table following:

	Jan.	Feb.	March
Number of new memberships sold	200	300	100
Number of renewals	500	200	100
Number of expirations (including members who renewed)	500	400	100
Total number of active members at end of month	6,000	6,100	6,200

Members who renew their contracts must also pay the $240 annual fee in advance of their membership year.

Monthly costs of operating the health facilities are approximately as follows:

Rent	$ 10,000
Salaries	50,000
Advertising and promotion	30,000
Depreciation and other operating costs	15,000
	$105,000

The company controller and an independent CPA disagree over the basis on which revenues should be recognized. The CPA argues that since members can use the facilities over a 12-month period, revenues from each member should be spread over a 12-month period (i.e., $20 per month per member). The controller, on the other hand, asserts that the entire membership fee should be recognized in the month the member either joins or renews. A major portion of the corporate effort, he argues, is exerted *before* and *at* the time a new member actually joins the club. He points out that the company spends over $30,000 per month in direct advertising and promotion costs, and, in addition, a significant portion of the time of several club employees (whose salaries are included in the $50,000 of salary costs) is directed to promoting new memberships and processing both new applications and renewals.

a. Determine, for the three-month period for which data are provided, the monthly income that would result from adopting each of the two positions.

b. Which position do you favor for external financial reporting purposes?

c. Is a compromise between the two positions possible? Would such a compromise be consistent with what you believe to be sound principles of financial reporting?

d. Suppose that you were the president of the firm. Why might you prefer to receive internal reports that reflect as revenue the full amount of a membership fee in the month that the member either joins or renews?

14. *Changing conditions require changes in accounting practices.*

The following statement appeared in the footnotes to the financial statements of Macmillan Publishing Company, Inc.

> During the year, the Company changed its definition of the unit of sale for the domestic home-study business from the entire contract amount to each individual cash payment, which is generally made when the lesson is delivered. Changing industry regulations affecting refund and cancellation policies and changing patterns of payment were proving to have such unpredictable effects on ultimate contract collectibility that the continued use of prior historical patterns to establish allowances for cancellations and doubtful accounts could have caused serious distortions in the matching of revenues and costs.

a. Which of the two definitions of unit of sale would result in the more "conservative" practice of revenue recognition?

b. Assume that in a particular month a customer contracts to take a home-study course consisting of 20 lessons. Total contract price for the entire course is $500. The customer remits $25 for the first lesson.

   (1) If the unit of sale is considered to be the entire contract and the entire amount of revenue is to be recognized at time of sale, prepare one entry to recognize the signing of the contract and another to recognize the delivery of the first lesson and the collection of cash. Ignore the costs applicable to the revenues.

   (2) If the unit of sale is considered to be each individual cash payment, prepare an entry to recognize the delivery of the first lesson and the collection of cash. Is it necessary to record the signing of the contract?

15. *On what basis should revenue from the sale of home-study courses be recognized?*

Computer Learning, Inc., develops and sells home-study courses on the use of Worksheet I, a sophisticated spreadsheet program. Each course consists of 10 lessons on computer disks with an accompanying manual. The manual and one disk are mailed to a student upon registration for the course. Thereafter one lesson is shipped to a student every two weeks over a period of approximately five months. After completing the program, the student takes an examination and, if successful, is awarded a certificate.

In 1993 the company developed the course at a cost of $120,000. The development costs were charged to expense accounts as incurred.

The cost of duplicating the manual is $10 per unit. That of copying a disk is $3 per unit ($30 for the set of 10). These costs are incurred as the materials are needed. The cost of administering the exam is $20 per course. Hence the cost per course, excluding development costs, is $60. (Shipping costs are immaterial.)

The price of the course is $400, payable as follows:

> $120 when student registers for course and receives the manual and first disk
> $180 ($20 every two weeks) as the student receives the remaining nine lessons
> $100 when the student takes the examination

The company estimated that it would sell 500 courses and that all 500 students would complete the course.

In 1994 the company sold 100 courses. It shipped 100 manuals and lesson 1 disks and a total of 400 additional disks. It collected the entire amount due on the materials shipped (a total of $20,000).

The company is undecided as to a proper basis of revenue recognition.

a. Suppose the company recognized all revenue from the course when a student registered for the course.
   (1) How much revenue should it recognize in 1994? Justify this basis of revenue recognition.
   (2) How much in expenses should it charge in 1994? Justify your response.
   (3) Prepare the journal entries to record the sale of the 100 courses and the shipment of the manuals and the additional disks.

b. Suppose, alternatively, the company recognized 10 percent of anticipated revenue each time it shipped a lesson.
   (1) How much revenue should it recognize in 1994? Justify this basis of revenue recognition.
   (2) How much in expenses should it charge in 1994? Justify your response.
   (3) Prepare the journal entries to record the sale of 100 courses and the shipment of the manuals and the additional disks.

c. Is there some other basis on which you would recommend that revenue be recognized? Explain.

16. *Financial statements can be cast and recast—from a limited amount of information.*

A management consulting firm contracts with clients to undertake specific projects. It recognizes revenues on a *percentage of completion basis*. Clients are required to pay for an engagement at the time it is completed. The company bills clients at an amount equal to $133\frac{1}{3}$ percent of costs.

As of January 1, 1993, a summarized version of the firm's balance sheet reflected the following (in millions):

Cash	$ 9.0
Work in progress, contract value	5.0
Total assets	$14.0
Capital stock	$10.0
Retained earnings	4.0
Total equities	$14.0

In the year ended December 31, 1993, the firm collected $10 million in cash from customers. It expended $6 million in cash on work related to customer projects.

a. Prepare an income statement for 1993 and a balance sheet for the year ended December 31, 1993.

b. Another firm in the industry recognizes revenues only upon completion of a project. Convert the two statements required in part (a) to a completed project basis (which for this company is the same as a cash basis). Be sure to take into account adjustments required in the balance sheet of January 1, 1993.

17. *It is often possible to convert statements from one basis to another with little more information than is included in the basic financial statements. This problem may provide a rigorous test of your understanding of the relationships among the accounts reported in the financial statements.*

Mogul Studios, Inc., produces films for television. The company signs a contract with a network prior to beginning production of a film. The contract gives the network the right to broadcast the film over a specified period of time for a flat fee. The license period begins as soon as the film is completed and usually extends for three to five years. The network is required to pay its fee over the period in which it is entitled to broadcast the film.

The company recognizes revenues from the production and licensing of films on a percentage of completion basis. The schedules that follow are summarized versions of the firm's balance sheets for 1993 and 1994 and its income statement and statement of cash receipts and disbursements for 1994.

The firm matches all costs associated with the production of films to license revenues. The ratio of costs to revenues has remained constant for several years.

When the firm completes a film, it relieves its inventory of the film (stated at the amount for which it will be licensed) and recognizes a receivable in the same amount.

For simplicity, it may be assumed that all production costs are paid in cash as incurred. Income taxes may be ignored.

Recognition of revenues on a percentage of completion basis is not in accord with a FASB pronouncement which indicates that revenues should be recognized no earlier than the beginning of the license period.

a. Convert the firm's income statement and balance sheet for 1994 to a basis by which revenues are recognized at the start of license periods (when production is completed).

b. Convert the same two statements to a cash collection basis.

Balance Sheets as of December 31
(in millions)

	1994	1993
Cash	$ 22	$ 18
Films in process, contract value	36	54
License fees receivable	54	30
Total assets	$112	$102
Common stock	$ 20	$ 20
Retained earnings	92	82
Total equities	$112	$102

Income Statement for Year Ended December 31, 1994
(in millions)

Revenues	$30
Costs applicable to revenues	20
Income	$10

Statement of Cash Receipts and Disbursements
for Year Ended December 31, 1994
(in millions)

Collections from broadcasters	$24
Less: Costs incurred in production of films	20
Net increase in cash	$ 4

18. *Licensing practices in the record and music industry present special problems of revenue and expense recognition. This problem enables you to compare your solutions with those of the FASB.*[8]

River City Records created a star. In 1993 the small Texas recording studio produced a record featuring Nelly Wilson, a local Austin talent. Much to its surprise, the record went to the top of the charts.

Because River City Records did not have the distribution channels necessary for the record to realize its worldwide sales potential, it licensed the production and distribution rights to Long Island Sounds, a prominent label in country and western music.

a. Prepare journal entries to recognize River City Records' 1993 revenues from its new hit, assuming each of the three different sets of circumstances presented below. Briefly justify the amount of revenue that you think should be recognized.

(1) The license agreement provides that River City Records is to receive $2 for each record sold by Long Island Sounds. In 1993 Long Island Sounds sold 1.5 million records.

(2) In 1993, per the license agreement, Long Island Sounds made a one-time payment to River City Records of $10 million. This payment entitles Long Island Sounds to unlimited production and distribution rights. Long Island Sounds has no additional obligation to River City Records.

(3) In 1993, as required by the license agreement, Long Island Sounds paid River City Records a minimum guarantee of $6 million. The contract stipulates that River City Records is to receive $2 for each record sold. Hence the $6 million covers the first 3 million in sales. In 1993 Long Island Sounds sold 2.0 million records. River City Records is reasonably certain that sales in future years will exceed 1.0 million.

b. River City Records spent $200,000 to produce the "record master" (including outlays for equipment, vocal background, technicians, and supplies) which it provided to Long Island Sounds.

(1) When, in your opinion, should the costs be charged as expenses? Consider each of the three sets of circumstances.

(2) Would your response differ if, when the initial recording was made, the artist was a proven talent and there was a basis for estimating the cost that would be recovered from future sales?

19. *How should revenues and expenses in the shipping industry be recognized?*

The Cromwell Co. was organized on June 1 for the specific purpose of chartering a ship to undertake a three-month, 10,000-mile voyage. On June 1 the founders of the company contributed $600,000 to the company in exchange for common

---

[8]In 1981, the FASB issued a pronouncement, "Financial Reporting in the Record and Music Industry," *Statement No. 50,* which established revenue recognition guidelines. You need not refer to this statement. Instead, use your best judgment as to the most appropriate basis for determining revenue in this problem.

stock. On the same day, the company paid the entire $600,000 to the owners of a ship for the right to use it for a period of three months.

During the three-month period, the chartered ship made several stops.

Indicated in the table following are the number of miles traveled and the amount of cargo, in terms of dollar billings to customers, that the firm loaded and unloaded. (For example, in June the company loaded cargo for which it billed customers $500,000. During that same month it unloaded $300,000 of that same cargo.)

	Loaded	Unloaded	Number of Miles Traveled
June	$ 500,000	$ 300,000	4,000
July	300,000	100,000	2,500
August	200,000	600,000	3,500
	$1,000,000	$1,000,000	10,000

Operating and administrative expenses, in addition to the charter fee, were $100,000 per month (to be accounted for as a period cost).

The Cromwell Co. was liquidated on August 31. At that time all expenses had been paid and all bills collected.

a. Determine the income of the company over its three-month life.
b. Determine the income of the company during *each* of the three months. Make alternative decisions as to the methods used to recognize revenues and charge expenses.
   (1) Revenue is recognized when cargo is loaded; charter costs ($600,000) are amortized evenly ($200,000 per month) over the three-month period.
   (2) Revenue is recognized when cargo is unloaded; charter costs are amortized evenly over the three-month period.
   (3) Revenue is recognized when cargo is loaded; charter costs are amortized in proportion to number of miles traveled.
   (4) Revenue is recognized when cargo is unloaded; charter costs are amortized in proportion to number of miles traveled.
c. Which methods are preferable? Why?
d. The Cromwell Co. was unable to estimate, *in advance,* the total *revenues* to be earned during the voyage. If it could, is there another basis, preferable to the other two, by which the $600,000 in charter costs might be allocated?

20. *In the shipping industry revenue may be recognized at the start, during, or at the completion of a voyage.*

   The notes that follow are adopted from annual reports of three shipping companies. Each describes a different basis of revenue recognition.[9]

   > Revenues from vessel operations are recognized upon unloading inbound cargoes—that is, on a terminated voyage basis.

   > Revenue . . . is recorded on a pro rata basis over a specified period of time.

   > Transportation revenues and related voyage expenses are generally recognized at the commencement of a voyage.

   Consider three sets of circumstances under which a shipping company may operate. Which basis of revenue recognition would you recommend for each of the circumstances? Justify your response.

---

[9]The companies are the Lykes Corporation, the Trans Union Corporation, and R. J. Reynolds Industries, Inc., respectively.

a. The company time-charters its vessels for a specified number of months.

b. It operates "tramp steamers" which pick up cargo wherever it is found and discharge it wherever required.

c. It operates a cargo shuttle service between two ports.

21. *The trading stamp industry poses particularly interesting questions of revenue recognition.*

In the trading stamp industry, a company such as Sperry and Hutchinson (S&H Green Stamps) sells stamps to retailers. It bills the retailers for the stamps upon delivery. The retailers give the stamps to their customers according to the amount of their purchases. The customers redeem the stamps for merchandise at outlets operated by the trading stamp company.

Assume that a trading stamp company sells $500 million in stamps to retailers. It estimates that 80 percent of the stamps will actually be redeemed for merchandise. The cost of the merchandise is 75 percent of the stamp redemption value. All other operating expenses are $120 million per year. These costs are accounted for as period costs.

A key question facing the trading stamp industry is whether revenue (and related expenses) should be recognized upon sale of stamps to the retailer or upon redemption of the merchandise by the customer.

a. Present arguments in favor of each of the two points of revenue recognition; indicate the circumstances or assumptions under which each would be appropriate.

b. Prepare two sets of journal entries to record the sale of stamps, the acquisition of merchandise inventory, and the redemption of the stamps. Also give recognition to the operating costs. First recognize revenues and related expenses when the stamps are sold and then when the stamps are redeemed. Assume that the sales of stamps are for cash, that inventory is purchased for cash, and that the other operating costs are paid in cash. Assume also that the stamp redemption rate is as estimated.

22. *Income as determined for one purpose may not be appropriate for another.*

Tom Ogden celebrated Christmas by purchasing a new car. In his first year as sales manager of the newly formed industrial equipment division of the Shakespeare Manufacturing Co., Ogden and his sales force had generated $7.5 million in noncancelable orders for equipment.

Ogden's employment contract provided that he receive an annual bonus equal to 3 percent of his division's profits. He was aware that costs of manufacturing the equipment were approximately 60 percent of sales prices and that the company had budgeted $2.0 million for administrative and all other operating costs. He could afford to splurge on a new car since, according to his rough calculations, his bonus would total at least $30,000.

In mid-January, Ogden received a bonus check for $12,000. Stunned, but confident that a clerical error had been made, he placed an urgent call to the company controller. The controller informed him that no error had been made. Although costs were in line with those budgeted, reported sales were only $6 million.

The equipment produced by Shakespeare is special-purpose polishing equipment. Since it must be custom-made, customers must normally wait for delivery at least two months from date of order.

a. Demonstrate how the amount of the bonus was calculated by *both* Ogden and the company controller. What is the most likely explanation of the difference in their sales figures?

b. The company president has asked for your recommendations with respect to the bonus plan. Assuming that the objective of the company is to give reasonably prompt recognition to the accomplishments of its sales manager, on what basis do you think revenue should be recognized for the purpose of computing the sales manager's bonus? Do you think the company should use the same basis for reporting to shareholders? Explain.

23. *Unusual risks assumed by a construction company may justify conservative accounting principles—for some, though not necessarily all, purposes.*

In 1993 a real estate company established a division, Devco, Inc., to develop and construct shopping centers. Upon forming the new company, it contributed $25 million in equity capital.

To attract a few key executives, Devco, Inc., offered them employment contracts stipulating that a portion of their compensation would be based on divisional earnings. The contracts did not, however, specify the principles by which earnings would be computed.

In 1993 Devco, Inc., contracted with a group of investors to construct two shopping centers, one in New York and the other in New Jersey. The contract price of each was to be $20 million. Payment for each was to be according to the following schedule (in millions):

When shopping center is completed and turned over to purchaser	$ 2.0
Over the following six years ($3.0 million per year, plus interest on outstanding balance)	18.0
Total	$20.0

From the time a shopping center was delivered to its purchaser until the balance of the purchase price was paid, Devco, Inc., would have a security interest in the property. If the purchaser defaulted on its obligation, the company would repossess its center. Ultimately, however, the financial wherewithal of the purchaser to meet its obligation would depend on its ability to generate rental revenues by leasing the stores in the center to creditworthy tenants. Until the shopping center became well established, there was considerable risk of the purchaser's having to default on the required payments.

In 1994 Devco, Inc., began construction on the two shopping centers. By year end, it had completed work on the New York center, turned it over to the purchaser, and collected the contractually required payment. It had also completed work on 60 percent of the New Jersey center.

The company estimated (correctly, it turned out) that construction costs would be $15 million per shopping center.

At the close of 1994 Devco, Inc., and its vice-president of construction disagreed as to the amount of earnings on which his compensation would be based. The company planned to base his compensation on the amount of earnings to be reported in its general-purpose financial statements. Revenues were to be recognized only when their realization would be assured with a high degree of certainty. The vice-president of construction argued that such earnings were an inappropriate basis on which to base his compensation.

a. On what basis do you think the company planned to recognize revenues for purposes of general reporting? In a few sentences, defend this basis. Prepare an appropriate income statement and balance sheet (prior to taking into account the amount to be paid to the vice-president). Assume that all construction costs were paid in cash as incurred.

b. Suppose that you were called upon to represent the vice-president for construction. On what basis might you assert that revenues should be recognized? Indicate why you believe that such basis is more appropriate for the specific decision at hand. Prepare an income statement and balance sheet that you would present to the company.

(*Note:* Should preparation of the balance sheets prove difficult, you might find it helpful to journalize the transactions described.)

24. *How should a computer software company, in the face of uncertainty as to whether its productive efforts will provide returns, recognize revenues and expenses?*

The University Systems Co. developed a series of computer programs designed to simplify the "back office" operations of stock brokerage firms. All costs of developing the programs have been charged to expense accounts as incurred. Although the programs can readily be applied to the operations of all firms in the industry, certain features of the programs must be custom-designed to meet the specific requirements of each customer. It is generally possible to estimate with reasonable reliability the costs of developing the custom features.

In January analysts of University Systems made a preliminary study of the "back office" operations of Conrad, Roy, Atwood, Smith, and Harris (CRASH), a leading brokerage firm. University Systems hoped that as a result of the study it could demonstrate the savings in costs and increases in efficiency that its programs could bring about and that it could thereby sell its programs to CRASH. It was agreed that the entire costs of the preliminary study would be borne by University Systems; CRASH was under no obligation to either purchase the programs or pay for the preliminary study. Cost of the preliminary study was $100,000.

The preliminary study was successful; on February 2, CRASH placed an order with University Systems for its series of programs; the contract price was $1.5 million.

During February and March, University Systems developed the custom features of the program for CRASH. Costs incurred in February were $80,000 and in March, $120,000. These costs were equal to amounts previously estimated.

On March 15 University Systems delivered the completed series of programs to CRASH, and they were reviewed and accepted by CRASH management.

On April 4, University Systems received a check for $500,000 plus a two-year, 8 percent note for the balance.

a. Prepare journal entries to record the events described.

b. Prepare comparative income statements for the months ending January 31, February 28, March 31, and April 30.

c. In a short paragraph, justify your choice of basis of revenue and expense recognition. Indicate any assumptions that you may have made.

25. *Unconditional guarantees create special problems of revenue recognition.*

Western Art, Inc., produces and sells bronze sculptures of cowboys and other characters associated with the western United States. The company contracts with a well-known artist to sculpt an original work of art; from the original, the company produces a mold from which castings are taken.

The company produces a casting only upon receipt of an order from a customer accompanied by full payment. It offers a buyer an unconditional guarantee of satisfaction for a period of four months from date of sale. During the four months, the customer is entitled to a full refund, no questions asked.

In 1993 the company commissioned artist Frank Winslow to sculpt "Cowboy and His Horse." The contract with the artist stated that his compensation was to be "40 percent of the income (before commissions and taxes) attributable directly to the production and sale of the sculpture during 1993 and 30 percent thereafter." The contract did not specify principles of revenue and expense recognition.

In 1993 the company incurred costs of $60,000 to produce a mold from which to cast "Cowboy and His Horse." Because the company forecast that sales of the sculpture would take place evenly over a period of three years, it decided that the cost of the mold would be depreciated over three years.

The company determined that the cost of producing each casting (not including any share of the cost of the mold) would be $700.

Sales price for each casting was set at $2,000.

In 1993 the company produced and shipped 70 castings. By year end, the four-month guarantee period had expired on 50 of the castings.

Shortly after the close of the year the company prepared and sent to Frank Winslow the following income statement and balance sheet pertaining to "Cowboy and His Horse":

Income Statement for the Year Ended December 31, 1993

Revenues		$100,000
Less: Cost of castings	$35,000	
Depreciation of mold	20,000	55,000
Income before commissions		$ 45,000
Commissions @ 40%		18,000
Income		$ 27,000

Balance Sheet as of December 31, 1993

Cash		$31,000
Company interest in castings shipped on which revenues have not been recognized		14,000
Mold	$60,000	
Less: Accumulated depreciation	20,000	40,000
Total assets		$85,000
Commissions payable		$18,000
Unearned revenue on castings shipped		40,000
Accumulated earnings to date		27,000
Total liabilities and equities		$85,000

a. On what basis has the company recognized revenues? Can this basis be justified? Comment.

b. In the following year, 1994, the company shipped 50 units. The guarantee period expired on 40 of them. It paid the 1993 commissions due the artist, but not the 1994 commissions. Assuming that the company adhered to the same accounting principles in 1994 as in 1993, prepare an income statement and balance sheet for 1994. (Remember that commissions in 1994 are only 30 percent of income.)

c. Frank Winslow was surprised at the amount of his commissions in 1993. He thought they would be much greater. He asserted that when he produced other sculptures for similar firms, virtually none were ever returned. Prepare an income statement and a balance sheet for 1993 using a basis of revenue recognition that would better serve the interests of Frank Winslow. Justify the basis selected.

1. a. Construction in progress $500,000
      Cash (or accounts payable) $500,000
      To record construction costs incurred

   b. The percentage of total revenues to be recognized equals 40 percent (two-fifths); 40 percent of $1 million is $400,000.
   c. The percentage of total expenses to be recognized must also equal 40 percent; 40 percent of $800,000 is $320,000.
   d. Completed pools must be carried at contract value—$400,000.
   e. Construction in progress must be reduced by $320,000.

   f. Completed pools at contract value $400,000
      Revenues from construction $400,000
      To record revenues from construction

      Expenses relating to revenues
        from construction $320,000
        Construction in progress $320,000
      To record expenses relating to revenues

2. a. Construction in progress $300,000
      Cash (or accounts payable) $300,000
      To record construction costs incurred

      Completed pools at contract value $600,000
      Revenues from construction $600,000
      To record revenues from construction

      Expenses relating to revenues
        from construction $480,000
        Construction in progress $480,000
      To record expenses relating to revenues

   b. Accounts receivable $1,000,000
      Completed pools at contract value $1,000,000
      To record delivery of pools to the city

6

Valuation of Assets; Cash and Marketable Securities

NIK
PRESENT VALUE

PART I.   Valuation of Assets

Chapters 6 through 10 are directed primarily to questions of asset and liability valuation—that is, to the problems of determining the most meaningful amounts to be assigned to the various balance sheet accounts. This chapter is divided into two sections. The first provides an overview of the valuation process, the second considers two specific assets—cash and marketable securities.

Although accountants have been unable to derive a definition of an asset upon which there has been complete agreement, almost all proposed definitions stress the notion that assets represent rights to future services or economic benefits. The question facing the accountant is what value—what quantitative measure—should be assigned to the resources or claims which are to yield future services or benefits. (This question is, of course, directly related to that discussed in the previous chapter: When should increases or decreases in the value of net assets—those associated with revenues and expenses—be recognized?)

The leading objective of this chapter is to provide insight into the nature of value. *Value,* as it is used in accounting, can have at least three distinctive meanings:

1. An *assigned* or calculated *numerical quantity;* as in mathematics, the quantity or amount for which a symbol stands

2. The *worth* of something sold or exchanged; the worth of a thing in money or goods at a certain time; its fair market price
3. Worth in *usefulness* or *importance* to its possessor; utility or merit

The accounting profession has not yet reached consensus on criteria of valuation. In fact, in accord with generally accepted accounting principles, assets may be stated at amounts reflective of any one of the three definitions of value.

From the perspective of managers and investors, the distinctions among the three concepts of value are crucial. The "value" assigned to an asset on a financial statement may not—indeed is *unlikely* to—be indicative of the amount for which the asset could be sold or of its ultimate worth to the party owning or using it. As a consequence, decisions that will maximize the *reported* value of assets may not always maximize their true economic worth and may be counter to the financial well-being of a firm and its investors.

HISTORICAL COST

The first definition, that value is nothing more than an assigned or calculated numerical quantity, implies that value need have nothing to do with inherent worth; it is simply a numerical quantity assigned on a basis that is, presumably, logical and orderly. It is, in fact, this first meaning that is most consistent with current accounting practice.

Financial statements are *cost-based*. Most assets are initially recorded at the amounts paid for them. Subsequent to date of purchase, assets are, in general (some exceptions will be pointed out later in this chapter), reported at either initial cost or depreciated cost. Depreciation cost is initial cost less the portion of initial cost (often indicated in a contra account) representing the services of the asset already utilized. Land is an example of an asset that is reported at initial cost; plant and equipment are examples of assets that are reported at depreciated cost.

Except at the date assets are purchased, the cost-based amounts reported on a firm's balance sheet do not represent (unless by coincidence) the prices at which they can be either purchased or sold. The reported amounts cannot be viewed as approximations of either the fair market value or the worth of the services that the assets will provide. They designate nothing more than initial cost less the portion of initial cost already absorbed as an expense.

Because historical cost financial statements are cost-based, the income of any particular year is influenced by events that took place in prior years, perhaps before current managers assumed their positions. Correspondingly, the income of any year fails to capture all relevant events taking place in the current year. Thus, a gain attributable to increases in the value of marketable securities would be recognized in the year the securities are sold, even though the increases may have taken place in previous years.

The Going Concern

Once assets have been initially recorded, they are thereafter valued on the assumption that the firm is a *going concern*—one that will continue in operation indefinitely. Assets are measured with respect to the particular firm reporting them—not with respect to the general marketplace. Thus certain assets, "organizational costs," for example, can be expected to benefit the firm on whose books they are recorded, even though they are not readily marketable. The going-concern concept implies that the firm will survive at least long enough to realize the benefits of its recorded assets.

The corollary to the going-concern concept is that when there is evidence that a firm will be unable to survive, its assets should be reported at their *liquidation* values—the amounts that could be realized if the firm were to be dissolved and its assets put up for sale. Thus, if a firm is expected to be dissolved, perhaps as the result of bankruptcy proceedings, the conventional balance sheet would be inappropriate; instead, a balance sheet that indicates net realizable values should be prepared.

The Principle of Matching

Why do accountants "value" assets at amounts that have nothing to do with either market value or inherent worth? Historical cost valuations are consistent with the concepts of income determination discussed in the previous chapters. The cost of a long-lived asset is charged as an expense as the asset is consumed. The cost is thereby *matched to* the benefits (revenues) that it produces. The portion of cost that has not yet been charged to expense is reported on the balance sheet, awaiting transfer to the income statement in a future accounting period. In this sense, the balance sheet is a statement of *residuals*—costs that have not yet been charged as expenses. In fact, until recently the primary focus of financial reporting was upon *earnings* rather than assets and liabilities. The *statement of income,* not the balance sheet, was the foremost financial statement. Today, however, the FASB is showing increased concern with the balance sheet, gradually trying to assure that it is a useful statement in its own right rather than merely an adjunct to the income statement.

Concerns over Objectivity

It is often asserted that historical cost valuations are *objective*. This is true but only to a limited extent. Purchase price of a long-lived asset or initial amount of an account receivable can be determined with reliability. But the other factors which determine the values assigned to an asset cannot. Useful life, salvage value, and estimates of uncollectible accounts are subject to managerial judgment. Hence the objectivity of historical cost-based statements may be more illusory than real—arbitrary rules being substituted for judgments required.

Usefulness for Investors and Managers

To managers as well as investors, who are called upon to make decisions that will affect the future, not the past, historical costs are of little significance. There are virtually no decisions for which historical costs are necessary or even useful.[1] Assets, by definition, provide benefits that will be realized in the future.

[1]Historical costs are, of course, necessary to make decisions that must, by statute or policy, be based on them. The tax laws, for example, require that the gain on sale of an asset be calculated as the difference between selling price and historical cost. Banks sometimes insist (unwisely in the view of many accountants and lending specialists) that in order to be eligible for a loan, a borrower must maintain a specified ratio of assets (stated at historical cost) to liabilities.

The historical cost of an asset offers no insight into the resources that could be derived by either retaining or selling the asset. It furnishes no basis on which to assess cash flows that the asset will generate in the future or to evaluate the efficiency of management in using the asset.

Three Alternatives to Historical Cost

Three of the most frequently proposed alternatives to historical cost are (1) current cost, (2) net realizable value, and (3) net present value. The first two are market-based. They are consistent with the second definition of value—the worth of a thing in money or goods at a certain time, its fair market price. The third alternative expresses value as the cash to be generated by an asset and is thereby consistent with the third definition of value—its worth in usefulness to the asset's particular owner.

MARKET VALUES

Current Cost

Current cost is an asset's replacement cost—the amount that would have to be paid to obtain the same asset or its equivalent. It is an *input* cost. For inventory it would be the cost either to manufacture or to purchase the goods from a supplier. For fixed assets it would be the outlays to construct or to purchase. Current cost indicates the amount that a firm could save by owning an asset rather than having to acquire it, the cost that it would have to incur if it were deprived of the asset. Underlying current costs is the presumption of a going concern, a firm that will continue to use the asset or will otherwise replace it with a similar asset.

Net Realizable Value

Net realizable value is the amount for which an asset could be sold less any costs that must be incurred to bring it to a salable condition. It is an *output* price. For inventory it would be the expected selling price less any costs to complete and sell the product. The difference between an item's current cost and its net realizable value would ordinarily be the seller's margin of profit. For fixed assets, net realizable value would be the price for which it could be sold or salvaged less any disposal costs.

Net realizable value is essential in determining whether a firm should continue to retain an asset. It indicates the sacrifice the firm incurs by holding rather than selling an asset. Such sacrifice is referred to as an *opportunity cost*—the cost of using an asset in its ''next-best'' alternative.

Market Values in Practice

Revenue Recognition prior to Sale

Even though conventional accounting is primarily cost-based, in selected situations firms do report assets at market values. In general, whenever revenue is recognized prior to the point of sale, the related asset is reported at the amount that is expected to be realized, a market value. For example, when revenue is recognized upon completion of production (e.g., upon the removal of a precious mineral from the ground), the completed products are valued at their anticipated selling price. To avoid the distortions in income that would result from delaying recognition of revenue until point of sale, firms estimate the amount of revenue that they will realize. The best projection of this is the current output price as indicated by either a sales contract or trades in the marketplace.

FASB *Statement No. 89* encourages firms to report replacement cost of their assets in the notes to their financial statements. It also urges that they indicate what income would have been had it been determined on the basis of replacement values rather than historical costs.[2]

Lower of Cost or Market Rule

The concern of accountants with conservatism also leads them to report market values whenever the prevailing price of an asset intended for sale falls below its acquisition cost. Following the rule of *lower of cost or market,* the accountant compares the historical cost of an asset—that which the company paid either to purchase or produce it—with what it would cost to *replace* it (a current *input* cost). If the market—the replacement—price is less than the historical cost, then the asset is *written down* to the market price and the corresponding loss recognized on the income statement. The lower of cost or market rule is applied only to assets, primarily inventories and marketable securities, that the firm actually expects to sell in the normal course of business. It is grounded on the assumption that financial statements would be misleading if assets were reported at prices higher than those for which the company expects to sell them. The rule is not ordinarily applied to assets, such as plant and equipment, that are not intended for resale. The lower of cost or market rule will be examined in greater detail in the second part of this chapter when we deal with marketable securities and again in Chapter 8 in connection with a discussion of inventories.

NET PRESENT VALUE, OR VALUE TO USER

The third definition of value relates value to worth in terms of usefulness or importance to the individual possessor. It suggests that the value of an asset be determined with respect to the particular party that owns it.

This third concept of value is of utmost concern to managers and investors as it underlies virtually all decision models pertaining to assets. Moreover, it is of interest to all persons involved with business and economics because the factors that contribute to the worth of an asset to a particular individual or firm provide insight into the nature of both assets and market prices.

Value to individual owners has not, in the past, been the common basis for stating assets in general-purpose financial reports. This is mainly because of the difficulty of assessing the future benefits that assets will provide. However, accountants are increasingly taking into account the worth of the services to be rendered by the asset in determining how it should be reported. This is particularly true when neither an exchange transaction nor a market price is available to indicate value.

---

[2]"Financial Reporting and Changing Prices," Financial Accounting Standards Board, *Statement of Financial Accounting Standards No. 89,* 1986.

The economic benefits of an asset ordinarily are cash receipts. An individual invests in the common stock of a corporation in anticipation of cash receipts greater than the cash disbursement required by the initial purchase. The cash receipts will be from periodic cash dividends paid by the company, from the proceeds resulting from the sale of the stock, or from both. Similarly, a manufacturer purchases a machine with the expectation that it will contribute to the production of goods which will be sold for cash. The value of an asset to its owner is, therefore, the value of the net cash receipts that the asset is expected to generate. The challenge to the accountant or manager is, first, to identify and measure the cash receipts. This may be difficult considering that most assets generate cash only when used in conjunction with other assets and that, in a world of uncertainty, future sales and costs cannot easily be estimated. And, second, the challenge is to determine the present value of those cash receipts.

Although it might appear as if the value of expected cash receipts is simply the sum of all anticipated receipts, an analysis of some fundamental concepts of compound interest will demonstrate that this is not so. Since cash may be placed in interest-bearing bank accounts or used to acquire securities that will provide a periodic return, it has a value in time. Funds to be received in distant years are of less value than those to be received at present. An economically rational person would prefer to receive $1 today rather than in one year, since the $1 received today can be invested so as to increase to some greater amount one year from today.

TIME VALUE OF MONEY: PRESENT AND FUTURE VALUES

Future Value of a Single Sum

Suppose that an individual deposited $1 in a savings bank. The bank pays interest at the rate of 6 percent per year. Interest is *compounded* (computed) annually at the end of each year. To how much would the deposit have grown at the end of one year?

The accumulated value of the deposit at the end of one year would be $1 × 1.06 = $1.06.

In more general terms,

$$a = (1 + i)^n$$

where a represents the final accumulation of the initial investment of $1 after
  n interest periods
  i indicates the rate of interest

As indicated in Exhibit 6-1, after two years the initial deposit would have accumulated to $1.12—the $1.06 on deposit at the beginning of the second year

EXHIBIT 6-1

Future Value of $1 Invested Today, 6% Return
(rounded to nearest cent)

Year

0	1	2	3	4	5	6
$1.00 →	$1.06 →	$1.12 →	$1.19 →	$1.26 →	$1.34 →	$1.42

times 1.06. After three years it would have accumulated to $1.19—the $1.12 on deposit at the beginning of the third year again times 1.06.

Employing the general formula (and rounding to the nearest cent), we find:

At the end of two years,

$$a = (1 + i)^n$$
$$= (1 + .06)^2 = \$1.12$$

At the end of three years,

$$a = (1 + i)^n$$
$$= (1 + .06)^3 = \$1.19$$

At the end of six years,

$$a = (1 + i)^n$$
$$= (1 + .06)^6 = \$1.42$$

If an amount other than $1 was deposited, the accumulated amount could be computed simply by multiplying the future value of $1 by that amount. Thus $200 deposited in a bank at a rate of 6 percent would grow to $200 times $(1.06)^6$, or $283.70, at the end of six years.

Common notation for compound interest is

$$a_{\overline{n}|i} = (1 + i)^n$$

To facilitate computations of compound interest, tables have been developed and are available in almost all accounting textbooks as well as numerous books of financial tables. Moreover, many business calculators and computer software packages are programmed with time value of money routines. Table 1 in the Appendix of this volume indicates the amounts to which $1 will accumulate at various interest rates and at the end of different accounting periods. The number at the intersection of the 6 percent column and the 6 periods row indicates that $1 would accumulate to $1.4185. Two hundred dollars would accumulate to $200 times that amount, or $200 × 1.4185 = $283.70.

The following examples illustrate the concept of future value.

Example 1

A company sells a parcel of land for $50,000. The purchaser asks to be allowed to delay all payments for a period of three years. The company agrees to accept a note from the purchaser for $50,000 plus interest compounded at an annual rate of 8 percent. What amount would the purchaser be required to pay at the end of three years?

As indicated in Table 1 (8 percent column, 3 periods row), $1 will accumulate to $1.2597. Hence $50,000 will grow to $50,000 times 1.2597, or $62,985. The purchaser would be required to pay $62,985:

$$\$50,000a_{\overline{3}|.08} = \$50,000(1 + .08)^3$$
$$= \$62,985$$

Example 2

An individual deposits $30,000 in a savings bank certificate of deposit. The bank pays interest at an annual rate of 12 percent *compounded semiannually*. To what amount will the deposit accumulate at the end of 10 years?

If interest is compounded semiannually and the *annual* rate of interest is 12 percent, then interest is computed *twice* each year at 6 percent—*one-half* the annual rate. (Interest is almost always stated at an *annual* rate even when compounded semiannually or quarterly.) Each interest period would be six months, rather than a year, so that over a 10-year span there would be 20 interest periods. Table 1 in the Appendix indicates that at an interest rate of 6 percent $1 will accumulate to $30,000 times 3.2071, or $96,213. As a general rule, whenever interest is compounded semiannually, the interest rate must be halved and the number of years doubled:

$$\$30,000a_{\overline{20}|.06} = \$30,0000(1 + .06)^{20}$$

$$= \$96,213$$

Example 3

A corporation invests $10,000 and expects to earn a return of 8 percent compounded annually for the next 60 years. To how much will the $10,000 accumulate over the 60-year period?

Table 1 does not indicate accumulations over 60 years. However, the table does indicate that $1 invested at 8 percent for 50 years would accumulate to $46.9016. Over 50 years $10,000 would accumulate to $469,016. The table also indicates that $1 invested at 8 percent for 10 years would accumulate to $2.1589. If at the end of 50 years $469,016 were invested for an additional 10 years, it would increase in value to 2.1589 times $469,016, or $1,012,558:

$$\$10,000a_{\overline{50}|.08} = \$10,000(1 + .08)^{50}$$

$$= \$469,016$$

$$\$469,016a_{\overline{10}|.08} = \$469,016(1 + .08)^{10}$$

$$= \$1,012,558$$

Example 4

A corporation reached an agreement to sell a warehouse. The purchaser agreed to pay $800,000 for the warehouse but only if payment could be delayed for four years. The corporation, however, was in immediate need of cash and agreed to accept a lesser amount if payment was made at time of sale. The corporation estimated that it would otherwise have to borrow the needed funds at a rate of 15 percent. What amount should the corporation be willing to accept if cash payment was made at the time of sale rather than delayed for four years?

The question can be stated in an alternative form. What amount if invested today at an interest rate of 15 percent would accumulate to $800,000 in four years? From Table 1 it may be seen that $1 invested today would increase to $1.7490. Hence some amount (x) times 1.7490 would increase to $800,000:

$$1.7490x = \$800,000$$

Solving for x (i.e., dividing $800,000 by 1.7490) indicates that amount to be $457,404. Thus the company would be equally well off if it accepted payment of $457,404 today as it would be if it waited four years to receive the full $800,000. In other words, $457,404 deposited in a bank today at a 15 percent annual interest rate would increase in value to $800,000 after four years:

$$xa_{\overline{4}|.15} = \$800.000$$

$$a_{\overline{4}|.15} = (1 + .15)^4$$

$$= 1.7490$$

$$1.7490x = \$800.000$$

$$x = \$457.404$$

Present Value of a Single Sum

As implied in Example 4, it is frequently necessary to compute the *present value* of a sum of money to be received in the future. That is, one may want to know the amount which if invested today at a certain rate of return would be the equivalent of a fixed amount to be received in a specific number of years hence.

In simple terms, an example can be formulated as follows. If a bank pays interest at the rate of 6 percent annually, how much cash would an individual have to deposit today in order to have that amount accumulate to $1 one year from now? Example 4 illustrated one means of computation. In more general terms, the present value of a future sum can be calculated by taking the reciprocal of the basic formula for future value—$a_{\overline{n}|i} = (1 + i)^n$. Thus, for $1,

$$p_{\overline{n}|i} = \frac{1}{(1 + i)^n}$$

where n indicates the number of periods

i indicates the rate of interest (which when used in connection with present value computations is often referred to as a *discount* rate, since a future payment will be *discounted* to a present value)

p indicates the required initial deposit or investment

$$p_{\overline{1}|.06} = \frac{1}{(1 + .06)^1} = \$.94$$

The present value of $1 to be received two years in the future would be

$$p_{\overline{2}|.06} = \frac{1}{(1 + i)^n}; \ p_{\overline{2}|.06} = \frac{1}{(1 + .06)^2} = \$.89$$

The present value of $1 to be received six years in the future would be

EXHIBIT 6-2

Present Value of $1 to Be Received in the Future, 6% Return (rounded to nearest cent)

Year

0	1	2	3	4	5	6

$.94 ← $1
.89 ← $1
.84 ← $1
.79 ← $1
.75 ← $1
.71 ← $1

$$p_{\overline{3}|.06} = \frac{1}{(1 + i)^n}; \quad p_{\overline{3}|.06} = \frac{1}{(1 + .06)^6} = \$.71$$

In other words, as illustrated in Exhibit 6-2, 71 cents invested today at 6 percent interest compounded annually would increase to $1 at the end of six years.

As with future value, if an amount other than $1 were to be received, then its present value could be determined by multiplying the present value of $1 by that amount. Thus, if an individual wanted to receive $200 six years from the present, then the amount he or she would have to invest today at 6 percent interest would be

$$\$200 p_{\overline{6}|.06} = \$200 \frac{1}{(1.06)^6} = \$141$$

Table 2 in the Appendix indicates the present value of $1 for various discount rates and time periods. The present value of $1 to be received six years from today discounted at the rate of 6 percent would be $.7050. The present value of $200 would be $200 times .7050, or $141.

Concepts of present value are demonstrated in the examples that follow.

Example 1

Assume the same facts as in Example 4 of the previous section. A corporation agreed to sell a warehouse. The purchaser was willing to pay $800,000 four years hence or some lesser amount at time of sale. Assuming that the corporation would have to borrow the needed funds at a rate of 15 percent, what equivalent amount should it be willing to accept if payment were made at time of sale?

Per Table 2, the present value of $1 to be received in four years, at an annual rate of 15 percent, is $.5718. The present value of $800,000 is $800,000 × .5718, or $457,440. Except for a $36 rounding difference, the result is identical to that computed in the earlier illustration:

$$\$800,000 p_{\overline{4}|.15} = \$800,000 \left[\frac{1}{(1 + .15)^4} \right]$$

$$= \$457,440$$

Example 2

A man wishes to give his nephew a gift of the cost of a college education. The nephew will enter college in six years. It is estimated that when he enters college, tuition and other charges will be approximately $80,000 for a degree program. The gift will be placed in a certificate of deposit, which pays interest at an annual rate of 16 percent, compounded *quarterly*. What size gift is required if the full $80,000 is to be available to the nephew at the start of his college career?

Since interest is compounded quarterly, the question to be answered is as follows: What is the present value of $80,000 to be received 24 (4 times six years) periods away if discounted at a rate of 4 percent per period? Per Table 2, the present value of $1 to be received 24 periods in the future, discounted at a rate of 4 percent, is $.3901. The present value of $80,000 is, therefore, $80,000 times .3901, or $31,208. That is,

$$\$80,000 p_{\overline{24}|.04} = \$31,208$$

(*Check:* Per Table 1, the future value of $1 to be received in 24 periods if invested at a rate of 4 percent is $2.5633. We find that $31,208 times 2.5633 is, with allowance for rounding, $80,000.)

Future Value of an Annuity

Commercial transactions frequently involve not just a single deposit or future payment but a series of equal payments spaced evenly apart. For example, a company interested in accumulating a specified amount of cash would be concerned with the deposit that it would be required to make during each of a certain number of years to attain its goal. A series of *equal* payments at fixed intervals is known as an *annuity*. An annuity in which the payments are made or received at the *end* of each period is known as an *ordinary annuity* or an *annuity in arrears*. One in which the payments are made or received at the *beginning* of each period is known as an *annuity due* or an *annuity in advance*. Unless otherwise indicated, the examples in this chapter will be based on the assumption that payments are made or received at the *end* of each period. (Annuity tables in the Appendix contain interest factors for ordinary annuities.)

Suppose that at the *end* of each of four years a person deposits $1 in a savings account. The account pays interest at the rate of 6 percent per year, compounded annually. How much will be available for withdrawal at the end of the fourth year?

As shown in Exhibit 6-3, the $1 deposited at the end of the first period will accumulate interest for a total of three years. As indicated in Table 1, it will increase in value to $1.19. The deposit at the end of the second year will grow to $1.12, and that at the end of the third year will grow to $1.06. The payment made at the end of the fourth year will not yet have earned any interest. As revealed in the diagram, the series of four $1 payments will be worth $4.37 at the end of the fourth year.

The mathematical expression for the future value (A) of a series of payments of $1 compounded at an interest rate (i) over a given number of years (n) is

EXHIBIT 6-3

Future Value of $1 Invested at the End of Each of Four Periods, 6% Return (rounded to nearest cent)

	Year			
	1	2	3	4
	$1.00 →	$1.06 →	$1.12 →	$1.19
		$1.00 →	1.06 →	1.12
			1.00 →	1.06
				1.00
Amount available for withdrawal	$1.00	$2.06	$3.18	$4.37

$$A_{\overline{n}|i} = \frac{(1 + i)^n - 1}{i}$$

(Note that the uppercase A signifies an annuity, while the lowercase a denotes a single sum.) The value at the end of four years of $1 deposited at the end of each of four years compounded at an annual rate of 6 percent is

$$A_{\overline{4}|.06} = \frac{(1 + .06)^4 - 1}{.06} = \$4.37$$

Table 3 in the Appendix indicates the future values of annuities of $1 for various rates of return. The next three examples illustrate the concept of an annuity.

Example 1

A corporation has agreed to deposit 10 percent of an employee's salary into a retirement fund. The fund will be invested in stocks and bonds that will provide a return of 8 percent annually. How much will be available to the employee upon retirement in 20 years, assuming that the employee earns $30,000 per year?

The future value of an annuity of $1 per year compounded at a rate of 8 percent per year for 20 years is $45.7620. Hence the future value of an annuity of $3,000 (10 percent of $30,000) is $3,000 times 45.7620, or $137,286. That is,

$$\$3,000A_{\overline{20}|.08} = \$137,286$$

Example 2

An individual invests $1,000 every three months in securities that yield 20 percent per year compounded quarterly. To how much will these investments accumulate at the end of 15 years (60 quarters)?

Table 3 in the Appendix does not specifically indicate values for 60 periods. However, per Table 3, $1,000 deposited at the end of each of 50 periods and compounded at a rate of 5 percent per *quarter* will accumulate to $1,000 times 209.3480, or $209,348. At the end of 50 quarters, therefore, the individual will have $209,348 invested in securities. Per Table 1, that sum will increase to $209,348 times 1.6289, or $341,007, by the end of the 10 additional quarters. The $1,000 deposited at the end of quarters 51 through 60—an ordinary annuity for 10 periods—will accumulate, per Table 3, to $1,000 times 12.5779, or $12,578. The total amount that will have accumulated over the 15-year (60-quarter) period is the sum of the two amounts, $341,007 and $12,578, or $353,585. In notation,

$$\$1000A_{\overline{50}|.05} = \$209,348$$

$$\$209,348a_{\overline{10}|.05} = \$341,007$$

$$\$1,000A_{\overline{10}|.05} = \underline{12,578}$$

$$\text{Total} \quad \underline{\underline{\$353,585}}$$

Example 3

A municipality has an obligation to repay $200,000 in bonds upon their maturity in 20 years. The municipality wishes to make annual cash payments to a fund to assure that when the bonds are due it will have the necessary cash on hand. The municipality intends to invest the fund in securities that will yield a return of 8 percent, compounded annually.

The required payment of $200,000 can be interpreted as the future value of annuity. That is, some amount (x) deposited annually to return 8 percent must accumulate at the end of 20 years to $200,000. From Table 3, it can be seen that $1 invested annually would accumulate in 20 years to $45.7620. Therefore some amount (x) times 45.7620 would accumulate to $200,000:

$$45.7620x = \$200,000$$

$$x = \frac{\$200,000}{45.7620}$$

$$= \$4,370$$

If deposited annually into a fund that earns a return of 8 percent, $4,370 would accumulate to $200,000 in 20 years.

Present Value of an Annuity

Just as it is sometimes necessary to know the present value of a single payment to be received sometime in the future, so also there is sometimes interest in the present value of a stream of payments. An investor or creditor may wish to know the amount to be received today that would be the equivalent of a stream of payments to be received in the future.

The present value, discounted at 6 percent, of $1 to be received at the end of each of the future four periods is depicted diagrammatically in Exhibit 6-4. The present value of the stream of receipts, $3.46, is the sum of the present values of the individual receipts. The present values of the individual receipts, which are indicated in the left-hand column, could be taken directly from Table 2.

EXHIBIT 6-4

Present Value of $1 to Be Received at the End of Each of Four Periods, 6% Return (rounded to the nearest cent)

Year

0	1	2	3	4
$ .94 ←	$1			
.89 ←		$1		
.84 ←			$1	
.79 ←				$1
$3.46				

The mathematical formula for the present value P of an annuity of $1 per period compounded at a rate of i for n periods is

$$P_{\overline{n}|i} = \frac{1 - (1 + i)^{-n}}{i}$$

The present value of an annuity of $1 per period for four periods compounded at a rate of 6 percent is

$$P_{\overline{4}|.06} = \frac{1 - (1 + .06)^{-4}}{.06} = \$3.46$$

Consistent with the notation for future values, the uppercase P signifies an annuity, the lowercase p a single amount.

Table 4 in the Appendix indicates the present values of annuities in arrears (i.e., payments received at the *end* of each period) at various rates of return. Each amount in Table 4 is simply the sum, up to that period, of the amounts in Table 2.

The application of the concept of the present value of an annuity is demonstrated in the examples that follow.

Example 1

A mother wishes to give her daughter a gift of a sum of money, so that if the daughter deposits the sum in a bank, she would be able to withdraw $8,000 at the end of each of four years to meet her college expenses. The bank pays interest at the rate of 5 percent per year compounded annually. What is the single amount that the mother should give her daughter that would be the equivalent of four annual payments of $8,000 each?

The present value of an annuity of $1 per year for four years compounded at a rate of 5 percent is, per Table 4, $3.5460. The present value of an annuity of $8,000 is $8,000 times 3.5460, or $28,368. That is,

$$\$8,000P_{\overline{4}|.05} = \$28,368$$

The result can be verified as follows:

Initial deposit	$28,368
First-year earnings (5%)	1,418
Balance at end of first year before withdrawal	$29,786
First-year withdrawal	(8,000)
Balance at end of first year	$21,786
Second-year earnings (5%)	1,089
Balance at end of second year before withdrawal	$22,875
Second-year withdrawal	(8,000)
Balance at end of second year	$14,875
Third-year earnings (5%)	744
Balance at end of third year before withdrawal	$15,619
Third-year withdrawal	(8,000)
Balance at end of third year	$ 7,619
Fourth-year earnings (5%)	381
Balance at end of fourth year before withdrawal	$ 8,000
Fourth-year withdrawal	(8,000)
Balance at end of fourth year	$ 0

Example 2

A corporation has a choice: it can either lease its new plant at an annual rental fee of $30,000 for 20 years or it can purchase it. Assuming that the company estimates that it could earn 14 percent annually on any funds not invested in the plant, what would be the equivalent cost of purchasing the plant? Assume also that the plant would have no value at the end of 20 years.

The present value of a stream of payments of $1 per year, compounded at a rate of 14 percent, for 20 years, is, per Table 4, $6.6231. The present value of a stream of payments of $30,000 is $30,000 times 6.6231, or $198,693. The company would be as well off renting the plant for $30,000 per year as it would be purchasing it for $198,693 (ignoring, of course, both tax and risk factors).

Example 3

A corporation issues a security (e.g., a bond) that contains the following provision: The corporation agrees to pay the purchaser $20,000 every six months for 20 years and make an additional single lump-sum payment of $500,000 at the end of the 20-year period. How much would an investor be willing to pay for such a security, assuming that if he did not purchase the security he could, alternatively, invest the funds in other securities which would provide an annual return of 10 percent compounded semiannually?

The company promises to pay an annuity of $20,000 per period for 40 six-month periods. The present value of such an annuity when discounted at a rate of 5 percent (the *semiannual* alternative rate of return) is, with reference to Table 4,

$$\$20,000 \times 17.1591 = \$343,182$$

The present value of a single payment of $500,000, 40 periods hence, discounted at a semiannual rate of 5 percent is, with reference to Table 2,

$$\$500,000 \times .1420 = \$71,000$$

The present value of the stream of payments *and* the single lump-sum payment is therefore $343,182 plus $71,000, or $414,182. This is the amount the investor would be willing to pay:

$$\$20,000P_{\overline{40}|.05} = \$343,182$$

$$\$500,000p_{\overline{40}|.05} = \underline{71,000}$$

$$\text{Total} \quad \underline{\underline{\$414,182}}$$

Similar examples will be presented in Chapter 10; they help to explain why a bond with a certain face value (e.g., $500,000) might sell in the open market at a greater or lesser amount (e.g., $414,182).

Example 4

A company wishes to contribute an amount to a pension fund so that each employee will have an annual income of $24,000 upon retirement. The firm's consulting actuary estimates that an average employee will survive 15 years after his or her retirement and will be employed 20 years prior to retirement. The company anticipates that it will be able to obtain a return of 12 percent per year on contributions to the fund. How much should the company contribute each year, per employee, to the pension fund?

Upon the retirement of an employee, the company must have in its pension fund an amount equivalent to a stream of payments of $24,000 for 15 years. Per Table 4, the present value of a stream of payments of $1 per year, for 15 years, discounted at a rate of 12 percent is $6.8109. The present value of the stream of $24,000 is $24,000 times 6.8109, or $163,461:

$$\$24,000P_{\overline{15}|.12} = \$163,461$$

The company must therefore make equal annual payments so that the accumulated value of the payments after 20 years (the expected number of years an employee will work prior to retirement) will be $163,461. According to Table 3, a stream of payments of $1, invested to yield a return of 12 percent, will accumulate to $72.0524 after 20 years. That is,

$$P_{\overline{20}|.12} = 72.0524$$

Hence, some amount (x) times 72.0524 will accumulate to $163,461:

$$72.0524x = \$163,461$$

$$x = \$2,269$$

The firm would have to make 20 annual payments of $2,269 to be able to withdraw $24,000 per year for 15 years.

Discounted Cash Flow as a Means of Determining the Value of Assets

The procedures described in the preceding section in which a stream of future cash flows is *discounted* back to the present can be employed to determine the value to a particular firm of either individual assets or groups of assets.

Example 1

A firm is contemplating the purchase of new equipment. The company has determined that a new machine will enable it to reduce out-of-pocket production costs, after taxes, by $8,000 per year. If the machine will have a useful life of five years and the firm requires a return of at least 10 percent per year on all invested funds, what is the maximum amount it should be willing to pay for the machine?

The present value of the stream of equal cash savings is (per Table 4) 3.7908 times $8,000, or $30,326. The company should be willing to pay no more than that for the new machine.

Example 2

A company is evaluating the feasibility of acquiring another firm. Management estimates that the firm to be acquired will provide after-tax cash receipts to the purchasing company of $11 million per year for the first four years after it is acquired. Thereafter, however, it will lose certain competitive advantages, and the cash that it will be able to generate will be reduced to $7 million per year. It may be assumed that the $7 million annual cash flow will be permanent. What is the most that the company should be willing to pay for the new business, assuming that the company requires a return of 14 percent (compounded annually) on invested capital?

The stream of cash receipts can be evaluated in two parts: a permanent (infinite) flow of $7 million and a temporary "bonus" flow of $4 million for each of four years. The amount that the company would pay for the infinite flow can be calculated simply by dividing the annual flow by the appropriate discount rate.[3] Thus

$$\frac{\$7,000,000}{.14} = \$50,000,000$$

Were the company to pay $50 million, $7 million would provide a return of exactly 14 percent.

The amount that the company would pay for the temporary flow of $4 million for four years would be the present value of the anticipated cash receipts, that is, the present value of an annuity of $4 million for four years discounted at a rate of 14 percent. Per Table 4, the present value of

---

[3]The formula for the present value of an annuity is $P_{\overline{n}|i} = [1 - (1 + i)^{-n}]/i$. As n approaches infinity, $(1 + i)^{-n}$ approaches 0. Thus if $(1 + i)^{-n} = 0$, $P_{\overline{\infty}|i} = (1 - 0)/i = 1/i$.

---

an annuity of $1 for four years discounted at a rate of 14 percent is $2.9137. Hence the present value of an annuity of $4 million is $4 million times 2.9137, or $11,654,800.

For the business as a whole, the firm should be willing to pay the sum of what it would pay for the permanent and the "bonus" cash receipts:

$$\$50,000,000 \; + \; \$11,654,800 \; = \; \$61,654,800$$

Example 3

Although the market prices of common stocks, especially those that are traded on national exchanges, may appear to fluctuate irrationally, changes in market prices can be explained (though by no means predicted) by the present values of expected cash flows. The maximum amount that an investor will pay for a share of stock is that which will allow for an acceptable return. An *acceptable return* is one for which the present value of the expected cash inflows is no less than the security's purchase price. The expected cash flows would typically come from two sources: periodic dividends and single-sum proceeds upon sale or redemption.

Suppose, for example, an institutional investor is considering the purchase of a security that yields dividends of $6 per year. The investor expects to hold the security for five years and anticipates that sales proceeds will be $140. What is the maximum that the investor will be willing to pay for the security, assuming an expected return on investment of 12 percent per year?

The present value of the dividends, an annuity of $6P_{\overline{5}|.12}$, is, per Table 4,

$$\$6 \; \times \; 3.6048 \; = \; \$21.63$$

The present value of the cash from sale, a single sum, $140p_{\overline{5}|.12}$, is, per Table 2,

$$\$140 \; \times \; .5674 \; = \; \$79.44$$

The present value of both sources of cash, and therefore the maximum amount that the investor would be willing to pay, is $101.06.

Similar analyses on the part of other investors would establish the amounts that they would bid for the security and, through the interaction of supply and demand, would determine actual market price. Investors would, of course, incorporate into their analyses their own unique parameters for dividends, selling price, length of time until sale, and discount rate. These parameters would be continually reassessed to take into account the latest economic and corporate developments, such as actual or forecast changes in prevailing interest rates, market trends, and corporate earnings.

Deprival Value as a Means of Choosing between the Alternatives to Historical Cost

This chapter has identified three alternatives to historical costs: current cost (what it would cost to replace an asset), net realizable value (the amount for which the asset could be sold), and net present value (the discounted value of anticipated cash receipts or savings). Each of these alternatives has its advocates, but some accountants urge that the choice among the three should be dictated by the asset's *deprival value*. *Deprival value* is the amount that a firm would be willing to pay for an asset if it were deprived of it.

In almost all situations, an asset's current cost (CC) would exceed its net realizable value (NRV). As anyone who has tried to sell a house, car, or other asset shortly after acquiring it is aware, the amount that can be realized from the sale of an asset is usually much less than the amount paid for it. The difference can typically be ascribed to "middleman" profits and transaction costs, such as advertising and commissions. Both these amounts may be greater or less than the asset's present value (PV) (the discounted value of net cash receipts or savings). Thus, three possibilities remain:

$$(1) \quad PV > CC > NRV$$

$$(2) \quad CC > PV > NRV$$

$$(3) \quad CC > NRV > PV$$

If, as in possibility (1), the present value exceeds the current cost (purchase price), then if suddenly deprived of the asset the company would be expected to replace it since the present value of expected returns is greater than the amount required to replace it. The asset would be valued at *current cost*, the amount the company would have to pay to reacquire the asset if deprived of it.

If, however, as in possibility (2), current cost exceeds present value, which exceeds net present value, the firm would not replace the asset when deprived of it since the acquisition price would be greater than its value in use. The maximum that it would be willing to pay would be the present value. If it could obtain the asset at a price equal to the present value, it would use it, rather than sell it, since the value in use would be greater than the net realizable value, the amount that could be realized if it were to sell the asset. The asset would therefore be stated at *net present value*, the maximum the firm would be willing to pay if deprived of it.

If, as in possibility (3), current cost exceeds net realizable value, which exceeds present value, the maximum the firm would pay to replace the asset would be net realizable value. Once it acquired the asset, it would immediately sell it, for its net realizable value from sale is greater than its value in use. Hence, the asset would be reported at its *net realizable value*.

The notion of deprival value as a means of reporting assets has *not* gained general acceptance, mainly because deprival values are dependent upon subjective judgments as to what a company might do, but has no intention of actually doing. Nevertheless, the concept of deprival value may provide managers and investors with analytical insight into many actual and potential business transactions. Suppose, for example, an investment group is assessing a proposed acquisition of a multidivision company. In calculating the maximum price to be paid, it would have to consider current costs (prices for which the comparable divisions could be purchased elsewhere), net realizable values (the amounts for which the divisions could be sold if it were to break up the company), and net present values (the cash flows that could be generated by continuing to operate each of the divisions).

In accord with conventional financial reporting, the value assigned to an asset is ordinarily based on its *historical cost*—the amount paid to acquire it less that portion of initial cost representing the services of the asset already consumed (i.e., allowance for depreciation or amortization).

Values based on historical costs are consistent with the *matching* concept, by which costs are matched with the revenues that they generate. The portion of asset cost that has not yet been charged as an expense (i.e., matched with revenues) is carried forward on the balance sheet to be expensed in future accounting periods. Thus the historical cost balance sheet is not a statement of current values; it is, instead, a statement of *residuals*—actual costs that have not yet been charged as expenses.

Historical cost values are frequently said to be *objective*. This characterization is correct only as it applies to the initial value assigned to an asset. Thereafter the reported amount of an asset may be affected by managerial judgments. For example, the reported value of plant and equipment depends upon management's estimate of the assets' useful lives and salvage values; the reported value of accounts receivable is influenced by management's estimate of uncollectible accounts.

The *market value* of an asset has the advantage over its historical-cost value of being more relevant for most managerial and investor decisions, because it is indicative of either the enterprise's economic sacrifice in holding and using the asset or the cost the company would have to incur to replace it. Market value can take one of two forms: current cost or net realizable value. *Current (purchase) cost* is an *input (entry) value*, the amount that the firm would have to pay to replace the asset. *Net realizable (sale) value* is an *output (exit) value*, the amount that the firm would have to be paid to replace it.

Market value, however, fails to take into account the utility of an asset to its particular user. An asset may be worth more to a company than either its selling price or replacement cost. A slightly used vehicle, for example, may be almost as valuable to a company as a new one, although its market value will almost certainly be considerably less.

Moreover, the general use of market values (particularly output values) may be inconsistent with the concept that costs should be charged as expenses in the periods associated with the benefits that they provide. Start-up or organizational costs, for example, may not be considered to be assets at all, since they cannot readily be sold in the open market. Under a market-value system, the entire amounts of such costs would be charged as expenses in the periods in which they were incurred.

The value of an asset could also be stated in terms of its *utility* to a specific user. The worth of an asset to a particular user may be defined as the present value of the anticipated cash receipts with which it is associated. The present value of the cash receipts must take into account the "time value of money"—the fact that a dollar received today is worth considerably more than one to be received in the distant future. Determination of the present value of cash flows requires an understanding of the fundamental concepts of compounded interest—hence the extended discussion of that topic in this chapter. It is often impractical, however, to determine the present value of a particular asset, since individual assets are not generally associated with specific cash receipts. Thus conventional financial statements seldom express asset values in terms of worth to the individual possessor Nevertheless, an understanding of the concepts of present values of cash flows provides an appreciation of the underlying forces that determine the market values of assets and is the key to making rational decisions as to whether to purchase or sell assets.

In Part II of this chapter, as well as in the next several chapters, we deal with problems of valuing specific assets, such as cash, marketable securities, accounts receivable, inventories, and plant and equipment.

PART II. Cash and Marketable Securities

CASH

Cash is ordinarily reported at its face value. *Cash* includes currency on hand and funds on deposit in banks that are subject to immediate and unconditional withdrawal (i.e., amounts in checking accounts). It does not in a strict sense include amounts that may be subject to withdrawal restrictions, such as funds in the form of savings accounts, which may technically require advance notification for withdrawal, or certificates of deposit. Most companies maintain several general ledger accounts for cash. In statements made available to the public, however, most cash and ''near-cash'' balances are summarized into a single figure.

There are several characteristics of cash that make it of distinctive interest to a manager or accountant. It is the ultimate asset of concern to investors as it is the medium of exchange in our society. The business cycle begins and ends with cash. Owners and creditors contribute cash to a firm. The firm, in turn, uses the cash to acquire other assets. It expects that by providing goods and services, it will eventually be able to reconvert these other assets into more cash than was contributed. It then distributes this greater amount of cash to the owners and creditors.

Cash is the most liquid of assets. Indeed, liquidity is a measure of how easily an asset can be converted into cash. Because of its liquid nature, cash must be the subject of especially tight safeguards and controls. As a general rule, for example, the number of persons handling currency should be kept to a minimum, all currency should be deposited in a bank as soon as feasible, and accounting recognition should be given immediately to all cash receipts via a cash register tape or a manual listing. The responsibility for particular cash funds should be assigned to particular individuals, and whenever possible, to assure better that the payments are made to the parties for whom they are intended, disbursements should be made by check rather than with currency.

Cash is the accepted medium of paying bills and satisfying obligations. It is essential that a firm have an adequate amount of cash available to meet its debts as they come due and to make the day-to-day payments required of any operating enterprise. Management, as well as financial analysts and creditors, must, therefore, be continually alert to whether the firm's available cash—or assets that can readily be turned into cash—is sufficient to meet foreseeable needs.

Unproductive Asset

Cash, however, is an *unproductive asset*. Cash on hand or on deposit in a checking account earns little or no interest. If there is inflation in the economy, cash loses its purchasing power. Unlike many other assets, it produces no services and provides no return to its owner. As a consequence, it is to the advantage of a firm to keep as little cash as possible either on hand or in checking accounts. Cash that is needed for a *safety reserve* or is being held for future purchase of other assets, distribution to shareholders, or payment of outstanding obligations should be invested temporarily in common stocks, short-term government notes, certificates of deposit, or other dividend- or interest-bearing securities.

Cash on Hand; Imprest Basis

Cash on hand includes customer receipts that have not yet been deposited, currency necessary to conduct routine business, and petty cash. *Petty cash* represents small amounts of cash maintained to meet disbursements of insufficient size to justify the time and inconvenience of writing a check. Petty cash funds are frequently accounted for on an *imprest* basis. That is, the general ledger balance of petty cash will always reflect a fixed amount, $100, for example. At all times the fund itself should contain either cash or payment receipts for that amount. Periodically the fund is restored to its original amount by a transfer from general cash, and at that time accounting recognition is given to the particular expenses that had been incurred. The following journal entry might be made to restore $70 to the petty cash fund:

Postage expense $30
Entertainment expense 40
    Cash in bank $70
To replenish petty cash fund

Cash in Bank

The balance of cash reported in a firm's general ledger is unlikely to be that actually available for withdrawal at a particular time. Conventional practice dictates that a firm reduce the general ledger cash balance when it writes a check. However, a period of several days or even weeks may elapse before a check reaches and clears the firm's bank. During that period, the balance per the records of the bank will be greater than the balance in the books of the firm by the amount of the check. Similarly, a firm may record deposits at the time it mails or delivers them to its bank. The bank will credit the firm's account only when it actually receives the deposit or, if the receipt is after hours, on the next business day. As a consequence, the amount of cash that a firm reports may be either greater or less than that actually available for withdrawal per the records of the bank. Periodically, upon receiving a statement of its account from the bank, the firm must *reconcile* its balance with that of the bank; that is, it must account for any differences between the balance as indicated by its own records and that of the bank. At the same time, it must update its own books to give recognition to any transactions about which it learns from the bank statement. An example and explanation of a bank reconciliation (in one of many possible forms) are provided in Exhibit 6-5.

EXHIBIT 6-5

Bank Reconciliation
December 31

	Per Firm's Own Books	Per Bank Statement
Balance, December 31 (Note 1)	$20,020.53	$16,160.30
Items that explain differences between firm's and bank's balance		
Add: Deposit in transit (Note 2)		12,176.25
Subtract: Outstanding checks (Note 3)		(6,562.19)
Subtract: Bank service charge (Note 4)	(10.00)	
Subtract: N.S.F. check (Note 5)	(236.17)	
Add: Note collected by bank (Note 6)	2,000.00	
Adjusted balance, December 31 (Note 7)	$21,774.36	$21,774.36

Note 1. The firm's records indicate a cash balance of $20,020.53; the bank's records indicate a balance of $16,160.30. Assuming that neither is in error, the difference can be explained by transactions about which one party or the other has no knowledge.

Note 2. The firm made a deposit in the bank on, or shortly before, December 31, the date of the bank statement. The company recorded the deposit, but the bank has not, most likely because it was received after the close of business on December 31.

Note 3. The company has written checks on its account that have not yet "cleared" the bank. The bank is unaware of them since these checks have not yet been presented for payment. As the company wrote the checks, it credited (reduced) its recorded cash balance. The bank will reduce the balance in the firm's account when it makes the required disbursements on behalf of the firm.

Note 4. The bank reduced the firm's balance in the amount of a service charge. The company, perhaps because it learns of such charge by way of the monthly bank statement, has not yet recorded it.

Note 5. The bank also reduced the firm's balance to reflect an N.S.F. (not sufficient funds) check. An N.S.F. check is one returned by the bank to the depositor because it has been dishonored by the bank on which it was drawn. When the firm initially deposited the check, the bank, assuming that the check would be collectible, credited (increased) the firm's account. Upon learning that the party that wrote the check had insufficient funds in its account to cover the payment, the bank returned the dishonored check to the firm and reduced the balance in its account. The firm, when it first deposited the check, had also recorded an increase in its cash balance. Unlike the bank, however, it has not yet recorded the return of the dishonored check by reducing the balance in its cash-in-bank account.

Note 6. The bank collected the proceeds of a customer note for the company and has given the company credit for it. As with the N.S.F. check, it did not yet notify the company (or if it did, the company has not yet recorded it by increasing its cash balance).

Note 7. The cash-in-bank available to the firm is $21,774.36. The company must now record the bank service charge and the N.S.F. check. In the normal course of events, the bank will routinely record the deposit in transit and the outstanding checks. Then (disregarding all subsequent transactions), the records of both the firm and the bank would agree; they would show a balance of $21,774.36.

EXHIBIT 6-5 Continued

The reconciliation points to the need of the firm to update its records to take account of the information provided by the bank statement. The following entry would give effect to that information:

Cash $1,753.83
Bank service charge (expense) 10.00
Accounts receivable 236.17
    Notes receivable $2,000
To update the cash account for information indicated by the bank reconciliation
(Accounts receivable has been debited by the amount of the N.S.F. check because the party which wrote the check is now indebted to the company for the amount of the check.)

Classification of Cash

Cash is ordinarily classified as a current asset. In fact, cash is the fundamental current asset in that current assets are defined as those that will be converted into cash within the operating cycle of a business. Nevertheless, there are exceptions. Cash should be considered a current asset only when there are no restrictions—either those imposed by contract or by management intent—upon its use as a medium of exchange within a single operating cycle. Suppose, for example, that a company is required by terms of a bond agreement to maintain a *sinking fund* for the retirement of debt that will mature in 10 years. A sinking fund consists of cash or other assets segregated in the accounts to repay an outstanding debt when it comes due. All such assets, although normally considered current, when set aside in a sinking fund should be classified on the balance sheet as *noncurrent* assets since management has earmarked them for a specific, noncurrent, purpose. The intent of management should be the key criterion for classification.

MARKETABLE SECURITIES

In an effort to obtain a return on what would otherwise be temporarily idle cash, many corporations use such cash to purchase stocks, bonds, or commercial paper (short-term certificates of debt). Temporary investments are ordinarily grouped together in the current asset section of the statement of position under the heading ''marketable securities.'' Marketable securities are distinguished from the corporate investments by corporate intent. The firm ordinarily expects to hold the securities for a relatively short period of time, until a need for cash arises, and does not anticipate exercising any significant degree of control over the company whose shares it may own. If the company has other intentions with respect to the securities, they should ordinarily be classified as ''long-term investments,'' a noncurrent asset (to be discussed in Chapter 13).

As with most other assets, marketable securities are reported on the balance sheet at their original cost. However, because the company is likely to sell them in the near future, the current market value is disclosed parenthetically on the face of the statement. Thus

Cash		$ 80,000
Market securities (current market value, $350,000)		335,000

Gains and losses on the sale of individual securities are ordinarily recognized at the time of sale. No recognition is given to fluctuations in market value. Assume, for example, that a company had purchased 100 shares of IBM at $110 per share. The stock would be reported on the statement of position at $11,000. Should the company sell the stock for $125 per share, it would record the sale as follows:

Cash	$12,500
Marketable securities	$11,000
Gain on sale of marketable securities	1,500

To record the sale of marketable securities

Revenues from dividends or interest on marketable securities are ordinarily recognized upon receipt. Thus, had IBM declared and paid a dividend of $5 per share before the company had sold the shares, the following entry would have been appropriate.

Cash	$500
Dividend revenue	$500

To record receipt of dividend

Lower of Cost or Market Rule

The one critical exception to the general rule that marketable securities be reported at historical cost is that, where the market price of an entire portfolio of equity securities (i.e., stocks) is less than cost, the carrying value of the securities should be reduced to the market value, and a corresponding loss should be recognized. The exception represents an application of the guidelines of conservatism. Unfavorable events should be recognized at the earliest possible time.

This "lower of cost or market" rule according to a pronouncement of the FASB should not be applied to individual securities: it must be applied to all current marketable securities taken as a group.[4]

Assume, for example, that during 1993 a firm acquired a portfolio of three stocks. As shown, by year end, two of the stocks had declined in value and one had increased:

	Original Cost	Market Value 12/31/93	Lower of Cost or Market
Stock A	$10,000	$12,000	$10,000
Stock B	12,000	8,000	8,000
Stock C	15,000	9,000	9,000
Total	$37,000	$29,000	$27,000

[4] "Accounting for Certain Marketable Securities," Financial Accounting Board *Statement of Financial Accounting Standards No. 12,* 1975.

The FASB requires that the portfolio be written down to the market value of the three securities combined, $29,000. Were the lower of cost or market rule to be applied on the basis of individual securities, the portfolio would be written down to $27,000. The portfolio method is less conservative than the individual security method in that gains in some securities are permitted to offset losses in others.

The FASB also mandates that the decline in market value be recognized in the statement of income as a loss. Although reported like other losses or expenses, the loss would be unrealized—"unrealized" because it has not been affirmed by an actual sale. Correspondingly, the difference between the cost and the market value of the portfolio would be reported in a "valuation allowance." The valuation allowance would be a contra account to marketable securities. The original cost of the securities would be retained in the marketable securities account. The marketable securities account, less the amount in the valuation allowance, would indicate the market value (if lower than cost) of the portfolio.

The following journal entry would record the decline in the value of the portfolio.

Loss on valuation of marketable securities (expense) $8,000
    Allowance for excess of cost of marketable securities
      over market value (asset contra account) $8,000
To recognize a loss equal to the excess of cost ($37,000) over market value ($29,000) of marketable securities

If, in subsequent years, the value of the portfolio increased, then the balance in the allowance account would be reduced. Correspondingly, a gain on recovery would be reported in the statement of income. However, a gain on recovery would be recognized only to the extent that unrealized losses were previously recognized. The carrying value of the portfolio must never exceed cost.

Suppose, for example, that during 1994 the market prices of the securities changed to:

	Original Cost	Market Value 12/31/94
Stock A	$10,000	$11,000
Stock B	12,000	10,000
Stock C	15,000	13,000
Total	$37,000	$34,000

The market value of the portfolio increased since year-end 1993 by $5,000 from $29,000 to $34,000. Hence the valuation allowance must be reduced by $5,000 and a recovery gain in that amount recognized as revenue:

Allowance for excess of cost of marketable
   securities over market value (asset contra account) $5,000
      Recovery of previously recognized losses on
       valuation of marketable securities (revenue) $5,000
To recognize increase in market value of security portfolio (i.e., recovery of previously recognized losses)

The balance in the valuation allowance would now be $3,000—the difference between cost of $37,000 and market value of $34,000.

Should the company sell a security, it would record a gain or loss on the individual security, just as illustrated previously. Suppose, for example, that in 1995 the firm sells stock C for $14,000. The original cost of stock C was $15,000; hence it would recognize a loss (now a "realized loss") of $1,000:

```
Cash . . . . . . . . . . . . . . . . . . . . . . . . . . . . . . . . . . . . . . . . . . . . . . . . . . . . . $14,000
Loss on sale of marketable securities . . . . . . . . . . . . . . . . . . . . . . . . .    1,000
     Marketable securities . . . . . . . . . . . . . . . . . . . . . . . . . . . . . . . . . . . . . $15,000
```
To record the sale of marketable securities at a loss

At the conclusion of 1995, the firm would compare the cost and market values of the securities that remain in its portfolio. It would adjust the allowance account to reflect the difference between the two and record a corresponding valuation loss or recovery gain for the amount that must be added to, or subtracted from, the allowance account. If, for example, the combined market value of stocks A and B increased to $25,000, an amount in excess of original cost of $22,000, then the balance in the valuation allowance should be zero. Since the balance at the end of 1994 would have been $3,000, the following entry would be in order:

```
Allowance for excess of cost of marketable
   securities over market value (asset contra account) . . . . . . . . . . . . . . . . $3,000
     Recovery of previously recognized losses on
        valuation of marketable securities (revenue) . . . . . . . . . . . . . . . . . . . . . $3,000
```
To recognize increase in market value of security portfolio (i.e., recovery of previously recognized losses)

VALUATION OF MARKETABLE SECURITIES— A PROPOSED ALTERNATIVE

The current practice of generally reporting marketable securities at original cost is consistent with that for other assets. Two characteristics of marketable securities may justify an alternative approach. First, the current market value of marketable securities (at any particular time) can ordinarily be objectively determined. This is especially true of securities that are widely traded, since current prices are available in either newspapers or through electronic services. Second, there is always a market in which to sell the securities. Unlike fixed assets or inventories, marketable securities can be disposed of at the market price by a single telephone call to a stockbroker. As a consequence of these two characteristics, critics of current practice assert that the dual accounting goals of providing information that is both relevant and objective can best be achieved by valuing securities on the balance sheet at market values rather than historical costs.

Historical costs detract from the utility of both the balance sheet and the income statement. The stated value of the marketable securities may bear no relationship to their selling prices. In fact, shares in the same company—which could be converted to the same amount of cash—may be valued at different amounts if not acquired at the same time.

Gains or losses from holding an individual security are recorded only when the security is actually sold. In an accounting sense, at least, management is neither credited nor discredited for holding a security as it increases or decreases in market value until the period of sale. The period of sale may be one subsequent to that in which the increase or decrease in value actually took place.

If a firm has in its portfolio one or more securities that have increased in value since they were purchased, management can easily manipulate reported earnings. If management wishes to improve earnings on the current period, it simply sells those securities that have appreciated in value. If, on the other hand, it wishes to give the earnings of the following year a boost, it delays the sale until then. It is questionable, given the ease by which it can be done, that the sale of a security is of greater economic significance than the changes in its market value while it is being held.

The problem of reporting marketable securities is of special concern to industries, such as banking, mutual funds, and insurance, in which all or a sizable portion of assets consists of marketable securities. In those industries it is vital that an investor be concerned with unrealized gains or losses. As a consequence, firms in such industries either already give effect to unrealized gains or losses on both the balance sheet and the income statement or otherwise make prominent disclosure in footnotes.

Although the issue of cost versus market value can conveniently be highlighted in a discussion of marketable securities, it is one that bears upon all assets and liabilities. It will be alluded to again in several subsequent chapters.

SUMMARY OF PART II

In Part II of this chapter we have dealt with problems of accounting for and reporting cash and marketable securities, both of which are ordinarily classified as current assets. Cash includes currency on hand as well as demand deposits in banks.

Cash is the asset of greatest interest to managers and investors as it is the means by which goods and services are acquired. Indeed, the paramount objective of most investors is to maximize cash returns. Cash is also the most liquid of assets. As such it must be the subject of especially tight safeguards and controls.

Cash, although generally classified as a current asset, should be grouped with the noncurrent assets in those situations in which it is subject to restrictions upon its withdrawal, regardless of whether the restrictions are imposed by contract or by management itself.

Marketable securities include those securities which a firm holds as temporary investments. The key issue with respect to marketable securities pertains to the value at which they should be reported on the balance sheet and the point at which increases or decreases in value should be recognized on the income statement. Marketable securities are conventionally reported at cost. Increases or decreases in market value are recognized only upon the sale of a security. An exception is made, however, when the market value of an entire portfolio is less than its cost. In accord with the "lower of cost or market" rule, the portfolio is written down to its overall market value. Alternatively, however, many accountants argue that all changes in the market values of securities should be given accounting recognition and all gains or losses, both *realized* and *unrealized,* should be reflected immediately in enterprise earnings.

Exercise for Review and Self-Testing

Try to complete this exercise without using the interest tables in the Appendix.

Assume that today is January 1, 1994. Further assume that the prevailing rate of interest paid by banks on deposits is 8 percent, compounded annually.

1. *Future value of a single amount.* A corporation deposits $100,000 in a bank today.
   a. How much will it have in its account on December 31, 1994?
   b. How much will it have in its account on December 31, 1995?
   c. How much will it have in its account on December 31, 1996?
2. *Future value of an annuity.* A corporation deposits $100,000 in a bank on December 31, 1994.
   a. How much will it have in its account on December 31, 1994, immediately after making the deposit?
   b. It makes another deposit of $100,000 on December 31, 1995. How much will it have in its account after making the deposit?
   c. It makes yet another deposit of $100,000 on December 31, 1996. How much will it have in its account after making the third deposit?
3. *Present value of a single amount.* A corporation wants to be able to withdraw from its account $100,000 on December 31, 1994.
   a. How much should it deposit today?
   b. Assume instead that it wants to be able to withdraw $100,000 on December 31, 1995. How much should it deposit today?
   c. Assume alternatively that it wants to be able to withdraw $100,000 on December 31, 1996. How much should it deposit today?
4. *Present value of an annuity.* A corporation wants to be able to withdraw from its account $100,000 on December 31, 1994, $100,000 on December 31, 1995, *and* $100,000 on December 31, 1996. How much should it deposit today?

Questions for Review and Discussion

1. What is meant by *value* as the term is used in connection with assets reported on the conventional balance sheet?
2. The balance sheet, it is often asserted, provides little indication of a company's inherent worth. Instead, it is nothing more than a compilation of *residuals*. Do you agree?
3. Historical cost values of assets are of little relevance to most decisions faced by management, creditors, or investors. Why, then, do accountants resist efforts to convert to a market-value-oriented balance sheet?
4. Market values can be interpreted as either *input* or *output* prices. What is the distinction between the two? Give an example of each.
5. What are the economic benefits associated with an asset? How can they be quantified?

6. Current assets are defined as those which are reasonably expected to be *realized in cash,* sold, or consumed during the normal operating cycle of the business. Yet cash itself is not always classified as a current asset. Why is this so?

7. The owner of a small corporation was recently advised by her CPA that she "has too much cash in her checking account." The company has a checking account balance of $100,000, and the CPA told the owner that the account was costing the company "about $10,000 per year." The owner of the corporation insisted that this could not be so; the money was deposited in a "no-charge" checking account. What do you think the CPA had in mind when he made his comment?

8. The general managers of two of a large firm's subsidiaries each reported operating earnings in 1993 of $100 million, excluding income from the sale of marketable securities. The manager of company A also indicated that on January 5, 1993, his subsidiary purchased but had not yet sold 1 million shares of United Mining Co. common stock at $15 per share. On December 31, 1993, United Mining was traded at $45 per share. By contrast, the manager of company B revealed that his subsidiary had purchased 1 million shares of United Mining Co. common stock on April 18, at $35 per share and had sold them on November 25 at $38 per share. If conventional accounting principles are adhered to, which subsidiary would report the higher income? Excluding all factors other than those discussed, which subsidiary do you think had the superior performance in 1993?

========= **Problems** =========

1. *Problems 1–8 are intended to facilitate understanding of the four basic concepts of compound interest.*

   Assuming an interest rate of 8 percent compounded annually, $300,000 is
   a. The present value of what amount to be received in five years?
   b. The value in five years of what amount deposited in a bank today?
   c. The present value of an annuity of what amount to be received over the next five years?
   d. The value in five years of an annuity of what amount deposited in a bank at the end of each of the next five years?

2. The board of directors of a printing company decided that the company should take advantage of an unusually successful year to place in a reserve fund an amount of cash sufficient to enable it to purchase a new printing press in six years. The company determines that the new press would cost $200,000 and that funds could be invested in securities that would provide a return of 8 percent, compounded annually.
   a. How much should the company place in the fund?
   b. Suppose that the return would be compounded quarterly. How much should the company place in the fund?

3. In anticipation of the need to purchase new equipment, a corporation decided to set aside $40,000 each year in a special fund.
   a. If the amount in the fund could be invested in securities that provide an after-tax return of 5 percent per year, how much would the company have available in eight years?
   b. Assume instead that the company knew that it would require $500,000 to replace the equipment at the end of eight years. How much should it contribute to the fund each year, assuming an annual return of 5 percent?

4. A corporation wishes to provide a research grant to a university so that the university can withdraw $10,000 at the end of each of the next three years. The university will deposit the amount received in an account that earns interest at the rate of 5 percent per year. How much should the corporation give the university? Prepare a schedule in which you indicate the balance in the account at the end of each of the three years.

5. On the day of a child's birth, the parents deposit $1,000 in a savings bank. The bank pays interest at the rate of 6 percent each year, compounded annually.
   a. How much will be on deposit by the time the child enters college on her eighteenth birthday?
   b. Assume instead that the interest at an annual rate of 6 percent is compounded semiannually. To how much will the original deposit increase in 18 years?

6. A corporation borrows $5,000 from a bank. Principal and interest are payable at the end of five years.
   a. What will be the amount of the corporation's payment, assuming that the bank charges interest at a rate of 10 percent and compounds the interest annually?
   b. What will be the amount of the corporation's payment if interest at an annual rate of 10 percent is compounded semiannually?

7. You deposit a fixed amount in a bank. How long will it take for your funds to double if the bank pays interest at a rate of
   a. 4 percent compounded annually?
   b. 8 percent compounded annually?
   c. 8 percent compounded semiannually?
   d. 8 percent compounded quarterly?

8. A company wishes to establish a pension plan for its president. The company wants to assure the president or his survivors an income of $40,000 per year for 20 years after his retirement. The president has 15 years to work before he retires. If the company can earn 7 percent per year on the pension fund, how much should it contribute during each working year of the president?

9. *Effective interest rates can be adjusted in a number of different ways.*
   U.S. savings bonds differ from conventional government or corporate *coupon* bonds in that they do not have attached to them coupons that can periodically be redeemed for interest payments. Instead, they carry a face value of a fixed amount, for example, $25, $50, or $100. The purchaser buys the bonds at a discount. For example, he or she might pay $75 for a $100 bond that will mature in 10 years. The difference between what is paid for the bond and its face value represents the interest for the entire period during which the bond is outstanding. Upon maturity the purchaser will present the bond to the government and receive its full face value. The government can adjust the effective interest rate that it pays by varying either the initial selling price of the bond or the number of years the purchaser must hold the bond before he or she can redeem it.
   a. Suppose that the government sells a $100 face value bond for $75 and establishes a holding period of 10 years. What is the approximate effective rate of interest (assume that interest is compounded annually)?
   b. Suppose instead that the government wishes to establish an effective rate of 8 percent and a holding period of 10 years. At what price should it sell the bond?
   c. If the government wishes to establish an effective rate of 8 percent and a price of $75, how long a holding period should it require?

10. *Truth-in-lending laws are designed to eliminate the type of deception suggested by this problem.*

    The Helping Hand Loan Co. placed an advertisement in a local newspaper that read in part, "Borrow up to $10,000 for 5 years at our low, low rate of interest of 6 percent per year." When a customer went to the loan company to borrow the $10,000, he was told that total interest on the five-year loan would be $3,000. That is, $600 per year (6 percent of $10,000) for five years. Company practice, he was told, requires that the interest be paid in full at the time a loan is made and be deducted from the amount given to the customer. Thus the customer was given only $7,000. The loan was to be repaid in five annual installments of $2,000.

    Do you think that the ad was misleading? What was the actual amount loaned to the customer? Determine what you consider to be the "true" rate of interest.

11. *Rates of discount determine firms' preferences for alternative financing arrangements.*

    Company A is presently negotiating with company B to purchase a parcel of land. Three alternative sets of terms are under consideration:
    a. Company A will pay $400,000 at time of sale.
    b. Company A will pay $50,000 at time of sale and give company B a note for $500,000 that matures in five years.
    c. Company A will make five annual payments of $100,000 each commencing one year from the date of sale.

    Company A can obtain an after-tax return of 7 percent per year on any funds that it has available for investment; company B can obtain a return of 9 percent. Both firms use discount rates to evaluate potential investments that are equal to the rates of return that they can obtain.

    Rank the three sets of terms as you would expect them to be preferred by each of the two companies.

12. *Present value techniques can be used to develop a mortgage schedule.* (This problem is intended for solution using an electronic spreadsheet.)

    On December 31, 1992, a bank lends a corporate customer $500,000 to acquire a building. The loan is for a period of 10 years and bears interest at the rate of 12 percent. As is typical of mortgage loans, the borrower will be required to repay the loan in equal installments. In this case, the borrower will make 10 annual payments, the first on December 31, 1993. Each payment will comprise two elements: interest at the rate of 12 percent on the outstanding balance and a reduction of the principal (the loan balance) that is equal to the total payment less the amount applied to interest.
    a. Determine the amount of each required payment (i.e., the amount of an annuity with a present value of $500,000).
    b. Prepare a schedule in which you show in appropriate columns:
       (1) The balance on the loan at the end of each of the ten years
       (2) The annual payment as computed in part (a)
       (3) The portion of each payment that is applied to interest (This amount will decrease each year as the balance in the loan is reduced.)
       (4) The portion of each payment that is applied to the principal and thereby reduces the outstanding balance (This amount will increase each year as the amount applied to interest decreases.)

13. *Present value analysis can be used to support a taxpayer claim for loss on an investment.* (This problem is intended for solution using an electronic spreadsheet.)

    Wertimer, Inc., has claimed a deduction on its state tax return, which the state controller has challenged. Under state tax law, a corporate taxpayer is entitled to write down an investment from cost to market value when there is evidence that its market value has been permanently impaired. In 1987 Wertimer Co. acquired Gambs, Ltd., for $200 million and until December 31, 1992, stated its investment at cost. Effective January 1, 1993, Wertimer wants the asset to be written down to market.

Gambs, Ltd., has sustained substantial operating losses since being acquired. An independent consultant has determined that for Gambs, Ltd., to be profitable it would have to upgrade its facilities substantially. The required funds would have to be provided by Wertimer, Inc. The consultant estimates that if Wertimer, Inc., elects to modernize the facilities, then (under the most optimistic scenario) it can expect cash flows from Gambs (taking into account the modernization costs) to be as follows for the next 20 years (in millions):

1993	($15)
1994	(10)
1995	(3)
1996	2
1997	5
1998–2002	8 per year
2003–2012	12 per year

Suppose that you are asked to assist Wertimer in preparing a legal brief in support of its deduction. Wertimer has not received any offers to purchase Gambs; hence there are no offers on which to base an estimate of market value. However, the state controller is willing to accept alternative evidence of market value.

a. Based on the present value of cash flows for the period 1993–2012, what is the maximum value that you would place on Gambs, Ltd.? Apply a discount rate of 15 percent.

b. Suppose the state controller claims that the estimates of cash flows for the years 2003–2012 are unrealistically low. Recalculate the present value, assuming that the cash flows for that period would be increased by 100 percent from $12 to $24 million per year.

c. Suppose instead that the state controller challenged the cash flows for the years 1998–2002 and said that they should be increased by 100 percent, from $8 million to $16 million per year. Recalculate the present value. Comment on the relative significance of an $8 million increase per year in years 6 to 10 as compared with an increase of $12 million per year in years 11 to 20.

14. *The impact of alternative tax proposals can be assessed by discounting resultant cash savings.*

Congress is considering three alternative tax incentives to encourage investment in certain types of plant and equipment. Your company is planning to acquire a plant, which would be eligible for the benefits. The plant would cost $100 million and is expected to provide a cash return, before taxes, of $10 million per year for 10 years. The proposed changes, and their impact on the investment, would be as follows:

(1) Provide an investment tax credit of 10 percent of the cost of eligible plant. This would save the company $10 million at the time of acquisition.

(2) Reduce the tax on income from the plant from 40 to 30 percent. This would save the firm $1 million per year over the 10-year life of the plant.

(3) Reduce the tax on gains from the sale of the plant. This would save the company $10 million when it disposed of the plant at the end of year 10.

The company applies a discount rate of 12 percent to all investment proposals.
a. Calculate the present value of the savings that would result from each of the three proposals.
b. Suppose that Congress rejected option 1. What would be the amount of annual savings (for option 2) or savings upon sale (for option 3) that would be necessary to provide the equivalent benefits of option 1?

15. *The market value of a firm's common stock is likely to be affected by changes in anticipated cash flows.*

    The common stock of the North Sea Oil Company is presently trading at $48 per share. There are 10 million shares outstanding.

    The company will soon announce a major new oil find. The new discovery is expected to have the following impact on the firm's cash flows (in millions, per year):

Years 1 and 2 (as the fields are developed)	($10)
Years 3 through 10	18
Years 11 through 20	12

    Historically the firm's dividend policy has been directly associated with net cash receipts. Annual dividend payout has been approximately 40 percent of net cash receipts. In valuing the common stock of North Sea, investors as a group have discounted anticipated cash dividends at a rate of 8 percent. Focusing strictly on the limited amount of information provided in the problem, what would you anticipate to be market price of North Sea common stock immediately following the announcement of the new find?

16. *Alternative bases of asset valuation affect both earnings and assets.*

    In 1993 the 47th Street Diamond Mart acquired a gem for resale. The cost of the jewel to the firm was $1 million. By the end of 1993, the firm would have had to pay $1.2 million to acquire a stone of comparable size and quality, and it could have sold the stone to a retail customer for $1.5 million. However, it was certain that if it would wait an additional year to sell the jewel, it could do so for $1.8 million.
a. Indicate the amount at which the firm should report the gem on its balance sheet of December 31, 1993, if it elects to wait one year to sell it, assuming each of the following bases of valuation:
   (1) Historical cost
   (2) Current cost (an input price)
   (3) Net realizable value (an output price)
   (4) Value to user (the firm determines the present value of expected cash receipts using a discount rate of 7 percent)
b. Indicate the amount of any gain associated with the stone that the firm would report in 1993, assuming each of the bases indicated.

17. *The basis of asset valuation determines the basis for revenue recognition.*

    During 1993, in its first year of operations, the Mann Company purchased, for $60 per unit, 1,000 units of a product. Of these, it sold 800 units at a price of $100 per unit. On December 31, 1993, the company was notified by its supplier that in the following year the wholesale cost per unit would be increased to $70 per unit. As a consequence of the increase, Mann Company determined that the retail price would increase to $120 per unit.

    Ignoring other revenues and expenses, determine the ending inventory balance and compute income, assuming that ending inventories are to be valued at
a. Historical cost (generally accepted basis)

b. Current cost (an *input* price)

c. Net realizable value (an *output* price)

In computing income, distinguish between revenue from the actual sale of product and yet to be realized gains from *holding* the product in inventory. Remember that any recorded increases in the value of the inventory must also be reflected in the determination of income (and, more specifically, of revenues).

18. *Present value techniques can be used to determine the value of a business.*

The general ledger of the Odessa Co. reflected, in summary form, the following balances (there were no material liabilities):

Current assets (accounts receivable, inventory, etc.)	$ 40,000
Equipment	80,000
Building	120,000
Land	60,000

The Geneva Company purchased the company for a total of $400,000 (cash). Immediately after purchase an independent appraiser estimated the value of the individual assets as follows:

Current assets	$ 40,000
Equipment	100,000
Building	160,000
Land	100,000

a. Prepare a journal entry to record the acquisition on the books of the Geneva Company.

b. Assume instead that the Geneva company is willing to pay for the Odessa Company an amount such that its return on investment will be 10 percent per year. Geneva estimates that the earnings (net cash inflow) of Odessa will be $50,000 for the first five years following the acquisition and $40,000 for an indefinite period thereafter.

   (1) How much would the Geneva Company be willing to invest to receive a net cash inflow of $40,000 per year for an infinite number of years?

   (2) How much would it be willing to invest in order to receive a net cash inflow of $10,000 (the "bonus" earnings) for a period of five years?

   (3) How much would it be willing to pay for the Odessa Company?

19. *Rental charges can be established so that lease arrangements are, in economic substance, equivalent to sales.*

At the request of several of its customers, a heavy equipment manufacturer has decided to give them the option of leasing or buying its products. The company expects a rate of return of 12 percent on all investments. The useful life of its equipment is eight years. Each lessee (that is, customer) will pay all operating costs including taxes, insurance, and maintenance.

a. The company establishes an annual rental charge of $12,000. What would be the sale price that would leave the company equally well off as if it had leased the equipment for the entire useful life of the equipment?

b. The company establishes a price for the equipment of $75,000. What annual rental charge would leave the company as well off as if it had sold the equipment?

20. *Businesses, as well as individuals, should at least once a month compare the cash balance per a bank statement with that per their own records, account for all differences, and adjust their books as required. The next two problems are exercises in preparing bank reconciliations.*

On December 31, 1993, the general ledger of the Lincoln Company indicated that the cash balance in the firm's checking account at the First National Bank was $108,753. A statement received from the bank, however, indicated that the balance in the account was $145,974. Investigation revealed the following:

(1) The company had drawn checks totaling $53,186 that had not been paid by the bank.

(2) The company made a deposit on the evening of December 31 of $26,102. This deposit was included by the bank in its business of January 2, 1994.

(3) On December 10, the company had deposited a check given to it by a customer for $103. On December 31, the bank returned the check to the company marked "N.S.F." (not sufficient funds in customer's account). The company had given no accounting recognition to the return of the check.

(4) The bank debited the account of the company for a monthly service charge of $10. The company had not yet recorded the charge.

(5) On December 31, the bank collected a customer note of $10,250 for the company. The company did not receive notification of the collection until January 4.

a. Prepare a schedule that reconciles the balance per the general ledger with that per the bank statement and indicates the balance that should be shown in the general ledger.

b. Prepare a journal entry to bring the general ledger up to date.

21. The general ledger of the McGuire Corp. indicated cash in bank of $3,822.81 as of December 31. A statement from the bank, as of the same date, indicated cash in bank of $5,666.00.

As of December 31, the company has outstanding checks of $1,800.00. On December 29, it mailed a deposit of $465.81 to the bank. As of year end, it had not yet been received. On December 31, the bank collected for the company a note from a customer. As of year end, the bank had not yet notified the company. The amount of the note was $500.

On December 18, the company made a deposit in the amount of $423.50. The bank recorded it as $432.50.

a. Prepare a schedule in which you account for the difference between the balance per the company books and that per the bank statement and determine the amount of cash in bank that should be reported in the firm's end-of-year financial statements.

b. Prepare a journal entry to adjust the present balance.

22. *This problem describes a common banking arrangement, whereby a borrower is required to maintain a* compensating balance *with a lending institution. It suggests an accounting issue associated with the arrangement.*

Indicated as follows are year-end balances from selected general ledger accounts of the Jefferson Co.:

Cash, First State Bank	$ 50,000
Note payable, First State Bank	500,000
Interest (expense)	70,000

The interest represents borrowing charges for one year on the note payable to First State Bank. Per terms of the loan agreement, the company will maintain in a special interest-free account an amount equal to 10 percent of any loans outstanding to the First State Bank.

The controller of the Jefferson Co. has proposed to include the following comment among the footnotes to its published financial statements: "As of December

31, 1993, the company was indebted to First State Bank for $500,000. The note to the bank matures in 1995. The company pays interest at the prime rate of 14 percent per year.''

The controller indicated that she intends to classify the cash in the special interest-free account with First State Bank as a current asset.

a. Inasmuch as the note payable with which the special interest-free account is associated will be classified as a noncurrent liability, do you think that the compensating cash balance should be classified as a current asset?

b. How much money did the company really borrow from the bank; how much did it have available for use?

c. How much interest did it pay each year? What was the effective interest rate paid?

23. *The lower of cost or market rule can be applied on two different bases, each having a different effect on both assets and earnings.*

The following table indicates the marketable securities (all common stocks) owned by the Colorado Co. on December 31, 1993. All securities were purchased within the previous 12 months. Also shown are the original purchase prices and the current market rates.

Securities	Number of Shares	Purchase Price	Current Market Price
Caesar's World	100	35 ¼	40
Fairchild	200	14 ½	10
Circle K	100	6	16
General Home	50	5 ½	2
Capitol Cities	20	250	240

a. Prepare a schedule indicating the lower of cost or market value of each security.

b. Prepare a journal entry to apply the lower of cost or market rule.

   (1) Assume that the rule is to be applied on an individual security basis.

   (2) Assume that the rule is to be applied on a portfolio basis (as recommended by the FASB).

c. Which basis is likely to be more conservative in that it results in lower asset values? Which minimizes the inconsistency of recognizing decreases in market values but not increases?

24. *Do earnings as computed in accord with established conventions always provide the best measure of economic performance?*

At the start of 1993, a corporation had in its portfolio of marketable securities 100 shares of each of stocks A, B, and C. Acquisition cost per share and unit market prices as of the end of 1993 and 1994 were as follows:

| | Acquisition Cost | Market Price | |
		12/31/94	12/31/93
Security A	$100	$80	$150
Security B	50	70	80
Security C	60	63	90

During 1993 the company engaged in no securities transactions. During 1994 it sold 100 shares of security C for $65 per share.

---

a. Determine reported earnings related to securities for 1993 and 1994. Be sure to take into account the lower of cost or market rule applied on a portfolio basis.

b. Do you think that reported earnings is an appropriate measure of economic performance? Why?

25. *The lower of cost or market rule affects both the income statement and the balance sheet.*

Security	Date Acquired	Cost	Market Value 12/31/94	Market Value 12/31/93	Sales Date	Sales Price
A	1/23/93	$140,000	$120,000	$130,000		
B	3/11/93	50,000	40,000	55,000		
C	9/16/93	40,000	—	—	11/5/93	$30,000
D	9/25/93	80,000	60,000	70,000		
E	1/5/94	110,000	170,000	—		

a. Prepare a schedule in which you show, as of December 31, 1993 and 1994, the cost, market value, and lower of cost or market value of each security on hand.

b. Prepare journal entries to reflect all events and transactions that would have affected the securities portfolio during 1993 and 1994. Value securities using the principles required by the FASB. For convenience, combine all 1993 purchases into a single entry.

c. Show how information pertaining to marketable securities would be presented on the balance sheets and income statements for both 1993 and 1994.

d. Repeat part (c), assuming instead that the lower of cost or market rule was to be applied on the basis of individual securities rather than the entire portfolio.

e. Which basis, the portfolio or individual securities, is the more conservative? What results in greater income from the time the first security is purchased to that when the last security is sold?

26. *Measures of performance based on amounts reported in the income statement may be misleading.*

On January 1, the Grey Corporation acquired 100 shares of common stock of company A and 100 shares of company B. Price per share of both securities was $200.

During the year companies A and B declared dividends of $16 and $12 per share, respectively. As of December 31, the market price of the stock of company A was $210 per share; that of company B was $230 per share.

a. Determine return on investment of each security based on the dollar amounts that would be reported on the firm's balance sheet and income statement.

b. Determine return on investment taking into account any "unrealized" gains or losses. Use *average* market value as the denominator.

c. Which security do you think was the better investment? Which basis for calculating return on investment do you think provides the better measure of economic performance? Why do you suppose that the market values of marketable securities must be disclosed in financial reports?

27. *Reported earnings may be a poor reflection of "economic" earnings.*

A company has divided its portfolio of marketable securities into two sections. In one, the market value exceeds the cost; in the other, the cost exceeds the market value. Data pertaining to the two sections for a period of three years are presented in the following schedule:

	December 31		
	1995	1994	1993
Market exceeds cost			
Cost	$ 8,000	$ 8,000	$10,000
Market	8,000	17,000	12,000
Cost exceeds market			
Cost	$10,000	$10,000	$10,000
Market	9,000	8,000	6,000

The securities that were eliminated from the portfolio during 1994 were sold for $1,000, an amount equal to their market value as of year end 1993.

a. Prepare all journal entries relating to marketable securities for 1994 and 1995 that would be required to apply generally accepted accounting principles.

b. Prepare comparative income statements for 1994 and 1995 and comparative balance sheets (assets only) for 1993, 1994, and 1995. Assume that the firm had no assets other than the marketable securities and the cash received upon the sale of the securities in 1994. Assume also that the firm received no dividends from the securities.

c. Repeat part (b), assuming that all securities were to be stated at market value and that all changes in market values were to be incorporated into income.

d. Compare the statements and comment upon the differences.

28. *Underlying transactions in marketable securities may be deduced from balance sheet and supplementary information.*

The balance sheet of the Clark Corporation indicated the following (in thousands):

	December 31	
	1994	1993
Marketable securities at cost	$280	$300
Less: Allowance for excess of cost over market value	10	60
Marketable securities, net	$270	$240

During 1994 the company sold for $70,000 marketable securities that had a market value at December 31, 1993, of $60,000. The company reported a realized loss of $30,000 on the transaction.

a. Reconstruct all entries relating to marketable securities that the company would have made during 1994.

b. Compute the amount of unrealized gain or loss during 1994 on the securities that were not sold during the year.

Solutions to Exercise for Review and Self-Testing

1. a. $100,000 × 1.08 = $108,000.
   b. $108,000 × 1.08 = $116,640.
   c. $116,640 × 1.08 = $125,971.
   Verify your answers by referring to Table 1 in the Appendix, "Future Value of $1."
2. a. $100,000.
   b. $100,000 + ($100,000 × 1.08) = $208,000.
   c. $100,000 + ($208,000 × 1.08) = $324,640.

Verify your answers by referring to Table 3 in the Appendix, "Future Value of an Annuity of $1 in Arrears."

3. a. $100,000 ÷ 1.08 = $92,593.
   b. $ 92,593 ÷ 1.08 = $85,734.
   c. $ 85,734 ÷ 1.08 = $79,383.

Verify your answers by referring to Table 2 in the Appendix, "Present Value of $1."

4. It should deposit the sum of the amounts determined in Exercise 3:

$$\$92,593 + \$85,734 + \$79,383 = \$257,710.$$

Verify your answer by referring to Table 4 in the Appendix, "Present Value of an Annuity of $1 in Arrears."

Receivables
and Payables

This chapter is directed to accounts and notes receivable and payable. It also includes a brief section on accounting for payroll transactions. The primary focus of the chapter is on issues of measurement—those relating to the amounts at which receivables and payables as well as the related revenues and expenses should be reported on the financial statements.

Definitions

Receivables

Receivables represent claims arising from sale of goods, performance of services, lending of funds, or some other type of transaction which establishes a relationship whereby one party is indebted to another. Claims resulting from the sale of goods or services and not supported by a written note are categorized as *accounts receivable*. They are distinguished from amounts backed by written notes (which may or may not arise out of a sales transaction) called *notes* receivable and those arising out of myriad other day-to-day business activities, such as *deposits receivable* (e.g., amounts to be received upon return of containers), *amounts due from officers* (perhaps as a consequence of loans), *dividends receivable, rent receivable,* and *interest receivable.* Accounts receivable often do not require payment of interest; notes receivable almost always do.

Payables

Payables represent the corresponding obligations on the part of the recipient of the goods or services. Many of the issues pertaining to the valuation of payables are mirror images of those relating to receivables. The discussion in this chapter will center largely around receivables, with the expectation that, as appropriate, the reader can generalize to payables.

Current and Noncurrent Receivables and Payables

Receivables and payables that mature within one year (or sometimes one operating cycle of the business if it is greater than one year) are classified as *current* assets or liabilities. Those that mature in a longer period are classified as *noncurrent*.

Significance

Receivables are important to managers and investors for a number of reasons. First, receivables are assets, and financial reports must reflect their value. Second, issues relating to receivables are fundamental to those of income determination and thus performance measurement. Receivables, particularly accounts receivable, often arise out of sales or other revenue-generating transactions. They may be written off as "bad debts." The question of when to recognize increases or decreases in receivables may be viewed alternatively as when to recognize revenues or expenses.

Third, accounts receivable may be unproductive or underproductive assets. They may provide either no return or a return less than could be earned on other types of assets. It is generally to the advantage of a firm to collect its non- or low-interest-bearing accounts as soon as possible and to minimize the resources "tied up" in such accounts.

Correspondingly, the concern of investors and managers with *payables* is that the obligations are fairly presented, that the expenses with which they are associated are recorded in an appropriate accounting period, that payment is made when the liability is due, and that the firm avails itself of all discounts for prompt payment.

AN OVERVIEW

Receivables, like other assets, are reported on the balance sheet in accordance with generally accepted accounting conventions. The resultant values may not necessarily be the same as their face values, their "economic" values, or their market values.

Face versus Economic Values

The *face,* or *stated, value* of a receivable is that which is indicated in the underlying promissory note, sales agreement, or comparable document. The *economic value* (value to user) is the *present value* of the cash that it will provide. It is the cash that the company will receive, discounted to take into account the time value of money. The *market value,* by contrast, is the amount for which the receivable can be sold. Many types of receivables are negotiable; they may be sold or transferred. Companies that prefer not to wait until their receivables mature can exchange them for cash with banks or similar financial institutions.

In general, accepted accounting principles require receivables to be recorded initially at amounts that reflect their economic values. Both the economic values of receivables and the amounts at which they are first recorded may differ from their face values for two reasons. First, not all receivables will be collectible. The face values of receivables must therefore be reduced by an estimate of the amounts that will be uncollectible. One of the major causes of corporate bankruptcy is the failure to transform outstanding receivables into cash. Not surprisingly, a considerable number of legal actions against CPA firms have resulted from alleged overstatements of receivables.

Second, the face value of a receivable may include an element of interest. Face value may indicate the actual amount of cash to be received rather than the present value of such cash. For example, a promise of $100 plus 10 percent interest in one year may sometimes be reflected in a note with a face value of $110. The present value would be the cash to be received less the interest, in this case only the $100. The amount of the interest may be set forth explicitly in the document supporting the receivable, or it may have to be imputed from the circumstances surrounding the transaction from which the receivable arose. As was indicated in previous chapters, interest receivable is not given accounting recognition until it is actually earned. Hence, to arrive at the amount at which a receivable should be recorded initially, the face value must be discounted to eliminate unearned interest. The means by which face values can be reduced to allow for both bad debts and unearned interest are described in sections of this chapter that follow.

Financial accounting is based on historical costs. Therefore, once receivables have been recorded, their values are adjusted only to take into account payments on outstanding balances, interest earned, and (if required) changes in the estimate of the portion that will be uncollectible. They are not adjusted to reflect changes in prevailing rates of interest. Increases in prevailing rates above those incorporated into particular receivables will reduce both the economic value and the market value of those receivables. They will be less desirable both to the firm itself and to other parties to whom they could be sold because they will be providing a return to their holder less than could be obtained from alternative investments.

Basic Journal Entries

The basic journal entries to establish and to relieve a receivable account are straightforward. Upon the sale of goods and services for $100, for example, the appropriate journal entry would be

Accounts receivable $100
    Sales revenue $100
To record the sale of goods and services

And upon subsequent receipt of customer payment,

Cash $100
    Accounts receivable $100
To record the collection of cash

Variations in the terms of sales and the nature of the transactions resulting in the creation of the receivable necessitate considerable modification in the basic entries to accommodate specific circumstances.

UNCOLLECTIBLE ACCOUNTS RECEIVABLE

There are two ways of accounting for uncollectible accounts receivable. The first, and generally *unacceptable,* is the *direct write-off* method. It is described here mainly as a basis for comparison with the second, the *allowance* method.

Deficiencies of the Direct Write-Off Method

Per the direct write-off method, when it becomes obvious that an account receivable is uncollectible, it is *written off,* and a *bad-debt expense* is charged. For example, upon learning that a customer from whom it held a receivable of $100 is likely to default on its obligation, a company might give accounting recognition to its loss with the following journal entry:

Bad-debt expense $100
        Accounts receivable $100
To write off an uncollectible account

Concurrently, the firm would also credit the account of the individual customer in the accounts receivable subsidiary ledger. The accounts receivable subsidiary ledger is nothing more than a book or file of the amount owed by each customer. Each element of the file is maintained as a "mini" general ledger account for a specific customer, with debits indicating additional debts incurred by the customer and credits signifying payments made by the customer. The sum of the balances due from all customers should, at all times, be equal to the balance in the accounts receivable ledger account (often called the accounts receivable *control* account). If it is not, an error has been made. In other words, the accounts receivable ledger provides the support—or the detail—for the general ledger account.

The direct write-off method, however, is inconsistent with the matching concepts discussed in Chapter 5. For the reasons suggested below, it may lead to misstatements of *both* income and accounts receivable in the period of sale as well as in subsequent periods.

Rationale for the Allowance Method

The *allowance* method overcomes these deficiencies.

Consider, for example, a company in the retail furniture industry. To attract business, the company grants credit to relatively poor credit risks. The policy results in extensive losses on uncollectible accounts, but the increase in sales which it generates more than offsets the losses. Based on several years' experience, management estimates that for every dollar of credit sales 10 cents will be uncollectible. The company vigorously pursues its delinquent debtors and writes off accounts only after it has made every reasonable attempt at recovery. Few accounts are written off before at least a year has elapsed since a customer has made a payment.

Under the circumstances, it would be inappropriate for the company to include among its assets the entire balance of accounts receivable. After all, only a portion of the balance is likely to be collectible. Similarly, and equally significantly, if in 1993 the company had $5 million in credit sales, it would not be justified in reporting revenues of $5 million when only $4.5 million (90 percent of $5 million) would, in all probability, be fully realized. The individual accounts related to the sales in 1993 would not be written off for at least one or two years subsequent to 1993. But these losses would be the result of decisions—the decisions to sell to customers who prove to be unworthy of credit—made in 1993. The losses would relate directly to sales made in 1993; they should be matched therefore with revenues of 1993.

There are, however, two obstacles to assigning credit losses to the year in which the sales takes place. First, the amount of the loss cannot be known with certainty until several years subsequent to the sales. Normally, however, it can be estimated with reasonable accuracy. Based on the past collection experience of the company—or on that of other firms in similar industries—it is possible to predict the approximate amount of receivables that will be uncollectible. The inability to make precise estimates of the anticipated losses can hardly be a justification for making no estimate at all. For even the roughest of estimates is likely to be more accurate than no estimate—the equivalent of a prediction of zero credit losses.

Second, even though a firm may be able to predict with reasonable precision the overall percentage of bad debts, it certainly is unable to forecast the *specific* accounts that will be uncollectible. After all, if it knew in advance that a particular customer would be unable to pay his or her debts, it would never have made the sale in the first place. If a company were to recognize bad debts as expenses and correspondingly reduce its accounts receivable balance, then which subsidiary ledger accounts would it credit? Since the sum of the balances of the subsidiary ledger accounts must equal the balance in the accounts receivable control account (i.e., the general ledger balance), the firm cannot reduce the balance in the control account without, at the same time, reducing the balances in the accounts of specific customers.

A firm can circumvent this second obstacle by establishing a *contra account*, "accounts receivable, allowance for uncollectibles." The contra account will normally have a credit balance (the opposite of the accounts receivable balance) and will always be associated with, and reported directly beneath, its *parent* account, accounts or notes receivable. Instead of reducing or crediting accounts receivable directly, the firm will credit "accounts receivable, allowance for uncollectibles."

Example

To illustrate the procedure, continue the assumption that a firm in 1993 made $5 million in credit sales. At year end the firm estimates that 10 percent ($500,000) of the credit sales will be uncollectible. The following adjusting entry would give accounting recognition to its estimate:

(a)

Sales, uncollectibles (or bad-debt expense)[1] $500,000
    Accounts receivable, allowance for uncollectibles.................$500,000
To establish an allowance for uncollectibles

The relevant T accounts would appear as follows:

Accounts receivable		Accounts receivable, allowance for uncollectibles		
5,000,000			**(a)**	500,000

	Sales, uncollectibles	
(a)	500,000	

On the balance sheet, accounts receivable (assuming none of the $5 million has yet been collected) and its related contra account would be reported as

Accounts receivable..........................$5,000,000
    Less: Allowance for uncollectibles......... 500,000 4,500,000

As soon as the company is aware that a specific account cannot be collected, it is then able to credit the accounts receivable control account as well as the specific accounts receivable subsidiary ledger account. Since the allowance for uncollectibles was established to accommodate future bad debts, it would now be debited.

Assume that in 1994 accounts totaling $70,000 are determined to be uncollectible. The appropriate entry would be

(b)

Accounts receivable, allowance for uncollectibles..................$70,000
    Accounts receivable $70,000
To write off specific accounts

At the same time, the specific accounts to be written off would be credited in the accounts receivable subsidiary ledger. It is noteworthy that at the time specific accounts are written off *no entry is made to "sales, uncollectibles." The effect of the uncollectible accounts on income would already have been recognized in the year the sales were made.* Hence no further entries to revenue or expense accounts are justified. Moreover, the entry to write off the specific accounts has no effect on current assets or working capital. The *net* accounts receivable (accounts receivable less allowance for uncollectibles) remains unchanged by the entry because both the parent account and the related contra account have been reduced by identical amounts. Thus

---

[1]Many, perhaps even most, companies debit "bad-debt expense" and report the amount among the other expenses. Other firms debit "sales, uncollectibles" and show the account as a reduction of revenues. The authors prefer the latter approach. The firm has not incurred an expense. Instead, anticipated revenue has been lost; the firm will realize less than the full amount for which it billed customers.

	Before Write-off	After Write-off
Accounts receivable	$5,000,000	$4,930,000
Less: Allowance for uncollectibles	500,000	430,000
Net receivables	$4,500,000	$4,500,000

If the company wishes to restore a receivable after it has been written off, only the receivable account and the allowance account need be adjusted. The company can simply reverse the entry that was made to write off the account. Suppose that a customer whose receivable of $10,000 has been written off signifies a willingness and ability to make good on his account. The following entry would be in order:

Accounts receivable $10,000
    Accounts receivable, allowance for uncollectibles $10,000
To restore an account previously written off

The customer's account in the subsidiary ledger would, of course, also be restored.

VERIFYING THE ADEQUACY OF THE ALLOWANCE FOR UNCOLLECTIBLES

The virtue of calculating the annual addition to the allowance account as a percentage of revenues is that the corresponding charge to earnings is a direct function of, and match to, revenues. If, however, the net receivables reported on the balance sheet are to be indicative of actual amounts to be collected, then the allowance must be periodically assessed. If anticipated uncollectibles will be greater than the allowance, then the allowance must be increased. If they will be less, then it can be reduced.

One means of testing the adequacy of the allowance is by use of an *aging schedule,* which indicates what its name implies—the "age" of each account receivable. That is, it reveals the status of the various accounts—are they current, up to 30 days past due, up to 60 days past due? An aging schedule is illustrated in Exhibit 7-1.

EXHIBIT 7-1
Aging Schedule as of 12/31/93

Customer Name	Total Balance	Current	No. of Days Past Due 0–30	31–60	61–90	Over 90
J. Faulkner	$ 634,780	$ 634,780				
F. Fitzgerald	602,500	261,390	$ 290,000	$ 51,110		
A. Hawthorne	82,220					$ 82,220
G. Brown	116,500				$116,500	
C. Ryder	928,110	292,060	339,300	260,000	36,750	
D. Deming	372,200		372,200			
G. Hawkins	1,101,000	1,101,000				
F. Cohen	1,162,690					1,162,690
	$5,000,000	$2,289,230	$1,001,500	$311,110	$153,250	$1,244,910

Based on the aging schedule, the firm estimates the dollar amount of accounts that will be uncollectible. This amount is indicative of the *total* balance required in the allowance for uncollectibles account.

As a rule, the longer an account is outstanding, the longer a debtor goes without paying, the less likely it is that the account will be collectible. Thus a considerably greater proportion of accounts that are 120 days past due than those that are current will in all probability be uncollectible. A larger percentage of the balance of accounts 120 days past due must be added to the allowance for uncollectibles than for accounts that are current. The following summary based on the aging schedule in Exhibit 7-1 reveals the total balance required in the allowance for bad debts:

Summary of Accounts Receivable as of 12/31/93			
Number of Days Past Due	Amount	Percent Likely to Be Uncollectible	Required Provision
0 (current)	$2,289,230	2	$ 45,785
1–30	1,001,500	8	80,120
31–60	311,110	12	37,333
61–90	153,250	20	30,650
Over 90	1,244,910	50	622,455
	$5,000,000		$816,343

The total required provision less the balance that is currently in the account is the amount that must be added to the account. Suppose, for example, that the balance in the allowance for bad debts as of December 31 is $500,000. The amount that must be added is $316,343 ($816,343 less $500,000).

The key distinction between the percentage of sales and the aging schedule methods is that under the percentage of sales method the annual addition is determined by multiplying credit sales by a preestablished percentage. The amount of the addition is thereby computed independently of the existing balance in the allowance for uncollectibles account. Under the aging schedule method, the annual addition is determined by first estimating the *required* balance in the allowance for uncollectibles account (as revealed by the aging schedule) and then subtracting from the required balance the actual balance in the account.

Over the life of an enterprise (as illustrated in problem 3 at the end of the chapter), the two methods would result in the same charge to income—the actual accounts that are written off. The charges from year to year, however, would be the same only if sales, collections, and write-offs remained constant.

CORRECTING MISESTIMATES

If the aging schedule indicates that allowance for uncollectibles becomes too high or low, then income of the past also has been misstated; the charges to "sales, uncollectibles" have been too high or too low. The only conceptually pure way to correct the errors is to restate the financial statements of the years in which the charges were made. The accounting profession, however, frowns upon prior-period adjustments, except in a very limited number of circumstances. It fears that continual revisions of previously reported amounts would undermine user confidence in financial statements. Moreover, it believes that the impact of a correction would be diminished if made only to the statements of previous periods, those to which investors pay little attention compared with current-period reports. A statement of the Accounting Principles Board, ''Accounting Changes,'' requires that adjustments to the allowance account be made only in a current period, not retroactively.[2] To get the allowance account back in line, a greater or smaller amount than would otherwise be dictated by the current sales volume should be added to the account in the year the out-of-line condition becomes known. Correspondingly, a greater or smaller charge should be made to ''sales, uncollectibles.''

If, as in the illustration in the previous section, the aging schedule indicated that the allowance was $316,343 too low, the following entry should be made:

Sales, uncollectibles $316,343
    Accounts receivable, allowance for uncollectibles $316,343
To correct underestimates of bad debts of prior years

This practice has the undesirable effect of correcting prior-period errors by distorting earnings of the year of change. But it serves the positive cause of providing an up-to-date balance sheet without the confusion and complexity that would result from frequent changes in previously issued statements.

Industry Example: Savings and Loans

The experiences of savings and loan institutions (''thrifts'') in the 1980s illustrate the need for a healthy skepticism toward allowances for uncollectibles. Obviously, receivables are more significant for lending institutions than for firms in other industries because receivables constitute their primary assets. But the caveats are no less applicable to all firms.

In the 1970s and 1980s the thrifts lent heavily to the real estate industry. Many of them, particularly those in Texas, directed their funds to ventures that provided high rates of return but were exceedingly risky. Default rates were initially low and, correspondingly, the thrifts established small allowances for bad debts. Moreover, the thrifts were confident that their loans were adequately secured since the properties held as collateral were appraised at values that far exceeded the loan balances.

In the mid 1980s, however, the real estate economy spiraled downward, propelled by falling oil prices. The default experiences of the past were rendered irrelevant by the new economic realities. As real estate prices plummeted, borrower defaults forced the thrifts to foreclose on the properties held as security. But market values were now far less than the loan balances, resulting in massive losses to the industry and scores of bank failures. *The New York Times* labeled the debacle ''the biggest financial disaster of the post-war era.''[3]

Why hadn't the savings and loans adequately reserved against the loan losses even as they became foreseeable? One explanation is that federal and state regulations mandated that savings and loans maintain minimum asset-to-capital ratios. Were the institutions to slip below those minimums, the regulators would

---

[2]''Accounting Changes,'' *Accounting Principles Board Opinion No. 20,* 1971.
[3]''Who to Thank for the Thrift Crises,'' *The New York Times,* Sunday, June 12, 1988, Section 3, page 1.

---

have been forced to shut them down. Like a captain striving to save a sinking ship by disconnecting the alarm bells, the regulators tried to keep the troubled thrifts afloat by permitting them to understate their losses and overstate their assets. Their policies did nothing, of course, to enhance the collectibility of the loans. They did, however, enable the thrifts to unobtrusively circumvent the government guidelines.

The savings and loan fiasco teaches accountants and financial analysts at least two important lessons. First, in evaluating the adequacy of an allowance for uncollectibles, it is risky to rely solely on historical rates of default; the allowance must be sufficient to cover losses of the future, not the past.

Second, the inherent worth of receivables may differ from the balance in either the receivables account or the related allowance for uncollectibles account. Bookkeeping adjustments do nothing to affect the collectibility of the loans. Nevertheless, the *reported* balances of receivables (or any other account, for that matter) can have substantive economic consequences. In the case of the thrifts, the excessive values attached to the net receivables permitted the thrifts to meet the regulatory guidelines and thereby remain legally, if not financially, solvent.

SALES RETURNS

Sales returns are accounted for in much the same way as bad debts. If goods that have been sold are expected to be returned in a subsequent accounting period, the anticipated returns must be recognized in the same period as the sales. Financial statements that fail to take into account goods to be subsequently returned and refunds to be given to customers would clearly overstate revenues and hence earnings. But as with allowances for bad debts, the necessary accounting entries must reflect the uncertainty, until the returns are actually made, of both the amount of the returns and the specific customers who will make them. Thus, as with bad debts, firms must establish an allowance for returns based on an estimate.

Example

Assume that at year end a firm estimates that merchandise that was sold for $1 million will be returned in the following year. An appropriate journal entry would be

(a)

Sales, returns $1,000,000
    Accounts receivable, allowance for returns $1,000,000
To record the estimate of sales returns

Both of the accounts are *contra accounts*. "Sales, returns" would be reported on the income statement as a reduction of sales. "Accounts receivable, allowance for returns" would be reported on the balance sheet as an additional reduction of accounts receivable along with the allowance for uncollectibles.

If the merchandise to be returned can be resold, then it is necessary to recognize that cost of goods sold, in addition to sales revenue, has been overstated in the year of sale. Assume that the merchandise to be returned had an original cost of $800,000. The required entry to record the anticipated returns would be

(b)

```
Merchandise to be returned (asset) ...........................$800,000
    Cost of goods sold (expense)................................$800,000
    To record the cost of goods to be returned
```

When the merchandise is actually returned, only balance sheet accounts need to be adjusted; the impact on revenues and expenses would have been accounted for in the year of sale:

(c)

```
Accounts receivable, allowance for returns (asset; contra)........$1,000,000
    Accounts receivable (asset)................................$1,000,000
    To give the customer credit for merchandise returned
```

(d)

```
Merchandise inventory (asset) ...............................$800,000
    Merchandise to be returned (asset) ..........................$800,000
    To record the receipt of returned merchandise
```

If the merchandise returned cannot be resold and has no value, then entries **(b)** and **(d)** need not be made.

The entries as illustrated in the example above are appropriate when a firm expects that returns will be relatively small in relation to sales and it is able to estimate the volume of returns. As indicated in Chapter 5 in the section pertaining to the installment basis of accounting, when a company grants uncommonly liberal rights of return and cannot make reasonable estimates of the amount of returns, then it should delay recognition of revenue until the rights of return expire. In such a situation, there would be no need to record estimates of returns; the sales themselves would not be recognized until it was certain that there would be no further returns.

Industry Example: Sales with Rights of Return

Policies on sales returns form a continuum. At one end are those in which the seller grants no right of return; the sale is final, the merchandise is sold "as is," and the seller provides no warranties as to its condition. At the other end are those in which unlimited rights of return are permitted. Under a *consignment* arrangement, for example, the buyer accepts merchandise which it intends to resell. The buyers are obligated to pay for the goods only if they are able to resell them. Until resale, title remains with the seller, who bears virtually all risks of ownership (e.g., theft, damage, and loss of market value), and the buyer has an unconditional right of return.

When a seller grants no right of return, it is clear that revenue can be recognized upon sale (assuming, of course, that the other criteria of revenue recognition are met). When a seller "sells" on consignment, it is equally obvious that recognition of revenue must be delayed until the buyer has resold the merchandise and no longer has an unrestricted right of return. As with many accounting controversies, it is the "in-between" transactions that challenge the profession's standard setters.

A simple example can be used to illustrate the issue. Clones, Inc., a manufacturer of personal computers, sells its machines to independent computer retailers. The retailers are required to pay for the merchandise within 30 days of receipt. To encourage retailers to stock and display its products, Clones, Inc., grants a one-year unconditional right of return on unsold (and undamaged) goods. Company experience indicates that approximately 10 percent of goods shipped are returned.

Should the company recognize revenue from sales when it ships its computers to the retailers or should it delay recognition until rights of return have expired?

On the one hand, the main criteria for revenue recognition (substantial portions of production and sales effort have been exerted, revenues can be objectively measured, and collection of cash is reasonably assured) appear to be met when the company ships the goods to the retailers. That would suggest recording the sale at the time the goods are shipped.

On the other hand, a critical event in the earnings process is the sale by the retailer to the ultimate consumer. Until that sale is made (or the one-year return period expires), the company is obligated to accept for refund all unsold goods. The company, not the retailer, bears the risks of the marketplace. That would suggest that revenue recognition be delayed until the goods have been resold or the return period has expired.

Prior to 1981, there were no specific accounting guidelines as to when, in such circumstances, revenue should be recognized. Some firms took advantage of this gap in standards to artificially inflate reported earnings. They would ship merchandise at the end of one year, fully expecting that it would be returned early in the next. They recorded the shipments as sales of the first year and failed to establish an adequate allowance for returns.

Now, per a 1981 FASB pronouncement, when rights of return exist, revenue can be recognized only when the return privilege has expired *or* all of the following conditions are met:

1. The sales price has been fixed.
2. The buyer has paid the seller, or its obligation to pay the seller is not contingent upon resale of the product.
3. The buyer would have to pay for the goods even if they are stolen or damaged.
4. The amount of future returns can be reasonably estimated.[4]

Applied to the facts as presented, the guidelines indicate that revenue should be recognized at time of shipment and need not be delayed. To be sure, the conditions for revenue recognition are not as rigorous as some accountants would prefer. Nevertheless, the guidelines have made reporting more uniform and eliminated the more abusive practices of premature revenue recognition.

[4]"Revenue Recognition When Right of Return Exists," Financial Accounting Board *Statement of Financial Accounting Standards No. 48,* 1981.

It is common business practice for companies to offer discounts for prompt payment. For example, a firm may sell under terms such as "2/10, n/30." That is, the total amount is due within 30 days; however, if the customer pays within 10 days, he receives a discount of 2 percent. In economic substance it is difficult to interpret the discount as a true price reduction. A more acceptable explanation is that the customer is penalized for not paying on time.

Suppose that a customer buys merchandise with a *stated* price of $100 on terms 2/10, n/30. A customer who pays on the thirtieth day following purchase rather than on the tenth day will retain cash for an additional 20 days. Losing the 2 percent discount, the customer pays $100 instead of $98, thereby incurring a cost of $2 to use $98 for 20 days—an effective annual interest rate of 37 percent (365 days/20 days × $2/$98 = .37) Only a company with a severely impaired credit rating would be willing to pay such an extraordinarily high rate. An unbiased observer might suspect therefore that the merchandise had a fair market value not of the stated sales price of $100 but rather of $98, the stated sales price less the discount of $2.

The proper accounting for cash discounts is *not* one of the critical issues facing the accounting profession. It is of interest primarily because it is another example of the importance of distinguishing substance over form.

Net Method and Gross Method

Both purchasers and sellers account for cash discounts in either of two basic ways: the net method or the gross method. The *net* method is theoretically preferable. It requires that both purchases and sales be recorded at the fair market value of the goods traded—that is, sales price *less* the discount—and that payments in excess of the discounted price be recorded separately as a penalty for late payment or as a financing cost.

The *gross* method, by contrast, permits purchases and sales to be recorded at the stated price rather than the fair market value. It thereby inflates both purchases and sales. Purchase discounts taken are credited to an account "purchase discounts."

Example

A company purchases merchandise that has a sale price of $100,000 on terms 2/10, n/30:

Net Method	Gross Method
Inventory $98,000	Inventory $100,000
Accounts payable........$98,000	Accounts payable.......$100,000
To record the purchase of merchandise	

It pays within the discount period:

Net Method	Gross Method
Accounts payable $98,000	Accounts payable $100,000
Cash $98,000	Cash $98,000
	Purchase discounts 2,000
To record the purchase of merchandise	

Or, alternatively, it fails to pay within the discount period:

Net Method	Gross Method
Accounts payable $98,000	Accounts payable $100,000
Purchase discounts	Cash $100,000
lost (expense) 2,000	
Cash $100,000	
To record payment after the discount period	

The gross method overstates inventory because goods acquired are recorded at gross purchase price, which exceeds the fair market value by the amount of the discount. As a consequence, upon sale of the goods, cost of goods sold is also overstated. The gross method can be justified as a bookkeeping convenience, but only if at year end the overstatements in inventory and cost of goods sold are eliminated. The required entries would have the effect of converting the gross method to the net method.[5]

Additional Advantage of the Net Method

The net method, but not the gross method, contributes to management control. The net method results in a charge to the expense account, "purchase discounts lost," whenever the firm fails to avail itself of the discounts. Management is thereby explicitly made aware of the cost of its negligence in, or policy of, not paying on time. The gross method, by contrast, "buries" the penalty charge in inventory, and it is eventually reflected in cost of goods sold.

The entries recording the sales and subsequent collection from the standpoint of the seller would correspond to those of the purchaser. The gross method would result in the overstatement of both sales and accounts receivable.

PROMISSORY NOTES

When a firm extends credit beyond a short period (two or three months) or makes a loan, it usually requests formal written documentation of the borrower's obligation to make timely payment. The legal instrument that provides such documentation is known as a *promissory note*. A typical promissory note is illustrated in Exhibit 7-2.

A promissory note, unlike an account receivable, generally requires that the maker (the borrower) agree to pay a fee, known as *interest*, for the right to

---

[5]The adjustment would be a credit in the amount of the discount to "merchandise inventory" (or "cost of goods sold" to the extent that the merchandise has been resold) and a debit either to "purchase discounts" (if the discount were taken) or to "purchase discounts lost" (if the discount were lost).

EXHIBIT 7-2
Typical Promissory Note

NationsBank

NationsBank of Texas, N.A.

Note #   Acct #

Promissory Note
(Installment)

Name and Address of Lender *(Including County)*	Officer	Date
	Maturity Date	Amount of Note $

	Annual Rate of Interest (AR): *(Check and Complete one)*	☐ 1. Fixed Rate of %, or ☐ 2. Lender's Business Base Rate plus %, or ☐ 3. Lender's Prime Rate plus %, or ☐ 4. See Below.*	☐ Payments Include Interest *(X if applicable)* Payments will be the greater of the Amount of Each Payment or interest due.
(Lender)			

Amount of Each Payment	First Payment Date	Subsequent Payment Dates	AR Computed Using Days Per Year

Terms used in this Note shall have the meanings indicated herein and in the boxes above. On demand, or if prior demand is not made then on Maturity Date, unless payment is earlier required herein, Maker promises to pay to the order of Lender at Lender's address shown above the Amount of Note plus interest. Unpaid Amount of Note shall bear interest from Date to maturity at the AR over the elapsed term of Note provided that the amount of interest payable shall not exceed the maximum amount Lender lawfully may charge on this Note and at each Payment Date and at Maturity Date interest then payable shall be calculated from Date on the unpaid Amount of Note outstanding from time to time at the AR over the elapsed term of Note, provided that (1) any interest previously paid shall be deducted from the interest then payable, and (2) the total interest payable through such date shall not exceed the maximum amount of interest Lender lawfully may charge on this Note from Date to such date. If the AR is stated in terms of Lender's Business Base Rate, Lender's Prime Rate or such other variable Rate described under the * below, the AR shall change with each change in such named Rate as of the date of any such change without notice. "Lender's Business Base Rate" shall mean the Business Base Rate charged by Lender as announced or published by Lender from time to time. "Lender's Prime Rate" shall mean the Prime Interest Rate charged by Lender as announced or published by Lender from time to time. The two rates may not be related and either may not be the lowest interest rate charged by Lender. Unpaid and past due Amount of Note and interest shall bear interest at the highest rate Lender lawfully may charge on this Note. Interest paid or agreed to be paid shall not exceed the maximum amount permissible under applicable law and, in any contingency whatsoever, if Lender shall receive anything of value deemed interest under applicable law which would exceed the maximum amount of interest permissible under applicable law, the excessive interest shall be applied to the reduction of the unpaid Amount of Note or refunded to Maker.

Before Maturity Date , this Note shall be payable in instalments in the Amount of Each Payment beginning on the First Payment Date and continuing on the Subsequent Payment Dates thereafter until Maturity Date, when all unpaid Amount of Note and interest shall be due. Unless Payments Include Interest, interest in addition to the Amount of Each Payment shall be payable as it is due on the dates payments are due. If Payments Include Interest each payment shall be applied first to interest due and then to Amount of Note. The Amount of Note, or any part thereof, may be prepaid at any time without penalty. However, at Lender's option all voluntary prepayments shall be applied to future installments in inverse order of maturity.

Each Maker, guarantor, surety, and endorser waives demand, presentment, notice of dishonor, protest, notice of intent to accelerate, notice of acceleration and diligence in collecting sums due hereunder; agrees to application of any debt of Lender to payment hereof; agrees that extensions and renewals without limit as to number, acceptance of any number of partial payments, releases of any party liable hereon, and releases or substitution of collateral, before or after maturity, shall not release or discharge his obligation under this Note; and agrees to pay in addition to all sums due hereunder reasonable attorney's fees if this Note is placed in the hands of an attorney for collection or if it is collected through probate, bankruptcy, or other judicial proceeding, plus all court costs and other collection expenses incurred by Lender. Reasonable attorney's fees shall be ten percent (10%) of the unpaid balance unless either party shall plead and prove otherwise. As used herein, where appropriate, the masculine gender includes the feminine and neuter and the singular number includes the plural . All payments hereunder shall be made in lawful tender of the United States of America. This Note is executed in the county and state stated above.
*

_____

_____

_____
(Maker)

43 20534 (Rev. 1/92) TX-04 (4/88)

use the funds provided. The promissory note is a legally binding contract. It would specify the following:

- The parties involved in the contract—the payor, who is the person or organization that agrees to make the payment, and the payee, who is the person or organization to whom the money is owed. (Sometimes a note may be drawn to bearer—that is, payment is made to whomever presents the note to the maker.)
- The date the note was issued and the date payment is due. (Some notes state that payment is due in a specific number of days from the date it was issued.)
- The principal of the note (the amount of credit being extended), often referred to as the face value of the note.
- The rate of interest.
- Any collateral or property that the borrower either pledges or surrenders as security for the note.

Interest on a note is expressed as an annual percentage rate. The formula for translating the percentage rate into the actual dollar amount is[6]

$$\text{Interest} = \text{Principal} \times \text{Rate} \times \frac{\text{Days of loan}}{\text{Total days in one year}}$$

If, for example, a company issues a note for $100,000 that bears interest at a rate of 8 percent and is payable in 90 days, the actual interest that it will be required to pay can be computed as

$$\$100,000 \times .08 \times \frac{90}{360} = \$2,000$$

Notes are reported on the balance sheet at their principal, or face, amount. This convention confuses many students since the total obligation of the maker is not only the principal but the interest as well. In the foregoing illustration, for example, the total amount to be paid after 90 days is $100,000 plus $2,000 interest. Yet the note would be recorded on the balance sheet at only $100,000. The logic beyond the convention becomes apparent, however, when the impact of notes and interest on the balance sheet is viewed in conjunction with that on the income statement. Interest is a charge imposed on a borrower for the use of funds over a period of time. From the standpoint of the borrower, therefore, the interest cannot be considered an expense—and hence not a liability—until the borrower has actually used the funds over time. With the passage of time, the borrower will recognize the expense associated with the use of funds—interest expense—and correspondingly the liability—accrued interest payable. Similarly, the lender will periodically recognize the earnings attributable to the funds that it has provided the debtor and concurrently acknowledge the enhancement of an asset, interest receivable.

A brief example may clarify the relationship between income and balance sheet accounts.

---

[6]To facilitate computation, it is common in practice to use 360 days as "total days in one year." We will observe that practice in the examples that follow.

Example

On June 1, Echo Co. informs Foxtrot Corp. that it will be unable to make payment on its open account, which on that date has a balance of $20,000. Echo requests that Foxtrot accept instead a 60-day note that will bear interest at the rate of 6 percent. Foxtrot agrees.

Upon accepting the note on June 1, Foxtrot Corp. would make the following entry to record the exchange of an account receivable for an interest-bearing note receivable:

Notes receivable $20,000
    Accounts receivable $20,000
To record acceptance of the note

Thereafter, over time Foxtrot Corp. must account for the revenue that it is earning on its note. Most companies, considering the clerical costs of making frequent journal entries, update their accounts quarterly or at best monthly. Assuming that Foxtrot Corp. updates its accounts monthly, the following entry would be appropriate on June 30:

Accrued interest receivable $100
    Interest revenue $100
To record monthly interest revenue from the note

The $100 represents interest for a period for 30 days computed as

$$\$20{,}000 \times .06 \times \frac{30}{360} = \$100$$

On July 30, the note would fall due. Assuming that both the note and the interest are paid in full, two entries are required to record collection. The first is identical to that made on June 30; it recognizes the interest earned during the one-month period since interest revenue was previously recorded:

Accrued interest receivable $100
    Interest revenue $100
To record monthly interest revenue from the note

The balance in the accrued interest receivable account now stands at $200 and that in the notes receivable account at the original $20,000. Upon collection of both interest and principal, the appropriate entry would be

Cash $20,200
    Accrued interest receivable . . . . $ 200
    Notes receivable 20,000
To record the collection of the note and interest (Note that this entry has no effect on revenues or expenses.)

From the position of the payor—the maker of the note—the journal entries would be a mirror image of those of the payee.

NOTES WITH INTEREST INCLUDED IN THE FACE VALUE

A note may not specifically indicate a rate of interest. Instead, the face value of the note may include not only the amount originally borrowed but also the applicable interest charges as well. A borrower, for example, may give to a bank or other creditor a note for $1,000 in exchange for a 90-day loan. The bank, however, would not give the borrower the full $1,000. Instead, if the agreed-upon interest rate was 12 percent, it would give the borrower only $970.87. If the annual rate of interest was 12 percent, then the interest on a loan of $970.87 for 90 days would be

$$\$970.87 \times .12 \times \frac{90}{360} = \$29.13$$

The interest of $29.13, plus the principal of $970.57, exactly equals the face value of the note, $1,000.

Regardless of how the terms of the loan are stated, the difference between the amount actually received by the borrower and the amount that must eventually be repaid at the maturity of the note represents the cost of borrowing (i.e., interest). In the present example, the actual amount of the loan as well as the interest could have been calculated as follows:

Let x = the actual amount of the loan

If interest is to be at an annual rate of 12 percent, then interest for the 90-day period, approximately one-fourth of a year, would be a total of 3 percent of the actual amount of the loan. The total amount to be repaid is the actual amount of the loan, x, plus the interest, $.03x$. The total amount to be repaid has been established (the face amount of the note) at $1,000. Hence

$$\$1,000 = x + .03x$$

$$\$1,000 = 1.03x$$

$$x = \frac{\$1,000}{1.03} = \$970.87$$

The interest must be the difference between the face amount of the note and the amount actually borrowed: $1,000 minus $970.87, or $29.13. Interest for each of the three 30-day periods is therefore $9.71.

When the amount actually loaned is less than the face amount of the note—that is, when the face amount includes both principal and interest—the note is known as a *discount note* and the interest rate as a *discount rate*. The journal entries required to record discount notes and the associated interest charges are similar to those for conventional interest-earning instruments.

Assume, for example, that on July 1 a lending institution accepted a three-month discount note of $1,000 in exchange for an actual cash loan of $970.87. The entry to record the loan would be

Notes receivable, face value		$1,000.00
Cash		$970.87
Notes receivable, discount (asset contra account)		29.13

To record acceptance of the note

The overall effect of the entry is to record the asset, notes receivable, at the amount actually loaned. "Notes receivable, discount" is a contra account associated with the account, "notes receivable, face value." If a balance sheet were to be drawn up immediately after the loan was made, the relevant accounts would be reported on the balance sheet (among current assets) as

Notes receivable, face value	$1,000.00	
Less: Discount on notes	29.13	$970.87

As with conventional interest-bearing notes, interest must periodically be taken into account. On July 31, the appropriate entry would be (making the simplifying assumptions that one-third of the overall interest charges will be recorded during each of the three months regardless of the actual number of days in the month)

Notes receivable, discount $9.71
    Interest revenue $9.71
To record interest on the note for one month

The effect of this entry is to recognize the interest revenue and also to increase the value of the note (by decreasing the value of the contra account) by the amount of revenue recognized. The entry is similar to that which would have been made had the note had a stated interest rate. The main difference is that with the discount note the recognition of the interest results in the net increase of an asset, notes receivable, whereas with the interest-bearing note it results in the increase of a different asset, interest receivable.

An entry identical to that of July 31 would also be made on August 31 and September 30 to record the interest revenue earned during August and September.

On September 30, the balance in the "notes receivable, discount" account would be reduced to zero. Collection of the note would be recorded as follows:

Cash $1,000.00
    Notes receivable, face value $1,000.00
To record collection of the note

If the period of the loan were greater than one year, the present value formulas described in Chapter 6 would have to be used to determine the amount to be advanced to the borrower.

Example

A finance company makes a loan to a customer on a discount basis. The company accepts from the customer a two-year note for $5,000. The actual cash advanced is based on a 12 percent annual rate of interest.

Per Table 2 in the Appendix, the present value of $5,000 discounted at a rate of 12 percent for two years is

$$\$5,000 \times .7972 = \$3,986$$

The finance company would advance the customer $3,986 and record the loan as follows:

Notes receivable $5,000	
Notes receivable, discount $1,014	
Cash 3,986	

To record the loan to the customer

Interest revenue for the first year would be 12 percent of the *net* balance of the outstanding customer obligation, that is, 12 percent of $3,986, or $478. An appropriate journal entry after the note has been outstanding for one year would be

Notes receivable, discount $478	
Interest revenue $478	

To record interest for the first year

Since the customer did not actually remit an interest payment, the effective balance of its obligation would increase after the first year by $478. The increase in the effective balance is accounted for by a decrease in the discount. After the first year, the note would be reported as follows:

Notes receivable	$5,000	
Less: Discount on notes	536	$4,464

Interest for the second year would be based on the effective customer obligation at the end of the first year. Thus it would be 12 percent of $4,464, or $536. The entry at the end of the second year to record both interest revenue and collection of the full $5,000 would be

Cash $5,000	
Notes receivable, discount 536	
Notes receivable $5,000	
Interest revenue 536	

To record second-year interest and collection of the note

The interest revenue on a discount note would increase from year to year, corresponding to an increase in the effective obligation of the customer. Interest must be paid not only on the original amount borrowed but on any unsatisfied obligations for interest as well. (If the loan is for a relatively short period of time—less than one year—the "interest on the interest" is often ignored because it would be immaterial.)

"NONINTEREST-BEARING NOTES" AND IMPUTED INTEREST

Firms sometimes appear to sell on especially generous terms of credit—so generous, in fact, as to defy credibility.

Assume, for example, that a company sells for $100,000 equipment that it no longer needs. The company accepts from the purchaser a five-year "interest-free" note for the full sales price. As emphasized in Chapter 6, $100,000 to be received in five years is worth considerably less than the same amount to be received today. Indeed, per Table 2, the present value of a single payment of $100,000 five years hence, discounted at a rate of 8 percent, is

$$\$100,000 \times .6806 = \$68,060$$

Recognizing Substance over Form: Impact on Timing and Classification of Revenues and Expenses

It is hardly reasonable to expect a company to provide an interest-free loan to a customer for five years. A more believable interpretation of the transaction is that interest charges are included in the $100,000 selling price. If the prevailing rate for similar types of loans is 8 percent, the "true" selling price of the equipment would be only $68,060. The difference ($31,940) between this amount and the stated selling price of $100,000 represents interest on a five-year loan of $68,060.

If firms are to be concerned with the substance rather than merely the form of transactions, they must divide the $100,000 into its components. They must account separately for the sales price and the interest. They must *impute* interest of $31,940. If the equipment had been recorded on the books of the seller at $50,000, then the following entry would be appropriate:

Notes receivable		$100,000
Equipment		$50,000
Notes receivable, discount		31,940
Gain on sale of equipment		18,060
To record the sale of the equipment		

During each year that the note was outstanding, the company would accrue interest on the effective balance of the "loan"—the note receivable less the unamortized portion of the discount. Thus, to record interest after one year,

Notes receivable, discount		$5,445
Interest revenue		$5,445
To record interest for one year on a note of $68,060 at a rate of 8 percent		

And after the second year,

Notes receivable, discount		$5,880
Interest revenue		$5,880
To record interest for one year on a note of $73,505 at a rate of 8 percent ($73,505 represents the face value of the note less unamortized discount of $26,495—original discount of $31,940 less first-year amortization of $5,445.)		

Over the life of the note, the firm will recognize earnings on the transaction of $50,000—$100,000 received in cash less the recorded value of the equipment of $50,000—regardless of how the $100,000 is divided between "true" sales price and interest. If the transaction were accounted for in accordance with its form (selling price of $100,000), then a gain of $50,000 would be realized at time of sale. If accounted for in accordance with substance (selling price of $68,060), then a gain of only $18,060 would be recognized in the year of sale. The remaining $31,940 would be recognized as interest and taken into income over the five-year period of the note.

EXHIBIT 7-3
Impact on Income: Interest Imputed versus Interest Not Imputed

Assumptions:
Stated selling price of equipment: $100,000
Total imputed interest (8% per year): $31,940
Selling price if interest is imputed: $68,060 ($100,000 less $31,940)
Useful life of equipment: 10 years
Seller's book value of equipment at time of sale: $50,000

Perspective of Seller

Period	Interest Imputed	Interest Not Imputed	Difference
0 (time of sale) Gain on sale	$18,060	$50,000	($31,940)
1 Interest revenue	$ 5,445		$ 5,445
2 Interest revenue	5,880		5,880
3 Interest revenue	6,350		6,350
4 Interest revenue	6,858		6,858
5 Interest revenue	7,407		7,407
Total interest revenue	$31,940		$31,940
Total	$50,000	$50,000	$ 0

Perspective of Buyer

Period	Interest Imputed	Interest Not Imputed	Difference
0–10 Annual depreciation	$ 6,806	$ 10,000	
Years of useful life	× 10	× 10	
Total depreciation	$ 68,060	$100,000	($31,940)
1 Interest expense	5,445		5,445
2 Interest expense	5,880		5,880
3 Interest expense	6,350		6,350
4 Interest expense	6,858		6,858
5 Interest expense	7,407		7,407
Total interest expense	$ 31,940		$31,940
Total	$100,000	$100,000	$ 0

On the books of the purchaser of the equipment, if the entire $100,000 is assigned to the cost of the equipment, then that amount would be subject to depreciation and recognized as an expense over the remaining useful life of the equipment—perhaps 10 years. If, however, the interest of $31,940 was taken into account, then only $68,060 would be assigned to the cost of the equipment and expensed as depreciation over its useful life. The interest, $31,940, would be charged as an expense over the five-year period of the note. The manner in which the transaction is accounted for has no effect on *total* earnings of either the purchaser or the seller; it does, however, have a significant impact on the timing and classification of such earnings. Exhibit 7-3 indicates the differences in revenues and expenses from the perspective of both buyer and seller.

Industry Example: Retail Land Sales Companies

The issue of imputed interest is especially important as it applies to retail land sales companies. Retail land sales companies purchase large tracts of land and subdivide them into small parcels for sale to consumers. They plan communities; install streets, sewers, and utilities; and sometimes construct amenities such as golf courses, clubhouses, motels, and restaurants. Often they engage in extensive promotional efforts (e.g., free dinners or trips to the site), and frequently they direct their sales efforts at those who are interested in either retirement or vacation homes. Retail land sales companies seldom accept interest-free notes. Sometimes, however, they charge relatively low rates of interest. For example, they might charge a purchaser 8 percent interest annually at a time when the *prime rate* (that charged by banks to their most select customers) is 10 percent and the firms' own cost of borrowing is 12 percent.

At one time, it was standard procedure in the industry to record sales at the face value of the note received. This practice, however, overstated sales revenue and understated interest revenue. Since sales revenue is recognized at the time a sales contract is signed and interest revenue is recognized over the term of the note, the effect was to speed up recognition of revenue and to overstate earnings in the year of the sale. Considering that the notes were often for 10 years and that the difference between the rate actually charged and that normally charged for "loans" of similar types may have been as much as 10 percent, the difference in first-year revenues on sales of $1 million could be almost $350,000. To eliminate such overstatements in earnings, the Accounting Principles Board prescribed that the required payments on notes receivable that bear unreasonably low rates of interest be *discounted* by the *prevailing* rate for similar types of credit instruments and that a portion of the stated sales price of the land be accounted for as interest rather than sales revenue.[7]

Example

New Mexico Land Co. sells parcels of land for $50,000. Purchasers must pay $5,000 down and can give a 10-year note, which bears interest at a rate of 4 percent for the $45,000 balance. The note must be paid in 10 annual installments of $5,548, the annual payment required to repay a loan of $45,000 in equal installments if interest is charged at a rate of 4 percent per year.

If the company's customers had attempted to borrow the funds from a traditional lending institution, they would have had to pay the prevailing interest rate of 12 percent.

The present value of the consideration—that is, the "true" selling price of the land—can be determined by discounting *all* required payments (both principal and interest) by the *effective* rate of interest, in this example 12 percent:

Present value of $5,000 down payment	$ 5,000
Present value of 10 annual payments of $5,548 discounted at a rate of 12 percent:	
Per Table 4, $5,548 × 5.6502	31,347
Present value of all payments	$36,347

[7]"Accounting for Retail Land Sales," American Institute of Certified Public Accountants, 1972, now incorporated into "Accounting for Sales of Real Estate," Financial Accounting Board *Statement of Financial Accounting Standards No. 66,* 1982.

As a consequence, the firm would recognize sales revenue of only $36,347, which represents the worth at time of sale of all the payments to be received by the company. The difference between that amount and $50,000 represents interest revenue and must be reported as such over the 10-year period that the note is outstanding.

Industry Example: Franchise Companies

The financial arrangements in the franchise industry highlight some of the key issues pertaining to valuation of receivables as well as recognition of revenue.

Franchisers sell to franchisees the right to operate a specific kind of business, to use the name of the franchiser, and to provide goods or services associated with the franchiser. Companies such as McDonald's and Burger King may be among the best-known franchisers, but thousands of establishments throughout the world bear franchised names. Franchisees may be individual businesspersons or may themselves be large corporations.

The revenue of a franchiser ordinarily comes from several sources. First, the franchiser sells franchises to the parties who will operate them. The franchiser receives a small down payment and accepts from the franchisee long-term notes. Second, it receives royalties based on the sales volume of the franchisee. Third, it sells to the franchisee all or a portion of the business's product (e.g., the seasonings for the fried chicken). In return for the payments from the franchisees, the franchiser provides advertising and promotional support, training and business counseling, assistance in site selection, and financial support.

The issues of valuation of receivables and recognition of revenue are especially vexing because the financial well-being of the franchiser and the franchisees is so tightly intertwined. The franchiser can be profitable only if the individual franchisees are successful. The franchisees, however, are dependent upon the goodwill generated, and support provided, by the franchiser. In particular, the franchiser can expect payment on its notes and receivables from franchisees (often a substantial portion of its assets) only as long as it has the financial capacity to promote its name and nurture the franchisees.

The source of revenue that presents the most difficult accounting problems is that from the sale of the franchise. A franchisee may purchase a franchise many months before it is ready to begin operations. During the intervening period and sometimes for years afterward, the franchiser may be obligated to provide services (advertising and management training, for example) to the franchisee. The question arises as to the point at which the revenue from the sale should be recognized and the related receivable should be recorded as an asset. Consistent with the principle that revenue should be related to productive effort, it could be recognized at the time the contract is signed, when the outlet first commences operations, or in the one or more periods in which various services are performed.

Because eventual collection of cash cannot always be reasonably assured, it has sometimes been suggested that revenue be recognized only as the notes are actually collected, that is, on the cash collection or installment basis. This approach would eliminate the possibility that the assets of the franchiser are overstated by the amounts that will prove uncollectible; it would make certain that revenues are not prematurely realized. But it would also be inconsistent with the general accounting practice of recognizing revenue when a transaction is substantially completed (and, as necessary, making appropriate provisions for uncollectible accounts). The installment method of accounting is ordinarily reserved for exceptional cases in which there is no reasonable basis for estimating the degree of collectibility of outstanding receivables. This approach has been rejected in favor of one permitting recognition prior to collection of cash but not as early as when the contract is signed.

Current accounting rules require that the recognition of revenues from the sale of a franchise be delayed until the franchiser has performed substantially all of the initial services set forth in the sales agreement.[8] Because of the variety of contractual arrangements, there can be no one specific condition or event that is the sole criterion for revenue recognition. The test of substantial performance may be met at a number of different times. Nevertheless, the applicable pronouncement stipulates that "conservatism justifies that *commencement of operations by the franchisee* is the earliest point at which substantial performance has occurred." As a rule, the pronouncement recommends, revenues should therefore be recognized at the time that the franchise starts its operations.

PAYROLL TRANSACTIONS

Although payroll transactions present few conceptual considerations that have not already been dealt with, they are worthy of discussion because they are engaged in by almost all profit and nonprofit organizations and are of major magnitude.

Characteristic of payroll transactions is that the wage or salary expense pertaining to an individual employee may be considerably *greater* than the amount indicated by his or her wage or salary rate but that the amount actually paid to the employee may be considerably *less*. The business firm must pay payroll taxes that are specifically levied on the employer and, commonly, must provide for *fringe benefits* in addition to regular wage and salary payments. Moreover, the employer must withhold from each employee's wages and salary the employee's share of payroll taxes as well as amounts for other designated purposes. Amounts withheld from the employee ordinarily represent a liability of the employer; they must be remitted either to the government or to a specific fund.

Example

An employee is paid at the rate of $4,000 per month. From her salary must be withheld (either by law or by employee election) the following: federal income taxes (according to a schedule published by the Internal Revenue Service)—$805; Federal Insurance Contribution Act deductions

[8]"Accounting for Franchise Fee Revenue," American Institute of Certified Public Accountants, 1973, now incorporated into "Accounting for Franchise Fee Revenue," Financial Accounting Standards Board *Statement of Financial Accounting Standards No. 45,* 1981.

(abbreviated FICA and commonly referred to as Social Security payments)—7.5 percent of gross salary, or $300; health insurance contribution—$168; savings bond plan—$180. As a consequence of the deductions, monthly *take-home* pay of the employee is $2,627.

In addition, the employer incurs the following voluntary or statutory charges: employer share of FICA contributions—7.5 percent of gross salary, or $300; contribution to company pension fund—8 percent of gross salary, or $320; state and federal unemployment insurance taxes—3 percent of gross salary, or $120.

The following entry would be appropriate on the payroll dates for a group of 1,000 employees, making the simplifying assumption that the payroll deductions for each employee are the same:

Salaries (expense)	$4,000,000
FICA expense, employer's share	300,000
Unemployment insurance (expense)	120,000
Pension expense	320,000
Salaries payable	$2,627,000
Liability for income taxes withheld	805,000
Liability for FICA (both employee's and employer's share)	600,000
Liability for medical insurance	168,000
Liability for savings bonds	100,000
Liability for pensions	320,000
Liability for unemployment insurance	120,000

To record payroll

When cash payments are made to the employee or to the appropriate funds or government agencies, the various liability accounts would be debited; cash would be credited.

When employees take their vacations, the expense of their salaries during the vacations should be allocated to those accounting periods in which they are actually performing services. If, in the example, the employee takes a one-month annual vacation, then the $4,000 that she would be paid while on vacation should be charged as an expense during the 11 months in which she worked. The monthly expense would be $363.63 ($4,000 divided by 11 months). The accrual of vacation pay could be recorded by the following additional entry each month for the employee group:

Vacation pay (expense)	$363,636
Provision for vacation pay (liability)	$363,636

To accrue vacation pay—one-eleventh of monthly salaries

When an individual employee takes a vacation, the appropriate entry (which, for simplicity, omits consideration of payroll withholdings and other deductions) would be:

Provision for vacation pay	$4,000
Salaries payable	$4,000

To record the amount due an employee for vacation pay

It is particularly important for organizations to spread the costs of vacation pay over the production periods of their employees if they prepare quarterly or semiannual financial reports in addition to annual reports. If they neglect to *accrue* vacation pay, then cost of operations in the summer months may appear to be considerably higher than in other months. The increase in cost is attributable to the large number of employees who take their vacations in the summer. When they do so, substitute workers must be hired if production levels are to be maintained.

The more interesting and controversial issues pertaining to employee compensation relate to retirement benefits such as pensions, to health insurance, and to bonuses in common stock and other securities. Consideration of these will be delayed until later in the text.

RATIOS

This section is directed to two ratios that are useful in the control and evaluation of accounts receivable.

Accounts Receivable Turnover

Accounts receivable turnover is an activity ratio. *Activity ratios* measure the effectiveness of management in utilizing specific resources under its command. Activity ratios are often referred to as *turnover ratios*. They relate specific asset accounts to sales or to some other revenue or expense accounts with which they are logically associated.

Accounts receivable turnover is the ratio that measures the number of times that receivables are generated and collected during a period. It is computed by dividing sales by average accounts receivable:

$$\text{Accounts receivable turnover} = \frac{\text{Sales}}{\text{Average accounts receivable}^9}$$

The greater the number of times that accounts receivable turn over, the smaller the amount of funds that the company has "tied up" in accounts receivable and the greater the amount of funds that it can invest in other assets.

The balance sheet and income statement of American Home Products Corporation, a manufacturer of pharmaceuticals, medical supplies, other health care products, foods, and household products, are shown in Exhibit 7-4. The company's statement of cash flow is presented in Exhibit 14-1 in the chapter directed to cash flows. In 1991 American Home Products had net sales (in millions) of $7,079. As of December 31, 1991, it held accounts receivable of $1,024; as of December 31, 1990, $1,021. Average accounts receivable were thus $1,023—($1,024 + 1,021)/2

$$\text{Accounts receivable turnover} = \frac{\$7,079}{\$1,023} = 6.9 \text{ times}$$

[9] Refinements in the calculation of ratios, such as questions of whether installment contracts receivable should be included among receivables or whether the allowance for doubtful accounts should be deducted, are beyond the scope of this text. Suffice it to say that the specific way a ratio is computed must depend on the analytical function that it will serve. What is most important is that the analyst strive for consistency among firms and over time. This objective is not always possible to achieve because firms are not uniform in their practices of data aggregation and classification.

EXHIBIT 7-4

Consolidated Balance Sheets and Statements of Income
American Home Products Corporation and Subsidiaries

Consolidated Balance Sheets

December 31	1991	1990
	(Dollar amounts in thousands except per share amounts)	
Assets		
Cash and cash equivalents	$2,064,603	$1,788,534
Accounts receivable less allowances (1991—$37,419 and 1990—$34,248)	1,024,163	1,021,407
Inventories	842,044	795,869
Other current assets	188,247	220,265
Total current assets	4,119,057	3,826,075
Property, plant and equipment:		
Land	61,433	51,787
Buildings	1,076,708	1,046,677
Machinery and equipment	1,521,091	1,434,358
	2,659,232	2,532,822
Less accumulated depreciation	1,182,391	1,095,432
	1,476,841	1,437,390
Goodwill	254,551	283,214
Other assets	88,348	90,428
	$5,938,797	$5,637,107
Liabilities		
Loans payable to banks	$ 5,260	$ 13,331
Commercial paper	—	665,157
Trade accounts payable	314,453	240,039
Accrued expenses	838,165	639,817
Accrued federal and foreign taxes on income	112,257	135,508
Total current liabilities	1,270,135	1,693,852
Long-term loans payable	104,710	111,430
Deferred compensation payable under Management Incentive Plan	49,283	51,689
Other noncurrent liabilities	1,214,122	1,104,914
Shareholders' equity		
$2 convertible preferred stock, par value $2.50 per share; 5,000,000 shares authorized	$ 128	$ 143
Common stock, par value $.33⅓ per share; 600,000,000 shares authorized	105,208	104,676
Additional paid-in capital	838,099	683,504
Retained earnings	2,316,555	1,802,658
Currency translation adjustments	40,557	84,241
Total shareholders' equity	3,300,547	2,675,222
	$5,938,797	$5,637,107

EXHIBIT 7-4 Continued

Consolidated Statements of Income

Years Ended December 31	1991	1990
	(In thousands except per share amounts)	
Net sales	$7,079,443	$6,775,182
Cost of goods sold	2,390,463	2,453,469
Selling, administrative and general expenses	2,971,941	2,806,045
Other (income) expense, net	(42,771)	30,012
Gain on sale of household and depilatory businesses	—	(999,528)
Special charges	—	656,906
	5,319,633	4,946,904
Income before federal and foreign taxes on income	1,759,810	1,828,278
Provision for taxes on income:		
Federal	163,217	369,552
Foreign	221,320	228,129
	384,537	597,681
Net income	$1,375,273	$1,230,597
Net income per share of common stock	$ 4.36	$ 3.92

Ideally, average receivables should be based on 12 individual months rather than beginning and end-of-year values. Otherwise, the average may be distorted by seasonal fluctuations. Indeed, many companies intentionally choose to end their fiscal years when business activities are at their slowest.

The same relationship can be expressed in an alternative form, *number of days' sales in accounts receivable* (sometimes called the *average collection period*). Assuming that all sales were made on account, then on average, American Home Products made $19.4 million in sales per day.

$$\text{Average sales per day} = \frac{\text{Total sales}}{365}$$

$$= \frac{\$7,079}{365}$$

$$= \$19.4$$

The number of days' sales in accounts receivable may be determined by dividing accounts receivable as of *any particular day* by average sales per day:

$$\frac{\text{Number of days' sales in accounts receivable}}{\text{(Average collection period)}} = \frac{\text{Accounts receivable}}{\text{Average sales per day}}$$

Number of days' sales in accounts receivable as of December 31, 1991

$$= \frac{\$1,023}{\$19.4} = 52.7 \text{ days}$$

Expressed in another way, based on average sales it takes 52.7 days for the company to collect its accounts receivable. Should the collection period increase from one year to the next, or should it be greater than the number of days in the payment period specified in the company's terms of sales, then there would be reason to investigate whether the firm is experiencing difficulty in collecting from its customers.

Current and Quick Ratios

Liquidity ratios measure the ability of a firm to meet its obligations as they mature. As indicated in Chapter 4, the primary measure of liquidity is the *current ratio*. The current ratio compares current assets with current liabilities. The higher the ratio of current assets to current liabilities, the less likely the company will be to default on its obligations. Current assets, however, commonly provide either no direct return to the company or a return smaller than could be obtained if funds were invested and producing assets. If the current ratio is high, therefore, the company may be incurring an *opportunity cost*—it could be losing revenue by tying up funds in current assets rather than by taking advantage of other financial opportunities.

A test of liquidity more severe than the current ratio is the *quick ratio*. The quick ratio compares cash and cash equivalents (such as marketable securities) and accounts receivable to current liabilities. It provides an indication of the ability of the company to satisfy its obligations without taking into account both inventories, which are less readily transformed into cash than other current assets, and prepaid expenses, which save the company from having to disburse cash in the future but which are not themselves transformed into cash. The ratio of American Home Products as of December 31, 1991, is 2.4 to 1:

$$\text{Quick ratio} = \frac{\text{Cash and cash equivalents } + \text{ Current receivables}}{\text{Current liabilities}}$$

$$= \frac{\$2,065 + \$1,024}{\$1,270}$$

$$= 2.4$$

Caveats

Both the current and quick ratios are of special interest to short-term creditors, those who are concerned about the firm's ability to meet its obligations within a period of one year. Both ratios, however, should be viewed with considerable care. They are ratios that can readily be manipulated by management. For example, by paying off short-term loans just prior to year end (and subsequently reborrowing at the start of the next year), management may be able to increase its year-end current and quick ratios. It is important to bear in mind that an identical change in both current assets and current liabilities will, in fact, alter the two ratios. If, for example, a firm had current assets of $400,000 and current liabilities of $200,000 and subsequently repaid an outstanding current obligation of $100,000, its current ratio would increase from 2 : 1 prior to repayment to 3 : 1 after payment. The practice of taking deliberate steps to inflate the current and quick ratios is known as *window dressing*.

At the same time, an increase in the current and quick ratios may be symptomatic of financial deterioration rather than improvement. The numerator of the quick ratio includes accounts receivable; that of the current ratio includes accounts receivable as well as inventories. Suppose that a firm's inventory balance is increasing because of an inability to sell its products and its accounts receivable balance is increasing because of a failure to collect outstanding debts. Both the current and quick ratios would also increase, even though the financial condition of the firm is weakening. This increase points to the danger of focusing on individual rather than groups of relationships. If, for example, ratios of sales to inventory and sales to accounts receivable were computed, then the unhealthy buildup of receivables and inventory would become apparent. It would be clear that both balances were increasing at the same time that sales were decreasing.

Summary

Three main ideas pervaded the discussion of receivables and payables:

1. Questions of the amounts at which receivables and payables should be stated are directly related to those of when revenues and expenses should be recognized.

If an enterprise grants credit to customers, it is doubtful that all its receivables will be transformed into cash. "Losses" on bad debts are an expected deduction from revenues. They should be charged as a reduction of sales (or an expense) in the same accounting period in which the related sales are made. Correspondingly, accounts receivable should be reduced by the amount likely to be uncollectible.

Both sales and receivables should be reduced also by the amount of expected returns, allowances, and discounts of which customers may avail themselves, and interest included in the face of the receivable but not yet earned. Notes receivable, for example, often include in the stated value an element of interest to be earned during the period over which the notes will be held.

2. The substance of a transaction must take precedence over its form. Accountants and managers must look to the economic rather than the stated values of goods or services exchanged. It is not unusual, for example, for firms to allow customers to delay payments for months or even years and make no explicit charges for interest. Money, however, has a time value, and the right to use funds for an extended period of time is not granted casually. Whenever the sales price of an item is *inflated* by unspecified interest charges, the firm must impute a fair rate of interest and account for the revenue from the sale of the item apart from the revenue from the interest.

3. Proper accounting for receivables and payables requires the good judgment of both managers and accountants. The "correct" value of receivables can never be known with certainty. It is dependent on the amounts that customers will fail to pay, the amount of goods returned, and the amount of cash discounts taken. Reported receivables and revenues are, at best, only estimates.

Exercise for Review and Self-Testing

The LJG Company sells equipment to a customer for $1,000. The customer is permitted to defer payment for one year but is to be charged interest at a rate of 4 percent. The company accepts a note from the customer with a face value of $1,040. This amount represents principal of $1,000 and interest of $40.

The prevailing rate of interest—the rate normally charged similar customers in similar circumstances—is 12 percent, and the company often sells its equipment for less than $1,000.

1. Determine the fair market value of the equipment, taking into account the prevailing rate of interest. What is the present value of the note (both principal and interest) to the company?
2. Prepare a journal entry to record the sale of the equipment. Be sure that the amount of revenue recognized reflects the value of the consideration received. Any difference between the face amount of the note and the amount of revenue recognized should be classified as "notes receivable, discount."
3. After one year the company collects the entire $1,040 from the customer. Prepare a journal entry to record the collection of the note and to recognize interest revenue for the year. Be sure that the amount of interest revenue recognized reflects the "true" (prevailing) rate of interest.
4. The firm estimates that of the total sales for the year for which notes were accepted, $7,000 will be uncollectible. Prepare a journal entry to add that amount to "notes receivable, allowance for uncollectibles."
5. A review of notes on hand indicates that $2,500 is presently uncollectible. Prepare a journal entry to write off the notes against the allowance provided.

Questions for Review and Discussion

1. Why is it preferable for a firm to maintain an allowance for uncollectible accounts rather than simply to write off bad accounts as soon as it is known which specific accounts will be uncollectible?
2. On December 29 a company purchases for $100,000 merchandise intended for resale. The company is granted a 5 percent discount for paying cash within 10 days of purchase. The company records the purchase using the gross method. As of year end, the company has not yet paid for the goods purchased but has resold half of them. The company intends to pay within the specified discount period. Assuming that no adjustment to the accounts has been made, in what way is it likely that the financial statements as of year end are misstated?
3. A company borrows $1,000 for one year at the prevailing interest rate of 6 percent. The note issued to the lender promises payment of $1,000 plus interest of $60 after one year. Upon borrowing the funds, the company records a liability for $1,060. Do you approve of this accounting practice? Explain.
4. A finance company loaned an individual $1,000 on a discount basis. The actual cash given to the borrower was only $940; interest was taken out in advance. At the time of the loan, the company recorded its receivable at $1,000, reduced its cash by $940, and recognized revenue of $60. Do you approve of this practice? How would you record the loan? Explain.
5. A retail store places the following ad in a newspaper, "Complete Room of Furniture; $1,000; no money down; take up to 2 years to pay; no interest or finance charges." During a particular month the firm sells 10 sets of the advertised furniture. The company records sales of $10,000. If you were the firm's independent CPA what reservations would you have about the reported sales?
6. A firm acquires a building at a cost of $200,000 but gives the seller a five-year interest-free note for the entire amount. Assuming that the firm would otherwise have had to borrow the funds at a rate of interest of 10 percent compounded annually, at what amount should the building be recorded? What would be the impact of failing to take into account *imputed* interest on reported earnings of the years during which the note is outstanding as well as on those of the remaining years of the useful life of the building?

7. After operating successfully in a single city, the owners of Big Top Ice Cream Parlors decide to sell franchises to individual businesspeople in other cities. Within one year the firm signs contracts and receives down payments for 20 franchises. The total sales price of each franchise is $50,000. The required down payment is a small fraction of total sales price. During the first year only five outlets are actually opened. The company reports revenues from sale of franchises of $1 million. What warnings would you give an investor with respect to first-year earnings?

8. The supervisor of a large clerical department in a government agency finds that efficiency in his department always seems to drop during the summer months. He determines efficiency by dividing total payroll costs by the number of documents processed. Total payroll costs include amounts paid to employees on vacation. The department charges all salaries—both those of workers actually on the job and those on vacation—as an expense in the month paid. Why do you suspect efficiency appears to be low during the summer months? What improvements to the accounting system might you recommend?

9. A finance company charges customers 12 percent interest on all balances outstanding. The company continues to accrue interest revenue on outstanding loans (that is, it debits interest receivable and credits interest revenue) even though loan payments might be past due. Only when it writes off a loan does it cease to accrue interest. What dangers are suggested by such practice?

10. The *quick ratio* of a firm has increased substantially from one year to the next. The treasurer of the firm cites the increase as evidence of improved financial health. Why can an increase in the quick ratio be as much of a sign of financial deterioration as of improved financial health? What other ratio or relationship would you look to for insight as to the significance of the increase.

Problems

1. *This is a simple exercise in accounting for uncollectibles.* The trial balance of the Elton Co. indicates the following:

Sales	$486,000
Accounts receivable	63,000
Allowance for uncollectibles	11,000

In the current year, bad-debt expense has not yet been recorded.

The firm estimates that approximately 5 percent of sales will be uncollectible. A review of accounts receivable reveals that $21,500 of accounts presently on the books are unlikely to be collected and should therefore be written off.

Prepare any entries that you believe are necessary in light of the facts as presented.

2. *Neither the entries to write off accounts receivable nor to restore accounts that were previously written off have a direct impact upon earnings.*

Transactions involving accounts receivable and related accounts of Warner's Department Store for 1992 and 1993 can be summarized as follows (in millions):

	1993	1992
Credit sales	$30.00	$40.00
Cash collections on accounts receivable	31.00	28.00
Accounts deemed uncollectible and written off	.65	.30

The firm estimates that 2 percent of annual credit sales will be uncollectible.

Included in the $31 million of cash collections in 1993 is $30,000 from customers whose accounts were written off in 1992. The balances in the accounts when they were written off totaled $80,000. It is the policy of the company to restore in their entirety accounts previously written off upon collection of a partial payment from a customer, since a partial payment is often an indication that payment of the remaining balance will be forthcoming.

a. Prepare journal entries to record the activity reported.

b. Compare the impact of credit losses on reported earnings of 1992 with those of 1993.

c. Comment briefly on how your answer to part (b) would differ if the amount to be added to the allowance for doubtful accounts were based on an aging schedule instead of a flat percentage of sales.

3. *In the long run though not in any particular year, charges for bad debts based on an aging schedule should be equal to those based on dollar volume of credit sales.*

The Melrose Co. began operations in January 1990. The following schedule indicates credit sales and end-of-year balances in accounts receivable for 1990 through 1993. The end-of-year balances are broken down by the "age" of the receivables.

Credit Sales and End-of-Year Balance in Accounts Receivable (in thousands)

| | | Accounts Receivable | | | | |
| | | | | No. of Days Past Due | | |
Year	Credit Sales	Total	Current	1–30	31–60	Over 60
1990	$12,000	$1,080	$ 800	$100	$150	$ 30
1991	14,000	1,500	1,100	300	50	50
1992	16,000	1,600	900	400	200	100
1993	18,000	1,820	1,280	220	200	120

The company estimates that approximately 5 percent of all credit sales will be uncollectible. It has also determined that of its accounts receivable balance at any date the following percentages will likely be uncollectible:

Current	15%
1–30 days past due	40
31–60 days past due	50
Over 60 days past due	60

The balance in the "allowance for uncollectibles" account was zero prior to the adjustment at the end of 1990. Actual write-offs of accounts receivable were as follows:

1990	260
1991	580
1992	815
1993	893

a. Determine bad-debt charges for each of the four years, assuming first that the company bases its addition to the allowance for uncollectibles on credit sales and alternatively on a schedule of *aged* accounts receivables. Bear in mind that when the sales method is used, the bad-debt charge is determined directly. When the aged accounts receivable method is used, it is necessary to first determine the required balance in the allowance for uncollectibles account.

b. Compare total bad-debt charges over the combined four-year period under each of the two methods. (They should be the same in this example.) Which method results in the more erratic pattern of bad-debt charges? Why?

4. *Journal entries can be prepared once the missing data are derived.*

The financial records of a firm reveal the following (in thousands):

	1993	1992
Accounts receivable	$ 4,520	$ 3,980
Allowance for uncollectibles	226	201
Sales (all on account)	54,200	47,500
Restoration of accounts previously written off	27	18

It is the practice of the company to charge "sales, uncollectibles" with an amount equal to 3 percent of sales. Prepare journal entries to summarize all activity in accounts receivable and the related allowance for uncollectibles in 1993.

5. *Interest on troublesome loans should not be accrued.*

The following comment was included in the notes to the financial statements of the Equitable Life Mortgage and Realty Investors:

> Nonaccrual of Interest. When it is not reasonable to expect that interest income will be received, its recognition is discontinued. At that point, interest accrued but not received is reversed, and no further interest is accrued until it is evident that principal and interest will be collected.

a. Why should the company "reverse" interest accrued but not yet received?

b. What is the most likely journal entry made to effect the reversal?

6. *This problem provides an illustration (adapted from an actual annual report) of a firm whose allowance for uncollectibles was inadequate to cover loan losses.*

The annual report of First Houston Corporation contained the following comment and table regarding its provision for loan losses:

> One of the most significant factors adversely affecting 1993 results was the $126.5 million provision for loan losses, up from $118.5 million in 1992. Net loan charge-offs were $145.8 million, exceeding the provision for loan losses by $19.3 million.

	1993	1992
Balance, beginning of period	$ 121,352	$ 95,766
Additions (deductions)		
Loans charged off	(153,688)	(95,583)
Recoveries	7,874	2,669
Net charge-offs	$(145,814)	$(92,914)
Provisions charged to operating expenses	126,500	118,500
Balance, end of period	$102,038	$121,352

a. Prepare journal entries to reflect the activity in the account, "provision for loan losses," in 1993.

b. Based only on the limited information provided, do you think that the balance in the account at the end of 1993 will be adequate to cover losses on loans to be incurred in the future? Explain.

7. *Bad-debt problems can easily be masked by rapid increases in sales.* (Solution of this problem would be facilitated by use of an electronic spreadsheet.)

Throughout the 1980s sales of Atlanta Co. were level at $100 million per year. Bad debts were approximately 5 percent of annual sales, and the firm maintained an allowance for uncollectibles equal to one year's write-offs ($5 million). The company made extensive efforts to collect on all receivables, and accounts were typically not written off until three years after the year of sale. Thus receivables from sales of 1987 would not be written off until 1990.

Starting in 1990, the company changed its previously conservative merchandising policies and sales improved dramatically. From 1990 through 1994 they increased at a compound rate of 20 percent per year ($1.2 million in 1990, $1.44 million in 1991, etc.). As a consequence of more liberal credit policies, bad debts increased from 5 percent of sales to 7 percent. Nevertheless, the company continued to add to its allowance for bad debts at the rate of only 5 percent of sales. As in the previous decade, accounts were not actually written off until three years after the year of sale. Thus, beginning in 1993, the company was forced to write off 7 percent of the previous years' sales, but had provided an allowance for bad debts of only 5 percent.

In 1995 sales leveled off and from 1995 to 2001 remained constant at $248.83 million per year.

a. Determine the balances in the allowance for uncollectibles at year end 1987 through 2001. Calculate the balance as a percentage of sales for the year.

b. Comment on the pattern of changes in the balances and on its significance for financial analysts concerned with the adequacy of the allowance.

8. *In some industries it is especially critical that allowances be made for anticipated returns of merchandise sold.*

Division Products had gross sales in 1992 (its first year of operations) of $4 million and in 1993 of $6 million. As of December 31, 1992, the company had accounts receivable of $2 million and as of December 31, 1993, $3 million. The business of the company is highly seasonal; most of its sales are made in the last three months of the year.

The company follows standard practice in its industry. It permits the retailers with whom it deals to return for full credit any merchandise that they are unable to sell within a reasonable period of time. In January 1993, the company accepted for return merchandise that it had sold for $400,000. None of the merchandise had yet been paid for by the retailers. A return rate of 10 percent of sales is typical for the industry.

The firm's cost of goods sold is approximately 60 percent of sales. In financial statements prepared for internal use only (and not in accord with generally accepted accounting principles of reporting to the general public), the firm gives accounting recognition to merchandise returned only when it is actually received; it establishes no year-end allowances.

a. Determine for both 1992 and 1993 the difference in income and assets that would result if the company were to establish an allowance for returned merchandise. Assume that all goods returned would be resold at standard prices.

b. Suppose that the company was in a business, such as toys, in which it is extremely difficult to predict the rate of return from pre-Christmas sales. Do you think the company should recognize revenue at time of sale? What alternative point of revenue recognition might be preferable?

c. How else can companies in high seasonal industries, such as toys, eliminate the danger of misestimating returns in their annual financial reports? Why do you suppose that many department stores report on the basis of a fiscal year ending July 31 rather than on a calendar year?

9. *In mail-order companies, the financial impact of returns may be significant.*

The financial statements of New Process Company (an actual company), which sells clothing by direct mail, contained the following footnote:

> Returns: A provision for anticipated returns is recorded monthly as a percentage of gross sales; the percentage is based upon historical experience. Actual returns are charged against the allowance for returns, which is netted against accounts receivable in the balance sheet. The provision for returns charged against income in 1987 and 1986 amounts to $69,470,047 and $68,759,379, respectively.

The financial statements also revealed the following:

	1987	1986
Sales	$362,576,000	$359,609,000
Accounts receivable	71,069,000	66,291,000
Allowances for doubtful accounts and returns	(19,776,737)	(21,785,543)

a. Based on the information provided, prepare the journal entries made by the company in 1987 to provide for anticipated returns and to account for actual returns. Assume that, of the allowances for doubtful accounts and returns, 20 percent is for returns and 80 percent for doubtful accounts.
b. Based on the information provided (there is no other with respect to returns included in the financial statements), do you think that the merchandise returned has significant value? Explain.
c. How many days' sales are in accounts receivable as of year end 1987?

10. *Minor differences in return policies may necessitate major differences in accounting practices.*
  a. University Textbooks, Inc., sells textbooks to college bookstores. Based on information provided by course instructors, the bookstores order only as many copies as they estimate will be sold. Occasionally, however, they overorder and, as an accommodation, University Textbooks allows them to return unsold books as long as it will be able to resell them. The company estimates that returns are approximately 4 percent of sales.

In December 1993, University Textbooks sold, on account, $10 million in textbooks. Cost of books sold was $6 million.
  (1) Prepare the appropriate entries.
  (2) In January and February 1994, University Textbooks accepted for return books that it had sold in December for $300,000. Prepare the appropriate entries.
  b. Universal Paperbacks sells paperbacks to supermarkets, newsstands, and airport bookstands. To get maximum exposure for its books, the company allows the retailers to return any books that remain unsold 60 days after they have been received and placed on display racks. The company estimates that returns *on average* are 40 percent of sales. However, the range of returns, by title, varies considerably. If a book catches on, there will be few, if any, returns. If it doesn't, almost all copies will be returned.
  (1) In December 1993, Universal Paperbacks shipped $10 million in books. Cost of books was $6 million. Prepare the appropriate entries.
  (2) In January and February 1994, Universal Paperbacks accepted for return books that it had sold in December for $800,000. Prepare the appropriate entries.

c. Justify your entries and comment on any similarities and differences between parts (a) and (b).

11. *The means of accounting for cash discounts may not be the critical issue of our time, but they point up the importance of recognizing substance rather than form.*

Indiana Industrial Supplies reported accounts receivable of $1 million as of December 31, 1993. Of that amount, $800,000 represents sales of the final 20 days of the year. The company allows its customers to take a cash discount of 4 percent of sales price on all merchandise paid for within 20 days.

The company has consistently accounted for cash discounts by the *gross* method. Annual sales and year-end balances in accounts receivable have remained generally constant over the last several years. Approximately 90 percent of the customers take advantage of the cash discount. Comment on whether the firm's sales and accounts receivable are likely to be fairly presented at year end. Indicate the amount of any possible overor understatement.

12. *The gross method of accounting for cash discounts may not reflect the fair market value of goods traded.*

The Grimm Co. purchases all of its merchandise from the Anderson Co. Terms of sale are 1/15, n/30. In the month of December the following transactions took place:

    12/1   Grimm purchased $80,000 of merchandise on account.
    12/10   Grimm remitted payment for the goods purchased.
    12/12   Grimm purchased $50,000 of merchandise on account.
    12/31   Grimm remitted payment for the goods purchased.

a. Record the transactions on the books of the Grimm Co. using first the net method and then the gross method.
b. Record the transactions on the books of the Anderson Co. using first the net method and then the gross method. The entries from the standpoint of the seller were not illustrated in the text. They correspond closely to those of the purchaser, however.
c. Assuming that no additional adjustments were made to the accounts and that none of the merchandise acquired by Grimm has yet been sold, comment on any distortions of the accounts that might result from use of the gross method. Suppose that Grimm had sold all or part of the merchandise that it had acquired. What accounts might be misstated? What information, useful for management control, is highlighted by the net method but obscured by the gross method?

13. *Compute simple and compound interest.*

In each of the following situations, determine the interest revenue that a firm should recognize.
a. It holds for 180 days a $3,000 note that earns interest at an annual rate of 8 percent.
b. It holds for 30 days a $10,000 note that earns interest at an annual rate of 6 percent.
c. It holds for 400 days a $1,000 note that earns interest at an annual rate of 12 percent (interest is not to be charged on interest accrued at the end of the first year).
d. It holds for five years a $5,000 note that earns interest at a rate of 7 percent compounded annually.

14. *The stated price of merchandise is not always the "true" price.*

A firm sells merchandise for a supposed price of $1,000 but sometimes grants unusually generous terms of credit. Prevailing rates of interest are 10 percent. De-

termine the amount most indicative of "true" selling price of the merchandise if the buyer
a. Pays $1,000 cash today.
b. Pays $1,000 cash one year from today.
c. Pays $1,000 cash plus interest at 6 percent (that is, $1,060) one year from today.
d. Pays $500 six months from today and $500 one year from today.

15. *Compute the amount of discount notes.*
A bank makes a loan to a customer on a discount basis. Determine the amount that should be advanced to the customer in each of the following situations, assuming that the face amount of the note is $10,000 and the rate of discount is 12 percent per year.
a. The period of the loan is 1 year.
b. The period of the loan is 60 days.
c. The period of the loan is 4 years.

16. *The effective rate of interest on discount loans may be substantially higher than the stated rate.*
The Confidential Loan Co. placed an advertisement in a local newspaper. It read, in part, "Borrow up to $15,000. Take up to 3 Years to Repay. Low, Low, 6% Interest Rate."
Upon visiting the loan company you learn that on a three-year, 6 percent loan of $15,000, interest of $2,700 ($900 per year) is taken out in advance; you would receive only $12,300 cash. You would be required to repay the loan in three annual installments of $5,000.
Indicate the main points that you might make in a letter to the local consumer protection commission. Be sure to specify the approximate effective rate of interest charged by the company.

17. *This problem illustrates a borrowing arrangement that, although not specifically discussed in the text, represents an application of the principles which were described.*
Sometimes a firm will "discount" with a bank an interest-bearing note that it has received from a customer. The bank will advance the firm the amount to be received from the customer, less interest charges for the number of days until the note matures. When the note matures, the customer will make payment to the firm and the firm will transfer the amount received to the bank.
Suppose that a firm receives a one-year note from a customer in the amount of $1,000. The note bears interest at the rate of 8 percent. Immediately upon receipt of the note, the firm discounts it with a bank. The bank, however, accepts notes only at a discount rate of 10 percent.
a. Upon the maturity of the note, how much will the customer be required to remit to the firm?
b. What is the amount that the bank will be willing to advance to the firm based on its discount rate of 10 percent?

18. *Even banks and finance companies face difficult questions of revenue recognition.*
Sunrise Finance Co. loaned a customer $10,000 for two years on a discount basis. The customer was to repay $5,000 at the end of each year. The rate of discount (the *effective* rate of interest) was 12 percent.
a. How much cash would the company actually advance the customer? Prepare a journal entry to record the loan and the receipt by the company of a note for $10,000.
b. How much revenue should the company recognize during the first year of the loan? Prepare a journal entry to record receipt of the first payment of $5,000. At what value will the note be reported (net of discount) after the first year? How much revenue should the company recognize during the second year?

c. Many bankers and managers of finance companies assert that a portion—perhaps 15 percent—of the total revenue to be earned over the two-year period should be recognized at the time the loan is made, without waiting for interest to accrue with the passage of time. In light of the costs of obtaining customers (advertising) and processing loan applications, why do you suspect they feel as they do?

19. *In the real estate industry, it is not uncommon for the selling price of property to include an element of interest.*

   The Lincoln Co. purchased a building from the Polk Co. The stated selling price of the building was $10 million. Polk Co. agreed to accept from the Lincoln Co. an *interest-free* note, which was payable in full five years from the date the transaction was closed.

   The building has an estimated useful life of 20 years and zero salvage value after that period. At time of sale, it had been recorded on the books of the Polk Co. at $4 million. Had Lincoln Co. been required to pay cash for the building, it would have had to borrow the funds from a bank at an annual rate of interest of 10 percent.

   a. Prepare a journal entry to record the purchase of the building on the books of the Lincoln Co. Be certain that the entry recognizes substance over form.

   b. Prepare any journal entries that would be required after the first year of ownership to recognize both interest expense and depreciation.

   c. Determine the difference in Lincoln Co. earnings of the first year that would result from taking into account, as opposed to ignoring, the *imputed* interest.

   d. Determine the difference in Polk Co. earnings of both the first year and second year that would result from taking into account the *imputed* interest. What would be the total difference in earnings in years 1 through 5? (You should not have to compute earnings in each of the five years to answer the question.)

20. *The apparent value of a hotel may be greater than its real value.*

   Resorts, Inc., recently acquired the Flamingo Palace, a luxury hotel, at a stated price of $100 million. Two days after the transaction was completed, the hotel was destroyed by fire. Resorts, Inc., has submitted a claim to its casualty insurance company for $100 million.

   Assume that you are a claims agent of the insurance company. By examining the purchase contract, you learn that Resorts, Inc., had made a down payment of only $20 million and had given a 4 percent mortgage note for the remaining balance of $80 million. The mortgage note required that the loan be repaid in five annual installments. As with a conventional household mortgage, the installments were to be of equal amounts, each representing the repayment of principal plus interest at the rate of 4 percent on the remaining principal balance. With each subsequent payment, the principal balance would decrease. Correspondingly, the proportion of each payment representing principal rather than interest would increase.

   You also learn that the prevailing interest rate on comparable types of loans is 10 percent.

   a. Determine the dollar amount of each required installment.

   b. What is the maximum amount that you would recommend that the insurance company offer in settlement of the claim? Explain and show all computations.

   c. Assume instead that the hotel was not destroyed by fire. The estimated life of the hotel is 20 years (with no residual value). What would be the difference in earnings between what Resorts, Inc., would report if it imputed interest and if it did not (1) in year 1, (2) in year 20, and (3) over the life of the hotel.

21. *Determination of the real value of a business acquired by another may be complex.*

The following note appeared in the 1973 financial report of United Brands Company:

> On December 31, 1973, the Company sold its 83% interest in Baskin-Robbins Ice Cream Company to J. Lyons & Company Limited, a British food company, for a total of $37,600,000 including $30,300,000 in notes. The notes bear interest at 4% per annum and mature in 3 equal annual installments of $10,100,000 commencing on December 31, 1974. The notes have been recorded in the financial statements at an imputed interest rate of 12%.

a. Determine the present value, discounted at 12 percent, of *all* payments (both principal and interest) that United Brands will receive over the three-year period. Be sure to determine the interest payments as 4 percent of the outstanding balance of the notes at the time of each payment.

b. Prepare a journal entry to record the sale of the 83 percent interest in Baskin-Robbins. Assume that the 83 percent interest had been valued on the books of United Brands at $20 million. To simplify the journal entry and subsequent computation of interest, record the present value of the expected principal and interest payments to be received in a single account, "notes receivable."

c. Prepare an entry to record the first receipt of principal and interest. Be sure to base the computation of interest earned on the effective rate of 12 percent and the effective balance in the notes receivable account.

d. How much greater or less would the reported income of United Brands have been in both the year of sale and year of collection of the first principal and interest payment had the company not imputed the additional 8 percent interest?

22. *"Interest-free" loans may mislead customers as well as distort financial statements.*

The Davis Land Development Co. sells real estate on terms of 10 percent down, the balance to be paid in annual installments over a three-year period. Customers are not specifically charged interest on their outstanding balances.

During 1993 the company sold several lots at a stated price of $80,000 each. The original cost to the company of each of the lots was $4,000. The annual interest rate on similar "loans" would be 10 percent.

a. How much *income* do you think the company should recognize at time of sale (upon collection of the 10 percent down payment) assuming recognition of all *sales* (but not *interest*) revenue at time of down payment? Prepare a journal entry to record the transaction.

b. How much income should be recognized at the time of each of the three installment payments? What would be the balances in notes receivable and the related discount account immediately following each payment?

23. *Information that is essential to an evaluation of a franchise is likely to be omitted from the franchiser's financial statements.*

A headline in *The Wall Street Journal* warned, "Jiffy Lube Raises Some Eyebrows with Loans to Its Franchisees for Their Up-Front Expenses." The accompanying column reported that some savvy investors thought the stock of the company, a franchiser of quick-oil-change auto centers, was overpriced. The main concern of the investors was $49 million of notes receivable from franchisees that the company reported as assets. The company had lent franchisees that amount to assist them in paying start-up costs, such as franchise purchase fees, as well as ongoing royalties to the company.

a. Explain why the analysts might be especially skeptical of large amounts of receivables from franchisees? Why are such receivables especially risky?

b. The article also indicated that documents other than Jiffy Lube's financial statements reveal that the company's largest franchisee, which owns 67 outlets,

reported a substantial loss in the year that had just ended. Why is this information critical to an assessment of Jiffy Lube's fiscal capability, even if its receivables include no amounts due from the franchisee?

c. Franchisers are not required to report on the financial health of their franchisees,
either individually or collectively. In light of the obvious significance of this information, do you believe that they should be? If so, how should the data be
presented? What are the major obstacles that a franchiser would face in satisfying such a requirement?

24. *Should a franchiser always recognize revenue at the time it signs a sales contract or are there*
circumstances that justify a delay?

The Peter Pan Cheese Co., after successfully operating a single retail cheese
store for several years, decided to expand its operations. It offered to sell Peter
Pan franchises in several cities for $100,000 each. For that amount, a franchisee
acquired the right to sell under the name "Peter Pan" and to purchase from the
franchiser several products bearing the company name.

Upon signing a contract, a franchisee gave the company an interest-bearing
note for $100,000. The franchisee was required to pay $25,000 upon the opening
of the outlet and could pay the $75,000 balance over a period of three years.

The company estimated that the cost of initial services it would be required
to provide the franchisee prior to the opening of an outlet would be $80,000. In
accord with the provisions of generally accepted accounting principles, it elected
to recognize revenue from the sale of a franchise *at the commencement of an outlet's*
operations.

In 1993 the company signed sales contracts with 10 franchisees. It estimated
that of the $1 million in notes that it received, 6 percent would be uncollectible.

Of the 10 new franchisees, 6 began operations during the year. From these six
the company collected a total of $150,000 in cash on the notes that they had signed.

During the year the company incurred $480,000 in costs in connection with
the outlets actually opened and $350,000 in connection with those expected to open
in the following year. In addition, the company had cash sales of merchandise to
the new outlets of $500,000; the cost of merchandise sold was $400,000. The company also collected interest of $35,000.

a. Prepare an income statement for 1993 to reflect the company's franchise operations. Be sure to match expenses with revenues.

b. Prepare a balance sheet as of year end. Assume that the company began the
year with $500,000 in cash and contributed capital. All costs were paid in cash.

c. Suppose instead that the franchisees were not required to make any payment
on their notes when an outlet was opened. Instead they would have to pay off
10 percent of sales each year until the balance was reduced to zero. Moreover,
the company was unable to make a reliable estimate of the amounts that would
be uncollectible. Do you think the company should recognize revenue on the
sale of franchises at the time an outlet commences operations? On what basis
do you think it should recognize revenue? Explain.

25. *Reported wage expense is generally greater than the amounts actually disbursed to employees.*

Wellman Manufacturing Co. has 100 hourly employees, each of whom worked
40 hours in a week and was paid $6.50 per hour.

Total federal income taxes that the company was required to withhold for
the week were $3,900.

The Social Security (FICA) rate applicable to both employer and employee
was 8 percent.

The company is required to pay 3 percent of gross wages into the State Unemployment Insurance Fund.

The company has a matching pension plan. Employees contribute 5 percent of their wages; the company contributes an equal amount.

The firm is required by union contract to withhold from each employee union dues of $2.50 per week.

Twenty employees have elected to join the savings bond program. Each week $18 is withdrawn from wages and used to purchase a government bond.

The company contributes to medical insurance for each employee. The cost is $8 per week per employee.

a. Prepare a journal entry to record the weekly payroll.

b. Prepare a journal entry to record disbursement of all required payments to the various government agencies, insurance companies, pension funds, etc.

26. *The impact of an accounting change on the balance sheet may be substantially greater than on the income statement. An event may have a significant impact on the interim statements but no effect on the annual statements.*

The Sonora Co. has an annual payroll of approximately $2 million. This amount does *not* include $120,000 paid to employees on vacation. The company does not accrue vacation pay; it charges it to expense as employees take their vacations. The controller has rejected the suggestions of the company's independent CPA that vacation pay be recognized on a week-by-week basis; he claims that such recognition would have no effect on the financial statements; it would only increase clerical costs.

The payroll of the company has remained constant for a number of years. Employees are entitled to three weeks of vacation each year based on work performed in the previous fiscal year, and the vacations must be taken during July and August. Employees receive their regular wages while on vacation, and all employees must be replaced by temporary employees at the same wage rate. The company's fiscal year ends June 30.

a. Is the controller correct in his assertion that accrual of vacation pay would have no impact on the financial statements? Estimate the impact of a change in policy on both the income statement and the balance sheet.

b. Suppose the firm were to issue *interim* financial statements on December 31 for the six months ending on that date. What would be the impact of accruing vacation pay on the income statement and the balance sheet?

27. *An increase in the current ratio may not necessarily be indicative of an improved financial position.*

The president of a company, in requesting a renewal of an outstanding loan, wrote to an officer of a bank: "In spite of a decline in sales and earnings, we were able to strengthen our working capital position." She went on to cite the increase in the current ratio as evidence of the improvement.

The balance sheet of the company reported the following current assets and liabilities:

	December 31, 1993	December 31, 1992
Cash	$ 60,000	$120,000
Accounts receivable	270,000	190,000
Inventories	420,000	300,000
Total current assets	$750,000	$610,000
Accounts payable	$370,000	$330,000
Notes payable	140,000	140,000
Total current liabilities	$510,000	$470,000

The income statement (in summary form) revealed the following:

	1993	1992
Sales	$1,400,000	$1,560,000
Cost of goods sold	$ 840,000	$ 936,000
Other expenses	240,000	260,000
Total expenses	$1,080,000	1,196,000
Net income	$ 320,000	$ 364,000

a. Determine the current ratio for both years.
b. (1) Determine the quick ratio.
   (2) Calculate number of days' sales in accounts receivable.
c. Provide a possible explanation for the increase in accounts receivable and inventories that would undermine the contention of the president that the firm's working capital position has improved. Has the current position of the company really improved?

28. *The manner in which a ratio is computed depends on the purpose to which it is put; conclusions from ratios must be drawn with care.*

The following data (in millions of dollars) were taken from an annual report of a manufacturer of vacuum cleaners:

	1993	1992
Sales	$754.3	$691.8
Notes and accounts receivables less allowances for bad debts (in millions) of $2.4 in 1993 and $2.0 in 1992	143.6	143.7

a. On the basis of accounts receivable turnover, in which year did the firm employ its receivables more effectively? (Compute receivables turnover *gross*—that is, without reduction for allowances—and use year-end rather than average sales.)
b. Suppose that the firm sells on terms 2/10, n/30. What concern would be raised by a calculation of number of days' sales in accounts receivable? Inasmuch, however, as the data combine notes receivable and accounts receivable, why might your concern be unwarranted?
c. A question is often raised as to whether ratios involving accounts receivable, such as the current ratio and the quick ratio, should incorporate accounts receivable gross or net of allowances for bad debt. Why might your response be different if you were providing an answer to a banker who is interested primarily in the ability of the firm to collect on its outstanding receivables and repay its debts than if you were responding to a manager who is concerned with minimizing the amount of funds tied up in "unproductive" assets?

Solutions to Exercise for Review and Self-Testing

1. The fair market value of the equipment may be obtained by calculating the value *today* of the note. Per Table 2 in the Appendix, the present value of $1 to be received in one year, discounted at a rate of 12 percent, is $.8929. The present value of the note therefore is $1,040 × .8929, or $928.62. The fair market value of the equipment therefore would also be $928.62.

2. Notes receivable $1,040.00
     Notes receivable, discount $111.38
     Sales revenue 928.62

   To record sale of equipment

3. Cash $1,040.00
 Notes receivable, discount 111.38
     Notes receivable $1,040.00
     Interest revenue 111.38

   To record collection of the note and to recognize interest revenue for one year (Interest of $111.38 is 12% of the initial net balance of the note, $98.62.)

4. Sales, uncollectibles $7,000
     Notes receivable, allowance for uncollectibles $7,000

   To record estimate of bad debts

5. Notes receivable, allowance for uncollectibles $2,500
     Note receivable $2,500

   To write off specific notes that are uncollectible

8

Inventories and Cost of Goods Sold

The term *inventory* refers to goods that are awaiting sale or are in the various stages of production. It includes the merchandise of a trading concern as well as the finished goods, the work in process, and the raw materials of a manufacturer. In addition, the term embraces goods that will be consumed indirectly as the enterprise manufactures its product or provides its service. Thus stores of stationery, cleaning supplies, and lubricants would also be categorized as inventories. Proper accounting for inventories is critical not only because they often compose a substantial portion of a firm's assets but also because they relate directly to what is frequently the firm's major expense—the cost of goods sold. The beginning inventory balance plus purchases minus the ending inventory balance equals the cost of goods sold. This chapter is directed to several key accounting issues pertaining to inventory, some of which are currently at the center of active controversy. Among the questions raised are

What are the objectives of inventory measurement and valuation?
What costs should be included in inventory?
How should inventory quantities be determined?
What assumptions regarding the flow of costs are most appropriate in particular
    circumstances?
When and how should changes in the market prices of inventories be recog-
    nized?

The discussion of inventories is in the context of generally accepted accounting principles—how inventories are accounted for in practice. But consideration is also given, in a concluding section, to alternatives that have been proposed but are not presently viewed as acceptable.

The overriding objective of conventional inventory accounting is to match the costs of acquiring or producing goods with the revenues that they generate. The emphasis is decidedly on income determination rather than on balance sheet valuation. It is to assure that the resultant measure of income is useful for evaluating performance of the past and making predictions of the future. An unfortunate consequence is that the amounts reported on the balance sheet are indicative of costs incurred in the past—sometimes, in fact, in the very distant past. They provide information on neither the prices that would have to be paid to replace the goods on hand nor those for which they could be sold.

In a typical operating cycle of a firm, the costs of goods that are either manufactured or purchased are included in inventory and reported as an asset. Even though the goods may have been paid for, their costs are not considered to be expenses. Instead the costs are *stored* on the balance sheet until the goods are sold and the costs can be associated with specific revenues. At the end of a year, a portion of the *goods* remains on hand; the rest have been sold to outsiders. A portion of the costs therefore must be assigned to the goods that remain on hand and the rest to the goods that have been sold. That portion of the costs that is assigned to the goods on hand will continue to be carried on the balance sheet, while that assigned to the goods that have been sold will be charged to an expense account, cost of goods sold, and reported on the income statement. The question facing the firm is "How much of the total costs should be assigned to the goods on hand and how much to the goods that have been sold?" The issue is depicted in Exhibit 8-1.

Insofar as a greater value is placed on the goods in inventory, a lesser amount will be charged as an expense. Insofar as a greater amount is charged as a current expense, then smaller amounts will remain on the balance sheet to be charged as expenses in future years.

EXHIBIT 8-1

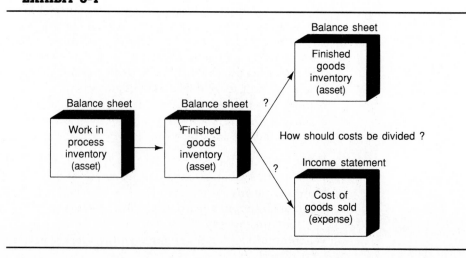

Chap. 8 Inventories and Cost of Goods Sold

Inventories are ordinarily stated at historical cost—that of acquisition or production. Cost, as applied to inventories, "means in principle the sum of the applicable expenditures and charges directly or indirectly incurred in bringing an article to its existing condition and location."[1] If goods are purchased from outsiders, then cost would include not only the invoice price but also costs of packaging and transportation. Trade, cash, or other special discounts or allowances must be deducted from the stated price.

As a rule, all costs that can reasonably be associated with the manufacture or acquisition, with the storage, or with the preparation for sale of goods should be included as part of the cost of such goods. In determining whether a particular item of cost should be added to the reported value of inventory, the impact on both the income statement and the balance sheet should be taken into account. If costs are added to the reported value of goods on hand, they will be charged as expenses (as part of cost of goods sold) in the period in which the merchandise is actually sold. By contrast, if the costs are not assigned to particular items of inventory, they will be charged as expenses in the periods in which they are incurred, regardless of when the merchandise is sold.

Example

A company purchased 100 units of product at $20 per unit. It was permitted a trade discount (one granted to all customers in a particular category) of 5 percent but had to pay shipping costs of $300. Cost per unit would be computed as follows:

Base price (100 units @ $20)	$2,000	
Less trade discount (5%)	100	$1,900
Plus shipping costs		300
Total cost of 100 units		$2,200
Number of units		÷ 100 units
Cost per unit		$ 22

If goods are produced by the company itself, the problem of cost determination is considerably more complex. Cost includes charges for labor and materials that can be directly associated with the product as well as *overhead* such as rent, maintenance, and utilities that may be common to several products produced in the same plant. To determine the cost of a particular product, a company has to allocate these common charges among the various products. In addition, however, the firm has to decide whether certain costs should be considered *product* costs, and thereby added to the carrying value of the goods produced, or *period* costs, and thereby charged off as an expense as incurred. The implications of classifying an

---

[1]*Accounting Research Bulletin No. 43,* Committee on Accounting Procedure, American Institute of Certified Public Accountants, 1961.

outlay as a product rather than a period cost were discussed earlier in Chapter 4 in connection with the discussion of the manufacturing cycle.

ACCOUNTING FOR QUANTITIES ON HAND

Periodic versus Perpetual Bases

In Chapter 4 it was pointed out that inventories may be maintained on a perpetual or a periodic basis. A *perpetual basis* implies that accounting recognition is given to the diminution of inventories each time a sale is made, supplies are consumed, or raw materials are added to production. When goods are removed from inventory upon a sale, for example, the following journal entry would be made:

Cost of goods sold xxxx
    Inventory xxxx

The *periodic method,* on the other hand, recognizes the reduction in inventory resulting from the sale or use of goods only periodically, perhaps once a year. The sum of the beginning inventory and the goods added during the year constitutes a pool of costs that at year end will be divided between the income statement (cost of goods sold) and the balance sheet (inventory).

As goods are added to inventory during the year, the inventory account is debited with their cost.[2] As goods are removed, however, no entry is made. Throughout the year, therefore, the inventory account misstates the cost of the goods actually on hand. At the end of the period, a physical count of goods on hand is taken. The goods are assigned their acquisition cost, and the inventory account is adjusted to reflect the resultant dollar amount. Goods not on hand are assumed to have been sold, and their cost is charged to cost of goods sold.

Assume that a firm begins the year with a balance in inventory of $1 million. During the year it purchases goods of $9 million and debits the purchases to its inventory account. At year end the inventory account would have a balance of $10 million. A physical count, however, reveals only $500,000 of goods on hand. Hence, $9.5 million of the $10 million must be charged to cost of goods sold. The following entry (in millions) would be appropriate:

Cost of goods sold $9.5
    Inventory $9.5
To adjust the year-end inventory account to reflect goods actually on hand

Although this text is not primarily directed toward the record-keeping procedures of enterprises, the two alternative methods of accounting for inventories are explained here because they *may* have an impact on the reported value of

---

[2]As noted in Chapter 4, many firms, as they acquire inventory, debit an account entitled "purchases" rather than the inventory account itself. At year end, they transfer the balance in the purchases account to the inventory account by debiting "inventory" and crediting "purchases." See page 126 for an example.

inventories at year end. The circumstances in which a difference may occur will be identified in the following discussion of the flows of costs.

FLOWS OF COSTS

The critical issue of inventory accounting, that of flows of costs, arises because the acquisition or production costs of goods do not remain constant. As a consequence, it is sometimes necessary to make assumptions as to which goods have been sold and which remain on hand—those with the higher costs or those with the lower. (Recall the example in the first chapter of the text pertaining to the cost of a chemical solvent.) In some situations, identification of specific costs with specific goods presents no problem. The goods have sufficiently different characteristics that they can readily be tagged with specific costs. The costs to retailers of automobiles, appliances, or rare pieces of jewelry, for example, can easily be associated with specific units. Not so, however, with *fungible* (interchangeable) goods such as grains or liquids, purchases of which made at different times are mixed together, or with most small items, such as canned goods or items of clothing for which it is inconvenient to account for each unit independently. Moreover, for reasons to be indicated shortly, accountants sometimes find it desirable to make assumptions regarding the flow of *costs* that are in obvious conflict with available information regarding the flow of *goods*.

SPECIFIC IDENTIFICATION

The specific identification inventory method requires the enterprise to keep track of the cost of each individual item bought and sold. Ordinarily, a firm would either code the cost directly on the item itself or otherwise tag each item with a control number and maintain a separate record of costs.

Refer, for example, to the data provided in Exhibit 8-2, which indicates quantities of an item purchased and sold on various dates. Also indicated are the opening balance, the prices at which the various acquisitions were made, and the total cost of each acquisition. Assume that of the 200 items that were sold on 4/20, 100 units were taken from the lot that was on hand on 1/1 and 100 were taken from that purchased on 3/2. Of the 300 items sold on 11/8, 100

EXHIBIT 8-2
Purchases and Sales of a Particular Item

	Purchases				
Date	No. of Units	Unit Cost	Total Cost	No. of Units Sold	No. of Units on Hand
1/1 (bal. on hand)	300	$5	$1,500		300
3/2	100	6	600		400
4/20				200	200
5/25	400	8	3,200		600
9/18	200	7	1,400		800
11/8				300	500
Total	1,000		$6,700	500	

were taken from the lot on hand on 1/1 and 200 from that purchased on 5/25. The cost of goods sold would be computed as follows:

Sale of 4/20			
From lot of 1/1	100 @ $5	$ 500	
From lot of 3/2	100 @ $6	600	
	200	$1,100	
Sale of 11/8			
From lot of 1/1	100 @ $5	$ 500	
From lot of 5/25	200 @ $8	1,600	
	300	$2,100	
Cost of goods sold	500	$3,200	

Total merchandise costs to be accounted for during the year (initial balance plus purchases) are $6,700. If the cost of goods sold is $3,200, then the balance of the total costs must be that of the goods still on hand at year end—$6,700 minus $3,200 = $3,500. This amount can be verified by the following tabulation of ending inventory:

From lot of 1/1	100 @ $5	$ 500
From lot of 5/25	200 @ $8	1,600
From lot of 9/18	200 @ $7	1,400
Ending inventory	500	$3,500

The specific identification method is most appropriate for dealers, such as those of automobiles and appliances, who sell relatively few items of large unit cost. It becomes burdensome to firms that sell large quantities of low-cost items. The specific identification method is rational in that it assures that the amounts charged as expenses are the actual costs of the specific goods sold. But at the same time, especially if the goods sold are similar to one another, it permits the firm to manage income. If, in the example, management wanted to report a higher income, it could simply have made certain that the units sold were taken from a lot of lower cost (e.g., the goods sold on 11/8 were taken from the $7 lot of 9/18 rather than from the $8 lot of 5/25).

FIRST IN, FIRST OUT

Most well-managed businesses sell goods in the order in which they have been acquired. This practice minimizes losses from spoilage and deterioration. In the absence of the ability or the willingness to expend the required time and effort to identify the cost of specific units sold, the assumption that goods acquired first are sold first is likely to provide a reasonable approximation of the actual flow of goods. Under the *first-in, first-out* approach, commonly abbreviated *FIFO,* the flow of *costs* (that which is of primary concern to the accountant) is presumed to be the same as the usual flow of *goods.* The FIFO method can be demonstrated using the data presented in Exhibit 8-2.

To compute the cost of goods sold, the items sold on 4/20 would be assumed to have come from the lot that was purchased first—that on hand on 1/1, assuming a perpetual inventory system. The items sold on 11/8 would be assumed to have come from the balance of the 1/1 lot and lots of 3/2 and 5/25. Cost of goods sold therefore would be $2,900:

Sale of 4/20		
From lot of 1/1	200 @ $5	$1,000
Sale of 11/8		
From lot of 1/1	100 @ $5	500
From lot of 3/2	100 @ $6	600
From lot of 5/25	100 @ $8	800
	300	$1,900
Cost of goods sold	500	$2,900

If 500 units were sold at a cost of $2,900, then still to be accounted for are the remaining 500 units, at a cost of $6,700 minus $2,900, or $3,800. These items—the ones still on hand—would be assumed to be those that were purchased most recently (and calculated first under a periodic system):

From lot of 5/25	300 @ $8	$2,400
From lot of 9/18	200 @ $7	1,400
Ending inventory	500	$3,800

An Evaluation

Proponents of the FIFO method point out that not only is the underlying assumption that goods purchased first are sold first in accord with conventional management practice but that the method eliminates the opportunities for income manipulation that are possible if costs are identified with specific units.[3] Regardless of which items are actually sold, for accounting purposes it will be assumed that those purchased first have been sold first. Moreover, FIFO provides a balance sheet value that comprises those items purchased last. In most instances the most recent acquisitions are more indicative of current replacement costs than are those purchased earlier. Insofar as current values are of interest to investors and other readers of financial statements, then FIFO provides a more useful balance sheet valuation than do any of the other methods to be discussed. (But as pointed out previously, the balance sheet, in the context of currently accepted accounting principles, should be viewed as a compendium of *residuals,* unexpired costs, as opposed to current market values.)

WEIGHTED AVERAGE

The weighted average inventory method is based on the assumption that all costs can be aggregated and that the cost to be assigned to any particular unit should be the weighted average of the costs of the units held and available for sale during the accounting period. The weighted average method assumes no particular flow of goods. The cost of any unit sold is simply the average of those

---

[3]In some industries, of course, goods sold first may be those that are acquired last. A gravel company, for example, might reasonably place newly acquired gravel at the top of a pile and remove the gravel from the top as it is sold.

available for sale—an average that is weighted by the number of units acquired at each particular price.

In the discussion of both the specific identification and FIFO methods, no distinction was made between the methods as they would be applied by firms that maintain perpetual inventory records and those which update their records only periodically after taking a physical count of goods on hand. It would make no difference in either cost of goods sold or ending inventory whether the firm followed perpetual or periodic procedures. In applying the weighted average method, however, the results would not be the same. The weighted average cost of goods on hand at the end of the year may differ from those calculated at various times throughout the year. Hence the costs assigned to the various quantities sold would also differ.

Weighted Average—Periodic Basis

To apply the weighted average method on a *periodic* basis, the firm would assign a cost to all goods—both those that were sold and those in inventory at year end—that represents the weighted average of the cost of *all* goods available for sale during the period. The cost of the goods on hand at the beginning of the year as well as those purchased during the year would be considered in the calculation of the average. The weighted average, based on the information in Exhibit 8-2, would be calculated as follows:

Balance 1/1	300 @ $5	$1,500
Lot of 3/2	100 @ $6	600
Lot of 5/25	400 @ $8	3,200
Lot of 9/18	200 @ $7	1,400
	1,000	$6,700

The average cost of goods available for sale would be $6,700/1,000 = $6.70.

Inasmuch as 500 units were sold during the period, the cost of goods sold would be 500 times $6.70, or $3,350. Since, by coincidence, 500 units remain unsold at year end, the closing inventory would also be 500 times $6.70, or $3,350.

Weighted Average—Perpetual Basis

If the weighted average method were to be applied on a perpetual basis (see Exhibit 8-3), then a new weighted (or *moving*) average of the cost of goods available for sale would have to be computed after each purchase at a different price. This average cost would be assigned to both the goods sold and those that remain in inventory. For example, the total cost of goods available for sale, after the purchase of 3/2, would be

Cost of goods available for sale on 4/20		
Balance 1/1	300 @ $5	$1,500
Lot of 3/2	100 @ $6	600
	400	$2,100

EXHIBIT 8-3
Perpetual Inventory Record Weighted (Moving) Average Method

Date	Purchases Units	Unit Cost	Total Cost	Sales Units	Unit Cost	Total Cost	Balance Units	Total Cost	Unit Cost
1/1							300	$1,500.00	$5.00
3/2	100	$6.00	$ 600				400	2,100.00	5.25
4/20				200	$5.25	$1,050.00	200	1,050.00	5.25
5/25	400	8.00	3,200				600	4,250.00	7.0833
9/18	200	7.00	1,400				800	5,650.00	7.0625
11/8				300	7.0625	2,118.75	500	3,531.25	7.0625

Average cost of goods available for sale would be $2,100/400 = $5.25.

The cost assigned to the 200 units sold on 4/20 would be 200 times $5.25, or $1,050. That assigned to the 200 units that remain in inventory after the sale of 4/20 would also be $1,050.

The average cost of goods available for the next sale, that of 11/8, would be based on the average cost of goods on hand immediately following the last sale (i.e., 200 units at $5.25 per unit) plus that of the subsequent acquisitions. Thus

Cost of goods available for sale on 11/8		
Balance of 4/20	200 @ $5.25	$1,050
Lot of 5/25	400 @ $8.00	3,200
Lot of 9/18	200 @ $7.00	1,400
	800	$5,650

Average cost of goods available for sale would be $5,650/800 = $7.0625.

The cost assigned to the 300 units sold on 11/8 would be 300 times $7.06256, or $2,118.75, and that to the 500 units remaining on hand at year end would be 500 times $7.0625, or $3,531.25 (or $5,650 minus the $2,118.75 assigned to the goods sold). The total cost of goods sold for the year would be the sum of the costs assigned to each of the two lots sold:

Total cost of goods sold during the year	
Goods sold on 4/20	$1,050.00
Goods sold on 11/8	2,118.75
Total	$3,168.75

This compares with $3,350 calculated using the periodic procedures.

An Evaluation

The weighted average method can be set forth as representing the physical flow of goods when all goods available for sale are mixed together with one another—as would be the case with liquids or other fungible goods. When applied on a periodic basis, however, this justification becomes tenuous. If goods are purchased subsequent to the last sale of the year, then their cost will enter into the average cost of the goods sold during the year, even though they could not possibly have been sold. Suppose that in the example presented, the firm on 12/1, well after the last sale of the year, acquired 1,000 units at $20 per unit. The 1,000 units at $20 per unit would be included in the computation of the average cost of the units sold, even though it is obvious that none of them were actually sold. The weighted average method, as applied on a periodic basis, owes its popularity to its convenience. However, if cost of goods sold is affected by merchandise purchased after the final sale of the year, it is decidedly lacking in theoretical support.

LAST IN, FIRST OUT

In recent years the last-in, first-out method has been the focus of accounting controversy pertaining to inventory valuation. As its name implies, the *last-in, first-out* method (*LIFO*) assigns to goods sold the costs of those goods that have been purchased last. It is based on the assumption that, irrespective of the actual physical flow of goods, the goods sold are those that have been acquired last and the goods that remain on hand are those that have been acquired first. No pretense is made that the flow of costs even approximates the usual flow of goods.

As with the weighted average method, there will be significant differences in the cost of goods sold, as well as in the ending inventory, if a firm follows periodic as opposed to perpetual inventory procedures. If the firm determines ending inventory and cost of goods sold based on a *periodic* (i.e., annual) inventory count, then the cost of goods sold will be the cost of products that were purchased *closest to the year end*. If the firm maintains *perpetual* records, then the cost of the goods sold will be considered to be the cost of units that were purchased *closest to each individual sale*. Only LIFO assuming periodic procedures will be illustrated here as firms seldom use LIFO in association with perpetual systems.[4]

As indicated in Exhibit 8-2, the firm sold 500 units during the year. The cost to be assigned to those 500 units will be that of the 500 units purchased most recently, i.e., those purchased on 9/18 and 5/25:

Cost of goods sold		
From lot of 9/18	200 @ $7	$1,400
From lot of 5/25	300 @ $8	2,400
Cost of goods sold	500	$3,800

Since there was a total of 1,000 items available for sale at a total cost of $6,700, the costs that would be assigned to the ending inventory would be $6,700 minus the $3,800 assigned to the goods sold, or $2,900. Ending inventory would be composed of the 500 items, including those that were on hand at the beginning of the year, that were purchased first:

[4]For guidance on applying LIFO on a perpetual basis, see problem 2 at the conclusion of this chapter.

Ending inventory		
From lot of 1/1	300 @ $5	$1,500
From lot of 3/2	100 @ $6	600
From lot of 5/25	100 @ $8	800
Ending inventory	500	$2,900

Exhibit 8-4 summarizes the costs of goods sold and the ending inventories under the FIFO, weighted average, and LIFO methods.

The Rationale for LIFO

Very few firms sell or use first the goods that they have acquired last. In some situations, a company might indeed store certain commodities in a pile and remove goods as needed from the top of the heap—that portion of total goods that presumably has been added last. This would be the case in firms maintaining stores of coal or sand. But LIFO is not used only when the physical flow of goods follows a last-in, first-out pattern. It is applied even when goods acquired first are sold first. The justification for the use of LIFO must be found in reasons other than that it is representative of the physical flow of goods.

Matching Current Costs with Current Revenues

The objective of inventory accounting, it was previously indicated, is to *match* the costs of acquiring or producing goods with the revenues that they generate. The more specific objective of the LIFO method is to match the *current costs* of acquiring or producing the goods with the current revenues from sales. Under LIFO the cost of goods sold is considered to be that of the goods most recently acquired.

Eliminating "Inventory" Profits

Proponents of LIFO point out that a business must maintain a minimum supply of goods on hand. This basic stock of goods is as essential to the firm's continued operations as are its fixed assets, such as machinery and equipment.

Suppose, for example, that a business must have a minimum inventory of 100 units. At the start of a year it has on hand 100 units which had cost $1,000 each. During the year it sells 100 units at a price of $1,200. At year end it re-

EXHIBIT 8-4
Summary of Cost of Goods Sold and Ending Inventory

	Cost of Goods Sold	Ending Inventory	Total Costs Accounted for
First in, first out (FIFO)*	$2,900.00	$3,800.00	$6,700
Weighted average			
Periodic	3,350.00	3,350.00	6,700
Perpetual	3,168.75	3,531.25	6,700
Last in, first out (LIFO)			
Periodic	3,800.00	2,900.00	6,700

*Cost of goods sold and inventory would be the same regardless of whether inventory records were maintained on a periodic or a perpetual basis.

EXHIBIT 8-5
LIFO Eliminates ''Inventory Profits''

Assumptions

Inventory balance at start of year	100 units @ $1,000	$100,000
Purchases	100 units @ $1,200	120,000
Sales	100 units @ $1,200	120,000
Minimum required inventory, 100 units		

Cash Flow

Sales	$120,000
Less purchases	120,000
Net inflow	$ 0

	Income	
	FIFO	**LIFO**
Sales (100 units @ $1,200)	$120,000	$120,000
Cost of goods sold		
100 units @ $1,000	100,000	
100 units @ $1,200		120,000
Income	$ 20,000*	$ 0

*Is the company really $20,000 better off at the end of the year than it was at the beginning?

plenishes its inventory, purchasing an additional 100 units. The purchase price, however, has increased to $1,200. Exhibit 8-5 summarizes these assumptions and indicates alternative computations of income.

If inventory and cost of goods sold were to be determined on a FIFO basis, then ending inventory would be valued at $1,200 per unit; the cost of goods sold would be $1,000 per unit. The firm would report a profit of $200 per unit—a total of $20,000. Is the firm really $20,000 better off than it was at the beginning of the period?

Since the firm deemed it necessary to maintain an inventory of 100 units, it would be unable to distribute to owners any funds from the business without contracting operations. It would be required to use the entire $20,000 gain to replace the goods that it had sold. The $20,000, according to proponents of LIFO, is not a ''true'' profit; rather, it represents an *inventory profit*. The inventory profit is nothing more than the difference between the initial cost of the minimum stock and its current cost.

Under LIFO, ending inventory would be reported at $1,000 per unit and cost of goods sold at $1,200. Since the items were sold at a price of $1,200 per unit, the firm would report zero profit for the year. Inventory would be valued on the balance sheet at the amount initially invested in the 100 units. The firm would not appear to be $20,000 better off when, as the advocates of LIFO point out, it is in the identical position at the end of the year that it was at the beginning.

Reducing Distortions in Income Attributable to Inflation

LIFO represents an attempt to reduce distortions in the income statement attributable to inflation. In a period of stable prices, both inventory and cost of goods sold would be identical under FIFO and LIFO. In a period of rising prices, compared with FIFO, LIFO would ordinarily result in a lower reported value for inventory (since goods are being valued at the earliest prices paid) and correspondingly a lower reported income (since the cost of goods sold is being determined on the basis of the most recent purchases—those at the higher prices).

Exhibit 8-6 compares reported cost of goods sold and year-end inventory for a five-year period. It is based on the assumption that at the start of 1992 a firm had on hand 1,000 units at $100 each. During each of the next five years, the firm sold 1,000 units and purchased 1,000 units. The cost of the units purchased increased at a compound rate of 10 percent per year.

As indicated in Exhibit 8-6 the difference each year in cost of goods sold is equal to the difference between the cost of goods purchased in the previous year and the cost of those purchased in the current year. Under FIFO, goods

EXHIBIT 8-6
Five-Year Comparison between FIFO and LIFO

Table 1: FIFO

	Cost of Goods Purchased	FIFO Cost of Goods Sold		FIFO Ending Inventory	
	Per Unit	Per Unit	Total (1,000 units)	Per Unit	Total (1,000 units)
1991				$100.00	$100,000
1992	$110.00	$100.00	$100,000	110.00	110,000
1993	121.00	110.00	110,000	121.00	121,000
1994	133.10	121.00	121,000	133.10	133,100
1995	146.41	133.10	133,100	146.41	146,410
1996	161.05	146.41	146,410	161.05	161,050
Total			$610,510		

Table 2: LIFO

	Cost of Goods Purchased	LIFO Cost of Goods Sold		LIFO Ending Inventory	
	Per Unit	Per Unit	Total (1,000 units)	Per Unit	Total (1,000 units)
1991				$100.00	$100,000
1992	$110.00	$110.00	$110,000	100.00	100,000
1993	121.00	121.00	121,000	100.00	100,000
1994	133.10	133.10	133,100	100.00	100,000
1995	146.41	146.41	146,410	100.00	100,000
1996	161.05	161.05	161,050	100.00	100,000
Total			$671,560		

Table 3: Differences between FIFO and LIFO
(Table 1 minus Table 2)

	Cost of Goods Sold		Ending Inventory	
	Per Unit	Total (1,000 units)	Per Unit	Total (1,000 units)
1992	$10.00	$10,000	$10.00	$10,000
1993	11.00	11,000	21.00	21,000
1994	12.10	12,100	33.10	33,100
1995	13.31	13,310	46.41	46,410
1996	14.64	14,640	61.05	61,050
Total	$61.05	$61,050		

sold in 1992 are assumed to be purchased in 1991; under LIFO, goods sold in 1992 are assumed to be purchased in 1992. Proponents of LIFO argue that because FIFO matches the current revenues with the cost of goods acquired in a previous period, it consistently understates the "true" cost of goods sold and as a result overstates income.

The difference in ending inventory is considerably more striking. Under FIFO, goods on hand at the end of 1996 are assumed to have been purchased in 1996; under LIFO, they are assumed to have been purchased in 1991 (each year's sales are assumed to have been taken from the current year's purchases; the stock on hand at the start of 1992 is assumed never to have been depleted). The difference in ending inventory at the end of 1996 ($61,050) is the equivalent of the cumulative difference in cost of goods sold for the five-year period ($671,560 versus $610,510).

LIFO—The Objections

The effects of LIFO on both the balance sheet and the income statement are, in the view of some managers and accountants, unacceptable. LIFO results in a reported inventory that is continually out of date. If the firm never dips into its base stock (for example, in Exhibit 8-6, the inventory was never reduced below 1,000 units), then the reported inventory would be reflective of prices that existed at the time LIFO was first adopted, decades earlier perhaps. The balance sheet, as continually emphasized in this text, is not purported to be representative of current values. Nevertheless, many accountants feel uncomfortable when values that are preposterously out of date are assigned.

More serious, however, is the impact of LIFO on reported income when the firm is required to dip into its base stock. If the firm is required to sell goods that are valued on the balance sheet at decades-old prices, then the cost of goods sold will be based on the same ancient prices. Refer back to Exhibit 8-6. Suppose that in 1996 the firm was unable to purchase its required 1,000 units. Instead, it sold its goods on hand and thereby reduced its end-of-year inventory to zero. The cost of goods sold would be $100 per unit—the price of the goods on hand when the company first adopted LIFO in 1992—this at a time when the current replacement cost of the goods is $146.41 per unit. If the cost of goods sold is misleadingly low, then reported income would, of course, be correspondingly high. Whatever its advantages when the firm is able to meet current sales out of current purchases, LIFO produces results that are absurd when it becomes necessary to reduce inventory below a level that is historically normal. Many accountants who are opposed to LIFO recognize the need to account for rapid increases in the replacement costs of inventories. They believe, however, that it should be done directly, by adjusting both cost of goods sold and goods on hand to reflect current values. Current cost accounting as it applies to inventories will be discussed later in this chapter.

LIFO—Its Recent Popularity

From the mid-1970s on, several hundred major U.S. firms shifted from either a FIFO or a moving average to a LIFO inventory valuation method. The shifts were motivated almost entirely by the opportunities to reduce the federal income tax burden.

Since 1938, the Internal Revenue Code has recognized the acceptability of LIFO. In periods of rapid inflation, such as those experienced in many industrial nations in the 1970s and early 1980s, LIFO has been particularly popular. By basing the cost of goods sold on the most recent purchases, LIFO reduces taxable income. The difference in taxable income between that determined on a FIFO or average cost as opposed to a LIFO basis may not be trivial. Du Pont, for example, estimated that its shift from average cost to LIFO reduced income by over $250 million and reduced its earnings per share by $3.02 (from $11.22 to $8.20). Other major corporations effected similar reductions in earnings and hence in taxes. Estimates of the overall loss in tax revenues to the federal government range up to $40 billion per year.

As a rule, when there are alternative accounting methods that are generally accepted, businesses are not required to use the same method in reporting to the Internal Revenue Service as they do in reporting to their stockholders. With respect to the method of determining inventories, however, the tax code makes an exception. If a company adheres to one method in reporting to the general public, it usually must use the same method in reporting to the IRS. As a consequence of this ruling, firms that wish to take advantage of the tax-savings opportunities provided by LIFO are ordinarily required to switch to LIFO for general reporting purposes.

Quite apart from the tax advantages of LIFO, some financial analysts consider earnings of LIFO-based companies to be of higher "quality" than those of FIFO or average cost firms. What they mean is that were it not for the "inflated" value of their inventories, the earnings of the non-LIFO firms may have been considerably lower and growth trends somewhat more flat.

LIFO—Can a Firm Afford Not to Adopt It?

Many accountants, in particular accounting researchers, assert that in periods of inflation, the use of any inventory method other than LIFO cannot be justified. LIFO permits a company to postpone tax payments and thereby to increase the amount of cash available for other corporate purposes. Failure to switch to LIFO, some say, is the equivalent of making a donation to the taxing authorities. They assert that fears of adverse consequences of the decline in *reported* earnings that results from a switch to LIFO are unwarranted. The benefits of higher reported earnings attributable to non-LIFO methods are at best illusory. There is highly persuasive, if not conclusive, evidence to indicate that investors as a group are not influenced by the higher earnings that would generally be reported by a company using a non-LIFO inventory method. A number of empirical studies have revealed that use of LIFO has no discernible negative impact on the market value of a firm's common stock. Investors are apparently able to "discount" the higher earnings caused solely by choice of inventory method.

It is ironic that non-LIFO methods may enable a firm to report higher earnings and correspondingly greater net worth than LIFO methods. In economic substance, the non-LIFO methods may leave the company worse off. LIFO has no effect on *actual* cost of goods sold (i.e., the cash outlays) or the value (replacement costs or expected selling prices) of the goods on hand. It may enable a company to delay the payment of taxes and thereby to reduce the present value of future tax payments. In economic substance therefore, the use of LIFO may enhance the net worth of the company in the amount of the present value of the difference in expected tax payments.

Nonetheless, many large firms, including such large and well-managed companies as IBM and ITT, do not account for the major portion of their inventories on a LIFO basis. Several explanations have been offered by executives of these firms as well as by outside observers:

1. The firms are in industries in which prices are declining. Despite the widespread inflation of recent years, not all goods have increased in price. Prices of electronic equipment, such as computers and calculators, are among the more notable examples.
2. Because of special features of the tax laws, firms may not have taxable income even if they have reportable earnings. Thus the firms may not currently be paying taxes and see no need to switch until such time as they are.
3. Firms are fearful of having to sell goods being carried on the books at artificially low values. A "dip into the LIFO base" may be caused by strikes, general economic downturns, or cyclical movements within an industry. This may result in inordinately large increases in taxable income and correspondingly large increases in taxes. The taxes postponed in several previous years may have to be paid in a single year. Although the firms would have benefited over the years from the cash that would otherwise have been paid to the government, their executives believe that the additional problems of cash management (and perhaps costs) are not offset by the present value of the taxes postponed.
4. The reduction in *reported* earnings owing to a shift to LIFO may have adverse *economic consequences* for the firm or its managers. This would be the case when contractual arrangements with lenders or other parties specify that to be eligible for continued funding or other benefits, the firm must maintain its reported earnings or net worth above an established level. Similarly, the shift might reduce the salaries and bonuses of employee groups (including the executives responsible for selecting the inventory method) if compensation is tied to reported earnings. Thus a mere *accounting* change would have genuine *economic* consequences.

LOWER OF COST OR MARKET RULE

Regardless of which of the previously described inventory methods a firm adopts, the application of generally accepted accounting principles requires a departure from cost whenever the utility of the goods on hand has diminished since the date of acquisition. Loss of utility might be the result of physical damage or deterioration, obsolescence, or a general decline in the level of prices. Loss of utility should be given accounting recognition by stating the inventories at *cost* or *market, whichever is lower*. In this expression *market* is *replacement cost* where this is *bounded* by a *ceiling* based on sales price at normal profit and a *floor* based on sales price without profit. This lower of cost or market rule is grounded in the convention of *conservatism,* which holds that firms should recognize losses as soon as possible but delay recognition of gains.

Example

Suppose that a jewelry retailer purchases a lot of 100 digital watches for $100 each, with the intention of selling them at a price of $125. Prior to sale, however, the wholesale price of the watches drops to $80 and the corresponding retail price to $105. Application of the lower of cost or market rule would require that the stated value of the watches on hand be reduced from original cost of $100 to the current market (replacement) price of $80. The following journal entry would record the decline in price:

Loss on inventory (expense) $2,000
    Inventory (asset) $2,000
To record the loss attributable to the decline in the replacement cost of 100 digital watches from $100 to $80 (Many firms would credit a contra asset, such as "inventory—allowance for decline in market value" instead of "inventory" itself.)

The lower of cost or market rule may be applied to inventories on an individual (item-by-item) or a group basis. If applied on an individual basis, then the cost of each item in stock is compared with its current replacement cost. If the replacement cost of an item is lower than its original cost, then the item is written down to its replacement cost. If applied on a group basis, then the original cost of the inventory pool (which may be either the entire inventory or a collection of similar items) is compared with its market value, and a reduction in book value is required only if total market value is less than total initial cost. The group basis is likely to result in a considerably higher inventory valuation than the individual basis since it permits the increases in the market prices of some items to offset the decreases in others. The two bases were illustrated in Chapter 6 as part of a discussion regarding the values to be assigned to portfolios of marketable securities.

Some Questions

The lower of cost or market rule has been adopted by the rule-making bodies of the profession, but it has been the subject of widespread attack by accounting theoreticians. Critics assert that the rule sacrifices consistency for conservatism. The rule introduces a measure of inconsistency into financial reports, since it gives prompt recognition to decreases in market values but not to increases. Moreover, they contend that the rule requires that losses be recognized even though not really incurred. In the previous example, the firm purchased watches for $100 and will sell them for $105. Although it will not earn the full $25 profit that was expected, it will nevertheless realize a gain (excluding all other operating costs) of $5 per unit. If the lower of cost or market rule is adhered to, the accounts will reflect a loss of $20 per unit in the period of the write-down and a gain of $25 in the period of sale.[5] Critics contend that, as a consequence, earnings of both periods are distorted. In fact, they assert, the company earned a profit of $5 at the time of sale, not a loss of $20 in one period and a gain of $25 in the next.

[5]Authoritative pronouncements provide that inventory should never be reduced to a level that will lead to recognition of an unusually high profit in a subsequent period. Thus, if in the example the firm estimated that it would be able to sell the watches at retail for $115 rather than $105, it should reduce inventory to no less than $90, which is the *floor* as discussed above. If it reduced inventory below $90, its profit in the period of sale would be greater than its "normal" profit of $25 per unit.

Application of the lower of cost or market rule would be advantageous for tax purposes. It would enable a taxpayer to report an expense (the loss on inventory) in a period before goods are actually sold and a loss realized. The U.S. tax code, however, denies the benefits of the lower of cost or market rule to firms that are on a LIFO basis. The conceptual rationale for the lower of cost or market rule is no less sound for the LIFO than for the FIFO or the weighted average flow of cost assumptions. The taxing authorities do not look to any particular accounting theory for support in denying the benefits of the lower of cost or market rule to LIFO taxpayers. Instead, they contend merely that LIFO itself provides a tax advantage which should not be further enhanced by applications of the lower of cost or market rule. Generally accepted accounting principles, in contrast to the tax code, require that the lower of cost or market rule be applied, irrespective of inventory method. Thus inventory values may differ between financial statements and tax filings.

PROPOSED ALTERNATIVE: USE OF CURRENT COSTS

Many accountants have proposed that inventories be stated at their current costs. In this way, they suggest, many of the deficiencies of each of the alternative assumptions regarding flow of costs, as well as the inconsistencies of the lower of cost or market rule, can be overcome. Their suggestions are worth attention, not so much because they are likely to be accepted in the foreseeable future— although there is unquestionably a trend in the direction of current value accounting—but rather because they provide an insight into the components of gains or losses attributable to the sale of goods included in inventory.

Assume that on September 1, 1992, a sporting goods outlet purchases 30 cans of tennis balls at $2.00 per can. In the remainder of 1992 it sells 20 cans at $3.00 per can. On December 31, 1992, the wholesale price of tennis balls increases to $2.50 per can. As a consequence, the business raises the retail price to $3.50 per can. In 1993 it sells the 10 cans that remain from 1992. These facts are summarized in Exhibit 8-7. Per conventional practice, the company will record a gain of $1.50 for each can (sales price of $3.50 minus cost of $2.00). The $1.50 is composed of two types of gains—a *holding* gain of 50 cents and a *trading* gain of $1.00.

The trading gain arises out of the normal business activities of the firm. It represents a return to the merchant for providing the usual services of a retailer—providing customers with the desired quantity of goods at a convenient time and place. The holding gain, on the other hand, can be attributed to the increase in price between the times the merchant purchased and sold the goods. The magnitude of the holding gain depends on the quantity of goods held in inventory and the size of the price increase. Most merchants are required to maintain a stock of goods adequate to service the needs of their customers—that is, to make certain that they have a sufficient number of goods on hand to minimize the risk of outages and to provide customers with an ample choice of styles, sizes, and colors. Some merchants, however, intentionally maintain an inventory greater than necessary to meet their operating needs. Hoping to take advantage of increases in price, they employ inventory as a means of speculation. Speculative holding gains (and of course losses) are espe-

EXHIBIT 8-7
Trading Gains versus Holding Gains

Assumptions

Sept. 1, 1992	Company purchases	30 cans @ $2.00
Sept. 1 – Dec. 31, 1992	Company sells	20 cans @ 3.00
Dec. 31, 1992	Wholesale price increases to $2.50; company increases retail price to $3.50	
Jan. 1–Dec. 31, 1993	Company sells remaining	10 cans @ 3.50

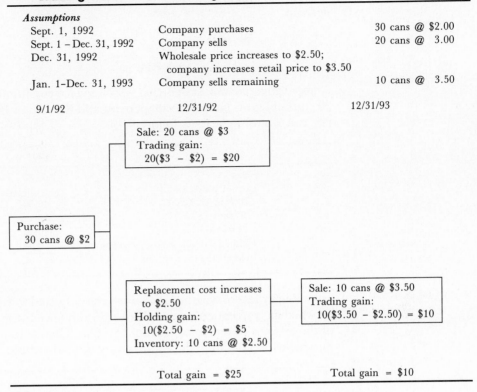

cially common in industries that deal in commodities that are subject to frequent and substantial fluctuations in prices—for example, grains, cocoa, and metals.

Were inventories to be stated at their current values, it would be relatively easy to distinguish—and report separately—the holding gains from the trading gains. And more significantly, the holding gains could be identified with the accounting period in which the increase in prices actually took place, rather than delayed until the period of sale. In the example, the holding gain actually occurred in 1992, the year in which the price increase was announced. Management control and evaluation of performance would be facilitated because the elements of profit that are within the control of specific managers could be set forth. Gains or losses arising from changes in prices could be taken into account in appraising the record of management only when they are relevant to its accomplishments.

Exhibit 8-7 depicts the economic substance of the transactions.

The following journal entry would recognize the holding gain of 50 cents per can of tennis balls that took place during 1992.

Inventory $5.00
    Holding gains on inventory (revenue). $5.00
To record the 50 cents holding gain on 10 cans of tennis balls that remained on hand at year end (replacement cost of $2.50 less original cost of $2.00)

When the 10 cans were sold in the following year, the cost of goods sold would be charged, and inventories credited, with their adjusted carrying value of $2.50 per can:

Cost of goods sold $25.00
Inventory $25.00
To record the cost of goods sold

Comparative income statements which give recognition to the sale in 1990 of 20 cans of tennis balls at $3.00 per can and the sale in 1993 of 10 cans at $3.50 per can would appear as follows:

	1992	1993
Sales	$60.00	$35.00
Cost of goods sold		
20 cans @ $2.00	40.00	
10 cans @ $2.50		25.00
Operating income	$20.00	$10.00
Holding gain on goods inventory	5.00	—
Comprehensive current income	$25.00	$10.00

Regardless of whether inventory was adjusted to reflect the holding gains or whether conventional procedures were followed, the total gain on the sale of the 30 cans of tennis balls would be $35. Conventional income statements, in which the holding gains were not identified, would appear as follows:

	1992	1993
Sales	$60.00	$35.00
Cost of goods sold		
20 cans @ $2	40.00	
10 cans @ $2		20.00
Income	$20.00	$15.00

The effect of increasing the carrying value of the 10 cans in inventory and of concurrently recognizing a holding gain of 50 cents per can would be to shift $5 of income from 1993, the year in which the cans were sold, to 1992, the year in which the price increase took place.

An Advantage of the Current Cost Method

Current cost accounting underscores the limitations of the methods presently used. The example that follows demonstrates how income, computed using either FIFO or LIFO, can be deceiving. It shows how reported income may increase even in the face of both a *decline in sales* and an *increase in costs*. It is designed to warn that increases in income as reported under generally accepted accounting principles may *not* necessarily indicate a true improvement in performance.

The example compares three different inventory procedures—FIFO, LIFO, and current cost. It shows their impact on the earnings of two firms in a single period. The activities of the two firms are the same, with a single exception. Whereas Firm A has sold 100 percent of the merchandise that it purchased, Firm B has sold only 80 percent.

Firm A and Firm B each start the year with 5,000 units of inventory purchased the previous year at $10 per unit. For simplicity, assume they have no other assets. During the year, a period of rising prices, each of the firms acquires inventory as shown in the following schedule:

	Units	Unit Cost	Total
Beginning inventory	5,000	$10.00	$50,000
Purchases			
1	10,000	10.50	105,000
2	10,000	11.00	110,000
3	10,000	11.50	115,000
4	10,000	12.00	120,000
5	10,000	12.50	125,000
6	10,000	13.00	130,000
7	10,000	13.50	135,000
Total purchases	70,000		$840,000
Total beginning inventory and purchases	75,000		$890,000

Note: Year-end current cost is $14.00 per unit.

Firm A sells 70,000 units at an *average price* of $12.50. Sales revenue is $875,000. Firm B sells only 56,000 units at the same price. Its revenue is $700,000. Purchases and sales are for cash.

In this example, unlike the sporting goods outlet example, prices increase *during* the year, not just at the end. Under current cost procedures, inventory must be adjusted for each price increase. Cost of goods sold is based on the replacement value of the inventory at time of sale. Operating income is the difference between sales and the *revalued* cost of the goods sold.

Exhibit 8-8 indicates ending inventory, cost of goods sold, and income under each of the three inventory procedures.

The sales of Company A are 25 percent *greater than* those of Company B. Yet under FIFO, the income of Company A is 15 percent *less*—$52,500 versus $62,000. Under LIFO, the income of Company A is 288 percent *greater*—$35,000 versus $9,000. Only under current cost does the percentage difference in operating income (25 percent, or $35,000 versus $28,000) correspond to the percentage difference in sales.

The example can be used to note some additional features of current cost accounting. As emphasized in previous chapters of the text, irrespective of accounting methods, the income statement must *articulate with* the balance sheet. Income for the period (plus owner contributions minus owner withdrawals) must equal the change in net assets. In this example the change in net assets equals the change in inventory plus the change in cash (the net cash receipts). This relationship holds for FIFO and LIFO but not, apparently, for current cost.

The current cost income statement and balance sheet accounts fully articulate, however, when the *realizable* holding gain is taken into account—that is, when income is specified as *comprehensive current income*, not merely current operating income. Comprehensive current income consists of the current operating income (in essence the *trading gain*) plus the realizable holding gain.

EXHIBIT 8-8

	Company A			Company B		
Beginning Inventory						
(which equals net assets)	5,000 @ $10.00	= $ 50,000		5,000 @ $10.00	= $ 50,000	
Purchases (for cash)	70,000	840,000		70,000	840,000	
Sales (for cash)	70,000 @ $12.50	= 875,000		56,000 @ $12.50	= 700,000	
Net cash receipts						
(sales less purchases)		$ 35,000			($140,000)	
Ending Inventory						
FIFO	5,000 @ $13.50	= $ 67,500		10,000 @ $13.50	$135,000	
				+ 9,000 @ $13.00	117,000	
				19,000	$252,000	
LIFO	5,000 @ $10.00	= $ 50,000		5,000 @ $10.00	$ 50,000	
				+ 10,000 @ $10.50	105,000	
				+ 4,000 @ $11.00	44,000	
				19,000	$199,000	
Current cost	5,000 @ $14.00	= $ 70,000		19,000 @ $14.00	$266,000	
Cost of Goods Sold						
FIFO						
Beginning inventory	$ 50,000			$ 50,000		
+ Purchases	840,000			840,000		
− Ending inventory	(67,500)	$822,500		(252,000)	$638,000	
LIFO						
Beginning inventory	$ 50,000			$ 50,000		
+ Purchases	840,000			840,000		
− Ending inventory	(50,000)	$840,000		(199,000)	$691,000	
Current cost*						
70,000 units @ $12		$840,000				
56,000 units @ $12					$672,000	
Operating Income (Sales minus Cost of Goods Sold)						
FIFO		$ 52,500			$ 62,000	
LIFO		35,000			9,000	
Current cost		35,000			28,000	
Ending Net Assets (Ending Inventory plus Net Cash Receipts)						
FIFO		$102,500			$112,000	
LIFO		85,000			59,000	
Current cost		105,000			126,000	

* Upon each purchase during the year, the goods in inventory are revalued to reflect the higher cost. Cost of goods sold is based on the most recent acquisition cost. The goods are sold *uniformly throughout the year*. The *average* acquisition cost—and also therefore the *average* cost of goods sold—is $12.

The realizable holding gain is the difference between the *outputs* into the trading or manufacturing process (the ending inventory and the cost of goods sold) and the *inputs* (the beginning inventory plus purchases). It is the total holding gain in that it includes the gains on goods sold during the year *and* goods remaining in year-end inventory.

The realizable holding gain for Company A is $20,000; that for Company B is $48,000:

Realizable holding gain = Outputs − Inputs

Realizable holding gain = (Ending inventory + Cost of goods sold) − (Beginning inventory + Purchases)

For Company A,

$$\text{Realizable holding gain} = (\$70,000 + \$840,000) - (\$50,000 + \$840,000)$$
$$= \$20,000$$

For Company B,

$$\text{Realizable holding gain} = (\$266,000 + \$672,000) - (\$50,000 + \$840,000)$$
$$= \$48,000$$

The realizable holding gain can also be interpreted as a realizable *cost saving*. It is the amount the firm *saved* by judiciously acquiring the goods in advance of price increases.

Comprehensive income captures both the trading gain and the holding gain:

$$\text{Comprehensive current income} = \text{Current operating income}$$
$$+ \text{ Realizable holding gain}$$

For Company A,

$$\text{Comprehensive current income} = \$35,000 + \$20,000 = \$55,000$$

For Company B,

$$\text{Comprehensive current income} = \$28,000 + \$48,000 = \$76,000$$

For both firms therefore comprehensive income is equal to the change in net assets:

$$\text{Comprehensive current income} = \text{Ending net assets} - \text{Beginning net assets}$$

For Company A,

$$\$55,000 = \$105,000 - \$50,000$$

For Company B,

$$\$76,000 = \$126,000 - \$50,000$$

Under current cost accounting, reported income would mirror economic performance. Holding gains would be captured in the period in which they actually occurred, not when the goods happened to be sold. Cost of goods sold would reflect worth at time of sale.

In the discussion to this point, current cost has been used to mean replacement cost, an *input* value. As indicated in an earlier chapter, however, current cost can be viewed as an *output* value as well as an input value. Thus some theoreticians suggest that inventories be stated at a current *output* value, such as the amount for which they could currently be sold, or at *net realizable* value (the amount for which they are *likely* to be sold in the future, less any costs of bringing the goods to a salable condition).

Regardless of which particular current value is employed, the suggestion that inventories be valued at some current value should not be viewed as particularly radical. Recall the discussion in Chapter 5 pertaining to recognition of revenue. It was pointed out then that when, in unusual circumstances, revenue is recognized in the course of production (as in long-term construction contracts) or upon completion of production (as in the mining of precious metals), inventory is, in effect, stated at a current value as it also is in "cost or market, whichever is lower." Our example in this section suggests cogent reasons for developing a *generalized framework* for reporting the current values of inventories. At the very least it indicates that changes in current costs are too important for either managers or investors to ignore.

History of the Idea in Practice

In 1979 the FASB issued *Statement No. 33,* which required firms larger than a specified size to disclose the replacement value of inventories. The stipulated data on inventories were part of a comprehensive package of current cost information intended to supplement the historical cost statements. The disclosures proved unpopular with the affected companies, who maintained that the cost of the data far exceeded their benefits to statement users. Indeed, several studies indicated that the disclosures were not widely used. In 1986 the FASB rescinded its 1979 pronouncement, replacing it with one "encouraging" but not requiring the current value disclosures.

The elimination of the disclosures should add to, rather than detract from, the importance that analysts place upon understanding and interpreting current value models of accounting. The latest pronouncement of the board does nothing to eliminate the deficiencies of historical cost accounting, to reduce the differences between historical and current values, or to diminish the utility of current value information. Instead it shifts the burden of compiling the current value data from the preparer—who presumably can do so at least cost and inconvenience—to the user—who must now not only interpret the data but estimate it as well.

INVENTORY TURNOVER

The effectiveness with which a firm uses its inventory to support sales can be measured by an activity ratio, *inventory turnover.* Inventory turnover is the number of times the annual cost of sales exceeds average inventory. It is computed by dividing cost of goods sold by average inventory:

$$\text{Inventory turnover} = \frac{\text{Cost of goods sold}}{\text{Average inventory}}$$

The greater the number of times per year the inventory *turns over,* the more efficiently the inventory is being used. The smaller the inventory in relation to cost of goods sold, the greater the sales activity that the inventory is able to sustain.

Because inventory is more closely related to cost of goods sold than it is to sales, cost of goods sold rather than sales is the numerator. This is in contrast to the accounts receivable turnover ratio (discussed in Chapter 7) and the fixed asset turnover ratio (to be discussed in Chapter 9). As with the accounts receivable turnover ratio, the denominator should ideally be based on a 12-month average (as opposed to a beginningand end-of-year average) to avoid distortions resulting from seasonal fluctuations.

Per its statements included in Chapter 7, American Home Products reported cost of goods sold in 1991 (in millions) of $2,390. Average inventory (based on beginning and ending inventory, the only data provided in the annual report) was $819. Inventory turnover was therefore 2.9 times:

$$\text{Inventory turnover} = \frac{\$2,390}{\$\ 819} = 2.9 \text{ times}$$

It should be obvious that when a firm uses LIFO to account for its inventory, the usefulness of the inventory turnover ratio as a technique of management control or investment analysis is severely limited. If the inventory is being reported at values representing prices of a distant past, then a comparison of LIFO inventory with cost of goods sold (based on current prices) is of little or no significance.

Summary

In this chapter we have dealt primarily with accounting issues pertaining to inventory within the traditional historical cost framework. Because of the overriding importance of inventories to most manufacturing and retail companies, selection of accounting alternatives may have a critical impact on both reported assets and earnings.

The primary objective of conventional accounting is to match the costs of acquiring or producing goods with the revenues that they generate and thereby produce a useful measure of income. To realize this objective, it is necessary to make assumptions as to the flow of costs—whether the cost of goods acquired first, or last, for example, should be associated with the revenues of a particular period. Persuasive arguments can be advanced in favor of or against each of the assumptions, and choice of assumption may have a significant effect on reported cost of goods sold as well as ending inventories.

Regardless of assumption, however, inventories should be restated at the lower of cost or market to reflect declines in their replacement cost. Although some accountants have suggested that accounting recognition be given to increases in market prices as well as to decreases, current practice favors conservatism over consistency, and gains from holding inventories are realized in the accounts only as they are sold.

Exercise for Review and Self-Testing

The inventory records of the Simon Corp. indicate the following with respect to a particular item:

Date	Purchases No. of Units	Unit Cost	Total Cost	No. of Units Sold	No. of Units on Hand
1/01/93*	400	$20	$8,000		400
2/24/93	200	21	4,200		600
6/16/93				300	300
9/23/93	100	22	2,200		400
11/15/93				300	100
12/28/93	100	23	2,300		200

*Beginning balance.

1. Determine the total number of units as well as the total costs to be accounted for during the year.
2. The firm maintains its records on a *periodic* basis. Determine year-end inventory and cost of goods sold, assuming each of the following cost flows:
   a. First in, first out
   b. Weighted average
   c. Last in, first out
3. Suppose that the firm values its inventory on the FIFO basis. On December 31, the price per unit of the item falls to $21 and the anticipated selling price falls by $2. At what amount, in accord with the lower of cost or market rule, should year-end inventory be stated? What would be the effect of the write-down on earnings of 1993? What would be the effect on earnings of 1994 when the goods are sold?
4. Assume alternatively that the firm were to report inventory at current replacement cost (a practice *not* in accord with ''generally accepted accounting principles'') and that the price at year end remained at $23 per unit. At what amount should year-end inventory be stated? How much ''holding gain'' should be recognized? What would be the effect on cost of goods sold in 1994 of recognizing the holding gain in 1993, assuming that the goods are sold in 1994?
5. Determine inventory turnover. Assume the firm uses the FIFO inventory method. For convenience, consider average inventory to be one-half the sum of beginning- and end-of-year values.

Questions for Review and Discussion

1. ''Since it is the objective of asset accounting to assign fair values to goods owned by a firm, LIFO is an inappropriate means of accounting for inventories. LIFO may result in values that are far out of date.'' Do you agree? Comment.
2. ''Firms make assumptions as to the flows of goods only because it is costly and inconvenient to keep records of specific items actually sold. The specific identification method is theoretically superior to any of the other methods and eliminates the possibilities of income manipulation associated with those methods.'' Do you agree? Comment.
3. The president of a firm whose shares are traded on a national stock exchange has asked you for advice on whether the company should shift from FIFO to LIFO. The company is in an industry in which prices have been continually increasing. What is the primary benefit to be gained by a switch to LIFO? Are there any potential costs or risks?
4. Suppose that the president referred to in question 3 expresses concern that a switch to LIFO would make it more difficult for her company to raise capital. She points out that LIFO results in lower reported earnings, and she is fearful that the reduction in earnings would have an adverse impact on the market price of her firm's stock. Are her reservations justified? Comment.
5. It is sometimes asserted that LIFO provides a more meaningful income statement, albeit not necessarily a more meaningful balance sheet. Why does LIFO provide a more meaningful income statement? Does it always? Provide an example of a situation in which it may seriously distort income.
6. What is meant by the term *market* as it is used in the expression *cost or market, whichever is lower*? The lower of cost or market rule is often cited as an example of the possible conflict between conservatism and consistency. Why? Over a period of several years, is the lower of cost or market rule likely to decrease the overall income of a firm? Explain.

7. Suppose that inventories were to be stated on the balance sheet at current replacement cost (which may exceed historical costs). What would be the impact on earnings of the year in which an increase in replacement cost was first recognized? What would be the impact on earnings of the year in which the goods were sold?

8. Conventional accounting requires that inventories be stated at historical cost. How could a financial analyst obtain information on the replacement cost of a firm's inventory?

9. Why does the use of LIFO limit the utility of the inventory turnover ratio?

10. A firm acquires a substantial quantity of inventory on December 31, subsequent to the last sale of the year. The price paid is considerably greater than that of previous purchases. Why might use of the weighted average method, applied on a periodic basis, produce a cost of goods sold that many accountants would claim is overstated?

Problems

1. *Frequency of calculations may affect earnings.*

As of the start of a year, a firm had 700 units of product on hand. The stated value was $1,400. During the year the firm had two sales—the first on January 17 of 600 units, and the second on November 11 of 700 units. On March 9 the firm received a shipment of 1,600 units at a cost of $4,800. Assume that the purchases were for cash.

a. Prepare those journal entries that would affect inventory assuming that the firm uses
   (1) Periodic inventory procedures:
       (a) FIFO
       (b) Weighted average
   (2) Perpetual inventory procedures:
       (a) FIFO
       (b) Weighted average

b. Compare the total cost of goods sold and the ending inventory under each of the alternatives.

2. *This exercise illustrates the three fundamental inventory valuation methods, each applied on both periodic and perpetual bases.*

During a year the Whitman Co. engaged in the following purchases and sales of an item:

| | Purchases | | Sales |
	No. Units	Cost per Unit	(No. Units)
Jan. 1 (beg. bal.)	400	$5.00	
Feb. 11			150
May 6	200	5.10	
Sept. 8			220
Sept. 30	300	5.20	
Oct. 17			310
Nov. 26	100	5.25	
Dec. 16			50
	1,000		730

Determine December 31 inventory and cost of goods sold for the year, assuming first that the company maintains inventory on a periodic basis and then on a perpetual basis. Assume also each of the following flows of costs: FIFO, weighted average, LIFO.

LIFO, applied on a perpetual basis, is not specifically illustrated in the text. The procedures are not difficult, however. Compute the cost of goods sold upon each sale. The goods sold would be assumed to be those that were acquired most recently up to the date of sale. For example, the 220 units sold on September 8 would be considered to be the 200 units acquired on May 6 plus 20 from the balance on hand as of January 1.

3. *The specific identification method, even if clerically feasible, may not be theoretically preferable.*

As of December 1, Big Sam Appliance Co. has 300 refrigerators in stock. All are identical; all are priced to sell at $900. Each is tagged with a card indicating in code its cost to Big Sam. Of the 300 refrigerators on hand, 100 were acquired on June 15 at a cost of $800 each, 100 on November 1 at a cost of $650 each, and 100 on December 1 at a cost of $700 per unit. Big Sam estimates that, in the month of December, 200 refrigerators will be sold.

a. Determine cost of goods sold on a FIFO basis, assuming that 200 refrigerators were in fact sold.

b. Suppose that Big Sam uses the specific identification method and wishes to maximize reported earnings for the year. How can it accomplish its objective by judicious selection of the units to be sold?

c. Suppose that Big Sam uses the specific identification method and, to minimize taxes, wishes to minimize reported earnings. How can it accomplish its objective?

4. *The impact of inventory method depends on the direction of price changes.*

Fill in the table that follows with the cost flow assumption—FIFO, LIFO, or average cost—that would produce the results indicated in the rows under the conditions indicated by the columns:

	Inflation	Deflation
Cost of Goods Sold		
Highest		
Lowest		
Ending Inventory		
Highest		
Lowest		
Cash Flow before Taxes		
Highest		
Lowest		
Cash Flow after Taxes		
Highest		
Lowest		

5. *Is the impact of LIFO upon earnings the same in periods of falling prices as in those of rising prices?*

The Simmons Co. began operations on January 1. In its first year the company produced 85,000 units at a cost of $12 per unit and sold 80,000 units. In each of the next three years, it produced 80,000 units and sold 80,000 units. Costs of production were $14, $16, and $18, respectively, in each of the years.

a. Compute both cost of goods sold and year-end inventory for each of the four years, using first FIFO and then LIFO.

b. Do the same as in part (a), assuming this time that production costs were $12, $10, $8, and $6 in each of the four years. (Omit application of the lower of cost or market rule.)

c. What generalizations can be made regarding the impact of LIFO as compared with FIFO on cost of goods sold and inventories in periods of rising prices versus periods of falling prices?

6. *In the long run, choice among accounting principles seldom makes a difference.*

The Pittsfield Co. existed in business for a period of four years. During that period, purchases and sales were as follows:

| | Purchases | | Sales | |
Year	Units	Unit Cost	Units	Sales Price
1	12,000	$10	8,000	$15
2	14,000	11	15,000	16
3	9,000	12	9,000	17
4	10,000	11	13,000	17

a. Determine income for each of the four years, assuming first that the company uses FIFO and then that it uses LIFO.

b. Determine total income for the four-year period. Over the life of the business, does it matter which method of inventory is used?

7. *Earnings based on LIFO are said to be "higher quality" than those based on FIFO.*

In December 1992, L. Minton established a door-to-door sales company. He invested $10,000 and purchased 2,000 units of inventory at $5 per unit—the minimum number of units required to sustain his business. He made his purchase at a propitious time, for the next day, before he had a chance to make a single sale, the price per unit of his inventory increased to $6.

During 1993 Minton purchased an additional 10,000 units at $6 per unit and sold 10,000 units at $7 per unit. He withdrew from the business for his personal use *all* cash except that necessary to assure that his inventory was maintained at its minimum level of 2,000 units.

a. Prepare journal entries to reflect the foregoing transactions. First assume that Minton maintained his inventories on a FIFO basis; then assume that he maintained them on a LIFO basis, and indicate any entries that would be different. Prepare income statements and balance sheets comparing results under the two methods.

b. How much cash was Minton able to withdraw during 1993? Compare his cash withdrawals with income as determined by both the FIFO and the LIFO methods. What do you suppose that some financial observers mean when they say that in periods of inflation LIFO results in earnings that are of "higher quality"?

8. *An invasion of the LIFO base may seriously distort earnings.*

As of January 1, 1992, the Byron Co. had 50,000 units of product on hand. Each unit had cost $.80 to produce. During each of the next three years the company produced 100,000 units and sold the same number. In the fourth year, as the result of a strike, the company was able to produce only 50,000 units, though it was able to maintain sales at 100,000. In the fifth year the company, in order to replenish its inventory, produced 150,000 units and continued to sell 100,000 units. Unit production costs and sales prices are indicated in the accompanying table. The company maintains its inventory on a periodic LIFO basis.

	Units Produced		Units Sold	
	No. Units	Unit Cost	No. Units	Unit Price
1992	100,000	$1.00	100,000	$1.40
1993	100,000	1.20	100,000	1.60
1994	100,000	1.40	100,000	1.80
1995	50,000	1.60	100,000	2.00
1996	150,000	1.80	100,000	2.20

a. Determine the net income *after taxes* for each of the five years. Assume a tax rate of 40 percent of income.

b. Determine the *cash flow* for each of the five years. That is, determine total cash receipts less total cash disbursements. Assume that all sales were for cash and that all production costs and taxes were paid in cash.

c. In the view of a manager or a financial analyst, of what significance is the income of the firm for 1995?

d. Compare the total cash flow for 1995 and 1996 with that of the prior two-year period. Why is it lower?

9. *Problems 9 and 10 illustrate the advantages—and disadvantages—of a shift from FIFO to LIFO.*

The annual report of a leading U.S. chemical company contained the following footnote (figures are stated in millions):

> If inventory values were shown at estimated replacement or current cost rather than at LIFO values, inventories would have been $489.9 and $410.6 higher than reported at December 31, 1991, and December 31, 1990, respectively.

a. In periods of rising prices, which valuation method, FIFO or LIFO, results in inventory values which most closely approximate current market prices?

b. Assume that replacement costs are approximately equal to inventory as computed on a FIFO basis. Ignoring the impact of income taxes, how much more, or less, as of December 31, 1990, and 1991, would retained earnings have been had the company remained on FIFO?

c. Considering the effect of the change in valuation method on retained earnings of 1990 and 1991, how much more or less would earnings before taxes have been in 1991 if no change had taken place?

d. Based on your response to part (c) and assuming a tax rate of 40 percent, how much more or less would the tax obligation of the firm have been in 1991?

e. Comment on why, in a period of rising prices, a firm would deliberately select a method of accounting that would adversely affect reported earnings.

10. The same annual report contained the following footnote pertaining to inventories:

> During 1990 inventory quantities were reduced from the abnormally high year-end 1989 level. This reduction resulted in a liquidation of LIFO inventory quantities carried at lower prices prevailing in prior years as compared with 1990 costs, the effect of which increased the 1990 net income by approximately $38.9 million, or $.81 per share.

a. Explain in your own words why a liquidation of inventory increased net income.

b. If the liquidation increased the reported after-tax income by $38.9 million, by how much greater or less was the value of the goods sold based on current (1990) costs than on the historical costs at which they were actually carried on the books? Assume a tax rate of 40 percent.

c. It is clear that in 1990 the use of LIFO seriously distorted the firm's reported income. In fact, management felt compelled to include in its financial statements the previously cited footnote to warn readers of the aberrant earnings. Why did not the company shift to FIFO for 1990 and than shift back to LIFO in subsequent years when earnings would not be distorted by inventory liquidations?

11. *A CPA firm points out that there are no generally accepted standards of "preferability."*

In 1992 (dates changed), the Susquehanna Corporation, a firm whose securities are traded on the American Stock Exchange, changed from the FIFO to the LIFO method of accounting for inventories. The change, according to a footnote to the financial statements, was made "to better match the most recent inventory acquisition costs against current sales, thereby minimizing the effects of inflation on earnings."

In a letter to the firm's board of directors, the company's auditors, Price Waterhouse & Co., wrote the following:

> Note 2 to the consolidated financial statements of The Susquehanna Corporation, included in the Company's Annual Report to its stockholders for the year ended December 31, 1992, and incorporated by reference in the Company's Annual Report on Form 10-K for the year then ended, describes a change from the first-in, first-out method of accounting for inventories to the last-in, first-out method. We concurred with this change in our report dated February 10, 1993, on the consolidated financial statements referred to above. It should be understood that preferability of one acceptable method of inventory accounting over another has not been addressed in any authoritative accounting literature and in arriving at our opinion expressed below, we have relied on management's business planning and judgment. *Based upon our discussions with management and the stated reasons for the change, we believe that such change represents, in your circumstances, adoption of a preferable accounting principle in conformity with Accounting Principles Board Opinion No. 20.*

a. What makes one accounting method preferable to another?
b. If a method of accounting, such as LIFO, is considered preferable to another method, such as FIFO, by both a company and its auditors, how can the use of the alternative method by a company in the same industry, whose financial statements might be examined by the same firm of auditors, be justified?

12. *By shifting to FIFO from LIFO, a company may increase reported earnings but incur a substantial economic cost.*

In November 1970, the president of a "Big Three" U.S. automobile manufacturer became concerned that actual earnings for 1970 would fall short of predicted earnings. In discussions with the corporate controller, he suggested that one way to boost earnings would be to shift from the last-in, first-out method of reporting inventories, which the company was presently using, to the first-in, first-out method.

Upon investigation, the controller found that anticipated inventories at year end would be approximately $100 million if stated on a LIFO basis. If valued on the basis of the cost of the most recent purchases (FIFO), they would be approximately $180 million.

a. What would be the effect on cost of goods sold if inventories for the year 1970 were stated on a FIFO rather than a LIFO basis? Explain.
b. What would be the impact on income tax obligations? Assume a combined federal and state tax rate of 50 percent. (In practice the Internal Revenue Service is likely to allow the company to pay the additional taxes attributable to the shift over a 20-year period.)
c. Comment on any advantages and disadvantages to the company of making the shift.

13. *The LIFO method permits income manipulation.*

As of January 1, the Elliot Corp. had 10,000 units of product on hand. Each had a carrying value of $20. In November of the same year the president estimated that sales for the year would total 80,000 units. To date, the company had produced 70,000 units, at a cost of $25 per unit. If additional units were to be produced in the remainder of the year, they would cost $26 per unit. The company determines inventory on a periodic LIFO basis.

Determine cost of goods sold if
a. The president ordered that no additional units be produced during the year.
b. The president ordered that 10,000 additional units be produced.
c. The president ordered that 40,000 additional units be produced.

14. *Did General Motors really benefit from LIFO?*

The 1987 financial statements of General Motors contained the following note:

> Inventories are stated generally at cost, which is not in excess of market. The cost of substantially all domestic inventories is determined by the last-in, first-out (LIFO) method. If the first-in, first-out (FIFO) method of inventory valuation had been used for inventories valued at LIFO cost, such inventories would have been $2,359.9 million higher at December 31, 1987, and $2,203.8 million higher at December 31, 1986. As a result of decreases in LIFO U.S. inventories, certain LIFO inventory quantities carried at lower costs prevailing in prior years, as compared with the costs of current purchases, were liquidated in 1986 and 1985. These inventory adjustments favorably affected income before income taxes by approximately $38.2 million in 1986 and $20.9 million in 1985.

Major Classes of Inventories	1987	1986
	(in millions)	
Productive material, work in process, and supplies	$3,876.0	$4,042.5
Finished product, service parts, etc.	4,063.7	3,192.6
Total	$7,939.7	$7,235.1

a. By how much greater or less would pre-tax income have been in 1987 had the company used FIFO rather than LIFO?
b. By how much greater or less would retained earnings have been as of December 31, 1987, had the company used FIFO? Ignore the consequences of income tax benefits.
c. The note indicates that the liquidation of inventories in 1986 and 1985 had a favorable impact on income before taxes. Was the company really better off as a result of the liquidation? What would the adverse consequence have been? What was the main advantage to the company of using LIFO in 1987?

15. *Are differences between ''book'' and ''tax'' values a boon or a bane?*

The 1987 annual report of the Dana Corporation reported the following:

> Inventories are valued at the lower of cost or market. Cost is determined on the last-in, first-out basis for domestic inventories and on the first-in, first-out or average cost basis for international inventories. If all inventories were valued at replacement costs, inventories would be increased by $68,532,000 at December 31, 1987. The valuation of LIFO inventories for financial reporting purposes is $19,166,000 in excess of the valuation for federal income tax purposes.

Total reported inventories of the company on December 31, 1987, were $726 million.

Difference between tax and book inventory valuations can result from various technical features of the tax code pertaining to the application of LIFO.
a. Was the company better or worse off because the book value of its inventory exceeded the tax value? Did the tax regulations which led to the discrepancy work to the benefit or detriment of the company? Explain.

b. Suppose that in 1988 Dana had been required to substantially reduce its inventory. What would have been the most probable impact, relative to 1987, on
   (1) Cost of goods sold as a percentage of sales? (Would this percentage be useful as a measure of performance?)
   (2) Income tax expense as a percentage of sales?

16. *The advantages of postponing taxes can be expressed in a single dollar amount.*

    Gilling, Inc., is considering shifting from FIFO to LIFO. The change would be effective January 1, 1992.

    The controller's staff of the company has determined that beginning-of-year inventory on January 1, 1992, will be $100 million, irrespective of accounting method.

    Company sales for 1992 were $600 million and cost of goods sold $500 million. The controller's staff forecasts that the number of *units* manufactured and sold will remain constant over the next five years but that manufacturing *costs* and *selling prices* will increase at a compound rate of 10 percent per year.

    The company pays taxes on income at a rate of 40 percent. It uses a discount rate of 8 percent to perform all analyses in which the time value of money must be taken into account.

    Based on the limited information provided (some of which may be extraneous), determine the present value of the tax "savings" that will accrue over the five years beginning January 1, 1992.

17. *An increase in reported earnings may not necessarily be reflected in the market price of a firm's common stock.*

    The president of a publicly held corporation was considering switching from the FIFO to the LIFO method of accounting for inventory. The shift would enable the firm to reduce its annual income tax payments. The president was reluctant to authorize the shift, however, because it would result in an immediate decline in reported earnings. Such a decline, he thought, might adversely affect the market price of the company's stock and thereby antagonize the shareholders.

    As of January 1, 1992, the company had 1,000 (000s omitted) units of product on hand. They were carried on the books at $20 per unit, and because the company had recently reduced its inventory to zero, they would be valued at $20 regardless of whether the company remained on FIFO or switched to LIFO.

    As of January 1, 1992, the president made the following estimate of purchases and sales for the following three years (000s omitted from quantities):

1992	Purchase 1,000 units @ $22; sell 1,000 units @ $30
1993	Purchase 1,000 units @ $24; sell 1,000 units @ $32
1994	Purchase 1,000 units @ $26; sell 1,000 units @ $34

    a. Determine annual earnings after taxes for each of the three years, assuming first that the company maintains its inventory on a FIFO basis and second that it shifts to LIFO. The effective rate of taxes is 40 percent. For convenience, disregard all costs other than cost of goods sold and taxes.
    b. Determine the annual cash flows after taxes for each of the three years under both FIFO and LIFO. Compare them with annual earnings. Cash flows should represent sales minus purchases and taxes.
    c. Assume that the market price of the firm's stock is based on anticipated corporate cash flows. The total market value of all shares outstanding is equal, at any time, to the present value of expected cash flows for a number of years into the future (in this case assume three years). In calculating the present value

of expected cash flows, use a discount rate of 8 percent. Determine the total market value of all shares outstanding, assuming first that the company remains on FIFO and second that it shifts to LIFO. (For convenience assume that all cash flows occur at year end.)

d. Suppose that the company has 100,000 shares of stock outstanding. Determine the expected market price per share under both FIFO and LIFO.

e. If the capital markets are "efficient" (if they recognize or are able to distinguish between economic earnings and reported accounting earnings), are the reservations of the president justified?

18. *A change in inventory method may not have the same impact on flows of cash as on flows of working capital.*

The following table provides selected data from the financial statements of a company that engages in retail sales (all amounts in millions):

	Period		
	1	2	3
Ending inventory	$100	$120	$115
Sales	600	768	732
Cost of goods sold	500	640	610
Accounts receivable	300	340	330

The company maintains its inventory on a FIFO basis. The company pays for all goods in the period following purchase (e.g., goods acquired in period 1 are paid for in period 2).

a. Prepare for period 3 a statement in which you indicate the inflows and outflows of cash attributable to the purchase and sale of merchandise.

b. Prepare for period 3 a statement in which you indicate the inflows and outflows of working capital (current assets less current liabilities).

c. Assume that the company shifts its inventory method from FIFO to LIFO at the start of period 2. Assume also that the quantity of inventory remains constant over the three-year period; the difference from one year to the next in inventory values can be attributed entirely to changes in prices. Convert the inventory and cost of goods sold to a LIFO basis.

d. Repeat parts (a) and (b) based on the values calculated in part (c). Comment on whether cash or working capital is the more *objective* measure of financial resources.

19. *The difference between reported and replacement values of inventory gives a clue as to accounting method; inventory turnover is altered dramatically when basis of inventory valuation is changed.*

The financial statements of Deluxe Check Printers, a company whose shares are listed on the New York Stock Exchange, reported the following (dates changed):

	1993	1992
Costs of sales, exclusive of depreciation	$280,894,000	$246,873,000
Inventory (December 31)	14,092,000	13,420,000

A note to the statements indicated that inventories at December 31, 1993, and 1992, were approximately $8,482,000 and $6,272,000, respectively, less than replacement cost. By contrast, costs of sales, based on replacement values, were approximately equal to those reported.

   a. Calculate inventory turnover for 1993 based on the average of reported beginning and ending inventories.

   b. On which basis, LIFO or FIFO, is it more likely that the company maintained its inventories? Why? There is a substantial difference between inventories as reported and their replacement values. Yet costs of sales as reported and those based on replacement values are approximately the same. Can you explain why?

   c. Recalculate inventory turnover based on replacement values of inventory. Which calculation do you think would be the more useful for most decisions to be made by investors and managers?

20. *Ratios must be adjusted to take into account inventory basis; often a considerable amount of information pertaining to changes in prices and quantities can be derived from the data in the financial statements.*

     The data that follow were taken from the annual reports of Hasseldine Industries (all dollar amounts in millions). The company accounts for inventory on the basis of LIFO, which it applies periodically (rather than perpetually). The inventory consists almost entirely of a single product.

	Inventory		Cost of	Pretax
Year	LIFO	Replacement Value	Goods Sold	Income
1	$100	$120	$ 960	$48
2	110	132	1,088	54
3	105	131	1,030	20
4	120	144	1,152	72
5	121	157	1,256	98

   a. In which year, if any, did inventory *quantities* decline? Explain.

   b. In which year, if any, did the *prices* of goods included in inventory decline? Explain.

   c. You wish to compare the current ratio of this company in year 5 with that of another firm that reports on a FIFO basis. Hasseldine Industries in year 5 reported current assets of $432 million and current liabilities of $280 million. Based on the information provided, adjust the inventory of Hasseldine so that it would be comparable to that of the other firm. Defend your adjusted inventory as being a reasonable approximation of that which would be reported if the company were on FIFO. Compute the current ratio on both an unadjusted and an adjusted basis.

   d. By approximately what percentage did prices increase in year 5? Explain.

   e. Suppose that inventory is to be accounted for on the basis of FIFO and that the replacement value of the inventory is approximately equal to its FIFO value. How much greater or less than the reported LIFO amount would cost of goods sold be in year 5? If the tax rate were 40 percent, what would be the impact on after-tax income? Disregarding taxes, what would be the impact on reported retained earnings at the end of year 5? What would be the impact if taxes were taken into account?

21. *The lower of cost or market rule does not reduce the total profits to be realized on the sale of inventories; it only transfers them from one year to the next.*

     The Roscoe Corp. started business on January 1, 1992. Its purchases and sales, as well as the replacement cost of goods on hand at year end, for its first three years of operations are

	Purchases		Sales		Unit Replacement Cost at Year End
	Units	Unit Cost	Units	Unit Price	
1992	12,000	$20	10,000	$30	$15
1993	12,000	15	10,000	25	10
1994	6,000	10	10,000	20	5

The company stated its inventory on a FIFO basis and applied the lower of cost or market rule.

a. Determine income for each of the three years.

b. Comment on the effect of the lower of cost or market rule on earnings over an extended period of time.

22. *The lower of cost or market rule provides that declines in the value of inventory be given prompt recognition.*

Indicated in the table following is the December 31 inventory of the Albany Company, along with current replacement costs and expected selling prices:

Items	Units	Unit Cost	Replacement Cost	Expected Selling Price
A	6,000	$10	$12	$18
B	4,000	8	6	9
C	12,000	6	4	6
D	2,000	4	2	6

It is the policy of the company to sell at 50 percent above cost, but sometimes market conditions force (or enable) the company to sell at a lower (or higher) price.

Apply the lower of cost or market rule to determine the value at which December 31 inventory should be stated. Assuming that replacement cost determines "market value," apply the rule first on an item-by-item basis and then on a group basis. (In assigning a value to item D, be sure to refer to footnote 5 in this chapter (page 319), which indicates that inventories should never be reduced to a level that will lead to recognition of an unusually high profit in a subsequent period.)

23. *A recent Supreme Court decision restricted the application of the lower of cost or market rule as it applies to federal income taxes. Henceforth, a firm will be able to write down its inventory to net realizable value only when it actually intends to make sales at the prices used to determine net realizable value. This ruling may have a significant impact on inventory practices in certain industries. Publishers, for example, may now find it advantageous to sell their books as soon as possible, even if only at greatly reduced prices, rather than retain them in inventory for sale at later dates at standard prices. There would be no financial incentive for them to carry in stock works of academic and literary merit that are "slow-moving" because of their limited market appeal.*

Art Books, Inc., printed, at a cost of $20 per copy, 20,000 copies of a scholarly art text. In the year of publication, it sold 10,000 copies at a price of $25 per copy. It estimates, however, that sales in the future will be limited to a relatively few collectors and scholars. It predicts that it will be able to sell, at $25 per copy, 1,000 copies per year for 10 years.

The prevailing income tax rate is 40 percent.

a. In your view, is the inventory still worth $20 per copy? What, for example, is the *maximum* amount a buyer would pay for the entire remaining stock of 10,000 books if the decision criterion is present value of expected cash receipts? Assume a discount rate of 15 percent. In other words, what is the present value of the cash receipts (ignoring taxes) to be received from sales over the period of 10 years?

b. Suppose that Art Books, Inc., has a choice. It could retain the books in inventory and sell them over the period of 10 years. It would be permitted no immediate tax deduction to reflect the loss of the inventory value suggested by your response to part (a). Over the 10-year period, it would, of course, be taxed on profits from the sale of the books (revenue less cost of goods sold) as they are earned. Alternatively, the firm could sell its entire stock of books to a cut-rate bookstore for $10 per copy. The tax loss on the sale (revenue less cost of goods sold) could be used to offset other corporate income. As a consequence, the firm would realize a cash saving equal in amount to 40 percent (the tax rate) of the loss. In an analysis of this course of action, the cash saving could be considered a cash receipt.

   (1) What is the present value, after taxes, of the cash to be received from the sale of books at the standard price of $25 over the period of 10 years? Assume a discount rate of 15 percent. The cash receipts for each year are equal to the *revenues* to be received less the taxes to be paid. Cost of goods sold, although an expense, does not require an outlay of cash inasmuch as the books to be sold have already been produced.

   (2) What is the present value, after taxes, of the total amount to be received from the immediate sale of the books to the cut-rate bookstore? Because the cash will be received immediately, no discounting is necessary. Be sure to include the tax saving as a cash receipt.

   (3) Which course of action is likely to be chosen by management? To simplify the illustration, no mention has been made of the costs of holding the inventory, such as storage and insurance, and of selling and distributing the books. What impact would these costs have on the course of action decided upon? Comment on why the decision of the court would encourage firms to destroy, or sell as salvage, slow-selling works rather than to retain them.

24. *In the precious metals industry, holding gains may dramatically alter operating earnings.*

Engelhard Corporation is a world leader in the development of specialty chemicals and metals. The following data were drawn from its annual report of December 31, 1987:

	1987	1986
	(in thousands)	
Inventories		
Precious metals	$ 104,213	$ 107,021
Nonmetallic minerals and products	57,308	50,640
Other	43,624	30,339
Total inventories	$ 205,145	$ 188,000
Total sales	$2,479,230	$2,289,531
Cost of goods sold	2,177,317	2,021,257
Operating earnings		
Specialty chemical business	87,397	76,975
Specialty metals business	22,173	18,644
Other	(4,582)	
Total operating earnings	$ 104,988	$ 95,619
Total current assets	$ 700,095	$ 603,940
Total current liabilities	$ 297,499	$ 315,976

The financial statements contain the following note:

> All precious metals inventories are stated at LIFO cost. The market value of these inventories exceeded the cost by $138.2 million at December 31, 1987, and $118.6 million at December 31, 1986.

a. Determine the approximate value of the precious metals inventory of December 31, 1987, at prices of December 31, 1986. By how much, and by what percent, did the market value of the 1986 inventory increase during 1987?

b. Suppose that the company were to base cost of goods sold on market values of inventories rather than on historical cost. To what extent would cost of goods sold have been different in 1987? Explain. (You need not make specific calculations.) Would your response be the same if the company assumed a FIFO flow of costs?

c. Suppose that the holding gain computed in part (a) was taken into account in determining operating earnings. By how much (in percent) would each of the following have been greater or less?
   (1) Total operating earnings in 1987
   (2) Operating earnings of the specialty metals business in 1987

d. Determine the current ratio as of December 31, 1988, based on historical values. Then recompute, incorporating the current rather than the historical value of the inventories.

e. In your opinion, do the operating earnings and current ratio based on historical costs or on market values provide a more useful measure of corporate performance? Explain.

25. *Identical fiscal performance in different years results in differences in reported income under both LIFO and FIFO. Hence interperiod comparisons are difficult, even within a single firm.*

   The following are selected data as to a firm's sales, purchases, and inventory for a period of four years (number of units and dollar sales are in millions):

	Year 1	Year 2	Year 3	Year 4
Sales				
No. units	24	28	30	24
Sales price	$ 22	$ 21	$ 22.50	$ 22
Dollar sales	$528	$588	$675	$528
Beginning inventory				
No. units	10	6	8	10
Replacement cost	$ 17	$ 16	$ 17.50	$ 17
Purchases				
No. units	20	30	32	20
Unit price	$ 17	$ 16	$ 17.50	$ 17
Ending inventory				
No. units	6	8	10	6
Unit replacement cost	$ 16	$ 17.50	$ 17	$ 16

a. Determine income for each of the four years under both FIFO and LIFO cost-flow assumptions. You need not apply the lower of cost or market rule. Assume that the inventory at the start of year 1 is to be valued at $20 per unit under both FIFO and LIFO.

b. Compare income for years 1 and 4 under each of the assumptions. Note that sales, purchases, and replacement value of beginning and ending inventory were the same in both years. How do you account for differences in reported income in those years under both the FIFO and LIFO cost-flow assumptions?

c. Suppose instead that the firm were to value inventories on the basis of current (i.e., replacement) costs. Would there still be a difference in earnings between years 1 and 4? Explain.

26. *In Great Britain, unlike the United States, changes in replacement values are incorporated into the primary financial statements.*

The following data are from the 1987 statement of income of the British Petroleum Company. They are expressed in millions of pounds.

Turnover	£ 27,578
Replacement cost of sales	(20,758)
Production taxes	(901)
Gross profit	£ 5,919
Distribution and administrative expenses	(3,449)
Exploration expenditures	(469)
	£ 2,001
Other income	784
Replacement cost operating profit	£ 2,785
Stock holding gain	133
Historical cost operating profit	£ 2,918

The following are from a note (amounts also in millions of pounds):

Stocks	1987	1986
Historical cost	£2,716	£2,899
Replacement cost	2,694	3,015

The financial report also contains the following explanation:

Replacement Cost

> Replacement cost operating results exclude stock holding gains or losses and reflect the average cost of supplies incurred during the year. Stock holding gains or losses represent the difference between the replacement cost of sales and the historical cost of sales calculated using the first-in, first-out method.

a. What is meant by the terms *turnover* and *stock*?
b. Does "Replacement cost operating profit" include gains or losses from changes in the replacement values of goods held in inventory at year end? Explain.
c. Did replacement values of the firm's products increase or decrease during 1987? Explain.
d. In light of your response to part (c), explain how the company could have a stock holding gain in 1987.

27. *Historical cost accounting may not properly reflect propitious acquisitions of inventory.*

The president of Carolina Textiles, Inc., was disappointed to learn from his controller that preliminary data indicated that his firm had suffered a loss of $25,000 in 1994. The president was surprised by the report of the controller since the price of print cloth, the product in which the company trades, had increased substantially during the year.

As of January 1, 1994, the company had on hand 400,000 yards of print cloth, for which it had paid 25 cents per yard. The replacement cost of the cloth as of that date was 27 cents per yard. As of December 31, 1994, the company had in inventory 600,000 yards of cloth for which it had paid 30 cents per yard. If it were to replace the cloth on December 31, it would have to pay 45 cents per yard.

The president believed that creditors would be misled by financial reports on which inventories were valued, and income determined, strictly on the basis of historical cost. He requested that the controller prepare supplementary reports in which inventories were valued at market values and *holding gains* were specifically recognized in the computation of income.

Determine income for 1994, assuming that inventories were stated at replacement cost in *both* 1993 and 1994.

28. *Given sufficient company information, an analyst can readily modify the conventional income statement to give effect to changes in inventory replacement costs.*

The F. C. Miller Co. trades in scrap metal. The company purchases the scrap from small dealers and sells it in bulk to the major steel manufacturers. As a matter of policy, the company sells the scrap to the manufacturers for $5 per ton more than the current price it pays the individual dealers. The price of scrap steel is volatile. The following table indicates several price changes that occurred during the year and the transactions engaged in by the F. C. Miller Co. in the periods between the price changes.

Period	Price Paid to Dealers	No. of Tons Purchased	Total Cost	No. of Tons Sold	Price per Ton	Total Revenue
1/1	$ 82	5,000*	$ 410,000			
1/2–3/11	85	16,000	1,360,000	18,000	$ 90	$1,620,000
3/12–6/4	87	25,000	2,175,000	22,000	92	2,024,000
6/5–9/26	93	5,000	465,000	9,000	98	882,000
9/27–12/30	104	17,000	1,768,000	13,000	109	1,417,000
12/31	106	-0-		-0-		0
		68,000	$6,178,000	62,000		$5,943,000

*Opening inventory.

During the year F. C. Miller incurred operating costs of $325,000.
a. Prepare a conventional income statement in which gains or losses are recognized only upon actual sales of goods. Use the FIFO method of inventory valuation.
b. Prepare an income statement in which gains or losses are recognized upon increases in wholesale prices. Cost of goods sold should be based on replacement costs applicable at the time the goods are sold. Be sure to indicate the realizable holding gain (ending inventory plus cost of goods sold less beginning inventory and purchases).

Solutions to Exercise for Review and Self-Testing

1. The total number of units to be accounted for is the sum of beginning balance and the purchases throughout the year—800 units. Similarly, the total cost to be accounted for is $16,700.

2. a. *FIFO*

Ending inventory			
From purchase of 12/28	100 @ $23	$2,300	
From purchase of 9/23	100 @ 22	2,200	$ 4,500
Cost of goods sold			
From balance of 1/1	400 @ $20	$8,000	
From purchase of 2/24	200 @ 21	4,200	12,200
Total	800		$16,700

b. *Weighted average:* Average cost = $16,700/800 units = $20.875

Ending inventory	200 @ $20.875	$ 4,175
Cost of goods sold	600 @ $20.875	12,525
Total	800	$16,700

c. *LIFO*

Ending inventory			
From balance of 1/1	200 @ $20		$ 4,000
Cost of goods sold			
From purchase of 12/28	100 @ $23	$2,300	
From purchase of 9/23	100 @ 22	2,200	
From purchase of 2/24	200 @ 21	4,200	
From balance of 1/1	200 @ 20	4,000	12,700
Total	800		$16,700

3. The 200 units on hand would have to be written down to $21 per unit—$4,200. The write-down from $4,500 would cause earnings to decrease by $300. Inasmuch as the carrying value of the inventory would be reduced, cost of goods sold, when the goods are actually sold, would be reduced by $300 and earnings thereby increased by that amount.

4. The entire inventory must be stated at $23 per unit. The 100 units that would otherwise be reported at $22 per unit would have to be increased in value by $1 per unit—a total of $100. Thus a holding gain of $100 would be recognized. The effect of writing up the inventory by $100 in 1993 would be to increase reported cost of goods sold and reduce reported income in 1994 by the same amount.

5. Beginning inventory is given as $8,000. Ending inventory is calculated in part 2(a) as $4,500. Cost of goods sold is computed in part 2(a) as $12,200:

$$\text{Average inventory} = \frac{\$8,000 + \$4,500}{2} = \$6,250$$

$$\text{Inventory turnover} = \frac{\text{Cost of goods sold}}{\text{Average inventory}}$$

$$= \frac{\$12,200}{\$6,250}$$

$$= 1.95 \text{ times}$$

9

Long-Lived Assets and Depreciation

This chapter is directed to long-lived assets of the firm—assets that are not consumed within a single operating cycle of the business. Long-lived assets include plant assets (such as land, buildings, and equipment, often referred to as *fixed* assets), natural resources (such as minerals), intangible assets (such as copyrights), and deferred charges (such as organizational costs). Long-lived assets can be thought of as "bundles of services" that the firm will consume over time. Although they may be purchased and paid for in a single year, they will be used to generate revenues over a number of years.

THE FUNDAMENTAL ISSUES: WHAT IS THE VALUE OF AN ASSET? HOW SHOULD ITS COST BE ALLOCATED OVER ITS USEFUL LIFE?

The Economic Value of a Fixed Asset to Its Owner

Fixed assets may differ considerably in physical form from marketable securities and notes receivable. In economic substance, however, they are quite similar. The value of a note receivable is in the stream of cash flows that it provides. Suppose, for example, a company holds a note that entitles it to annual cash receipts of $100,000 per year for 10 years. This amount includes elements of both interest and principal. The value of the note is the present value of an annuity of $100,000 for 10 years. Assuming a discount rate of 12 percent, we find (per Table 4 in the Appendix) that the asset is worth $565,020:

$$\$100,000 \times 5.6502 = \$565,020$$

Suppose instead that the company owns a building that has a remaining useful life of 10 years. The company rents the building to a tenant under a non-cancelable 10-year lease. Annual rent is $100,000. The building's economic value to the company is identical to that of the note—the present value of 10 cash receipts of $100,000, or $565,020.

Most fixed assets cannot be as clearly identified with specific cash flows as can a note receivable or a building on which there is a noncancelable lease for a term exactly equal to remaining useful life. Hence their economic values cannot easily be determined. This pragmatic obstacle, however, in no way alters the substantive economic characteristics that the fixed assets have in common with the other assets.

Generally accepted accounting principles stipulate that fixed assets (like marketable securities, receivables, and inventories) be stated on the balance sheet at amounts based on their *historical* costs rather than their economic values. Of course, other alternatives have been proposed, and they will be addressed later in this chapter. As discussed in Chapter 6, these include current cost, net realizable value, and present value.

Allocation of Cost

A long-lived asset, by definition, is purchased in one accounting period but consumed over several. Therefore its cost must be allocated among the periods in which it provides its economic benefits. As the asset is used, a portion of cost must be charged as an expense. The share that has not yet been expensed must be "stored" on the balance sheet.

The cost to be allocated is the original cost of the asset less its *residual* or *salvage* value—the amount to be recovered when the asset is sold or salvaged. If an asset cost $12,000, but is expected to be sold at the end of its useful life for $2,000, the net amount to be allocated would be $10,000.

The process of allocating the cost of an asset over several accounting periods is referred to as *depreciation* if the asset is plant and equipment; *depletion,* if natural resources; and *amortization,* if intangible or a deferred charge.

Most of this chapter is directed to two related questions: When, and in what amount, should net asset cost be charged as expense? What amount of net cost should remain, and be reported, on the balance sheet?

The basic journal entry to record the acquisition of a long-lived asset such as equipment is (assuming the equipment to have cost $12,000)

Equipment $12,000
    Cash (or notes payable) $12,000
To record the purchase of equipment

The basic entry to record the periodic allocation of the cost of the asset over its useful life (assuming a life of 10 years and a residual value of $2,000) is

Depreciation (expense) $1,000
    Equipment, accumulated depreciation $1,000
To record periodic depreciation expense

Fixed assets are reported on the balance sheet at original cost less accumulated depreciation or amortization.

The account for accumulated depreciation or amortization (sometimes called *allowance* for depreciation or amortization) is a contra account and is always reported directly beneath the particular group of assets to which it pertains. Use of the contra account enables the firm to provide information that is more complete than if the balance in the asset account were reduced directly. Thus, after one year, the equipment might be shown on the balance sheet as

Equipment	12,000	
Less: Accumulated depreciation	1,000	$11,000

The standard pattern of accounting for long-lived assets suggests several subsidiary issues which need to be addressed:

1. What should constitute the *acquisition cost* of an asset? What should constitute appropriate adjustments to acquisition cost?
2. How should *useful life* and *residual value* be determined?
3. What basis of *depreciation* (or *amortization* or *depletion*) should be used to allocate acquisition cost over the asset's useful life?
4. How should the *sale, trade-in,* or *retirement* of an asset be accounted for?

We will discuss these issues as they apply to plant assets, but the general concepts apply to all long-lived assets. Toward the conclusion of the chapter, however, we shall address issues unique to selected other long-lived assets.

ACQUISITION COST OF PLANT ASSETS

The acquisition cost of a plant asset is, in general, its stated purchase price. But it is often more, and occasionally less, than that. It includes all costs that are necessary to bring the asset to a usable condition. Therefore the cost would include, in addition to actual purchase price, amounts paid for freight, installation, taxes, and title fees. The costs that are included as a part of the fixed asset are said to be *capitalized*. They are incurred to benefit several periods, not just one, and should be charged as expenses over the useful life of the asset rather than in the year in which they are incurred.

Interest Excluded

The acquisition cost of an asset generally excludes interest, both implicit and explicit (although some exceptions are noted in a section that follows). Suppose that a firm acquires an asset for $1 million but is permitted to delay payment for one year. It is charged interest of $80,000. The asset would be recorded at $1 million; the $80,000 would be reported as interest expense. Suppose, alternatively, that a firm agrees to pay $1 million for an asset but is permitted to delay payment for one year with no interest charges. As was pointed out in previous chapters, money has a time value, and businesses cannot be expected to make interest-free loans. Hence the true purchase price can be assumed to be something less than $1 million. If the prevailing rate of interest is 8 percent, then the asset would be recorded at $925,900. That amount is the present value of $1 million discounted at 8 percent. The difference of $74,100 between the stated price of $1 million and the value of the consideration, $925,900, would be accounted for as interest expense.

The catalog or advertised price of an asset may not always be the relevant purchase price. Often the stated price of an asset is nothing more than the starting point of the bargaining process. Frequently, dealers give trade discounts (not to be confused with trade-in allowances) to customers of a certain category and cash discounts for prompt payment. Such discounts must be deducted from the originally stated price, since the purchase price must be determined on the basis of value actually surrendered by the buyer and received by the seller— that is, the *current cash equivalent*.

Example

Assume that a firm purchases a machine for $10,000 under terms 2/10, n/30 (the company will receive a 2 percent discount if it pays within 10 days, but, in any event, must pay within 30 days). Transportation costs are $300, and the wages of the two workers who install the machine amount to $150. In addition, while the machine is being installed, three employees who work in the vicinity of the new machine are idled for two hours, since power to other machines has to be disconnected. The wages paid to the workers while they are idle are $90. The cost of the new machine would be computed as follows:

Purchase price	$10,000	
Less: 2% discount	200	$ 9,800
Freight		300
Installation costs		150
Payment for idle time		90
		$10,340

It may appear illogical to add the wages of the idle employees to the cost of the machine (and in practice many firms would not bother to do so). But could the machine have been installed without such loss of time? Was the cost necessary to bring the asset to a performing state? If the answer in each case is yes, then such costs have been incurred to benefit future periods, rather than the current period, and should rightfully be capitalized as part of the asset and should be allocated (i.e., depreciated) over the useful life of the new machine. If the answer is no, then the wages of the employees should be charged in full as an expense in the period of installation.

Purchases of Land

The same general principle applies to purchases of land. If a company purchases a parcel of land on which it intends to erect a new building, then all costs necessary to make the land ready for its intended use should be capitalized as part of the land. Thus, should a firm purchase land on which stands an old building that must first be torn down before a new building can be constructed, the demolition costs must be added to the purchase price of land; they will benefit future accounting periods.

Example

A company purchases land for $1 million, with the intention of constructing a plant. Before construction can begin, however, an old building on the land must be removed. Demolition costs amount to $100,000, but the firm is able to sell scrap from the old building for $30,000. Title and legal fees incurred in connection with the purchase total $10,000. At what value should the land be recorded?

Purchase price		$1,000,000
Add: Demolition costs	$100,000	
Less: Sale of scrap	30,000	70,000
Title and legal fees		10,000
Net cost of land		$1,080,000

Land is somewhat different from other fixed assets in that it does not ordinarily lose either service potential or value with the passage of time. Indeed, most often it *appreciates* in value. Thus the cost of the land should not be depreciated or allocated over time as long as there is no evidence of a decline in its service potential or value. If the land does not decline in value and the firm can, at any time, sell the land for the amount that it originally paid, then there is no real cost to the firm and thus no expense need be charged. Land, therefore, is not ordinarily considered a *depreciable* asset.

Construction of Assets

When a firm constructs its own assets, the *theoretical* guidelines to determine cost are quite clear. The firm should include in the cost of the asset all costs necessary to bring it to a serviceable state. Thus the materials used, as well as the wages of all employees who work on the construction project, should be capitalized as part of the asset. It is the *operational* questions that are the most difficult for many firms and their accountants to answer. How should a company account for those costs that are common to a number of activities that are carried out within the firm and cannot be traced directly to the construction of the asset? For example, how should it treat the salary of a general manager who devotes only a portion of his time to supervising the construction project? Or the wages of administrative personnel who maintain records pertaining to both the construction project and other activities of the company? Should these costs be included as part of the asset constructed by the firm or should they be charged to expense as incurred?

The general answer is that the firm should allocate such costs between the fixed asset and the other activities. It should make estimates of the proportion of time that the general manager and the administrative personnel performed services relating to the construction project as opposed to the other activities. Only that proportion of overall costs should be added to the cost of the fixed asset.

Example

The cost of constructing a minor addition to a plant might be computed (in oversimplified fashion) as follows:

Wages of employees directly associated with construction	$25,000
Materials and supplies used in project	40,000
Salary of plant supervisor (80% of salary for 1 month)	10,000
Wages of administrative personnel (10% of wages for 1 month)	600
	$75,600

Decisions as to what proportions of such *joint* (common) costs should be added to the cost of fixed assets are by no means either trivial or academic, especially if the projects involve large dollar amounts. Costs that are included as part of a fixed asset will be charged as expenses, through the process of depreciation, over the life of the asset. The remaining costs that are allocated to other activities are likely to be charged as expenses in the year in which they are actually incurred. Thus, in this example, if the decision had been made that no portion of the salary of the plant supervisor should be included as part of the asset, then overall company expenses for the year would have been greater, since the entire $10,000 would have been deducted from revenues. As it is, only a small portion of the $10,000 (one year's depreciation) would be charged against this year's revenues; the remainder would be spread out over the useful life of the asset.

Capitalization of Interest

The question of which costs related to the construction of fixed assets should be capitalized is reflected in a long-standing dispute among accountants. When a company constructs a major fixed asset, such as a new plant, it often has to borrow funds to finance the construction. On the amounts borrowed, it must pay interest. Should the interest be charged as an expense during all the years in which the loan is outstanding, or should the interest, like all other costs of construction, be capitalized as part of the fixed asset and charged off, in the form of depreciation, over the life of the asset? Some accountants argue that interest costs are no different from labor costs or material costs. They are a necessary cost of construction and should therefore be added to the cost of the asset. Moreover, they assert, the company earns no revenues from the plant while it is under construction; hence the matching principle dictates that it should charge no expenses. The interest costs, they say, will benefit future periods; they should therefore be expensed in future periods.

Other accountants, however, maintain that interest is a special kind of expense. The firm borrows money, they say, for all sorts of purposes. Just as it is impossible to trace capital contributed by stockholders to specific assets, so also is it impossible to trace the proceeds from the issue of bonds or other instruments of debt to particular assets. Thus, they argue, it would be improper to associate the related interest charges to specific construction projects. Interest, they say, should be expensed in the periods during which the loans are outstanding, regardless of the reason for the borrowing.

Opponents of interest capitalization also point out that the practice results in similar assets, both used within the same industry, being recorded at different values because they are financed from different sources. Suppose, for example, that each of two companies constructs identical plants at a cost of $20 million. One finances the new plant by issuing bonds, the other common stock. The company that issues bonds incurs $2 million in interest costs during the period of construction. The other incurs no interest costs (but, it can be assumed, incurs costs of capital in another form, such as dividends). When the two plants are put into service, the one financed with bonds would be reported at $22 million, the one financed with common stock at $20 million.

The issue of interest capitalization is of particular importance to public utilities, whose rates are established by regulatory commissions, and to their customers. It is the policy of most regulatory commissions to set user charges at levels that permit the utilities to earn specified rates of return. Rates of return are typically calculated by dividing income by assets.

Public utilities, such as electric, telephone, and gas companies, require large amounts of plant and equipment. The construction of new facilities often takes many years. The firms often incur substantial interest costs while building is in progress.

If a utility were to charge interest as an expense as it is incurred, then expenses during construction periods would be higher than if interest were capitalized. To compensate for the added expenses (and reduced earnings), regulatory commissions would permit the company to increase rates as soon as construction begins. In effect, therefore, the interest costs would be paid by the customers of the utility during the period of construction. If, by contrast, the interests were to be capitalized, then it would be added to the cost of the plant and charged as an expense (depreciation) over the life of the plant. The interest charges would not be an allowable expense to be incorporated into the rates until the new facilities were on line and the firm began to charge depreciation on them. Thus the capitalization of interest would permit the customers to delay having their rates increased to pay the interest costs. Existing consumers usually benefit from capitalization of interest in two ways: first, because the present value of dollars to be paid later is less than that to be paid currently, and second, because the customers of the future may be greater in number than those of the present, thereby enabling the company to spread the costs over a greater number of parties. The latter benefit is particularly important if the new plant is being constructed to extend service into new areas.

The FASB, in *Statement No. 34,* "Capitalization of Interest" (1979), ruled that interest should be capitalized on assets requiring an extended period to get them ready for their intended use. *Intended use* means either "sale" or "use within the business." Thus interest may be capitalized on plant assets as well as on those that will be sold to outsiders. It should be capitalized, however, only on discrete projects, such as ships and planes, not on inventories that are routinely produced in large numbers.

ADDITIONS TO ACQUISITION COST: BETTERMENTS BUT NOT REPAIRS AND MAINTENANCE

Betterments (costs incurred to "better" an asset during its useful life) should be accounted for in the same way as initial acquisition costs. They should be added to the original cost of the asset and depreciated over the remaining asset life.

Betterments must be distinguished from repairs and maintenance. Betterments extend an asset's useful life, increase its normal rate of output, or lower its operating costs. Maintenance and repairs, by contrast, keep an asset in good operating condition and merely keep up its efficiency. The distinction between the two is not always obvious, but the accounting implications are consequential.

Maintenance and repair costs are charged off as expenses as they are incurred. Betterment costs are capitalized and charged off as expenses in the periods that they will benefit.

Example

The Z Company expended $900 to air-condition the cab of one of its trucks. At the same time, it spent $220 to replace a worn-out clutch. The journal entry to record the repair/betterment combination would be

Trucks (fixed asset) $900
Truck, repairs (expense) 220
    Cash $1,120
To record repairs and betterments

If the remaining useful life of the truck was five years, then during each of the five years, depreciation expense on the truck would be $180 (one-fifth of the air-conditioning costs) greater than what it was previously.

The gray area of maintenance involves those costs that routinely recur. Airlines, for example, overhaul engines every several years. Some airlines charge the full cost of an overhaul as an expense in the year in which it is performed, even though the procedure benefits several years. Others capitalize the cost of the overhaul, setting up the repair job as an independent asset. The cost is then depreciated over the expected number of years between overhauls; the expense is thereby allocated to the several years benefited by the cost.

USEFUL LIFE AND RESIDUAL VALUE

Useful life is a key determinant of annual depreciation charges as well as of the net asset value reported on the balance sheet. In textbook examples, *useful life* is typically stated so cavalierly that a reader can easily be lulled into believing either that its influence upon reported income and assets is insignificant or that it is easy to estimate. Neither is correct.

Annual depreciation charges are extremely sensitive to differences in estimates of useful life. Suppose, for example, a firm has $120 million in depreciable equipment. Annual straight-line depreciation charges based on a four-year useful life will be $30 million, on a six-year life only $20 million—a difference of 50 percent!

The number of years that a firm will keep an asset depends on more than the ability to maintain it in working order. Physical deterioration is, of course, a relevant consideration, but one of decreasing importance. Of greater significance is technological obsolescence. Improvements in production equipment may permit a company to reduce manufacturing costs. If the company is to remain competitive, it may have no choice but to replace old, but perfectly serviceable, equipment with new. Or advances in the same or related industries may reduce or eliminate the demand for the firm's product—and thereby make many of its production facilities obsolete. The challenges to meaningfully estimating useful life cannot be overstated, but unfortunately neither accountants nor managers are uniquely endowed with powers of prophecy.

The depreciation practices of major airlines highlight the subjective nature of estimates of useful life. Whereas Delta depreciates substantially all of its flight equipment over a 10-year period, American does so over periods of up to 20 years. The estimates are not necessarily inconsistent. One company may *plan* to use its planes for a shorter time than the other. Airlines, however, are both competitive and capital-intense. Thus the seemingly conflicting policies at the very least raise questions as to the reliability of their estimates and detract from the overall credibility of their financial statements.

In the last decade it has been become common for companies to report write-offs of large amounts of assets. These losses often result from closings of entire plants or elimination of product lines. Each write-off is representative of a misestimate of a useful life. If the company had perfect foresight, the plant or equipment would have been depreciated down to its residual value at the time it was sold or abandoned, and no write-off would have been necessary.

The problems of estimating *residual value*—the amount to be recovered when an asset is retired—are essentially the same as those of predicting useful life. Residual value is one element of the formula (one exception will be discussed later in this chapter) used to compute depreciation. In many industries, the estimates of residual values tend to be only a small percentage of original asset costs. Hence annual depreciation charges are not greatly affected by the residual values. In some industries, however, estimates of residual values can be critical. In rental businesses (autos, for example), assets are held for only a short period and sold for a substantial portion of initial purchase price. Residual values are therefore a significant parameter in the depreciation calculation.

DEPRECIATION

Depreciation in accordance with generally accepted accounting principles is the process of allocating (in a systematic and rational manner) the cost of a tangible asset, less residual value, if any, over the estimated useful life of the asset. Allocation of cost is necessary if costs are to be matched with the revenues that they help to generate.

Depreciation is a process of *allocation,* not *valuation*. The original cost of an asset less the accumulated depreciation (the amount of depreciation taken on an asset up to a given time) is often referred to as the *book value* of an asset. Accountants do not purport that the book value of an asset represents the value of the asset in the open market. The potential for conflict between the two values can be demonstrated in a simple example involving an automobile.

A company purchases an automobile for $31,000 with the intention of using it for five years. It estimates that the trade-in value of the auto after that time will be $6,000. The amount of depreciation to be charged each year can be calculated to be $5,000:

EXHIBIT 9-1
Comparison of Book and Market Values for a Typical Automobile

End of Year	Original Cost	Depreciation Taken to Date	Cost Less Accumulated Depreciation ("Book" Value)	Estimated Market Value
1	$31,000	$ 5,000	$26,000	$23,000
2	31,000	10,000	21,000	17,000
3	31,000	15,000	16,000	12,000
4	31,000	20,000	11,000	8,000
5	31,000	25,000	6,000	6,000

$$\frac{\text{Original cost } - \text{ Residual value}}{\text{Useful life}} = \frac{\$31,000 - \$6,000}{5} = \$5,000$$

Exhibit 9-1 shows a comparison of book values at the end of each of the five years of estimated useful life. The market value represents a "typical" pattern of the decline in value of an automobile.

Merely because the amounts in the last two columns are not the same, it cannot be said that the decision to depreciate the asset at the rate of $5,000 per year was in error. It is *not* the objective of depreciation accounting existing under generally accepted accounting principles to indicate what the asset could be sold for at the end of a year.

It is also not the objective of the depreciation process to provide funds with which to replace assets when they must be sold or retired. The absurdity of contending that it is becomes evident by examining the basic journal entry for depreciation:

Depreciation expense xxxx
    Accumulated depreciation xxxx

Cash is neither debited nor credited; it is neither received from outsiders nor moved from one bank account into another. It is not possible for an accountant to assure that a firm will have sufficient cash on hand to purchase a new asset when an old one is retired merely by making an end-of-month or end-of-year adjusting entry.

Only in the most indirect sense can it be said that depreciation accounting provides funds for the future replacement of assets. Depreciation, like other expenses, is deducted from revenues to calculate annual income. To the extent that it reduces taxable income, it also reduces income taxes. Insofar as it reduces income taxes, it enables the firm to save for asset replacement more cash than it would if it had not recorded depreciation. In the same vein, the reduction in income attributable to depreciation expense may discourage some firms from declaring cash dividends of the amount they might have if income were greater. In neither case is it the depreciation that provides cash. At best, the depreciation expense influences decisions that affect cash—cash which may be used to replace assets or for any other corporate purpose.

ACCELERATED DEPRECIATION METHODS

Until this point, the annual depreciation charge has been calculated by dividing the total amount to be depreciated (cost less residual value, if any, usually called the *depreciable base*) by the number of years that the asset is expected to be in use. The depreciation charges are thereby the same during each year of the asset's life. This way of calculating depreciation is known as the *straight-line* method. There are, however, other means of allocating the cost of an asset to the various periods during which it will be used that result in unequal annual charges. Two of the most popular are known as the *sum-of-the-years'-digits* method and the *declining balance* method. Both of these result in depreciation charges which decline over the life of the asset. That is, depreciation expenses are greater in the beginning years of the asset's life than they are at the end. Both are referred to as *accelerated* methods of depreciation.

Sum-of-the-Years'-Digits Method

By the *sum-of-the-years'-digits* method, a fraction of the asset's net depreciable cost is charged off each year. The denominator of the fraction remains constant over the life of the asset. It is determined by taking a sum of numbers starting with 1 and continuing to the estimated life of the asset. Thus, if the life of the asset is three years, the denominator will be $1 + 2 + 3 = 6$. If it is five years, it will be $1 + 2 + 3 + 4 + 5 = 15$. A shortcut technique eliminates the need to add the digits. The life of the asset (n) may be multiplied by the life of the asset plus 1 (that is, $n + 1$) and the product divided by 2. For example, the denominator to be used for an asset with five years of useful life would be

$$\frac{n(n + 1)}{2} = \frac{5(6)}{2} = 15$$

The numerator of the fraction would vary over the life of the asset. Each year it would be equal to the number of years remaining in the asset's life at the *beginning* of that year. Thus, in the first year of the life of a five-year asset, $5/15$ of the asset's cost (less residual value) would be depreciated. In the second year, when the asset has a remaining life of only four years, $4/15$ would be depreciated. In subsequent years, $3/15$, $2/15$, and $1/15$, respectively, would be charged to depreciation expense.

Example

A firm purchases an auto for $31,000. It estimates that the auto has a useful life of five years, after which it can be sold for $6,000. The net amount to be depreciated for $25,000 (original cost less estimated salvage value). Depreciation charges using the sum-of-the-years'-digits method would be as follows:

Year	Net Depreciable Amount	Depreciation Fraction	Depreciation Charge
1	$25,000	$5/15$	$ 8,333
2	25,000	$4/15$	6,667
3	25,000	$3/15$	5,000
4	25,000	$2/15$	3,333
5	25,000	$1/15$	1,667
		$15/15$	$25,000

Declining Balance Method

The *declining balance* method consists of applying to the current book value of the asset (cost less accumulated depreciation to date) a percentage rate equal to some proportion of the straight-line depreciation rate. If the rate is twice the straight-line rate, it is referred to as the *double declining balance* method.

In the earlier example of straight-line depreciation in which the asset had a useful life of five years, one-fifth or 20 percent of the net depreciable cost was charged off each year. Hence the depreciation rate could be said to have been 20 percent. The appropriate rate for the double declining balance method would therefore be twice that, or 40 percent. The appropriate rate for 150 percent declining balance depreciation would be 1.5 times the straight-line rate, or 30 percent. Unlike the straight-line or sum-of-the-years'-digits methods, *the declining balance procedure requires that the rate be applied initially to the original cost of the asset—not original cost less residual value.*

Example

Again, the asset to be considered cost $31,000 and has a useful life of five years and an estimated residual value of $6,000. Depreciation charges using the double declining balance method are based on a rate of 40 percent (twice the straight-line rate of 20 percent). The calculations are shown in Exhibit 9-2.

EXHIBIT 9-2
Double Declining Balance Depreciation

Year	Cost Less Accumulated Depreciation (End-of-Year Book Value)	Depreciation Rate (%)	Depreciation Charge	Remaining Book Value End of Year
1	$31,000	40	$12,400	$18,600
2	18,600	40	7,440	11,160
3	11,160	40	4,464	6,696
4	6,696	—	696	6,000
5	6,000	—	0	6,000

The declining balance method does not automatically assure that an asset will be depreciated exactly down to its estimated residual value at the end of its forecasted useful life. Most frequently, residual value is reached before the end of estimated useful life. When that occurs, an asset should not be depreciated below its estimated residual value. In the example, depreciation in year 4 is limited to $696, rather than $2,278, the full 40 percent of beginning balance of $6,696. This figure ($696) reduces the remaining book value to an estimated residual value of $6,000. In year 5, no depreciation is taken.

For assets for which it is a small percentage of original cost, residual value may not be reached by the end of estimated useful life. In fact, if residual value is zero, then it will never be reached, no matter how long the asset is retained. If a firm holds an asset beyond its originally estimated useful life, then it should continue to depreciate the asset until it disposes of the asset or depreciates it to its estimated residual value.

The Accelerated Cost Recovery System

The Internal Revenue Service Code stipulates that depreciation charges on property placed in service after 1980 can be determined using the *accelerated cost recovery system (ACRS)*. Under this system, which was modified by the Tax Reform Act of 1986, most types of property are divided into several classes indicative of the number of years over which depreciation may be charged—for example, 3 years, 5 years, 7 years, 10 years, 15 years. Property in the three-, five-, seven- and ten-year classes may be depreciated using the 200 percent declining balance method. Assets in the 15- and 20-year classes are limited to the 150 percent declining balance method, while those in longer-lived classes are restricted to straight-line depreciation. For taxpayers who apply the accelerated methods, the code provides an added benefit. Taxpayers are permitted to switch to the straight-line method in the course of an asset's life. It would be advantageous to make the change when the deduction under the straight-line method exceeds that under the accelerated.

WHICH METHOD IS PREFERABLE?

Official accounting pronouncements permit companies broad discretion in selecting a depreciation method. Any method is acceptable as long as it allocates costs in a "systematic and rational manner." The straight-line method is the most widely used for general-purpose financial reporting. Accelerated methods are commonly used for tax reporting because they result in stiff charges to income in the early years of asset life. Whereas the tax provisions require taxpayers who take advantage of LIFO in computing their cost of goods sold to adopt it for financial reporting, they place no comparable demands on taxpayers who use accelerated depreciation methods. Hence firms can reap the benefits of accelerated deductions on their tax returns while taking only straight-line deductions on their financial statements.

Accelerated Methods

Many accountants who have given thought to the issue believe that depreciation charges should be tied to asset efficiency and productivity. In the periods in which an asset provides the greater output or cost savings, its depreciation charges should also be the greater. The efficiency and productivity of most assets decline with age. Vehicles and equipment, for example, are subject to increasing repair costs and "downtime." Residential and commercial buildings are less able to attract premium rents. In the face of declining efficiency and productivity, the accelerated methods provide the closer match between asset benefits and costs. A larger proportion of an asset's cost is expensed in the early years of asset life when the asset output is the greatest.

EXHIBIT 9-3
Example: Rate of Return Based on Double Declining Balance Depreciation, Assuming Constant Asset Efficiency and Productivity

Asset cost: $10,000
Useful life: 5 years
Residual value: $0
Depreciation rate: 40 percent
Revenues represent contributions of asset after deduction of all related expenses other than depreciation, assumed to be $2,638 per year.

| | Period | | | | |
	1	2	3	4	5
Revenues	$2,638	$2,638	$2,638	$2,638	$2,638
Depreciation	4,000	2,400	1,440	864	518
Income	($1,362)	$ 238	$1,198	$1,774	$2,120
Net book value, beginning of period	$10,000	$6,000	$3,600	$2,160	$1,296
Rate of return (income/book value)	(13.6%)	4.0%	33.3%	82.1%	163.5%

Straight-Line Method

Even though, as emphasized earlier, the objectives of depreciation are more closely tied to the income statement than to the balance sheet, the relationship between depreciation and book value cannot be ignored. After all, return on investment, which relates income to net assets (or to stockholders' equity, which is the equivalent of net assets) is one of the most pervasive measures of organizational performance.

When either depreciation or net income (which is directly affected by depreciation) is related to the book values of assets, the straight-line method of depreciation produces a more stable return on investment than do the accelerated methods. As shown in Exhibit 9-3, if the net revenues (revenues less operating expenses) generated by an asset remain constant, the double declining balance method causes rates of return to increase dramatically over the years of asset life. The increasing return on investment gives the highly misleading impression that the profitability of a firm improves with the age of its assets.[1]

The straight-line method considerably alleviates, but by no means eliminates, the anomaly of rates of return that increase with asset age. As shown in the first part of Exhibit 9-4, when net revenues remain constant, rates of return again rise substantially over the life of the asset. However, in the more realistic case, when net revenues *decline* over asset life (as illustrated in the second part of Exhibit 9-4), the straight-line method yields a reasonably constant return on investment.

[1]The focus herein is on the return of the plant assets alone. The book values of plant assets alone must be distinguished from the book value of the entire firm. If the firm retains, and invests, funds equal to the depreciation charges, then both the value of its total assets as well as its income will be greater than what is shown in Exhibit 9-3. The trend of return on investment (total income as a percentage of book value of all assets) will be considerably flatter than what is indicated in the exhibit.

EXHIBIT 9-4

Example: Rate of Return Based on Straight-Line Depreciation When Asset Efficiency and Productivity Are Constant and When They Are Decreasing

Asset cost: $10,000
Useful life: 5 years
Residual value: $0
Annual straight-line depreciation: $2,000
Revenues represent contributions of asset after deduction of all related expenses other than depreciation.

Constant Asset Efficiency and Productivity
(Net Revenues Assumed to Be $2,638 per year)

	Period				
	1	2	3	4	5
Revenues	$2,638	$2,638	$2,638	$2,638	$2,638
Depreciation	2,000	2,000	2,000	2,000	2,000
Income	$ 638	$ 638	$ 638	$ 638	$ 638
Net book value, beginning of period	$10,000	$8,000	$6,000	$4,000	$2,000
Rate of return (income/book value)	6.4%	8.0%	10.6%	16.0%	31.9%

Decreasing Asset Productivity and Efficiency
(Net Revenues Assumed to Be $3,000 in Year 1 and $200 Less Each Year)

	Period				
	1	2	3	4	5
Revenues	$3,000	$2,800	$2,600	$2,400	$2,200
Depreciation	2,000	2,000	2,000	2,000	2,000
Income	$1,000	$ 800	$ 600	$ 400	$ 200
Net book value, beginning of period	$10,000	$8,000	$6,000	$4,000	$2,000
Rate of return (income/book value)	10%	10%	10%	10%	10%

The constant rate of return is desirable because it reflects the economic decision made by the firm to acquire the asset. As was illustrated in Chapter 6, the value to the firm of an asset is the present value of its cash inflows (or savings). *Present value* is determined by discounting the cash flows of each year by a constant discount rate. A firm will be willing to acquire an asset as long as the present value of the cash flows, based on that discount rate, is greater than the present value of the cash outflows required to obtain it.

Suppose, that as in the first part of Exhibit 9-4, an asset will provide annual cash returns of $2,638. The discount rate of the firm is 10 percent. Per Table 4 in the Appendix, ''Present Value of an Annuity,'' the value of the asset to the firm is $10,000:

$$\$2,638 \times 3.7908 = \$10,000$$

The $10,000 in this example also happens to be the purchase price. This coincidence is not by chance. In a competitive economy, one might expect the value of an asset to a particular user to approximate its value to the market, at least over the long haul.

Compound Interest Depreciation

A depreciation method known as the *compound interest* method assures that the rate of return on an asset remains constant over its useful life, when the revenues do not decline but rather are constant. It provides for annual depreciation charges that *increase* from year to year. It has never been widely accepted in practice because it is counter to both accepted tax methods and the accountant's regard for conservatism. The compound interest method reports as depreciation each year's decline in the present value of expected benefits. When the firm acquires the asset described in the first part of Exhibit 9-4, it expects to receive the equivalent of five cash receipts of $2,638. Based on a discount rate of 10 percent, these are worth $10,000. After one year, the firm anticipates only four receipts of $2,638. These are worth only $8,362:

$$\$2,638 \times 3.1699 = \$8,362$$

Hence the value of the asset to the firm declines by $1,638. This, therefore, is the amount that would be recorded as depreciation in the first year.

EXHIBIT 9-5
Example: Depreciation and Rate of Return Based on Compound Interest Depreciation, with Annual Decline in Present Value of Anticipated Cash Flows

Asset cost: $10,000
Useful life: 5 years
Residual value: $0
Anticipated annual receipts of $2,638 represent contributions of asset after deduction of all related expenses other than depreciation.

Depreciation

End of Year	No. of Payments Remaining	Amount of Each Payment	Present Value of Annuity Remaining Payments (10%)	Present Value of Asset	Decline in Value during Year (Depreciation)
0	5	$2,638	3.7908	$10,000	—
1	4	2,638	3.1699	8,362	$1,638
2	3	2,638	2.4869	6,561	1,801
3	2	2,638	1.7355	4,579	1,982
4	1	2,638	.9091	2,390	2,180
5	0	—	—	0	2,398
Total depreciation					$9,999

Rate of Return Assuming Constant Asset Efficiency and Productivity

	Period 1	2	3	4	5
Revenues	$2,638	$2,638	$2,638	$2,638	$2,638
Depreciation	1,638	1,801	1,982	2,180	2,398
Income	$1,000	$ 837	$ 638	$ 458	$ 240
Net book value, beginning of period	$10,000	$8,362	$6,561	$4,579	$2,399
Rate of return (income/book value)	10%	10%	10%	10%	10%

After two years, the firm anticipates three more receipts of $2,638. These are worth $6,560:

$$\$2,638 \times 2.4869 = \$6,560$$

The $1,801 decline in value from $8,362 to $6,460 will be the depreciation charge for year 2. The complete depreciation schedule is shown in Exhibit 9-5. As can be seen from the second part of the table, return on investment is constant at 10 percent (the discount rate). Were the assumed revenues (which indicate asset productivity) not constant, then a different depreciation schedule would have to be developed. In such a schedule, as in the one shown, the depreciation charges would be the differences in the present values of the expected cash receipts from one year to the next. Nevertheless, the return on investment would remain constant and be equal to the discount rate used to determine the present values.

ALLOCATION BASED ON HISTORICAL COSTS VERSUS MARKET VALUES

Advantages of Historical Costs

Each of the methods discussed so far is based on historical costs. The amount paid for an asset is allocated to the years it will be in service. As will be discussed (and was indicated in earlier chapters), there are many disadvantages to historical costs. The advantages, however, should be appreciated.

The historical costs to be allocated are objective. In the case of fixed assets, they are transaction-based; the amount paid for an asset can be verified by its purchase documents. Total charges to depreciation are equal to the actual net cost (cost less salvage value, if any) of the asset. Resultant financial statements present a historical record based, at least initially, on verifiable arm's-length exchanges.

It is incontrovertible that financial statements based on historical costs do not provide *all* information required for investment or management decisions. It is doubtful, however, whether financial statements prepared on any single basis could do that. The use of historical costs by no means precludes the preparation and release of supplementary statements on other bases.

Limitations of the Historical Cost Basis

The limitations of historical costs with regard to fixed assets are similar to the limitations of historical costs as applied to inventories, marketable securities, and other assets. But they are especially pronounced when applied to fixed assets, which have long lives and are slow to turn over. Hence (as with LIFO inventories) the gap between historical and market values is often substantial.

Insofar as the financial reports fail to account for changes in market values, *both* the balance sheet and the income statement may be of limited utility to managers as well as investors. The balance sheet fails to provide information on the total amount of resources available to management for which it should be held accountable. It serves inadequately, therefore, as a basis on which to determine the return generated by the assets. Corporate performance can be meaningfully measured only in current values—not historical values. Current values indicate the alternative uses to which the assets could be put—the amount for which they could be sold and the proceeds invested in other ventures.

"Stealth" Assets

Historical cost accounting permits firms to maintain a reserve of hidden values and profits. If market values exceed book values, then the corporation can capture additional income merely by selling off the understated assets.

Assets that have especially long lives, such as land and buildings, are the most likely to exhibit wide differences between market and book values. One business journal referred to corporate real estate as a "stealth" asset—its value hidden from all but insiders and a few savvy investors.[2] It pointed out that on their books the largest 500 U.S. companies own real estate worth $350 billion, but that is only a fraction of its potential yield. Under pressure to generate short-term gains, many companies sell their properties, fearing that if they do not do so, they will be acquired by corporate raiders who will use the assets as sources of immediate cash. In recent years, the financial press has contained any number of stories of companies that were acquired for their real estate rather than their worth as going concerns. Examples include bus companies, restaurant chains, and department stores whose main business segments were well past their prime, but whose land and buildings were in choice downtown locations.

Distorted Earnings

The historical cost–based income statement provides no information as to the market value of the services consumed as an asset is used. Depreciation expense represents the cost of a portion of an asset's service potential. If the annual depreciation charge is determined on the basis of outdated historical costs, then in a period in which market values exceed historical costs the charge will understate the market value of the services consumed. A reader of the financial report may be led to infer that the firm is being operated with greater efficiency (less cost) than is in fact the case.

Similarly, a naïve manager may improperly conclude that one plant is more cost-effective than another. In fact, its lower costs may be the consequence of lower depreciation charges, which are attributable to the use of older and less costly assets. If, however, the current market values of the assets are the same, then the value of resources consumed will also be the same, despite the differences in the accounting numbers assigned to them.

The income statement also fails to provide information on the periodic increases in the value of assets (and thus of corporate net worth) over time. If income is to be a measure of how much "better off" a firm is from one period to the next, then changes in the amount for which assets could be bought or

[2]"More Companies Are Living Off the Fat of Their Land," *Business Week*, November 7, 1988, p. 156.

sold may be as important in determining income as actual exchange transactions. Decisions to hold or to sell fixed assets may be critical to the long-run welfare of the company. Since historical cost–based income statements omit *holding* gains or losses until the assets are sold or retired, they fail to account for an important dimension of corporate performance.

One of the more telling ironies of the failure to recognize holding gains as they occur is that the reported earnings of airlines actually increase as the result of major air disasters. Airlines, of course, insure their planes for their market values, not their book values. When a plane crashes, the company collects from the insurance company the full market value of the lost plane. It recognizes a gain in the amount of the excess of insurance proceeds over book value. In fact, by virtue of its DC-10 disaster in 1979 American Airlines increased its earnings by $26 million—from $1.25 per share to $2.63 per share.

An Alternative Basis: Replacement Cost

There are several market-based substitutes for historical costs. One proposed alternative is *current replacement cost*. The current replacement cost of an asset can be one of two values. First, it can be the amount necessary to acquire an asset that is identical to the existing one. The asset would be of the same age and condition and hence have the same *service potential*. This value is easily available for assets (such as motor vehicles and many types of equipment) for which there is an active "used" market. Second, it can be the cost of a similar *new* asset. If this value is used, it must be adjusted for any improvements in design and technology that make the new asset more productive than the old. From this cost must be deducted an allowance for depreciation to reflect the portion of the existing asset already consumed.

Under a replacement cost system of asset valuation, income would incorporate not only an expenditure (depreciation) indicative of asset consumption, but also a *holding* gain or loss based on the change in the asset's market value.

Replacement cost systems have the obvious advantage of reporting on the balance sheet values that are more useful than historical costs for most investment and management decisions. They are likely to be a better measure of an asset's earning potential from either continued use or sale. Current replacement costs do *not* directly indicate the value of an asset to a particular user—that is, the present value of the cash flows that it will generate. The value of an asset to a company that uses it with unusual efficiency might far exceed the price at which it is being traded in current markets. Nevertheless, the price that independent purchasers are willing to pay would, in general, be a reasonable approximation of the present value of the anticipated services. Certainly it is likely to be a more reliable surrogate than historical cost.

Equally important, replacement cost systems result in a depreciation charge that indicates the current value of resources consumed. Historical cost depreciation, by contrast, is analogous to historical cost of goods sold, particularly that on a FIFO basis. It values resources expended based on prices that pertained in what might be the distant past.

The following example shows how replacement costs can be incorporated into the accounts.

Example

A company owns a building that originally cost $1.8 million when purchased 10 years ago. The building has an estimated useful life of 40 years and no salvage value. It is currently reflected on the balance sheet as follows:

Building	$1,800,000
Less: Accumulated depreciation ($\frac{10}{40}$ of $1,800,000)	450,000
	$1,350,000

During each of the 10 years, depreciation has been recorded with the conventional journal entry

Depreciation expense	$45,000	
Accumulated depreciation		$45,000
To record annual depreciation expense		

Replacement cost has remained constant for the first 10 years of asset life.

At the end of this tenth year, however, owing to increases in construction costs, the replacement cost of the building has increased by $300,000. The following entry would recognize the increase in replacement cost:

Building	$300,000	
Accumulated depreciation		$ 75,000
Realizable holding gain (gain from appreciation)		225,000
To record the increase in replacement cost		

The necessity for crediting accumulated depreciation for $75,000 may not be obvious. The useful life of the building has not changed. Thus 25 percent of the building must still be considered as having been depreciated, regardless of the value placed on it. The new value of the building is $2.1 million; hence 25 percent (10 years worth—$525,000) of replacement cost must be reported in the accumulated depreciation account.

In each of the following 30 years, depreciation would be recorded in the standard manner, except that the charge would be $\frac{1}{40}$ of $2.1 million:

Depreciation expense	$52,500	
Accumulated depreciation		$52,500
To record depreciation expense		

This example is based on the assumption that there is no market for comparable used buildings. At the end of its tenth year of life the building will be reported at a net value of $1,575,000 million (replacement cost of $2.1 million for a *new* building less depreciation of $525,000). The amount, of course, is only an estimate of what would be required to obtain a comparable 10-year-old facility.

If there were a market for used assets, then the net value assigned to the building would be the market value of a 10-year-old asset. The net charge to income (depreciation expense combined with the holding gain or loss) would equal the change in the value during the period.

Objections to Replacement Cost

A primary objection to the use of replacement costs is the difficulty of measuring them. Many assets are unique and market prices are not readily available.

How, for example, would you determine the current replacement cost of a tract of land? In some cases it may be possible to derive a value based on a recent purchase offer. In others, a reasonable value could be obtained by determining the amount for which similar tracts in the same neighborhood have recently been sold or by using price indices that reflect a general increase in commercial real estate value. Consider the problem, however, of estimating the value of land on which Ford Motor Company's River Rouge plant is located. The track of land comprises several square miles, and the industrial influence of the plant is felt for many miles around the plant. Whatever value (or lack of it) the surrounding land has is attributable to the activities of Ford. It would be impossible to determine the value of the land either by looking at other recent offers (the plant is of such enormous value that it is reasonably certain that there have been few serious offers) or by looking at the sales prices of surrounding land (the Ford land determines the value of the surrounding land, not the other way around). Current replacement costs may be relevant for many decisions, but they are not often objectively determinable.

The difficulty of establishing replacement costs for some assets cannot be denied. But the issue that accountants face is whether an approximation, however subjective, of a useful value is to be preferred to an exact measure of a useless one. Replacement values, even if arbitrary, convey information that is pertinent to many managerial and investment decisions. Historical values do not.

A second objection is that the firm may have no intention of either selling the assets or replacing them. Moreover, even if it were to dispose of the assets, it might replace them with ones that are more technologically advanced. The significance of information on amounts that are unlikely to be either paid or received is at best problematic.

The response to this objection is that replacement cost systems do not presuppose that firms intend to sell or replace their assets. Replacement values express the worth of resources within the command of an entity as measured by criteria of the marketplace, not the individual user. Value to the user, as discussed earlier, requires specification of the cash flows to be generated by the assets, either by sale or by use.

A third objection is that, irrespective of theoretical merit, current values have not proved to be of concern to statement users. Perhaps, as implied in this chapter, they *should* use them. But apparently they do not. Thus it is questionable whether the cost of obtaining and gathering the data equals the benefit. This is the objection that was persuasive to the Financial Accounting Standards Board. As discussed in Chapter 8 in relation to inventories, the board at one time mandated extensive supplementary current value disclosures. Citing lack of interest, however, it has since reduced the disclosure of the information from the level of "required" to that of "encouraged."

RETIREMENT OF FIXED ASSETS

Upon the retirement of an asset, either by sale or by abandonment, the asset *as well as the related accumulated depreciation* must be removed from the books. If the asset is sold for the amount and at the time originally estimated, then the retirement entry is especially simple.

Return once again to the auto that originally cost $31,000 and had an estimated residual value after five years of $6,000. At the end of five years, the fixed asset account would have a debit balance of $31,000 (regardless of the choice of depreciation method), and the accumulated depreciation account a credit balance of $25,000 (slightly less if the double declining balance method was used). If the asset is, in fact, sold for $6,000, then the appropriate journal entry would be

Cash	$ 6,000	
Accumulated depreciation, autos	25,000	
Fixed assets, autos		$31,000

To record the sale of the asset

If, at any time during its life, the asset is either sold or abandoned for an amount greater or less than its book value, then a gain or loss on retirement would have to be recognized.

Example

The firm had charged depreciation on the auto using straight-line depreciation. At the end of three years, after $15,000 of depreciation had been charged, the firm sold the auto for $12,000. The book value of the asset at time of sale would have been $16,000, or $31,000 less $15,000. Hence the firm has suffered a loss of $4,000:

Cash	$12,000	
Accumulated depreciation, autos	15,000	
Loss on disposal	4,000	
Fixed assets, autos		$31,000

To record the sale of the asset

Bear in mind that if an asset is sold anytime before the close of the year, depreciation for the portion of the year that the asset was actually held must first be recorded before any gain or loss can be computed.

The nature of gains or losses on retirement merits comment. Such gains or losses arise only because a company may not have perfect foresight when it acquires the asset as to the time of retirement and the selling price. If it had such foresight, it would determine its depreciation schedule accordingly and hence there would be no gain or loss upon retirement.

In the previous example, the $4,000 loss on retirement indicates that insufficient depreciation of $1,333 per year for the three years that the asset was held had been charged. If the firm had known that it would sell the asset (that cost $31,000) for $12,000 after using it for three years, then it would have allocated $19,000 of asset cost ($31,000 cost less $12,000 salvage value) to each of the three years—instead of the $15,000 actually allocated. Annual depreciation would thereby have been $6,333 instead of $5,000.

Proper accounting might therefore dictate that, rather than recognizing a loss on retirement in the year of sale, the company should correct the earnings of the prior years for the insufficient depreciation charges. This type of correction would reduce retained earnings without burdening reported income in the year of retirement. In practice, such an approach is not permitted because it would require an excessive number of prior adjustments and thereby complicate the process of financial reporting.

TRADE-INS

A special problem is presented when a firm *trades in* an old asset for a new one. For example, a firm surrenders an old car, plus cash, for a later model. One convenient way of handling a trade-in is to view it as two separate transactions. In the first, the old asset is sold—not for cash but for a *trade-in allowance*. In the second, the new asset is purchased—for cash plus the trade-in allowance. The critical step in implementing such a procedure lies in determining the price for which the old asset was sold. In many instances, the amount that the dealership says it is offering as a trade-in allowance bears no relationship to the actual fair market value of the old asset. In the auto industry, for example, it is common for new car dealers to offer unusually high trade-in allowances on the used vehicles of prospective new car purchasers. If purchasers accept the high trade-in allowance, they may be unable to avail themselves of discounts that are generally granted to purchasers who come without used cars. They may, in effect, have to pay full, or nearly full, *sticker* price for the new car, something they would not ordinarily have to do if they came to the dealer without an old car to trade.

If a meaningful gain or loss on retirement is to be computed, it is essential therefore that the company determine as accurately as possible the actual fair market value of the asset given up. This amount, irrespective of representations by the dealer, is the true trade-in allowance. It can usually be derived—or at least estimated—by consulting industry publications, such as the car dealers' ''blue book'' of used car prices, or by obtaining data on transactions involving similar assets.

Example

The auto which originally cost $31,000 (estimated life of five years, $6,000 salvage) is traded in for a new car after three years. The dealer grants a trade-in allowance of $18,000, but according to a book of used car prices, the car is worth no more than $13,000. The true trade-in allowance is therefore only $13,000. Correspondingly, the sticker price of the new car is $41,000 but, in fact, an astute buyer would not normally pay more than $36,000. In addition to giving up its old car, the company pays cash of $23,000, thereby surrendering cash and a car with a total value of $36,000.

The book value of the old car, assuming straight-line depreciation, would at the time of trade-in be

Original cost	$31,000
Accumulated depreciation (3 years × $5,000)	15,000
Book value	$16,000

Loss on the sale of the old car would therefore be $16,000 less $13,000 (fair market value of the old car), or $3,000.

The "sale" of the old car could be recorded as follows:

(a)

Loss on retirement	$ 3,000	
Accumulated depreciation, autos	15,000	
Trade-in allowance (a temporary account)	13,000	
Fixed assets, autos		$31,000
To record the "sale" of the asset		

The entry to record the purchase of the new auto would be

(b)

Fixed assets, autos	$36,000	
Cash		$23,000
Trade-in allowance		13,000
To record the purchase of the new asset		

Clearly, the two entries could be combined (and the trade-in allowance account eliminated).

This method of accounting for trade-ins allows the new asset to be recorded at its fair market value, which is equal to the cash price that an independent buyer would have to pay. At the same time, it permits the gain or loss on retirement of the old asset to be based upon its fair market value. It thereby gives recognition to the economic substance of the transaction, regardless of what amounts the buyer and seller arbitrarily assign to the trade-in allowance and the price of the new asset.

The transaction just illustrated resulted in a reported loss on retirement. If, however, application of the accounting procedure described had resulted in a *gain* rather than a loss, then the Accounting Principles Board (in *Opinion No. 29*) prescribes the use of a slightly different method. Under the APB method, no gain on retirement would be recognized. The new asset would be recorded at an amount equal to the sum of

1. The book value (cost less accumulated depreciation) of the old asset
2. Any additional cash paid

Suppose, for example, a firm were to exchange the old auto having a book value of $16,000 (cost $31,000, accumulated depreciation $15,000) plus cash of $15,500 for a new auto that has a fair market value of $36,000.

These facts imply that the old auto had a market value of $20,500 inasmuch as the dealer was willing to accept it plus $15,500 cash for a new auto worth $36,000. Since the book value of the old auto was only $16,000, the trade-in resulted in an economic gain of $4,500. Nevertheless, the following entry would be in order:

Accumulated depreciation (old auto) $15,000
Automobile (new) 31,500
    Automobile (old)..$31,000
    Cash 15,500

To record trade-in of automobile

The entry gives no recognition to either the fair market value of the new asset or the obvious economic difference at the time of the trade between the fair market value and the book value of the old asset. The new balance in the automobile account would be depreciated over the useful life of the new auto.

The APB method applies only to trades of similar assets—an auto for an auto, for example, but not an auto for a computer. As with many accounting rules, it was legislated to eliminate abusive reporting practices. Prior to *Opinion No. 29,* firms in some industries, such as utilities, were exchanging assets whose market values exceeded their book values. These trades enabled the utilities to report increases in both the book values of their assets and in annual depreciation charges. The higher depreciation charges (a noncash expense) could then be passed on to customers in the form of increased rates.

The contrast between the two methods is another reminder that many current accounting issues can be attributed to the practice of reporting assets on the basis of historical cost rather than market value. If the reported value of an asset were periodically increased to reflect changes in market conditions, then at the time of retirement or trade there would be little need to recognize a gain or a loss. The reported value of the asset would be nearly identical to the amount for which it could be sold or traded.

PLANT AND EQUIPMENT TURNOVER

The efficiency with which plant and equipment is utilized may be measured by the *plant and equipment turnover ratio,* determined by comparing sales to average book value (cost less accumulated depreciation) of plant and equipment:

$$\text{Plant and equipment turnover} = \frac{\text{Sales}}{\text{Average plant and equipment}}$$

For example, American Home Products in 1991 had average plant and equipment (in millions) of \$1,457 (the average of the beginning balance of \$1,437 and the ending balance of \$1,477) and sales for the year were \$7,079.

$$\text{Plant and equipment turnover} = \frac{\$7,079}{\$1,457} = 4.9 \text{ times}$$

The greater the turnover ratio, the more effectively plant and equipment are being employed. In years when sales are down and physical facilities are not being used to capacity, the ratio will decline. In years when sales are up and the plant is being used to the fullest extent possible, the ratio will increase.

Although plant and equipment are conventionally stated in the ratio at book values, there is no reason why market values could not be used instead. Indeed, if management is concerned with comparing asset utilization among plants of different ages, then market values may provide a more appropriate measure of the resources over which plant executives have stewardship.

Natural resources, or *wasting assets,* as they are often referred to, are accounted for in a manner similar to plant and equipment. They are recorded initially at acquisition cost, and this value is subsequently reduced as service potential declines.

Units of Output Basis

The process of allocating the cost of natural resources over the periods in which they provide benefits is known as *depletion.* The service potential of natural resources can ordinarily be measured more meaningfully in terms of quantity of production (such as tons or barrels) than number of years. Hence depletion is generally charged on a *units of output* basis. As with other types of long-lived assets, the initial cost of a natural resource may be reported on the balance sheet for as long as it is in service. The accumulated depletion may be indicated in a contra account. In practice, however, a contra account is not always used; often the balance in the natural resource account itself is reduced directly by the amount of the accumulated depletion.

Example

A firm purchases mining properties for $2 million cash. It estimates that the properties will yield 400,000 usable tons of ore. During the first year of production, the firm mines 5,000 tons.

The following entry would be appropriate to record the purchase of the properties:

Mineral deposits $2,000,000
     Cash $2,000,000
To record the purchase of the ore deposit

Since the deposit will yield an estimated 400,000 tons of usable ore, cost assignable to each ton is

$$\frac{\$2,000,000}{400,000 \text{ tons}} = \$5 \text{ per ton}$$

Depletion cost of the first year is

$$5,000 \text{ (tons mined)} \times \$5 \text{ per ton} = \$25,000$$

The entry to record the depletion would be

Depletion (expense) $25,000
    Mineral deposits, accumulated depletion. $25,000
To record first-year depletion

After the first year, the mineral deposits would be reported on the balance sheet as

Mineral deposits	$2,000,000
Less: Accumulated depletion	25,000
	$1,975,000

Depletion is a cost of production, to be added along with other production costs (labor, depreciation of equipment, supplies) to the carrying value of the minerals inventory. It should be charged as an expense (cost of minerals sold) in the accounting period in which the inventory is sold and the revenue from the sale is recognized.

Depreciation of Location-Specific Equipment

A mining or drilling company may have to purchase or build equipment or structures that can be used only in connection with the recovery of a specific deposit. If the structures or equipment will be used for as long as the property continues to be exploited (and only so long), then depreciation charges should logically be determined using the same units of output basis as used to compute depletion.

Suppose, for example, that mining equipment costs $80,000 and can be used exclusively at a site with estimated ore content of 400,000 tons. Depreciation would be charged at a rate of 20 cents per ton mined ($80,000 divided by 400,000 tons) regardless of useful life in terms of years. If in the first year of operation 50,000 tons was mined, the depreciation charge would be $10,000 (50,000 tons @ 20 cents per ton). Depreciation, if based on output, is more likely in such circumstances to assure that the cost of equipment or structures is matched with the revenues realized from the sale of the minerals than if based on useful life in terms of time.

INTANGIBLE ASSETS AND DEFERRED CHARGES

Intangible assets are those assets characterized by the rights, privileges, and benefits of possession rather than by physical existence. Examples of intangible assets are patents, copyrights, trademarks, licenses, and goodwill. Often the service potential of intangible assets is uncertain and exceedingly difficult to measure. As a consequence, intangible assets frequently are the subject of controversy.

Closely related to intangible assets are deferred charges. *Deferred charges* are expenditures not recognized as a cost of the period in which incurred but carried forward as assets to be written off in future periods. Examples of deferred charges that are categorized as long-term assets (because they will be written off over a period greater than one year) are certain product development costs, organization costs, costs of drilling unsuccessful oil wells, and store preopening costs. The distinction between intangible assets and deferred charges is at best vague; in fact, deferred charges can be considered as a type of intangible asset. The basic accounting principles and issues pertaining to them are the same.

In this section we shall deal with only a few selected intangibles and deferred charges. But the principles and issues set forth can be generalized to a wide range of other assets with similar characteristics. (A discussion of goodwill, one of the more controversial intangible assets, will be deferred until the chapter pertaining to ownership interests among corporations, since goodwill conventionally arises only out of the acquisition of one company by another.)

Intangibles are considered to be assets either because they represent rights to future benefits or because the expenditures that were made to acquire or develop them will benefit a number of accounting periods in the future. Hence the costs must be allocated to the periods in which the benefits will be realized.

Intangibles are recorded initially at their acquisition or development costs. The costs are then amortized over (allocated to) the periods in which the benefits will accrue. The general accounting approach to intangibles may be illustrated with respect to copyrights.

Copyrights

A *copyright* is an exclusive right, granted by law, to publish, sell, reproduce, or otherwise control a literary, musical, or artistic work. Since January 1, 1978, in the United States, copyrights on most new works have been granted for the life of the creator plus 50 years. The cost to secure a copyright from the federal government is minimal; however, the cost to purchase one from its holder on a work that has proved successful—on a best-selling novel or musical recording, for instance—may be substantial.

If a firm were to purchase a copyright, it would record it initially as it would any other asset. Assuming a cost of $20,000, for example, an appropriate journal entry might be

```
Copyright . . . . . . . . . . . . . . . . . . . . . . . . . . . . . . . . . . . . . . . . . . . $20,000
    Cash . . . . . . . . . . . . . . . . . . . . . . . . . . . . . . . . . . . . . . . . . . . $20,000
To record the purchase of the copyright
```

If the remaining useful life was 10 years, then the following entry would be appropriate each year to record amortization:

```
Amortization of copyrights . . . . . . . . . . . . . . . . . . . . . . . . . . . . . . $2,000
    Copyrights, accumulated amortization . . . . . . . . . . . . . . . . . . . . . . $2,000
To record amortization of copyright
```

Accounting practices as to copyrights focus attention on a question that is raised with many intangibles—that of the number of years over which cost should be amortized. Although the legal life of a copyright may be firmly established, the copyright may be of significant economic value for a considerably shorter period of time. Actual useful life may depend on a multitude of factors such as public taste, critical acclaim, or future success of the author, none of which can readily be assessed. As with other long-lived assets, carrying value of the assets as well as amortization charges (the periodic decline in value) must be based, in large measure, on subjective judgments of corporate management and accountants.

Costs of Drilling Unsuccessful Oil Wells

Accounting practices in the oil and gas industry raise other important issues relating to intangible assets. What is the nature of the costs to be included as part of the asset? How directly must a cost be associated with a future benefit before it should properly be capitalized? How broadly should an asset be defined?

Despite highly sophisticated geological survey techniques, it is usually necessary for oil and gas companies, in their search for new reserves, to drill unsuccessfully in several locations before actually striking oil or gas. Obviously, the cost of drilling the productive wells should be capitalized and amortized over the years during which oil or gas will be withdrawn from the ground. But what about the costs of drilling the dry holes? Should they be written off as incurred, or should they also be capitalized and amortized over the period in which oil is withdrawn from the successful wells? Should they be considered losses (corporate errors in a sense) as opposed to expenditures that are statistically necessary to discover the productive locations? The dry holes may produce no direct benefits to the company, but they are an inevitable cost of finding the productive wells.

If an asset is defined narrowly as a single hole, then there would be little justification for capitalizing it. It clearly has no future service potential. But if the asset is defined more broadly as an entire oil field, then the dry hole can be interpreted as an element of cost required to bring the field to a serviceable state.

In past years, some companies capitalized costs associated with unsuccessful prospects (dry hole costs), while others did not. Those that did were known as *full-cost* companies, since the costs of the proven mineral reserves included the costs of drilling the unsuccessful as well as the successful wells. Those that did not were referred to as *successful-efforts* firms, because only the costs of drilling successful wells were added to the costs of the oil and gas properties; outlays associated with unsuccessful drilling efforts were charged as expenses as soon as it was concluded that the efforts at a particular location were a failure.

Economic Consequences of Accounting Methods in Establishing Drilling Costs

The use of one method rather than the other has no direct economic consequences for a firm. It has no impact on tax liabilities; as with depreciation, the allowable tax deductions are independent of the method used for reporting. It has no effect on either the amount of proven reserves or their anticipated selling prices. Reported earnings, of course, would differ, but because the firm is required to disclose the method used, knowledgeable analysts can easily convert earnings to the other basis. One might think therefore that a standard that prescribed one method rather than the other would generate neither controversy nor emotion. In fact, however, it did.

In 1977, the Financial Accounting Standards Board, in *Statement No. 19,* prescribed that all firms must use *only* the *successful-efforts* method. The decision of the FASB was a source of consternation to those firms that had been using the full-cost method and the federal agencies concerned with administering the antitrust statutes. The full-cost method had been used by many small exploration firms. The switch to the successful-efforts method resulted, at least in the short run, in reductions in their reported earnings because the costs of unsuccessful wells were written off in the year of failure rather than over a number of succeeding years. The small firms argued that the reduction in reported earnings would make them less attractive to investors and lenders and thereby less able to acquire the capital necessary to compete with the giants of the industry, many of which were already using the successful-efforts method. The FASB and its defenders, however, asserted that fears of reduced competition were groundless because the change would affect only *reported* earnings. In terms of economic wealth—the present value of actual oil and gas reserves—the firms would be neither better nor worse off merely because they made use of one accounting method rather than another.

The Securities and Exchange Commission failed to support the directive of the FASB that mandated the use of the successful-efforts method. It took the position that both the successful-efforts and the full-cost methods were deficient because they failed to provide adequate information on the economic worth of the oil and gas reserves that had been discovered. The SEC proposed that a third method, *reserve recognition accounting,* be developed. The new method required that proven reserves be reported at the present value of the cash flows that they were likely to generate. It required firms not only to estimate the quantities of oil and gas in their fields, but also to make assumptions as to the prices at which they would be sold and the cost of lifting them from the ground.

Owing in large measure to the difficulties of making the necessary estimates, reserve recognition accounting never gained the support of firms in the oil industry, and eventually the SEC abandoned efforts to impose it upon them. In light of the initial opposition to successful-efforts accounting on the part of the SEC, the FASB suspended the key provisions of *FAS 19*. Since 1982, firms can use either the full-cost or the successful-efforts method but must disclose the extent of their reserves.

Accounting researchers have conducted several studies as to whether the small firms were correct in asserting that the lower earnings resulting from the successful-efforts method would increase their cost of capital. The results have been mixed, with no clear answer as to whether, in fact, there are indirect economic consequences of choice of accounting method.

Research and Development Costs

Accounting procedures for research and development costs are illustrative of an additional issue common to intangible assets: To what extent must theoretical concepts of intangible assets be tempered by "practical" considerations? Research and development costs are, by nature, incurred to benefit future accounting periods. Expenditures for research and development are made with the expectation that they will lead to new or improved products or processes that will in turn increase revenues or decrease expenses. The matching concept suggests that research and development costs be capitalized as intangible assets and amortized over the periods in which the additional revenues are generated or cost savings effected.

In practice, however, it has proved exceedingly difficult to match specific expenditures for research and development with specific products or processes. Some expenditures are for basic research; they are not intended to produce direct benefits. Others produce no benefits at all or result in benefits which could not have been foreseen at the time they were incurred.

The FASB, in *Statement No. 2* (1974), prescribed that expenditures for most types of research and development costs be charged to expense in the year incurred rather than capitalized as intangible assets. The board was motivated by the great variety of practice among corporations as to the nature of costs that were capitalized and the number of periods over which they were amortized. Given almost unlimited flexibility in accounting for research and development, some firms capitalized costs that were unlikely to provide future benefits; others wrote off large amounts of previously capitalized costs in carefully selected periods so as to avoid burdening other accounting periods with amortization charges.

As a consequence of the board's actions, uniformity of accounting practice among companies has been enhanced. But research and development costs must now be charged as an expense as if they benefit but a single accounting period. And the period in which they are to be charged off—that in which they are incurred—is that which is, in fact, least likely to benefit from the expenditures, since research and development costs are almost always future- rather than present-oriented.

The approach of the board is inconsistent with the concept that costs should be matched to the revenues with which they are associated. It substitutes a precise accounting rule for the professional judgment of managers and accountants. It can hardly be viewed as an ideal solution to the accounting problems related to intangibles. But the board's approach does represent an attempt to ensure greater consistency among firms and to eliminate abusive reporting practices.

Start-Up Costs

A problem common to numerous industries is how to account for start-up costs. *Start-up costs* are outlays incurred prior to the point at which a venture is fully operational.

The issues pertaining to start-up costs are further demonstrative of the practical difficulties of applying the matching concept. The matching concept requires that costs be charged as expenses in the same period as the revenues that they generate are recognized. Start-up costs are incurred before the revenues that they are expected to generate are earned. Therefore they should be recorded as assets and amortized over the periods to be benefited by them. But there is seldom a direct link between the start-up costs and the anticipated revenues. Hence it is almost never obvious what outlays should be capitalized and over how many periods they should be charged as expenses.

The examples that follow show how start-up costs are dealt with in two specific industries.

Retail Industry

Prior to the opening of a new store, retail chains incur costs of site selection, rent, advertising, stocking shelves, and training new employees. Since the store produces no revenues before it opens, the costs will provide benefits only in periods thereafter.

There are no specific authoritative pronouncements as to how preopening costs should be accounted for, and practice in the industry is diverse. Some chains (e.g., F. W. Woolworth & Co.) charge preopening costs to expense in the year incurred. This policy is conservative and convenient (the company avoids having to account for the costs for over more than one period), but it otherwise has little to recommend it. It is contrary to the matching principle, since expenses are charged in periods before revenues are earned. Other chains (e.g., J. C. Penney) capitalize the preopening costs and charge them to expense in their entirety in the year in which the store is opened. Still others capitalize the costs and amortize them over an arbitrary period, such as three years.

Cable Television Industry

Cable television firms can expect cash outflows to exceed cash inflows for some time after they initiate service in a new market. They must incur costs not only for the capital equipment required to receive and transmit signals, but also for advertising, promotion, general administration, and programming. Many of their costs are "fixed"; they do not vary significantly, regardless of the number of subscribers.

Some types of start-up costs will be incurred in their entirety before revenue is earned from the first subscriber. But others will continue even after the system goes on line. Most cable companies can expect to incur cash deficits until a target number of subscribers have been signed up and the system is operating at a specific level of capacity.

There is no question that equipment costs should be capitalized in full and depreciated over their expected useful lives. But advertising, promotion, general administration, and programming costs, especially those incurred after the system goes on line, are usually considered period costs. They are commonly expensed as incurred. When service is extended to a new area, however, they are clearly intended to benefit the future, not the present. Should they nevertheless be expensed as incurred, or should they be capitalized? And if they are to be capitalized, then how should the start-up costs that will benefit the future be distinguished from the normal operating costs that will benefit only the present? What is an acceptable length for the start-up period? Over how many years should the costs that have been capitalized be amortized?

The Financial Accounting Standards Board responded to diversity of practice within the industry by establishing arbitrary (though seemingly quite reasonable) guidelines.[3] The guidelines require a cable firm to establish a "prematurity" period of not more than two years when it begins service to a new geographic area. During the period, "subscriber-related and general and administrative expenses" must be expensed as incurred. Programming and other system costs (including property taxes and costs of renting equipment) must be allocated between current and future operations. The portion allocated to current operations must be expensed as incurred; the remainder capitalized and amortized over the same period used to depreciate the main cable television plant. The allocation must be based on a formula developed by the board that relates current to anticipated number of subscribers.

Summary

Long-lived assets are used over a number of accounting periods. They are recorded initially at *acquisition cost,* which is the amount necessary to bring them to a serviceable condition. Interest, whether implicit or explicit, is generally excluded from acquisition

[3]"Financial Reporting by Cable Television Companies," Financial Accounting Standards Board *Statement of Financial Accounting Standards No. 51*, 1981.

cost but may be included on that of certain long-term construction proj
quent to acquisition, costs of *betterments,* but not of repairs and maintenar
added to initial cost.

Because long-lived assets provide services over more than one perio
must be allocated to all the periods that benefit from them. The process
is referred to as *depreciation, depletion,* or *amortization.* Among the several b
of allocation are *straight-line, sum of the years' digits,* and *declining balance.* An additional
method, *compound interest,* provides insight into the economic benefits of assets. However,
unlike the others, it results in increasing charges and for that reason is seldom used
in practice.

Long-lived assets are reported at historical cost, less the allowance representing
the portion of services consumed. This value has the virtue of being based on actual
transactions in which the firm engaged but does not provide information that is useful
for investment or management decisions. Market values, by contrast, provide more
relevant information but must be based on transactions external to the firm.

When an asset is sold or traded at an amount that differs from its book value,
a gain or loss must be recognized. This gain or loss results because the firm did not
have perfect foresight and failed to correctly predict useful life or residual value.

Irrespective of how a long-lived asset is accounted for—its basis of depreciation,
the estimate of useful life, whether changes in market values are recognized—its impact on reported earnings over its entire useful life will be the same. The total cost—
the amount to be charged as an expense—will be the price paid less the amount received
when it is sold or retired. "Only" the allocations of costs among periods will differ.
It is because financial statements must be prepared periodically—and income for each
individual period determined—that long-lived assets are the cause of as many issues
and controversies as they are.

Exercise for Review and Self-Testing

Airline Freight acquires a cargo plane. The company pays $3 million cash and gives
the seller marketable securities with a fair value of $500,000. The company incurs ad-
ditional costs of $6,000 to have the plane delivered to its home airport and $94,000
to have it fitted with special equipment. The firm plans to keep the plane for 10 years;
it estimates that it will be able to sell the cargo plane at the end of 10 years for $900,000.

1. At what amount should the plane be initially recorded?
2. What is the total dollar amount to be allocated as depreciation expense over
   the period during which the plane will be in service?
3. What should be the charge for depreciation for each of the 10 years of useful
   life if the firm were to use the straight-line method?
4. What should be the charge for depreciation for each of the first three years
   of useful life if the firm were to use the double declining balance method?
5. Suppose that the firm used the double declining balance method and that at
   the end of the sixth year of useful life the book value of the plane was
   $943,718—that is, depreciation of $2,656,282 had been charged to date. How
   much depreciation should the firm charge in the seventh year of service? How
   much in the eighth? Be sure your answers are consistent with your response
   to part 2.
6. Suppose that after the third year of using the plane the company elected to
   trade in the old plane for a new one. The company paid $7 million cash for
   the new plane and surrendered the old cargo plane. Immediately prior to the
   trade, the firm had received offers from parties who were willing to buy the
   plane outright. All were willing to pay approximately $1.5 million cash. At

the time of the trade, the old plane had a book value of $1,843,200 (initial cost less accumulated depreciation of $1,756,800) based on use of the double declining balance method. How much gain or loss should the firm report on the transaction? At what amount should it record the new plane?

Questions for Review and Discussion

1. "Because fixed assets are stated on the *balance sheet* at values that are based on historical costs, the *income statement* is of limited value in evaluating corporate performance." Do you agree? Explain.

2. What is the value of an asset to a particular user? Why is it seldom feasible to measure the value of a fixed asset to a particular user?

3. It is generally agreed that market values of fixed assets are more relevant than are historical values for decisions that must be made by both investors and managers. Why, then, do accountants persist in reporting historical values?

4. A company recently purchased for $350,000 a parcel of land and a building with the intention of razing the building and using the land as a parking lot for employees. The land had an appraised value of $300,000 and the building, $50,000. The company incurred costs of $10,000 to remove the building. The firm recorded the parking lot on its books at $360,000. Can such value be justified?

5. A company purchased a parcel of land for $100,000, but was permitted by the seller to delay payment for one year with no additional interest charges. The prime lending rate at the time was 12 percent per year. Do you think that the company should record the land at $100,000 or at a greater or lesser amount? Explain.

6. The term *reserve* for depreciation is sometimes used instead of *accumulated* depreciation. Some managers point out that it is essential that firms, through the process of depreciation, make periodic additions to such reserve to make certain that they have the wherewithal to replace assets when they must be retired. Explain why (or why not) depreciation assures that a firm will have sufficient resources to acquire new assets as old ones wear out.

7. "Accelerated methods of depreciation are generally preferable to the straight-line method because most assets decline in market value more rapidly in the early years of their useful lives than in later years." Do you agree?

8. A taxi company owns a fleet of vehicles. The president of the company recently observed that the older cabs seemed to be more efficient than the newer ones. He based his conclusion on "return on investment," which he calculated by dividing net revenues (revenues minus expenses, including depreciation) by beginning net book value. The firm uses the straight-line method to compute depreciation. What might be an explanation, other than greater efficiency, for the older assets providing the greater return on investment?

9. A company incurred $1 million in advertising costs for radio and television ads broadcast during the year. It elected to *capitalize* such costs as an intangible asset and charge them off as expenses over a five-year period. This practice is *not* in accord with generally accepted accounting principles. What arguments might the firm make, however, in defense of the practice? Why do you suppose that the practice is not generally accepted?

10. As an executive of a firm with two manufacturing plants, you are required to evaluate the effectiveness with which the managers of the plants utilize the resources within their control. One criterion by which you judge is plant and equipment turnover. The two plants are of substantially different ages. In computing turnover, why might you find it advantageous to state plant and equipment (including land) at market rather than book values?

Problems

1. *Depreciation, regardless of the method used, is a means of allocating the cost of an asset over its productive life.*

   The Valentine Construction Corp. purchased a crane for $150,000. The company planned to keep it for approximately five years, after which time it believed it could sell it for $30,000.
   a. Determine depreciation under each of the following methods for the first four years that the crane is in service:
      (1) Straight-line
      (2) Sum-of-the-years' digits
      (3) Double declining balance
   b. At the start of the fifth year the company sold the crane for $60,000. Determine the gain under each of the three depreciation methods.
   c. Determine for each of the methods the net impact on earnings (total depreciation charges less gain) of using the crane for the four-year period.

2. *Costs incurred at the end of an asset's useful life may be associated with revenues of previous accounting periods.*

   National Auto Company agrees to participate as a major exhibitor at the North American Trade Fair. The company constructs and furnishes its exhibit hall at a cost of $8 million. The fair will last for three years, after which National Auto will be required to remove its building from the fairgrounds. National estimates that removal costs will be approximately $100,000 but that the building materials and the exhibits can be sold for $300,000.
   a. Record the construction of the exhibit hall on the books of National Auto. Assume all payments are made in cash.
   b. Calculate first-year depreciation using the straight-line method.
   c. Record the removal of the exhibit hall at the completion of the fair. Assume that removal costs are as estimated.
   d. Suppose instead that removal costs were estimated to be approximately $700,000 and that the building materials and exhibits could be sold for $300,000. Prepare journal entries to record the exhibit hall, to account for the hall during the three-year period, and to remove it from the books after the three-year period. Over how many periods should the removal costs (net of the amount to be salvaged) be charged as an expense?

3. *The useful life of one asset may depend upon that of another.*

   The James Co. purchases a small plant for $2.5 million. The plant has an estimated useful life of 25 years with no salvage value. Included in the plant is specialized climate-control equipment. At the time of purchase the company is aware that the remaining useful life of the equipment is 15 years. The firm estimates the value of the equipment to be $250,000.
   a. Record the purchase of the plant.
   b. Record depreciation on a straight-line basis during the first year.
   c. At the end of 15 years the climate-control equipment requires replacement, and the firm purchases new equipment for $400,000. The estimated useful life of the new equipment is also 15 years.
      (1) Record the replacement of the old equipment with the new.
      (2) Record depreciation during the sixteenth year.
      (3) Over how many years did you decide to depreciate the new equipment? What assumptions did you make?

4. *Periodic maintenance costs that benefit more than one accounting period may be accounted for in at least two different ways.*

Treetop Airlines conducts maintenance overhauls on all aircraft engines every three years. The cost of each overhaul is approximately $120,000. The company owns 24 engines. In 1992 the company overhauls 10 engines, in 1993, 8 engines, and in 1994, 6 engines.

a. How much expense should the company report in 1994 in connection with engine overhauls?

b. A financial report of one major U.S. airline indicates that "expenditures for maintenance overhauls of aircraft engines and airframes are charged to expense as incurred." Is the policy of this airline consistent with your response in part (a)? If it is, can you think of, and justify, an alternative policy that might be as acceptable or even preferable? If it is not, then defend your response.

c. Suppose instead that it was company practice to overhaul eight engines each year. Would it matter, as far as reported expense is concerned, which accounting procedure the company used?

5. *It is often unclear whether certain types of costs are necessary to bring an asset to a serviceable condition.*

On January 2, National General Corporation purchased for $10,000 an *option* on a tract of land on which it hoped to construct a plant. The option gave the company the right to purchase the land itself within a given time period and for a fixed price—in this case within 10 months and for $2 million. If the company decided to exercise its option, it would pay the seller an additional $2 million and receive title to the land. If it decided not to purchase the land, then it would let the option lapse and would be unable to recover the $10,000. The option arrangement allows the company additional time to decide whether to make the purchase and at the same time compensates the seller for giving the company the exclusive right to purchase the property.

a. On July 2, National General decided to purchase the tract of land for $2 million. Prepare journal entries to record both the purchase of the option and the subsequent purchase of the land. Should the cost of the option be added to the cost of the land?

b. Suppose instead that on January 2, National General purchased three options—each for $10,000—on three tracts of land. The company expected to purchase and build on only one of the three tracts; however, it wanted to locate its new plant by the side of a proposed highway, and the exact route of the highway had not yet been announced. The company purchased the three options in order to assure itself that the plant could be built adjacent to the road, regardless of which three routes under consideration was selected for the highway. On July 2, the company exercised its option on one of the three tracts and purchased the land for $2 million. It allowed the other two options to lapse. Prepare journal entries to record the purchase of the three options, the purchase of the land, and the expiration of two of the options. Consider carefully whether the cost of all three options should be included as part of the cost of the land. Present arguments both for and against including the expired options as part of the cost of the land.

6. *The impact on earnings of both alternative depreciation practices and errors may depend upon a firm's replacement pattern and growth trend.*

Collins Manufacturing Corporation, established in 1992, uses 18 lathes, each of which costs $10,000 and has a useful life of three years (with no residual value). Each year the company retires six machines and replaces them with six others.

a. Compute total depreciation charges on the 18 lathes for the three-year period 1996, 1997, and 1998 using

(1) The straight-line method

(2) The sum-of-the-years'-digits method

b. Suppose the company used an incorrect useful life in calculating depreciation charges. Even though it replaced the machines after a three-year period, it charged depreciation over a two-year period. It made no adjustments in the accounts for the "error"; it simply charged zero depreciation in the machines' third year. Compute depreciation using the straight-line method for the same three-year period.

c. In 1999 the company undertook an expansion program. In each of the next three years (1999, 2000, and 2001) the company purchased seven machines and retired six. Thus in 1999, 2000, and 2001 the firm had in operation 19, 20, and 21 machines, respectively. Compute depreciation charges for the three-year period using

(1) The straight-line method

(2) The sum-of-the-years'-digit method

d. Assume again that the firm used an incorrect useful life and depreciated the machines over a two-year period instead of three. Compute depreciation charges for the three-year period using the straight-line method.

e. What conclusions can you draw regarding the impact of choice of depreciation method and estimate of useful life on the income of a firm that is expanding its asset base as opposed to one that is maintaining it at a constant level?

7. *Complete journal entries can be reconstructed from limited amounts of data; annual reports sometimes contain misleading assertions.*

The following information relating to plant, warehouse, and terminal elevator equipment was taken from a 10-K report of General Mills, Inc. (in thousands):

Equipment	
Balance at beginning of period	$346,838
Additions and miscellaneous adjustments	70,305
Balance at end of period	384,406
Equipment, accumulated depreciation	
Balance at beginning of period	173,964
Depreciation expense and miscellaneous adjustments	32,267
Balance at end of period	186,668

a. Based on the data provided, plus any other amounts that it may be necessary to derive from them, prepare a journal entry that summarizes the retirement of equipment during the period. Assume that the equipment was sold for $10 million.

b. In a discussion of replacement cost information, the report contains the following comment: "While inflation's annual impact on replacement of existing productive capacity is minimal because of the long time span over which replacements occur, its long-run result is that accumulated depreciation is insufficient to replace fully depreciated productive capacity."

(1) Prepare a journal entry that summarizes depreciation expense for the period.

(2) Is it the purpose of depreciation accounting to provide for the replacement of equipment? In what way, if any, does the entry you proposed enable the company to accumulate funds for replacement?

8. *Compound interest depreciation results in a depreciation charge indicative of the decline in the present value of anticipated cash flows.*

Machine Rentals, Inc., is considering purchasing a new computer that it will be able to rent to a customer for $10,000 per year for four years. The machine has a useful life of four years and no salvage value. The company expects a rate of return of 6 percent on all its assets.

a. What is the maximum amount the firm would be willing to pay for the machine? That is, what is the present value, discounted at a rate of 6 percent, of anticipated future cash receipts?

b. What is the present value of anticipated cash receipts at the end of each of the four years?

c. Suppose that the firm was able to purchase the machine for the amount computed in part (a). It elects to charged depreciation on the basis of what the machine is worth to the company (the present value of anticipated cash receipts) at the end of a year as compared with what it was worth at the beginning. How much depreciation should it charge during each of the four years? Determine total depreciation charges for the four-year period.

d. Comment on the trend of charges by this method of depreciation as compared with other methods. This method is not widely used in practice, but is regarded with favor by many theoreticians for assets whose efficiency remains constant. How can it be justified?

9. *Straight-line depreciation provides a level return on investment only when cash flows decline. (This problem is intended for solution using an electronic spreadsheet.)*

Computer Rentals, Inc., acquires a computer at a cost of $379,080. It immediately leases the computer to a customer for a term of five years. Annual rent is $100,000. The company believes that the machine will have no significant value when the lease expires.

a. Determine annual return on investment (i.e., income as a percent of the book value, net of accumulated depreciation).

(1) Assume that the company computes depreciation on a straight-line basis.

(2) Assume instead that the company computes depreciation using compound interest depreciation. Use a discount rate of 10 percent. Depreciation each year should represent the difference between present value of the anticipated cash flows at the beginning and end of the year.

(3) Comment on the trends in rate of return. Would the apparent problem with straight-line depreciation be alleviated or exacerbated by an accelerated method?

b. Suppose instead that the computer is used internally; it is not leased to outsiders. The company estimates that cash savings attributable to the machine will be $120,000 the first year and will decline by $10,000 per year over the remaining four years.

(1) Compute return on investment, using the straight-line method. Comment on the difference in return on investment when cash flows decline as the asset ages.

(2) Comment on the trend in return on investment that would result form use of the compound interest method. You should not have to actually carry out the computations.

(3) Which pattern of cash flows—equal or declining over asset life—do you think is characteristic of most assets? Consider specifically when and why a company would retire an asset.

10. *Financial analysts must be watchful of depreciation practices, especially in capital-intensive industries such as steel.*

Prior to 1969 most major steel firms depreciated their assets on an accelerated basis. In that year several companies shifted to the straight-line basis. Some firms, however, currently use a modified version of the straight-line method. The

"Summary of Principal Accounting Policies" in a recent annual report of U.S. Steel, for example, brings out the following:

> For the most part, depreciation expense is related to rates of operation, within a limited range.

In other words, the charge for depreciation is determined, in part, by the units of output method. The greater the use of the assets, the greater the charge for depreciation.

In 1977, Bethlehem Steel closed several of its plants. It wrote off the undepreciated value of assets at the facilities, charging earnings for $167 million. In 1979, U.S. Steel did the same, writing off $218.7 million in plant and equipment. Both firms blamed foreign imports and environmental regulations that would have required substantial capital expenditures to clean up what the firms believed to be marginally profitable facilities.

a. Neither the foreign competition nor the environmental regulations sprung up in a single year. In retrospect, what do the write-offs suggest about the depreciation practices of the two companies? How might the firms defend their practices?

b. In light of rapid technological developments in the steel industry, what dangers do you see in the policy of basing depreciation, even in part, on units of output? Comment specifically on the adequacy of depreciation charges in periods of low output.

c. On what basis can a shift from accelerated to straight-line depreciation be justified? What do you suspect was the real motive behind the change?

11. *The method of depreciation selected should provide the best possible match of costs to revenues.*

The Strip Mining Co. decides to remove coal from a deposit on property it already owns. The company purchases for cash mining equipment at a cost of $850,000 and constructs a building on the site at a cost of $90,000. The equipment has a useful life of 10 years and an estimated salvage value of $50,000 and can readily be removed to other mining locations. The building has a potential useful life of 12 years but will have to be abandoned when the company ceases operations at the site.

The mine contains approximately 1 million tons of coal, and the company plans to remove it over a four-year period according to the following schedule:

Year 1	400,000 tons
2	250,000 tons
3	250,000 tons
4	100,000 tons

The property will be abandoned at the end of the fourth year.

a. Record the purchase of the equipment and the construction of the building.

b. Compute depreciation charges for the first year on both the building and equipment. Justify in one or two sentences your choice of depreciation method(s) and lives.

12. *Depreciation and depletion costs, like those of labor and materials, may be considered production, rather than period, costs if they can be associated directly with the minerals recovered.*

Wildcat Minerals, Inc., was incorporated in 1992 for the specific purpose of mining a tract of land. The company acquired the tract at a cost of $6.2 million. It estimated that the tract contained 700,000 tons of ore and that after the property was completely mined (in approximately four years) it could be sold as farmland for $600,000.

The company built various buildings and structures at a cost of $1.4 million. Such improvements have a potential life of 15 years but have utility only when used at the specific mining site; they cannot be moved economically to other locations. In addition, the company purchased other equipment at a cost of $400,000. This equipment has a useful life of five years and an estimated salvage value of $50,000.

In 1992 the company incurred labor and other production costs of $357,700 and selling and administrative costs of $224,000. It paid taxes of $105,000.

The company mined 100,000 tons and sold 80,000 tons of ore. The selling price per ton was $19.

The company elected to charge depreciation on a unit of output basis.

a. Determine total depreciation and depletion costs for 1992.
b. Determine the cost per ton of ore sold.
c. Determine net income.
d. Determine the ending inventory.

13. *The information in annual reports as to fixed assets may enable an analyst to estimate average useful life of assets but is otherwise quite limited.*

The 1987 financial statements of Bristol-Myers contained the following information regarding fixed assets and depreciation:

From a Footnote, "Property, Plant, and Equipment":

| | December 31 | | |
| | (in millions of dollars) | | |
	1987	1986	1985
Land	$ 44.8	$ 36.4	$ 31.3
Buildings	640.3	517.8	407.2
Machinery, equipment, and fixtures	1,083.3	984.0	875.8
Construction in progress	111.1	187.7	180.6
	$1,879.5	$1,725.9	$1,494.0
Less: Accumulated depreciation	737.6	655.9	560.0
	$1,141.9	$1,070.0	$ 934.9

From the "Statement of Changes in Financial Position":

Depreciation and amortization	$115.9	$104.9	$ 88.0
Additions to fixed assets, net of disposals	180.5	216.3	210.7

From a Note on Accounting Policy as to Property and Depreciation:

> Expenditures for additions, renewals and betterments are capitalized at cost. Depreciation is generally computed by the straight-line method based on the estimated useful lives of the related assets.

There was no additional information in the financial statements regarding either fixed assets or depreciation. However, the "financial review" section of the annual report (which is not part of the financial statements) contained (without explanation) the graph on the following page.

a. Based on the information provided, estimate the average useful life of buildings, machinery, equipment, and fixtures.

**Capital Expeditures
and Depreciation**

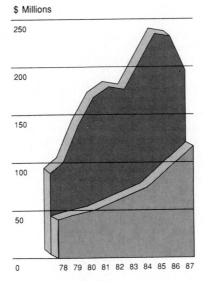

$ Millions

- ☐ Capital expenditures
- ■ Depreciation

b. Assume that all assets retired or otherwise disposed of had been fully depreciated.
  (1) What was the initial cost of the assets retired in 1987?
  (2) What were the total additions to fixed assets? (Note that the statement of changes in financial position provides data on "additions, *net of* disposals.")
c. (1) Discuss the significance of the graph, which compares outlays for fixed assets (i.e., "capital" expenditures) with depreciation expense. What useful information, if any, does it convey? Can it be inferred from the graph that the company is expanding its stock of fixed assets?
  (2) Why has depreciation expense increased steadily over the years, even though capital expenditures has fluctuated?

14. *A footnote provides insight into depreciation and capitalization practices.*

The following note is from an annual report of Boise Cascade Corporation, a leading supplier of timber and related products.

Property

> Property and equipment are recorded at cost. Cost includes expenditures for major improvements and replacements and the net amount of interest cost associated with significant capital additions. Capitalized interest totaled $1,326,000, $1,200,000, and $5,320,000 in 1987, 1986, and 1985. Substantially all paper and wood products manufacturing facilities determine depreciation by the units-of-production method, and other operations use the straight-line method.
>
> Cost of company timber harvested and amortization of logging roads are determined on the basis of the annual amount of timber cut in relation to the total amount of recoverable timber. Timber and timberlands are stated at cost, less the accumulated total of timber previously harvested.

Start-Up Costs

> Preoperating costs incurred during the construction and start-up of major new manufacturing facilities are capitalized and amortized over the shorter of 15 years or the life of the constructed equipment. At December 31, 1987, the remaining unamortized balance of start-up costs amounted to $37,747,000 and is included in "Other assets" on the Balance Sheets. Amortization of start-up costs totaled $5,021,000, $5,184,000, and $5,053,000 during 1987, 1986, and 1985. No significant amounts of start-up costs were capitalized during any of these periods.

Research and Development Costs

> Research and development costs are expensed as incurred. During 1987, 1986, and 1985, research and development expenses were $6,837,000, $7,936,000, and $7,802,000.

a. Prepare journal entries for 1987 to reflect the information provided as to
   (1) Interest
   (2) Start-up costs
   (3) Research and development costs
b. Would you characterize the company's policies as to start-up costs as being "liberal" or "conservative"? How do you explain the apparent inconsistency in that interest and start-up costs are capitalized but research and development costs are not?
c. What is the probable rationale for depreciating paper and wood products manufacturing facilities by the units of production basis but other facilities on a straight-line basis? What is the rationale for depreciating the logging roads on the basis indicated?

15. *Tax laws, as they affect depreciation, may encourage firms to sell assets long before the expiration of their useful lives.*

Commuter Airlines, Inc., issued common stock for $12 million and used the funds to purchase six small passenger jets at a total cost of $12 million. The firm plans to use the planes for 10 years, after which it believes they can be sold for a total of $4 million.

a. Compute depreciation for the first three years under each of the following methods:
   1. Straight-line
   2. Sum-of-the-years' digits
   3. 150 percent declining balance
b. Assume that income before depreciation and taxes during each of the first three years is $3 million. Compute income taxes for those years if the tax rate is 40 percent. Which method results in the least tax burden in the early years of asset life?
c. Suppose that at the end of the second year the planes are sold for $10 million. The remaining useful life of the assets is eight years. If the new owner charged depreciation for tax purposes using the 150 percent declining balance method, what would be the first-year deduction for depreciation? Compare such deduction to that which would be permitted Commuter Airlines if it used the 150 percent declining balance method. Why might it be said that the asset is "worth" more to the new owner than to the previous one?

16. *Depreciation methods differ considerably in the economic value of the tax savings that they provide.* (This problem is intended for solution using an electronic spreadsheet.)

Suppose that you are an executive of an equipment manufacturer. The equipment that your firm sells costs approximately $100,000 and has a useful life of 10 years (with no residual value).

Assume further that the current tax laws require purchasers of the equipment to depreciate it using the 150 percent declining balance method. A Congressional committee, however, is considering a proposal which would permit firms to use the double (200 percent) declining balance method. You have been asked to provide evidence as to the economic value of the change to your customers. *Economic value* is interpreted as the difference in the present values of the depreciation deductions. The current tax rate is 30 percent.

a. Prepare two schedules, one for double declining depreciation and the other for 150 percent declining depreciation. In each, show annual depreciation charges that would be permitted the equipment purchaser. Determine the present values of the two series of depreciation deductions and the difference between them. Use a discount rate of 12 percent. Calculate the after-tax value of the difference.

b. In your testimony to the committee you plan to advocate an additional "technical" adjustment to the proposal. Firms would be permitted to switch from the 200 percent declining balance method to the straight-line method when the deduction under straight-line depreciation became greater than that under the accelerated method. In shifting to straight-line depreciation, a taxpayer would be required to amortize the undepreciated balance of the asset over the remaining useful life of the asset. Thus, if the shift was made at the *start* of year 5 and the undepreciated asset balance was $42,000, then the firm could write off $7,000 over each of the remaining six years of asset life.

Prepare a schedule in which you determine the optimal year in which a taxpayer would shift to straight-line depreciation and show the additional economic benefit of the switch.

17. *Utility rates are affected by interest capitalization policies.*

The rates that Northern Electric and Gas is permitted to charge customers are fixed by a state utility commission. The commission has a policy of establishing rates so that the company realizes a pretax return on assets of 12 percent per year. That is, rates are established that permit the company to generate annual revenues of an amount so that revenues less expenses will equal 12 percent of reported assets.

Prior to 1991, the reported value of the company's assets was $80 million. It earned revenues of $29.6 million and incurred expenses (excluding taxes) of $20 million. Operating profit was therefore $9.6 million—12 percent of $80 million. The book value of these assets, and the earnings thereon, is expected to remain constant through 1993.

In 1991, to extend its service area, the company began construction of a new plant. The estimated cost of the plant is $50 million. It will be completed by the end of 1992. During construction, the company will pay a total of $6 million in interest costs on funds borrowed to finance the new plant. They will be incurred as follows:

1991	$2 million
1992	$4 million

On average, the company will have $20 million recorded as construction in progress in 1991 and $40 million in 1992. For purposes of determining rates, construction in progress is included in the asset base.

The company estimates that once the new plant goes "on line" in January 1992, annual operating expenses, excluding depreciation but including interest, will be $8 million.

Depreciation on the new assets will be charged on a straight-line basis. Estimated life of the new plant is expected to be 40 years (with no salvage value).

An important accounting issue is whether interest costs related to the construction of assets should be *capitalized* (added to the cost of the assets constructed). Interest costs that are not capitalized are charged as expenses in the years incurred.

  a. Prepare a table, assuming that interest is not capitalized. Show the following for each of the three years, 1991, 1992 (the two years of construction), and 1993 (the first year the plant goes on line).
     (1) The asset base (on existing and new facilities combined)
     (2) The income that the utility commission will permit
     (3) The expenses on the existing plant
     (4) The new interest
     (5) The new depreciation
     (6) The new operating expenses
     (7) The total expenses
     (8) The allowable revenues

     In determining asset base, assume that new assets, with a cost equal to the annual charge for depreciation, are acquired each year. Thus, for purposes of calculating the asset base, ignore any reduction that would result from depreciation.

  b. Do the same, assuming that interest is capitalized.

  c. Suppose, first, that you represent a consumer group concerned with holding utility rates to a minimum; suppose, next, that you represent Northern Electric and Gas, which is interested in obtaining maximum revenues as soon as possible. What recommendations would you make to the public utility commission as to a policy of capitalization of interest? What arguments would you make in support of your position?

18. *Changes in useful life can have a potent impact on depreciation charges and earnings per share.* The 1987 annual report of TWA contained the following note:

   > Effective January 1, 1988, the estimated remaining useful service lives of TWA's owned wide-body aircraft fleets will be extended and the estimated residual values will be reduced to recognize that these aircraft are physically capable of being actively flown into the 21st century. The change reflects an approximate increase in average depreciable lives of six years for owned L1011 aircraft, four years for owned B747 aircraft and nine years for owned B767 aircraft. Such change in estimate does not affect the provision for depreciation expense computed for 1987 and prior years.

   > Estimated useful service lives in effect for the three years ended December 31, 1987, for purposes of computing the provision for depreciation, of flight equipment (aircraft and engines, including related spares) were sixteen to twenty-three years.

   The firm's balance sheet indicates that the book value of flight equipment, before depreciation, was $2.89 billion. Assume that the average useful life of flight equipment, prior to the change, was 20 years. After the change it would be 28 years.

   Determine the approximate impact that the change would have on
   a. Earnings before taxes
   b. Earnings per share before taxes (The company had 30,506,000 shares outstanding.)

   To put the magnitude of the change in perspective, it should be noted that in 1987 TWA had net income (after taxes) applicable to common shares of $50,400,000 and earnings per share of $1.65.

19. *As illustrated by an actual annual report, companies have broad discretion in accounting for long-lived assets. Taken together, the policies that they adopt can have a formidable impact on reported earnings.*

The following notes were taken from the 1987 annual report of Simmons Airlines, a commuter airline. To its credit, Simmons Airlines (an actual company) discloses substantially more about its long-lived asset accounting practices than do most companies.

Property and Equipment

Flight and other property and equipment are carried at cost including capitalized interest, if any, and depreciated to residual values over their estimated useful lives on a straight-line basis. Estimated useful lives are five to twenty-four years for flight equipment and three to fifteen years for other property and equipment.

In the quarter ended July 31, 1986, the estimated useful lives and residual values of the Shorts 360 aircraft owned by the Company were revised, effective August 1, 1985, resulting in an increase of six years in the estimated useful lives and a decrease of ten percent in the estimated residual values. The effect of these changes on depreciation expense in fiscal 1986 was a reduction of approximately $547,00 and an increase of approximately $509,000 in net income ($.11 per common share).

Aircraft Overhaul Charges

The Company uses the deferral method of accounting for certain aircraft overhaul costs. Under the deferral method, the incurred costs of engine overhauls and certain major component overhauls are capitalized and amortized over the estimated time between overhauls.

Deferred Development and Preoperating Costs

Costs related to the introduction of new types of aircraft are deferred and amortized over five years and are presented net of accumulated amortization ($329,000 in 1987, $285,000 in 1986). Preoperating costs related to the Company's joint services agreements with major airlines were deferred and amortized over one year and were classified as current assets. Costs associated with inaugurating service over new routes are expenses as incurred.

Acquisition Costs of Landing Slots

Costs related to the acquisition of landing slots are capitalized and amortized over a 40 year period and are presented net of accumulated amortization ($34,000 in 1987, $7,000 in 1986).

Capitalized Interest Costs:

Interest costs relating to deposits on aircraft and interest costs incurred in readying aircraft for service are added to the cost of the flight equipment and amortized over the estimated useful lives of the related aircraft.

Review each of the notes and identify any policies and practices that are within the discretion of the company. Indicate any alternatives which the company might have selected. Comment on whether the policies and practices adopted by the company appear to be "liberal" (i.e., result in later recognition of expenses) or "conservative" (i.e., result in earlier recognition of expenses).

20. *Trade-in transactions must be accounted for in a manner that reflects economic substance rather than form.*

In January 1991 the Jarvis Co. purchased a copy machine for $6,000. The machine had an estimated useful life of eight years and an estimated salvage value of $500. The firm used the double declining balance method to record depreciation.

In December 1993 the company decided to trade in the machine for a newer model. The new model had a *list* price of $12,000, but it is common in the industry for purchasers to be given a 15 to 20 percent trade discount off of list price. The manufacturer offered the company a trade-in allowance of $4,000 on its old machine. The company accepted the offer since it was considerably above the several offers of approximately $2,000 that the firm had received from other parties interested in purchasing the machine. The company paid $8,000 in addition to giving up the old machine.

Record the trade-in of the old machine and the purchase of the new. Assume that depreciation had already been recorded for 1993.

21. *Disasters can result in increased earnings.*

On October 26, 1992, the Great Hotel was destroyed by fire. Best Hotels, Inc., had purchased the hotel exactly three years earlier at a cost of $50 million. The company had been depreciating the hotel by the double declining balance method, based on an estimated life of 25 years.

The hotel was insured for only 80 percent of its market value. At the time of the fire, market value was $62 million.
a. Indicate the impact of the fire on the financial statements of Best Hotels, Inc.
b. Comment on why seemingly unfavorable events result in reported gains. Assume that Best Hotels, Inc., is a publicly held company whose shares are traded on a major stock exchange. What impact do you think the fire would have on the market price of the firm's stock? How can you reconcile the effect on market price with your response to part (a).

22. *Revaluation of assets to reflect changes in market values would affect not only their recorded values but also the allocation of earnings among the years that the assets were in service.*

The Rhinegold Chemical Co. constructed a new plant at a cost of $20 million. The plant had an estimated useful life of 20 years, with no salvage value. After the plant had been used for four years, its replacement cost had increased to $24 million. The company decided to recognize in its accounts the increase in the fair market value of the asset. (Such practice is not, of course, in accord with currently acceptable accounting principles.)
a. Prepare the journal entry to record depreciation for each of the first four years.
b. Prepare an entry to record the revaluation of the plant.
c. Prepare an entry to record depreciation in the fifth year, the first year subsequent to the revaluation.
d. At the *start* of the eighth year the company accepted an offer to sell the plant for $19 million. Prepare an entry to record the sale.
e. Suppose that the company had not readjusted its accounts after the fourth year to recognize the increase in market value. How much gain would it have reported upon sale of the plant? Compare total depreciation expense and total gains recognized if the company recognized the increase in market value with those that would have resulted if it had adhered to conventional practice and not recognized the increase.

23. *Two principal accounting practices employed in the oil industry may result in substantial differences in reported earnings and assets, but neither reflects "true" economic values.*

Panhandle, Inc., in 1992 drilled three exploratory oil wells at a cost of $300,000 each. Of the three, only one proved successful. The company estimates that the property on which the successful well is located will provide a cash inflow of $600,000 per year, after taking into account recovery costs, royalties, and other cash outlays for each of the next 10 years, including 1992. The firm uses a discount rate of 12 percent to evaluate investments.
a. Determine earnings for 1992, assuming that the firm uses
  (1) The full-cost method
  (2) The successful-efforts method

b. Assume that the firm uses the successful-efforts method. It does not own the property on which it discovered oil; instead it pays a per barrel royalty to the owner of the property.
   (1) At what value should the oil reserves (including the capitalized drilling costs) be reported on the balance sheet as of the end of 1992?
   (2) Do you think that such value fully and fairly reflects the value of the asset? What is your estimate of the "economic value" of the reserves? What supplementary disclosures would you recommend?

24. *This problem deals with title insurance, an issue recently addressed by the FASB, but not discussed in the text.*

    Title insurance guarantees that the rights to property are properly established. A title insurance policy indemnifies the policyholder against losses incurred in the event that the title (ownership right) to the covered property is deemed invalid. Home buyers, for example, almost always insure against defects in the titles on their homes. Should a purchaser have to surrender a home because the seller did not have authority to sell it (perhaps because many years earlier an owner had not made all tax or mortgage payments), the insurance company covers the losses up to the amount specified by the policy.

    Title insurance companies must maintain a *title plant,* a historical record of all matters affecting titles to real estate within a particular area. It contains maps, contracts, copies of prior title insurance policies, and numerous other legal documents. To be useful, the title plant must not only cover an extended period of time but it must be continually kept up to date.

    United Title Insurance Co. has decided to extend its service area to a new town. It is able to purchase an existing title plant from another company which is abandoning the title business. Purchase price is $5 million.

    The purchased title plant, however, contains numerous gaps and is therefore inadequate. To bring it to a usable condition, United incurs $3 million in research-related costs.

    To maintain the title plant during its first year of operations, United spends an additional $1 million. These costs are incurred to add documents on sales and transactions that take place during the year.
    a. In your judgment (and without reference to the relevant FASB pronouncement), which, if any, of the costs to acquire and develop the title plant should be capitalized (i.e., recorded as a long-lived asset)? Which should be expensed?
       (1) The $5 million to purchase the existing title plant
       (2) The $3 million to bring the plant up to standard
       (3) The $1 million to maintain the plant
    b. If you proposed that the some or all of the costs be capitalized, then over how many years do you recommend the costs be amortized?
    Justify your responses in the context of the general principles discussed in this chapter.

25. *The practices of one company are illustrative of ambivalence toward start-up costs.*

    The note that follows was included in a recent financial report of Ball Corporation, a manufacturer of glass jars and other packaging materials:

    Deferred Preoperating Costs

    > Preoperating costs of new manufacturing facilities are charged to income as incurred except for those facilities and major expansions or modifications thereof which are constructed primarily to serve customers under contractual supply arrangements. The costs deferred, which represent principally training and other startup costs, are amortized over the terms of the related supply contracts of generally five to seven years commencing with commercial production.

The same financial report provided the following additional data about deferred preoperating costs (thousands of dollars).

From the balance sheet, noncurrent assets (dates have been changed):

	1993	1992
Deferred preoperating costs	$5,902	$4,118

From the statement of changes in financial position:

	1993	1992
Amortization of deferred preoperating costs	$1,126	$1,158
Use of financial resources for deferred preoperating costs	2,910	2,270

a. Prepare summary entries to record all activity relating to deferred preoperating costs in 1993.
b. What justification is there for deferring preoperating costs of facilities constructed to serve customers under contractual supply contracts but not other preoperating costs?

26. *Accounting for start-up costs varies among, as well as within, industries.*

    Indicate how each of the costs described here should be accounted for. Express an opinion as to whether the cost should be recorded as an asset or an expense. If as an asset, explain how it should be depreciated or amortized. State the period of depreciation or amortization or tell how it should be determined. For some of the costs, there are no authoritative pronouncements that provide specific guidance as to how they should be handled. Use your own judgment.

    a. A chain of discount stores opens an outlet at a new location. Prior to beginning operations, it incurs $800,000 in advertising, promotion, training, and general administration costs.
    b. To celebrate the first anniversary of the opening of its store at the new location, the aforementioned discount chain incurs $100,000 in advertising costs to announce a new line of products. Although the advertisements will be run toward the end of 1992, the new products will not be sold until 1993.
    c. On February 1, 1991, an established cable television company acquires franchise rights to provide service to a city in west Texas. In the two years following the award of the franchise, the company incurs $10 million in programming, rental, and advertising costs in addition to amounts it spends on plant and equipment. Although the company's system goes on line in December 1992, as is expected it does not reach a profitable level of operations until February 1994.
    d. In 1995 the same cable television company upgrades the level of its service to the city by adding additional programs to those previously available. It incurs $5 million in programming and advertising costs to improve the system. It estimates that the costs will be recovered through additional revenues within a period of five years.
    e. A hotel chain purchases a rundown hotel with the intention of modernizing it by renovating its rooms and adding new restaurants and convention facilities. Although the physical changes are made within three months of acquisition, the company, consistent with its plans, incurs $2 million in net operating losses in its first two years of operations. The losses were anticipated since it takes at least two years for the hotel to build up its clientele. The losses are in addition to outlays for furniture, fixtures, and other changes to the facilities, which of course have been capitalized.

27. *Under generally accepted practices of cost capitalization, comparable assets are not necessarily reported at comparable values.*

In each of the following situations, indicate whether the outlay described gives rise to an asset that would be reported on the balance sheet. If it does, indicate the amount. Provide a brief explanation of your response.

a. A drug firm incurs $2 million in research costs to develop a new cold tablet. The tablet is brought to the market and is a highly successful product.

b. The same firm purchases the patented formula for a new skin cream from an independent research laboratory. Purchase price is $2 million.

c. A publishing company contracts with an unknown author for the rights to publish his first novel. The author is to receive as royalties 15 percent of sales. The book becomes a best-seller, and the company is offered (but has not yet accepted) $5 million for paperback and movie rights.

d. A paperback publisher purchases for $2 million the rights to publish the paperback version of the novel cited in part (c).

e. A computer firm custom-designs and installs a computer system for an airline. As of the end of a year, the computer firm has incurred $2.5 million for labor and materials and an additional $300,000 in interest on funds borrowed to finance the project. The project is not yet complete and has not been turned over to the customer.

f. The same firm manufacturers microcomputers for sale to the general public. As of the end of the year, it has in inventory 1,000 computers awaiting sale. Cost of the inventory is $2.5 million. This amount excludes interest of $300,000 on funds borrowed to finance the manufacture of the computers.

Solutions to Exercise for Review and Self-Testing

1. The amount at which the plane should be recorded must include the fair market value of all consideration (cash and property) paid to bring the asset to a usable condition. In this case, it includes all amounts indicated: $3 million cash payment; $500,000 in marketable securities; $6,000 in delivery charges; $94,000 in furnishing costs—a total of $3.6 million.

2. The total cost of using the plane for 10 years—the amount to be allocated—is the initial amount recorded ($3.6 million) less the anticipated residual value ($900,000)—$2.7 million.

3. If the straight-line method is used, annual depreciation charges will be $2.7 million divided by 10, or $270,000 per year.

4. The straight-line rate of depreciation is 10 percent; twice that is 20 percent. This rate would be applied each year to the current book value (cost less accumulated depreciation) *without* regard to residual value (except as suggested in part 5 of this exercise). Thus

Year	Book Value, Start of Year	Depreciation Rate (%)	Depreciation Charge	Book Value, End of Year
1	$3,600,000	20	$720,000	$2,880,000
2	2,880,000	20	576,000	2,304,000
3	2,304,000	20	460,800	1,843,200

5. Depreciation must never be charged so as to reduce the remaining book value below expected salvage value—in this case $900,000. In the seventh year of service,

---

therefore, the firm would charge only $43,718 of depreciation ($943,718 less $900,000); in the eighth year, zero.

6. In economic substance the firm sold an asset with a book value of $1,843,200 for $1.5 million—the apparent fair market value of the old plane. Hence it should report a loss of $343,200. The new plane should be recorded at an amount representative of the fair market value of the consideration paid—$7 million cash plus $1.5 million, the fair market value of the plane surrendered—a total of $8.5 million.

10

Liabilities and Related Expenses

Liabilities are claims upon assets. They are as significant to the financial health and performance of an entity as the assets themselves. As with assets, the questions of balance sheet valuation are intertwined with those of income measurement.

Within the past several years, issues relating to liabilities have become the center of accounting concern and controversy. This new focus can be traced to several ongoing financial developments. First, worldwide corporations have gone on a debt binge, financing with borrowed money activities that previously would have been paid for with funds from investors. Second, owing to the magnitude of their obligations, the accounting profession has demanded that companies give explicit accounting recognition to liabilities that previously were recorded "off the balance sheet" (i.e., in footnotes, if at all). Prime among this category of debt are pensions and other benefits promised to retired employees. Third, the tax code has become increasingly complex and has thereby made the calculation of tax liabilities and expenses even more tangled than it had been previously. Fourth, many new types of financing instruments have been developed and widely adopted. Some, in fact, have been designed specifically to circumvent existing measurement and disclosure rules. Each creates its own unique accounting problems.

In a previous chapter, liabilities were defined as

Obligations of an entity at the account date to make future transfers of assets or services (sometimes uncertain as to timing and amount) to other entities

Liabilities obviously encompass amounts that an entity is legally obligated to pay others. But the accounting and legal concepts of a liability are quite different. Liabilities as interpreted by the accountant include *probable* sacrifices of resources stemming from past events or transactions whether or not there is a binding obligation to make payment.

The accounting issues relating to liabilities mirror those associated with assets. Key questions center upon the circumstances that give rise to liabilities and the values to be assigned to them.

Issues of Recognition

Liabilities usually result from agreements between the parties to business transactions. The transactions may involve loans, purchases of goods, or the provision of services. Liabilities may also be imposed upon a business by statute (e.g. taxes) and by court action or threat of court action (e.g., lawsuits).

As pointed out in an earlier chapter, accountants do not record as liabilities all expected future sacrifices of resources even if the amount and dates of payment are known with certainty. Obligations arising from contracts in which neither side has yet fulfilled its side of the bargain are generally not recognized as liabilities. A company may sign a five-year employment contract with an executive for $500,000 per year. At the time the contract is signed, the company need not record a liability. Only as the executive provides the expected services and the company receives the expected benefits must the company report a liability and, of course, a related expense.

As a rule, a firm must record a liability as soon as (1) it has received a benefit from an event or transaction and made an obligation to make a future transfer of assets or services, (2) the amount of the required sacrifice of resources is known, and (3) the due date has been established. But it can also do so even if all the criteria have not been satisfied. The tough accounting questions arise when one or more of these criteria have not yet been met.

Lease arrangements under present-day generally accepted accounting principles are illustrative of the difficulties of determining when to recognize that assets and liabilities have actually been created. As indicated in the previous chapter on long-lived assets, when a business rents a store on a year-by-year basis, it does not record the rights to the property as an asset. Neither does it record the required rent payments as a liability. It is assumed that the company will receive the benefits and incur the obligations from the transactions over the course of the lease. But when a long-term lease is structured so that the business acquires virtually all rights of ownership—when it has in economic substance purchased the property—it must record the property as an asset when the lease is first signed. So also, therefore, must it record the lease payments as a liability as if it had borrowed the funds to buy the property. The troublesome accounting issue is: When should a lease be considered an ordinary rental arrangement, a contract in which the business obtains the rights to use the property and incurs the obligation to pay for it over the life of the lease? When should it be considered a purchase-borrow transaction, a contract in which the business obtains the rights and incurs the obligations at the inception of the lease?

Repair warranties and income taxes are illustrative of potential obligations that must be recorded as liabilities, even though it is uncertain whether and in what amount a future sacrifice of resources will be required. Generally accepted accounting principles state that when a firm provides repair warranties, the firm should credit a liability account at the time of sale in the amount of the expected cost to fulfill them. Obviously, the firm cannot be sure what the eventual sacrifice will be, but any estimate is likely to be better than none—which would be an implicit estimate of zero. The practice of setting up a liability for warranty costs is consistent with the matching concept. The cost of the repairs should be reported in the same period as the sales revenue with which it is associated.

As will be discussed later in this chapter, the tax code permits a firm to postpone the payment of taxes on earnings recognized in a particular period. The taxes will have to be paid only if certain conditions are satisfied or events take place. A source of long-standing conflict among accountants is the extent to which payment must be probable before the tax liability should be recognized. Whereas there is widespread agreement that potential warranty costs should be recorded as liabilities, there is considerable controversy over how deferred taxes should be accounted for.

Issues of Measurement

The economic value of a liability is the present value of the cash that will be required to settle it. As with assets, the expected cash flows must be discounted at an appropriate rate. Assuming a discount rate of 10 percent, a liability of $100 to be paid in two years has a value of $82.64 ($100 × .8264, the present value of $1 discounted at 10 percent for two years). This is the amount that the firm could set aside today in an account that earns interest at 10 percent and be able to pay off the loan when due without having to contribute anything additional.

As with assets, the manner in which liabilities are *reported* may not necessarily reflect their economic values. Liabilities, like assets, are reported at historically based amounts. Long-term liabilities are generally stated at the present value of payments to be made in the future. (Current liabilities are usually reported at actual, rather than present, values, only because the difference between the two is immaterial.) The present value at any time a liability is outstanding is determined by discounting required future payments by the *historical* rate of interest—that which was in effect at the time the liability was initially recorded. Only at the time the liability is first recorded will its reported value necessarily be equal to its economic value. Thereafter, prevailing interest rates will change. The present value of the future payments discounted at the prevailing rate may be greater or less than that discounted at the historical rate. The prevailing rate is the relevant rate for determining economic value. If the firm wanted to discharge the claim at any time prior to its due date, it could place in an interest-bearing bank account funds equal to the present value of the future payments of principal and interest. Assuming that the rate of interest paid by the bank was equal to the prevailing rate and was guaranteed from date of deposit to when the liability matures, the firm would have to make no further payment. The principal and interest could be paid from the funds placed in the bank and the interest that was earned on them.

The Issue of Market Value

Liabilities, like assets, have market values. In previous chapters, it was noted that bonds and similar certificates of indebtedness are often held by firms as marketable securities. Accounts receivable may be purchased and sold. Obviously what is a bond or note receivable to one party is a payable to another. The market for receivables can be viewed, with equal logic, as a market for payables.

Under generally accepted accounting principles, the amounts at which liabilities are stated are seldom adjusted to reflect fluctuations in market prices. The market price of a liability has as much significance as that of an asset, and the arguments in favor of reporting liabilities at market values may be as compelling as those for assets. The market price of a liability represents the amount that would be required for a firm to discharge its debt at a particular time. The firm could purchase the debt from its holder at the prevailing market price. For reasons to be explained shortly, such price may be greater or less than the book value of the debt. By not purchasing the debt in the market, the firm (like the corresponding asset holder) is taking the risk that subsequent price movements will be in its favor.

BONDS

Corporations, as well as governmental units and nonprofit organizations, borrow funds to finance *long-term* projects, such as plant and equipment and major public works projects. Conventionally, borrowers provide the lender with bonds or notes as evidence of their obligations to repay the funds and to make periodic interest payments. A bond is a more formal certificate of indebtedness than a note. Bonds are usually evidence of long-term indebtedness (five years or more), while notes may be issued in connection with shortor long-term borrowings.

Corporate bonds are most commonly issued in denominations of $1,000. The *par* or *face* value of a bond indicates the *principal* amount due at the *maturity*, or due, date of the bond. Bonds ordinarily carry a stated annual rate of interest, expressed as a percentage of the principal. Most bond *indentures* (agreements that set forth the legal provisions of the bonds) require that interest be paid semiannually. Thus a corporation that has issued $1,000-denomination bonds that specify an annual rate of interest of 12 percent would pay the holder of a single bond $60 on each of two interest dates six months apart.

Corporate bonds may be secured (collateralized) by property, such as a plant or land. Or they may be unsecured, with the lender relying primarily upon the good faith and financial integrity of the borrower for repayment. Secured bonds may be categorized by the type of legal instrument used to provide the lien on the property that is pledged (e.g., mortgage bonds and equipment trust bonds). Unsecured bonds are commonly called *debentures*.

Virtually all corporate bonds specify a maturity date. However, many corporate issues provide for the early retirement of the debt at the option of the *borrower* (the corporation). Such a *call provision* ordinarily requires the company to pay the lender (the bond holder) a *call premium,* an amount in addition to the par value of the bond, as a penalty for depriving the lender of its ''right'' to interest payments for the original term of the loan.

Bonds are generally freely negotiable—they can be bought and sold in the open market subsequent to original issue. An active market for corporate bonds is maintained by both the New York and American Stock Exchanges. A lender who no longer wishes to have its funds tied up in a loan to the issuer of a bond can sell the bond to an investor who is seeking the type of return provided by that type of bond. The price at which the bond is sold would not be that for which the bond was initially issued. Rather, it would be at a price based on interest rates prevalent at time of sale.

The Nature of Bonds

Bonds provide for interest payments of a fixed amount. Ordinarily, the more financially sound the lender, the lower the rate of interest. Interest rates for securities *within* the same category of risk are determined by the forces of supply and demand—the amount of funds being sought by borrowers, the amount being made available by lenders. Rates of interest that prevail throughout the world fluctuate from day to day and even from hour to hour. Although corporations conventionally set the coupon rate of interest—the amount that will be paid to the lender each interest period—and print it in the bond indentures several weeks prior to the date on which they are to be issued, the actual interest rate is determined at time of sale. The actual interest rate is called the *yield rate*. It is established not by changing the coupon rate but rather by adjusting the price at which the bond is sold. Suppose, for example, that a $1,000 bond has a coupon rate of 8 percent—that is, the holder of the bond will be entitled to two payments of $40 each year. At the time of sale, however, the prevailing interest rate for that type of bond is 8¼ percent. Would purchasers be willing to pay $1,000 for such a bond? Obviously not. They could lend their money to another similar company and receive $82.50 per year rather than $80. Therefore the purchaser would be willing to pay something less than $1,000 for the bond. How much less will be considered in the next section. Similarly, if the prevailing interest rate was lower than 8 percent—7½ percent, for example—rational buyers would be willing to pay more than $1,000 for the bond. If they were to purchase the bonds of similar companies, the buyers would receive only $75 per year in interest. They would be willing to pay something above $1,000 to receive a return of $80 per year. If purchasers pay less than the face amount for a bond, then the difference between the face amount and what the purchasers actually pay is referred to as a bond *discount*. If the purchasers pays more than the face amount, then the additional payment is referred to as a *premium*.

Rational purchasers would undertake a similar analysis in deciding how much to pay for a bond that had been issued several years earlier, one to be purchased not from the issuing company directly but rather from the current holder of the bond. If prevailing interest rates are greater than the coupon rate of the bond, the purchasers would be willing to pay *less* than the face value of the bond, for they could receive the prevailing rate by purchasing a different bond on which the coupon rate is equal to the prevailing rate. If prevailing rates are less than the coupon rate, the purchasers would be willing to pay more, since the semiannual interest payments would be greater than what they could obtain elsewhere.

> *As prevailing rates of interest (yields) increase, the market prices of outstanding bonds with fixed coupon rates of interest decrease.*

> *As prevailing rates of interest (yields) decrease, the market prices of bonds with fixed coupon rates of interest increase.*

Determination of Discount or Premium[1]

Determining the amount that a rational purchaser would pay for a bond requires an understanding of the promises inherent in the bond agreement.

Suppose that on a particular day a corporation seeks bids on two bonds. Bond A bears a coupon rate of 12 percent and bond B a coupon rate of 10 percent. Both bonds will mature in two years. Both pay interest semiannually. The prevailing annual rate of interest is 12 percent.

Both bonds contain a promise to pay the purchaser $1,000 upon maturity after two years—four semiannual periods hence. The present value of a single cash payment four semiannual periods away, given an interest rate of 6 percent, is, per Table 2 in the Appendix, $1,000 × .7921, or $792.10. The 6 percent rate is one-half the annual rate of 12 percent; it reflects the semiannual rather than the annual payment of interest. The 12 percent rate is the *prevailing* rate for bonds of that type, not necessarily the coupon rate on either of the two bonds in question. It is the rate that is relevant to prospective purchasers since it is that which they could receive if they were to turn to alternative investments of comparable risk.

Bond A also promises four semiannual payments of $60. The present value of four semiannual payments, discounted at 6 percent per period (one-half the *prevailing* annual rate), is, per Table 4, $60 × 3.4651, or $207.90. The total present value of the two promises—the promise to pay principal of $1,000 plus the promise to make semiannual interest payments—discounted at the prevailing rate of 6 percent per semiannual period—is $1,000 ($792.10 plus $207.90). The rational buyer would be willing to pay $1,000—in this instance, the face value—for the bond.

Bond B, on the other hand, promises four semiannual payments of only $50, since the coupon rate is 10 percent per year. The present value of four semiannual payments of $50, discounted at 6 percent is, again per Table 4, $50 × 3.4651, or $173.25. The rate of 6 percent is one-half the *prevailing* rate of 12 percent. The *prevailing rate is the one that must be used to evaluate an investment opportunity,* since it (rather than the coupon rate) is indicative of the return that the investor can expect to receive. The present value of the two promises

---

[1]The reader is strongly urged to review the material on compound interest and present value contained in Chapter 6.

combined is therefore $792.10 plus $173.25, or $965.35. A rational purchaser would be willing to pay only $965.35 for the bond with a face value of $1,000 and a coupon rate of 10 percent. The discount of $34.65 would assure him or her a *yield* of 12 percent per year, even though the coupon rate is only 10 percent per year. The analysis can be summarized as follows:

	Bond A (12% coupon, $6 per period)	Bond B (10% coupon, $5 per period)
Present value of $1,000 to be received at the end of 4 periods, discounted at prevailing per period rate of 6% ($1,000 × .7921 per Table 2)	$ 792.10	$792.10
Present value of $60 to be received at the end of each of 4 periods, discounted at prevailing per period rate of 6% ($60 × 3.4651 per Table 4)	207.90	
Present value of $50 to be received at the end of each of 4 periods, discounted at prevailing per period rate of 6% ($50 × 3.4651 per Table 4)		173.25
Present value of bond	$1,000.00	$965.35

Diagramatically, the two bonds can be depicted as in Exhibit 10-1. Both bonds are evaluated at a rate of 6 percent per period—the prevailing yield on

EXHIBIT 10-1

Bond A
12% Coupon: 12% Yield

Present value	1/1/92	6/30/92	12/31/92	6/30/93	12/31/93
$ 56.60	.9434	$60			
53.40	.8900		$60		
50.38	.8396			$60	
47.52	.7921				$60
792.10	.7921				$1,000
$1,000.00					

Bond B
10% Coupon; 12% Yield

Present value	1/1/92	6/30/92	12/31/92	6/30/93	12/31/93
$ 47.17	.9434	$50			
44.50	.8900		$50		
41.98	.8396			$50	
39.60	.7921				$50
792.10	.7921				$1,000
$965.35					

comparable securities. It is assumed that the bonds were sold on January 1, 1992. All discount factors are per Table 2. Bond A would sell at face value because its coupon rate is identical to the yield rate. Anytime there is a difference between the coupon and the yield rates, the bonds would be sold at an amount other than face value.

Alternative View

The discount of $34.65 on bond B can be viewed from a slightly different perspective. If a purchaser can obtain a yield of 12 percent per year elsewhere, then from a $1,000 bond he or she expects interest payments of $60 every six months. In fact, bond B will pay only $50 per six months. The purchaser is ''losing'' $10 per period. The present value of $10 lost for four periods, discounted at a rate of 6 percent per period (one-half the prevailing yield of 12 percent), is, per Table 4, $10 × $3.4561, or $34.65.

Computation of the bond premium or discount can be facilitated by asking four simple questions.

1. How much interest per period (based on the *coupon rate*) is a purchaser of the bond actually going to receive?
2. How much interest (based on the prevailing *yield* of comparable securities) would the purchaser expect to receive?
3. What is the difference between the two amounts?
4. What is the present value, discounted at the prevailing *yield rate,* of the difference?

The present value of the difference between the amounts a purchaser would expect to receive and what he or she will actually receive represents either a premium or a discount:

Interest to be received each period, based on an annual coupon rate of 10%	$50
Less: Interest expected each period, based on an annual yield rate of 12%	60
Interest ''lost'' each period	$(10)
Present value of an annuity of $1 for 4 periods at a per period yield rate of 6 percent	× 3.4651
Present value of ''lost'' interest, or bond premium (discount)	($34.65)

RECORDING OF BOND ISSUES

The issue of bond B for a price of $965.35 could be recorded by the following journal entry:

Cash (asset) $965.35
Discount on bonds
(contra account to bonds payable) 34.65
Bonds payable (liability) $1,000
To record issuance of the bond

If financial statements were prepared immediately after the issuance, the liability would be reported as follows:

Bonds payable	$1,000.00	
Less: Discount	34.65	$965.35

The *net* liability to be reported would be only $965.35, not the $1,000 face value of the bond.

Nature of Premium or Discount

The net liability of the company at the time of issuance of bond B is only $965.35. That is the amount of cash actually received. It may be argued that the company will have to repay $1,000, the face value of the bond, and that that amount therefore is the liability to be reported. The company will, of course, have to pay $1,000 at time of maturity. But if it only borrowed $965.35, then the "extra" $34.65 must represent interest, in addition to the semiannual coupon payments, to be paid to the lender. The additional $34.65 has the effect of increasing the rate of interest paid by the company from 10 percent to 12 percent. Interest is not ordinarily reported as a liability and recorded as an expense until the borrower has had use of the funds. Just as the liability for each of the periodic coupon payments of $50 will not be recorded until the interest has accrued, neither should the liability for the additional interest of $34.65 to be paid upon maturity of the bond. Instead, it should be added to the liability account over the remaining life of the bond issue—as the firm has use of the funds borrowed.[2] Similarly, if the bonds were sold at a premium, at a price of $1,020, for example, then the amount borrowed by the company is the amount actually received, $1,020. The company, will, of course, have to repay only $1,000. The $20 represents a reduction, over the life of the issue, of the firm's borrowing costs and should be accounted for as such.

Recording the Accrual and Payment of Interest

As a consequence of the price adjustments attributable to the premium or discount at which the bonds were sold, the effective rate of interest to be paid by the company is that established not by the coupon rate but rather by the *yield rate* (the effective rate at time of issue). *The reported interest expense should be based on the yield rate.*

In the previous example, the company borrowed $965.35 at an effective interest rate of 12 percent (6 percent per interest period). Each interest date, however, it must pay the bondholder only $50. On the first interest date, its effective interest expense is 6 percent of $965.35, or $57.92, an amount that is $7.92 greater than the actual payment of $50 to be made to the bondholder. The $7.92 represents the first interest period's share of the $34.65 in additional interest to be paid upon the maturity of the loan. It is therefore the amount of the discount that must be amortized and charged as additional interest expense in the first period. The following journal entry would reflect this interpretation of the bond discount:

[2]It could, of course, be asserted that the company has a legal liability for the full $1,000. Should the company go bankrupt, however, soon after the sale of the bonds, it would be unreasonable for a bankruptcy court to award the full $1,000 to a bondholder who recently had loaned the company only $965.35.

Interest expense	....	$57.92
Cash	....	$50.00
Discount on bonds	....	7.92

To record payment of interest

As a result of this entry, the unamortized portion of the bond discount has been reduced from $34.65 to $26.73. The bond would be reported in the liability section of the balance sheet as follows:

| Bonds payable | $1,000.00 | |
| Less: Discount | 26.73 | $973.27 |

The effective liability of the company has increased from $965.35 to $973.27 because the company now owes not only the original amount borrowed ($965.35) but also a portion of the interest which the bondholder has earned during the first period. The additional interest now owed is equal to the effective interest for the period ($57.92) less the amount actually paid ($50.00).

At the end of the second interest period, the interest expense would again be based on the effective interest or yield rate that prevailed at the time the bond was issued. But now the effective liability is not $965.35 as at the end of the first period but rather $973.27, an amount reflective of the amortization of a portion of the original discount. Hence the effective interest expense is 6 percent of $973.27, or $58.40. As in the first period, the actual payment to the bondholder would be only $50.00. The difference between the two represents the portion of interest earned by the bondholder but not yet paid to him or her—the amount that must be subtracted from the bond discount and thereby added to the effective liability. The following journal entry would be required on the second interest date:

Interest expense	....	$58.40
Cash	....	$50.00
Discount on bond	....	8.40

To record payment of interest

As a result of this entry, the unamortized portion of the bond discount has been reduced from $26.73 to $18.33. After the second payment of interest the bond would be reported as follows:

| Bonds payable | $1,000.00 | |
| Less: Discount | 18.33 | $981.67 |

A history of the bond is summarized in Exhibit 10-2.

The effective liability, as of any date, can be determined by following the same procedures used to calculate the initial issue price of the bond. For example, as of 12/31/92, there are two interest payments of $50 remaining. The present value of the payments discounted at the effective interest or yield rate of 6 percent per period is, per Table 4, $50 × 1.8334, or $91.67. The present value of the $1,000 to be received at maturity is, per Table 2, $1,000 × .8900, or $890.00. The present value of the two sets of payments combined is $91.67 plus $890.00, or $981.67.

EXHIBIT 10-2

$1,000 Bond Issued on January 1, 1992; Matures on December 31, 1993;
10% Coupon; Sold to Yield 12% (6% per Semiannual Period)

Date	Interest (6% of Effective Liability)	Coupon Payment	Discount	Effective Liability
1/1/92	—	—	$34.95	$ 965.35
6/30/92	$57.92	$(50.00)	(7.92)	7.92
			26.73	973.27
12/31/92	58.40	(50.00)	(8.40)	8.40
			18.33	981.67
6/30/93	58.90	(50.00)	(8.90)	8.90
			9.43	990.57
12/31/93	59.43	(50.00)	(9.43)	9.43
			$ 0.00	$1,000.00

The following example deals with a bond to be sold at a premium rather than a discount.

Example

A company wishes to sell 10-year debentures that bear a coupon rate of 10 percent. At the time of sale, bonds of comparable risk are being sold to yield 8 percent.

1. For how much will the company be able to sell each $1,000 bond?
   The present value at the effective *yield* rate of 4 percent per half-year period (8 percent per year) of a single payment of $1,000, twenty periods hence, is, per Table 2, $1,000 × .4564, or $456.40.
   The present value of a stream of 20 payments of $50 each (the required *coupon payment* discounted at the *yield* rate of 4 percent per period) is, per Table 4, $50 × 13.5903, or $679.52. The sum of the two present values is $1,135.92, the amount for which the company will be able to issue the bond:

Present value of $1,000 to be received after 20 periods, discounted at prevailing rate of 4% per period ($1,000 × .4564 per Table 2)	$ 456.40
Present value of $50 to be received at the end of each of 20 periods, discounted at prevailing rate of 4% per period ($50 × $13.5903 per Table 2)	679.52
Present value of bond	$1,135.92

Alternatively, the same result could have been obtained by focusing on the premium. The company is offering the purchaser 20 payments of $50 each. The purchaser, based on the prevailing interest rate of 8 percent, would be willing to accept 20 payments of $40 each. The present value of the series of the $10 "bonuses" is, per Table 4, $10 × 13.5903, or $135.90. The latter figure represents the bond premium; hence the sale price would be the face value of $1,000 plus a premium of $135.90—the same (with allowance for rounding discrepancies) $1,135.92 as computed earlier.

2. Prepare a journal entry to record the sale of one bond.

Cash $1,135.92
    Bonds payable $1,000.00
    Premium on bonds payable 135.92
To record sale of the bond

3. How would the bonds be reported on the balance sheet immediately after sale?

Bonds payable	$1,000.00	
Premium	135.92	$1,135.92

4. Prepare a journal entry to record the first interest payment. The total amount borrowed by the company is $1,135.92. The effective annual rate of interest, the yield rate, is 8 percent. The effective semiannual interest would therefore be 4 percent times the outstanding balance of $1,135.92, or $45.43. The amount of interest actually to be paid at the time of the first payment is, based on the coupon rate, $50:

Interest expense $45.43
Premium on bonds payable 4.57
    Cash $50.00
To record payment of interest

This entry reduces the premium to $131.35.

5. How would the bonds be reported immediately after the first payment of interest?

Bonds payable	$1,000.00	
Premium	131.35	$1,131.35

6. Prepare a journal entry to record the second interest payment. The effective liability just prior to the second payment of interest is $1,131.35. Effective interest charges, based on the yield rate at the time of sale, are $1,131.35 × .04, or $45.25:

Interest expense $45.25
Premium on bonds payable 4.75
    Cash $50.00
To record payment of interest

The net liability will now be $1,131.35 less that portion ($4.75) of the premium just amortized—$1,126.60.

7. For how much could the bondholder sell the bond immediately after the second payment of interest, assuming that the prevailing interest rate is still 8 percent?

Present value of $1,000, 18 periods away, discounted at 4%, per period (per Table 2), $1,000 × .4936	$ 493.60
Present value of 18 coupon payments of $50 each (per Table 4), $50 × 12.6593	632.97
Price at which the bond could be sold	$1,126.57

This amount is the same amount that would be reported on the books of the issuing company as calculated for part 6 of this example (save for a minor rounding discrepancy). It is the same only because the prevailing interest rate is the same as it was at the time when the bond was first issued—8 percent.

End-of-Year Accruals

If a bond interest date does not occur exactly at year end, it is necessary to accrue interest for the expense incurred from the time of either the issue date or the last payment date to the year end. Suppose, for example, that a 12 percent, 20-year coupon bond were sold on December 1, 1992, for $866.68—a price that would result in a yield of 14 percent. Interest is payable each year on May 31 and November 30. Interest expense for the first full six-month period would be 7 percent of $866.68, or $60.67. That portion of the discount amortized would be the difference between the interest expense of $60.67 and the actual coupon payment of $60.00, or 67 cents. The accrual entry on December 31, 1992, would reflect one-sixth of these amounts:

Interest expense (⅙ of $60.67)		$10.11
Discount on bonds payable (⅙ of 67)	$ .11	
Accrued interest payable (⅙ of $60.00)	10.00	
To record accrual of interest		

The entry on May 31, 1993, when the first payment was made, would be reflective of the remaining five-sixths (note that, consistent with conventional practice, the interest expense on May 31 is *not* based on the effective liability at December 31—after the *partial* amortization of the discount—but rather on the liability as of December 1):

Interest expense (⅚ of $60.67)		$50.56
Accrued interest payable		10.00
Discount on bonds payable (⅚ of 67)	$ .56	
Cash	60.00	
To record payment of interest		

The Deficiencies of Straight-Line Amortization

Some firms, instead of determining interest charges and amortization of discount or premium as described in the preceding paragraphs, have in the past amortized the premium or discount on a straight-line basis. Total interest charges for the month are calculated by adding to the cash coupon payment (or subtracting from, in the case of a premium) the portion of the discount (or premium) amortized. The amount of the discount or premium amortized each period is determined simply by dividing the initial discount or premium by the total number of periods for which the bond will be outstanding. As a consequence, effective interest charges remain constant over the life of the issue. In the illustration used earlier, a 10 percent coupon bond was issued at a price of $965.35—a discount of $34.65. Since the bond would be outstanding for four periods, one-fourth of $34.65, or $8.66, would be amortized each period. Total interest costs each period would be $58.66—the portion of the discount amortized plus the $50 coupon payment. The straight-line method is convenient; it eliminates the need to recompute interest each period. But it is deficient in that it results in a constantly changing *rate* of interest when interest expense is compared with effective liability (face value plus or minus discount or premium). Since, in the example, the effective liability would increase by $8.66 each period, the effective interest rates over the life of the bond (interest expense ÷ effective liability) would decline as follows:

$$\frac{\$58.66}{\$965.35} = 6.08\%\,;\, \frac{\$58.66}{\$974.01} = 6.02\%\,;\, \frac{\$58.66}{\$982.67} = 5.97\%\,;\, \frac{\$58.66}{\$991.33} = 5.92\%$$

The effective rate of interest tends to increase over time when a bond is sold at a premium. Because of such distortions, the Accounting Principles Board, in *Opinion No. 21,* "Interest on Receivables and Payables," specifically prohibited firms from using the straight-line method for their reports to the public if it would result in interest charges that were materially different from those obtained by the effective interest method.

The concern over varying rates of interest is similar to that over the increasing rates of return on assets generated by the straight-line method of depreciation. The straight-line method is proscribed for bonds but is the most popular method for fixed assets. This inconsistency makes it clear that, whereas long-lived assets and liabilities have much in common, accounting principles do not treat them as mirror images of each other.

REDEMPTION OF BONDS

When a firm redeems its bonds outstanding upon their maturity, no special accounting problems are presented. Once the interest expense of the final period is recorded, the discount or premium should be amortized to zero. Thus for a single bond, the following entry would be appropriate:

Bonds payable $1,000.00
    Cash $1,000.00
To record redemption of the bond

If, however, the firm decides to redeem the bonds before they mature, then the accounting questions are more complex.

Assume that a company 20 years ago had issued 30-year, 7 percent coupon bonds at a price of $1,025.50 to yield 6.8 percent. With 10 years remaining until maturity, the firm decides to redeem the bonds since it no longer needs the funds that it borrowed. According to the bond agreement, the company has the right to call the issue any time after 15 years of issuing date at a price of $102. (Bond prices are frequently quoted in terms of $100 even though they are conventionally sold in denominations of $1,000. Thus the company would have to pay $1,020 to redeem a single bond.) The bond was originally issued at a price of $1,025.50; if the company had amortized the premium correctly, the net value of the bond after 20 years (10 years remaining) per the corporate books would be $1,014.34. If the company exercised its option to redeem the bond for $1,020.00, the following entry could be appropriate:

Bonds payable	$1,000.00	
Premium on bonds payable	14.34	
Redemption costs (call premium)	5.66	
Cash		$1,020.00

To record redemption of the bond

The redemption costs represent a penalty payment that management has elected to make to the bondholders in return for depriving them of the return that their investment in the bonds was providing them.

A corporation may also realize a gain by redeeming its bonds prior to maturity. This is especially true if the company does not officially *call* its outstanding issue but instead purchases its bonds in the open market. The company would pay the current bondholders the prevailing price for the security. By purchasing the bonds outstanding, the company would eliminate its liability to outsiders, and it would recognize as a gain the difference between the book value of the bonds and the purchase price.

Fluctuating Nature of Bond Prices

Bond prices, as pointed out earlier, are determined by the relationship between the coupon rate and the prevailing return that an investor is able to obtain elsewhere. It is believed by many that bonds are a relatively riskless investment— that bond prices remain reasonably stable. This is untrue. If, for example, prevailing interest rates increase from 12 percent to 14 percent, then the market price on a bond that bears a coupon rate of 12 percent and has 30 years remaining until maturity could be expected to decline from $100.00 to $85.96—a 14 percent change. If a company had initially issued such a 12 percent coupon bond at a price to yield 12.2 percent, then after 10 years (with 20 years—40 periods— until maturity), the bond would be recorded on its books at a net value of $98.51 (a discount of $1.49 per hundred dollars). The purchase (i.e., the redemption) of a single $1,000 bond at a price of $86.67 (which reflects a market rate of interest of 14 percent) would be recorded as follows:

Bonds payable	$1,000.00	
Cash		$866.70
Discount on bonds payable		14.90
Gain on redemption		118.40

To record redemption of the bond

Interpreting Gains and Losses on Redemptions

Gains or losses on the redemption of bonds must necessarily be interpreted with care by both managers and independent financial analysts. Such gains or losses are recognized and reported on the income statement in the year in which the redemption takes place. As a result, corporate management can easily time its redemptions so as to provide a source of discretionary income whenever it believes that a boost in reported earnings would be helpful. Assume, for example, that in 1978 a firm issued (at par) $10 million in 5 percent coupon bonds payable in 45 years. In 1993, 15 years later, the prevailing rate of interest for similar securities was 7 percent. A 5 percent bond with 30 years remaining until maturity would be traded in the open market for approximately $75. The company could purchase the entire issue for $7.5 million and thereby realize a $2.5 million gain. If management believes that interest rates will continue to remain substantially above the level of the period in which the bond was issued, it is free to select the year in which it redeems the bonds and thereby reports the gain.[3]

Viewed from another perspective, a gain or loss on redemption of bonds may be seen as being very similar to a gain or loss on the sale of long-term assets. If a company were blessed with perfect foresight and were able to predict exactly when and for how much it will redeem its bonds, it would calculate its periodic charges or credits for the amortization of the bond discount or premium in a manner that would assure that the net book value of the bonds at time of redemption is exactly equal to the redemption price. Thus there would be no gain or loss on redemption. If a company does not have perfect foresight, then, upon redeeming its bonds, it must make adjustment for its failure to amortize correctly the discount or premium in the years that the bond was outstanding. The gain or loss on the retirement of long-lived assets may be interpreted as a correction of depreciation expense. Similarly, the gain or loss on redemption of bonds may be considered to be a correction of the amortization of the bond discount or premium and, thus, as an adjustment to the interest charges of previous periods.

The gain on redemption that will be reported on the financial statements does not accrue to the corporation without a price. If the corporation must reborrow the funds used to redeem the outstanding issue, it will have to do so at the prevailing rates of interest—rates that are higher than those that it had been paying in the past. The new rates will, of course, be reflected on income statements of the future as greater interest expenses.

Times Interest Earned

Insight into the ability of a company to satisfy its fixed obligations to creditors may be obtained by comparing earnings with interest charges. Although the *times interest earned* ratio may be expressed in a variety of ways, the simplest form indicates the relationship between interest and income, *before* deducting both interest and income taxes. The objective of the ratio is to indicate the margin of safety afforded bondholders and noteholders. If earnings only barely cover interest charges, then the creditors' promised interest payments are in jeopardy. If, however, earnings are several times greater than interest charges, then in the absence of a business reversal their return is reasonably assured.

Since the objective of the ratio is to indicate the earnings available for the payment of interest, it is important that the interest charges themselves be added back to net income. Moreover, since interest payments are a deductible expense in the determination of taxable income, income taxes should also be added back. In a sense, the payment of interest takes precedence over the pay-

---

[3]The advantages of redeeming bonds to inflate ''artificially'' reported earnings has been tempered by FASB *Statement No. 4*, ''Reporting Gains and Losses from Extinguishment of Debt.'' The statement requires that gains and losses from debt redemption be classified as *extraordinary* items.

ment of federal, state, and local income taxes. Required income tax payments are calculated after deducting payments to creditors. If the firm, after payment of interest, has zero income or a net loss, then the tax liability is zero.

As indicated in the financial statements presented in Chapter 7, American Home Products Corporation had net income (after taxes, in millions) of $1,375 in 1991. Income taxes, both federal and foreign, were $384. Interest expense, not broken out separately in the income statement but reported in a footnote, was $31. Times interest earned was

$$\text{Times interest earned} = \frac{\text{Net income + interest + income taxes}}{\text{Interest}}$$

$$= \frac{\$1,375 + \$31 + \$385}{\$31}$$

$$= \frac{\$1,791}{\$31} = 58 \text{ times}$$

The company covered its interest expense 58 times and, based on this ratio, is in no danger of being unable to meet its interest payments.

As will be indicated in the next section, many companies are increasing the amount of their debt and correspondingly decreasing the ratio of income to interest. It is common to find firms with coverage ratios only slightly better than 1 to 1. Whether these companies will, in fact, be able to meet their interest and debt payments is an open question, and the jury is still out as to whether the fiscal guidelines of the past were unduly conservative and restrictive.

JUNK BONDS AND LBOS

In the mid- and late 1980s, a new wave of corporate acquisitions swept over the U.S. economy as well as several other Western economies. These buyouts differed from traditional takeovers in that they were financed mainly by debt rather than by equity (stock). In a conventional acquisition, the purchasing company exchanges shares of its common stock, often newly issued, for those of the target firm. Alternatively, the purchaser might issue new shares of its own stock in the open market and then use the cash proceeds to buy the stock of the target.

In the new type of transaction, the purchaser puts up little of its own money, perhaps 10 percent or less of the purchase price. The remainder is borrowed.

Transactions that are financed primarily with debt are referred to as *leveraged buyouts* (*LBOs*). They can be extremely profitable to the buyers because, as their name implies, they make use of financial *leverage*. *Leverage* is the use of debt to increase the earnings of the stockholders. The benefits of using debt to finance an acquisition can be explained and illustrated with a simple example.

Suppose Company P has 20 million shares of common stock outstanding and has annual earnings after taxes of $15 million, or 75 cents per share. Company P proposes to acquire Company S at a cost $400 million. Earnings of Company S have been, and will continue to be, $60 million per year (after taxes).

Company P has two options available to obtain the necessary $400 million for acquisition of Company S: (1) issue 80 million shares of stock at a price of $5 per share or (2) issue 8 million shares at $5 per share (for $40 million) and borrow the remaining $360 million at an interest rate of 10 percent. Exhibit 10-3 shows the effect of each of the alternatives on the earnings per share of Company P's common stock.

As can be seen, if the company finances the acquisition entirely with additional stock, earnings per share of Company P remain at 75 cents per share; if it finances the acquisition with 90 percent debt and 10 percent equity, earnings increase to $1.84 per share. The leverage is positive in this example because Company P borrowed $360 at a rate of 10 percent ($40 million before taxes, $23.6 million after taxes) and Company S provided $60 million in earnings. However, leverage is not without risks. The interest is a *fixed* cost; it must be paid irrespective of actual earnings. Were earnings of Company S to drop below the required payments, then earnings of Company P shareholders would be leveraged downward and the shareholders would be worse off for having financed the acquisition with debt.

As is shown in Exhibit 10-3, the advantages of debt over equity financing are greatly enhanced by provisions of the tax code which allow interest payments to be tax-deductible. Thus the after-tax cost of interest is significantly less than the before-tax cost. By contrast, payments of dividends (the returns to stockholders) are not tax-deductible. Since many acquiring companies assume formidable amounts of debt, they are able to lighten considerably their tax burdens, often down to zero.

EXHIBIT 10-3
Example of Effective Use of Leverage

P to acquire S for $400 million
Option 1: Issue 80 million shares of stock at $5 per share
Option 2: Issue 8 million shares of stock at $5 per share and borrow $360 million at an
interest rate of 10%

	Earnings per Share of P	
	Option 1 100% Stock	Option 2 10% Stock
	(dollars in millions)	
Projected earnings of P (independent of S)	$15.0	$15.0
Earnings to be contributed by S	60.0	60.0
Total earnings of P before interest	$75.0	$75.0
Interest on debt of $360 (after taxes)*	—	(23.4)
Projected net income	$75.0	$51.6
Number of shares of stock of P currently outstanding (millions)	20	20
Number of additional shares to be issued (millions)	80	8
Projected total shares of P outstanding (millions)	100	28
Projected earnings per share of P (projected net income divided by projected shares outstanding)	$0.75	$1.84

*Assume a corporate tax rate of 35 percent. Total interest is $36.0, but effective interest cost, after taxes, is only $23.4:

Interest cost (10% of $360)	$36.0
Tax deduction @ 35%	12.6
Interest after taxes	$23.4

Because of their risk, the bonds issued in LBOs have been dubbed *junk* bonds. They command high rates of interest and are not considered to be of "investment grade" (i.e., suitable for investors unwilling to take high risks). Junk bonds were extremely popular when the economy was strong in the 1980s. But they lost their luster in the early 1990s when a weakened economy resulted in several well-publicized bond defaults. Leverage is all to the good when corporate earnings are sufficient to cover interest costs; it can spell fiscal disaster when they are not.

LEASES

A financial arrangement that is of special concern to managers and accountants is *leasing*. In a strict sense a lease involves the right to use land, buildings, equipment, or other property for a specified period of time in return for rent or other compensation. In practice, however, many lease arrangements are the equivalent of installment loans or other forms of borrowing.

Acquisition by Purchase

Suppose that a construction firm is in need of equipment. The cost of the equipment is $100,000; the estimated useful life is 10 years. Since the company does not have sufficient cash on hand to purchase the equipment, it borrows its full cost. The terms of the loan are that principal and interest will be paid in 10 annual installments of equal amount. The amount of each payment will be determined on the basis of an annual interest rate of 12 percent. If $100,000 is viewed as the present value of an annuity for 10 periods, discounted at a rate of 12 percent, then the annual payment required to amortize the loan can be determined (per Table 4 of the Appendix) as follows:

$$\$100,000 = 5.6502x$$

$$x = \$17,698$$

Upon purchasing the equipment and borrowing the necessary funds, the company would make the following journal entries:

```
Cash ...........................................................$100,000
        Note payable ...............................................$100,000
To record the loan of $100,000

Equipment......................................................$100,000
        Cash ......................................................$100,000
To record the purchase of the equipment
```

Each year the company would make the required payment on the note and would record depreciation on the equipment. The division of the payment between principal and interest would, of course, vary from year to year. As the balance of the loan declines, a smaller portion of the payment would be for interest and a larger portion for reduction of the principal. The interest expense for the first year would be 12 percent of the $100,000 balance of the note, or $12,000. The remainder of the total payment of $17,698 would be a repayment of the principal. The entry for the payment of the first year would be

Interest expense	....	$12,000
Note payable	....	5,698
Cash	....	$17,698

To record the first payment of the note

The entry for depreciation (assuming the straight-line method is being used) would be

Depreciation expense	....	$10,000
Allowance for depreciation	....	$10,000

To record depreciation for one year

Acquisition by Lease

Suppose instead, however, that the transaction took a slightly different form. The manufacturer of the equipment, upon arrangement with the construction company, sold the equipment to a financial institution, such as a bank or an insurance company. The financial institution thereupon leased the equipment to the construction company. The agreement specified that the term of the lease was to be for 10 years, after which time the construction company would have the option to purchase the equipment for $1. Annual rental charges would be $17,698, and the construction company (the lessee) would have to pay all insurance, maintenance costs, and license fees on the equipment. In economic substance, all parties are in the identical position that they would have been had the company purchased the equipment outright and borrowed the required funds from the financial institution. Annual cash payments by the construction company would be the same $17,698.

Compare, however, the manner in which the lease, as opposed to the borrow-purchase, transaction might be accounted for. At the time the lease agreement was signed no entry would be required. Each year upon payment of the "rent" the following journal entry would be made:

Rent expense	....	$17,698
Cash	....	$17,698

To record payment of rent for one year

Depreciation, of course, would not be taken on the equipment, since the equipment itself would never be recorded on the books of the lessee (the construction company).

The fundamental accounting distinction between the transaction as a purchase-borrow arrangement and as a lease is that when considered as a lease the company records on its books neither the asset nor the accompanying liability. From the standpoint of the company, the omission of the liability may represent an important advantage of the lease transaction. Potential creditors and investors may view with disfavor excessive amounts of debt appearing on a balance sheet. Moreover, some loan arrangements specify the maximum amount of debt that a company is permitted to incur. The leasing arrangement would be a convenient means of circumventing such restrictions. In effect it would permit the company to arrange for "off the balance sheet" financing of its equipment acquisitions.

Accounting for Capital Leases

There would be little justification for permitting two transactions, the purchase-borrow arrangement and the lease, which are in economic substance identical, to be accounted for differently. The construction company, as a lessee, has the same rights and obligations as it would if it were the legal owner of the equipment. The company bears all risks and has acquired all rights of ownership. If the equipment lasts for longer than the estimated 10 years, the company has the option to purchase it for a negligible amount. If it suffers a major breakdown, the construction company has the obligation to repair it. Moreover, the company has both a legal and a moral obligation to make the specified payments over the life of the lease. The firm that holds title to the equipment, the financial institution, is the owner in name only.

The Committee on Accounting Procedure, a predecessor of the Accounting Principles Board, ruled (in 1949) that leases that are clearly in substance purchases of property (capital or leases) should be recorded as such. The position of the committee has been affirmed by both the Accounting Principles Board and the Financial Accounting Standards Board. The acquisition of the construction equipment would be recorded as a purchase. The transaction would be accounted for in the same way as the purchase illustrated previously except that appropriately descriptive account titles would be used for both the asset and the liability:

> Equipment held under lease (asset) $100,000
>   Present value of lease obligations (liability) $100,000
> **To record acquisition of equipment under a lease arrangement**

The asset, "equipment held under lease," would be amortized over the useful life of the equipment;[4] the liability, "present value of lease obligations," would be accounted for as if it were an ordinary interest-bearing note:

> Amortization of equipment held
>   under lease (expense) $10,000
>   Equipment held under lease,
>   allowance for amortization $10,000
> **To record first-year amortization** (straight-line method, useful life of 10 years)

> Interest expense (12% of $100,000)............................$12,000
> Present value of lease obligations 5,698
>   Cash $17,698
> **To record the first lease payment**

In the remaining years of the lease, the entries would be similar. The entries for the second year would be

> Amortization of equipment held
>   under lease (expense) $10,000
>   Equipment held under lease,
>   allowance for amortization $10,000
> **To record second-year amortization**

---

[4]This asset can be amortized over the life of the lease if ownership of the property is not likely to be transferred to the lessee or if lease life is shorter than useful economic life.

Interest expense (12% of $94,302,
which is $100,000 − $5,698)..................................$11,316
Present value of lease obligation................................ 6,382
  Cash $17,698
To record the second lease payment

Many lease agreements indicate only the amount of annual payments; they do not reveal either the actual purchase price (i.e., the fair market value) of the property transferred or the interest rate used to determine the required amounts of the annual payments. If the lease agreement is silent on these points, the accountant must look to other borrowing arrangements into which the firm has entered to identify an appropriate rate at which to discount the periodic payments or to comparable purchase transactions to derive the value of the property.

Accounting for Operating Leases

Not all lease agreements are the equivalent of purchases. Businesses enter into rental agreements for a variety of reasons: They need property for only a short period of time; they do not wish to accept the risks of ownership; they do not have the cash necessary to make a purchase and are unable or unwilling to incur additional debt; they want the service and maintenance that might be provided by the lessor.

Traditionally, *operating* leases, those that cover merely the right to use property for a limited time in exchange for periodic rental payments, have been accorded no balance sheet recognition. No entry is made at the time the lease is executed; entries to record the rent expense are made periodically. Many accountants argue, however, that *all* lease agreements (assuming that they are not cancelable) create property rights as well as obligations that deserve to be reported on the balance sheet. A lessee has most of the rights of an owner, with the exception of the right to dispose of the property at its discretion. At the same time, it has the obligation to make rental payments as they come due. The present value of the rights obtained in a lease agreement, according to many accountants, should be *capitalized* and recorded as an asset; the corresponding present value of the obligation should be recorded as a liability. The asset should be amortized (depreciated) over the life of the lease. The stated value of the obligation should be reduced as the periodic rental payments are made. Each rental payment would be considered in part a payment of *principal,* the initial liability being equal to the present value of the property rights, and in part a payment of interest on the unpaid balance of the original obligation.

There are, however, serious obstacles to *capitalizing* (recording as an asset) the value of the property rights inherent in *all* noncancelable lease commitments. It is exceedingly difficult to measure the value of such property rights. Many leases, for example, provide not only for the right to *use* the property but also for services on the part of the lessor. The lessor of an office building, for example, may provide heat, electricity, and janitorial and security services. Consistent with other accounting principles, the rights to receive those types of services are not capitalized as assets—no more than accounting recognition is given to an employment contract at the time it is signed. The task of allocating the lease payments between the right to use the property and the other services provided is likely to be inordinately difficult. Moreover, determination of an appropriate rate at which to discount the lease payments to arrive at their present value is also likely to present difficulties. Whereas in transactions involving purchase-type leases the effective interest rate is often a subject for negotiation, in those pertaining to *operating* (nonpurchase) leases the question of interest is unlikely to be specifically considered.

Distinguishing Criteria

In 1977 in *Statement No. 13,* the FASB set forth criteria for distinguishing between capital leases and operating leases. According to the board, a lease should be considered a capital lease if it meets *any one* of the following tests:

1. The present value of the required lease payments is equal to at least 90 percent of the fair market value of the lease property.
2. The term of the lease is 75 percent or more of the leased property's estimated useful life.
3. The lessee has the right either during or at the expiration of the lease agreement to purchase the property from the lessor at an amount less than what the property is actually worth.
4. Ownership is transferred to the lessee by the end of the lease term.

If the agreement meets none of these tests, it should be considered an operating lease and not capitalized. Disclosure of the terms of the lease should be made in a footnote to the financial statements.

The economics of lease financing should be understood by managers, accountants, investors, and lenders. Lease financing may provide a firm with an opportunity to conserve working capital, to avoid some of the risks of ownership, and to take advantage of favorable provisions of the tax regulations. It should not, however, be permitted to result in financial statements which obscure its underlying nature and which imply substantive differences from purchase arrangements where none, in fact, exist.

INCOME TAXES

For many companies, taxes based on income represent their single largest recurring expenditure. The combined federal, state, local, and foreign income tax rate is sometimes over 40 percent of earnings. Income taxes must obviously be a major factor to be accounted for in any business decision. The proper determination of tax liability is also a critical element of financial reporting.

Permanent as Distinguished from Temporary Differences

As a general rule, corporate earnings on which income taxes are based are determined in the same manner as for general financial reporting. There are, however, a number of exceptions. The exceptions fall into two broad categories:

permanent differences and temporary differences. A *permanent difference* is one in which, because of special legislative consideration, particular revenues or expenses are omitted from computation of taxable income. Interest on municipal bonds, for example, is not taxed by the federal government and hence, in calculating the income on which the federal income tax is based, it would be omitted from the revenues. Similarly, under certain circumstances charitable contributions, officers' salaries, and life insurance premiums may be corporate expenses which are not deductible in the determination of taxable income and would therefore be excluded from expenses.

A *temporary difference,* on the other hand, is one in which an item is reflected in income for tax purposes in one period but in income for general reporting purposes in another. For example, a dance studio may sell a series of dance lessons to a customer. The customer pays for the lessons in advance. As illustrated previously in the text, for purposes of general reporting, the company would properly record the revenue in the periods in which the lessons were actually taken. In the computation of taxable income, however, the revenue would be taken into account in the period in which the cash was collected. An oil company, in searching for new oil, incurs costs of drilling dry holes. For general reporting purposes the costs may be considered unavoidable for discovering the actual location of the oil and thereby capitalized and written off over the period during which the oil is removed from the producing wells. For tax purposes, however, they may be considered expenses in the year in which they were actually incurred.

Allocating Taxes to Related Revenue or Expense

Because of the magnitude of the tax rate, reported income can easily be distorted if the tax expenditure or deduction associated with a particular revenue or expense is reported in a period other than that in which the revenue or expense is recorded. This distortion can be avoided by *interperiod tax allocation,* a procedure which causes the reported tax expense to be based on *reported,* rather than taxable, income.

The objective of interperiod tax allocation is to recognize an obligation for all unpaid taxes *arising from earnings reported on the financial statements.* Accordingly, a firm would base its tax liability on income that has been recognized in the financial statements, even if that income differs from what has been reported on the firm's tax returns. The liability is classified as either current or deferred, depending on whether it is payable currently or will likely have to be paid in the future.

The Accounting Principles Board first mandated interperiod tax allocation in *Opinion No. 11,* ''Accounting for Income Taxes'' (1967). In *Statements No. 96* (1987) and *109* (1992), all three with the same title, the Financial Accounting Standards Board reaffirmed the essentials of *Opinion No. 11,* though it modified many of its provisions.[5] The rationale for interperiod tax allocation can be explained by the following example, which is detailed in Exhibit 10-4.

A company has a single asset. The asset cost $100,000 and has a useful life of four years, with a residual value of $20,000. It will generate annual

---

[5]Owing to strong opposition from influential constituents, the FASB delayed the effective date of *Statement No. 96* until 1992 and then superceded it with *Statement No. 109.* Hence, it was never implemented.

revenues, after all operating expenses other than depreciation and taxes, of $38,000 per year. The firm, like most companies, depreciates its assets on a straight-line basis for purposes of financial reporting, but takes advantage of an accelerated method in calculating its actual tax obligation. The specific accelerated method that it uses is the 150 percent declining balance method.

Straight-line depreciation is $20,000 per year (cost of $100,000 less residual value of $20,000, divided by useful life of 4 years). Declining balance depreciation, as indicated in Part I of Exhibit 10-4 ranges from $37,500 to $4,414.

EXHIBIT 10-4
Example: Interperiod Income Tax Allocation

Assumptions

Asset cost:	$100,000
Useful life:	4 years
Residual value:	$ 20,000
Depreciation for financial reporting:	Straight-line, i.e., 25% per year
Depreciation per tax return:	150% declining balance, i.e., 37.5% (150% of 25%)
Annual revenues, net of expenses other than taxes and depreciation:	$38,000

I. Annual Depreciation Charges, 150% Declining Balance Method

	Year 1	Year 2	Year 3	Year 4
Balance, start of year	$100,000	$62,500	$39,063	$24,414
Depreciation, 37.5%	37,500	23,438	14,648	4,414*
Balance, end of year	$ 62,500	$39,063	$24,414	$20,000

*Depreciation is only $4,414 since under the declining balance method an asset cannot be depreciated to less than residual value.

II. Taxable Income, Required Tax Payments, and Net Cash Inflow*

	Year 1	Year 2	Year 3	Year 4	Total
Net revenue	$38,000	$38,000	$38,000	$38,000	$152,000
Depreciation (150% per above)	37,500	23,438	14,648	4,414	80,000
Income before taxes	500	14,562	23,352	33,586	72,000
Tax @ 40%	200	5,825	9,341	13,434	28,800
Cash inflow	$37,800	$32,175	$28,659	$24,566	$123,200

*Net cash inflows are net revenues less taxes; cash flows relating to the purchase and retirement of the asset have been excluded.

III. Reported Accounting Income, Assuming That Taxes Are *Not* Deferred*

	Year 1	Year 2	Year 3	Year 4	Total
Net revenue	$38,000	$38,000	$38,000	$38,000	$152,000
Depreciation (straight-line)	20,000	20,000	20,000	20,000	80,000
Income before taxes	18,000	18,000	18,000	18,000	72,000
Tax (required payment)	200	5,825	9,341	13,434	28,800
Net income	$17,800	$12,175	$ 8,659	$ 4,566	$ 43,200

*That is, taxes represent the required tax payment.

(continued)

EXHIBIT 10-4 Continued

IV. Reported Accounting Net Income, Assuming That Taxes Are Deferred

	Year 1	Year 2	Year 3	Year 4	Total
Net revenue	$38,000	$38,000	$38,000	$38,000	$152,000
Depreciation (straight-line)	20,000	20,000	20,000	20,000	80,000
Income before taxes	18,000	18,000	18,000	18,000	72,000
Tax @ 40%	7,200	7,200	7,200	7,200	28,800
Net income	$10,800	$10,800	$10,800	$10,800	$ 43,200
Balance in deferred tax liability account, start of year	$ 0	$ 7,000	$ 8,375	$ 6,234	
Tax expense (per above)	7,200	7,200	7,200	7,200	
Required tax payment (per Part III)*	(200)	(5,825)	(9,341)	(13,434)	
Amount to be added to (deducted from) deferred tax liability account	7,000	1,375	(2,141)	(6,234)	
Balance in deferred tax liability account, end of year	$ 7,000	$ 8,375	$ 6,234	$ 0	

*Note that the required tax payments, and hence all cash flows, are the same whether or not income taxes are deferred.

V. Journal Entries to Record Tax Expense*

Year 1

Income tax expense		$7,200
Taxes payable in current year		$ 200
Taxes deferred until future years		7,000

Year 2

Income tax expense		$7,200
Taxes payable in current year		$5,825
Taxes deferred until future years		1,375

Year 3

Income tax expense		$7,200
Taxes deferred until future years		2,141
Taxes payable in current year		$9,341

Year 4

Income tax expense		$7,200
Taxes deferred until future years		6,234
Taxes payable in current year		$13,434

*Each year as tax payments are actually made, "taxes payable in current year" would be debited, "cash" would be credited.

Part II of Exhibit 10-4 presents the required tax payments. As tax depreciation decreases over the years, the required tax payments increase—from $200 in year 1 to $13,434 in year 4. Correspondingly, the net cash flow (revenues less taxes) decreases.

Part III of the exhibit indicates reported income, assuming that the tax expense represents the required tax payment. As indicated, for reporting purposes the company uses the straight-line method of depreciation. Since tax expense increases from year to year, income decreases.

The data of Part III raise substantive questions as to whether the reported earnings over the four-year period is a meaningful and useful representation of the company's performance. Has the company's performance really deteriorated from year 1 to year 4? Can the reported earnings of year 1 be used as a basis of predicting future cash flows (and thereby fulfilling a prime function of financial reporting)? Prevailing accounting thought answers both questions in the negative.

The company acquired the asset knowing that it would be permitted tax deductions (in the form of depreciation) over the four-year period of $80,000, the net cost of the asset. The tax deductions can be interpreted as reductions of asset cost—reductions to be realized over asset life rather than at time of acquisition. It would seem logical, therefore, that the tax benefits should be reflected in income on the same basis as the asset cost—evenly over the life of the asset—irrespective of the timing of the cash flows.

Correspondingly, the asset can be expected to provide total income before taxes of $72,000, which will be allocated equally to the four years. Total taxes will be $28,800. The taxes are directly associated with these earnings and hence should be matched to them. The tax rate is 40 percent and, therefore, 40 percent of earnings should be charged as tax expense. To be sure, the taxing authorities, through special provisions of the tax laws (i.e., the privilege of using accelerated depreciation), permit the company to postpone a portion of the taxes from year 1 and year 2 to year 3 and year 4. Nevertheless, per the well-established principles of accrual accounting, the timing of the tax payments should have no bearing on the tax expense. The difference between the tax expense and the taxes to be paid should be recorded as a noncurrent liability, "taxes deferred until future years."

Part IV of Exhibit 10-4 illustrates interperiod tax allocation. The tax expense "follows" the reported income before taxes and is thus 40 percent of reported income, regardless of the required tax payments. In years 1 and 2, such tax expense ($7,200) exceeds the required payments of $200 and $5,825. The excess would be recorded as a deferred tax liability. In years 3 and 4 the tax expense (again, $7,200) is less than the required tax payments of $9,341 and $13,434. The deficiency would now be deducted from the deferred tax account. By the end of year 4, the balance in the deferred tax account would be reduced to zero. The total tax expense would be the same as if taxes had not been deferred; only the allocation among periods differs.

Part V of Exhibit 10-4 presents the journal entries required to give effect to interperiod tax allocation.

Reported Tax Expense Based on Reported Pretax Income

In essence, tax allocation requires that the reported income tax expense be based on pretax accounting income. The reported tax liability is divided into two parts: (1) the portion that is currently payable and (2) that which can be deferred until future periods.

The portion that is currently payable is based on the liability per tax return (that is, on *taxable* income). The deferred portion is the difference between the reported tax expense and the portion of the liability that is currently payable. In years in which the firm is able to postpone taxes, the deferred portion of the liability is credited (that is, the deferred liability is increased); in years in which the firm must ''repay'' the taxes that had been postponed, the deferred liability is debited (and thereby decreased). The following example illustrates a temporary difference in which *revenue* is included in years subsequent to those in which it is included in accounting (reported) income.

Example

In 1992 the Ann Arbor Bridge Co. receives a $40 million contract to construct a bridge across the Huron River. The company estimates that construction costs will total $36 million and that the bridge will be built over a two-year period.

The company estimates that construction and collection of cash will adhere to the following timetable:

	Percent Completed in Year	Percent Cash Collected in Year
1992	20	—
1993	80	25
1994	—	75

The company decides to report earnings from the contract on a percentage of completion basis in its financial statements but elects to report the earnings on an installment basis (i.e., as cash is collected) on its income tax return.

The tax rate is 40 percent. The required tax payments and income statement are shown in Exhibit 10-5.

In the income statement, the tax expense is based on the reported income before taxes, irrespective of the required tax payment. *The tax expense follows the income.*

The following journal entries give effect to the appropriate *allocation* of taxes. It is assumed for convenience that the required tax payment (the current portion of the liability) is made entirely in the year to which it is applicable, although in practice a part of the payment is likely to be delayed until the following year:

Year 1992

Tax expense $320,000
        Taxes deferred until future years $320,000
To record tax expense (No tax payment need be made in 1992; tax expense represents 40 percent of reported income before taxes of $800,000.)

EXHIBIT 10-5

Required Tax Payments
(Installment Basis)

	1992	1993	1994
Revenue	$ 0	$10,000,000 (25%)	$30,000,000 (75%)
Expenses applicable to revenues ($^{36}/_{40}$ of revenues)	0	9,000,000 (25%)	27,000,000 (75%)
Taxable income	$ 0	$ 1,000,000	$ 3,000,000
Tax rate	40%	40%	40%
Tax	$ 0	$ 400,000	$ 1,200,000

Income Statement for Purposes of Financial Reporting
(Percentage of Completion Basis)

	1992	1993	1994
Revenue	$8,000,000 (20%)	$32,000,000 (80%)	$ 0
Expenses applicable to revenues ($^{36}/_{40}$ of revenues)	7,200,000 (20%)	28,800,000 (80%)	$ 0
Income before taxes	$ 800,000	$ 3,200,000	$ 0
Tax expense (40%)	320,000	1,280,000	0
Net income	$ 480,000	$ 1,920,000	$ 0

Year 1993

> Tax expense $1,280,000
>   Taxes payable in current year $400,000
>   Taxes deferred until future years 880,000
> **To record tax expense** (Required tax payment is $400,000; tax expense represents 40 percent of reported income before taxes of $3,200,000.)
>
> Taxes payable in current year $400,000
>   Cash $400,000
> **To record payment of taxes**

Year 1994

> Taxes deferred until future years $1,200,000
>   Cash $1,200,000
> **To record payment of taxes** (Required tax payment is $1,200,000; reported income is zero so no tax expense need be charged.)

The liability, "taxes deferred until future years," would be reported on the balance sheet among the current or noncurrent liabilities, depending on when it is likely to be reversed. The balance in the account will increase in those years in which the tax expense (the amount added to the liability) exceeds the required tax payments (the amounts deducted from the liability) and decrease in those years in which required tax payments exceed the tax expense.

Taxes deferred until future years		
(1994) 1,200,000	(1992)	320,000
	(1993)	880,000

Controversial Nature of Tax Allocation

The issue of tax allocation continues to be controversial and there are many accountants who reject the very concept of tax allocation for some of the reasons outlined below.

Lack of Direct Relationship

Tax allocation is rooted in the matching concept; it assumes that there is a cause-and-effect relationship between income and tax expense. It is intended to prevent companies from reporting a relatively high income in one period only to have to report a correspondingly low income when taxes that have been postponed from the earlier years must be paid. Many accountants maintain, however, that the relationship between required tax payments and reportable income is sufficiently indirect that attempts to associate the two detract from, rather than add to, the usefulness of the resultant tax expense and after-tax earnings. They contend that the tax code is designed to advance a number of economic policy objectives. It is a package of subsidies and penalties intended to encourage certain types of corporate behavior (e.g., investment in long-lived assets) and discourage others. It is neither feasible nor beneficial to associate specific payments of tax with specific revenues.

To some degree, the FASB addressed this concern in *Statement No. 109*. In that statement the FASB shifted the emphasis of tax allocation from the income statement to the balance sheet and made the deferred tax liability a more meaningful indicator of taxes that will actually have to be paid. One of the main distinctions between the requirements of *Opinion No. 11* and *Statement No. 109* is that under the latter the balance in the deferred tax account must be adjusted to take into account changes in tax rates as well as other provisions of the tax laws. Thus, if the tax rates were to be reduced, the balance in the deferred tax account would also be diminished. Correspondingly, the full benefit of the rate reduction would be recognized with a credit to income in the year of the change. As a consequence, earnings may be more volatile than they were under *Opinion No. 11*. In previous chapters it was pointed out that over the years rule-making authorities have focused more on the income statement than on the balance sheet, that the balance sheet has become little more than a statement of residuals (costs not yet charged off as expenses). *Statement No. 109* clearly runs counter to that trend.

Buildup of Liability

Opponents of tax allocation further assert that neither the tax expense nor the deferred tax liability is a useful indicator of future tax outlays. They argue that allocation causes firms to report tax expenses that are unrealistically high and deferred tax liabilities that may never have to be paid. They admit, of course, that the temporary differences that result from purchases of individual assets will eventually reverse, requiring a firm to pay the taxes that had previously been postponed. But they point out that unless the firm cuts back its size, new temporary differences will arise and reduce taxable income. The deferred tax balance will continue to grow and, in a sense, never have to be repaid. To support their position, they cite a number of empirical studies that show that since the adoption of the APB opinion requiring tax allocation, the deferred tax liabilities of major corporations have continued to expand. For some companies, they have ballooned to a point where they are their single greatest liability.[6]

Inordinate Complexity

The U.S. tax law is a tangled web of U.S. tax code provisions, implementation regulations, and judicial decisions. Net taxable income may bear little relation to net reportable earnings, and the differences between the two are often not easily categorized between "temporary" and "permanent." Indeed, the computation of reported tax expense is far more intricate than has been indicated by the discussion so far. Among the questions addressed in *Statement No. 109* are the following:

1. Should a company report a deferred tax *asset* when it may be able to offset losses of a current year against income of future years? If a firm incurs a loss in a particular year, the tax code permits it to apply the loss first against income of up to five past years and then against three future years. The firm could thereby receive a refund of taxes previously paid or reduce taxes of future years. The value of the "carry forward" rights are dependent upon earnings in the future. Unless the firm is profitable in the following three years, the rights would have no value.

   Simple answer: Yes, the firm may report a deferred tax *asset* to the extent that it is likely to be realized (that is, to reduce taxes to be paid in the future).

2. Should the deferred tax liability be affected by "tax planning strategies," legitimate means by which the firm can reduce its apparent tax obligations?

   Simple answer: Yes, if they satisfy specified conditions.

3. What tax rate should the firm use to measure its deferred tax liability or asset when its income taxes (either in the U.S. or other countries) are based on graduated tax rates (i.e., taxes on income above specified amounts are taxed at higher rates)?

   Simple answer: The *average* graduated rate applicable to the amount of estimated income in the periods in which the deferred tax liability or asset will be settled.

Statement No. 109 alleviates several of the problems that the business community had with *Opinion No. 11*. Most significantly, it leads to a liability that better expresses the actual taxes to be paid in the future. It has done so, however, in exchange for increases in both complexity and record-keeping costs.

---

[6]The counter to the argument that the deferred tax liability will continuously "roll over" and thus be postponed indefinitely is that accounts payable also continuously roll over. As long as a firm continues to function at its present level or to expand, then its liability for accounts payable, like that for deferred taxes, is unlikely to ever be liquidated. Few, if any, accountants would argue that accounts payable should not be reported on the balance sheet.

A *pension* is a sum of money paid to retired or disabled employees owing to their years of employment. At one time, pensions were viewed as discretionary payments made by an organization to its loyal and dedicated workers. Today they are contractual obligations of companies, are incorporated into almost all collective bargaining agreements, and are regulated under federal legislation.

Under typical pension plans, an employer makes a series of contributions to a special fund over the working lives of its employees. Under some plans, the employees must also contribute to the fund. If both the employer and the employees are required to contribute, the plan is called a *contributory* plan; if only the employer, then it is referred to as a *noncontributory* plan. The fund is often maintained by an independent trustee. The contributions are invested so as to earn a return. If employees work a specified number of years for the employer, then upon their retirement they are entitled to periodic payments until their or their spouses' deaths.

Defined Contribution Plans

There are two primary types of pension plans. The first, and more simple to account for, is the *defined contribution* plan. Under a defined contribution plan, the employer agrees to make a series of contributions of a specified amount. Often the amount is stated as a percentage of employee earnings. For example, a company might contribute to a fund 12 percent of each eligible employee's wage or salary. The contributed funds are invested, and each employee's interest in the total fund is determined by his or her proportionate share of total contributions. Upon retirement, the employees can withdraw their funds, usually in a series of monthly payments. The employer makes no promises as to how much employees will receive upon their retirement. The actual benefits to be received are dependent upon the investment performance of the fund. The employer guarantees only inputs; it makes no representation as to outputs.

Upon making its promised contribution to the fund, the employer has no further liability to the employees. Thus no accounting liability need be recognized. If the employer made a cash contribution of $2 million, the following entry would be in order:

Pension expense..	$2,000,000	
Cash		$2,000,000

To record contribution to the pension fund

Defined Benefit Plans

In contrast to a defined contribution plan, a *defined benefit* plan requires the employer to provide each employee with specific benefits upon his or her retirement. Usually, the promised benefits will vary according to length of service and salary. For example, a company might agree to pay an employee a percentage of his or her final salary. The percentage might be equal to 2 percent times the number of years of service. Thus an employee who had 30 years of service and had earned $100,000 in his or her last year of employment would be entitled to an annual pension of $60,000 (30 years × 2% × $100,000). The employer must set aside sufficient funds during each year of employee service so that its contributions plus the earnings on the fund will be sufficient to make the promised pension payments. The employer guarantees outputs; it is obligated to have the financial wherewithal to make good on its promises.

Until recently, many employers failed to set aside sufficient funds to assure that they could satisfy their pension obligations. Some operated their plans on a pay-as-you-go basis. They set aside no funds; instead they paid the retired employees out of what was available from current operations. Others only partially *funded* (set aside funds for) their pension obligations. To eliminate pension abuses and to help assure that retirees receive what is promised to them, Congress, in 1974, passed the Employee Retirement Income Security Act (ERISA). This act requires employers to fund their plans at specified minimum levels and provides various other safeguards to employees.

The discussion in this chapter is directed to defined benefit, rather than defined contribution, plans.

Accrual Basis

As are other costs, pensions must be reported on an accrual basis. As a result, the accounting for defined benefit plans becomes complex.

Regardless of when a company actually makes the required payments to the employees or to the pension fund, the company receives the benefit of an employee's services in the years in which he or she has actually worked. Pension costs, like other directed wage payments, must be recorded as expenses in the periods in which the employees provide their services. But the actual expense cannot be known for certain until the employee has received all the benefits to which he or she is entitled. This will not be known until the employee's death and that of survivors who may also be entitled to benefits. Among the uncertainties that will affect the actual expense for an employee population are the following:

1. Life expectancy of employees
2. Turnover rates (employees who leave the firm prior to retirement may be entitled to no or only partial benefits)
3. Future wage and salary rates on which pensions will be based
4. Rate of earnings on amounts in the pension fund

The amount that a company must provide each year to meet its future pension obligations can be calculated *actuarially*. An actuary is a statistician who computes insurance risks and premiums. But the amount determined by the actuary necessarily depends upon estimates, assumptions, and an actuarial cost method. An *actuarial cost method* is a procedure for allocating the total cost of expected benefits to the periods in which the employees perform their services. It has much in common with a depreciation method. Whereas a depreciation method allocates the cost of long-lived assets over the periods that they are in service, an actuarial cost method distributes the costs of pensions over the periods that employees contribute their efforts.

The Pension Fund

The pension fund is ordinarily a distinct legal and accounting entity that is separate from the company that sponsors the plan. The fund must maintain its own accounting records and issue periodic financial statements. The assets of a pension fund consist of cash, securities, and other income-earning investments. The main liability of the fund is the estimated pension benefits of current and retired employees. This liability is called the *accumulated plan benefit.* It includes *vested* benefits as well as *nonvested* benefits that are expected to vest in the future. Benefits that are *vested* are amounts to which employees are entitled even if they leave the company. *Nonvested* benefits are those that employees would have to surrender if they quit the company prior to completing a minimum eligibility period. The liability must, of course, be determined on an actuarial basis, and it should be stated at the present (discounted) value of the benefits earned by the employees. The difference between the liability for future benefits and the assets available to pay these benefits is referred to as the *unfunded liability.* It represents the amount that must be contributed to the fund to pay all benefits which employees have already earned. The accounting guidelines for defined benefit pension funds were originally set forth in FASB *Statement No. 35,* ''Accounting and Reporting by Defined Benefit Pension Plans'' (1980).

Economic Ties to the Fund's Sponsoring Employer

Although in legal form the pension fund is a separate entity, the fund and the employer are inextricably associated. In economic substance the employer is ultimately responsible for the promised benefits to its retired employees. Should the actuarial variables, such as investment income, be less favorable than anticipated, the employer would have to make up the deficiency. Should they be more favorable, the employer could reduce expected contributions to the fund. In an economic sense therefore, the assets as well as the liabilities of the fund are those of the employer, not of an independent entity. The boundaries between the fund and the employer are illusory.

Until the FASB issued ''Employers' Accounting for Pensions'' (*Statement No. 87*) in 1985, accounting standards maintained the fiction that the fund was separate from the employer. *Statement No. 87* breaks down the walls between the employer and the fund by requiring that the resources and obligations of the fund be reported on the financial statements of the employer.

As a general principle, the employer is required to report as a liability the difference between the actuarial liability of the pension fund and the market value of the assets in the fund. As noted previously, this difference is called the unfunded projected benefit obligation. Thus, if the employer has made sufficient contributions to keep the fund fully funded, its reported liability would be zero. Unfortunately, *Statement No. 87* is extraordinarily complex and the unfunded obligation is subject to a number of adjustments. The adjustments take into account events and transactions which are given delayed recognition on the income statement. Some of these adjustments can be quite substantial.

The Employer's Pension Expense

An employer's pension expense consists of six components. The first three compose the ongoing pension expense. The remaining three represent the amortization of adjustments to the unfunded projected benefit obligation.

The Three Components of Ongoing Pension Expense

The three components of ongoing pension expense are service cost, interest cost, and investment income.

1. *Service cost.* Service cost is the actuarial present value of the benefits earned by employees for their service *in the current period.* It is similar to wages and salaries. It differs, however, in two ways. First, it will be paid in the future, when the employees retire. Therefore it must be discounted to its present value. Second, it can only be estimated, since the actual amount to be paid is unknown. The amount to be paid will depend on actuarial factors such as employee turnover and mortality rates.

2. *Interest cost.* Interest cost is the increase in the liability to the employees due to the passage of time. As just indicated, the service cost is the present (discounted) value of the benefits earned. The interest cost represents the annual increase in the present value of the benefits earned *in earlier periods.*

3. *Investment income.* Investment income is the *expected* return on the fund assets. It includes projections of dividends, interest, and gains in value.

   To avoid abrupt changes in annual pension expense, investment income is based on expected rather than actual earnings. As will be explained in the discussion of the fifth component of the employer's pension expense, pension gains and losses, the difference between actual and expected investment earnings (or losses) will be charged or credited to income over a number of periods, not just one.

In determining net ongoing pension expense, investment income must be *deducted* from service cost and interest cost. Ongoing pension expense is recorded by a standard payroll-type entry. Suppose, for example, that the ongoing pension expense is $50 million. The following entry would be necessary:

Pension expense $50,000,000
    Accrued pension cost (liability) $50,000,000
To record ongoing pension expense

As the employer *funds* the liability by contributing to the fund, the liability would be reduced. If, for example, the employer contributed $40 million, the entry would be

Accrued pension cost (liability) $40,000,000
    Cash $40,000,000
To record contributions to the pension fund

Thus the remaining liability would express the *unfunded* pension obligation.

Three Additional Elements of Employer Expense

Each of the three remaining components represents the amortization of a deferred charge or deferred credit. These assets or liabilities are established so that certain economic costs or gains will have an impact on reported pension expense over several periods instead of one. This practice causes income to be smoother than if the costs or gains were fully recognized in a single period.

The pattern of accounting for each of the costs or gains to be deferred is similar. Assume the element is a cost (the accounting for gains is a mirror image). The employer would add the full amount of the cost to its accrued pension liability. It would offset the liability with a deferred charge (asset) of the same amount. For purposes of balance sheet display, the asset and liability would be combined, so initially there would be no net effect on the reported accrued pension liability.[7]

Then, over a predetermined number of years, the deferred charge would be amortized. The amortization would be a component of pension expense. As the offsetting deferred charge is reduced, the net reported pension liability would increase. The reported pension liability itself would be reduced only as it was funded.

4. *Prior service costs arising from benefit enhancements.* When a company enhances pension benefits, the projected benefit obligation of the pension fund typically increases immediately. That is because the plan amendments generally apply to all employees presently on the payroll, including those who are near retirement age. The new benefits will be based primarily on these employees' *prior service* to the firm.

Statement No. 87 requires that the employer add to its pension liability the actuarial present value of the new benefits. To avoid a major shock to its earnings, the employer does not, however, have to recognize a corresponding expense immediately. Instead, it would debit a deferred charge, ''unrecognized prior service costs.'' This asset would be amortized over the remaining service periods of the employees eligible to receive benefits.

Suppose that the employer amended its pension plan. The resultant increase in the actuarial present value of its pension obligation was $5 million. The following entry would be in order:

Unrecognized prior service costs (deferred charge) $5,000,000
    Accrued pension cost (liability) $5,000,000
To recognize the liability and corresponding deferred charge arising from improvements to pension plan

For purposes of reporting, the asset and liability would be combined. Therefore the entry would have no impact on the pension liability shown on the balance sheet.

If the unrecognized prior service costs were to be amortized over 25 years, then each year, 1/25th would be reported as an expense:

Pension expense $200,000
    Unrecognized prior service costs (deferred charge) $200,000
To amortize unrecognized prior service costs

This entry would reduce the deferred charge and thereby increase the net (reported) accrued pension liability.

As indicated previously, the liability ''accrued pension cost'' would be reduced only as the company ''funds'' the obligation by making contributions to the pension fund.

[7]In practice, much of the accounting for pensions is accomplished by ''memo'' entries. The only entries that are actually ''booked'' are those that will affect the net amounts to be reported on the balance sheet or income statement.

5. *Pension gains and losses.* Pension gains and losses are of two types: (1) actuarial gains and losses and (2) unexpected returns on plan assets. Like prior service costs, they are accorded delayed recognition.

Actuarial gains and losses result from changes in actuarial assumptions. As indicated previously, actuarial assumptions are used to estimate the employer's projected benefit obligation. Changes in actuarial assumptions increase or decrease this liability. For example, an increase in life expectancy would increase the obligation because the pension benefits would have to be paid for a longer period of time.

Unexpected returns on plan assets result whenever actual earnings are greater or less than the previously projected rate. They could be caused by changes in prevailing interest or dividend rates or by unusual shifts in the values of marketable securities.

Pension plans are accounted for from a long-term perspective. Small changes in an actuarial assumptions can have a relatively large impact on the projected benefit obligation. So too can swings in the stock and bond markets. *Statement No. 87* is grounded on a premise that the year-to-year pension expense should not fluctuate widely in the face of changes in the projected benefit obligation. The effect of any changes should be spread out over a number of periods.

Pension gains and losses are accounted for similarly to prior service costs. Suppose that, because of a broad-based fall in securities prices, the actual return on plan assets was $3 million less than the projected return. The following entry would be in order:

Unrecognized pension loss (deferred charge).................$3,000,000
    Accrued pension cost (liability) $3,000,000
To record a pension loss

As with the unrecognized prior service cost, the unrecognized pension loss (a deferred charge) would be netted against the accrued pension cost and thereby have no immediate impact on the reported pension liability.

Assuming that the deferred charge was to be amortized over 10 years, the following entry would be appropriate each year:

Pension expense $300,000
    Unrecognized pension loss (deferred charge) $300,000
To amortize the unrecognized pension loss

This entry would increase pension expense and, at the same time, increase the accrued pension costs (the liability) reported on the balance sheet.[8]

6. *Transition gains and losses. Statement No. 87* imposed new rules as to how to compute the projected benefit obligation. Thus a firm might have had to increase or decrease its pension liability in the year it first applied *Statement No. 87*. To avoid a sudden jolt to earnings, the FASB prescribed that the change be treated similarly to unrecognized prior

[8]In fact, *Statement No. 87* stipulates that, unlike the prior service cost, the unrecognized pension loss need only be amortized if it becomes sufficiently large to satisfy stipulated criteria. This unusual approach (i.e., establishing a deferred charge and then amortizing it only when it becomes excessively large) has little conceptual merit. It represents a compromise. Some members of the FASB wanted unusual gains and losses in the pension fund to be recognized immediately in the income statement of the employer. Others, fearing that the pension expense would be excessively volatile, sought to modulate it by allowing the gains and losses to "even out" over time.

service costs. The employer would offset the change in the liability with a deferred charge or credit, *unrecognized net transition loss or gain.* It would then amortize the deferred charge or credit over the remaining service period of active employees.

Suppose that as a consequence of adopting *Statement No. 87,* the projected benefit obligation *decreases* by $4 million. The following entry would be appropriate:

Accrued pension cost (liability) $4,000,000
    Unrecognized transition gain (deferred credit) $4,000,000
To record the transition gain

As with the entries to record the prior service costs and the pension loss, this entry has no immediate balance sheet effect, since the unrecognized transition gain or loss is combined with the accrued pension cost liability.

As the unrecognized transition gain is amortized (assume over a period of 10 years), both the annual pension expense and the unrecognized transition gain are reduced. So also, therefore, is the net pension liability to be reported on the balance sheet:

Unrecognized transition gain (deferred credit) $400,000
    Pension expense $400,000
To amortize the transition gain

Summary of Pension Expense

In summary, the pension expense as defined by *Statement No. 87* captures two categories of costs. The first is the "normal," ongoing costs:

1. Service costs, the benefits earned by the employees during the period
2. Interest cost, the annual increase in the present value of the pension liability
3. Investment income, the *expected* return on pension fund assets

The second is the "unusual" costs:

1. Prior service costs, enhancements of pension benefits
2. Pension gains and losses, changes in actuarial assumptions and unexpected returns on pension assets
3. Transition gains and losses, the gains and losses from the initial adoption of *Statement No. 87*

The unusual costs are not taken into income all in one year. Instead, they are amortized over time.

Summary of Impact on Reported Pension Liability

The accounting for pensions is driven by the expense, not the liability. The reported liability is an artificial accounting construct. It comprises the *unfunded* projected benefit obligation plus or minus the three deferred charges or credits. The unfunded projected benefit obligation is the difference between the projected benefit obligation and the market value of the fund's investments.[9] The three deferred charges or credits are

[9]*Statement No. 87* requires that under certain circumstances an employer must recognize a *minimum* pension liability that is greater than that which would otherwise be recorded. Recognition of the minimum liability limits the extent to which the deferred items can reduce (or even eliminate) the reported pension liability.

1. Unrecognized prior service costs
2. Unrecognized pension gains and losses
3. Unrecognized transition gains and losses

Exhibit 10-6 summarizes the impact of this section's illustrative transactions on both the pension expense and the pension liability.

Exhibit 10-7 compares the economic and reporting consequences of selected events and transactions. Note that some have an economic impact on either or both the projected benefit obligation or the fund assets. Nevertheless, they are given no immediate accounting recognition in that they have no effect on the reported pension expense or liability. They affect the reported pension expense or liability only over time through the process of amortization.

Required Note Disclosures

A typical corporate income statement and balance sheet may reveal nothing of the company's pension fund, since the various pension accounts are aggregated and often combined with nonpension accounts. The information of significance is revealed in the notes to the financial statements. Exhibit 10-8 illustrates the disclosures required by *Statement No. 87.*

EXHIBIT 10-6
Effect of Journal Entries on Pension Expense and Liability
(in millions)

Pension Expense

Net ongoing expense for year (includes service costs and interest cost less investment income)		$50.0
Add: Amortization of deferred charges and credits		
Prior service costs (plan amendments)	$ 0.2	
Pension loss (less than expected return on plan assets)	0.3	
Transition gain	(0.4)	0.1
Net pension expense		$50.1

Pension Liability

Increase owing to ongoing pension expense		$50.0
Add: Increases owing to nonroutine events		
Plan amendments	$ 5.0	
Pension loss	3.0	
Transition gain	(4.0)	4.0
		54.0
Subtract: Increases in offsetting deferred charges and credits, net of amortization		
Prior service costs	$ 4.8	
Pension loss	2.7	
Transition gain	(3.6)	3.9
Increase in pension liability prior to employer contributions		50.1
Employer contribution to plan		(40.0)
Net increase in pension liability		$10.1

EXHIBIT 10-7

Comparison of Economic and Reporting Consequences of Selected Transactions and Events

Transaction or Economic Event	Economic Impact[1]			Impact on Financial Statements of Employer		
	Projected Benefit Obligation –	Assets of Fund	Unfunded Projected Benefit = Obligation	Reported Pension Expense	Reported Pension Liability[2]	Net Deferred Charge[3]
Employees earn benefits	I	NE	I	I	I	NE
Interest on pension obligation increases with passage of time	I	NE	I	I	I	NE
Fund investments increased by interest and dividend earnings (at expected rate)	NE	I	D	D	D	NE
Employer makes cash contribution to pension fund	NE	I	D	NE	D	NE
Plan pays benefits to retired employees	D	D	NE	NE	NE	NE
Benefits attributable to prior service are enhanced by changes to plan	I	NE	I	NE	NE	I
Prior service costs are amortized	NE	NE	NE	I	I	D
Actuary changes assumptions to increase actuarial obligation	I	NE	I	NE	NE	I
Actuarial changes are amortized	NE	NE	NE	I	I	D
Plan investments earn returns greater than expected	NE	I	D	NE	NE	D*
Greater than expected returns are amortized	NE	NE	NE	D	D	I*
Actuary reports adoption of SAS No. 87 increases actuarial obligation	I	NE	I	NE	NE	I
Transition costs are amortized	NE	NE	NE	I	I	D

I = Increase; D = Decrease; NE = No effect.

[1]Calculations of the projected benefit obligation will made by the plan's actuary. Information on the market value of the plan's assets will be provided by a trustee who administers the fund. The difference between the projected benefit obligation and the market value of the assets is the unfunded projected benefit obligation.

[2]The reported pension liability is the obligation that will be reported on the employer's balance sheet. It represents the unfunded projected benefit obligation plus or minus the net deferred charge. The deferred items are disclosed in the notes to the financial statements but on the balance sheet they are netted against the unfunded projected benefit obligation. As a result, transactions and events that increase or decrease both the unfunded projected benefit obligation and the net deferred charge have no effect on the reported pension liability. The reported pension liability is affected only by events or transactions that affect *either* the unfunded projected benefit obligation *or* the net deferred charge—but not both.

[3]This column indicates the deferred items. An increase (I) represents either an increase in a deferred cost (charge) or a decrease in a deferred credit. A decrease (D) denotes either a decrease in a deferred charge or an increase in a deferred credit. The items marked by an asterisk (*) would affect deferred credits.

Part 1 of Exhibit 10-8 disaggregates the pension expense into the three elements of current service cost and the net amortization of the deferred charges and credits.

The second table shows both the *accumulated benefit obligation* and the *projected benefit obligation*. The *accumulated benefit obligation* (an obligation not previously discussed) is similar to the projected benefit obligation. It is the actuarial present

EXHIBIT 10-8
Example of Pension Note Disclosures

1. Pension costs of a corporation's domestic operations aggregated $8,819,000 in 1993:

	(in thousands)
Service cost (benefit earned during period)	$12,636
Interest cost	25,454
Actual return on plan assets	(7,799)
Net amortization of transition items and deferrals	(21,472)
Net periodic pension cost	$ 8,819

2. The actuarial present value of benefit obligations and the funded status for the corporation's domestic plans at December 31, 1993, was

	(in thousands)
Projected benefit obligations:	
Accumulated benefit obligation:	
Vested benefits	$254,200
Nonvested benefits	14,400
	268,600
Projected compensation increases	48,400
Total projected benefit obligations	$317,000
Fair value of plan assets available for benefits, primarily	
U.S. government and equity securities	299,500
Projected benefit obligations in excess of plan assets	$ 17,500
Unrecognized prior service cost (a deferred charge)	(23,300)
Unrecognized net gain (a deferred credit)	7,500
Unamortized transition gain (a deferred credit)	5,200
Net pension liability	$ 6,900

3. The actuarial assumptions used in accounting for the corporation's domestic plans at December 31 were as follows:

Weighted average discount rate	8.5%
Rate of increase in compensation	5.5%
Expected long-term rate of return on plan assets	9.0%

value of all benefits that have been earned. It differs from the projected benefit obligation in that the projected benefit obligation is based on estimated increases in wage and salary levels. Future compensation is relevant to the pension obligation because pension benefits are almost always based on earnings throughout an employee's career. The accumulated benefit obligation, by contrast, incorporates no assumptions as to future rates of compensation. The difference between the two measures, as shown in the second table, is therefore the actuarial value of the benefits attributable to the compensation increases.

Part 2 of Exhibit 10-8 also indicates the investments of the fund, valued at market, that are available for the payment of benefits. Added to, or subtracted from, the investments are the deferred charges and credits. The difference between the accumulated benefit obligation and the net assets available for benefits, plus or minus the deferred items, is the *net pension liability*.[10] This is the amount that will be reported as a long-term liability on the balance sheet.

---

[10]If the net assets available for benefits, plus or minus the deferred items, *exceed* the projected benefit obligation, then the firm would report a net pension *asset*.

The note also sets forth (see part 3 of Exhibit 10-8) key actuarial assumptions: the rate used to discount the benefits to be paid in the future, the rate of compensation increases used to calculate the projected benefit obligation, and the expected rate of return on fund investments.

Pension accounting is another example of a problem that has proved exceedingly intractable. The discussion in this text, as was true of that on income taxes, only hints at the complexity of both the issues and the resultant pronouncement. Moreover, because it proved so difficult to implement, the effective date of *Statement No. 87,* like its counterpart on income taxes, had to be delayed so as to give corporations sufficient time to obtain the required data.

OTHER POSTEMPLOYMENT BENEFITS

Many progressive companies provide retired employees benefits in addition to pensions. The most common of these are health care and life insurance. These benefits present accounting challenges that are exceedingly similar to pensions but even less surmountable. Employees earn these benefits, like wages, salaries, and pensions, during their working years. The payment is deferred, however, until they retire. As with pensions, the eventual cost to the employer will depend on actuarial variables such as employee turnover, mortality rates, and investment earnings. Unlike pension benefits, however, the annual amount to be paid on behalf of each employee is beyond the control of the company. The amount that an employee receives each year in pension benefits is a function of salary earned and number of years of service. By contrast, the annual medical insurance premiums paid on behalf of the employee will depend on the cost of medical services at the time. Technological and scientific changes in the field of health care make it beyond the capabilities of employers to predict reliably the form that health care will take in the distant future, let alone its cost.

In December 1990, the FASB issued *Statement No. 87,* "Employers' Accounting for Postretirement Benefits Other Than Pensions." In this statement the FASB recognizes that postretirement health care and life insurance benefits are conceptually similar to pensions. Therefore, the statement mandates that these benefits, like pensions, be recognized as expenditures as they are earned by a firm's employees during their working years. They can no longer be accounted for on a pay-as-you-go basis. As with pensions, the annual charge must consist of the "normal" costs (service costs, interest cost, and investment income) plus a portion of unamortized "unusual" costs (prior service costs, gains and losses from changes in assumptions, and transition gains and losses).

The FASB's pronouncement on other postemployment benefits is likely to have a more profound impact on the financial statements of corporations than any other statement that it has issued. Some sources have estimated that the change will add $1 trillion dollars of debt to the balance sheets of U.S. companies. The effect will be so great—greater even than that of the statement on pensions—because most companies have not funded their postemployment benefits as they have been earned by their employees. Thus they will have to "book" the entire obligation when the new rules are adopted and will have no assets set aside to offset the new liability.

Summary

In this chapter we have reviewed the accounting for several types of liabilities—bonds, leases, taxes, pensions, and other postemployment benefits. Each of the liabilities is directly related to an expense—interest expense, income tax expense, and pension and other postemployment expense. The amount at which a liability is stated on the balance sheet is tied to the related expense.

In economic substance, the value of a liability, like that of an asset, is the present value of what will have to be paid. Liabilities, like assets, however, are not necessarily reported on the balance sheet at their economic value. "Deferred taxes," for example, need not be discounted to reflect a present value. Bonds, by contrast, are shown at an amount indicative of their present value (although the present value is based on the discount rate that determined the initial value of the bond, not the discount rate that prevails on the balance sheet date).

Some liabilities, such as for pensions and postemployment health benefits, are subject to especially thorny problems of measurement. The amount to be paid is dependent on a number of actuarial variables, such as employees' turnover and mortality, and on earnings on amounts in the fund established to pay the liabilities.

The guiding principle in accounting for liabilities and their related expenses is that both should be recognized when the obligation is first established and the firm has benefited from the cost. Timing of cash payment should not dictate recognition of either the liability or the expense. Nevertheless, of the liabilities discussed in this chapter, those associated with at least four costs—income taxes, leases, pensions, and postemployment benefits—were not until recently even recorded on the balance sheet. Instead, the costs were accounted for on a pay-as-you-go basis. In large part, the reluctance of the accounting profession to require that they be recorded can be ascribed to the need to estimate their values, since the amount of payment cannot always be known until the distant future. Efforts on the part of the standard-setting authorities to mandate timely recognition of these liabilities and expenses have met with considerable resistance and controversy. Nonetheless, the trend in standard setting is clear. Corporations can no longer keep their obligations off the balance sheet. They must bring them into the light.

Exercise for Review and Self-Testing

On January 1, 1992, a company issued bonds. The bonds had a coupon rate of 14 percent, but they were issued at a price that provided bondholders a return of only 12 percent. The bonds were to mature in 20 years.

1. For each $1,000 bond, how much interest will the company be required to pay each six months?
2. For each $1,000 bond held, how much interest would a bondholder expect to receive semiannually based on the prevailing yields of comparable securities?
3. What is the difference between the two amounts?
4. What is the present value of the difference based on the effective yield rate (compounded semiannually) and the number of periods until maturity?
5. What is the premium or discount at which the bond will be issued? What is the issue price of each $1,000 bond?
6. What is the interest, based on the effective yield rate, that the company should record as an expense when, on June 30, 1992, it is required to make the first interest payment?

7. What is the actual required payment?
8. What is the difference between the interest expense and the required payment? By how much should the recorded value of the bond premium be reduced?
9. What is the effective liability of the company, per bond, on July 1, 1992?
10. What is the interest expense that the company should record on December 31, 1992, when it is required to make its second payment of interest?

Questions for Review and Discussion

1. A friend recently purchased $10,000 of AT&T bonds. The company is considered as financially sound as any major U.S. corporation. The bonds are scheduled to mature in 30 years, but your friend intends to sell them within two or three years to provide funds for her child's education. She wants a ''safe'' investment. She decided not to purchase the common stock of the same company because she viewed it as too risky. Do you think she made a wise decision? Would she have been better off buying AT&T bonds that matured in only three years? Explain.

2. The account ''discount on bonds payable'' ordinarily has a debit balance. It has sometimes been argued that bond discount, like most other accounts which have debit balances, should be reported as an asset rather than as *contra* (as an adjustment) to a long-term liability. Considering the nature of bond discounts, do you agree?

3. For many years there has been controversy over the accounting for gains and losses that may arise when a company repurchases or redeems its own bonds at a price different from the value at which they are recorded on its books. Why have some financial observers charged that major corporations have engaged in repurchases or redemptions to give an artificial boost to earnings? How is this possible?

4. Why are some lease arrangements accounted for as if they were installment purchases? Why do some accountants believe that almost all long-term noncancelable lease agreements should be *capitalized* (i.e., assets and corresponding liabilities recorded) on the balance sheet? Why might a company believe that it is able to present a more favorable balance sheet by leasing, rather than purchasing, plant or equipment?

5. Why might a company report a tax expense on its income statement that is greater or less than the required tax payment indicated on its income tax return?

6. Why do some financial experts contend that interperiod tax allocation results in an overstatement of liabilities, in that amounts that may never have to be paid are included among reported obligations?

7. Distinguish between a defined *contribution* and a defined *benefit* pension plan. Why do defined benefit plans present the more difficult accounting issues?

8. What are the three elements of *ongoing* pension expense? What other elements of cost are incorporated into a firm's total pension expense?

9. As a consequence of a rapid increase in stock prices, the return on investment of a pension fund greatly exceeds expectations. How would the rise in the value of the fund assets affect the pension expense to be reported by the employer in the year of the increase? In subsequent years?

10. Why do postemployment benefits, such as life and health insurance, present virtually the same accounting problems as pension benefits? Why might many companies have to report a net liability for postemployment benefits that exceeds that for pension benefits?

11. What is a leveraged buyout? What are ''junk bonds''?

Problems

1. *The amount for which a bond is issued, as well as subsequent charges to income, is dependent upon the prevailing yield rate at the time of issue.*

   On January 2, 1992, the Green Company issued 12 percent coupon bonds at a price that provided purchasers a yield of 10 percent. The bonds paid interest on June 30 and December 31 and were scheduled to mature on December 31, 1993.
   a. Record the sale of a single $1,000 bond.
   b. Determine interest expense for each of the four periods and record the first payment of interest.
   c. Record the redemption of the bond (including final interest payment).

2. *The prices at which outstanding bonds can be resold fluctuate with changes in the prevailing rates of interest.*

   The Baltimore Co. issued at par (i.e., at a price of $100) $10 million in 8 percent, 20-year coupon bonds. Interest is payable semiannually.
   a. Within two years, prevailing interest rates increased to 10 percent. At what price could a bondholder sell a single $1,000 bond in the open market?
   b. By the fourth year, prevailing interest rates had increased to 12 percent. At what price could a bondholder now sell a single $1,000 bond?
   c. What impact would the increase in prevailing interest rates have upon the reported interest expense of the Baltimore Co.?
   d. "In comparison with common stocks, bonds provide a relatively risk-free investment." Do you agree?

3. *Call provisions may establish a ceiling on the prices at which outstanding bonds are traded.*

   In 1980 the Universal Drilling Co. issued $100,000 of 6 percent, 30-year bonds. The bond indentures provided that the company could redeem the bonds any time after 1990 at a price of $102.

   In 1995, with 15 years remaining until maturity, the company decided to retire the bonds. Since the prevailing interest rate was 8 percent, the company repurchased the bonds in the open market at the prevailing price.
   a. Determine the price that the company would have to pay for the bonds.
   b. Assume instead that the prevailing annual interest rate in 1995 was 4 percent. Determine the price that the company would have to pay for the bonds. Be sure to consider the maximum price at which the bonds are likely to trade in light of the call provision.

4. *Years to maturity is a primary influence on bond value—but only up to a point.* (This problem is intended for solution using an electronic spreadsheet.)

   As the treasurer of a company, you are estimating the amount of cash your firm will receive from a pending issue of 30-year bonds. The bonds will bear a coupon rate of 9 percent and will pay interest semiannually. The issue price of the bonds will depend on prevailing yields on the date the bonds are actually issued.
   a. Prepare a table in which you indicate the issue price of each $1,000 bond, assuming the following yield rates: 8.8 percent; 8.9 percent; 9.0 percent; 9.1 percent; 9.2 percent.
   b. Assume instead that the bonds (with the coupon rate of 9 percent) are to be issued to yield 8.8 percent.
      (1) Determine the issue price, assuming the following maturities: 10 years, 20 years, 50 years, 100 years.

(2) Comment on why years to maturity has a critical impact on issue price (or bond value)—but only up to a point. As the number of years increases, the significance of years to maturity diminishes.

5. *Bonds may also be issued between interest dates, and, although not specifically discussed in the text, the accounting problems associated with such issues are not overly complex.*

    The city of Highland Hills on January 31, 1992, issues 6 percent coupon bonds to mature in 20 years. The bonds are sold, at par, to yield 6 percent. The bonds require the payment of interest on June 30 and December 31.

    a. What will be the required interest payment on June 30, 1992, on a single $1,000-denomination bond? (All coupons, including the first, require the payment of the same amount of interest.)
    b. Since the bondholder on June 30 has held the bond for only five months, how much interest would he have earned (i.e., actually "deserve" to receive)?
    c. Suppose the bondholder agreed to *advance* the company the portion of the first interest payment that he did not actually earn. How much would he advance the company?
    d. Prepare a journal entry to record the issue of one bond, assuming that the company received the principal plus the unearned portion of the first interest payment.
    e. Prepare a journal entry to record the first interest payment. The interest expense should represent the cost of borrowing funds only for the period during which the company had the use of such funds.

6. *Principles of accounting for financial reporting may not be appropriate for managerial decisions.*

    In January 1967, the Bowman Co. issued $100,000 of 6 percent, 30-year coupon bonds. The indentures stipulate that the company has the right to *call* (redeem) the bonds at a price of $103 any time after the bonds have been outstanding for 10 years. In 1990 the bonds were stated on the company's books at a value of $98,300; there was a reported discount of $1,700.

    In January 1992, when five years remained until maturity, the company controller debated whether or not the company should refund the entire bond issue—that is, whether it should redeem the bonds and reborrow the entire cost of redemption. The controller determined that the company could acquire the entire $103,000 necessary to call the outstanding issue by issuing, at par, bonds that paid interest at an annual rate of 5 percent and matured in five years.

    The company uses a discount rate of 8 percent to evaluate all financial opportunities.

    a. Prepare a journal entry to record the redemption of the bonds.
    b. Because the company would have to report a loss on the redemption of the bonds, the controller decided against redeeming the bonds. Do you agree with the decision? (*Hint:* Identify all cash receipts and disbursements that would result in the next five years—10 semiannual periods—under both of the alternatives. Determine their present value to the company.)

7. *The straight-line method of bond amortization distorts the cost of borrowing.*

    In the past, companies wishing to avoid the complexities of the *effective interest* means of accounting for bond premium or discount used the *straight-line* amortization method.

    Suppose a company issues 12 percent coupon bonds at a price that will provide a return to the bondholders of 10 percent. The bonds will mature in 20 years.

    a. Prepare a journal entry to record the issue of a single $1,000 bond.

b. Prepare journal entries to record both the *first* and the *last* payments of interest. Assume first that the company uses the effective interest method and second the straight-line method. Be sure to determine the *effective* liability outstanding at the *start* of each of the periods.

c. Determine the effective rate of interest recorded as an expense under each of the two methods for both the first and the last payments. That is, express the recorded interest expense as a percentage of the reported effective liability (bonds payable plus unamortized premium).

8. *By redeeming its debt at a "bargain" price, a firm is able to realize a substantial gain.*

Suppose the financial statements of a company contained the following note:

> During 1993 [the company] purchased $11.6 million principal amount of its 4½% convertible debentures due 2020 at a price of $550 each under a tender offer. The resulting net gain was $2.6 million after related deferred federal income taxes of $2.4 million.

a. The firm is financially sound. Why do you suspect that it is able to redeem its outstanding debt at a "bargain" price?

b. The note makes reference to *deferred* federal income taxes. What does the use of the term *deferred* suggest about the provisions of the tax laws pertaining to gains on the redemption of bonds?

c. Suppose that the company is unable to pay off its debt without reducing the scale of its operations. It therefore has to reborrow the amount that it paid to the holders of the 4½ percent debentures. How do you think the rate of interest on the new debt would compare with that on the old (much higher, much lower, etc.)? Will the company really be better off as a consequence of having "refunded" (paid off and reborrowed) its debt? What is the real nature of the gain of $5 million (before taxes)? When did the gain really occur—at the time of refunding or in the several previous accounting periods?

9. *An important issue facing banks and other financial institutions is whether they should give immediate accounting recognition to unfavorable modifications in the terms of debt arrangements.*

A bank acquired $1 million of the bonds of Gotham City. The bonds paid interest at a rate of 10 percent and were sold to yield 10 percent (that is, they were sold "at par"). The bonds were to mature in five years.

Shortly after the bank made its investment, Gotham City faced a fiscal crisis. After a series of complex legal maneuvers, it was able to "restructure" its debt. The city was permitted to extend the maturity of the debt from five years to ten years and to reduce the rate of interest paid from 10 percent to 6 percent. The amount of principal owed (the face value of the bonds) was to remain unchanged.

a. What is the value to the bank of its Gotham City bonds immediately following the restructuring? That is, what is the present value, discounted at the prevailing yield rate of 10 percent per year (5 percent per period), of the anticipated payment of $1 million in principal and the anticipated 20 semiannual payments of $30,000 in interest?

b. Do you think that the bank should "write down" the carrying value of the bonds from $1 million to the amount determined in part (a) and thereby recognize an immediate loss? If it did, what would be the impact on earnings of the current year and future years as compared with that if it did not? How would total earnings, over the remaining life of the issue, be affected by a decision to recognize an immediate loss?

(*Note:* The question of how to account for "restructured debt," although not specifically dealt with in the text, was an important issue in the mid-1970s as a consequence of fiscal crises that faced New York City as well as a large number of firms in the real estate industry. The FASB, in *Statement No. 15,* ruled that in situations similar to the one described in this problem no write-down would be required. However, in cases where total anticipated receipts of both principal and interest, without regard to their *present* value, are less than the carrying value of the debt, an immediate loss would have to be recognized.)

10. *Bonds can provide substantial returns to their holders—even if they pay zero interest.*

    The Wall Street Journal reported that PepsiCo, Inc., planned "to take out a 'loan' on which it won't have to pay any interest for 30 years." According to the *Journal,* the company would issue bonds that would pay no annual interest. Instead the bonds, known as "zero coupon" securities, would be sold at a "deep discount" from face value and would then be redeemed at the full amount upon maturity. The difference between the two would be the investors' return.

    The *Journal* indicated that PepsiCo would issue $25 million of the new securities. Initially, each bond with a face value of $1,000 would be priced at $270.

    a. Suppose that a 30-year bond was priced to sell for $270. What would be the effective percentage yield (within 1 percent) to the purchaser? (To be able to make use of the tables in the Appendix, assume that interest is compounded annually rather than semiannually).

    b. What would be the primary advantage to the borrower in issuing zero coupon bonds?

    c. Suppose, as in part (a), that a bond was issued for $270. What journal entry would you propose that the firm make to record

       (1) Issuance of the bond?

       (2) First-year interest expense?

       (3) Second-year interest expense?

11. *Principles of liability valuation are essential to assessing the assets of thrifts (savings and loan associations) as well as financial institutions in general.*

    A letter to *The Wall Street Journal* stated,

    > "Threat to Thrifts" [a previous article] skirts the real, present, financial plight of not only thrifts but of banking institutions in general. So-called "net worth" is only an illusion, a distortion of reality resulting from the treatment of 8% mortgage loans with 15 years amortization as being worth the principal balance due on them rather than the market value, in today's 15% mortgage market, of less than 70% of the unpaid balance. (The Penn Central also had an impressive net worth prior to its bankruptcy.)

    The author went on to suggest that a more meaningful measure of the assets (i.e., the mortgage loans outstanding) of a thrift institution would be their current market values.

    Suppose that a thrift institution issued a 30-year mortgage loan of $100,000 at an annual rate of interest of 8 percent. Annual payments on the loan were $8,883. (Although mortgage notes often require monthly payments, assume for convenience in this problem that only one payment per year is required.) Each yearly payment would contain an element of interest (8 percent of the remaining loan balance) and an element of principal.

    a. What would be the "book value" (i.e., the remaining principal balance) of the loan after 15 years?

    b. What would be the most likely market value of the loan, assuming that prevailing interest rates on mortgage loans had increased to 15 percent?

    c. Is the letter writer correct in asserting that market value is likely to be less than 70 percent of the book value (unpaid principal balance)?

12. *The distinction, in economic substance, between an installment purchase and a financial lease may be trivial.*

The covenants incorporated into the outstanding bonds of the Eastern Machine Co. stipulate the maximum amount of debt that the company can incur. The company wishes to expand its plant and purchase new equipment but has insufficient funds to purchase the equipment outright. Since the company is prohibited by the existing covenants from borrowing the needed funds, its controller has suggested that the firm arrange for the manufacturer of the equipment to sell the equipment to a lending institution. The lending institution would, in turn, lease the machine to the company. The lending institution would provide no maintenance or related services, and the company would have responsibility for insuring the equipment. Upon the expiration of the lease, the company would have the option of purchasing the equipment. If the company were to acquire the equipment outright, its cost would be $500,000. If it were to borrow the funds, it would be required to pay interest at the rate of 8 percent per year. The financial institution has agreed to a noncancelable lease with a term of 15 years, a term corresponding to the useful life of the equipment.

a. If the company decides to lease the equipment, what would be the most probable annual rental payments?

b. How do you suspect the controller intends to account for the acquisition of the equipment? What journal entries do you think she would propose at the time the equipment is acquired? At the time the first payment of rent is made?

c. Do the proposals of the controller in your opinion reflect the substance of the transaction? Are they in accord with provisions of the Financial Accounting Standards Board? What alternative journal entries would you propose?

13. *Ownership arrangements that are very different in form may be very similar in economic substance.*

Deception, Inc., currently has a loan outstanding from the Gibraltar Insurance Co. that requires that Deception, Inc., maintain a "debt-to-equity ratio" no greater than 1:1. That is, the balance in all liability accounts can be no greater than that in the capital stock and retained earnings accounts. As of December 31, Deception, Inc., had total liabilities of $3 million and total capital stock and retained earnings of $3,150,000.

The vice-president of production of Deception, Inc., has proposed that the company purchase new equipment that would cost $257,710. The equipment would have a three-year useful life and no salvage value and during its life would allow for substantial cost savings to the company. Aware that the company is short of cash, the vice-president arranged with the manufacturer of the equipment to give a three-year note for the purchase price. Interest would be at the rate of 8 percent on the unpaid balance. Payments would be made at the end of each of the three years as follows:

Year	Remaining Balance	Payment of Interest at 8%	Payment of Principal	Total Payment
1	$257,710	$20,617	$ 79,383	$100,000
2	178,327	14,266	85,734	100,000
3	92,593	7,407	92,593	100,000
			$257,710	

When the company controller was informed of the proposed purchase, he advised the vice-president that the additional debt would increase the firm's debt-to-equity ratio above the maximum permitted in its loan agreement with Gibraltar Insurance.

As an alternative, he recommended an arrangement whereby Deception, Inc., would *lease* the new equipment from the manufacturer. The lease could not be canceled and would be for a term of three years. Annual rent would be $100,000, but Deception, Inc., would have to pay all maintenance and insurance costs. At the expiration of the lease, Deception, Inc., would have an option to purchase the machine for $1.

a. Prepare all journal entries that would be required on the books of Deception, Inc., if it agreed to *purchase* the machine and issued the note for $257,710. The company records depreciation on a straight-line basis.

b. Prepare all journal entries that would be required if the firm agreed to *lease* the machine and accounted for it as an operating lease.

c. What are the total charges associated with the acquisition of the machine under each of the two alternatives?

d. Comment on the difference, if any, in the *substance* of the two transactions. Viewing the transactions from the point of view of Gibraltar Insurance Co., how would you propose that the firm record the transaction if it decided to *lease* the equipment? What changes would you make to the entries in part (a) above?

14. *Pronouncements of the FASB are intended to prevent firms from avoiding balance sheet disclosure of financial obligations by leasing rather than purchasing long-lived assets.*

The managers of Business Services, Inc., are debating whether to buy or to rent a computer. A computer manufacturer has offered the company the opportunity to lease a machine for $100,000 per year over a period of 15 years. Alternatively, the company would purchase the machine outright and could borrow the purchase price from an insurance company at an annual rate of 10 percent. The note to the insurance company would be repaid in 15 equal installments, each installment representing both a repayment of principal and a payment of interest on the unpaid balance.

Costs of operating the equipment would be the same under either alternative; the salvage value after 15 years would be negligible.

Currently the company has total assets of $5 million, total liabilities of $2 million, and total owners' equity of $3 million.

a. What is the maximum that the company should be willing to pay to purchase the machine?

b. Suppose that the company paid the maximum amount. Compare total expenses that would be reported during the first year if the company purchased the machine as opposed to leasing it, assuming that it accounts for the transaction as an operating lease (although under current FASB pronouncements the lease would satisfy the criteria of a capital lease). The company uses the straight-line method of depreciation.

c. Determine the ratio of total debt to total owners' equity under each of the alternatives immediately upon acquisition of the asset (prior to giving effect to first-year expenses).

15. *With the most commonly used methods of depreciation, capitalized leases may result in expenses that decline over the life of the lease.* (This problem is intended for solution using an electronic spreadsheet.)

A company leases equipment that has a market value of $800,000. The term of the lease is 10 years, which is also the useful life of the equipment. Annual lease payments are to be based on an implicit interest rate of 12 percent. At the end of the period, the company will have the option to acquire the equipment for a nominal amount.

a. Determine the annual lease payments.
b. Prepare a schedule in which you show
   (1) "Loan" balance at start of year
   (2) Interest expense for year
   (3) Reduction of principal
   (4) Amortization of leasehold (on a straight-line basis)
   (5) Total expense for year
c. Compute total expense for the entire 10-year period. How does it compare with what the total expense would have been had the lease been accounted for as an *operating* lease?
d. Comment on the trend over the 10-year period in annual expenses (interest plus amortization). Is there a depreciation method that would result in level annual expenses? Explain.

16. *The perceptive financial analyst would adjust for differences between companies relating to the means of financing and accounting for long-term assets and obligations.*

As a financial analyst, you are reviewing the 1993 annual reports of two discount department store firms. The reports indicate that one of the two companies owns all its stores; the other leases them. A footnote to the financial statements of the firm that leases contains the following information:

The company operates principally in leased premises. The terms of the leases range from 10 to 20 years. The leases meet the criteria of noncapitalized leases (operating leases) as defined by the Financial Accounting Standards Board and accordingly have not been included among long-term liabilities. Total minimum rental commitments are as follows (in thousands):

1994–1998	$30,000 per year
1999–2008	$25,000 per year
2009–2013	$10,000 per year

An additional note to the financial statements indicates that the company's cost of borrowing is 12 percent.

What adjustments to the assets and liabilities of the firm that leases its stores would make its financial reports comparable to those of the firm that owns the stores?

17. *The leasing note of K Mart highlights the difference between capital and operating leases.*
The following is adapted from the notes of K Mart (1987):

Description of Leasing Arrangements

The company conducts operations primarily in leased facilities. K Mart store leases are generally for terms of 25 years with multiple five-year renewal options which allow the company the option to extend the life of the lease up to 50 years beyond the initial noncancelable term. The majority of specialty retail units are leased generally for terms varying from 5 to 25 years with varying renewal options. Certain leases provide for additional rental payments based on a percent of sales in excess of a specified base. Also, certain leases provide for the payment by the lessee of executory costs (taxes, maintenance and insurance). Some selling space has been sublet to other retailers in certain of the company's leased facilities.

Lease Commitments

Future minimum lease payments with respect to capital and operating leases are

| | Minimum Lease Payments (in millions) ||
	Capital	Operating
Fiscal year		
1988	$ 334	$ 365
1989	328	355
1990	324	343
1991	321	329
1992	312	310
Later years	3,110	2,738
Total minimum lease payments	4,729	4,440
Less: Minimum sublease rental income		(279)
Net minimum lease payments	$4,729	$4,161
Less:		
Estimated executory costs	(1,429)	
Amount representing interest	(1,658)	
Obligations under capital leases, of which $85 million is due within one year	$1,642	

Reconciliation of Capital Lease Information

The impact of recording amortization and interest expense versus rent expense on capital leases in millions is as follows:

	1987
Amortization of capital lease property	$ 97
Interest expense related to obligations under capital leases	174
Amounts charged to earnings	271
Related minimum lease payments net of executory costs	(254)
Excess of amounts charged over related minimum lease payments	$ 17

a. How much debt owing to capital leases is presently recorded on the balance sheet as lease liabilities? Explain. What is meant by ''amount representing interest'' in the schedule of lease commitments?

b. Suppose that the firm were to capitalize all operating leases. How much additional debt would that add to the K Mart balance sheet? Assume a discount rate of 12 percent and that the $2,738 in payments for ''later years'' will be spread evenly ($273.8 per year) over a period of 10 years starting in 1993.

c. Explain each of the lines in the schedule ''Reconciliation of Capital Lease Information.''

18. *By the time an asset is fully depreciated, the balance in the deferred tax account related to that asset should be reduced to zero.*

The Frost Co. purchased equipment in 1992 at a cost of $100,000. The equipment had an estimated useful life of four years with zero salvage value. The company elected to use straight-line depreciation for general reporting purposes but decided to take advantage of the provisions of the tax code which permit use of the 200 percent declining balance method.

In each of the four years from 1992 through 1995 the company had earnings of $50,000, before both depreciation on the equipment and taxes. The tax rate is 40 percent.

a. Determine taxable income and taxes for each of the four years. Assume that the asset is depreciated to zero in the fourth year.

b. Determine reported tax expense and net income for each of the four years, assuming that tax expense is based on reported rather than taxable income.

c. Prepare journal entries to give effect to the allocation of taxes for each of the four years. Assume that all taxes are paid in the year in which they are incurred. Determine, and keep track of, the year-end balances in the deferred taxes account.

19. *As long as a company continues to expand, the balance in its deferred tax liability account will continue to increase.*

A company made purchases of fixed assets as follows (in millions):

Year	
1	$ 60
2	90
3	120
4	120
5	0
6	0
7	0

The useful lives of all assets are four years. They have no residual value. The income tax rate is 40 percent.

The company uses the straight-line method of depreciation for reporting purposes and the double declining balance method for tax purposes.

a. Determine, for each of the seven years, total depreciation that would be reported on the financial statements and that which would be deductible for tax purposes. Indicate the difference each year.

b. Determine the taxes that would be *saved* (postponed) or would have to be *repaid* during each of the seven years.

c. Determine the amount that would be reported as a deferred tax liability each year.

d. Suppose that the firm continued to increase its purchases of fixed assets after the third year. What would be the effect on the deferred tax liability? Why do you suppose some managers and accountants are opposed to interperiod tax allocation?

20. *A liability for taxes that will have to be paid in the future should be established whenever a company is permitted to recognize revenue for financial reporting purposes in one period and for tax purposes in a later period.*

The Arizona Land Co. was organized on January 1, 1992. The corporation issued 10,000 shares of common stock for $1 million cash. The company elected to recognize revenue on the installment basis (i.e., upon collection of cash) for income tax purposes but at time of sale for general accounting and reporting purposes.

In 1992 the company purchased a parcel of land for $600,000 cash. In the same year it sold the land for $1 million; the buyer made a down payment of $500,000 and paid the balance in 1993.

In 1993 the company purchased another parcel of land for $1.8 million cash and sold it for $2 million. The buyer paid the entire amount in cash at the end of sale.

The effective tax rate is 40 percent. The company pays all taxes in the year to which they are applicable. The company allocates taxes as appropriate. Prepare a statement of income and a balance sheet for 1992 and 1993.

21. *Information about a corporation's pension costs and obligations is to be found in notes, not the income statement or the balance sheet.*

The following are excerpts from the pension note of Georgia-Pacific Corporation. Observe how the company, which has numerous independent plans, has elected to combine them. This form of display, while not typical, is not uncommon.

Effective January 1, 1986, the Corporation adopted Statement of Financial Accounting Standards No. 87. This change in accounting principle reduced pension expense by approximately $22 million before income taxes in 1986, principally due to the initial excess of plan assets over the projected benefit obligation being amortized over the estimated remaining service periods from 10 to 17 years.

| | Year Ended December 31, 1987 | |
| | Plans Having Assets in Excess of Accumulated Benefits | Plans Having Accumulated Benefits in Excess of Assets |
	(in millions)	
Accumulated benefits obligation		
Vested portion	$308	$ 20
Nonvested portion	30	2
	338	22
Effects of projected future compensation		
levels	38	5
Projected benefit obligation	376	27
Plan assets at fair value	515	7
Plan assets in excess of (less than)		
projected benefit obligation	139	(20)
Unrecognized net (gain) loss	(11)	2
Unrecognized prior service cost	12	3
Unrecognized net (gain) loss from		
initial application of SFAS No. 87	(114)	1
Prepaid (accrued) pension cost		
at December 31	$ 26	$(15)
Service cost of benefits earned	$ 30	$ 22
Interest cost on projected benefit		
obligation	32	26
Actual return on plan assets	(10)	(79)
Net amortization and deferral	(43)	38
	$ 9	$ 7

The discount rates and rates of increase in future compensation levels used in determining the projected benefit obligation were, respectively, 9.0% and 6.0%.

The expected long-term rate of return on plan assets used in determining net periodic pension cost was increased to 8.5% in 1987, from 7.5% in 1986. The increase reduced 1987 pension expense by approximately $5 million.

a. Would Georgia-Pacific report a net pension asset or liability on its balance sheet? In what amount?

b. Has the company's actuarial experience been better or worse than anticipated, or has the company made actuarial changes that increased or decreased its projected benefit obligation? Explain.

c. Did Georgia-Pacific's projected benefit obligation increase or decrease as a result of the company's having adopted *Statement No. 87?* How can you tell?

d. What was the amount of the pension benefits earned by employees in 1987 attributable to their service of that year?

e. By how much does the company expect wages and salaries to increase each year in the future?

22. *Some, but not all, changes in an employer's pension obligation are incorporated into pension expense.*

   In reviewing your company's earnings forecast, you became aware of several factors that may influence pension costs. Indicate as best you can from the information provided how each of the following is likely to affect *reported* pension expense. The company maintains a defined benefit plan. It amortizes deferred pension debits and credits over 10 years.

   a. Employees will earn benefits of $20 million attributable to service of the current year. The company plans to contribute only $15 million to the pension fund.

   b. The company expects to improve its plan. The change will increase the plan's projected benefit obligation attributable to prior employee service by $25 million.

   c. The company will earn $2 million on pension investments during the year (as previously projected).

   d. The company will change its actuarial assumptions as to investment earnings and employee turnover. The change will decrease its projected benefit obligation by $6 million.

23. *This problem tests and reviews the terminology used in a typical pension footnote.*

   The information that follows was excerpted from the pension note of Fleming Companies, a food distribution firm whose shares are traded on the New York Stock Exchange.

	Dec. 26, 1987	Dec. 27, 1986
	(in thousands)	
Accumulated benefit obligation, including vested benefits of $46,556 and $45,696	$50,461	$50,647
Projected benefit obligation	$66,616	$67,229
Plan assets at fair value	61,673	72,597
Unfunded projected benefit obligation	4,943	4,632
Unrecognized net asset being recognized primarily over eight years	4,123	5,383
Unrecognized net loss	(3,207)	(6,753)
Unfunded accrued pension expense included in current liabilities	$ 5,859	$ 3,262
Net pension expense included the following components:		
Service cost	$ 3,871	$ 2,989
Interest cost	6,050	5,121
Actual return on plan assets	(1,651)	(6,067)
Net amortization and deferral	(5,386)	463
	$ 2,884	$ 2,506
Weighted average discount rate	9.5%	9.0%
Rate of increase of future compensation levels	6.5%	6.5%
Long-term rate of return on assets	10.0%	9.0%

a. Does the information in the note relate to a defined benefit plan or a defined contribution plan? Explain.

b. What is represented by the difference between the total accumulated benefit obligation of $50,461 and the share of the obligation comprising vested benefits ($46,556)?

c. What is represented by the difference between the accumulated benefit obligation of $50,461 and the projected benefit obligation of $66,616?

d. What is the "unrecognized net loss" of $3,207? Why is it *subtracted* from the unfunded projected benefit obligation in arriving at the net unfunded accrued pension expense?

e. What is the unrecognized net asset of $4,123? Why is it *added* to the unfunded projected benefit obligation in arriving at the net unfunded accrued pension expense?

f. What would be the impact on both the accumulated benefit obligation and the projected benefit obligation of the increase in 1987 in
   (1) The weighted average discount rate?
   (2) The long-term rate of return on assets?

24. *Why would an individual company, and indeed the nation at large, adopt an accounting rule that would severely diminish its net worth?*

On November 21, 1988, the LTV Corporation announced that it would take a special charge of $2.26 billion to reflect estimated costs of health and insurance benefits promised to retirees. The company indicated that it was taking the charge in anticipation of a rule change by the Financial Accounting Standards Board that would require companies to include postemployment obligations on their balance sheets. According to *The New York Times*,[11]

> Instead of forcing companies to recognize all the costs immediately as LTV has done, the standards board will permit companies to average the costs over 15 years. Still, many companies have argued that the rule is too drastic and will bite heavily into the net worth of the nation's industrial base.

a. In the year it recorded the charge for postemployment benefits, LTV was in bankruptcy proceedings and attempting to renegotiate its debt with its creditors. It expected to emerge from the proceedings in reorganized form and to be able to continue operations. Why do you think that LTV voluntarily recorded an obligation when generally accepted accounting principles did not require it to do so?

b. *The New York Times* article implies that the FASB's standard on postemployment benefits may severely reduce the nation's industrial net worth. In what way will the nation be worse off as a consequence of the new accounting rule?

Solutions to Exercise for Review and Self-Testing

1. 7 percent (½ of 14%) of $1,000, or $70 interest payable each six months.
2. 6 percent (½ of 12%) of $1,000, or $60 interest expected each six months.
3. $10 difference.
4. The present value of an annuity of $10 for 40 semiannual periods at a discount rate of 6 percent is, based on Table 4 in the Appendix,

$$\$10 \times 15.0463 = \$150.46$$

[11]*New York Times*, November 22, 1988, p. 29.

5. Each bond will be issued at a premium of $150.46 and at a total price of $1,150.46.
6. 6 percent of $1,150.46, or $69.03.
7. $70 (see part 1).
8. $70.00 − $69.03 = 97 cents amortization of bond premium.
9. $1,150.46 − $.97 = $1,149.49 effective bond liability on July 1, 1992.
10. 6 percent of 1,149.49, or $68.97 interest expense.

11

Transactions Between a Firm and Its Owners

This chapter is the first of two that are addressed primarily to transactions between a firm and its owners. In this chapter we shall compare partnerships with corporations and identify the issues that are unique to partnerships. We shall also consider the characteristics of common and preferred stock and the problems and issues of accounting for transactions involving those instruments of ownership.

PROPRIETORSHIPS AND PARTNERSHIPS

There are three major types of business enterprises: the individual proprietorship, the partnership, and the corporation. The *proprietorship* is a business firm owned by a single party. The *partnership* is one owned by two or more parties. The *corporation* is a separate legal entity that operates under a grant of authority from a state or other governmental body and is owned by one or more stockholders.

The proprietorship is far and away the most common type of business in the United States. Indeed, proprietorships compose approximately 70 percent of the over 16 million enterprises. Partnerships account for about 10 percent and corporations 20 percent. However, proprietorships generate only 7 percent of business receipts and partnerships only 4 percent. Corporations generate the remaining 89 percent. Moreover, the largest .3 percent of corporations generates approximately 62 percent of corporate business receipts.

No Limits on Size

Corporations are often thought of as large enterprises, proprietorships and partnerships as small. While it is true that most proprietorships and partnerships are small businesses, *most* corporations are also relatively small, often family-owned firms. The corporation is associated with bigness because most large businesses—those that account for the major part of industrial output—are corporations. Nevertheless, many large enterprises are organized as partnerships. Service organizations such as brokerage firms and CPA firms may be organized as partnerships even though they generate hundreds of millions of dollars in annual revenues.

No Limits on Owner Liability

Proprietorships and partnerships are, in a legal sense, extensions of their owners. One or more parties simply establish a business. They purchase or rent whatever equipment or space is needed, acquire supplies or inventory, and obtain any local operating licenses that might be required. No formal charter or state certificates are required. If the business is to be operated as a partnership, it is generally wise to have an attorney draw up a partnership agreement that specifies the rights and obligations of each partner—how profits will be distributed, who will perform what services, how much each partner must contribute initially, what rights of survivorship will accrue to each partner's estate, what limitations there will be upon sale of a partner's interest in the business. But a partnership agreement is for the protection of the individual partners; it is not ordinarily required by law.

A proprietor, as well as each partner of a partnership, is usually personally responsible for all obligations of his or her business. If the enterprise suffers losses, the owners are jointly and severably responsible for all debts incurred. Partners will generally be held liable not only for their own individual shares of the debts but, should their fellow partners be unable to meet their shares of the claims against the business, for the debts of those partners as well. As a consequence, few investors are as willing to purchase an equity interest in a partnership as they might be to purchase one in a corporation. In the event the partnership is liquidated and fellow partners are unable to meet their share of obligations, the personal assets of the investors might be subject to the claims of creditors. Their assets at risk are unlimited, extending beyond their orginal investment.

There are no limits to the number of parties who might compose a partnership. Because of the extended liability to which each partner is subject, most partnerships are small—two or three members. However, many partnerships are considerably larger. Some CPA firms that are organized as partnerships have *thousands* of partners who are located throughout the world.

Tax Liabilities

Neither proprietorships nor partnerships are subject to federal or state taxes on income. Instead, the tax is assessed on the individual owners. If the organization is a partnership, then each partner is taxed on his or her own share of partnership earnings. The rate of tax is determined by the tax bracket in which the individual partner falls after taking into account earnings from nonpartnership sources. Each partner is taxed on his or her individual share of the entire earnings of the partnership, not just on withdrawals from the business. Thus, especially if the partnership requires capital for expansion, a partner may be taxed on earnings that are retained in the business and are not available for his or her discretionary use, as well as on funds actually taken from the business.

CORPORATIONS

A Legal "Person"

A corporation, by contrast, is a legal entity separate and distinct from its owners. It is a legal "person" created by the state. A corporation is owned by its stockholders, but its stockholders are not compelled to take an active role in its management. In many corporations there is a distinct separation of ownership and operating control, with managers typically holding only a small fraction of total shares outstanding. A corporation has an indefinite life. It continues in existence regardless of the personal fortunes of its owners. Its owners are commonly free to transfer or sell their shares of stock to anyone they wish.

Corporations, unlike proprietorships or partnerships, are creatures of the state. A corporation has the right to own property in its own name, and it can sue or be sued. Upon its formation, it must be chartered by the state. Although at one time charters were granted only upon special acts of the legislature, today they are routinely issued upon submission of certificates of incorporation and supplementary application forms, and payment of necessary fees. The certificate of incorporation specifies the name of the proposed corporation, its purposes (most certificates of incorporation are drawn so as to allow the company to engage in an unlimited range of business activities), the number of shares authorized to be issued, and the number of directors.

Once the charter has been issued, the corporation has to adopt formal bylaws, which govern a number of critical areas of operation. They cover such matters as the issuance and transfer of stock and the conduct of meetings of directors and stockholders.

Limited Liability

The single most significant distinction between corporations and proprietorships or partnerships is that the liability of stockholders of a corporation is limited to the amount of their initial investment in the company, whereas that of the owners of proprietorships or partnerships is unlimited. With few exceptions, the maximum loss that a stockholder can sustain on the purchase of an interest in a corporation is the amount of his or her initial investment. Should the corporation fail, creditors can avail themselves of only the assets of the corporation: they cannot seek redress against the personal assets of the individual stockholders. Only in rare circumstances—the involvement of corporate stockholders in fraud, for example—is it possible for creditors or others who may have judgments against the corporation to "pierce the corporate veil" and bring a successful legal action against the individual stockholders. Because it is able to protect investors against unlimited loss, the corporation is a vehicle that is well suited to raise large amounts of capital. Investors may be willing to purchase an ownership interest in a company knowing that they can share in the gains of the company to an unlimited extent but that their losses will be limited by the amount of their direct contributions. They need not be overly concerned with the day-to-day operations of their business, since neither the managers nor their fellow owners can so mismanage the business as to put their personal assets in jeopardy.

Tax Liabilities

Corporations, like other legal persons, are subject to both federal and state income taxes. Earnings of a corporation are taxed regardless of whether or not they are distributed to its owners, albeit at rates different from those of individuals. The individual owners of the corporation, unlike those of a partnership, are not taxed on their shares of the earnings that are retained in the business; they are, however, taxed on the earnings when corporate assets are distributed to them in the form of dividends. Earnings of a corporation are taxed twice—once when earned by the corporation and again when "earned" as dividends by the stockholders.

CORPORATIONS VERSUS PARTNERSHIPS: DISTINCTIONS IN PERSPECTIVE

It is easy to place too much emphasis on the distinctions between partnerships and corporations. For some businesses, especially smaller enterprises, the differences may be more of form than of substance.

Capital Formation

For a small business the corporate form of organization is unlikely to facilitate acquisition of required capital any more than would the partnership form. Most small enterprises have difficulty obtaining equity capital, not so much because potential investors are concerned about subjecting all of their personal assets to possible loss, but rather because they are unwilling to risk any funds on the venture. Small businesses are inherently hazardous, and the corporate form of organization does not by itself enhance prospects for success.

Equally significant, the limited liability feature of the corporate form of organization may actually deter potential suppliers of capital. To a bank or other lending institution, the limitation on owners' liability is an obstacle rather than an inducement to making a loan. The bank, after all, wants assurance that in the event of default it can have access to all the assets of owners, not merely those devoted to the business. As a consequence, many lenders circumvent the limitations on stockholder liability by requiring that the stockholders personally cosign any notes issued by the corporation.

Partners' Liability

The distinction between the corporate and partnership form of organization has been diminished further in recent years by legislation in some states that provides for the limitation on the liability of certain partners in selected circumstances. As long as there exists one *general* partner whose liability is unlimited, the liability of other partners, particularly those who take no part in the day-to-day management of the enterprise, may be limited.

Stock Transferability

The advantage of a corporation over a partnership in that shares of ownership are readily transferable may also be more illusory than real. Although the shares of major corporations can be sold without difficulty, those of companies that are *closely held* by a small number of stockholders could probably not be sold any more easily than could a similar interest in a partnership. Indeed, agreements among stockholders of smaller companies sometimes provide that all sales of shares to outsiders must meet the approval of existing owners.

Tax Distinctions

The tax distinctions between partnerships and corporations have also been diminished greatly by statute. The current federal tax code provides that if certain criteria are met, small corporations may elect to be taxed as partnerships. As a consequence, small corporations can avoid the burden of "double" taxation; only stockholders, not the corporation, will be taxed on corporate earnings.

DISTINCTIVE FEATURES OF PARTNERSHIP ACCOUNTING

There are relatively few differences between accounting for a proprietorship or partnership and a corporation. What differences there are relate primarily to the owners' equity accounts and are more of form than of substance. For accounting purposes the proprietorship may be viewed as a special case of a partnership—a "partnership" with only a single partner.

The owners' equity section of a partnership general ledger usually consists of one capital account for each partner. Each capital account is credited (increased) by the amount of a partner's contributions to the firm and by his or her share of partnership profits. It is debited (decreased) by a partner's withdrawals from the firm and by that individual's share of partnership losses.

Lee and Grant decide to form a partnership. Lee contributes $2 million cash, and Grant contributes a building that has been appraised at $1.5 million but on which there is a mortgage of $500,000. The building had been carried on Grant's personal books at a value of $750,000. The partnership agrees to assume the liability for the mortgage. The following entry would be required to establish the partnership:

(a)

Cash		$2,000,000
Building		1,500,000
Mortgage note payable		$ 500,000
Capital, Lee		2,000,000
Capital, Grant		1,000,000

To record formation of the partnership

Property contributed is recorded at its *fair market value*, regardless of the value at which it might have been carried on the books of the individual partners prior to being assigned to the partnership.

The partners agree to share profits and losses in the same ratio as their initial capital contributions, 2 to 1. During the first year of operations the partnership has revenues of $2.4 million and expenses (including partner salaries) of $1.8 million—income of $600,000. The following *closing entry* would be required, assuming that revenues and expenses were properly recorded throughout the year:

(b)

Revenues (various accounts)		$2,400,000
Expenses—(various accounts)		$1,800,000
Drawings, Lee		400,000
Drawings, Grant		200,000

To close the revenue and expense accounts

The partner "drawings" account will be used to record the partners' shares of income as well as their withdrawals during the period. They will enable the partnership to keep track of changes in the partners' capital balances. At year end the drawings accounts will be closed to the partners' capital accounts.

During the year Lee withdraws $280,000 in cash and Grant $320,000. The appropriate entry would be

(c)

Drawings, Lee		$280,000
Drawings, Grant		320,000
Cash		$600,000

To record partner withdrawals

The year-end entry to close the partners' drawings accounts and transfer the balances to the capital accounts would be

(d)

Drawings, Lee		$120,000
Capital, Grant		120,000
Capital, Lee		$120,000
Drawings, Grant		120,000

To close the partners' drawings accounts

Exhibit 11-1 shows in T account form the partners' capital and drawings accounts.

At the conclusion of the year, Lee has a capital balance of $2,120,000 and Grant only $880,000. The capital balances are no longer in the original ratio of 2 to 1.

Whether a partner is permitted to draw his or her capital account below a specified level is a question that must be addressed in the partnership agreement. Some partnership agreements provide for the payment of interest *to* any partner who maintains an *excess* capital balance in relation to the other partners or *by* any partner who has a *deficiency*.

It is also essential that a partnership agreement set forth any amounts that the individual partners are to receive in salaries, apart from the percentage of earnings to which they are entitled. Payments of salaries to partners should be accounted for as they would be if they were ordinary expenses. They have no direct impact on the drawings accounts or the individual capital accounts.

Generally, it is advantageous for partnerships to establish salaries for active partners and to record these salaries as expenses. The partners will thereby be able to distinguish the return to their capital from that to their labor. Partners incur an "opportunity cost" (in this case, the opportunity to be employed elsewhere) by working in their own business. The profits of the business would be overstated if this went unrecognized.

Admission of New Partners

The difficult conceptual issues pertaining to partnership accounting relate to the sale of partnership interests and the admission of new partners. The critical question—one to which there is no widespread agreement on an answer—is

EXHIBIT 11-1
Partners' Drawings and Capital Accounts

Capital, Lee				Capital, Grant			
	(a)	2,000,000		(d)	120,000	(a)	1,000,000
	(d)	120,000					
							880,000
		2,120,000					

Drawings, Lee				Drawings, Grant			
(c)	280,000	(b)	400,000	(c)	320,000	(b)	200,000
(d)	120,000					(d)	120,000

whether such events demand an overall revaluation of partnership assets. Suppose, for example, that at the conclusion of its first year of operations the Lee-Grant partnership decides to admit a third partner, Sherman. Sherman agrees to pay $2 million for a one-third interest in the partnership. Just prior to his admission, the combined balance in the capital accounts of the two partners is $3 million. Hence reported net assets must also be $3 million. After admission of Sherman and acceptance of his contribution of $2 million, net assets of the partnership will be $5 million.

Sherman is willing to pay $2 million for a one-third interest in the partnership. In his eyes—and probably those of the marketplace, assuming an arm's-length transaction—the total value of the partnership must be three times $2 million, or $6 million. Yet the reported net assets of the company after his admission will be only $5 million. Should the additional $1 million in value be recognized? If so, how?

Revaluation Approach

There are two probable explanations for the apparent $1 million excess of *market* value over *reported* value. First, the market value of one or more specific assets is worth more than its reported value. For example, plant and equipment recorded at a value net of depreciation of $2 million may, in fact, have a market value of $3 million. Or, second, the company possesses assets that have not been recognized. More than likely, such assets are intangible—the good name of the firm, special skills of management, an advantageous location or economic environment. Such intangible assets could be grouped together in a broad category of *goodwill*.

The market value of the "new" asset, goodwill, or the increase in the existing assets, plant and equipment, as well as the corresponding increase of the equity of the two original partners can be recorded with the following journal entry:

Goodwill (or plant and equipment) $1,000,000
    Capital, Lee.. $666,667
    Capital, Grant... 333,333
To record admission of a new partner

The increase in owners' equity is divided among the two partners *in proportion to the agreed-upon* profit/loss sharing ratio, 2 to 1, even though their capital balances are not in such ratio.

The admission of the new partner can now be recorded as follows:

Cash $2,000,000
    Capital, Sherman $2,000,000
To record admission of a new partner

After his admission, the balance sheet of the partnership would reveal net assets of $6 million and owners' equity as follows:

Capital, Lee	$2,786,667
Capital, Grant	1,213,333
Capital, Sherman	2,000,000

The revaluation approach is based on the assumption that the transfe. the partnership interest in an arm's-length transaction provides an objective means of determining the fair market value of partnership assets. Proponents of the approach assert that the transfer is of sufficient economic significance to justify a restatement of assets. Indeed, they argue, the admission of a new partner is the equivalent of the dissolution of one business entity and the formation of another.

Those who object to the revaluation approach contend that the admission of a new partner may create a new legal entity, but not a new economic one. Hence, they say, the revaluation approach is inconsistent with the historical cost basis of accounting. Assets of an enterprise are generally reported at original cost, less any allowances for depreciation or amortization. Goodwill developed by the enterprise is never recognized. The balance sheet indicates unexpired costs, not current market values. Moreover, the approach is in violation of accounting principles as applied by corporations. In corporate accounting, neither the sale of existing shares nor the issue of new shares at a price reflective of a market value in excess of book values is considered to be proper occasion for an overall revaluation of corporate assets.

Bonus Approach

As an alternative to recognizing the increase in fair market value, the partnership can account for the additional payment by the new partner as a *bonus* paid to the existing partners. After the admission of the new partner, the net assets of the partnership will be $5 million (the $3 million in assets prior to his admission plus the new partner's contribution of $2 million). For his contribution of $2 million, the new partner will receive a one-third equity in a partnership that has total equity of $5 million. He will be credited, therefore, with a capital interest of one-third of $5 million, or $1,666,667. The difference of $333,333 between his contribution of $2 million and the capital interest with which he will be credited ($1,666,667) may be interpreted as a bonus to be divided among the existing partners *in proportion to the profit/loss sharing ratio* of 2:1. Thus the admission of Sherman could be recorded as follows:

Cash	$2,000,000
Capital, Sherman	$1,666,667
Capital, Lee	222,222
Capital, Grant	111,111

To record admission of a new partner

After his admission, the balance sheet of the partnership would reveal net assets of $5 million (as compared with $6 million under the *goodwill* approach), and partners' capital accounts would be reported as follows:

Capital, Lee	$2,342,222
Capital, Grant	991,111
Capital, Sherman	1,666,667

The issue of accounting for the admission of a new partner is not one that is currently under consideration by the rule-making authorities. It is of interest to students of accounting primarily because it is yet another example of the problem that arises when book values are inconsistent with market values.

RPORATE CAPITAL ACCOUNTS

In contrast to the owners' equity section of a partnership balance sheet, in which the capital balances of the partners are reported, that of a corporation indicates the par values of different classes of stock, the amount received by the corporation in excess of such par values, and the earnings retained in the business. Exhibit 11-2 illustrates the stockholders' equity section as might be presented by a typical company.

There are two major categories of capital stock: common stock and preferred stock. *Common stock* is the ''usual'' type of stock; when only one class of stock is issued, it is almost certain to be common stock. *Preferred stock*, when issued, ordinarily has certain preferences as to dividend payments and rights in liquidation.

As indicated in Exhibit 11-2, the balance sheet includes, often parenthetically, information on the numbers of shares of each class of stock authorized, issued, and outstanding. The number of shares *authorized* is the maximum number of shares, per its corporate charter, that the company is permitted to issue; the number of shares *issued* is the amount that has actually been put into circulation; the number of shares *outstanding* indicates those currently in circulation. It represents the number of shares issued less those that have been repurchased

EXHIBIT 11-2

Armstrong World Industries, Inc.
December 31, 1993
(dollar amounts in thousands)

	1993	1992
Shareholders' equity		
Preferred stock, $3.75 cumulative, no par value:		
Authorized 161,821 shares, issued 161,522 shares		
(at redemption price of $102.75 per share)	$ 16.6	$ 16.6
Class A preferred stock: Authorized 20 million shares		
Common stock, $1 par value per share:		
Authorized 90 million shares, issued 51,878,910		
shares	51.9	51.9
Capital in excess of par value	21.1	19.7
Retained earnings	899.3	791.2
Foreign currency translation*	31.8	(.4)
	1,020.7	879.0
Less treasury stock, at cost:		
Preferred stock, $3.75 cumulative: 1993, 58,173 shares;		
1992, 43,373 shares	4.7	4.0
Common stock: 1993, 5,632,321 shares; 1992,		
4,360,256 shares	102.2	62.0
	106.9	66.0
Total shareholders' equity	$ 913.8	$813.0

*To be discussed in Chapter 15.

by the company. Shares held by the company, called *treasury* shares, are considered to be issued but not outstanding.

COMMON STOCK: CHARACTERISTICS AND RIGHTS OF SHAREHOLDERS

Common stock is characterized by rights to income and control. Common stockholders receive distributions of the assets of the corporation if and when dividends are declared by its board of directors. Common stockholders, however, have a *residual* interest in their company. Upon dissolution of the corporation, they have the right to share in the remaining assets of the company after all claimants, including preferred stockholders, have been satisfied.

Common stockholders ordinarily possess rights to vote. They can elect members of the board of directors and can vote on such matters of corporate policy as are specifically reserved in corporate bylaws for decision by the stockholders-at-large. Corporate voting is conducted on the basis of one *share* (not one shareholder), one vote.

PREFERRED STOCK: CHARACTERISTICS AND RIGHTS OF SHAREHOLDERS

Preferred stock has the characteristics of both common stock and bonds. It combines some of the benefits—and limitations—of both. Preferred stock ordinarily stipulates that a fixed or minimum dividend will accrue to the holder each year. The dividend may be stated as a dollar amount (e.g., $5 per share) or as percentage of the par value (e.g., 5 percent). In this regard, preferred stock is similar to bonds. However, the obligation to pay dividends on preferred stock is not as binding on the corporation as that to pay interest on bonds. The company would not typically be in default if it failed to make a single dividend payment. Instead, it would be prohibited from making any dividend payments to common stockholders until it satisfied its current and, in some instances, accumulated obligations to the preferred stockholders. Similarly, in the event of liquidation, the preferred stockholders would have preference over the common stockholders. Before the company could distribute assets to the common stockholders, it would have to return to the preferred stockholders both their initial investment as well as any accumulated dividends.

As a rule, companies can omit a preferred dividend only for specified reasons (e.g., corporate earnings are less than the required dividend). Stock in which the shareholders are entitled to dividends even if they are not declared in a particular period is referred to as *cumulative preferred* stock. That in which the holders are entitled to dividends only if the company declares them is referred to as *noncumulative*.

The specific features of preferred stock vary from issue to issue. Generally, preferred stockholders do not have voting rights, except when the company has failed to pay preferred stock dividends for a specified number of periods.

Some issues, called *participating* issues, entitle the preferred stockholders to share in distributions in excess of the stipulated dividend. For example, an issue may carry a minimum dividend. It may provide that once the preferred stockholders have received their minimum dividend—and usually once the common shareholders have received a dividend of a stated amount—any additional funds available for distribution will be divided, in a specified proportion, between the two groups of stockholders.

Preferred stock can be both participating and cumulative.

Unlike bonds, preferred stock does not mature on a particular date. Usually, however, the corporation has the option to *call* (redeem) the stock at a stipulated price after a number of years have elapsed. Many issues (approximately 40 percent in recent years) provide that preferred shares can be *converted*, at the option of the holder, into shares of common stock. Accounting issues pertaining to convertible securities are addressed later in this chapter.

Dividends Not Deductible

From the standpoint of the issuing corporation, preferred stock has one critical disadvantage over bonds or other pure debt securities. The dividends on preferred stock (like those on common stock) are not deductible from corporate income for tax purposes, whereas interest payments are. The effective cost of the capital acquired through the issue of preferred stock is therefore magnified substantially. Suppose, for example, that a company wishes to raise $1 million in capital. It could issue bonds that could be sold to yield 6 percent or preferred stock that would bear a dividend rate of 8 percent. Preferred stock, especially if it is not convertible into common stock, often provides the holder with a higher return since interest takes precedence over dividends. The interest would require an outlay of $60,000 per year, and the dividends, $80,000. If, however, the combined state and federal tax rate was 40 percent, then the *effective* outlay for the dividends would be $80,000/(1 − .40), which equals $133,333. That is, the company would have to earn $133,333 to meet its preferred stock dividends of $80,000:

Income before taxes	$133,333
Tax at 40%	53,333
Income available for dividends	$ 80,000

By contrast, the company would have to earn only $60,000 to meet its required interest of $60,000. Since the interest is fully deductible, if the corporation earned $60,000 and paid interest of $60,000, it would have no taxable income and hence no tax liability. The full $60,000 of earnings could be used to meet the interest:

Income before taxes	$60,000
Taxes	0
Income available for interest	$60,000

The mechanics of forming a corporation are straightforward; the central accounting problems relate to the values to be placed upon the assets or services contributed by its organizers.

A corporation is ordinarily formed by one or more individuals known as promoters. The *promoters* organize the corporation, apply for a charter, and establish the bylaws under which the corporation will initially operate. A promoter may itself be a corporation. The promoters contribute cash, other assets, or services to the company in exchange for all or a portion of the capital stock to be issued. If additional equity (ownership) financing is required, then the promoters arrange for shares of the stock to be sold either to the general public or to specific parties known to the promoters. The promoters are in a *fiduciary relationship*—one of trust—to the corporation. They are prohibited from benefiting at the expense of those who will subsequently purchase shares of corporate stock. They are entitled to an interest in the new corporation no greater than the value of the assets or services which they have contributed.

Par Value

Corporate stock traditionally bears an indication of par value per share. *Par value* is the nominal value of the stock, a value that has been arbitrarily assigned. Common stock can be sold for an amount above or below par value. If sold above, it is said to have been sold at a *premium*, and if below, at a *discount*. Originally par value was intended to protect creditors. It was to assure them that stockholders had contributed assets worth at least as much as the par value of the shares. If the stockholders had not—that is, if they had purchased their shares at a discount—and the corporation was dissolved, they could be held responsible for the difference between what they paid for the stock and its par value, despite the usual limitations on stockholder liability.

Par value did not prove to be an effective means of protecting creditors because a new corporation could assign to its shares a par value far below the price at which it expected the shares to be sold. Many states have substituted a concept of *stated* or *legal* capital for par value. Stated or legal capital is either an amount established by the company (similar to par value) or that for which the stock was actually issued. Typically, stated or legal capital establishes a limit on the payment of dividends; the corporation is prohibited from paying dividends that will reduce its owners' equity below its stated or legal capital.

Fair Market Value

When a corporation issues common stock for cash or other assets, either upon formation or anytime thereafter, a simple journal entry is in order. Asset accounts are debited and owners' equity accounts are credited for the *fair market value* of the property received by the corporation. The credit to the capital account is divided into two parts—the par (or stated) value of the stock issued and the amount in excess of par (or stated) value. Suppose, for example, that a corporation issues 10 million shares of $1 par value stock at $8 per share. The appropriate entry would be (in thousands of dollars):

Cash $80,000
    Common stock, par value $10,000
    Contributed capital in excess of par value, common stock 70,000
To record the issue of common stock

The two credited accounts combined indicate the capital contributed by common stockholders.

ISSUANCE OF ADDITIONAL SHARES OF COMMON STOCK

Should a firm issue additional shares of stock subsequent to its formation, similar entries would be in order. The resultant increase in owners' equity would be reflected first in the "common stock, par value" account, and then, to the extent of amounts received above par, in the account, "contributed capital in excess of par value."

The price at which additional shares of stock are issued would depend on the market value as opposed to the book value of the company's existing shares outstanding.

Example

After several years of operations, the same firm has reported assets of $170 million, liabilities of $30 million, and owners' equity of $140 million. Owners' equity is composed of the following accounts (in thousands):

Common stock, $1 par value,	
10 million shares issued and outstanding	$ 10,000
Contributed capital in excess of par value	70,000
Retained earnings	60,000
Total owners' equity	$140,000

The book value per share is $140 million divided by 10 million shares, or $14 per share.

The company wishes to raise $100 million in capital. The market price of the company's stock is $20 per share. (Large discrepancies between book value and market value are common. Book value is based on historical costs; market value is based on investor expectations as to future earnings.) Assuming that the market price is unaffected by the impending issue of the new stock (a major financial event which may itself affect investor expectations of future earnings), the company could acquire the $100 million in needed capital by issuing an additional 5 million shares at $20 per share.

The journal entry to record the issue would be (in thousands):

```
Cash . . . . . . . . . . . . . . . . . . . . . . . . . . . . . . . . . . . . . . . . . . . . . . $100,000
    Common stock, par value . . . . . . . . . . . . . . . . . . . . . . . . . . . . . . . . . . $ 5,000
    Contributed capital in excess of par value . . . . . . . . . . . . . . . . . . . . . . 95,000
To record the issue of additional stocks
```

Owners' equity would now be made up as follows (in thousands):

Common stock, $1 par value,	
15 million shares issued and outstanding	$ 15,000
Contributed capital in excess of par value	165,000
Retained earnings	60,000
Total owners' equity	$240,000

Book value per share would now be $16 ($240 million divided by 15 million shares), compared with $14 prior to the sale of additional shares.

The increase in book value can be attributed to the willingness of the new investors to pay $20 per share for stock that had a book value of only $14 per share. The new investors contributed $100 million in return for a one-third interest (5 million shares out of 15 million shares) in a company that will have *reported* net assets of $240 million. In effect, existing shareholders received a ''bonus'' reflecting the market's assessment of the company.

TRANSACTIONS IN A CORPORATION'S OWN SHARES OF COMMON STOCK

Companies may purchase their own outstanding shares of stock for a number of reasons. They may plan to reissue the shares to executives or other employees in connection with stock-option or related compensation plans. They may intend to invest temporarily in their own shares, just as they might invest in shares of other corporations. Or they may want to reduce the scale of their operations—to return to stockholders a share of the capital they had contributed. In the 1980s, many United States corporations did, in fact, buy back substantial amounts of their own stock in the market, often as part of what was in effect a *restructuring* of equities. Sometimes this was financed by newly issued debt, the restructuring not infrequently being linked to antitakeover efforts. Stock that is acquired and retained by the issuing corporation is known as *treasury stock*. Treasury shares may not be voted, do not receive dividends, and carry none of the usual rights of ownership.

The manner in which treasury stock is accounted for has a direct impact on a firm's reported capital structure. There are two primary methods of accounting for treasury stock. One method is referred to as the *cost* method and the other as the *par value* method. Under the cost method, treasury shares are accounted for in a separate account. Under the par value method, treasury shares are treated as stock to be permanently retired.

Cost Method

In general, if a corporation expects to reissue the shares acquired, it would most likely account for them by the cost method. Under the *cost method*, the treasury shares are reported in a separate account, which is shown on the balance sheet *contra* to the other equity accounts. The amount recorded in the treasury stock account represents, as suggested by the name of the method, the *cost* of the shares acquired. The cost would be dictated by market conditions at the time of acquisition.

Using the data from the previous example, assume that the firm purchases 1.5 million shares of its own common stock at a price of $22 per share. Under the cost method, the acquisition could be recorded with a simple journal entry (in thousands of dollars):

Treasury stock...$33,000
    Cash..$33,000
To record the purchase of treasury stock (1.5 million shares at $22 per share)

Treasury stock would be reported in the equity contra account as follows:

Common stock, $1 par value, 15 million shares issued, 1.5 million shares held in treasury	$ 15,000
Contributed capital in excess of par value	165,000
Retained earnings	60,000
	$240,000
Less: Shares held in treasury (at cost)	33,000
Total owners' equity	$207,000

Some companies report treasury stock among the current assets—along with other marketable securities. They would justify this practice by asserting that the stock could be converted to cash at any time, even more readily, perhaps, than most other current assets. Those who reject this position point out that it is illogical for a corporation to own itself. When a company purchases its own shares, it *reduces* its assets and correspondingly the equity of its owners. Moreover, the firm has the potential to sell for cash an unlimited number of *unissued* shares as well as the treasury shares. Yet few would argue that unissued shares should be reported as assets. The position of those who maintain that treasury stock should be accounted for as a reduction in stockholders' equity, rather than as an asset, prevails in practice.

When a company sells the treasury shares, the treasury stock account should be reduced by the amount of their original reacquisition cost. If the selling price exceeds (or is less than) the original cost, then any difference is added to (or subtracted from) contributed capital in excess of par.[1] Assume, for example, that the 1.5 million shares, originally purchased at $22 per share, were resold for $24 each. The following entry would be made:

Cash...$36,000
    Treasury stock...$33,000
    Contributed capital in excess of par value 3,000
To record the sale of treasury stock (1.5 million shares at $24 per share)

---

[1] There is an exception as to sales of treasury stock where selling price is less than original cost. *Losses*, according to APB *Opinion No. 6*, should be subtracted from capital contributed in excess of par only to the extent that previous net *gains* from sales or retirements of the same class of stock are included therein; otherwise, they should be subtracted from retained earnings. The rationale behind this approach is that contributed capital (an amount that often has legal significance) should not be dissipated by purchases and sales of treasury stock.

The entry reflects the widely held view among accountants that ny should not include in reported income gains or losses on transac own securities. Such transactions involve nothing more than increases o in the amount of contributed capital. Thus the purchase and sale stock, like the issue or retirement of other shares, should not result i or expenses to be included in the computation of net income.

Par Value Method

If a corporation does not expect to reissue the shares acquired, then it should use the par value method. Under the *par value method*, the acquisition of the treasury shares is accounted for as a retirement of the stock purchased. First, both the common stock, par value, and the contributed capital in excess of par accounts are reduced (debited) by amounts indicative of the percentage of shares being retired. Then retained earnings are reduced (debited) by any amounts in excess of the reduction in both common stock and contributed capital in excess of par.[2]

Using the data previously presented, for example, we see that the purchase of 1.5 million shares at a price of $22 per share represents the retirement of 10 percent (1.5/15 million) of the outstanding shares. Common stock ($1 per share par value) would be reduced by 10 percent of $15 million—$1.5 million. Contributed capital in excess of par, previously $165 million, would be reduced by 10 percent of $165 million or $16.5 million. Retained earnings would be reduced by the difference between the total amount paid for the shares ($33 million) and the sum of the reductions to the other two accounts ($18 million) or $15 million. Thus (in thousands)

Common stock..	$ 1,500
Contributed capital in excess of par..........................	16,500
Retained earnings.......................................	15,000
Cash..	$33,000

To record the purchase of treasury stock (1.5 million shares at $22 per share)

Subsequent to the retirement, the capital accounts would appear as follows (again in thousands)

Common stock, $1 par value, 13.5 million shares issued and outstanding	$ 13,500
Contributed capital in excess of par value	148,500
Retained earnings	45,000
Total owners' equity	$207,000

[2] Generally accepted accounting principles are quite flexible as to how the excess of reacquisition cost over par value can be allocated between common stock, par value, and contributed capital in excess of par. The main restriction is that the ''contributed capital in excess of par'' account cannot be reduced by more than the sum of the proportionate share of the stock retired and any additional amounts added to the account as a result of previous treasury stock transactions involving the same class of stock.

If the price paid to acquire the stock is *less* than the original issue price, then, for each share, common stock would be debited with par value, and contributed capital in excess of par would be debited by the difference between par value and purchase price.

Were the treasury shares to be reissued in the future, the sale would be accounted for as any other issue of new shares of stock.

Comparison of Methods

Both the cost and the par value methods are accepted means of accounting for treasury stock. The par value method is the theoretically preferable method, especially if the company does not intend to reissue the shares in the foreseeable future. It results in the retirement of the acquired shares and is thereby consistent with the proposition that a company cannot ''own itself.'' But the cost method is the more widely used of the two, mainly because companies generally acquire their own common shares with the expectation that they will eventually reissue them. The differences between the two methods are not critical. Both result in the same reported assets, liabilities, and total owners' equity. Neither method affects reported revenues or expenses. They vary only in their impact on the components of owners' equity.

ISSUANCE OF PREFERRED STOCK

The mechanics of recording the issuance of preferred stock is almost identical with that of recording common stock. However, the amount received in excess of or below par value is more similar to the premium or discount associated with bonds than with common stock.

The amount that investors will pay for a corporation's common stock is dependent on their expectations of the firm's earnings in the future. Because investors will share in the *residual* income of the company—that which remains after the claims against earnings of bondholders and preferred stockholders are satisfied—the price that they are willing to pay for a share of common stock will rise and fall with their assessment of the company's earning potential.

Owners of preferred stock, however, are less concerned with anticipated profits of the company. Their dollar share in the income of the company is contractually fixed. They will receive only the dollar amount of the dividend specified on their shares. As long as the company has sufficient earnings to meet its required dividend payments, they will be unaffected by swings in income.

The primary concern of the purchasers of preferred stock is the yield that they will obtain from one company as opposed to another with similar risk characteristics. Suppose, for example, the preferred stock of a company has a par value of $100 per share and a dividend rate of $6 per year. If similar securities are being sold to yield 7 percent per year, then rational purchasers would be willing to invest in the shares only if they could purchase them at a discount sufficiently great to assure a return equivalent to the rate prevailing in the market. If similar securities are being sold to yield only 5 percent, then they would be willing to pay a premium of such magnitude as to reduce the return to that which they could obtain elsewhere.

Example

The ABC Co. wishes to issue 1 million shares of $100 par value preferred stock, which will pay dividends of $10 per year. On the day of issue the prevailing yield on similar types of securities is 9 percent.

For how much is each share likely to be sold?

Let

$$x = \text{Amount for which each share will be sold}$$

$$.09x = \$10$$

$$x = \frac{\$10}{.09}$$

$$x = \$111.11$$

If the stock that pays dividends of $10 per year is to be sold to yield 9 percent, then it would be sold at $111.11. Since, unlike bonds, there is no maturity date, the return can be assumed to be a *perpetuity* (one for an infinitely long duration); hence there is no need to refer to present value tables to determine the selling price. Similarly, there is no need to amortize the premium ($11.11 per share in this case), which is commonly classified on the balance sheet as "contributed capital in excess of par."[3]

CONVERTIBLE SECURITIES

Convertible securities, usually bonds or preferred stock, are hybrids. They have the characteristics of both debt and equity financial instruments. They can be changed, usually at the option of the holder, into the issuer's common stock. The security indentures would specify a *conversion ratio*, which is the number of shares into which the security may be converted. If a $1,000 bond can be tendered for 50 shares of common stock, then the conversion ratio is 50 to 1. The principles and issues pertaining to convertible securities are illustrated here with reference to bonds; the examples and discussions can easily be generalized to preferred stock.

Convertible bonds pay interest, although the rate is generally lower than that on conventional bonds. There are two main features of the conversion right that make it attractive to investors. The first is that it allows the investors to realize the benefits of appreciation in the issuer's common stock. If the value of the common stock into which the bonds can be converted exceeds that of the bonds, then the investors can exchange the bonds for the stock. As a consequence, the market value of the bonds is tied directly to that of the stock. As the stock appreciates, so also do the bonds. If the stock does not increase in value, then the bondholders need not convert, and they can still be assured of fixed payments of interest and a return of principal.

Consider, for example, the $1,000 bond with the 50-to-1 conversion ratio. If the market price of the stock was to rise to $20, conversion would yield stock with a value of $20 × 50 = $1,000. Any market price for the stock above $20

[3] For a different perspective on perpetuities, see footnote 3 in Chapter 6, page 233.

would yield conversion values exceeding $1,000. Hence it would be in the interest of the bondholders to convert prior to the maturity of the bonds. When the stock price goes above $20, the market value of the bonds can be expected to increase by approximately $50 for every $1 increase in the value of a share of stock over $20.

The second advantage of the conversion right is that it allows the bondholders to share in the rewards of corporate ownership without the corresponding risks. Convertible securities are therefore often used by both new corporations seeking start-up capital and by failing firms attempting to reestablish themselves. Should an issuing company become financially successful, bondholders can exchange their interests as creditors for those of owners. They can thereby share in the subsequent corporate earnings. Should the company fail or become only marginally profitable, the bondholders can continue as creditors. They would be assured payments of interest and principal before any dividends or other distributions of corporate assets were made to stockholders.

The primary benefits of convertible bonds to the issuer are a lower rate of interest and the possible opportunity to avoid repaying the debt by forcing conversion to common stock. The latter can be accomplished by making the bonds *callable*. A call provision included in the bond indenture permits the company to redeem the bonds at a specified price, one that is usually above the face value of the bond. Should the aggregate market value of the stock to be issued on conversion of a bond increase to where it is above the call price of the bond, then the rational investor would have to convert from bonds to stock. Otherwise, the company could redeem the bonds at the call price, leaving the investor worse off than if he or she had taken the stock.

If, for example, in our above illustration, the bond was callable at $1,200, the rational investor would automatically convert if the share price ever went above $24, for $24 × 50 = $1,200, and any share price above $24 would lead to a bond-conversion value exceeding the call value of the bond.

Accounting for the Issuance

When a firm issues convertible bonds, the *generally accepted* entry to record the transaction is identical to that for conventional bonds. Suppose, for example, that a firm issues $100,000 of 8 percent convertible bonds at a premium of $3,000. Each bond has a face value of $1,000 and is convertible into the firm's common stock ($1 par value) at a ratio of 50 to 1. Thus the firm has issued 100 bonds that are convertible into a total of 5,000 shares (100 bonds times 50). The market price of the firm's common stock at the time the bonds are issued is $15 per share. The generally accepted entry to record the issuance of the bonds would be

Cash	$103,000	
Bonds payable		$100,000
Premium on bonds payable		3,000
To record the issuance of bonds		

The theoretical deficiency of this entry is that it assigns the entire amount received to the debt. It is almost certain, however, that the purchasers paid at least a portion of the issue price for the conversion rights—the possibility of sharing in the future earnings of the company and of obtaining other benefits of corporate ownership.

Suppose, for example, that the prevailing yield on bonds that are comparable in all respects to those just described, except that they are not convertible, is slightly *more* than 8 percent. If, like the convertible bonds, their coupon rate was 8 percent, then they would sell at less than the face value of $100,000. Assume that they sold for $98,500, at a *discount* of $1,500. The most plausible explanation as to why the investors were willing to pay the additional $4,500 (the difference between $103,000 and $98,500) for the convertible bonds is that they placed that value upon the conversion rights. Many theoreticians would assert that the $4,500 should be assigned to owners' equity—either capital in excess of par or some other appropriately described account. Thus

Cash	$103,000	
Discount on bonds payable		
($100,000 − $98,500)	1,500	
Bonds payable		$100,000
Contributed capital from		
issuance of convertible bonds		4,500

To record the issuance of convertible bonds

This entry is *not*, however, in accord with generally accepted accounting principles. The Accounting Principles Board ruled that *no portion* of the proceeds of convertible debt should be accounted for as attributable to the conversion feature. The board pointed to the *practical difficulties* of valuing the conversion rights as well as to the inseparability of the debt and the conversion rights. Neither the debt nor the conversion rights, it argued, can exist independently of one another; the holder cannot sell one right and retain the other.[4]

Accounting for the Conversion

Assume that the issuance was recorded in accord with generally accepted accounting principles.

After several years the market price of the firm's common stock increases to $22 per share. By this time, the company has amortized the bond premium down to $2,000; hence the book value of the bonds is $102,000. The market value of the bonds, because of their convertibility feature, could be expected to be $22 × 50 = $1,100 × 100 bonds = $110,000. The investors would exercise their option to convert.

Under generally accepted accounting principles, the conversion may be accounted for on the basis of *either book value or market value.*

Book Value

If the conversion is to be accounted for on the basis of *book* value, then the new common stock to be issued will be recorded at the book value of the bonds that they will replace—in this exchange, $102,000. No gain or loss will be recognized on the trade. Thus

Bonds payable	$100,000	
Premium on bonds payable	2,000	
Common stock, par value (5,000 shares @ $1)		$ 5,000
Contributed capital in excess of par ($102,000 − $5,000)		97,000

To record conversion of bonds (book value method)

---

[4]"Convertible Debt and Debt Issued with Stock Purchase Warrants," Accounting Principles Board *Opinion No. 12*, 1966.

The book value method accounts for the conversion as an extension of the previous transaction in which the bonds were first issued. The value assigned to the stock is that of the *bonds* and may bear no relation to the market value of the stock at the time the stock is issued.

Market Value

If the conversion is to be accounted for on the basis of market value, then the new securities will be recorded at their current market prices—in this case $22 per share and a total of $110,000 for the 5,000 shares to be issued. The firm would recognize a loss of $8,000 on the exchange, the difference between the market value of the stock issued and the book value of the bonds retired:

Bonds payable		$100,000
Premium on bonds payable		2,000
Loss on conversion		8,000
Common stock, par value (5,000 shares @ $1)	$ 5,000	
Contributed capital in excess of par ($110,000 − $5,000)	105,000	

To record conversion of bonds (market value method)

The market value method accounts for the conversion as an independent event, assigning to the new securities a value reflective of what would have been recorded had they been issued for cash at the time of the exchange. The market value method, however, typically requires recognition of a loss. This loss can best be interpreted as an *opportunity cost*. It indicates how much better off the firm would have been had it been able to redeem the bonds at book value and separately issue the common stock at its prevailing market price.

A Comparison

Although the market value method results in what many accountants believe to be a more meaningful presentation of the equity accounts on the balance sheet, the recognition of the loss is understandably objectionable to many firms. After all, it is attributable to *increases* in the market value of the firm's common stock—the higher the market value, the greater the reported loss. Gains in the market value of a firm's common stock are not, of course, otherwise given ongoing accounting recognition. In practice, the book value method is used almost exclusively, in large measure, no doubt, because of the necessity of reporting conversion losses under the market value method.

NEW FINANCIAL INSTRUMENTS

One of the significant ongoing challenges to the accounting profession is how to account for and report the new, nonconventional financial instruments. Over the last decade, corporate financing has become exceedingly innovative, with new types of securities being created each year. This trend is almost certain to continue. Many of the new instruments are hybrids. Like convertible securities, they have elements of both debt and equity. Some contain promises that are conditional upon future earnings or appreciation in stock prices.

To cite but one example: When General Motors acquired EDS Company in 1984, it issued to EDS shareholders a new class of common stock (called "Class E" stock) as well as promissory notes. Dividends on the Class E stock were to be paid out of the earnings only of the EDS company, not General Motors at large. Moreover, the promissory notes were payable at an "amount equal to

.2 times the excess of $125 over the market price of the Class E common stock at the maturity date of the note."

No general rules have yet been established as to how a new financial instrument should be accounted for. As this text goes to press, the Financial Accounting Standards Board has a major project underway to develop guidelines applicable to a broad range of new types of financial instruments. Pending completion of the project, one key to analysis is to determine the economic nature and market value of each of its components. Often that will make clear how the components should be categorized on the balance sheet and what values should be assigned to them. The market-based means of accounting for both the issuance and the conversion of convertible bonds are illustrative of this approach. Although market-based approaches may need to be modified to take into account "practical" realities, they can generally be expected to capture the economic substance of a transaction.

DEBT-TO-EQUITY RATIO

Financing ratios, one of which is the debt-to-equity ratio, compare claims of creditors with the equity of stockholders.

The debt-to-equity ratio relates capital provided by creditors to that supplied by owners. Debt includes all outstanding liabilities, both current and noncurrent. Equity includes balances in all owners' equity accounts—common and preferred stock, capital provided in excess of par, and retained earnings.

Example

The total debt of American Home Products (see its statements in Chapter 7), composed of both the current and the noncurrent liabilities, is (in millions) $2,638. Total stockholders' equity is $3,301. The debt-to-equity ratio as of December 31, 1991, therefore, is 0.79 to 1:

$$\text{Debt-to-equity ratio} = \frac{\text{Total debt}}{\text{Stockholders' equity}} = \frac{2,638}{3,301} = 0.79$$

The debt-to-equity ratio is of particular concern to creditors. The claims of creditors against the assets of a firm have priority over those of the stockholders. The higher the debt-to-equity ratio, the greater the amount of the *priority* claims against the assets, and in the event the firm is unable to meet all its outstanding obligations, the less likely that any individual claim will be liquidated in full. Moreover, a high debt-to-equity ratio suggests the obligation to make high periodic interest payments. As a consequence, there is an increased risk that corporate earnings will be insufficient to cover all required principal and interest payments.

The debt-to-equity ratio is also of interest to managers and the stockholders they represent. Stockholders can expect no return on their investment, either periodically in the form of dividends or upon liquidation, until all senior claims of creditors have been satisfied. The lower the debt-to-equity ratio, the less the risk of loss assumed by stockholders. But in contrast to the possible preference of stockholders to be assured a return on their investment, there may be a conflicting desire to make use of *leverage*—the ability to take advantage of other people's money to enhance the return on their invested capital. Any earnings on borrowed capital above required interest payments increase the return to stockholders. As discussed in Chapter 10, however, leverage works both ways. Any interest payments in excess of the earnings on the borrowed captial reduce the return to stockholders.

Summary

In this chapter we have focused on the equity accounts of *proprietorships, partnerships,* and *corporations*. Although there are important legal and organizational differences between proprietorships, partnerships, and corporations, the accounting distinctions are relatively minor, affecting primarily the accounts composing the owners' equity section of the balance sheet.

A corporation's transactions involving its own shares are seldom reported on its statement of income. Yet they can have a profound impact on its earnings per share as well as on the value of outstanding shares.

In the 1960s, for example, many companies took advantage of relatively high stock market prices to issue additional shares. Since the prices that the new investors were willing to pay were substantially above the *book* values of the new shares, the added premiums increased the book values of the existing shares. Inasmuch as the cost of the capital acquired was low in relation to the returns that could be generated by the additional capital, sales of the new shares increased overall earnings per share. Numerous firms that were previously privately owned went public to benefit from the ease of obtaining capital through the sale of common stock.

In the 1970s and 1980s, when stock market prices were depressed, a number of companies engaged in the reverse process; they reacquired shares that they had issued previously. If the market prices of the shares acquired were less than their intrinsic values, then the proportionate values of the remaining shares increased. Since relatively little capital had to be surrendered to reacquire the shares, the overall earnings capacity of the firms may have declined only slightly. But since earnings now had to be divided among a significantly smaller number of shares, earnings per share may have increased substantially.

The late 1980s was a period of financial restructuring. There were numerous mergers and acquisitions as well as divisions of firms into smaller, independently owned units. Often the changes were accompanied by new "creative" financial instruments.

Perceptive investors and financial analysts examine carefully the transactions between a company and its owners and the manner in which they are accounted for. This can have a critical effect on a stockholder's interest in past and future corporate earnings. The skilled manager and perceptive investor must be aware of the opportunities and pitfalls inherent in corporate dealings between a company and its owners and must be cognizant of how they are reflected in the financial reports.

Exercise for Review and Self-Testing

Scopus, Inc., decides to reorganize its corporate structure. To facilitate additional financing, it elects to incorporate one of its divisions. Scopus will transfer to the new corporation plant and equipment that is presently recorded on its books at a cost of $8.9 million, less accumulated depreciation of $4 million, and patents that were developed by the company itself and have not been recognized in the accounts. The fair market value of the plant and equipment is $8.2 million; that of the patents, $2 million.

1. The new company issues 100,000 shares of common stock, par value $50. Initially, all the shares will be held by the parent company.
   a. What value should the new company assign to the plant and equipment? To the patents?
   b. What value should the new company assign to "common stock, par value"? To "common stock, capital in excess of par"?
   c. Prepare a journal entry to record the issuance of the common stock.
2. The new company also issues 10,000 shares of preferred stock. The preferred stock is assigned a par value of $100 and pays dividends at a rate of 9 percent per year. At the time the stock is issued, comparable securities are being sold to yield 8.5 percent.
   a. What is the dollar amount per share that the firm will pay in dividends?
   b. How much is an investor likely to pay for a share of stock that pays a dividend of such amount if he or she expects a return of 8.5 percent?
   c. Prepare a journal entry to record the issuance of the preferred stock, assuming that the stock is issued for cash at the price determined in part (b).
3. After a year, the new company acquires 1,000 of its outstanding shares of common stock for the purpose of reissuing them to employees as part of a stock option plan. The company acquires the shares for cash at a price of $180 per share.
   a. Do you think that the acquisition of the treasury stock should be accounted for by the cost or the par value method?
   b. Based on your answer to part (a), prepare a journal entry to record the acquisition of the stock.
4. Shortly after reissuing the shares described in part 3, the company reacquires an additional 20,000 shares of common stock with the intention of retiring them. The company purchases the shares for $160 each. At the time of purchase the company has a balance in its retained earnings account of $2 million.
   a. Should the acquisition be accounted for by the cost or par value method?
   b. By what percentage would the number of shares outstanding be reduced?
   c. By what percentage and by what amount should the balance in the account "common stock, par value" be reduced?
   d. By what percentage and by what amount should the balance in the account "common stock, capital in excess of par" be reduced?
   e. By what amount—the difference between total amount paid and the sum of the reductions in the other capital accounts—should the balance in "retained earnings" be reduced?
   f. Prepare a journal entry to record the retirement of the shares.

Questions for Review and Discussion

1. The risks of being a *silent partner* (one who takes no active role in management) of a business organized as a partnership are far greater than those of being a silent stockholder of a firm organized as a corporation. Do you agree? Explain.
2. It is often pointed out that the limitations on liability afforded stockholders of a corporation make it easier for a corporation as opposed to a partnership to raise capital. Cite an example of a situation where the limitations of liability may, in fact, make it more difficult for a corporation to acquire needed funds.
3. A corporation, it is said, is a legal "person." Why is a corporation, but not a partnership or a proprietorship, so described?
4. Why is *preferred* stock preferred? What preferences attach to it?
5. A friend wants to purchase "safe" securities for a period of two to three years. He wants assurance that the original amount of his investment will remain intact.

Assume that you are satisfied that the company in which he is considering investing is sound—that it is highly unlikely that it will be unable to pay required preferred stock dividends or interest. Would you suggest to him that the preferred stock of the company is necessarily a safer investment than the common stock? What factors are most likely to influence the market price of the preferred stock, assuming that it is not convertible into common stock?

6. What are the critical accounting problems involved in the formation of a corporation? What warnings would you give to someone who is about to purchase the common stock of a newly organized corporation?

7. The financial statements of RCA Corporation contained the following footnote:

> At December 31, 52,967 shares of treasury stock, included in Other Assets [a noncurrent asset] at cost to RCA of $1.3 million, were available to cover undistributed awards payable to RCA common stock.

What objections might there be to classifying treasury stock as a noncurrent *asset*?

8. Describe the way in which the issuance of convertible bonds is accounted for. Why can it be said that the entry required by GAAP does not allocate the proceeds of the issue in a way that reflects the benefits acquired by the investors?

9. Distinguish between book value and market value methods of accounting for security conversions. What is the rationale for each? What is the weakness of each?

10. What is meant by *leverage*? Which financial ratio provides a measure of leverage? What are the risks of leverage?

Problems

1. *The method of financing used by a "closely held" corporation must take into account the distinctions in the tax code between dividends and interest.*

   William Elton is the sole stockholder of the Elton Co. Mr. Elton intends to contribute $1 million of his personal funds to the corporation to finance expansion of a plant. He expects that the added capacity of the plant will enable the company to earn $300,000 per year additional income, before federal and state taxes. Mr. Elton has asked your advice as to whether he should have the corporation issue common stock or bonds in return for the $1 million. Mr. Elton intends to withdraw $100,000 of the additional earnings each year, either in the form of interest on bonds or dividends on the common stock. The corporation pays combined federal, state, and local taxes at a rate of 40 percent. Mr. Elton personally pays at a rate of 50 percent. Mr. Elton would be required to pay taxes on all returns from the corporation, regardless of whether in the form of interest or dividends.

   What advice would you give to Mr. Elton?

2. *Accounting principles applicable to partnerships are essentially the same as those applicable to corporations.*

   Simmons and Ross decided to form a partnership to engage in the purchase and sale of real estate. Simmons contributed land that had an appraised value of $400,000; Ross contributed cash of $100,000. The land was subject to a liability of $100,000, which the partnership agreed to assume. The land had been recorded on the personal books of Simmons at a value of $200,000. The partners agreed that profits and losses would be shared in proportion to the initial contributions of the owners, after allowing for all expenses, including a management fee of $10,000 per year paid to Ross.

During its first year of operation, the partnership purchased additional land for $800,000, paying $150,000 cash and giving a note for the balance. It sold for $300,000 land that it had acquired for $200,000. The buyers paid cash of $90,000 and agreed to assume liabilities of $210,000 that the partnership had incurred when it had acquired the land.

During the first year the partnership borrowed $80,000 from Simmons. It agreed to pay Simmons interest at the rate of 6 percent per year. As of year end the loan had been outstanding for six months, but the partnership had neither paid nor accrued any interest.

The firm incurred additional interest expenses, paid in cash, of $40,000. At year end, Ross withdrew $30,000 cash from the partnership and, in addition, was paid his management fee; Simmons withdrew nothing. (Assume that all other operating expenses are negligible.)

a. Prepare all necessary journal entries to record the formation of the partnership and to summarize all transactions in which it engaged during its first year of operations. Prepare also any required adjusting and closing entries.

b. Prepare a balance sheet as of year end.

3. *Distributions to partners upon liquidation of a partnership must be based upon the balances, after appropriate adjustments, in the partners' capital accounts.*

After 10 years, Freeman Brothers Men's Shop is going out of business. Freeman Brothers is operated as a partnership. Just prior to liquidation, its balance sheet reflected the following:

Cash	$ 200,000
Merchandise inventory	800,000
Total assets	$1,000,000
Current liabilities	$ 50,000
Capital, J. Freeman	450,000
Capital, L. Freeman	500,000
Total liabilities and owners' equity	$1,000,000

The two Freeman brothers share profits and losses equally.

The firm holds a "going-out-of-business" sale and sells its entire merchandise inventory for $1 million. It pays the creditors and distributes the remaining cash between the two partners.

a. Prepare the required journal entries to record the sale of the merchandise and payment of the liabilities. (Prepare closing entries with respect to revenues and expenses associated with the sale of the merchandise.)

b. Determine the balances in the partners' capital accounts immediately prior to the final distribution of cash between the partners. Explain why, even though the partners share profits and losses equally, their capital balances are not also equal.

c. How much cash should be distributed to each of the partners? Prepare a journal entry to record the final distribution to the partners.

4. *Partners' capital accounts are basically the same as owners' equity accounts of corporations.*

The accompanying table is an excerpt from the annual report of Price Waterhouse & Co., one of the major international CPA firms (dates have been changed).

Worldwide Statement of Changes in Partners' Capital and Undistributed Income, Years Ended June 30, 1992 and 1991
(thousands of dollars)

	1992	1991
Partners' capital		
Balance, beginning of year	$ 65,900	$ 53,500
Additional capital provided	10,700	17,900
Repayment of paid-in capital	(3,500)	(5,500)
Balance, end of year	$ 73,100	$ 65,900
Undistributed income		
Balance, beginning of year	$129,200	$119,300
Payments to retired partners	(1,300)	(3,300)
Net income of active partners	186,100	154,800
Distributions to active partners	(164,800)	(141,600)
Balance, end of year	$149,200	$129,200

a. To what corporate account would "partners' capital" be comparable?

b. To what corporate account would "undistributed income" be comparable?

c. What were the net assets of Price Waterhouse as of December 31, 1992?

d. If Price Waterhouse had 1,487 partners worldwide, what would the average earnings per active partner be in 1992? What would the average amount of payments (presumably in cash) be to each of the active partners?

5. *The initial values assigned to the assets of a newly established corporation must be indicative of their fair market values.*

You have recently been offered 1,000 shares of the common stock of Computer Service Corporation at a price of $15 per share (a price well below book value). The company has just been formed; it has not yet commenced operations. It was organized by three computer systems analysts, who are presently the only stockholders. The company intends to lease office space and computers; it will provide electronic accounting services to small businesses.

A balance sheet provided you by the company reveals the following:

Cash	$100,000
Inventories and supplies	20,000
Goodwill	150,000
Total assets	$270,000
Common stock, par value $1 (20,000 shares authorized, 10,000 shares issued and outstanding)	$ 10,000
Common stock, contributed capital in excess of par	260,000
Total equities	$270,000

A footnote to the financial statements indicates that the $150,000 of goodwill represents the accumulated expertise of the founders of the corporation. All three promoters have had extensive experience with a leading computer manufacturer and have held management positions with other computer service companies. The goodwill was authorized by the firm's board of directors.

a. What reservations might you have about purchasing the stock of the company?

b. Assume instead that you were an independent certified public accountant called upon to audit the company shortly after its formation. What adjusting journal entry might you propose?

6. *The amounts for which shares of common stock were issued can be derived from information provided upon their retirement.*

The financial report of Warner Communications, Inc., contains the following note:

> During the year, 9,000,000 Common treasury shares, $1 par value, having an aggregate cost of $157,798,000 were retired resulting in charges of $9,000,000 to capital stock, $36,440,000 to paid in capital and $112,358,000 to retained earnings.

a. How much did the company pay to acquire each share?
b. What was the initial issuance price per share?
c. Prepare a journal entry to record the retirement of the shares, assuming that just prior to their retirement they were recorded at acquisition cost in a treasury stock account.

7. *The price at which preferred stock, like bonds, is issued is reflective of the relationship between prevailing yields and the promises inherent in the security.*

The Board of Directors of the Thoreau Electric Co. has voted to issue 100,000 shares of preferred stock that will pay an annual dividend of $6 per share. The preferred stock will have a stated value of $100 per share. At the date of issue, similar grades of preferred stock are being sold to provide a return to investors of 7 percent.
a. At what price is the preferred stock of Thoreau likely to be issued?
b. Prepare a journal entry to record the sale of the preferred stock.
c. Prepare an entry to record the payment of the first annual cash dividend.
d. Suppose instead that the preferred stock will have a stated value of $1 per share. Prepare an entry to record the issuance of the stock.

8. *Preferred stock dividends are usually "cumulative."*

The *Wall Street Journal* reported that Cenco, Inc., which had missed all but one of its preferred dividend payments for five years, now planned to pay the accumulated dividends. According to the *Journal*, "the dividends, totaling about $933,000 at $1.40 a share, will be payable April 27 to stockholders of record February 28." Cenco, the *Journal* indicated, "said the payment is subject to the condition that it won't violate the company's debenture agreements, which call for Cenco to have about $31.4 million in retained earnings before it can pay its preferred dividends." That requirement was the reason that Cenco had been unable to pay its preferred dividends in the past.

Cenco's financial problems were attributable to a $25 million phony profit scheme that involved inflating both inventories and earnings. Several executives had been convicted of conspiracy and fraud.
a. What is meant by the term *accumulated dividends*?
b. How many shares of preferred stock did the company have outstanding?
c. What entries, if any, does *The Wall Street Journal* report suggest that the firm made in those years that it failed to pay its dividends? Explain.

9. *Prices at which securities are issued and acquired can be derived from changes in the balances of owners' equity accounts.*

The stockholders' equity section of the balance sheet of the Intercontinental Corp. reveals the following:

	1993	1992
Common stock, $10 par value	$ 1,200,000	$ 1,000,000
Preferred stock, $100 par value, 8%	500,000	450,000
Contributed capital in excess of par		
Common stock	11,500,000	8,900,000
Preferred stock	8,000	—
Retained earnings	18,143,000	20,220,000
Less: Common stock held in treasury		
(1,300 shares in 1993, 1,000 shares in 1992)	(173,000)	(130,000)
	$31,178,000	$30,440,000

No treasury stock was retired or reissued during 1993.

a. How many shares of common stock did the company issue in 1993? What was the issue price per share?

b. How many shares of preferred stock did the company issue in 1993? What was the issue price per share?

c. What would you estimate to be the prevailing yield rate for comparable types of securities at the time the preferred stock was issued? That is, what was the yield rate used to determine the issue price of the preferred stock?

d. What was the price paid for the 300 shares of common stock acquired by the company in 1993?

10. *The price at which common stock of a newly formed corporation is issued should reflect the fair market value of the corporate assets.*

   Filmore and Francis are partners in a firm that operates a chain of drugstores. They decide to incorporate their business and sell shares in the enterprise to the general public. Filmore has a 60 percent interest in the partnership and Francis a 40 percent interest.

   The net assets (assets less liabilities) of the partnership are recorded on the books of the partnership at $8 million. However, after considerable study and consultation with independent appraisers, the partners decide that the fair market value of their business is $12 million. Indeed, just prior to their decision to incorporate they received an offer to sell the firm to an independent party for that amount.

   The partners intend to issue 200,000 shares of common stock. They plan to keep 60 percent of the shares for themselves and sell the rest to the public. Each share of stock will have a par value of $20.

   a. At what price should the shares be sold to the public?

   b. Prepare any journal entries required to record the formation of the new corporation.

11. *A shift from partnership to corporate status is an event of sufficient economic and legal significance to justify revaluing assets and liabilities.*

   Bryan and Moore are partners in a retail stereo business. After several successful years of operation as a partnership, the two decide to incorporate their business as Stereo, Inc. Bryan and Moore share profits and losses in the ratio of 3:1. Prior to the liquidation of the partnership and its subsequent incorporation, the balance sheet of the partnership indicated the following:

Assets		
Cash		$ 120,000
Accounts receivable		260,000
Inventory		830,000
Furniture and fixtures	$ 750,000	
Less: Allowance for depreciation	220,000	530,000
Land		180,000
Building	$1,020,000	
Less: Allowance for depreciation	600,000	420,000
Total assets		$2,340,000

Liabilities and owners' equity	
Accounts payable	$ 290,000
Notes payable	800,000
Capital, Bryan	937,500
Capital, Moore	312,500
Total liabilities and owners' equity	$2,340,000

Prior to transferring the assets to the corporation, the partners decide to adjust the books of the partnership to reflect current market values.

The building has a current market value of $850,000; the land, $260,000; and the furniture and fixtures, $300,000.

The firm has not previously provided for uncollectible accounts. However, it is estimated that $40,000 of the accounts are uncollectible. It is also determined that $80,000 of inventory is obsolete. The new corporation is to assume the liabilities of the partnership except as noted below.

The new corporation is authorized to issue 100,000 shares of $100 par value common stock. Common stock is to be issued at par value, with the number of shares proportionate to the fair market value of one's contribution.

Shares will also be issued to the following parties in addition to the partners:

To an attorney for providing services pertaining to the organization of the corporation; the fair market value of the services is $80,000.

To the party holding the note payable, who has agreed to accept common stock in full payment of his $800,000 note.

To a venture-capital financial institution, which has agreed to invest $500,000 cash in the new corporation.

a. Prepare journal entries to revalue the partnership, to transfer the assets to the new corporation in exchange for common stock, and to distribute the shares of the common stock to the partners.
b. Prepare journal entries to organize the new corporation.
c. Indicate the number of shares each investor will receive.

12. *Transactions involving a firm's own stock are often based upon the price at which the shares are being traded in the open market.*

The Frost Co. was organized on June 1, 1992. According to the terms of its charter, the firm was authorized to issue capital stock as follows:

Common stock: $2 par value, 100,000 shares
Preferred stock: $100 par value, 5 percent dividend rate, 10,000 shares

During the first year of operation the following transactions that affected capital accounts took place. Prepare journal entries to record the transactions.

a. The corporation issued for cash 50,000 shares of common stock at a price of $30 per share.
b. The corporation issued for cash 10,000 shares of preferred stock at $90 per share.
c. The company purchased a building, giving the seller 10,000 shares of common stock. At the time of the purchase, the common stock of the company was being traded in the open market at $25 per share.
d. The firm's advertising agency agreed to accept 3,000 shares of common stock, rather than cash, in payment for services performed. At the time of payment the market price of the stock was $28 per share.
e. The firm agreed to purchase the stock of a dissident shareholder. The firm purchased 3,000 shares at a price of $30 per share.
f. The company subsequently sold the shares to another stockholder at a price of $31 per share.

13. *United Parcel Service explains why it accounts for treasury stock as an asset.*

The balance sheet of United Parcel Service includes the following current asset:

	1987	1986
	(in thousands)	
Treasury stock, at cost	$370,734	$322,153

The company explains this unusual classification in a footnote:

> UPS generally accounts for treasury stock as an asset because it is held for distribution pursuant to awards under the UPS Managers' Incentive Plan and the UPS Incentive Stock Option Plan. The liability for the amount of the annual managers' Incentive award is included in Accrued Wages and Withholdings. Treasury stock in excess of anticipated future requirements, if any, is treated as a reduction of shareowners' equity.

a. Why is treasury stock rarely reported as an asset?

b. Comment on the company's explanation as to why treasury stock is shown as an asset. Is it reasonable?

14. *Union Camp Corporation accounts for treasury stock transactions in an atypical way.*

The December 31, 1987, balance sheet of Union Camp Corporation disclosed the following:

	1987	1986
	(in thousands)	
Stockholders' equity		
Common stock, par value $1.00 per share:		
Shares outstanding: 1987, 71,752,077;		
1986, 73,616,410	$ 71,752	$ 73,616
Capital in excess of par value	24,688	83,353
Retained earnings	1,355,577	1,213,600
Stockholders' equity, net	$1,452,017	$1,370,569

A note reported the following:

> During the fourth quarter of 1987, the company purchased 2,000,000 shares of its common stock. The purchase reduced common stock, par value, by $2 million and capital in excess of par value by $61.2 million. During the period January 1 through February 9, 1988, the company purchased an additional 879,600 shares of its common stock at a cost of $29.2 million.

Other 1987 transactions reported in the note (issuance of new shares as part of a stock option plan) increased the balance in common stock, par value, by $136,000 and in capital in excess of par by $2,535,000.

a. Prepare the entry that the company apparently made to record the purchase of its shares in the fourth quarter of 1987. Assume that no portion of the excess of purchase price over par value was allocated to retained earnings.
  (1) How might you explain the reduction in "capital in excess of par value" in an amount that greatly exceeded the proportion of shares retired?
  (2) What was the purchase price per share?

b. Prepare the entry that the company would make in 1988 to record the purchase of the additional 879,600 shares. Assume this time that "capital in excess of par" would be reduced only by an amount in proportion to the number of shares retired.

(1) What was the purchase price per share?

(2) The purchase of these additional shares took place in 1988. Why should they be reported in the *1987* financial statements (a point not discussed in the text)?

15. *A corporation can increase the equity of existing (and remaining) stockholders by judiciously issuing and retiring shares of its own common stock.*

In 1992 Mary Bells, Inc., reported earnings of $6 million. Its owners' equity at the end of the year was $30 million. The firm had 1 million shares of common stock issued and outstanding.

At the start of 1993 the company decided to expand its operations. To raise an additional $15 million in capital, it issued additional common stock at a price of $100 per share. The additional capital enabled the firm to increase earnings by $3 million per year after taxes to $9 million.

a. Determine the *book* value per share and earnings per share both before and after the issue of the additional common stock.

b. In 1996 the market price of the firm's common stock fell to $50 per share. The firm decided to reacquire, at market price, $7.5 million of common stock. To avoid having to reduce its scale of operations, the firm decided to issue long-term bonds for $7.5 million. The bonds could be sold at a price such that the effective interest cost to the company, after taxes, would be 5 percent. Determine the book value per share and earnings per share after the reacquisition of the shares and the issue of the bonds. Assume that in the intervening years, including 1996, the firm declared dividends in the amount of earnings and that income in 1996, before taking into account interest on the new bonds, was the same as that in 1993—$9 million.

16. *The value of a business which is about to be acquired by another firm can be established in a number of different ways.*

Alliance Department Stores, Inc., has agreed to purchase McKay Bros. Discount Store. McKay Bros. is operated as a partnership. The owners' equity accounts on the books of the partnership indicate that each of the two partners has a recorded capital balance of $10 million. An independent appraiser has determined that the value of the individual assets of the company (there are no significant liabilities) is $25 million. The partners, however, have had several offers to sell the entire business for $30 million.

Alliance Department Stores, Inc., has offered to purchase the store for shares of its own common stock. The number of shares to be issued is currently being negotiated between the two parties. Alliance currently has 5 million shares of common stock outstanding. The par value of each share is $2. The company has $30 million in capital in excess of par and $60 million in retained earnings. The current market price for shares of Alliance is $25 per share.

Six possible ways of determining the number of shares to be issued to the McKay Bros. partners are under consideration. The value of a share to be issued by Alliance can be based on either its *book* or its *market* value. The value of the interest to be purchased by Alliance can be based on the book value of McKay Bros.' assets, the appraised value of its assets, or its market value as a going concern.

a. Determine the number of shares to be issued by Alliance under each of the five combinations:

> **Value of Alliance shares based on (1) book value or (2) market value** and
> **Value of McKay Bros. based on (1) book value, (2) appraised value, or
> (3) market value**

b. How do you account for the differences between book value, appraised value, and market value?

c. On which basis do you recommend the number of shares should be determined?

17. *Prevailing tax laws are a key factor in a corporation's decision as to whether it should issue bonds or preferred stock.*

A firm wishes to construct a new plant. The estimated cost of the plant is $5 million. The firm is undecided as to whether to raise the required capital by issuing bonds or preferred stock. The current prevailing yield on bonds of similar grade is 7 percent, and that on preferred stock is 9 percent.

What would be the minimum earnings, before taxes, that the firm would have to realize, under both alternatives, if it were to break even on the proposed project? The effective combined state and federal tax rate is 40 percent.

18. *In choosing between alternative instruments of financing, a firm must take into account its expectations as to future earnings.*

A corporation has decided to construct an addition to its plant. The cost of the addition is $5 million; it is expected to increase earnings by $900,000 per year before taking into account income taxes.

The firm is considering three means of acquiring the needed $5 million capital:

- The firm can sell bonds; current yield rates are 8 percent per year.
- The firm can issue preferred stock; current yield rates are 12 percent per year.
- The firm can issue common stock; There are currently 600,000 shares outstanding. The firm estimates that additional shares could be sold at a price of $10 per share. The company has not paid any dividends on common stock in recent years and does not plan to do so in the foreseeable future. The current tax rate is 48 percent.

a. Prepare a table that has one column for each of the three options and the following captions for its rows:
(1) Anticipated additional earnings (before taxes)
(2) Required interest or dividend payments
(3) Additional "earnings" less direct cost of capital [(1) − (2)]
(4) Income taxes
(5) Net additional earnings [(3) − (4)]
(6) Shares of common stock outstanding
(7) Additional earnings per share of common stock [(5) − (6)]

Which alternative do you think the company ought to select if impact on earnings per share of common stock is to be the most important criterion?
b. Suppose that anticipated earnings from the new addition is $1.5 million per year. Which alternative do you think the firm ought to select? (You need not recompute earnings per share; simply use judgment.)
c. Suppose that estimated additional earnings is $900,000 per year but that the market price of the firm's common stock is $20 per share. Which alternative should now be favored?

19. *Market-based relationships suggest an alternative means of recording the issuance of convertible bonds.*

Dunedin Corp. issues $1 million of 8 percent coupon bonds at a price of $110 (i.e., $1.1 million). The bonds are convertible, after three years, into the firm's $10 par value common stock at a ratio of 40 to 1. The bonds mature in 20 years.

At the time the bonds are issued, the prevailing rate of interest on bonds with the same characteristics, but lacking the conversion feature, is 10 percent.
a. Prepare an entry to record the issuance of the bonds.
b. For what amount would the bonds most probably have been issued if they were not convertible?

c. Why should the purchasers of the bond be willing to pay an amount in addition to that determined in part (b)? Do you think that the extra amount should be classified as "debt"? How else might it be classified?

d. Prepare an alternative entry to record the issuance of the bonds, one that is consistent with your response to part (c). (Note that this entry is *not* in accord with generally accepted accounting principles.)

20. *Choice of accounting method for convertible bonds affects the classification of owners' equity.*

Rotorua Industries, Inc., issues $1 million of 8 percent convertible bonds at a premium of $200,000. The bonds may be exchanged, any time after four years from the date of issuance, for shares of the firm's common stock ($5 par value) at a ratio of 20 to 1. At the time the bonds are issued, the common stock has a market value of $48 per share.

After four years, the market price of the firm's stock has increased to $60 per share. The bond premium has been amortized down to $180,000. The bondholders elect to convert.

a. Prepare a journal entry to record the issuance of the bonds.

b. Prepare a journal entry to record the conversion using first the book value method and then the market value method.

c. Suppose instead that the market price of the securities at the time of conversion is $63 per share. What is the difference, if any, in each of the entries?

d. What difference in the firm's *total* owners' equity would result from using the market value rather than the book value method? What difference would result in the distribution among the categories of owners' equity? Explain.

21. *The conversion of preferred stock to common stock requires an adjustment only to owners' equity accounts.*

The annual report of Chromalloy American Corporation contains the following note:

> Preferred Stock—*The Company's preferred stock is issuable in series and is entitled to one vote per share. The outstanding $5 Cumulative Convertible Preferred Stock is convertible at the rate of 3.888 shares of common for each share of preferred stock.*

The stockholders' equity section of the balance sheet indicates the following:

Preferred stock, authorized 1,825,000 shares, par value $1 per share; $5 cumulative convertible preferred stock; outstanding 561,164 shares	$ 561,164
Common stock, authorized 20,000,000 shares, par value $1 per share; issued 10,748,462 shares	10,748,462
Other capital ascribed to others	42,930,965
	$ 54,240,591
Retained earnings	122,696,044
	$176,936,635

Suppose that all 561,164 shares of preferred stock were converted into common stock. Prepare a journal entry to record the exchange.

22. *This problem illustrates common provisions of convertible securities. It also raises the question of whether the premium or discount on preferred stock should be amortized.*

The financial statements of USF&G Corporation describe its two classes of stock:

The corporation has two classes of capital stock authorized: 12,000,000 shares of $50 par value preferred stock and 120,000,000 shares of $2.50 par value common stock.

In 1986, the corporation completed the sale of 4,000,000 shares of $4.10 *Series A Convertible Exchangeable Preferred Stock* ("preferred stock"), yielding proceeds of approximately $194,000,000. The holder of each share of the preferred stock is entitled to an annual cumulative dividend of $4.10 per share and a liquidation preference of $50 per share plus accrued and unpaid dividends. Each share is convertible into 1.087 shares of the corporation's common stock at the option of the holder subject to adjustment under certain conditions. The stock can be exchanged in whole at the option of the corporation on any dividend payment date beginning in October 1989, for the corporation's 8.20 percent Convertible Subordinated Debentures due in October 2011, at a rate of $50 principal amount per share. The shares are redeemable for cash in whole or in part at the option of the corporation commencing in October 1989, at redemption prices declining to $50 per share in October 1996, plus accrued and unpaid dividends to the redemption date.

Holders of the preferred stock are not entitled to vote except that they may vote separately with respect to certain matters including the authorization of any additional classes of capital stock which would rank senior to the preferred stock. In the event that six quarterly dividends are unpaid, the Board of Directors of the corporation will be increased by two and holders of preferred stock may elect two directors until all such dividends in arrears have been paid.

a. Prepare the entry most probably made to record the issue, in 1986, of the Series A preferred stock.
b. Record the payment of the first annual dividend.
c. As indicated in the text, it is generally not necessary to amortize a discount or premium on preferred stock. Could you make an argument that in this case the discount or premium should be amortized?
d. Assume that the market value of the preferred stock is $50 per share. What would the approximate market value of the common stock have to be in order to induce holders of the preferred stock to convert to common stock?
e. Would you characterize the issue of the preferred stock as *cumulative* or *noncumulative*?
f. Prepare the entry that would be made to record the conversion of the entire issue of Series A preferred stock to the *subordinated debentures*. Assume the conversion is to be based on book values.
g. Prepare the entry that would be made to record the conversion of the entire issue of Series A preferred stock to *common stock*. Assume the conversion is to be based on book values.

23. *The journal entry to record conversion of preferred to common stock can be reconstructed from the information provided in the owners' equity section of the balance sheet and in accompanying notes.*

The 1988 financial statements of Conagra, Inc., included the following note:

Preferred Shares Subject to Mandatory Redemption

	1988	1987
	(in thousands)	
Class D, Outstanding		
$2.50 cumulative convertible, outstanding 3,850,650 shares in 1988 and 5,331,550 shares in 1987	$9,627	$13,329

The Company shall call the voting, convertible, cumulative Class D, $2.50 preferred stock for redemption on or prior to July 20, 1988, and on each July 20 thereafter a number of shares of $2.50 cumulative, convertible preferred stock equal to 5 percent and at the option of the Company up to 10 percent of the aggregate number of shares issued by paying in cash $25.00 per share plus accrued dividends. All or any portion of the $2.50 cumulative, convertible preferred stock may be called for redemption by the Company at any time at prices ranging from $25.75 (1989) to $25.00 (1992 and thereafter) plus accrued dividends. The holders of the Class D, $2.50 preferred stock have the option at any time to convert their shares to common stock at the rate of 3.08 shares of common stock for each share of $2.50 cumulative, convertible preferred stock.

During 1988 and 1987, 148,689 and 35,956 shares of $2.50 cumulative, convertible preferred stock were converted into 458,075 and 110,702 shares of common stock, respectively. Conversions are applied against redemption requirements.

The owners' equity section of the 1988 balance indicated the following:

	1988	1987
	(in thousands)	
Preferred shares subject to mandatory redemption	$ 9,627	$ 13,329
Common stockholders' equity		
Common stock of $5 par value, authorized 300,000,000 shares; issued 78,998,845 and 78,875,818, respectively	394,994	394,379
Additional paid-in capital	883	165
Retained earnings	444,298	352,672
	$849,802	$760,545

a. What was the amount per share at which the Class D stock was issued? How can you tell?
b. Prepare the entry that was most likely made to record the conversion in 1988 of the Class D stock to common stock.
c. What would you estimate to be the minimum market value per share of the common stock at the time of conversion, assuming that the market value of the Class D shares was equal to or greater than their book value?

Solutions to Exercise for Review and Self-Testing

1. a. The assets should be recorded at their fair market values. Hence plant and equipment, $8.2 million; patents, $2 million.
   b. Common stock, par value: 100,000 shares × $50 per share = $5 million. Common stock, capital in excess of par: $10,200,000 − $5,000,000 = $5.2 million.
   c. Plant and equipment....................................$8,200,000
      Patents 2,000,000
           Common stock, par value $5,000,000
           Common stock, capital in excess of par..................... 5,200,000
      To record issuance of common stock

2. a. The firm will pay $9 per share in dividends.
   b. $9 ÷ 0.85 = $105.88, which equals the market value per share of preferred stock.

---

c. Cash $1,058,800

     Preferred stock, par value $1,000,000

     Preferred stock, capital in excess of par 58,800

To record issuance of preferred stock

3. a. Because the company intends to reissue the shares in the near future, they should be accounted for by the cost method.

  b. Treasury stock $180,000

     Cash $180,000

     To record acquisition of 1,000 shares of common stock

4. a. Because the company intends to retire the shares, they should be accounted for by the par value method.

  b. 20 percent.

  c. 20 percent; 20% of $5,000,000 = $1,000,000.

  d. 20 percent; 20% of $5,200,000 = $1,040,000.

  e. 20,000 shares × $160 per share − $2,040,000 = $1,160,000.

  f. Common stock, par value $1,000,000

    Common stock, capital in excess of par 1,040,000

    Retained earnings 1,160,000

     Cash $3,200,000

    To record retirement of 20,000 shares of common stock

12

Special Problems of Measuring and Reporting Dividends and Earnings

This chapter, as did the previous one, focuses on transactions between a corporation and its owners. Specifically, it considers the means of measuring and reporting distributions of earnings—dividends in cash, "in kind," and in stock—as well as stock splits.

It also deals with four seemingly unrelated accounting issues:

1. Measuring employee compensation in the form of the employer's common stock or options to acquire the common stock
2. Recognizing losses
3. Calculating earnings per share
4. Determining income for an *interim* period, one that is shorter than a full accounting cycle

The issues, however, are tied together by a common thread: "Correct" accounting is dependent upon future events. Hence the accounting of the present must be governed by estimates or assumptions as to eventual outcomes.

The issues dealt with are of immediate concern to investors inasmuch as they affect directly both the magnitude and the proportion of their claims to corporate assets. They are of equal importance to managers because managers are the agents (representatives) of investors and their performance is likely to be evaluated on how competently and equitably they represent their interests.

Moreover, the corporations that managers administer may themselves be investors, owning shares in other companies.

CASH DIVIDENDS AND RETAINED EARNINGS

Retained earnings are the total accumulated earnings of a corporation less amounts distributed to stockholders as dividends and any amounts transferred to other capital accounts.

Dividends are distributions of *assets* (or shares of common stock) that reduce retained earnings. They are *declared* by a formal resolution of a firm's board of directors. The announcement of a dividend indicates the *amount per share* to be distributed, the *date of record* (that on which the stock records will be closed and ownership of the outstanding shares determined), and the *date of payment*. A typical announcement reads as follows: ''The board of directors of the XYZ corporation, at its regular meeting of December 9, 1993, declared a quarterly dividend of $2 per share payable on January 24, 1994, to stockholders of record on January 3, 1994.''

Basic Entries

The entry to record the declaration of a dividend is straightforward. On the date of declaration, when the liability for payment is first established, the entry (in this case to record a dividend of $2 per share on 1 million shares outstanding) would be

```
Common stock dividends . . . . . . . . . . . . . . . . . . . . . . . . . . . . . . . . . . . $2,000,000
      Dividends payable . . . . . . . . . . . . . . . . . . . . . . . . . . . . . . . . . . . . . . $2,000,000
      To record declaration of the cash dividend on common stock
```

At year end, ''common stock dividends'' would be *closed* to retained earnings. When payment is subsequently made, it would be recorded as follows:

```
Dividends payable . . . . . . . . . . . . . . . . . . . . . . . . . . . . . . . . . . . . . . . . $2,000,000
      Cash . . . . . . . . . . . . . . . . . . . . . . . . . . . . . . . . . . . . . . . . . . . . . . . . . . $2,000,000
      To record payment of the dividend
```

Dividends and Availability of Cash or Other Assets

Although conventional (nonstock) dividends are *charged* to retained earnings, they are *paid* in cash or other tangible assets. It does not follow that merely because a company has a balance in retained earnings it has the wherewithal to make dividend payments. Retained earnings are a part of owners' equity. Owners' equity is the excess of assets over liabilities. It cannot be associated with specific assets to which stockholders have claim.

The nature of retained earnings is a common source of misunderstanding. At one time the term *earned surplus* was used in place of retained earnings. ''Surplus'' implies something extra—an amount over and above what is needed. Retained earnings rarely, in fact, represent surplus. Rather, a balance in retained earnings is indicative of earnings that have been reinvested in the corporation. By not distributing its earned assets to stockholders, the corporation may have internally financed expansion. The retained earnings, therefore, may not denote the availability of cash or other assets that can readily be distributed to stockholders; instead, the company may have used its available resources to acquire land, buildings, and equipment. The owners' equity section of a recent General Motors Corporation balance sheet, for example, comprised the following accounts (in millions):

Preferred stock	$ 236.4
Common stock	532.8
Capital in excess of par	6,764.6
Retained earnings	25,771.7
	$33,305.5

Retained earnings, in this case, accounted for 77 percent of owners' capital. It is obvious that distribution of assets represented by the entire $25.8 billion in retained earnings would have forced the company to retrench its operations back to the scale of its "horseless carriage" days.

When and how much of a dividend to declare depends on financial requirements and opportunities as well as legal constraints.

The company must first determine whether available and projected cash is sufficient to meet its other operating requirements—the need to meet payrolls, maintain inventories, and replace worn-out equipment. In addition, however, the corporation must consider the interests of shareholders. Insofar as assets are not distributed to stockholders, the stockholders are being forced to increase their investment in the corporation. Whether they wish to increase their investment will depend largely on the return they could obtain from competing investments. If the funds to be retained in the corporation are likely to provide a return greater than stockholders could obtain elsewhere, then stockholders should be willing to permit the company to retain all or a portion of its assets. In fact, many corporations, particularly *growth* companies, omit payment of dividends for years at a time. Stockholders of these companies are willing to forgo immediate cash returns for long-term corporate expansion and enhancement of their investment.

The payment of dividends is sometimes constrained by statute. The corporation laws of some states prohibit firms from paying dividends "out of capital"; they can pay them only "out of earnings." That is, the payment of dividends cannot reduce the stockholders' equity of the company beneath the amount contributed by the stockholders. The motive behind these restrictions is protection of creditors. The state laws are designed to make certain that corporations repay their debts before they distribute assets to stockholders. The stockholders, because of their limited liability, are not individually responsible for the obligations of the corporation.

DIVIDENDS IN KIND

Although dividends are usually paid in cash, it is not uncommon for a company to distribute other types of assets.

A company may own all or a portion of the outstanding stock of a subsidiary. Wishing to divest itself of that firm, it distributes the stock to its own stockholders. The stockholders can then choose to retain their interest in the subsidiary or sell the shares in the open market. Such a transaction is referred to as a *spinoff*. In the 1980s, spinoffs were used extensively by major corporations to rid themselves of unwanted lines of business.

Example

Suppose, for example, the Gamma Co. owns 1 million shares of XYZ Corporation stock. It declares and pays a *dividend in kind* (as such dividends in property are known) of 4 shares of XYZ stock for each of its own 250,000 shares outstanding. If the stock of the XYZ Corporation has been recorded on the books of the Gamma Co. at $5 per share but has a fair market value of $8 per share, then the following two entries would be required:

XYZ Corp. stock $3,000,000
 Gain on investment. $3,000,000
To write up XYZ Corp. stock to reflect market value

Common stock dividends $8,000,000
 XYZ Corp. stock $8,000,000
To record declaration and payment of dividend in kind

As a consequence of the dividend, the corporation will report a holding gain in the amount of the difference between book value and market value of the property distributed.

Many accountants assert, however, that a corporation should *not* be permitted to realize gains or losses as the result of discretionary, nonarm's-length transactions with stockholders. If it were, they contend, it could readily manipulate earnings by distributing to shareholders assets that it could not otherwise sell to outsiders at the value assigned to them. Other accountants point out, however, that "market value" implies an ability to sell the assets to outsiders at the value assigned. Moreover, they observe, a corporation should not have to incur the transaction costs of selling its assets to outsiders to realize a gain. It could as easily transfer them directly to its shareholders, who could sell them for as much cash as they would otherwise receive. The Accounting Principles Board, in *Opinion No. 29,* held that dividends in kind should generally be accounted for at market values and appropriate gains or losses recognized.[1]

Distributions of the stock of other companies (*dividends in kind*) should not be confused with *stock dividends,* which will be discussed in a following section.

STOCK SPLITS

Corporations will sometimes *split* their stock; that is, they will issue additional shares for each share outstanding. A firm might, for example, split its stock

---

[1]An exception to this general rule is made when a company distributes to its stockholders *all* of the shares of another corporation as part of a reorganization or rescindment of a prior business combination. In this type of transaction, *the distribution of shares should be based on their recorded* value. Hence no gains or losses are recognized.

3 for 1, meaning that, for each one share presently held, a shareholder will receive an additional two.

Stock splits are ordinarily intended to reduce the market price per share, to obtain a wider distribution of ownership, and to improve the marketability of the outstanding shares. The common stock of a corporation might be trading at $150 per share. The board of directors determines that at such a high price the stock is less attractive to investors than it would be at a lower price. Many investors like to acquire stock in round lots of 100 shares since brokerage commissions are relatively higher when fewer shares are purchased. The board might, therefore, vote a 3-for-1 stock split. Each shareholder will end up with three times as many shares as previously, but the market price per share can be expected to fall to nearly one-third its previous price. Neither the corporation nor the individual stockholder will be intrinsically better or worse off as a result of the split.

Commonly, the corporation would reduce the par value of the common stock to reflect the split and would so notify shareholders. If the stock previously had a par value of $10, it would subsequently have a new par value of $3.33. Common stock, par value, will in total remain unchanged. So too will capital contributed in excess of par and retained earnings. A stock split is the equivalent of an exchange of one $5 bill for five $1 bills. As a consequence, no accounting entries are required to effect the split.

Alternatively, the corporation might elect to retain the same par value per share. Then it is necessary to adjust the par value account so that it is equal to par value per share times the number of shares outstanding. The amount that must be added to, or subtracted from, the par value account is transferred from "common stock, contributed capital in excess of par." Assume a company has 1 million shares of $10 par value common stock outstanding. If it splits the stock 3 for 1 and does *not* change the par value, then it will be necessary to increase the balance in the par value account by $20 million. Whereas previously the required balance was $10 million (1 million shares @ $10), now it will be $30 million (3 million shares @ $10). The following entry would be required:

Common stock, contributed capital in
  excess of par $20,000,000
    Common stock, par value $20,000,000
To adjust the par value account for a 3-for-1 stock split

STOCK DIVIDENDS

Motivation

A special form of stock split is known as a *stock dividend*. As with a stock split, a stock dividend results in the issuance of additional shares. Ordinarily the ratio of new shares to outstanding shares is lower for a stock dividend than for a stock split. Seldom does the number of new shares to be issued exceed 20 percent of previously outstanding shares; generally it is less than 5 percent. More significantly, the motivation for a stock dividend is considerably different from that for a stock split. A corporation would not issue a stock dividend to improve the marketability of its shares, but instead to provide its shareholders with tangible evidence of an increase in their ownership interest. A company may view a stock dividend as a substitute for a dividend in cash or other property. Lacking the available cash, it would distribute to each shareholder, on a pro rata basis, additional shares of its own stock. Sometimes, for example, a company that has consistently paid cash dividends may experience a cash shortage. Rather than omitting the dividend entirely, the company would distribute additional shares of stock. A stock dividend may also provide a means for a company to *capitalize* a portion of accumulated earnings. The company would transfer a portion of accumulated earnings from the "retained earnings" account (which is sometimes viewed as a temporary capital account) to "common stock, par value," and "capital received in excess of par" accounts (which are considered to be of a more permanent nature). This type of transfer provides formal evidence that resources have been permanently retained in the business and are no longer available for the payment of dividends.

In Essence a Stock Split

A stock dividend, like a stock split, has no effect on the intrinsic worth of the corporation. It leaves the shareholders neither better nor worse off than previously. A stock dividend has no effect on corporate assets and liabilities. As a result of the dividend, additional shares of common stock are outstanding. But since the net worth of the corporation remains the same, each share of common stock represents a proportionately smaller interest in the corporation.

Suppose, for example, that a corporation, prior to declaration of a stock dividend, had net assets of $100 million and 1 million shares of common stock outstanding. A stockholder who owned 100,000 shares would have held a 10 percent interest in a company with a book value of $100 million. If the corporation declared a 3 percent stock dividend, then the stockholder would receive 3,000 additional shares. He would now own 103,000 shares out of a total of 1,030,000 shares—still a 10 percent interest in a company with a book value of $100 million. Insofar as the market price for the stock is determined rationally, then the market price per share can be expected to be reduced proportionately.

The underlying nature of a stock dividend has been well expressed by the U.S. Supreme Court. In a case in which the court was called upon to rule whether stock dividends constituted income subject to tax under the provisions of the Sixteenth Amendment, Justice Pitney affirmed a judgment in a previous case in which it was held

> A stock dividend really takes nothing from the property of the corporation, and adds nothing to the interest of the shareholders. Its property is not diminished, and their interests are not increased. . . . The proportional interest of each shareholder remains the same. The only change is in the evidence which represents that interest, the new shares and the original shares together representing the same proportional interest that the original shares represented before the issue of the new ones.[2]

But Accounted for Differently

Although stock dividends are, in essence, a form of stock split, the rule-making authorities of the accounting profession have determined that they should be

[2]Eisner v. Macomber, 252 U.S. 189, 40 S. Ct. 189.

accounted for differently. Whereas a stock split is accounted for as *renumbering* of selected ownership accounts, a stock dividend is handled as a *reclassification* of the owners' equity accounts.

According to a pronouncement of a committee on accounting procedures, a predecessor of the Accounting Principles Board, when a corporation issues less than 20 to 25 percent additional shares as a dividend, it should transfer from retained earnings to "permanent" capital an amount equal to the *fair value* of the shares issued.[3] Assume, as before, a company which previously had 1 million shares of stock outstanding declared a 3 percent stock dividend. Assume additionally that each share had a par value of $10 and that the market price at the time of the declaration was $150 per share. The fair value of the 30,000 shares to be issued and the accumulated earnings to be capitalized would be 30,000 times $150, or $4.5 million. Because of the relatively small percentage of additional shares to be issued, a company would usually *not* reduce the par value of its shares. Instead, it would transfer from retained earnings to "common stock, par value," an amount reflective of the par value of the new shares to be issued—in this example, $300,000—and to "common stock, contributed capital in excess of par," the remaining amount—in this example, $4.2 million.

The following entry would give effect to the stock dividend:

```
Dividends in common stock..............................$4,500,000
        Common stock, par value ................................$  300,000
        Common stock, contributed
          capital in excess of par ..................................  4,200,000
To record the issue of a stock dividend
```

The stock dividends account would then be "closed" to retained earnings:

```
Retained earnings .........................................$4,500,000
        Dividends in common stock...............................$4,500,000
To close stock dividend account
```

Rationale Behind Generally Accepted Practice

The rationale behind the *capitalization* of retained earnings rests largely with the interpretation supposedly placed upon stock dividends by the recipients. The professional committee that issued the official pronouncement noted that a stock dividend does not, in fact, give rise to any change whatsoever in either the corporation's assets or its respective shareholders' proportionate interests. However, it said, "it cannot fail to be recognized that, merely as a consequence of the expressed purpose of the transaction and its characterization as a *dividend* in related notices to shareholders and the public at large, many recipients of stock dividends look upon them as distributions of corporate earnings and usually in an amount equivalent to the fair value of the additional shares received."[4]

Moreover, the committee pointed out, in many instances the number of shares issued is sufficiently small in relation to shares previously outstanding so

---

[3]American Institute of Certified Public Accountants, *Accounting Research Bulletin No. 43,* Chapter 7, New York, 1961.
[4]Ibid.

that the market price of the stock does not perceptibly decline. Hence the overall market value of a stockholder's interest may increase by the amount of the market value of the new shares. Because both recipients and the investing public *think* that the dividend shares are of value, the committee said, the corporation should account for them as if they were of value. It should transfer a portion of accumulated earnings from "temporary" to "permanent" capital accounts so as to indicate that such portion of earnings is no longer available for the payment of dividends. Whatever merit the rationale of the committee might have had when it was first set forth has unquestionably been reduced by the increased sophistication of investors. Today, only the most naïve of investors would see the new shares per se as having value—although they do, of course, recognize that the earnings that they represent have enhanced the value of their investment.

WHEN IS A LOSS A LOSS?

Inherent in almost all accounting issues is the question, "When is a company better off than it was previously?" Implicit in this question is its corollary, "When is a company worse off?" Or, to phrase it somewhat differently, "When should a loss be recognized as a loss?"

Suppose, for example, that a U.S. company that has interests abroad has been threatened with the expropriation of its foreign manufacturing facilities. Unquestionably, the mere threat of the expropriation leaves the firm worse off than it was previously. No doubt, the market price of the firm's outstanding common stock would fall in reaction to such a threat. But should the mere possibility of expropriation be a cause for the firm to write off its foreign assets and charge income with a "loss from expropriation"?

Consider also a company that has been accused by federal authorities of having engaged in price-fixing activities. Learning that they have been overcharged, its customers sue for recovery of damages. At what point should the firm recognize an impairment of its value: When the suit is actually filed; when an initial judgment against the firm is rendered; or when all available appeals have been exhausted?

Contingencies

The question of when to recognize *contingencies* (losses that are uncertain as to both occurrence and amount) is particularly troublesome. On the one hand, the convention of conservatism dictates that prompt recognition be given to losses. But, on the other, financial statements must be objective. The probability of many types of losses does not suddenly go from remote to certain. It increases gradually over a period of time. Firms cannot be permitted unlimited discretion in selecting the period in which to recognize losses. If they were, then reported income would be nothing more than an arbitrary determination of corporate management.

The difficulty of establishing guidelines as to when a loss should be recognized arises in large measure because the types of losses that firms incur form a continuum from "reasonably certain and estimable" to "remotely possible and not estimable." On one end of the continuum are losses such as those arising from warranty obligations and uncollectible accounts. As indicated previously, such losses are conventionally recognized at the time of the related sale of merchandise. They are statistically certain to occur, and the amount of the loss is subject to reasonable estimation, even though the particular account that will have to be written off or the party to whom payment might have to be made is unknown at the time of sale. On the other end of the continuum are losses from fires and natural disasters, which, although sure to occur at some time, are random happenings.

Criteria for Recognizing Loss

The Financial Accounting Standards Board, in *Statement No. 5,* ''Accounting for Contingencies,'' has prescribed that a loss may be charged to income only when

(1) information available prior to issuance of the financial statements indicates that it is probable that an asset had been impaired or a liability had been incurred at the date of the financial statements, and

(2) the amount of loss can be reasonably estimated.

These guidelines are, of course, nonspecific, but the complete statement of the board provides a number of examples as to when various types of losses should be recognized. The statement directs that, even if a loss contingency does not satisfy the criteria for formal recording within the accounts, the contingency must nevertheless be *disclosed* in a footnote to the financial statements. The disclosure must indicate the nature of the contingency and give, if possible, an estimate of, or range of, the possible loss.

In keeping with the convention of conservatism, *gain* contingencies are not usually recognized in the accounts until the cash or other resources are actually received. They may, of course, be disclosed in the footnotes of periods prior to those when they are recognized.

COMPENSATION IN STOCK OR STOCK OPTIONS

Corporations frequently compensate their employees in shares of stock or in options which permit them to purchase stock on favorable terms. Stock plans take a variety of forms. They have become popular for several reasons. First, they provide employees with tax advantages over straight cash wages in that they permit employees to defer the tax on the compensation. Second, by making the employees corporate owners, stock plans can increase loyalty, efficiency, and productivity. Third, they enable the employer to conserve cash by permitting it to substitute stock for cash.

Accounting for Compensation Expense

The guiding accounting rule for compensation in stock or stock options is that the total compensation cost is to be measured by the fair market value of the stock or options at the date of the grant. The compensation expense is to be recognized over the period during which the employees perform the related services and thereby earn the stock or option.

Compensation in Stock

The accounting for compensation in stock is relatively straightforward because the value of the stock is known at the time it is earned by the employees.

Example

Assume that in abbreviated form the balance sheet of a corporation is (in millions)

Assets (net of liabilities)	$300
Capital stock (300 million shares)	$200
Retained earnings	100
Total capital	$300

The corporation, in addition to paying its employees standard cash wages and salaries, grants them 25 million shares of its own common stock. Market value of the shares (which in this example is the same as book value) is $1 per share.

The corporation would report wage and salary expense of $25 million—the market value of 25 million shares at $1 per share and a corresponding increase in capital stock:

Wage and salary expense $25
    Capital stock $25
To record employee compensation and the issuance of additional shares of common stock

At year end, wage and salary expense would be closed to retained earnings, thereby reducing retained earnings by $25 million.

Note, however, an anomaly. The reported wage expense will be greater than the likely value of the shares to be given the employees. After the new shares have been issued, and wage and salary expense has been closed to retained earnings, the total assets, as well as the total capital, will remain at $300 million. There will now, however, be 325 million shares outstanding. The value per share (both book and market) can be expected to decline to $.9231 per share ($300 million in capital divided by 325 million shares). Thus from their perspective, the employees receive compensation of only $23.07 million rather than $25 million.

Compensation in Stock Options

The issues of accounting for compensation in stock options are considerably more complex than those for the stock itself because of the uncertainty that attaches to the compensation.

Stock options take many forms, but typically they permit employees to purchase shares of a company's stock at a fixed price at some date in the future. Although the employees will have to pay for their shares, the price to be paid remains constant regardless of fluctuations in market value. Should the market value of the shares increase above the set price (the *exercise* price), employees could acquire the shares at a considerable savings over what they would otherwise have to pay. Should the market price fall below the exercise price, then they need not exercise their options, but can allow them to lapse.

Measuring Compensation Expense and Determining Share Values

The difficult accounting issues with respect to employee stock options are how to measure the compensation paid and how to value the shares of stock to be issued. If the employees had to exercise the options immediately upon receipt, then the problems of valuation would be reasonably straightforward. The approximate value of each option would be the number of shares that could be purchased times the difference between the current market price of the stock and the exercise price of the option. If, for example, options permitted employees to purchase 100 shares of stock at $40 per share at a time when the stock was being traded at $45 per share, then the employees could "save" $5 per share. The value of each option would be

Current market price	$45	
Less: Exercise price	40	$5
Times number of shares that could be purchased		× 100
Value of options		$500

Most stock option plans stipulate that an option can be exercised only after a specified number of years has elapsed and only if the employee has remained with the company during that period. Indeed, one of the primary objectives of stock-option plans is to reduce employee turnover. As a result, at the time the option is granted, neither the number of shares to be issued nor the total amount to be received from an employee as payment for the shares is known.

Moreover, once an option plan has been adopted, the *exercise price*—the price that the employees will have to pay for their shares—is adjusted only periodically. Because of fluctuations in the market price of the firm's shares, the exercise price may sometimes be *greater* than the market price. For example, the options may allow employees to purchase shares of stock at a price of $40 even though the current market price is only $35. If the value of the options is to be based on the excess of the exercise price over the market price, then it would appear to be negative.

The options, however, clearly have positive value, regardless of the relationship between exercise and market prices. The recipients have the *right* to purchase the shares at $40 per share. If in the period during which they are eligible to exercise the options, the market price increases to more than $40, they can purchase the shares at a *discount* price. If the price remains below $40 per share, they need not exercise the options; they have lost nothing.

Matching Compensation Expense with Employee Service

Despite these problems of measurement, the Accounting Principles Board has ruled that stock options should be recorded as compensation expense in the periods in which an employee performs the services for which the option is granted.

The dictum of the board is intended to ensure that the cost of employee services is matched with the benefits (revenues) that they generate. The value of the option should be determined as of the date that the option is granted.

The board prescribed that the value of each option be measured by the difference between the exercise price and the market price so long as the market price exceeds the exercise price. But, if, as in the situation just described, the exercise price is greater than the market price, then the option and the related compensation should be assumed to have a zero value. The board recognized that there is, in fact, value to options that are granted when the exercise price is greater than the market price. However, it considered the practical difficulties of determining such value to be insurmountable.

Example

On December 31, 1993, a firm grants an executive the option to purchase 1 million shares of $1 par value common stock at a price of $8 per share. The option is in recognition of service performed during 1993. It can be exercised during the five years beginning January 1, 1996, providing the executive is still employed by the firm. The market price of the stock on December 31, 1993, is $10 per share.

The compensation and the option would be assigned a value of 1 million times $2 ($10 minus $8), or $2 million, and would be recorded on the date granted as follows:

Executive compensation (expense) $2,000,000
    Capital received, stock options $2,000,000
To record the issue of the employee stock options

The account "capital received, stock options," would be reported among the other owners' equity accounts. It would represent capital contributed by the executive in the form of services rather than cash or other property. When the option is actually exercised, the receipt of the $8 million cash from the executive and the issue of the 1 million shares would be recorded as follows:

Capital received, stock options $2,000,000
Cash 8,000,000
    Common stock, par value $1,000,000
    Common stock, contributed
      capital in excess of par value 9,000,000
To record the issue of 1,000 shares of common stock

If, alternatively, the executive elects not to exercise the option and it lapses, then no entry would be required (although "capital received, stock options," could be reclassified to an account with a title indicative of the lapsed status of the option).

Now suppose that on December 31, 1994, the firm grants the executive an identical option. The market price of the stock has now fallen to $7 per share, however. Since the exercise price is greater than the market price, the option, for accounting purposes, is deemed to have a zero value; no journal entry is required to record the grant of the option.

When the option is actually exercised, the issue of the 1 million shares would be recorded with the following entry:

Cash $8,000,000
    Common stock, par value $1,000,000
    Common stock, contributed
      capital in excess of par value 7,000,000
To record issue of 1,000 shares of common stock

Note that the recorded value of the capital received is directly dependent on the market price of the common stock on the *date the options are granted* rather than the date on which the options are exercised and the shares issued.

The board's approach to valuing options oversimplifies an intricate economic question. The valuation of options involves more than merely subtracting exercise price from market price. Academic researchers have developed sophisticated mathematical models to determine the value of options. They are widely used by professional option traders. They take into account a number of variables in addition to market price of stock and exercise price of option. Among them are time to expiration, prevailing rates of interest, and the variability in the market price of the stock. The board, of course, recognizes that the prescribed method is simplistic, but continues to support it because it believes that the benefits of the more elegant methods are outweighed by the implementation costs imposed by their complexity.

EXTRAORDINARY ITEMS

Extraordinary items are those that are *unusual in nature and infrequent in occurrence.* In *Opinion No. 9* and *Opinion No. 15,* the Accounting Principles Board directed that extraordinary items be segregated from other revenues and expenses and reported separately on the income statement. The board recommended that they be included as part of the income statement as follows:

Income before extraordinary items	$xxxx
Extraordinary items (less applicable taxes	
of $_____) (Explanatory note:____)	xxxx
Net income	$xxxx

As indicated by the suggested presentation, the taxes associated with the extraordinary items should be presented along with those items. The taxes applicable to the extraordinary items should therefore be excluded from the tax expense reported in the main body of the income statement.

To help assure uniformity of practice, the board established rigorous criteria as to what constitutes an extraordinary item. To qualify as extraordinary, an item (as set forth in *Opinion No. 30*) must be *unusual in nature* in that "the underlying event or transactions should possess a high degree of abnormality and be of a type clearly unrelated to or only incidentally related to the ordinary and typical activities of the entity." It must also be *infrequent in occurrence* in that it should be "of a type not reasonably expected to recur in the foreseeable future."

Examples of events or transactions that would ordinarily be categorized as extraordinary items are losses resulting from major casualties such as earthquakes, expropriations of property by foreign governments, or governmental prohibitions against the sale or use of products which the company had previously manufactured.

Examples of events or transactions that would *not* be categorized as extraordinary items and should thereby be reported along with ordinary expenses are write-offs of receivables, losses on the sale of plants, and losses from foreign currency revaluations.

EARNINGS PER SHARE

If there is any one single measure of corporate performance that is of primary concern to common stockholders and potential investors, it is unquestionably earnings per share (EPS). In its simplest form, calculation of earnings per share is straightforward:

$$\text{EPS} = \frac{\text{Net income} - \text{Preferred stock dividends}}{\text{Number of shares of common stock outstanding}}$$

Net earnings should be those after taxes. Preferred stock dividends must be deducted from earnings whenever the ratio is being computed for the benefit of common stockholders, since preferred dividends reduce the equity of common stockholders.

Basis: Average Number of Shares Outstanding

The number of shares outstanding should be based on the *average* number of shares outstanding during the year. The average should be weighted by the number of months the shares may have been outstanding. The *average* number of shares outstanding, rather than simply the number outstanding at year end, must be used in the denominator. That is because the corporation would have had the use of the capital associated with any additional shares issued during the year only for a part of the year. The company's opportunity to generate earnings on the additional capital would have been limited by the number of months it had the use of the capital.

Example

A firm had earning after taxes of $800,000. It paid preferred stock dividends of $200,000. It had 200,000 shares of common stock outstanding since January 1. On October 1, it issued an additional 100,000 shares of common stock.

Earnings available to common stockholders would be $600,000 (earnings after taxes less preferred dividends paid).

The average number of shares outstanding would be

200,000 shares × 9 months	1,800,000
300,000 shares × 3 months	900,000
	2,700,000
Divided by 12 months	÷ 12
	225,000 shares

Earnings per share of common stock would be

$$\frac{\$600,000}{225,000} = \$2.67$$

Accounting for Potential Dilution

Because of the complex capital structures of many firms, the straightforward computation of earnings per share may be misleading. Although the average number of shares actually outstanding during a year is, by year end, a historical fact, many firms have commitments to issue additional shares in the future. If earnings per share are to have predictive value—if they are to be useful in forecasting future earnings—then the number of shares reasonably expected to be issued in the future must also be taken into account. Otherwise, earnings per share may take a precipitous drop in the period in which the additional shares are issued.

The obligation to issue the additional shares of common stock stems largely from commitments contained in other securities that may be outstanding: stock rights, warrants, and options as well as bonds and preferred stock that might be converted into common stock.

Stock rights, often called *preemptive rights,* represent commitments on the part of a company to issue, at an established price, a specified number of shares of common stock. A company typically grants stock rights to existing shareholders whenever it intends to issue new shares of stock. The rights give the existing stockholders first opportunity to acquire the new shares and thereby to preserve their proportionate interests in the company.

Warrants, like rights, are promises on the part of a company to issue a stated number of shares at a set price. Warrants, however, are usually issued by companies in connection with the sale of bonds to make the bonds more attractive to prospective purchasers.

When a firm has a complex capital structure—one that includes securities that could result in the *dilution* of earnings per share—the calculation of earnings per share becomes both subjective and complicated: subjective because it must necessarily be based on a number of estimates and assumptions; complicated because the issue of the additional shares will affect not only the number of shares outstanding but overall corporate earnings as well. The Accounting Principles Board, in *Opinion No. 15,* established specific guidelines for the computation of earnings per share. An overview of these guidelines will indicate some of the difficulties of determining earnings per share when the capital structure is complex.

Must Present Primary and Fully Diluted Earnings per Share

Opinion No. 15 requires that a firm with a complex capital structure present two types of earnings per share data on the face of its income statement. The first would indicate *primary earnings per share* and the second *fully diluted earnings per share.* The calculation of *both* of the earnings per share figures would take into account the impact of additional shares of common stock that might be issued.

The items differ, however, in that the primary earnings per share calculation assumes the conversion to common stock of only some outstanding securities, while fully diluted earnings assumes the conversion of virtually all.

In *primary* earnings per share, the number of shares outstanding includes:

1. All common shares presently outstanding
2. Potential common shares to be issued if all securities that meet the criteria, set forth below, of a *common stock equivalent* are converted

In *fully diluted* earnings per share, the number of shares outstanding includes:

1. All common shares presently outstanding
2. Potential common shares to be issued if all convertible securities that meet the criteria of a common stock equivalent are converted
3. Potential common shares to be issued if *all other* convertible securities (with a few exceptions) are converted

Must Adjust Number of Shares vis-à-vis Common Stock Equivalents

Securities that are in substance *common stock equivalents* are those that are not, in form, common stock but contain provisions that enable their holders to convert them into common stock. They are securities that derive their value from that of the common stock in that they can readily be converted into common stock. The holders of such securities can expect to participate in the appreciation of the value of the common stock and share in the earnings of the corporation. An option to purchase shares of common stock, for example, will ordinarily be considered a common stock equivalent as long as the exercise price is less than the prevailing market price of the common stock. As the common stock appreciates in value, so also will the option, since it can be converted into common stock.

Issue: When Are Convertible Securities Common Stock Equivalents?

Preferred stock and bonds that are convertible to common stock may or may not be a common stock equivalent. Convertible preferred stock that provides its holders with a return approximately equal to one that they could obtain by purchasing similar securities without the conversion privilege would *not* be considered a common stock equivalent. It has a value in its own right; holders receive periodic dividend payments sufficient to provide them with a return comparable to one that they could obtain elsewhere. Convertible preferred stock that provides its holders with a yield significantly less than they could obtain elsewhere *would,* however, be considered a common stock equivalent. Holders can be presumed to have purchased such securities to be able to convert their shares into common stock. The security derives its value primarily from the common stock into which it can be converted.

Suppose, for example, that the prevailing rate of return that an investor could expect to receive is 12 percent. If an issue of convertible preferred stock is sold at a price to yield 12 percent, then it would *not* be considered a common stock equivalent; it does not derive its value primarily from the common stock. The potential number of shares of common stock to which it could be converted would not be taken into account in determining primary earnings per share. If, however, the stock is sold at a price to yield only 4 percent, then it would be considered a common stock equivalent. The number of shares to which it could be converted would be included in the calculation of primary earnings per share. The convertible preferred stock that is not considered to be a common stock equivalent would, however, be taken into account in the calculation of fully diluted earnings per share. *Opinion No. 15* sets forth, in detail, rules to be adhered to in determining whether a particular security is a common stock equivalent and whether the number of shares of common stock into which it can be converted should thereby be included in the computation of primary earnings per share. The rules apply to both bonds and preferred stock. In general, a security is considered a common stock equivalent if its yield *at the time it is issued* is less than two-thirds of prevailing interest rates (the average Aa corporate bond yield[5]).

Example

A company had outstanding 10 million shares of common stock and 5 million shares of convertible preferred stock. The preferred shares had a par value of $100 and were convertible into common stock at a rate of one share for one share. The preferred shares were issued when prevailing rates of interest were 12 percent.

Earnings of the company *before* payment of preferred dividends were $200 million. Two assumptions can be made:

Assumption 1: The preferred stock pays dividends at a rate of 12 percent ($12 per share; $60 million per year on 5 million shares). In this case, the stock would *not* be considered a common stock equivalent since its yield when issued was greater than two-thirds the prevailing interest rate.

Assumption 2: The preferred stock pays dividends at a rate of 4 percent ($4 per share; $20 million per year on 5 million shares). In this case, the stock *would* be considered a common stock equivalent since its yield when issued was less than two-thirds the prevailing interest rate.

Exhibit 12-1 illustrates the computation of the number of shares outstanding on the basis of both assumptions.

Must Adjust Earnings to Reflect Interest and Preferred Dividends Saved and Income to Be Received from Additional Capital

If, in computing earnings per share, both primary and fully diluted, it is assumed that certain securities will be converted into common stock and thereby

[5]The designation *Aa* refers to a rating of bond quality assigned by Moody's or Standard & Poor's, the leading bond rating services. Aa bonds are considered by both services to be high-quality obligations of firms having a strong capacity to pay interest and repay principal.

EXHIBIT 12-1
Computation of Number of Shares: EPS Denominator (in millions)

	Assumption 1 Stock Is *Not* a Common Stock Equivalent (Dividends = 12%)	Assumption 2 Stock *Is* a Common Stock Equivalent (Dividends = 4%)
Primary EPS		
Common shares	10	10
Additional common shares assumed to be issued upon conversion of preferred stock	0	5
Total shares in EPS denominator	10	15
Fully Diluted EPS		
Common shares	10	10
Additional common shares assumed to be issued upon conversion of preferred stock	5	5
Total shares in EPS denominator	15	15

increase the number of common shares outstanding, it is also necessary to consider the impact of the conversion on the *earnings* of the company that are available to common stockholders. For example, if outstanding bonds or preferred stock will be converted to common stock, the firm will no longer have to pay interest or dividends on these securities. The amounts saved will increase the earnings in which the common stockholders have an equity interest. In determining the numerator (earnings) of the EPS fraction, one must add to the actual earnings for the year the interest or dividends of preferred stock or bonds that are assumed to be converted into common stock.

Exhibit 12-2 illustrates the computation of the earnings, as well as the earnings per share, assuming both of the factors: first, the preferred stock is *not* a common stock equivalent and then that it *is* an equivalent.

Issue: How to Take into Account the Cash to Be Received upon the Exercise of Warrants and Options

Outstanding stock warrants or options permit the holder to *purchase* (for cash) shares of common stock. If, in computing number of shares outstanding, it is assumed that warrants and options will be exercised and additional shares of common stock issued, it is also necessary to take into account the cash that will be received in exchange for the additional shares. Few firms will permit cash to remain idle in a checking account. Instead, they will invest it in income-producing projects. If the shares to be issued are added to those outstanding, it will also be necessary to add the potential increase in corporate earnings to actual earnings for the year.

The Accounting Principles Board recognized the practical difficulties of estimating the additional income that would be derived from the cash received from the exercise of warrants and options. To assure comparability among

EXHIBIT 12-2

Computation of Earnings (EPS Numerator) and Earnings per Share (Shares and Earnings in Millions)

	Assumption 1 Preferred Stock Is *Not* a Common Stock Equivalent (Dividends = 12%)	Assumption 2 Preferred Stock *Is* a Common Stock Equivalent (Dividends = 4%)
Primary EPS		
Earnings before preferred dividends	$200	$200
Subtract preferred dividends ($12 and $4, respectively, on 5 million shares)	(60)	(20)
Earnings after preferred dividends	$140	$180
Add back preferred dividends that would not have to be paid if shares were converted	*	20
Earnings available to common stockholders	$140	$200
Number of shares assumed to be outstanding (per Exhibit 12-1)	10	15
EPS (earnings available to common stockholders divided by number of shares)	$14.00	$13.33
Fully Diluted EPS		
Earnings after preferred dividends	$140	$180
Add back preferred dividends that would not have to be paid if shares were converted	60	20
Earnings available to common stockholders	$200	$200
Number of shares assumed to be outstanding (per Exhibit 12-1)	15	15
EPS (earnings available to common stockholders divided by number of shares)	$13.33	$13.33

*Since the preferred stock is not a common stock equivalent, it is assumed for purposes of primary EPS that it will not be converted.

firms, the board required that each firm make a common assumption. That is, each firm must assume that it would *not* invest the proceeds from the exercise of the warrants and options in income-producing projects. Instead, it would use the proceeds *to purchase and retire shares of its own common stock.*

The number of shares to be purchased and retired would be based on the present market price of the stock. If, for example, a company had 10,000 warrants outstanding, each of which could be used to acquire one share of common stock at a price of $54 per share, it would be assumed that the firm would receive $540,000 in cash. If the current market price of the common stock was $60 per share, then it would be assumed also that the $540,000 would be used to purchase and retire 9,000 shares of common stock ($540,000 ÷ $60). The effect of this method would be that 1,000 shares (10,000 shares issued less 9,000 assumed to be retired) would be added to the outstanding common shares but there would be no change in earnings.

Thus

Shares to be issued upon exercise of options		10,000
Cash to be received (10,000 shares @ $54)	$540,000	
Divided by current market price per share	÷ $60	
Equals number of shares assumed to be purchased and retired		9,000
Shares to be issued less shares assumed to be purchased and retired equals net additional shares		1,000

The board recognized that few firms would, in fact, use the proceeds from the exercise of warrants or options to retire common stock outstanding. It viewed the assumption as a practical means of taking into account the earning potential of the funds received in exchange for the new shares of common stock.

Example

The capital structure of a firm included the following throughout all of 1994.

Common stock: 200,000 shares issued and outstanding.

Preferred stock, Class A: 50,000 shares issued and outstanding. Each share is convertible into one share of common stock. Each share pays a dividend of $2. The stock was initially sold to yield shareholders a return of 3 percent—a yield substantially below (less than two-thirds) the bond yields of 6 percent that prevailed at the time.

Preferred stock, Class B: 100,000 shares issued and outstanding. Each share is convertible into one share of common stock. Each share pays a dividend of $6. The stock was initially sold to yield shareholders a return of 7 percent—a yield approximately equal to the rate that prevailed at the time.

Executive stock options outstanding: Options to purchase 9,000 shares at a price of $40 per share are outstanding.

The current market price of common stock is $60 per share.

The firm had net earnings of $3 million. Of this amount, $100,000 was paid in dividends to holders of preferred stock, Class A, and $600,000 was paid in dividends to holders of preferred stock, Class B. Earnings available to common stockholders were, therefore, $2.3 million.

Preferred stock, Class B, would *not* be considered a common stock equivalent, since it has value in its own right—its yield at time of initial issue was greater than two-thirds of prevailing bond yields.

Preferred stock, Class A, would be considered a common stock equivalent, since it apparently would derive its value directly from the common stock—its yield at time of initial issue was less than two-thirds of prevailing bond yields.

The computation of earnings per share, both primary and fully diluted, is shown in Exhibit 12-3.

EXHIBIT 12-3
Computation of Earnings per Share: A Comprehensive Example

Primary Earnings per Share

Number of shares outstanding		
Common stock		200,000 shares
Common stock equivalents		
Preferred stock, Class A (convertible into 50,000 shares of common stock)		50,000
Options	9,000 shares	
Less: Shares of common stock assumed to be purchased and retired with proceeds of $360,000 ($40 × 9,000); $360,000 ÷ $60 (market price)	6,000	3,000
Shares outstanding for primary EPS calculation		253,000 shares
Earnings		
Earnings available to common stockholders (per information provided)		$2,300,000
Add: Dividends on preferred stock, Class A, considered to be a common stock equivalent (50,000 shares @ $2)		100,000
Income for primary EPS calculation		$2,400,000

$$\text{Primary EPS} = \frac{\$2,400,000}{253,000 \text{ shares}} = \$9.49$$

Fully Diluted Earnings per Share

Number of shares outstanding	
Per primary EPS calculation	253,000 shares
Add: Preferred stock, Class B (not a common stock equivalent but nevertheless convertible into 100,000 shares common stock)	100,000
Shares outstanding for fully diluted EPS calculation	353,000 shares
Earnings	
Income for primary EPS calculation	$2,400,000
Add: Dividends on preferred stock, Class B assumed in calculation of number of shares outstanding to be converted into common stock	600,000
Income for fully diluted EPS calculation (100,000 @ $6)	$3,000,000

$$\text{Fully diluted EPS} = \frac{\$3,000,000}{353,000 \text{ shares}} = \$8.50$$

Publicly traded corporations are required, and many other firms elect, to issue interim financial reports. *Interim financial reports* are those that cover less than a full year. Commonly they cover a quarter- or half-year period. The interim reports of most companies are not nearly as detailed as their annual reports. Usually they note only a few key indicators of performance, such as sales or net income and earnings per share.

The accounting principles to be followed in calculating income for a period of a quarter or half year are the same as those followed for a full year. Nevertheless, meaningful determination of income for short periods presents inherent difficulties. In an earlier chapter it was pointed out that over the life of an enterprise determination of income is relatively simple. Most accounting problems arise because of the need for financial information on a periodic basis. Revenues and expenses must be assigned to specific accounting periods long before the full consequences of a transaction are known with certainty. Prepaid and deferred costs must be stored in asset and liability accounts pending allocation to earnings of particular years. To the extent that interim periods are shorter than annual periods, the related problems of income determination and asset valuation are correspondingly greater. It becomes considerably more difficult to associate revenues with productive effort and to match costs with revenues.

Revenues and Expenses May Be Based on Annual Measures

A period of one year will often correspond to a firm's natural business cycle. However, periods shorter than a year may be characterized by seasonal fluctuations in both revenues and expenses, thereby compounding the problems of financial reporting. Indeed, some revenues and expenses are determined on an annual basis; they cannot be calculated accurately for a period less than a year until results for the entire year are known. As a consequence, meaningful interim reports cannot be prepared for any one period without consideration of anticipated financial activities in subsequent periods.

A corporate compensation plan may require a firm to pay year-end bonuses to employees based on annual measures of performance, such as corporate earnings or a salesperson's gross sales. The amount of the bonus cannot be determined, and will not be paid, until the end of the fourth quarter. Yet the bonus unquestionably represents compensation for services rendered throughout the year, not just the final quarter.

Some firms permit customers quantity discounts based on cumulative purchases during the year. The discount may not take effect until the customer has reached a specified level of purchases—a level not likely to be attained until the third or fourth quarter of the year. Prices—and revenues—will appear to be higher in the earlier quarters than the later ones. Unless an adjustment to revenues is made to take into account the discounts to be granted in the future, the interim reports will overstate earnings.

In the same vein, firms may incur certain costs in a particular season. Major repairs, for example, may be undertaken during a firm's "slow" season, but they benefit the entire year. Property taxes may be paid at year end, but they represent an operating cost for the entire year. Unless these expenditures are spread over the entire year, the interim reports for each individual period may be misleading.

Each Interim Period Should Be Viewed as Part of an Entire Year

Opinion No. 28 of the Accounting Principles Board deals specifically with interim reports. It emphasizes that each interim period should be viewed as an integral part of an annual period and that, as appropriate, adjustments should be made to expenses and revenues for benefits received or costs incurred in other periods.

Although the opinion helped to provide for greater uniformity of practice among firms, it did not (and, of course, could not) eliminate the underlying weaknesses of interim reports. Interim reports necessarily are based on an even greater number of subjective assumptions, estimates, and allocations than are annual reports. They provide financial information for a relatively short period of time. Especially if a business is seasonal, they cannot be relied upon as predictors of earnings for the remaining periods of the year. If carefully prepared, they are a useful means of comparing performance in one quarter with that in a corresponding quarter of a prior year, though usually not among quarters of the same year.

Example

The accounting records of a firm indicate (in summary form) the following *first-quarter* data:

Sales		$10,000,000
Cost of goods sold	$6,000,000	
Other expenses	2,500,000	8,500,000
Income before taxes		$ 1,500,000

Several adjustments to the recorded amounts are necessary to make the first quarter an integral part of the entire year.

1. *Sales Discounts.* The company grants discounts to customers on annual purchases above specified amounts. Customers are allowed a discount of 10 percent on cumulative purchases during the year of more than $100,000. As of the end of the first quarter, no customer has purchased more than $100,000 of goods. Hence no discounts have been granted. However, the company estimates that on average over the entire year, sales discounts will be 1.5 percent of sales. Because discounts are as much associated with purchases of the first quarter as of subsequent periods, sales of the first quarter must be adjusted to take into account discounts that will actually be taken in later periods. Sales must be reduced by 1.5 percent, or $150,000.
2. *LIFO Inventory.* The company maintains its inventory on a LIFO basis. In the first quarter of the year, sales exceed production, and the company has to dip into its LIFO base. Hence cost of goods sold in-

cludes items acquired at relatively low cost. Of the goods sold, 100,000 units have been carried at $6 per unit. Current replacement cost is $8 per unit. The company is certain that by year end the LIFO base will be restored. Since cost of goods will be determined on a periodic basis at year end, all goods sold will be assumed to have been acquired at current-year prices of $8 per unit.

Cost of goods sold must be increased by $2 for each of the 100,000 units taken out of the LIFO base—thus $200,000.

3. *Expenses That Benefit the Entire Year.* Each year, in the third quarter, the company overhauls certain of its equipment at a cost of $600,000. The overhaul is required because of production carried out throughout the year. Hence 25 percent of the cost, $150,000, must be added to expenses of the first quarter.

4. *Income Taxes.* The company estimates that because it is able to take advantage of various special credits and deductions, its effective tax rate will be only 24 percent, a rate considerably below the firm's marginal combined federal and state rate of 36 percent. The reported tax expense for the quarter must be based on this rate, even though all the conditions for the special tax benefits might not be satisfied until later in the year.

Summary of Adjustments

Sales ($10,000,000 less 1.5%)		$9,850,000
Cost of goods sold ($6,000,000 plus LIFO adjustment of $200,000)	$6,200,000	
Other expense ($2,500,000 plus share of overhaul, $150,000)	2,650,000	8,850,000
Income before taxes		$1,000,000
Taxes @ 24%		240,000
Income after taxes		$ 760,000

Summary

In this chapter we have dealt with distributions of assets, stock options, losses and contingencies, earnings per share, and interim reports. Although we discussed several diverse accounting problems, the general approach to resolving them must, in essence, be the same as the approach to the issues discussed in previous chapters. Accountants must discern the substance, as well as the form, of a transaction; they must measure and assign values to the goods, services, or securities exchanged; and then must make a judgment as to the appropriate accounting period in which to give recognition to the impairment or enhancement of company resources.

Exercise for Review and Self-Testing

A corporation had earnings of $500,000 after taxes and preferred dividends. It had 100,000 shares of common stock outstanding for the entire year.

The company also had outstanding 10,000 shares of preferred stock. The shares were issued at par ($100) and provide the holders with a return of 4 percent. Each share is convertible into one share of common stock. At the time the shares were issued, the prevailing rate of interest, as measured by Aa corporate bond yields, was 10 percent.

The firm's capital structure also includes 2,000 convertible bonds, each of which is convertible into 15 shares of common stock—a total of 30,000 shares of common stock. Each bond pays interest at a rate of 8 percent per year. The bonds were issued at a time when the Aa corporate bond yield was also 8 percent. Total annual interest costs are $160,000, but after-tax interest costs are only 60 percent (1 minus an assumed tax rate of 40 percent) of that amount, or $96,000.

1. Which of the two issues of convertible securities would be considered a *common stock equivalent?* Why?
2. In determining *primary* earnings per share, how many shares of common stock should be considered outstanding? Such amount would include the actual number of shares of common stock plus the number of shares of common stock into which the common stock equivalent could be converted.
3. If the common stock equivalent were converted into common stock, by how much would interest or preferred dividends be reduced? What would be total earnings available to common stockholders?
4. Based on the calculations in (2) and (3), what would be *primary* earnings per share?
5. How many additional shares of common stock would the company be required to issue if the convertible security that is not considered a common stock equivalent were converted? How many shares of common stock should be considered outstanding in determining *fully diluted* earnings per share?
6. If the bonds were converted into common stock, by how much more would interest (after taking into account tax costs) be reduced? What would now be total earnings available to common stockholders?
7. Based on the calculations in (5) and (6), what would be *fully diluted* earnings per share?

Questions for Review and Discussion

1. *The Wall Street Journal* reported that Gulf & Western Industries, Inc., declared a 100 percent stock dividend, said it intends to raise its quarterly dividend by the equivalent of 2.5 cents a current share, and predicted record earnings for the coming fiscal year. Explain the significance of each of the three elements of the announcement. Which of the three is of most significance to the economic welfare of the stockholders? Which is of the least?
2. Dividends are sometimes said to be "paid out of retained earnings." Yet for many corporations, especially those that have been in existence for, and have expanded over, a period of several years, the balance in retained earnings is of little consequence in the decision as to the amount of dividends that can be declared. Why?
3. A firm owns 10,000 shares of stock in another corporation. It wishes to distribute the stock to its shareholders as a dividend in kind. The stock was purchased by the company as a temporary investment at a price of $4 per share. It has a present market value of $10 per share. If the company were to distribute the shares to its stockholders, how much gain on the transaction should the company report? Some accountants oppose recognizing gains or losses on distributions to stockholders. Why?
4. The following excerpt of a conversation was overheard in a crowded elevator in a Wall Street office building: "I just heard that IBM is going to split its stock 2 for 1. The announcement will be made later this week so you'd better purchase a few hun-

dred shares before everyone else hears about it and the price skyrockets." Assuming that the tip is reliable, is there any reason for the price of IBM to "skyrocket"?

5. Why is it important that accounting recognition be given to executive stock options in the period that they are first issued? Why would it not be preferable to wait until the period in which the options are exercised—and the company actually receives cash and issues the additional shares—to record the option transaction?

6. In calculating earnings per share, why is it necessary to make assumptions as to what a firm will do with any cash received when options are exercised? Why not simply add the potential number of shares to be issued to the number of shares currently outstanding?

7. What is the distinction between primary earnings per share and fully diluted earnings per share? Are primary earnings per share necessarily based on the average of the actual number of shares outstanding during the year?

8. A firm incurred unusual losses on two of its six plants. Each plant had a book value, prior to the loss, of $100 million. One plant was destroyed by flood. Insurance covered only $60 million of the loss. The other plant was sold for $60 million. Should either of the losses be considered *extraordinary?* Explain.

9. Under what circumstances would income taxes for the current year be reported as an extraordinary item? Why?

10. "The deficiencies and limitations of financial statements are magnified many times when they are prepared on a quarterly rather than annual basis." Do you agree? Explain.

Problems

1. *Are stockholders really better off if they receive a cash, rather than a stock, dividend?*

   As of January 1, 1992, the owners' equity section of Arrow Industries contained the following balances:

Common stock ($2 par value, 12,500,000 shares issued and outstanding)	$ 25,000,000
Capital in excess of par value	230,000,000
Retained earnings	300,000,000
	$555,000,000

   In 1992 the company had earnings of $20,000,000.

   In 1991 the company had declared cash dividends of $1.50 per share. In 1992, however, the board of directors wished to use all available cash to expand facilities. It decided instead to issue a stock dividend "equivalent in value" (based on market prices) to the cash dividend.

   The market price for the firm's common stock on December 31, 1992, was $60 per share.

   a. How many additional shares of common stock should the company issue?

   b. Prepare a journal entry to record the distribution of the additional shares.

   c. Comment on whether the stockholders are as well off for having received the stock rather than the cash dividend.

2. *You be the judge. Does a stock dividend represent income to the recipient? Does a cash dividend?*

   The case before the court presents the question whether, by virtue of the Sixteenth Amendment, Congress has the power to tax, as income of the stockholder, a *stock dividend* made lawfully and in good faith against earnings accumulated by the corporation since March 1, 1913.

The facts are as follows:

> On January 1, 1916, the Standard Oil Company of California declared a stock dividend; the company issued additional shares to its stockholders and transferred a portion of its retained earnings to permanent capital (common stock and capital received in excess of par).

> Plaintiff, a shareholder of Standard Oil Company of California, received her pro rata number of additional shares. She was called on to pay, and did pay under protest, a tax imposed on the shares. The amount of the supposed income was her proportionate share of the retained earnings transferred to the other capital accounts.

> Plaintiff has brought action against the Collector of taxes to recover the tax. In her complaint she contends that the stock dividend was not income within the meaning of the Sixteenth Amendment.

a. Put yourself in the position of a judge hearing the case. Outline an opinion in which you decide whether the shareholder can recover the tax paid. The only issue you need to consider is whether a stock dividend constitutes income. Make certain that in your outline you summarize the arguments most likely to be made by *both* plaintiff (shareholder) and defendant (tax collector).

b. Suppose that the court held that a stock dividend does *not* constitute earnings to the recipient. What arguments could you now make to support a contention that, if a stock dividend does not constitute earnings, then neither does a *cash dividend*. Indeed, when is a stockholder "better off" because of the activities of the corporation in which he or she has an interest? (Recall your response to these questions when you study the cost and equity methods of accounting for intercorporate investments in the next chapter. As you will see, the rationale for the equity methods is that a cash dividend does not, in economic substance, enhance the well-being of the recipient when the recipient has substantial influence over the fiscal policies of the company that pays the dividend.)

3. *The economic as well as the accounting impacts of three types of dividends of "equal value" may be somewhat different.*

The balance sheet of Cannon Industries reports the following amounts:

Cash		$ 2,000,000
Marketable securities		4,000,000
Other assets		14,000,000
Total assets		$20,000,000
Liabilities		$ 7,000,000
Common stock		
($1 par value, 500,000 shares issued and outstanding)	$ 500,000	
Common stock, capital in excess of par	3,500,000	
Retained earnings	9,000,000	13,000,000
Total liabilities and owners' equity		$20,000,000

Marketable securities include 300,000 shares of Consolidated Industries, which were purchased for $6 per share.

In past years the company has paid annual dividends of $4 per share. This year the company is considering two other alternatives to a cash dividend that it hopes will have "equal value" to shareholders:

(1) A *dividend in kind* of shares of Consolidated Industries. The market value of the shares is $8 per share. The company would distribute to stockholders one share of Consolidated for each two shares of Cannon—a total of 250,000 shares.

(2) A *stock dividend*. The market value of Cannon Industries stock is $80 per share. The company would distribute one additional share for each 20 shares—a total of 25,000 shares.

    a. Prepare journal entries that would be required if the company were to issue (1) the dividend in kind, (2) the stock dividend, (3) the cash dividend of $4 per share.

    b. Comment on any problems the company might face in issuing the cash dividend.

4. *Although a stock dividend is comparable in economic substance to a stock split, it is not accounted for in the same manner.*

    The owner's equity section of the Cortland Co. includes the following balances as of June 30:

Common stock (80,000 shares par value $20, issued and outstanding)	$ 1,600,000
Common stock, capital in excess of par	9,200,000
Retained earnings	30,000,000
	$40,800,000

On June 30 the market price of the firm's stock is $700 per share. On that date the firm issues to its stockholders an additional 16,000 shares.

    a. Record the issuance of the additional shares if the transaction is to be accounted for as (1) a 6-for-5 stock split and (2) a stock dividend.

    b. At what price would you anticipate the common stock would be traded subsequent to the issuance of the new shares?

    c. Comment on how the individual stockholders should account for the additional shares received in their own books and records. How much income should they report for federal tax purposes?

5. *The evidence suggests that stocks that split outperform those that do not.*

    A column in *Newsweek* ("The Lure of Stock Splits," October 31, 1983) pointed out that companies, in record numbers, were splitting their stocks—engaging in a "splendid orgy of reproduction." The column raised the question of whether a stock split increases the market value of a company's stock and thereby benefits its shareholders.

    According to the column, "The brokerage community generally insists that you can make money buying into splits." This position seems to run counter to the incontrovertible argument that a stock split, by itself, has no economic significance. It does not change the company's assets, liabilities, or prospects for the future.

    The column cited a 1981 New York Stock Exchange study that asked whether companies that split their stock do better than companies that do not. "The answer was a resounding yes," the column reported. "Between 1963 and 1980, stocks that split rose 2½ times faster in price than nonsplitting stocks." The evidence of the study clearly points to the conclusion that "companies with a history of splits are better buys, on average, than companies that rarely, if ever, split their stocks."

    The column did not, however, recommend that shareholders urge their boards of directors to split their shares. Quite the contrary. It explained why academic experts, while not disputing the evidence or conclusions of the New York Stock

Exchange study, have shown that splits per se have little or no impact on the value of a firm's shares.

    a. Which companies, those with the more favorable or less favorable trends in the market values of their shares, would you expect to be more likely to split their shares? Why?

    b. Provide an explanation, consistent with the view that a stock split per se is of no economic significance, as to why stock splits may be *associated with,* although not necessarily *cause,* strong market performance.

    c. Outline in general terms a study in which you would investigate whether stock splits are, in fact, the prime cause of increases in the market values of companies' shares.

6. *The distinction between a stock split and a stock dividend may be a source of confusion.* Barron's *contained the following two news items in the same article:*

> McQuay-Perfex, Inc., declared a 50% stock dividend and raised its quarterly cash dividend to 24 cents a share from 20 cents.

> Stanley Works directors declared a three-for-two stock split and boosted the cash dividend on presplit shares to 40.5 cents from 36.0 cents.

    a. Assume that the stockholders' equity of both firms comprised the following:

Common stock, par value $3	
(100,000 shares outstanding)	$ 300,000
Additional paid-in capital	800,000
Retained earnings	2,000,000
	$3,100,000

Prepare the journal entry, if any, that each of the firms should make to record the stock "dividend" or stock split.

    b. Comment on why accountants, businesspeople, and journalists are sometimes accused of using needlessly confusing jargon.

7. *Restrictions on the payment of dividends that are based on balances in retained earnings may be inappropriate for some companies.*

The Mineral Wells Mining Co. has been organized for the sole purpose of extracting ore from a deposit that the company intends to purchase. It is anticipated that after the property is mined, the company will be dissolved.

The company issues 10,000 shares of common stock ($1 par value) at a price of $110 per share. It purchases the properties for $1 million cash.

During its first year of operations the company extracts 25 percent of the available ore. It has sales revenue of $400,000 and operating expenses and taxes of $100,000, *excluding* depletion. All revenues are received, and all operating expenses are paid, in cash.

The company estimates that it requires an operating cash balance of $100,000.

    a. Prepare an income statement and a balance sheet that would reflect the results of operations for the first year.

    b. Based entirely on the cash requirements of the firm, what is the maximum cash dividend it can pay?

    c. Prepare a journal entry to record payment of such "dividend." (Debit owners' equity accounts directly rather than "dividends.")

d. The statutes of many states prohibit companies from paying dividends in amounts greater than the existing balance in retained earnings. The purpose of the restriction is to assure that distributions of corporate assets are not made to stockholders at the expense of creditors. Do you think that such restrictions should apply to companies organized to extract minerals from specific properties? What would be the impact, over time, of such restrictions on the assets of the companies?

8. *The question of how best to report litigation and resultant claims is a troublesome one for accountants.*

Assume the following facts:

In 1990 a major manufacturer of electrical equipment is charged by a group of customers with engaging in pricing practices that are in violation of antitrust statutes. The alleged illegal activities took place in the years 1987 to 1989. The customers file suit in federal court; they seek treble damages totaling $36 million. Attorneys for the defendant confidentially advise their client to "be prepared for a final judgment between $10 million and $20 million."

In 1993, after a lengthy trial, the company is found liable to the plaintiffs for $20 million in damages. The company announces its intention to appeal.

In 1994 an appeals court reverses the decision of the lower court and orders a new trial.

In 1995 the company agrees to an out-of-court settlement with the plaintiffs. The firm will pay damages of $6 million.

In 1996 the company pays the agreed-upon amounts to the plaintiffs.

How do you think the company should account for the litigation? Indicate any specific journal entry that the company should make during or at the end of each of the years in question. Consider the possibility of making supplementary disclosures in footnotes to the financial statements. Bear in mind that the financial statements will be public documents, available to the plaintiffs and their attorneys.

9. *When is a gain a gain?*

The following is an excerpt from a financial magazine report:

Samson International Corp. said net income of 71 cents a share reported for the fiscal fourth quarter included 30 cents a share of what it expects to recover from litigation against two subcontractors. That's about 44% of the earnings.

The company, in its first quarter report to shareholders, also disclosed that the Securities and Exchange Commission is investigating the inclusion in earnings of the hoped-for court awards.

As reported earlier this year, Samson is seeking damages exceeding $2,766,000 against Norcomp Systems, Inc. and more than $1,477,000 against Unito, Inc., two subcontractors Samson terminated on a contract in Peublo, Colo. Samson filed suits against them in federl court in Denver, which are still pending.

Based on the 10.5 million Samson shares outstanding, the expected awards totaled more than $4 million of Samson's earnings of $6.8 million for the fiscal fourth quarter, ending Sept. 30.

a. Based on the limited information provided in the article, what do you think is the basis of the Securities and Exchange Commission investigation? In what other way might the litigation have been accounted for and reported?

b. How do you think Norcomp Systems, Inc., and Unito, Inc., accounted for and reported the suit?

10. *One firm's loss may not be another's gain.*

The following were taken from the notes to the 1987 financial statements of Pacific Resources Corp.

Note 12. Contingencies

> In February 1988, the U.S. Court of Appeals for the Ninth Circuit reversed in full the antitrust judgment rendered in 1985 against PRI and its subsidiary, GASCO, Inc. In October 1987, the same court had reversed about 75% of the 1985 judgment. As discussed in Note 4, PRI recorded an extraordinary loss in 1985 to reflect the 1985 judgment and, in 1987, an extraordinary gain to record the partial reversal. The plaintiff is appealing from the Ninth Circuit's decision. Special Counsel has advised the Company that it is unlikely that the court will modify its decision or that the U.S. Supreme Court will review this matter if appealed.

Note 4. Extraordinary Item

> As a result of the antitrust action discussed in Note 12, the Company recognized an extraordinary loss provision of $3,375,000 in 1985, net of a $3,277,000 deferred income tax benefit. In 1987, as a result of a reversal of part of this antitrust judgment by the U.S. Court of Appeals, the Company reversed $2,086,000 of this extraordinary loss provision, net of $1,614,000 in deferred income taxes. In February 1988, the U.S. Court of Appeals reversed the remainder of the antitrust judgment. The Company will determine the advisability of reversing the remaining provision in 1988.

a . Suppose that you were the independent CPA of the company which was the beneficiary of the antitrust judgment against Pacific Resources Corp. in 1985. Knowing that Pacific Resources would appeal the judgment, would you have recommended that the company recognize the amount of the award as income of that year? Explain. Are your recommendations "symmetrical" to the way in which the litigation was accounted for by Pacific Resources? If not, explain and justify any inconsistencies.

b. Based on the information provided, do you think that Pacific Resources Corp. should record a gain in 1988 to recognize the February 1988 ruling of the U.S. Court of Appeals, or should it defer any further recognition until the appeals process is completed?

11. *Lawsuits that raise "going-concern" questions present special problems of accounting and reporting.*

    The 1987 annual financial statements of Union Carbide explain in considerable detail the status of litigation attributable to the tragedy at its Bhopal, India, chemical plant. The disaster left thousands dead, injured, or homeless. What follows is a brief excerpt from the relevant note.

> Numerous lawsuits were brought against the Corporation and/or Union Carbide India Limited (UCIL) (50.9% of the stock of which is owned by the Corporation) in Federal and state courts in the United States and in Indian courts alleging, among other things, personal injuries or wrongful death, property damage and economic losses from the emission of gas at UCIL's Bhopal, India, plant in December 1984. Most of the actions in United States courts were field on behalf of individual plaintiffs and as a purported class action in which plaintiffs claimed to represent large numbers of claimants seeking unspecified compensatory and punitive damages for injuries and deaths, property damage and economic losses from the gas emission

> The Union of India also brought suit against the Corporation in the District Court in Bhopal, India. In that suit, the Union of India seeks punitive damages, damages for injury to the environment, amounts paid for emergency aid provided by the Union of India, economic losses suffered by businesses and individuals, and all personal injury damages recoverable by its citizens. The Corporation is vigorously defending the pending litigation. In its Amended Complaint, the Union of India estimates that the approximate value of the total claims would exceed $3 billion if the suit is tried to judgment.

> Given the Corporation's numerous defenses and the evidence that the tragedy was caused by employee sabotage, liability is in dispute.

a. The financial statements of 1987 report that the book value of Union Carbide's assets is $7.9 billion and net worth is $1.25 billion. In light of the magnitude of the potential liability, how would you recommend that the litigation be reflected in the financial statements? Explain. If you believe that additional information is required for you to make a judgment, specify what you would need and how it could be obtained.

b. Suppose that corporate attorneys provided you with the following probability estimates of the eventual amount for which the case will be resolved. They assert that they are unable to be more precise in their estimates.

Probability, %	Amount of Settlement
5	$2 billion or greater
25	$1 billion or greater but less than $2 billion
50	$500 million or greater but less than $1 billion
20	$250 million or greater but less than $500 million

Would the additional information change your response?

12. *Unusual events present unusual problems of accounting and reporting.*

The following four notes were adapted from published financial statements. They differ from the notes as they actually appeared in that the published notes indicated how the issues raised in this problem were resolved.

For each of the notes, discuss the issues of accounting and reporting that the situations present. For example, do you think the companies should recognize a gain or loss in the year of the statements? If you do, should it be ordinary or extraordinary? If you do not, what events must take place before you would recommend that a gain or loss be recognized? If you believe that more information is necessary to resolve an issue, specify what you would need and where you would obtain it.

a. *Intel Corporation:* In July 1987 two former officials of Great Lakes (a wholly owned subsidiary) pleaded guilty to conspiring prior to 1985 to eliminate competition on certain government dredging projects. The company estimates that it will cost $7.3 million to resolve the antitrust charges against Great Lakes.

b. *Georgia Bonded Fibers, Inc.:* In November 1985 a flood damaged the company's domestic manufacturing facility and certain other assets. Substantially all assets and flood-related costs were insured. The company settled its claim with the carrier for an amount that was $354,000 (net of income taxes of $329,000), or 25 cents per share, in excess of the flood-related costs and the net book value of the damaged assets.

c. *Johnson & Johnson:* As a result of criminal tampering with Tylenol Extra-Strength Capsules in February 1986, the company announced the withdrawal of all capsule products made directly available to the consumer. The company also announced that it will no longer manufacture or sell these capsule products and that it has no plans to reenter this business in the foreseeable future. The costs associated with these decisions are estimated at $140 million ($80 million after income taxes), and include customer returns, inventory handling and disposal costs, and communication expenses to reassure consumers of the safety of non-capsule Tylenol products.

d. *Public Service Company of Colorado:* As of the quarter ended September 30, 1986, the company expected to incur a sizable loss resulting from an anticipated writing down of a substantial portion of the total investment in Fort St. Vrain (a nuclear generating station), recognizing estimated future decommissioning expenses and recognizing estimated unrecoverable operating and capital expenditures. The estimated loss at September 30, 1986, was $93.7 million (net of $89.4 million in related income taxes) and was subsequently increased to $101.4 million (net of $101.5 million in related income taxes) at December 31, 1986. The estimate of amount of the investment in Fort St. Vrain that would have to be written down was based on the assumption that the plant would remain operational until all existing fuel in the reactor and on-site was utilized (approximately three to four years, assuming a continued average annual capacity factor of about 45 percent) and that the reactor would then be decommissioned and the plant converted to a fossil-fuel-burning plant.

Realization of the company's remaining investment in Fort St. Vrain (approximately $70.3 million at December 31, 1987), and the reliability of the estimated future decommissioning expenses and unrecoverable operating and capital expenditures, was dependent on future events, including sustained operations at levels significantly greater than in the past, achieving and maintaining a cost-effective relationship between expenses and revenues from Fort St. Vrain, and satisfactory resolution of various alternatives regarding Fort St. Vrain after the on-site nuclear fuel was utilized.

13. *Employee stock options are a cost of compensating employees. They should be recorded as an expense in the accounting period during which the employees perform the related services.*

The Warwich Co. adopted a stock option plan that entitled selected executives to purchase shares of its common stock for $40 per share, the price at which the stock was being traded in the open market on the date the plan was adopted.

The plan stipulated that the options could be exercised one year after being received, provided the executive was still employed by the company. The options were to lapse, however, 2½ years after they were issued.

Each option entitled the executive to purchase one share of common stock, which has a par value of $5.

The following transactions or events with respect to the option plan took place over a period of three years:

Dec. 31, 1990: The company issued 1,000 options to its executives. Market price of the stock on that date was $52.

Dec. 31, 1991: The company issued an additional 2,000 options. Market price of the stock was $35.

July 1, 1992: Executives exercised 800 of the options issued in 1990. Market price of the common stock was $42.

March 6, 1993: Executives exercised 1,000 of the options issued in 1991. Market price of the common stock was $48.

June 30, 1993: The remaining 200 of the options issued in 1990 lapsed. Market price of the common stock was $47.

Prepare journal entries, as required, to record these transactions and events.

14. *Owing to outstanding stock appreciation rights, an increase in the market price of a firm's shares caused a decrease in reported earnings.*

The Wall Street Journal called Texas International, an Oklahoma City–based exploration company, one of the year's "hottest trading stocks." In 1991 (dates changed) and the first quarter of 1992, the price of the stock increased more than fourfold. It traded as high as 46⅞, which, as *The Wall Street Journal* indicated, was "not bad" for a company that had 1991 earnings of only 76 cents a share.

But the *Journal* pointed to a dark cloud in front of the silver lining. Both the chairman and the president of the company held "stock appreciation rights." These rights entitled the officers to *cash payments* based on the increase in the market value of the company's shares. For each right held, the officers would receive the difference between the per share selling price as of specified dates and a stated exercise price ($4^3/_8$).

Every fiscal quarter, according to *The Wall Street Journal,* the company must charge as an expense an amount reflective of the stock's rise and the corresponding increase in the firm's obligation to the officers. In the first quarter of 1992, the firm had to charge about $5.2 million to earnings—earnings which, after the charge, were less than $3 million.

a. Distinguish between the stock appreciation rights described in this problem and the employee stock options described in the chapter.

b. Why must Texas International charge an expense each period to reflect the increase in the market price of the shares? Why can't the company record the full amount of compensation expense at the time the rights are granted, as it would if it had granted stock options?

c. Does the charge of $5.2 million against earnings represent a true economic sacrifice? Or could the firm take advantage of the increase in the market price of its shares to acquire, at small cost, the cash to make the required payments to the holders of the rights?

Suppose that first quarter 1992 earnings, prior to charges relating to stock appreciation rights, were $8.2 million. The firm's obligation to holders of stock appreciation rights increased during the quarter by $5.2 million. The firm had outstanding 9.5 million shares of common stock.

d. The firm decides to acquire the $5.2 million in cash needed to satisfy the rights obligations by issuing new shares of common stock. Assume that the market price per share is $50. How many new shares would the firm have to issue?

e. What would be earnings per share, assuming no charge to earnings for stock appreciation rights, based on 9.5 million shares of common stock outstanding?

f. What would be earnings per share, assuming no charge to earnings for stock appreciation rights, based on the number of shares outstanding after the additional shares had been issued?

15. *A firm's footnote pertaining to stock options permits reconstruction of journal entries and determination of their impact on earnings per share.*

A note pertaining to stock options of Flowers Industries reads as follows:

| | Number of Shares | | |
	Authorized	Granted	Available
Balance at June 28, 1986	1,650,024	423,788	1,226,236
Granted		1,006,554	(1,006,554)
Exercised	(4,089)	(4,089)	
Expired		(6,153)	6,153
Balance at June 27, 1987	1,645,935	1,420,100	225,835
Exercised	(106,748)	(106,748)	
Balance at July 2, 1988	1,539,187	1,313,352	225,835

Option price must be 100% of the market value of the common stock at the time of the grant and is exercisable when granted. For all options granted, the exercise period is ten years.

At July 2, 1988, the options yet to be exercised are as follows (amounts in thousands except share data):

	Number of Shares	Option Price per Share	Total Value
Granted in fiscal 1984	72,192	$ 7.61	$ 549
Granted in fiscal 1985	87,475	9.00	787
Granted in fiscal 1986	72,678	16.25	1,181
Granted in fiscal 1987	1,006,554	15.00	15,098
Total	1,313,352		$18,508

Information with respect to options exercised is as follows (amounts in thousands except share data):

	Number of Shares	Option Price per Share	Total	Per Share Average Market Price
For the year ended June 27, 1987				
Granted in fiscal 1984	4,089	$ 7.61	$ 31	$19.53
For the year ended July 2, 1988				
Granted in fiscal 1984	37,271	$ 7.61	$ 284	$19.53
Granted in fiscal 1985	37,431	9.00	337	19.53
Granted in fiscal 1986	19,740	12.00	237	19.53
Granted in fiscal 1987	12,306	16.25	200	19.53
	106,748		$1,058	

Proceeds received from the exercise of stock options are credited to the Company's capital accounts.

a. Prepare all journal entries pertaining to stock options that the company would have made in the fiscal years ending in 1987 and 1988. Assume that the common stock has a par value of $1 per share.

b. How would the outstanding options affect the computation of earnings per share for the fiscal year ending 1988? Indicate the impact upon the numerator (earnings) and the denominator (number of common shares and common stock equivalents). Assume that the market price of the common stock at year end was $20 per share.

16. *This problem provides a review of several types of transactions that affect owners' equity.*
    As of January 1, the owners' equity section of the Green Mountain Co. contained the following balances:

Common stock, $4 par value (100,000 shares issued and outstanding)	$ 400,000
Common stock, capital received in excess of par	600,000
Retained earnings	800,000
	$1,800,000

During the year, the following events took place:

a. On January 7, the company issued to executives options to purchase 2,000 shares of common stock at a price of $25 per share. The market price of the common stock on that date was $28 per share.

b. On February 1, the company purchased 2,000 shares of its own stock in the open market at a price of $20 per share. The firm intended to use the stock to satisfy obligations on outstanding options.

c. On February 10, the company declared a cash dividend of 50 cents per share. The dividend was paid on February 23.

d. On March 7, executives exercised options to purchase 2,000 shares. The market price of the common stock on that day was $26 per share.

e. On May 10, in lieu of its usual quarterly cash dividend, the company declared and paid a dividend in kind. The company distributed to shareholders 5,000 shares of Pacific General Co. common stock that had been held as an investment. The prevailing market price for the shares was $10 per share; they had been purchased previously, and recorded on the books of Green Mountain Co., at a price of $2 per share.

f. On August 10, the company declared and paid a stock dividend equal in value (based on the current market price of the shares issued) to the 50 cents per share of its traditional quarterly dividend. The market price of the shares on that date was $25.

g. On December 17, the company declared a stock split. For each old share owned, stockholders would be given *two* new shares.

h. On December 28, the company issued to executives the options to purchase 4,000 shares at a price of $12.50 per share. The market price of the common stock on that date was $10 per share.

Prepare journal entries to record these events. (Debit any dividends directly to the owners' equity accounts affected rather than to "dividends.")

17. *This problem, based on the statements of a large food company, reviews the impact of key events that affect owners' equity accounts.*

The April 30, 1988, financial statements of Bob Evans Farms, Inc., indicated the following as to owners' equity of April 30, 1985 (*dollar* amounts are in thousands):

Common stock, par value	$ 669
Capital in excess of par	$48,421
Retained earnings	$67,238
Number of shares of common stock outstanding	16,506,378

The financial statements also reported net income and dividends declared per share for each of three years ending April 30:

	Net Income	Dividends per Share (See Note F)
1986	$20,575	$0.18
1987	$21,470	$0.22
1988	$29,329	$0.24

The financial report of April 30, 1988, also contained the following note:

Note F—Stockholders' Equity

On December 16, 1985, the stockholders of the company approved a plan of reorganization. As a result of this reorganization, the par value of common stock was adjusted to $.01 per share.

On August 12, 1985, the Board of Directors authorized a 10% stock dividend on all the company's issued common stock as of August 16, 1985. On August 11, 1986, the Board of Directors authorized a 5-for-4 stock split on the company's issued common stock as of September 5, 1986. On August 10, 1987, the Board of Directors authorized a 5-for-4 stock split on the company's issued common stock as of September 11, 1987. *All data as to per share cash dividends have been adjusted for the stock splits.*

When the company split its shares, as well as when it declared a stock dividend, it did not change the par value of its shares. Hence it made an appropriate transfer from "capital in excess of par" to "par value."

For convenience, assume that cash dividends were paid at year end and were based on number of shares outstanding at year end. As a consequence, the dividend per share in the year ending April 30, 1988, was in the amount reported; there is no need to adjust it for the stock split in August 1987. By contrast, the dividends for the years ending April 30, 1986 and 1987, must be restated to their original amounts. (There is no need to adjust dividends per share for the 10 percent stock dividend.)

The reduction in retained earnings attributable to the stock dividend was based on market value per share. The market value on the date of the dividend was $22 per share.

Prepare a schedule which indicates the impact of the information provided on number of shares outstanding and the balances in each of the owners' equity accounts over the three-year period between April 30, 1985, and April 30, 1988.

18. *Beginning and ending balances in owner's equity accounts can be reconciled from information on the face of the balance sheet as well as in notes.*

The stockholders' equity section of Norfolk Southern Corporation balance sheet reported the following:

	December 31	
	1987	1986
	(thousands of dollars)	
Common stock, $1.00 per share par value, 450,000 shares authorized; issued 195,302,488 shares and 196,575,003 shares, respectively	$ 195,302	$ 196,575
Other capital	458,173	455,310
Retained income	4,346,542	4,439,473
Less treasury stock at cost, 7,252,844 shares and 7,255,611 shares, respectively	(20,566)	(20,607)
Total stockholders' equity	$4,979,451	$5,070,751

From other sections of the financial statements you learn:
(1) Net income for 1986 was $518,688,000 and for 1987 was $172,377,000.
(2) In 1986 the company declared dividends for that year of $3.40 per (presplit) share. The average number of shares outstanding was 63,041.
(3) In 1986 the company issued 70,000 (presplit) shares of stock for $1,820,000.
(4) In 1986 it sold, for $3,080,000, shares which had been held in the treasury. The carrying value of these shares was $2,954,000.
(5) The board of directors declared a 3-for-1 stock split effective December 31, 1986. The company elected *not* to change the par value of the shares from $1.00.

(6) In 1987, following the split, the company issued 418,000 shares for $7,301,000.

(7) In 1987 it sold treasury stock for $11,000. The carrying value of these shares was $41,000. In previous years the company had recognized sufficient "gains" on sales of treasury stock so that the 1987 "loss" could be charged to "capital in excess of par."

(8) In 1987 the company also purchased and retired 1,691,000 shares. The amount paid for these shares was $43,469,000. Assume that this transaction took place at year end. (Owing to this assumption, you will be unable to reconcile to the dollar; you will have a "discrepancy" of $23,000.)

(9) In 1987 the company declared dividends of $1.20 per (postsplit) share. The average number of shares outstanding was 189,600.

Prepare a schedule in which you reconcile the January 1, 1986, balance in the owner's equity accounts with both the December 31, 1986, and December 31, 1987, balances. Use the form that follows. The balances for January 1, 1986, are provided in the schedule.

	Common Stock Par Value	Capital in Excess of Par	Retained Earnings	Treasury Stock	Total
Balance, Jan. 1, 1986	$ 65,455	$584,484	$4,135,126	$(23,561)	$4,761,504
Balance, Dec. 31, 1986	$196,575	$455,310	$4,439,473	$(20,607)	$5,070,751
Balance, Dec. 31, 1987	$195,302	$458,173	$4,346,542	$(20,566)	$4,979,451

19. *End-of-year changes in number of shares outstanding will have but little effect upon earnings per share.*

In November 1992 the controller of a firm estimated that net earnings for the year ending December 31 would be approximately $500,000, an amount considerably less than the $600,000 for the previous year. Aware that the financial press commonly focuses on earnings per share, the controller devised a scheme to boost EPS. On December 1, the firm would acquire in the open market 20,000 shares of its own common stock. It would immediately retire those shares. The acquisition and retirement would reduce the denominator of the EPS ratio and thereby boost EPS. Throughout 1991 and the first 11 months of 1992, the firm had 100,000 shares of common stock outstanding.

a. Determine EPS for 1991 and 1992, based on 100,000 shares outstanding.

b. Determine EPS for 1992 as the controller apparently expects it will be computed.

c. Will the scheme of the controller be successful? Determine EPS for 1992 in accord with generally accepted accounting principles.

20. *An understanding of the principles underlying the computation of earnings per share helps in interpreting information contained in a firm's annual report.*

The following information pertaining to earnings per share appeared in an annual report of the Monsanto Company. Income and the number of shares used in the computation of earnings per common and common equivalent shares were determined as shown.

Earnings per Common Share

	Primary	Fully Diluted
Income (millions of dollars)		
Net income	$366.3	$366.3
Preferred dividends	(2.2)	
Interest (less tax) on		
Loan stock of Monsanto Limited	0.3	0.3
Debentures of Monsanto International		
Finance Company		0.5
	$364.4	$367.1
Number of shares		
(thousands of shares)		
Weighted average shares outstanding	35,835	35,835
Incremental shares for outstanding		
stock options	161	167
Shares issuable upon conversion		
Loan stock of Monsanto Limited	276	276
Debentures of Monsanto International		
Finance Company		269
$2.75 preferred stock		983
	36,272	37,530

a. Is the firm's $2.75 preferred stock a common stock equivalent? How can you tell?

b. Why were preferred dividends of $2.2 million deducted in the computation of primary earnings but not fully diluted earnings?

c. Are the debentures (bonds) of Monsanto International Finance Company (a consolidated subsidiary) common stock equivalents? How can you tell?

d. Why is the term *incremental* used in describing the shares to be issued in connection with outstanding stock options?

21. *The procedure for determining earnings per share, although complex, is designed to make certain that potential dilution is taken into account.*

    The Sutton Company had earnings after taxes and before dividends of $300,000. The company has 100,000 shares of common stock outstanding. The corporate income tax rate is 40 percent.

    In addition, the company has issued $500,000 of bonds that are convertible into common stock at a rate of 40 shares for each $1,000 bond. The bonds were sold to yield 4 percent. When they were issued, corporate Aa bond yields were 8 percent.

    The company also has outstanding 3,000 shares of $100 par value convertible preferred stock. Each share of preferred stock may be exchanged for five shares of common stock. The preferred stock carries a dividend rate of $10 per share. The stock was issued at par (no discount or premium) at a time when the prevailing Aa corporate bond yields were 7 percent.

a. Determine primary earnings per share.

b. Determine fully diluted earnings per share.

22. *In computing earnings per share, a firm must make an assumption as to what it does with cash received when outstanding stock options are exercised.*

    Riggs Corporation had earnings after taxes of $800,000. The company had 200,000 shares of common stock outstanding. The current market price of the common stock was $25 per share.

Years earlier the company had adopted a stock option plan. Outstanding as of current year end were 5,000 options that would enable the holder to purchase one share each at $20 per share and 10,000 options which could be exercised for one share each at $10 per share.

The company had 10,000 shares of 8 percent convertible preferred stock outstanding. Par value of the stock was $100; each share was convertible into *three* shares of common stock. The year-end market price of the preferred stock was $105. The preferred stock was issued at a time when the prevailing Aa corporate bond yields were 6 percent.

a. Determine primary earnings per share.

b. Determine fully diluted earnings per share.

23. *Published financial statements seldom provide sufficient information for the user to independently compute earnings per share. This example is illustrative of an exception.*

Various notes to the 1987 financial statements of Unisys Corporation indicated the following:

> On September 16, 1986, stockholders approved the issuance of up to 30,000,000 shares of the Company's Series A Cumulative Convertible Preferred Stock, par value $1 per share. Each share of Convertible Preferred Stock (i) receives cumulative dividends of $3.75 per share per annum, payable quarterly, (ii) has a liquidation preference of $50.00 plus accrued and unpaid dividends, (iii) is convertible into 1.67 shares of the Company's common stock.

> Primary earnings per common share are based on the weighted average number of outstanding common shares and common share equivalents. The number of shares used in the computations for the year ended 1987 were (in thousands):

Primary	151,023
Fully diluted	198,745

The income statement reported (in millions except for per share amounts):

Net income	$578.0
Dividends on preferred shares	106.9
Earnings on common shares	$471.1
Earnings per common share	
Primary	$ 3.12
Fully diluted	$ 2.91

a. Based on reported dividends, how many share of preferred stock were issued and outstanding?

b. Were the preferred shares common stock equivalents? How can you tell?

c. Show how primary earnings per share were computed.

d. Show (as best you can) how the number of common shares and common stock equivalents used in the computation of fully diluted earnings per share was determined.

e. Show how fully diluted earnings per share was computed.

24. *Seasonal businesses have special problems of interim reporting.*

Lakeview, Inc., operates a summer resort. The resort is open for guests during the summer months only. All its revenue is earned during the summer months. In the first quarter (January 1 through March 31) of its fiscal year, the company has zero revenues but makes cash disbursements as follows:

Property taxes for the period		
January 1 to December 31	$ 60,000	
Administrative salaries for the		
first quarter	30,000	
Advertising	12,000	
Repair and maintenance (annual		
overhaul of boats and docks)	7,000	
Total disbursements	$109,000	

a. For each disbursement, consider whether, for purposes of interim reporting, (1) it should be charged as an expense as incurred, (2) it should be allocated evenly to each of the four quarters, or (3) it should be allocated on some other basis. (Use your judgment; the answer cannot be found in the text.)

b. Comment on the special difficulties faced by seasonal businesses in preparing interim reports. (In practice, policies as to the allocation of costs such as those indicated in this problem vary from firm to firm. There are no specific professional guidelines that deal with seasonal industries.)

25. *First-period "interim" earnings must be adjusted to take into account events of subsequent periods.*

For the first three months of the year, the Warwick Company, according to its president, had earnings before taxes of $140,000, determined as follows:

Sales		$420,000
Cost of goods sold	$200,000	
Other expenses	80,000	280,000
Income before taxes		$140,000

The following additional information has come to your attention:

a. The company gives quantity discounts to its customers based on total purchases for the year. No quantity discounts have been allowed to date. The firm estimates that total sales for the year, at *gross* sales prices, will be $2 million. After taking into account quantity discounts, $200,000 of the sales will be at 95 percent of gross sales prices (a discount of $10,000) and $400,000 will be at 90 percent of gross sales prices (a discount of $40,000). Average selling prices for the year are thus somewhat lower than those implied by sales revenue of the first quarter.

b. The company uses the LIFO inventory method and determines year-end inventory and the annual cost of goods sold on the basis of a periodic inventory count, which is taken on December 31 of each year. The cost of goods sold for the quarter ending March 31 was calculated as follows:

Goods on hand, January 1:		
30,000 units @ $5	$150,000	
Production, 1st quarter:		
10,000 units @ $10	100,000	$250,000
Estimated goods on hand,		
March 31: 10,000 units @ $5		50,000
Cost of goods sold, 30,000 units		$200,000

The company estimates that it will complete the year with an inventory of 30,000 units. As a consequence, the ending inventory will be stated at $5 per unit;

the firm will not have to "dip into" its LIFO stock. The cost of goods sold for the entire year will be based on current production costs of $10 per unit.

c. The company overhauls its plant once a year in July at a cost of $20,000. The cost of the overhaul has not been taken into account in computing first quarter expenses.

d. Each December the company gives its salaried employees a bonus equal to approximately 10 percent of their annual salaries. First-quarter salaries (included in other expenses), without adjusting for the bonus, amounted to $75,000.

e. Assume that the current federal income tax rate is 20 percent of the first $75,000 of taxable income and 34 percent on all earnings above that amount. The company estimates that taxable income for the entire year will be $120,000. Thus its average effective rate for the year will be different from that based on first-quarter earnings alone.

Determine earnings after taxes for the first quarter of the year as they should be reported to the general public.

Solutions to Exercise for Review and Self-Testing

1. A convertible security is considered a common stock equivalent if it derives its value from the common stock. The test specified in official pronouncements is whether its yield at the time it was issued was less than two-thirds of the Aa corporate bond rate. The preferred stock was issued to yield 4 percent at a time when the Aa rate was 10 percent. It would therefore be considered a common stock equivalent. The convertible bonds were issued to yield 8 percent at a time when the prevailing rate was also 8 percent. It would not therefore be considered a common stock equivalent.

2. 100,000 shares of common stock + 10,000 shares that would be issued if the preferred stock were converted = 110,000 shares.

3. Preferred dividends would be reduced by $40,000. Total earnings available to common stockholders would be $540,000.

4. Primary earnings per share = $540,000/110,000 shares = $4.91.

5. An additional 30,000 shares would be issued; 140,000 shares would now be outstanding.

6. Interest would be reduced by $96,000, after taking into account income taxes. Total earnings available to common stockholders would be $540,000 + $96,000 = $636,000.

7. Fully diluted earnings per share = $636,000/140,000 shares = $4.54.

13

Intercorporate Investments and Earnings

In this chapter we consider issues of accounting for and reporting intercorporate investments. They are often of major magnitude, and they are a source of continuing controversy. The means by which an investment in another company is recorded initially and updated subsequently are of considerable consequence for the valuation of assets and the determination of income.

It is, therefore, of utmost importance that both managers and investors understand how intercorporate activity is reported. The impact on the financial statements of intercorporate events will affect policies not only of companies that own or may in the future own other firms, but also of those that are already owned by or may be an acquisition target of another.

MOTIVATION FOR, AND MEANS OF, OWNERSHIP

A corporation may acquire an *equity interest* (ownership of common or preferred stock) in another company for a number of reasons. A company may have cash that is temporarily idle. It may use this cash to purchase a relatively small number of the shares of another company to obtain a short-term return—as an alternative, perhaps, to purchasing short-term government notes or certificates of deposits. Such securities are categorized on the books of the acquiring corporations as "marketable securities." The accounting for current marketable securities was discussed in Chapter 6. On the other hand, a company may purchase the stock of another corporation as a long-term investment.

It may do so for several reasons:

1. *To expand into new markets.* A consumer food products company sees an opportunity to tap the restaurant market. Although it can easily adapt its products for sale to restaurants, it has no direct ties with restaurants. Therefore it acquires an existing company with strong channels of distribution in the restaurant industry.
2. *To develop sources of supply.* An appliance manufacturer purchases electric motors from a number of different suppliers. It believes it could improve the quality and lower the cost of motors if it had greater control over a motor manufacturer. To achieve the greater control, it purchases one of its suppliers.
3. *To secure a return on capital greater than it could obtain through internal expansion.* A cigarette manufacturer recognizes that the long-term profit outlook for its product is bleak. To reduce its dependence on a single product, it invests available funds in firms in other industries. Sometimes it acquires controlling influence in a company; other times it merely holds a minority position.

This chapter pertains to long-term, as opposed to temporary, investments.

A company may acquire the stock of another company by purchasing it for cash or other assets. Or it may exchange shares of its own common stock for those of the company it seeks to acquire. Moreover, a firm may obtain shares of another company simply by organizing such a company and retaining all, or a portion of, the new shares issued.

When a company owns 100 percent of another firm, it can, if it wishes, dissolve the subsidiary firm and combine its assets with its own. There are several reasons, however, for operating as separate legal entities rather than as a single combined corporation. Among them are

1. *To take advantage of tax benefits.* Although separate corporations are permitted to file consolidated returns, there may be benefits to having separate businesses taxed independently.
2. *To take advantage of the limitations on corporate liability.* Shareholders of a corporation, be they individuals or other corporations, are generally not liable for losses of the company they own in amounts greater than their original investment. By dividing its operations into several legal entities, a company may be able to protect general corporate assets against liabilities arising from unprofitable operations of a single unit.
3. *To enhance organizational efficiency.* By dividing its operations into separate legal entities, a firm may be able to make the subsidiary units more autonomous than if the company were operated as a single corporation. For example, the individual units might have greater flexibility in obtaining bank loans or in issuing common or preferred shares to outsiders. In many situations, decentralization may contribute to increased performance.

4. *To make it easier to satisfy government regulations.* Federal, state, or local regulations can often be more efficiently and effectively met by carrying out certain types of activities in separate corporations. Sometimes a company will find it necessary to maintain separate corporations for activities conducted in each of the 50 states in which it does business. Almost always, separate corporations are established for specialty activities, such as banking and insurance.

LEVEL OF INFLUENCE

The critical determinant of the means by which intercorporate investments are accounted for is the degree of influence that the investor corporation exerts over the acquired company.

If the investor corporation exerts relatively minor influence, the investment would generally be accounted for by the *cost method*.

If it exerts substantial influence, the investment would be accounted for by the *equity method*. (Both these methods will be defined and evaluated shortly.)

If the investor company is able to *control* the other company (control ordinarily being defined as ownership of over 50 percent of the voting stock), the investment is commonly reported by means of *consolidated financial statements*. Consolidated financial statements report the financial positions and earnings of two or more corporations as if they were a single entity.

The three methods of accounting for corporate investments—the cost, the equity, and the consolidated statement method—are not, it should be emphasized, categorically consistent. *Since each corporation is a separate legal entity, a separate set of accounting records must, by law, be maintained for it. On the books of the investor corporation, the shares of the other company must be accounted for by either the cost or the equity method. If, however, the investor company has control over another corporation, then, for purposes of reporting, and only for purposes of reporting, the individual financial statements of the two companies can be combined into a single, consolidated set of statements.*

The relationships and distinctions between the methods will be brought out in the next several sections.

Criteria for Presumption of Significant Influence

Where an investor corporation is unable to maintain significant influence over the company in which it owns an interest because of the small proportion of its holdings or for other reasons, then it should account for its investment by the cost method. Evidence of an ability to influence significantly the key financial and operating policies of an investee company can be made manifest by several factors: percentage of shares owned, representation on the corporate board of directors, membership on key policy-making committees, interchange of managerial personnel, material purchases or sales between the two companies, and exchanges of technological information. Even though a company may not own a majority of a corporation's outstanding shares, it can nevertheless exercise a predominant impact on that company's policies. The Accounting Principles Board recognized that degree of influence cannot be objectively measured.

To make practice more uniform, however, it prescribed (in *Opinion No. 18*, 1971) that an investment of 20 percent or more should lead to a presumption that the investor has the ability to significantly influence the investee. It therefore directed that investments of less than 20 percent of voting stock should be accounted for by the *cost method*. Those of 20 percent or more should generally be accounted for by the *equity method*. But if an investor company can demonstrate that even though it owns 20 percent or more of a firm's stock it has, in fact, little or no influence over the investee's operating and financial policies, then it should use the cost rather than the equity method.[1]

COST METHOD

Under the cost method, a company records its investment in the stock of another company at cost—the amount paid to acquire the stock. It recognizes revenue from its investment only to the extent that the investee company actually declares dividends. In the absence of unusual declines in market values, the investment would be maintained on the books of the investor at original cost. The carrying value of the investment would be unaffected by changes either in the market value of shares owned or in the net worth of the company that they represent.

Example

On January 2, 1993, the Adams Company purchases 10,000 of 100,000 (10 percent) shares of the outstanding common stock of the Cain Company. It pays $30 per share. The following entry would be required on the books of the *investor* company, the Adams Company:

Investment in Cain Company $300,000
    Cash $300,000
To record the purchase of 10,000 shares of Cain Company common stock

On December 31, 1993, the Cain Company announces that earnings for the year were $500,000 ($5 per share of common stock).

No entry is required to record the announcement of the annual earnings. The Adams Company recognizes revenue from its investment only upon the actual declaration of dividends by the company whose shares it owns.

On the same date, December 31, 1993, the Cain Company declares dividends of $2 per share, payable on January 20, 1994:

Dividends receivable $20,000
    Dividend revenue from investment in Cain Company $20,000
To record dividends to be received from the Cain Company

[1]"Criteria for Applying the Equity Method of Accounting for Investments in Common Stock: An Interpretation of APB *Opinion No. 18*," Financial Accounting Standards Board *Interpretation No. 35*, 1981.

Lower of Cost or Market

Financial Accounting Board *Statement No. 12*, "Accounting for Certain Marketable Securities" (1976), provides that long-term investments accounted for by the cost method be stated at the *lower of cost or market*, just as short-term investments are (see Chapter 6). Long-term securities should not, however, be combined with short-term securities. They should be placed in a separate portfolio, and whenever the market value of the entire portfolio is less than cost, it should be written down to market. Because day-to-day fluctuations in market prices are of less significance in valuing long-term than short-term securities, the board prescribed a somewhat different method of applying the lower of cost or market rule. Unrealized losses, and subsequent recoveries, on short-term securities are reported as income statement items, similar to other expenses or revenues. Unrealized losses, and subsequent recoveries, on long-term securities, by contrast, should be carried directly to the balance sheet. Bypassing the income statement, they should be charged or credited to a special owners' equity account, "unrealized loss on long-term investments in equity securities." This account, which would always have a debit balance, would be reported "contra" to the other owners' equity accounts.

Assume, for example, that on December 31, 1993, the market value of the investment in Cain Company is $276,000, which is $24,000 less than cost. The appropriate entry would be

Unrealized loss on long-term equity
  securities (an equity contra account)..........................$24,000
    Allowance to reduce investment in Cain Company
      to market (an asset contra account) $24,000
To record decline in market value of investment in Cain Company

The unrealized loss on long-term equity securities would be recognized as a realized loss either when the securities are sold or when the decline in market value is deemed permanent. Suppose that on January 15, 1994, the investment in Cain is sold for $270,000. The following two entries would be in order:

(1)

Allowance to reduce investment in Cain Company
  to market (asset contra account) $24,000
    Unrealized loss on long-term equity securities
      (equity contra account) $24,000
To reverse entry of December 31, 1993, which recorded decline in market value

(2)

Cash $270,000
Realized loss on sale of long-term
  investments ($300,000 – $270,000) 30,000
    Investment in Cain Company................................$300,000
To record sale of shares in Cain Company

The cost method of maintaining investments is in essence that illustrated in previous chapters in connection with marketable securities and recognition of dividend revenue. Dividends are recognized as revenue when they are declared, and the lower of cost or market rule is applied.

EQUITY METHOD

Under the equity method, a company records its investment in another company at cost (the same as under the cost method). But it periodically adjusts the carrying value of its investment to take into account its share of the investee's earnings and dividends. It recognizes its share of increases or decreases in the book value net worth of the investee as soon as it knows of them.

If net worth increases as a result of investee earnings, then the investor recognizes promptly, on its own books, revenue in the amount of its proportionate share of such earnings; it does not wait until the earnings are distributed in the form of dividends. Since earnings of the investee company benefit the investor, the investor will increase the carrying value of its investment by its share of investor earnings.

If net assets of the investee decrease, then the investor will also recognize a decrease in its investment. Net assets will decrease as a consequence of operating losses. But they will also decrease whenever dividends are declared (a liability for the payment of a dividend is established; retained earnings are decreased). Hence, when the investee declares a dividend, the investor recognizes the dividend receivable and at the same time adjusts the carrying value of its investment to reflect the decline in the net assets of the investee. An example may help to clarify the accounting procedures.

Example

Assume the same facts as in the previous example, except that this time, on January 2, 1993, the Adams Company purchases 20,000 of 100,000 (20 percent) shares of the common stock outstanding of the Cain Company. Again, it pays $30 per share. This time, however, since Adams has acquired 20 percent of the shares outstanding, it may be presumed that it exerts substantial influence over the Cain Company. Hence it is required to account for the investment by the equity method:

(a)

Investment in Cain Company...............................$600,000
   Cash $600,000
To record the purchase of 20,000 shares of Cain Company common stock for $30 per share

This entry is identical (except in amounts) to that illustrated previously in connection with the cost method.

On December 31, the Cain Company announces that earnings for the year were $500,000 ($5 per share of common stock):

(b)

Investment in Cain Company................................$100,000
    Revenue from investment in Cain Company....................$100,000
To record the proportionate share of the 1993 income reported by the Cain Company

The net worth of the Cain Company increased by $500,000 as a consequence of 1993 earnings. The Adams Company must recognize 20 percent of that amount as its own revenue. Since the Adams Company receives no cash or other assets as a direct result of the Cain Company having realized the income, its share of the earnings would be reflected by an increase in the carrying value of its investment.

When the Cain Company declares a dividend of $2 per share, the Adams Company would establish a receivable account for the dividends but would recognize a corresponding *decrease* in the carrying value of its investment:

(c)

Dividends receivable..$40,000
    Investment in Cain Company................................$40,000
To record dividends to be received from the Cain Company

Upon learning that the Cain Company has declared a dividend, the Adams Company would *not*, under the equity method, recognize revenue. Revenue representing the earnings of the Cain Company was recognized at the time it was first reported. To recognize it again when assets are distributed to shareholders in the form of dividends would be to count it twice. The carrying value of the investment in the Cain Company would be reduced by the amount of the dividend received because, as a result of cash distributions to its shareholders, the Cain Company has reduced both its assets and its retained earnings. The share of the Adams Company in the retained earnings has thereby been proportionately reduced.

As indicated in the accompanying T accounts in Exhibit 13-1, the net effect of the last two entries [(**b**) and (**c**)] has been to increase the assets of the

EXHIBIT 13-1

Investment in Cain Company				Revenue from investment in Cain Company		
(a)	600,000	(c)	40,000		(b)	100,000
(b)	100,000					

Dividends receivable			Cash		
(c)	40,000			(a)	600,000

The investment account of a corporation is increased (debited) when the net assets of the company that it owns increase as a consequence of periodic earnings.

The investment account is decreased (credited) when the net assets of the company it owns decrease as a consequence of dividend declarations.

Adams Company by $100,000 (investment in Cain Company, $60,000; dividends receivable, $40,000). Correspondingly, the Adams Company recognized $100,000 in revenue from its investment in the Cain Company. The $100,000 represents, of course, 20 percent of the reported earnings of the Cain Company.

Under the equity method, the investor is continually adjusting the carrying value of its investment for its share of investee profits, losses, and dividends. There is no need to adjust further for changes in the market value of the securities owned. The investor is not required to apply the lower of cost or market rule.

COST AND EQUITY METHODS COMPARED

The rationale for the cost and the equity methods and the distinctions between them can readily be appreciated when the two methods are viewed within the context of issues of revenue recognition. A company owns stock in another company. If the investee is profitable, the investor is obviously better off than if the investee is not. Since, in the long run, earnings of a company represent revenue to its owners, earnings of the investee signify revenue to the investor. The question facing the accountant of the investor relates to the time at which such revenue should be recognized.

Under the cost method, the investor recognizes as revenue its share of investee earnings only as the investee actually declares dividends—that is, as it announces its intention to distribute assets to shareholders.

If the investee is profitable, the cost method is more conservative than the equity method. Under the cost method, revenue is recognized by the investor only as cash (assuming that the dividend is to be paid in cash) is about to be received. The cost method makes sense when an investor has but little influence on the dividend or other operating policies of the company in which it owns shares. Although the investee may be profitable, it need not necessarily declare dividends, and the investor cannot compel it to do so. It may be many years, therefore, before earnings of the investee company are translated into liquid assets of the investor company.

If the investee sustains losses, then the cost method may be less conservative than the equity method. The equity method requires that the investor give immediate recognition to its share of investee losses. The cost method permits recognition of losses to be delayed. Losses would be reported only when the investor sells its shares in the investee for less than what it paid for them or a decline in their market value is deemed permanent.

Cost Method Permits Income Manipulation

Under the equity method, the investor recognizes as revenue its share of investee earnings as soon as the earnings are reported, regardless of when assets will be distributed to shareholders in the form of dividends. The equity method is appropriate when the investor can have a significant impact on the dividend policy of the investee. The rationale for the equity method can be easily understood if the consequences of *not* using it are considered. If the investor had sufficient influence over the investee to control if and when the investee could declare dividends, then it could readily control its own earnings. If the investor otherwise had an unprofitable year, it could direct the investee to increase its dividends. Its share of the dividends would be reflected immediately as higher reported revenues. If the investor otherwise had an unusually profitable year and did not need additional revenues, it could request that the investee firm delay payment of dividends until future periods. In Chapter 5 it was pointed out that revenue should be recognized only when it can be objectively measured and when eventual collection of cash can reasonably be assured. When one firm is able to exert substantial influence (characterized by the Accounting Principles Board as ownership of 20 percent or more of voting stock) over another, then the two criteria are reasonably satisfied when the investee reports its earnings. The equity method is then more appropriate. When the firm is unable to exert such influence, then the criteria are not reasonably satisfied until the investee declares a dividend. Then the cost method is more appropriate.

CONSOLIDATED REPORTS

When a company is able to control, as opposed to merely influence, the financial and operating policies of another company, then the information requirements of investors as well as other users of financial statements are usually best served by consolidated financial statements. Consolidated financial statements report the financial position and results of operations of two or more corporations, each a separate legal entity, as if they were a single economic entity. They are designed to show the economic substance as opposed to the legal form of the corporate relationship. They combine the assets, liabilities, equities, revenues, and expenses of the two or more companies into a single balance sheet and income statement.

Consolidated statements are a means of *reporting*. The preparation of consolidated financial statements does not preclude the preparation of individual financial statements for specific purposes. Indeed, each member of a group of corporations whose financial statements may be combined into a single consolidated set of statements must maintain separate accounting records. An investor corporation must therefore use either the cost or the equity method—although, as will be seen shortly, choice of method becomes unimportant, since both the investment accounts and the revenue from investment accounts are eliminated in the process of consolidation.

The usual condition for consolidated statements is voting control—that is, ownership of more than 50 percent of the voting stock. There are, however, exceptions to this rule. Consolidated statements would not generally result in the most meaningful presentation and are therefore not required when the two or more companies are not, in fact, a single economic entity (if, for example, voting control is likely to be only temporary).

As a general rule, if an investor company owns less than 20 percent of the voting stock of another company, it should *account for* its investment on the cost basis; if it owns 20 percent or more, then it should *account for* its investment on an equity basis; if it owns over 50 percent, it should *report* to stockholders on a consolidated basis, unless because of special circumstances consolidation is inappropriate.

A company that has control (over 50 percent ownership) of another company is referred to as the *parent company*; the controlled company is known as the *subsidiary*.

PRINCIPLES OF CONSOLIDATION—BALANCE SHEET

In simplest form, consolidated statements represent the sum of the balances in accounts of the individual companies that are to form the consolidated entity. However, as is demonstrated in the discussion and examples to follow, certain eliminations and adjustments are required if double counting is to be avoided.

The objective of consolidated statements is to depict the financial position and results of operations of two or more companies as if they were a single economic entity. It is necessary, therefore, to adjust for the effect of certain intercompany transactions on both the income statement and the statement of position.

Consider the following: If a parent company sells merchandise for $100 to a subsidiary company, which in turn sells it to outsiders for $120, then the sum of the sales of the two companies would be $220. But if the two companies were viewed as a single entity, then the sale from the parent to the subsidiary would be accounted for as an internal transfer rather than a sale. Total sales—those to outsiders—would be only $120. The sale from parent to subsidiary must therefore be eliminated. Moreover, if the subsidiary is still indebted to the parent for the goods which it purchased, so too would the account receivable (on the books of the parent) and the account payable (on the books of the subsidiary) have to be eliminated.

The examples to follow focus upon the effects of consolidation on the balance sheet; in the next section we shall consider the effects on the income statement.

Intercompany Investments and Debts

Assume that a parent company purchases 100 percent of the common stock of a subsidiary company. Immediately after acquisition, the trial balances of the two individual companies appear in condensed form as follows (all dollar amounts in thousands):

	Parent	Subsidiary
Cash	$ 20,000	$10,000
Account receivable (from subsidiary)	10,000	
Investment in subsidiary	40,000	
Other assets	80,000	40,000
	$150,000	$50,000
Account payable (to parent)		$10,000
Common stock	$ 30,000	10,000
Retained earnings	120,000	30,000
	$150,000	$50,000

Since the balances are those immediately following acquisition, it is clear that the parent company must have paid $40,000 to acquire the subsidiary—

the amount in its investment in subsidiary account. If the two companies are to be combined, there is no need for an investment in subsidiary account. From a consolidated standpoint, a company cannot have an investment in itself. At the same time, if the two sets of statements are to be combined, it would be inappropriate to report $40,000 owners' equity of the subsidiary (common stock, $10,000, plus retained earnings, $30,000), since it is the parent company which is the sole owner of the subsidiary and which has such equity in it. To effect a consolidation, it would be necessary to eliminate *both* the investment in the subsidiary *and* the equity of the owners. For convenience, the eliminations can be expressed in journal entry form:

(*a*)

Common stock (of subsidiary) $10,000
Retained earnings (of subsidiary)...............................30,000
    Investment in subsidiary (by parent)...........................$40,000
To eliminate the investment in subsidiary and corresponding subsidiary owners' equity accounts

The trial balance also indicates that the subsidiary company owes the parent company $10,000. From the standpoint of the combined enterprise, both accounts receivable and payable would be overstated if assets and liabilities were simply added together; a company cannot have a payable to or a receivable from itself. The payable and receivable must be eliminated:

(*b*)

Account payable (to parent) $10,000
    Account receivable (from subsidiary)...........................$10,000
To eliminate intercompany payable and receivable

The two adjustments would be made to the books of neither *the parent nor the subsidiary. They are nothing more than* worksheet *eliminations to effect a combination of the two individual sets of statements.* Thus the consolidated balance sheet would appear as indicated in the far right-hand column in Exhibit 13-2.

EXHIBIT 13-2
Eliminating Intercompany Investments and Debts

	Original Statements		Adjustments		Combined Statements
	Parent	Subsidiary	Debit	Credit	
Cash	$ 20,000	$10,000			$ 30,000
Account receivable (from subsidiary)	10,000			(b) $10,000	
Investment in subsidiary	40,000			(a) 40,000	
Other assets	80,000	40,000			120,000
	$150,000	$50,000			$150,000
Account payable (to parent)		$10,000	(b) $10,000		
Common stock	$ 30,000	10,000	(a) 10,000		$ 30,000
Retained earnings	120,000	30,000	(a) 30,000		120,000
	$150,000	$50,000	$50,000	$50,000	$150,000

Interests of Minorities

A firm does not always acquire 100 percent of the outstanding common stock of another firm. *Minority stockholders* may also own an equity interest in an investee firm. Assume facts similar to those in the previous example, but this time suppose that the parent company purchases only 80 percent of the common stock of the subsidiary. The parent company pays $32,000 for its interest, an amount exactly equal to 80 percent of the *book value* of the subsidiary. Book value of the subsidiary is represented by common stock of $10,000 and retained earnings of $30,000.

The parent company's investment in subsidiary of $32,000 must be eliminated against $32,000 of the $40,000 owners' equity of the subsidiary:

Common stock (of subsidiary) . . . . $ 8,000
Retained earnings (of subsidiary) 24,000
    Investment in subsidiary (by parent) $32,000
To eliminate investment in subsidiary and corresponding amounts in subsidiary's owners' equity account

But that leaves $8,000 remaining in the owners' equity accounts of the subsidiary. This amount represents the equity of the minority shareholders—those who hold the remaining 20 percent interest in the firm. Consolidated financial statements are prepared from the perspective of the *majority* stockholders, those of the parent company. From the standpoint of a majority stockholder, it would be both confusing and misleading to report on the balance sheet common stock and retained earnings of two companies—those of the parent and those of the subsidiary. Hence the minority interest in each of the owners' equity accounts (the amounts that remain after the majority interest has been eliminated) are reclassified into a single account, "minority interest in subsidiary":

Common stock (of subsidiary) $2,000
Retained earnings (of subsidiary) 6,000
    Minority interest in subsidiary $8,000
To reclassify the equity of minority shareholders in the subsidiary

The minority interest in subsidiary account represents the equity of the minority shareholders in the consolidated corporation. It is, in a sense, the minority's portion of the residual interest in the subsidiary. Common practice is to report minority interest in subsidiaries on a single line between long-term liabilities and owners' equity. The amounts reported in the owners' equity section of the consolidated balance sheet represent only the equity of the parent company stockholders.

Acquisition Price in Excess of Investment Book Value

In the discussion so far, the price paid by the parent to acquire its investment in the subsidiary was exactly equal to its proportionate share of the *book value* (which is equal to the *owners' equity*) of the subsidiary. If, as is common, the parent company acquires its interest at an amount greater than the book value of the assets acquired, then such excess must be transferred to an account indicative of its nature.

Assume now that the parent company pays $45,000 to acquire a 100 percent interest in the subsidiary but that the net assets of the subsidiary, as recorded on its own books, are only $40,000 (see Exhibit 13-3). As in the previous examples, if the financial positions of the two individual companies are to be shown as a single economic entity, then both the investment of the parent and its corresponding owners' equity as recorded on the books of the subsidiary must be eliminated. This time, however, although the investment would be recorded on the books of the parent at $45,000, the corresponding equity would be recorded on the books of the subsidiary at only $40,000.

The portion of the investment ($40,000) that represents value as recorded on the books of the subsidiary can be eliminated against the corresponding owners' equity with an entry identical to that made in a previous example. Thus

(a)

Common stock (of subsidiary)	....	$10,000
Retained earnings (of subsidiary)	....	30,000
Investment in subsidiary (by parent)	....	$40,000

To eliminate investment in subsidiary and corresponding amounts in subsidiary's owners' equity accounts

That leaves $5,000 (the excess of $45,000 paid over the corresponding book value of $40,000) of the investment still to be accounted for.

Specific Tangible or Intangible Assets

This excess of cost over book value is often a source of confusion and misunderstanding. There are at least two reasons a firm may pay for an interest in a subsidiary an amount in excess of its book value. First, the book value of individual assets (and hence the recorded owners' equity) is based on historical cost—the amount initially paid to acquire the assets, less amortization and depreciation. Book value, as frequently emphasized in this text, is not necessarily indicative of market value. Thus the price paid by the company to acquire its shares of stock in the subsidiary may be indicative of the market value of the individual assets represented by such shares. If this is the case, then the excess of cost over book value should be assigned to the particular assets acquired.

Consistent with the historical cost basis of accounting, assets should be valued at purchase price. The mere fact that the parent company may not have purchased the assets directly, but instead acquired the common stock of the company that has title to the assets, does not change the substance of the transaction. Nor should it change the manner in which the assets are accounted for. Sometimes, in fact, as is the case with intangible assets, the assets acquired may not even be recorded on the books of the subsidiary. In accord with generally accepted accounting principles, patents, copyrights, and trademarks when developed internally (as opposed to purchased from outsiders) are not given accounting recognition. When such assets are obtained in connection with the purchase of a subsidiary, they should be stated at their fair market values and an appropriate share of the excess of the cost over the book value assigned to them. The following additional adjustment is required if the entire excess of cost over book value is to be allocated to specific assets:

(b)

```
Specific assets (land, buildings, equipment, patents, etc.) ............$5,000
    Investment in subsidiary .....................................$5,000
```
To allocate the excess of cost over book value of investment to specific assets

Subsequent to the acquisition, the consolidated enterprise should base its charges for depreciation and amortization on the amounts at which the assets are recorded on the consolidated balance sheet. Thus depreciation and amortization charges may be greater on the consolidated income statement than the sum of the separate depreciation charges on the financial statements of the two individual companies. The acquired subsidiary, on its own financial statements, will maintain its assets and continue to base depreciation and amortization at their original values.

Goodwill

A firm may also pay an amount in excess of recorded book value to acquire another company because the company possesses certain intangible assets that cannot be specifically identified. These assets may be favorable customer attitudes toward the company, unusual talents of corporate managers, advantageous business locations, or special monopolistic or political privileges. Or they may exist because the individually identifiable assets when used together are worth considerably more than the sum of the fair market values of the assets employed independently. Whatever their attributes, they enable the firm to earn amounts in excess of "normal" returns. Such assets—that is, the amount in excess of book value that cannot be specifically allocated to other assets—may be classified as *goodwill*:

(b, alternative)

```
Goodwill.....................................................$5,000
    Investment in subsidiary .....................................$5,000
```
To allocate the excess of cost over book value of investment to goodwill

Goodwill is a residual. It represents that portion of the cost of acquiring a subsidiary that cannot be assigned directly to any specific assets. Goodwill is one asset that arises *only* out of business combinations. Although firms may develop the attributes that compose goodwill over a number of years, they may not, under conventional accounting principles, recognize them. Goodwill may be recorded only when one firm purchases another and the excess of cost over book value cannot be specifically assigned to other assets.

Because of the very nature of goodwill—it is a residual asset—its useful life is not readily determinable. Nevertheless, the Accounting Principles Board has prescribed that firms should make their best efforts to estimate the useful lives of all intangible assets, including goodwill, and that they should be amortized over their useful lives.[2] In no event, however, should the amortization

---

[2] "Intangible Assets." AICPA Accounting Principles Board *Opinion No. 17*, 1970. *One* type of intangible, that generated by R&D expenditures, is normally expensed as incurred, as indicated in Chapter 9.

EXHIBIT 13-3
Acquisition Price in Excess of Book Value of Investment

| | Original Statements | | Adjustments | | Combined |
	Parent	Subsidiary	Debit	Credit	Statements
				$40,000 (a)	
Investment in subsidiary	$ 45,000			5,000 (b)	
Various assets	105,000	$40,000			$145,000
Specific tangible or intangible assets or goodwill			$ 5,000 (b)		5,000
	$150,000	$40,000	$ 5,000	$45,000	$150,000
Common stock	$ 30,000	$10,000	$10,000 (a)		$ 30,000
Retained earnings	120,000	30,000	30,000 (a)		120,000
	$150,000	$40,000	$40,000		$150,000

period exceed 40 years. Therefore, if a consolidated entity records goodwill, it must each year reduce the balance in the goodwill account (a credit to goodwill) and increase expenditures by a like amount (a debit to amortization of goodwill) by no less than one-fortieth of the initial amount recorded. Both the goodwill itself and the charge for amortization would appear only on the consolidated statements, not on those of either the parent or the subsidiary balance sheet. Exhibit 13-3 highlights the required adjustments when acquisition price exceeds the subsidiary's book value.

PRINCIPLES OF CONSOLIDATION—INCOME STATEMENT

In essence, the consolidated income statement, like the consolidated balance sheet, presents the sum of the balances in the accounts of the component corporations. However, as with the balance sheet, numerous adjustments and eliminations may be necessary to give effect to transactions among the individual companies.

The consolidated income statement indicates the change in enterprise welfare between two dates as if the various components of the enterprise were a single economic entity. Principles of revenue and expense recognition must be applied as if the individual companies were, in fact, combined into a single company. Thus revenues and expenses, if they are to be recognized, must be the result only of arm's-length transactions with parties *outside* of the consolidated entity.

Intercompany transactions take many forms; the specific eliminations and adjustments that might be required must be determined in light of their particular nature. The general approach to consolidations may be illustrated with some typical intercompany transactions.

Assume the following statements of income of the parent company and the subsidiary company:

	Parent	Subsidiary
Sales	$400,000	$300,000
Gain on sale (to subsidiary) of fixed assets	6,000	
Interest revenue (from subsidiary)	7,000	
Total revenues	$413,000	$300,000
Cost of goods sold	$240,000	$210,000
Interest expense (to parent)		7,000
Other expenses	80,000	53,000
Total expenses	$320,000	$270,000
Income	$ 93,000	$ 30,000

The parent company owns 80 percent of the subsidiary.

Interest

The individual components of a company may enter into arrangements which result in revenues to one and expenses to another but involve no transactions with outsiders. Suppose, for example, that a parent makes a loan to its subsidiary. Interest on the loan would be recognized as a revenue to the parent and as an expense to the subsidiary. From the standpoint of the consolidated entity, the "loan" is nothing more than an intracompany transfer of funds from one "division" to another. Just as any intercompany payable and receivable outstanding at year end would be eliminated from the consolidated balance sheet, so too must the interest revenue and expense be eliminated from the income statement. If $7,000 of the interest revenue and expense reported on the individual statements were intercompany interest, then the following elimination would be required:

(a)

```
Interest revenue (parent) ....................................... $7,000
        Interest expense (subsidiary) ................................... $7,000
To eliminate intercompany interest
```

Sales and Cost of Goods Sold

From the standpoint of a consolidated enterprise, a sale of merchandise by one member of a consolidated group to another is not an event worthy of revenue recognition. A sale takes place only when merchandise is sold to a party outside of the consolidated enterprise. Intercompany sales should, of course, be given accounting recognition on the books of the individual companies; they must, however, be eliminated when reporting on the operations of the companies as a consolidated economic entity.

Assume, for example, that included in the revenues of the parent are $100,000 in sales to the subsidiary. The goods sold to the subsidiary were manufactured by the parent at a cost of $80,000. The subsidiary company in turn sold the goods to outsiders at a price of $120,000. The transactions would be reflected on the books of the two companies as follows:

	Parent (Sales to Subsidiary)	Subsidiary (Sales to Outsiders)
Sales revenue	$100,000	$120,000
Cost of goods sold	80,000	100,000

From the standpoint of the consolidated firm, sales to outsiders were $120,000 and the cost of goods sold only $80,000. It is necessary to eliminate $100,000 in both sales revenue (the sale by the parent to the subsidiary) and cost of goods sold (the cost of the goods sold by the subsidiary to outsiders):

(b)

Sales revenue (parent) $100,000
    Cost of goods sold (subsidiary) $100,000
To eliminate intercompany sales

The required adjustments for intercompany sales become considerably more complex when, at year end, one member of the corporate group has not yet sold to outsiders its entire stock of goods purchased from another member. It then becomes necessary to reduce the value of inventory in the amount of any profit recognized on the sale from one company to another. Inventory must be stated at its cost to the consolidated entity, rather than at the intercompany selling price.

Sales of Fixed Assets

Fixed assets must be reported on the consolidated statements on the basis of their initial cost to the consolidated enterprise. If a fixed asset has been sold by one member of the consolidated group to another, then the amount at which the asset is carried on the books of an individual company may be greater or less than that based on original cost.

Assume, for example, that the $6,000 in the account of the parent company, "gain on sale of fixed assets," represents in its entirety the gain on the sale of land to the subsidiary. The land was sold to the subsidiary at a price of $45,000; it had originally cost the parent $39,000. After the sale, the land would be recorded on the books of the subsidiary at its purchase price of $45,000—an amount $6,000 greater than that paid for it by the two companies viewed as a single, consolidated entity.

To report the consolidated results of operations and financial positions of the two companies, it is necessary to eliminate the effects of transactions that would be considered nothing more than internal transfers if the two companies were viewed as a single economic entity. Thus

(c)

Gain on sale of fixed assets (by parent) $6,000
    Land (of subsidiary) $6,000
To adjust for gain on intercompany sale of land

This adjustment, as is the case with many consolidation adjustments, would affect both the income statement and the balance sheet.

The intercompany sale of land will have to be accounted for in the preparation of consolidated statements in years subsequent to that in which the sale took place—in fact, for as long as the asset remains on the books of the subsidiary. The land will continue to be "overvalued" by the amount of the gain recognized by the parent. Since, on the books of the parent, the gain will have been *closed* at year end to retained earnings, retained earnings also will be permanently overstated.

The adjustments for the sale of fixed assets are substantially more complex when the assets transferred are subject to depreciation. From the standpoint of the consolidated enterprise, depreciation charges must be based on the original cost of the asset to the first member of the consolidated group that acquired it. On the books of the company on which the asset is presently recorded, however, it would be maintained on the basis of the price paid to the seller company, a member of the consolidated entity. If, for example, the fixed asset sold was equipment rather than land, then the subsidiary would properly depreciate, on its own books, an asset that had cost $45,000. If the useful life was 10 years and salvage value was zero, annual depreciation charges would be $4,500. For purposes of consolidated reporting, however, the asset initially cost only $39,000, the original acquisition cost of the parent (seller). Hence annual depreciation charges would be only $3,900. An adjustment would be required to reduce annual depreciation charges by $600. But, in addition, adjustments would also be required in each year after the first to "correct" for the cumulative effect on "accumulated depreciation" of the previous "overstatements" of depreciation charges.

Amortization of Goodwill

As was indicated in the discussion relating to the interpretation of the excess of investment cost over book value, *goodwill* is an asset that arises exclusively out of the process of consolidation. Goodwill is recorded only on a consolidated balance sheet, not on the balance sheets of the component companies of a consolidated group. When goodwill is amortized, the amortization expense is reported only on the consolidated income statement, not on the income statements of the individual companies.

Assume that the parent company pays $200,000 for an 80 percent interest in the subsidiary company and that the book value of the subsidiary company is $225,000. The book value of the 80 percent interest is therefore $180,000. The excess of cost over book value—assumed in this case to represent goodwill—is, at time of acquisition, $20,000.

If the goodwill is to be amortized over 40 years, the maximum amortization period permitted by current professional pronouncements, then the following consolidation adjustment would be made:

(d)

Amortization of goodwill (expense)	$500
Goodwill (asset)	$500
To amortize goodwill	

EXHIBIT 13-4
Income Statement Adjustments

Parent Company
Consolidated Statement of Income

	Individual Statements		Adjustments That Affect Income Statement		Consolidated Statement of Income
	Parent	Subsidiary	Dr. (Cr.)		
Sales	$400,000	$300,000	$100,000	(b)	$600,000
Gain on sale of fixed assets	6,000		6,000	(c)*	
Interest revenue	7,000		7,000	(a)	
Total revenues	$413,000	$300,000	$113,000		$600,000
Cost of goods sold	$240,000	$210,000	($100,000)	(b)	$350,000
Interest expense		7,000	(7,000)	(a)	
Other expenses	80,000	53,000			133,000
Amortization of goodwill			500	(d)†	500
Total expenses	$320,000	$270,000	($106,500)		$483,500
Total income	$ 93,000	$ 30,000	$ 6,500		$116,500
Less: Minority interest in earnings of subsidiary					6,000
Consolidated income					$110,500

*Corresponding credit would be to land, which would be reported on the balance sheet.
†Corresponding credit would be to goodwill, which would be reported on the balance sheet.

Minority Interests in Earnings of Subsidiary

Consolidated statements, as already emphasized, are prepared from the perspective of the stockholders of the parent corporation. The parent corporation, however, is entitled to only a portion of the earnings of its subsidiary. The minority stockholders of the subsidiary are entitled to the remaining earnings. Therefore the portion of subsidiary earnings that can be ascribed to the minority stockholders must be deducted from total consolidated income to arrive at net consolidated income.

The earnings of the subsidiary company as indicated in its income statement are $30,000. Inasmuch as the parent company owns only 80 percent of the outstanding shares of the subsidiary, the minority share of subsidiary earnings would be 20 percent of $30,000, or $6,000.

By summing the amounts reported in the income statements of the individual companies, taking into account the consolidating adjustments, and giving recognition to the minority interest in the earnings of the subsidiary, a consolidated statement of income can be prepared. A worksheet is shown in Exhibit 13-4.

COMPREHENSIVE EXAMPLE

Exhibits 13-5 through 13-8 illustrate in a single example the essentials of preparing both the income statement and the balance sheet. Exhibit 13-5 contains the individual financial statements of a parent (Texas, Inc.) and its subsidiary

EXHIBIT 13-5
Financial Statements of Individual Companies and Additional Information as to Intercompany Transactions

Balance Sheets
December 31, 1993

	Texas, Inc.	Austin, Inc.
Assets		
Cash	$ 10	$ 5
Accounts receivable	80	12
Notes receivable	60	90
Property, plant, and equipment (net of depreciation)	400	110
Investment in Austin, Inc.	152	
Total assets	$702	$217
Liabilities and owners' equity		
Accounts and notes payable	$150	$ 57
Common stock	10	10
Capital in excess of par	40	75
Retained earnings	502	75
Total liabilities and equities	$702	$217

Statements of Income
Year Ended December 31, 1993

	Texas, Inc.	Austin, Inc.
Sales	$700	$ 90
Interest revenue	12	9
Gain on sale of land	28	0
Total revenues	$740	$ 99
Cost of goods sold	600	58
Interest expenses	15	6
Other expenses	48	15
Total expenses	$663	79
Net income	$ 77	$ 20

Other Information

On January 1, 1993, Texas, Inc., acquired an 80 percent interest in Austin, Inc., for $152 million. The excess of price paid over book value cannot be assigned to specific assets.

During the year, Texas, Inc., made sales to its subsidiary of $25 million.

Texas, Inc., made several loans to its subsidiary during the year. At year end the balance in notes from Austin, Inc., was $10 million. During the year, Texas, Inc., earned $4 million in interest on notes from its subsidiary.

During the year Austin, Inc., purchased land from its parent at a price of $15 million. Texas, Inc., had paid $10 million for the land.

It is the policy of Texas, Inc., to amortize goodwill over a period of 40 years.

EXHIBIT 13-6
Consolidating Worksheet

	Individual Statements				Adjustments		Consolidated Statements	
	Texas, Inc.		**Austin, Inc.**					
	Dr.	Cr.	Dr.	Cr.	Dr.	Cr.	Dr.	Cr.
Cash	10		5				15	
Accounts receivable	80		12				92	
Notes receivable	60		90			10 (e)	140	
Property, plant, and equipment (net of depreciation)	400		110			5 (g)	505	
Investment in Austin, Inc.	152					40 (a) 112 (b)	0	
Goodwill					40 (a)	1 (h)	39	
Accounts and notes payable		150		57	10 (e)			197
Minority interest in Austin, Inc.						28 (c)		28
Common stock		10		10	8 (b) 2 (c)			10
Capital in excess of par		40		75	60 (b) 15 (c)			40
Retained earnings, 1/1/93		425		55	44 (b) 11 (c)			425
Sales		700		90	25 (d)			765
Interest revenue		12		9	4 (f)			17
Gain on sale of land		28		0	5 (g)			23
Cost of goods sold	600		58			25 (d)	633	
Interest expense	15		6			4 (f)	17	
Amortization of goodwill					1 (h)		1	
Other expenses	48		15				63	
	1,365	1,365	296	296	225	225	1,505	1,505

EXHIBIT 13-7
Consolidating Journal Entries

(a)

Goodwill $40		
Investment in Austin, Inc $40		

To assign excess of cost over book value to goodwill

Investment in Austin, Inc.		$152
Book value of Austin:		
Common stock	$ 10	
Capital in excess of par	75	
Retained earnings, 1/1/93	55	
Total book value	140	
Percent of ownership	× 80%	
Book value of Texas' interest		112
Excess of cost over book value		$ 40

(b)

Common stock . . . . $ 8	
Capital in excess of par 60	
Retained earnings 44	
Investment in Austin, Inc $112	

To eliminate remaining balance in investment in Austin, Inc., against corresponding equity in Austin, Inc.

(c)

Common stock . . . . $ 2	
Capital in excess of par 15	
Retained earnings 11	
Minority interest in Austin, Inc $28	

To reclassify minority interest in Austin, Inc.

(d)

Sales $25	
Cost of goods sold $25	

To eliminate intercompany sales (of Texas) and corresponding cost of goods sold (of Austin)

(e)

Accounts and notes payable $10	
Notes receivable $10	

To eliminate intercompany receivable and payable

(f)

Interest revenue $4	
Interest expense $4	

To eliminate intercompany interest revenue and expense

(g)

Gain on sale on land $5	
Property, plant, and equipment $5	

To eliminate gain from intercompany sale on land

(h)

Amortization of goodwill $1	
Goodwill $1	

To amortize goodwill of $40 over 40 years

EXHIBIT 13-8
Consolidated Financial Statements of Texas, Inc., and Subsidiary

Consolidated Statement of Income
Year Ended December 31, 1993

Sales	$765	
Interest revenue	17	
Gain on sale of land	23	$805
Cost of goods sold	633	
Interest expense	17	
Amortization of goodwill	1	
Other expenses	63	714
Consolidated income		91
Less: Minority interest in earnings of subsidiary (20% of $20,000)		4
Net consolidated income		$ 87

Consolidated Balance Sheet
As of December 31, 1993

Assets	
Cash	$ 15
Accounts receivable	92
Notes receivable	140
Property, plant, and equipment (net of depreciation)	505
Goodwill	39
Total assets	$791
Liabilities and owners' equity	
Accounts and notes payable	$197
Minority interest in Austin, Inc. (see note 1)	32
Common stock	10
Capital in excess of par	40
Retained earnings (see note 2)	512
Total liabilities and equities	$791

Note 1: Minority Interest in Austin, Inc.

Minority interest in Austin per worksheet	$28
Minority interest in 1993 earnings per statement of income	4
Minority interest in Austin, Inc.	$32

Note 2: Retained Earnings

Retained earnings per worksheet	$425
Net consolidated income	87
Total consolidated retained earnings	$512

(Austin, Inc.) as of December 31, 1993. (All dollar amounts are in millions.) It also provides essential information as to intercompany transactions.

Exhibit 13-6 illustrates a worksheet that can be used to prepare both the consolidated income statement and the consolidated balance sheet. The trial balances in the columns to the left are *preclosing* trial balances. Therefore the balances in retained earnings differ than those shown in the balance sheets. They are less by the amount of earnings of 1993.

Exhibit 13-7 shows the journal entries required to make the consolidating adjustments and eliminations. They have been posted to the worksheet in Exhibit 13-6.

Exhibit 13-8 displays the consolidated balance sheet and income statement of Texas, Inc., and its subsidiary.

INSTANT EARNINGS

A company may, of course, purchase all, or a portion, of the outstanding stock of another corporation for *cash*. But quite often interests in other companies are obtained in exchange for the common stock of the acquiring corporation. If the investment is accounted for as a purchase (an alternative means will be discussed shortly), no special accounting problems are presented. Suppose, for example, Alpha Company acquired 500,000 shares of Beta Company at a price of $10 per share. In exchange for the shares, Alpha Company issued to Beta Company stockholders 50,000 shares of its own common stock, each share having a market value of $100. The common stock has a par value of $1 per share. The following journal entry would be required:

```
Investment in Beta Co. ....................................$5,000,000
        Common stock, par value .................................$    50,000
        Common stock, capital in excess of par.......................  4,950,000
To record purchase of Beta Co. by Alpha Co.
```

An acquisition for stock, rather than cash, may have a striking impact on the reported earnings of the parent company. Indeed, acquisitions may result in instant increases in reported profits even in the absence of any substantive improvements in the operations of either the parent or the subsidiary company. Consider the following additional information pertaining to the acquisition of Beta by Alpha:

Selected Financial Data Immediately Prior to Acquisition		
	Alpha	Beta
Number of shares outstanding	100,000 shares	500,000 shares
Net assets	$1,000,000	$5,000,000
Capital stock ($1 par value)	$100,000	$500,000
Retained earnings	$900,000	$4,500,000
Book value per share	$10	$10
Latest annual income	$200,000	$500,000
Latest earnings per share	$2	$1
Market price of common stock	$100 per share	$10 per share

Alpha Company is the smaller of the two companies in terms of assets and total earnings. Yet investors obviously consider its prospects for future earnings to be more promising than those of Beta. The price/earnings (P/E) ratio (market price of common stock to earnings per share) of Alpha is 50 to 1 and that of Beta is only 10 to 1. Suppose that the exchange of stock was to be based on the market prices of the shares of the two companies. The 500,000 shares of Beta Company have a total market value of $5 million (500,000 shares at $10 per share). Since each share of Alpha has a market value of $100, the number of shares that Alpha would be required to issue would be $5 million divided by $100, or 50,000.

If Alpha Company was to issue 50,000 additional shares to the owners of Beta Company, then it would have outstanding a total of 150,000 shares. Consolidated earnings, assuming no substantive improvement in the operations of either firm, would be the sum of the earnings of the two individual companies—$700,000 ($200,000 plus $500,000). No amortization of excess of cost over book value is required since the total market price of Beta Company stock is exactly equal to its book value. Earnings per share of Alpha Company, reported on a consolidated basis, would now be $4.66 ($700,000 divided by 150,000 shares)—233 percent of previously reported earnings of $2 per share.

The ramifications of this simplified example are critical to an understanding of the merger movement of the 1960s and 1970s. Many of the acquisitions of that era were for common stock rather than cash, and often, as in the example, a whale of a firm was swallowed up by a minnow. Today, mergers and acquistions tend to take forms that are both different and more varied than those of the earlier periods. Many acquisitions are for cash, rather than stock; consider, for example, leveraged buyouts. In the case of acquisitions, new and creative financial instruments are issued. In almost all, however, the impact on *reported* income, assets, and liabilities is a prime consideration in premerger analyses.

The acquisition in the example above, as is common in practice, was facilitated by the substantial difference in the price-earnings ratios of the two firms. The P/E ratio of Alpha was considerably higher than that of Beta. Alpha was able to acquire Beta by giving up shares with a market value that exceeded by a considerable amount their book value. Because the number of shares issued was based on market value, not book value, Alpha had to issue only a relatively small number of new shares. It was thereby able to add a relatively large amount of earnings without substantially adding new ownership claims to those earnings.

Stock market prices are likely to be influenced by the trend in earnings over a number of years. The relatively high P/E ratio of Alpha might be explained, at least in part, by a trend of rapidly increasing earnings. The acquisition of Beta would likely help sustain that trend or even accentuate it. The P/E ratio of Alpha may thereby remain high or even increase, thus making it even easier for the firm to acquire additional firms in the future. And future acquisitions may further add to reported earnings per share. To a considerable degree, the merger movement was supported by the circle of acquisition, increase in earnings, increase in market price of stock, additional acquisitions, and so on.

It must be pointed out, however, that the increase in earnings is seldom as dramatic as in the example. If the acquiring corporation pays a price in excess of a firm's book value, then the excess might have to be amortized over a number of years (exceptions will be discussed in the paragraphs that follow), and the charge for amortization would reduce reported earnings.

Description and Rationale

In the discussion of business combinations to this point it has been assumed that one company acquires another. The combinations have been accounted for as purchase-type transactions—one company purchases, either for cash or common stock, the outstanding common stock of another. In those instances where a business combination is effected by an exchange of common stock— where one company, be it a new or existing company, acquires substantially all of the voting stock of another in return for its own common stock—the transaction may be accounted for as an alternative type of business combination, a *pooling of interests*.

A pooling is a union of two companies, with neither acquiring the other. Whereas in a purchase a new basis of accountability is established for the acquired firm, in a pooling both firms carry over the asset and liability values from their own books.

The financial consequences of accounting for a business combination as a pooling of interests rather than a purchase may be profound; reported earnings as well as values assigned to assets may be significantly different.

Underlying the pooling of interests method of accounting for business combinations is the rationale that two firms join together to operate as a single economic enterprise. Neither of the two purchases the other, and the owners of both of the component companies are granted a proportionate interest in the combined enterprise. The combination represents a marriage of equals, or if not exactly of equals, then at least a marriage where one party does not clearly dominate the other.

No Increase in Asset Values

The key feature of the pooling of interests method is that each of the component companies retains its former basis of accounting. That is, the assets and liabilities of neither company are revalued at the time of combination. The recorded assets and liabilities of both companies are carried forward to the consolidated enterprise at their previously recorded amounts. So also are their retained earnings. *No accounting recognition is given to goodwill, nor are other assets written up to their fair market values.* Retention of the former basis of accounting is justified because there has been no sale of the assets of one firm to another; there has merely been a fusion of two companies into one.

The pooling of interests method has great appeal to combining firms in that in most circumstances it permits the consolidated enterprise to report higher earnings than if the combination were accounted for as a purchase. The pooling of interests method may result in higher reported earnings because it does not require the consolidated enterprise to increase the carrying values of the assets of the acquired firm to reflect an excess of purchase price over book value. No goodwill need be recorded. Therefore the firm does not have to charge either depreciation or amortization on the amounts by which the fair market values of either of the two firms exceed their book values. An example can be used to illustrate the pooling of interests approach and to highlight the differences between the pooling of interests and the purchase methods of accounting for business combinations.

Example

Indicated in the table following is selected information about two firms, Delta Corp. and Echo Corp., prior to their merger:

	Balance Sheet	
	Delta Corp.	Echo Corp.
Net assets (assets less liabilities)	$1,000,000	$5,000,000
Common stock, par value $1	100,000	500,000
Contributed capital in excess of par	300,000	700,000
Retained earnings	600,000	3,800,000
Total owners' equity	$1,000,000	$5,000,000
Number of shares outstanding	100,000	500,000
Net income, in year prior to merger	$200,000	$500,000
Earnings per share	$2	$1
Recent market price per share	$100	$20

Delta and Echo agree to combine their operations. Delta Corp. will issue to the current stockholders of Echo Corp. new shares of its own common stock in exchange for their existing shares in Echo Corp. The number of shares to be issued by Delta will be based on the relative market prices of the shares just prior to the negotiations leading to the merger. Since the shares outstanding of Echo Corp. have a current market value of $10 million (500,000 shares at $20 per share), Delta Corp. will have to issue 100,000 shares ($10 million divided by $100, the market price of Delta Corp. stock).

Under the pooling of interests method, the accounting entries are a bit tricky. The consolidated balance sheet, however, would reflect the sum of the assets and liabilities of each of the two companies. A revised "common stock, par value," account would indicate the par value of the shares outstanding (those of the parent company, in this example, Delta Corp.). The balance in the "retained earnings" account would represent the sum of the previous balances of the two individual companies. The balance in the "contributed capital in excess of par" account would, in essence, be a "plug"—whatever amount required to assure that assets less liabilities were equal to owners' equity.

Delta Corp. and Subsidiary Consolidated Balance Sheet	
Net assets	$6,000,000
Common stock, par value $1 (200,000 shares outstanding)	$ 200,000
Contributed capital in excess of par	1,400,000
Retained earnings	4,400,000
Total owners' equity	$6,000,000

The assets and liabilities are stated on the same basis as on the books of the component companies. In contrast to the purchase method, no adjustment has been made to asset values—either by revaluation of specific assets or by the addition of goodwill—to reflect the difference between the market value of the common stock issued by Delta Corp. ($10 million) and the value at which the assets were recorded on the books of the Echo Corp. ($5 million).

If there were no substantive increases in the earnings of the two firms as a consequence of the merger, then earnings after the merger would be the sum of the earnings of the two individual firms—$200,000 contributed by Delta, $500,000 contributed by Echo, a total of $700,000.

The earnings per share, based on 200,000 shares of Delta Corp. stock outstanding would be $3.50—an increase of $1.50 per share from the premerger EPS. This increase in EPS can be attributed entirely to the *instant earnings* effect described earlier. The shares of Delta were selling at a price/earnings ratio of 50 to 1; those of Echo at only 20 to 1. Delta was thereby able to increase total earnings 3.5 times (from $200,000 to $700,000) by only doubling the number of its outstanding shares (from 100,000 shares to 200,000).

By contrast, if the combination had been accounted for as a purchase, then the combined entity would either have reported goodwill of $5 million or increased the carrying value of specific assets by that amount. If the $5 million in additional assets or in goodwill were depreciated or amortized over a period of, say, 20 years, then earnings would be $250,000 per year lower than under the pooling method. If earnings of the two individual firms after the merger were the same as those prior to the merger, then consolidated earnings, if the combination was accounted for as a purchase, would be only $450,000. By contrast, they would be $700,000 if the combination was accounted for as a pooling. Hence earnings per share would be only $450,000 divided by 200,000 shares, or $2.25.

Exhibit 13-9 highlights these differences.

Abuses and Reforms

The term *pooling of interests* was at one time used to describe a type of business combination rather than an accounting method. Two corporations of similar size joined together to carry out their operations. The owners of the two firms obtained, and retained, an interest in the new firm proportionate to their respective contributions, and the new company was managed jointly by the previous managers of the two firms. A pooling of interests was viewed as a merger of two great rivers, as contrasted with a purchase, which was seen as a stream feeding into a river.

In the late 1950s and early 1960s, the traditional criteria for a pooling of interests began to erode. Business combinations that were not in spirit poolings of interests were accounted for as if they were. First, the relative size test was abandoned. Combinations of giant firms with much smaller firms were treated as poolings of interests. Then the criteria of continuity of ownership and management were disregarded. One of the two firms involved in the combination may have paid sizable amounts of cash, rather than common stock, for a portion of the common stock of the other firm. Thus the owners of one of the firms were, to the extent that they received cash payments, *bought out* by those of the

EXHIBIT 13-9
Example of Differences between Pooling and Purchase Accounting

Reported Net Assets

	Pooling	Purchase
Reported net assets (assets less liabilities) per individual statements		
Book value of Delta	$1,000,000	$ 1,000,000
Book value of Echo	5,000,000	5,000,000
Total book value:	$6,000,000	$ 6,000,000
Excess of cost over book value	—	5,000,000*
Consolidated net assets	$6,000,000	$11,000,000

*Market value of stock issued by Delta	
(500,000 shares @ $20)	$10,000,000
Book value of Echo	5,000,000
Excess of cost over book value	$ 5,000,000

This amount would be assigned, if possible, to specific assets. If, however, it cannot be associated with specific assets, then it is assigned to goodwill.

Reported Earnings

	Pooling	Purchase
Delta	$200,000	$200,000
Echo earnings	500,000	500,000
Total individual company earnings	$700,000	$700,000
Amortization of goodwill	—	250,000*
Net consolidated earnings	$700,000	$450,000
Number of shares of stock outstanding	200,000	200,000
Earnings per share	$ 3.50	$ 2.25

*Assuming that excess of cost over book value is amortized (or depreciated) over 20 years.

Note: Companies do not have a choice as to whether to account for a merger or acquisition as a pooling or a purchase. If the transaction qualifies as a pooling, then it must be accounted for as one.

other. Eventually, almost any combination could be accounted for as a pooling. Poolings of interests and purchases came to be recognized as accounting alternatives from which managements could select, rather than as types of business combinations.

Today, as set forth in *Opinion No. 16*, "Business Combinations," issued by the Accounting Principles Board in 1970, a business combination may be accounted for as a pooling of interests only if a number of specific conditions are satisfied. Primary among the criteria for a pooling of interests is that the merger must be carried out almost entirely by an exchange of common stock. Purchases of stock for cash (except in minor amounts) are prohibited, and one company must acquire substantially all (at least 90 percent) of the common stock of the other. Moreover, stockholders who receive the newly issued shares must either retain them or sell them to outsiders; they cannot redeem them for cash to the issuing operation.

Opinion No. 16 does not require adherence to the spirit of the traditional pooling of interests in the sense that the two combining companies must be of similar size. One company is permitted to dominate another. But *Opinion No. 16* does restrict the freedom of firms to choose whether a combination should be accounted for as a purchase or as a pooling of interests. If it satisfies certain criteria, it *must* be accounted for as a pooling of interests; if it does not it *must* be accounted for as a purchase.

Despite the issuance of *Opinion No. 16*, the issue of business combinations remains controversial. The critical issue on which attention is focused relates to the values that should be assigned to the assets of the combining companies—and most particularly those of a company acquired by another. The values assigned to the assets have, of course, a direct bearing on depreciation and amortization charges and hence on reported earnings. In a pooling, the assets of each company are stated at their previous bases; in a purchase, assets are restated to reflect the consideration paid for them.

SHOULD ALL MAJORITY-OWNED SUBSIDIARIES BE CONSOLIDATED?

A key question that faces the accounting profession is whether a company should consolidate majority-owned subsidiairies that are in unrelated industries.

When companies are in different industries, consolidated statements become less meaningful. This is especially true when one or more of the firms are in specialized industries such as insurance, banking, and real estate, which engage in unique accounting practices. There is a risk that unrelated numbers will be combined into a meaningless hodgepodge. For the 30 years prior to 1989 firms were not required to consolidate heterogeneous subsidiaries. The presumption was that when the companies had little in common, other than common ownership, separate statements would be more informative.

During that period manufacturing and merchandising concerns used "non-homogeneity" as a basis for selectively excluding subsidiaries from their consolidated statements. Often the real motive for not consolidating the subsidiaries was to escape having to report sizable liabilities on the parent's balance sheet. Sometimes, in fact, the subsidiaries were established for the main purpose of providing "off the balance sheet" financing.

In 1987, to eliminate the abuses, the FASB issued *Statement No. 94*, which took effect late in 1988. This pronouncement stipulates that all majority-owned subsidiaries must be consolidated, except where control is likely to be temporary or where control does not rest with the majority owner.

ECONOMIC CONSEQUENCES OF ACCOUNTING PRACTICES

For the most part, the way a merger or acquisition is accounted for has little impact on corporate cash flows. Hence in economic substance, one accounting method leaves a company no better or worse off than another.[3]

---

[3]The federal tax consequences of mergers and acquisitions are generally independent of the accounting methods used for general reporting. In some states, however, franchise or income taxes may be affected by financial reporting method. If they are, there would be some direct economic consequences.

Nevertheless, many investment bankers are convinced that impact on reported earnings has been the driving force behind many mergers and acquisitions. They contend, in fact, that U.S. accounting standards place domestic companies at a competitive disadvantage relative to firms in other countries. In the United States, mergers have to satisfy rigid criteria before they can be accounted for as poolings of interest. If a merger does not meet the criteria, then it must be reported as a purchase. Under the purchase method, the excess of purchase price over book value must be assigned either to specific assets or to goodwill. If assigned to specific assets, it must be amortized over their useful lives; if to goodwill, it must be depreciated over a maximum of 40 years. In Great Britain, goodwill must also be amortized. However, in contrast to U.S. conventions, it need not be expensed. Instead, it can be charged directly to owners' equity. Thus no matter how great a premium over book value a company pays for an acquisition, the premium will never affect reported income.

Forbes magazine, in a story entitled "Ill Will,"[4] claimed that the U.S. goodwill amortization rules make acquisitions more attractive for foreign companies than for domestic companies. "By making it tough for U.S. public companies to buy, the rule limits the number of potential bidders when a corporate asset goes on the market. The fewer the bidders, the less the final price."

The contention that the amortization rules have unfavorable economic consequences for U.S. companies is consistent with criticisms that have been cast at other income-reducing provisions: those pertaining to pensions, deferred income taxes, postemployment benefits, and intangible oil drilling costs, to cite but a few. It raises, in yet another context, the issue of whether investors can "see through" variations in *reported* earnings that result solely from differences in accounting practices. As indicated previously, the academic evidence, while by no means either uncontested or conclusive, suggests that investors do take note of the accounting differences. At the very least, therefore, the charges that the FASB is undermining the U.S. economy should be met with skepticism. The anecdotal evidence of the investment bankers is still unsubstantiated.

Summary

Intercorporate ownership may take a variety of forms. The objective of accounting is to reveal the economic substance of the relationship between the parties involved.

As a general rule, the manner in which the interest of one company in another is accounted for is determined by the degree of control that it is able to exercise. If an investor company is unable to exert substantial influence over the company whose shares it owns, it would account for its interest on the *cost basis*. If it is able to exercise substantial influence, it would account for its interest on the *equity basis*.

When a corporation has control over another, then the information needs of the stockholders of the controlling company are usually best served by combining the financial positions and results of operations of the merging firms into a single set of *consolidated* financial statements. If the business combination results entirely from an exchange of common stock, then the consolidated statements would ordinarily be prepared on a pooling of interests basis. If, on the other hand, one company acquires the outstanding stock of another for cash or other assets, the combination would be accounted for as a purchase.

[4]"Ill Will," *Forbes*, January 23, 1989, p. 41.

EXHIBIT 13-10
Summary of Investor Decisions

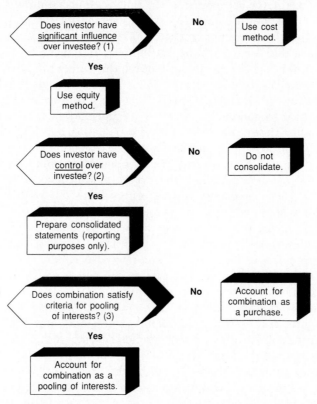

(1) General test is whether investor owns 20% or more of stock of investee.

(2) General test is whether investor owns 50% or more of stock of investee.

(3) Among the tests are whether merger was carried out only by exchange of common stock (i.e., no cash paid for stock) and whether investor owns at least 90% of stock of investee.

Exhibit 13-10 summarizes in a flowchart the possible intercorporate-ownership relationships and their accounting ramifications for the investor company.

Exercise for Review and Self-Testing

Parent Co. acquired 90 percent of the outstanding common stock of Subsidiary Co. On January 1, 1993, immediately following the acquisition, the balance sheets of the two firms revealed the following:

	Parent Co.	Subsidiary Co.
Investment in Subsidiary Co.	$320,000	—
Other assets	500,000	$300,000
Capital contributed by stockholders	200,000	120,000
Retained earnings	620,000	180,000

Subsidiary Co. reported earnings for the year ending December 31, 1993, of $30,000 and declared dividends of $10,000. Parent Co. reported earnings, *excluding* any revenues attributable to Subsidiary Co., of $100,000.

1. Parent Co. maintains its investment in Subsidiary Co. on the equity basis.
   a. What would be the amout that it should report in 1993 as earnings from subsidiary?
   b. At what amount should it value "investment in Subsidiary Co." on December 31, 1993, after the declaration of the dividend?
2. If the financial statements of Parent Co. and Subsidiary Co. were to be consolidated, what amount should be reported on the balance sheet as excess of cost over book value (goodwill) prior to amortizing such excess in 1993? What would be total reported assets?
3. What would be the amount of Subsidiary Co.'s 1993 earnings that could be ascribed to minority stockholders?
4. If the excess of cost over book value were to be amortized over a period of 40 years, by how much would the combined earnings of the two companies be reduced when the income statements of the two firms were consolidated?
5. What would be the consolidated income of the two companies, assuming that the earnings of the subsidiary company owing to minority stockholders was considered as an expense?
6. Suppose alternatively that Parent Co. acquired 100 percent of the stock of Subsidiary Co. in exchange for shares of its own common stock. At time of acquisition, the common stock issued by Parent Co. had a fair market value of $400,000 and the book value of Subsidiary Co. was $300,000. What would now be the consolidated income of the two companies for 1993 assuming that the merger satisfied the conditions of the pooling of interests accounting method? What would be total reported assets?

Questions for Review and Discussion

1. Under what circumstances should a firm account for an investment in another company by the cost method? By the equity method? When should it prepare consolidated financial statements?
2. Why is the cost method considered inappropriate for investments in which the investor can exert significant influence over the operating policies of the investee?
3. Why, under the equity method, does a firm *reduce* its balance in its investment account upon declaration of a dividend by the investee?
4. When, under the equity method, does an investor recognize revenue attributable to the earnings of the company in which it maintains an investment? When under the cost method? When is revenue recognized if consolidated statements are prepared?
5. Why do consolidations relate only to corporate *reports* rather than to the underlying corporate books and records? On which set of books—those of the parent, those of the subsidiary, those of both, or those of neither—are consolidation adjustments made?
6. From the standpoint of which group of stockholders—that of the parent, of the subsidiary, or of both—are consolidated statements prepared?
7. Under what conditions may a company improve its earnings per share simply by acquiring controlling interest in another company?
8. What is *goodwill*? When is it recorded? From what does it arise? Suppose that a firm acquires an interest in a subsidiary for an amount in excess of its book value. What difference might it make on consolidated net income if the excess was classified as goodwill rather than assigned to specific assets?

9. What is the underlying rationale of a pooling of interests? What critical differences arise in terms of asset valuation and income determination if a combination is accounted for as a pooling rather than as a purchase?
10. What four accounts—two income statement accounts and two balance sheet accounts—appear only on consolidated financial statements, never on those of individual companies?
11. General Cinema Corp. announced that it had purchased 18.9 percent of the outstanding shares of Heublein, Inc. According to *The Wall Street Journal*, "General Cinema's decision to stop buying Heublein stock with a holding of 18.9 percent came as a surprise." Most analysts thought that General Cinema would want a 20 percent holding. What is significant about the 20 percent figure?

Problems

1. *The equity method provides for more timely recognition of subsidiary earnings and losses than does the cost method.*

   On January 2 the Colorado Co. purchased for $60 per share (cash) 2 million of the 10 million outstanding shares of the Denver Corp.

   On July 5 the Denver Corp. reported earnings of $40 million for the first six months of the year.

   On July 15, the board of directors of the Denver Corp. declared and the company paid, a $1 per share cash dividend.

   On December 31, the Denver Corp. reported a loss of $15 million for the second six months of the year.

   a. Prepare journal entries to account for the investment of the Colorado Co. in the Denver Corp. using first the *cost* method and then the *equity* method.

   b. Compare total revenues of the Colorado Co. attributable to its investment under the two alternative methods. Compare the year-end carrying values of the investment.

2. *The earnings of a subsidiary can be derived from information on the carrying value of the investment and dividends declared.*

   On January 1, 1990, the Eagleton Co. purchased for $80 million a 40 percent interest (4 million of 10 million shares) in the common stock of Alexander, Inc.

   On December 31, 1992, the Eagleton Co. sold 1 million of the shares at a price of $25 per share. It recorded a gain of $2 million on the sale.

   On December 31, 1994, the remaining shares were reported on the books of Eagleton at a value of $78 million.

   During the five-year period from 1990 through 1994, Alexander, Inc., paid annual dividends of $1.50 per share.

   a. Determine the earnings of Alexander, Inc., during the period January 1, 1991, to December 31, 1992.

   b. Determine the earnings of Alexander, Inc., during the period January 1, 1993, to December 31, 1994.

3. *The equity method prevents an investor company from regulating its own earnings by manipulating the dividend practices of the investee firm.*

   The Maine Co. owned 40 percent (10 million shares) of the voting stock of the Bangor Corp. and controlled a majority of seats on the latter's board of directors. Toward the end of 1992, the controllers of the two firms estimated that Maine Co. would have earnings for the year of approximately $10 million (exclusive of earnings attributable to Bangor Corp.) and that Bangor Corp. would have earnings of approximately $50 million.

The president of Maine Co. was disappointed that his firm would earn only $10 million plus its share of Bangor Corp. earnings. Prior to 1992, Maine Co. had increased its earnings by 10 percent each year; consistent with that trend, Maine Co. would have to report total earnings in 1992 of $45 million.

a. In accord with APB guidelines, Maine Co. accounts for its interest in Bangor Corp. on the equity basis. If Bangor Corp. were to declare its usual dividend of 50 cents per share, what would be the total reported income of Maine Co.?

b. The president of Maine Co. suggested to his controller that Bangor Corp. be directed to declare a special dividend of $3 per share in addition to the 50 cents per share. What impact would the additional dividend have on earnings of Maine Co.?

c. Suppose that Maine Co. accounted for its investment in Bangor Corp. on the cost basis. What would be the total reported earnings of Maine Co. if the latter declared its regular dividend of 50 cents per share? What impact would the additional dividend specified in part (b) have on earnings of Maine Co.?

d. Comment on why the equity rather than the cost method is considered appropriate for firms that can exert substantial influence over companies in which they have an interest.

4. *A firm is ordered to pay its earnings from a subsidiary to the U.S. Treasury.*

The Federal Trade Commission held that Beatrice Food Co.'s 1978 acquisition of Tropicana Products, Inc., violated federal antitrust laws. The acquisition had been valued at about $490 million.

According to the financial press, an FTC hearing officer ordered Beatrice Foods to divest itself of Tropicana Products, Inc., and "pay its profits to the U.S. Treasury." Although Beatrice did not break out Tropicana's earnings in its financial statements, industry sources estimated that Tropicana contributed about $57 million to Beatrice's income in 1979.

Antitrust specialists speculated that the unusual penalty was imposed in order to discourage other firms from engaging in questionable takeovers. Some companies, they suggested, were willing to make acquisitions that they knew would be challenged by federal authorities because of the profits that could be earned even while a case was in litigation.

a. By which method, cost or equity, is it likely that Beatrice accounted for its interest in Tropicana?

b. Suppose that after being acquired by Beatrice, Tropicana declared dividends of an amount less than annual earnings. Would recorded *earnings* from the subsidiary be a reasonable measure of economic value of the benefits that Beatrice received from Tropicana during the period of ownership? What might be a better measure?

c. Is it really possible for a firm to "pay its *profits* to the U.S. Treasury"? Comment.

5. *Consolidating adjustments may have varying effects on consolidated earnings.*

The consolidated income of two companies is the sum of their individual earnings after certain adjustments have been made. For each of the transactions listed, indicate with a brief explanation whether the required adjustments would increase, decrease, or have no effect upon consolidated income as determined simply by summing the earnings of the two individual companies. Assume that Company A owns 100 percent of the outstanding shares of common stock of Company B.

a. Company B acquired $100,000 of bonds issued by Company A. Company A paid Company B interest of $8,000.

b. Company B sold $100,000 of merchandise to Company A. The goods had cost Company B $80,000 to produce. By year end, Company A had resold all of the goods to outsiders.

Chap. 13 Intercorporate Investments and Earnings **567**

c. Company A sold $50,000 of merchandise to Company B. The goods had cost Company A $30,000 to produce. At year end, all the goods remained in the inventory of Company B.

d. Company B owned 5,000 shares of the preferred stock of Company A. Company A paid dividends of $3 per share on the preferred stock.

e. Company A sold Company B land for $25,000. The land had cost Company A $40,000.

f. Two years earlier, Company A sold Company B equipment for $10,000. The equipment had cost Company A $6,000. The equipment had an estimated useful life of 10 years and zero salvage value. Company B has been charging depreciation based on its cost of $10,000—$1,000 per year.

6. *Consolidated income represents the sum of the earnings of individual firms plus or minus any revenues or expenses that would not have been recognized had the individual firms been divisions of a single entity.*

   Chicago Corp. owns 100 percent of the outstanding stock of the Woodlawn Co. Chicago Corp. has earnings of $200,000 (exclusive of its share of Woodlawn Co. earnings) and Woodlawn Co. has earnings of $80,000. Given the additional information that follows, determine consolidated earnings:

   a. Chicago Corp. sold merchandise to Woodlawn Co. at a price of $60,000. The cost of the merchandise was $48,000. Woodlawn Co. has not yet resold any of the merchandise.

   b. Chicago made a loan of $100,000 to Woodlawn, which paid interest of $6,000 on the loan.

   c. Chicago Corp. purchased equipment from Woodlawn for $25,000. The equipment has a remaining useful life of 10 years and no anticipated salvage value. The equipment had a net value on the books of Woodlawn of $15,000 (cost of $30,000 less accumulated depreciation of $15,000). Woodlawn had been depreciating the equipment over a period of 20 years ($1,500 per year). Chicago Corp. charged a full year's depreciation (based, of course, on its cost).

   d. Woodlawn Co. leased office space from Chicago Corp. and made rent payments of $500 per month—a total of $6,000.

   e. Chicago Corp. paid for its interest in Woodlawn an amount that was $60,000 in excess of Woodlawn's Co.'s book value. The $60,000 was allocated entirely to goodwill and is being amortized over a period of 20 years.

7. *The sale of equipment by one member of a consolidated group of firms to another may result in complex adjustments to a number of accounts for as many years as the equipment is used.*

   The Wayside Co. purchased manufacturing equipment from its subsidiary, The Gardner Co. The Wayside Co. paid $40,000. The equipment had been recorded on the books of the Gardner Co. at its cost of $50,000 less accumulated depreciation of $25,000. The Gardner Co. had been depreciating the asset over a period of 10 years. The Wayside Co. will depreciate the asset over its remaining useful life of five years.

   a. At what amount should the Wayside Co. record the asset on its own books? How much depreciation should it charge each year?

   b. At what amount should Wayside Co. report the asset on its consolidated balance sheet? How much depreciation should it report?

   c. Suppose that depreciation charges on the equipment enter into the computation of cost of goods sold. Explain the nature of any adjustments to cost of goods sold that might have to be made when a consolidated income statement is prepared. Suppose that not all goods manufactured in the course of a year are actually sold. Explain the nature of any adjustments to year-end inventory that might have to be made.

8. *Intercompany sales may require the adjustment of inventory as well as sales and cost of goods sold.*

Retail Co. serves as the marketing division of Manufacturing Co. It purchases all the goods that it sells to outsiders from Manufacturing Co. Manufacturing Co. sells only to Retail Co., at prices that exceed costs by 66⅔ percent.

The following data were taken from the year-end balances of the two firms:

	Manufacturing Co.	Retail Co.
Sales revenue	$200,000	$216,000
Cost of goods sold	120,000	180,000
Ending inventory	—	20,000

Neither company had inventory on hand at the beginning of the year. The financial statements of the two firms are to be consolidated.

a. What is the total amount that should be reported as sales (i.e., sales to outsiders)?

b. What is the cost to the consolidated entity of the goods sold?

c. What is the amount at which the ending inventory should be reported (i.e., what is its cost to the consolidated entity)?

d. Prepare a journal entry to eliminate intercompany sales and cost of goods sold and to eliminate any "unearned" profit from the ending inventory. Your entry should reduce the combined trial balances of the two firms to the amounts computed in parts (a), (b), and (c).

9. *By way of intercorporate investments, control over corporate giants can be obtained with small commitments of financial resources.*

Condensed balance sheets of three companies, A, B, and C, are as follows:

	A	B	C
Miscellaneous assets	$500,000	$140,000	$80,000
Investment in B (80 percent)	190,000		
Investment in C (60 percent)		60,000	
	$690,000	$200,000	$80,000
Common stock	$ 50,000	$ 5,000	$10,000
Retained earnings	640,000	195,000	70,000
Total owners' equity	$690,000	$200,000	$80,000

Company A just acquired its interest in Company B; Company B just acquired its interest in Company C.

a. Make any necessary adjustments to eliminate, for purposes of consolidation, the investment of B in C, to recognize goodwill, and to reclassify the interest of the minority stockholders.

b. Make any necessary adjustments to eliminate the investment of A in B, to recognize goodwill, and to reclassify the interest of the minority stockholders.

c. Combine the remaining balances into a consolidated balance sheet.

Suppose that Company A is controlled by a small group of investors. Because the stock of the company is disbursed among many small shareholders, they have been able to establish their control with an ownership interest of only 20 percent of outstanding shares.

The investors wish to obtain control of Company D. They believe that they could do so by purchasing 10 percent of its outstanding shares. The market value of all outstanding shares of Company D is $8 million. The investors plan to have

Company C buy the 10 percent interest for $800,000. The stockholders of Company C will contribute the necessary cash in proportion to their ownership interest. Then, in turn, the stockholders of Companies B and A will make appropriate proportionate contributions to their firms.

d. What will be the required cash contribution by the group of investors to obtain control of Company D?

10. *This exercise reviews the various types of adjustments that are generally required to consolidate financial statements.*

Indicated in the table that follows (dollar amounts in thousands) are the pre-closing trial balances of X Co. and its subsidiary Y Co. as of December 31, 1992.

	X Co.		Y Co.	
	Dr.	Cr.	Dr.	Cr.
Cash	$ 20,200		$ 3,000	
Accounts and notes receivable	50,000		16,000	
Interest receivable	4,000		3,000	
Inventory	25,000		10,000	
Fixed assets	185,000		30,000	
Investment in Y Co.	29,000			
Accounts and notes payable		$ 44,000		$ 17,000
Interest payable		2,000		1,000
Common stock		10,000		10,000
Capital contributed in excess of par		50,000		20,000
Retained earnings		181,200		10,000
Sales		100,000		40,000
Interest and other revenues		12,000		2,000
Cost of goods sold and related expenses	80,000		32,000	
Interest expense	6,000		6,000	
	$399,200	$399,200	$100,000	$100,000

The following information suggests adjustments to the accounts of the two firms that must be made before they can be summed (dollar amounts in thousands):

(1) X Co. owns 60 percent of the common stock of Y Co. It acquired its interest in Y Co. on January 1, 1992. The difference between what it paid for its interest ($29,000) and the book value of its interest ($24,000) can be attributed entirely to land owned by Y Co., which was worth more than its recorded value. (Be sure to eliminate the entire investment in Y Co. against fixed assets and the three owners' equity accounts of Y Co. Also, reclassify the equity of Y Co.'s minority stockholders as "minority interest in subsidiary.")

(2) In 1992 X Co. made $20,000 of sales to Y Co. None of the goods purchased by Y Co. remains in its inventory. Hence, from a consolidated perspective, sales and cost of goods sold are overstated by $20,000.

(3) Y Co. still owes X Co. $6,000 for the merchandise purchased.

(4) In the course of the year, X Co. made loans to Y Co. X Co. charged Y Co. $2,000 of interest on the loans. Although there was no outstanding balance on the principal of the loans at year end, Y Co. was still indebted to X Co. for $1,000 of interest. Both companies have properly accrued the interest revenue or expense.

(5) During the year, X Co. sold land to Y Co. Selling price was $6,000. The land had originally cost X Co. $3,000. X Co. included the gain on the sale of land in "interest and other revenues."

(6) In preparing a consolidated balance sheet from the adjusted trial balance, it is important to remember that the balance in X Co.'s "retained earnings"

does not reflect earnings for 1992. Correspondingly, the balance in "minority interest in subsidiary" (an account established by your journal entries) does not include the interests of the minority stockholders in the earnings of the subsidiary in 1992. It will be necessary, therefore, to add to the balance sheet account, "minority interest in subsidiary," the minority share of 1992 earnings and to add to "retained earnings" net consolidated income of 1992.

a. Make all adjustments necessary to prepare consolidated financial statements.

b. Prepare a consolidated income statement and balance sheet. Be sure to include minority share of subsidiary earnings as a deduction from consolidated income. You will probably find it useful to prepare a worksheet in which you establish columns for original balances, adjustments, and consolidated balances.

11. *This problem requires the preparation of a consolidated income statement and balance sheet.*

On January 1, 1993, Britain, Inc., acquired 90 percent of the outstanding stock of London, Inc., a manufacturer of scientific instruments. The balance sheet and income statement of the two companies are shown below. Britain, Inc., made no entries to reflect its share of London's 1993 earnings.

The primary reason why Britain, Inc., paid more than the book value for its acquisition of London was that London, Inc., had developed patents for technologically advanced equipment. In keeping with generally accepted accounting principles, London had assigned only nominal value to the patents. The remaining economic lives of the patents is 11 years.

During 1993 Britain made sales of $110 million to its new subsidiary.

It also made several loans to London, the year-end balance on which was $50 million. It charged London $10 million in interest.

Britain sold a parcel of land to its subsidiary for $30 million. It was its only sale of land during the year.

Prepare a consolidated statement of income and a consolidated balance sheet. You will probably find it helpful to make consolidating adjusting and elimination entires and to prepare a worksheet. Remember to take into account the interests of the minority shareholders. Remember also that the balances in retained earnings shown in the balance sheets are at year end 1993, not at date of acquisition. Assume that neither company declared dividends during the year.

Balance Sheets
December 31, 1993
(in million of dollars)

	Britain, Inc.	London, Inc.
Assets		
Cash	$ 50	$ 15
Accounts receivable	270	60
Notes receivable	300	100
Property, plant, and equipment		
(net of depreciation)	1,200	380
Investment in London, Inc.	404	
Total assets	$2,224	$555
Liabilities and owners' equity		
Accounts and notes payable	$ 440	$130
Common stock	100	40
Capital in excess of par	900	210
Retained earnings	784	175
Total liabilities and equities	$2,224	$555

Income Statements
1993

	Britain, Inc.	London, Inc.
Sales	$2,200	$270
Interest revenue	35	17
Gain on sale of land	14	0
Total revenues	$2,249	$287
Cost of goods sold	1,400	197
Interest expense	45	15
Other expenses	450	50
Total expenses	$1,895	$262
Net income	$ 354	$ 25

12. *If management were not required to amortize goodwill, it could avoid "income statement responsibility" for amounts paid to acquire assets.*

Shortly after the Accounting Principles Board (APB) imposed the requirement that goodwill be amortized over a period of not longer than 40 years. International Telephone & Telegraph Corporation (ITT) indicated in a footnote to its financial statements that it disagreed with the position of the board because, it asserted, the value of goodwill does not necessarily diminish over time.

a. If an asset, such as goodwill or land, does not diminish in value over time, do you think that it should be amortized?

b. Suppose that a company such as ITT wishes to acquire a plant that manufactures solar energy cells. Solar Energy, Inc., offers to sell the company such a plant, its only asset, for $100 million. The remaining useful life of the plant is 40 years. Its value on the books of Solar Energy, Inc., is $10 million.

Alternatively, the owners of Solar Energy, Inc., offer to sell their *stock* (not the plant) to ITT for $100 million.

(1) Assume that ITT acquires the *plant* for $100 million. How much depreciation would it charge each year?

(2) Assume instead that ITT acquires the *stock* for $100 million. Based on the "judgment" of management it allocates the entire excess of cost of its investment in Solar Energy, Inc., over its book value of $10 million to goodwill. If the company were not required to amortize goodwill, how much depreciation would it charge each year? If, instead, it were required to amortize goodwill over a period of 40 years, what would be the combined charge for depreciation and amortization?

(3) Why do you suppose the APB decided that goodwill must be amortized?

13. *A merger or acquisition, particularly if accounted for as a pooling, may provide "instant earnings" to the firm whose shares remain outstanding.*

The following information pertains to the Cambridge Co. and the Leeds Co. as of December 31.

	Cambridge Co.	Leeds Co.
Number of shares of common stock outstanding	1,000,000	500,000
Net assets	$15,000,000	$5,000,000
Latest annual income	$ 2,000,000	$1,000,000
Recent market price of common stock (per share)	$40	$20
Earnings per share	$2	$2

The Cambridge Co. and the Leeds Co. have agreed to a business combination. Cambridge Co. will acquire 100 percent of the common stock of Leeds Co. at the recent market price of $20 per share.

a. Suppose that Cambridge Co. were to purchase all 500,000 shares of Leeds Co. for $20 per share in cash. Cambridge Co. would borrow the required funds at an interest rate (after taxes) of 5 percent per year. The combination would be accounted for as a purchase, and the excess of cost over book value would be amortized over a period of 20 years. Determine anticipated earnings per share of Cambridge Co. after the acquisition, assuming no substantive changes in the earnings of either company.

b. Suppose alternatively that Cambridge Co. were to acquire all 500,000 shares in an exchange of stock. The number of shares to be issued would be based on relative market values, and the combination would be accounted for as a pooling of interests. Determine the anticipated earnings per share of Cambridge Co.

14. *Alternative means of merging may have differing impacts upon reported assets and equities.*
   Indicated as follows are condensed balance sheets of the MNO Co. and PQR Co:

	MNO Co.	PQR Co.
Assets	$5,000,000	$2,000,000
Common stock, par value $10	$1,000,000	$ 500,000
Contributed capital in excess of par	1,500,000	650,000
Retained earnings	2,500,000	850,000
Total owners' equity	$5,000,000	$2,000,000

Prepare balance sheets of the MNO Co. (consolidated as appropriate) to reflect the acquisition of the PQR Co. by the MNO Co. under each of the following conditions:

a. The MNO Co. purchases the assets of the PQR Co. at a price of $2.5 million cash. To raise the necessary cash, MNO Co. issues 50,000 shares of common stock at $50 per share.

b. The MNO Co. purchases 100 percent of the outstanding stock of the PQR Co. at a total price of $2.5 million cash. To raise the necessary cash, MNO Co. issues 50,000 shares of common stock at $50 per share.

c. The MNO Co. issues 50,000 shares of its own common stock in exchange for 100 percent of the outstanding shares of the PQR Co. The market price of the MNO Co. stock at the time of the exchange is $50 per share. The transaction is to be accounted for as a pooling of interests.

15. *Alternative means of accounting for excess of cost over book value can have substantially different effects on reported earnings.*

   In 1992, the National Products Company acquired 100 percent control of State Industries, Inc., for $200 million in common stock. At the time of the acquisition the net assets (assets less liabilities) of State Industries were recorded on its books at $120 million. In 1992, National Products had earnings of $90 million, exclusive of earnings of State Industries, Inc., which had earnings of $20 million. There were no material intercompany transactions during the year. Determine the consolidated earnings of National Products Company and its subsidiary under the following alternative assumptions:

a. The combination is accounted for as a purchase, and the excess of acquisition cost over book value is allocated to various fixed assets that have an average remaining useful life of 10 years.

b. The combination is accounted for as a purchase, and the excess of acquisition cost over book value is allocated entirely to "goodwill." The goodwill is to be amortized over the maximum period allowed by Accounting Principles Board guidelines—40 years.

c. The business combination is accounted for as a pooling of interests. (A firm cannot in practice choose whether to account for a merger as either a purchase or a pooling. If, and only if, an acquisition satisfies the criteria for a pooling can it be accounted for as such. Otherwise, it must be accounted for as a purchase.)

16. *The equity method of accounting for an investment will have an effect on parent company earnings comparable to that of a full-scale consolidation.*

    The preclosing trial balances of the Mann Co. and the Rudolph Co. as of December 31, 1992, are as follows (in millions):

	Mann Co.	Rudolph Co.
Cash	$100	$20
Investment in Rudolph Co.	54	
Other assets	76	75
Common stock	10	10
Retained earnings	190	80
Sales	140	60
Cost of goods sold	95	50
Other expenses	15	5

The Mann Co. owns 60 percent of the outstanding stock of the Rudolph Co. It acquired its investment in January 1992 for $54 million at a time when the net worth of Rudolph Co. was $90 million. Mann maintains its investment in Rudolph on the equity basis. Mann Co. has not yet taken into account its share of Rudolph Co.'s 1992 earnings.

a. Prepare a 1992 income statement and balance sheet for Mann Co., assuming that it is *inappropriate* to consolidate its accounts with those of Rudolph.

b. Prepare a *consolidated* income statement and balance sheet. Be sure that the last line of the income statement excludes the minority share of Rudolph Co. earnings.

c. Compare net worth and income under the two procedures. Why is the equity basis of accounting for business combinations sometimes referred to as a *one-line consolidation*?

17. *The "value" of shares received by stockholders of a firm being acquired may be less than apparent.*

    Octopus Corp., a conglomerate, decided to acquire controlling interest in Meek Co.

    The common stock of Octopus Corp. had been trading at $20 per share and that of Meek Co. at $60 per share. Octopus had 1 million shares outstanding, and Meek had 300,000 shares outstanding.

    The management of Meek Co. was opposed to the takeover. To circumvent the opposition, Octopus offered to purchase all outstanding shares of Meek Co. stock for $80 per share—a price that was $20 greater than the market price prior to the announcement of its offer. Octopus would not, however, pay cash for the stock. Instead it would issue to Meek stockholders common stock of Octopus Corp., with a market value of $80 for each share that it received. Hence, it would issue four shares of Octopus stock for each share of Meek.

In the year prior to the offer, Octopus Corp. had earnings of $500,000; Meek had earnings of $1 million. At the time of the offer, Meek Co. had a book value (net worth) of $15 million.

a. Determine the earnings per share of Octopus Corp. in the year prior to the acquisition.

b. Determine the earnings per share of Octopus in the year immediately following the acquisition. Assume that Octopus will prepare consolidated financial statements and that the operating earnings of the two individual companies will remain unchanged. Any excess of cost over book value will be assigned to goodwill and amortized over a period of 40 years. Assume also that only 80 percent of the outstanding shares of Meek were tendered (sold) to Octopus. The remainder were retained by minority shareholders.

c. Suppose an investor owned 1,000 shares of Meek. How much better off was he in terms of market value of his holdings after he sold his shares to Octopus than before?

d. How much better (or worse) off was he with respect to earnings that could be ascribed to his shares?

18. *This problem was suggested by the merger of General Electric and Utah International. It is intended to highlight the significance of the distinction between purchase and pooling accounting.*

Colonel Electric, a multinational manufacturer of both industrial and commercial products, has recently acquired Arizona International, a mining company with oil, gas, copper, uranium, and coal reserves. Colonel Electric issued 41 million shares of its common stock in exchange for all outstanding shares of Arizona International. The Colonel Electric stock had a market value of $53 per share.

Shown in the table that follows are aggregated balance sheet accounts of Arizona International immediately following the takeover. They are shown both at historical cost-based values (per the firm's financial statements) and at estimated fair market values. All dollar amounts are in millions.

Arizona International		
	Per Books	Market Values
Current assets	$ 193	$ 283
Plant and equipment, net of accumulated depreciation	615	2,027
Investments	108	198
Other assets	131	151
Total assets	$1,047	$2,659
Current liabilities	$ 282	$ 282
Noncurrent liabilities	224	224
Total liabilities	506	506
Owners' equity	541	2,153
Total liabilities and owners' equity	$1,047	$2,659

At the time of the merger, Colonel Electric had assets of $11,002, liabilities of $6,172, and owners' equity of $4,830.

The next table shows amounts taken from individual income statements of the two firms in the year following the acquisition. The data of Colonel Electric exclude the earnings of Arizona International.

	Colonel Electric	Arizona International
Sales	$14,697	$1,001
Less: Expenses		
Cost of goods sold	11,074	407
Other expenses	2,874	350
Income taxes	299	98
Total expenses	14,247	855
Net income	$ 450	$ 146

a. Compute consolidated assets, liabilities, and owners' equities that would result upon acquisition under both purchase and pooling accounting. (From the limited information presented, it would appear as if the acquisition should be accounted for as a pooling.)

b. Prepare a schedule in which you show consolidated income of the first year after the acquisition that would be reported if the combination were accounted for first as a purchase and then as a pooling. In the first two columns of the schedule, indicate revenues and expenses as reported by the individual companies (i.e., as presented). In the third, show consolidated revenues and expenses assuming purchase accounting. In the fourth, show consolidated revenues and expenses assuming pooling accounting. Make the following assumptions:

(1) The excess of cost of investment over book value that is assigned to plant and equipment should be depreciated over 13 years. That assigned to goodwill should be amortized over 20 years. That assigned to any other assets need not be amortized.

(2) Income taxes will remain the same irrespective of whether the merger is accounted for as a pooling or as a purchase.

c. Compute return on investment assuming both purchase and pooling accounting based on the earnings and equities calculated in the previous part of the problem.

19. *This problem was inspired by the experience of Datapoint Corp., a computer manufacturer, which for a time was a "high flyer" on Wall Street. It reported increases in earnings in 17 consecutive quarters. Then, following the acquisition of one of its distributors, earnings declined. The purpose of this problem is to demonstrate the special analytical care that must be taken in evaluating postconsolidation earnings.*

Compucorp, Inc., a manufacturer of computers, has reported quarter-to-quarter increases in sales and earnings over a period of several years. The company sells all the computers that it produces to Distributor Corp., a company that deals exclusively in the products of Compucorp.

As soon as Compucorp manufactures its products, it ships them to Distributor Corp. Hence Compucorp maintains no inventory of finished goods. Distributor Corp. is able to sell all the computers it receives. However, there is ordinarily a two-month delay between the date Compucorp ships a computer to Distributor Corp. and that when Distributor sells it. As a consequence, increases in sales of Compucorp are reflected two months later as increases in sales of Distributor, Inc. At the end of any quarter, the inventory of Distributor Corp. is equal to two-thirds (two of three months) of the sales of Compucorp for that quarter.

Compucorp sells to Distributor Corp. at a price 33⅓ percent above its own cost. Distributor sells to outsiders at a price 10 percent above the price it pays to Compucorp.

Compucorp recently acquired for cash all the outstanding stock of Distributor Corp. Prior to the acquisition, its earnings, consolidated with those of its other subsidiaries, had increased by 10 percent per quarter. In the quarter of the acquisition, earnings flattened to an increase of only 3 percent.

Compucorp borrowed the cash required to purchase the stock of Distributor Corp. Quarterly interest costs are $16.50 million (an amount exactly equal to fourth-quarter earnings of Distributor Corp.). Compucorp acquired the stock at a price equal to its book value; hence no amortization of goodwill is necessary.

The following schedule indicates selected data from the four quarterly reports of (1) Compucorp not consolidated with Distributor Corp., (2) Distributor Corp., and (3) Compucorp consolidated with Distributor Corp. Compucorp acquired Distributor Corp. in the fourth quarter. All amounts are in millions of dollars.

Compucorp (excluding Distributor Corp.)

	Quarter			
	I	II	III	IV
Sales	$132.00	$145.20	$159.72	$175.69
Less: Cost of goods sold	99.00	108.90	119.79	131.77
Gross margin	33.00	36.30	39.93	43.92
Plus: Earnings of subsidiary	.00	.00	.00	16.50
Less: Interest expense	.00	.00	.00	16.50
Income before taxes	$ 33.00	$ 36.30	$ 39.93	$ 43.92

Distributor Corp.

	I	II	III	IV
Sales	$136.40	$150.04	$165.04	$181.55
Less: Cost of goods sold	124.00	136.40	150.04	165.04
Income before taxes	$ 12.40	$ 13.64	$ 15.00	$ 16.50
Ending inventory	$ 88.00	$ 96.80	$106.48	$117.13

Compucorp. (consolidated with Distributor Corp. in fourth quarter)

	I	II	III	IV
Sales	$132.00	$145.20	$159.72	$181.55
Less: Cost of goods sold	99.00	108.90	119.79	123.78
Gross margin	33.00	36.30	39.93	57.77
Less: Interest expense		.00	.00	16.50
Income before taxes	$ 33.00	$ 36.30	$ 39.93	$ 41.26

Analysts were puzzled by the flattening of Compucorp consolidated earnings for the fourth quarter, that in which the acquisition of Distributor was recorded. Executives of Compucorp assured them that production had increased by 10 percent, just as it had in the previous quarters. Correspondingly, Distributor continued to sell all the computers that it received, subject as before to the two-month delay. The analysts were particularly confused because the leveling of consolidated earnings was in the face of an increase in consolidated sales (14 percent) greater than that in previous quarters. At the same time, cost of goods sold as a percentage of sales decreased.

For purposes of this problem, expenses other than cost of goods sold and interest are to be ignored.

a. How do you account for the fourth-quarter increase in consolidated sales?

b. How do you account for the fourth-quarter decline in consolidated cost of goods sold as a percentage of sales?

c. One analyst noted that if you adjust fourth-quarter consolidated statements to remove the markup of Distributor Corp., then consolidated sales were up only slightly over those of the third quarter (3.3 percent per his calculations). He concluded that corporate growth was beginning to level off. In light of the 10 percent increase in sales of Compucorp itself (not taking into account those of Distributor Corp.), is his explanation plausible? What else might account for the apparent leveling off in sales? At what point in the entire process of earnings (production, shipment to distributor, and sales to customer) would Compucorp as an independent company recognize sales revenue? At what point as a consolidated company?

d. Based on the trends apparent in the data presented, prepare a statement in which you indicate for the two quarters following those shown in the table projected consolidated sales, cost of goods sold, interest expense (to be held constant), and income. Has the growth of the company really slowed?

20. *In the late 1970s and early 1980s (prior to the debacle in the industry in the late 1980s), many financial institutions such as savings and loan associations experienced severe financial stress. The period was one of rapidly rising interest rates. The institutions were locked into loans made at low interest rates, but at the same time had to pay high rates on customer deposits. Ironically, despite reported losses, they became popular takeover candidates. This problem is intended to show how the alchemy of purchase accounting can turn losses of an acquired company into gains of the acquirer.*

Great Eastern Savings and Loans, Inc., has outstanding a portfolio of loans with a book (face) value of $100 million. Most were made when rates of interest were substantially lower than they are at present. Most are long-term, made to finance the purchase of personal homes. On average, they bear a rate of interest of 8 percent. They must be repaid in equal annual installments over a period of 10 years. Each year total receipts from the loans, including both interest and principal, are $14.903 million ($100 million divided by $6.7101, the present value of a 10-year annuity of $1 discounted at 8 percent).

The firm has no major sources of revenue other than interest on its mortgage loans. In the next year it expects to incur annual expenses of $9 million. This amount includes both interest paid on customer deposits and other expenses.

Because of its losses, the firm is being acquired by New York Industries, Inc. New York Industries will purchase the outstanding stock of the company for an amount equal to the *market value* of its loan portfolio, less outstanding liabilities (mainly customer deposits). Market value of the loan portfolio may be determined by discounting the portfolio at the prevailing rate of interest, which is 12 percent. The company has outstanding liabilities of $75 million. For purposes of this problem, other assets of Great Eastern may be considered immaterial and therefore need not be taken into account. The stock will be purchased for cash; hence the acquisition must be accounted for as a purchase, not a pooling.

a. Determine the losses of Great Eastern in the year after acquisition as they would be calculated by Great Eastern (as an independent company).

b. Compute the amount paid for Great Eastern by New York Industries. Prepare the journal entry that New York Industries would make to record the acquisition.

c. Prepare also a consolidation entry to eliminate the investment in the subsidiary. Notice that in this example the amount paid for the acquired company is less than its book value. Whereas an excess of cost of over book value must be added to the assets to which it applies, a deficiency must be subtracted.

d. Prepare a journal entry to record the next year's receipts from borrowers. Be sure to allocate the amounts received between principal and interest.

e. Calculate the net earnings that the acquisition will add to New York Industries on a consolidated basis. How do you explain the apparent transformation of losses into profits?

21. *The consolidation of finance and insurance subsidiaries may have a major impact on financial ratios.*

The data that follow were taken from the 1987 financial statements of ITT. (All dollar amounts are in millions.) Until 1988 (in accord with applicable recording standards of the time), ITT did *not* consolidate its insurance and finance subsidiaries. The data that are presented in the column "ITT" are those of the parent and the many subsidiaries that it did consolidate. The data in the column "Insurance and Finance Subsidiaries" were taken from the consolidated financial statements of the subsidiaries that were excluded from the consolidated statements of their parent.

The assets and liabilities of the insurance and finance subsidiaries were not classified in the annual report as to whether they were current or noncurrent. Hence the classification presented here is somewhat arbitrary. The assets of the insurance and finance subsidiaries are primarily investments in marketable securities and related financial instruments.

Balance Sheet
December 31, 1987

	ITT	Insurance and Finance Subsidiaries
Cash and equivalents	$ 802	$ 98
Investments and other current assets	2,842	25,359
Total current assets	$ 3,644	$25,457
Investment in insurance and finance subsidiaries	3,987	—
Other assets	5,723	5,158
Total noncurrent assets	$ 9,710	$ 5,158
Total assets	$13,354	$30,615
Current liabilities	$ 2,259	$21,893
Other liabilities	3,276	4,735
Stockholders' equity	7,819	3,987
Total liabilities and stockholders' equity	$13,354	$30,615

Income Statement
Year Ended December 31, 1987

	ITT	Insurance and Finance Subsidiaries
Sales and other revenues	$9,161	$11,043
Earnings of insurance and finance subsidiaries	532	—
Total revenues	$9,693	$11,043
Expenses and other charges	8,675	10,493
Net income	$1,018	$ 550

a. As best the data permit, prepare a balance sheet that consolidates ITT with its insurance and finance subsidiaries.

b. Compute the current ratio and the debt-to-equity ratio (total debt to stockholders' equity) of (1) ITT independently and (2) ITT consolidated with the insurance and finance subsidiaries.

c. Comment on the impact that consolidation would have on the reported earnings of ITT. As is required, ITT accounts for the subsidiaries on the *equity* basis.

1. a. In 1993 Parent Co. would report as earnings from subsidiary 90 percent of Subsidiary Co. income of $30,000, or $27,000.

   b. It would value "investment in Subsidiary" at $338,000. This amount is the original investment of $320,000 plus $27,000, its share of subsidiary earnings, less $9,000 of dividends received (or recognized as receivable) from the subsidiary.

2. Parent Co. paid $320,000 for a 90 percent interest in a firm with a book value of $300,000. The excess of cost over 90 percent of total book value ($270,000) is $50,000. Total reported assets would be $850,000 ($800,000 of other assets plus $50,000 excess of cost over book value).

3. Subsidiary Co. had earnings of $30,000. The minority share would be 10 percent of earnings—$3,000.

4. Inasmuch as excess of cost over book value is $50,000, consolidated earnings would be reduced by one-fortieth of that amount—$1,250.

5. Consolidated earnings would be the combined earnings of the two firms, $130,000, less the minority interest in earnings of $3,000 and less amortization of the excess of cost over book value of $1,250, or $125,750.

6. If an acquisition is accounted for as a pooling, then the investment in the subsidiary is recorded on the books of the parent at the book value of its equity in the subsidiary—in this case, $300,000. The market value of the stock exchanged is not taken into account. No goodwill is recognized; none needs be amortized. Consolidated earnings would therefore simply be the sum of the earnings of the two individual companies—$130,000. Total reported assets would be $800,000, the sum of each firm's other assets.

14

Statement of Cash Flows

The statement of cash flows is the third of the three primary financial statements. It is equal in status to the income statement and the balance sheet by way of official pronouncement, although not by tradition. The forebear of the statement of cash flows, the statement of "changes in financial position," first became a required element of financial reports in 1971 by virtue of Accounting Principles Board *Opinion No. 19.* In that opinion the board prescribed that the statement of changes in financial position be presented for each period in which an income statement is shown. The statement of changes in financial position reported on changes in "funds," and *Opinion No. 19* allowed for considerable flexibility in the definition of funds. Many firms interpreted funds to mean working capital—that is, current assets less current liabilities. An increasing number, however—and by 1986 a majority—construed funds as cash or near-cash.

In 1987 the Financial Accounting Standards Board affirmed the trend toward reporting cash rather than working capital. In *Statement No. 95,* "Statement of Cash Flows," the board stipulated that the statement of changes in financial position be replaced by a statement directed exclusively to cash and cash equivalents.

EXHIBIT 14-1
Consolidated Statements of Cash Flow
American Home Products Corporation and Subsidiaries

	(Dollars in thousands)	
Years Ended December 31	1991	1990
Operating Activities		
Net income	$1,375,273	$1,230,597
Adjustments to reconcile net income to net cash provided from operating activities:		
Depreciation and amortization	167,166	179,761
Deferred income taxes	(15,459)	152,220
Gains on sales of businesses	(10,336)	(999,528)
Provisions for special charges	—	656,906
Changes in working capital, net of businesses acquired or sold:		
Accounts receivable	(2,997)	74,388
Inventories	(51,554)	(7,329)
Trade accounts payable and accrued expenses	270,865	23,319
Accrued taxes	(23,251)	(11,181)
Other current assets	34,728	34,179
Other items, net	153,624	(19,024)
Net cash provided from operating activities	$1,898,059	$1,314,308
Investing Activities		
Purchases of property, plant, and equipment	$ (227,911)	$ (247,693)
Proceeds from sales of businesses	14,000	1,255,050
Proceeds from sales of assets	30,947	22,005
Purchases of other assets	(8,470)	(17,956)
Net cash (used for) / provided from investing activities	$ (191,434)	$1,011,406
Financing Activities		
Dividends paid	$ (749,138)	$ (674,178)
Net (repayments) / proceeds of commercial paper and other debt	(665,039)	(1,106,445)
Purchase of treasury stock	(123,898)	(40,091)
Exercise of stock options	127,873	67,455
Net cash used for financing activities	(1,410,202)	(1,753,259)
Effects of exchange rates on cash balances	(20,354)	8,279
Increase in cash and cash equivalents	276,069	580,734
Cash and cash equivalents, beginning of year	1,788,534	1,207,800
Cash and cash equivalents, end of year	$2,064,603	$1,788,534

Exhibit 14-1 shows the consolidated statements of cash flows of American Home Products Corporation and its subsidiaries.

OBJECTIVES OF THE STATEMENT OF CASH FLOWS

The statement of cash flows reconciles cash at the beginning of the year with that at the end. Its objective is to provide information about an enterprise's cash receipts and disbursements. As repeatedly emphasized throughout this text, cash is the premier of assets. Cash is what is needed by a business to satisfy its obligations as they come due, to meet day-to-day operating expenses, and to pay interest and dividends. Cash is the medium of exchange in our economy, and stockholders contribute cash to a business with the ultimate objective of receiving more cash than they have given up. As discussed in previous chapters, the value of individual assets and liabilities, as well as that of a firm as a whole, is determined by anticipated flows of cash. Investors and managers need to know why cash has increased or decreased in the past. It helps them to predict the cash that the firm will generate in the future, that it will require to satisfy its commitments to outsiders, and that it will have available for distributions to stockholders. The FASB, in its *Concepts Statement No. 5,* ''Recognition and Measurement in Financial Statements of Business Enterprises'' (1984), stressed the importance of information about cash receipts and disbursements in assessing an entity's liquidity, financial flexibility, profitability, and risk. *Statement No. 95* sets forth the objective of a statement of cash flows. Those objectives are to help investors, creditors, and others to assess

1. The enterprise's ability to generate positive future net cash flows
2. The enterprise's ability to meet its obligations, its ability to pay dividends, and its needs for external financing
3. The reasons for differences between net income and associated cash receipts and payments
4. The effects on an enterprise's financial position of both its cash and noncash investing and financing transactions during the period

THE STATEMENT OF CASH FLOWS AS A COMPLEMENT TO THE STATEMENT OF INCOME

The statement of cash flows complements the statement of income. A central theme of this text has been that *income* is superior to cash flow as a measure of overall organizational performance. Income, unlike cash flow, registers changes in the overall level of economic resources, not just selected assets.

Income, however, is a relatively subjective indicator. It is determined on an accrual basis. Revenues and expenses may be recognized before or after corresponding cash receipts and disbursements. The timing of recognition depends both upon guidelines established by rule-making authorities and upon the judgment of management. Moreover, income is constructed upon a framework of estimates, assumptions, and allocations. Depreciation requires that asset life and salvage value be estimated. Cost of goods sold necessitates an assumption as to flows of costs (LIFO, FIFO, etc.).

Cash flow, by contrast, is objective. It focuses exclusively upon changes in cash. It is uncontaminated by estimates, allocations, and assumptions. Cash presents few problems of definition and measurement. The net change in cash for a period can be determined simply by subtracting the ending cash balance from the beginning.

The statement of cash flows also reports on activities that would not be shown on the income statement. Financing and investing activities, for example, do not increase or decrease the overall level of a firm's resources. Therefore they are not categorized as either revenues or expenses. When a corporation issues bonds or common stock, only balance sheet accounts are affected. No income is generated. Yet the transaction may be critical to the fiscal well-being of the enterprise.

WHAT IS CASH?

The balance sheet classification "cash" typically encompasses currency on hand as well as deposits in banks. There are valid reasons, however, to expand the focus of the statement of cash flows to include other assets as well. No well-managed enterprise maintains a significant balance in currency or in non-interest-bearing checking accounts. Instead, it places its funds in short-term investments such as Treasury bills, commercial paper, and money-market funds. These investments are easily interchangeable with cash. Indeed, many companies transfer funds between cash and other investments on a daily basis. Because they are the virtual equivalent of cash, these "near-cash" assets must be incorporated into any meaningful analysis of cash.

The question arises, however, as to how broad the definition of cash should be. Should it encompass marketable securities, such as stocks and bonds, which are also held as temporary investments and can be easily sold for cash? Should it include accounts receivable, which can be expected to be transformed into cash in a short time? Should it be reduced by accounts payable, which will soon necessitate cash payments? As the definition of cash is expanded, the statement of cash flows become less affected by arbitrary management decisions (e.g., whether to purchase or sell investments or to delay payments to suppliers). Correspondingly, however, it becomes less focused on cash itself, which is, after all, the asset of ultimate concern.

The FASB, in *Statement No. 95*, opted for a narrow definition of cash. It required that the statement of cash flows focus only on *cash and cash equivalents*. *Cash equivalents* are investments that are readily convertible into cash. They must be convertible to known amounts of cash and so near their maturity that they present insignificant risks of changes in value because of changes in interest rates. Examples are Treasury bills and shares in money-market funds. Investments in marketable securities such as stocks and bonds, even if they are publicly traded and can be easily sold, are excluded.

CLASSIFICATION OF CASH FLOWS

Statement No. 95 specifies how cash inflows and outflows should be classified. The statement of changes in financial position that firms prepared before *Statement No. 95* was issued was called the statement of *sources and uses* of funds because it was divided into two main sections. The first showed sources of funds (inflows), the second uses of funds (outflows). The disadvantage of a "sources and uses'' classification is that related inflows and outflows are not grouped together.

The FASB believed that the statement would be more useful if it classified cash flows by the activities in which firms engage. It specified three primary categories of activities:

1. Operating activities
2. Investing activities
3. Financing activities

Operating Activities

Operating activities include producing and selling the firm's goods and services and performing its administrative functions. In fact, operating activities encompass all transactions that are not categorized as investing and financing activities.

The operating classification includes both interest and dividends received and interest disbursed. Many accountants believe that interest paid should be shown as a financing activity and interest and dividends received as an investing activity. Interest is paid as a result of having borrowed financial resources; both interest and dividends are received as returns on investments in debt or equity securities. But in specifying that interest and dividends received and interest paid be classified as operating activities, the FASB was persuaded by the overwhelming proportion of companies that showed interest and dividends received as an operating inflow and interest paid as an operating outflow under *Opinion No. 19.* In addition, it cited widespread support for the notion that the items included in the cash from operating activities classification should be the same as those incorporated in the computation of operating income. Almost all companies, it noted, currently take in dividends received as well as interest both paid and received as part of operating income.[1]

The main cash *inflows* from operating activities are

1. Cash receipts from the sale of goods or services, including the collection of accounts and notes receivable arising from sales
2. Interest and dividends from loans and investments
3. All receipts not included among financing and investment activities, including proceeds of settlements of lawsuits, proceeds of insurance settlements, and refunds from suppliers

The main cash *outflows* from operating activities are

1. Purchases of inventory and other goods and services
2. Wages and salaries
3. Taxes
4. Interest paid to lenders and other creditors

---

[1]This rationalization, however, failed to convince three of the seven members of the FASB. These three dissented to the classification of interest and dividends as an operating activity, arguing that they should be shown as financing and investment activities.

5. All payments not included among financing and investment activities, including payments to settle lawsuits, contributions to charities, and cash refunds to customers

Investing Activities

Investing activities include acquiring and selling property, plant, and equipment; making and collecting loans; and purchasing and selling the equity securities (stock) of other companies.

The main cash *inflows* from investment activities are

1. Receipts from the collection of loans made by the company or from the sales of notes and bonds (excluding interest, which is classified as an operating activity)
2. Receipts from the sale of the stock of other companies
3. Receipts from the sale of the property, plant, and equipment.

The main cash *outflows* are

1. Amounts loaned to others, including the purchase of bonds and notes
2. Payments to acquire the stock of other companies
3. Payments made to acquire property, plant, and equipment and other assets

Only payments made at the time of purchase or shortly thereafter are included in the third category. Those made afterward are considered to be repayments of loans and included among financing outflows.

Financing Activities

Financing activities include borrowing and repaying loans and issuing and redeeming stock.

The main cash *inflows* from financing activities are

1. Proceeds from issuing stock
2. Proceeds from issuing bonds, notes, and other instruments of debt

The main cash *outflows* are

1. Payments of dividends
2. Payment to redeem stock
3. Repayments of amounts borrowed

Effect of Changes in Foreign Currency Exchange Rates

A company that has cash flows in foreign currencies must combine them with the flows in U.S. dollars. The foreign flows would be translated using the exchange rate in effect at the time of the flows. If the beginning-of-year balance in foreign currency (translated at beginning-of-year exchange rates) is to reconcile with the end-of-year balance (translated at end-of-year exchange rates), an adjustment must be made for the changes in the rates. This adjustment is reported on a single line in the statement of cash flows. It is captioned, ''effect of exchange rate changes on cash.''

REPORTING NONCASH INVESTING AND FINANCING ACTIVITIES

One of the principal ways in which the statement of cash flows supplements the statement of income is by reporting on the investing and financing transactions indicated in the previous section. These transactions do not affect income in the period in which they take place and therefore would not be reported on the income statement. There are still other financing and investing transactions that do not involve cash receipts or disbursements. Therefore they would not naturally be reported on either the income statement or the statement of cash flows. The following are examples:

A firm acquires property, plant, and equipment in exchange for a long-term note.
A firm acquires another company in exchange for shares of its own stock.
A firm redeems bonds payable by issuing common stock.
A firm trades in one asset for another.
A firm acquires property by entering into a capital lease.

To make the statement of cash flows a complete report on investing and financing activities, the FASB stipulated that such transactions should be disclosed, either in a supplemental schedule or in a narrative note. Some transactions are part cash and part noncash. For example, a firm might acquire new equipment in exchange for both cash and used equipment. The cash portion should be included in the body of the statement; the noncash portion should be reported in the supplemental schedule or note.

DIRECT VERSUS INDIRECT PRESENTATIONS

Changes in cash flow may be presented in either of two ways: the *direct* method or the *indirect* method. The difference in the two methods relates only to the manner in which *operating* cash flows are presented; the presentation of investing and financing activities is the same under both methods.

The Direct Method

The direct method reports all operating receipts and payments. The payments are subtracted from the receipts. The operations section of a statement of cash flows might appear as follows:

Cash received from customers	$47,000
Cash paid to suppliers	(21,000)
Cash paid to employees	(12,000)
Net cash provided by operating activities	$14,000

The Indirect Method

The indirect method reconciles reported income to cash flow. The indirect method starts with net income as a cash flow. It then adjusts income for revenues and expenses that do not provide or use cash. Depreciation, for example, is a noncash expense. The sales revenue of a firm may be greater or less than cash collected from customers. The amounts paid to purchase merchandise inventory may be greater or less than cost of goods sold.

Suppose the income statement of a company is as follows:

Sales revenue		$50,000
Less: Cost of goods sold	$25,000	
Wages and salaries	10,000	
Depreciation	5,000	40,000
Net income		$10,000

Assume further that

1. The firm collected only $47,000 of the sales revenue. (The $3,000 difference between sales and collections was added to accounts receivable.)
2. The firm paid suppliers only $21,000. (The $4,000 difference between cost of goods sold and payments to suppliers was added to accounts payable.)
3. The firm paid employees $12,000 ($10,000 of current-year wages and salaries plus $2,000 from the previous year).

The operations section of the statement of cash flows, in the indirect format, would appear as follows:

Cash Flows from Operating Activities		
Net income		$10,000
Adjustments to reconcile net income		
to cash flow		
Depreciation expense	$5,000	
Increase in accounts receivable	(3,000)	
Increase in accounts payable	4,000	
Decrease in wages and salaries payable	(2,000)	4,000
Net cash provided by operating activities		$14,000

Compare this presentation with the direct format. Both reflect the same operating activities.

The Two Methods Compared

The *direct* method is the conceptually simpler and more informative of the two. It shows the inflows and outflows of cash from operating activities. The indirect method, by contrast, shows only the *net* cash provided by operations. It does not show the collections from customers, the payments to suppliers, and the payments to employees.

The main virtue of the *indirect* method is that it shows the difference between income and cash flow. Many analysts use income to help predict cash flow of the future. The reconciliation between income and cash flow may thereby be particularly informative in that it highlights the extent to which cash leads or lags the related revenues and expenses.

Another asserted advantage of the indirect method is that, for many companies, it is easier to prepare. In theory, the amounts of all cash receipts and payments can be derived by analyzing the cash account and the related cash journals. After all, the statement of cash flows, in concept, is nothing more than summary of checkbook entries. In practice, however, the accounting systems of many companies are not designed to classify the cash entries in the categories required by the statement of cash flows. Hence, to obtain the required data, companies may have to reclassify thousands of transactions, an obviously costly process.

This contention may have merit in the short term, but certainly not in the long term. If accounting systems of today do not provide the necessary data, it is only because until *Statement No. 95* was issued there was no reason why they should. There are no serious obstacles to modifying the systems, particularly those that are built around large computers, so that the information is routinely available.

Moreover, even if the required data on individual cash flows cannot be determined directly from the cash accounts, they can almost always be derived indirectly. As will be shown in the section that follows, cash receipts can be calculated from the receivables and sales accounts; payments to suppliers can be established from the cost of goods sold, inventory, and payables accounts.

FASB Preference

The FASB *encourages* firms to use the direct method, mainly because it shows the operating cash receipts and disbursements, while the indirect method does not. However, the FASB stipulates that firms which use the direct method should reconcile (in a supplemental schedule) net income from operating activities to net cash flow from operating activities. This reconciliation contains the information that would be available if the indirect method were used. Thus statement users reap the benefits of both methods.

Although the FASB *advocates* the direct method, it *permits* the indirect method.[2] It was persuaded by the arguments that the information required by the direct method would be too costly for some firms to collect. Despite the board's preference for the direct method, an overwhelming majority of firms use the indirect method. The most likely explanation is that they prefer less disclosure to more. In contrast to the direct method, the indirect method does not require that they report receipts from customers or payments to suppliers and employees. In concept, an independent analyst should be able to convert from the indirect to the direct method. In practice, however, that is seldom possible because the required information is lost through aggregation.

PREPARATION OF THE STATEMENT OF CASH FLOWS ON THE DIRECT BASIS

This section illustrates the preparation of the statement of cash flows on a direct basis since it is the basis preferred by the FASB. The procedures used to prepare the statement are presented for two primary reasons. First, they

[2]Two members of the Board dissented to the option provision.

provide an opportunity to review the means of accounting for several types of transactions discussed in other chapters. Second, and more importantly, they provide a different perspective on the relationships between accounts—one that focuses on cash rather than income.

Statement of Cash Flows as a Statement of Changes in Other Accounts

By the nature of the accounting equation, changes in cash can be associated with changes in the other balance sheet accounts.

The basic accounting equation indicates that assets (A) equal liabilities (L) plus owners' equity (OE). Assets are composed of cash (C) and other assets (OA). Therefore

$$C + OA = L + OE$$

By rearranging the terms in the equation, it is apparent that cash is equal to liabilities plus owners' equity minus other assets:

$$C = L + OE - OA$$

Therefore changes in cash are equal to changes in the noncash accounts. Increases in cash are associated with increases in liabilities and owners' equity and with decreases in other assets. Decreases in cash are associated with decreases in liabilities and owners' equity and increases in other assets.

The key to preparing a statement of cash flows is in making certain that all changes in noncash *balance sheet* accounts have been explained. When this has been accomplished, there is logical assurance that all changes in cash have also been accounted for. This can be done by reconstructing, in summary form, all entries that affect the balance sheet accounts. By posting them to a worksheet, you can be sure that all changes have been explained.

Setting Up a Worksheet

The preparation of a statement of cash flows will be illustrated using the balance sheet and income statement of the Taconic Corp. These, along with supplemental information, are presented in Exhibit 14-2.

We recommend the following approach:

1. Set up a worksheet. (See Exhibit 14-3.) Use the following column headings:

   Column 1. Accounts/Reasons for Cash Flows
   Column 2. Beginning-of-Year Balances
   Column 3. Transactions (Debits)
   Column 4. Transactions (Credits)
   Column 5. End-of-Year Balances

EXHIBIT 14-2
Data for Preparation of Statement of Cash Flows

Taconic Corp.
Comparative Statement of Financial Position
December 31, 1993 and 1992
(all amounts in millions)

	1993	1992		1993	1992
Assets			*Liabilities and Owners' Equity*		
Current assets			Current liabilities		
Cash	$ 40	$ 30	Accounts payable	$ 62	$ 56
Accounts receivable	76	80	Other liabilities		
Marketable securities	160	50	Deferred income taxes	69	62
Inventory	60	62	Bonds payable	378	261
Total current assets	$336	$222	Bond premium	3	
			Total other liabilities	$450	$323
Other assets					
Building and equipment	403	328	Owners' equity		
Accumulated depreciation	(90)	(72)	Common stock ($1 par value)	13	12
Land	67	67	Capital in excess of par	127	122
Investment in subsidiary	6	0	Retained earnings	70	32
Total other assets	$386	$323	Total owners' equity	$210	$166
			Total liabilities and		
Total assets	$722	$545	owners' equity	$722	$545

Taconic Corp.
Statement of Income
Year Ended December 31, 1993
(in millions)

Sales	$1,045	
Gain on sale of equipment	6	$1,051
Cost of goods sold	895	
Depreciation	51	
Interest expense	11	
Tax expense	30	
Other expenses	4	991
Net income		$ 60

Other Information (from Journal Entries or Specific Accounts)

1. The company acquired equipment for $112 million.
2. It sold equipment for $10 million. The equipment had originally cost $37 million. At the time of sale, depreciation of $33 million had been accumulated.
3. The company paid $23 million in taxes. The difference between taxes paid and tax expense was credited to ''deferred income taxes.''
4. It purchased marketable securities for $110 million.
5. It acquired a subsidiary in exchange for 1 million shares of its own newly issued common stock ($1 par value). The shares had a market value of $6 per share.
6. It declared and paid dividends of $22 million.
7. It issued for $120 million bonds having a face value of $117 million.

2. In column 1, list all of the accounts; in column 2, post beginning-of-year balances; and in column 5, post end-of-year balances.
3. Beneath the balance sheet accounts, list each of the income statement accounts. Include an additional line designated "net income." Do not, however, post the amounts. These will be added as the reconstructed journal entries are made.
4. Beneath the income statement accounts, indicate the three categories of cash flows (operating, investing, and financing activities). Leave space between each for the specific cash flows. This section of the worksheet will provide the information needed for the actual statement of cash flows.

Reconstructing the Transactions

The reconstructed transactions will be expressed in journal entries that are similar to those that would have been made during the year. There is one exception, however. Whenever cash is affected, the debit or credit will *not* be made to the cash account. Instead it will be to an account descriptive of the reason for the cash flow. These amounts will be posted to the last section of the worksheet, that from which the statement of cash flows will be derived. The journal entries will be marked OA (for operating activities), IA (for investing activities), and FA (for financing activities).

The statement of income is the most convenient starting point for reconstructing the transactions. It is the prime source of information about changes that affected cash as well as the other balance sheet accounts.

Sales
Sales would typically have been recorded as follows:

(a)

Accounts receivable $1,045
    Sales $1,045
To record sales

This entry increases accounts receivable, but it has no impact on cash. The collections from customers will be accounted for in a subsequent entry.

Gain on Sale of Equipment
The income statement reports a gain on sale of equipment of $6. The supplementary information reveals that the equipment was sold for $10. It had cost $37, and depreciation of $33 had been accumulated. Thus the sale would have been recorded as follows:

EXHIBIT 14-3
**Worksheet for Preparation of Statement of
Changes in Cash Flows**

| | | Year Ended December 31 Reconstructed Entries | | |
	1992	Debits	Credits	1993
Balance Sheet				
Cash	30	10 (q)		40
Accounts receivable	80	1,045 (a)	1,049 (h) *OA*	76
Marketable securities	50	110 (k)		160
Inventory	62	893 (i)	895 (c)	60
Building and equipment	328	112 (l)	37 (b)	403
Accumulated depreciation	(72)	33 (b)	51 (d)	(90)
Land	67			67
Investment in subsidiary	0	6 (m)		6
Accounts payable	(56)	887 (j) *OA*	893 (i)	(62)
Deferred income taxes	(62)		7 (f)	(69)
Bonds payable	(261)		117 (n)	(378)
Bond premium			3 (n)	(3)
Common stock ($1 par value)	(12)		1 (m)	(13)
Capital in excess of par	(122)		5 (m)	(127)
Retained earnings	(32)	22 (o)	60 (p)	(70)
Total (check)	0			0
Income Statement				
Sales			1,045 (a)	
Gain on sale of equipment			6 (b)	
Cost of goods sold		895 (c)		
Depreciation		51 (d)		
Interest expense		11 (e) *OA*		
Tax expense		30 (f)		
Other expenses		4 (g)		
Net income		60 (p)		
Cash Flows				
From operating activities				
Payment of interest			11 (e) *OA*	
Payments of taxes			23 (f) *OA*	
Payments of other expenses			4 (g) *OA*	
Collections from customers		1,049 (h) *OA*		
Payments to suppliers			887 (j) *OA*	
From investing activities				
Sale of equipment		10 (b) *IA*		
Purchase of equipment			112 (l) *IA*	
From financing activities				
Purchase of marketable securities			110 (k)	
Issuance of bonds		120 (n)		
Payment of dividends			22 (o)	
Net increase in cash			10 (q)	
Total (check)		5,348	5,348	

Handwritten annotations: ASSETS, LIABILITY OR OB, OA, IA, FA

(b)

Cash from sale of equipment (IA)................................$10	
Accumulated depreciation.. 33	
Gain on sale of equipment ....$ 6	
Buildings and equipment 37	
To record sale of equipment	

The sale of the equipment caused cash to increase by $10. This amount is therefore posted to the cash flow (investing activities) section of the worksheet.

Cost of Goods Sold

The following entry would have recorded cost of goods sold:

(c)

Cost of goods sold $895	
Inventory...$895	
To record cost of goods sold	

Cost of goods sold reduces inventory but not cash. The purchase of, as well as the payment for, the goods acquired will be accounted for in other entries.

Depreciation

Depreciation is another expense that does not affect cash:

(d)

Depreciation expense..$51	
Accumulated depreciation..$51	
To record depreciation	

Interest Expense

In this example, we can assume that the interest payments for the year were equal to the interest expense. If they were not, then there would have been an increase or a decrease in (1) either a prepaid interest or an interest payable account or (2) either a bond premium or a bond discount account. The balance sheet in Exhibit 14-2 contains neither a prepaid interest nor an interest payable account. It does, however, contain a bond premium account. But the increase of $3 can be explained fully by the issuance of new bonds (see entry **n** below). Therefore the following entry would summarize both the cash payments and the interest expense:

(e)

Interest expense $11	
Interest payment (OA) $11	
To record interest	

Tax Expense

Tax expense, per the income statement, was $30. As indicated in the supplementary information, however, the actual tax payment was only $23. As emphasized in Chapter 10, the reported tax expense is based upon reported income rather than taxable income as calculated under the tax code. The difference between the tax that is payable for the current year and that recognized as a tax expense is added to, or subtracted from, the deferred tax account. Thus

(f)

Tax expense	$30	
Deferred income taxes		$ 7
Payment of taxes (OA)		23
To record taxes		

Other Expenses

Other expenses required the disbursement of cash. We know this because, as with interest, there are no asset or liability accounts related to the expenses. Hence the expenses were equal to the cash payments:

(g)

Other expenses	$4	
Payment of other expenses (OA)		$4
To record other expenses		

Collections from Customers

Neither the financial statements nor the supplementary data reveal the collections from customers. The collections can be derived, however, from the related balance sheet (accounts receivable) and income statement (sales) accounts:

Accounts receivable, 12/31/92 + Sales − Collections

= Accounts receivable, 12/31/93

Therefore

Collections = Sales + Accounts receivable, 12/31/92

− Accounts receivable, 12/31/93

For 1993, collections were $1,049:

$$\text{Collections} = \$1,045 + \$80 - \$76$$
$$= \$1,049$$

The following entry summarizes the collections:

(h)

Collections from customers (OA)	$1,049	
Accounts receivable		$1,049
To record collections		

Payments to Suppliers

Payments to suppliers are also not reported in the income statement, balance sheet, or supplementary data. They too must be derived. Payments to suppliers relate, first, to the amount of goods purchased and, second, to the amount of goods paid for. Unlike collections from customers, they must be derived from two, rather than one, balance sheet accounts—inventory and accounts payable.

Goods purchased can be calculated from the beginning and ending balances in inventory and from cost of goods sold:

Inventory, 12/31/92 + Purchases − Cost of goods sold = Inventory, 12/31/93

Therefore

$$\text{Purchases} = \text{Cost of goods sold} + \text{Inventory, 12/31/93} - \text{Inventory, 12/31/92}$$

$$= \$895 + \$60 - \$62$$

$$= \$893$$

The purchase of inventory increases accounts payable; it has no impact on cash:

(i)

```
Inventory...................................................$893
    Accounts payable.........................................$893
To record purchases of inventory
```

Once the purchases are known, the actual cash payments can be derived by analyzing accounts payable:

Accounts payable, 12/31/92 + Purchases − Payments

= Accounts payable, 12/31/93

Therefore, based on the purchases as just determined ($893) and beginning and ending balances in accounts payable:

$$\text{Payments} = \text{Purchases} + \text{Accounts payable, 12/31/92}$$

$$- \text{Accounts payable, 12/31/93}$$

$$= \$893 + \$56 - \$62$$

$$= \$887$$

The entry to reflect the payments would be:

(j)

```
Accounts payable...............................................$887
    Payment to suppliers (OA)..................................$887
To record payments to suppliers
```

Many companies keep track of both collections from customers and payments to suppliers. Therefore they do not have to resort to the analysis just illustrated. The analysis is presented here to demonstrate that companies need not forsake the direct for the indirect presentation simply because their accounting systems do not keep track of collections from customers and payments to suppliers. These amounts can be derived from the income statement and the beginning- and end-of-year balance sheets. Indeed, the cash flows associated with any revenue and expense can be calculated by adding to it the net change in the related balance sheet account.

Purchase of Marketable Securities

The company purchased marketable securities for $110. Purchases of securities are classified as investing activities:

(k)

Marketable securities		$110
Purchase of marketable securities (IA)		$110

To record the purchase of marketable securities

Purchase of Equipment

The company purchased equipment for $112. Purchases of property, plant, and equipment are categorized as investing activities:

(l)

Buildings and equipment		$112
Purchase of equipment (IA)		$112

To record purchase of equipment

Investment in Subsidiary — A Noncash Acquisition

The company acquired a subsidiary in exchange for 1 million newly issued shares of its own common stock. Since the stock had a fair market value of $6 per share, the investment in the subsidiary would have been recorded at $6 million. Inasmuch as the par value of the stock is $1 per share ($1 million for 1 million shares), the difference between the acquisition price of $6 million and the par value ($1 million) would have been added to "contributed capital in excess of par":

(m)

Investment in subsidiary		$6
Common stock ($1 par value)		$1
Contributed capital in excess of par		5

To record acquisition of subsidiary

The acquisition of the subsidiary is an investing activity, but unlike the purchase of marketable securities and equipment, it did not require the payment of cash. Therefore it will not be reported in the main part of the statement of cash flows. Instead, it will be shown in either a supplementary schedule or a narrative note.

Issuance of Bonds

The firm received $120 in cash by issuing bonds. The bonds had a face value of $117. The difference between the two amounts would have been credited to a bond premium account. The issuance of bonds is classified as a financing activity:

(n)

Issuance of bonds (FA)	$120	
Bonds payable		$117
Bond premium		3
To record issuance of bonds		

Payment of Dividends

The company paid $22 in dividends. Dividends are generally charged to "dividends," an account that has the characteristics of an expense account but is not incorporated into the calculation of income. The dividends account is "closed" into retained earnings at year end. The entry that follows gives effect to the payment of dividends. Dividends paid are classified as a financing activity:

(o)

Retained earnings	$22	
Payment of dividends (FA)		$22
To record payment of dividends		

Completing the Worksheet

After the entries that have been made so far have been posted to the worksheet, it is apparent that, with the exception of two accounts, all changes in the balance sheet during the year have been accounted for. That is, beginning balance, plus or minus adjustments, equals ending balance. The two accounts that do not yet reconcile are retained earnings and cash.

Retained earnings is decreased during the year when dividends are declared and increased at year end when revenue and expense accounts are closed out, thereby transferring net income to retained earnings. To this point, an entry has been made to recognize the declaration of dividends but not to transfer the net income. This omission can be remedied with the following entry:

(p)

Net income	$60	
Retained earnings		$60
To transfer net income to retained earnings		

The difference between beginning- and end-of-year cash balance ($10) has been accounted for by the entries to the changes in the cash section of the worksheet. The last entry completes the worksheet and serves as a check on our analysis:

(q)

Cash	$10	
Net increase in cash		$10
To reconcile cash		

If no errors have been made, then the $10 increase in cash will be equal to the difference between the cash receipts and payments that have previously been identified.

Preparing the Statement

The main body of the statement of cash flows can be prepared directly from the section of the worksheet indicating the cash flows. Exhibit 14-4 contains the same information as the worksheet with only minor rearrangement of some of the items.

EXHIBIT 14-4
Statement of Cash Flows on a *Direct* Basis

Taconic Corp.
Statement of Cash Flows
Year Ended December 31, 1993
(all amounts in millions)

Increase (Decrease) in Cash

Cash Flow from Operating Activities		
Collections from customers		$1,049
Payments to suppliers		(887)
Payments of interest		(11)
Payments of taxes		(23)
Payments of other expenses		(4)
Net cash provided by operating activities		$ 124
Cash Flow from Investing Activities		
Proceeds from sale of equipment		$ 10
Purchases of equipment		(112)
Net cash used in investing activities		$ (102)
Cash Flow from Financing Activities		
Proceeds from issuing bonds		$ 120
Purchases of marketable securities		(110)
Payment of dividends		(22)
Net cash used in financing activities		$ (12)
Net increase in cash		$ 10

Reconciliation of Net Income with Cash Provided by Operating Activities

Net income		$ 60
Adjustments to reconcile net income to cash provided by operating activities		
Depreciation	$51	
Gain on sale of equipment	(6)	
Decrease in accounts receivable	4	
Decrease in inventory	2	
Increase in accounts payable	6	
Increase in deferred income taxes	7	$ 64
Net cash provided by operating activities		$124

Supplemental Information on Noncash Investing Activities

Taconic acquired a subsidiary in exchange for 1 million shares of its own newly issued common stock ($1 par value). The shares had a market value of $6 per share.

Reconciling Cash from Operating Activities with Net Income

Statement No. 95 requires that the statement of cash flows contain, in a supplemental schedule, a reconciliation of net income to net cash flow from operating activities. This schedule can be prepared by comparing each of the items in the "cash from operating activities" section of the worksheet with the related revenue or expense on the income statement.

Change in Accounts Receivable

Cash collections from customers exceeded sales by $4. Sales are associated with increases in accounts receivable, cash collections with decreases. Hence accounts receivable decreased during the year. The $4 *decrease in accounts receivable* (i.e., the amount by which collections exceeded sales) must be added to net income if net income is to be considered a source of cash from operations.

Changes in Inventory and Accounts Payable

Cost of goods sold exceeded payments to suppliers by $8. This is because (1) the company sold $2 more goods than it purchased, thereby reducing inventory by $2; and (2) it purchased $6 more goods than it paid for, thereby increasing accounts payable by $6.

The $2 *decrease in inventory* and the $6 *increase in accounts payable* must be added to net income to show the cash provided by income-producing activities.

Depreciation Expense

Depreciation is an expense that did not require an outflow of cash. Hence to reconcile income with cash from operations, it must be added to income.

Gain on Sale of Equipment

Gain on sale of equipment is a noncash revenue. The entry to record the sale of the equipment was

Cash	$10	
Accumulated depreciation	33	
Gain on sale of equipment		$ 6
Buildings and equipment		37

The sale of the land was a source of $10 in cash. It would be reported as cash from investing activities. But included in reported income would be the $6 gain on the sale. If income, including the gain of $6, is to be shown as a source of cash, and so also is the $10, then total sources of cash would be overstated by $6; the gain would be counted twice. If income is to be presented as a source of cash, any reported gains must be deducted. Similarly, any losses must be added to income. The losses, like the gains, would have had no impact on cash. Therefore they must be restored to income.

Increase in Deferred Income Taxes

Income taxes charged as an expense exceeded those actually paid. The difference of $7 was added to deferred income taxes. The *increase in deferred income taxes* must be added to income.

In the reconciling schedule, the difference between a revenue or expense and the cash received or paid is typically expressed as a change in the related asset or liability (e.g., "increase in accounts receivable"). There is no reason, however, why the change could not be described so as to indicate the reason behind it (e.g., "amount by which sales exceeded collections from customers").

Exhibit 14-5 summarizes the differences. The differences are also reported as part of the statement of cash flows (Exhibit 14-4).

Supplemental Schedule of Noncash Investing and Financing Activities

The final element of the statement of cash flows is the report on *noncash* investing and financing activities. Per the supplementary data (and journal entry **m**), the company acquired a subsidiary in exchange for 1 million shares of its own common stock. This transaction did not involve cash. Nevertheless, it had a significant impact on the assets and equities of the company and would not

EXHIBIT 14-5
Summary of Differences between Net Income and Cash Flow from Operating Activities

	Per Statement of		Difference: Amount to Be Added to Income*
	Cash Flow	Income	
Collections from customers/sales revenue (note 1)	$1,049	$1,045	$ 4
Payments to suppliers/cost of goods sold (note 2)	(887)	(895)	8
Depreciation	0	(51)	51
Gain on sale of equipment	0	6	(6)
Tax payments/tax expense (note 3)	(23)	(30)	7
Total	$ 139	$ 75	$ 64
Net income			60
Cash from operating activities			$124

*Amount by which cash inflow (outflow) per income statement is less than (greater than) that per statement of cash flows.

Note 1. The $4 by which cash collections exceeds sales revenue resulted in a decrease of the same amount in accounts receivable. On the reconciliation that is part of the statement of cash flows this is shown as "decrease in accounts receivable, $4."

Note 2. The $8 by which cost of goods sold exceeds payments to suppliers resulted in (1) a decrease in inventory of $2, as cost of goods sold exceeds purchases, and (2) an increase in accounts payable of $6, as purchases exceeds payments to suppliers. On the reconciliation this is shown as "decrease in inventory, $2" and "increase in accounts payable, $6"

Note 3. The $7 by which tax expense exceeds cash payments resulted in an increase in deferred income taxes. On the reconciliation this is shown as "increase in deferred income taxes, $7."

otherwise be reported on one of the three primary financial statements. It must be reported either on the same page as the main schedule of cash flows or in an accompanying note.

Exhibit 14-4 presents the completed statement.

PREPARATION OF THE STATEMENT OF CASH FLOWS ON THE INDIRECT BASIS

The procedures for preparing the statement of cash flows on a indirect basis are sufficiently similar to those used for preparing the statement on a direct basis that they need not be illustrated here. The main difference is in the worksheet entries affecting cash from operating activities. The entries reconstructing the various revenue and expense accounts would be replaced with a single entry:

Retained earnings $60
  Net income (OA) $60
To report net income as a cash inflow

Thereafter entries would be made to adjust net income for each of the items required to reconcile net income to cash from operating activities. These are the same items, of course, that are reported on the reconciliation schedule that is part of the statement of cash flows prepared on the direct basis. Indeed, the cash from the operating activities section of the statement is virtually identical to the reconciliation. Examples of the entries would be

Decrease in accounts receivable (OA) $4
  Accounts receivable $4
To adjust net income for the decrease in accounts receivable

Depreciation expense (OA) $51
  Accumulated depreciation $51
To adjust net income for depreciation, a noncash expense

Similar entries would be made to record the increase in accounts payable, the decrease in inventory, the increase in deferred income taxes, and the gain on sale of equipment.

If the statement of changes in cash flow is presented on an indirect basis, then the cash flows relating to individual revenues and expenses are not reported. However, the FASB believed that, because of their importance, the amounts paid for both interest and taxes should be disclosed. These amounts should be reported on the statement itself or in a related note.

Exhibit 14-6 illustrates the presentation on an indirect basis.

EXHIBIT 14-6
Statement of Cash Flows on an *Indirect* Basis

Taconic Corp.
Statement of Cash Flows
Year Ended December 31, 1993
(all amounts in millions)

Increase (Decrease) in Cash

Cash Flow from Operating Activities		
Net income		$ 60
Adjustments to reconcile net income to cash provided by operating activities		
Depreciation	$ 51	
Gain on sale of equipment	(6)	
Decrease in accounts receivable	4	
Decrease in inventory	2	
Increase in accounts payable	6	
Increase in deferred income taxes	7	$ 64
Net cash provided by operating activities		$124
Cash Flow from Investing Activities		
Proceeds from sale of equipment	$ 10	
Purchases of equipment	(112)	
Net cash used in investing activities		(102)
Cash Flow from Financing Activities		
Proceeds from issuing bonds	$120	
Purchases of marketable securities	(110)	
Payment of dividends	(22)	
Net cash used in financing activities		(12)
Net increase in cash		$ 10

Supplemental Disclosures of Cash Flow Information

Amounts paid for interest	$ 11
Amounts paid for taxes	23

Supplemental Information on Noncash Investing Activities

The Company acquired a subsidiary in exchange for 1 million shares of its own newly issued common stock ($1 par value). The shares had a market value of $6 per share.

WORKING CAPITAL

Changes in Working Capital as Changes in Nonworking Capital Accounts

Statement No. 95 directed that all firms issue a statement of cash flows rather than, as many had previously presented, a statement of changes in working capital. Working capital has long been used by financial managers, investors, and creditors as a measure of *liquidity. Statement No. 95* obviously diminished its accounting significance in that it will no longer be specifically reported upon in a separate financial statement. But *Statement No. 95* is unlikely to reduce the emphasis that financial analysts and managers place on working capital. Many regard working capital as a fundamental indicator of a firm's ability to meet its short-term obligations as they come due.

Working capital is generally defined as current assets less current liabilities. It comprises the cash and other assets that will be transformed into cash, sold, or consumed within the normal operating cycle of a business. From these assets are subtracted the obligations that will have to be satisfied out of those assets.

Current assets includes cash, marketable securities, accounts receivable, and inventories. *Current liabilities* includes accounts payable, wages and salaries payable, notes payable, and other short-term obligations. *Working capital*—the difference between the current assets and the current liabilities—is the margin of safety between a firm's liquid resources and the demands upon them.

Just as changes in cash are associated with changes in all noncash accounts, changes in working capital are associated with changes in all nonworking capital accounts. The basic accounting equation provides that current assets (*CA*) plus other assets (*OA*) are equal to current liabilities (*CL*) plus other liabilities (*OL*) plus owners' equity (*OE*). That is,

$$CA \ + \ OA \ = \ CL \ + \ OL \ + \ OE$$

When the terms in the equation are rearranged, it is clear that working capital (current assets minus current liabilities) must equal other liabilities plus owners' equity minus other assets:

$$\frac{\text{Working Capital}}{CA \ - \ CL} = \frac{\text{All Other Accounts}}{OL \ + \ OE \ - \ OA}$$

Increases in working capital result from *increases* in noncurrent liabilities or owners' equity and from *decreases* in noncurrent assets. *Decreases* in working capital result from *decreases* in noncurrent liabilities or owners' equity or *increases* in noncurrent assets. Thus

Sources of Working Capital (Events Associated with Increases in Working Capital)	Uses of Working Capital (Events Associated with Decreases in Working Capital)
Increases in noncurrent liabilities	*Decreases in noncurrent liabilities*
Issuance of notes or bonds	Repayment of notes or bonds
Increases in owners' equity	*Decreases in owners' equity*
Periodic income	Periodic losses
Issuance of stock	Redemption of stock
	Declaration of dividends
Decreases in noncurrent assets	*Increases in noncurrent assets*
Sale of fixed assets	Purchases of fixed assets

For most companies, the main source of working capital is income-producing activities. To reconcile income with working capital from operating activities requires far fewer adjustments than to reconcile income with cash from operating activities. Sales, for example, increase working capital irrespective of how much cash is actually collected (since both cash and accounts receivable are components of working capital). Similarly, cost of goods sold is associated with an equivalent decrease in working capital, irrespective of how much merchan⌐ is purchased and how much is paid for (since inventory, cash, and account⌐ payable are all elements of working capital).

Exhibit 14-7 compares the impact of several common transactions on both cash and working capital.

A Caveat

Working capital, unlike cash, is not directly comparable among firms. Working capital includes both accounts receivable and inventories. Accounts receivable may be influenced by accounting policies as to revenue recognition, bad debt expense, and write-offs of uncollectible accounts. Inventories are affected by choice of inventory method and policies as to inventory write-downs.

Moreover, an increase in working capital can be as much a sign of fiscal weakness as of fiscal strength. It is not uncommon for a firm undergoing fiscal

EXHIBIT 14-7
Comparison of Impact of Selected Transactions on Cash and Working Capital

Transaction	Working Capital	Cash
Sales on account (Dr. accounts receivable; Cr. sales)	Increase	No effect
Recognition of cost of goods sold (Dr. cost of goods sold; Cr. inventory)	Decrease	No effect
Collection of account receivable (Dr. cash; Cr. accounts receivable)	No effect	Increase
Purchase of inventory on account (Dr. inventory; Cr. accounts payable)	No effect	No effect
Payment to suppliers (Dr. accounts payable; Cr. cash)	No effect	Decrease
Purchase of inventory for cash (Dr. inventory; Cr. cash)	No effect	Decrease
Declaration of a dividend (Dr. dividends; Cr. dividends payable)	Decrease	No effect
Payment of the dividend (Dr. dividends payable; Cr. cash)	No effect	Decrease
Purchase of equipment for cash (Dr. equipment; Cr. cash)	Decrease	Decrease
Recognition of depreciation (Dr. depreciation; Cr. accumulated depreciation)	No effect	No effect
Sale of equipment at a loss (Dr. accumulated depreciation, loss on sale, cash; Cr. equipment)	Increase	Increase
Recognition of bad debt expense (Dr. bad debt expense; Cr. allowance for uncollectible accounts)	Decrease	No effect
Write-off of an uncollectible account (Dr. allowance for uncollectible accounts; Cr. accounts receivable)	No effect	No effect
Purchase of a subsidiary in exchange for bonds (Dr. investment in subsidiary; Cr. bonds payable)	No effect	No effect

stress to experience increases in both accounts receivable and inventory—and therefore working capital. Accounts receivable increases as customers become slow in paying; inventory increases as merchandise which is difficult to sell builds up.

Summary

The statement of cash flows is third of the three main statements that compose an annual financial report. Cash is the asset that is of primary concern to a business and its constituents. Cash is required to pay obligations as they come due, to meet daily operating costs, and to pay dividends and interest. Cash is the medium of exchange in our society, and it is the objective of a business to return more cash to its owners than they contribute.

The statement of cash flows is conceptually straightforward. It is a listing of cash receipts and disbursements classified into several categories. The three main groupings are cash from operating activities, cash from financing activities, and cash from investing activities.

The statement of cash flows can be prepared by analyzing a firm's cash receipts and disbursements journals. The journals of most firms, however, are not set up to provide the required data; time-consuming analysis of individual transactions would be required. However, the change in cash during the year is equal to the sum of the changes in all other balance sheet accounts. It is generally more convenient to prepare the statement by identifying the changes in all the other accounts.

The FASB recommends that firms present the statement of cash flows on a *direct* basis, but permits them to report on the *indirect* basis. The difference between the two is in the way cash from operating activities is shown. The direct basis itemizes each of the cash flows associated with income. The indirect basis, by contrast, shows net income as a single source of cash. Income is then adjusted for the noncash components of the revenues and expenses. Most firms have elected to report on the indirect basis.

The statement of cash flows is no less important to managers, investors, and creditors than the balance sheet or income statement. It not only completes the picture of financial status and performance painted by the other two, but adds another dimension.

Exercise for Review and Self-Testing

A firm's condensed balance sheets for the years ending December 31, 1994 and 1993, and statement of income for 1994 are as shown in the accompanying table (all amounts in millions).

1. By how much did cash increase during 1994?
2. a. By how much did sales increase accounts receivable assuming all sales were "on account"?
   b. How much cash was collected from customers?
3. a. By how much did cost of goods sold *decrease* inventory?
   b. How much inventory was purchased?
   c. By how much did purchases increase accounts payable assuming all accounts payable are to suppliers?
   d. How much cash was paid to suppliers?
4. a. How much did depreciation add to accumulated depreciation?
   b. By how much was accumulated depreciation reduced when equipment was sold?

c. Assume that the equipment that was sold had been acquired for $12. For how much cash was the equipment sold?

d. How much cash was paid to acquire new equipment?

5. a. By how much did deferred income taxes increase?

   b. How much cash was paid in income taxes?

6. a. By how much did the bond discount decrease?

   b. What journal entry was made to record interest expense?

   c. How much cash was paid in interest?

7. a. By how much did retained earnings increase? Why?

   b. Have all changes in balance sheet accounts now been accounted for?

   c. Summarize all cash receipts and disbursements. Do they account for the change in cash?

		1994		1993
Balance Sheet				
Assets				
Cash (and equivalents)		$100		$ 90
Accounts receivable		150		92
Inventory		39		18
Equipment	$245		$250	
Less: Accumulated depreciation	(36)	209	(30)	220
Total assets		$498		$420
Liabilities and owners' equity				
Accounts payable		$100		$ 60
Deferred income taxes		11		4
Bonds payable	$200		$200	
Less: Bond discount	(4)	196	(5)	195
Contributed capital		15		15
Retained earnings		176		146
Total liabilities and owners' equity		$498		$420
Statement of Income				
Sales revenue			$278	
Cost of goods sold		$200		
Depreciation		10		
Loss on sale of equipment		2		
Interest		17		
Income taxes		19	248	
Net income			$ 30	

Questions for Review and Discussion

1. A statement of cash flows is usually thought to be more objective than an income statement. Why?

2. Why is cash of greater concern to investors, creditors, and managers than are other assets?

3. When negotiating with its union, management argued that even though reported earnings were at record highs, the company was unable to afford even a small in-

crease in wages. By contrast, a union in negotiating with its management asserted that even though earnings were at record lows, the company could well afford even a large increase in wages. What is likely to be the common basis for both contentions?

4. What are the primary objectives of the statement of cash flows?

5. Why does the statement of cash flows focus on temporary investments such as Treasury bills and commercial paper as well as on cash? Why does it not focus upon other temporary investments such as stocks and bonds?

6. What are the three main classifications of cash flows required by the FASB? Why did the FASB switch from the traditional classifications of "sources" and "uses" of cash?

7. Under which classification would interest be reported? Why?

8. What is the main advantage of the *direct* presentation over the *indirect?* Why is the indirect method permitted? Does the indirect presentation have any merits in and of itself?

9. Why are some transactions reported on the statement of cash flows even though they result in neither an increase nor a decrease in cash? Provide examples of such transactions.

10. What warnings would you give an analyst who wants to compare the working capital position of one company with that of another?

11. The president of Presidential Realty Corporation, a firm whose shares are traded on the American Stock Exchange, made the following comment in a letter to stockholders:

> In our opinion, however, conventionally computed "operating income" has never adequately measured the performance of real estate development and investment companies such as ours. We believe that the best measure of our performance is the "Sum" of the operating income, the noncash charges against such income (consisting of rental property depreciation, write-off of mortgage origination costs, and deferred federal income taxes), and the funds generated from net gains from capital transactions. It is this "Sum" that is available for all corporate purposes, such as payment of mortgage debt, reinvestment in property replacements and new properties and enterprises, and distributions to shareholders.

The president of the company is, in essence, advocating a cash basis of reporting. Why, in light of his comments, has the accounting profession insisted that financial statements be prepared on the accrual basis and that noncash as well as cash charges be deducted from revenues in determining income? Do you believe that a better measure of performance is obtained if noncash expenses are added back to income? Can you think of any special characteristics of the real estate industry that may have influenced the president?

Problems

1. *"Missing" information on cash receipts and disbursements may be deduced by analyzing the changes in accounts other than cash.*

    The following account balances appeared on the financial statements of the Rackham Corp.:

	1993	1992
Buildings and equipment	$475,000	$400,000
Accumulated depreciation	125,000	100,000
Depreciation	40,000	35,000
Gain on sale of equipment	12,000	57,000

During 1993 the Rackham Corp. purchased $134,000 in new equipment.

a. Compute the increase in cash attributable to the *sale* of equipment in 1993 (*Hint:* Analyze the changes in the buildings and equipment and related accumulated depreciation accounts, giving consideration to the types of events that cause their balances to increase or decrease.)

b. Indicate any additions to, or deductions from, 1993 income that would be required if income were to be reconciled to cash from operating activities.

2. *Careful analysis of owners' equity accounts can provide considerable information on cash from investing as well as other activities.*

The owners' equity section of the Driscoe Corp. balance sheet as of December 31, 1993 and 1992, contained the following balances:

	1993	1992
Common stock (par value $10)	$105,000	$100,000
Contributed capital in excess of par	43,000	40,000
Retained earnings	256,000	244,000

At the start of 1993, the company declared and paid a cash dividend of 50 cents per share and a stock dividend of 20 cents per share (200 shares). Reported earnings of the firm included a loss of $20,000 attributable to a fire at a company plant, depreciation of $10,000, and a gain of $2,000 on the retirement of outstanding bonds.

The company issued for cash 300 shares of common stock.

Based on this information, determine, as best you can, the increase in cash associated with changes in the owners' equity accounts.

3. *A statement of changes in cash, on the direct or the indirect basis, can be prepared by analyzing all accounts other than cash.*

Comparative income statements and the balance sheets for the Rushmore Sales Corp. for the years ended December 31, 1993 and 1992, are as follows:

Rushmore Sales Corp.
Balance Sheet
as of December 31, 1993 and 1992

	1993	1992
Assets		
Cash	$ 40,000	$ 19,000
Accounts receivable	60,000	45,000
Inventories	20,000	28,000
Fixed assets (net of accumulated depreciation)	107,000	112,000
	$227,000	$204,000
Equities		
Accounts payable	$ 89,000	$ 85,000
Common stock	100,000	100,000
Retained earnings	38,000	19,000
Total equities	$227,000	$204,000

Rushmore Sales Corp.
Income Statement
for Years Ending
December 31, 1993 and 1992

	1993	1992
Sales	$100,000	$85,000
Cost of goods sold	$ 70,000	$50,000
Depreciation	5,000	5,000
Other expenses	6,000	8,000
Total expenses	$ 81,000	$63,000
Net income	$ 19,000	$22,000

[Handwritten marginal notes, left side:]

AR 92 + SALES – COLLECTIONS = AR 93
DYS – 100 – COLLECT = 60
  COLLECT = 100 – 45 – 60
  COLLECT = 85

I 92 + PURCHASE – COGS = I 93
28 + PURCHASE – 70 = 20
PUR = 20 + 70 – 28
PUR = 62

AP 92 + PUR – PAY = AP 93
85 + 62 – PAY = 89
PAY = 85 + 62 – 89
PAY = 58

DIR
COLLECTIONS   85
PAYMENTS MERCHANDISE PUR.   (58)
PAYMENTS OTHER OPERATIONS   (6)
                                              21

INDIRECT
NET INCOME   19
ADJUSTMENTS
  AR   (15)
  INV   8
  AP   4
  DEP   5
                      21

[Printed text:]

a. All sales were made on account. By analyzing "accounts receivable," determine the amount of cash collected in 1993.

b. All "other expenses" were paid directly in cash. Indicate the amount of cash applied to the payment of "other expenses." *6,000*

c. Determine the amount of inventory purchased during 1993. Then, by analyzing "accounts payable," determine the amount of cash payments to suppliers made during the year. *IND ⟶ +5,000 TO NI*

d. Indicate any other expenses not requiring an outlay of cash. *DEPRECIATION*

e. Prepare two statements of cash flows. In the first, indicate directly all cash receipts and disbursements. In the second, start with net income as a source of cash and indicate any required adjustments (e.g., for changes in inventories and accounts receivable).

4. *For some decisions information on changes in cash may be more relevant than that on income.*

The Badlands Mining Co. was organized to remove ore from a specific tract of land over a period of five years. In its second year of operations the company incurred a loss of $200,000, determined as follows:

Sales of ore		$2,000,000
Less: Depletion of ore	$1,000,000	
Depreciation on equipment	200,000	
Wages and salaries	400,000	
Other operating costs	600,000	2,200,000
Net loss		$ 200,000

In spite of the loss, the president of the company recommended to the board of directors that it declare a dividend of $300,000. One member of the board declared the recommendation to be nonsense. "How can we justify declaring a dividend in a year when we took a financial beating?"

a. How, in fact, might the board justify the declaration of a dividend?

b. Why would a statement of cash flows provide a better indication of the ability of the company to declare dividends than would a statement of income?

c. Suppose that the company had to acquire $400,000 of equipment during the year. Prepare a schedule that would support the position of the president that the company could "afford" to declare a dividend despite the required outlay for the equipment.

5. *In some industries changes in cash may provide a better measure of corporate performance than income.*

In January 1993 Real Estate Investors Corp. purchased an apartment building for $1 million. The company paid $100,000 in cash and gave a 10-year note for the balance. The company was required to pay only interest on the note for the first five years. In years 6 through 10 it was required to make principal payments of $180,000 per year.

In 1994 (the second year after the purchase of the property) the income statement of the company appeared as follows:

Revenues from rents		$200,000
Less: Depreciation	$90,000	
Interest	54,000	
Other expenses	60,000	204,000
Net loss		$ 4,000

Depreciation was based on the double declining balance method with an estimated useful life of 20 years.

a. Determine net cash inflow during 1994.

b. Compute return on investment on a cash basis (cash inflow divided by company investment in the apartment building).

c. Comment on why some real estate experts believe that the statement of cash flows provides a better indication of corporate performance in the real estate industry than does the statement of income. Consider the fact that many properties are sold long before the end of their useful (depreciable) lives.

6. *After only one year of a firm's operations it is relatively easy to identify the sources of cash and the uses to which it was put.*

The Earl Company began operations in 1993. Its income statement and balance sheet for its first year of operations follow (all amounts are in thousands):

Earl Company
Statement of Income
Year Ended December 31, 1993

Sales		$ 94,000
Less: Cost of goods sold	$48,000	
Depreciation	3,000	
Amortization of organization costs	2,000	
Taxes	7,000	
Interest*	1,000	
Other expenses	20,000	81,000
Net income		$ 13,000

*The reported interest expense of $1,000 represents, in its entirety, amortization of discount on the note payable.

Balance Sheet
as of December 31, 1993

Assets		
Cash		$ 17,000
Accounts receivable		12,000
Inventories		8,000
Plant and equipment	$53,000	
Less: Accumulated depreciation	3,000	50,000
Land		20,000
Organization costs	$10,000	
Less: Accumulated amortization	2,000	8,000
Total assets		$115,000
Equities		
Accounts payable		$ 19,000
Income taxes deferred until future years		2,000
Note payable	$40,000	
Less: Discount	6,000	34,000
Common stock		50,000
Retained earnings		10,000
Total liabilities and stockholders' equity		$115,000

Reconstruct as necessary the transactions of the year and prepare a statement of cash flows. (*Hint:* Be sure to account for the change in each noncash account. Make assumptions that are consistent with the information presented and with standard accounting practice. For example, income was $13,000, but the ending balance in "retained earnings" is only $10,000; thus it may be assumed that dividends of $3,000 were paid.)

7. *It is possible to derive a statement of cash flows entirely from comparative balance sheets and a statement of income.*

Comparative income statements and balance sheets of the Hassel Corp. are as follows:

Hassel Corp.
Statement of Income
Years Ended December 31
(in thousands)

	1993	1992
Sales	$160,000	$146,000
Gain on sale of land sold	8,000	
	$168,000	$146,000
Less: Cost of goods sold	$108,000	$ 86,000
Depreciation	10,000	9,000
Other expenses	20,000	10,000
Income taxes	8,000	11,000
	$146,000	$116,000
Net income	$ 22,000	$ 30,000

Balance Sheet
as of December 31

	1993	1992
Assets		
Cash	$ 30,000	$ 20,000
Accounts receivable	20,000	19,000
Inventory	10,000	8,000
Total current assets	$ 60,000	$ 47,000
Equipment	$150,000	$120,000
Less: Accumulated depreciation	(40,000)	(30,000)
	$110,000	$ 90,000
Land	35,000	50,000
Total assets	$205,000	$187,000
Liabilities and owners' equity		
Trade accounts payable	$ 20,000	$ 31,000
Income taxes deferred until future years	9,000	7,000
Notes payable	30,000	25,000
Common stock	100,000	100,000
Retained earnings	46,000	24,000
Total liabilities and owners' equity	$205,000	$187,000

a. Determine the net change in cash.
b. Analyze each of the noncash accounts. Determine the most likely reason for the change in each of the accounts and reconstruct the journal entries that af-

fected each account. Identify the entries associated with receipts or disbursements of cash.

c. Prepare a statement of cash flows.

8. *This a is comprehensive exercise in preparing a statement of cash flows.*

Comparative balance sheets and an income statement of the Inman Company are presented below. Additional information is also provided. Prepare a statement of cash flows.

Inman Corp.
Balance Sheet
as of June 30, 1993 and 1992

	1993	1992
Assets		
Current		
Cash	$ 46,000	$ 13,000
Accounts receivable	65,000	12,000
Inventories	66,000	54,000
Total current assets	$ 177,000	$ 79,000
Noncurrent		
Property, plant, and equipment	$ 925,000	$1,090,000
Less: Accumulated depreciation	228,000	298,000
	$ 697,000	$ 792,000
Investment in subsidiary	230,000	219,000
Other assets	120,000	140,000
Total noncurrent assets	$1,047,000	$1,151,000
Total assets	$1,224,000	$1,230,000
Liabilities and shareholders' investment		
Current		
Accounts payable	$ 40,000	$ 35,000
Notes payable	145,000	15,000
Total current liabilities	$ 185,000	$ 50,000
Noncurrent		
Notes payable	74,000	280,000
Shareholders' investment		
Common stock ($2 par value)	$ 20,000	$ 20,000
Contributed capital in excess of par	80,000	80,000
Retained earnings	865,000	80,000
Total shareholders' investment	$ 965,000	$ 900,000
Total liabilities and shareholders' investment	$1,224,000	$1,230,000

Statement of Income
Year Ended June 30, 1993

Sales	$555,000	
Proportionate share of subsidiary earnings	26,000	$581,000
Less: Cost of goods sold	236,000	
Interest	20,000	
Taxes	30,000	
Depreciation	90,000	
Other expenses	140,000	516,000
Net income		$ 65,000

(1) The company incurred an uninsured loss at its plant. Equipment that had a book value of $80,000 (original cost $240,000, accumulated depreciation $160,000) was destroyed. The loss is included among "other expenses." No other "property, plant, and equipment" was sold or retired. The remaining change in the account balance ($75,000) can be attributed to the purchase of new equipment.

(2) Other assets include patents of $40,000 in 1993 and $60,000 in 1992. Amortization expense of $20,000 is included in other expenses.

(3) The company owns a 30 percent interest in another company. It accounts for its investment by the equity method. The subsidiary paid cash dividends of $15,000 to Inman Corp. during 1993.

(4) The entire increase in "notes payable" (current) is the result of additional borrowings.

(5) The entire decrease in "notes payable" (noncurrent) is attributable to debt repayment.

9. *This is a comprehensive exercise in preparing a statement of cash flows.*

   The consolidated balance sheets of the Sorrells Co. as of December 31, 1993 and 1992, and the income statement for 1993, are as given in the accompanying tables. Additional information is as follows:

   (1) The company declared cash dividends of $30,000.
   (2) "Other expenses" includes a loss of $2,000 on equipment sold. The equipment had cost $17,000 and had a book value at time of sale of $8,000 (cost less accumulated depreciation of $9,000). It was sold for $6,000.
   (3) The balance of other expenses was paid in cash.
   (4) The reduction in other current liabilities was attributable to the repayment of loans.
   (5) The company acquired a 15 percent interest in the unconsolidated subsidiary in exchange for 10,000 shares of common stock. There were no other changes in the common stock accounts during the year.
   (6) The company credits the difference between taxes reported on the income statement and those actually payable within one year to "deferred income taxes."

Sorrells Co.
Statement of Income
Year Ended December 31, 1993
(in thousands)

Sales		$883,000
Less: Expenses		
Cost of goods sold	$596,000	
Depreciation	87,000	
Amortization of goodwill	9,000	
Interest	13,000	
Other expenses	8,000	
Income taxes	76,000	789,000
Net income		$ 94,000

Sorrells Co.
Consolidated Balance Sheet
as of December 31, 1993 and 1992
(in thousands)

	1993	1992
Assets		
Current		
Cash	$ 88,000	$ 61,000
Accounts receivable	250,000	211,000
Inventory	269,000	245,000
Total current assets	$ 607,000	$ 517,000
Other assets		
Plant and equipment	$ 950,000	$ 958,000
Less: Accumulated depreciation	180,000	102,000
	$ 770,000	$ 856,000
Investment in unconsolidated		
subsidiary	50,000	-0-
Goodwill	65,000	74,000
Total other assets	$ 885,000	$ 930,000
Total assets	$1,492,000	$1,447,000
Liabilities and owners' equity		
Current liabilities		
Accounts payable	$ 218,000	$ 179,000
Other current liabilities	63,000	176,000
Total current liabilities	$ 281,000	$ 355,000
Other liabilities		
Deferred income taxes	$ 24,000	$ 20,000
Bonds payable	$ 200,000	$ 200,000
Less: Unamortized discount	13,000	14,000
	$ 187,000	$ 186,000
Total other liabilities	$ 211,000	$ 206,000
Owners' equity		
Common stock ($1 par value)	$ 110,000	$ 100,000
Contributed capital in excess of		
par	340,000	300,000
Retained earnings	550,000	486,000
Total owners' equity	$1,000,000	$ 886,000
Total liabilities and owners'		
equity	$1,492,000	$1,447,000

Prepare a statement of cash flows (direct basis). Reconstruct journal entries as required. You may find it helpful to prepare a worksheet, although one is not required.

10. *An ending balance sheet can be derived from a statement of cash flows and a beginning balance sheet.*

The following are the 1993 statement of cash flows (indirect method) and the beginning-of-year balance sheet of Hamilton Industries, Inc. (All dollar amounts are in millions.) In addition, the records of the company reveal that the equipment that was sold during the year had cost $52 million when it was acquired.

Based on the beginning balance sheet and the statement of cash flows, prepare a year-end balance sheet.

Hamilton Industries, Inc.
Statement of Cash Flows
Year Ended December 31, 1993

Cash from Operating Activities	
Net income	$ 84
Adjustments to income	
Increase in accounts receivable	(25)
Decrease in inventory	4
Increase in accounts payable	10
Increase in deferred income taxes	10
Depreciation	71
Gain on sale of equipment	(8)
Total from operating activities	$ 146
Cash from Investing Activities	
Purchase of equipment	$(157)
Sale of equipment	14
Total from investing activities	$(143)
Cash from Financing Activities	
Proceeds from issuance of bonds	$ 168
Payment of dividends	(31)
Total from financing activities	$ 137
Total increase in cash	$ 140

Note: The company acquired an interest in a subsidiary in exchange for 1 million shares of newly issued common stock valued at $8 million.

Balance Sheet
as of January 1, 1993

Assets	
Cash	$ 100
Accounts receivable	90
Inventories	75
Building and equipment	459
Accumulated depreciation	(101)
Land	94
Total assets	$ 717
Liabilities and owners' equity	
Accounts payable	$ 33
Deferred income taxes	87
Bonds payable	365
Common stock, par value $1	17
Capital in excess of par	171
Retained earnings	44
Total liabilities and owners' equity	$ 717

11. *An income statement and an end-of-year balance sheet can be derived from a statement of changes in cash and a beginning-of-year balance sheet.*

Maryland Co.'s 1993 statement of cash flows and January 1, 1993, balance sheet are presented below (all dollar amounts are in millions).

a. Prepare a statement of income for 1993.

b. Prepare a balance sheet as of December 31, 1993.

Maryland Co.
Statement of Cash Flows
Year Ended December 31, 1993

Cash from operating Activities

Net income	$ 90
Adjustments to income	
Increase in accounts receivable	(75)
Increase in inventory	(60)
Increase in accounts payable	18
Increase in deferred income taxes	21
Depreciation	30
Amortization of bond discount	3
Gain on sale of equipment	(6)
Total from operating activities	21

Cash from Investing Activities

Sale of equipment	9
Total increase in cash	$ 30

Notes:

(1) The equipment sold during the year had been purchased for $15.

(2) Interest payments were $48.

(3) Tax payments were $36.

(4) Payments made for the purchase of merchandise were $642.

(5) Revenue consisted entirely of sales and the gain on the sale of equipment.

Balance Sheet
as of January 1, 1993

Assets	
Cash	$ 180
Accounts receivable	285
Inventories	111
Building and equipment	750
Accumulated depreciation	(90)
Total assets	$1,236
Liabilities and owners' equity	
Accounts payable	$ 156
Deferred income taxes	12
Bonds payable	600
Discount on bonds payable	(15)
Contributed capital	45
Retained earnings	438
Total liabilities and owners' equity	$1,236

12. *This problem illustrates the practical problems of converting from the direct to the indirect basis as well as of reconciling related amounts reported on the statement of cash flows to those on the balance sheet and income statement.*

The 1987 financial statements of Georgia-Pacific Corporation, including a footnote pertaining to an acquisition, are presented below. All dollar amounts are in millions. The statement of cash flows does not include all the data that the FASB currently requires, since it was prepared prior to the mandatory implementation date of *Statement No. 95.*

Georgia-Pacific Corporation
Balance Sheets
December 31

	1987	1986
Assets		
Current assets		
Cash	$ 70	$ 80
Receivables (less allowances of $24 and $21)	771	618
Inventory	837	681
Other current assets	51	41
	1,729	1,420
Timber and timberlands, net	915	844
Property, plant, and equipment		
Land and improvements, buildings,		
machinery and equipment, at cost	5,702	5,052
Accumulated depreciation	(2,654)	(2,361)
	3,048	2,691
Other assets	178	159
	$5,870	$5,114
Liabilities		
Current liabilities		
Bank overdrafts, net	$ 104	$ 79
Commercial paper and other short-term notes	85	100
Current portion of long-term debt	153	134
Accounts payable	355	295
Accrued compensation	109	87
Other current liabilities	190	142
	996	837
Long-term debt, excluding current portion	1,298	893
Deferred income taxes	744	695
Other long-term liabilities	152	124
Redeemable preferred equity	—	113
Common stockholders' equity		
Common stock, par value $.80 (111,187,000		
and 107,987,000 shares issued)	89	86
Additional paid-in capital	1,215	1,101
Retained earnings	1,645	1,304
Less common stock held in treasury	(263)	(19)
Accumulated translation adjustments	(6)	(20)
	2,680	2,452
	$5,870	$5,114

Georgia-Pacific Corporation Statement of Income
Year Ended December 31, 1987

Net sales	$8,603
Costs and expenses	
Cost of sales	6,777
Selling, general, and administrative	583
Depreciation and depletion	387
Interest	124
	7,871
Income before extraordinary items and taxes	732
Unusual items	66
Income before taxes	798
Provision for taxes	340
Net income	$ 458

Georgia-Pacific Corporation Statement of Cash Flows
Year Ended December 31, 1987

Cash Provided by (Used for) Continuing Operations	
Income from continuing operations before	
extraordinary item	$458
Items in income not affecting cash	
Depreciation	351
Depletion	36
Deferred income taxes	49
Gain on sale of assets	(4)
Gain on liquidation of investments	(66)
Other	46
	870
Cash Provided by (Used for) Working Capital	
Receivables	(78)
Inventories	(70)
Other current assets	(10)
Accounts payable and accrued liabilities	69
	(89)
Cash provided by operations	(781)
Cash Provided by (Used for) Financing Operations	
Repayments of long-term debt	(339)
Additions to long-term debt	683
Decrease in short-term liabilities	(16)
Common stock purchased for treasury	(255)
Cash dividends paid	(115)
Cash (used for) financing activities	(42)
Cash Provided by (Used for) Investment Activities	
Capital expenditures	
Property, plant, and equipment	(592)
Timber and timberlands	(107)
	(699)
Investment in U.S. Plywood	(208)
Proceeds from sale of assets	11
Proceeds from liquidation of investments	125
Other	22
Cash (used for) investment activities	(749)
Increase (Decrease) in Cash	
Balance at beginning of year	(10)
Balance at end of year	80
	$ 70

619

Georgia-Pacific Corporation
Note on Acquisition

On June 12, 1987, the Corporation acquired all of the outstanding stock of U.S. Plywood Corporation for $208 million in cash in a transaction accounted for as a purchase. The assets acquired and liabilities assumed at the acquisition date were as follows:

Receivables	$ 75
Inventories	86
Property, plant and equipment	126
Other assets	91
	378
Bank overdrafts, net	26
Accounts payable	28
Other current liabilities	33
Current portion of long-term debt	81
Other long-term liabilities	2
	170
	$208

a. Determine, as best you can, the amounts that follow. If you believe that necessary data are lacking, indicate the information you would need.
   (1) Collections from customers
   (2) Payments to suppliers
   (3) Payments to employees
   (4) Payments of interest
b. A footnote indicates that the company paid $255 in taxes. Can you reconcile this amount with ''deferred income taxes'' and ''provision for taxes''? What might account for any discrepancy?
c. What would you estimate to be the original cost of the property, plant, and equipment sold? What would you estimate to be the accumulated depreciation on those assets? Are you able to account for all transactions affecting accumulated depreciation?
d. Can you account for all activity in the ''timber and timberlands'' account?

13. *This problem requires that a beginning balance sheet be constructed from an ending balance sheet and a statement of cash flows.*

    Canadian Marconi is a manufacturer of avionics, communications and radar systems, and specialized components. As a Canadian company it is not subject to pronouncements of the FASB. Its statement of cash flows deviates slightly from the requirements of the FASB. Shown below are a balance sheet as of March 31, 1988, and a statement of cash flows for the year ending March 31, 1988. All dollar amounts are in thousands.

    Reconstruct, as best the data permit, the firm's balance sheet as of March 31, 1987. It will be necessary for you to combine all noncash elements of working capital (current assets less current liabilities) into a single account.

Canadian Marconi Company
Balance Sheet as of March 31, 1988

Assets

Current assets

Cash and temporary investments		$127,338
Accounts receivable		54,336
Income taxes refundable		4,908
Inventories		44,186
Prepaid expenses		699
		231,467
Other investments, at cost		37,147
Fixed assets at cost	$89,303	
Less: Accumulated depreciation	(51,926)	37,377
		$305,991

Liabilities and Shareholders' Equity

Current liabilities

Accounts payable and accrued liabilities	$ 65,747
Income taxes payable	24
	65,771
Deferred income taxes	6,998
Long-term debt	986
	73,775

Shareholders' equity

Stated capital	10,216
Retained earnings	222,020
	232,236
	$305,991

Canadian Marconi Company
Statement of Changes in Cash Flow
Year Ended March 31, 1988

Cash Provided by (Used in)

Operating activities

Net income	$ 22,039
Depreciation	9,295
Deferred income taxes	3,651
Gain on sale of surplus land	(2,237)
Net change in noncash working capital balances	(14,640)
	18,108

Financing activities

Reduction of long-term debt	(1,840)
Dividends	(6,656)
	(8,496)

Investment activities

Increase in other investments	(37,147)
Additions for fixed assets, net	(14,319)
Proceeds from sale of fixed assets	2,344
	(49,122)
Net cash (used) provided in year	(39,510)
Cash and temporary investments, beginning of year	166,848
Cash and temporary investments, end of year	$127,338

14. *Although U.S. firms no longer prepare a statement of changes in working capital, many non-U.S. firms do. Hence it is useful to be able to convert from a statement of working capital to a statement of cash flows.*

The statement of changes in financial position presented below was taken (with minor modifications) from an annual report of Binney and Smith, Inc., the manufacturers of crayons and toys. (All dollar amounts are in thousands.)

Recast the statement, as best the data permit, into a statement of cash flows. Use the indirect method, as sufficient data are not available for the direct method.

Sources of Working Capital	
Current operations	
Net earnings before extraordinary charge	$ 9,107
Charges not affecting working capital	
Depreciation and amortization	2,291
Provision for deferred income taxes	138
Treasury stock provided to employees and	
charged to compensation expense	280
Working capital provided from operations	$11,816
Working capital used for extraordinary charge	(350)
Increase in long-term debt	111
Property, plant, and equipment sold	276
Proceeds from exercise of stock options	404
Other (net)	288
Total sources of working capital	$12,545
Applications of Working Capital	
Additions to property, plant, and equipment	$ 4,627
Cash dividends on common stock	3,341
Reduction of long-term debt	726
Changes in exchange rates	240
Increase in investment in unconsolidated subsidiary	81
Total uses of working capital	$ 9,015
Increase in working capital	$ 3,530
Changes in Components of Working Capital	
Increase (decrease) in current assets	
Cash	$ 6,131
Accounts receivable	1,959
Inventories	1,558
Prepaid taxes	(148)
Prepaid expenses and other current assets	61
	$ 9,561
Increase (decrease) in current liabilities	
Bank loans	(265)
Payables and accrued expenses	2,586
Accrued income taxes	3,695
Current portion of long-term debt	15
	$ 6,031
Increase in working capital	$ 3,530

15. *The reason for a change in working capital is more important than the magnitude of the change.*

Crown Industries is contemplating acquiring Omega Co. Although Omega reported a loss in 1993, management of Crown is impressed with its increase in working capital.

Comparative balance sheets and income statements of Omega are shown below.
a. By how much did working capital increase during 1993?
b. What were the sources of the increase?
c. Comment on whether the increase in working capital is more likely indicative of financial strength or weakness.
   (1) Compute and compare accounts receivable turnover for 1993 and 1992 (based on year-end accounts receivable balances).
   (2) Compute and compare inventory turnover for 1993 and 1992 (based on year-end inventory balances).
   (3) What is a possible reason for the increases in accounts receivable and inventory?

	1993	1992
Balance Sheet (millions)		
Assets		
Cash	$ 1	$ 2
Accounts receivable	12	6
Inventory	14	8
Long-lived assets	50	50
Accumulated depreciation and amortization	(17)	(10)
Total assets	$60	$56
Equities		
Accounts payable	$12	$10
Long-term debt	25	21
Owners' equity	23	25
Total equities	$60	$56

	1993	1992
Income Statement (millions)		
Sales	$80	$70
Cost of goods sold (including depreciation and amortization)	62	50
Gross margin	$18	$20
Other expenses	20	18
Net income (loss)	($ 2)	$ 2

16. *Seemingly similar types of transactions may have very different effects on working capital.*
    Indicate whether each of the following transactions would increase (I), decrease (D), or have no effect on (NE) the working capital and cash of a company.
    a. Declaration of a $150,000 stock dividend
    b. Declaration of a $150,000 cash dividend
    c. Purchase of marketable securities for $12,000 cash
    d. Sale, for $15,000 cash, of marketable securities that had initially cost $12,000
    e. Declaration of $8,000 in dividends by a firm in which the company has a 5 percent interest
    f. Declaration of $8,000 in dividends by a firm in which the company has a 40 percent interest
    g. Write-off of an uncollectible account of $3,000 against the allowance provided
    h. Acquisition of another company in exchange for $1 million in long-term notes
    i. Acquisition of treasury stock for $4,500 cash
    j. Sale for $600 cash of merchandise that had cost $400

17. *Transactions that affect working capital may not affect cash; those that affect cash may not affect working capital.*

The following describes several transactions in which the Ramara Corp. engaged.

(1) Sold merchandise, on account, for $6,000. Cost of the goods sold was $5,000

(2) Collected $3,200 of the amount owed by customers

(3) Purchased additional inventory for $1,700 (on account)

(4) Paid $1,500 of the amount owed to suppliers

(5) Purchased marketable securities for $700 cash

(6) Sold the marketable securities for $500 cash

(7) Recorded one month's interest on notes payable, $50

(8) Paid one month's interest on the notes payable, $50

(9) Recorded one month's rent due from tenant, $200

(10) Received payment of one month's rent from tenant

a. Indicate whether the transactions would increase (I), decrease (D), or have no effect on (NE) the working capital of the corporation.

b. Indicate whether the transactions would increase (I), decrease (D), or have no effect on (NE) the cash balance of the corporation.

Solutions to Exercise for Review and Self-Testing

1. Cash increased by $10.
2. a. Sales increased accounts receivable by $278.
   b. By analysis of accounts receivable, collections from customers were $220:

   Beginning balance + Sales − Collections = Ending balance

   Collections = Beginning balance − Ending balance + Sales

   $$= \$92 - \$150 + \$278$$

   $$= \$220$$

3. a. Cost of goods sold *decreased* inventory by $200.
   b. By analysis of inventory, purchases were $221:

   Beginning balance + Purchases − Cost of goods sold = Ending balance

   Purchases = Ending balance − Beginning balance + Cost of goods sold

   $$= \$39 - \$18 + \$200$$

   $$= \$221$$

   c. Purchases increased accounts payable by $221.
   d. By analysis of accounts payable, payments to suppliers were $181:

   Beginning balance + Purchases − Payments = Ending balance

   Payments = Beginning balance − Ending balance + Purchases

   $$= \$60 - \$100 + \$221$$

   $$= \$181$$

4. a. Depreciation added $10 to accumulated depreciation.
   b. By analysis of accumulated depreciation, equipment on which depreciation of $4 had been accumulated was sold during the year:

$$\text{Beginning balance} + \text{Depreciation} - \text{Accumulated}$$
$$\text{depreciation on equipment sold} = \text{Ending balance}$$
$$\text{Accumulated depreciation on equipment sold}$$
$$= \text{Beginning balance} - \text{Ending balance} + \text{Depreciation}$$
$$= \$30 - \$36 + \$10$$
$$= \$4$$

   c. The equipment had a book value of $8 (cost of $12 less accumulated depreciation of $4). It was sold at a loss of $2, per the statement of income. Therefore it was sold for $6.

   d. By analysis of the equipment account, purchases of equipment were $7:

$$\text{Beginning balance} + \text{Purchases} - \text{Sales} = \text{Ending balance}$$
$$\text{Purchases} = \text{Ending balance} - \text{Beginning balance} + \text{Sales}$$
$$= \$245 - \$250 + \$12$$
$$= \$7$$

5. a. Deferred income taxes increased by $7.

   b. By analysis of the deferred income tax account, tax payments were $12:

$$\text{Beginning balance} + \text{Tax expense} - \text{Tax payments} = \text{Ending balance}$$
$$\text{Tax payments} = \text{Beginning balance} - \text{Ending balance} + \text{Tax expense}$$
$$= \$4 - \$11 + \$19$$
$$= \$12$$

6. a. Bond discount decreased by $1.

   b. Interest expense would have been recorded as follows:

Interest expense		$17
Bond discount		$ 1
Cash		16

   c. The cash interest payment was $16.

7. a. Retained earnings increased by $30. The entire increase is attributable to earnings.

   b. All changes in balance sheet accounts have been accounted for by the analysis above.

   c. Summary of cash receipts and disbursements:

Collections from customers	$220
Payments to suppliers	(181)
Payments of interest	(16)
Payments of taxes	(12)
Sale of equipment	6
Purchase of equipment	(7)
Net increase in cash	$ 10

This summary accounts for the net change in the cash balance.

15

Accounting for Changes in Prices

This chapter is directed to two related areas. First, it addresses changes in prices—changes in *specific prices* as well as changes in the *general price level*. Second, it deals with a particular aspect of changing prices, foreign currency translation—how to convert financial measurements from one currency to another.

In previous chapters, such as those concerned with marketable securities, inventories, and long-lived assets, we demonstrated how changes in prices of *specific* resources can be taken into account. In this chapter we illustrate a full set of statements that reflect not only changes in prices of specific resources but also the effects of general inflation.

In the first major section of this chapter, we present a *current cost/constant dollar* model of accounting. This model is *not* today an integral part of generally accepted accounting principles (GAAP). It is therefore *not* widely used by corporations in their reports to the public.

Why should students in a basic financial accounting course be concerned with accounting practices that are not used today and may thereby seem to be of no more than academic interest? For at least two reasons: First, by understanding the alternative practices, one will obtain greater insight into the accepted practices. The discussion to follow highlights the limitations of historical cost–based statements. The rationale for the presentation is not that current cost/constant dollar accounting is necessarily preferable to historical cost accounting. Instead, it is that each model has positive and negative features. The historical cost model is the one that is "generally accepted." Nevertheless, both managers and investors (to the extent they can obtain the necessary data) should be able to convert to a current cost model when the information provided is better suited to the specific decisions at hand.

Second, it is widely recognized that the accounting profession has not yet dealt adequately with the issues of changing prices. As discussed in Chapter 8, in 1979 the FASB issued *Statement No. 33* requiring firms to present current cost data in notes that supplement their financial statements. In 1986, in the face of evidence that the information was not widely used, it downgraded the current value disclosures from "mandatory" to "encouraged." Since then, the board has not actively pursued other ways of reporting the effects of price changes. During the 1980s and early 1990s, however, the rate of inflation was relatively low in most industrialized countries. Hence the absence of concern on the part of both statement users and rule-making authorities is understandable. Nevertheless, there are inevitably "carry-over" effects from years when price changes were substantial to years when they were small. For example, current cost depreciation would continue to be considerably greater than historical cost depreciation. Should the rate of price increases accelerate in the future, there is sure to be renewed attention to the issues of current value accounting. Accountants, investors, and managers are certain to be affected by any new accounting remedies that will then be proposed.

THE ISSUES IN PERSPECTIVE

The central issues underlying almost all accounting problems turn on *recognition* and *measurement*. *When* does a firm recognize the *existence of or changes in the values of assets or liabilities*? *How* does a firm *measure* what it wishes to recognize? Or (inasmuch as the balance sheet must *articulate with* the income statement), when and how should *revenues* and *expenses* resulting from the value changes be measured and recognized?

The earliest—and indeed simplest—accounting systems recognized changes in values (and hence revenues and expenses) only on the basis of formal *exchanges*, most typically transactions involving cash. As discussed in Chapter 3, however, cash-based accounting fails to capture significant economic events in the period in which they have their primary impact. For example, rent is reported as revenue when received rather than when earned.

Modern-day accounting systems are accrual-based and thereby reflect economic events in addition to these involving transactions. They thereby better meet the criteria that accounting information be both *relevant* and *reliable*.

A Matter of Timing

The issue of whether to recognize changes in the value of assets and liabilities due to changes in prices is simply an extension of revenue and expense recognition problems as applied to normal accruals. Should a firm record changes in values consequent upon changes in prices even though no transaction *by the firm* has taken place? Should accountants try to incorporate the impact of price changes into the basic accounts? These are questions which have split accountants over the years. Some have asserted that the reliability of financial statements will suffer if changing prices are accounted for as they occur; others insist that the *relevance* and *representational faithfulness* of statements will be diminished if changing prices are *not* accounted for.

Consider the Schaefer Bookstore example of Chapter 2. Suppose that corporate management elected to locate a store in the center of town rather than in a suburban shopping mall. They chose the in-town site anticipating that the City would undertake an economic revitalization plan for the area surrounding the store. Having forecast correctly, they saw the value of their property increase by over 25 percent immediately upon the decision of the City Council to undertake its improvement program.

The bookstore will reap the benefits (cash flows) of the revitalization either through *use* of the property and enhanced sales over its years of operation or through *sale* of its property. The accounting issue is one of timing—when to recognize the gain. Current value advocates would say that it should be recognized when there is measurable evidence that the property increased in value. In that way the gain would be assigned to a period within the tenure of the management team that made the correct location decision. It was in that period, after all, that there was an increase in the value of the company's assets (resources that are expected to yield future economic benefits). Countering objections that the property values might subsequently fall, they would contend that a loss should be recognized when the values decline. Thus income should not be smoothed by offsetting gains of one period with losses of another.

Changes in Specific Prices versus Changes in the General Price Level

Prices of goods and services increase or decrease for at least two reasons. First, there might be a change in either the demand for or supply of a specific product. A change in either would affect market value. Second, the purchasing power of the monetary unit (e.g., the dollar) may change. On average, taking into account all goods and services bought and sold in the economy, the monetary unit might buy more or less today than in a previous period. Although the number of monetary units required to buy a product might change, the price relationship between the product and that of other goods or services will remain the same. Increases in the number of monetary units required to purchase a typical *basket* of consumer goods is referred to as *inflation*.

Example

Suppose that in December 1993 a company acquired land at a cost of $100,000 and sold it in 1994 for $125,000—an apparent gain of $25,000 dollars. Assume further, however, that during the year, the general level of prices increased by 15 percent. That is, a basket of typical consumer items that could have been purchased in December 1993 for $1,000 would have cost $1,150 in December 1994. In terms of goods and services—the only terms in which a dollar has meaning—it can be said that 1.00 1993 dollar was the equivalent of 1.15 1994 dollars:

$$\$^{93}\ 1.00\ =\ \$^{94}\ 1.15$$

Most often the general price level is stated as an index value. One widely cited index is the *Consumer Price Index (CPI)*, maintained by the U.S. Department of Labor. The CPI expresses prices of various years as percentages of prices of a selected base year. The base year is assigned a value of 100. If, for example, 1993 is the base year, then the price level of 1994, in which prices are 15 percent higher, would be 115.

Thus, the land acquired for $100,000 nominal (unadjusted) 1993 dollars must be thought of as having been acquired for 115,000 *1994 dollars*. The $115,000 was derived by multiplying the acquisition cost by the ratio of the 1994 price index value to that of the 1993 value:

$$\$100,000\ \times\ 115/100\ =\ \$115,000$$

The gain on sale, expressed in *constant* dollars—in this case, dollars of December 1994—is therefore only $10,000, rather than $25,000 in *nominal* (unadjusted) dollars:

Sales price, 1994 dollars	$125,000
Acquisition cost, 1994 dollars	115,000
Gain on sale, 1994 dollars	$ 10,000

FOUR POSSIBLE ACCOUNTING MODELS

The distinction between changes in *specific prices* (or values) and changes in the *general price level* suggests that accounting models can take at least four forms:

1. *Historical costs/nominal dollars*. This is the traditional accounting model, with resources stated at historical costs, without adjustment for changes in price levels.
2. *Historical costs/constant dollars*. In this model, resources are stated at their historical costs, expressed in dollars of the balance sheet (current) date rather than dollars of acquisition date.
3. *Current costs/nominal dollars*. In this model, resources are adjusted to take into account changes in market values, but no recognition is given to changes in the purchasing power of the dollar.
4. *Current costs/constant dollars*. Under this structure, resources are stated at market values, adjusted for changes in the purchasing power of the dollar.

Example

A company purchased land for $100,000 in December 1993. The land rose in value to $125,000 by December 1994. Retaining the land for another year, the firm then sold it on December 31, 1995, for $130,000. The price level was 100 when the company acquired the land. It was 115 on December 31, 1994; it was 127 on December 31, 1995.

EXHIBIT 15-1
Comparison of Four Accounting Models

Acquisition cost of land	$100,000
Market value of land, December 31, 1994	$125,000
Market value of land, December 31, 1995	$130,000
Constant dollars are those of December 31, 1995	
Consumer Price Index, December 31, 1993	100
Consumer Price Index, December 31, 1994	115
Consumer Price Index, December 31, 1995	127

	Historical Costs/Nominal Dollars	Historical Costs/Constant (1995) Dollars	Current Costs/Nominal Dollars	Current Costs/Constant (1995) Dollars
Acquisition cost of land, December 31, 1993	$100,000	$127,000[1]	$100,000[2]	$127,000[1]
Book value of land, December 31, 1994	100,000	127,000[1]	125,000[3]	138,043[4]
Gain on land, 1994	0	0	25,000	11,043
Sale price of land, December 31, 1995	130,000	130,000	130,000	130,000
Gain on land, 1995[5]	30,000	3,000	5,000	(8,043)

[1]$100,000 × 1.27/1.00.
[2]Market value of land on December 31, 1993.
[3]Market value of land on December 31, 1994.
[4]Market value of $125,000 × 1.27/1.15—the ratio of the purchasing power of the dollar on December 31, 1995 (1.27) to that of December 31, 1994 (1.15).
[5]Sale price of land less book value of land on December 31, 1994.

Exhibit 15-1 compares the value of the land under each of the four models. It also shows the reported income (gain on land) for 1994 and 1995 using each model. Income is the difference between the selling price of the land on December 31, 1995, and its stated value on December 31, 1994. Notice that under the two nominal-dollar models, the firm earned income for the two years combined of $30,000, whereas under the two constant-dollar models it had income of only $3,000 (expressed in the monetary unit of 1995). Thus, in actual purchasing power, the firm gained only $3,000. Further, the *division* of the total gains (both nominal and real) between the two years differs sharply by model. Under the current cost models a portion of the income is assigned to 1994, whereas under the historical cost models, the entire income is allocated to 1995. Under the historical cost models the management team of 1994 would have received no credit for the increase in value that occurred during that year.

DOES IT MAKE A DIFFERENCE?

FASB *Statement No. 33* required what was, in essence, *current cost/constant dollar* information. Exhibit 15-2 illustrates the disclosures of Quaker Oats. Current cost *operating* income for 1986 was $134.0 million as compared to historical cost income of $174.2—a disparity of 30 percent! Net current cost assets were $1,197.9 compared with historical cost assets of $831.1—a variation of 44 percent!

EXHIBIT 15-2

The Quaker Oats Company and Subsidiaries

Consolidated Statement of Income from Continuing Operations
Adjusted for Changing Prices

Dollars in Millions

Year Ended June 30, 1986	As Reported in the Primary Statements	Adjusted for Changes in Specific Prices (Current Costs)
Net Sales	$3,670.7	$3,670.7
Cost of goods sold (excluding depreciation expenses)	$2,061.8	$2,063.0
Depreciation expense	76.9	119.4
Selling, general and administrative expenses (excluding depreciation expense)	1,171.1	1,171.1
Interest expense—net	33.3	33.3
Other expense	12.0	15.4
Provision for income taxes	141.4	141.4
Income from Continuing Operations	174.2	127.1
Gain from decline in purchasing power of net amounts owed		6.9
Total	$ 174.2	$ 134.0
Increase in current cost of inventories and property, plant, and equipment held during the year*		$ 94.0
Effect of increase in general price level†		25.6
Excess of increase in specific prices over the general price level		$ 68.4

*At June 30, 1986, current cost of inventory was $433.6 million and current cost of property, plant, and equipment, net of accumulated depreciation, was $1,123.8 million.

†Based on the U.S. Consumer Price Index for all Urban Consumers.

As with most companies, a substantial portion of the difference in income results from the greater depreciation charged under the current cost/constant dollar model. The additional depreciation is attributable to the restated value of long-lived plant assets, which had been acquired many years earlier. However, a considerable part of the increase in the current cost of inventories, plant, and equipment ($25.6 of $94.0 million) results from increases in the general level of prices rather than specific price changes.

A few companies, McDonald's Corporation (''billions sold'') being especially notable, went considerably beyond the standard format for *Statement No. 33* information illustrated by the Quaker Oats statement. McDonald's, over the years 1980 through 1985, presented a complete set of current cost/constant dollar statements. These statements reconciled income with the change in ownership equity on a comparative current cost/constant dollar balance sheet along the lines illustrated in the Daniel Gee example that follows.

The extent of differences between traditional statements and current cost statements are not the same for all firms. They are affected by the average asset age, rate of turnover, and proportion of assets and liabilities that are monetary (having a specified dollar amount, such as accounts receivables and payables) rather than nonmonetary.

EXHIBIT 15-2 Continued

Five-Year Comparison of Selected Supplementary Financial Data
Adjusted for Effects of Changing Prices*
Dollars in Millions (Except Per Share Data)

Year Ended June 30	1986	1985	1984	1983	1982
Net					
Constant dollar	$3,670.7	$3,622.3	$3,575.5	$2,895.5	$2,980.2
Historical	3,670.7	3,520.1	3,344.1	2,611.3	2,576.2
Income from continuing operations					
Current cost	$ 127.1	$ 86.1	$ 73.5	$ 73.8	$ 76.7
Historical	174.2	156.6	138.7	119.3	117.3
Income from continuing operations					
per common share					
Current cost	$ 3.33	$ 2.01	$ 1.72	$ 1.75	$ 1.84
Historical	4.35	3.76	3.35	2.91	2.90
Gain from decline in purchasing					
power of net amounts owed	$ 6.9	$ 15.6	$ 18.3	$ 11.0	$ 31.2
Net assets at year end					
Current cost	$1,196.9	$1,194.5	$1,548.7	$1,184.6	$1,239.7
Historical	831.1	824.8	758.6	680.7	675.9
Increase in the general price level					
over/(under) increase in specific					
prices of inventories and property,					
plant, and equipment	$ (68.4)	$ (48.7)	$ (12.8)	$ (32.2)	$ (27.4)
Exchange adjustment					
Current cost	$ 53.1	$ 28.1	$ 36.5	$ 27.3	$ 53.8
Historical	35.3	20.0	22.1	20.7	27.9
Dividends declared per common					
share					
Constant dollar	$ 1.40	$ 1.28	$ 1.17	$ 1.11	$ 1.05
Historical	1.40	1.24	1.10	1.00	.90
Market price per common share					
at year end					
Constant dollar	$ 78.13	$ 53.64	$ 34.08	$ 28.22	$ 21.93
Historical	78.13	52.13	31.88	25.44	19.44
Average U.S. consumer price index					
(1967 = 100)	326.0	316.8	304.9	294.0	281.8

*All constant dollar and current cost amounts are stated in average fiscal year 1986 dollars.

ADJUSTING HISTORICAL COST STATEMENTS FOR CHANGES IN SPECIFIC PRICES

In this section we demonstrate a general approach to adjusting historical cost accounts for changes in *specific* prices. Thus we illustrate a model based on *current costs/nominal dollars.* In a following section we extend the model to encompass changes in the overall level of prices (inflation), thereby transforming it into a *current costs/constant dollar* model. *Current cost* is used to mean an *input value*—the amount that it would cost to *replace* an asset.[1]

[1]In a variation of the model presented, current cost could be defined as an *exit* value—the amount for which an asset could be sold. See Phillip W. Bell, *CVA, CCA and CoCoA: How Fundamental Are the Differences?* Australian Accounting Research Foundation, Melbourne, 1982, pp. 35–36, for a discussion of the two approaches.

Historical cost statements of Daniel Gee, Inc., are presented in Exhibits 15-3 through 15-5. Exhibit 15-6 contains additional information relating to the firm. The company was incorporated on December 31, 1993, and all assets and liabilities are stated at their current costs as of that date. The fashioning of current cost/nominal dollar statements, shown as an end product in Exhibits 15-7 and 15-8, proceeds as illustrated in the section that follows.

EXHIBIT 15-3

Daniel Gee, Inc.
Balance Sheets as of December 31, 1994 and 1993

		1994			1993
Assets					
Cash		$ 46,000			$180,000
Accounts receivable		300,000			0
Merchandise inventory		260,000			100,000
Land		60,000			60,000
Building	$400,000			$400,000	
Less: Accumulated depreciation	20,000	380,000		0	400,000
Equipment	250,000			250,000	
Less: Accumulated depreciation	50,000	200,000		0	250,000
Total assets		$1,246,000			$990,000
Liabilities and owners' equity					
Accounts payable		$ 160,000			$ 0
Bonds payable		400,000			400,000
Common stock, par value		300,000			300,000
Additional paid-in capital		290,000			290,000
Retained earnings		96,000			0
Total liabilities and owners' equity		$1,246,000			$990,000

EXHIBIT 15-4

Daniel Gee, Inc.
Statement of Income and Change in Retained Earnings
Year Ended December 31, 1994

Sales revenue		$1,890,000
Less expenses		
Cost of goods sold	$1,400,000	
Depreciation, building	20,000	
Depreciation, equipment	50,000	
Interest	64,000	
Selling and administrative	90,000	1,624,000
Net income		$ 266,000
Dividends		170,000
Increase in retained earnings		$ 96,000

EXHIBIT 15-5

Daniel Gee, Inc.
Statement of Cash Flows
Year Ended December 31, 1994

From Operating Activities	
Collections from customers	$ 1,590,000
Payments to suppliers	(1,400,000)
Payment of selling and administrative costs	(90,000)
Payment of interest	(64,000)
Total from operating activities	$ 36,000
From Financial Activities	
Payment of dividends	$(170,000)
Net change in cash	$(134,000)

EXHIBIT 15-6
Additional Information Relating to Daniel Gee, Inc.

Analysis of Inventory, 1994 (FIFO Basis)

Beginning inventory (5,000 units @ $20)	$ 100,000
+ Purchases (65,000 units @ an average price of $24)	1,560,000
= Goods available for sale (70,000 units)	1,660,000
− Ending inventory (10,000 units @ $26)	(260,000)
= Cost of goods sold (60,000 units)	$1,400,000

Building and Equipment, Useful Life and Depreciation

Building: 20 years; $20,000 per year ($400,000/20 years)
Equipment: 5 years; $50,000 per year ($250,000/5 years)

Bonds

On December 31, 1993, company issued $400,000 10-year, 16 percent bonds at par. Required interest payments are $32,000 every six months.

Year-End Current Cost Information

Inventory: During the year 65,000 units were purchased at an average price of $24. Year-end price lists indicate that the market value of the 10,000 units in ending inventory is $27 per unit—$270,000.

Land: Records of area transactions indicate that during 1994 the market value of land increased by 30 percent from $60,000 to $78,000.

Building: Government-prepared indices of construction costs suggest that the replacement cost of the firm's building increased from $400,000 at acquisition date to $460,000. The building has an economic life of 40 years.

Equipment: Price lists of used equipment indicate the following replacements costs as of December 31, 1993 and 1994:

	1994	1993
New equipment	$280,000	250,000
One-year-old equipment	210,000	250,000

Bonds: Interest rates on comparable bonds declined from 16 percent to 12 percent. The decline took place at midyear, after the first interest payment had been made. The decline caused the market value of the bonds to increase to $489,263. On December 31, 1994, after the second payment of interest, the bonds had a market value of $486,619.

Values of a Leading Consumer Price Index

December 31, 1993	100
June 30, 1994	105
December 31, 1994	110

The Current Cost/Nominal Dollar Balance Sheet

Under current cost/nominal dollar accounting, the balance sheet is conceptually straightforward. Both assets and liabilities are stated at their current values.

Cash, Accounts Receivable, and Accounts Payable

Cash, accounts receivable, and accounts payable are stated at the same value as on historical cost statements. Their current value is typically face value (less allowances for uncollectibles or discounts for unearned interest).[2]

Other Nondepreciable Assets: Inventory and Land

Both merchandise inventory and land are recorded at current values. Thus for Daniel Gee, Inc., merchandise inventory would be stated at current replacement cost of $270,000 (10,000 units at $27 and land at $78,000).

Buildings and Equipment

Depreciable assets such as buildings and equipment are reported at current cost *less* an allowance for accumulated depreciation. In our example, buildings will be accounted for slightly differently than equipment. For buildings, we are provided information on the amount required to *construct* a *new* building; there are no direct data available on what it would cost to *acquire* a comparable building of the same age and condition as the one owned.

The current cost of constructing the new building is $460,000. It is one year old and is being depreciated over 20 years. Current cost accumulated depreciation after one year must be 5 percent of its current cost new—$23,000.

For equipment we know not only the cost of *new* equipment, but also the market value of *used* equipment. The replacement cost of the new equipment is $280,000, that of one-year-old used equipment is $210,000. Thus on a current cost basis, the depreciation for the first year of use, in terms of market value, is $70,000. The current cost balance sheet would show accumulated depreciation as the difference between the current values of the new and the used equipment:

Equipment (current value, new)	$280,000
Less: Accumulated depreciation	70,000
Equipment (current value, used)	$210,000

Bonds Payable

There is an active market for bonds and hence the issuer can retire its bonds by purchasing them in the open market. Daniel Gee, Inc., issued its $400,000 of bonds at face value. Therefore at issue date, the coupon rate of 16 percent was equal to prevailing interest rates. Six months later, however, interest rates dropped from 16 percent to 12 percent. Consequently, the market price in-

---

[2]In some firms, such as banks and finance companies, accounts receivable are assets comparable to marketable securities. They are freely bought and sold. In those situations, the receivables should be stated at market value rather than adjusted face value.

creased to $489,263.[3] By December 31, 1994, the market price had fallen to $486,619. But this decline in value did not reflect a further change in interest rates. Instead, it resulted only from the passage of time which made the bonds one period closer to maturity.[4]

On the December 31, 1994, current cost balance sheet, the bonds would be shown at current market value of $486,619.

Owners' Equity

Owners' equity, because it is a residual, is reported as the difference between assets and liabilities. The paid-in portion is stated at historical cost amounts; the change in ownership equity, incorporating current cost adjustments, is made to retained earnings. The change in retained earnings is the net sum of the adjustments to the other accounts. The current cost balance sheet of Daniel Gee, Inc., is presented in Exhibit 15-7.

Current cost retained earnings must, of course, reconcile with current cost retained earnings of the previous period (i.e., be equal to beginning balance plus income less dividends). This reconciliation represents a fundamental check between the income statement and the comparative balance sheets.

The Income Statement

Two main types of adjustments are required to convert a historical cost income statement to a current cost income statement. First, *realizable* holding gains or losses must be recorded for each asset and liability that has been adjusted. Second, expenses must be amended to express the sale or consumption of resources based on their current, rather than their historical, costs.

---

[3]The value of $400,000 in 16 percent coupon bonds (8 percent or $32,000 per period), with 19 periods remaining, sold to yield 12 percent (6 percent per period) would be

Present value of principal (per Table 2, present value of a single payment), 6%, 19 periods, $400,000 × .33051	$132,204
Present value of interest (per Table 4, present value of an annuity), 6%, 19 periods, $32,000 × 11.15811	357,059
Total present value	$489,263

[4]The value of $400,000 in 16 percent coupon bonds (8 percent or $32,000 per period), with 18 periods remaining, sold to yield 12 percent (6 percent per period) would be

Present value of principal (per Table 2, present value of a single payment), 6%, 18 periods, $400,000 × .35034	$140,136
Present value of interest (per Table 4, present value of an annuity), 6%, 18 periods, $32,000 × 10.82760	346,483
Total present value	$486,619

EXHIBIT 15-7

Daniel Gee, Inc.
Current Cost Balance Sheets as of December 31, 1994 and 1993

		1994		1993
Assets				
Cash		$ 46,000		$180,000
Accounts receivable		300,000		0
Merchandise inventory		270,000		100,000
Land		78,000		60,000
Building	$460,000		$400,000	
Less: Accumulated depreciation	23,000	437,000	0	400,000
Equipment	280,000		250,000	
Less: Accumulated depreciation	70,000	210,000	0	250,000
Total assets		$1,341,000		$990,000
Liabilities and owners' equity				
Accounts payable		$ 160,000		$ 0
Bonds payable	$400,000		$400,000	
Plus: Current cost adjustment	86,619	486,619	0	400,000
Common stock, par value		300,000		300,000
Additional paid-in capital		290,000		290,000
Retained earnings		104,381		0
Total liabilities and owners' equity		$1,341,000		$990,000

A *realizable* holding gain is the total gain on assets or liabilities that takes place during the year on resources that both remain on hand at year end and were sold or consumed during the year. It is based exclusively on changes in prices that took place during the current year. As the assets which increased in value are "used up" through consumption or are sold, a portion of the realizable holding gain is *realized*. The portion *realized* through use is the amount by which the asset-related expense based on current costs exceeds the expense based on historical costs. *Realizable* gains on depreciable assets are realized by way of additional depreciation; *realizable* gains on merchandise inventory are realized through additions to cost of goods sold.

To digress briefly from the Daniel Gee, Inc., case, suppose, for example, that in 1994 a firm acquired 1,000 units of merchandise at $100 per unit. At the beginning of the year the current value of the goods suddenly increased to $120 per unit. The *realizable* holding gain for 1994 would be $20 per unit—$20,000, in total. If the firm now sells the merchandise, current cost of goods sold would be $120 per unit—$20 more than historical cost of goods sold—and the *realizable* gain would thereby be *realized*. If the firm sold 750 units in 1994, it would *realize* $15,000 of the realizable gain—$20 times 750. If it sold the remaining 250 units in 1995, it would then realize the remaining $5,000 of the realizable gain—$20 times 250. The table that follows shows how the holding gain affects income both at the time it takes place and in the periods in which it is realized. The table incorporates the further assumption that the selling price of the goods was $150 per unit.

Total income over the two years under each of the two models is the

	Current Cost		Historical Cost	
	1994	1995	1994	1995
Sales revenue (750 and 250 units sold @ $150)	$112,500	$37,500	$112,500	$37,500
Realizable holding gain	20,000	0	—	—
Total revenue	132,500	37,500	112,500	37,500
Cost of goods sold:				
Historical ($100 per unit)	75,000	25,000	75,000	25,000
Realized holding gain ($20 per unit)	15,000	5,000	—	—
Total cost of goods sold	90,000	30,000	75,000	25,000
Net income	$ 42,500	$ 7,500	$ 37,500	$12,500

same. The realizable gain under the current cost model is offset by its subsequent realization.

In the income statement of Daniel Gee, Inc., realizable gains and losses are reported in a separate section of the income statement. The realized portions are included in their related expenses (e.g., cost of gods sold, depreciation, interest).

Realizable Holding Gain on Inventory and Current Cost of Goods Sold

As illustrated in Chapter 8, the *realizable holding gain* can be determined by subtracting the period's *inputs* into the trading process (beginning inventory plus purchases), computed at current cost, from the period's *outputs* (ending inventory plus costs of goods sold), also computed at current cost. The formula for realizable holding gain is based on the traditional equation for cost of goods sold:

Cost of goods sold = Beginning inventory + Purchases − Ending inventory

The realizable holding gain has been added:

Cost of goods sold = Beginning inventory + Purchases

+ Realizable holding gain − Ending inventory

The terms have been rearranged and expressed in current costs:

Realizable holding gain

= (Ending inventory at current cost + Current cost of goods sold)

− (Beginning inventory at current cost + Purchases)

For Daniel Gee, Inc., we have

Outputs		
Ending inventory at current cost	$ 270,000	
Current cost of goods sold	1,440,000	$1,710,000
Less: Inputs		
Beginning inventory at current cost	100,000	
Purchases	1,560,000	1,660,000
Realizable holding gain on inventory		$ 50,000

The realizable holding gain is the *cost saving* achieved by company management by purchasing goods prior to a price increase.

Ending inventory of $270,000 is the amount reported in the current cost balance sheet in Exhibit 15-7. The current cost of goods sold of $1,440,000 is the 65,000 units sold times the average 1994 purchase price of $24. Because the company began operations in December 1993, the current cost ($100,000) of beginning inventory is the same as historical cost. Similarly, the current cost of 1994 purchases ($1,560,000) is also the same as historical cost.[5]

Realizable Holding Gain on Land

Land increased in value by $18,000 during the year. This amount is the realizable holding gain. No land was consumed through either sale or depreciation during the year. Hence no portion of the holding gain was *realized* during the year. It will be realized only when the land is sold.

Realizable Holding Gain on Depreciable Assets and Current Cost Depreciation

The current cost of the building new is $460,000; its historical cost is $400,000. The realizable holding gain is therefore $60,000.

The realizable holding gain for the building, like that for the inventory, is equal to the current year's outputs minus inputs. For depreciable assets, *outputs* are the current value of the building (net of depreciation) at the end of the year and the portion of the building consumed during the year (i.e., current cost depreciation). *Inputs* are the current value of the building at the beginning of the period plus additions during the year. Thus

$$
\begin{aligned}
\text{Realizable holding gain} = \ & (\text{Ending balance at current cost} \\
& + \text{Current cost depreciation}) \\
& - (\text{Beginning balance at current cost} \\
& + \text{Additions})
\end{aligned}
$$

[5]The adjustments required to convert the historical inventory and related accounts to a current cost basis can be made by journal entries:

Merchandise inventory, current cost increment	$50,000	
Realizable holding gain		$50,000
To recognize the realizable holding gain		

Cost of goods sold, current cost increment	$40,000	
Merchandise inventory, current cost increment		$40,000
To recognize the using up (i.e., the realization) of the holding gain		

The $10,000 balance in "merchandise inventory, current cost increment" is carried over as a balance sheet debit to be added to the historical cost inventory balance of $260,000. This yields the $270,000 appearing in the current cost balance sheet in Exhibit 15-7

For Daniel Gee, Inc., then we have

Outputs		
Ending balance at current cost	$437,000	
Current cost depreciation	23,000	$460,000
Less: Inputs		
Beginning balance at current cost	400,000	
Additions	0	400,000
Realizable holding gain on building		$ 60,000[6]

Annual *current cost* depreciation charges for the building, which has an expected useful life of 20 years, would be $23,000—current cost of $460,000 divided by 20 years. This compares to historical cost depreciation of $20,000. Hence $3,000 of the realizable holding gain would be realized each year.

The current value of the equipment, net of depreciation, is $210,000. Beginning balance at market (which in this example is the same as historical cost) is $250,000. The realizable holding gain is therefore $30,000:

Outputs		
Ending balance at current cost	$210,000	
Current cost depreciation	70,000	$280,000
Less: Inputs		
Beginning balance at current cost	250,000	
Additions	0	250,000
Realizable holding gain on equipment		$ 30,000

As pointed out in the section which addressed the balance sheet valuation of the equipment, current cost accumulated depreciation at year end is the $70,000 difference between the current cost of new equipment and the current cost of one-year-old equipment. We assume that viable markets exist for both new and used equipment and quotes of current prices are readily available.

Inasmuch as this is the first year of operations, the accumulated depreciation account had a zero balance at the start of the year. Therefore the entire $70,000 must be added to accumulated depreciation and correspondingly charged as depreciation expense. Historical cost depreciation would be only $50,000. The $20,000 difference is the portion of the realizable holding gain that is realized in the current year.[7]

[6]These calculations, for both current cost depreciation and realizable holding gain, are based on the assumption that prices "jumped" at the start of the year. If we were to make the more realistic assumption that prices rose gradually throughout the year (or jumped by the full amount *after* a half-year's depreciation was charged, which has the same effect) then current cost depreciation would be only $21,500 ($10,000 for the first half-year based on an asset value of $400,000, and $11,500 for the second based on an asset value of $460,000). The realizable holding gain would be only $58,500. In effect, a half-year-old asset, valued at $390,000 (net of depreciation), is assumed to rise in price at midyear by 15 percent to $448,500 (net of depreciation).

[7]In this example, $20,000 of the total realizable gain of $30,000 will be realized in the current year, even though the anticipated useful life of the equipment is five years. The disproportionately large charge in the current year can be attributed to the relationship between the prices for new and used equipment. One-year-old equipment is selling for only 75 percent of the price of new equipment. By contrast, historical cost accounting would assign a net book value to the equipment after one year of 80 percent of initial cost.

Realizable Holding Loss on Bonds Payable and Current Cost Interest Expense

Interest rates dropped gradually over the period from 16 percent to 12 percent. This is equivalent to assuming a sudden drop in rates at midyear (after the payment of interest for the first six-month period). Thus it can be assumed that the bonds increased in value from $400,000 to $489,263 at midyear. This increase resulted in a realizable holding *loss* of $89,263, the added amount that the company would now have to pay to retire the bonds by purchasing them in the open market.

Current cost interest expense must be based on the current value of the bonds and the prevailing rates of interest. Under these assumptions, current cost interest for the first half of the year (prior to the change in interest rates) would be 8 percent of $400,000 (thus $32,000), while current cost interest for the second half of the year would be 6 percent of $489,263 (thus $29,356). Total current cost interest would therefore be $61,356.

Historical cost interest expense would be the same in both periods—$32,000 ($64,000 for the year). The $2,644 difference between current cost and historical cost interest is the portion of the realizable holding loss that is *realized* in the current period because the firm is using money that has been borrowed at more than the current rate of interest.

From a more general perspective, realizable holding losses or gains on bonds, like those on assets, can be determined by comparing outputs and inputs. In this example, for instance, we have

Outputs		
Ending balance of bonds at current cost	$486,619	
Cash paid in interest	64,000	
Cash paid for bond retirements or additions	0	$550,619
Less: Inputs		
Beginning balance of bonds at current cost	$400,000	
Current cost of bond interest	61,356	461,356
Realizable holding loss (gain) on bonds payable		$ 89,263

Bonds are liabilities. Therefore, if the current worth of outputs (what the firm *owes* at year end plus what it has paid during the year) *exceeds* the current worth of the inputs (what it *owed* at the beginning of the year plus the *current cost* of what it paid out), then the firm has incurred a *loss*. In this example, therefore, the firm incurred a realizable holding loss.

Other Expenses

Sales and administrative expenses require adjustment only insofar as they include the consumption of resources for which there was a difference between cost and market value (e.g., long-lived assets and inventories). In this example we assume that the expenses represent primarily wages and salaries, which would have been based on current market rates when they were incurred.

Daniel Gee's current cost income statement is presented in Exhibit 15-8. Note that the current cost income statement articulates with the current cost balance sheet. Not only can each of the revenues and expenses be reconciled with their related balance sheet accounts, but so too can comprehensive net income. Indeed, net income of $274,381, less the dividends of $170,000, is equal to December 31, 1994, retained earnings of $104,381.

ADJUSTING FOR CHANGES IN THE GENERAL PRICE LEVEL

In this section we extend our example to incorporate changes in the general level of prices. The resultant statements will be stated in *current cost/constant dollars*. The "constant dollars" will be those of December 31, 1994.

The overriding rationale for converting nominal-dollar statements into constant-dollar statements is that transactions that take place in different times cannot meaningfully be summarized in a single statement unless expressed in the same monetary unit. Combining transactions that took place in dollars of today with transactions that took place with dollars of past years makes no more sense than intermingling transactions stated in dollars with those expressed in francs or pounds.

The general approach to translating nominal-dollar financial statements (irrespective of whether they are in current or historical costs) to constant-dollar statements is to multiply both balance sheet and income statement values by an adjustment ratio. The numerator of the ratio will be the value of a price index as of the balance sheet date. The denominator will be the value of the index when the transaction that created the value took place.

EXHIBIT 15-8

Daniel Gee, Inc.
Current Cost Statement of Income and
Change in Retained Earnings
Year Ended December 31, 1994

Sales revenue		$1,890,000
Less current cost expenses		
Cost of goods sold	$1,440,000	
Depreciation, building	23,000	
Depreciation, equipment	70,000	
Interest	61,356	
Selling and administrative	90,000	1,684,356
Current operating income		$ 205,644
Plus realizable holding gains and losses		
Inventory	$ 50,000	
Land	18,000	
Building	60,000	
Equipment	30,000	
Bonds payable	(89,263)	68,737
Comprehensive current income		274,381
Dividends		170,000
Increase in retained earnings		$ 104,381

To digress again from Daniel Gee, Inc., for a simpler illustration, suppose that a firm's 1993 historical cost statements show the following as to a building:

Building	$10,000,000
Less accumulated depreciation	2,000,000
	$ 8,000,000

The building was acquired in 1990 and is being depreciated over 20 years ($500,000 per year). At the time of acquisition, a consumer price index was at 220. At year end 1993 it was at 280.

The historical cost of the building and the accumulated depreciation can be stated in 1993 dollars by multiplying the unadjusted (i.e., 1990) dollars by the ratio of the price index in 1993 to that of 1990:

Building	$10,000,000 × 280/220	=	$12,727,272
Accumulated depreciation	2,000,000 × 280/220	=	2,545,454
	8,000,000	=	$10,181,818

Annual depreciation, since it is based on the cost of the building, would be translated by the same ratio:

Depreciation expense, 1993	$500,000	×	280/220	=	$636,363

There are two categories of end-of-year balance sheet items, however, that are automatically expressed in year-end dollars: (1) monetary assets and liabilities and (2) assets and liabilities that are stated in current values. These items need *not* be translated. They are already stated in constant (year-end) dollars.

Monetary versus Nonmonetary Items

We will define *monetary* items as assets and liabilities that are contractually fixed or which are convertible into a fixed number of dollars regardless of changes in prices. Suppose, for example, that in 1987 a company (again, not Daniel Gee, Inc.) deposited $1 million in a noninterest-bearing checking account. Between 1987 and 1993 a price index increased from 100 to 140. If the company elected to withdraw its funds in 1993, it would still receive only $1 million. Over the period, the company incurred a loss in purchasing power, but the bank will not compensate the company for its loss by returning more than $1 million. It would be inappropriate, therefore, to state the cash at a value other than $1 million.

Other monetary items include accounts and notes receivable as well as corresponding payables. If a firm holds a note receivable, it will receive no more or less than its stated value, irrespective of changes in the purchasing power of the dollar. Correspondingly, if a firm has obligations to make contractually fixed payments, its nominal liability is unaffected by changes in the value of the dollar. In periods of inflation, creditors incur purchasing power losses, however, because they will be repaid with dollars worth less than initially contracted for. Debtors, on the other hand, derive purchasing power gains because they will be able to satisfy their debts in the devalued currency.

Nonmonetary items are assets and liabilities which are *not* contractually fixed in terms of a specific dollar amount. Assuming that their intrinsic worth remains constant, their value expressed in nominal dollars will depend on the purchasing power of the nominal dollars. As the purchasing power of the nominal dollars decreases, it will require a greater number of nominal dollars to constitute the same intrinsic value. Nonmonetary items include all items which are not classified as monetary. Among nonmonetary assets are

- Common stocks held as marketable securities
- Inventories
- Most prepaid costs, such as insurance, advertising, and rent
- Property, plant, and equipment
- Goodwill

Among nonmonetary liabilities and equities are

- Deferred revenues (e.g., obligations to perform services)
- Common stock
- Contributed capital in excess of par
- Retained earnings
- Bonds payable

Note that bonds payable, which are traded in a market and which can be acquired (and retired) by the firm at market prices, are also nonmonetary liabilities by our definition.

Current Values

Assets and liabilities that are stated in current values are also automatically stated in year-end dollars. Prices established by buyers and sellers as of a specific date (i.e., the balance sheet date) are expressed in dollars of that date, not those of an earlier time. Therefore balance sheet items stated in current values, like monetary items, need not be translated.

On a current cost balance sheet, all assets and liabilities would be stated in current values. Therefore the conversion process is relatively simple, with only paid-in capital having to be translated. On a historical cost balance sheet, most nonmonetary assets and liabilities would have to be converted. However, even on a historical cost balance sheet some assets may be stated at market values. For example, in accordance with the lower of cost or market rule, both inventories and marketable securities may have been written down to market.

Translating the Balance Sheet

Balance Sheet as of Statement Date

The December 31, 1994, current cost/nominal dollar balance sheet of Daniel Gee, Inc., can be converted to a current cost/constant dollar (often called a current cost *real* balance sheet) simply by adjusting the owners' equity accounts. The other accounts are either monetary assets and liabilities or are stated in current values.

As indicated in Exhibit 15-6, the price level, per a leading consumer price index, was 100 at December 31, 1993, 105 at midyear 1994, and 110 at December 31, 1994.

The common stock was issued on December 31, 1993, when the price level index was at 100. Both common stock (at par) and additional paid-in capital can be translated by multiplying the historical amounts by the ratio of the price level as of the balance sheet date (110) by that as of the issue date (100):

Common stock, at par	$300,000 × 110/100	$330,000
Additional paid-in capital	290,000 × 110/100	$319,000

The adjustment to retained earnings is most conveniently handled as a "plug," the amount required to assure that the equities equal the assets. More properly, it can be calculated as the net of the adjustments to the other accounts. The retained earnings balance can be verified, however, by making certain that it equals the balance in the account at the end of the prior period plus the income earned and less the dividends declared—all expressed in dollars as of December 31, 1994.

Previous-Period Balance Sheet

To state the current cost/nominal dollar balance sheet of the end of the previous period in current costs/constant dollars, it is necessary to adjust *all* current values so that they are in dollars as of the statement date (in this example, dollars of December 31, 1994). The adjustment process is straightforward: Multiply each of the balance sheet amounts by the ratio of the index value as of the end of the current year to that as of the end of the previous year. In this example, that requires each value to be multiplied by the ratio of 110 (the index value as of December 31, 1994) to 100 (the index value as of December 31, 1993).

Monetary as well as nonmonetary items must be translated. Monetary items must be translated because they have constant-dollar equivalents, just as do nonmonetary items. Daniel Gee, Inc., had $180,000 cash in a bank as of December 31, 1993. This amount is the equivalent of $198,000 dollars as of December 31, 1994. To be sure, if it had this same balance as of December 31, 1994, the bank would not return to the company a dollar more than $180,000. The $18,000 difference would be a loss in purchasing power, to be captured in the computation discussed in the section that follows entitled, "Purchasing power gains and loss from holding monetary items."

Thus the required adjustments to state the December 31, 1993, current cost balance sheet in dollars of December 31, 1994, are

Cash	$180,000 × 110/100 =	$ 198,000
Merchandise inventory	100,000 × 110/100 =	110,000
Land	60,000 × 110/100 =	66,000
Building	400,000 × 110/100 =	440,000
Equipment	250,000 × 110/100 =	275,000
Total assets	$990,000	$1,089,000
Bonds payable	$400,000 × 110/100 =	$ 440,000
Common stock, par value	300,000 × 110/100 =	330,000
Additional paid-in capital	290,000 × 110/100 =	319,000
Retained earnings	0 × 110/100 =	0
Total equities	$990,000	$1,089,000

Comparative current cost/constant dollar ("real") balance sheets are presented in Exhibit 15-9.

EXHIBIT 15-9

Daniel Gee, Inc.
Current Real Cost Balance Sheets as of December 31, 1994 and 1993
(current costs/constant dollars)

	1994		1993	
Assets				
Cash		$ 46,000		$ 198,000
Accounts receivable		300,000		0
Merchandise inventory		270,000		110,000
Land		78,000		66,000
Building	$460,000		$440,000	
Less: Accumulated depreciation	23,000	437,000	0	440,000
Equipment	280,000		275,000	
Less: Accumulated depreciation	70,000	210,000	0	275,000
Total assets		$1,341,000		$1,089,000
Liabilities and owners' equity				
Accounts payable		$ 160,000		$ 0
Bonds payable	$400,000		$440,000	
Plus: Current cost adjustment	86,619	486,619	0	440,000
Common stock, par value		330,000		330,000
Additional paid-in capital		319,000		319,000
Retained earnings		45,381		0
Total liabilities and owners' equity		$1,341,000		$1,089,000

Translating the Income Statement

Translating the income statement is more complicated. Three types of adjustments are required.

Ordinary Revenues and Expenses

First, the ordinary revenues and expenses must be translated from nominal to end-of-year dollars. Assuming that they were earned or incurred evenly throughout the year, when on average the price index was at 105, they can be translated by multiplying by 110/105. Thus

Sales	$1,890,000 × 110/105 =	$1,980,000
Cost of goods sold	1,440,000 × 110/105 =	1,508,571
Interest	61,356 × 110/105 =	64,278
Depreciation, building	23,000 × 110/105 =	24,095
Depreciation, equipment	70,000 × 110/105 =	73,333
Selling and administrative	90,000 × 110/105 =	94,286

Realizable Holding Gains and Losses

Second, the realizable holding gains and losses must be adjusted to eliminate the portions attributable to inflation. For example, the current cost income statement reports a realizable gain of $18,000 from holding land. This gain results from the increase in the market value of the land from $60,000 to $78,000. In dollars of year-end 1994, however, the value of the land at the beginning of the year was $66,000:

$$\$60,000 \times 110/100 = \$66,000$$

Hence the "real" gain is only $12,000 ($78,000 less $66,000). The rest of the gain of $6,000 can be attributed to an amount necessary simply to keep pace with inflation. This can be thought of as a "fictional" gain, in contrast to the "real" gain of $12,000.

For other assets, which have been added to and consumed during the year, the realizable holding gain must be recomputed using "dated" dollars. Thus for inventories the translated holding gain would be only $34,285 rather than $50,000 as computed previously:

	Unadjusted Amounts	Conversion Factor	Adjusted Amounts (12/31/94 Dollars)
Outputs			
Ending inventory at current cost	$ 270,000	110/110	$ 270,000
Current cost of goods sold	1,440,000	110/105	1,508,571
	1,710,000		1,778,571
Less: Inputs			
Beginning inventory at current cost	100,000	110/100	110,000
Purchases	1,560,000	110/105	1,634,286
	1,660,000		1,744,286
Realizable holding gain on inventory	$ 50,000		$ 34,285

Comparable computations would be made for the holding gains or losses on the building, equipment, and bonds payable.[8]

Purchasing Power Gains and Losses from Holding Monetary Items

Third, the purchasing power gain or loss from holding monetary assets must be computed. This is one of the most significant measures derived by adjusting the financial statements for changes in the overall level of prices. If a company holds monetary assets during a period of rising prices, it incurs a monetary (purchasing power) loss. Its monetary assets are worth less at the end of the period than at the beginning. If it holds monetary liabilities (i.e., is indebted to others), it realizes a monetary (purchasing power) gain. It can satisfy its obligations in dollars that are worth less than when the debts were initially assumed.

To digress once again from Daniel Gee, Inc., suppose that throughout a year a firm held $100,000 in cash and accounts receivable. At the beginning

[8]

	Unadjusted Amounts	Conversion Factor	Adjusted Amounts (12/31/94 Dollars)
Building			
Outputs			
Ending balance at current cost	$437,000	110/110	$437,000
Current cost depreciation	23,000	110/105	24,096
	$460,000		$461,096
Less: Inputs			
Beginning balance at current cost	400,000	110/100	440,000
Additions	0		0
	400,000		440,000
Realizable holding gain on building	$ 60,000		$ 21,096
Equipment			
Outputs			
Ending balance at current cost	$210,000	110/110	$210,000
Current cost depreciation	70,000	110/105	73,333
	$280,000		$283,333
Less: Inputs			
Beginning balance at current cost	250,000	110/100	275,000
Additions	0		0
	250,000		275,000
Realizable holding gain on equipment	$ 30,000		$ 8,333
Bonds Payable			
Outputs			
Ending balance at current cost	$486,619	110/110	$486,619
Cash paid in interest	64,000	110/105	67,048
Cash paid for bond retirements or additions	0		0
	550,619		553,667
Inputs			
Beginning balance at current cost	400,000	110/100	440,000
Current cost of bond interest	61,356	110/105	64,278
	461,356		504,278
Realizable holding loss (gain) on bonds payable	$ 89,263		$ 49,389

of the year, a price index was at 200; at the end of the year it was at 240. Had it held assets that could have been transformed into year-end dollars, the firm would have been able to exchange the assets (assuming no change in intrinsic values) for $100,000 times 240/200, or $120,000. It would thereby have retained the same purchasing power. Instead, however, at year end it had only $100,000 in purchasing power, when $120,000 was needed to acquire the same goods and services. In terms of year-end dollars, it incurred a purchasing power loss of $20,000.

The overall gain or loss in purchasing power resulting from holding monetary items can be determined by subtracting the face amount of the items from the amount of current dollars that would be required to achieve the same purchasing power if there had been no decline in the value of the dollar. However, insofar as the monetary items are acquired in the middle of a period, then the purchasing power gain or loss must be measured from the date the item was acquired to the end of the year. If monetary items are disposed of during the year, then the gain or loss must be determined from the start of the year to the date of disposal.

For Daniel Gee, Inc., we will assume (to simplify the calculations) that all increases and decreases in monetary items occurred evenly throughout the year, with the exception of the decrease in cash associated with dividends. Dividends were paid at the end of the year.

The beginning balance of monetary assets will be converted using the price index as of December 31, 1993. The cash flows that took place during the year will be converted using the price index as of midyear. The dividends will be converted using the price index as of year end.

The loss from holding monetary items (cash and accounts receivable less accounts payable) would be calculated as follows:

	Unadjusted Amounts	Conversion Factor	Adjusted Amounts (12/31/94 Dollars)
Balance in net monetary assets, December 31, 1993	$ 180,000	110/100	$ 198,000
Add: Sales	1,890,000	110/105	1,980,000
	2,070,000		2,178,000
Deduct:			
Merchandise purchases	1,560,000	110/105	1,634,285
Selling and administrative costs	90,000	110/105	94,286
Interest payments	64,000	110/105	67,048
Dividends	170,000	110/110	170,000
	1,884,000		1,965,619
Net monetary assets necessary to be as well off on December 31, 1994, as on December 31, 1993			212,381
Less: Actual net monetary assets, December 31, 1993 (unadjusted)	$ 186,000		186,000
Difference: Loss (gain) in purchasing power			$ 26,381

The complete current cost/constant dollar income statement is presented in Exhibit 15-10.

EXHIBIT 15-10

Daniel Gee, Inc.
Current Cost Real Statement of Income and Changes in Retained Earnings
Year Ended December 31, 1994
(current costs/constant dollars)

Sales revenue		$1,980,000
Less: Current cost expenses		
Cost of goods sold	$1,508,571	
Depreciation, building	24,095	
Depreciation, equipment	73,333	
Interest	64,278	
Selling and administrative costs	94,286	1,764,563
Current operating income		215,437
Plus realizable holding gains and loss on		
Inventories	$ 34,285	
Land	12,000	
Building	21,096	
Equipment	8,333	
Bonds payable	(49,389)	26,325
Comprehensive current income before loss in purchasing power from holding monetary items		241,762
Loss in purchasing power from holding monetary items		(26,381)
Comprehensive current income		215,381
Dividends		(170,000)
Increase in real retained earnings		$ 45,381

ASSESSMENT OF CURRENT COSTS AND CONSTANT DOLLARS

There are numerous characteristics of the current cost/constant dollar financial statements that make them useful for both managers and investors:

- The income statement separates earnings into three components: revenues and expenses from ongoing operations; currently accruing holding gains and losses from changes in the market value of assets and liabilities; gains and losses caused by inflation. Current operating income serves as a long-run benchmark from which to project future earnings assuming that prices will remain stable. This projection can then be adjusted to incorporate separate forecasts of changes in both specific prices and the general price level.
- Revenues and expenses of a current period are uncontaminated by gains and losses that may have occurred in prior periods. They reflect flows of resources based on current values. Income is therefore a more useful measure of current performance, particularly in comparing one firm in different years or several firms in a single year.

- Price-level adjustments increase the internal consistency of the statements. They assure that all amounts are stated in dollars of the same value rather than a hodgepodge of values from different years.
- Assets and liabilities are stated at current values, which are more likely than historical values to indicate an enterprise's earning potential. Moreover, they may even be less subjective than historical costs, which may be based upon estimates of useful life and salvage value and arbitrarily selected cost allocation formulas (e.g., FIFO versus LIFO; straight-line versus accelerated depreciation).

The model, however, is not without its limitations:

- The values assigned to resources may be highly subjective. In an era of rapid technological change, it is exceedingly difficult to determine the "current" values of assets for which no viable used-asset market exists and hence that may not be replaceable in their current form.
- In a period of rising prices, current operating income may lead to overly conservative projections of future earnings. In many firms, increases in the prices at which it sells its output may lag increases in the replacement costs of its input. Current operating income may reflect increases in replacement costs of the input immediately (through depreciation and cost of goods sold) but capture related changes in output selling prices only belatedly as they take place.
- The cost of the additional information may be greater than the benefits. Information is not a free good. The evidence, while at best clouded, suggests that the data that would be presented in general-purpose reports might not be sufficiently used to justify their cost.

The controversy as to whether supplementary current cost statements should be included in general-purpose financial reports is certain to continue for years to come. What is beyond debate, however, is that current cost data are essential for many specific decisions that both managers and investors are required to make.

ACCOUNTING FOR TRANSACTIONS IN FOREIGN CURRENCY

Overview of Issues

Similar to the issue of accounting for assets and liabilities stated in dollars of different years is that of accounting for assets and liabilities expressed in foreign currencies. Both issues center around changing units of measurement. Today, virtually all major U.S. corporations have interests in other countries, and in recent years the value of the dollar has been subject to wide fluctuations against other major currencies. The problem of accounting for transactions in foreign currencies can be illustrated by way of an example (with dollars, and deutschemarks expressed in thousands).

Suppose that a U.S. firm invested $8,840 and formed a subsidiary company in Germany. At the time the new firm was organized, one U.S. dollar was equivalent in value to 1.92 German deutschemarks (DMs). Conversely, 1 DM was the equivalent of 52 cents. Immediately after the new company was organized, its balance sheet, expressed in deutschemarks and translated into dollars, appeared as follows:

	DMs	Translation Factor	$US
Assets			
Cash	DM 1,000	.52	$ 520
Accounts receivable	3,000	.52	1,560
Plant and equipment	15,000	.52	7,800
	DM 19,000		$9,880
Equities			
Accounts payable	DM 2,000	.52	$1,040
Owners' equity	17,000	.52	8,840
	DM 19,000		$9,880

Shortly after the company was formed, the value of the deutschemark increased against the dollar. Whereas previously one deutschemark could be acquired for 52 cents, it would now cost 60 cents.

The parent company clearly has benefited from the increase in the value of deutschemarks. It holds in cash DM 1,000. In addition, it holds accounts receivable for DM 3,000. The receivables are stated in deutschemarks, not dollars. The company will receive payments in deutschemarks, which can be converted into a greater number of dollars than when the receivables were first recorded. By contrast, the advantage of holding DM 4,000 in cash and accounts receivable is offset in part by the obligation to make payment of DM 2,000—deutschemarks that are more costly in terms of dollars than when the obligation was established.

Thus the company holds net assets of DM 2,000 (cash of DM 1,000 plus receivables of DM 3,000 less payables of DM 2,000) that can be said to be *denominated* in deutschemarks. Assets and liabilities that are *denominated* in a foreign currency are very much like monetary assets and liabilities as described in the section on price-level adjustments. They are contractually fixed; the number of monetary units to be received or paid will remain the same regardless of whether the value of these units increases or decreases. Inasmuch as the company holds DM 2,000 in denominated net assets and the value of each deutschemark increased by 8 cents (60 less 52 cents), the company is $160 (DM 2,000 times 8 cents) better off as a result of the change in the rate of exchange.

The company also holds plant and equipment, which is recorded on its balance sheet at DM 15,000. Unlike that of cash or accounts receivable, the value of plant and equipment is not contractually fixed. The firm cannot automatically sell the plant and equipment for an established number of either deutschemarks or dollars. The plant and equipment have an intrinsic value apart from that of any particular currency. As the value of the deutschemark, relative to the dollar, increases, the number of deutschemarks for which the plant and equipment can be sold may remain the same—thereby increasing their value in terms of dollars—or may decline in proportion to the increase—thereby causing their value in terms of dollars to remain the same. (Note that the magnitude of any price change will depend on a wide array of international economic factors.) Thus it cannot be said with assurance that the firm has benefited from the change in exchange rates because of its ownership of plant and equipment.

The key accounting issues as to assets and liabilities in foreign currencies relate to the rates of exchange at which they should be translated into dollars and to the timing of gains or losses associated with the adjustments in their balance sheet values. Should balance sheet accounts be translated at the current rate of exchange or the rate of exchange that existed when assets were first acquired and liabilities first incurred? Should a distinction be made between assets and liabilities that are denominated in a foreign currency and those that are not? Should gains or losses on currency fluctuations be recognized in the periods in which the exchange rates increase or decrease, or only as assets and liabilities are actually liquidated?

FASB Position

In 1975 the FASB issued *Statement No. 8*, which set forth specific rules for translating currency transactions. In essence, the FASB stated that assets and liabilities that are *denominated* in foreign currencies must be translated at the current rate of exchange; other assets and liabilities must be translated at the rate in existence when the asset or liability was first acquired or incurred. Thus cash, payables, and receivables should generally be translated at the current exchange rate; inventory and fixed assets should be translated at the rate in effect when the assets were first acquired. Gains or losses arising from the "revaluation" of the denominated assets should be reported in the period of the change in the rate of exchange.

Per the guidelines of the FASB, if a balance sheet of the illustrative company were prepared immediately after the rate of exchange changed from 52 cents to 60 cents per each deutschemark, it would be translated as follows:

	DMs	Conversion Factor	$US
Assets			
Cash	DM 1,000	.60	$ 600
Accounts receivable	3,000	.60	1,800
Plant and equipment	15,000	.52	7,800
Total assets	DM 19,000		$10,200
Equities			
Accounts payable	DM 2,000	.60	$ 1,200
Owners' equity	17,000	(residual)	9,000
Total equities	DM 19,000		$10,200

Cash, accounts receivable, and accounts payable would be translated at the current rate of exchange. Plant and equipment would be translated at the "historical" rate of exchange—that which was applicable when the assets were acquired. Owners' equity is a residual; it reflects the original owners' equity of $8,840 plus the gain of $160 from holding the denominated assets. The gain of $160 would be reported on the statement of income as a currency translation gain.

Modifications to FASB Position

Statement No. 8 was one of the more controversial pronouncements issued by the FASB. Most objectionable to many corporations was the requirement that a firm continually recognize gains or losses from holding net assets denominated in foreign currencies as the rate of exchange fluctuates, even if it has no intention of actually selling those assets or converting them into dollars. Many firms pointed out that their foreign subsidiaries require a stock of assets and liabilities denominated in foreign currencies to carry out normal operations. Changes in the exchange rate have no immediate effect on the ability of the parents to withdraw funds from their foreign subsidiaries and thus to benefit from the changes in the exchange rates. The firm's holdings in foreign currencies are, in essence, they said, long-term investments, not significantly different from those in plant and equipment. Fluctuations in prices of foreign currency, they argued, should no more be recognized as they occur than should those in the prices of fixed assets.

Realizing that reported earnings may be distorted by currency fluctuations, particularly when they are volatile, the FASB, in 1981 (*Statement No. 52*), changed to a functional currency approach. A *functional currency*, as defined by the board, is the currency of the primary economic environment in which a foreign unit operates. It is distinguished from a *foreign currency*, which is defined as any currency other than a functional currency.

Under the new approach taken by the board, a firm must determine a functional currency for each entity included in its financial statements. If an entity's operations are relatively self-contained and integrated within a particular country, then its functional currency would ordinarily be the currency of that country. Otherwise, its functional currency would likely be that of its parent. The U.S. dollar would generally be the functional currency of subsidiaries of U.S. companies that are *not* self-contained and integrated within a particular foreign country. If a U.S. company owns a British subsidiary that manufactures and sells its products primarily within Great Britain, then the functional currency of the subsidiary would be the British pound. But if, by contrast, the same U.S. company operates a sales office in Mexico that sells products manufactured in the United States, then the functional currency of that unit would be the U.S. dollar. If the Mexican unit held pesos, then the peso would be considered a foreign currency.

Per the 1981 FASB pronouncement, a company must first convert the financial statements of all foreign units into an appropriate *functional* currency. The adjustment from foreign currency to functional currency must be done according to the guidelines set forth in *Statement No. 8*. Thus, for example, the statements of the Mexican unit cited previously must be converted from pesos to dollars. The statements of the British subsidiary need not be converted into a functional currency; it would already be in one.

But according to *Statement No. 52*, once a company has converted the statements of all foreign units into functional currencies, it must then translate all functional currency statements into U.S. dollars (assuming that the dollar is the *reporting currency*). The translation would be done using the *current* rate of exchange for *all* assets and liabilities. The company would not incorporate gains or losses from the translation into income. Instead, it would carry the translation adjustments directly to the balance sheet and show them as a component of stockholders' equity. This procedure is a major change from that required by *Statement No. 8* in that long-term assets must now be translated at the current exchange rate rather than those in effect when the assets were acquired. Moreover, gains and losses from currency fluctuations must be excluded from the calculation of income. The net impact of currency gains and losses must be accumulated on the balance sheet and can flow through to income only upon sale or liquidation of the foreign subsidiary.

Suppose that a U.S. firm invested in the German subsidiary described previously. As before, assume that immediately upon acquisition, the deutschemark strengthened against the dollar, increasing from 1 DM = 52 cents to 1 DM = 60 cents. This time, however, assume that under FASB *Statement No. 52*, the deutschemark satisfies the criteria of functional currency. The balance sheet of the firm would now be translated using the current exchange rate of 60 cents for all assets and liabilities (not only those assets and liabilities denominated in deutschemarks, as was done previously). Thus

	DMs	Translation Factor	$US
Assets			
Cash	DM 1,000	.60	$ 600
Accounts receivable	3,000	.60	1,800
Plant and equipment	15,000	.60	9,000
Total assets	DM 19,000		$11,400
Equities			
Accounts payable	DM 2,000	.60	$ 1,200
Owners' equity	17,000	.52*	8,840
Equity adjustment from translation			1,360
Total equities	DM 19,000		$11,400

*Statement No. 52 is silent as to the exchange rate that should be used to translate owners' equity accounts. However, if the statements of the subsidiary are to be consolidated with those of the parent, it is necessary to use historical rather than current rates. Otherwise, the consolidating entry in which the subsidiary's owners' equity accounts and the parent's investment in subsidiary are eliminated could not be made without additional adjustments.

The equity adjustment from translation ($1,360) represents the net gain from translating the assets and liabilities at the current exchange rate (60 cents) rather than that in effect at the time the assets were acquired and the liabilities incurred (52 cents). In this example, it was derived simply by subtracting total liabilities and equities from total assets. The equity adjustment would be reported only on the balance sheet. It would *not* flow through the income statement. This is in contrast to the way in which the currency translation gain would have been accounted for under FASB *Statement No. 8* and the way in which it would still be accounted for under FASB *Statement No. 52* if the currency were considered a foreign currency rather than a functional currency.

As indicated in the discussion pertaining to the previous illustration, the translation gain (then $160) would be reported on the income statement and reflected on the balance sheet as part of retained earnings.

Summary

Our economic world is one of changing tastes, resources, and technology. This inevitably means an environment of changing prices. In a market economy the intrinsic worth of goods or services is governed by forces of supply and demand. Prices, however, may change as a consequence not only of increases or decreases in intrinsic worth; they may also be affected by instability in the economy which results in changes in the purchasing power of the monetary unit. The accounting issues presented by these changes are variations of issues addressed throughout the text. Should these changes be recognized? If so, when and how?

In the first part of this chapter we presented an accounting model in which changes in specific prices are recognized as they take place—even if the changes are not authenticated by transactions in which the firm itself has engaged. In this model, assets and liabilities are stated at their current values, and gains and losses from holding the assets and liabilities are included in income in the period in which they occur. Correspondingly, revenues and expenses are measured by the current values of the resources received or consumed.

In the second part of the chapter, we extended the model to adjust for changes in the general price level. All transactions are thereby expressed in a common monetary unit—dollars of the balance sheet date. The result is financial statements that are internally consistent. An added benefit, however, is that the gain or loss from holding monetary assets and liabilities is specifically identified and reported.

In the third part of the chapter, we addressed the issue of accounting for changes in the monetary unit from a different, although related, perspective. We considered the accounting problems that arise when financial statements in one currency must be translated into those of another. Changes in the relationships between currencies affect the well-being of the reporting entity. The accounting issues of whether, when, and how to recognize these changes are similar to those involving changes in the value of a single currency.

This chapter has emphasized general concepts rather than specific rules of practice. The accounting policies for changes in prices, values, and foreign currencies are certain to remain controversial for many years to come.

Exercise for Review and Self-Testing

J. Bear, Inc., a retail store, was established on December 31, 1992. Common stock and bonds were issued on that date.

Comparative balance sheets for December 31, 1993 and 1992, as well as an income statement for 1993, are presented in Exhibit 15-11. The company needs to convert the 1993 statements to both a current cost/nominal dollar basis and a current cost/constant dollar basis.

Part I. Preparing Statements in Current Costs/Nominal Dollars

1. What value should be placed upon cash, accounts receivable, and accounts payable, assuming that there is no active market for the firm's accounts receivable and payable? At what amount should sales revenue and selling and

EXHIBIT 15-11

J. Bear, Inc.
Balance Sheets as of December 31, 1993 and 1992

		1993	1992
Assets			
Cash		$270,000	$580,000
Accounts receivable		300,000	0
Merchandise inventory		180,000	0
Furniture and fixtures	$250,000		
Less: Accumulated depreciation	50,000	200,000	0
Total assets		$950,000	$580,000
Liabilities and owners' equity			
Accounts payable		$100,000	$ 0
Bonds payable		250,000	250,000
Common stock, par value		100,000	100,000
Capital in excess of par		230,000	230,000
Retained earnings		270,000	0
Total liabilities and owners' equity		$950,000	$580,000

J. Bear, Inc.
Income Statement for Year Ended December 31, 1993

Sales revenue		$900,000
Less expenses		
Cost of goods sold	$500,000	
Depreciation	50,000	
Selling and administrative	60,000	
Interest	20,000	630,000
Net Income		$270,000

administrative expenses be reported, assuming that their recorded amounts are indicative of their current values at the time of the underlying transactions?

2. Prices on the goods carried by the firm increased throughout the year. The average *current cost* of the merchandise sold was the same as its average purchase cost—$520,000. This compares with the historical cost of $500,000. At year end the current cost of merchandise held in inventory was $240,000 (versus historical cost of $180,000).

   a. At what amount should inventory be reported? At what amount should cost of goods sold be reported?

   b. Based on a comparison of outputs (ending inventory at current costs plus current cost of goods sold) and inputs (beginning inventory at current cost plus purchases), what was the *realizable* holding gain for the year? Of this amount, how much was *realized* (i.e., incorporated into cost of goods sold)? How much remains on the balance sheet as an addition to inventory? (Note that this example involves a company that has just begun operations. In a continuing company *realized* holding gains for a particular year could exceed *realizable* gains for that year. That is because the *realized* gains can relate to gains that were *realizable* in previous years. For example, *realizable gains* on inventory would be recognized in the period of a price increase. The *realized* gain on those goods would be reported when the goods are sold.)

c. Of what use might the figures for current cost of goods sold and ending inventory be to managers and investors? (*Hint*: Refer back to the discussion of current costs toward the end of Chapter 8.)

3. The estimated useful life of the furniture and fixtures is five years, with no residual value. They were acquired on January 1, 1993. The current cost (new) of these items on December 31, 1993, was ascertained from suppliers to be $325,000 (compared with the historical cost of $250,000). It was also determined that identical items one year old could be purchased for $260,000.

a. At what amount should the furniture and fixtures be reported? What should be reported as accumulated current cost depreciation?

b. Assume (for simplicity, as in the text) that the entire 30 percent increase in the current cost of the furniture and fixtures occurred at the start of 1993. What amount should be reported on the income statement as depreciation expense?

c. Based on a comparison of outputs (ending balance at current cost plus current cost depreciation) with inputs (beginning balance at current cost plus additions), what was the *realizable* holding gain for the year? Note that, in this example, beginning balance at current cost is the same as historical cost.

d. What portion of the realizable holding gain was *realized* (through use) during 1993, the first year of the useful life of the furniture and fixtures?

e. Of what use to managers and investors are the data on current cost depreciation and realizable holding gains (which could also be called cost savings)?

4. The bonds payable were issued at par on December 31, 1992. They paid interest at a rate of 8 percent (4 percent per period) and were to mature in 10 years. During 1993, interest rates on comparable securities rose steadily and by year end were at 10 percent. As a consequence, on December 31, 1993, the company's bonds were being quoted at a price of $220,776.

a. At what amount should the bonds be reported? Verify that this value is consistent with the yield rate of 10 percent (5 percent per period) and the remaining maturity of 18 periods.

b. What is the amount that should be reported as current cost interest? [*Note*: The uniform increase in interest rates and the corresponding decline in market value are the equivalent to a one-time increase in interest rate and decline in market value at midyear. Hence interest charges can be computed in two parts: The first would be based on market values and interest rate for the first half of the year (which in this case are the same as historical values and rates); the second would be based on the market value and interest rate for the second half of the year. The market value of the bonds at midyear, immediately after the increase in interest rates, would have been $219,786. This represents the present value of $250,000 in 8 percent coupon bonds (4 percent per period) with *19* periods until maturity sold to yield the 10 percent (5 percent per period) market rate of interest.]

c. Based on a comparison of outputs (ending balance at current cost plus cash paid in interest plus any cash paid to retire bonds) and inputs (beginning balance at current cost plus current cost of interest charges), what was the *realizable* holding gain for the year on the bonds? (Note that although the outputs are less than the inputs, the company realized a gain; it could retire its debt at year end for less than it could at the start of the year. Moreover, it gained because it had the foresight to borrow at rates lower than those which subsequently prevailed.)

d. How much of the realizable gain was *realized* during the year?

e. Of what use to managers and investors are the data on the market values of the bonds, current cost interest, and realizable holding gains?

5. Prepare a current cost/nominal dollar income statement and balance sheet. Since 1993 is the first year of operations, be sure that ending retained earnings equals income.

Part II. Adjusting the Current Cost/Nominal Dollar Statements to Reflect Current Costs/Constant Dollars

Relevant values of a general price index were as follows:

December 31, 1992	100
Average for 1993	110
December 31, 1993	121

The firm's revenues were generated and expenses incurred evenly throughout the year.

1. At what amounts should the firm's monetary items (cash, accounts receivable, and accounts payable) be stated on the December 31, 1993, balance sheet? Is any adjustment required? At what amounts should they be reported on the December 31, 1992, balance sheet? (Be sure they are reported at an amount reflective of their purchasing power expressed in dollars of December 31, 1993).

2. At what amount should the other assets and liabilities be expressed on the December 31, 1993, balance sheet? Inasmuch as they are already stated at current costs, which are automatically expressed in dollars of December 31, 1993, are any adjustments necessary?

3. At what amount should the other assets and liabilities be expressed on the December 31, 1992, balance sheet? These items must be shown at their current costs of December 31, 1992 (which in this example is the same as historical cost), expressed in dollars of December 31, 1993.

4. What adjustments are required to state capital stock and paid-in capital (items which were reported at historical cost because they have no meaningful current costs) in dollars of December 31, 1993?

5. What adjustments are required to express each of the revenues and expenses (all of which were generated or incurred evenly throughout the year) in dollars of December 31, 1993?

6. Recompute the realizable holding gains for inventories, furniture and fixtures, and bonds payable by "dating" each of the elements that entered into the previous calculation of these gains. That is, multiply each of the elements by the ratio of the price index on December 31, 1993, to that on the date of the underlying transaction or balance.

7. Determine the purchasing power gain or loss from holding net monetary items (cash plus accounts receivable, less accounts payable).

a. Prepare a schedule in which you reconcile the beginning balance in net monetary assets with the ending balance.

b. Adjust each of the elements in the reconciliation by multiplying it by the ratio of the price index on December 31, 1993, to that on the date of the underlying transaction or balance. The resultant balance will indicate the net monetary items that the company should have had on hand to have avoided a loss in purchasing power.

c. Subtract the net unadjusted monetary items (the amounts actually on hand) from the net adjusted monetary items (the amounts required to keep pace with inflation).

8. Prepare the financial statements. Be sure that retained earnings equals income.

1. It has been suggested that any move away from historical cost to current cost accounting will inevitably compromise "objectivity." Is current cost accounting necessarily less objective than historical cost accounting? How objective, in fact, is historical cost accounting? To what extent, for example, do "subjective rules objectively applied" govern the accounting for both inventory and plant?

2. "If prices rose substantially over the life of a business, then historical cost (nominal-dollar) financial statements would understate reported income relative to current cost (nominal-dollar) statements." Do you agree? Explain.

3. The manager of a gasoline distribution business anticipates a significant rise in wholesale prices and acquires a substantial amount of inventory prior to the price increase. Under historical cost accounting models, when would the manager's sagacious insight be reflected in the firm's reported income? Under current cost accounting, when would it be reflected?

4. "Price-level adjustments in no way undermine the historical transaction–based underpinning of financial accounting. Constant dollar statements must be distinguished from current cost statements because the former may be based on historical costs while the latter are not." Comment.

5. "Current cost accounting makes sense, if at all, only in times of inflation. Once a protracted period of price increases ends there is no longer any reason to account for price changes." Discuss, commenting specifically on the statement's implication that *past* price changes have no effect on *present* accounting reports.

6. What is meant by a *realizable* holding gain? How, in general terms, is it computed? How is a realizable holding gain on the following assets and liabilities "realized"?
   a. Buildings and equipment
   b. Merchandise inventory
   c. Bonds payable

7. It has been suggested that holding gains distort income. Income, after all, is a measure of how much better off a firm is at the end of a period than at the beginning. How can increases in the prices of inventories or other resources, which will have to be replaced at these higher prices, enhance the well-being of a firm? Comment.

8. "The realizable holding gains on assets in current cost/constant dollar accounting may be both misleading and irrelevant if a company has no intention of selling its assets prior to the conclusion of their economic lives. Further, a realizable holding gain or loss on bonds payable may be illusory if the firm plans not to pay off its debt until maturity." Discuss, considering the merits, if any, of having a framework for assessing managerial performance that attributes gains and losses to the periods in which they are "earned."

9. What is the difference between monetary and nonmonetary items? Is it necessary to convert monetary items into constant dollars?

10. In converting the current cost/nominal dollar balance sheet into a current cost/constant dollar balance sheet at the end of a period, neither monetary nor nonmonetary assets and liabilities must be adjusted. Why?

11. What are purchasing power gains and losses? How are they computed?

12. Bonds payable, like accounts payable, have a "face value," which is indicative of the amount for which the obligation can be satisfied. Yet in our illustrations, bonds were accounted for as if they were nonmonetary rather than monetary items. Why?

13. What are the primary advantages and disadvantages of the current cost/constant dollar model over the historical cost/nominal dollar model? Over the historical cost/constant dollar model?

14. Suppose that a U.S. company owns a subsidiary located in a foreign country. Why will currency fluctuations have a different impact on monetary assets and liabilities denominated in the foreign currency than on other assets?

15. What were the primary criticisms directed at Financial Accounting Standards Board *Statement No. 8*? How were they addressed by *Statement No. 52*?

Problems

1. *Increases in prices must be distinguished from increases in value.*

   In 1990 a certain grade of lumber sold for $115 per 1,000 board feet. In 1995 the same grade of lumber sold for $165 per 1,000 board feet. In 1990, a widely used general price index was at 135; in 1995 it was at 188. By how much did the cost of lumber actually increase, after taking into account the decline in the overall value of the dollar? Express your answer in terms of 1995 dollars.

2. *In adjusting for changes in price levels, monetary items must be distinguished from nonmonetary items.*

   Indicate whether each of the following items should be considered a monetary (M) or a nonmonetary (N) item:
   a. Cash on hand
   b. Cash in bank
   c. Marketable securities (e.g., common stocks)
   d. Accounts and notes receivable
   e. Inventories
   f. Refundable deposits
   g. Property, plant, and equipment
   h. Accumulated depreciation
   i. Goodwill
   j. Patents, trademarks, licenses
   k. Accounts and notes payable
   l. Dividends payable
   m. Bonds payable
   n. Common stock, par value
   o. Common stock, capital contributed in excess of par
   p. Retained earnings

3. *"Earnings" from marketable securities may, in fact, be more than offset by losses in purchasing power.*

   As of the beginning of 1994, an investor had $200,000 in cash. On the first day of the year she purchased a certificate of deposit for $100,000 and 2,000 shares of common stock (a nonmonetary asset) of a well-known company for $50 per share.

   In the course of the year, the investor earned interest of $6,000 on the money placed in the certificate of deposit. She earned dividends of $3,000 on the common stock which she held. At year end, she sold the 2,000 shares of common stock at a price of $52 per share.

   A general-purpose price index at the start of 1994 was at a level of 159. On average during the year it was at 170, and at year end it was at 178.
   a. Determine income for the year on a conventional basis.

b. Determine the gain or loss in purchasing power for the year. Be sure to take into account (and translate using appropriate price-index ratios) each of the receipts and disbursements of cash.

c. Determine the real gain or loss (on a price-level-adjusted, or constant-dollar, basis) from the sale of the common stock.

d. Determine price-level-adjusted earnings for the year, including the gains or losses in purchasing power and from the sale of common stock.

e. Reconcile, on a price-level-adjusted basis, the equity of the investor at the start of the year with that at the end. (Express beginning-of-year equity in terms of end-of-year dollars.)

4. *Current cost inventory and cost of goods sold data can help in decision making.*

The Monzi newspaper chain is considering investing in one of two major paper mills to ensure its raw materials supply. Both mills produce the same product using machinery of the same type and vintage. Mill B is about 50 percent larger than Mill A. Mill B can be bought for $60 million, Mill A for $40 million. The income statements for the last year for the two mills are shown below (in millions of dollars). The revenues and expenses seem to reflect reasonably well the relative performances of previous years.

	Mill A			Mill B		
Revenue			$200			$300
Expenses						
Cost of goods sold						
Pulp	$150			$195		
Wages	30			50		
Other	15	$195		30	$275	
Selling and administration		5	200		10	285
Net income			$ 0			$ 15

On the face of it, Mill B would appear to be the more efficient operation. It is earning a 25 percent profit on the value of its ownership equity, while Mill A's rate of return is 0 percent. The primary reason for Mill B's better performance would appear to be its more efficient use of pulp.

Mill A reports cost of goods sold on a FIFO periodic inventory basis, while Mill B uses a LIFO periodic inventory method. Monzi's analysts decide to put both income statements on a current cost basis so far as of goods sold is concerned, using the following (historical cost) facts provided by the two mills (units, hence values, in millions):

	Mill A	Mill B
Sales, paper	10 units @ $20.00 = $200.00	15 units @ $20.00 = $300.00
Purchases, pulp	15 units @ $10.00 = $150.00	21 units @ $10.00 = $210.00
Beginning inventory	1 unit @ $15.00 = $ 15.00	1 unit @ $ 7.50 = $ 7.50
Ending inventory	2 units @ $ 7.50 = $ 15.00	1 unit @ $ 7.50
		+ 1 unit @ $15.00 = $ 22.50

a. Assuming the average purchase price of $10 is the current cost of pulp for the year, put Mill A's and Mill B's income statements into current cost/nominal dollar terms so far as the cost of goods sold is concerned.

b. Which mill do you think is the better investment for Monzi Publishers, all things other than profitability being equal? Why?

5. *Current cost/constant dollar adjustments have varying effects upon firms in different industries.*

Two companies, A and B, are in different industries. Both, however, are of the same size and do the same volume of business. The 1993 income statements and balance sheets for the two are as follows (in thousands):

Income Statements
Year Ended December 31, 1993

	Firm A	Firm B
Sales	$1,000	$1,000
Cost of goods sold	700	850
Depreciation	200	50
Total expenses	900	900
Net income	$ 100	$ 100

Balance Sheets as of December 31, 1993

	Firm A	Firm B
Inventory	$ 200	$ 800
Fixed assets	1,200	300
Less: Accumulated depreciation	400	100
Net fixed assets	800	200
Total assets	$1,000	$1,000
Owners' equity	$1,000	$1,000

The fixed assets have a useful life of six years; they were acquired in January 1992. The prices of fixed assets increased by 10 percent in each of the two years since they were acquired. Hence fair market values (new) as of year ends were as follows:

	Firm A	Firm B
December 31, 1992	$1,320	$330
December 31, 1993	$1,452	363

The inventory of both firms turns over rapidly. Their historical values are approximately the same as their market values.
a. Determine for both firms:
   (1) Current cost depreciation expense for 1992 and 1993.
   (2) Current cost of the fixed assets (net of accumulated depreciation) as of both December 31, 1992 and 1993
   (3) Realizable holding gain on fixed assets for 1993
b. Prepare current cost/constant dollar income statements for 1993. (Assume that no general price-level adjustments are required.)
c. Comment on why the two companies differ in current cost/constant dollar earnings even though their historical cost earnings are the same and their fixed assets increased in market value by the same percentage.

6. *In some industries current cost statements may be especially useful.*

LJG Associates is a real estate firm whose only major assets are downtown office buildings. Historical cost financial statements (in millions) are presented in the accompanying tables.

The firm's buildings have a useful economic life of 20 years (no residual value). As of year end 1992 they had a current value (new) of $700 million. By year end 1993 their current value (new) had increased to $800 million.

The current values of the firm's other assets and liabilities were the same as their historical values.

a. Convert the 1993 income statement and *both* the December 31, 1993 and 1992, balance sheets to a current cost basis. Be sure to adjust retained earnings for both years.

    (1) Be certain that depreciation expense for 1993 and accumulated depreciation for both years reflect the year-end current costs of the building.

    (2) Determine the realizable holding gain for 1993 by comparing outputs with inputs (with both being valued at *current costs*).

    (3) Verify your adjustments by making certain that retained earnings of December 31, 1992, reconciles with that of December 31, 1993.

b. Suppose, as is typical in the real estate industry, that the firm does *not* intend to hold its properties until the expiration of their economic lives. Which income statement, the historical or the current cost, provides the more useful and complete measure of performance? Explain.

LJG Associates
Historical Cost Balance Sheets as of December 31

		1993		1992
Assets				
Cash		$ 69		$ 30
Accounts receivable		12		10
Buildings	$400		$400	
Less: Accumulated depreciation	120	280	100	300
Total assets		$361		$340
Liabilities and owners' equity				
Bonds payable		$200		$200
Contributed capital		50		50
Retained earnings		111		90
Total liabilities and owners' equity		$361		$340

Income Statement for Year Ended December 31, 1993

Rent revenue		$80
Less expenses		
Depreciation	$20	
Interest	24	
Other expenses	15	59
Net income		$21

7. *Current cost financial statements can easily be converted into current cost/constant dollar statements. (This problem shows how to reconcile the beginning- and end-of-year balances in retained earnings.)*

    The current cost financial statements (in millions) of WXY Associates are presented below. A leading consumer price index was at the following levels:

December 31, 1992	200
Average, 1993	210
December 31, 1993	231

a. Recast the December 31, 1993, current cost balance sheet into a "real" (i.e., constant-dollar) balance sheet. Assume that the firm's common stock (reported as contributed capital) was issued on December 31, 1992. In adjusting the statements, remember that the firm's assets and liabilities, both monetary and nonmonetary, are already stated in dollars of December 31, 1993, and therefore need not be adjusted. Retained earnings can be adjusted as a "plug."

b. Recast the 1993 current cost income statement into a real income statement. Assume that all revenues and expenses, other than depreciation, were recorded evenly throughout the year. Therefore they must be translated using the average index value for the year. Depreciation was recorded at year end and based on the year-end current value of the building. Therefore it need not be translated.

  (1) Determine the purchasing power gain or loss from holding *monetary* assets and liabilities during the year.

  (2) Recalculate the realizable holding gain on the building (net of depreciation). In comparing outputs with inputs, be sure to express the net current value of the building at the beginning of the year in constant (December 31, 1993) dollars. (That is, multiply the net *current* value by the ratio of the price index of December 31, 1993, to that of December 31, 1992.)

  (3) Translate other revenues and expenses into December 31, 1993, dollars.

c. Verify your income statement and balance sheet computations by reconciling December 31, 1992 and 1993, constant dollar retained earnings.

  (1) Recast the December 31, 1992, current cost balance sheet into dollars of December 31, 1993, by adjusting all amounts by the ratio of the value of the December 31, 1993, price index to that of the December 31, 1992, index.

  (2) Make certain that retained earnings of December 31, 1992, plus income equals retained earnings of December 31, 1993.

WXY Associates
Current Cost Balance Sheets as of December 31

	1993		1992	
Assets				
Cash		$ 69		$ 30
Accounts receivable		12		10
Buildings	$800		$700	
Less: Accumulated depreciation	240	560	175	525
Total assets		$641		$565
Liabilities and owners' equity				
Bonds payable		$200		$200
Contributed capital		50		50
Retained earnings		391		315
Total liabilities and owners' equity		$641		$565

Current Cost Income Statement
Year Ended December 31, 1993

Rent revenue		$80
Less expenses		
Depreciation	$40	
Interest	24	
Other expenses	15	79
Net operating income		1
Realizable holding gain		75
Net income		$76

---

8. *The next two problems are intended to provide perspective on the relationship between realizable holding gains and depreciation. In the first, information as to value of used assets is available; in the second, it is not.*

On January 1, 1992, a company acquires equipment at a cost of $90,000. It has a three-year useful life with no anticipated residual value. Over the three-year period the cost to replace the equipment (new) is as follows:

December 31, 1992	$ 96,000
December 31, 1993	102,000
December 31, 1994	111,000

a. Prepare a table in which you indicate for each year:
   (1) The current value (i.e., replacement cost) of the equipment at year end
   (2) Depreciation expense, based on year-end current value
   (3) Current cost accumulated depreciation at year end
   (4) Net current value (i.e., current value less accumulated depreciation) at year end
   (5) Realizable holding gain (i.e., end-of-year net current value plus depreciation less beginning-of-year net current value)
   (6) Net cost of using the equipment during the year (i.e., current cost depreciation expense less realizable holding gain)

b. Compare the net cost of using the equipment over the three-year period with what would be reported in a historical cost model. Is total cost the same? Comment on the reason for differences in the pattern of charges

9. A company acquires the equipment described in the previous problem. The replacement cost of the equipment (new) is as indicated in the problem. Now, however, there is also an active market for used equipment. The fair market values of the used equipment is as follows:

December 31, 1992 (one-year-old equipment)	$50,000
December 31, 1993 (two-year-old equipment)	$20,000
December 31, 1994 (three-year-old equipment)	$ 0

Complete the requirements of the previous problem. (You might find it helpful, however, to compute year-end accumulated depreciation before you calculate depreciation expense. Depreciation expense can then be calculated as the difference between beginning- and end-of-year accumulated depreciation.)

10. *This problem shows the impact of changes in both specific prices and the general level of prices on the income statement and balance sheet. It also indicates how beginning balances are tied to ending balances.*

On January 1, 1993, Greenlawn, Inc., a lawn service company, had $80,000 in working capital (all monetary items) and vehicles and equipment that had cost, in total, $600,000. Book value of the vehicles and equipment, after taking into account accumulated depreciation, was $150,000.

The following table indicates the replacement value of the vehicles and equipment, both new and used, as of the start and the end of 1993:

	January 1	December 31
New	$1,000,000	$1,100,000
Used	300,000	320,000

During 1993 the firm reported cash sales of $700,000 and incurred cash expenses of $550,000. In addition, it charged depreciation expense of $60,000. Hence historical cost income was $90,000. The sales and expenses, including depreciation, were recognized evenly throughout the year.

The consumer price index for the year was as follows:

January 1	130
Average for the year	140
December 31	150

In its current cost/constant dollar balance sheet the firm states vehicles and equipment so that the gross value is the current cost of the assets new and the net value is the current cost of the assets used. The difference is accumulated depreciation. On its current cost/constant dollar income statement, "annual depreciation charges" is the difference between beginning and ending accumulated depreciation (adjusted for any asset retirements).

a. What would reported accumulated depreciation be at both January 1 and December 31? What would current cost depreciation expense be for the year (i.e., the difference between the two amounts)?

b. What would be the realizable holding gain for the year, expressed in *real* terms? (*Hint*: Compute the realizable holding gain using "dated" dollars. That is, adjust each of the components by the appropriate price index ratio. For example, current cost depreciation would be multiplied by 150/140, beginning balance by 150/130.)

c. Compute the gain or loss from holding monetary items during the year (i.e., the purchasing power gain or loss).

d. Prepare a current cost/constant dollar income statement. Be sure to adjust current cost depreciation as well as the other revenues and expenses by the appropriate price index ratio.

e. Prepare a current cost/constant dollar balance sheet as of December 31. Remember, neither monetary items nor assets that are already stated in current values need be adjusted.

f. Verify your computations by reconciling beginning and ending retained earnings. To do this, you must prepare a current cost/constant dollar balance sheet as of January 1. In this balance sheet, *both* the monetary items and the vehicles and equipment must be expressed in constant (i.e., December 31) dollars. Multiply both assets and contributed capital by the ratio of 150/130. Assume that the firm started the year with contributed capital (based on historical costs) of $100,000. Consider retained earnings of January 1 to be a plug.

11. *Use of LIFO may compensate, in part, for failure to adjust for changes in current costs.*

   Three companies, the LIFO Company, the FIFO Company, and the Current Cost Company, engage in identical operations. Each maintains its inventory on the basis indicated by its name.

   At the start of 1993, each firm had 5,000 units of inventory on hand, stated on its books as follows:

LIFO	5,000 @ $34	$170,000
FIFO	5,000 @ $48	$240,000
Current Cost	5,000 @ $50	$250,000

During 1993 each company purchased 24,000 units as follows:

12,000 @ $52	$ 624,000
12,000 @ $56	$ 672,000
	$1,296,000

The purchases were made evenly throughout the year and the average price was $54. The final purchase of the year was made on December 31, at a price of $56. During the year each company sold 21,000 units.

a. Compute cost of goods sold for each of the three companies as well as the realizable holding gain for the Current Cost Company.

b. Comment on the extent to which LIFO is a reasonable substitute for current cost accounting.

12. *For a start-up company, the separation of holding gains into realized and unrealized portions facilitates an understanding of the relationship between income statement and balance sheet accounts.*

A firm began operations on January 1, 1993. On that date it had $1 million in cash and a corresponding amount of paid-in capital. At the start of the year the firm acquired fixed assets at a cost of $400,000. The assets have an estimated useful life of four years, with no salvage value. Depreciation is recorded at year's end. Throughout the year the firm made purchases of inventory for $900,000.

The historical cost income statement of the firm for its first year of operations indicates the following:

Income Statement (historical costs)

Sales revenue		$1,200,000
Cost of goods sold	$700,000	
Depreciation	100,000	
Other expenses	100,000	900,000
Income		$ 300,000

By December 31, 1993, the replacement cost of the fixed assets acquired at the start of the year had increased by 15 percent, to $460,000. The replacement cost of inventory on hand at year end had increased by 5 percent, from $200,000 to $210,000. The replacement costs of the $700,000 in goods that were sold were, at times of sales, $735,000. All sales and purchases of goods and services were for cash. There was no general inflation during the year; hence all holding gains were ''real.''

Assume that the firm will prepare current cost financial statements.

a. What was the total holding gain related to inventory and cost of sales during the year? Of this amount, how much was realized (reflected in cost of goods sold) and how much unrealized (reflected in ending inventory)?

b. What was the total holding gain related to fixed assets? Of this amount, how much was realized (reflected in depreciation) and how much unrealized (reflected in year-end fixed assets)?

c. Prepare a current cost statement of income.

d. Prepare a current cost balance sheet.

13. *Current cost adjustments may alter return on investment and, as a consequence, utility rates.*

A state public utilities commission establishes rates so that utilities within its jurisdiction are permitted to earn a return of 10 percent on total invested capital. A condensed balance sheet and an income statement of Atlantic Gas and Electric Co. for the year ended December 31, 1993, appear as follows:

Atlantic Gas and Electric Co.
Balance Sheet as of December 31, 1993
(in millions)

Assets		
Cash and accounts receivable		$ 250
Inventories and supplies		16
Plant and equipment	$1,200	
Less: Accumulated depreciation	300	900
Total assets		$1,166
Equities		
Current liabilities		$ 100
Long-term debt		500
Stockholders' equity		566
Total equities		$1,166

Statement of Income
Year Ended December 31, 1993

Revenues		$417
Operating expenses and taxes	$240	
Depreciation	60	
Interest	35	335
Net income		$ 82

Return on investment is defined as net income before interest divided by total assets. Thus $82 million in income plus interest of $35 million is approximately 10 percent of $1,166 million in total assets.

As of December 31, 1992, the plant and equipment had a market value new of $1,520 million. Accumulated depreciation based on current costs was $304. As of December 31, 1993, market value new had increased to $1,600 million. There was no viable market for used plant and equipment. The average useful life of the plant and equipment was 20 years.

The market value of supplies and inventories is approximately the same as their book value. There were no changes in inventory quantity or value during the year. The market value of long-term debt was also was equal to its book value both at the beginning and the end of the year.

Revenues and expenditures, with the exception of depreciation, were reflective of current costs at the time they were recognized.

a. Prepare a current cost balance sheet and income statement for 1993. Be sure to take into account the holding gains on the plant and equipment.

b. Determine the rate of return on the basis of current costs. What would be the impact on utility charges if the commission were to base rates on current costs, assuming no change on allowable percentage return?

14. *Adjustments for changes in prices may alter assessments of corporate efficiency as measured by financial ratios.*

Shown below are the disclosures of a leading manufacturer of trucks as required originally by FASB *Statement No. 33*. (These disclosures are no longer required; they are merely "encouraged.")

a. For each of the three "models" for which data are presented, compute (1) inventory turnover and (2) plant and equipment turnover. Since data are presented for one year only, use year-end rather than average values in the denominator of the ratio. Comment on which model makes the company appear most efficient.

b. Have the values, as opposed to merely the nominal prices, of the goods sold by the company increased? How can you tell?

c. The reported value of inventories is greater under both constant-dollar accounting and current cost accounting than under historical cost accounting. Does this seem inconsistent with your response to part (b)? If so, what is a possible explanation?

Consolidated Statements of Operations and Selected Balance Sheet Data Adjusted for Changing Prices (in thousands)

	As Reported in the Primary Statements	Adjusted for General Inflation (Constant Dollars)	Adjusted for Changes in Specific Prices (Current Costs)
Revenues	$1,913,082	$1,913,082	$1,913,082
Costs and expenses			
Cost of sales	$1,565,406	$1,583,668	$1,559,658
Depreciation	96,874	135,698	129,525
Other costs and expenses	331,393	331,393	331,393
Taxes on income (credit)	(50,200)	(50,200)	(50,200)
	$1,943,473	$2,000,559	$1,970,376
Net earnings (loss)	$ (30,391)	$ (87,477)	$ (57,294)
Inventories	$ 238,057	$ 379,322	$ 356,558
Net properties and equipment leased to customers	$ 731,007	$1,105,280	$1,059,759
Effect of increase in general price level on cost of inventories; property, plant, and equipment; and equipment leased to customers held during year			$ 30,312
Decrease in specific prices (current costs)			19,316
Excess of increase in general price level over decrease in specific prices			$ 49,628

15. *Forest product firms have special problems of determining current cost.*

The table on the following page is an excerpt from the supplementary inflation accounting information in an annual report of Champion International Corporation, a producer of paper, building materials, and other forest-related products. (Amounts are in millions of dollars.)

a. Has the cost of the products sold increased in *value* (as opposed to price) since the products were acquired? Explain.

b. Did the firm, on average, hold net monetary assets, or was it obligated for net monetary liabilities during the year? Explain.

c. Did the current cost adjustments pertaining to inventories and property, plant, and equipment increase or decrease income (after taking into account real holding gains) relative to historical cost income?

d. A substantial portion of the firm's assets are in standing timber (i.e., trees). Many of the trees are too young for sale. How would you propose that the firm determine the current cost of its standing timber?

Champion International Corporation

	As Reported in the Historical Dollar Statements	Adjusted for General Inflation	Adjusted for Changes in Specific Prices
Net sales	$3,753	$3,753	$3,753
Cost of products sold (excluding depreciation and cost of timber harvested)	2,985	3,032	3,011
Depreciation and cost of timber harvested	148	218	230
Selling, general, and administrative expenses (excluding depreciation)	369	369	369
Interest and debt expense	58	58	58
Other (income) expense, net	(31)	(31)	(31)
	3,529	3,646	3,637
Income before income taxes	224	107	116
Income taxes	42	42	42
Income from continuing operations	$ 182	$ 65	$ 127
Gain from decline in purchasing power of net amounts owed		$ 127	$ 74
Increase in specific prices (current cost) of inventories; property, plant, and equipment; and timber and timberlands held during the year			$ 446
Effect of increase in general price level (constant dollar)			478
Excess of increase in general price level over increase in specific prices			$ 32

16. *The main reason for controversy over currency conversion is uncertainty as to when a company will actually reap the benefits from, or incur the costs of, changes in exchange rates.*

Exports, Inc., a U.S. company, purchased for 10 million baht (B) the entire outstanding common stock of a firm in Thailand. At the time of acquisition, $1 = 23 B. The balance sheet of the subsidiary, in baht, appeared as follows (in thousands):

Assets	
Cash	8,600 B
Accounts receivable	11,200
Inventory	4,500
Plant and equipment	25,700
Total assets	50,000 B
Equities	
Accounts payable	4,900 B
Notes payable	35,100
Common stock	10,000
Total equities	50,000 B

Shortly after the acquisition, the Thai government devalued the baht so that the exchange rate was now $1 = 40 B.
a. What do you think was the value of the inventory, plant, and equipment, expressed in dollars, prior to the devaluation (assume that book values are rep-

resentative of market values)? What do you think will be the value of the same assets subsequent to the devaluation? Explain.

b. What do you think was the value of the net liabilities denominated in baht (cash and receivables less accounts and notes payable), expressed in dollars, prior to the devaluation? What do you think will be their value subsequent to the devaluation? Explain.

c. Do you think that Exports, Inc. (the parent company), has benefited from the devaluation? Discuss, making alternative assumptions as to the relationship between the parent and the subsidiary and the nature of the business carried out by the subsidiary. Under what circumstances do you think that the consolidated entity should report a gain or loss from the change in the exchange rate?

d. Assume that the subsidiary is a fully integrated company that conducts business primarily in Thailand. Convert the balance sheet of the subsidiary to dollars. Justify the conversion factors used and the manner in which you accounted for any gains or losses.

17. *The nature of the foreign unit determines the way in which its currency is converted.*

America, Inc., established a New Zealand subsidiary, Rotorua Industries Ltd. Shortly after the new firm was organized, it prepared the following balance sheet (in thousands of New Zealand dollars):

Rotorua Industries Ltd. Balance Sheet as of January 1, 1993 (New Zealand dollars, in thousands)	
Assets	
Cash	$ 7,000
Notes receivable	9,000
Inventory	12,000
Property, plant, and equipment	26,000
Total assets	$54,000
Equities	
Accounts payable	$10,000
Bonds payable	15,000
Contributed capital	29,000
Total equities	$54,000

At the time the subsidiary was formed, the rate of exchange was $NZ 1 = $US .70. Shortly after the company was organized, the U.S. dollar strengthened against the New Zealand dollar to $NZ 1 = $US .65.

Rotorua Industries Ltd. is a fully integrated manufacturing and sales subsidiary and conducts business entirely in New Zealand.

a. Convert the balance sheet of Rotorua Industries Ltd. to U.S. dollars so that it can be consolidated into the financial statements of its parent. What would be the effect of the conversion on income of the parent?

b. Assume instead that Rotorua Industries Ltd. is merely a sales agent for the parent and that many of its transactions are conducted in U.S. dollars. Convert the balance sheet to U.S. dollars and indicate the effect of the conversion on income of the parent.

c. How can you justify the differences in conversion rates used for parts (a) and (b)?

Part 1. Current Costs/Nominal Dollars

1. None of these items have to be adjusted. Their historical values are also their current values.

2. a. Inventory should be reported at $240,000, its current cost at year end. Cost of goods sold should be reported at $520,000, the current cost of the goods sold at time of sale.

    b.

Outputs		
Ending inventory at current cost	$240,000	
Current cost of goods sold	520,000	$760,000
Inputs		
Beginning inventory at current cost	$ 0	
Purchases	680,000	680,000
Realizable holding gain on inventory		$ 80,000

    Realized holding gains of a period are the excess of the current cost of inputs consumed in a period over their historical cost. Thus, in this example, the realized gain is the $520,000 current cost of goods sold less the $500,000 historical cost—$20,000.

    c. In Chapter 8 it was noted that managers and investors can be misled by traditional historical cost inventory procedures such as FIFO and LIFO. We presented an example in which sales declined and inventory prices increased. Under FIFO the company reported an increase in income. Under LIFO it reported a decline in income that far exceeded the decline in sales. The reason for the anomaly is that both LIFO and FIFO inventory costs do not reflect all events of the present period but do reflect events of prior periods. The current cost framework captures *all* events of the present period and *only* events of the present period.

3. a. Furniture and fixtures should be reported gross, at $325,000, the current cost of new assets. They should be reported net at $260,000, the current cost of one-year-old assets. The difference of $65,000 should be reported as accumulated depreciation.

    b. Inasmuch as 1993 was the first year of operations, depreciation expense would also be $65,000.

    c.

Outputs		
Ending balance (net) at current cost	$260,000	
Current cost depreciation	65,000	$325,000
Inputs		
Beginning balance (net) at current cost	$ 0	
Purchases	250,000	250,000
Realizable holding gain on furniture and fixtures		$ 75,000

    d. The realized portion of the realizable gains in the difference between current cost depreciation of $65,000 and historical cost depreciation of $50,000—thus

$15,000. As with inventory, this represents the excess of the current cost of inputs consumed in the period over their historical cost.

e. Managers should be held accountable (by investors and other managers) for the efficiency and effectiveness with which they control and consume resources each period. The value of the resources on hand, as well as the portion consumed, can most meaningfully be determined with reference to current market prices, not historical costs. Historical costs incorporate into income decisions and events of the past. At the same time, managers should also be assessed on their purchase decisions. They should be rewarded for having the foresight to acquire and hold assets prior to increases in prices. The cost savings from wise early purchases will be reflected in realizable holding gains.

4. a. The bonds should be reported at their current market value of $220,776.

Present value of principal (per Table 2, present value of a single payment) 5%, 18 periods, $250,000 × .41552	$103,880
Present value of interest (per Table 4, present value of an annuity) 5%, 18 periods, $10,000 × 11.6896	116,896
Present value of payments	$220,776

b.
Beginning-of-year market value of $250,000 × .04	$10,000
Midyear market value of $219,786 × .05	10,989
Total current cost interest	$20,989

c.
Outputs		
Ending balance at current cost	$220,776	
Cash paid in interest	20,000	
Cash paid to retire bonds	0	$240,776
Inputs		
Beginning balance at current cost	$250,000	
Current cost of interest on bonds	20,989	270,989
Realizable holding loss (gain) on bonds payable		($ 30,213)

d. Of this amount $989 was realized. This is the difference between current interest cost of $20,989 and historical interest cost of $20,000.

e. Managers should be held accountable for financing a firm's assets as well as for using them. Current cost data on market values of bonds and rates of interest as well as realizable holding gains provide information as to whether the company effected cost savings by borrowing on favorable terms when interest rates were low and market prices high. Such data are extremely useful in evaluating and controlling a firm's borrowing activities. As has sometimes been pointed out, "one manages what one measures; one does not and cannot manage what one does not measure."

EXHIBIT 15-12

J. Bear, Inc.
Current Cost Balance Sheets as of December 31
(current costs/nominal dollars)

		1993	1992
Assets			
Cash		$ 270,000	$580,800
Accounts receivable		300,000	0
Merchandise inventory		240,000	0
Furniture and fixtures	$325,000		
Less: Accumulated depreciation	65,000	260,000	0
Total assets		$1,070,000	$580,000
Liabilities and owners' equity			
Accounts payable		$ 100,000	$ 0
Bonds payable		220,776	250,000
Common stock, par value		100,000	100,000
Capital in excess of par		230,000	230,000
Retained earnings		419,224	0
Total liabilities and owners' equity		$1,070,000	$580,000

J. Bear, Inc.
Current Cost Income Statement for Year Ended December 31, 1993
(current costs/nominal dollars)

Sales revenue		$900,000
Less expenses		
Cost of goods sold	$520,000	
Depreciation	65,000	
Selling and administrative	60,000	
Interest	20,989	665,989
Current operating income		234,011
Plus realizable holding gains		
Inventory	80,000	
Furniture and fixtures	75,000	
Bonds payable	30,213	185,123
Comprehensive current income		$419,224

5. The current cost/nominal dollar statements are shown in Exhibit 15-12.

Part 2. Current Costs/Constant Dollars

1. On the December 31, 1993, balance sheet the firm's monetary assets and liabilities should be shown at face value; they need not be adjusted. They are already expressed in dollars of 1992. Hence

Cash	$270,000
Accounts receivable	300,000
Accounts payable	100,000

By contrast, the monetary assets and liabilities of December 31, 1992, which are expressed in dollars of that date, must be adjusted so that they are in dollars of December 31, 1993. The index on December 31, 1993, was 121; that on December 31, 1992, was 100. The only monetary item on hand at December 31, 1992, was cash of $580,000. Thus

$$\text{Cash} = \$580,000 \times 121/100 = \$701,800$$

2. Other assets and liabilities need not be adjusted. Their current costs are based on dollars of December 31, 1993. Thus

Inventory		$240,000
Furniture and fixtures	$325,000	
Less: Accumulated depreciation	65,000	260,000
Bonds payable		220,776

3. The other assets and liabilities of December 31, 1992, must be adjusted so that they are expressed in dollars of December 31, 1993. In this example, there are no other assets, only bonds payable. Thus for bonds payable December 31, 1992,

$$\$250,000 \times 121/100 = \$302,500$$

4. Capital stock was issued on December 31, 1992. The required adjustment to express capital stock and paid-in capital in dollars of December 31, 1992, is the same for both the December 31, 1992 and 1993, balance sheets:

Capital stock, par value	$100,000 × 121/100 = $121,000
Capital stock in excess of par	230,000 × 121/100 = 278,300

5. Revenues and expenses would be adjusted by the ratio of the price index at December 31, 1993 (121), to that of when the revenues were generated or expenses incurred (110). Hence

Sales revenue	$900,000 × 121/110 = $990,000
Cost of goods sold	520,000 × 121/110 = 572,000
Depreciation	65,000 × 121/110 = 71,500
Selling and administrative	60,000 × 121/110 = 66,000
Interest	20,989 × 121/110 = 23,088

6. The realizable gains would be recomputed as follows:

	Unadjusted Amounts	Conversion Factor	Adjusted Amounts (12/31/93 dollars)
Inventories			
Outputs			
Ending inventory at current cost	$240,000	121/121	$240,000
Current cost of goods sold	520,000	121/110	572,000
	760,000		812,000
Inputs			
Beginning inventory at current cost	0	121/121	0
Purchases	680,000	121/110	748,000
	680,000		748,000
Realizable holding gain on inventories	$ 80,000		$ 64,000
Furniture and Fixtures			
Outputs			
Ending balance (net) at current cost	$260,000	121/121	$260,000
Current cost depreciation	65,000	121/110	71,500
	325,000		331,500
Inputs			
Beginning balance (net) at current cost	$ 0	121/100	0
Purchases	250,000	121/100	302,500
	250,000		302,500
Realizable holding gain on furniture and fixtures	$ 75,000		$ 29,000
Bonds Payable			
Outputs			
Ending balance at current cost	$220,776	121/121	$220,776
Cash paid in interest	20,000	121/110	22,000
Cash paid to retire bonds	0		0
	240,776		242,776
Inputs			
Beginning balance at current cost	250,000	121/100	302,500
Current cost of interest on bonds	20,989	121/110	23,088
	270,989		325,588
Realizable holding loss (gain) on bonds payable	($ 30,213)		($ 82,812)

7. The purchasing power loss would be calculated as follows:

	Unadjusted Amounts	Conversion Factor	Adjusted Amounts (12/31/93 dollars)
Balance in net monetary assets, December 31, 1992	$ 580,000	121/100	$ 701,800
Add: Sales	900,000	121/110	990,000
	$1,480,000		$1,691,800
Deduct:			
Purchase of furniture and fixtures	250,000	121/100	302,500
Merchandise purchases	680,000	121/110	748,000
Selling and administrative costs	60,000	121/110	66,000
Interest payments	20,000	121/110	22,000
	$1,010,000		$1,138,500
Net monetary assets, necessary to be as well off on December 31, 1993, as on December 31, 1992			553,300
Less: Actual net monetary assets, December 31, 1992 (unadjusted)	$ 470,000		470,000
Difference: Loss (gain) in purchasing power			$ 83,300

8. The current cost/constant dollar statements are shown in Exhibit 15-13.

EXHIBIT 15-13

J. Bear Inc.
Current Cost Real Balance Sheets as of December 31
(current costs/constant dollars)

	1993		1992
Assets			
Cash		$ 270,000	$701,800
Accounts receivable		300,000	0
Merchandise inventory		240,000	0
Furniture and fixtures	$325,000		
Less: Accumulated depreciation	65,000	260,000	0
Total assets		$1,070,000	$701,800
Liabilities and owners' equity			
Accounts payable		$ 100,000	$ 0
Bonds payable		220,776	302,500
Common stock, par value		121,000	121,000
Capital in excess of par		278,300	278,300
Retained earnings		349,924	0
Total liabilities and owners' equity		$1,070,000	$701,800

EXHIBIT 15-13 Continued

J. Bear Inc.
Current Cost Real Income Statement for Year Ended December 31, 1993
(current costs/constant dollars)

Sales revenue		$990,000
Less expenses		
Cost of goods sold	$572,000	
Depreciation	71,500	
Selling and administrative	66,000	
Interest	23,088	732,588
Current operating income		257,412
Plus realizable holding gains		
Inventory	64,000	
Furniture and fixtures	29,000	
Bonds payable	82,812	175,812
Loss in purchasing power from		
holding monetary items		(83,300)
Comprehensive current real income		$349,924

16

Financial Reporting and Analysis in Perspective

In studying and evaluating specific accounts and procedures, it is easy to lose sight of the purposes of financial accounting and the reasons why it is so seemingly complex. The overriding goal of this chapter is to place in perspective the key ideas that have been developed in the earlier chapters.

In the first part of this chapter we examine the objectives of financial reporting and show why accrual accounting is necessary to achieve them. Correspondingly, we consider some of the adverse consequences of accrual accounting as it is practiced today. We shall be particularly concerned with the limitations of accrual accounting as they relate to the decisions that managers and investors are called upon to make. We also summarize the types of information that firms are required to report in notes supplementary to the three primary financial statements. In large measure the additional disclosures are intended to overcome the constraints of the primary statements.

In the second part of the chapter we discuss the relationship between financial reporting and financial analysis. We describe and evaluate in detail a ratio that has been cited previously—*return on investment*. Return on investment is considered the single most significant measure of financial performance, and as such it is focused upon by both managers and investors. Yet, as we demonstrate, efforts on the part of managers to maximize return on investment may not necessarily be in the interests of corporate owners.

OBJECTIVES OF FINANCIAL REPORTING

In 1978 the FASB published a statement of objectives of financial reporting by business enterprises. The objectives were intended as the foundation on which a logical and orderly set of accounting standards could be constructed.

According to the board, financial reports should be directed primarily to potential *investors* and *creditors*. They should provide information that is useful in making investment, credit, and similar decisions. By implication, financial reports should not be specifically directed to managers and parties internal to the organization. Managers and other internal parties, unlike investors and creditors, have the authority to prescribe the information they want and can obtain it from sources other than general-purpose financial reports.

The board stated that financial reports should provide information that will help users to assess the amounts, timing, and uncertainty of *cash* that they will receive. Investors and creditors contribute cash to a business in the expectation of receiving more cash than they give up. Their cash returns will be in the form of dividends, interest payments, and proceeds from the sale, redemption, or maturity of securities and loans. Obviously, the prospects of investors and creditors receiving cash are dependent upon the ability of the enterprise itself to generate cash through its income-producing activities. Thus financial reporting must facilitate predictions of enterprise cash flows.

In addition, financial reporting should help investors, creditors, and others to assess an enterprise's financial performance during a period. It should serve as a basis for evaluating how well management has carried out its stewardship responsibilities to the owners of the business.

NEED FOR ACCRUAL ACCOUNTING

Although a key objective of financial reporting is to assist investors and creditors to predict the *cash* that an enterprise will generate, financial statements that reported merely changes in cash balances would inadequately satisfy that objective. The amount of cash to be generated depends mainly on the economic resources available to the firm. The resources include the complete array of assets controlled by the firm—tangible as well as intangible. Moreover, the performance of an organization over a specified period of time must be measured by the changes in those resources. *Accrual accounting* captures the changes in many more of a firm's resources than does cash accounting. Financial events are recorded when they have their substantive economic impact, not only when cash is received or disbursed. Accrual accounting, for example, records an increase in level of resources when a firm makes a sale, regardless of whether the proceeds are received before or after the date of sale. It records a decline in resources when equipment is consumed over time, not when it is acquired and not necessarily when it is paid for. Accrual accounting is generally seen as providing more useful information than cash accounting for both predicting cash flows and assessing the periodic performance of the firm and its managers.

CONSEQUENCES OF ACCRUAL ACCOUNTING

Complexity

Because accrual accounting reports upon changes in the full scope of a firm's resources and not just cash, it is necessarily more complex than cash accounting. Cash accounting involves little more than the identification, classification, and summarization of cash inflows and outflows—something that could be accomplished by an analysis of a firm's checkbook. Comparability of practices among firms could be achieved by merely establishing reasonable categories for classifying cash receipts and disbursements. There would be no issues of asset valuation; the only asset to be valued would be cash. There would be no questions of revenue or expense recognition; revenues or expenses would be concurrent with receipts or disbursements of cash.

Accrual accounting, by contrast, is concerned with *income*, not cash flows. The process of resource enhancement in a firm takes place over time and involves a series of related activities. In a manufacturing enterprise, for example, it includes the purchase of plant and equipment, the acquisition of raw materials, the manufacture and sale of the product, and the collection of cash. Accrual accounting requires a firm to determine (or make assumptions about) how much each particular activity contributes to increases in the firm's well-being—what the firm's resources are at any particular time and how much they have changed between two times.

If accounting reports are to be comparable, then guidelines of income measurement must be established. But the commercial activities in which firms engage are both diverse and complicated. Financial arrangements that are similar in substance may differ considerably in form. It has proved impossible to promulgate a set of simple accounting principles that captures the economic essence of all transactions in which firms engage.

As recently as 35 years ago, however, guidelines of accrual accounting were few in number and broad in scope. Individual firms had considerable freedom in reporting upon their activities. The resultant diversity of practice decreased the comparability of reports and allowed for some clear-cut instances of intentional deception. In the last quarter century, the rule-making authorities of the accounting profession have narrowed the range of reporting options. But they have also made the set of rules to which firms must adhere more detailed and cumbersome. Greater comparability of reports has been achieved at the cost of greater complexity.

The trade-off between greater comparability and less complexity has proved especially difficult to avoid because *uniformity* of practice does not necessarily ensure comparability. The value of a firm's resources—the extent to which they will generate cash in the future—depends upon circumstances that are unique to each firm. The benefits to be derived from a fixed asset in the control of one company may differ considerably from those from an identical asset in the control of another. Accounting rules that were to require identical useful lives and patterns of depreciation may make the financial reports of the two firms uniform, but certainly not comparable.

Opportunities to Influence Reported Earnings

Despite the strides in recent years toward greater uniformity of practice, individual firms still have opportunities to influence *reported* (as opposed to substantive economic) earnings. These opportunities exist because of the inherent characteristics of accrual accounting. Over time they may be reduced in number, but they will likely never be eliminated. It is essential that managers and investors be cognizant of them, not only so they can spot blatant attempts at income manipulation, but more importantly, so that they can compensate for differences in reporting policies among firms.

The section that follows summarizes the ways in which management can influence reported earnings. Although the emphasis is on *earnings*, it must be remembered that any actions that affect earnings must necessarily affect assets, liabilities, or owners' equity.

There are three primary ways in which management can have an impact on reported earnings:

1. By choosing judiciously among acceptable accounting methods
2. By making biased estimates
3. By timing transactions so that changes in value that have occurred over time are given accounting recognition in the most opportune periods

Choosing between Available Accounting Methods

In the preceding chapters a number of areas were discussed in which alternative accounting methods may be used. Among them are

1. *Revenue recognition.* Although most businesses recognize revenue at time of sale, they may do so at other times as well. For example, revenue on a long-term project may be recognized as work is carried out (a percentage of completion basis), when the project is completed, or when cash is collected.
2. *Cost of goods sold.* Cost of goods sold and inventory values may be established by a number of methods, the most popular of which are first-in, first-out and last-in, first-out.
3. *Depreciation.* Firms may select among straight-line and various patterns of accelerated depreciation.
4. *Matching of costs to revenues.* Costs should be charged as expenses in the periods in which the revenues that they generate are recognized. Management, however, has considerable latitude in determining whether a cost should be considered a period cost to be charged as an expense as it is incurred, a product cost to be inventoried and charged as an expense as part of cost of goods sold, or a capitalizable cost to be amortized over several accounting periods.
5. *Cost of drilling unsuccessful oil wells.* Costs of drilling unsuccessful wells may be written off as incurred (the successful-efforts method) or capitalized as part of the cost of the successful wells (the full-cost method).

Some accountants and analysts characterize earnings in terms of their *quality*. The higher the quality of earnings, the more conservative are the accounting methods on which they are based. Conservative accounting methods are those that recognize revenues as late as possible and expenses as early as possible.

Making Estimates

Accrual accounting requires that numerous management estimates be incorporated into the financial reports. Among them are

1. *Useful lives.* Management must determine the number of years over which to amortize the cost of fixed assets and intangibles, including goodwill.
2. *Losses on bad debts.* Management must estimate the percentage of sales or accounts receivable that will be uncollectible, and credit such amount to an allowance for uncollectibles contra account.
3. *Warranties.* Expenses must be matched with revenues. Therefore management must estimate repair and replacement costs that will be incurred subsequent to the period in which revenue is recognized, and it must establish appropriate allowances.

Selecting the Period to Recognize Gains and Losses

Gains or losses from changes in the value of assets or liabilities are ordinarily recognized when the assets or liabilities are sold or liquidated, not in the periods in which the changes take place. Thus a firm that owns assets that have appreciated in value or owes liabilities that have depreciated has a ''reserve'' of earnings that it can draw upon at its discretion. It can engage in two types of transactions to realize the earnings in the reserve:

1. It can sell appreciated assets (such as marketable securities). The gain would be recognized entirely in period of sale, regardless of when the increase in value actually took place.
2. It can retire long-term bonds that have depreciated in value. Bonds would be traded at a price less than book value if interest rates have increased since the bonds were issued. The firm could purchase, and then retire, the bonds at an amount less than that at which they are recorded, and thereby recognize a gain in the period of retirement.

Both these types of transactions may be economically insubstantial because the assets surrendered by the firm (such as the marketable securities or the cash used to repay the debt) may be replaceable without loss of economic utility. The assets may be repurchased at the price for which they were sold; the cash may be reborrowed at a rate of interest reflective of the price at which the debt was retired.

Limitations for Managers

Financial statements based on the principles of accrual accounting are designed for investors and creditors, not managers. Managers are responsible for planning and controlling the activities of an enterprise. Seldom do they focus on predicting cash flows or evaluating the performance of the firm as a whole. Instead, they are concerned with the cash flows that can be generated by *specific* projects, activities, and assets; they evaluate the performance of *individual* managers or corporate segments.

Managers need information that is tailor-made for the decisions at hand. Reports intended for investors and creditors are often inappropriate because they fail to isolate the changes in the resources that will be affected by the decision. Revenues and expenses as reported in the income statement, for example, are usually poor predictors of the cash consequences of any particular management action. They are "contaminated" by the estimates, allocations, and choices of accounting principles required by accrual accounting. Suppose that a manager must decide whether to increase production volume. The expense, "cost of goods sold," would provide little guidance as to the additional manufacturing costs that would be incurred. "Cost of goods sold" includes allocations of fixed costs (such as those for plant maintenance) that will be unchanged by the increase in volume. Moreover, it is influenced by estimates (such as that of the useful life of existing plant and equipment) and choice of inventory method (such as that between LIFO or FIFO) that will affect reported expense, but not actual manufacturing costs. Management would require a report that focuses directly upon the incremental cash flows attributable to the increase in production volume.

Similarly, when managers review the accomplishments of departments or divisions of the firm, they must focus attention exclusively on the components of performance over which the unit has control. Earnings, as computed in accordance with accepted principles of accrual accounting, incorporate elements that are likely to be beyond the influence of the managers of a specific unit. Depreciation expense, for example, reflects decisions of the past. It is based on the amount paid to acquire an asset—an asset that may have been purchased in a period prior to that in which present managers took charge. Over time, of course, present managers can decide to dispose of old assets and buy new ones. But in the short run they are saddled with depreciation charges that they can do little or nothing to reduce.

Correspondingly, units may be credited with revenues or charged with expenses that are established "arbitrarily" at corporate headquarters. The revenues of a production unit may represent intracompany "sales" to a marketing division. The sales price (in actuality a *transfer* price since it represents the price at which goods are transferred from one unit of the firm to another) would be determined by the company itself. Its expenses may include allocations of common corporate costs (such as administrative and financing costs), also decided upon by company executives. Insofar as the unit lacks control over one or more key components of income, income cannot be used as a valid indicator of performance.

It would be incorrect to infer that financial reports based on accrual accounting are useless to managers and completely adequate for investors and creditors. Managers are themselves investors or creditors when they acquire securities of, or make loans to, other firms. And investors and creditors must make analyses similar to those of management when they decide whether to provide financial support for proposed corporate projects. On balance, however, accrual accounting is considered the preferred means of communicating financial information to investors and creditors. Reports that are specifically designed for the decisions at hand are required by managers.

The three basic financial statements are not a satisfactory means of conveying financial data to *all* investors and creditors. Users differ in their information requirements and preferences. The accounting and reporting practices that underlie the statements are the product of compromises and arbitrary decisions by rule-making authorities, the firm's managers, and its independent auditors. Moreover, the quantitative, tabular form of accounting statements can never fully capture all the events and circumstances that bear upon a firm's financial health. They must be supplemented by verbal reports and explanations.

In recent years there has been a sharp increase in the amount of information contained in notes that accompany the three basic statements. These notes form an integral part of the financial report and are intended, in large measure, to reduce the inherent deficiencies of the statements themselves. The information contained in the supplementary notes varies from company to company. The following, however, are among the more significant types of disclosures and an indication of the deficiencies that they are intended to reduce:

1. *A summary of significant accounting policies.* The flexibility allowed firms in selecting accounting principles diminishes the objectivity and comparability of financial statements. The importance of the principles chosen is reduced, however, when the firm describes the principles used and provides the particulars of the transactions reported on. The user of the report is then able to adjust the statements to reflect his or her own preferred principles. The accounting policies a firm must describe in the supplementary notes are those over which a firm has discretion. They include those relating to inventories and cost of goods sold, depreciation, income taxes, revenue recognition, retirement plans, and consolidations. Presently, firms are not required to provide sufficient details of most types of transactions to permit accurate adjustments. But the information on accounting policies facilitates at least estimates of what the adjustments would be.

2. *Details of transactions.* The three primary statements may not reveal all important aspects of transactions in which a firm engages. For example, if a firm "defers" a portion of its income taxes, then the income statement would not indicate the amount of taxes actually paid. Similarly, if a firm capitalizes its lease obligations, then the reported lease (or interest) expense would differ from the actual cash paid. Typical of transactions about which additional information should be provided in supplementary notes are those involving income taxes, leases, research and development costs, and employee stock options.

3. *Breakdown of reported amounts.* The main body of each statement summarizes groups of accounts into single figures. But there is no optimum level of data aggregation. What is necessary detail to one user may be information overload to another. A firm can best satisfy differing preferences of users by indicating summary balances on the

face of the statements and supporting amounts in supplementary notes. In this way, the firm is able to present the necessary data both clearly and completely. Among the accounts for which supporting detail is often provided are long-term debt, interest expense, fixed assets, and owners' equity.

4. *Outstanding commitments.* Accepted accounting principles do not require that all commitments be recognized. Yet some commitments may have a material impact on a firm's financial well-being and should therefore be disclosed. Examples are obligations for rent payments under noncancelable leases, promises to redeem preferred stock, and pledges to issue stock under employee stock options.

5. *Contingent losses.* Contingent losses are potential losses. They would be transformed into actual losses only if certain unfavorable events were to occur. They frequently result from pending litigation, threats of expropriation, and guarantees of the indebtedness of others. Contingent losses are reported on the income statement only if the outcome of the related event can be predicted with a reasonable degree of certainty. But the consequences of an unfavorable event may overwhelm the information contained in the main body of the financial statements. If, for example, an unfavorable antitrust ruling were to cause the firm to be divided into several smaller units, then reported asset values (based on the concept of the going concern) would have little meaning. Firms are required (by FASB *Statement No. 5*) to explain the nature of a contingency and to give an estimate of the possible range of loss even if the criteria for income statement recognition are not met.

6. *A 5- or 10-year summary of operations.* The body of a financial statement generally covers the fiscal year just ended plus only one (and sometimes two) preceding periods. Evaluations of past performance, as well as prediction of future results, require analysis of trends over time. Consequently, firms are required to summarize the financial statements of 5 to 10 years. Among the key figures the summaries indicate are sales, net income, working capital, and owners' equity.

7. *Information on lines of business and classes of products.* Many firms are engaged in a number of different types of business endeavors. Some companies are *conglomerates*: they are composed of divisions in a number of unrelated industries. Their consolidated financial statements combine the financial position and results of operations of all their activities. They indicate neither corporate resources devoted to any particular industry nor the profits derived from them. Yet financial analysis is meaningful only when one firm is compared with others in the same industry. If the financial statements fail to provide data by industry, then comparisons are impossible.

Firms have been reluctant to disclose financial information for individual lines of business. They cite the inherent difficulties of allocating common expenditures, such as headquarters' costs, to the separate businesses and of classifying all products into lines of business. They have also feared that the additional data on product lines might aid their competitors. Nonetheless, both FASB and SEC pronouncements now require that firms report revenues, income, and assets for each major line of business.

8. *Particulars of employee pension and postretirement health benefits.* These must include information on accounting and funding policies as well as the assumptions underlying any estimates of future costs.

9. *Management explanations and interpretations.* The numbers in the primary financial statements describe quantitatively a firm's results of operations and financial position. But they fail to explain and interpret them. Managers can be expected to have insights into the firm's financial history and prospects that extend beyond the reported data. They can increase the usefulness of the reported information—and in fact are required to do so—by identifying transactions, events, or circumstances that have a bearing on the firm's financial well-being but are not obvious from the statements themselves. Among the matters that management should address in notes to the financial statements are favorable and unfavorable trends, changes in product mix, the acquisition and disposal of major assets or lines of business, and unusual gains and losses.

FINANCIAL ANALYSIS: AN OVERVIEW

Financial reports assist investors, creditors, and other users in predicting cash flows of the future and assessing enterprise performance of the past. They do not, however, include actual forecasts or evaluations. Investors, creditors, and other users must do their own forecasting and evaluating.

Two contradictory assessments can be made as to the role that financial reports play in facilitating forecasts and evaluations. The first is that financial statements provide an abundance of information about the company whose financial affairs they describe. The financial statements of a company enable an analyst to gain an insight into its economic well-being with a clarity that cannot be matched by any other documents or sources of information. A measure of expertise, however, may be required to discern the true nature of the firm's financial situation.

Financial statements are comparable to aerial photographs. An untrained observer may not only learn considerably less from an examination of the photographs than a skilled analyst, but the conclusions that he or she draws from them may be erroneous. A layperson, for example, may see in a series of aerial photographs nothing more than a pastoral landscape of rolling hills and farms dotted with residential homes and barns. An expert, however, by carefully focusing on changes over time and relationships among the various structures, roadways, and power lines, may detect the presence of underground missile batteries. Similarly, a casual observer may see in a set of financial statements a seemingly stable, financially sound corporation. A skilled manager or analyst, however, by studying trends over time and relationships among accounts, may discern the existence of financial factors that point to fiscal turbulence.

The second assessment is that the importance of financial statements can be easily overemphasized. For any decisions in which the financial prospects of a company must be taken into account, an analysis of the data contained in the financial statements is unquestionably necessary. But it is hardly sufficient.

Financial statements do not explicitly provide information on a number of factors that are likely to have an effect on the future success of a company. Financial statements, for example, do not generally report upon scientific or technological breakthroughs. And they are generally silent about changes in the economic or social environment in which the firm operates. Changes in the real income or in the tastes of the consumers served by the firm could have a major impact on its profitability, but even a detailed examination of financial reports may not provide a hint of such changes.

Expertise in accounting must be recognized as being of limited utility. It enables one to prepare and interpret financial statements. But financial statements are only one source (albeit a crucial source) of information among many that must be taken into account in deciding whether to invest in a corporation. For every millionaire whose investment success can be attributed to a keen ability to interpret financial statements, there is undoubtedly another who cannot distinguish a debit from a credit.

Financial analysis is founded upon ratios and similar measures. No accounting numbers, including net income, have meaning in and of themselves. Therefore ratios are necessary to extricate information of significance from financial reports. Measures have been developed to describe quantitatively a firm's solvency and liquidity, its profitability, and its effectiveness in employing all, or selected categories of, the resources within its control. The financial measures discussed throughout this text are summarized in Exhibit 16-1. Managers and investors should never forget, however, that a ratio can be no more significant than the underlying data in the numerator and denominator. If the data are not representationally faithful to the underlying economic phenomena they purport to explain, then the ratios themselves will be inconsequential.

RETURN ON INVESTMENT

Return on investment is the single most important measure of corporate profitability and efficiency. It encompasses all revenues and expenses as well as all assets and liabilities, and it is widely used as an evaluative criterion by managers as well as investors and creditors. Return on investment was discussed briefly in Chapter 4. In this section we shall expand upon its significance and indicate its limitations.

First, return on investment may be calculated so as to indicate enterprise profitability without regard to how it has been financed. Income, excluding a deduction for interest, is related to total capital employed in the business. Interest is excluded because, like dividends, it is a distribution to the parties which provided the capital. Total capital may be represented by either total assets (the left-hand side of the accounting equation) or total liabilities plus total owners' equity (the right-hand side).

Second, return on investment may be computed so as to signify profitability from the perspective of all the stockholders, both common and preferred. Net income (with interest included along with all other operating expenses) is related to the equity of the stockholders.

Third, return on investment may be determined so as to denote profitability

EXHIBIT 16-1
Summary of Selected Financial Measures

Name	Formula	Objective
I. Profitability and activity measures		
A. Return on investment (all capital); see Chapter 16	$$\frac{\text{Net income} + \text{Interest after taxes}}{\text{Average assets}}$$	To indicate the effectiveness of a business in employing *all* resources within its command
B. Return on investment (stockholders' equity); see Chapter 16	$$\frac{\text{Net income}}{\text{Average stockholders' equity}}$$	To indicate the effectiveness of a business in employing capital provided by stockholders
C. Return on equity of common stockholders; see Chapter 16	$$\frac{\text{Net income} - \text{Preferred stock dividends}}{\text{Average equity of common stockholders}}$$	To indicate the effectiveness of a business in employing capital provided by common stockholders
D. Price/earnings ratio; see Chapter 4	$$\frac{\text{Market price per share}}{\text{Earnings per share}}$$	To measure the return on the market value of common stock
E. Inventory turnover; see Chapter 8	$$\frac{\text{Cost of goods sold}}{\text{Average inventory}}$$	To measure the efficiency of inventory
F. Accounts receivable turnover; see Chapter 7	$$\frac{\text{Sales}}{\text{Average accounts receivable}}$$	To measure the efficiency of accounts receivable
G. Number of days' sales in accounts receivable; see Chapter 7	$$\frac{\text{Accounts receivable}}{\text{Average sales per day}}$$	To determine the average number of days in which accounts receivable are outstanding
H. Plant and equipment turnover; see Chapter 9	$$\frac{\text{Sales}}{\text{Average plant and equipment}}$$	To measure the efficiency of plant and equipment
II. Liquidity ratios		
A. Current ratio; see Chapter 4	$$\frac{\text{Current assets}}{\text{Current liabilities}}$$	To measure a firm's ability to meet current obligations as they come due
B. Quick ratio; see Chapter 7	$$\frac{\text{Cash} + \text{Marketable securities} + \text{Accounts receivable}}{\text{Current liabilities}}$$	To measure, by a more severe test, a firm's ability to meet current obligations as they come due
III. Financing measures		
A. Debt-to-equity ratio; see Chapter 11	$$\frac{\text{Total debt}}{\text{Total ownership equity}}$$	To indicate the proportion of capital provided by creditors rather than by owners
B. Times interest earned; see Chapter 10	$$\frac{\text{Net income} + \text{Interest} + \text{Income taxes}}{\text{Interest}}$$	To measure a firm's ability to meet fixed interest charges

to the common stockholders alone. Net income, less the dividends to the preferred stockholders, is related to the equity of the common stockholders (that is, capital contributed by the common stockholders plus retained earnings).

Return on Investment (All Capital)

During 1991 American Home Products (see Exhibit 16-2) employed on *average* $5,788.0 million in capital. This was determined by summing the *total assets* at the end of 1991 and 1990 and dividing by 2. It is preferable to base the computation on the average capital rather than that at a single date to avoid distortions that would result if capital had been acquired or returned to investors during the year. Since the firm would not have had use of such capital for an entire year, it should not be expected to have earned a return on it for a full year.

In 1991 American Home Products had earnings *after taxes* of $1,375.3 million. Deducted from revenues in the calculation of net income was interest expense of $31.4 million. This amount had been paid to the parties that supplied debt capital. The interest must be added back to net income if total income available to suppliers of capital is to be related to total capital employed by the company.

Interest, however, is a tax-deductible expense. The cost to the company of the interest paid was not the amount charged as interest expense; it was the interest expense less the tax saving. Notes to the statements indicate that American Home Products paid taxes at a rate of 34 percent. Its effective interest cost was $31.4 million less 34 percent of $31.4 million—a net of $20.7 million.

American Home Products in 1991 had a return on investment (all capital) of 24.1 percent:

$$\text{Return on investment (all capital)} = \frac{\text{Net income} + \text{Interest after taxes}}{\text{Average assets}}$$

$$= \frac{\$1,375.3 + 20.7}{\$5,788.0} = 24.1\%$$

Return on Investment (Stockholders' Equity)

The firm's entire net income (after interest and tax expenses) of $1,375.3 million will accrue to its owners, the common and preferred stockholders. The average equity of the stockholders during 1991 (calculated by averaging *total* stockholders' equity for year ends 1991 and 1990) was $2,987.9 million. Return on investment (stockholders' equity) was therefore 46.0 percent:

$$\text{Return on investment (stockholders' equity)} = \frac{\text{Net income}}{\text{Average stockholders' equity}}$$

$$= \frac{1,375.3}{2,987.9} = 46.0\%$$

Return on Equity of Common Stockholders

Earnings applicable to common stockholders represent net income less dividends declared to preferred stockholders. The equity of common stockholders includes common stock at par value, capital received in excess of par, and retained

EXHIBIT 16-2
Selected Data from the Financial Statements of American Home Products

	1991	1990
	(in millions of dollars)	
Total assets (or total liabilities and stockholders' equity	$5,938.8	$5,637.1
Total liabilities	$2,638.3	$2,961.9
Stockholders' equity:		
Preferred stock (convertible)	$ 0.1	$ 0.1
Common stock	105.2	104.7
Other paid-in capital	838.1	683.5
Retained earnings	2,316.6	1,802.7
Currency translation adjustments	40.6	84.2
Total common stockholders' equity	3,300.5	2,675.1
Total stockholders' equity	$3,300.6	$2,675.2
Interest expense	$ 31.4	$ 136.2
Income before taxes	1,759.8	1,828.2
Income taxes	384.5	597.7
Net income after taxes	1,375.3	1,230.6
Preferred stock dividends	0.1	0.1
Incremental tax rate	34%	34%

earnings—that is, total stockholders' equity less preferred stock. American Home Products declared preferred stock dividends in 1991 of only $0.1 million. Average equity of common stockholders (based on the average of 1991 and 1990) was $2,987.8 million. The return to common stockholders was therefore 46 percent—in this case about the same as the return to all stockholders:

Return on equity of common stockholders

$$= \frac{\text{Net income} - \text{Preferred stock dividends}}{\text{Average equity of common stockholders}}$$

$$= \frac{\$1,375.3 - \$0.1}{\$2,987.8} = 46.0\%$$

Return on Investment as an Indicator of the Successful Use of Leverage

As discussed in Chapter 10 in the section pertaining to junk bonds, the extent to which common stockholders use capital supplied by lenders and preferred stockholders is known as *leverage*. Common stockholders benefit whenever the firm earns a return on funds acquired from outsiders that is greater than their cost. Interest and preferred stock dividends are fixed in amount; any earnings in excess of the stipulated payments accrue entirely to the common stockholders.

American Home Products made successful use of leverage. This is evident by comparing the return on investment (all capital) with return on investment (stockholders' equity). Return on investment (all capital) was 24.1 percent; return on investment (stockholders' equity) was 46.0 percent. The company earned more on the funds from bondhonders and preferred stockholders than it had to pay in interest and preferred dividends.

Success in employing leverage can be measured by the ratio of return on investment (stockholders' equity) to return on investment (all capital). The higher the ratio, the more effective the use of leverage. However, as long as the ratio is greater than 1 to 1, the leverage is positive and has been used effectively. The ratio for American Home Products is

$$\text{Leverage effectiveness ratio} = \frac{\text{ROI (stockholders' equity)}}{\text{ROI (all capital)}}$$

$$= \frac{46.0\%}{24.1\%} = 1.9 \text{ to } 1$$

Pitfalls of Return on Investment as an Evaluative Criterion

Return on investment is a comprehensive measure of performance. But taken by itself, it is not an adequate measure, since it is based upon accrual accounting and thereby has all of its limitations. What is more, it may not always reflect the interests of *existing* corporate owners.

Has Same Deficiencies as Accrual Accounting

Return on investment, in that it relates earnings to resources, is appropriate as an evaluative criterion only to the extent that the accounting measures of earnings and resources are appropriate. As indicated previously in this chapter, earnings—particularly over a short period of time—may not be a valid indicator of either management or enterprise accomplishments. Both reported earnings and resources may be subjective in that they are dependent upon arbitrary choices between accounting principles; they can readily be manipulated by nonsubstantive management actions; they may be influenced by unreliable or biased estimates; and they may be reflective of decisions that were made prior to the period under review. Moreover, because assets are generally stated at historical costs, the denominator of the ratio is likely to be an unsatisfactory indicator of the economic value of the resources which are committed to the enterprise.

May Lead to Dysfunctional Management Decisions

Management decisions taken with a view toward maximizing return on investment can lead to a *reduction* in the earnings per share of common stockholders. Actions taken to increase return on investment may therefore be counter to the interests of existing owners. By way of illustration, assume that a firm has the opportunity to acquire a parcel of land that it would lease to outsiders. It would finance the acquisition by issuing 50,000 shares of common stock. The following data are relevant to the proposed acquisition:

Cost of land	$1,000,000
Expected rent revenue per year (after taxes)	120,000
Number of shares of common stock that the firm would issue to acquire necessary capital ($20 per share issue price)	50,000

Other factors that affect return on investment and earnings per share are as follows:

Present assets	$10,000,000
Present liabilities	4,000,000
Present stockholders' equity	6,000,000
Expected income (after taxes), prior to taking into account rent revenue from proposed acquisition	1,100,000
Interest (after taxes) on outstanding debt (10% of $4 million)	400,000
Present number of shares of common stock outstanding	1,000,000 shares

If the firm decided *not* to acquire the land, then return on investment (all capital) would be

$$\frac{\text{Net income} + \text{Interest after taxes}}{\text{Assets}} = \frac{\$1,100,000 + \$400,000}{\$10,000,000}$$

$$= 15\%$$

Return on investment (stockholders' equity) would be

$$\frac{\text{Net income}}{\text{Stockholders' equity}} = \frac{\$1,100,000}{\$6,000,000} = 18.3\%$$

Earnings per share of common stock would be

$$\frac{\text{Net income}}{\text{Number of shares outstanding}} = \frac{\$1,100,000}{1,000,000}$$

$$= \$1.10$$

If the firm elected to acquire the land and finance the purchase by issuing 50,000 shares of common stock at the market price of $20 per share, then income would increase by $120,000 and stockholders' equity by $1 million. Return on investment (all capital) would decline:

$$\frac{\$1,100,000 + \$400,000 + \$120,000}{\$10,000,000 + \$1,000,000} = \frac{\$1,620,000}{\$11,000,000}$$

$$= 14.7\%$$

So too would return on investment (stockholders' equity):

$$\frac{\$1,100,000 + \$120,000}{\$6,000,000 + \$1,000,000} = \frac{\$1,220,000}{\$7,000,000} = 17.4\%$$

Yet earnings per share of common stock would *increase*:

$$\frac{\$1,100,000 + \$120,000}{1,000,000 + 50,000} = \frac{\$1,220,000}{1,050,000} = \$1.162$$

Were the firm to use return on investment, regardless of whether all capital or stockholders' equity, it would turn down the proposed land acquisition. But by doing so, it would be passing up an opportunity to increase the dollar return to existing stockholders. The anomaly occurs because the percentage return on the additional investment of $1 million would be less than the *average* return that the firm was earning on previously invested capital. Nevertheless, the additional return of $120,000 would be greater than the cost of the additional capital. The cost of the additional capital would be $58,100—the dollars of earnings assigned to the newly issued shares (50,000 shares times income per share of $1.162). Thus the existing shareholders would be better off by $61,900 ($120,000 – $58,100).

Residual Income as a Means of Avoiding Dysfunctional Decisions

The danger that corporations will inadvertently maximize return on investment at the expense of returns to existing stockholders is especially pronounced in divisionalized firms. Corporations commonly permit their divisions broad discretion in making investment decisions. The divisions receive capital from the corporation and are charged interest for it; they have no control over how the capital is obtained. Their performance is evaluated on the basis of return on investment. Therefore there are decided risks that the divisions will reject any projects that do not increase their returns on investment, even if acceptance would work to the benefit of existing shareholders.

One means of avoiding this danger is to substitute residual income for return on investment as an evaluative criterion. *Residual income* is defined as *net income* (excluding any actual interest costs) *less an imputed cost of capital*. The imputed cost of capital would be determined by multiplying total assets by the minimum rate of return that top corporate managers or owners demand on invested capital.

Assume that in the previous illustration the company demands a minimum return of 11 percent on invested capital. If it did not acquire the land, the company would have $10 million in invested capital. It would therefore be charged $1.1 million in imputed capital costs (11 percent of $10 million). Its residual income would be $400,000, determined as follows:

Net income (given)	$1,100,000	
Plus: Interest after taxes (given)	400,000	$1,500,000
Less: Imputed cost of capital (11% of $10,000,000)		1,100,000
Residual income		$ 400,000

Were the firm to acquire the land, then it would earn an additional $120,000 in revenue. It would be charged with an additional $110,000 in capital costs (11 percent of $1 million). Residual income would increase by $10,000. Aware that its performance is being evaluated on the basis of residual income, management would elect to acquire the land—a decision consistent with the interests of stockholders.

Measures of Performance That Supplement Return on Investments

In light of the limitations of return on investment—or any other individual income-based measure—it is necessary for firms to develop supplementary criteria of performance. These criteria can be tailored to the specific objectives of the firm. Among criteria that are widely used are *profit margin* (net income as a percent of revenues), *gross margin* [1 minus (cost of goods sold as a percentage of revenues)], *share of market, innovations in product and manufacturing processes, productivity of labor*, and *rate of growth*. Although these measures cannot be summed to provide an overall performance "score," and may be even more subjective than return on investment, taken together they may provide a fairly complete accounting of firm or divisional accomplishment.

RATIOS IN FINANCIAL ANALYSIS

Until the 1960s, financial analysis was generally not carried beyond the calculation of ratios. Today, however, ratios serve as the starting point of financial analysis. The following are merely suggestive of the ways in which ratios are used:

Ratios are incorporated into statistical models that are intended to predict financial distress.
They are used in making forecasts of earnings and cash flows.
They are integral elements in investment models of asset valuation.
They are used in assessing the risk of individual securities and portfolios of securities.
They serve as the basis of comparing one firm with others in the same industry. Statistical tests have been developed to assess the significance of deviations from industry norms.

Financial statement analysis has become a specialized area within the disciplines of both accounting and finance. There is an abundant body of literature on the topic in textbooks, scholarly journals, and practice-oriented magazines.

Summary

Financial reporting is directed primarily to investors and creditors. It should enable them to assess future cash receipts and to evaluate the fiscal performance of firms in which they have an interest. Accrual accounting, in that it captures the periodic changes in the full range of a firm's resources, better serves the objectives of financial reporting than does cash accounting, a far simpler and more objective form of accounting. But accrual accounting requires the development of an elaborate set of principles and rules and affords firms considerable leeway to influence the earnings that they report, which they do in selecting among acceptable principles, in making required estimates, and in timing planned transactions. Moreover, because reported amounts are based upon allocations, estimates, and choices among accounting principles, they may be inappropriate for many types of decisions required of managers. Managers usually need reports specially tailored to the decisions at hand—reports that focus upon cash flows associated with proposed projects and assets or upon activities under the control of specific organizational units.

Because of inherent constraints, the three primary statements can never fully report upon all events and circumstances relevant to a firm's fiscal well-being. They must be supplemented by notes that explain accounting policies and give details of balances and transactions, indicate commitments and contingencies, and interpret the numerical data.

Financial analysis begins with the calculation of ratios. Return on investment is the most encompassing of the ratios discussed in this text. But it incorporates all of the weaknesses of the underlying accounting numbers. Although the performance of corporations and their divisions is often evaluated using return on investment as a criterion, efforts on the part of managers to maximize return on investment can run counter to the interests of stockholders.

Exercise for Review and Self-Testing

The following are balance sheets and income statements of General Mills, Inc. (as of May 29, 1988), and Kellogg Company (as of December 31, 1987). They have been recast slightly to make them comparable. All amounts, except earnings per share, are in millions.

Balance Sheets		
	General Mills	Kellogg
Assets		
Current assets		
Cash	$ 11.4	$ 126.2
Short-term investments	3.2	
Accounts receivable		
(net of allowance for		
doubtful accounts)	230.0	275.1
Inventories	423.5	310.9
Prepaid expenses	60.8	89.7
Other current assets	257.0	—
Total current assets	$ 985.9	$ 801.9
Land, buildings, and equipment		
(net of accumulated depreciation)	1,376.4	1,738.8
Intangible assets	72.9	77.4
Other assets	236.7	62.8
Total noncurrent assets	$1,686.0	$1,879.0
Total assets	$2,671.9	$2,680.9
Liabilities and Stockholders' Equity		
Current liabilities		
Accounts payable	$ 460.8	$ 311.9
Notes payable	371.6	151.4
Miscellaneous accruals	185.4	351.7
Other	173.6	38.4
Total current liabilities	$1,191.4	$ 853.4
Other liabilities and deferred credits		
Long-term debt	361.5	290.4
Deferred income taxes	407.1	256.4
Other	63.4	69.3
Total other liabilities and deferred		
credits	$ 832.0	$ 616.1
Total liabilities	$2,023.4	$1,469.5
Stockholders' equity		
Common stock	223.3	96.6
Retained earnings	1,067.9	1,717.9
Less: Treasury stock	(608.2)	(598.2)
Cumulative foreign currency adjustment	(34.5)	(4.9)
Total stockholders' equity	$ 648.5	$1,211.4
Total liabilities and stockholders'		
equity	$2,671.9	$2,680.9

Income Statements

	General Mills	Kellogg
Net sales	$5,178.8	$3,798.7
Cost of goods sold	2,987.8	1,939.3
Selling, general, and administrative costs	1,692.8	1,162.5
Interest expense	37.7	31.2
Total expenses, excluding income taxes	$4,718.3	$3,133.0
Income before taxes	460.5	665.7
Income taxes	177.4	269.8
Net income	$ 283.1	$ 395.9
Net income per share	$ 3.25	$ 3.20

1. Which of the two firms had greater earnings, prior to taking into account the cost of capital, in relation to all the resources within its command? That is, which provided the greater return on investment (all capital)? Base your response to this and the following questions on year-end (rather than average) values. Assume, in calculating interest after taxes, that each firm paid taxes at an incremental rate of 34 percent.
2. Which of the firms provided the greater return to common stockholders as measured by income available to them as a percentage of their equity?
3. Which of the two firms was the more highly leveraged as measured by the ratio of total debt to total stockholders' equity?
4. Which of the two firms made more effective use of leverage?
5. Which of the firms appeared to be better able to meet its fixed interest obligations; that is, which firm "covered" interest the greater number of times with earnings?
6. Which of the firms was more likely to be able to meet its current obligations as they came due as indicated by the current ratio?

Questions for Review and Discussion

1. Per the objectives of the FASB, to which main groups of potential users should financial reports be directed? What two main functions should financial reports facilitate?
2. Why is accrual accounting more consistent with the objectives of financial reporting than is cash accounting?
3. Why is accrual accounting necessarily more complex than cash accounting?
4. What are three ways in which the management of a firm can exercise discretion over reported earnings?
5. Financial statements report the financial history of an organization. Managers as well as investors and creditors are concerned with what the organization has accomplished in the past. If accounting is to be objective, how can there be justification for presenting the history differently to investors and creditors than to managers?
6. What is meant by a *transfer price*? Why do transfer prices introduce additional elements of subjectivity into the determination of earnings of a corporate division?
7. Supplementary notes reduce some of the deficiencies of the basic financial statements. Provide illustrations of several types of disclosures made in supplementary notes and indicate the deficiencies that they reduce.

8. "The manner in which a ratio is determined should depend on the specific decision at hand." Illustrate this statement by comparing return on investment using total investment with that computed using stockholders' equity.

9. What is meant by *residual income*? In what way does it overcome a deficiency of return on investment?

10. *The Wall Street Journal*, in a story about Federated Department Stores, Inc., reported that the newly appointed chief executive officer said that Federated would continue to keep an eye on the bottom line. He noted, however, that the company was also making a concerted effort, particularly at the divisional level, to stress such other yardsticks as return on investment, share of market, and gross profit margin. Why is the "bottom line" (net income), by itself, an inadequate indicator of corporate or divisional performance?

═══════════ **Problems**

1. *A forward-looking management should understand the impact of its actions upon widely used financial ratios.*

   What effect would each of the following transactions have on a firm's (1) current ratio, (2) quick ratio, (3) debt-to-equity ratio? Indicate whether each transaction would cause the ratio to increase (I), decrease (D), or have no effect (NE). Assume that any transactions involving revenues or expenses have an immediate impact upon retained earnings. Assume that all ratios are initially *greater* than 1:1.
   a. The firm sells goods on account. It maintains its inventory records on a perpetual basis, and the price at which the goods are sold is greater than their initial cost.
   b. The firm collects the amount receivable from the customer to whom it made the sale.
   c. It issues long-term bonds.
   d. It issues preferred stock in exchange for cash.
   e. It declares, but does not pay, a dividend on common stock.
   f. It pays the previously declared dividend.
   g. It purchases merchandise inventory on account.
   h. It pays for the merchandise previously purchased.
   i. It purchases equipment, giving the seller a three-year note for the entire amount payable.
   j. It recognizes depreciation for the first year.
   k. It writes off an uncollectible account receivable against the allowance for uncollectibles.
   l. It writes off inventory as obsolete.

2. *The factors that affect return on investment may be depicted graphically.*

   Return on investment may be computed several ways. One way, often associated with the Du Pont Company, is illustrated in the accompanying diagram. The diagram is intended to direct the attention of management to the various elements that have an impact upon return on investment.
   a. Refer to the 1987 financial statements of Anheuser-Busch in Problem 5. Determine return on investment (all capital). Base your computations on year-end rather than average values and assume a tax rate of 40 percent.
   b. Determine return on investment (all capital) by filling in each of the boxes in the diagram and carrying out the required operations. "Other expenses excluding interest" should include income taxes. However, to income taxes must be added the tax "saving" on the excluded interest.

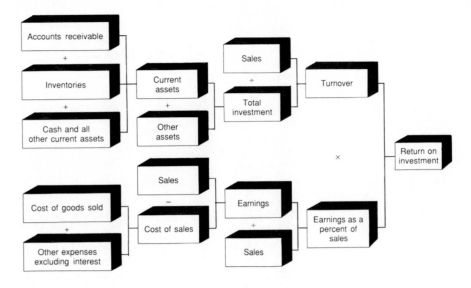

3. *Financial ratios incorporate all of the deficiencies of the underlying accounting data.*

A friend, who is president of Statistical Software, Inc., invites you to acquire an interest in his company. In explaining to you the advantages of such an investment, he points to the firm's profitability as evidenced by a high rate of return on stockholders' equity and the security of the investment as measured by *times interest earned*.

The firm develops and sells customized computer programs to industrial firms. The programs are intended to enable a firm to generate statistical information about its operations.

The president provides you with the company's 1992 financial statements. The statement of cash flows and the income statement are as follows:

Statistical Software, Inc.
Statement of Cash Flows
Year Ended December 31, 1992

Cash Flow from Operating Activities		
Net income		$ 1,200,000
Adjustments to income to reconcile net income to cash provided by operating activities		
Depreciation	$ 600,000	
Gain on sale of land	(1,600,000)	
Increase in accounts receivable	(1,700,000)	
Increase in advertising and promotion costs expected to benefit future periods	(300,000)	
Increase in program development costs applicable to software to be delivered in the future	(1,200,000)	(4,200,000)
Net cash provided by operating activities		$(3,000,000)
Cash Flow from Investing Activities		
Sale of land		2,200,000
Net increase (decrease) in cash		$ (800,000)
Cash balance beginning of year		4,100,000
Cash balance, end of year		$3,300,000

Statistical Software, Inc.
Statement of Income
Year Ended December 31, 1992

Sales	$5,400,000	
Other revenues	2,600,000	$8,000,000
Cost of programs developed	$5,300,000	
Other expenses	900,000	
Interest	200,000	
Taxes	400,000	6,800,000
Net income		$1,200,000

The balance sheet reveals that average stockholders' equity during the year was $6 million.

a. Determine the rate of return on stockholders' equity and the times interest earned measure of coverage of fixed charges.

b. Review carefully the two statements presented. Recognizing that no investment decisions can be made on the basis of statements for a single year, what questions would you raise (or what reservations would you have) pertaining to the firm's *quality* of earnings?

4. *The three problems that follow require that you compare and evaluate the performance of two national breweries.*

The income statement and balance sheet of Adolph Coors Company, a leading brewery, are presented below. (All amounts, except per share data, are in millions.)

a. Compare the company's 1987 and 1986 financial performance in regard to the measures that follow. Use year-end, rather than average, balance sheet values.
   (1) Return on investment (all capital) (Assume a tax rate of 40 percent.)
   (2) Return on investment (stockholders' equity)
   (3) Debt-to-equity ratio
   (4) Inventory turnover
   (5) Current ratio
   (6) Number of days' sales in accounts receivable
b. Explain, as best you can from the limited information contained in the financial statements, why income declined in 1987.

Adolph Coors Company
Income Statements

	1987	1986
Net sales	$1,351	$1,281
Cost of goods sold	878	848
Selling, general, administrative, and other costs	384	318
Interest expense	3	3
Total expenses, excluding income taxes	1,265	1,169
Income before taxes	86	112
Income taxes	38	51
Net income	$ 48	$ 61
Net income per share	$ 1.32	$ 1.65

Adolph Coors Company
Balance Sheets

	1987	1986
Assets		
Current assets		
Cash and temporary investments	$ 113	$ 150
Accounts receivable (net of allowance for doubtful accounts)	109	100
Inventories	155	157
Other current assets	74	66
Total current assets	451	473
Land, buildings, and equipment (net of accumulated depreciation)	976	901
Costs in excess of assigned value of businesses acquired	3	4
Other assets	26	18
Total noncurrent assets	1,005	923
Total assets	$1,456	$1,396
Liabilities and Stockholders' Equity		
Current liabilities		
Accounts payable	$ 86	$ 75
Taxes and other accrued liabilities	123	126
Total current liabilities	209	201
Other liabilities and deferred credits		
Deferred income taxes	189	181
Other	26	18
Total other liabilities and deferred credits	215	199
Total liabilities	424	400
Common stockholders' equity		
Common stock, par value	12	12
Other paid-in capital	29	24
Retained earnings	1,014	984
Less: Treasury stock	(23)	(24)
Total common stockholders' equity	1,032	996
Total liabilities and stockholders' equity	$1,456	$1,396

5. The income statement and balance sheet of Anheuser-Busch, another leading brewery, are presented below. (All amounts, except per share data, are in millions.)

   a. Compare the company's 1987 and 1986 financial performance using the measures that follow. Calculate the ratios with year-end rather than average balance sheet values.

   (1) Return on investment (all capital) (Assume a tax rate of 40 percent.)
   (2) Return on investment (stockholders' equity)
   (3) Debt-to-equity ratio
   (4) Inventory turnover
   (5) Current ratio
   (6) Number of days' sales in accounts receivable

   b. Explain, as best you can from the limited information in the financial statements, why income rose in 1987.

Anheuser-Busch Companies
Balance Sheets

	1987	1986
Assets		
Current assets		
Cash and temporary investments	$ 111	$ 69
Accounts receivable		
(net of allowance for		
doubtful accounts)	383	373
Inventories	452	428
Other current assets	180	150
Total current assets	1,126	1,020
Land, buildings, and equipment		
(net of accumulated depreciation)	4,914	4,427
Investments	161	117
Costs in excess of assigned value of		
businesses acquired	120	138
Other assets	171	132
Total noncurrent assets	5,366	4,814
Total assets	$6,492	$5,834
Liabilities and Stockholders' Equity		
Current liabilities		
Accounts payable	$ 540	$ 492
Taxes and other accrued liabilities	502	524
Total current liabilities	1,042	1,016
Other liabilities and deferred credits		
Deferred income taxes	1,161	1,091
Long-term debt	1,397	1,127
Total other liabilities and deferred		
credits	2,558	2,218
Total liabilities	3,600	3,234
Convertible preferred stock	0	287
Common stockholders' equity		
Common stock, par value	327	295
Other paid-in capital	332	6
Retained earnings	2,929	2,473
Less: Treasury stock	(696)	(461)
Total common stockholders' equity	2,892	2,313
Total liabilities and stockholders'		
equity	$6,492	$5,834

Anheuser-Busch Companies
Income Statements

	1987	1986
Net sales	$8,258	$7,677
Cost of goods sold	5,310	4,969
Selling, general, administrative, and		
other costs	1,821	1,714
Interest expense	71	53
Total expenses, excluding income taxes	7,202	6,736
Income before taxes	1,056	941
Income taxes	441	423
Net income*	$ 615	$ 518
Net income per share	$ 2.04	$ 1.69

*The company declared preferred stock dividends in 1986 of $20 million.

6. *Compare the 1987 financial statements of Adolph Coors and Anheuser-Busch contained in the two preceding problems.*
   a. Which of the two firms would you characterize as more "conservative" based on capital structure (i.e., relationship of debt to equity)?
   b. Which of the firms successfully took advantage of leverage? Explain.
   c. Which of the firms more effectively employed its
      (1) Inventory?
      (2) Accounts receivable?
   d. As of December 31, 1987, the market price per share of Adolph Coors was $16.87; that of Anheuser-Busch was $33.37. Which of the two had the higher price/earnings ratio? Based on the ratios that you computed in the preceding problems, do you agree with the market's assessment as to which firm is fiscally more sound?

7. *Differences in return on investment may be more apparent than real.*

   Rent-a-Truck, Inc., was founded in January 1993. The company issued 300,000 shares of common stock at $10 per share.

   The company acquired trucks at a cost of $3 million. The useful lives of the trucks were estimated to be five years, with zero salvage value.

   During its first year of operations, the revenues of the firm, less all expenses other than depreciation and income taxes, were $1.3 million.

   The applicable income tax rate is 40 percent. The company *defers* its tax expense; that is, reported tax expense is based on *reported* income; it is not indicative of the required current tax *payment*.
   a. Determine the first year's return on investment (stockholders' equity) under each of the following assumptions;
      (1) The firm uses straight-line depreciation for book purposes and straight-line depreciation for tax purposes.
      (2) The firm uses double declining balance depreciation for book purposes and double declining balance depreciation for tax purposes.
      (3) The firm uses straight-line depreciation for book purposes and double declining balance depreciation for tax purposes.
   Base your computation on year-end stockholders' equity instead of average stockholders' equity.
   b. Comment on any substantive (that is, "real" economic) differences in rate of return under each of the three methods.

8. *Use of return on investment as a criterion of corporate performance may lead to dysfunctional management decisions.*

   The president of Burnside, Inc., is faced with the decision as to whether to expand the corporation by acquiring a new plant. The cost of the new plant would be $500 million. The necessary capital could be acquired by issuing bonds which would provide a return to lenders of 12 percent per year. The new plant would increase corporate pretax earnings by $70 million prior to taking into account required interest payments of $60 million.

   In recent years, Burnside, Inc., has had annual pretax income, after deducting $50 million in interest payments, of $250 million. As of year end, the firm had outstanding debts of $500 million and owners' equity of $1.5 billion.

   The financial vice-president favors acquisition of the new plant, arguing that corporate earnings would be increased by $10 million. The corporate controller opposes acquisition, maintaining that it would result in reduction of the firm's return on invested capital.
   a. Determine return on investment (all capital) if (1) the plant is not acquired and (2) the plant is acquired for cash. Assume that earnings on the old facilities will

be the same in the future as they were in the past. Disregard income taxes (i.e., add back to income the full amount of interest costs). Base your computations on year-end instead of average values. Assume also that all earnings are distributed as dividends.

b. Calculate earnings per share under the two alternatives. The company has 10 million shares of common stock outstanding.

c. Suppose instead that the company could acquire the necessary $500 million in capital by issuing 2 million shares of common stock. Compute return on investment (stockholders' equity) and earnings per share, assuming first that the company did not expand and then that it did.

d. Do you think the company should acquire the plant? Explain.

e. Comment on the potential dangers of using return on investment as a criterion for making investment decisions.

f. What criterion might be preferable to return on investment?

9. *The advantages of debt as opposed to equity financing may be illusory.*

The Dement Corporation has $30 million in total assets. It has $10 million in current liabilities outstanding and $20 million in stockholders' equity. There are presently 100,000 shares of common stock outstanding. After-tax earnings over the past several years have averaged $2.1 million per year.

The company has decided to expand its operations by constructing a new plant. The new plant will cost $6 million, and it is estimated that it will increase earnings by $360,000 after taxes, not taking into account costs of financing.

The company has two options available to it to finance the plant. First, it can issue additional shares of stock. The additional shares could be sold for $400 per share.

Alternatively, it can raise the required $6 million by issuing bonds. The bonds would be sold to yield purchasers 10 percent per year. The interest costs would be tax-deductible to the company. The applicable tax rate is 40 percent. The company "pays out" 100 percent of earnings as dividends.

a. Assume that the company will construct the new plant. For each of the alternatives, determine anticipated (1) return on investment (all capital), (2) return on investment (stockholders' equity), and (3) earnings per share.

b. After reviewing the figures just computed, the president of the company stated, "It is obvious that we are better off financing expansion with debt rather than equity. In the future, let's finance all additions by issuing bonds rather than stock." Comment on the president's logic.

10. *A balance sheet and an income statement can be derived from selected financial ratios.*

The Ventnor Company had net earnings in a particular year of $50,000.

a. Its return on investment based on stockholders' equity as of year end was 10 percent. Determine year-end stockholders' equity.

b. The firm's debt-to-equity ratio was 0.4:1. Determine year-end debt.

c. Ventnor Company's return on investment (all capital) was 7.6571 percent based on year-end capital. It paid taxes at an incremental rate of 40 percent. Determine interest expense for the year.

d. Its *times interest earned* ratio was 13:1. Determine income taxes.

e. The company's net earnings as a percentage of sales was 5 percent. Determine sales.

f. Its gross margin was 40 percent. Determine cost of goods sold.

g. Its inventory turned over six times. Determine inventory.

h. The firm's accounts receivable turned over 25 times. Determine accounts receivable.
i. Its fixed assets turned over two times. Determine fixed assets.
j. Its only remaining asset was cash. Determine year-end cash.
k. Its current ratio was 2:1. Determine current liabilities.
l. All expenses not yet determined may be classified as "sales and administration." Reconstruct, as best you can, Ventnor Company's income statement and balance sheet.

11. *If financial statements fail to take into account current costs, so also do the financial ratios.*
    The financial statements of the Yorkville Bottling Co. revealed the following data for a recent year.

Current assets	$ 420,000
Other assets (property, plant, and equipment)	6,580,000
Current liabilities	670,000
Other liabilities	2,308,000
Sales	11,500,000
Interest expense, net of taxes	350,000
Net income	1,400,000

a. Determine the following relationships (based on year-end balances):
   (1) Return on investment (all capital)
   (2) Current ratio
   (3) Debt-to-equity ratio
   (4) Plant and equipment turnover
b. Investigation reveals that included in current assets are marketable securities that are recorded at a cost of $100,000. Their current market value is $350,000. Moreover, the company's plant is located on land that had originally cost $500,000. The land currently has a fair market value of $1 million. Recompute the foregoing relationships to take into account the additional information. Which set of relationships do you think is more relevant to most decisions required of both managers and investors?
c. Comment on how the revised ratios may affect the analyst's view of both financial position and operating performance.

12. *Ratio analysis may assist an investor in predicting whether a firm will "turn around" or go bankrupt.*
    The financial statements presented here were adapted from those of W. T. Grant, which operated a chain of low-priced department stores in 42 states. Most of its merchandise was priced under $10, but the stores also carried a line of major appliances.
    a. Explain as best you can the reason for the decline in earnings in year 2.
    b. Compare the liquidity of the company in year 2 with that of year 1.
    c. Compare the debt-to-equity ratio of year 2 with that of year 1.
    d. Comment on the firm's ability to meet fixed interest charges.
    e. Comment on the critical problems facing the firm in the following year. Do you see any bright spots? Do you believe that the ability of the firm to survive is in question?

W. T. Grant
Consolidated Statement of Income for Year ended January 31
(in thousands)

	Year 2	Year 1
Net sales	$1,761,952	$1,845,802
Other revenues	10,700	5,617
Total revenues	$1,772,652	$1,861,419
Cost of goods sold	$1,303,267	$1,282,944
Selling and other expenses	726,420	546,202
Interest	37,771	18,082
Income tax expense (refund)	(117,466)	3,289
Total expenses	$1,949,992	$1,850,517
Net income (loss)	$ (177,340)	$ 10,902

W. T. Grant
Consolidated Balance Sheet as of January 31
(in thousands)

	Year 2	Year 1
Assets		
Current		
Cash and equivalents	$ 79,642	$ 45,952
Accounts receivable (net)	431,191	540,802
Inventories	407,357	450,636
Other current assets	6,591	7,299
Total current assets	$ 924,781	$1,044,689
Noncurrent		
Property and equipment (net)	$ 101,932	$ 100,983
Investment in subsidiaries	49,764	44,251
Other assets	5,790	5,063
Total noncurrent assets	$ 157,486	$ 150,297
Total assets	$1,082,267	$1,194,986
Liabilities and stockholders' equity		
Current		
Accounts payable	$ 50,067	$ 58,192
Notes and other payables	600,995	453,096
Miscellaneous accruals	79,144	46,691
Taxes payable	9,700	103,078
Total current liabilities	$ 749,906	$ 661,057
Noncurrent		
Notes payable	$ 99,005	$ 100,000
Bonds payable	117,336	120,336
Other liabilities	2,183	18,845
Total noncurrent liabilities	$ 218,524	$ 239,181
Stockholders' equity		
Preferred stock	$ 7,465	$ 7,464
Common stock ($1.25 par value)	18,599	18,599
Capital in excess of par	83,914	18,599
Less: Stock held in treasury	(33,815)	(36,696)
Retained earnings	37,674	219,472
Total stockholders' equity	$ 113,837	$ 294,748
Total liabilities and stockholders' equity	$1,082,267	$1,194,986

13. *Analysis of financial data is necessary. But is it sufficient?*

The table that follows contains selected financial data of a leading U.S. airline for a period of four years. The data were taken from the firm's 10-year summary of operations that was included in one of its annual reports. The trends that are evident in the four-year period are, for the most part, extensions of ones established earlier. Earnings per share for the six years prior to the first year shown in the exhibit were $.32, $(.15), $.43, $.85, $.69, and $1.35.

A Leading U.S. Airline:
Excerpts from 10-Year Financial Review
(in thousands except for income per share)

	Year 4	Year 3	Year 2	Year 1
Operating revenues				
Airline				
Passenger	$845,353	$678,177	$582,715	$509,894
Other transport revenues	95,161	84,062	70,332	66,031
Transport-related	24,789	21,795	20,482	18,619
Military contract services	—	—	—	—
Nonairline subsidiaries	6,805	7,123	6,190	4,312
	$972,108	$791,157	$679,719	$598,856
Operating expenses				
Airline flying, maintenance/ground operations	682,013	543,925	468,116	403,499
Nonairline subsidiaries	2,992	2,965	3,177	2,618
Sales and advertising	108,737	83,416	72,989	65,677
Depreciation and amortization	60,980	55,593	51,388	48,360
General and administrative	37,227	36,230	25,257	24,382
	$891,949	$722,129	$620,927	$544,536
Operating income	80,159	69,028	58,792	54,320
Interest expense	29,209	25,997	25,222	26,024
Other nonoperating (income) and expenses, net	(4,285)	(6,428)	(1,812)	1,897
Provision for income taxes	10,005	12,767	9,043	6,411
Income	$ 45,230	$ 36,692	$ 26,339	$ 19,988
Per share income	$ 2.26	$ 1.83	$ 1.00	$ 1.00
Weighted average number of shares and equivalents (thousands)	20,016	20,008	20,127	19,950
Cash dividends declared	$ 6,906	$ 5,703	$ 4,594	$ 3,991
Stock dividends	—	—	—	—
Selected balance sheet items				
Current assets	$141,519	$134,028	$113,238	$113,445
Current liabilities	155,543	124,008	114,634	114,032
Working capital	$(14,024)	$ 10,020	$ (1,396)	$ (587)
Property and equipment, net	612,189	493,319	466,674	446,849
Total assets	855,165	699,523	627,839	602,411
Senior debt	320,985	235,312	193,816	180,410
Subordinated debt	27,692	37,307	48,083	54,503
Total long-term debt	$348,677	$272,619	$241,899	$234,913
Common stock and paid-in capital	56,792	56,732	56,575	56,221
Retained earnings	193,359	155,035	124,046	102,301
Total shareholders' equity	$250,151	$211,767	$180,621	$158,522

a. Evaluate the performance of the airline during the four-year period. Based on the information provided, indicate whether the outlook for the company appears favorable. Compute whatever financial ratios you think would provide insight into the firm's results of the past and prospects for the future.

b. Despite the apparently favorable trends, are there any warnings, drawn from the data, that you might offer to a prospective investor or creditor of the company?

14. *One of these two airlines filed for bankruptcy within seven years.*

The financial statements of two actual airlines, given the fictitious names Northern and Southern, are presented below. Answer the following questions, providing support with appropriate ratios. Assume a combined federal, state, and local tax rate of 48 percent.

a. Which of the two companies used the total resources within its command more effectively?

Balance Sheet
(in thousands)

	Northern	Southern
Assets		
Current		
Cash	$ 21,512	$ 45,549
Short-term investments, at cost	149,100	—
Accounts receivable (net allowance for uncollectibles)	332,979	318,506
Materials and supplies	180,803	47,493
Prepaid expenses and other current assets	28,407	76,650
Total current assets	$ 712,801	$ 488,198
Noncurrent		
Property, plant, and equipment	$3,839,212	$3,535,416
Allowance for depreciation	(1,537,198)	(1,590,955)
	$2,302,014	$1,944,461
Advance payments for new equipment	116,958	197,596
Other assets	93,114	27,625
Total noncurrent assets	$2,512,086	$2,169,682
Total assets	$3,224,887	$2,657,880
Liabilities and owners' equity		
Current		
Accounts payable	$ 459,426	$ 231,999
Notes payable	156,300	279,283
Other	232,712	232,711
Total current liabilities	$ 848,438	$ 743,993
Noncurrent		
Long-term debt (including obligations for leases)	$1,910,897	$ 362,774
Deferred tax credits and other liabilities	70,727	527,462
Total noncurrent liabilities	$1,981,624	$ 890,236
Preferred stock	$ 139,551	—
Common stock (par value and additional contributed capital)	$ 358,024	$ 199,371
Retained earnings (deficit)	(102,750)	824,280
Equity of common stockholders	$ 255,274	$1,023,651
Total liabilities and owners' equity	$3,224,887	$2,657,880

Income Statement
(in thousands)

	Northern	Southern
Operating revenues	$3,769,237	$3,617,523
Operating expenses	3,788,017	3,625,679
Operating profit (loss)	$ (18,780)	$ (8,156)
Nonoperating revenues (expenses)		
Interest expense	$ (178,274)	$ (60,438)
Gain on disposal of aircraft	32,735	1,570
Other (net)	79,063	51,819
Total nonoperating revenues (expenses)	$ (66,476)	$ (7,049)
Income (loss) before taxes	$ (85,256)	$ (15,205)
Provision for (reduction in) income taxes	(10,329)	(36,019)
Net income (loss)	$ (74,927)	$ 20,814

b. Which provided the greater return to stockholders?

c. Which was more highly leveraged? Which made the more effective use of leverage?

d. Which appeared to be the better able to meet its fixed interest obligations?

e. Which was better able to meet its current obligations with available current resources?

f. Based on the very limited information presented (i.e., financial data for one year only), which of the two do you think went bankrupt in seven years?

15. *The following news report highlights the deficiencies of accounting information as a basis for investor decisions.*

Depending on who was doing the analysis, *The Wall Street Journal* reported, the value of American Financial Corporation's common stock was somewhere between $5 and $70 a share. It was not surprising, therefore, that some shareholders did not find the company's proposed offer of $28 very enticing.

The *Journal* went on to relate that Carl Lindner, chairman, president, and founder of American Financial, who along with his family owns 45 percent of the firm's outstanding shares of common stock, was seeking to take over the company by acquiring the 55 percent of the stock held by parties other than the Lindner family.

Within days after Lindner offered to purchase the outstanding shares, minority stockholders filed suit, charging that the price of $28 was unfair and inadequate. One suit, the *Journal* indicated, charged that the offer did not consider future profits of American Financial and that it was less than the company's worth as a going concern. The latter assertion was backed by a financial analyst who estimated what American Financial would get for its assets if the firm were to be broken up and sold. Among the assets were insurance companies, convenience stores, savings and loan institutions, and investment positions in several companies. The analyst said that he based his estimates of the subsidiaries' values on the percentage amounts above or below book value that companies in their industries had recently received in the market. He valued American Financial's investment positions in other companies at current market prices. On the basis of these estimates, he calculated the company's worth at between $54 and $70 per share.

The *Journal* reported that American Financial belittled the estimate of the analyst. In fact, the company claimed its book value of $23.53 a share was deceptively high. The company believed tangible book value of its assets was more like $5 a share, in large part because the goodwill of its subsidiaries acounted for over half of the common stock's book value.

a. Comment on why book values cannot serve as the basis for establishing a fair value of the company, despite the assertion of the firm's auditors that the "financial statements present fairly" its financial position.

b. How would you assess the reliability of the procedure used by the financial analyst to estimate the values of the firm's subsidiaries?

c. Evaluate the explanation of American Financial as to why the book value of $23.53 was deceptively high.

16. *Leveraged buyouts do not always work out as intended.*

In 1986, to fend off the advances of a hostile corporate raider, the management of Fruehauf Corp. acquired the company in a leveraged buyout. The financial statements that follow are for 1987, the first full year of operations subsequent to the buyout, and 1986, the year of the buyout.

Fruehauf Corporation Balance Sheets		
	1987	1986
Assets		
Current assets		
Cash and temporary investments	$ 75	$ 124
Accounts receivable (net of allowance for doubtful accounts)	201	343
Inventories	228	343
Other current assets	188	126
Total current assets	692	936
Land, buildings, and equipment (net of accumulated depreciation)	755	582
Investments	58	291
Equipment leased to customers (net of accumulated depreciation)	46	194
Other assets	187	0
Total noncurrent assets	1,046	1,067
Total assets	$1,738	$2,003
Liabilities and Stockholders' Equity		
Current liabilities		
Accounts payable	$ 196	$ 388
Taxes and other accrued liabilities	199	312
Total current liabilities	395	700
Other liabilities and deferred credits		
Deferred income taxes	183	77
Long-term debt and capital leases	780	206
Other liabilities	152	516
Total other liabilities and deferred credits	1,115	799
Total liabilities	1,510	1,499
Preferred stock	255	0
Common stockholders' equity		
Common stock, par value	1	23
Other paid-in capital	28	305
Retained earnings	(56)	275
Treasury stock	0	(99)
Total common stockholders' equity	(27)	504
Total liabilities and stockholders' equity	$1,738	$2,003

Fruehauf Corporation
Income Statements

	1987	1986
Net sales	$1,854	$2,759
Cost of goods sold	1,539	2,271
Selling, general, administrative, and other costs	184	323
Interest expense	106	80
Depreciation	101	96
Total expenses, excluding income taxes	1,930	2,770
Income before taxes	(76)	(11)
Income taxes (tax benefit)	(34)	9
Income before extraordinary loss	(42)	(20)
Extraordinary loss (net of taxes)		(41)
Net income	$ (42)	$ (61)

The statements are not directly comparable because the buyout was accompanied by a major reorganization and recapitalization. As is apparent from the statements, for example, the new company had significantly more long-term debt, and less stockholders' equity, than the old. Moreover, to finance its acquisition, management sold off key divisions.

Fruehauf manufactures trucks and auto parts. It is in an industry that is considered highly cyclical. That is, sales tend to increase when the economy is strong and decrease when it is weak.

By mid-1989, it was clear that the buyout was unsuccessful. Management was struggling to keep the company afloat by selling its most profitable divisions—those for which it could obtain the highest prices.

a. Compare the capital structures of the company before and after the buyout. Compute appropriate ratios.

b. What do you see as the major reason for the increase in losses (before the extraordinary item) in 1987? Compute appropriate ratios.

c. In 1987 the company declared $27 million in preferred stock dividends. From the perspective of the common stockholders, would you characterize these dividends as more like common stock dividends or interest payments?

d. Comment on the dangers of leveraged buyouts in cyclical industries.

17. *Are reported earnings a measure only of short-term, not long-term, well-being?*

The Wall Street Journal of April 14, 1981, described a proxy fight in which a group of dissident shareholders attempted to unseat the existing board of directors of American Bakeries Co. Although the firm was small, the effort to oust the directors raised an important issue, according to the *Journal*. The main problem was the extent to which managers of publicly held companies dared to sacrifice short-term profits and dividends for long-term growth. This is what Japanese companies often did.

The dissident shareholders cited several measures of what they considered the firm's dismal performance: a decline in net income to $2.1 million in 1980 from $5.8 million in 1977; omission of the past two quarterly cash dividends in 1980; uneven sales growth from 1976 to 1981; and a decline in profitability to 0.39 percent of sales in 1980 from 1.38 percent in 1975.

According to the *Journal*, the chairman of American Bakeries objected to the suggestion that declining financial results of the past five years reflected mismanagement. He said that the decline stemmed from the biggest capital spending program—$84 million—in their history; the program had spanned the five years that ended in 1980. He thought that effort critically important for competitiveness and growth prospects.

There was no question, the *Journal* said, that the depressed earnings over the past five years was a result of the company's big capital spending program. The American Bakeries' executives acknowledged that the company's annual depreciation expense rose nearly 40 percent during the period to more than $11 million in 1980 and that interest expenses increased to $6.1 million in 1980 from $2.1 million in 1976.

a. Reported earnings are supposed to be a measure of corporate well-being. Is it not a deficiency of financial reporting that if a firm takes actions such as increasing capital spending, which are admittedly in its long-run interests, it may have to report lower earnings?

b. Comment on the dangers of using reported earnings alone to evaluate management performance.

c. Would the firm be saddled with the lower reported earnings if it adhered faithfully to the *principle of matching*? Explain. What changes in accounting practices would enable a firm to avoid having to report lower earnings in periods prior to those in which the benefits of a capital spending program were realized?

Solutions to Exercise for Review and Self-Testing

1. Return on investment (all capital):

$$\frac{\text{Net income + Interest after taxes}}{\text{Assets}}$$

Interest after taxes = (1 − incremental tax rate) interest expense:

a. General Mills

$$\frac{\$283.1 + (1. - .34)\$37.7}{\$2,671.9} = 11.5\%$$

b. Kellogg

$$\frac{\$395.9 + (1. - .34)\$31.2}{\$2,680.9} = 15.5\%$$

Kellogg had the greater earnings relative to the resources within its command.

2. Return on investment (common stockholders' equity):

$$\frac{\text{Net income − Preferred stock dividends}}{\text{Equity of common stockholders}}$$

a. General Mills

$$\frac{\$283.1 - \$0}{\$648.5} = 43.7\%$$

b. Kellogg

$$\frac{\$395.9 - \$0}{\$1,211.4} = 32.7\%$$

General Mills, even though its ROI (all capital) was less than Kellogg's, provided the greater return to common stockholders.

3. Debt-to-equity ratio:

$$\frac{\text{Total debt}}{\text{Total equity}}$$

a. General Mills

$$\frac{\$2,023.4}{\$648.5} = 3.120 \text{ to } 1$$

b. Kellogg

$$\frac{\$1,469.5}{\$1,211.4} = 1.213 \text{ to } 1$$

General Mills was the more highly leveraged, a position consistent with its ROI (all capital) being less than Kellogg's and its ROI (stockholders' equity) being greater.

4. General Mills made the more effective use of leverage. It was able to increase the return to stockholders 3.8 times that of the return to all capital (43.7% divided by 11.5%). Kellogg, which also used leverage quite effectively, increased it only 2.1 times (32.7% divided by 15.5%).

5. Times interest earned:

$$\frac{\text{Net income} + \text{Interest} + \text{Income taxes}}{\text{Interest}}$$

a. General Mills

$$\frac{\$283.1 + \$37.7 + \$177.4}{\$37.7} = \frac{\$498.2}{\$37.7} = 13.2 \text{ times}$$

b. Kellogg

$$\frac{\$395.9 + \$31.2 + \$269.8}{\$31.2} = \frac{\$696.9}{\$31.2} = 22.3 \text{ times}$$

Both firms covered their interest costs by many more times than is considered the minimum margin of safety.

6. Current ratio:

$$\frac{\text{Current assets}}{\text{Current liabilities}}$$

a. General Mills

$$\frac{\$985.9}{\$1,191.4} = .83 \text{ to } 1$$

b. Kellogg

$$\frac{\$801.9}{\$853.4} = .94 \text{ to } 1$$

The ratios of both firms are considered reasonably strong.

Overall, the ratios that have been computed describe two firms that are generally healthy. General Mills is the slightly more risky of the two as its capital structure contains relatively more debt.

17

Focus on Costs

With this chapter we begin a new section of this text. So far we have focused primarily on how accounting information is presented to parties *external* to the organization. We have seen that in reporting to outsiders, the need to assure that information is verifiable has sometimes led accountants to compromise their equally important objective of assuring that their descriptions of transactions and events faithfully represent economic reality.

In the remainder of this text we shall concentrate on accounting information as it can be used by *insiders*. We shall focus mainly on the information requirements of managers, who are responsible for determining the goods and services that their organizations will manufacture or provide, acquiring the necessary productive and financial resources, planning and controlling the required activities, and establishing the prices at which the goods or services will be sold.

Two considerations dominate *managerial* accounting in a way that distinguishes it from *financial* accounting. These are depicted in Exhibit 17-1. First, managers must *plan* the activities of the entity. Planning involves establishing the organization's internal objectives, assessing its strengths and limitations

EXHIBIT 17-1
Illustration of Management Activities:
Relationship between Planning and Control

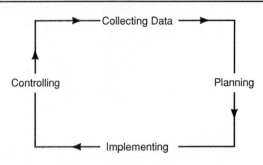

and the competitive economic environment in which it operates, and forecasting future events and conditions by which it will be affected and budgeting for each of its activities. Second, managers must *control* all aspects of their operations. Control incorporates the procedures that are established to identify and measure deviations from plans, to affix responsibility for these deviations, and either to remedy the deviation or amend the plans. As we shall see, effective control inevitably requires careful and comprehensive *performance assessment* of both the organization as a whole and its individual components.

Because cost information is central to the management functions involving planning and control, Chapters 17 and 18 will be directed to the *nature and behavior of costs* and the means by which costs can be assigned both to organizational units and to particular products and services. Chapter 19 discusses the way in which *incremental* costs underlie most managerial decisions—how the basic information on the costs developed in Chapters 17 and 18 can be determined and put to work in the various *ad hoc* planning and control activities in which managers take part. Next, in Chapters 20 and 21, we discuss the ways in which accounting information can be used in *managerial planning* in a more comprehensive and formal sense—first in planning for the longer run in which size of plant is subject to change, and then in the shorter run in which plant size is fixed. Chapter 20 addresses *investment decisions*, and Chapter 21 pertains to year-by-year *budgeting procedures*. Chapter 22 is concerned with *control*—specifically with the analysis of deviations from plans.

It is both convenient and common to distinguish between management activities that involve planning and those that involve control. In fact, however, as illustrated in Exhibit 17-1, the two functions are intertwined and, in practice, often inseparable. Moreover, they are continuous. Similarly, it may be useful analytically and pedagogically to classify management activities as affecting either the long term or the short term. In reality, the time span affected by a management decision can seldom be known for sure, and to a great extent the ultimate direction that an organization takes is the result of a series of seemingly short-term maneuvers. Management is an ongoing, continuous process in which executives take action in response to information about the results of past performance as well as anticipated conditions of the future. Management accounting is an inherent part of the management process. As such, it too is not as neatly divisible into topics of planning and control, or time frames of long and short terms, as is often implied.

Basic Themes

Underlying the remaining chapters will be several related themes.

1. *Information must be relevant to decisions at hand.* Accounting information is intended to facilitate management decisions. The ultimate criterion in determining the nature and form of accounting data is their utility. In presenting information to parties within the organization, accountants are unconstrained by pronouncements of outside regulatory authorities. Calculations and reports can be tailor-made for the individual managers who will use them.

2. *Decisions should focus on incremental receipts and disbursements.* For virtually all decisions that managers are called upon to make, only *incremental* revenues and expenses should properly be taken into account. Incremental receipts and disbursements are those that will be affected by the outcome of the decision. They are distinguished from those that will remain the same regardless of course of action selected and need not therefore be given analytical consideration.

   A corollary to this theme is that only future receipts and disbursements can be affected by a decision made today. Past receipts and disbursements are relevant only to the extent that they serve as a guide to those of the future.

3. *Time value of money and uncertainty must be taken into account.* In evaluating cash flows, both the time value of money and the uncertainty surrounding the cash flows must be taken into account. A dollar to be paid or received sooner is worth more than one to be paid or received later. In assessing the financial impact of alternative courses of action, the analyst must "discount" all future inflows and outflows by a factor (such as the firm's "cost of capital") that equates dollars of the future with those of the present.[1] Similarly, a dollar to be paid or received with certainty is worth more than one to which there is risk attached. Anticipated cash flows must, therefore, be adjusted to take into account the degree of uncertainty with which they are associated.

4. *Focus should be on cash and other liquid assets, more than income.* Insofar as it is the objective of the organization to maximize economic well-being (with economic well-being defined in the conventional monetary terms that exclude consideration of environmental, psychological, and sociological factors), then managers should focus mainly on cash and near-cash, rather than *income*. Cash, not income, can be used to acquire goods and services or earn additional returns. Whereas income may be an acceptable measure of organizational performance and may be the most reliable predictor of future cash flows, management must be concerned with when cash is actually received or paid.

---

[1]It is common, and perfectly reasonable, to ignore the time value of money when the time frame of a decision is sufficiently short so that the effect of discounting will be immaterial. When interest rates are high, as they were in the early and mid-1980s, the period of immateriality is, however, exceedingly short.

Nevertheless, managers must be careful not to become captives of terminology. While cash flow quite properly plays a primary role in management decisions, other assets, such as marketable securities and short-term accounts and notes receivable, are available to, or can be expected to, be transformed into cash within a short period of time. Correspondingly, accounts payable are a short-term claim of others upon the firm's cash. Hence, in practice many managers key upon *net current monetary assets*, rather than cash itself. Moreover, as shall be discussed in Chapter 20, it is to management's advantage to be aware of the impact of its decisions on income as well as on cash or on net current monetary assets.

5. *Accountability should be confined to matters over which a party has control.* In evaluating the performance of managers or the units of the organizations for which they are responsible, accountability should be confined to those costs or revenues over which they have control. It is common, and for some types of reports appropriate, to allocate the costs incurred by one unit of an organization to those of other units to which it provides services. The costs, for example, of operating a maintenance department may be allocated to manufacturing units. Under some allocation schemes, the costs assigned to an individual manufacturing unit may depend not only on the amount of service that it requests from the maintenance department but also on the overall costs incurred by the maintenance department. The amount of such costs may be a function of both the efficiency of the maintenance department and the amount of service provided to all other manufacturing units—factors which are beyond the control of any individual manufacturing unit. In evaluating the performance of any individual manufacturing unit, costs which it can control must be distinguished from those which it cannot.

Each of these themes, which serve as premises for many management accounting applications and concepts, will be developed in several different contexts. An appreciation of them will tie together and facilitate an understanding of much of the material that follows.

NATURE OF COSTS AND COST COMPONENTS

Fixed versus Variable Costs

Of all the ways that costs can be classified, unquestionably the most significant, from the perspective of managers, is by degree of variability. Managers must be able to estimate the effect of their actions on costs to be incurred in the future.

Fixed costs are those which will remain the same over fairly broad ranges of volume. They exist (at least in theory) when volume is zero and are constant in the absence of significant changes in volume.

Variable costs are those which change in direct proportion to changes in volume. In both definitions, "volume" refers to the quantity or output of the activity under consideration. In a manufacturing enterprise volume may be expressed in terms of physical units or dollar value of production. In service organizations or support units it could be expressed in units of service performed, such as customers called upon, patients or clients seen, documents processed, or miles driven. In sales departments it could be expressed as dollars of sales.

Fixed costs are *not unchanging*. Air conditioning and heating costs are almost always categorized as fixed costs, in spite of their volatility. They vary, however, with the weather, not with the volume or output of the organization. Costs of repairs are usually classified as fixed, even though they may also vary considerably from period to period. The magnitude of repair costs frequently depends on unpredictable breakdowns, which are random occurrences perhaps due to age, rather than on number of units produced.

The levels of some costs that are categorized as fixed are within the discretion of management. Expenditures for advertising, research and development, and community relations can be altered by management directive. Such programmable or discretionary costs are considered fixed because they vary at the option of management, rather than in response to changes in output or volume.

Fixed costs can be depicted graphically, as in Exhibit 17-2, which indicates the fixed costs incurred by a restaurant in relation to number of customers served. The horizontal line reveals that the costs (on the vertical axis) remain constant at $30,000 regardless of output (the horizontal axis).

Variable costs can be shown graphically, as in Exhibit 17-3, which indicates the cost of food in a restaurant. The upward-sloping straight line signifies that food costs are directly proportional to number of customers served.

Costs which contain both a fixed and a variable element are referred to as *mixed* costs. Electricity costs, for example, sometimes contain a fixed element, a monthly service charge, plus a variable element, a charge for each kilowatt used. The broader the classification of costs, the more likely is a particular category of cost to have both fixed and variable elements. Shipping costs will have both fixed and variable components in relation to number of packages shipped. The salaries of mailroom personnel and the depreciation on mailroom equipment will be primarily fixed. The cost of packaging materials will, however,

EXHIBIT 17-2

Illustration of Fixed Costs: Rent Expense in Relation to Number of Customers Served by a Restaurant

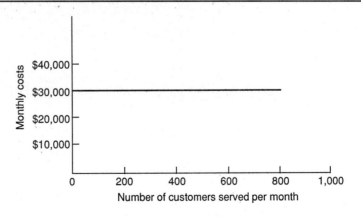

EXHIBIT 17-3

Illustration of Variable Costs: Food and Waiters' Costs in Relation to Number of Customers Served by a Restaurant

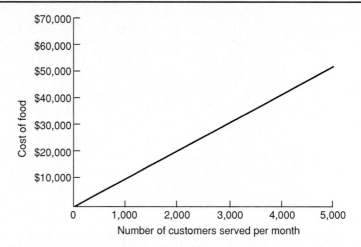

likely be variable. Mixed costs present no conceptual problems. For analytical purposes they can be viewed as consisting of two independent elements of cost, one fixed, the other variable.

The combination or summation of fixed and variable costs may now be shown in a graphical format as in Exhibit 17-4. This graph shows a bottom layer of fixed costs with variable costs added on top of the fixed cost layer. This graph, therefore, represents total costs, which may also be shown algebraically as

$$\text{Total costs} = \text{Fixed costs} + \text{Variable costs}$$

At 1,000 customers, total costs will be $30,000 plus $10,000, where the $10,000 is obtained from 1,000 customers multiplied by $10 per customer. In symbols, this can be represented and calculated as total costs of $40,000:

$$TC = FC + VC$$

$$TC = FC + \text{average } VC \text{ per customer} \times \text{Number of customers}$$

$$TC = \$30,000 + (\$10 \text{ per customer} \times 1,000 \text{ customers})$$

$$TC = \$40,000$$

More generally, if Y = total cost and X = number of customers,

$$Y = \$30,000 + \$10 \cdot X$$

This graphical and algebraic expression of total costs and its two components of fixed and variable costs will be referred to again in later discussions of cost behavior and in the analysis of changes in costs pertaining to various planning and control decisions by managers. While this model of cost behavior may be overly simplistic, it is a powerful and useful representation of cost components and their interaction.

EXHIBIT 17-4

Illustration of Total Costs: Combined Fixed and Variable Costs from Exhibits 17-2 and 17-3

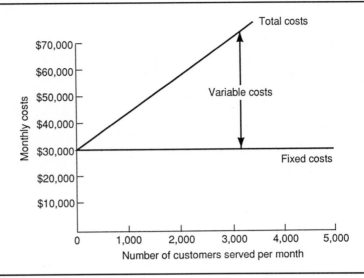

Variability and the Relevant Range

In practice, no costs are completely fixed. They are fixed only within a particular range of output. Among costs that are often thought of as fixed are rent, executive and supervisory salaries, and janitorial costs. Each of these costs will change if output expands or contracts to a point where the firm must make changes in its capacity. In the example of the restaurant, rent is fixed only as long as the firm can operate within the same amount of space. Should it require additional space, then rental costs would, of course, increase. Fixed costs, therefore, are defined as being fixed within a *relevant* range. The relevant range is simply the range that is appropriate for the decision at hand.

No costs can be inherently categorized as being either fixed or variable. For a decision as to whether to serve an additional eight customers per day, the cost of waiters may be fixed; no additional employees need be hired nor additional hours worked. For a decision as to whether to serve an additional 100 customers, the cost of waiters and food may be variable; experience may indicate that one additional waiter, costing $40, along with $60 of food is required for each 10 customers. Within the range of 100 customers, the cost of waiters alone would, when shown graphically, appear in the form of a series of steps (Exhibit 17-5). This series of steps can be approximated by a straight line.

In fact, all costs, both fixed and variable, usually can be described by a step function. Exhibit 17-6 depicts rent costs over a range of 3,000 customers, with the assumption that the maximum capacity of a single restaurant (or wing) is 1,000 customers. For each increment of 1,000 customers, additional space must be leased.

EXHIBIT 17-5
Illustration of Stepped Costs: Expenditures for Waiters in Relation to Customers Served

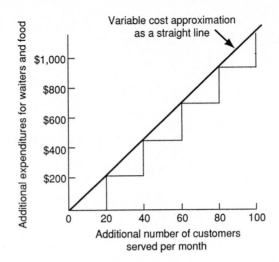

The primary distinction, therefore, between fixed and variable costs, is in the size of the step. If, within the range relevant for a particular decision, the costs are confined to a single step, then they are considered as fixed. If they increase by a sufficiently large number of steps that for the degree of accuracy required the steps can be depicted as an upward-sloping line, then they are classified as variable. If within the relevant range the costs are not confined to a single step and the steps are sufficiently large so that they cannot be considered

EXHIBIT 17-6
Alternative View of Fixed Costs: Rent Expense in Relation to Number of Customers Served (Range of 0 to 3,000 Customers)

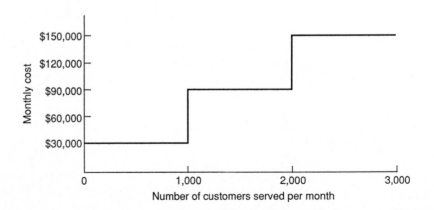

as an upward-sloping line, then they must be described as being in a step function and, accordingly, cannot be represented or analyzed by simple linear equations.

Cost per Unit, or Average Cost

Average (per unit) cost is arrived at by dividing the relevant total costs for a specified number of units of output by the number of units of output (customers, automobiles, etc.). Average, or per unit cost is the *slope (tangent) of a ray from the origin* to the point where this ray intersects the relevant cost curve depicted in Exhibits 17-2, 17-3, or 17-4. Thus, average total (fixed and variable) cost when there are 2,000 customers is, per Exhibit 17-4, $50,000 ÷ 2,000 = $25. Average fixed cost when there are that many customers is, per Exhibit 17-2, $30,000 ÷ 2,000 = $15. And average variable cost when there are that many customers is, per Exhibit 17-3, $20,000 ÷ 2,000 = $10. Average total cost should always equal average fixed plus average variable cost.

The *behavior* of *per unit cost* must be carefully distinguished from the behavior of *total cost*. As volume increases and resultant increasing *total costs* are spread over a larger number of units, the *cost per unit* decreases. This is shown in Panel A of Exhibit 17-7. Like total cost per unit, *fixed cost per unit* is always a downward-sloping curve approaching, but never reaching, the *X* axis, as shown in Panel B. In contrast, costs which are *variable* and related to output in a linear manner can be represented graphically on a *per unit basis* as a horizontal straight line. Panel C in Exhibit 17-7 shows that as volume increases, *per unit variable cost* remains constant.

Although average total cost may seem like a useful measure, it actually has very *little* applicability to the decisions that managers make. Indeed, there are *few*, if any, decisions for which use of average total cost is appropriate and for which a manager would not be better served by disaggregating average cost into its fixed and variable elements.

Managerial decisions in which costs must be taken into account invariably require forecasts of costs that will be incurred in the future. As long as total number of units produced will be different from that of a previous period, average unit cost will also be different. Thus, it would be incorrect to estimate future costs simply by multiplying total number of units by average cost. In forecasting costs of the future, the manager must be cognizant of the stability of some elements of unit cost and of the variability of others. Use of average cost, unfortunately, is an unacceptable shortcut to relevant cost analysis. For almost all of the decisions to be discussed in the remainder of this text, a breakdown of costs into fixed and variable portions is required and *incremental costs* will prove to play more of a role in managerial decision making than *average costs*.

Product versus Period Costs

As discussed in Chapter 4, costs may also be classified as *product* or *period* costs. Product costs are for labor, materials, or other production elements that can be associated with specific products. Period costs, by contrast, are recognized as expenses strictly on the basis of time, irrespective of the number of units produced in a period. Most fixed costs are period costs, and most variable costs are product costs.

EXHIBIT 17-7
Illustration of Unit Costs

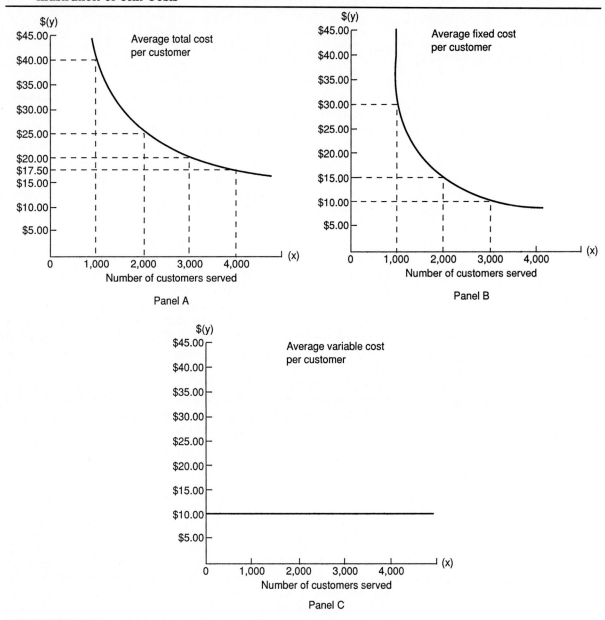

Panel A — Average total cost per customer

Panel B — Average fixed cost per customer

Panel C — Average variable cost per customer

Direct versus Indirect Costs

Costs can be further classified according to whether they are *direct* or *indirect*. Direct costs are those which are clearly and easily traceable to, and identified with, a specific product, activity, client, or service. Indirect costs, on the other hand, are not readily traceable to, or identified with, the firm's output—at least not without incurring costs of monitoring and analysis that exceed the value of the information.

In a manufacturing firm, *direct materials* (with respect to the product) are the components and subassemblies that are transformed into the final product and are an integral part of it. *Indirect materials* are those manufacturing ingredients that cannot be readily associated with specific units of product. They include cleaning supplies and machine lubricants. In a service organization, most materials are indirect because there is little tangible output with which to associate them.

Similarly, in a manufacturing firm, *direct labor* (with respect to the product) is the services of personnel that can be ascribed directly to the product. It typically includes the services of machine operators and assemblers. *Indirect labor* is the services of personnel which have only an oblique connection to the product. It includes the wages and salaries of supervisors (particularly those whose responsibilities encompass more than one product), most maintenance personnel, and factory accountants and other administrative employees. Indirect manufacturing costs, in addition to labor and materials, typically include power, heating, rent, and depreciation.

Although the distinction between direct and indirect costs is most often made with reference to manufacturing companies, it is equally valid as it applies to service organizations. In a law firm, for example, the salaries of most professional attorneys would be classified as direct labor with regard to clients, since their billable hours can be ascribed to specific cases. In contrast, the salary of an administrator who manages the office and has no client responsibilities would be classified as an indirect cost. In a hospital, the costs associated with nurses are usually considered direct labor with respect to patient care. However, that of orderlies and clerks is considered indirect labor. The difference would be ascribed to the ease with which their activities can be related to specific patients.

Indirect manufacturing costs are often called *factory overhead, burden*, or simply *overhead*.

Costs Classified for a Specific Cost Object

The classification of costs into direct and indirect categories must always be made in relation to the specific *cost object*—the costing unit under consideration. Whereas the salary of an assembly department supervisor may be an indirect cost of the products being assembled, it may nevertheless be a direct cost of the assembly department. This would be the case where the services of the supervisor are clearly identifiable with the assembly department but not with any of the specific products being assembled.

New Manufacturing Techniques Require New Cost Classifications

Traditional notions as to how certain costs should be classified are rapidly being rejected in light of technological changes. Most factory labor, for example, used to be classified as both direct and variable. In a robotics-based factory that uses computer integrated manufacturing (CIM) processes, labor has both diminished in significance and changed in role. Instead of being directly involved in conventional production activities, employees now spend their time monitoring and adjusting complex equipment and controls, performing machine maintenance, and conducting quality control inspections. In the modern factory, labor costs are a relatively small percentage of total costs and less variable with product output than they were in older manufacturing environments. On the other hand, machine costs are considerably more significant, although they too are relatively fixed.

In later sections of this text, the distinctions as well as the overlaps among these terms will be considered in the context of specific organizations. What appear to be variable and direct costs in one factory may be treated quite differently in another factory producing what may appear to be quite similar products. Similarly, in nonprofit and service organizations, these typical definitions cannot be applied without first inquiring as to the purpose of the costing (i.e., what is the cost object, and how is the variability or traceability of those costs different in the particular organization or unit?).

Other terms that are frequently used in management accounting, particularly in a manufacturing setting, include:

Prime costs—usually defined as direct materials plus direct labor
Conversion costs—usually defined as direct labor plus factory overhead (i.e., the cost of converting raw materials to final products)

Many organizations use hybrid terms that denote other combinations of direct and indirect costs. For example, Hewlett-Packard uses only the term *conversion costs* and does not separately analyze direct labor and factory overhead.

Standard Costs

The discussion of costs and cost concepts so far has related to *actual costs*—costs which occurred, or are at least reported as having occurred, during a given period. The expiration of assets which generates the reported expense is assumed to be a fact, and we measure the quantity and value of those expirations as best we can.

A quite different phenomenon is the concept of *standard costs*. Standard costs are *hypothetical costs* established by management. We deal with standard costs in Chapter 22. Standard costing procedures are likely to be based upon many of the aforementioned actual cost concepts—direct and indirect labor, fixed and variable costs, etc. And they are likely indeed to bear a close relationship to actual costs. But they will not be something that accountants have actually measured. They will rather consist of targets set by management derived from past experience or special statistical or engineering studies.

DETERMINING THE BEHAVIOR OF COSTS

The importance of distinguishing between fixed and variable portions of cost cannot be overemphasized; neither unfortunately can the difficulties of establishing specific relationships between costs and volume.

Although certain types of costs are often considered to be either fixed or variable, there is considerable risk in making assumptions about costs without examining historical data and making adjustments for changes that may take place in the future. Direct labor, for example, by definition can be traced to units of product. Direct labor is a prime example of a cost that varies with volume of output, particularly when employees are paid on an hourly basis. But as the proportion of compensation paid as "fringe benefits" increases, direct labor becomes more of a fixed cost and less of a variable cost. If, for example, a company pays the medical insurance premiums of its employees, then the portion of compensation representing the insurance premiums may be fixed; changes in hours worked will have no effect on medical insurance costs. Similarly, in some industries, owing to Supplementary Unemployment Benefits (SUB) employees are guaranteed a specified percentage of their earnings, regardless of number of hours actually worked. Temporary reductions in the size of the workforce, therefore, will have only a minimal impact on labor costs.

In relating costs to volume, the variable selected to represent volume must depend on the decision at hand. If management needs to estimate production costs at various levels of output, then number of units produced may serve as an appropriate indicator of volume. In that case, total costs of production, including labor, materials, depreciation, and maintenance, may be compared to number of units produced. But if, on the other hand, management wishes to establish a pattern of maintenance costs for purposes of control, then machine hours may be a more useful indicator of volume. The amount of maintenance required is more likely to be influenced by the number of hours that machinery is in use than it is by the number of units produced.

There are several methods of determining relationships of costs to volume. The methods range widely in both accuracy and sophistication; selection of method must be based on comparison of the added cost of using a particular method to the value of the incremental accuracy to be obtained.

Each of the following methods, with the exception of the first, involves analysis of data of the past. They are appropriate for making decisions that will affect the future, therefore, only insofar as conditions of the future will be similar to those in the past.

Deductive Analysis

Deductive analysis may be used to indicate the way costs in theory *should* behave in relation to volume. Deductive reasoning with respect to costs is often associated with, and carried out by, industrial engineers.

Deductive analysis requires the study of each element that goes into producing the goods or providing the service. A team of industrial engineers, for example, might determine the number of units of raw materials and minutes of labor required to produce the desired output, assuming that production was carried out in a reasonably efficient manner. It would take into account the time and materials required to start up and shut down a process as well as the elements of production, such as maintenance and supervision, that do not vary directly with output. It would also make allowance for normal waste and errors. Working with budget analysts or accountants, it would assign appropriate costs to the units of material or hours of labor. The result of its efforts would be a schedule of anticipated costs at various levels of output or a formula that expresses the relationships between costs and output.

Deductive analysis is particularly suited for production processes that are repetitive and exhibit a close relationship between inputs and outputs. It is not very useful where the product or service must be customized or where a high percentage of costs is "indirect" and cannot readily be traced to output. It would be more suitable for determining cost relationships on an automobile assembly line than in an automobile repair shop.

Deductive analysis rests on the assumption that the engineers or others making the analysis have taken into account all factors that affect the input–output relationships. People or processes seldom operate as they should, however; at the very least, therefore, normative relationships should be tested against actual experience before they are considered reliable.

Scatter Diagram

One can work more directly from empirical data to arrive at relationships of cost to volume. Historical data can be plotted on a graph. Relationships between cost and volume can be observed visually, or a curve can be fitted by hand and eye with a straight edge and graph paper.

Suppose that Rapid-Lube, a chain of auto service stations specializing in lubrication and oil changes, wishes to establish the relationship between labor costs and number of cars serviced. In one district, the data that follow were observed over a period of 12 months.

Operating Costs at Various Levels of Activity

Month	Number of Cars Serviced	Labor Costs
January	15,000	$372,000
February	15,400	382,000
March	21,600	495,000
April	21,300	500,000
May	20,700	480,000
June	12,600	325,000
July	15,800	381,000
August	18,000	435,000
September	22,200	513,000
October	21,600	501,500
November	19,200	462,000
December	12,000	307,000

Exhibit 17-8 indicates the data plotted on a scatter diagram. The curve that runs through the points reflects a linear relationship between volume and labor costs. At a volume of 14,000 cars serviced, the line indicates that labor costs were approximately $350,000. At a volume of 19,000, costs were approximately $450,000. For each change of 5,000 cars served (19,000 − 14,000) labor costs increased by $100,000 ($450,000 − $350,000). It appears, therefore, that average variable costs are approximately $20 ($100,000 ÷ 5,000 cars) per car serviced. Since total labor costs comprise a variable and a nonvariable element, once the variable element is known, the nonvariable can readily be deduced. At a volume of 14,000 cars serviced, the curve indicates that total costs would be approximately $350,000. Variable costs would be $280,000 (14,000 × $20). Hence, the nonvariable element would be $70,000 ($350,000 − $280,000). The relationship between costs and volume can be expressed in equation form as

$$\text{Total labor costs} = \$70,000 + \$20 \times \text{No. of cars serviced}$$

EXHIBIT 17-8
Illustration of Scatter Diagram: Relationship of Labor Costs to Number of Cars Serviced

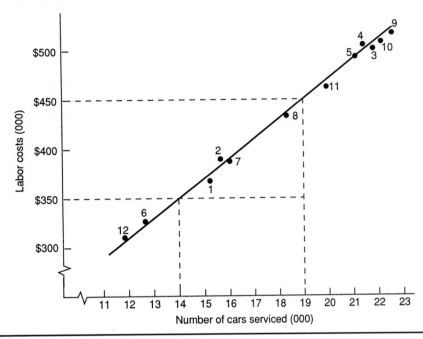

Note: Curve has been fitted visually. Numbers refer to months of the year.

High–Low Method

The high–low method establishes cost–volume relationships based on only two points—a high-volume point and a low-volume point. In the data presented the highest volume was in September; the lowest, in December. The following table indicates activity, costs, and changes:

Month	Volume	Cost
September	22,200	$513,000
December	12,000	307,000
Change	10,200	$206,000

Variable costs would be approximately $20.20, determined as follows:

$$\frac{\text{Change in costs}}{\text{Change in volume}} = \frac{\$206,000}{10,200} = \$20.196$$

This analysis is equivalent to finding the slope of a line and can be expressed as

$$b = \frac{\Delta y}{\Delta x} = \frac{\text{Rise}}{\text{Run}}$$

where b = slope = $20.196. It is then the average variable cost. The remaining (nonvariable) costs are depicted as the intercept of the line whose equation is

$$y = a + bx$$

where the costs not explained by changes in volume would be approximately $64,650:

Total costs at volume of 22,200	$513,000
Variable costs (22,200 × $20.196)	448,350
Remaining costs (a)	$ 64,650

In equation form,

$$\text{Total costs} = \$64,650 + \$20.196x$$

where x is the number of cars serviced.

A danger of using the high–low method is that either the high or low points may be "outliers," atypical of normal cost relationships. It is useful, therefore, to use the high–low technique in conjunction with the scatter diagram approach. Should either the high or low point be inordinately far from the plotted line, then that point should be replaced by one that is closer to the line. In addition, results of the high–low method can be verified for reasonableness by carrying out the same analysis using selected other points, such as the second highest and the second lowest. These modifications or adjustments are often called a *representative high–low method*.

It must also be recognized that no conclusions regarding the behavior of costs can be inferred for levels of activity above the high point or below the low point. The constant in the cost equation—the amount that cannot be explained by the changes in level of activity—is often thought of as representing fixed costs. Such costs would, however, represent true fixed costs only if the linear relationship established between the high and low points extended to zero volume. If the data include no points near the zero level of activity, there are no grounds for assuming that the relationship is constant. Sometimes, high–low analysis will indicate that fixed costs are negative. *Negative fixed costs* should be interpreted as indicating nothing more than a situation wherein if the line described by the equation were extended to zero activity it would cross the y axis at a negative point.

Linear Regression Analysis

Linear regression is a mathematical means of relating changes in one variable to changes in one or more variables on which its value depends. For example, changes in costs may be associated with changes in production volume. The variable whose value depends on the other variable is known as the dependent variable; the one or more variables that have an influence on the dependent variable are referred to as independent variables. Linear regression analysis in which only one independent variable is taken into account is called *simple* regression; that in which more than one independent variable is examined is called *multiple* regression.

Simple linear regression establishes a mathematical expression of the relationships between dependent and independent variables by taking into account all available data points—not just two as does the high–low method. The resultant equation is of a line that best fits between the points as plotted on a scatter diagram—one that minimizes the distances between the points and the line. The "goodness of fit" can be measured and expressed as the coefficient of determination (r^2). The coefficient of determination (r^2) is the square of the correlation coefficient (r) and should usually exceed .8 or 80% if the relationship is to be considered reliable.

In simple linear regression, the relationship between dependent and independent variable is expressed as an equation of the form

$$y = a + bx$$

where y is the dependent variable, such as total costs

$\quad\quad$ x is the independent variable, such as volume

$\quad\quad$ a is the y intercept, indicative, for example, of fixed costs

$\quad\quad$ b is the regression coefficient, indicative of the slope of the line or the unit variable cost

The regression coefficient (b) representing the variable portion of cost can be determined by solving the following equation:

$$b = \frac{n\Sigma xy - \Sigma x \Sigma y}{n\Sigma x^2 - (\Sigma x)^2}$$

where n is the number of observations. Then, using the results of that equation, the y intercept (a) can be determined by solving

$$a = \frac{\Sigma y}{n} - b\left(\frac{\Sigma x}{n}\right)$$

Exhibit 17-9 indicates the computation of the regression equation based on the data pertaining to the chain of auto service stations presented earlier. While these computations appear complex, the use of computers or even pocket calculators can dramatically simplify the calculation of regression coefficients.

The derivation of the formulas used to determine the regression equation as well as an adequate discussion of the uses and limitations of regression analysis is beyond the scope of this book. The example is provided merely to put readers on notice that there are available a variety of statistical techniques, many of which are exceedingly sophisticated and reliable, that can assist the manager in establishing historical relationships between costs and volume. Basic regression algorithms are readily available to managers, as they are incorporated into all the major personal computer spreadsheet programs.

Economists' versus Accountants' Views of Costs

There are two quite different views about the behavior of costs in the manufacturing firm—that of the managerial accountant on the one hand, and that of the economist on the other. The two views of cost are contrasted in Exhibit 17-10.

EXHIBIT 17-9

Example of Regression Analysis: Relationship between Labor Costs and Number of Cars Serviced in a Chain of Auto Service Stations

Month	X Number of Cars Serviced	Y Labor Costs	X^2 (000s omitted)	XY (000s omitted)
1. January	15,000	$ 372,000	225,000	5,580,000
2. February	15,400	382,000	237,160	5,882,800
3. March	21,600	495,000	466,560	10,692,000
4. April	21,300	500,000	453,690	10,650,000
5. May	20,700	480,000	428,490	9,936,000
6. June	12,600	325,000	158,760	4,095,000
7. July	15,800	381,000	249,640	6,019,800
8. August	18,000	435,000	324,000	7,830,000
9. September	22,200	513,000	492,840	11,388,600
10. October	21,600	501,500	466,560	10,832,400
11. November	19,200	462,000	368,640	8,870,400
12. December	12,000	307,000	144,000	3,684,000
	215,400	$5,153,500	4,015,340	95,461,000

$$b = \frac{n\Sigma xy - \Sigma x\Sigma y}{n\Sigma x^2 - (\Sigma x)^2}$$

$$= \frac{12(95,461,000) - 215,400(5,153,500)}{12(4,015,340,000) - (215,400)^2} = 19.84873$$

$$a = \frac{\Sigma y}{n} - b\left(\frac{\Sigma x}{n}\right)$$

$$= \frac{5,153,500}{12} - 19.84873\left(\frac{215,400}{12}\right) = 73,170$$

$$y \text{ intercept } (a) = \$73,170$$

Variable element of cost (b) = $19.85

In equation form, labor costs (y) are related to number of cars serviced (x) as follows:

$$y = \$73,170 + \$19.85X$$

The coefficient of determination (r^2) of this linear cost function (computation not shown) is .99. This means that 99 percent of the variance of labor costs around its mean can be explained by changes in volume. The remaining 1 percent is attributable either to other variables or to random variation.

The managerial accountant has traditionally viewed fixed costs as a straight horizontal line and variable costs as a straight upward-sloping line, as in Exhibits 17-2, 17-3, and 17-4. Variable costs *per unit* are generally perceived as remaining constant. Total costs, being the simple sum of fixed and variable costs, are thereby also seen as a straight upward-sloping line. Average total (fixed and variable) cost, by contrast, is seen by the accountant as a downward-sloping curve that is relatively steep at lower levels of activity but that flattens out at higher levels. Average total cost decreases as volume increases because the fixed costs are spread over a larger number of units, as was described in connection with Exhibit 17-7. The curve flattens out as volume increases because the dollar change in fixed costs per unit gets continually smaller as the number of units increases. If, for example, fixed costs are $1,000, then an increase in number of units produced from 10 to 20 would decrease fixed costs per unit from $100 to $50—a decrease of $50. In contrast, an increase in number of units from 20 to 30 would decrease fixed costs per unit from $50 to $33.33—a decrease of only $16.67.

An accountant's versus an economist's view of costs is shown in Exhibit 17-10. Like the accountant, the economist views fixed cost as a straight horizontal line (at least in the short run). Unlike the accountant, however, the economist tends to view variable costs as a curve that rises, first at a decreasing rate, then at a constant rate, and finally at an increasing rate. Variable costs *per unit*, according to the economist (depicted as the slope of a ray from the origin where such a line intersects the variable cost curve), decrease at first because a firm is able to take advantage of economies of scale both in the purchase of raw materials and in production processes. As the firm reaches its optimum capacity, the economies of scale are eliminated and variable costs per unit are at a minimum. Then, as the firm goes beyond optimum capacity, it faces increases in the price of raw materials and inefficiencies in production processes, and variable costs per unit increase. The economist's view of average total cost is similar to that of the accountant, except that the curve turns upward (at the point that variable costs per unit begin to increase) rather than continuing downward.

EXHIBIT 17-10
Accountant's versus Economist's View of Costs

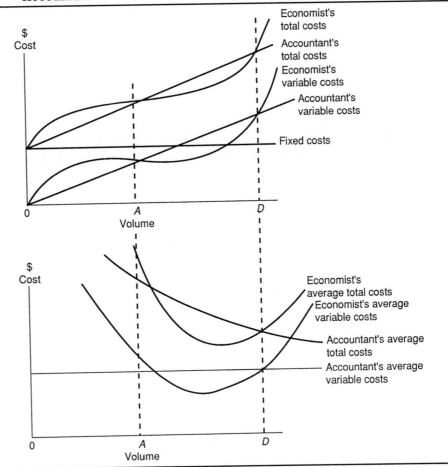

The economist's and accountant's views about the behavior of costs can be thought of as consistent one with another in the following sense. The accountant provides information for decisions for which the relevant range is one in which variable costs per unit remain relatively constant and the total variable cost curve can be thought of as linear—over the distance between *A* and *D* in Exhibit 17-10. The relevant range for the economist is considerably broader and includes those ends of the curves which represent both decreasing and increasing variable costs per unit.

A more realistic view of these relationships is shown in the three panels of Exhibit 17-11. In this situation, a step function for fixed costs is shown with two steps. A curvilinear function is shown for variable costs with two changes in slope. The firm is most efficient whenever the curve flattens and per unit

EXHIBIT 17-11
Realistic View of Cost Relationships

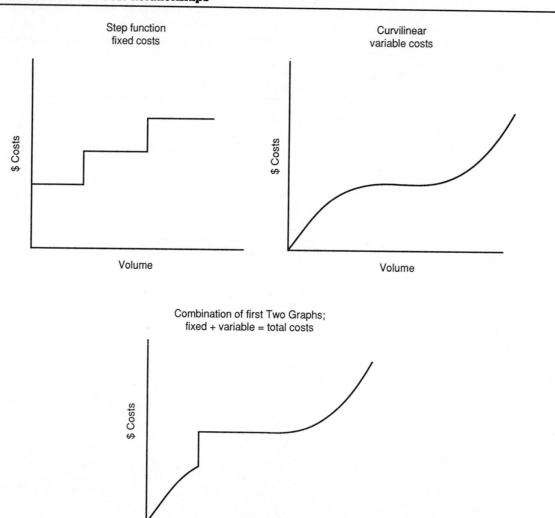

costs are thereby low. These two cost behavior patterns are then combined into total costs in the third panel, such that total costs are shown with two major step increases at the points where the fixed costs have step increases. This more realistic view is often taken in actual practice, where large changes in volume or output are being considered. However, where only small segments of each relationship are under consideration, then a linear approximation of that small segment of volume may be treated as a linear relationship. In the remainder of this chapter, we will be analyzing only simple linear segments of the total cost curve.

COST–VOLUME–PROFIT ANALYSIS

The basic relationship that total costs equal fixed cost plus variable costs, with variable costs being equal to variable cost per unit times number of units sold, can be used to facilitate a number of common types of management decisions.

The Basic Framework

Suppose that the Rapid-Lube Company mentioned in our previous example incurs monthly fixed costs of $48,000. This amount includes not only the fixed component of labor costs (the previous example dealt only with labor costs) but also rent, advertising, supervision, interest, and supplies. Total variable cost of changing oil and providing lubrication service, including materials and the variable portion of labor, is $28 per car. The standard charge for the service is $32 per car.

Total revenue earned by the company will be equal to selling price per unit ($32) times number of cars serviced.

Income will be equal to total revenue minus total costs, or

Income = (Selling price × Number of cars serviced)

  − Fixed costs − (Unit variable costs

  × Number of cars serviced)

Based on this relationship, the types of questions that follow can readily be answered.

1. How many cars must be serviced each month in order for the company to break even (earn profit of zero)?

Let Q = the unknown, number of cars that must be serviced

Desired income = (Selling price per unit)Q
  − Fixed costs
  − (Unit variable costs)Q
$0 = \$32Q - \$48{,}000 - \$28Q$
$\$48{,}000 = 4Q$
$Q = 12{,}000$ cars

2. What number of cars must be serviced each month in order for the company to earn a profit of $40,000?

$$\text{Let } Q = \text{number of cars that must be serviced}$$

$$\text{Desired income} = \$40,000$$

$$\$40,000 = \$32Q - \$48,000 - \$28Q$$

$$\$88,000 = 4Q$$

$$Q = 22,000 \text{ cars}$$

In solving each of the equations in the two illustrations, the variable cost per unit ($28) was subtracted from the revenue per unit ($32). The difference between the two represents the *contribution margin*. Contribution margin is defined as the excess of sales price over *variable* costs. Each unit of service *contributes* $4 toward covering overhead and realizing the profit objective. Also, in each of the illustrations, this contribution margin of $4 was divided into the sum of desired income and fixed costs in order to determine required volume of unit sales. Thus, to look at the relationship from a slightly different perspective:

Required output (in units)

$$Q = \frac{\text{Fixed costs} + \text{Desired income}}{\text{Contribution margin}}$$

The break-even point (i.e., zero desired income) may be determined as

$$\text{Break-even point} = \frac{\$48,000 + 0}{\$4} = 12,000 \text{ units}$$

The contribution margin is often expressed as a ratio or percentage rather than an absolute dollar amount. The ratio is calculated as follows:

$$\text{Contribution margin ratio} = \text{CMR}$$

$$\text{CMR} = 1 - \frac{\text{Variable costs per unit}}{\text{Selling price per unit}}$$

or:

$$\text{CMR} = \frac{\text{Contribution margin per unit}}{\text{Selling price per unit}}$$

In the example,

$$\text{Contribution margin ratio} = 1 - \frac{\$28}{\$32}$$

$$\text{CMR} = 1 - .875 = .125$$

$$\text{CMR} = 12.5\%$$

or:

$$\text{CMR} = \frac{\$4}{\$32} = .125 = 12.5\%$$

Unit variable costs are 87.5% of unit selling price. Therefore, the remaining 12.5% is a contribution toward fixed costs and desired income. These two components must always sum to 100%.

The contribution margin expressed in decimal or percentage form facilitates questions relating to the *dollar* volume of sales required to achieve a particular level of earnings.

3. What is the dollar volume of sales (i.e., revenues) necessary for the firm to break even?

Desired income at the break-even point is, as before, zero.
Variable costs ($28 per unit) are 87.5 percent of revenues ($32 per unit).

$$\text{Desired income} = \text{Required revenues} - \text{Fixed costs}$$
$$- \text{Variable costs}$$
$$\$0 = \text{Required revenues} - \$48,000$$
$$- .875 \text{ (Required revenues)}$$
$$\$48,000 = \text{Required revenues} - .875 \text{ (Required revenues)}$$
$$\$48,000 = .125 \text{ (Required revenues)}$$
$$\text{Required revenues} = \frac{\$48,000}{.125}$$

Required revenues = $384,000

The required dollar volume of sales could have just as easily been computed by making direct use in the equation of the contribution margin ratio. In the final step of the solution, the sum of fixed costs and desired income ($48,000 + $0) could be divided by the contribution margin *ratio* (.125) to arrive at the required revenues. The equation could, therefore, be reformulated as

$$\text{Required revenues} = \frac{\text{Fixed costs} + \text{Desired income}}{\text{Contribution margin ratio}}$$

$$\text{Required revenues} = \frac{\$48,000 + 0}{.125} = \$384,000$$

Because the selling price is $32 per unit, revenues of $384,000 are the equivalent of 12,000 cars serviced; that is, $384,000 divided by $32.

The relationships between costs and revenues can be shown diagrammatically. Exhibit 17-12 indicates the fixed costs, variable costs, and total costs of servicing cars at various levels of volume. The line representing total costs indicates the sum of the fixed costs ($48,000) and the variable costs ($28 times units of service); hence it is parallel to the line representing variable costs and each point is $48,000 greater than the point for corresponding volume on the variable cost line.

Exhibit 17-13 illustrates a *cost–volume–profit* chart. It indicates total cost (from Exhibit 17-12) and total revenue ($32 times number of units of service). In the shaded area total cost exceeds total revenue; hence the firm incurs a loss. The point of intersection (at 12,000 units; $384,000) is the break-even point. Beyond the point of intersection the firm earns profits, the amount of which at any particular volume of service will be the dollar difference between the two lines.

EXHIBIT 17-12
Fixed Costs and Variable Costs per Number of Cars Serviced

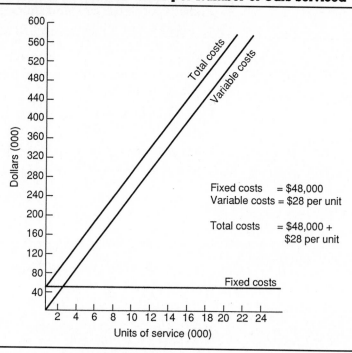

Fixed costs   = $48,000
Variable costs = $28 per unit

Total costs   = $48,000 +
                          $28 per unit

EXHIBIT 17-13
Cost–Volume–Profit Chart
Rapid-Lube Service Centers

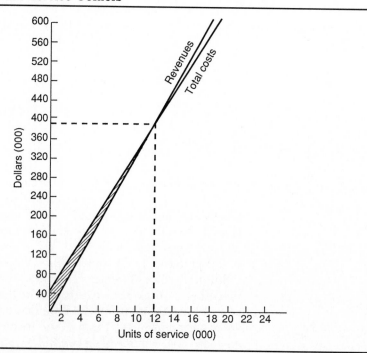

EXHIBIT 17-14
   Profit–Volume Chart
   Rapid-Lube Service Centers

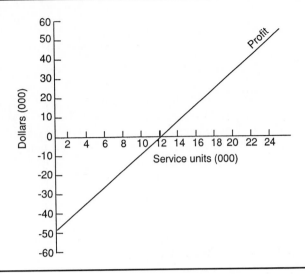

Exhibit 17-14, known as a *profit–volume* chart, focuses on profits rather than costs or revenues. The area below the horizontal axis represents a loss; that above, a profit. The income line indicates the profit at the various levels of volume. Each point along the income line represents the difference between the total cost and total revenue lines of Exhibit 17-13. The net income line crosses the horizontal axis (the zero income level) at the break-even point. It meets the vertical axis (the zero volume level) at – $48,000, an amount representing the fixed costs. Each of these last two graphs could be further constrained by a relevant range. If Rapid-Lube's capacity is only 18,000 units, its profit potential is relatively small.

Charts of this type are perhaps of greater interest to managers of the 1990s than they were to those of earlier years. Desktop computers, which are today components of comprehensive executive information systems (EIS), permit a manager to vary assumptions regarding prices and costs and instantaneously obtain a graphic display of anticipated profits at various levels of volume.

Balancing of Fixed and Variable Costs

The basic relationships between fixed costs and variable costs can be used to better understand other types of common issues facing managers. Balancing of costs between fixed and variable components is but one example. Suppose that Rapid-Lube has the opportunity to lease new equipment which would reduce variable labor costs by $.30 per car serviced. Equipment rental charges would be $4,200 per month. The effect of the acquisition would be to increase fixed costs from $48,000 to $52,200 and to decrease variable costs from $28.00 to $27.70 per car serviced. What volume of cars serviced per month would justify the added fixed costs?

The acquisition of the equipment would be justified as long as the volume of cars serviced is sufficiently great to make the cost saving of $.30 per car equal to or greater than the additional fixed costs of $4,200.

$$\text{Let } Q = \text{ the required volume of cars serviced}$$

$$\$.30Q = \$4,200$$

$$Q = 14,000 \text{ cars}$$

Under the existing configuration of inputs without the new equipment, total costs at a level of 14,000 cars would be $440,000—fixed costs of $48,000 plus variable costs of 14,000 times $28. Under the proposed configuration, total costs at a level of 14,000 would be the same $440,000—fixed costs of $52,200 plus variable costs of 14,000 times $27.70. At any volume greater than 14,000, total costs would be less under the proposed configuration. At 15,000 cars, for example, the *saving* in variable costs ($.30 × 15,000 = $4,500) would exceed the *addition* to fixed costs ($2,100).

Significance of the Break-Even Point and Opportunity Cost

Cost–volume–profit analysis is commonly referred to as break-even analysis, and discussions (such as those in this text) often focus on the break-even point. The break-even point unquestionably has dramatic appeal. An activity that results in losses is considered far more of a failure than one that reports at least some profits, no matter how meager. It is hard to see, however, why the break-even point, at least as traditionally calculated, has very much economic significance. A profit-oriented firm does not enter into ventures merely to break even. Rather, it does so to provide returns to owners greater than can be obtained from other investment opportunities.

A firm, for example, that earns a return of zero dollars on an investment of $1 million can hardly be considered to have broken even if, by purchasing risk-free Treasury notes, it could have earned a return of $80,000. At the very least, the loss of the opportunity forgone is $80,000. The difference in return that results from employing resources to less than their optimum advantage is an *opportunity cost*. In considering proposals for the investment of resources, the opportunity cost can readily be incorporated into cost–profit–value analysis either by including it as an additional expenditure (a cost of capital, for example) or by taking it into account in establishing "desired income." The amount of forgone income is a very useful benchmark for a variety of managerial decisions.

Cost–Volume–Profit Analysis: Some Caveats

Cost–volume–profit analysis requires the separation of costs into fixed and variable elements. Whatever specific form the analysis takes, it is a useful—indeed essential—element of the planning process. Its limitations, however, cannot be overlooked.

First, cost–volume–profit analysis is based on static relationships. It assumes that the association between costs and volume will remain constant, at least within the relevant range. But cost–volume relationships are, in fact, seldom stable. Management is, or at least should be, continually searching for ways to reduce cost and increase output. Similarly, in a dynamic economy—and most certainly in an inflationary one—the prices of either inputs or outputs seldom remain the same for long. Moreover, changes in costs, technology, and prices are intertwined, rather than independent as implied by the simple cost–volume–profit relationships illustrated in this text and often assumed by managers. Although accountants are careful to distinguish between the short run and the long run, changes evolve over time; they cannot empirically be categorized into convenient time divisions.

Second, the linear relationships of cost–volume–profit analysis imply that firms can freely move up or down the cost and revenue curves without altering the shape or position of the curves. Such may not be the case with respect to costs, as shown in Exhibit 17-11. There may, for example, be substantial costs associated with reduction of volume. These may take the form of supplementary unemployment benefits, loss of favorable relationships with suppliers, and hiring and start-up costs when volume is subsequently increased to previous levels.

But it is not only views on behavior of *costs* that separate accountants and economists. An equally important distinction between the two groups involves a difference in assumptions about *revenue*. In the accountant's cost–volume–profit analysis, total revenue is a straight line emanating from the origin; price is assumed to be constant. To the economist, this would be valid only if the firm is faced with a perfectly competitive market. Normally, firms, selling in imperfectly competitive markets, are assumed to be faced with downward-sloping demand (average revenue) curves. In order to increase sales volume, the firm may have to reduce prices, either across the board or by offering quantity or other special discounts. This implies that total revenue will grow with increasing volume, but at a constantly falling rate of growth, up to some maximum point and thereafter will fall with further increases in output. In other words, the total revenue curve will be a parabola, first rising, then falling. Needless to say, when one tries to build *both* curved total revenue and curved total cost lines into cost–volume–profit relationships, the problems are considerably more complex than can be depicted in the cost–volume–profit analysis of this introductory text.

Third, the cost and revenue functions used in cost–volume–profit analysis are no better than the underlying accounting data. They may be affected by all of the choices among accounting methods, estimates, and allocations that have been discussed in the text to this point and will be discussed in the chapters that follow.

Fourth, cost–volume–profit relationships may lead to inferences as to causal associations that are unwarranted. Changes in volume may require increases in some types of costs. If, for example, a firm is to produce a greater number of units, then it may have no choice but to purchase a greater amount of raw materials. But other types of costs, although analytically associated with changes in volume, may in fact vary with volume only because management elects to allow them to. As a matter of tradition or implicit policy decisions, for example, management may budget research and development costs as a percentage of sales. But the increase in volume does not "cause" an increase in research and development costs. Still other types of costs may be the moving force behind the changes in volume, rather than the other way around. Advertising costs, for example, may drive, as opposed to be driven by, sales volume. Thus, if cost–volume–profit relationships are to be analytically useful, it is essential that dependent and independent variables be correctly categorized. Causal relationships cannot be assumed, even where linear equations and graphs are used to analyze cost behavior patterns.

Time Series and Trends

Analyzing changes over time is one of the most important means of cost control. Knowledge of how and why costs vary over time is essential to effective planning and budgeting. A scatter diagram or plot is one easy and convenient way to display cost changes over time. Plotting total costs, as well as fixed and variable costs (on the vertical axis) with respect to time (on the horizontal axis) is another useful way of assessing cost behavior. In many cases, systematic shifts in costs will be visually evident from such graphs. These shifts may help in identifying possible steps in the fixed cost relationships or in the limits of the relevant range. Time series plots may also enable managers to discern data from prior time periods that are no longer relevant to the current decisions or to the current environment.

The analyst should always be aware of clusters or segments within any plots, but especially in a time series plot. These clusters or segments may indicate that the costs in those time periods are unique or represent other types of cost relationships. When those clusters are excluded, or analyzed separately, the stability and linearity of fixed and variable costs for the remaining time periods are often much more meaningful. Exhibit 17-15 indicates two clusters of heating costs, both of which are fixed but differ depending on the season. In other words, by being sensitive to patterns in the time series plots of cost data, the manager may be better able to decide which data to use in establishing fixed and variable cost relationships and which to use in preparing budgets and break-even analyses. Time series plots, especially of monthly or weekly data, can be very revealing and can indicate relationships that may otherwise only be known on an intuitive basis or may only be suspected by a few particularly astute managers.

EXHIBIT 17-15
Time Series Plot of Total Costs Representing Two Clusters

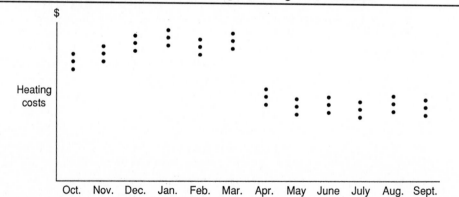

Several themes underlie the practice of management accounting, one of which is that only future, not past, costs are relevant to virtually all decisions that managers are called upon to make. In estimating costs that will be incurred in the future, managers must be able to discriminate between those that are likely to change as a result of managerial action and those that will remain the same. This chapter has focused on the distinction between fixed costs and variable costs. It has highlighted the means of classifying costs by degree of variability and of analyzing the impact of changes in volume upon costs and profits. The fundamental cost–volume–profit relationships set forth in this chapter underlie many of the principles of managerial accounting and analysis that are adhered to in practice and will be discussed in the remaining sections of this text.

Exercise for Review and Self-Testing

An analysis of a firm's monthly costs reveals the following:

	Fixed Elements	Variable Elements (per unit)
Direct labor	$11,000	$1.80
Direct materials		5.90
Power	400	
Rental of plant and equipment	5,000	
Maintenance	2,000	.20
Other costs	1,600	.10
Total	$20,000	$8.00

Selling price per unit is $10.
1. How much does the sale of each unit contribute toward covering fixed costs?
2. How many units must the firm produce and sell to break even—that is, to assure that total contributions to fixed costs are exactly equal to fixed costs?
3. How many units would the firm have to produce and sell in order to cover all costs and earn a profit of $6,000?
4. What would be the profit of the firm if it were to produce and sell
   a. 12,000 units?
   b. 8,000 units?
5. Suppose that the firm was able to rent additional equipment, at a cost of $2,000 per month, which would reduce variable costs by $.20 per unit. How would this change affect:
   a. The break-even point?
   b. Profit, if the firm were to produce and sell 12,000 units?
   c. Profit, if the firm were to produce and sell 8,000 units?
6. In general, what is the effect on the break-even point and the contribution margin (per unit contribution to fixed costs and earnings) of:
   a. An increase in fixed costs?
   b. An increase in selling price?
   c. An increase in variable costs?

1. Distinguish between "financial" and "management" accounting. With what types of questions is management accounting concerned?
2. What are four themes that underlie the practice and study of management accounting?
3. Fixed costs are fixed in amount. In the short run they are the same from month to month. Do you agree?
4. "There is no conceptual difference between fixed and variable costs. In fact, as is clearly evident when the two types of costs are displayed graphically, their behavior with respect to changes in volume is remarkably similar." Do you agree? Explain.
5. The most common expression of costs is "average" costs. For what types of decisions, if any, would a manager be better served by using average costs as opposed to fixed costs and variable costs?
6. Under what circumstances would deductive analysis of costs—the type of analysis performed by industrial engineers—be most appropriate? Why must deductive analysis usually be supplemented by other forms of analysis?
7. What is an important pitfall to be on guard against when performing a high–low analysis of costs?
8. Why are direct labor costs of less significance to managers of firms using computer integrated manufacturing processes than to those of traditional factories? Why do some firms combine direct labor and factory overhead into a cost category called "conversion costs"?
9. What are three critical limitations of break-even analysis?
10. "Accountants and economists have totally different views of the behavior of costs. Any effort to reconcile the two is likely to be an exercise in frustration." Do you agree? Explain.

Problems

1. *Changes in the fixed as opposed to the variable elements of earnings will have significantly different impacts on a profit–volume line.*

   Unsatisfied with its recent performance, the Deakin Co. is considering ways to reduce its operating losses. Presently, the firm faces a profit–volume relationship as indicated in the chart on page 747. This chart is based on monthly fixed costs of $40,000, variable costs of $22 per unit, and a selling price of $30 per unit.

   Prepare a profit–volume chart similar to the one illustrated. Include the line representing the present revenues and costs. Add additional lines to indicate the effect of each of the contemplated changes, considered independently:
   a. The firm will decrease fixed advertising costs by $10,000.
   b. It will decrease variable manufacturing costs by $2 per unit.
   c. It will increase selling price by $2 per unit.
   d. It will decrease selling price by $2 per unit and reduce advertising costs by $10,000.

2. *Some changes result in only a shift in the position of a cost or revenue curve; others, in a shift of slope.*

   A firm charges $140 per unit of its product. Fixed manufacturing costs are $200,000; variable costs are $100 per unit.

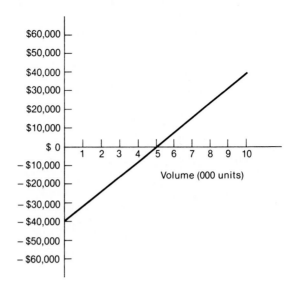

a. Plot two curves: one representing revenues in relation to sales volume; the other total cost in relation to sales volume. Determine the break-even point. Use algebraic procedures to verify your determination of the break-even point.

b. Suppose that the firm was able to increase sales price by 10 percent. Plot a new revenue curve and determine the revised break-even point. Verify algebraically.

c. Suppose alternatively that the firm was able to decrease fixed costs by 50 percent. Plot a new total cost curve and determine the revised break-even point. Verify algebraically.

d. Suppose instead that the firm was able to decrease variable costs by 70 percent. Plot a new total cost curve and determine the revised break-even point. Verify algebraically.

e. Which of the changes caused the curves to shift position yet retain the same slope? Which resulted in a shift in slope?

3. *In banks and related industries, output may best be measured by deposits or outstanding loans.*
    First City Savings Association pays its depositors interest at the rate of 6 percent. It is able to make loans at the rate of 10 percent. Fixed costs of operating one of its branches are $600,000 per year.

a. Assume that the bank is able to lend 100 percent of its deposits.
    (1) Prepare a cost–volume–profit chart in which you indicate, for various levels of deposits, fixed costs, variable costs, and revenues.
    (2) What is the break-even point? At what level of deposits will the branch realize income of $200,000? Verify your answer with appropriate computations.
    (3) Prepare a profit–volume chart in which you indicate income at various levels of deposits. Be certain that this graph is consistent with the cost–profit–volume chart; that is, at any particular level of deposits the difference between the revenue and total cost line per the first chart should be equal to the amount of profit per the second chart.

b. Assume that the bank is required by bank regulatory authorities to maintain reserves of 10 percent; that is, it is able to lend out only 90 percent of the amount on deposit. Repeat part a under the revised assumption. You need not redraw the charts. Simply add an alternate revenue line.

---

4. *Cost–volume–profit analysis can take various related forms.*

    Fairmont, Inc., incurs fixed costs of $270,000 and variable costs of $12 per unit. Selling price of its product is $20 per unit. The firm has established a monthly earnings objective of $30,000.

    a. Using the basic algebraic expression that includes price (*P*), fixed costs (*F*), variable costs (*V*), and desired income (*I*), determine the number of units (*u*) that Fairmont, Inc., would be required to manufacture and sell if it is to achieve its earnings objective. Calculate total sales revenue at that volume.

    b. Determine the contribution margin (*C*) expressed in dollar terms. Formulate a mathematical expression of the number of units (*u*) that must be manufactured and sold in order to achieve a profit objective that incorporates the contribution margin in place of selling price and variable costs. Apply the expression to the case at hand.

    c. Determine the contribution margin *ratio* (*R*)—a ratio which relates contribution margin to selling price. Formulate a mathematical expression of dollar sales volume for a firm to achieve a target income that incorporates such ratio in place of the contribution margin expressed in dollar terms. Apply the expression to Fairmont, Inc.

5. *Break-even analysis can be used to assist management in pinpointing changes that could have the greatest impact on earnings.*

    Management has been dissatisfied with the performance of a division because in the past month it was unable to do better than break even. A performance report for the month indicated the following:

Sales revenue (10,000 units @ $50)		$500,000
Costs		
Variable		
(10,000 units @ $20)	$200,000	
Fixed	300,000	500,000
Income		$ -0-

    Management has established an earnings goal of $20,000 for the next month. It is contemplating several measures to increase revenue and or reduce costs.

    a. Determine the number of units that the firm would be required to produce and sell in order to achieve the goal if the following changes (each to be considered separately) were made:
    (1) Sales price were increased by 10 percent.
    (2) Fixed costs were decreased by 10 percent.
    (3) Variable costs were decreased by 10 percent.
    (4) Fixed costs and variable costs were decreased by 10 percent.
    (5) No changes were made in costs or prices.

    b. Suppose instead that at a volume of 10,000 units total costs were, as before, $500,000, but that fixed costs were $200,000 and variable costs were $300,000 ($30 per unit). How many units would have to be sold to increase earnings to $20,000?

6. *Cost–volume–profit analysis facilitates equipment balancing decisions.*

    Flexi-Industries, Inc., was considering acquiring new manufacturing equipment which would enable it to substantially reduce direct labor costs. The equipment would cost $500,000 and would enable the firm to save $2 per unit in variable costs. The firm would have to borrow the amount required to purchase the equipment; as a result, interest costs would increase by $75,000. In addition, maintenance and miscellaneous costs would increase by $25,000.

In the past year, the firm produced and sold 100,000 units; sales price was $14 per unit. The actual income statement and year-end balance sheet, as well as *pro forma* statements indicating results as they would have been had the firm owned the new equipment, are shown here.

Balance Sheet

	Actual	Pro Forma
Assets		
Plant and equipment (net of allowance for depreciation)	$400,000	$ 800,000
Other assets	250,000	250,000
Total assets	$650,000	$1,050,000
Equities		
Notes payable	—	$ 500,000
Stockholders' equity	$650,000	550,000
Total equities	$650,000	$1,050,000

Income Statement

	Actual	Pro Forma
Sales revenue	$1,400,000	$1,400,000
Cost of goods sold	900,000	800,000
Gross margin	$ 500,000	$ 600,000
Administrative and other costs, including interest	400,000	500,000
Income before taxes	$ 100,000	$ 100,000
Cost of goods sold was determined as follows:		
Direct materials	$3.00	$3.00
Direct labor	5.00	3.00
Depreciation	1.00	2.00
	$9.00	$8.00
Number of units manufactured and sold	100,000 units	100,000 units
Cost of goods sold	$900,000	$800,000

Depreciation per unit was determined by dividing the *original cost* of plant equipment ($500,000 or $1,000,000) by useful life (five years) and by dividing the result ($100,000 or $200,000) by number of units manufactured and sold (100,000).

After reviewing the actual and *pro forma* financial statements, the vice-president for manufacturing commented, "Inasmuch as overall profits would not be improved by the acquisition, it would be senseless for us to undertake it. After all, why trade a decrease in variable costs for an increase in fixed costs? Our low fixed costs have always been our strength relative to our competitors. They have enabled us to adjust quickly to changes in demand."

a. In the schedule of cost of goods sold, should depreciation be considered a fixed or a variable cost? Explain.

b. If you knew for certain that volume in coming years would be 150,000 units per year, would you recommend acquisition of the equipment? Assume that your objective was to maximize *reported* earnings. Support your answer with an appropriate schedule.

c. If you knew for certain that volume would be only 70,000 units, would your response be the same? Prepare a supporting schedule.

d. What is the break-even point if the equipment is not acquired?

e. What is the break-even point if the equipment is acquired?

f. Do you agree with the vice-president for manufacturing that a relatively small proportion of fixed costs assures flexibility with regard to changes in demand? Comment.

7. *Contribution margin affects preferences for tax alternatives.*
   The annual revenues and expenditures of River View Hotel were as follows:

Revenues		$1,000,000
Expenditures		
Fixed	$300,000	
Variable	600,000	900,000
Income		$ 100,000

To finance the construction of a new convention center, the city in which the hotel is located is considering several alternative types of taxes to be imposed on hotels. Under one alternative, hotels would pay a per room franchise fee to the city. The annual cost to River View would be $85,000.

Under the other alternative, the city would levy a 10 percent tax on all hotel revenues. The tax would be paid entirely by hotel customers. However, since River View is in competition with similar hotels in an adjoining town, management estimates that the tax would result in a 15 percent decline in annual sales.

a. Which of the alternatives would River View prefer? Determine the effect on income of each of the two proposals.
b. Assume that the city elected to impose the per room franchise fee. The hotel decides not to increase the prices charged to customers. Instead, it endeavors to attract new business. By how much would revenues need to increase, assuming no increases in fixed costs other than the $85,000 franchise fee, for River View to maintain income at $100,000?
c. Assume instead that the city imposed the tax on revenues and that the hotel decided that to remain competitive, it must now reduce the prices charged to customers by approximately 10 percent. What would be the amount of revenue required to maintain income at its previous level of $100,000?
d. Assume instead that the city decided to impose a 2 percent tax on net income (revenues less expenditures). By how much would revenues need to increase, assuming no increase in prices charged to customers, for the hotel to maintain income at $100,000?

8. *Contribution margin affects profit potential of promotional strategy.*
   Two executives in related industries were discussing the merits of distributing free samples as a means of increasing sales. Both executives were from firms that sold their products to fashionable book and art shops. The first executive represented a publishing concern which produced and distributed expensive art books; the second represented a china firm which manufactured artistic plates, each of which was, in part, hand painted.

   Coincidentally, the selling price and cost of the two products were the same. Based on estimated production and sales volume of 10,000 units, the costs of the two products were as shown on page 751. Thus the average cost of both books and plates was $40 per unit. The selling price of each was $60 per unit.

   Both executives agreed that a sample of a product, given free to a retail store, could be expected to generate sales of 10 units. The executive representing the publishing firm asserted that sampling represented an effective means of promoting

Art Books

Costs of design and production of plates	$300,000
Costs of printing, binding, materials, and distribution; 10,000 books at $10 per book	100,000
Total costs	$400,000

Artistic Plates

Costs of design and molds	$ 50,000
Costs of labor, materials, and distribution; 10,000 plates at $35 per plate	350,000
Total costs	$400,000

sales and thereby increasing profits. The executive representing the china company was decidedly less enthusiastic about sampling, preferring to concentrate his firm's efforts on increasing the number of different plates available for sale.

a. Explain why each executive might view sampling as he does. Determine the impact on the earnings of each of the companies of distributing 100 free samples to the book and art stores with which they trade.

b. Indicate why it is to the relative advantage of the china company, as opposed to the publishing company, to introduce new products rather than concentrate on increasing sales of existing ones.

9. *In determining the impact of changes in volume on earnings, cost "step functions" must be taken into account.*

The Riverdale Transit Co. operates a commuter bus service between a suburban community and the downtown area of a major city.

The company presently operates 10 buses. Each bus has a practical capacity of 300 passengers (rides) per day. As the number of riders increases, the company can schedule more frequent service. However, each time the number of passengers increases by a multiple of 300, another bus must be added. The additional bus must be scheduled for the same number of daily trips as the others.

The company presently provides service for approximately 2,900 passengers per day. Inasmuch as the company does not operate on weekends or holidays, it bases all monthly calculations on the assumption that there will be 22 days of service per month. Thus, the company currently provides 63,800 rides per month.

The company leases, rather than purchases, its buses. Operating costs for a recent month were as follows:

Monthly costs per bus	
Lease charges	$ 1,500
Wages of drivers	3,000
Fuel costs	1,800
Variable maintenance and miscellaneous costs	600
Total costs per bus	$ 6,900
Number of buses	× 10
Total direct costs of operating buses	$69,000
Administration, general, and fixed maintenance costs	25,000
Total monthly costs	$94,000

The fare for each ride is $2. Monthly revenues are $127,600.

a. In making plans for future months, the president of the firm estimates that ridership will increase by 3 percent. He has estimated that earnings before taxes will also increase by 3 percent. Do you agree? If not, determine the amount by which you believe earnings will change.

b. The controller of the firm, somewhat more knowledgeable about accounting than the president, has estimated that ridership will increase by 5 percent. He has determined that earnings will increase by the difference between additional revenue and additional variable costs. He has computed variable costs to be $69,000 divided by average monthly ridership of 63,800—that is, $1.08 per rider. Do you agree with his computations? If not, determine the amount by which you believe earnings will change.

c. In light of your computations, do you believe that the firm should make an effort to increase ridership by 5 percent, or would it be better off by attempting to restrict ridership to its present level?

10. *Cost–volume–profit analysis is as applicable to nonprofit organizations as it is to private businesses.*

A nonprofit outpatient center for the elderly estimates that its variable costs per patient are $100 per week and fixed costs are $7,200 per week.

a. The center presently serves 80 patients. What is the least amount that it could charge each patient and still break even?

b. Suppose that the rate charged was $230 per week. What would be the minimum number of patients the center must serve in order to break even?

c. Assume, as in part b, that the rate is $230 per week. What is the number of patients that the center would be required to serve for it to realize a margin of $2,000 per week?

d. Assume that the center presently serves 80 patients. What is the rate per week that it should charge in order to realize a margin of 10 percent of patient revenues received?

e. In the current year the center expects its revenues to exceed total expenditures by $500 per week. It estimates that both fixed costs and variable costs will increase by 10 percent. Assuming that it will serve 80 patients per week, what rate should it charge next year if it is to continue to realize an excess of revenues over expenditures of $500 per week?

11. *Cost functions take a variety of forms, some of which appear to be inconsistent with the usual assumptions made by accountants.*

a. For each of the following descriptions of cost, draw a graph that indicates the relationship between dollar cost and an appropriate measure of level of activity (e.g., production, customers served, sales, etc.). In each case, put costs on the vertical axis. The first one is done for you as an example and is shown on page 753.

(1) Employer contributions to a state unemployment compensation fund are 2.2 percent of each employee's wages, with a maximum contribution of $348. The size and composition of the work force remained constant during the year.

(2) A commercial bank estimates that one teller is required for each 100 customers served per day.

(3) Copying costs are $.08 per page for the first 100 copies, $.07 for the next 100, $.06 for the next 100, and $.05 for all copies thereafter.

(4) Electric costs are $.031 for the first 10,000 kilowatt hours of electricity, $.032 for the next 10,000, $.033 for the next 10,000, and so on to a maximum charge of $.035 for each kilowatt hour over 50,000.

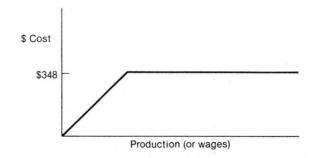

$ Cost

$348

Production (or wages)

(5) The salary of a company manager is $100,000 per year.
(6) Salary and bonus of the plant manager are $30,000 per year plus $.10 per unit for each unit of product over 100,000.
(7) Rent on a retail gas station is $4,000 per month plus $.12 per gallon of gasoline sold over 20,000 gallons. Maximum rental payment in any one month is $8,000.
(8) Depreciation on a factory building is calculated by the straight-line method.
(9) Depreciation on factory equipment is calculated by the units-of-output method.
(10) When acquiring raw materials, the company is allowed a discount of 2 percent once the total purchased during the year exceeds $100,000.

b. It is often convenient for the accountant to categorize costs as being either fixed or variable. He or she assumes that variable costs may be depicted as straight upward-sloping lines and fixed costs as horizontal lines. Yet many of the cost functions which you have just drawn do not conform to that pattern. Are the assumptions of the accountant unrealistic? How can you reconcile your graphs with the assumptions of the accountant?

12. *Analytical relationships will be affected by the accounting methods used to establish the underlying data.*

As a manager, you wish to determine the relationship between selling expenses and dollar sales. From the records of your company, you are able to abstract the following data for a period of 14 months:

Month	Sales	Selling Costs
December (1993)	$95,000	$5,600
January (1994)	85,000	5,700
February	74,000	5,100
March	63,000	4,400
April	90,000	3,800
May	92,000	5,400
June	67,000	5,500
July	69,000	4,000
August	88,000	4,100
September	86,000	5,300
October	79,000	5,200
November	83,000	4,700
December (1994)	62,000	5,000
January (1995)	80,000	3,700

a. Plot the data on a scatter diagram. Visually fit a curve to the points and, if possible, describe in equation form the relationships between sales and selling costs. Comment on the reliability of your equation; that is, how much of the variation in selling costs is explained by the equation?

b. You subsequently learn that the selling costs account is composed almost entirely of commissions of salespeople. Each month the account is increased by the amount actually paid to the salespeople. The amount paid is based on sales of the previous month. (At year end, when annual financial reports are to be prepared, an adjustment is made so that commission expense is matched to the sales revenue of the proper period.) Prepare a second scatter diagram in which selling costs are matched to the sales of the previous month. Visually fit a curve to the data points and describe the relationship in equation form.

c. Suppose that you were called upon to study the behavior of electricity costs in relation to production. Why might you face a problem similar to that suggested by this example?

13. *Relationships derived from correlations of one variable with another may be inappropriate for distinguishing the fixed from the variable elements of cost or for making predictions about costs to be incurred in the future.*

During the five-year period between 1989 and 1993, a firm reported advertising costs and sales revenue as follows:

Year	Sales	Advertising Costs
1989	$5,000,000	$220,000
1990	4,800,000	208,000
1991	5,700,000	262,000
1992	6,400,000	304,000
1993	6,200,000	292,000

a. Using the high–low method, express in equation form advertising costs as a function of sales.

b. Based on the equation, determine the variable and the nonvariable elements of costs at a sales volume of (1) zero; (2) $50,000.

c. Explain the significance (or lack thereof) of the nonvariable portion of the costs at sales volume of zero and $50,000. Is it possible for fixed costs to be negative?

d. In preparing a budget for the firm, you learn that the sales department estimates that sales volume in the following year will be $6,000,000. What is the amount that you would forecast for advertising costs?

e. Do you believe that the equation that you developed can really be used to make reliable predictions of advertising costs? Explain.

14. *This is a simple exercise in regression analysis which highlights the need for caution in drawing conclusions from it.*

A mail-order firm wishes to project the costs of packaging and shipping customer orders. It projects that sales for 1994 will be $87 million.

Sales and packaging and shipping costs for the previous five years were as follows:

Year	Sales (millions)	Packaging and Shipping Costs (millions)
1989	$70	$6.12
1990	89	6.70
1991	84	6.52
1992	97	6.91
1993	76	6.26

a. Following the form of the example in the text, prepare a table in which you determine the sums of x (sales), y (packaging and shipping costs), x^2, and xy.
b. Using the formulas in the example, determine (1) the y intercept and (2) the slope of the regression equation.
c. Based on the regression equation, estimate packaging and shipping costs for 1994.
d. Do you think that your equation could be used to predict packaging and shipping costs if sales were $300 million? Explain.
e. In this example, your analysis is based on only five data points. How would the small number of observations affect the conclusions that you can draw from your analysis?

15. *A spreadsheet program greatly enhances managers' analytical capabilities.*

Progressive Air Conditioning and Heating, a seasonal repair business, prepared the following schedule of total monthly operating costs and billable hours:

Month	Hours	Costs
January	6,200	$290,000
February	7,000	312,000
March	8,400	348,000
April	9,200	370,000
May	11,600	435,000
June	12,000	460,000
July	11,400	440,000
August	9,000	373,000
September	9,200	376,000
October	8,000	341,000
November	6,700	300,000
December	5,700	265,000

a. Prepare a scatterplot graph in which you relate billable hours (the X axis) to total operating costs (the Y axis).
b. Estimate monthly fixed costs and variable costs based on the graph. Confirm your estimate with regression analysis.
c. Suppose that the company anticipates that for a forthcoming month it will provide 9,800 hours of billable service. Based on your analysis, what would be your estimate of total operating costs?
d. Suppose instead that the company estimates that it will provide 20,000 billable hours. What would be your estimate of total operating costs? What reservations would you have as to the reliability of this estimate?

16. *The accountant's and the economist's perception of costs are not necessarily inconsistent. (This problem requires the use of a spreadsheet program with graphics capability.)*

A company's engineers and cost analysts made the estimates of production costs at various levels of volume that are shown on p. 756.
a. Prepare a graph in which you relate volume (on the X axis) with costs (on the Y axis).
b. Using regression analysis (i.e., the spreadsheet regression function), express the relationship between volume and costs in equation form (i.e., $Y = a + bX$).
c. Suppose that the only range in which the company would consider operating is between 20,000 and 34,000 units. Express the relationship between volume and costs within this range in equation form. Indicate anticipated fixed and variable costs.

Units Produced	Cost
10,000	$100,000
12,000	$104,400
14,000	$108,400
16,000	$113,200
18,000	$118,200
20,000	$124,000
22,000	$133,400
24,000	$142,800
26,000	$152,200
28,000	$161,600
30,000	$171,000
32,000	$180,400
34,000	$189,800
36,000	$206,400
38,000	$224,560
40,000	$244,400
42,000	$266,040
44,000	$294,000
46,000	$324,400
48,000	$366,000

d. Assume that the fixed costs will remain the same across the entire range of output (i.e., from 10,000 to 48,000 units). Prepare a schedule in which you compute for each level of output:
  (1) Fixed costs
  (2) Variable costs
  (3) Average costs
e. Prepare two additional graphs. In one, show fixed costs, variable costs, and total costs in relation to volume. In the other, show average costs in relation to volume. On both, indicate the relevant range.
f. Comment on the trend in fixed, variable, and average costs as seen by both the economist and the accountant.

Solutions to Exercise for Review and Self-Testing

1. Each unit contributes $2—the difference between selling price of $10 per unit and variable costs of $8 per unit.
2. Inasmuch as each unit contributes $2 toward covering fixed costs and there are $20,000 of fixed costs to be covered, the firm must produce and sell 10,000 units—$20,000 divided by $2.
3. In order to cover fixed costs of $20,000 and earn profits of $6,000, the firm must produce and sell 13,000 units—$26,000 divided by $2.
4. a. The production and sale of 12,000 units, each with a contribution margin of $2, would contribute $24,000 toward covering fixed costs of $20,000. Hence, profit would be $4,000.
   b. The production and sale of 8,000 units would contribute only $16,000 toward covering fixed costs of $20,000. Hence, the firm would incur a loss of $4,000.
5. a. The change would cause fixed costs to increase to $22,000 and the contribution margin to increase to $2.20. Since both the fixed costs and the contribution margin increased in the same proportion—10 percent—the break-even point would remain the same: $22,000/$2.20 = 10,000 units.

b. The production and sale of 12,000 units, each with a contribution margin of $2.20, would contribute $26,400 toward covering fixed costs of $22,000. Hence, profit would be $4,400.

c. The production and sale of 8,000 units would contribute only $17,600 toward covering fixed costs of $22,000. Hence, the firm would incur a loss of $4,400.

6. a. An increase in fixed costs would cause the break-even point to increase, but would have no effect on per unit contribution to fixed costs and earnings (the contribution margin).

b. An increase in selling price would cause the break-even point to decrease and would increase the per unit contribution to fixed costs and earnings.

c. An increase in variable costs would cause the break-even point to increase and would decrease the per unit contribution to fixed costs and earnings.

18

Establishing the Cost of a Product

One of the key functions of an accounting system is to establish the cost of the products that an organization manufactures and sells or the services that it provides. Determination of cost per particular product is not merely a matter of mechanically recording outlays and dividing total outlays by number of units produced. Cost is often difficult to trace to products or services. It is affected by choices among accounting procedures, methods used in allocations, and required estimates. We have seen in earlier chapters that the principles and procedures by which cost is determined have an impact on earnings as reported in general-purpose financial statements. Equally important, however, is that they may influence a wide range of *management* decisions, such as those involving pricing, production level, and further processing. It is essential, therefore, that managers understand the composition of particular product costs as well as the principles and procedures by which they have been computed.

OBJECTIVES

A sound cost accounting system can serve at least three objectives, each of which may require independent calculations of product cost:

- Establish inventory values and the cost of goods sold to be reported on external financial reports
- Facilitate control over operations and costs to promote efficiency
- Enable management to estimate product costs for purposes of pricing and bidding.[1]

Cost data on operations should permit management to identify out-of-line conditions and take prompt corrective measures. However, the data required to monitor and control operations are seldom in a form appropriate either for external financial reports or for pricing and bidding decisions. Consistent with the generally accepted historical cost model, inventory values must be stated at *full cost*, which encompasses direct as well as overhead costs. Overhead includes expenditures of all the production and service departments that contribute to making a product salable. Costs from the service departments must be combined into cost pools with the production departments' own overhead costs and then distributed to the various products produced by those departments. In contrast, in monitoring and controlling operations, management must focus separately on the cost of the specific elements of production and service. In general, as will be discussed in chapters to follow, *allocated* and *absorbed* costs undermine rather than promote management efforts to identify and correct aberrant operations.

For purposes of pricing and bidding, still different types of data are required. Managers must be aware not only of the full cost of the products, but also of the *incremental* costs of operating at various output levels. Further, they must be particularly concerned with costs to be incurred in the *future* rather than the *past*. Past costs are "sunk"; they cannot be reversed or changed by decisions yet to be made.

Moreover, cost data for purposes of external financial reporting need be collected and reported only as frequently as financial reports have to be prepared. Data for pricing and bidding need only be collected and reported whenever bids must be submitted or prices established or reviewed. Information for purposes of control, however, should be collected and reported as frequently as justified by its potential net cost savings (potential savings less the cost of providing the information). For some companies, especially those with computer-controlled production systems, this criterion dictates that information systems operate in "real-time" (i.e., instant-time) mode.

Product cost consists of three primary elements: direct labor, direct materials, and overhead. Direct materials and direct labor can, by definition, be readily identified with specific units of product. Overhead (indirect) costs, however, are those which cannot directly be ascribed to particular units of product. Overhead costs include expenditures for rent, power, supervision, lubricants, supplies, and overtime premiums. They are as essential to the manufacturing process as direct labor and materials. They must, therefore, be included in the total product cost, and procedures must be adopted to assign overhead costs to particular units of product.

[1]See Robert S. Kaplan, "One Cost System Isn't Enough," *Harvard Business Review*, January-February 1988, pp. 61–66.

This chapter will focus on principles of determining the cost of goods manufactured. Many of the concepts to be discussed are applicable also to services provided. As was pointed out earlier in the text, administration and selling, like manufacturing costs, are incurred to generate revenues. They should, therefore, be included in product cost and, in order to effect a proper matching of costs and revenues, charged as an expense in the period in which the goods are sold. However, in recognition of substantial difficulties of assigning them to particular units of product, and in respect to long-standing tradition, selling and non-factory administrative costs are conventionally accounted for as *period* costs. They are *omitted* from the cost of the product and thereby *excluded* from inventory. Instead, they are charged as expenses in the periods in which they are incurred. Some accountants have urged that indirect factory costs that cannot readily be identified with specific units of product should also be charged to expense as incurred—a method of accounting known as *direct costing*, which will be considered later in this chapter. Generally accepted accounting principles require, however, that for purposes of income determination, they be included in product cost and inventoried as assets until sold.

Most manufacturing firms are organized on a departmental basis. Some departments, known as *production* departments, engage directly in manufacturing operations. Assembly, molding, finishing, and painting departments are examples of production departments. Other departments, known as *service* departments, provide support services to the production departments. Among the functions carried out by service departments are personnel administration, warehousing and materials handling, telephone service, building maintenance, and equipment repair. Most departments, whether production or service, are also *cost centers*. A cost center is an organizational unit for which costs are accumulated. Some cost centers (or cost pools) do not directly produce goods or services. When certain costs, such as building occupancy costs, are difficult to trace and are common to a number of departments, they are assigned initially to a non-operating cost pool and then allocated to the user departments. In other words, costs are accumulated at the point incurred and are later assigned to other cost centers in order to achieve the three objectives noted earlier.

Allocation versus Absorption

The assignment of overhead costs to specific units of product is a two-stage process. First, since only production departments are directly associated with the manufactured products, costs that are accumulated in non-production cost centers must be assigned to the production departments. Second, the costs from the nonproduction cost centers must be combined with the overhead costs of the production departments themselves and assigned to particular units of product. The costs assigned from nonproduction departments are now treated as additional overhead costs of the production departments.

The process of assigning overhead costs from the service departments and other nonproduction cost centers to the production departments is referred to as *allocation*. That of assigning the augmented overhead costs from the production departments to the particular units of product is known as either *absorption*

EXHIBIT 18-1
Allocation and Absorption

Allocation

Assignment of Overhead Costs from Service Departments
(or Cost Centers) to Production Department Overhead

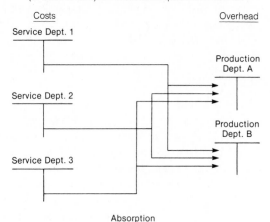

Absorption

Assignment of Augmented Overhead Costs from
Production Departments to Products

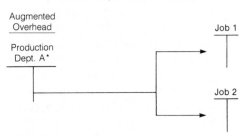

* Includes overhead costs of the department itself as well as those
allocated from service departments.

or *application*. Overhead costs are absorbed or applied to particular products or outputs. Some say they are "loaded" onto products.

The two parts of the product-costing exercise presented in the next section are depicted in Exhibit 18-1.

ALLOCATION OF SERVICE DEPARTMENT OVERHEAD COSTS TO PRODUCTION CENTER OVERHEAD

Our first problem is concerned with the *allocation* of costs from service departments or cost centers to the overhead cost of production departments. Examples of service departments that may be cost centers are maintenance, utilities, personnel, and data processing. It will be our objective not only to indicate widely used techniques of allocation but, more importantly, to comment upon their objectives and limitations. The discussion will center on the allocation of costs from service departments to production departments. It could readily be generalized to the allocation of any common costs (e.g., home office costs) to the various operating units of a corporation or other type of organization.

Overhead costs may be initially incurred by, or assigned to, nonproduction cost centers because they cannot be associated directly with specific production centers. Indirectly, of course, they have been incurred to benefit production departments and, ultimately, the product itself. But there may be no clear-cut measures of benefits received. Thus, there are no self-evident bases of allocation. In fact, there is no absolutely correct allocation base.

Objectives of Allocation

Allocation of costs may serve at least three purposes. These three purposes correspond with the three main objectives of product costing discussed earlier. First, and most prominently, allocation is a means of associating costs with the revenues that they produce. The matching principle requires that costs be charged as expenses in the same accounting period as the related revenues are realized. This principle is applied when manufacturing costs are held in inventory until point of sale and then charged off as costs of goods sold. The matching principle implies that *all* manufacturing costs—indirect as well as direct—be assigned to the product. If they are to be assigned to products, then they must first be assigned to the departments which produce them.

Second, allocation may serve as a means of motivating the employees of the production departments to assist in controlling overhead costs. If a department is charged for a service on the basis of amount used, it is likely that it will avail itself of the service only when the benefits that it will receive exceed their cost. But even if the department is charged for a cost (such as air conditioning) over which it may have no, or at best minimal control, it may do its best to put pressure on those departments which can influence the magnitude of the cost. At the very least, cost allocation serves to remind managers of the various production departments from which they are receiving the benefits and of the number of activities and services being carried out on their behalf.

Third, allocation may facilitate several types of management determinations. Foremost among these are the selling prices of the company's products. In a perfectly competitive market, a firm may be a "price taker"; it can sell only at the prevailing market price. But in less than perfectly competitive markets, and particularly when a firm negotiates contractual prices, product cost is an important element to be taken into account. Product costs are the starting point for most bids or negotiated contracts.

Nature and Characteristics of Overhead Costs

Two characteristics of overhead costs are especially relevant to a determination as to the most appropriate *means* of allocation from service cost centers to production departments. First, overhead costs may be classified as to *degree of variability*. Some overhead costs are fixed, having little or no relationship to level of activity. Examples are rent, depreciation of building and equipment, property taxes on plant, plant insurance, factory heat, air conditioning and light, most factory office costs, and many factory management costs (e.g., the salary of the plant manager). Others are, to some extent, variable. Indirect labor and supplies are typically influenced by volume. Machine maintenance and power costs are likely to be affected by machine usage, which in turn is affected by level of output. Fixed costs often provide basic operating capacity; they must be incurred for the firm to operate at even a minimum level of activity. Variable costs represent the portion of overhead costs that increases once the minimum level of activity has been exceeded.

Many types of overhead costs have both fixed and variable elements. A service department that repairs and maintains factory equipment must be sufficiently large to react to unforeseen equipment breakdowns. If the factory is to operate at all, the department must have the capability to provide assistance when called upon. But as volume increases, machines require greater amounts of maintenance, and hence the costs incurred by service departments increase.

A *second characteristic* of overhead costs that bears upon the appropriate means of allocation is that they may be classified by *degree* and *source of control*. Overhead costs may be controlled in two ways: by adjusting the *quantity* of service provided, and by monitoring the *efficiency* by which it is provided.

The *quantity* of some overhead services is beyond the scope of short-term decisions, subject to minimal influence by the firm, or, once established by company policy, resistant to change. In this category are heating and air conditioning, insurance, and building maintenance. The quantity of other services is subject to the control of the departments that benefit from them. Machine maintenance and repair service, for example, may be provided at the request of the various production departments. Purchasing services are rendered in response to requisitions of materials, supplies, or equipment. Personnel and payroll services are made available as new employees are added to the work force.

The *efficiency* with which services are provided is commonly under the control of the department that provides them. Given a specified or requested quantity of service, the costs of building maintenance, machine maintenance and repair, purchasing, and personnel services are dependent on the service departments rather than on production or beneficiary departments.

Guidelines for Overhead Allocations

There are two useful guidelines for the allocation of the overhead of service cost centers to production departments. First, allocations should reflect benefits received. This can usually be accomplished by a two-step process: (1) allocate fixed or capacity costs to the various departments in proportion to their long-range requirements for the service provided; and (2) allocate variable costs in proportion to actual usage.

Second, allocations should be made in such a way that the amount charged to a particular department does not vary from what is normal as a consequence of either (1) a change in quantity of service demanded by other departments or (2) a change in the efficiency with which the service is provided by the service department. Consistent with this guideline, it is generally preferable to base allocations on *estimated* rather than *actual* overhead costs and to use different bases for allocating the fixed and variable components of the costs.

Allocation of Fixed Costs

In allocating overhead costs, it is necessary to select a criterion by which to measure benefits received. For example, the benefits of building occupancy costs that are primarily fixed, such as rent, janitorial service, heat and air conditioning, and light, may be related to the number of square feet occupied. Suppose that monthly building occupancy costs in a plant are $12,000. There are three production departments: machining, assembling, and polishing. The number of square feet occupied by each of the departments and the resultant allocations based on square feet are as follows:

| | Production Department | | | |
	Machining	Assembling	Polishing	Total
Square feet	20,000	50,000	30,000	100,000
Percent of total	20%	50%	30%	100%
Share of cost ($12,000)	$2,400	$6,000	$3,600	$12,000

Some frequently used bases for allocating other overhead costs that are primarily fixed to production departments are as follows:

Type of Overhead Services Cost	Variable in Production Department Serving as Basis for Allocation
Personnel	Number of employees, dollar amount of payroll
Warehousing	Number of square feet occupied
Machinery repairs (fixed portion)	Number of machines
Telephone service (basic charge)	Number of telephones

The choice of allocation base is necessarily arbitrary and subjective. It should be based on causal or other logical relationships. In practice, however, it is often based on "fairness" or "ability to pay" criteria.

Allocation of Variable Costs

Where service unit overhead costs are variable, it is necessary to measure the actual quantity of services received. Some bases for allocating variable costs (or the variable portion of costs that have both fixed and variable elements) are as follows:

Type of Cost	Basis for Allocation
Power	Kilowatts consumed
Telephone (toll calls)	Actual billings
Machinery repairs (variable portion)	Number of machine hours
Purchasing Department services	Number of requisitions
Materials handling	Raw materials usage

If, for example, variable power costs are $.05 per kilowatt hour and a department uses 10,000 kilowatt hours in a period, then its charge for power would be $500 (10,000 hours @ $.05).

Advantages of Dual Allocation Schemes Based on Estimated Costs

The desirability of dual allocations based on *estimated* rather than actual costs can be demonstrated by way of an illustration. A division of an insurance company has two main clerical departments. One is responsible for life insurance policies, the other for pensions and annuities. Both rely on a central data processing service for computer support. The Life Insurance Department normally uses 240 hours per month of computer time; the Pensions and Annuities Department uses 160 hours. Monthly costs of operating the data processing center are as follows:

Fixed costs	$24,000
Variable costs	$ 30 per computer hour

Total normal costs of operating the center are thus $36,000:

Fixed costs	$24,000
Variable costs (240 hours for the Life Insurance Department plus 160 hours for the Pensions and Annuities Department)	
400 hours @ $30	12,000
Total normal operating costs	$36,000

A dual allocation scheme based on estimated costs will assure that the allocation to each department is unaffected by fluctuations in volume or efficiency of other departments. The charge to each operating department for the *fixed portion* of the costs incurred by the service center would be that of providing the capacity to fulfill normal requirements. The allocation would be based on *estimated normal costs* of the service center and normal hours of service required by the operating departments. In the example, normal fixed costs of the data processing center are $24,000. Inasmuch as the Life Insurance Department normally uses 60 percent (240 hours) of the services provided, its charge would be $14,400 (60 percent of $24,000). The Pensions and Annuities Department normally uses 40 percent (160 hours) of services provided; its charge would be $9,600 (40 percent of $24,000). The allocation of fixed costs would be constant from month to month, regardless of actual costs incurred by the service center or actual number of hours used by the operating departments.

The charge to each operating department for the variable costs would be the normal incremental cost of providing an hour of service. In the example at hand, it would be $30 per computer hour. The *amount per hour* would remain constant regardless of the actual costs incurred by the service center.

Consider the amounts to be allocated to the two departments under three sets of circumstances.

1. Actual costs of the data processing center are normal ($36,000); computer hours used by each of the operating departments are also normal (Life Insurance Department, 240 hours; Pensions and Annuities Department, 160 hours).

   In this case, since both actual costs and hours are as estimated, the costs allocated to each of the departments are in proportion to hours of service required and all costs are fully allocated. Thus,

	Life Insurance Department	Pensions and Annuities Department	Total
Allocation of fixed costs ($24,000)	$14,400[a]	$ 9,600[b]	$24,000
Allocation of variable costs ($12,000)	7,200[c]	4,800[d]	12,000
Total allocation	$21,600	$14,400	$36,000

[a]60 percent of total.
[b]40 percent of total.
[c]240 hours @ $30.
[d]160 hours @ $30.

2. Owing entirely to the inefficiency of the data processing center, its actual costs are $38,000 instead of $36,000 as estimated. Computer hours used by each of the two operating departments are as before. The allocation would be identical to that in situation 1. The amounts charged to both of the operating departments would be unaffected by the inefficiency of the service department. The amount ($2,000) representing the inefficiency of the service department would *not be allocated*; it would remain in the accounts of the service departments.[2]

3. Actual costs of the data processing department are less than normal ($34,800) owing entirely to decreased usage by the Life Insurance Department—hence a decline in the processing center's *variable* costs. The Life Insurance Department used 200 hours instead of its normal 240 hours. The Pensions and Annuities Department used exactly its normal 160 hours as expected.

   The allocation to the Pensions and Annuities Department is the same as it would have been had total hours been normal; it is unaffected by changes in hours of service used by other departments. The allocation to the Life Insurance Department is less than normal, reflecting less than normal use of service. The reduction in its allocation is exactly equal to the amount saved by the data processing center: $1,200, which represents 40 hours at *variable* cost per hour of $30. Thus,

	Life Insurance Department	Pensions and Annuities Department	Total
Allocation of fixed costs ($24,000)— based on normal hours and costs	$14,400	$ 9,600	$24,000
Allocation of variable costs ($10,800)—based on actual hours and standard cost per hour	6,000[a]	4,800[b]	10,800
Total allocation	$20,400	$14,400	$34,800

[a]200 hours @ $30.
[b]160 hours @ $30.

The dual allocation scheme results in charges to operating departments that reflect the benefits received. This is a desirable outcome for both managerial planning and evaluation. Each department is charged for the capacity that the service department makes available to it as well as for the actual services rendered.

[2]The unallocated balance could be analyzed and reported upon similarly to underabsorbed overhead: that is, prorated between cost of goods sold and ending inventory. The question of how to dispose of underabsorbed balances will be discussed in more detail in Chapter 22, which pertains to control.

Once the capacity charge and the per unit rate have been established, each department's share of costs is affected only by its demand for service. It is unaffected by the efficiency of the service department or the volume of service provided to other departments.

Allocations among Service Departments

In the discussion to this point, it has been assumed that all costs of service centers could readily be allocated directly to production departments. Commonly, however, allocation of some of these costs would be inappropriate as service centers themselves render and receive services from other service centers. A maintenance department, for example, occupies space in a building and uses heat, air conditioning, and power. At the same time, it maintains and repairs the equipment that provides these services.

Many companies do, in fact, allocate all costs directly from service centers to production departments and thereby ignore the services rendered among service departments. Alternatively, service department costs can be assigned using a step procedure. First, the costs of the department providing services to the greatest number of other service departments are allocated among all service departments and production departments. Then, the costs, including those which were just allocated to it, of the service department rendering services to the second greatest number of service departments are similarly allocated. The process continues until all service department costs are allocated. This step procedure takes into account services rendered by some service departments to others. But it is deficient in that it fails to give consideration to *reciprocal* relationships among service departments—those in which one service department both renders and receives services from another department. Insofar as the information requirements of a firm warrant such refinements, a firm can give recognition to reciprocal relationships by setting up and solving a series of linear equations in which the cost of each department is expressed as a proportional share of the costs of all other departments. For Medicare and Medicaid reimbursement of costs, hospitals have commonly based cost allocations on reciprocal relationships.

Need for Care in Making Cost Allocations

One of the central themes underlying our discussion of management accounting thus far, which will become even more pertinent as we move ahead, is that in deciding among alternative courses of action, managers must distinguish between those costs that will change as the result of a particular action and those that will not. In using financial data that include costs that have been allocated from one department to another, there is substantial risk that costs that are fixed—and thus not subject to change—will be mistakenly classified as variable. This is because the costs may be variable from the perspective of a department, yet fixed from the standpoint of the firm at large. Suppose a company must decide whether to abandon a particular production department. It may appear as if all costs of operating the department are, for purposes of this decision, variable. Included in the costs attributable to the department, however, may be those, such as building occupancy costs, that have been allocated from other cost centers. Assume, for example, that the department's share of rent, heat, air conditioning, and light is $10,000. If the department is abandoned, the *department* would obviously "save" $10,000, but there may be no appreciable saving to the firm as a whole. The $10,000 in building occupancy costs would now have to be real-located among the remaining departments in the plant.

Data that include allocations of cost must always be viewed as being tainted with arbitrariness. There is seldom a "correct" basis for allocations. Alternative allocation schemes may be equally logical yet yield dissimilar assignments of cost. Whereas allocations must be made for some purposes—e.g., product costs that are carried forward to external financial reports—they need not, and should not, be made for internally circulated reports unless they will indeed serve to facilitate the management decision for which the reports will be used.

Allocations for Advocacy

However limited their utility for many types of decisions made by managers, allocations are essential to a number of regulatory functions in our society in which outcomes are cost or income based. In the area of utility regulation, for example, rates are established at the level required to assure a fair return on investment. It is almost always necessary to determine the costs associated with providing service to a particular region, group of customers, or class of service. Because many costs are common to two or more regions, groups, or classes, appropriate means of allocating the common costs must be devised to establish "fair prices" for different customers. Similarly, in the field of taxation, both state and national levies may be based on the cost of products or on earnings within a particular jurisdiction. Again, costs must be allocated among products or jurisdictions.

Accounting data, presumably neutral and objective, are in fact the underlying cause of many disputes over taxes and regulated rates. Familiarity with the various means of allocating costs and knowledge of their limitations can serve as a potent weapon in the arsenal of those advocating a particular position. Disputes in which allocations of costs are a central issue are common:

- A multinational corporation is taxed on earnings at higher rates in one country than in others. In an effort to reduce the reported earnings in the country with the high tax rates, it allocates a disproportionately high share of common costs, such as home office costs, to that country. Tax officials of that country argue in favor of alternative allocation schemes that result in higher reported earnings.
- A multidivision firm is engaged in collective bargaining with employees of one of its divisions. It asserts that it cannot yield to union demands because the division is "unprofitable." The extent to which they are "unprofitable," however, is a function of the amount of firm-wide costs charged to the particular division.

ASSIGNMENT OF COSTS TO PRODUCTS

Having allocated central facility and other service department costs as overhead to production cost centers, we are now in a position to develop a framework wherein these and all other overhead costs can be *absorbed* into costs assigned to individual products, or product lines. How one goes about doing this, and in how much detail, in practice is very much a matter of choice within individual firms. The operations of every business firm are unique. Therefore, two issues arise.

The first is how to define a firm's product. One firm making the proverbial widget may define the product on which to center its product-costing procedures simply as a "widget." Another firm making similar, or even identical, widgets may decide that there are basically three kinds of widgets being produced—a standard variety and two special versions, each involving differing degrees of custom-design work. A third firm making widgets may decide to apply product-costing procedures individually to 10 separate varieties of widgets.

A second, crucial issue to be resolved in product costing, and one which is very much the subject of controversy and in the process of change today, lies in the *means* that are chosen to *absorb* overhead costs along with direct costs into a single product or product-line cost. The older, traditional treatment of the subject has, for the most part, overhead costs allocated to or absorbed into product costs in proportion to direct labor costs applied to each product (or occasionally in proportion to direct material costs). But as direct labor costs have steadily fallen in proportion to total costs, managerial accountants have tended to become dissatisfied with this procedure. They have turned to using varied bases for allocating the overhead costs, the choice depending upon individual production process circumstances, or to devising some sort of general "activity costing" basis for making these calculations.

There is now an extensive body of English-language literature on activity-based costing (ABC), but it nevertheless trails practice, perhaps because Japanese firms have been in the forefront of the changes. Activity-based costing is addressed later in this chapter.

The section that follows presents traditional product-costing procedures, primarily so that readers will have a basis for assessing future developments in the field. Readers should be warned that these procedures may soon be relegated from current texts to historical treatises.

The Extremes: Job Order versus Process Costing

In industries characterized by the production of customized units or batches of product, each of which requires different amounts of labor and materials, specific records must be maintained of the actual labor hours and materials used for each unit or batch. The method in which it is necessary to maintain cost records of the individual units or batches is known as *job order* costing. Job order costing, as the name implies, is used in those industries where each job is unique: construction, book publishing, shipbuilding, furniture and automobile repair. In general, it is used by those firms that accept orders for products that require some degree of customization.

In industries characterized by continuous processing of identical goods, all costs are simply accumulated by period in each production department. Cost per unit is calculated by dividing total costs by number of units produced during the period. This method of accumulating costs by department and then averaging them over the number of units produced in a period is known as *process costing*. Process costing is most closely identified with continuous processing industries, such as oil refining, chemicals, plastics, food processing, paper, and cement. It may also be used in service industries, such as banking and insurance, to account for the processing of checks, invoices, and similar documents.

Job order costing will be illustrated first; then process costing. In actual usage these product-costing methods will be adapted to particular circumstances. However, the basic elements of *either* job order or process costing will be used.

JOB ORDER COSTING

Direct Labor and Materials

Each job must be assigned three types of costs: direct labor, direct materials, and overhead. As each of the elements is assigned to a job, an appropriate cost is added to the account, *work in process*. Work in process, however, is a control account, which may encompass more than one job. Costs applicable to each specific job are recorded in a subsidiary ledger composed of *job cost sheets*, one for each job in process. The job cost ledger may be maintained manually or by computer.

Suppose that in a particular month the Production Department of Virginia Furniture Co. undertakes several jobs. Some are for chairs, some for tables, and some for cabinets. The example that follows focuses on one of those jobs, number 101, for 100 custom-designed tables. First, as materials which can be used for all jobs are purchased, journal entries similar to the following would be made:

(1)

Raw materials (or stores control, parts, etc.)	$800,000	
Accounts payable		$800,000

To record purchase of raw materials

Then, as some materials are requisitioned for job 101, the release of the goods from the storeroom would be recorded as follows:

(2)

Work in process	$60,000	
Raw materials (or stores control, parts, etc.)		$60,000

To record requisition of raw materials for job 101

The cost of the materials would also be recorded on a job cost sheet. Such a job cost sheet is illustrated in Exhibit 18-2.

Direct labor costs may be accounted for in a variety of ways. Under most systems, however, entries such as the following two would be made:

(3)

Direct labor	$900,000	
Payroll (or wages payable or cash)		$900,000

To record direct labor used on a number of jobs

(4)

Work in process	$40,000	
Direct labor		$40,000

To assign direct labor to work in process, job 101

EXHIBIT 18-2
Job Order Cost Sheet

Virginia Furniture Co.

Job Cost Sheet

Job. No. _101_   Date started _6/2_

Description _COLONIAL TABLES_   Date completed _6/30_

No. of units _100_

Direct Labor		Materials		Factory Overhead	
6/9	$ 8,200	6/9	$ 25,300	6/9	$ 5,125
6/16	7,680	6/11	10,615	6/16	4,800
6/23	12,912	6/19	12,650	6/23	8,070
6/30	11,208	6/24	8,945	6/30	7,005
		6/26	2,140		
		6/28	350		
Totals	$40,000		$60,000		$25,000

Total costs $ _125,000_   Per unit cost $ _1,250_

Direct labor could be accumulated directly in the work in process control account, thereby bypassing the direct labor account. The direct labor account, however, is utilized to maintain a record of total direct labor costs. As with direct materials, the entry to the work in process control account would be accompanied by a corresponding notation on each job cost sheet.

Overhead

Overhead, whether assigned from a service center or incurred in the production department itself, by its very nature cannot readily be traced to specific jobs. It cannot, therefore, be directly recorded or accumulated on each job or each job cost sheet. If product costs are to include overhead costs—which, in terms of magnitude may be as great as those of labor and materials—then they must be assigned indirectly.

Establishing an Overhead Charging Rate: General Principles

The most common mechanism for assigning overhead costs to specific jobs is the *overhead charging rate*, commonly referred to as the *application rate* or the *burden rate*. The overhead charging rate relates the overhead costs attributable to a production department to some measure of departmental volume, such as direct labor hours, direct machine hours, or direct labor dollars. Overhead costs are also affected by the complexity of the production process; the numbers of setups, inspections, and change orders; and the number of transactions engendered by the accounting system. If the measure of activity were to be direct labor hours, then the overhead charging rate for a production department would be

$$\frac{\text{Total overhead}}{\text{Total direct labor hours}}$$

The amount of overhead *charged to each job* would then be equal to the overhead charging rate times the number of direct labor hours worked on that job.

Predetermining Charging Rates

Overhead charging rates *could* be calculated to relate *actual* overhead costs to *actual* units of volume. Usually, however, overhead charging rates are *predetermined*, based on *estimates* of both costs and activity. There are at least two advantages to using predetermined overhead charging rates. First, predetermined overhead charging rates facilitate computation of unit cost prior to the end of an accounting period. Since some overhead costs (e.g., repair costs) are incurred only intermittently, the actual costs of a period may not be known at the time a job is completed and transferred to finished goods. Similarly, total volume into which costs must be divided may also be unknown. That is, the denominator in the overhead charging rate formula cannot be determined with certainty until the end of the period. Second, predetermined overhead charging rates assure a constant per unit overhead charge throughout the period covered by the rate. This advantage stems from the fixed nature of some overhead costs. Those costs, although not traceable directly to specific units of product, nevertheless vary with output. For example, costs of supplies, machine maintenance, and inspection may increase with increases in output. Other overhead costs, such as rent, taxes, heat, and light, are fixed; they bear no relation to volume. If the overhead charging rate for individual products were to be determined on the basis of actual volume, then per unit charges of fixed overhead costs would fluctuate in response to changes in volume. In periods of increased production, overhead cost per unit would decrease as the costs were spread over a larger number of units. In periods of decreased production, overhead cost per unit would increase. To avoid this type of fluctuation, a firm can determine its overhead charging rate at the start of its fiscal year and continue to use it throughout the year unless actual experience indicates that its estimates were acutely in error.

Overhead Rate and Associated Journal Entries

Suppose that Virginia Furniture estimates that annual overhead costs, including those allocated from service departments and other nonproduction cost centers, to be incurred by the furniture production department will be $4,000,000. The firm forecasts that it will utilize 800,000 hours of direct labor. The overhead charging rate will thus be $5 per direct labor hour:

$$\frac{\text{Estimated overhead costs}}{\text{Estimated direct labor hours}} = \frac{\$4,000,000}{800,000} = \$5$$

If on job 101 the firm used 5,000 hours of direct labor, then the amount of overhead charged to that job would be 5,000 × $5 = $25,000.

Overhead costs are accumulated initially in accounts that provide management with information as to their nature and origin (e.g., maintenance, depreciation, supervision). They are then transferred to, and summarized in, a control account, "factory overhead" or "factory overhead control." From the factory overhead account, by means of the overhead charging rate, the overhead costs are added to work in process. Extension of the Virginia Furniture Co. example illustrates the general approach to accumulation of overhead costs and their assignment to specific units.

Actual overhead costs in the furniture production department during the month of June were as follows:

Supervision	$ 60,000
Maintenance	50,000
Depreciation of equipment	20,000
Other overhead costs incurred by the department	90,000
Overhead costs allocated from other cost centers	110,000
Total overhead costs of the Production Department	$330,000

Based on annual estimates, the overhead charging rate has been originally established at $5 per direct labor hour. Since the Production Department applied 5,000 direct labor hours to job 101, the following journal entries would enter the overhead costs as costs of the production department and assign them to work in process:

(5)

Supervision	$ 60,000	
Maintenance (various specific accounts)	50,000	
Depreciation	20,000	
Other costs	90,000	
Overhead costs allocated from other cost centers	110,000	
Payroll and accounts payable		$200,000
Accumulated depreciation		20,000
Accounts of other departments		110,000

To record actual costs incurred and those allocated from other cost centers

(6)

Overhead control	$330,000	
Supervision		$ 60,000
Maintenance (various specific accounts)		50,000
Depreciation		20,000
Other costs		90,000
Overhead costs allocated from other cost centers		110,000

To summarize overhead costs in the overhead control account

(7)

Work in process $25,000
    Overhead control $25,000
To assign overhead to work in process, job 101

The amount actually assigned to work in process is determined by multiplying the 5,000 direct labor hours by the overhead charging rate of $5 per direct labor hour. As will be discussed in the section that follows, the total amount assigned to all jobs is not necessarily equal to the actual total of overhead costs incurred.

Upon completion of the job, its cost (including direct labor, direct materials, and overhead) would be transferred from work in process to finished goods:

(8)

Finished goods inventory $125,000
    Work in process $125,000
To record the completion of job 101 and its transfer to finished goods inventory

The amount transferred is equal to the sum of the direct materials, the direct labor, and the overhead assigned to job 101 and is shown on the job cost chart (see Exhibit 18-2).

Inasmuch as job 101 consists of 100 tables, the average cost per table would be $1,250 (that is, $125,000 divided by 100).

Exhibit 18-3 summarizes the flow of costs in a job order cost system. It uses the data for Virginia Furniture Co. and focuses on job 101.

EXHIBIT 18-3
Summary of Job Order Costing (with Focus on Job 101)

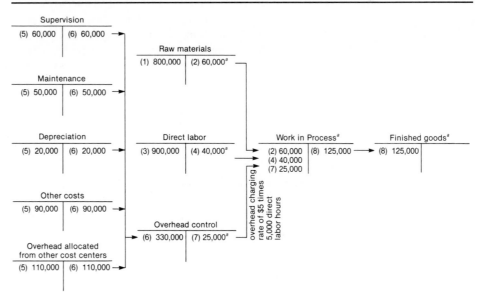

[a]Amounts shown are for job 101 only. Similar entries would be made for other jobs.

Alternative Bases for the Overhead Charge Rate

The basis for assigning overhead costs to product should be the variable that is most closely associated with overhead costs. For most organizations in the past, a significant portion of overhead costs was related to labor and therefore it was reasonable to base the overhead charging rate on either direct labor hours (DLH) or direct labor dollars. Today, however, especially in companies that use computer integrated manufacturing processes, direct labor is no longer a key element of production and may have only a marginal influence on overhead costs. In the electronics industry, for example, computer-controlled equipment and robotics are replacing human labor. In companies that continue to base the overhead charging rate on direct labor hours, the rate's numerator (overhead) is increasing whereas the denominator (direct labor hours) is decreasing. The obvious mathematical result of these two changes is that the overhead rate is spiralling upward, seemingly out of control.

Because of the likelihood that labor-based overhead rates will seriously overburden products that are the most labor intensive relative to other products, firms in which other factors of production have a more significant impact on overhead than does labor should look to alternative bases for the charging rate. For example, in firms in which much of the overhead is attributable to machine setups or maintenance, machine hours would be an appropriate basis for the overhead charging rate. In those in which warehousing or materials handling costs constitute the greater portion of overhead costs, then materials usage would be an appropriate basis for assigning overhead.

In recent years, however, managers of many firms have begun to recognize that overhead costs are not only tangentially associated just with direct labor, but also with the other conventional bases such as machine hours and direct materials. Hence, they are establishing new bases for overhead charging rates. Two such options are *cycle times* and *transactions*.

Cycle time is the total time necessary to process or manufacture a particular component. It is the elapsed clock time from the beginning of the manufacturing process until the completion of the final inspection. The rationale for basing overhead on cycle time is that overhead is more closely tied to time than to any of the traditional factors of production.

Transactions are the exchanges of information or materials required of an operating production process. Although not always traceable to specific physical units, they help to assure on-time delivery, high quality, and appropriate design. They would include, but are by no means limited to the following:

Logistical transactions—those involving the acquisition and movement of materials from one location to another that assure that supplies of goods and services are equal to demands for them. They may take in the services carried out by purchasing, receiving, shipping, data entry, and accounting departments.

Quality assurance transactions—those which assure that the product is properly designed and manufactured and which are conducted by engineers, inspectors, and statisticians.

Change transactions—those which update manufacturing systems to accommodate any changes in product design, scheduling, and manufacturing standards and may be performed by engineers, purchasing specialists, and data processing personnel.

This basis is grounded on the assumption that number of transactions best captures the amount of overhead for which a product is responsible. It helps assure, for example, that products that are sophisticated in design and production requirements, even if inexpensive in terms of labor and materials, get assigned their "fair" share of overhead.

Firms need not limit themselves to a single overhead charging rate. They can group homogeneous costs into cost pools and use different charging rates for each of the cost pools. In fact, the use of multiple bases for overhead distribution is one of the primary virtues of *activity-based costing* (discussed later in this chapter).

Over- or Underabsorbed Overhead

The overhead charging rate is based on estimates of annual overhead costs and direct labor hours or some other measures of activity. Should either of the estimates be in error—and in the absence of an uncommon degree of managerial prescience there is every likelihood that they will be—then either more or less than actual overhead costs will be assigned to products. Suppose, for example, that the actual annual overhead costs of the Production Department of Virginia Furniture Co. for the year were not $4,000,000 as estimated, but rather $4,300,000. Actual direct labor hours were not 800,000 as estimated but 820,000. Since the *predetermined* overhead charging rate was $5, only $4,100,000 ($5 × 820,000 direct labor hours, or DLH) of overhead costs would have been assigned or applied to the products manufactured during the year. At year end, a balance of $200,000 would remain in the overhead control account:

Overhead control		Work in process	
Actual		Amount absorbed	
costs 4,300,000	4,100,000	$5 × 820,000 DLH =	4,100,000
Balance 200,000			

If the amount applied to products (transferred to work in process) is less than actual costs, then a *debit* balance would remain in the overhead control account and overhead would be *underabsorbed*. If the amount applied to the products is greater than actual costs, then a credit balance would remain in the overhead control account and overhead would be *overabsorbed*. The question of how to dispose of the balance in the overhead control account—the amount that is over- or underabsorbed—is a particularly interesting one because it casts light on the relationship between "managerial" and "financial" accounting. Discussion of the issue will be postponed until Chapter 22, which deals with standard costs, so that it may be discussed as part of the broader question of how to account for all variances owing to management estimates and standards that are not met. Suffice it to say for now that many firms transfer the entire balance to an expense account, such as cost of goods sold, but that it is conceptually preferable to prorate it among cost of goods sold and ending inventories of finished goods and work in process.

Process costing is appropriate for mass production industries in which all units of product are essentially identical. Because all units are almost the same, there is no need to accumulate costs by job or batch. The total costs incurred in a period of time can be divided by the number of units produced, after accounting for partially completed goods in beginning and ending inventory.

Suppose, for example, a production department in a chemical plant has an output of 10,000 gallons of solvent in a particular month. Costs are incurred as follows:

Direct materials	$35,000
Direct labor	20,000
Overhead (including costs allocated	
from other cost centers)	10,000
Total costs	$65,000

Cost per gallon of output would be $6.50, determined by dividing total costs incurred by total output—$65,000 divided by 10,000 gallons. Conceptually, this calculation may be viewed as total costs divided by total output (or activity). For example:

$$\frac{\text{Monthly department costs}}{\text{Equivalent units of output (or activity)}}$$

Goods in Process and Equivalent Units

Process costing becomes considerably more complex when there are beginning or ending inventories that have been only partially completed and when labor and material are not added either concurrently or uniformly throughout the production process. For example, materials may be added first at the beginning of the production cycle but not again until the end; labor may be added uniformly throughout. It may be possible, therefore, for a product to be in differing stages of completion with respect to the different factors of production.

To account for goods that are partially complete, it is necessary to express production in terms of *equivalent units*. Equivalent units are the number of units that could have been completed by using all of the inputs that were used for partially completed units. Two units that are each one-half complete are the equivalent of one that is fully complete.

Suppose that costs in a particular month were, as in the previous example, $65,000. Assume this time that the firm completed and transferred to finished goods only 9,000 gallons. There was no work in process at the start of the year, but at year end 1,000 gallons remained in work in process inventory. These 1,000 gallons were 100 percent complete as to materials, but only 60 percent complete as to labor. One thousand gallons that are 60 percent complete are the equivalent of 600 units that are fully complete. With regard to labor, therefore, production of the period was 9,600 units—9,000 gallons completed and transferred to finished goods plus 600 equivalent units in work in process. With respect to materials, production was 10,000 gallons.

	Materials	Labor
Units completed and transferred to finished goods inventory	9,000 gal	9,000 gal
Equivalent units in inventory at year end	1,000[a]	600[b]
Total equivalent units to be accounted for	10,000 gal	9,600 gal
Less: Beginning inventory	-0-	-0-
Production during period (equivalent units)	10,000 gal	9,600 gal

[a]1,000 gallons 100 percent complete.
[b]1,000 gallons 60 percent complete.

For goods in process, then, costs per unit can be determined by dividing *costs incurred for each factor* during the period by equivalent production *contributed by that factor*. In process costing, overhead costs are assigned in essentially the same manner as in job order costing although overhead need not be assigned to specific jobs but is rather assigned to the single good "in process." Based on estimates of costs and activity (most commonly direct labor hours or direct labor dollars), an overhead charging rate is calculated. For each unit of activity used by a production department, a fixed dollar amount of overhead is added to product cost. In this example, assume that overhead is assigned on the basis of direct labor dollars. It is estimated that direct labor for the year will be $240,000 and that total overhead will be $120,000. Thus, for each $1.00 of direct labor charged to work in process, $.50 of overhead will be charged. For computational purposes direct labor and overhead costs can be grouped together; they will be referred to as *conversion costs*. Per unit costs can be determined as follows:

	Materials	Conversion Costs (direct labor and overhead)
Costs incurred during period	$35,000	$30,000[a]
Equivalent units of production	10,000 gal	9,600 gal
Cost per unit	$3.50	$3.125

[a]Direct labor	$20,000
Overhead ($20,000 × $.50)	10,000
	$30,000

Per unit cost of each completed unit would be the sum of the per unit materials and the conversion costs ($6.625). The $65,000 total costs incurred during the month may be divided between work still in process and that transferred to finished goods, where the costs of units transferred to finished goods can also be calculated as $59,625 (9,000 gal × $6.625):

	Work in Process	Transferred to Finished Goods	Total
Materials ($3.50 per gal)	(1,000 gal) $3,500	(9,000 gal) $31,500	$35,000
Conversion costs ($3.125 per gal)	(600 gal) 1,875	(9,000 gal) 28,125	30,000
Total	$5,375	$59,625	$65,000

This illustration is limited to a single processing department. Some products may have to be processed in two or more departments. In these situations, the accounting entries should reflect a transfer first from one department to another rather than directly to finished goods inventory. From the perspective of the receiving department, the goods transferred in are raw materials, and they should be accounted for as such (although they may be labeled "goods transferred from other departments"). They should be stated initially at the total cost (both materials and conversion costs) assigned in the previous department.

In-process inventories and transfers to other departments or to finished goods may be accounted for by any one of the basic inventory methods. The weighted-average method is the most widely used, with a modified version of FIFO a distant second.

In summary, the essential difference between job order costing and process costing is that in job order costing the focus is on the individual job, whereas in process costing it is on the production department. In a job order system, costs are accumulated initially by departments but then are assigned to particular jobs. Unit costs are determined by dividing costs assigned to a particular job by the number of units in that job. In a process costing system, unit cost is determined directly; costs incurred by a department are divided by the number of units produced, taking into account any adjustments for partially completed units in beginning or ending inventory. Under job order costing, overhead costs are assigned to each job, whereas under process costing, overhead costs are accumulated and applied to products at the departmental level.

ACTIVITY-BASED COSTING

The conventional costing system requires that overhead costs first be allocated from service departments to production departments and then distributed, using the overhead charging rate, to specific products. It was developed to support manufacturing processes in which overhead is mainly a function of direct labor, which, in turn, is dependent upon production volume. Moreover, in these processes the key manufacturing activities were carried out by clearly defined production departments, supported by service departments. The service departments performed functions that were decidedly ancillary to those of the production departments.

The conventional costing system has not been entirely successful in meeting the challenges of the modern, computer-driven, factory. In large measure, this is because in today's manufacturing environment direct labor is no longer the dominant production factor and production and service activities are not readily distinguishable.

To compensate for the deficiencies of the conventional system, some companies, as pointed out earlier in this chapter, now absorb overhead costs into their product on the basis of nontraditional measures, such as cycle time or number of transactions, rather than direct labor or direct materials. Others, however, have turned even farther from the conventional costing system and are collecting costs in specially designated "cost pools" rather than service departments or cost centers. In one variant of the traditional system, referred to as *activity-based costing* (ABC), overhead costs are first assigned to activity-based cost pools.

Each of these pools is homogeneous in that the costs assigned to it should be influenced or driven by a common factor. The activity pools can cut across departmental boundaries. They can include overhead costs incurred by production as well as service departments.

By not allocating overhead costs to departments, firms fail to realize at least one of the previously cited benefits of allocations—that of motivating employees of the departments receiving the cost allocations to assist in controlling the overhead costs. However, this limitation of activity-based costing can easily be overcome by any number of accounting mechanisms that will assure that the department that is best able to control a particular cost is charged with that cost *before* it is assigned to an activity pool.

After the firm collects the overhead costs in the activity-based cost pools, it distributes them to its various products by a *cost driver*. A cost driver is similar to an overhead charging rate, but it should represent the factor that has the greatest influence on the behavior of the overhead costs within a particular activity pool. It should not be based on direct labor or direct materials unless there is a causal relationship between those factors and the costs. Each activity pool may have its own cost driver—one that is most closely tied to its costs.

The following are examples of activity-based cost pools and cost drivers that might be used to distribute costs from the pools to the individual products:

Activity-Based Cost Pool	Cost Driver
Materials handing	Material transactions
Materials procurement	Number of orders
Maintenance	Maintenance hour
Depreciation on equipment	Machine hours
Quality control	Number of inspections

The total costs in each pool are distributed to the products on the basis of each product's cost driver volume. Thus, if a particular product required 60 percent of the quality control inspections (a cost driver), then it would be assigned 60 percent of the quality control costs (the related activity-based cost pool).

Exhibit 18-4 compares conventional and activity-based costing.

DIRECT (VARIABLE) VERSUS ABSORPTION (FULL) COSTING

Generally accepted accounting principles require that product cost include all manufacturing overhead costs. The deficiencies, as well as the attendant opportunities for income manipulation, of this *full* or *absorption* costing "model," which assigns all overhead costs to units produced, can be appreciated by comparing it to *direct (or variable) costing*. Direct costing is *not* an accepted alternative for general-purpose reporting to the public in the United States and most other countries. It is a means of presenting results of operations to internal management that provides substantially greater insight into cost behavior than does full costing. However, in some countries, such as Finland, direct costing is used to determine both inventory value and cost of goods sold for both tax and general reporting purposes.

EXHIBIT 18-4
Conventional versus Activity-Based Costing

Conventional

STAGE 1: Overhead departmentalization   STAGE 2: Application of absorption rates

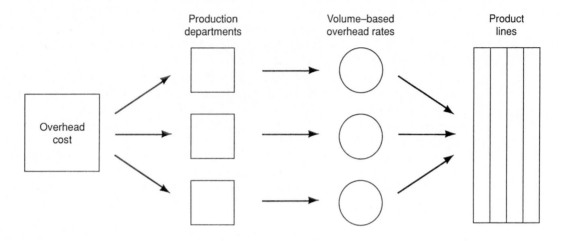

Activity Based

STAGE 1: Overhead pooling   STAGE 2: Application of cost driver rates

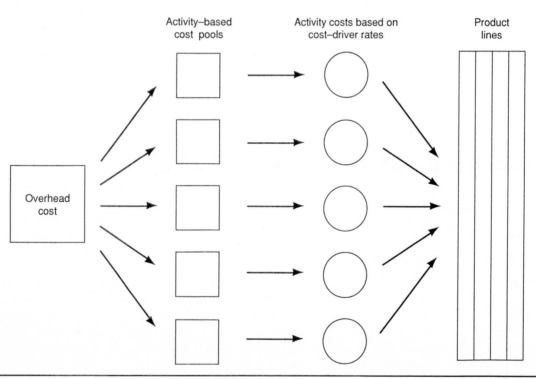

Source: J. Innes and F. Mitchell, ''Activity Based Costing, A Review with Case Studies'' (London: The Chartered Institute of Management Account-ants, 1990), pp. 6–7.

Direct costing is a procedure whereby only *variable* costs are included in product cost. *All* fixed costs are classified as period costs and thereby carried directly to the income statement. Product cost under direct costing would include direct materials, direct labor, and the portion of overhead that is variable. As distinguished from full costing, it would exclude the portion of the overhead that is fixed. Fixed overhead, along with selling and administrative costs (costs which are also considered as period costs under full costing, regardless of whether fixed or variable) would be reported in the year incurred irrespective of when the products to which they relate are actually sold.

Direct costing remedies two primary deficiencies of full costing. First, it eliminates the need to allocate fixed overhead from one department or cost pool to another and then to assign the overhead from the departments or pools to the products. Overhead allocations and assignments, in that they are based on criteria that are within the choice of management, are necessarily arbitrary and, as we have seen in a world of declining labor relative to total costs, there may be no generally accepted means of assigning overhead costs to product. Under direct costing, such allocations and assignments need not be made because all fixed costs are period costs and charged directly to earnings.

Second, direct costing eliminates fluctuations in product cost that are attributable to changes in volume. Under full costing, the cost assigned to each unit produced depends upon the number of units over which fixed costs can be spread. The greater the number of units produced, the less will be cost per unit.[3] As a consequence, management is able to reduce cost of goods sold, and thereby increase reported earnings, in any single accounting period, merely by increasing the volume of production. Even if sales decline, the decrease in cost per unit can cause income to increase. Under direct costing, in contrast, fixed costs do not enter into the determination of product cost; they are charged-off in full as they are incurred. Income, under direct costing, is driven entirely by sales. Assuming that selling prices, unit variable costs, and total fixed costs remain constant, the only way to increase reported income is by increasing sales.

Comparison With Full (Absorption) Costing Results

The example that follows compares income and ending inventory under full costing and direct costing. It covers a period of three years, one in which units produced equals units sold, one in which units produced exceeds units sold, and one in which units produced are less than units sold.

Example

A firm manufactures a single product. Its books and records reveal the following:

[3] This is true even if overhead is assigned by means of a predetermined overhead burden rate because any under- or overabsorbed burden must be prorated among inventory and cost of goods sold.

Fixed manufacturing costs *per year*		$100,000
Variable manufacturing costs *per unit*		
Direct labor	$5	
Direct materials	4	
Variable overhead	3	
Total variable manufacturing costs per unit	$12	
Selling price *per unit*	$25	

Selling and administrative costs shall be ignored in this example, as they are accounted for as period costs under both full and direct costing.

Exhibit 18-5 indicates volume, costs, and inventory over the three-year period. Income and ending inventory under direct and absorption costing is shown in Exhibit 18-6. Notice that because sales, price, volume, and per unit costs remain constant, income under direct costing (but not full costing) also remains constant. When production exceeds sales, income is greater under full costing than under direct costing. This is because under full costing a portion of the fixed costs is "stored" in inventory rather than charged in full against income. Correspondingly, when sales exceed production, income is less under absorption costing than under full costing because the fixed costs that were previously stored in inventory are now released and included in cost of goods sold. As with other circumstances in which there is a choice among accounting procedures, in the long run (in this case over any series of periods in which total sales are equal to total production) earnings will be the same under both direct and full costing.

A key advantage of direct costing from the perspective of managers is that it dovetails so naturally with cost–volume–profit analysis. Both contribution margin (sales less variable costs) and fixed costs are clearly set forth, and changes in earnings owing to changes in sales can readily be determined.

Another advantage of direct costing is that the basic costing information can be easily tailored and adapted to the second and third objectives of product costing identified at the beginning of this chapter. Direct costs, defined to include all variable costs which can be associated with volume of product, are more

EXHIBIT 18-5

	Year		
	1	2	3
Sales volume (in units)	10,000	10,000	10,000
Production volume (in units)	10,000	18,000	2,000
Fixed costs (per above)	$100,000	$100,000	$100,000
Variable costs ($12 × production volume)	$120,000	$216,000	$ 24,000
Total costs (fixed costs + variable costs)	$220,000	$316,000	$124,000
Cost per unit produced under absorption costing (total costs ÷ production volume)	$22.00	$17.5556	$62.00
Ending inventory (in units)	-0-	8,000	-0-

EXHIBIT 18-6

	Year		
	1	2	3
Direct or Variable Costing			
Income			
Sales @ $25	$250,000	$250,000	$250,000
Cost of goods sold (variable costs of $12 per unit)	120,000	120,000	120,000
Gross margin	$130,000	$130,000	$130,000
Fixed costs	100,000	100,000	100,000
Total income	$ 30,000	$ 30,000	$ 30,000
Ending inventory	$ -0-	$ 96,000[a]	$ -0-
Full or Absorption Costing			
Income			
Sales @ $25	$250,000	$250,000	$250,000
Cost of goods sold	220,000[b]	175,556[c]	264,444[e]
Total income	$ 30,000	$ 74,444	$(14,444)
Ending inventory	$ -0-	$140,444[d]	$ -0-

[a]8,000 units @ $12.
[b]10,000 units @ $22.
[c]10,000 units @ $17.5556.
[d]8,000 units @ $17.5556.
[e]8,000 units (from inventory) @ $17.5556 + 2,000 units @ $62.

useful for managerial planning and control because they are usually more relevant to an individual manager and an individual cost center's scope of responsibility. Such direct costs are easily understood and tend to have better acceptance in internal budgets and performance evaluation reports. The behavioral consequences of using direct or variable costing are usually more predictable and more favorable for the entire organization.

Direct costing can also be easily adapted to pricing or bidding activities. Direct costs can also be called *prime costs*, where materials and labor are the primary or only variable costs. Pricing models based on markups of prime costs can form easily understood and convenient pricing guides. Simple markup rules or procedures can be derived from the direct costing model and used in bidding and pricing in a way that avoids the misleading and often destructive effects of full absorption costing. The resultant prices can be easily changed to reflect alternative, or "what if," overhead relationships and different markup percentages. Using markup percentages on prime costs, or on all variable costs, avoids all of the problems identified earlier that may be associated with arbitrary allocations. Direct costing can also be easily adapted to a computer integrated manufacturing environment. This can be accomplished more expeditiously than under full or absorption costs because the impact of alternative allocation bases is minimized and because the need to find new cost drivers to reflect the environment is also minimized under direct costing. Direct costing can then form the basis for management planning, control, and pricing systems because such systems are more adaptable to a variety of managerial needs and objectives. Direct costing, or a customized variation of it, will then yield more useful managerial data about product costs.

One important function of an accounting system is to provide information on the cost of goods or services. Generally accepted accounting principles require that the cost of a unit of product—that to be matched with the revenue from sales—include not only those costs that can be directly associated with it, but also those that are common to other units of the same as well as different products.

If common costs are to be included in product cost, then they must be assigned in a rational and systematic manner. There are, regrettably, no perfectly objective means by which to associate common costs with particular units of output. The product values which result from application of the procedures and techniques described in this chapter are no more objective than the bases of allocation which underlie them. Different companies, as well as different managers and accountants within the same company, could justifiably allocate similar costs by dissimilar means.

Reports that are used solely within a firm, as opposed to those intended for parties external to the organization, do not require that product costs include a share of common costs. Allocations need be made only when they serve to facilitate the decisions for which the reports will serve as information. Direct costing, as opposed to full or absorption costing, is a costing procedure whereby all fixed costs—those which are usually the least directly tied to units of output—are charged-off as period costs and thereby excluded from product cost.

Reports based on direct costing procedures are untainted by allocations of fixed costs and, at the same time, they set forth separately fixed costs and variable costs. They are, therefore, especially helpful to managers in conducting cost–volume–profit analysis.

Exercise for Review and Self-Testing

The Community Health Clinic must determine the cost of serving individual patients in order to obtain reimbursement from both private insurance companies and sponsoring government agencies. The clinic is divided into several patient-care departments, one of which is pediatrics. Direct costs of treating each pediatric patient are:

Physicians' salaries, per hour	$90
Nurses' salaries, per hour	$20

Overhead costs of the *pediatrics* department for a *typical* month *excluding* allocations of costs of the clinic at large are:

Salaries of physicians and nurses applicable to activities other than patient care	$15,000
Depreciation of equipment	14,000
Supplies and medicines	11,000
Total	$40,000

In a typical month, the payroll of physicians and nurses applicable to direct patient care in the pediatrics department is approximately $132,000.

All costs of the clinic that cannot be directly assigned to the patient-care departments are assigned initially to two cost pools: occupancy costs and administrative costs. The following information relates to the allocation of the costs in these pools:

	Occupancy Costs	Administrative Costs
Basis of allocation	Floor space	Fixed amount[a] + $1 per patient served
Cost incurred during month of June (same as estimated costs per month)	$20,000	$22,500[b]

[a]Based on proportion of estimated number of patients served per month.
[b]$15,000 in fixed costs + $7,500 in variable costs

	Pediatrics Department	All Other Patient-Care Departments
Amount of floor space	4,000 sq ft	12,000 sq ft
Number of patients served in June (same as estimated number of patients per month)	1,500	6,000
Allocation of fixed administrative costs ($15,000)[a]	$3,000	$12,000

[a]Based on proportion of estimated number of patients served per month.

Overhead costs of the pediatrics department (including allocations of occupancy and administrative costs) are assigned to individual "jobs" (i.e., patients) by way of a predetermined overhead charging rate. The overhead charging rate is applied on the basis of patient-care payroll dollars (i.e., salaries of physicians and nurses) and is determined by dividing estimated monthly overhead costs by estimated monthly patient-care payroll dollars.

In the month of June, patient D. Short received 5 hours of physicians' services and 10 hours of nurses' services.

1. Allocation of at-large clinic costs to patient-care departments
   a. How much of the $20,000 in occupancy costs incurred in June should be allocated to the pediatrics department?
   b. How much of the $22,500 in administrative costs should be allocated to the pediatrics department?
2. Determination of overhead charging rate
   a. What would be the total estimated overhead costs of the pediatrics department, *including* its share of occupancy and administrative costs?
   b. What would be the predetermined overhead charging rate, based on $132,000 estimated patient-care payroll dollars?
3. Assignment of costs to a particular patient
   a. What would be the physicians' and nurses' costs assigned to D. Short?
   b. What would be the overhead costs assigned to D. Short?
4. Suppose that during the month of June, actual administrative costs of the clinic were $19,000 (instead of $22,500 as estimated) and actual patient-care payroll dollars were $135,000 (instead of $132,000 as estimated). How would these variances affect the dollar cost assigned to D. Short? Explain.

Questions for Review and Discussion

1. What is overhead? Why can it not be applied to a product in the same manner as direct labor or direct materials?
2. Distinguish between *allocation* and *absorption* as the terms are commonly used in the literature of accounting.

3. What is the essential difference between job order and process costing? If a firm produces a single product, all units identical to one another, which method would be most appropriate?
4. What is an *overhead charging rate*? What is the advantage of using a *predetermined* charging rate?
5. Under what circumstances would each of the following bases for an overhead charging rate be most appropriate:
   a. Direct labor hours?
   b. Direct labor dollars?
   c. Machine hours used?
   d. Machine setups?
   e. Number of material requisitions?
6. Suppose that a substantial portion of overhead costs was most directly associated with direct labor, but another equally substantial portion was most directly associated with direct materials. What would be the most appropriate basis for an overhead charging rate? Can the potential dilemma be resolved without conflict? At what price?
7. Many accountants aver that because of the arbitrary nature of the allocation process, little is accomplished by allocating service department costs to production departments. What purposes are, in fact, served by cost allocation?
8. What are the primary advantages of using a dual allocation scheme to distribute costs that have both a fixed and variable element?
9. In the long run, income as determined by direct or absorption costing will be the same. Under what circumstances will absorption cost income exceed direct cost income in a particular period? Under what circumstances will absorption cost income be less than direct cost income?
10. In a rate hearing before the utility commission of a northeastern state, representatives of a CPA firm engaged by the commission to undertake an independent study of costs testified that the cost to the electric company of providing electricity in that state was $.052 per kilowatt hour. The utility company serves a five-state area. The competence and integrity of the CPA firm is beyond dispute. Assuming that you are an attorney representing either the utility company seeking higher rates or a consumer group seeking lower rates, how could you impugn the cost figure provided by the CPA firm?
11. Why are some firms, particularly those employing computer integrated manufacturing systems, basing their overhead charging rates on nontraditional factors, such as cycle time and number of transactions?
12. What are activity-based cost systems (ABC)? How do they differ from conventional systems? What are their advantages?

======= **Problems**

1. *Journal entries can serve to describe the flow of costs in a job order cost system.*

   The data that follow relate to the manufacturing activities during May of Specialty Tools, Inc., and more specifically its finishing department. The firm uses a job order cost system to account for its production operations.
   (1) The finishing department incurred direct wage costs of $14,250. Of this amount, $6,000 was applicable to job 168. Job 168 was started in May.
   (2) The department received from the assembly department partially completed goods that had an assigned cost of $12,760. Of this amount, $9,000 was applicable to job 168.
   (3) The finishing department incurred the following overhead costs:

Indirect labor	$4,800
Supplies and materials (requisitioned from stores)	520
Depreciation	1,700
Total	$7,020

In addition, it was allocated $1,800 in overhead costs from other cost centers within the firm.

(4) The finishing department completed job 168 and transferred it to finished goods inventory.

The finishing department assigned overhead to work in process and specific jobs by means of a predetermined charging rate based on direct labor dollars. At the start of the year it estimated that total overhead costs (including those allocated from other departments) would be $112,500 and that total direct labor dollars would be $187,500.

Prepare all journal entries or T account entries necessary for the finishing department.

2. *Unless a predetermined rate is used to apply overhead, product cost may be subject to wide fluctuations.*

Manfred Industries, Inc., manufactures two types of products, Product A and Product B. The firm estimates that in the current year overhead costs (*all fixed*) will be as follows:

Rent and other fixed occupancy costs	$ 300,000
Depreciation	180,000
Supervision	240,000
Indirect labor costs	540,000
Total overhead costs	$1,260,000

The firm also estimates that production of the two products will require a total of 360,000 direct labor hours.

The present wage rate per direct labor hour is $15. Each unit of Product A requires 20 hours ($300) of direct labor and $1500 of direct materials. Overhead is applied on the basis of direct labor hours.

In a four-month period during the year, actual direct labor hours used in the manufacture of each of the two products were:

	Direct Labor Hours			
	June	July	August	September
Product A	20,000	20,000	10,000	20,000
Product B	10,000	10,000	10,000	15,000

In the same period, actual overhead costs were as estimated, $105,000 per month ($1,260,000/12 months), with the exception of July, in which they were $150,000. Number of units of Product A manufactured was 1,000 per month, with the exception of August, in which only 500 were manufactured.

a. Assuming that the company applies overhead based on *actual* overhead costs and *actual* direct labor hours used, determine cost per unit of Product A during each of the four months.

b. Assuming alternatively that the company applies overhead by way of a *predetermined* overhead charging rate, based on *estimates* of overhead costs and direct labor hours to be used in the course of an entire year, determine cost per unit of Product A during each of the four months.

c. Unless a *predetermined* overhead charging rate is used to apply overhead to products, cost per unit of product is subject to wide fluctuations. Based on your responses to parts a and b, indicate three factors which, if different in magnitude than anticipated, would cause product cost to deviate from that which is expected.

3. *Alternative bases of overhead absorption may have substantially different impacts on the amount to be paid by a customer.*

A sporting goods manufacturer has agreed to produce 10,000 units of camping equipment for the Air Force at a price that will be determined, to a considerable degree, by actual production costs.

The equipment to be sold to the Air Force is similar to that manufactured for sale through usual commercial channels, except that it is made of heavier and more durable materials. Comparative per unit labor and material costs of manufacturing the equipment are:

	For Commercial Use	For Military Use
Direct labor	$100	$100
Direct materials	600	900

The firm estimates that manufacturing overhead related to the equipment is approximately $4 million. It expects to produce a total of 20,000 units of the equipment—10,000 for the military and 10,000 for commercial sale.

a. In the past the company has used a predetermined overhead charging rate based on *direct material dollars* to apply overhead to the product. It intends to calculate costs of goods sold to the Air Force on the same basis. Determine per unit cost of equipment produced under the contract with the Air Force.

b. Air Force contract officers have argued that an overhead charging rate based on direct material dollars results in an allocation of costs that is unfair to the military. It asserts that the rate should be based instead on direct labor dollars. Determine the per unit cost of equipment sold to the Air Force based on the alternative charging rate.

c. How, in your opinion, should the difference be resolved? Under what circumstances can a rate based on materials as opposed to labor be justified?

4. *Some labor-related costs should be considered direct labor costs; others should be included in the pool of overhead costs.*

Precision Instruments, Inc., estimates that it will incur the following costs in the forthcoming year:

Direct labor (100,000 hours @ $19)	$1,900,000
Direct materials	2,500,000
Overtime premium (10,000 hours @ $9.50)	95,000
FICA (Social Security)	100,000
Pension contributions	114,000
Medical insurance	75,000
Vacation pay	130,000
Other overhead costs	800,000

The applicable FICA rate is 7.65 percent of wages to a maximum of $53,400 in wages.

Of the 100,000 hours of direct labor, 90,000 will be worked at the regular rate of $19; the remaining 10,000 at the overtime rate of $28.50. The overtime premium of $9.50 is charged to a separate overtime premium account. The firm's contribution to the employees' pension fund is, per union contract, a straight 6 percent of all direct labor costs (excluding overtime premiums). Medical insurance costs are approximately $2,400 per employee.

In the period December 27 to December 31, the firm began work on, and completed, job 56. The job ticket indicates the following charges:

Direct labor	400 hours
Direct materials	$16,700

Of the 400 hours worked on the job, 350 were paid at the overtime rate of $28.50, the remainder at the straight-time rate of $19. The overtime had been routinely planned. Job 56 was worked on during overtime hours only because it was scheduled for the end of the week, when several employees had already worked the number of hours beyond which overtime pay is required. Inasmuch as all employees who worked on job 56 had already surpassed $53,400 in earnings, the firm was not required to make FICA payments on their behalf during December.

The firm bases its overhead charging rate on direct labor hours.

a. Determine an appropriate overhead charging rate based on estimated costs for the year. Should all labor-related costs except for direct labor be included in the overhead pool, or should one or more be added to the direct labor rate? Explain.

b. Determine the cost, including overhead, of job 56.

c. In a sentence or two, justify the way in which you accounted for both overtime premium and FICA.

5. *The key to process costing is the determination of equivalent units of production.*

Love Chemical has determined that the cost of producing Florex, under standard conditions, should be $4.90 per gallon.

Love uses a process costing system to account for chemical production.

Raw materials are added only at the start of the production process. There should be no waste or shrinkage of raw materials.

As of July 1, there was no work in process. During July the company put into production 600,000 gallons of materials at a cost of $2,400,000.

It used 25,000 hours of direct labor. Direct labor is charged at a rate of $14 per hour. Overhead is charged at a rate of $8 per direct labor hour.

During July the firm completed and shipped out 560,000 gallons of Florex. At month end, 40,000 gallons of Florex remained in work in process inventory. The Florex in process was 25 percent complete with respect to labor.

Did the company operate efficiently during July? How much greater or less were actual per gallon costs than standard costs?

6. *Partially completed beginning and ending inventories add a measure of complexity to process costing calculations.*

Note: This exercise goes beyond the discussion in the text. However, with the help of the hints provided, it should provide insight into process cost calculations when there are beginning and ending inventories.

Kalman Chemicals, Inc., uses a process cost system to account for the manufacture of Blue Dye 1.

As of June 1, the company had in process 4,000 gallons of dye. The dye was fully complete with respect to materials but only one-fourth complete with regard to labor.

During the month of June, the company began work on, and added materials for, 60,000 gallons of dye. It completed and transferred to finished goods 58,000 gallons.

As of June 30, the company had in process 6,000 gallons of dye. The dye was fully complete with respect to materials and one-third complete with regard to labor.

Relevant cost data are as follows:

	Materials	Labor
Costs in beginning inventory	$ 8,000	$ 3,600
Costs added during month	110,000	168,000
Total costs to be accounted for	$118,000	$171,600

a. With regard to materials:
   (1) Determine the per gallon cost of materials added to production in June.
   (2) Determine the weighted-average cost per gallon of the dye transferred to finished goods and still in process at month end.
b. With regard to labor:
   (1) Determine the per gallon cost of labor added to production in June. *Hint*:
      (a) In addition to the gallons that were transferred to finished goods, what is the equivalent number of gallons in month-end work in process inventory that could be considered to have been produced during the month?
      (b) Of the goods that were transferred to finished goods, what is the equivalent number of gallons that were in beginning inventory and were thereby produced in a previous month?
   (2) Determine the weighted-average cost per gallon of the dye that was transferred to finished goods and still in process at month end. *Hint*:
      (a) What is the number of gallons that were transferred to finished goods?
      (b) What is the equivalent number of gallons that are in work in process inventory at month end?
c. Determine total (labor and materials) weighted-average cost per gallon of dye transferred to finished goods inventory.

7. *Under some allocation schemes, the amounts charged to a unit will be affected by factors beyond its control.*

A municipal fire department is divided into two primary divisions: operations, which includes all firefighting activities, and support services, which includes fire prevention, education, maintenance, and training. In addition, there is a clerical pool which prepares routine reports for each of the two divisions.

Studies have indicated that the cost of operating the clerical pool is $3,500 per month plus $4 for each document prepared.

The operations division has estimated that it will require the preparation of an average of 270 documents per month in the forthcoming year. The support services division has estimated that it will require 360 documents per month.

The fire department is considering three schemes for allocating the costs of the clerical pool to the two primary divisions.

a. Each division will be charged with a pro rata share of *estimated* monthly costs based on an *estimate* of the number of reports that it will submit to the clerical pool. Thus, the charge to each department will be the same each month.

b. Each division will be charged with a pro rata share of *actual costs* of the clerical pool based on the *actual* number of reports submitted to the clerical pool by the two divisions.

c. Each division will be charged with a pro rata share of *estimated fixed* monthly costs (i.e., $3,500) of the clerical pool based on *estimated* number of reports and, in addition, with a variable charge based on *estimated* per report variable costs (i.e., $4) and *actual* number of reports submitted.

(1) Prepare a schedule or spreadsheet in which you indicate the amount to be allocated to the operations division under each of the three allocation schemes and each of the following four sets of assumptions of actual numbers of reports and costs:

	Number of Reports		
	Operations Division	Support Division	Costs Incurred by Clerical Pool
1. Number of reports and costs as estimated	270	360	$6,020[a]
2. Number of reports as estimated; clerical division inefficient	270	360	7,000
3. Operations division submits greater than estimated number of reports; clerical division efficient	300	360	6,140[b]
4. Support division submits fewer than estimated number of reports; clerical division efficient	270	330	5,900[c]

[a]$3,500 + 630($4).
[b]$3,500 + 660($4).
[c]$3,500 + 600($4).

(2) In light of your results, evaluate each of the three allocation schemes in terms of equity and desired motivational effects on the two divisions.

8. *In the view of many accountants and managers, allocations of service department costs are both arbitrary and unnecessary for many types of decisions.*

Appliance Industries, Inc., has a separate department devoted to the manufacture of heavy-duty kitchen mixers. The variable costs of producing mixers are:

Direct labor	$48
Direct materials	52
Variable overhead	50
Total variable costs	$150

Fixed overhead costs of the mixer department excluding the two allocated costs discussed below are $260,000.

Within the company there is disagreement as to the basis for allocating factory office costs and warehousing costs. With respect to factory office costs, some managers assert that they should be allocated on the basis of number of employees; others, on the basis of total payroll dollars. The mixer department has 30 percent of factory employees, but since its employees are highly skilled, it pays 40 percent of payroll dollars. Annual factory office costs are $400,000.

With regard to warehousing costs, some managers maintain that the costs should be allocated on the basis of square footage occupied in the warehouse; others, on the basis of dollar value of goods stored. The mixer department occupies 20 percent of the square footage, but its goods account for 50 percent of the total dollar value. Annual warehouse costs are approximately $100,000.

The firm anticipates production volume of 10,000 units in the coming year.

a. Determine the total cost per mixer making four alternative assumptions as to the allocation of the office and warehouse costs (i.e., first office costs allocated one way and warehouse costs allocated each of the two ways, and then office costs allocated the other way and warehouse costs again allocated each of the two ways).

b. Suppose that the company was asked to enter into a contract with a retailer that required the sale of 2,000 mixers at a price of $191. The 2,000 units would be in addition to the 10,000 that the firm planned to produce. The company has the capacity to fulfill the contract, and the production of the additional units would in no way affect the production volume or selling prices of mixers or other products that the firm manufactures. All fixed costs would similarly remain unchanged. Should the firm accept the contract assuming each of the four combinations of allocation bases? Explain.

c. Suppose that the firm faced a "purely" competitive market for the sale of its mixers. As a consequence, it had no influence over sales price. Its only decision would be as to the number of units to produce and sell. Do you think that bases of allocation should affect the firm's determination of how many units to produce and sell? Explain.

d. By what criterion should the firm select between alternative bases of allocation? What other information would you recommend that the decision maker try to obtain?

9. *Can a department really incur a loss on a machine that is apparently profitable?*

The manager of a clerical department would like to install a snack vending machine for the convenience of employees. He believes that it would serve to boost morale. The machine would be owned, stocked, and maintained by a reputable vending service, which would pay the department a commission of $.04 for each item sold.

The machine, which measures 3 feet by 3 feet, would be placed in a corner which would otherwise be vacant. The manager estimates that approximately 5,000 items per year would be dispensed by the machine. Inasmuch as any "profits" would be contributed toward the annual company picnic, the manager thought that the machine would serve the interests of the department—that is, until he discussed the idea with the company accountant.

The accountant pointed out that (1) occupancy costs are allocated to the various corporate departments at an annual rate of $12 per square foot. (2) The machine would inevitably require some attention on the part of the manager in the way of bookkeeping time and calls to the vending service when the machine was inoperable. He estimates that the manager would spend at least 10 hours per year on matters pertaining to the machine. The salary of the manager is $40,000 per year; fringe benefits and related payroll costs amount to an additional $10,000 per year. The manager works an average of 2,000 hours per year.

a. Determine net income (or loss) as it would most probably be calculated by the accountant.

b. Based on financial considerations alone, do you think the department should install the machine?

10. *Utility rates are severely affected by allocation basis.*

Southwest Gas Co. serves a 12-county region in a southwestern state. Each municipality within that region has the authority to establish rates for the customers within its jurisdiction. The municipality of Burnt is presently holding hearings regarding the rates that it will charge. It has been generally agreed that the rates should be set so as to allow the company a return of 8 percent on assets. What is in dispute is the basis for allocating to Burnt both common costs and common assets. Burnt has no industry; virtually all of its customers are residential or small commercial establishments. As a consequence, the average consumption of gas per customer is substantially less than that for the entire 12-county region served by the company. Nearby municipalities are heavily industrialized and therefore have a number of customers who use many times more gas than the typical residential customer.

Southwest Gas Co. has provided the regulatory commission of Burnt with audited cost data. Costs and assets that are common to all customers within the 12-county area have been allocated to Burnt on the basis of its pro rata share of *number of customers*. Representatives of consumer groups assert, however, that the company's allocation of common costs and assets discriminates against the customers of Burnt. They say that common assets and costs should be allocated on the basis of *share of gas used* rather than number of customers.

The regulatory commission has been presented with the data that follow. Amounts in parentheses indicate Burnt's percentages of totals. (MCF = thousand cubic feet.)

	Burnt	12-County Area Including Burnt
Number of customers	10.000 (5%)	200,000
Number of MCF consumed annually	960,000 (3.33%)	28,800,000
Value of assets that can be associated with specific jurisdictions	$3,000,000 (5%)	$60,000,000
Annual depreciation and other fixed costs that can be associated with specific jurisdictions	$600,000 (5%)	$12,000,000
Annual direct cost of gas ($1.50 per MCF)	$1,440,000 (3.33%)	$43,200,000
Value of assets that are common to all jurisdictions		$90,000,000
Annual fixed costs that are common to all jurisdictions		$48,000,000

a. For each of the two alternative means of allocating common assets and costs, determine:
   (1) The total asset base of Burnt
   (2) The amount, based on the total asset base and the allowable earnings rate of 8 percent, that the company would be permitted to earn within Burnt
   (3) The total costs that would be attributable to Burnt
   (4) The total revenues that the company would be required to generate within Burnt
   (5) The allowable rate per MCF
b. Indicate briefly the primary arguments in favor of their positions that would be made by the representatives of both the company and the consumer groups.

11. *This problem illustrates the flow of costs from service departments to a particular job.*

The Ilan Co. has two service departments (Office and Materials Handling) and two production departments (A and B). At the start of the year, it made the estimates shown on p. 796.

Overhead costs of the service departments are allocated as follows. First, the costs of the office are allocated to each of the other departments (including materials handling) on the basis of number of employees. Then, the costs (including those allocated from the office) of the materials handling department are allocated to the two production departments. The fixed portion of the materials handling costs (including the share of office costs) are allocated on the basis of prior year purchases of materials. The variable portion is allocated on the basis of *actual* number of warehouse requisitions in a given month. Overhead costs of Department A are charged to specific jobs by means of a predetermined overhead charging rate. The rate is based on estimates of total annual overhead costs and direct labor hours.

	Service Departments		Production Departments	
	Office	Materials Handling	A	B
Annual fixed costs (prior to allocations from other departments)	$80,000	$60,000	$200,000[a]	$18,000[a]
Variable costs	—	$40 per requisition received	$10 per d.l.h.[b]	$12 per d.l.h.[b]
Number of employees	5	10	22	18
Annual number of warehouse requisitions	—	—	500	300
Annual number of direct labor hours	—	—	25,000	20,000
Materials purchases (prior year)	—	—	$350,000	$450,000

[a]Fixed overhead traceable to the department.
[b]Variable overhead traceable to the department (d.l.h. = direct labor hour).

  a. Determine the overhead charging rate of Department A for the year.
  b. During February, Department A was charged with 2,000 direct labor hours. It issued 40 warehouse requisitions. Actual fixed overhead costs traceable to the department (prior to allocations from the service departments) were $16,000. Department A's monthly share of the office department costs and the fixed portion of the materials handling costs is simply one-twelfth of its annual allocation (as calculated as part of the solution to item a).
    (1) Determine the total overhead costs to be charged to the overhead account of Department A during February.
    (2) Determine the amount of under- or over-absorbed overhead for the month.
  c. During February, Department A spent 150 direct labor hours on job 342. How much overhead should be charged to job 342?

12. *Universities sometimes adopt overhead allocation schemes that appear especially arbitrary.*

  A large state university permits its component academic departments, bureaus, and research institutes to enter into research contracts with outside organizations. Out of the negotiated price, the contracting unit must pay all direct costs pertaining to the project which it undertakes. In addition, however, it is charged by the university for "overhead." The charge is an amount equal to 60 percent of the direct wage and salary costs that will be incurred in fulfilling the contract.

  The university maintains an office of "contract research," whose mission is to assist the academic departments, bureaus, and research institutes in obtaining and administering contracts. The cost of maintaining the office is approximately $200,000 per year. For the most part, however, the overhead for which the units undertaking contract research are charged represents costs that are incurred to support the traditional academic functions of the university—buildings and grounds maintenance, libraries, laboratories, administration, athletic facilities, etc. These costs are fixed; they are unaffected by any single contract research project.

  Most contracts, particularly those with government agencies, are reimbursement-type agreements. A unit gets reimbursed for all costs, including overhead, that it incurs, but earns no "profit." Some contracts, however, are for a negotiated amount that provides for payments in excess of costs incurred. When such contracts are entered into, the unit performing the research is permitted to retain the excess of revenues over costs and use it to supplement university budget allocations. The primary motivation of conducting contract research is that it provides funding for projects that faculty and research associates want to conduct but which otherwise would have no financial support.

In recent years the contract value of sponsored research was $20 million.

Critically evaluate the policy of the university of imposing a charge for overhead.

a. What do you think are the primary purposes of the charge?
b. What effect do you think it has on the motivation of the various units to conduct research? On the ability of the units to obtain research contracts?
c. How do you think the 60 percent amount was arrived at?
d. What objections might be raised to the policy?
e. What are alternatives to the policy?

13. *The costs of a corporate consulting department should be allocated in a manner that is equitable and that encourages efficient distribution of its services.*

A multidivision corporation operates an internal consulting department. The department was organized for two primary reasons. First, it was recognized that many units within the organization were not operating at maximum efficiency and could thereby benefit from consulting services. Second, numerous units were continually spending large sums of money to obtain the services of outside management consulting firms. It was calculated, after extensive cost–benefit analysis, that the use of outside firms was sufficiently great that considerable savings could be effected by hiring consultants directly rather than paying their salaries (plus a premium) indirectly via a consulting firm.

The consulting department provides services in two ways. First, either on its own initiative or upon request of corporate management it surveys selected operations of the firm. It reports its findings to corporate management and, at the same time, advises division managers as to how their operations could be improved. Second, upon request of division managers, it undertakes specific consulting projects (e.g., assisting in instituting a computerized reporting system).

The budget for the consulting department has been established by corporate management at $1,500,000 per year. It is able to provide approximately 30,000 hours of consulting services.

On what basis do you think the costs of the consulting department should be allocated to the divisions that it serves? Be sure to take into account the objectives of the consulting department and the influence that any allocation scheme might have on the ability of the consulting department to fulfill its objectives.

14. *Direct costing facilitates cost–volume–profit analysis.*

A division prepared the following income statement, which is based on *direct costing:*

Sales		$1,350,000
Variable costs		
Manufacturing	$750,000	
Selling	150,000	900,000
Contribution margin		$ 450,000
Fixed costs		
Manufacturing	$300,000	
General and administrative	170,000	470,000
Loss		$ 20,000

During the period, the division produced 20,000 units and sold 15,000 units.

a. How many units would the division have to sell in order to earn a profit equal to 10 percent of sales revenue? Assume that production will equal sales.

b. Recast the income statement to one based on absorption costing.

c. Could the answer to part a have been derived solely from the absorption cost statements and the information on number of units sold and produced? Explain.

d. Determine end-of-period inventory that would be reported under both absorption costing and direct costing. Is the difference between the two amounts equal to that between the difference in reported earnings?

15. *Direct costing generally provides better guidance for management control.*

The president of a manufacturing concern has accused the vice-president for production of inefficiencies within his department. He has just received financial reports for February, and they indicate a $5,000 deficit for the month as opposed to an anticipated $35,000 surplus. Since sales as well as general and administrative costs were as budgeted, he concluded that the fault must lie with the production department.

Upon investigation, the vice-president for production was provided the report shown here.

	Actual	Budgeted
Sales (5,000 units @ $150)	$750,000	$750,000
Production (in units)	4,000 units	5,000 units
Fixed manufacturing costs	$248,000	$250,000
Variable manufacturing costs	$272,000	$350,000
General and administrative costs	$115,000	$115,000
Beginning of month inventory (1,000 units, each of which included direct manufacturing costs of $70 and fixed manufacturing costs of $50)	$120,000	$120,000

The financial statements that the president examined were prepared on a full-cost basis. Production for the month was less than budgeted because, owing to a severe snowstorm, the president had ordered the manufacturing plant closed for a few days.

a. Prepare a statement of income—as it was likely presented to the president—on a full-cost basis.

b. Recast the statement as it might have been prepared on a direct costing basis.

c. Was the production department inefficient during February? Explain. Which set of financial statements provides greater insight into the nature of the variance in costs from what was budgeted?

16. *Direct costing has obvious advantages over absorption costing; why then is it not generally accepted for purposes of external reporting?*

Electro-Games, Inc., began operations in 1991. In that year, it produced 1,000 electronic games, but its first shipments were not until the following year. Production, sales and year-end inventory (in units) for a four-year period were:

	Production	Sales	Year-End Inventory
1991	1,000	-0-	1,000
1992	1,000	1,000	1,000
1993	1,500	1,250	1,250
1994	250	1,500	-0-
Total for four years	3,750	3,750	

Production was curtailed for several months in 1994 owing to a labor dispute.

Fixed manufacturing costs during each of the four years were $100,000. Variable manufacturing costs were $300 per unit. Sales price per unit was $500.

a. Determine earnings and year-end inventory (in dollars) during each of the four years under:
   (1) Direct costing
   (2) Absorption costing
   Omit consideration of nonmanufacturing costs, as they will be accounted for the same under both methods. The firm maintains inventory on a FIFO basis.
b. Under which of the two methods is income most responsive to sales volume?
c. Suppose that a company attempts to artificially inflate reported earnings of a particular year by producing more units than it sells. Under which of the two costing methods would the scheme be effective? Explain.
d. In your opinion, which of the two methods results in the better match of costs with revenues? Explain, with reference to your calculation in part a.

17. *Activity-based costing can have a dramatic impact on product cost.*

An electronics company manufactures two components. Component A is extremely sophisticated, requiring technologically advanced equipment to assemble. Component B is mundane, put together mainly by unskilled workers. The direct costs of assembling the two components are:

	Component A	Component B	Total
	(dollar amounts in millions)		
Direct labor cost ($20 per hour)	$1.50 (30%)	$3.50 (70%)	$5.00
Direct materials	1.40 (50%)	1.40 (50%)	2.80
Total	$2.90 (37%)	4.90 (63%)	7.80

In addition, there are numerous types of indirect costs, which the company has divided into pools as follows:

	Cost (in millions)
Costs relating to equipment maintenance and ongoing control of operations	$2.40
Costs relating to engineering and design	3.00
Costs relating to acquisition and movement of materials	2.00
Costs relating to quality control	1.00
Total	$8.40

The schedule that follows indicates the factors that the company has determined have the greatest influence on each of the cost pools and the percentage of that factor associated with each of the components:

Cost Pool	Factor	Percentage of Factor Identified with	
		Component A	Component B
Equipment maintenance and control	Number of machine operations	70%	30%
Engineering and design	Number of design hours	80%	20%
Acquisition and movement of materials	Number of material transactions	60%	40%
Quality control	Number of inspections	70%	30%

During the year, the company assembles 100,000 units of Component A and 80,000 units of component B.

a. Compute the cost per unit of each component assuming that the company distributes overhead based on direct labor dollars.

b. Assume instead that the company uses an activity-based costing system and distributes costs based on the cost drivers (factors) indicated. Compute cost per unit.

c. Comment on the hazards of distributing overhead on the basis of direct labor when direct labor does not exert the prime influence on the behavior of overhead.

18. *Basic calculations associated with direct costing indicate relationships between fixed and variable revenues and costs.*

The Colorado Company produced 36,000 units of its product during a year. It had no beginning inventories. Its ending inventories consisted of 6,000 units of finished goods. The selling price was $8 per unit. Costs for the year were:

	Fixed Costs	Variable Costs
Direct materials		$72,000
Direct labor		$54,000
Overhead	$18,000	$18,000
Selling expenses	$39,000	10% of sales
Administrative expenses	$31,600	$12,000

Compute the following:
a. Sales revenue for the year
b. Contribution margin per unit
c. Contribution margin
d. Contribution margin ratio
e. Income under direct costing
f. Break-even point in dollars of sales revenue

19. *Contribution statements facilitate profitability comparisons among products.*

The Davis Company manufactures three principal products. During the past year, it had the following costs, revenues, and production:

	Product A	Product B	Product C
Units produced	5,000	10,000	1,000
Units sold	5,000	9,000	900
Unit sales price	$25	$15	$50
Direct material per unit	$5	$5	$20
Direct labor per unit	$6	$4	$10
Variable overhead per unit	$2	$1	$5
Fixed overhead per year	$5,000	$20,000	$5,000
Selling expenses (all fixed)	$5,000	$10,000	$1,000

a. Prepare for each product an income statement that shows its contribution margin.
b. Calculate the contribution margin per unit and the contribution margin ratio per unit for each product.
c. Prepare a schedule showing the ending inventory values for each product under both absorption costing and variable costing.
d. Discuss the value of the contribution margin in making incremental production decisions.
e. What recommendations might you make regarding each product and the prospects for the Davis Company? What additional information might be helpful?

Solutions to Exercise for Review and Self-Testing

1. a. The pediatrics department occupied 25 percent (4,000 of a total of 16,000 square feet) of the floor space of the clinic. It would be charged with 25 percent—$5,000 of the occupancy costs.
   b. The charge for administrative costs would be $3,000 plus $1 for each of the 1,500 patients typically served—a total of $4,500.
2. a. Total overhead costs of the pediatrics department:

Overhead directly attributable to pediatrics department (given)		$40,000
Overhead allocated from other cost pools		
Occupancy costs	$5,000	
Administrative costs	4,500	9,500
Total overhead costs		$49,500

   b. The overhead charging rate would be

$$\frac{\text{Estimated overhead costs (per part a)}}{\text{Estimated patient-care payroll dollars}}$$

$$= \frac{\$49,500}{132,000} = \$.375$$

3. a. Physicians' and nurses' costs assigned to D. Short:

Physicians (5 hours @ $90)	$450
Nurses (10 hours @ $20)	200
Total direct patient-care costs	$650

   b. Overhead costs assigned to D. Short:

Total direct patient-care payroll dollars assigned to D. Short	$650
Overhead charging rate	× .375
Overhead assigned to D. Short	$243.75

The total cost of services provided to D. Short would be $650 + $243.75 = $893.75.

4. A deviation of overhead costs or volume from those estimated would have no effect on the amount charged to any particular patient (or job) because the overhead absorbed is based on the predetermined rate. Indeed, the very purpose of using a predetermined rate is to avoid variations in "product" cost owing to fluctuations in either overhead costs or "production" volume.

19

Incremental Costs and Benefits: The Key to Management Decisions

Our purpose in this chapter is to set forth a general approach to *ad hoc* (that is, special purpose) managerial decisions. Our procedures will rely heavily on the types of cost information addressed in the two previous chapters. We shall center our attention on decisions in which the time value of money is not a significant factor either because the time horizon is too short or the discounting process will have the same relative impact on each of the alternatives. Our discussion will be constructed around a series of short cases, several of which, although simple, suggest choices that may not be intuitively obvious.

THE BASIC INGREDIENTS

Identifying Relevant Costs and Benefits

A decision involves a choice between two or more possibilities. Managers must strive to select the course of action that provides the greatest net *benefit*; that is, the greatest margin between *benefits* and *costs*. Although the term *cost–benefit analysis* is one that is conventionally associated with the nonprofit sector, it is equally applicable to commercial organizations. In fact, to a great extent, the art of management as it applies to making decisions involves the identification and the assessment of costs and benefits attributable to two or more options. Once the costs and benefits have been identified, measured, and assigned to the possibilities, the preferable courses of action can usually be determined quite readily.

The benefits associated with a course of action stem directly from the objectives of the organization. In making a decision, managers must specify what it is they expect to accomplish. For most corporate decisions, the operational objective is long-run maximization of cash inflow. As a consequence, the expected benefits are expressed in terms of net cash receipts. The course of action to be selected is that which provides the greatest *net cash inflow* (adjusted for the time value of money) after taking into account all relevant costs. Maximization of *accounting* income is ordinarily an inappropriate objective because, in the "short term," it can be tainted by arbitrary choices among accounting principles, estimates, and allocations of costs. In other words, accounting income or net income is often *not* the best decision criterion for managers to use in making decisions.

In theory, all benefits and costs, no matter how indirect, should be taken into account in making a decision as long as the cost of obtaining and processing the required information is less than the expected value of any loss that might be incurred by not taking them into account. Not all benefits and costs, however, can be easily identified, quantified, and monetarized. Whereas it may be appropriate to exclude from consideration those costs and benefits that are unlikely to affect the outcome of the decision, it is not acceptable to disregard a cost or benefit merely because it cannot be readily measured and expressed in dollars. If, for example, customer goodwill is an important benefit to be derived, it may be preferable to assign a dollar value to it—even if such an amount is nothing more than the most imperfect estimate—than to ignore it and thereby implicitly assign it a value of zero.

In practice, many managers are uncomfortable assigning dollar values to intangible benefits, such as customer goodwill. Therefore, they exclude intangible or subjective factors from consideration in the quantitative analysis of the various possibilities. In making the final selection among courses of action, however, they often temper the quantitative results of the analysis with the intangible costs and benefits and are willing to select an alternative with lesser quantifiable net benefits over one with greater. This, too, is a reasonable approach since the analytical techniques described in this text are unfortunately no better than the estimates of costs and benefits to which they are applied. Even in the face of highly sophisticated mathematical models and the computers to apply them, management remains very much an art rather than a science.

Focusing on Differential Costs

While the importance of identifying and quantifying the costs and benefits associated with alternative courses of action cannot be minimized, the burden on the analyst or manager is considerably less onerous than it might first appear. A decision model need not incorporate *all* costs and benefits associated with the various choices; it need include only those costs and benefits that will *differ* among the choices. Those costs and benefits that will be unaffected by the choice need not specifically be taken into account. Suppose, for example, that a firm is considering replacing one machine with another. The new machine will enable the firm to reduce its direct labor costs. If the firm can establish that sales and non-labor operating costs will be unaffected by the change, then the analysis can focus exclusively on the cost to acquire the machine and the savings in labor costs. Materials, maintenance, and power costs may be directly associated with the use of the machines. But, if they will remain the same irrespective of whether the new machine is acquired, they are irrelevant to the replacement decision. For many decisions, only *differential* or *incremental* costs and benefits need to be assessed.

Specifying A Time Horizon

A manager must give careful consideration to the period of time over which a decision will have its effect. For some types of decisions the time horizon that should be taken into account is fairly obvious. If a manager is selecting among firms with which to sign a contract to supply a part to be manufactured according to specification, then the appropriate time frame would ordinarily be the length of the contract. At the conclusion of the contract the firm presumably will be free to choose a new supplier, and its choice the second time can be independent of the supplier it selected the first time. For other types of decisions, the period of time over which to evaluate alternative courses of action is far less clear. Assume, for example, that a firm is engaged in collective bargaining with a union representing its employees. It must decide whether to offer an increase in the base wage rate or an improvement in a medical insurance program. Although the contract may be for a period of two years, a benefit once provided cannot usually be retracted except at considerable cost. Moreover, the wage rate in effect at the conclusion of one contract serves as the basis for negotiations on the next contract. And the wage in effect at the conclusion of the next contract in turn affects the subsequent contract.

DECISIONS AND FACTORS INVOLVED

Unavoidable Costs Are Irrelevant

Costs which a firm cannot avoid regardless of alternative selected are irrelevant and need not—*should* not—be incorporated into an analysis of costs and benefits. Unavoidable costs are often referred to as *sunk costs*. Sunk costs can be costs that have already been incurred. They can also be those that have yet to be incurred if they will be the same under all available courses of action. The cost of an asset already purchased is a sunk cost. It cannot be retrieved. So also are the costs to be paid in the future on an equipment lease that has already been signed, if the lease is noncancelable. The two cases that follow are intended to highlight the irrelevance of costs that have previously been incurred.

Case 1: The Foolish Overhaul
Recently, a firm spent $5,000 to repair and overhaul its copy machine. The machine makes copies at a cost of approximately $.05 per copy. This amount includes labor, supplies, power, and maintenance, all of which are variable costs.

The office manager of the firm has been approached by a salesman from a leading copy machine company. His company has offered to lease the firm a new, technologically improved, machine at a cost of $.02 per copy. Additional variable costs will bring the total cost per copy to $.04.

The old machine cannot be sold or leased out for a material amount (a reasonable assumption since the lease arrangement on the new machine is available to any prospective customer). For tax purposes, the old machine is fully depreciated and has a book value of zero.

The term of the lease on the new machine can be for a period equal in length to the remaining useful life of the old machine.

The office manager has refused to seriously consider leasing the new machine. "We just spent $5,000 to overhaul the old machine," he said, "There's no point in leasing a new machine until we've received some benefit from the expenditure."

Should the firm sign the lease agreement and abandon the machine that has just been overhauled?

In this case, the $5,000 paid to overhaul the old machine is a sunk cost. It cannot be recovered. As the title to the case suggests, in retrospect at least, it was a mistake to spend the $5,000. The issue that the case presents is whether the firm should now compound its error by continuing to use the old machine or whether it should take advantage of an opportunity to reduce future copying costs by $.01 per copy.

The relevant costs in this case are but two: (1) the $.05 per copy required to operate the old machine, and (2) the $.04 per copy required of the new. A comparison of these two amounts clearly indicates that the lease offer should be accepted.

Pointedly omitted from the case is the number of copies that the organization makes. This amount is irrelevant as long as it is within the capacity of the two machines. The savings attached to the lease agreement are $.01 per copy regardless of the number of copies made. The greater the number of copies made, the greater the amount of the savings, *but there will be savings as long as any copies are made.* If the facts of the case were different and the firm could sell, lease, or make use of the machine in some other manner, then the benefits of such actions (net of taxes) would, of course, have to be taken into account.

Case 2: The Unreported Loss

A firm has an opportunity to replace a machine with one that is more efficient. The new machine will enable the firm to realize *cash* operating savings of $6,000 per year.

The cost of the new machine is $20,000. It will have a useful life of five years, with no salvage value at the end of the five years.

The old machine cost $40,000 when it was acquired three years ago. It has a total useful life of eight years and a remaining useful life of five years. The old machine will have no salvage value at the end of its useful life. It could be sold today, however, for $7,000. The machine has a reported book value of $25,000, determined as follows:

Original cost	$40,000
Accumulated depreciation (three years @ $5,000)	15,000
Book value	$25,000

Were the machine to be sold today, the firm would have to report a loss on sale of $18,000—book value of $25,000 less sales price of $7,000.

The plant manager has rejected the opportunity to replace the old machine with the new, asserting that the annual cash operating savings are not sufficient to cover the cost of the new machine and citing the loss that will be incurred upon the sale of the old:

Annual cash savings ($6,000 per year for 5 years)		$30,000
Less: Purchase price of new machine	$20,000	
Loss on sale of old machine	18,000	(38,000)
Excess of cost of new machine and loss on old machine over annual cash savings on new machine		$ 8,000

Do you agree with the decision of the plant manager?

This case has much in common with "The Foolish Overhaul." The cost of the old machine, like that of the overhaul, is a sunk cost that cannot be recovered. It is therefore irrelevant to the analysis of the alternatives. The relevant factors are the cash flows that would be different if one alternative as opposed to the other were chosen. For an initial outlay of $13,000 ($20,000 purchase price of new machine less the $7,000 sales price of old), the firm can save $6,000 per year for five years—$30,000. Disregarding the time value of money, the acquisition is clearly favorable:[1]

Cash Flows

	Period	Replace	Do Not Replace
0	Sell old machine	$ 7,000	—
0	Purchase new machine	(20,000)	—
1–5	Cash operating savings (total)	30,000	—
	Net cash inflow	$17,000	

The $18,000 loss results because the firm purchased a machine three years earlier with the expectation that it would have a useful economic life of eight years. It has been depreciating—spreading the cost of—the machine over eight years. If it had correctly foreseen the future, the firm would have depreciated the machine over three years down to its salvage value of $7,000. No loss would then have to be reported; the full cost of using the machine over the three-year period would have been incorporated into the depreciation charges. Because the firm was unable to predict with accuracy the useful life and selling price of the old machine, it must now *recognize* a loss. But such loss is nothing more than the assignment of a portion of the cost of the asset to the period of sale.

Depreciation to be charged in the future on both the old and new machines has also been excluded from the analysis. Depreciation is nothing more than

[1]Because the time horizon for this decision is five years, the time value of money *cannot* properly be ignored. It is ignored here in order to concentrate on the key point which the example is designed to make: The cost of the machine to be disposed of is a sunk cost; neither depreciation charges nor losses, both of which represent the allocation of the cost to particular periods, should be incorporated into the replacement analysis. Even if time value of money is taken into account in this problem, the discount rate would have to be greater than 36 percent in order *not* to choose purchasing the new machine.

an allocation among accounting periods of the original purchase price of an asset. Depreciation on the old machine represents an allocation of a sunk—and therefore irrelevant—cost. Depreciation on the new machine, if incorporated into the analysis, would result in double counting because the cost of the asset has been accounted for directly.

To avoid complicating the analysis, the impact of income taxes has been disregarded. Tax considerations will be dealt with in Chapter 20.

Only Incremental Costs Are Relevant

The general notion that unavoidable costs are irrelevant can be applied in a number of situations, in each of which the unavoidable costs take a slightly different form. The case that follows pertains to a decision to manufacture and sell additional units of product. The focus is on *incremental* costs—those that will change if production is increased—rather than on unit average costs, which include elements that will remain unchanged.

Case 3: Accept or Reject an Unprofitable Offer?

Supertype, Inc., manufactures electronic word processors. They are sold to distributors for $3,000 each. Based on a monthly volume of 1,000 units, production costs are $2,000 per unit.

Radio World, a national chain of electronics stores, has offered to purchase and distribute 200 units of Supertype's word processors per month under its private label. The contract price would be $1,400 per unit. The sales manager has indicated that the contract with Radio World would have no impact on the quantity of existing sales, since the product would be directed to different types of customers. Supertype, Inc., has prepared the following analysis of costs both with and without the added new production required if the contract with Radio World is signed:

	Current costs @ 1,000 units	Proposed costs @ 1,200 units
Rent of plan offices	$ 150,000	$ 150,000
Administration and other fixed overhead costs	350,000	350,000
Design and engineering costs included in product cost	300,000	300,000
Direct labor @ $500 per unit	500,000	600,000
Materials @ $700 per unit	700,000	840,000
Total costs	$2,000,000	$2,240,000
Number of units	1,000	1,200
Average cost per unit	$ 2,000	$ 1,867

Should Supertype accept the offer from Radio World?

The contract price of $1,400 is considerably less than the new average production cost of $1,867. However, if the contract were accepted, the firm would receive an additional $1,400 per unit of revenue. It would incur additional direct labor costs of $500 per unit and additional materials costs of only $700 per unit—a total of only $1,200 per unit:

Incremental receipts (200 units @ $1,400)	$280,000
Incremental costs (200 units @ $1,200)	240,000
Net incremental receipts	$ 40,000

Incremental costs are relevant; average costs are not. Therefore, it is in the interest of the firm to accept the offer. Cash inflow, as well as earnings, would be increased by the sale of the additional 200 units at a price less than *average* production cost.

Whereas it may be inviting to assert that only *variable* costs as opposed to *fixed* costs should be taken into account, it is dangerous to do so unless it is made clear that the costs are being classified as fixed or variable with respect to only the decision at hand. Rent is ordinarily categorized as a fixed cost.

Other factors may also affect the analysis of Radio World's bid. Prime among these are how overhead costs are influenced by this new product line of private label word processors. Perhaps additional setup costs will be incurred in the manufacturing process, or additional warehousing transactions and shipping arrangements must be made for this new line. Perhaps the billing and collection transactions associated with the new line are significant in number, have a longer than usual lag time between billing and collection, and are more risky than normal sales activities. Each of these conditions may influence costs and thereby require that the assumption as to minimal or zero changes in fixed costs be reexamined.

To avoid running counter to the conventional classification of costs, it is preferable to generalize the analytical guidelines in terms of incremental versus static or unchanging costs rather than fixed versus variable costs: In making decisions about the future, only incremental costs should be taken into account; costs that are static and will remain unchanged regardless of the course of action taken need not be brought into the analysis.

Incremental costs may be associated with costs that are conventionally viewed as fixed, even though many of the effects on fixed costs of new products, new services, or new transactions costs appear to be inconsequential at first glance. As the complexity of product lines increases, and as the number of accounting transactions increases, overhead costs tend to increase in a manner that is not proportional to volume of output. Any analysis of incremental costs must be sensitive to cost changes that are not solely affected by volume changes.

Case 4: Engaging a Contractor to Perform a Service at Less Than Cost

A broad category of decisions which illustrates further the significance of focusing upon incremental costs is known as "make or buy" decisions. Decisions of this category involve a choice whether to manufacture goods or provide services internally, or to acquire them from outsiders. In essence, the approach to making this type of decision is similar to that illustrated previously in this chapter; it requires a determination as to which of two courses of action will enable the organization to maximize net benefits, net benefits being defined as cash inflows less cash outflows. The analytical means of resolving make or buy issues can be illustrated with regard to a service organization.

Homecheck is a division of Texas Home Sales, Inc. Homecheck inspects homes, prior to their sale, for mechanical and structural defects and certifies as to the condition of the homes. The certificate of the company is accepted by a buyer of a home for assurance, in lieu of seller warranties, that the home is in the state represented by the seller. The company charges the seller a fee for its service.

Homecheck has never been profitable; it does, however, support the sales division of Texas Home Sales, Inc., and enables it to provide a full range of services to its customers.

For a typical month, the financial report of Homecheck indicated the following costs:

Revenues		
(2,500 inspections @ $125)		$312,500
Expenses		
Salaries	$228,000	
Auto rental fees	24,000	
Rent of office space	6,000	
Other administrative costs	32,000	
Allocation of home office overhead	30,000	320,000
Operating profit (loss)		($ 7,500)

Texas Home Sales, Inc., has received an offer from an outside firm to conduct the inspections on its behalf. The outside firm would charge a fee of $120 per inspection, less than the $128 average cost (2,500 inspections at a total cost of $320,000) presently incurred by the firm. Were Texas Home Sales, Inc., to use the services of the outside contractor, it would retain the revenue of $125 per inspection that it derives from its customers. On the cost side, the alternative arrangement would eliminate all expenses associated with Homecheck except for two. First, home office overhead would be reduced by only $4,000 from $30,000 to $26,000. Second, instead of giving up the office space presently leased by Homecheck at a cost of $6,000, Texas Home Sales would move the accounting department of another division into those offices. That division presently pays $8,000 per year in rental costs to outsiders.

Assuming that volume of inspections and operating costs of the typical month are indicative of those to be incurred in the future, should Texas Home Sales, Inc., continue to permit its Homecheck division to provide the inspection service or should it acquire the service from the outside firm?

Because the revenues will be unaffected by course of action, the analysis need be directed only to differential costs. Salaries, automobile rental fees, and administrative costs will be incurred only if Homecheck continues to make the inspections, not if they are contracted-out. Of the home office costs, Texas Home Sales, Inc., will continue to incur $30,000 if the inspection services are performed internally, but only $26,000 if they are carried out by the external contractor. If the firm contracts with the outside company, then $30,000 of overhead will no longer be allocated to Homecheck; all but the $4,000 that will be saved will be reallocated to other corporate divisions.

If the firm continues to carry out the inspections itself, it will incur $6,000 per month in rent costs for the space occupied by Homecheck and $8,000 for that occupied by the accounting department of the other division—a total of $14,000. If it contracts with the outside firm, it will incur only the $6,000 per month in rent costs. That would be on the office space now occupied by Homecheck but into which the accounting department of the other division would move. The rental costs on both premises are relevant to the decision and must be incorporated into the analysis.

A comparison of differential costs is as follows:

	Accept Offer from Outside Firm	Reject Offer from Outside Firm
Salaries		$228,000
Auto rental		24,000
Other administrative costs		32,000
Rent (Homecheck)	$ 6,000	6,000
Rent (accounting department)		8,000
Home office costs	26,000	30,000
Fees paid to outside firm (2,500 inspections @ $120)	300,000	
Total cash outflows	$332,000	$328,000

The net outflow of the relevant costs is less if the firm continues to provide the service itself. It should reject the offer from the outside concern even though the outside company is willing to provide the service at a per unit cost that is less than the "full" cost that the firm must incur to provide the service itself.

Case 5: Discontinue a Losing Product?

The decision to abandon a line of business has many of the same characteristics as that of the make or buy decision. Those costs that the firm will be able to eliminate must be differentiated from those that it will not, and the analysis must focus exclusively on the former.

Green Thumb, Inc., is deciding whether to discontinue the production and sale of a garden tool that it manufactures. Management has determined that at an anticipated volume of 10,000 units per year and a competitive selling price of $14 per unit, the firm will lose $2.50 per unit sold:

Selling price			$14.00
Less: Standard manufacturing costs			
Direct labor	$4.00		
Direct materials	6.00		
Overhead ($.75 per direct labor dollar)	3.00	$13.00	
Selling costs		3.50	16.50
Profit (loss) per unit			($ 2.50)

The overhead charging rate of $.75 per direct labor hour was developed as follows:

Overhead costs	
Payroll-related fringe benefits and taxes	$ 6,000
Allocation of plant depreciation	5,000
Allocation of building occupancy costs	8,000
Allocation of factory administration and maintenance costs	2,000
Depreciation of manufacturing equipment	9,000
Total overhead costs	$30,000
Direct labor dollars	÷ $40,000
= Overhead charging rate	$ 0.75

Management has also made the following additional determinations pertaining to its decision whether to discontinue:

- Selling costs amount to $35,000. Of this amount, only $5,000 can be associated directly with the garden tool. The remaining $30,000 are costs that are common to other products. If the garden tool is discontinued, the costs will be spread among the other products.
- The manufacturing equipment would have to be abandoned; it has but negligible salvage value.
- Were the firm to continue to produce the garden tool, then on average $12,000 of equipment would have to be acquired each year.
- Of the overhead costs requiring cash outlays, only the payroll-related fringe benefits and taxes could be eliminated if the garden tool were discontinued. The other cash costs (building occupancy, factory administration, and maintenance) would be reallocated to other products.

The analysis that follows indicates those revenues that would be greater and costs that would be less if the product were continued:

	Product Continued
Sales revenue (10,000 @ $14)	$140,000
Direct labor (10,000 @ $4)	(40,000)*
Direct materials (10,000 @ $6)	(60,000)
Payroll-related fringe benefits and taxes	(6,000)
Replacement of manufacturing equipment	(12,000)
Selling costs	(5,000)
Net cash flow	$ 17,000

*Inflow (outflow)

Despite an apparent loss of $2.50 per unit—a total of $25,000—the firm would be $17,000 better off by continuing the product.

The differential costs that are incorporated into the analysis include manufacturing equipment to be acquired in the future. They exclude the depreciation charges on the existing equipment because those expenses are nothing more than the amortization of past—and therefore irrelevant—costs. Also excluded are the costs that will be reallocated to other departments or products. From the perspective of the company as a whole, they will be unaffected by the decision whether to discontinue the garden tool.

Case 6: Sell, or Process Further Despite Losses?

Another class of decisions in which the analytical focus must be on incremental revenues and costs is whether to sell a product at one stage of production or to continuing processing so that it may be eventually sold at a higher price. In general, the decision rule is simple: Continue to process as long as the additional revenues to be earned will be greater than the additional costs to be incurred.

As a consequence of producing its primary product, a liquid detergent, the Niagara Chemical Company must also produce an industrial solvent. A batch of 10,000 gallons of raw materials will ordinarily produce 6,000 gallons of detergent and 4,000 gallons of solvent. Total cost per batch is $40,000. The policy of the company is to allocate joint costs on the basis of physical units.

The detergent is sold at a price of $6 per gallon. The 4,000 gallons of solvent can be sold as a low-grade solvent for $3 per gallon. Alternatively, it can be processed further, at a cost of $3.75 per gallon, and sold as a high-grade solvent at a price of $7 per gallon.

	Do Not Process Further	Process Further	Dispose of as Waste
Receipts per gallon	$3.00	$7.00	$0.0
Additional costs to be incurred	0.00	3.75	0.0
Net incremental receipts	$3.00	$3.25	$0.0

Should the company sell the 4,000 gallons as a low-grade solvent, or should it process it further and sell it as a high-grade solvent? Alternatively, should it dispose of the 4,000 gallons as waste and not sell them at all?

As in the previous illustrations, an appropriate analysis focuses on the incremental receipts and costs associated with each of the courses of action to be considered. The costs and receipts associated with the 6,000 gallons of detergent are *not* introduced into the following analysis, as they will be the same regardless of the decision made with respect to the 4,000 gallons of solvent.

The analysis makes it clear that the firm would be best off by processing further. This course of action would leave it with a $.25 per gallon (a total of 4,000 times that amount, $1,000) advantage over not processing further.

The appropriate choice may seem obvious; indeed, the issue may seem trivial. It is clear that there would be no reason to dispose of goods that could be sold, with no incremental cost, for $3 per gallon; it is equally apparent that a firm should incur an additional $3.75 in costs in order to be able to earn additional revenue of $4 per gallon (the $7 per gallon selling price of high-grade solvent less the $3 per gallon selling price of low-grade solvent).

The analysis is straightforward only, however, because it focused on incremental costs and receipts. From the perspective of the manager concerned with *external reporting*, the $40,000 of common costs—those to produce the 10,000 gallons of both detergent and solvent—would have to be allocated between the two products. If applied on the basis of physical units, then the cost per gallon of solvent, before additional processing would be

Share of common costs (4,000/10,000 of $40,000)		$16,000	
Divided by number of gallons		÷ 4,000 gal	
Cost per gallon of solvent before additional processing		$ 4.00	

If the cost per gallon were $4.00 and the amount for which it could be sold in an unprocessed state were only $3.00 per gallon, it might appear that the firm should prefer to dispose of the product as waste rather than sell it "as a loss." Such a conclusion would clearly be unwarranted; the $40,000 of common costs must be incurred in order to produce the 6,000 gallons of detergent. Inasmuch as they will be incurred regardless of whether the solvent is disposed of as waste or sold as either low-grade or high-grade solvent, they are irrelevant to the decision at hand.

The irrelevance of the $40,000 common costs to the question of what to do with the 4,000 gallons of solvent can be emphasized further by pointing to the variety of bases, other than physical units, by which they could have been allocated between the two products. One popular basis of allocating joint costs is *net realizable value*. Net realizable value is the total revenues to be received, less any additional costs to be incurred. If the common costs were allocated on the basis of net realizable value, the per gallon cost of the solvent prior to further processing would be only $2.65, as indicated in the analysis that follows:

	Detergent	Solvent	Total
Total revenues	$36,000[a]	$28,000[b]	$64,000
Costs of additional processing	—	(15,000)[c]	(15,000)
Net realizable value	$36,000	$13,000	$49,000
% of combined total net realizable value	73.47%	26.53%	100%
Share of common costs (% of net realizable value applied to $40,000)	$29,388	$10,612	$40,000
Number of gallons of solvent		÷ 4,000	
Cost per gallon of solvent before additional processing		$ 2.65	

[a] 6,000 gallons @ $6.00.
[b] 4,000 gallons @ $7.00.
[c] 4,000 gallons @ $3.75.

Choice of an allocation basis is at the discretion of the firm. It is unreasonable to suppose that an arbitrary decision as to how costs among joint products are to be absorbed by, or applied to each type of product, could make it more or less economically desirable to sell or dispose of the products one way as opposed to others. The principles of financial accounting and reporting require that cost of goods sold include a share of all costs needed to manufacture a product. Hence, management *must* select a means of distributing joint costs to the common products. But since the total joint costs incurred will be the same regardless of how absorbed, they are irrelevant to decisions as to how best to sell or dispose of any one of the joint products.

Decisions pertaining to the prices at which goods are to be sold or services rendered are among the most common made by managers. Without question, cost must be a key element of any pricing analysis. Pricing decisions, however, necessarily involve numerous other considerations. Among them, to indicate but a few, are the extent of competition faced by the firm, the regulatory environment in which the organization does business, the shape of the product's demand curve (a graphic depiction of the number of units that can be sold at various prices), the image that a firm wants a product to project, and the role played by the product in supporting other products of the firm.

In both traditional literature and practice, prices are built upon costs, however determined. "Cost-plus pricing," in which a standard markup is added to cost, is a familiar means of setting prices. In recent years, many firms, inspired in part by Japanese companies, have been permitting prices to drive costs. They first determine the price necessary to establish a competitive niche in their market. Then they not only design the product to assure that it can be sold at this target price, but they also force the costs to assure a reported profit.

Pricing decisions are thus both complex and cross-disciplinary; they cannot be covered adequately in this text. Nonetheless, because of the importance attached to costs, a few caveats pertaining to full-cost pricing are in order.

In adopting pricing policies, it is common for companies to add a percentage markup to the cost of their products. The cost to which the markup is applied is generally the full cost. Full cost, as explained in previous chapters, includes direct labor, direct materials, and overhead. Overhead, commonly assigned by way of an overhead charging rate, includes variable overhead as well as fixed overhead. Fixed overhead may include costs, such as those of building occupancy, which have been allocated from service departments.

Inherent Flaw in Full-Cost Pricing Policies

Pricing policies that are based on full costs have an inherent flaw: They are based on a factor, full cost, that is not only unstable but is dependent on amounts that are to be determined: volume and prices affecting volume. The overhead charging rate is calculated by dividing *estimated* overhead costs by *estimated* volume. Hence, the fewer the number of units produced, the greater will be the overhead charging rate and the greater will be the full cost of the product. If price is to be established by adding a percentage markup to full cost, then the fewer the number of units produced, the greater will be the price. For most costs or services, however, the greater the price, the fewer will be the number of units sold. The consequences of adhering rigidly to a policy of adding a percentage markup to full cost can be appreciated by considering a manufacturing concern which, as a result of increases in direct materials, elects to raise the price of its product. The price increase causes a slight decline in sales volume. In response to the reduced sales, the manufacturer reduces output, thereby causing an increase in unit cost. If the manufacturer were to react by further increasing prices to reflect this increase in cost, then a spiral of price increases, volume decreases, and cost increases would be set into motion.

Unnecessary to Always Cover Full Cost

There is no need for a firm to cover full cost on all products at all times. This point was implied earlier in this chapter in the context of the decision as to whether to accept or reject a contract in which the selling price was less than full cost but greater than incremental cost (see Case 3, "Accept or Reject an Unprofitable Offer?"). A firm can realize maximum profitability even if it never covers the full cost of some of its products—as long as it covers the incremental cost of each of its products and the full cost of all of its products combined. Case 6, "Sell, or Process Further Despite Losses?" provided an example of a situation in which the market price for one of the firm's two products was insufficient to cover its full cost. Nonetheless, it was clearly in the interest of the firm to continue to sell the product because the combined revenue from the two products exceeded the combined cost.

Full cost is almost always a function of a number of management decisions as to how to allocate costs that are common to various departments and products. Different allocation decisions would result in different costs. If a pricing scheme based on percentage markups to full cost were truly to result in the establishment of optimum prices, then one arbitrary allocation decision would result in one "optimum" price; another arbitrary allocation decision in a different "optimum" price. It is unreasonable to suspect—and in fact can be easily demonstrated analytically—that optimality of price is independent of management decisions as to how to distribute common manufacturing costs.

Regardless of the pricing policy adopted by a firm, it is essential that management evaluate the impact upon profits that alternative prices will have. Management must estimate the number of units that will be sold at the various prices under consideration and determine the production costs at the volumes required to satisfy demand. Cost–volume–profit analysis, which was discussed in a previous chapter, is one means of assuring that a distinction is made between those costs that will remain fixed as output changes and those that will vary. Because it is so important to determine the contribution that each product is making toward covering fixed costs, some firms employ a form of direct costing to establish prices and evaluate their impact on profits. The "relevant" cost of a product is considered to be the variable cost—direct labor, direct materials, and *variable* overhead only. A percentage markup is added to the variable cost rather than the full cost. Any pricing formula that is entirely cost-based can be faulted as being simplistic in that it can never result in prices that are optimum in all economic circumstances. But a direct-cost pricing formula is likely to be preferable to a full-cost formula in that it at least assures that the focus of analysis is upon the incremental production costs.

Accountants' Cost

Marketing executives have been known to refer disparagingly to the "accountants' cost." By that they invariably mean full cost—that assigned on the financial statements to the goods sold or in inventory. They point out—quite correctly—

that such cost is inappropriate for making pricing and other marketing decisions. They err, however, in implying that there is a particular ''accountants' cost.'' Knowledgeable accountants (as well as knowledgeable marketing executives) are well aware of the limitations of full cost and of the importance of including in the determination of cost only those elements that are relevant to the decisions that it will be used to facilitate.

Accountants' and Economists' Models Contrasted

In truth, the traditional accountants' model or assumptions as to the behavior of costs and revenues are of only limited value in making profit-maximizing decisions relating to volume and price. This is mainly because, as discussed in Chapter 17, it focuses on a range of volume within which both prices and variable costs are constant. Its deficiencies are apparent when contrasted with the economists' model.

With respect to revenue, the constant price posited by the accountants' model implies, as illustrated by Exhibit 19-1,

- *Total revenue* increases at a constant rate and can therefore be depicted as a straight line emanating from the origin (Panel A).
- *Marginal revenue* (the added revenue from the sale of an additional unit) is always equal to both selling price ($\bar{P}_o$) and average revenue (AR). Therefore, it too can be shown by a single straight line, horizontal because it does not change with volume (Panel C).

With respect to cost, a constant variable cost implies that

- *Total cost* increases at a constant rate and, like total revenue, can also be depicted as a straight line. This line, however, emanates from the fixed cost point on the axis representing costs (Panel A).
- *Variable cost* varies with volume but is fixed per unit. Consequently, variable cost is always equal to the *marginal cost* (the added cost attributed to the production of an additional unit). Like price and marginal revenue, it too can be shown as a single straight line, horizontal because the costs do not change with volume (Panel C).
- *Average total cost* declines with increases in volume as the fixed costs are spread over a larger number of units.

Economists, in contrast, recognize that there is an inverse relationship between selling price and volume. Greater quantities can only be sold by lowering the price. Moreover, economists see average variable costs as continually changing with volume. They assume (an assumption supported by empirical evidence) that total costs initially increase with output at a *decreasing* rate, as the firm takes advantage of economies of scale and thereby becomes more efficient. Then, at greater volumes, costs increase at an *increasing* rate as the firm strains its physical and managerial capacity. Consequently, the key revenue and cost relationships take the form of curves rather than straight lines. With respect to revenue, this implies that

- *Total revenue* rises with volume but at a decreasing rate as increases in price cause a decrease in volume. At some point, total revenue begins

EXHIBIT 19-1

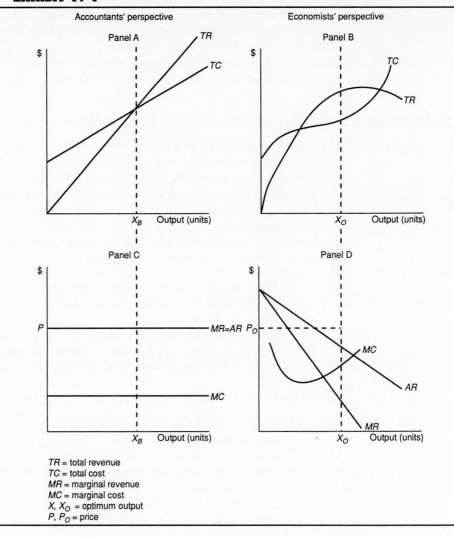

Accountants' perspective

Economists' perspective

Panel A

Panel B

Panel C

Panel D

TR = total revenue
TC = total cost
MR = marginal revenue
MC = marginal cost
X, X_O = optimum output
P, P_O = price

to decline as the increases in volume are more than offset by the decreases in price. Total revenue can therefore be shown as a curve emanating from the origin that eventually turns downward (Panel B).

- *Marginal revenue* is continually decreasing since an additional unit can be sold only by lowering the price per unit. Therefore, marginal revenue can be depicted by a downward-sloping line with twice the slope of average revenue (Panel D).

With respect to cost, the economist's model suggests that

- *Total cost*, because it is directly affected by marginal cost, rises at a decreasing rate as the firm takes advantage of economies of scale (and marginal cost decreases). Then, however, inefficiencies develop, so it rises at an increasing rate (when the marginal cost turns upward). This is shown by the curve emanating from the origin (Panel B).

- *Marginal cost* declines as the firm takes advantage of the economies of scale, but then rises as the inefficiencies develop. Accordingly, this curve (which is the slope of the total cost curve) declines at first and then rises (Panel D).

What guidance do these two models provide managers as to optimum price and output? The accountants' model posits a fixed and constant price. It dictates that as long as this price is greater than the average variable cost (which is equal to the marginal cost), the *contribution margin* is positive and the more the company produces the greater the income (or less the loss). Thus, as shown in Panel A, once the break-even point (X_B) is reached, the gap between total revenue and total cost widens with increases in volume. Thus, there is no unique income-maximizing price–output point. The accountants' model tells managers that if they produce more, they will earn more—hardly very realistic or practical advice.

In contrast, the economists' model suggests that a firm produce the output that will equate marginal (incremental) cost with marginal (incremental) revenue. Since the firm can control its price, it should establish the price so as to generate that particular volume. In Panel D, marginal cost equals marginal revenue at volume X_o, thereby dictating price (P_o). At that point, the gap between total revenue and total cost is the widest (Panel B). Thus, the economists' model tells managers that, other things being equal, whenever the expanded sales that result from a reduced price will increase revenue more than they will increase costs (i.e., marginal revenue is greater than marginal cost), then the firm should reduce its price and expand output.

Economists, like accountants, have no monopoly on marketing strategy, and their model presents as many problems as a guide to pricing as does the accountants'. First, marginal costs are not readily determinable. For most firms, their product's marginal cost (that of producing an additional unit of product) would not typically be the same as its variable cost—at least not as variable costs are classified as measured by their accounting systems. That is because over the volume range affected by a pricing decision, there may have to be changes in physical, administrative, and financial resources. The additional costs required by these changes may be difficult to estimate and are not typically incorporated in the accountant's computation of variable cost.

Second, the determination of marginal revenue (the net revenue provided by the sale of an additional unit of product) is equally challenging. Changes in prices may prompt reactions by competitors, which in turn necessitate shifts in marketing strategy, delivery schedules, and credit terms. Hence, the net revenue to be realized by a price change may be highly problematic.

Third, the economists' model focuses on a single product. Cost and revenue functions are significantly affected by product mix and the resultant interaction of manufacturing, warehousing, and shipping systems. For a company with several products the task of isolating the impact of a price change on overall revenues and costs may be daunting.

The economists' model is a useful means of conceptualizing the potential impact of price changes. However, modern-day accounting systems as well as techniques of estimating costs and revenue normally fail to provide the requisite information to make them operational.

SELECTING THE PRODUCT MIX

Decisions regarding the mix of products that a firm should produce are, like pricing decisions, interdisciplinary. The discussion that follows focuses on accounting aspects of the product-mix question and avoids issues conventionally considered within the domain of marketing, production, or other nonaccounting specialists. Underlying the illustrations, for example, will be the assumption that the sales volume of the various products produced by a firm are independent of one another. In practice, two or more products may be closely tied. One product may complement another. A manufacturer of shaving equipment may find that the profitability of blades is greater than that of razors. Accounting analyses might indicate that the firm should therefore devote all of its resources to the production of blades. Yet marketing considerations may dictate that to support the sale of blades, the firm must also produce and sell razors.

Case 7: Selecting the Optimum Product Mix

Ceiling Fans, Inc., has the capability of producing two styles of fans: modern and traditional. The following data pertain to each of the two styles:

	Traditional	Deluxe
Selling price per unit	$120	$145
Variable costs per unit	80	100
Contribution margin (selling price less variable costs) per unit	40	45
Number of direct labor hours required to produce each unit	2 hours	3 hours

The company must decide on a combination of the two styles to produce. It can produce all traditional fans, all deluxe fans, or a mix of the two.

The deluxe style is the more profitable of the two styles. Its contribution margin is $45 as opposed to $40 for the traditional style. A sale of one unit of the deluxe style will add $45 to the profits of the firm, while a sale of one unit of the traditional style will add only $40. This is true regardless of the amount of fixed costs or the means of allocating common costs (information on both having been omitted to emphasize their irrelevance to the decision at hand).

One Constraint

Assume that Ceiling Fans, Inc., can sell all the fans that it produces, but that the key factor that limits production is the number of available skilled employees. Direct labor hours is, therefore, the critical *constraint* on production.

> *When there is only one constraint, a firm can maximize contribution to profit by devoting its resources entirely to the production of the product for which the contribution margin of each unit of the constraining factor is the greatest.*

Regardless of the specific number of direct labor hours available to it, the firm could maximize its profits by manufacturing only the traditional-style fan. The contribution margin per the constraining factor will be greater for traditional-style than for deluxe-style fans:

	Traditional	Deluxe
Contribution margin (CM)	$40	$45
Number of direct labor hours required	÷ 2 hours	÷ 3 hours
Contribution margin per direct labor hour	$20	$15

Suppose that Ceiling Fans, Inc., can hire employees to provide a total of 180 direct labor hours per day. With 180 direct labor hours per day, it could produce any number of combinations of traditional- and deluxe-style fans. At the extremes, however, it could produce 90 traditional fans *or* 60 deluxe fans:

	Traditional	Deluxe
Number of direct labor hours available	180 hours	180 hours
Number of direct labor hours required to produce each unit	÷ 2 hours	÷ 3 hours
Maximum number of units that could be produced assuming zero hours directed to manufacture of other style	90 units	60 units

If the firm were to produce 90 traditional-style fans, then the contribution to profit would be $3,600—90 times the traditional-style fan contribution margin of $40. If the firm shifted any portion of available direct labor hours—the critical resource—to the manufacture of deluxe-style fans, then the overall contribution to profits would be decreased.

The combination that maximizes contribution margins can also be determined graphically. In Exhibit 19-2, the direct labor constraint line indicates the possible combinations of the two styles of fans that could be produced with 180 direct labor hours. Also indicated in Exhibit 19-2 are two lines (dashed), each point on which represents a combination of production that would yield the same contribution margin as any other point on that line. Each line (said to depict the *objective function* because it is the objective of the firm to maximize contribution margin) represents a particular fixed dollar amount of contribution margin from differing output combinations. Equal contribution margin line 1, for example, indicates the possible combinations of production that would yield a total contribution margin value of $720. A contribution margin of $720 could be achieved, for example, by producing 18 traditional-style fans and zero deluxe-style fans, zero traditional-style fans and 16 deluxe-style fans, or 9 traditional-style fans and 8 deluxe-style fans. Equal contribution margin line 2 indicates the possible combinations of production that would yield a total contribution margin of $3,600. The two lines are merely illustrative of an infinite number of other possible lines—all parallel to one another—that represent other contribution margins. The more distant a line is from the origin, the greater is the total contribution margin value that is represented and the greater the amount of resources required to achieve that contribution margin. A firm, however, must operate within the boundaries of its constraints. Equal contribution margin line 2 is the line

EXHIBIT 19-2

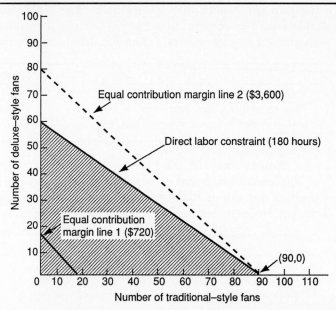

All combinations on equal contribution margin line 1 contribute $720 to firm profits.
All combinations on equal contribution margin line 2 contribute $3,600 to firm profits.
All combinations on the direct labor constraint line require 180 direct labor hours.
The shaded area represents all feasible combinations—those which satisfy the constraints.

that is farthest from the origin and still within (if only at a single point) the area bounded by the labor constraint. At that point, which indicates production of 90 traditional-style fans and zero deluxe-style fans, the contribution to profits is a maximum—$3,600. Any other point on the graph would be either outside the constraint line (and require the use of more than 180 hours of direct labor) or on an equal contribution margin line representative of smaller contribution margins. Graphically, therefore, the optimum combination is found by locating the point that is within the area bounded by the constraint and on the equal contribution margin line that is farthest from the origin.

Two Constraints

Assume now, in addition to the facts already presented, that each fan must undergo a machining process, the number of hours of which depends on the style:

Style	Required Machine Hours
Traditional	2.0
Deluxe	1.5

The maximum number of machine hours that are available per day is 150. At the extremes, therefore, the firm could produce either 75 traditional-style fans and zero deluxe-style fans or 100 deluxe-style fans and zero traditional-style fans:

	Traditional	Deluxe
Number of machine hours available	150	150
Number of machine hours required to produce each unit	÷2.0	÷1.5
Maximum number of units that could be produced assuming zero hours directed to manufacture of other style	75	100

The firm could no longer, under any circumstances, produce the 90 traditional fans that maximized contribution margin when there was only one constraint.

The objective of the firm is to maximize contribution margins, subject to two constraints. Algebraically, the total contribution margin value (CM) can be expressed as

$$\$40T + \$45D = CM$$

where T and D represent, respectively, the number of traditional and deluxe fans. The two constraints can be expressed as

1. Labor hours constraint $\quad 2T + 3D \leq 180$
2. Machine hours constraint $\quad 2T + 1.5D \leq 150$

When expressed in this form, the problem can readily be solved using a quantitative technique known as *linear programming*. Linear programming is described in standard texts on operations research. Diagrammatically, the product mix that maximizes contribution margin can be determined in the same manner as was illustrated with a single constraint.

Exhibit 19-3 incorporates two lines representing constraints, as opposed to only one in Exhibit 19-2. The area bounded by the constraints (the shaded area) represents the feasible solution. The firm can produce any combination within that region. The combination that maximizes contribution margin, however, is the one which lies on the equal contribution margin line farthest from the origin yet is still within the feasible region. The equal contribution margin line drawn in Exhibit 19-3 is, as in Exhibit 19-2, but one in a series of possible parallel lines, each of which represents a particular contribution margin. It was drawn by first selecting a convenient dollar amount (e.g., $3,600) and plotting the two extreme combinations of products that would provide this contribution margin. A line (not shown) connecting these points was drawn. A ruler was then placed on the line and moved downward to the corner of the feasible region where the two constraint lines intersect (point 60, 20) and a second line, parallel to the first, was drawn. This second line is the equal contribution margin line that is farthest from the origin and still within the feasible region. It is within the feasible region at only one point, that representing a combination of 60 traditional-style fans and 20 deluxe-style fans. It is this combination, therefore, that satisfies the two constraints and yields the maximum contribution margin. Since the contribution margin of traditional-style fans is $40 and that of deluxe-style fans is $45, the total contribution margin of this combination would be $3,300:

EXHIBIT 19-3

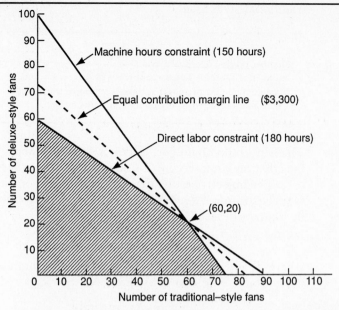

All combinations on the equal contribution margin line contribute $3,300 to firm profits.
All combinations on the machine hours constraint line require 150 machine hours.
All combinations on the direct labor constraint line require 180 direct labor hours.
The shaded area represents all feasible combinations—those which satisfy the
  two constraints.

$$\$40T \ + \ \$45D \ = \ CM$$
$$\$40(60) \ + \ \$45(20) \ = \ \$3,300$$

The graphic solution can be generalized to take into account any number of constraints. The optimum solution will be on the corner of the feasible region that is tangent to the equal contribution margin line located farthest from the origin but that still has a feasible combination on it. This solution may also be obtained using linear programming software and a personal computer.

Summary

In Chapter 17 we set forth several themes for the section of the text pertaining to management accounting. Two of them were as follows:

    1. For virtually all decisions managers are called on to make, only future receipts and costs matter and should properly be taken into account. Receipts and costs of the past are relevant only to the extent that they are a guide to, or affect the determination of, those of the future.

    2. Insofar as it is the objective of a manager to maximize the economic well-being of an organization, then *cash*—not income as it is reported today—is what matters. In evaluating the effect of decisions, a manager must focus on anticipated inflows and outflow of cash.

This chapter has served to develop these themes. In presenting the examples, we have emphasized the need to identify the *incremental* cash receipts and disbursements that will be associated with a course of action. We pointed out that while depreciation and gain or loss on sale might appear to be outlays of the future, they are in fact allocations of costs previously incurred. Generally, therefore (except to the extent that they may have an impact on future tax liabilities), they are irrelevant to most decisions that managers make. Similarly, allocations of factory, administrative, or other costs that will remain unchanged in total regardless of course of action selected need not be explicitly incorporated into an analysis of the choices faced by a manager.

A third theme set forth in Chapter 17 was that in evaluating cash flows, both the time value of money and the uncertainty surrounding the cash flows must be taken into account. In this chapter, however, the examples were structured so that the significance in differences in the timing of cash flows between alternative courses of action was minimized. In all cases we assumed that cash flows could be estimated with certainty. Moreover, in an effort to focus on a small number of concepts, we failed to take into account the income tax consequences of the decisions analyzed. Each of these gaps will be closed in forthcoming chapters.

Exercise for Review and Self-Testing

Pottsdam Paper, Inc., manufactures and sells a line of quality stationery to retailers. The firm also sells its products directly to consumers, soliciting mail orders through magazine advertisements. The stationery sold to retailers is not personalized; that sold directly to consumers is. Pottsdam maintains a small printshop, which imprints the stationery with a name and address as ordered by the customer. The company does not own a printing press; it rents one under a long-term lease arrangement. The lease agreement can be canceled by the lessee at any time.

The firm estimates that the cost of producing a single box of stationery, without printing, is $16. Printing adds an additional $4.25 per box. The company sells approximately 10,000 boxes of personalized stationery per year. Per box, as well as annual, printing costs are as follows:

	Per Box	Annual (10,000 boxes)
Direct labor	$3.00	$30,000
Ink and other supplies	.25	2,500
Lease of printing press	.40	4,000
Allocation of plant overhead	.60	6,000
Total	$4.25	$42,500

The company is considering discontinuing its printing operation and contracting the work to an outside firm. It would continue to carry out all other phases of its mail-order business. Were the firm to discontinue the printing operation, it could rent the space to outsiders at an annual rental charge of $3,000. The tenant would provide its own heating and air conditioning, thereby enabling Pottsdam to reduce its plant overhead by $1,000. The print shop is presently operated by a single employee, who earns $30,000 per year in salary. Were the printing operation to be discontinued, he would be transferred to another department and would draw his present salary. He would, however, be filling a position that is classified for a considerably lower salary—$24,000—and would ordinarily be filled with an employee who would be paid at that rate. What is the maximum price per box that Pottsdam should be willing to pay an outside contractor to perform the printing services? To simplify the analysis, income tax considerations may be ignored.

1. What, in general terms, is the most the company should pay to have a service performed by outsiders?
2. Would either revenues or the costs of manufacturing the stationery, excluding printing and other costs described previously, be affected by the decision to contract out the printing? Are such revenues and costs relevant to the determination of the price to be paid to an outside contractor?
3. Indicate for each of the following the relevant amounts to be paid or received under the alternative assumptions that the firm continues to personalize the stationery itself and that it contracts the service to an outside printer.
   a. Ink and other supplies
   b. Labor (taking into account any "extra" costs that the firm would incur in other departments if it were to abandon the printshop, transfer the printshop employee to another department, and pay him a premium above the rate at which it would have to compensate a different employee carrying out the same assignment)
   c. Rent on printing press
   d. Air-conditioning and heating costs
   e. Other plant overhead
   f. Rent received from tenant
4. Summarize the differences in costs and revenues and indicate the per box savings—the amount the company would be willing to pay to an outside contractor—that would be realized by discontinuing the printing operations.
5. Suppose that the company owned rather than leased its printing press. Book value (original cost less accumulated depreciation) of the press was $15,000. It could be sold for $10,000 cash. Annual depreciation was $5,000. Explain how the opportunity to sell the press would affect the analysis.

Questions for Review and Discussion

1. The costs and benefits associated with possible courses of action must be related to the objectives of the organization. What do managers ordinarily assume to be the objectives of a corporation? Why is maximization of *income* ordinarily an inappropriate objective for most types of decisions?
2. Why is it ordinarily unnecessary for a manager to identify and quantify *all* costs and benefits associated with alternative courses of action?
3. Why is the time horizon of a course of action sometimes uncertain or difficult to determine? Provide an example.
4. Why are *loss on sale of equipment* and *depreciation expense* generally irrelevant to most decisions (except insofar as they affect a firm's tax liability)?
5. In determining whether to make or to buy a product, how should administrative and factory costs that are common to more than one product be taken into account?
6. Why is the *average* unit cost of a product generally irrelevant in decisions as to whether a product should be discontinued, processed further, or sold at a "loss?"
7. It is the policy of a company to sell all goods that it produces at a price 20 percent above "full" cost. What is "full" cost, and what are the limitations of such a policy?
8. "*Accountants'* cost is inappropriate for most marketing decisions." Comment.

9. "In determining optimum product mix, it is generally to the advantage of the company to produce the maximum number of units possible of the product with the greatest contribution margin." Do you agree? Explain.
10. If optimum product mix is to be determined graphically, what point on the graph would represent optimum product mix? Explain.

Problems

1. *In deciding which of two or more products should be produced, only incremental revenues and costs are relevant.*

   Artform Printers, Inc., had planned to publish a calendar containing quality prints. The firm established that it would be able to sell 5,000 of the calendars at a price of $13 per calendar. It had already incurred $20,000 in art and design costs. It estimated that it would be able to earn a profit on the calendars of $18,150 ($3.63 per unit) computed as follows:

Sales revenue (5,000 @ $13.00)		$65,000
Cost of goods sold		
Direct labor (360 hours @ $15.00)	$ 5,400	
Direct materials ($.75 per unit)	3,750	
Overhead		
Fixed ($5.00 per direct labor hour;		
360 hours @ $5.00)	$1,800	
Variable ($2.50 per direct labor hour;		
360 hours @ $2.50)	900	2,700
Art and design costs		20,000	31,850
Gross margin		33,150
Selling and advertising costs		15,000
Income		$18,150

As the company was about to print the calendars, it received a special order to print 10,000 posters at a contract price of $30,000. The firm estimates the cost of the posters to be $10,750 ($1.075 per unit) determined as follows:

Direct labor (300 hours @ $15.00)		$ 4,500
Direct materials ($.40 per unit)		4,000
Overhead		
Fixed ($5.00 per direct labor hour; 300 hours @ $5)	$1,500	
Variable ($2.50 per direct labor hour; 300 hours @ $2.50)	750	2,250
Total cost		$10,750

Thus, its estimated profit on the posters will be $19,250—revenue of $30,000 less costs of $10,750. The order for the posters is "special rush"; the posters must be given priority over the calendars. However, if the firm postpones printing the calendars, it will be too late to distribute them on a timely basis and customers will refuse to accept them.

In light of the costs already incurred to produce the calendars, should the firm accept the order for the posters? Explain, show all calculations, and specifically identify the revenues and costs that are relevant to your analysis.

2. *Incremental costs can be greater rather than or less than average costs.*

Winter Sports, Inc., manufactures a line of fiberglass skis. Based on annual volume of 5,000 pairs, cost per pair is $185:

Direct labor ($75 per pair)		$375,000
Direct materials ($60 per pair)		300,000
Overhead		
Fixed	$100,000	
Variable ($.40 per direct labor dollar)	150,000	250,000
Total costs		$925,000
Annual volume		÷ 5,000 pairs
Cost per pair		$ 185

Winter Sports, Inc., sells its skis to retailers at a price of $225 per pair.

Sports Palace, Inc., a discount sporting goods store, has asked Winter Sports, Inc., to sell to it 1,000 pairs of skis, under a private brand, at a price of $200 per pair. The skis would be identical to those normally sold for $225.

Winter Sports has estimated that if it accepted the order, then Sports Palace, Inc., would reduce its usual order by 500 pairs and these sales could not be recouped elsewhere. It has also determined that to manufacture the additional skis that would result from accepting the order, all of the resultant direct labor hours would have to be compensated at overtime rates, which are 1½ times the base rates. Overtime premium is charged to an overhead account rather than to direct labor; variable overhead is based on direct labor dollars, excluding overtime premiums.

Should Winter Sports, Inc., accept the special order from Sports Palace, Inc.? Prepare a supporting analysis.

3. *Full-cost prices may lead to higher prices during periods of slack.*

Quality Worx produces specialty machine parts for industrial customers. Business is seasonal, with about five busy months and two slack months. Quality Worx uses a job order costing system, assigning overhead to jobs at the end of each month based on the labor cost of each job. Carole Worx, the owner, sets prices using the following format:

Estimated material cost	$34
Estimated labor cost	16
Subtotal	$50
Allowance for overhead at 60%	30
Subtotal	$80
Allowance for profit at 10%	8
Price	$88

This pricing formula is based on long experience and on the financial results of the past few years. Overhead has averaged about 60% of the sum of material and labor costs, and a 10% profit is reasonable in the industry. Similar jobs seem to be more or less profitable depending on the month in which they are done. This bothers Ms. Worx, and she wonders whether the pricing policy is sensible.

a. In which months, busy or slack, would jobs *appear* relatively more profitable? Why?

b. Should Ms. Worx modify the pricing policy? How? Why?

4. *Further processing may result in lower reported profits than sales without further processing but may nevertheless be in the best interests of the company.*

Real Timepiece Co. manufactures several lines of watches. The cost to manufacture one type of digital watch is $212:

Direct labor		$ 40.00
Direct materials		150.00
Overhead		
Fixed	$16.00	
Variable	6.00	22.00
Total cost per unit		$212.00

Fixed overhead is applied at the rate of $0.40 per direct labor dollar; variable overhead at the rate of $0.15 per direct labor dollar.

The company manufactured 10,000 units of this type of watch and has sold 9,000 of them at a price of $250. Owing to technological improvements in the industry and increased competition from other firms, the firm will have considerable difficulty in selling the remaining 1,000 units at the "standard" price of $250 unless it is willing to undertake an extensive advertising and sales campaign. Such a campaign would cost approximately $60,000. The firm is unwilling to reduce the price of the watch for fear that it would tarnish its image as a manufacturer of high-quality timepieces and thereby have a deleterious effect on sales of other products.

The firm has had an offer from a marketing concern that sells specialty items to university alumni associations. The concern would buy 1,000 watches at a price of $225 per watch if the firm would customize the watches with the crest of a particular university. Real Timepiece estimates that the customizing work would require $20 per watch in direct labor, $10 in direct materials, and $.15 per direct labor dollar in variable overhead. Consistent with company policies, overhead would be applied to the extra work at the standard overhead rates of $.40 (fixed) and $.15 (variable) per direct labor dollar.

a. The company is concerned about the negative effect that both of the alternatives (conducting the costly advertising campaign and selling without customizing, or selling after customizing) would have upon the quarterly income that it will be required to report. Which of the alternatives would have the more negative impact on earnings? Show all computations. (Do not include in your calculations any adjustments for under- or overabsorbed overhead; assume that they are made only at year end.)

b. Which of the alternatives would you recommend to the company if the selection criterion is to be net incremental revenue?

c. Suppose that the marketing concern offered the company only $50 per watch and that the firm's best other option was to sell the watches to a salvage dealer for $10 per watch. Should the company accept the offer from the marketing concern, assuming that it will have no effect on the prices at which other lines of watches are sold? What are the relevant revenues and costs for such a decision?

5. *The decision whether to process further must focus on incremental costs.*

Last month, April Seating Company began work on a large custom order for leather chairs. When the work was nearly complete, the retailer which had ordered the chairs went bankrupt and was not able to accept the order. The sales manager of April Seating immediately began to call other stores. While the original price was $210,000, the best price that the sales manager could get if the chairs were finished according to the original specifications was a $143,000 offer from the A-Mart chain. Sindle Company, which also operates a chain of stores, offered $168,000 for the chairs provided that different upholstery and trim were used. The sales manager obtained the following information as to costs incurred to date:

Materials	$ 31,500
Direct labor (7,000 hours @ $6)	42,000
Factory overhead ($10 per hour)	70,000
Total costs to date	$143,500

The factory overhead rate includes $4 variable overhead and $6 fixed overhead. The additional work required to complete the chairs was estimated by the production manager:

	A-Mart Specifications	Sindle's Specifications
Materials	$4,400	$9,500
Direct labor hours	1,000 hours	1,500 hours

a. Determine the total costs that would be charged to the job assuming (1) the work is completed to the original specifications or (2) the chairs are modified as required by Sindle Company.
b. Determine which offer April Seatings should accept.

6. *Full cost may be inappropriate for bidding decisions.*

Sainsbury Company manufactures industrial machines. The firm has been operating at well below capacity, and the sales manager has been trying to increase orders. She recently received an offer to bid on a large press and submitted the specifications to Sainsbury's pricing specialists. They prepared the following analysis:

Materials	$28,600
Direct labor at $9 per hour	19,800
Overhead at $12 per direct labor hour	26,400
Total manufacturing cost	74,800
Allowance for selling and administrative	
expenses @ 10% of manufacturing cost	7,480
Total cost	82,280
Standard allowance for profit at 15%	
of total cost	12,342
Suggested price	$94,622

The sales manager told Sainsbury's president that this estimate would not be low enough to secure the job. She said that the customer expected a price in the neighborhood of $75,000, which another company had already bid. The president consulted the controller, who said that the overhead rate was about 60% variable, 40% fixed, and that variable selling and administrative expenses were negligible. The president was reluctant to meet the $75,000 price but agreed to think it over and get back to the sales manager.

Advise the president. Should the company meet the $75,000 price? Explain.

7. *The decision to make or buy may be influenced by volume.*

Empire Engines is considering purchasing a part that it currently manufactures. Annual costs associated with the production of the part are as follows:

Variable		
Materials	$130,000	
Direct labor	90,000	
Supplies	4,000	
Power	3,000	
Other variable costs	16,000	$243,000
Fixed		
Indirect labor	30,000	
Depreciation	15,000	
Allocation of factory and administrative costs		
from other departments	20,000	
Other fixed costs	6,000	71,000
Total costs		$314,000

All fixed costs, with the exception of the allocated costs, are associated directly with the production of the part and could be eliminated if the firm ceased to manufacture it. Depreciation charges are approximately equal to annual expenditures required to replace plant and equipment.

Annual production of the part is 5,000 units.

An outside supplier has agreed to furnish the part for $55 per unit.

a. Determine the "full" cost of the part.
b. Prepare a schedule which compares the relevant costs of buying the part with those of manufacturing it. Should the company buy or manufacture the product?
c. Suppose that the annual production volume of the part was 10,000 units. Would your recommendation be the same? Explain and show any relevant computations.

8. *Only future costs are relevant to the decision whether to discontinue a business segment.*

Multiproducts, Inc., is considering selling the assets associated with one segment of its business. It would also retire the bonds for which the assets serve as collateral.

The assets and the bonds are reported on the firm's balance sheet as follows:

Plant and equipment	$6,000,000	
Less: Accumulated depreciation	(2,000,000)	$4,000,000
Patents and licensing agreements	$ 800,000	
Less: Accumulated amortization	(300,000)	500,000
Total assets		$4,500,000
Bonds payable	$1,000,000	
Add: Unamortized bond premium	70,000	1,070,000
Net book value of assets to be sold and bonds retired		$3,430,000

The firm anticipates that the reported income of the segment that would be discontinued would be approximately $420,000 per year comprising the following elements:

Sales revenue			$5,713,000
Less: Expenses			
Labor, material, and other manufacturing			
costs associated with the segment		$4,640,000	
Depreciation		500,000	
Amortization of patents and			
licensing agreements		100,000	
Interest on bonds	$60,000		
Less: Amortization of bond premium	(7,000)	53,000	5,293,000
Income of segment that			
would be discontinued			$ 420,000

The firm estimates that annual cash outlays of $800,000 would be required to replace and renew plant equipment, patents, and licensing agreements.

The firm has been offered $3,500,000 for the plant and equipment and $600,000 for the patents and licensing agreements. It would be able to redeem the bonds at their face value of $1 million.

Were the firm to sell the assets and retire the bonds, it would invest the net proceeds of $3,100,000 in securities that will provide an annual return of $465,000 (15 percent).

a. Determine the amount of net gain or loss that the firm would have to report at the time the assets were sold and the bonds retired if it elected to discontinue the business segment. For simplicity of analysis, ignore the impact of income taxes.

b. Prepare an analysis which would aid management in deciding whether to discontinue the business segment. Be sure that you identify the revenues and costs that are relevant to the decision at hand. Assume that all revenues and expenses associated with the segment would continue at their same level indefinitely. Of what relevance is the net gain or loss determined in part a?

9. *The decision to add a business segment, like that to discontinue one, requires incremental analysis.*

Fashion Shoes, Inc., manufactures quality men's shoes. The shoes are sold to retailers at $90 per pair; annual volume is 30,000 pairs. The cost to manufacture each pair of shoes is $72:

Direct labor		$40
Direct materials		10
Overhead		
Fixed	$14	
Variable	8	22
Total cost		$72

Fixed overhead, which totals $420,000, is applied at the rate of $.35 per direct labor dollar; variable overhead, which totals $240,000, is applied at the rate of $.20 per direct labor dollar.

The firm is considering adding a line of men's boots. It estimates that it could sell 5,000 pairs per year at a price of $130.

The company has determined that for the boots direct labor would be $70 per pair and direct materials would be $30 per pair. Variable overhead would remain proportional to direct labor costs ($.20 per direct labor dollar), but owing to the addition of new facilities fixed overhead would increase by $45,000 to

$465,000. Correspondingly, the fixed portion of the overhead charging rate would change to take into account the additional fixed overhead as well as the additional direct labor dollars.

Some managers of the firm have opposed adding the new product line, contending that cost per unit would exceed the selling price of $130.

a. Prepare an income statement for the existing line of *shoes*, assuming that the firm does *not* add the line of boots.
b. Determine the per unit cost, including both fixed and variable overhead, of manufacturing each pair of *boots*.
c. Prepare a statement of income for the line of boots.
d. Do you think that the company should add the line of boots, even if it would have to sell the boots at less than full cost? Explain and support your response with appropriate calculations.
e. Prepare an income statement for the two products combined. Include one column for shoes, one for boots, and one for the total of the two lines. In calculating cost of the *shoes* sold, be sure to use the revised overhead charging rate. Is the difference in income between that reported in the combined statement and that determined for the shoes alone (part a) consistent with your response to part d?

10. *Choice of depreciation method is irrelevant (ignoring taxes) to a decision as to whether to replace an asset.*

Nova, Inc., is presently using a stamping machine that it acquired two years ago at a cost of $40,000. The total estimated useful life of the machine is five years; estimated salvage value at the end of five years is $10,000. The firm charges depreciation using the double-declining balance method, and book value of the machine, with three years of useful life remaining, is $14,400. The machine could be sold today for $12,000.

Nova, Inc., has the opportunity to sell the old machine and replace it with a new one. The new machine would enable it to effect cash savings of $12,000 per year. The new machine would cost $30,000 and have a useful life of three years—same as the remaining useful life of the old machine. The company would charge depreciation on the new machine using the double-declining balance method. It estimates that the new machine would have zero salvage value at the end of its useful life. The full amount of the remaining book value of the new machine would be charged off as depreciation in the third and final year of useful life.

The company is reluctant to replace the old machine with the new because the new machine is almost fully depreciated. Nova, Inc., is a nonprofit organization and pays no income taxes.

a. Prepare a schedule in which you indicate the differences in *earnings* that would be reported during each of the next three years, as well as the three years combined, if the company were to replace the old machine with the new as compared to if it did not. Remember that depreciation should not be charged beyond the point at which the book value of an asset has been reduced to its salvage value. Be sure to take into account any gain or loss on the sale of the old machine if it were replaced with the new.
b. Prepare a schedule in which you indicate the differences in cash flows that would result over the period of three years if the firm were to replace the old machine with the new as opposed to if it did not.
c. Should the firm replace the old machine with the new? Explain.
d. Suppose that the firm used the straight-line method instead of the double-declining method. How would that affect the schedules which you prepared? Would it change your decision as to whether the machine should be replaced? Explain.

11. *Orders should not necessarily be filled at the plant with the lower apparent cost.*

Shore Industries, Inc., has two plants, one in Texas, and one in Michigan. Inasmuch as the Texas plant is considerably newer than the Michigan plant, fixed production costs in Texas are higher, but variable costs lower. Per unit costs at a volume of 8,000 units per month, the volume at which both plants are presently operating, are as follows:

	Per Unit Cost	
	Texas Plant	Michigan Plant
Fixed manufacturing costs	$ 50	$ 25
Variable manufacturing costs	55	80
Total	$105	$105

The firm has accepted an order from a customer in Ohio. Transportation costs of filling the order from the plant in Michigan would be $10 per unit; from that in Texas, $15 per unit. Both plants are presently operating at substantially less than full capacity.

a. What would be the per unit cost of manufacturing the product at each of the two plants? Consider "cost to be the *full* cost—that which would be reflected in cost of goods sold.

(1) Assume that the order was for 1,000 units.

(2) Assume alternatively that the order was for 4,500 units.

b. At which of the two plants should the order be filled?

(1) Assume that the order was for 1,000 units.

(2) Assume that the order was for 4,500 units.

12. *Incremental analysis can be used to estimate strike losses.*

Sturdman Valve Co. carries a strike insurance policy. The policy provides for reimbursement of all losses attributable to strikes. Losses are defined as the amount by which the excess of incremental revenues over incremental costs is less during the period of the work stoppage than it would have been had there been no strike.

The manufacturing operations of one division of Sturdman were discontinued for a month because of a strike. Management estimates that on account of the strike its production was reduced by 4,000 units, each of which could have been sold for $80. Cost of manufacturing each unit would have been $61, composed of the following costs:

Direct labor		$20
Direct materials		19
Overhead		
Fixed	$17	
Variable	5	22
Cost per unit		$61

Monthly fixed manufacturing overhead consists of the following:

Supervision	$16,000
Depreciation	17,000
Allocation of home office costs	3,000
Heat and power	8,000
Maintenance	21,000
Supplies	3,000
Total fixed overhead	$68,000

Variable overhead depends entirely upon the use of direct labor.

During the strike, supervisors reported to work and performed essential maintenance operations; they were paid their normal salaries. Heat and power costs during the strike were $4,000. Supply costs were $500. All nonmanufacturing activities were carried on as normal, with the exception that the firm canceled magazine ads which would have cost $2,500.

Determine the amount of the claim that Sturdman should submit to its insurer.

13. *Incremental cost analysis is appropriate for the decision as to the number of hours a supermarket should remain open.*

Save-More Supermarket is contemplating increasing the number of its business hours. Save-More is presently open from 9 A.M. to 8 P.M. Two proposals are under consideration. The first would extend the business hours until 1 A.M. The second would extend the hours until 9 A.M.; the store would be open 24 hours per day.

Management estimates that sales between 8 P.M. and 1 A.M. would be approximately $16,000; those between 1 A.M. and 9 A.M. would be $13,500. It believes that of the customers who would shop during the proposed new hours, 40 percent would make their purchases during the standard daytime hours if the store did not remain open; the other 60 percent would shop at other stores that were open at night.

On average, per the firm's annual report, net income is approximately 2 percent of sales. Of the merchandise that would be sold during the period 8 P.M. to 1 A.M., management estimates that the average markup from cost would be 15 percent. On that sold from 1 A.M. to 9 A.M. it would be 20 percent. The difference in markup can be explained by differences in product mix; purchases in the early morning hours tend to be specialty items.

During the period from 8 P.M. to 1 A.M. the store would require the services of 10 employees. Three of these ten, however, would ordinarily have to be in the store during those hours even if the store were to be closed for business, in order to restock the shelves. During the period 1 A.M. to 9 A.M. the store would have to be staffed by only three employees, inasmuch as certain services can be reduced. None of these three would otherwise be in the store. The average wage rate for the employees is $15 per hour.

Management estimates that by staying open from 8 P.M. to 1 A.M. it would incur $1,500 in additional electricity, air conditioning, heating, and miscellaneous costs; from 1 A.M. to 9 P.M. it would incur $2,000 in additional costs.

Were the store to remain open after 8 P.M., it would require the services of a security service. The cost of the security service is $150 per night. The firm would *not* be able to engage the security service for only a portion of the night at a fraction of the standard rate. If it remained open only until 1 A.M., it would still be required to engage the security service.

Based on the information provided, should the supermarket
a. Extend its hours to 1 A.M.?

b. Extend its hours to 9 A.M.?

c. Not extend its hours?

Support your response with an appropriate analysis.

14. *Sales-based commissions may be dysfunctional.*

Kitchen Products, Inc., manufactures a large number of household items. Among them are items 150 and 285. Both cost $15.20 to manufacture:

	Item 150	Item 285
Direct labor	$ 4.00	$ 8.60
Direct materials	10.00	4.02
Variable overhead	.40	.86
Fixed overhead	.80	1.72
Total cost	$15.20	$15.20

Fixed overhead is applied at a rate of $.20 per direct labor dollar; variable overhead is applied at the rate of $.10 per direct labor dollar.

It is the policy of the firm to price all items at an amount 25 percent above cost. Thus, both items are sold for $19.00.

a. Which of the two items contributes the greater amount to the profitability of the firm in both absolute dollars and as a percentage of selling price? Explain and show relevant calculations.

b. Suppose alternatively the firm had a policy of pricing all products at an amount 32 percent above *variable* cost. What would be the price at which each of the two products would be sold? What would be the contribution of each to the profitability of the firm? What would be the contribution of each as a percentage of selling price?

c. The salespeople of the firm receive a commission equal to 10 percent of dollar sales. Suppose that the price of item 150 was established at $19.00; that of 285 at $18.50. Which of the two products would the salespeople have the greater incentive to promote? Compare the contributions to profits that would result from the sale of each of the two products. Comment on possible dysfunctional consequences of basing salesperson's commissions on dollar sales.

15. *Allocations of joint costs may confound the decision as to whether to process further.*

The Salt Sea Chemical Works engages in a process that yields two chemicals, QX1 and QX2, from common raw materials. Joint costs of producing the two chemicals up to the split-off point are $24,000 per batch.

If processed beyond the split-off, at additional costs of $64,000 per batch, then QX1 can be sold to industrial customers for $70,400 per batch. If not processed further, then it has no value.

QX2, in contrast, can be sold to industrial customers without further processing for $25,600 per batch. If, however, it is processed further, then it can be sold as a consumer product for $121,600 per batch. The incremental processing costs would be $60,000 per batch, but in addition the firm would be required to incur $35,000 in advertising and selling costs.

The firm allocates joint costs in proportion to net incremental revenues beyond the split-off point. Net incremental revenues are defined as the selling price of the product less the additional *processing* costs (*excluding* advertising and selling costs). For example, assuming that QX1 is processed further but that QX2 is not, the $24,000 of common costs would be allocated as follows:

	QX1	QX2	Total
Selling price	$70,400	$25,600	$96,000
Less: Additional processing costs	64,000	-0-	64,000
Net incremental revenue	$ 6,400	$25,600	$32,000
Percent of net incremental revenue	20%	80%	100%
Proportionate share of $24,000 of common costs	$ 4,800	$19,200	$24,000

a. Determine the income, per batch, that would be attributable to QX2, assuming that it is *not* processed beyond the split-off point and is instead sold to industrial customers.

b. Determine the income attributable to QX2, assuming that it *is* processed further and sold as a consumer product. Be sure to recalculate the allocation of common costs.

c. Do you think that the company should sell the QX2 at the split-off point or should process it further even if further processing results in a decrease in the apparent profitability of the product? Explain and support your response with specific data.

16. *Pricing decisions must focus on incremental costs.*

Sundem Company maintains a job order costing system. It uses material supplied by its customers, so that virtually all of its manufacturing costs are direct labor and overhead. The controller prepared the following data for establishing the company's pricing policy for the next year.

Total budgeted direct labor hours	240,000
Total budgeted manufacturing costs	$4,800,000

Total budgeted manufacturing costs were developed using the formula:

Total manufacturing costs = $1,200,000 + ($15 × direct labor hours)

Total selling and administrative expenses are budgeted as $800,000 + ($0.10 × revenue). The company profit objective is $880,000.

a. Determine the total revenue that Sundem must earn to achieve its profit objective.

b. Determine the price per direct labor hour that Sundem must charge to achieve the objective.

c. Suppose that the company establishes the price you determined in part b and operates at a level of 230,000 direct labor hours. What will be its profit?

d. Suppose that the company establishes that price and operates at a level of 250,000 hours. What will be its profit?

17. *Cost-based prices may be convenient but simplistic.*

The sales manager and the controller of Victrola Company were discussing the price to be set for a new product with the following costs:

Variable costs	$8 per unit
Fixed costs	$80,000 per year

The sales manager had identified a target volume of 10,000 units per year. He estimated that average fixed cost would be $8 per unit. The firm follows a policy of setting prices at 200% of total cost, so the sales manager had a target price of $32 per unit.

The controller thought that $32 seemed high, especially as competitors were charging only $30 for essentially similar products. The sales manager agreed that only 8,000 units per year could be sold at $32. However, he was adamant that the price should be set at 200% of cost. "It is unfortunate that fixed costs are so high, because 10,000 units could definitely be sold if price were $30, and probably 12,000 at $28." However, it would not be possible to achieve the desired markup at those prices.

a. Evaluate the sales manager's logic.
b. Show what would happen at the $32 price. Would the firm achieve the desired profit?
c. Determine which three prices ($32, $30, $28) will result in the highest annual profit.

18. *Selection of product mix is guided by the critical constraint.*

Calculators Ltd. manufactures specialized calculators. It has recently developed three new types of calculators; for joggers, for auto race fans, and for dieters. The company has limited capacity. It has work stations for only 25 assemblers. It is certain, however, that it can sell all the calculators that it produces regardless of type. The following data pertain to the three types of calculators:

	Joggers	Race Fans	Dieters
Selling price	$17.00	$12.00	$24.00
Direct materials cost	3.20	2.80	7.20
Direct labor cost (assemblers)	5.00	2.50	5.00
Variable overhead ($.25 per direct materials dollar)	.80	.70	1.80
Required hours of assembly time	.50 hour	.25 hour	.50 hour

Because of the limitation in number of work stations, the company has available a maximum of 200 hours of assembly time per day. Fixed manufacturing costs are $3,500 per day. It is company policy to allocate fixed manufacturing costs on the basis of direct labor dollars.

The firm can produce any combination of the three types of calculators.

If it is the objective of the firm to maximize contribution to profits, how many of each type of calculator should it produce per day?

19. *Optimum product mix with two constraints can be determined graphically.*

Plas-Tec, Inc., is faced with the problem of determining the optimum mix of its two products, toy trucks and toy dolls. Both types of toys must be processed in a molding department and an assembly department. The following data pertain to the two products (based on batches of 100 units):

	Trucks	Dolls
Contribution margin	$100	$80
Required hours in molding department	2	3
Required hours in assembly department	4	2

The manufacturing facilities of Plas-Tec, Inc., including both the molding and assembly departments, are in operation 40 hours per week.

a. Prepare a graph, the horizontal axis of which represents the number of batches of trucks and the vertical axis of which represents the number of batches of dolls that can be produced each week. Scale the axes from zero to 20.

b. Draw lines representing the two constraints on production—the available hours in the molding and the assembly departments. Shade in the region of feasible combinations.

c. Add to the graph a line representing all combinations of the two products that would provide a contribution margin of a convenient dollar amount—$800, for example. Draw a second line, parallel to the first, that is as far from the origin of the graph as possible yet still within the region of feasible combinations (at one point at least).

d. What is the combination of products that maximizes contribution to profit? What is the total contribution to profits of that combination? Test your answer by shifting resources from one product to the other. If the shift increases the contribution to profit and does not cause the constraints to be violated, then your answer must be in error.

20. *A graphic determination of optimum product mix is feasible even with three or more constraints.*

Electronic Gadgets, Inc., has the capability of manufacturing in one of its plants two products: a digital bathroom scale and a digital household thermometer. The contribution margin of the scale is $15 per unit; that of the thermometer is $10 per unit. An important component of both products is Type B silicone chips. The scale requires two such chips; the thermometer one such chip. Owing to shortages in such chips, the company is able to acquire only 140 chips per day.

a. If it is the objective of the firm to maximize contribution to profits, what combination of the two products do you recommend be manufactured each day? Prepare a graph (with units from zero to 150) in which the horizontal axis represents number of scales and the vertical axis represents number of thermometers. Draw one line that depicts the critical production constraint and another which connects all possible combinations of products that will provide the same contribution to profits as the combination that you recommend be manufactured.

b. Suppose that the firm has available each day a maximum of 120 hours of assembly labor. Each scale requires 1.2 hours of assembly time; each thermometer requires 1.5 hours. Add to your graph an additional line representing the assembly labor constraint. What, per your graph, is the optimum product mix taking into account the additional constraint?

c. Suppose that the firm can sell no more than 40 scales per day. Add to your graph a line representing this third constraint. What, per your graph, is now the optimum product mix?

d. Suppose alternatively that the firm could sell no more than 60 scales per day. What impact would this constraint have on product mix?

Solutions to Exercise for Review and Self-Testing

1. The maximum price per box that Pottsdam should be willing to pay an outside contractor is the amount that it could save by discontinuing the printing operation. Thus, if it could truly save $4.25 per box, then it should be willing to pay up to $4.25 per box to an outside contractor.

2. Sales revenues and costs of manufacturing the stationery (except as noted in part 3) would be the same regardless of whether the printing is done within the company or outside. They are, therefore, irrelevant to the decision at hand.

---

3. a. The firm would have to incur $2,500 in ink and other supplies if it continued the printing operations; zero if it discontinued.
   b. It would incur $30,000 in labor costs if it continued the printing operations. It would, however, incur $6,000 in costs if it discontinued. The $6,000 (the excess of the $30,000 to be paid over the $24,000 that the job is worth) represents a cost that the firm elects to incur in order to satisfy an obligation—perhaps "moral," perhaps "legal"—to retain the printshop employee and pay him his printshop salary even if he were to work at a job that usually commands a lesser salary.
   c. Rent expense of $4,000 on the printing press would be incurred only if the printing operation were continued.
   d. If the firm were to continue the printing operations, it would incur $1,000 more in heating and air-conditioning costs than if it discontinued. The remaining heating and air-conditioning costs would be the same under each alternative and are therefore irrelevant.
   e. Other plant overhead costs would be the same regardless of the alternative selected. If the printing operations were discontinued, the amounts *allocated* to the remaining departments would increase since the departments would have to bear among them the costs previously allocated to the printing operation.
   f. Rent revenue would be $3,000 if the printing operation were discontinued; zero if it were continued.

4. (+ = inflow; − = outflow)

	Printshop Continued	Printshop Discontinued	Saving if Printshop Discontinued
Ink and other supplies	− $ 2,500	—	$ 2,500
Labor costs	− 30,000	− $6,000	24,000
Rent expense	− 4,000	—	4,000
Heating and air conditioning	− 1,000	—	1,000
Rent revenue	—	+ 3,000	3,000
Total	− $37,500	− $3,000	$34,500
Number of boxes per year			÷ 10,000 boxes
Savings per box			$ 3.45

The firm would be willing to pay no more than $3.45 per box to a printing contractor—considerably less than the apparent print cost per box of $4.25.

5. If the company owned the printing press, then the cash inflow—and only the cash inflow—resulting from the sale of the press should be taken into account. The amount to be realized upon the sale represents a *future* cash flow, one that would be affected by the decision to discontinue or continue printing operations. In contrast, both depreciation and loss on sales represent the allocation of a previously incurred cost to a particular accounting period. Neither depreciation expense nor loss on sales involves an outflow of cash and needs to be incorporated into the analysis of the decision.

20

Long-Run Planning, Investment Decisions, and Capital Budgeting

In Chapters 17 through 19, we focused on *costs*—their behavior, how they can be broken down for purposes of analysis, and how they are used to make *ad hoc* decisions. We now examine how managers use cost and revenue information for purposes of planning and control.

The focus of this chapter will be on *long-run* planning, involving capital expenditure decisions and capital budgeting. Capital expenditure decisions involve an investment of capital in the expectation of returns in the future. The characteristic of capital expenditures which warrants special attention is that future benefits associated with an investment can occur, as assets are used, over an extended period of time. To recognize the differences in value between benefits received and costs paid in different years, it is necessary to discount back to the present all anticipated future benefits and costs. Prominent among capital expenditure decisions are those involved in acquiring or replacing long-lived assets by purchase or construction. The approaches to capital expenditure analysis described in this chapter are generalizable, however, to virtually all courses of action in which benefits and/or costs will take place at different times.

The foundations for analysis of capital expenditure decisions and capital budgeting have been firmly established in earlier chapters—in particular in Chapter 6, where the concepts of time value of money and the techniques of equating dollars to be paid or received in the future with those to be paid or received in the present were described. Chapters 9 and 10 used this framework in analyzing plant asset acquisitions and depreciation, and long-run financing through issuance of bonds, respectively. Chapter 19 stressed the importance of these types of comparisons, illustrating the means of identifying incremental cash flows associated with alternative courses of action.

Our focus in this chapter is on *investment decisions* and the *capital budgeting planning process*. The approach to capital expenditure planning and analysis usually followed is termed the *discounted cash flow* (DCF) or *net present value* approach. It can be summarized as follows:

1. Estimate the timing and amount of incremental cash flows of each possible course of action aimed at achieving a specified objective—that is, those cash flows which would be different if one alternative as opposed to another were selected.
2. Choose an appropriate discount rate. This may be the firm's cost of capital, a lending opportunity cost rate, a target rate adjusted for risk, or some alternative to one of these which seems justifiable under the circumstances.
3. Using this rate, discount all expected cash receipts and disbursements back to the present. Sum the discounted cash receipts and disbursements for each alternative course of action.
4. Identify the course of action with the largest present value net cash inflow (or smallest net cash outflow).

Discounted Cash Flow Illustrated: Decision to Acquire a Machine

A firm has the opportunity to acquire a machine that would enable it to reduce overall operating costs of production by $75,000 a year, independent of any repair and maintenance costs associated with use of the machine. Repair and maintenance costs, it is estimated, will be $5,000 in year 1, $19,000 in year 2, $32,000 in year 3, and $44,000 in year 4. The initial cost of the machine will be $100,000. The discount rate used by the firm to evaluate investments is 10 percent. The expected useful life of the machine is four years.

Exhibit 20-1 indicates the actual as well as the discounted *cash* disbursements and receipts associated with the purchase and use of this machine. Cash savings are accounted for as if they were cash receipts. For computational convenience (so that the standard present value tables or formulas can be applied), it shall be assumed in this and subsequent examples that the cash disbursements and receipts occur at the end of an accounting period. Slight modifications to the present value formulas developed in Chapter 6 would be required to reflect a more realistic pattern in which operating savings occur uniformly throughout a period.

EXHIBIT 20-1
Capital Expenditure Analysis Using Discounted Cash Flows

	Relevant Cash Flows in Year					Present Value of $1 (10%)	Discounted Cash Flows (present value)
	0	1	2	3	4		
Acquire machine	($100,000)					$1.0000	($100,000)
Operating savings		$75,000	$75,000	$75,000	$75,000		
Cash outlays:							
Repair costs		(5,000)	(19,000)	(32,000)	(44,000)		
Net cash flows:							
Total, year 1		$70,000				.9091	63,637
Total, year 2			$56,000			.8264	46,278
Total, year 3				$43,000		.7513	32,306
Total, year 4					$31,000	.6830	21,173
Present value of total net cash receipts							$ 63,394

Discounted cash flow analysis yields a net present value for purchase and use of this asset of $63,394, as shown in Exhibit 20-1.

An appendix to this chapter describes a means of investment analysis in which excess current (or residual) income, rather than cash, is discounted. The excess current income approach is not widely used in practice, but it may have appeal to managers in that it explicitly forces consideration of options to use and replace assets beyond those addressed by the discounted cash flow procedures.

Determining the Discount Rate

A critical element in the analysis of investment opportunities is the rate of discount. The appropriate means of determining the rate of discount is the subject of ongoing controversy among economists and specialists in finance.

Many experts assert that the discount rate for all projects should reflect the *weighted average* of a firm's *cost of capital*. Cost of capital comprises the costs of bonds and other debts, common and preferred stock, and retained earnings. Because there are no required payments associated with common stock and retained earnings, intricate formulas have been developed to estimate the costs associated with these components of capital.

The literature of finance and economics of recent years, however, favors using a different rate of discount for each project under consideration. The rate selected would be dependent on the degree of risk associated with the project. The higher the risk, the higher the rate of discount. Support for a risk-related rate rests to a considerable extent on research pertaining to the value of investments (particularly stocks and bonds) and the selection of "portfolios" of assets that maximize returns at specified levels of risk.

In practice, it is not uncommon for managers to use a discount rate representing a target rate of return. A target rate would be based on executive judgment as to the minimum return that is expected of all investments.

Owing to its complexity, the issue of appropriate rate of discount is beyond the scope of this text. We can do no more than demonstrate how the discount rate can be applied in capital investment analysis.

Impact of Taxes on Cash Flows

In Chapter 19, we emphasized that only incremental cash receipts and disbursements should be taken into account in assessing the desirability of alternative courses of action. Neither depreciation expense nor gains or losses on the sale of assets can be included among the receipts or disbursements of cash. They represent the mere assignment of the cost of the assets to particular account periods. It may be recalled from Chapter 14 relating to cash flow statements that depreciation as well as losses on sales of assets must be "added back" to reported income to obtain cash provided by operations.

Both depreciation and gains or losses on the sale of assets are items of revenue and expense that enter into the determination of *taxable* earnings, however, and, hence, the amount *of cash* that will be *disbursed* to the taxing authorities. The example that follows is intended to emphasize that depreciation (or amortization) as well as gains or losses are not themselves cash items but do have a bearing on the net *after-tax* receipts or disbursements associated with a project. The tax consequences of gains and losses must be included in a comprehensive discounted cash flow analysis.

Another Example: A Replacement Decision, with Tax Consequences

A firm is deciding whether to replace an old machine with a new. The new machine will enable the firm to increase output. The data that follow relate to the new machine and the one that it will replace.

New Machine	
Cost	$180,000
Useful life	3 years
Salvage value	$30,000
Annual fixed operating costs, excluding depreciation	$27,000
Contribution margin on additional units that can be produced by the new machine (sales revenue less variable costs)	$82,000
Annual depreciation charges (straight-line method)	$50,000

Old Machine	
Amount for which machine could be sold if replaced by new	$70,000
Book value	60,000
Remaining useful life of old machine	3 years
Salvage value at the end of useful life	-0-
Annual fixed operating costs, excluding depreciation	$10,000
Annual depreciation charges (straight-line method)	$20,000

Tax and discount rates	
Tax rate on income	40%
Tax rate on gains on sale of plant and equipment	25%[1]
Discount rate for evaluating purchases of equipment (after-tax rate)	12%

[1]In this example, we assume different tax rates for ordinary income and capital gains—gains on the sale of assets held for an extended period of time. Although as of 1992, the U.S. rates were the same, in the past—and most likely again in the future—they differed. Moreover, the tax system of many other countries distinguishes between ordinary income and capital gains.

EXHIBIT 20-2

Incremental Net Cash Receipts from Replacing Old Machine with New

	Relevant Cash Flows in Year:				Present Value of $1 at 12%	Discounted Cash Flows (present value)
	0	1	2	3		
Disbursement for new machine	($180,000)					
Receipt from sale of old machine	70,000					
Tax on gain on sale of old machine	(2,500)					
Contribution margin on additional sales		$82,000	$82,000	$82,000		
Additional fixed operating expenses ($27,000 – $10,000)		(17,000)	(17,000)	(17,000)		
Additional tax expense		(14,000)	(14,000)	(14,000)		
Receipt upon sale at end of useful life				30,000		
Net disbursement, year 0	($112,500)				1.000	($112,500)
Net receipts, year 1		$51,000			.8929	45,538
Net receipts, year 2			$51,000		.7972	40,657
Net receipts, year 3				$81,000	.7118	57,656
Present value of net receipts						$ 31,351

Exhibit 20-2 indicates the incremental cash flows associated with the purchase of the new machine. Year 0 represents the date at which the new machine would be purchased and the old one sold. All other cash receipts or disbursements are assumed to occur at the *end* of the respective years. A few explanatory comments may be helpful.

1. All receipts and disbursements that would be the same regardless of whether the new machine is acquired are excluded from the analysis; they would be unaffected by the purchase decision.
2. The analysis could have been separated into two tables. In one would be indicated the cash flows associated with the purchase of the new machine; in the other, those associated with the retention of the old. The alternative in which the present value of the net cash inflows was the greater would be selected.
3. The tax on the sale of the old machine was calculated as follows:

Amount for which old machine could be sold	$70,000
Less: Book value of old machine	60,000
Gain on sale of machine	$10,000
Tax rate on gains on sale of plant and equipment	× .25
Tax	$ 2,500

4. The additional tax expense for each of the three years during which the new machine will be used was determined as follows:

Contribution margin on additional units to be produced by new machine		$82,000
Less: Additional fixed operating costs ($27,000 – $10,000)	$17,000	
Additional depreciation ($50,000 – $20,000)	30,000	47,000
Additional income before taxes		$35,000
Tax rate		× .40
Additional tax expense		$14,000

5. The rate by which the cash flows are discounted must be an *after-tax* rate. It should be indicative of the minimum acceptable return *after* allowance for tax expenditures. Clearly, the minimum acceptable return after taxes will be less than that before taxes.

The present value of the net receipts to be generated by replacing the old machine with the new is positive ($31,351 per Exhibit 20-2). Hence, it is to the advantage of the firm to undertake the proposed capital investment.

THE INTERNAL RATE OF RETURN AND CAPITAL BUDGETING

An alternative to the net present value approach to capital budgeting is an approach centering on use of the internal rate of return—an approach that is often used both to make the initial investment decision and to determine the asset book values needed for subsequent decision making as well. This alternative to present value analysis, employed often in the literature and espoused by many, deserves careful scrutiny.

As a Criterion for Investment Decision Making

The internal rate of return represents the rate which, when used to discount each of the cash receipts earned by an investment over time, equates the present value of those receipts with the initial outlay to acquire the asset (plus the present value of any subsequent outlays). The higher the internal rate of return, the more desirable a project, presumably because a higher internal rate of return implies higher cash receipts from a given investment outlay.

Example: Uniform Cash Flows

A firm has the opportunity to make an investment of $47,912 that will provide net cash receipts, after taxes, of $12,000 per year for five years. What is the internal rate of return?

The present value of the single cash outflow, inasmuch as it takes place at time zero, is $47,912 regardless of discount rate. The internal rate of return, therefore, is that rate which when used to discount the inflows—an annuity of $12,000 for five years—is exactly equal to $47,912. If x equals the internal rate of return, then

$$\$47,912 = \$12,000 \text{ times the present value of an}$$
$$\text{annuity of } \$1 \text{ for 5 years at } x\%$$

and

$$\frac{\$47,912}{\$12,000} = \text{the present value of an annuity of } \$1$$
$$\text{for 5 years at } x\%$$

Therefore,

$$\$3.9927 = \text{the present value of an annuity of } \$1$$
$$\text{for 5 years at } x\%$$

Per Table 4 in the Appendix, 3.9927 is equal to the present value of an annuity for five years at a discount rate of 8 percent. This rate can be determined by reading along the row for five periods until 3.9927 is reached; 3.9927 is under the column for 8 percent. The internal rate of return is therefore 8 percent. If the amount to be found fell between two rates of discount indicated in the table, then it would be necessary to estimate the internal rate of return by way of interpolation (see the next example).

Example: Nonuniform Cash Flows

Assume the same facts as in the previous example with the addition that at the end of the fifth year the firm will sell its interest in the investment for $10,000. Thus, the internal rate of return is that rate of discount which will equate the present value of a cash outflow of $47,912 in period zero with an annuity of $12,000 for five years and a single payment of $10,000 at the end of year five.

Because there is no simple algorithm to determine the internal rate of return when there are nonuniform cash flows, the trial and error method is used. Owing to the additional cash receipt at the end of the fifth year, the internal rate of return is obviously greater than the 8 percent calculated in the previous example. The following table indicates the present value of the cash flows discounted at a trial rate of 14 percent:

	Relevant Cash Flows	Discount Factor, 14%	Present Value
Initial investment, year 0	($47,912)	1.0000	($47,912)
Annual returns, years 1 through 5 (an annuity)	12,000	3.4331	41,197
Salvage value at end of year 5	10,000	.5194	5,194
Net present value			($ 1,521)

The objective is to determine a discount rate such that the net present value is zero. Since the net present value at 14 percent is negative, the trial rate of 14 percent is too high. The following table indicates the present value of cash flows discounted at a second trial rate of 12 percent:

	Relevant Cash Flows	Discount Factor, 14%	Present Value
Initial investment, year 0	($47,912)	1.0000	($47,912)
Annual returns, years 1 through 5			
(an annuity)	12,000	3.6048	43,258
Salvage value at end of year 5	10,000	.5674	5,674
Net present value			$ 1,020

The net present value at 12 percent is positive; therefore, the desired present value of zero is between 12 and 14 percent. The approximate internal rate of return is proportionately as far from 12 percent as the desired present value of zero is from the present value at 12 percent of $1,020. Thus, by way of interpolation, if x = the unknown actual internal rate of return,

$$\frac{\text{High rate } - \text{ Low rate}}{\left(\begin{array}{c}\text{Net present value} \\ \text{at high rate}\end{array}\right) - \left(\begin{array}{c}\text{Net present value} \\ \text{at low rate}\end{array}\right)}$$

$$= \frac{x - \text{Low rate}}{0 - \text{Net present value at low rate}}$$

$$\frac{.14 - .12}{(-1,521) - 1,020} = \frac{x - .12}{0 - 1,020}$$

$$\frac{.02}{(-2,541)} = \frac{x - .12}{-1,020}$$

By cross multiplying, we get

$$-20.4 = -2,541x + 304.92$$

$$2541x = 325.32$$

$$x = .128$$

The appropriate internal rate of return is 12.8 percent.

In actual practice, internal rate of return can be most conveniently established by using a commercially available electronic spreadsheet or even a reasonably advanced hand calculator. All of the major-brand spreadsheet programs incorporate a function which determines internal rate of return of a series of cash flows within a specified block. Both these programs and the hand calculators employ a trial-and-error algorithm. Consequently, to reduce computation time, they may require that the user specify an initial estimate of the rate of return as a starting point.

NET PRESENT VALUE VERSUS INTERNAL RATE OF RETURN

In selecting among alternative investments, a firm would normally choose the option with either the greater net present value or internal rate of return. Generally, but not always, the two will dictate the same choice. Differences are common when the internal rate of return is substantially greater than the applied rate of discount and when the projects differ in length of time.

Compare an investment outlay (Project A below) of $100,000 that provides a constant cash return of $53,000 for four years, with one (Project B below) having varying returns over the same period. With a discount rate or cost of capital of 10 percent, the present value of Project A is $67,999:

Period	Cash Flow	Present Value of Project A of $1 @ 10%	Present Value
0	$(100,000)	1.0000	$(100,000)
1	53,000	0.9091	48,182
2	53,000	0.8264	43,799
3	53,000	0.7513	39,819
4	53,000	0.6830	36,199
Total			$ 67,999

Period	Cash Flow	Present Value of Project B of $1 @ 10%	Present Value
0	$(100,000)	1.0000	$(100,000)
1	70,000	0.9091	63,637
2	56,000	0.8264	46,278
3	43,000	0.7513	32,306
4	31,000	0.6830	21,173
Total			$ 63,394

That of project B (as completed previously in Exhibit 20-1) is $63,394. Based on present value of cash flows, the clear choice is Project A. Project B, however, provides an internal rate of return of 41.772 percent, whereas that of Project A offers one of only 38.664 percent.[2] Hence based on internal rate of return, the choice would be Project B.

[2]*Proof*: When the cash flows associated with each of the projects are discounted by their internal rate of return, the present value is zero:

Period	Cash Flow	Present Value of Project A of $1 @ 38.664%	Present Value
0	$(100,000)	1.0000	$(100,000)
1	53,000	0.7212	38,222
2	53,000	0.5201	27,564
3	53,000	0.3751	19,879
4	53,000	0.2705	14,335
Total			$ 0

Period	Cash Flow	Present Value of Project B of $1 @ 41.772%	Present Value
0	$(100,000)	1.0000	$(100,000)
1	70,000	0.7054	49,378
2	56,000	0.4975	27,860
3	43,000	0.3509	15,089
4	31,000	0.2475	7,673
Total			$ 0

Exhibit 20-3 shows the net present value of the cash flows associated with each of the projects at varying discount rates. The x axis represents varying discount rates; the y axis, different present values. Thus, when discounted at its internal rate of return (i.e., 38.66 percent and 41.77 percent, respectively) the present value of each project is zero. When discounted at 10 percent, the present values (as per the preceding tables) are $67,999 and $63,394. When discounted at a rate of 20.43 percent, the two have approximately the same present value ($36,094).

When the two procedures yield different rankings, net present value should be preferred. Maximizing net present value is, after all, the *sine qua non* of investing.

Consider also Projects C and D, which have different lengths of life.

	Project C	Project D
Initial investment	$100,000	$100,000
Life of project	1 year	5 years
Annual cash returns	$ 20,000	$ 15,000
Return of investment at the end of project life	$100,000	$100,000

The internal rate of return that will be provided by Project C is 20 percent; that which will be provided by Project D is 15 percent. If internal rate of return were the decision criterion, the firm would select Project C over Project D.

EXHIBIT 20-3
Comparison of Net Present Values and Internal Rates of Return for Two Four-Year Investments, Project A and Project B

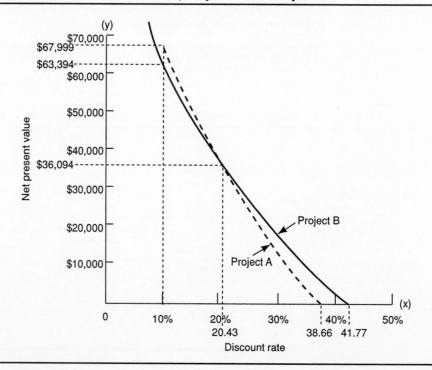

In contrast, suppose the firm uses a discount rate of 10 percent to evaluate investment opportunities. The net present value of the cash receipts and disbursements associated with Project C, discounted at a rate of 10 percent, is $9,091; that of Project D is $18,954. If present value of net cash receipts were the decision criterion, the firm would select Project D over Project C.

The different rankings here are a consequence of the differences in project life. Project C offers a higher rate of return, but for a shorter period of time than does Project D. The important question that management must address is what the firm will do with the funds that are returned to it at the end of one year, the conclusion of the life of Project C. If it were able to reinvest the principal of $100,000 in another project that would provide a return of $20,000 per year for four additional years, then it would be better off selecting Project C over Project D, which provides a return of only $15,000 per year. But if it were able to reinvest the principal in a project that would provide a return of only $10,000—that suggested by the discount rate of 10 percent—then Project C would be preferable.

If a firm were to select Project C over Project D on account of Project C's higher internal rate of return, then it would be assuming implicitly that its reinvestment rate on the funds from Project C subsequent to its termination was equal to that earned on the project during its life. If, however, it were to select Project D over Project C on account of Project D's greater net present value, then it would be assuming implicitly that the funds invested in Project C were, upon its termination, returned to the parties which provided them. The firm would no longer incur a cost of the capital; it would no longer earn a return on the capital.

Because both implicit assumptions may be contrary to the intentions of, or opportunities available to, the firm, it is best to avoid the dilemma of having to choose between the two techniques in circumstances in which they will provide different rankings. The firm should make every effort to equalize the useful lives of each competing proposal. This can be accomplished by making explicit reinvestment assumptions. Suppose, for example, that the $100,000 principal that will be returned to the firm at the expiration of Project C could be used to acquire marketable securities that would pay dividends and interest at a rate of 13 percent ($13,000) per year. The firm could incorporate into the cash flows of the project annual returns of $13,000 in years two through five and $100,000 at the end of year five, when for analytical convenience, it would assume that the securities would then be sold at no gain or loss.

OTHER CRITERIA FOR EVALUATING INVESTMENTS

Payback Period

A popular rule-of-thumb guide to investment profitability is *payback period*. Payback period indicates the number of years required to recover an initial outlay.

Payback period is conventionally calculated by dividing the initial investment outlay by the annual *cash* returns:

$$\text{Payback period} = \frac{\text{Investment outlay}}{\text{Annual net cash receipts}}$$

Previously in this chapter, we considered an investment of $47,912 that provided a return after taxes of $12,000 per year for five years. The payback period would be 3.99 years:

$$\frac{\$47,912}{\$12,000} = 3.99 \text{ years}$$

It would take the firm 3.99 years to get back its outlay of $47,912. In reality, it would take 4 years to recover this investment.

If the cash flows are not uniform in the years prior to that in which the initial outlay is recovered, then the cash flows of each year can be summed until an amount equal to the initial outlay is reached. If, for example, an investment required an initial outlay of $10,000 and the net cash receipts were $5,000 in year one, $4,000 in year two, and $3,000 in year three, then the payback period would be 2⅓ years; it would take the cash receipts in years one and two, plus one-third of the receipts in year three, to "pay off" the investment.

The payback period is useful when nothing more than an imprecise measure of the earnings potential of an investment is required. The shorter the payback period, the more desirable the investment. It is easily computed and understood, and it is particularly serviceable when managers are concerned with the length of time that funds will be "at risk."

The limitations of the payback period are that it does not take into account cash flows beyond the point where the initial investment has been recovered and it takes no account of the *timing* of receipts (i.e., of the time value of money). In the examples presented, neither the cash receipts of year five nor the pace of receipts and interest that can be earned on those receipts was incorporated into the analysis.

Suppose that a real estate developer had to select between two office complexes in which it could invest:

	Complex A	Complex B
Initial investment	$1,000,000	$1,000,000
Number of years that complex will be held	3 years	10 years
Estimated sale price when complex will be sold	$ 100,000	$1,000,000
Annual net cash receipts	$ 333,000	$ 250,000

The payback period for the investment in Complex A is three years—$1,000,000 ÷ $333,000; that for the investment in Complex B is four years—$1,000,000 ÷ $250,000. If payback were the decision criterion, then Complex A would be the more desirable. Yet internal rate of return, net present value, and common sense point to Complex B as preferable.

Because of its limitations, the payback period has been largely discredited by academics and others concerned with the theory of capital budgeting. Over the last four decades there has been a decided shift in practice away from the payback period method toward net present value and internal rate of return as investment decision criteria. Nevertheless, payback period remains in widespread use today, particularly in Japan.

Indeed, within the last several years, academic revisionists have come to view the payback period as not so bad after all. They have demonstrated analytically that for investments with certain characteristics, the *payback reciprocal* approximates the internal rate of return. *Payback reciprocal* is nothing more than the reciprocal of the payback formula; that is, annual net cash receipts divided by investment outlay, or 1 divided by payback period. For example, the payback reciprocal for a project with a payback of five years would be 1 divided by 5—20 percent. Payback reciprocal can be used as a surrogate for internal rate of return when the duration of the investment is at least twice the payback period and when the cash flows are uniform. It approaches internal rate of return as both the duration of the investment and the true internal rate of return increase.

Average Return on Investment

Another popular criterion for evaluating investment proposals is average return on investment. Average return on investment relates average net cash receipts after taxes *less* average depreciation to average lifetime investment:

Average return on investment

$$= \frac{\text{Average annual net cash receipts } - \text{ Average annual depreciation}}{\text{Average investment}}$$

$$= \frac{\text{Average net income}}{\text{Average investment}}$$

If straight-line depreciation is charged, average investment would be

$$\frac{\text{Initial investment } - \text{ Salvage value (or other recoverable amount)}}{2}$$

The average investment on the previously presented investment of $47,912 that provided annual net cash receipts of $12,000 and allowed for the recovery of $10,000 upon termination of the project at the end of five years would be

$$\frac{\$47,912 - \$10,000}{2} = \$18,956$$

(If accelerated depreciation were charged, this formula for computing average investment would be inappropriate inasmuch as the remaining book value of the investment would be less in each year of project life than if straight-line depreciation were charged. It would be necessary to determine the remaining book value of the investment at the end of each year and calculate the average book value over the life of the asset.) Using the straight-line method, annual depreciation charges would be

$$\frac{\$47,912 - \$10,000}{5 \text{ years}} = \$7,582$$

Average return on investment would be, therefore,

$$\frac{\$12,000 - \$7,582}{\$18,956} = 23\%$$

Average return on investment, unlike payback period, *does* take into account amounts received throughout the life of an investment. It is computationally convenient and, because it incorporates depreciation into the calculation, it is reflective of rate of return as it would be determined on the basis of data reported in financial statements intended for investors. One of the primary deficiencies of average return on investment as a decision criterion is that it does not give effect to the time value of money. Cash flows that occur early in the life of the project, and which are thereby of greater value to an organization, are weighted the same as those that occur later. Furthermore, average return on investment tends to approach the internal rate of return as both the investment period and the rate-of-return decrease.

CAPITAL RATIONING AND MUTUALLY EXCLUSIVE PROJECTS

When sufficient capital is not available or obtainable to finance all projects that either have a positive discounted cash flow or are above the internal rate of return cut-off, then capital must be *rationed*.

A means of *rationing* capital among *mutually exclusive* projects is a *profitability index*. The term *mutually exclusive* is used to characterize a project whose selection would exclude another project from also being selected. For example, when a firm has to decide among two or more plant locations, research projects, or acquisitions, each of the possibilities may be considered mutually exclusive. So also are those projects whose selection would consume enough of the available capital to prevent funding others. A profitability index can be developed by dividing the present value of each project's cash flows by the initial required investment. For each project, the outcome would be a ratio of discounted cash flow to required investment. The projects could then be ranked by their ratios, and projects would be funded in rank order. Obviously, this procedure is inappropriate when the required investment outlay must be made over several periods rather than up front. In this case, alternative, more sophisticated selection procedures would have to be employed.

TAKING INTO ACCOUNT RISK AND UNCERTAINTY

Characteristic of most expenditure decisions is risk—uncertainty about the outcome of the possible courses of action. The effectiveness of even the most sophisticated decision models is limited by the reliability of the underlying predictions of cash flows. There is an extensive body of literature on decision making in the face of uncertainty. Regrettably, it does not provide the guidance necessary for ordinary managers to become clairvoyant. It does, however, provide insight into how statistical probability, as well as managerial experience, judgment, or intuition can be explicitly incorporated into an evaluation of options under consideration.

Management decisions can be characterized by the number of independent events which determine the outcome of the course of action selected. When the outcome depends on a large number of independent events, management is able to benefit from the "certainty" that results from combining a large number of events, each of which individually is uncertain. In evaluating the cost of a proposed employee life insurance plan, for example, a manager has no way of predicting whether a particular employee will die during the period of coverage. But provided with sufficient demographic data about the employee population, an actuary could forecast with considerable accuracy the *total* number of employees who *will* pass away. In contrast, when the overall result depends on but a single event, the "law" of large numbers cannot be applied. A predictable number of favorable occurrences is not available to offset a predictable number of unfavorable occurrences. When an aircraft manufacturer undertakes the development of a unique commercial aircraft, there is no population of similar projects to support statistically defensible predictions of success. The project stands alone. Success in some projects cannot be counted on to offset failures in others.

If the return on an investment project will depend on the outcome of numerous independent events, then it is possible to compute an *expected value* of the return. The expected value is an average of the possible outcomes, weighted by the probability that each will occur. Suppose that a real estate developer is considering purchasing a resort complex that comprises a large number of apartments. The apartments are rented by the week. The cash flow for any individual month depends on the number of weeks that an apartment is rented. The firm has had extensive rental experience with similar properties and has been able to determine the probabilities of apartments being occupied for varying periods of time. The weekly rental charge is $300. The following table summarizes the probabilities of possible rental periods and the associated cash receipts:

Number of Weeks per Month of Occupancy	Expected Likelihood of Rental	Rental Receipts for Such a Period (Number of Weeks Times $300)
4 weeks	.20	$1,200
3 weeks	.35	900
2 weeks	.30	600
1 week	.10	300
0 weeks	.05	0
	100%	

The expected value (EV) of the rent receipts for any one apartment is the average of the possible rent receipts, weighted by the related probabilities. Thus,

$$EV = .20(\$1,200) + .35(\$900) + .30(\$600) + .10(\$300) + .05(\$0)$$

$$= \$240 + \$315 + \$180 + \$30 + \$0$$

$$= \$765$$

To the extent that the past experience of the real estate firm is relevant to the future, it can use the expected value of the per apartment receipts to approximate the total receipts for the entire project. Obviously, no one apartment can be expected to provide receipts of $765, but *on average* the receipts of the entire complex can be expected to be near $765 per apartment. The greater the number of apartments, the smaller will be the deviation from the expected mean (average) of $765.

If, on the other hand, the return on an investment depends on a single outcome, then the "laws" of probability cannot be relied on to produce an expected *average* outcome. The "average" outcome will be the actual outcome. Nevertheless, managers can incorporate uncertainty into an analysis *as if* there were a large number of recurring events by assigning to the outcomes *subjective probabilities*. Subjective probabilities represent a particular individual's assessment of the likelihood of a particular outcome. They may be developed on the basis of past experience, judgment, or merely "hunch." Based on subjective probabilities derived from its past experience, for example, the aforementioned real estate firm might assert that the subjective probabilities of any *single* apartment being occupied for four weeks is 20 percent; for three weeks 35 percent; and so on. Then, by weighting the possible outcomes by the subjective probabilities, it could compute an expected value of the rental receipts for a particular month. The expected value would, of course, be the same $765 as determined previously.

But such expected value has to be interpreted with care. If the developer were to acquire 100 apartments, then it could assert with reasonable assurance that the total receipts would be approximately $76,500 ($765 × 100 apartments). They might be somewhat greater or less, but if the past experience on which the company developed its probabilities was both reliable and relevant, then the deviation from an average of $765 per apartment should not be great. By contrast, if the developer were to acquire but a single apartment, then the actual cash receipts *cannot* be $765. They may be $0, $300, $600, $900, or $1,200. The expected value of $765 represents merely a weighted average of possible outcomes.

Subjective probabilities can be incorporated into an evaluation of capital projects by computing the *expected value* of their cash flows. The following example illustrates how this can be accomplished.

Example: Evaluating a Project in the Face of Uncertainty

A motion picture studio must decide whether to produce a film, the temperamental director of which, although creative, has little regard for accountants, their budgets, and their financial controls. The cost of the film is planned initially to be $20 million, but experienced studio executives view that amount with suspicion. If the film is successful, it could generate $60 million in film rentals over a three-year period. Studio executives consider that amount to be more of a goal than a prediction.

The financial planners have assigned the probabilities to costs and revenues that are shown in Part A of Exhibit 20-4.

The costs, it may be assumed, will have to be paid at the end of the first year after production begins. The revenues will be received at the end of the years indicated. The company applies a discount rate of 14 percent to all investment proposals. Part B of Exhibit 20-4 indicates the *expected* present value of the net cash receipts.

The expected present value of the cash receipts exceeds that of the cash disbursements by $6.66 million. Consistent with the criterion of expected present value of cash receipts, the company should undertake the production of the film.

An actual distribution of possible outcomes may contain an infinite number of points. In the example, however, the distribution was described by only three points (unfavorable, neutral, favorable). The company executives could obtain greater precision in the computation of expected value

EXHIBIT 20-4
Expected Value of Net Cash Flows

A. Probabilities of Costs and Revenues

	Costs		Revenues			
		Amount		Amount (millions)		
State	Probability	(millions)	Probability	Year 1	Year 2	Year 3
Unfavorable	.5	$40	.3	$15	$ 6	$ 2
Neutral	.4	30	.5	25	15	5
Favorable	.1	20	.2	30	20	10

B. Unadjusted Cash Flows (millions)

	Year 1	Year 2	Year 3	Total	Probability	Expected Value
Receipts						
Unfavorable outcome						
Unadjusted	$15.00	$ 6.00	$ 2.00			
Present value of $1 @ 14%	.8772	.7695	.6750			
Adjusted	$13.16	4.62	1.35	$19.13	.3	$ 5.74
Neutral outcome						
Unadjusted	$25.00	$15.00	$ 5.00			
Present value of $1 @ 14%	.8772	.7695	.6750			
Adjusted	$21.93	$11.54	$ 3.38	$36.85	.5	$18.43
Favorable outcome						
Unadjusted	$30.00	$20.00	$10.00			
Present value of $1 @ 14%	.8772	.7695	.6750			
Adjusted	$26.32	$15.39	$ 6.75	$48.46	.2	$ 9.69
Total receipts						$33.86
Disbursements						
Unfavorable outcome						
Unadjusted	$40.00					
Present value of $1 @ 14%	.8772					
Adjusted	$39.09			$35.09	.3	$10.53
Neutral outcome						
Unadjusted	$30.00					
Present value of $1 @ 14%	.8772					
Adjusted	$26.32			$26.32	.5	$13.16
Favorable outcome						
Unadjusted	$20.00					
Present value of $1 @ 14%	.8772					
Adjusted	$17.54			$17.54	.2	$ 3.51
Total disbursements						$27.20
Expected present value of net cash receipts (receipts less disbursements)						$ 6.66

by assigning probabilities to other possible outcomes (e.g., receipts of $25 or $35 million).

There is considerable risk to management in focusing exclusively on the "bottom line" of Exhibit 20-4, the expected present value of net cash receipts ($6.66 million). This amount represents only a weighted average of possible outcomes. Management should properly consider also the shape of the distribution of possible outcomes. A widely dispersed distribution of possible outcomes might suggest that the project is one of high risk; the net cash receipts could be considerably higher or lower than the expected average. A narrow distribution would suggest a project of less risk; the actual outcome is likely to be in the vicinity of the expected average. Management should also take into account the consequences of the possible outcomes, particularly the highly unfavorable ones. In the example, there is a 30 percent chance that the present value of the costs will be $35.09 and a 30 percent chance that the present value of the receipts will be only $19.13. There is, therefore, a combined probability of .09 (.30 times .30) that the company will incur a loss of $15.96. Corporate executives must question whether the firm could withstand a loss of this magnitude. If it could not, then the project should be rejected, even though "on average" it can be anticipated that the project will be profitable. Indeed, just as it is possible to drown in a stream with an average depth of only a few inches, so too it is possible to experience fiscal catastrophe by undertaking a project in which the weighted average of expected present values is positive.

Sensitivity Analysis

Sensitivity analysis is the generic term for examining the extent to which predicted outcomes are dependent upon assumed variables. It is often referred to as "what if" analysis.

Where uncertainty is involved, some estimates, of course, are more crucial to an investment analysis than others. A decision to construct a new plant is more likely to result in economic disaster because of major construction cost overruns than because revenues of the distant future (of equal total dollar amount) failed to live up to expectations.

There are numerous mathematical, linear programming, and statistical models available to measure the sensitivity of an analysis to the specified parameters. Typically, in these models the contribution margin associated with changes in any of the project inputs is identified. That is, the *opportunity cost of the next best alternative* is calculated and assessed. In some models, a break-even point is determined such that a specified percentage change in one of the key variables (e.g., a 10 percent decline in forecast sales volume) would cause a switch in the preferability ranking among competing projects.

Electronic spreadsheets, of course, also give managers the capability to ask "what if" questions and to readily test a range of potential scenarios. At the very least, in light of their convenience, managers should use them to examine a wide range of possibilities (e.g., pessimistic, most likely, and optimistic).

Taking into Account the Costs and Benefits of Indecision

The rapid pace of technological change adds complexity to capital budgeting. Firms may understandably be reluctant to lock themselves into a specific project or course of action knowing that technological developments in the near future may prove that their choice was misguided. Therefore, they would like to put off a decision until they have better information as to the anticipated developments. Yet at the same time, a delay is certain to involve costs. Not only might it postpone needed enhancements to existing systems or facilities, but it might foreclose other opportunities that must be acted upon immediately. For example, firms are almost always aware of more powerful and less expensive computer systems that are soon to be released. But postponing the acquisition decision requires that they continue to operate with their current, presumably inefficient, systems.

When the costs and benefits of delay are significant, managers should take advantage of mathematical models that enable them to incorporate these factors into their decision. These models are beyond the scope of this text. Nevertheless, even for decisions for which formal models are unnecessary, managers should recognize waiting as one possible alternative and assess its costs and benefits.

Attitudes Toward Risk

Corporations, like individuals, have personalities. Some are willing to assume risks; others are "risk adverse." Inasmuch as capital projects are inherently uncertain, it is especially important that the attitudes toward risk of the individual managers who will make the expenditure decisions are in harmony with those of the corporation as a whole. Attitudes toward risk are not merely a matter of subjective emotions. It may be perfectly rational, and in their respective self-interests, for individual managers and their companies to be willing to assume different levels of risk.

Suppose that a corporation is offered the opportunity to spend $50 million on a project that would provide a 50 percent chance of a total return of $0 and a 50 percent chance of a total return of $105 million. The expected value of the project would be $2.5 million:

Expected value of receipts .50($0) + .50 ($105)	$52.5
Less: Expected value of disbursement 1.0($50.0)	50.0
Expected value of project	$ 2.5

Because the expected value is positive, the decision model that has been presented in the preceding section would indicate that the investment is one that should be taken advantage of.

The analysis to this point, however, fails to take into account what would be gained or lost in terms of overall corporate well-being. If the outcome is successful, the corporation may achieve a significant increase in earnings which would allow for an increase in its dividend rate. If it is unsuccessful, it might be forced to terminate operations. If the costs of termination are greater than the benefits of the increase in earnings, then the investment opportunity may not, in fact, be as propitious as it first appeared. The *utility* of the dollars lost may be greater than those of the dollars to be gained.

As a rule, the more dollars a party has or stands to gain, the less the utility (i.e., value) of each incremental dollar. If the wealth of an individual or corporation is negligible, then a small number of additional dollars may facilitate substantial improvements in quality of life. If, however, the party is already affluent, then the same number of dollars would have but an insignificant impact on its well-being.

Whether or not the investment opportunity just referred to is advantageous will depend on the characteristics and objectives of the particular company to which it was offered. Of pervasive importance is likely to be the size of the company. If the company were large—several billion dollars in earnings—then the proposal would probably represent a sound business risk. The consequences of losing $50 million would not be substantial; the expected value of the possible increase in overall well-being would exceed the expected value of the potential decrease. In contrast, if the firm were a small business with earnings of only several million dollars, the consequences of failure may far outweigh the benefits of success. The expected value of the investment project in terms of well-being may well be negative and, hence, an unsound business risk.

In any organization, particularly a large one in which the managers are not owners, it is possible—perhaps even likely—that the managers who must make capital expenditure decisions will assess the "value" of potential gains and losses in the context of their own character traits and objectives rather than those of the corporation. As indicated, the aforementioned investment project may well represent a sound business risk from the perspective of a large corporation but not necessarily a small one. The manager of one unit of the corporation, however, could quite reasonably reject the proposal because the consequences of failure would be severe both to his unit and to him personally. At an extreme, for example, a substantial decrease in earnings could cause elimination of the organizational unit and the termination of the manager's position.

Procedures have been developed to explicitly incorporate into capital expenditure analysis the *utility* of incremental dollars to a particular company.[3] In essence, these techniques require that dollars be translated into a measure of utility (e.g., "utils") and that expected value be computed in terms of such measure rather than dollars. For example, selected dollar amounts may be expressed in utils as follows:

Dollars	Utils
$ 0	0
25,000	2,400
50,000	4,600
100,000	8,700
105,000	9,100

This table suggests that to a particular firm, $100,000 is "worth" not four times more than $25,000, but only 3.6 times (8,700 utils divided by 2,400 utils).

If a corporation is offered the opportunity to spend $50,000 on a project that would provide a 50 percent chance of a total return of $0 and a 50 percent chance of a total return of $105,000, then the expected return in utils would be negative, indicating that the opportunity should be forgone:

Expected value of receipts .50(0 utils) + .50 (9,100 utils)	4,550 utils
Expected value of disbursement 1.0 (4,600 utils)	4,600 utils
Expected value of project	(50 utils)

[3]See, for example, Ralph O. Swalm, "Utility Theory—Insights into Risk Theory," *Harvard Business Review*, vol. 44, No. 6 (November-December), 1966, pp. 123–136. Swalm describes techniques of eliciting from an individual his or her valuations of dollars in terms of utils.

Reference to this type of utility analysis is not made in this text because of its wide use in practice. In fact, it has proven difficult to implement and, as a consequence, is by no means an accepted managerial procedure. Awareness of it, however, should serve to sensitize a manager to the limitations of the conventional means of incorporating uncertainty into expenditure analysis. Monetary units, such as dollars, are an inadequate expression of either corporate or individual well-being. Merely because an investment has a positive expected dollar value, it is not necessarily likely to enhance the overall utility of the party assuming the risk.

THE IMPACT OF PRICE CHANGES

Future inflation represents another element of uncertainty and risk that often troubles the evaluation and assessment of long-term capital projects. First, inflation is likely to affect the future cash flows of alternative investment projects differently. In periods of a rising general price level (i.e., inflation), cash flows associated with some projects are likely to rise more than in proportion to the rate of general inflation; cash flows on other projects are likely to rise less than in proportion to the general inflation. The first task of the evaluator, then, is to take account of any and all expected changes of *specific prices* associated with expected cash flows. For example, suppose that the expected operating savings on the first project we analyzed in this chapter, summarized in Exhibit 20-1, were expected to rise only 6 percent per year even though inflation was expected to be 10 percent per year over each of the four years for which the project was to run. Repair costs, on the other hand, were expected to increase by 12 percent per year. The amended future cash flow projections, in nominal dollar terms, would then be

	Year			
	1	2	3	4
Operating savings	$79,500	$84,270	$89,326	$94,686
Repair costs	5,600	23,834	44,958	69,235
Net cash inflow	$73,900	$60,436	$44,368	$25,451

Notice that while the expected net cash inflows are higher in the first three years as compared to what they were before adjustments for specific price changes, they are actually lower in nominal terms in the last year because repair costs, expected to rise by more than the inflation rate, are increasing sharply—independently of price changes.

The second task is to adjust for expected *changes in the value of the dollar*. With expected general inflation of 10 percent per year, the analyst must deflate each of the aforementioned net cash inflow figures by $(1.10)^n$ to express each in terms of the value of today's dollar. Thus,

	Year			
	1	2	3	4
Net cash inflow adjusted for the change in the value of the dollar	$67,182	$49,947	$33,334	$17,383

The last task, then, is to decide how inflation is going to affect the cost of capital. One cannot assume automatically that the nominal rate of interest will rise to 20 percent simply because it was expected to be 10 percent without inflation and the inflation rate is expected to be 10 percent. Assume instead that the nominal rate is likely to lag inflation, and rise by only 18 percent. Thus, real cost of capital is expected to be 8 percent. It is this real cost of capital that must be used to discount the constant dollar, price-adjusted future cash flows at the real cost of capital. The present value of the future cash flows adjusted for the change in the value of the dollar would then be discounted at 8 percent:

$$\$62,206 + \$42,822 + \$26,462 + \$12,777 = \$144,267$$

$$(e.g., 62,206 = 67,182 \div 1.08 \text{ and } 42,822 = 49,947 \div (1.08)^2)$$

Net present value, after deducting the initial investment of $100,000, would be $44,267, rather than the $63,394 projected in Exhibit 20-1. The internal rate of return on the investment based on these adjusted amounts would be 22.069 percent, substantially less than the 41.77 percent calculated earlier in this chapter.

Summary

The essence of capital budgeting is the analysis of either cash flows or excess current incomes. Gains and losses as well as depreciation are elements of income that do not reflect either the receipt or disbursement of cash. They do, however, enter into the determination of income taxes, an expenditure which requires a disbursement of cash.

Receipts and disbursements take place at difference times throughout the life of a project. Owing to the time value of money, they must be discounted back to the present. The cash flow and excess current income approaches to project analysis take into account not only the time value of money but a specific cost of capital. Other techniques, such as the internal rate of return, average return on investment, and payback period, do not factor in a specific cost of capital, and the latter two take no account even of the time value of money in valuing the worth of cash flows.

Uncertainty may be incorporated into capital budgeting analyses by assigning probabilities to the various possible outcomes. The expected value of any particular receipt or disbursement would represent an average, weighted by the probabilities, of the possible receipts or disbursements. In general, in the absence of a need for capital rationing, a proposal should be accepted if the expected value of the net discounted cash receipts is positive. If capital rationing is required, a profitability index may aid in choosing among possibilities. However, in either case the consequences of the possible gains and losses must also be taken into account. Even though the expected value of a project is positive, the utility of the potential losses may exceed that of the expected gains. Further, inflation and other facets of uncertainty must also be incorporated into the decision process.

Appendix: An Excess Current Income Approach to Investment Decision Making

Even though, as we have emphasized repeatedly, present value techniques are based on flows of cash, not income, some firms use a procedure in which they discount *income* rather than cash. This procedure is not only acceptable, it may actually be preferable to that in which cash is discounted. If properly employed, the discounted income procedure will lead to the *exact same result* as the discounted cash routine. One of the virtues of the discounted income procedure, however, is that it highlights the financing costs implicitly tied up in the project under consideration. It may also incorporate into the analysis continuous changes in balance sheet values which, if properly computed, reflect current market values and so be useful in decisions to be made over the life of the asset.

Exhibit 20-5 illustrates the excess current income approach. A company is considering a machine that costs $100,000 and will provide operating savings, prior to repair costs and depreciation, of $75,000 per year for four years (the same as in Exhibit 20-1). Repair costs, as shown in Exhibit 20-1, increase from year to year.

As was evident from Exhibit 20-1, the present value of net *cash receipts* from the project, discounted at 10 percent, is $63,394.

The income analysis in Exhibit 20-5 starts with the cash savings after deducting repair costs. To arrive at the "excess" (or residual) income (actually excess of revenues over expenses), depreciation and financing costs must be deducted as expenses. *Only income, not the initial investment, is discounted since the initial investment is accounted for in the depreciation charges.* The finance costs are based on the beginning-of-year book values (cost less accumulated depreciation) of the investment, assuming the same rate as the discount rate. The finance costs must be included whether they are explicit (actually paid as interest) or implicit (the expected return to stockholders).

In Part I of Exhibit 20-5, the company uses straight-line depreciation. The discounted value of the excess income flows is $63,394, the same as that of the cash flows. In Part II the company uses deprival value depreciation, which takes into account the specific value of the asset to the company as indicated by what the company would

EXHIBIT 20-5
Capital Expenditure Analysis Using Present Value of Excess Current Incomes

	I. Straight-Line Depreciation Employed						
	Relevant Cash Flows and Excess Current Incomes in Year					Present Value of $1	Discounted Income Flows (present values)
	0	1	2	3	4		
Net cash flows after repairs (per Exhibit 20-1)		$70,000	$56,000	$43,000	$31,000		
Less: Straight-line depreciation		(25,000)	(25,000)	(25,000)	(25,000)		
Implicit or explicit interest costs*		(10,000)	(7,500)	(5,000)	(2,500)		
Excess current income Year 1		$35,000				0.9091	$31,818
Year 2			$23,500			0.8264	19,420
Year 3				$13,000		0.7513	9,766
Year 4					$3,500	0.6830	2,390
Present value of excess current incomes							$63,394
Book value of asset (cost less accumulated depreciation)	$100,000	$75,000	$50,000	$25,000	$0		

*10% of beginning of period book value.

EXHIBIT 20-5 Continued

II. Deprival Value Depreciation Employed

	Relevant Cash Flows in Year					Present Value of $1	Discounted Income Flows (present values)
	0	1	2	3	4		
Net cash flows after repairs (per Exhibit 20-1)		$70,000	$56,000	$43,000	$31,000		
Less:							
Deprival value depreciation		(40,000)	(30,000)	(20,000)	(10,000)		
Implicit or explicit interest costs*		(10,000)	(6,000)	(3,000)	(1,000)		
Excess current income							
Year 1		$20,000				0.9091	$18,181
Year 2			$20,000			0.8264	16,528
Year 3				$20,000		0.7513	15,025
Year 4					$20,000	0.6830	13,660
Present value of excess current incomes							$63,394
Book value of asset (cost less accumulated depreciation)	$100,000	$60,000	$30,000	$10,000	$0		

*10% of beginning of period book value.

be willing to pay for the asset if it were suddenly deprived of it. Whatever depreciation method is employed, the discounted value of the excess income stream remains the same, $63,394. But use of deprival values and deprival value depreciation, it turns out, is consistent with a *constant excess current income stream*.

The *deprival* value of an asset is the amount that a firm would be willing to pay for the asset if it were hypothetically deprived of it. Determination of deprival value requires comparing an asset's current cost (the amount that would be required to replace it), net realizable value (amount for which it could be sold), and net present value (present value of anticipated cash flows). If present value of future cash flows exceeds current purchase cost (entry value), which in turn exceeds net realizable value (sales price)— the normal case—the firm would pay only current purchase cost to replace an asset if "deprived" of it. If, on the other hand, an asset's current purchase cost exceeds its present value (its value in use), then the most it would be willing to pay if deprived of it would be the present value. At any amount above present value, the company would be paying more than the value of the returns.

Straight-line depreciation employed in Part I of Exhibit 20-5 would yield used asset values that simply would not represent what the market would be willing to pay for assets that were one, two, or three years old. Users of an asset such as that treated in Exhibit 20-5 would not pay $75,000 for a one-year-old asset, or $50,000 for a two-year-old asset. If, for example, a two-year-old asset were purchased initially, and another at the end of the second year of a four year period, for $50,000 each as suggested by straight-line depreciation valuation, the net present value of the cash flow stream would not match that gained by purchasing a new asset and using it for the full four years.

$$-\$50,000 + \$43,000 \times p_{\overline{1}|.10} + \$31,000 \times p_{\overline{2}|.10} - \$50,000 \times p_{\overline{2}|.10}$$
$$+ \$43,000 \times p_{\overline{3}|.10} + \$31,000 \times p_{\overline{4}|.10} = \$26,868,$$

which is considerably less than the $63,394 net present value that could be realized by purchase of a new asset in period 0 and using it for four years. If, on the other hand, the two-year-old asset could be purchased for its deprival depreciation value of $30,000, a user would be *indifferent* about the above option, for both choices would yield the same net present value of $63,394. Arriving at asset values by computing a *constant excess current income stream,*

$$X \times P_{\overline{4}|.10} = \$63,394, \text{ or}$$

$$X = \frac{\$63,394}{3.1699} = \$20,000,$$

and subtracting this along with the implicit or explicit interest costs on the beginning-of-the-period investment from net cash flows will yield a deprival value depreciation figure consistent with used asset values that should, in theory, logically prevail in the market place.

The present value of excess current income method serves just as well as the discounted cash flows method in making the initial investment decision. But the excess current income method has an additional advantage of highlighting changes in asset values.

While the method of depreciation chosen will not affect the *initial decision* to invest, it may well have an impact on *intermediate decisions* over the life of the asset. By electing to use a deprival value depreciation method, consistent with a *constant excess current income stream* over the life of the asset, managers can explicitly build into their analyses the "economic" cost of using an asset each year and thereby assess the optimum time either to sell the asset or trade it in for another.

For purposes of project evaluation, *deprival value depreciation* offers decided benefits. Under deprival value depreciation, the annual depreciation charge would be the decrease between beginning- and end-of-year deprival values. Consequently, managers would automatically have to make, and take into account, estimates of an asset's present value, current cost, and replacement value. These estimates would enable them to assess the advantages of acquiring, and then periodically replacing, a series of several used assets rather than a single new asset. Suppose, for example, that an asset has a four-year useful life. Depending on the relationship between new and used asset prices, the firm might be better off buying a series of one-year-old assets (and using them for three years) than new assets, which it could use for four years.[4] Hence, the excess current value approach, with depreciation based on deprival values, might open the door for consideration of options that might otherwise be ignored.

Exercise for Review and Self-Testing

A company has the opportunity to replace an old machine with a new. The following data pertain to the two machines:

	New Machine	Old Machine
Purchase price	$200,000	
Original cost		$120,000
Accumulated depreciation		$30,000
Remaining useful life	5 years	5 years
Amount for which machine could be sold today		$80,000
Salvage value in five years	$50,000	$40,000
Annual depreciation charges	$30,000	$10,000

[4]In some industries it may not be economically feasible to acquire used plant and equipment. In others, such as the airline industry, it is quite common for companies to acquire used equipment.

The old machine will require $92,000 in cash per year to operate. Company engineers believe that there is a 60 percent probability that the new machine will require $70,000 and a 40 percent chance that it will require only $50,000 per year in cash to operate.

The company evaluates investment proposals using a discount rate of 12 percent. Gains on the sale of equipment and ordinary income are both taxed at a rate of 30 percent. The firm expects to sell other equipment at a gain during the year; any losses incurred on the sale of the old machine could be used to offset those gains.

1. If the company elects to replace the old machine with the new, what would be the required initial outlay, taking into account the reduction in taxes owing to the loss on the sale of the old machine?
2. What is the expected value of the annual operating costs of the new machine prior to taking into account income taxes?
3. What are the expected values of the annual operating costs of the new machine and the old machine after taking into account the tax reductions associated with both the direct operating costs and the charges for depreciation? What are the *present* values of these amounts?
4. What are the present values of the amounts to be received upon the sale of both the new machine and the old machine at the end of their useful lives?
5. What are the net present values of the disbursements associated with the two alternatives? Based on the criteria of net present value, should the company replace the old machine with the new?
6. Determine the after-tax internal rate of return of the proposed expenditure. The cost of the new machine can best be represented by the net required outlay (as calculated in part 1). The annual return would be the difference between the per year after-tax operating costs of the new machine and the old (the cost indicated in part 3, prior to discounting). The relevant salvage value would be the difference between what would be received upon the sale of the new machine and the old. In attempting to find the rate that equates the present values of the inflows to the present value of the outflows, first try a rate of 7 percent.

<hr>

Questions for Review and Discussion

1. How would you determine an appropriate rate of discount or cost of capital?
2. Depreciation is a noncash expense. Yet it is an element to be considered in calculating the net present value of an investment project even with a discounted cash flow approach. Why, and to what extent, must depreciation be taken into account in determining the net present value of a project?
3. In calculating the net present value of an investment project, how should the interest payments associated with the loans made to finance the project be taken into account in a pure cash flow approach? In an excess current income approach?
4. Suppose that a firm must choose between two projects, one of which would provide a substantially greater internal rate of return than the other. Both projects entail the same degree of risk. Why might it be in the interest of the firm to select the project with the *lower* internal rate of return? Why might the project that provides the greater rate of return have the smaller net present value?
5. What is the common deficiency of both payback period and accounting rate of return as means of evaluating investment proposals? How can the use of either be defended?
6. What are *subjective probabilities*? What is subjective about them? Why must they be resorted to?
7. What is a significant limitation of *expected value* as a decision criterion? Indicate by way of an example how two proposals could have the same expected value, yet one would clearly be more consistent with a firm's objectives than the other.

8. A gambler has an opportunity to place two bets. The first would require an outlay of $45. There would be a .5 probability of a return of zero and a .5 probability of a return of $100. The second would require an outlay of $45,000. There would be a .5 probability of a return of zero and a .5 probability of a return of $100,000. Why might the gambler (quite rationally) accept the former and reject the latter?

9. Why is it generally preferable that a firm separate the decision to acquire an asset from that as to whether it should purchase or lease it; that is, why should a firm first decide whether to acquire an asset, based on the cash price, and then determine whether a lease arrangement is preferable to an outright purchase?

Problems

1. *Tax expenditures and savings must be taken into account in evaluating investment proposals.*

Mifflin Co. has the opportunity to acquire a new machine that would replace an old one. The machine would cost $80,000 and would have a useful life of 10 years with no salvage value. Acquisition of the new machine would necessitate special training for the operators at a cost of $7,000. It would enable the firm to reduce annual cash operating costs by $8,000.

The old machine has a remaining useful life of 10 years, and it is estimated that there will be no salvage value at the end of its life. The book value of the machine is presently $50,000 and annual depreciation charges are $5,000. If the new machine were purchased, the old machine would be sold for $30,000.

The tax rate is 40 percent on ordinary income and 20 percent on the sale of plant and equipment. The new machine would be eligible for an investment tax credit of 10 percent. The training costs would be amortized over the life of the asset, but for tax purposes they would be deductible immediately. The company takes depreciation on a straight-line basis. The firm has sufficient ordinary income and gains on the sale of plant and equipment to offset (and thereby benefit from) any taxable losses associated with the sale of the old machine and the acquisition of the new.

The firm accepts expenditure proposals only if they provide an after-tax return of 10 percent or greater.

a. Determine the net after-tax cash outlay (including training costs) that would be required if the machine were purchased.

b. Determine the annual net after-tax cash savings.

c. Determine whether the machine would provide an after-tax return on investment of 10 percent or more.

2. *Accelerated methods of depreciation, relative to the straight-line method, provide an investment incentive.*

Trans Texas Trucking Co. is considering the purchase of a new truck. The cost of the truck will be $100,000. It will have a useful life of four years and an estimated salvage value of $20,000. The firm estimates that the new truck would enable it to increase annual cash earnings, prior to depreciation and taxes, by $35,000. The firm would only purchase the truck if it would provide a return, after taxes, of 12 percent. The marginal rate of income tax for the firm is 46 percent.

a. Suppose that Internal Revenue Service regulations require that the firm use the straight-line method of depreciation. Should the firm accept the proposal to acquire the new truck?

b. Now suppose that the IRS requires the firm to use the accelerated cost recovery system and classifies these trucks as five-year property. The appropriate depreciation rates each year would be 15%, 22%, 21%, 21%, and 21%, respectively. Should the firm accept the proposal to acquire the new truck?

3. *The excess current income approach clarifies the relationship between cash flows and income. (This problem is intended for solution using an electronic spreadsheet.)*

A firm is contemplating the acquisition of an asset that will provide the following revenues (in cash) after deducting all operating costs other than depreciation (in millions):

Year 1	$700
Year 2	500
Year 3	300
Year 4	100

The asset would cost $900 million, the entire amount to be paid upon acquisition. The firm estimates its cost of capital at 10 percent and uses that percent as its discount rate.

a. Determine the present value of net cash flows.

b. Determine the present value of excess current income (revenues less depreciation and an imputed cost of capital based on the book value of the asset at the start of each year).

   (1) Assume first that the company uses the straight-line method of depreciation.

   (2) Assume instead that the company uses the sum-of-the-years' digits method.

   (3) Comment on why the present values are (or are not) the same.

c. Compute the internal rate of return.

4. *This exercise contrasts four means of evaluating investment proposals. Note particularly how the different criteria result in different rankings.*

A firm is evaluating three investment proposals. Each requires an initial outlay of $80,000. The net cash inflows associated with each are as follows:

	Net Cash Receipts under Proposal		
Year	A	B	C
1	$25,000	$10,000	$40,000
2	25,000	20,000	30,000
3	25,000	30,000	20,000
4	25,000	50,000	10,000

For each of the proposals, compute the measures of return indicated. Determine the order of preferability of the proposals using each of the measures as a criterion.

a. Payback period

b. Accounting rate of return

c. Net present value

   (1) Using a discount rate of 15 percent

   (2) Using a discount rate of 2 percent

d. Internal rate of return (within 1%). For convenience, in computing the rates of return of Proposals B and C, interpolate between the rates of 15 percent and 2 percent.

5. *Different investment criteria—including net present value and internal rate of return, which are similar in nature—may result in different rankings of proposals.*

Bexar Investment Co. is considering three mutually exclusive investment proposals.

Proposal A requires an initial outlay of $100,000 and provides a return of $26,380 for each of five years.

Proposal B requires an initial outlay of $50,000 and provides a return of $13,870 for each of five years.

Proposal C requires an initial outlay of $100,000 and provides returns as follows:

Year 1	$50,000	Year 4	$7,000
Year 2	40,000	Year 5	4,400
Year 3	10,000		

The firm's after-tax cost of capital is 5 percent.

a. For each of the three proposals, calculate:
  (1) Net present value
  (2) Internal rate of return
  (3) Payback period
b. Rank the proposals according to each of the three criteria.
c. Comment on why Proposal A has a greater net present value but lower internal rate of return than does Proposal B. Suppose that Proposal A and Proposal B were mutually exclusive. How should the firm decide between the two proposals? What other information must be incorporated into the analysis?

6. *Investment projects that have a positive net present value may not always be "profitable."*

Amerex, Inc., is evaluating a proposal to modernize its plant by acquiring new equipment. The equipment that it is considering would cost $600,000. It would have a useful life of four years and a salvage value of $200,000. It would result in cash savings, before financing costs and taxes, of $150,000 per year.

Amerex, Inc., uses the double-declining balance method of depreciation for tax purposes. The firm estimates that its average cost of capital, after taxes, is 9 percent.

a. On the basis of the net present value criterion, would you recommend that the equipment be acquired?
b. Were the firm to acquire the equipment, it would borrow the required cash ($540,000, after taking into account the investment tax credit of $60,000) at an annual rate of 15 percent (which is the equivalent of 9 percent after taxes). For financial reporting purposes, the firm charges depreciation on the straight-line basis. Determine the impact of the acquisition on earnings of the first year.
c. In light of your results in parts a and b, comment on why application of generally acceptable accounting principles may discourage investment decisions that are in the best interests of a company.
d. Now suppose that the IRS requires the firm to use the accelerated cost recovery system and classifies the equipment as three-year property. The required depreciation rates each year are 25%, 38%, and 37%, respectively. How would this change affect your response to part a?

7. *"Artificial" assumptions must sometimes be made to equalize project lives.*

Downtown University is in need of additional classroom space for its College of Business. Classes are presently conducted in a building that the University leases at an annual cost of $800,000. The required additional space could be rented for a 10-year period in a nearby building for $700,000 per year.

The University is studying the possibility of constructing a new building which would eliminate entirely the need to rent from outsiders. It would be located on land which the University owns and which is presently being operated as a commercial parking lot. The cost of constructing the new building would be $10 million. Annual operating costs would be $200,000. The useful life of the building would be 50 years (no salvage value).

The parking lot on which the new building would be constructed generates $250,000 in revenue each year; operating costs are $75,000 per year. The land could be sold today for $2 million cash.

The lease on the building that the University presently uses has 10 years remaining until expiration. The owners of the building have agreed, however, to terminate the lease upon completion of the new building, for a cash payment of $1,200,000.

University planners predict that after 10 years (the period remaining until expiration of the lease) the new building, including the land, could be sold for $8.5 million. The land alone, if the building were not constructed, could be sold for $2.5 million.

The University would construct the new building only if it would provide a "return" of 8 percent. Assume, for convenience, that construction of the building could be both started and completed in period 0.

Based on the criteria of net present value, should the University construct the building or, alternatively, should it continue to occupy the present quarters and lease additional space? Over how many years did you carry out the analysis? What assumptions did you make with respect to the disposition of the new building and land at the end of the period covered by the analysis? Is such assumption reasonable?

8. *How sensitive is present value analysis to errors of estimate and prediction?*

An executive of a company prefers "rule of thumb" evaluative techniques to net present value because of the unreliability of the estimates and predictions required by the net present value technique. In particular, the executive objects to the required estimates of cost of capital and predictions of cash flows and asset lives.

Assume that a firm is considering the acquisition of an asset that has an estimated useful life of 10 years and will provide cash receipts of $100,000 per year. The firm uses a discount rate of 10 percent.

a. Determine the present value of the cash receipts.

b. Suppose that the firm made the misestimates that follow. For each, indicate the percentage difference between the present value as computed in part a and the present value that would be computed based on the misestimates.

   (1) The firm estimated that cash receipts in years 6 through 10 would be 25 percent greater than they actually were (i.e., $125,000).

   (2) It used a discount rate 20 percent greater than was appropriate (i.e., 12 percent).

   (3) It predicted the useful life of the asset to be 20 percent longer than it actually will be (i.e., 12 years).

   (4) It predicted the useful life of the asset to be 100 percent longer than it actually will be (i.e., 20 years).

c. Based on your computations, what assertion might you make in defense of the net present value technique?

9. *Both payback reciprocal and average return on investment can be used in certain circumstances as surrogates for internal rate of return.*

The table that follows represents six independent investment projects, each of which provides the indicated net cash flow for the indicated number of years. Each of the projects requires an initial outlay of $100,000.

Net Cash Inflow	Number of Years		
	4	12	20
$30,159			
$26,262			

a. For each cell in the table, determine:
   (1) Internal rate of return (within 1 percent)
   (2) Payback reciprocal
   (3) Average return on investment (assume straight-line depreciation and zero salvage value)
b. Despite their theoretical limitations, both payback reciprocal and average return on investment can be used as appropriate surrogates for internal rate of return, if the investment proposals have certain characteristics. Based on the data that you calculated, under what circumstances (e.g., length of investment period, internal rate of return) would payback reciprocal provide a reasonable approximation of internal rate of return; under what circumstances would average return on investment provide a reasonable approximation?

The following represents the present value of an annuity of $1 discounted at rates that are not included in Table 4 of the Appendix:

Periods	\multicolumn{7}{c}{Rate}

Periods	24%	25%	26%	27%	28%	29%	30%
12	3.8514	3.7251	3.6059	3.4933	3.3868	3.2859	3.1903
20	4.1103	3.9539	3.8083	3.6726	3.5458	3.4271	3.3158

10. *The financing decision must be distinguished from the acquisition decision.*

Deborah, Inc., is contemplating the acquisition of a new machine. The machine would enable the company to realize manufacturing savings, after taxes, of $67,500 per year. The machine has an estimated useful life of five years (no salvage value). The machine could be purchased for $250,000.

Deborah, Inc., uses a discount rate of 12 percent. It could, however, obtain financing for the new machine from either a bank or the manufacturer at the current prime rate of 10 percent.

a. Based on the net present value criteria, should the firm acquire the new machine?
b. Suppose, alternatively, that the equipment manufacturer agreed to lease the machine to Deborah, Inc., for a period of five years (the useful life of the machine). The annual rental charge would be $65,950. Annual after-tax manufacturing savings would be the same as if the machine were purchased outright ($67,500). Using as a criterion the net present value of all anticipated cash inflows and outflows, should the company lease the machine?
c. Are your two answers in conflict? If so, explain the conflict and point to any flaws in your analysis.

11. *The time value of money can readily be incorporated into break-even analysis; it may alter significantly the break-even point.*

Danco, Inc., must decide whether to purchase conventional or technologically advanced equipment. The conventional equipment would cost $4 million; the technologically advanced, $10 million. The useful lives of both are 10 years, with no anticipated salvage value.

The firm manufactures a product that it sells for $400 per unit. If the conventional equipment is acquired, variable manufacturing costs would be $300 per unit; if the technologically advanced equipment is purchased, then variable costs would be $200 per unit. The only fixed cost that need be considered is depreciation, which is charged on a straight-line basis.

The firm uses a discount rate of 12 percent to evaluate equipment acquisitions.

a. Ignoring the time value of money, determine the number of units that will have to be manufactured and sold each year for the firm to break even assuming the purchase of, first, the conventional equipment and, second, the technologically advanced equipment. Use conventional break-even analysis, considering the fixed costs to be annual depreciation.

b. Suppose that the firm expects to produce and sell 5,000 units per year over a 10-year period. If net present value is the decision criterion, can the acquisition of either type of equipment be justified? If one type must be acquired, which is preferable?

c. Using net present value as a criterion, what is the minimum number of units that must be produced and sold each year to justify acquisition of the *technologically advanced* equipment?

12. *Owing to accelerated depreciation as well as to "leverage," investments in real estate can provide high rates of return even if appreciation in value is small and before-tax payments exceed rental receipts.*

Speculative Realty, Inc., is evaluating the earnings potential of an apartment complex. The firm can acquire the complex at a price of $5 million. The firm would be required to pay $500,000 cash and would assume a 12 percent 20-year mortgage for the balance.

The firm estimates that annual rent receipts would be $600,000 per year. Property taxes, insurance, and other cash operating costs would be $140,000 per year.

The firm plans to hold the property for three years and then sell it. Annual mortgage payments during each of the three years would be $602,455, divided between principal and interest as follows:

Year	Principal	Interest
1	$ 62,455	$ 540,000
2	69,950	532,505
3	78,344	524,111
Total	$210,749	$1,596,616

The firm estimates that at the end of three years it could sell the property for $5,600,000 (an amount reflecting an annual compound increase in value of less than 4 percent). At the time of sale, the firm would repay the outstanding mortgage balance, which would then be $4,289,251.

The tax rate on both ordinary income and on gains resulting from the sale of property is 30 percent. The company will charge depreciation using the double-declining balance method assuming a useful life of 20 years and no salvage value.

Speculative Realty has sufficient income from other properties to offset any tax losses attributable to the apartment complex that it is considering purchasing. Hence, any "negative" tax obligations can be viewed as cash receipts.

The firm will acquire the property only if it will provide an after-tax return on its required initial investment ($500,000 cash) of 15 percent.

a. Determine the net after-tax cash receipts (excluding those from the sale of the property) during each of the three years. Depreciation, property taxes, insurance, other operating costs, and that portion of the mortgage payment representing interest are expenses that are deductible for tax purposes. Calculate the present value of the net receipts.

b. Determine the net cash receipts upon sale of the property, and payment of both the balance on the mortgage and the required taxes on the resultant gain. Compute the present value of the net receipts.

c. Should the firm acquire the complex? Explain.

13. *Subjective probabilities may be assigned to possible useful lives.*

Posthaste Co. has decided to acquire a new delivery vehicle. The vehicle can be acquired outright for $72,000 or it can be leased for $20,000 per year. The minimum term of the lease is only one year. At the end of one year, the company has the right to extend the lease on a month-to-month basis for as long as it wishes at the same rental rate. Per terms of the lease agreement, Posthaste is responsible for all insurance and maintenance costs.

Posthaste managers are unsure of the useful life of the vehicle. They have assigned the following subjective probabilities to various possibilities:

Years of Useful Life	Probability
3	.10
4	.20
5	.25
6	.20
7	.15
8	.10
	1.00

Posthaste evaluates all expenditure proposals using a discount rate of 12 percent.

Ignoring the impact of income taxes, should the company buy the vehicle or lease it?

14. *Subjective probabilities can be assigned to anticipated receipts and disbursements to determine their expected values.*

Keys, Inc., manufactures a household product that sells for $40 per unit. Annual fixed manufacturing costs are presently $600,000; variable costs are $26 per unit.

The firm has the opportunity to acquire a new machine which would cause variable costs to be reduced by $2 per unit. The machine can be purchased for $200,000. It has a useful life of three years and no salvage value.

The firm has assigned subjective probabilities to annual sales for the next three years:

Probability	Sales per Year (units)
.20	40,000
.50	46,000
.30	48,000

The firm uses a discount rate of 10 percent to evaluate purchases of plant and equipment.
a. Using net present value as a criterion, should the firm acquire the new machine?
b. Suppose alternatively that company engineers estimate that there is a 10 percent probability that the machine will not perform satisfactorily. The firm will be able to determine whether the machine is acceptable immediately after it is installed. If it is unacceptable, the manufacturer will permit the firm to return the machine and will refund 85 percent of the purchase price. What is the maximum amount that the firm should be wiling to pay for the machine assuming cost savings and estimated sales as presented?

15. *Expected value of net receipts is not, by itself, a definitive decision criterion.*

A company has the opportunity to invest in a mining project. The amounts of both the required investment and the expected returns are uncertain.

The amount to be invested depends on excavation costs. Geologists and engineers have indicated that there is a .8 probability that the excavation costs will be $5 million and a .2 probability that they will be only $2 million.

The return on the investment depends on the price at which the mine can be sold. Company specialists believe that there is a .7 probability that it can be sold for $6 million and a .3 probability that it can be sold for only $4 million.

Any funds that the company does not invest in the project would be kept in government securities that return 6 percent per year. Thus, if the cost of the project is only $2 million, then the $3 million difference between such cost and the maximum cost of $5 million would be placed in the government securities.

The time span between the date of investment and the sale of the mine will be approximately one year. For computational convenience, it may be assumed that the anticipated receipts from the sale of the mine are expressed in dollars of the present; hence, there is no need to discount them.

a. Assuming that the decision criterion is expected value of net receipts, should the company invest in the mining project?

b. Suppose alternatively that the company wishes to maximize the expected value of net receipts subject to avoiding any possibility of a loss on its investment. Should it invest in the project?

16. *The expected value criterion fails to take into account the "worth" of dollar to be gained or lost.*

   Gamble, Inc., must decide which of two versions of a new product to introduce. Version A is similar to other products currently on the market. Version B has several features which make it unique. The initial cost of introducing the two versions will be the same, $33 million. The firm has assigned the following subjective probabilities to the potential net cash receipts during each of the next 10 years:

Version A		Version B	
Probability	Annual Net Cash Receipts (millions)	Probability	Annual Net Cash Receipts (millions)
.05	$3.0	.20	$ 0.0
.25	4.0	.25	4.0
.40	5.0	.25	6.0
.25	6.0	.15	10.0
.05	7.0	.05	20.0

The firm uses a discount rate of 10 percent to assess investment proposals.

a. Based on the information provided, should the firm introduce either of the two versions? If it had to choose one, which would it prefer? Which provides the opportunity of the greater gain? Which allows for the greater loss?

b. Suppose that the company recognizes that the more dollars it has, or is able to acquire, the less valuable is each incremental dollar. To account for this explicitly, it has developed a table in which various dollar amounts are translated into a measure of value, which it refers to as utils. The following are selected excerpts from the table:

Dollars (millions)	Utils
$ 0.0	0
3.0	320
4.0	400
5.0	477
6.0	550
7.0	622
10.0	830
20.0	1,430
33.0	2,080

Notice how as the dollar amounts increase, the value per dollar, in utils, decreases.

Recompute the expected present value of the two versions of the product using utils instead of dollars. That is, in place of each dollar amount substitute the equivalent number of utils. Taking into account the additional information, should the firm introduce either of the two versions? Which should it prefer?

Solutions to Exercise for Review and Self-Testing

1.

Tax Savings from Sale of Old Machine

Sales price of old machine		$ 80,000
Less: Book value of old machine		
Original cost	$120,000	
Accumulated depreciation	(30,000)	90,000
Loss on sale of old machine		$ 10,000
Tax rate on sale of equipment		× .30
Savings in taxes		$ 3,000

Required Outlay

Outlay to purchase new machine		$200,000
Less:		
Proceeds from sale of old machine	$ 80,000	
Savings in taxes owing to loss on sale of old machine (per previous computation)	3,000	83,000
Required net outlay		$117,000

2.

$$\text{Expected value} = .60(\$70,000) + .40(\$50,000)$$

$$\text{Expected value} = \$62,000$$

3.

	New Machine	Old Machine
Expected value of annual operating costs	$ 62,000	$ 92,000
Depreciation charges	30,000	10,000
Total deductible costs	92,000	102,000
Tax rate on ordinary income	× .30	× .30
Tax saving	$ 27,600	$ 30,600
Expected value of annual operating costs	$ 62,000	$ 92,000
Less: Tax saving	27,600	30,600
Expected value of annual operating costs after taxes	34,400	61,400
Present value of an annuity of $1 for 5 years discounted at 12 percent	× 3.6048	× 3.6048
Present value of expected annual operating costs	$124,005	$221,335

4.

	New Machine	Old Machine
Amount to be received upon salvage	$50,000	$40,000
Present value of $1 to be received in 5 years discounted at 12 percent	.5674	.5674
Present value of salvage proceeds	$28,370	$22,696

5.		New Machine	Old Machine
Net outlay upon acquisition of new machine (per part 1)		$117,000	
Present value of net operating costs (per part 3)		124,005	$221,335
Present value of salvage proceeds (per part 4)		(28,370)	(22,696)
Present value of net cash disbursements		$212,635	$198,639

Inasmuch as the present value of the net cash disbursements would be greater if the new machine were acquired than if it were not, the new machine should *not* be acquired.

6.	Amount	Present Value at 7%	Present Value at 8%
Initial outlay	($117,000)	($117,000)	($117,000)
Difference in operating costs (annuity for 5 years)	27,000 (a)	110,705	107,803
Difference in salvage value (single payment in 5 years)	10,000	7,130	6,806
Net present value		$ 835	($ 2,391)

(a) Per part 3, expected value of annual operating costs after taxes:

Old machine	$61,400
New machine	34,400
Difference	$27,000

The internal rate of return will be that rate which provides a net present value of zero. Since 7 percent results in a net present value greater than zero, a slightly greater rate, 8 percent, was tried. Because 8 percent provides a net present value less than zero, the actual rate of return must be between 7 percent and 8 percent. Interpolation would indicate a rate of 7.25 percent.

21

Budgeting for the Shorter Run

This chapter is directed to budgeting. A budget is a quantified plan of organizational activities. Effective budgeting is one major key to successful management because the budget is the primary managerial instrument for planning and control. The budget reflects virtually all management decisions having financial consequences. It serves as the benchmark by which the organization's progress in achieving its objectives is measured. The term *budgeting* is sometimes used synonymously with *profit planning*. It may sometimes be used, incorrectly, as a reference to *strategic planning* or *long-term planning*. Budgeting is an ingredient or input to strategic planning but is not as all-encompassing or pervasive as most strategic planning models.

Budgeting is one of the most important activities in any organization, whether it is profit, nonprofit, service, or governmental. At one point the director of the Office of Management and Budget (OMB) in the U.S. government was regarded as an obscure bureaucrat. Now that office is recognized as one of the most powerful in the federal government, and it is a choice assignment to be selected as an OMB staff member. The director of OMB determines, subject to the approval of the President and Congress, the extent to which the various federal programs will be funded. The relative influence of those directing the budget process in large corporations or large nonprofit organizations (e.g., United Way or Salvation Army) is no less great than at OMB. The direction in which an organization will move is determined in large measure by the amount of funds directed to each of the activities in which it engages.

TYPES OF BUDGETS

Budgets may be executed for the entire organization or for any of its component units. Budgets may encompass all activities or only specific types of revenues or expenses. An *operations* or *annual budget*, sometimes termed a *master budget*, is a comprehensive plan comprising a series of related schedules, each of which focuses on a particular function or phase of activities. A comprehensive operations budget will be illustrated later in this chapter. Another type of budget is a *financing budget*, which is used to evaluate capital structure and to determine future financing patterns. Other budgets may also be called *pro forma financial statements* because they are in the same format and with the same content as the organization's eternal financial statements. The term *pro forma* connotes a future orientation or a "what if" view of the financial statements. The operations budget, or annual budget, is often linked to a financial budget. A *cash budget*[1] is one type of financing budget which indicates anticipated cash receipts and cash disbursements. We will illustrate it later in this chapter. Many computer software packages facilitate preparation of the types of budgets described in this chapter and provide the flexibility for users to change headings and budget categories.

Some organizations use *continuous budgets*, which are updated every month or every quarter. These *rolling budgets* are updated to reflect new forecasts, and the data pertaining to the elapsed time periods are removed from the budget. *Project budgets* may also be prepared for activities or events that extend across several departments, legal entities, or time periods. Project budgets would also be linked to the operations budget. *Capital budgets* are usually prepared to reflect potential purchases of long-term assets, including land, buildings, equipment, or other companies or organizations.

The time period covered by budgets, as well as the length of the segment into which they are divided, reflect management's planning horizon for the decisions at hand. Capital expenditure budgets, in that they indicate major acquisitions that have to be planned for years in advance, may extend for five years or more and may be segmented into periods as long as a year. Long-range cash budgets, which must be closely coordinated with capital expenditures, may cover correspondingly long periods. Short-term cash or production budgets, which in contrast are used to plan and control activities for which there are short lead times, may cover quarters or months and contain projections by weeks or even days.

---

[1]In previous chapters we emphasized the significance of cash relative to income. In this chapter we refer to "profit planning" and suggest that maximization of profit is the primary objective of most commercial entities. The apparent contradiction is eliminated when it is recognized that as the length of the measurement period increases the difference between net cash inflow (excluding owner contributions and withdrawals) and net income approaches zero. Indeed, over the life of an enterprise net income is equal to the difference between the cash the owners withdrew from the business and that which they contributed.

The budgeting process serves at least five primary functions:

1. It provides a means of developing and expressing organizational objectives.
2. It facilitates the allocation of organizational resources.
3. It allows the organization to formulate and communicate its plans for realizing its objectives. Concurrently, it promotes coordination of the activities in which it engages.
4. It encourages increased productivity and other forms of behavior that are in the interests of the organization.
5. It establishes the criteria by which the performance of individuals as well as organizational units will be judged.

The first four of these functions will be discussed in this chapter. The last will be dealt with in Chapter 22, pertaining to performance evaluation.

THE BUDGET AS AN EXPRESSION OF OBJECTIVES

Although budgeting is often seen as little more than a perfunctory exercise in accounting intended to fulfill "paperwork" obligations, it provides an opportunity for an organization (or any of its subunits) to engage in periodic self-examination. In order to plan and allocate resources, an organization and its managers must consider what it is they are planning for and what it is that should be accomplished by the resources that will be expended.

Limitations of Profit Maximization as an Objective

The explicit goal of most corporations or other profit-oriented enterprises is generally that of maximizing income—of ultimately returning to their owners more cash than they contributed. The objectives of both the subunits of an entity as well as the individual managers and employees may, however, be quite different from that ascribed by top management to the organization as a whole. It is a challenge to both managers and accountants to recognize potential differences—even conflicts—in goals and to design systems of budgeting and performance measurement that encourage the subunits and individual employees to act and make decisions that are consistent with the stated goal of profit maximization.

Profit maximization is not generally the objective of a subunit of a corporation because the subunit is unlikely to be a *profit center*. Its objective may be to maximize or minimize one or more elements of profit, but not profit *per se*. A *profit center* is a unit of an organization that has responsibility for both revenues and expenses and can be evaluated on the basis of profit earned. In practice, relatively few components of a corporation have complete responsibility for both revenue and expenses. Those that come closest are usually major divisions of conglomerates. But even seemingly autonomous divisions seldom have control over *all* expenses that enter into the determination of profit. It is unusual, for example, for divisions to have the authority to acquire long-term capital independently. Thus, they have but limited influence on the entity's cost of capital (e.g., interest) or the quantity or quality of the fixed assets. As component units get smaller and more specialized (e.g., production centers, sales divisions, or service departments) the number of profit elements over which they have control is likely to be further reduced. A production department is generally concerned with output; it has substantial influence over manufacturing costs but little over selling prices or sales effort. A sales division can control selling prices and marketing programs but may have little impact on production costs or product design.

It is convenient, yet simplistic, to assume that the purpose of every corporate subunit or activity is to "maximize profit." While it may be true that, for the organization as a whole, all activities should be intended to enhance long-term profitability, the impact of some activities on overall profitability is so indirect that profitability cannot adequately serve as an *operational* or workable objective. The objectives of accounting, legal, personnel, advertising, and stockholder relations departments are all, in some way, related to profit maximization. But the day-to-day—or even year-to-year—performance of none of these departments can meaningfully be evaluated in terms of contribution to profit. Characteristic of each of these departments is the need to express its objectives in terms of output, other than profits, that can be quantified and measured.

In this regard, the problems of management accounting in profit-seeking corporations are remarkably similar to those in not-for-profit organizations. Many nonprofit organizations never seriously consider what it is they are seeking to accomplish. To be sure, they may have goals that are as vague as they are noble, e.g., "to improve the quality of life" within a particular area of human endeavor. Such statements of purpose are not *operational*. They fail to imply standards of accomplishment. As a consequence, they cannot serve as a basis for comparing the benefits to be achieved by alternative courses of action or for measuring the extent to which they have been realized. Both types of organizations must decide where it is they want to go before they can determine the best route to take or periodically assess whether they have made progress in getting there.

Link Between Goal Setting and Budgeting

Although it is often asserted that a firm must establish its objectives before it can prepare a budget that reflects those goals, goal setting and budgeting are, in fact, integrally linked. The wherewithal of a firm to achieve its objectives is dependent on the availability of resources and the competing demands on them. Suppose, for example, that a successful brewer sets as an objective diversification into products and services other than beer. It considers acquiring corporations in other industries, developing new products such as soft drinks and snack foods, and constructing "educational parks" which feature rides and amusements tied to a particular theme.

The transformation of the strategic goal, that of diversification, from a broad statement of aspirations to targets which the management of the firm can strive to accomplish, must be carried out within the constraints of the corporate budget. A long-term budget will indicate the sources and the amount of resources that can be directed toward the objective and will determine, to a great extent, the form that the diversification efforts will take. Whether or not, for example, the firm should, in fact, seek out new ventures depends very much on the return that existing products will generate in comparison to those which can be expected from the new lines of business, the amount of new investment that they will require, and the funds that they make available for diversification. At the same time, of course, the corporate goals affect corporate plans as reflected in the budget. Budgeting and goal setting are interactive processes; neither can be separated from the other. The budget must incorporate projections of revenues and expenditures. Insofar as the difference between the two is less than the firm's profit objective, then means must be developed either to increase revenues or reduce expenditures. As a consequence, the budget serves as an effective catalyst for creative thinking about new products, markets, production methods, administrative procedures, and financial policies.

The Budget as a Means of Allocating Resources

In any organization there are competing demands upon limited resources. Factions of managers believe that funds should be directed to projects or activities in which they have a special interest. However, there are often automatic claims upon a sizable proportion of resources. To the extent that a firm establishes a sales target for a particular product, for example, the funds required to satisfy production demands must be provided. There are inevitably, however, some resources for which different divisions or departments must contend with one another. The ultimate allocation of funds is the consequence of pleadings by, and negotiations among, responsible managers. The resultant budget, therefore, may be seen as very much of a political document.

The political nature of the budget, in an extreme form, can be appreciated by considering the budgetary process in a governmental organization, such as a municipality. In contrast to business organizations, which are to a considerable extent controlled by the forces of the "market," government organizations are regulated by their budgets. By way of the budgetary process municipal officials determine how much revenue the municipality will receive (e.g., they establish tax rates) and what its sources will be. They decide on the types and levels of services to be provided and the extent to which they will be funded. Whereas the revenues and expenditures incorporated in the budget of a business organization may only be estimates subject to the vicissitudes of the market, those settled on in the budget of a government organization can be backed by the authority of law. The revenue estimates see expression as enforceable tax levies; the expenditure estimates take the form of mandates from which little deviation may be permitted.

The similarity between business and government organizations with regard to budgeting should not be overlooked. Ultimately, of course, it is expected that each dollar expended by a business will provide a return. The budgetary process is designed to allocate resources to the activities from which the return per dollar will be the greatest. Insofar as the ultimate return associated with expenditures can be determined with reliability, the criteria for allocation in businesses are considerably more concrete and objective than those in nonbusiness organizations. There are, however, any number of projects undertaken or activities carried out by a business in which the association with profit is so tenuous as to limit the utility of financial return criteria. Funds expended on new office complexes, institutional advertising, legal services, public relations, and executive perquisites are expected to operate to the ultimate benefit of the firm. The extent to which they will succeed, however, defies measurement or even estimate. Thus, the amounts allocated to these projects or activities owe more to the persuasiveness and stature of the parties who have a vested interest in them than to their ability to meet quantitative tests of financial return. The ultimate budget of a business, therefore, like that of a government, is as much the product of internal political processes as of objective techniques of profit maximization.

THE BUDGET AS AN OPERATIONAL PLAN

The budgeting process enables the firm to set forth specifically how it intends to realize its objectives and to coordinate the various activities that it will be required to carry out. The process helps to assure that there will be goods on hand to satisfy projected sales, that there will be cash available to make required payments, that plant and equipment will be adequate to sustain the planned production, that the advertising and marketing strategies are consistent with anticipated sales, and that administrative and sales staffs are capable of supporting the forecasted sales and production.

Formulating the Revenue Objective

In business organizations, the key target that must be established is sales revenue. To a great extent, once sales revenue is projected, the other variables that affect profit can be determined as a function of sales.

Developing targets, be they for revenues or expenditures, requires concurrent consideration of what will be and what should be. Management must first forecast revenues or expenditures in the context of a given set of conditions and management policies. It must then determine if and how the firm can alter those conditions and policies so that the resultant revenues or costs will allow for the overriding profit objective to be met.

Sales forecasting is complex. Each of the broad categories of forecasting techniques that are indicated in the discussion that follows can be used independently; it is generally preferable, however, that they be used in conjunction with one another.

1. *Economic models*. Economic models are sets of equations representing selected segments of the economy. They are most useful in providing initial guidance as to future sales, especially in those industries which are affected by general economic conditions, such as automobiles, airlines, and housing. In the automobile industry, for example, economic models have been used to forecast with considerable accuracy the total number of cars that will be sold in the United States. Inasmuch as there are but a relatively small number of producers and each firm's share of the total market is predictable, each company can estimate its own most likely sales volume. The use of economic models need not, however, be limited only to giant firms. Firms that supply parts or services to the automobile manufacturers usually find that their revenues are tied directly to automobile sales. As a consequence, the models are as relevant to them as they are to the automobile manufac-

turers. Only a relatively few firms are of sufficient size to justify a full-time staff of economists; smaller firms can obtain the benefits of economic models by engaging the services of consulting economists.

2. *Statistical techniques*. Statistical procedures, such as regression and correlation analysis, can also be used to project sales. These techniques, which were discussed briefly in Chapter 17 with respect to behavior of costs, relate sales to the factors which cause them to vary. Some of these variables may be external to the company and beyond its control. Examples are economic factors, such as personal income, the level of unemployment and the level of consumer prices; the marketing efforts of competitors; and sales of products for which those of the company are either complements or substitutes. Other variables may be within the control of the company, such as advertising dollars and selling prices.

3. *"Ground-up" forecasts*. Sales forecasts based on either economic models or statistical techniques are commonly developed by staff departments associated with high levels of management. The more traditional and, in the view of many, still the more reliable means of projecting sales is by combining forecasts from field representatives. Individual salespersons who are the most familiar with their territories will indicate the sales volume that they believe they are capable of generating. Their estimates, modified by managerial judgments as to the extent to which salespersons are overly optimistic or cautious (perhaps out of reluctance to commit themselves to estimates to which they might later be held accountable), will be combined into district, regional, and eventually national forecasts. One advantage of this approach is that it benefits from the judgments of persons who, by being close to those who will make the purchasing decisions, have a sense of the market that may be lacking in those at corporate headquarters. Another is that it involves in the budgetary process the parties that will be required to fulfill the forecasts that are included in the budget. Budgets are widely perceived as a means of pressuring employees to meet targets imposed by higher levels of management. This feeling can be alleviated, at least in part, by widespread and genuine contributions to the budget by those who will be required to carry it out.

Formulating Expenditure Targets

Variable expenditures are, by definition, a function of volume. Hence, once revenue forecasts are made and translated into units of output, the procedures described in Chapter 17 in the section regarding cost behavior can be employed to predict variable costs. The budget process, however, provides the opportunity to review the historic relationships between cost and volume to see if cost reductions are feasible. In contrast, many types of fixed costs are discretionary; management determines the level of service for which it is willing to pay. Maintenance, clerical, advertising, and supervisory costs are within this category. The budgetary process is a means by which management can consider explicitly the levels of service that are optimum and, at the same time, examine ways in which the costs of obtaining the required services can be held to a minimum.

THE BUDGETARY PROCESS ILLUSTRATED

The example that follows is meant to illustrate the general approach to planning sales, production, income, and cash receipts and disbursements. The schedules presented can properly take any number of forms, and it should not be inferred that the forms shown are necessarily the most preferable. Each may be viewed as a summary of more detailed plans. Worthy of special note in the example is the extent to which it incorporates many of the principles of both financial and managerial accounting that have been discussed throughout this text. The budgeting process as illustrated begins with the balance sheet as it is expected to appear at the start of the period for which the plan is being formulated and concludes with one for the end of the period. The manner in which the two are linked together by the intermediate schedules is tribute to the simplicity, order, and logic of the double-entry accounting model.

The time frame of the illustrated budget is one year—a typical period for a comprehensive budget. In practice, however, many of the schedules would show details for each quarter or month. The detailed estimates are omitted from the illustration in order to focus on the relationships among the several schedules. For examples of more complete schedules, the reader is referred to a comprehensive text on budgeting.[2]

Town Lake Industries manufactures two products, 101 and 202. Exhibit 21-1 is its balance sheet as management *expects* it to appear at the start of 1994.

EXHIBIT 21-1

Town Lake Industries
Expected Statement of Position
January 1, 1994

Assets		
Cash		$ 2,450,000
Accounts receivable		1,800,000
Inventory—raw materials for product 101:		
97,000 lb @ $1.10 = $106,700		
raw materials for product 202:		
101,000 lb @ $1.30 = $131,300		238,000
Inventory—finished goods of product 101:		
60,000 units @ $13 = $780,000		
finished goods of product 202:		
20,000 units @ $21 = $420,000		1,200,000
Plant and equipment	$10,000,000	
Less: Accumulated depreciation	4,000,000	6,000,000
Total assets		$11,688,000
Liabilities and owners' equity		
Accounts payable		$ 1,400,000
Owners' equity		
Common stock	$ 5,000,000	
Retained earnings	5,288,000	10,288,000
Total liabilities and owners' equity		$11,688,000

[2]See, for example, Glenn A. Welsch, Ronald W. Hilton, and Paul N. Gordon, *Budgeting: Profit Planning and Control* (Englewood Cliffs, N.J.: Prentice-Hall, Inc., 1988).

The Sales Budget

The sales budget indicates management's projection of sales. It requires estimates of unit selling prices and number of units to be sold. It may reveal sales by regions or major categories of products. Schedule I represents a sales budget in summary form.

SCHEDULE I

| | Estimated Sales for 1994 | | |
	Unit Price	Total Units	Total Dollars
Product 101	$22.00	480,000	$10,560,000
Product 202	28.00	360,000	10,080,000
Total			$20,640,000

Production Budget

Production plans are derived from the sales budget. The number of units that the firm will produce depends on expected sales, the number of units on hand at the start of the period, and the number of units that the firm considers necessary to have in stock at the end. Assume that management estimates its end-of-year required stock to be approximately one month's sales, i.e., 40,000 units of product 101 and 30,000 units of product 202. Schedule II.A indicates *required number of units to be produced*.

Once the number of units to be produced has been determined, then the total costs of production can be calculated. The standard for direct labor is as follows:

Product 101   .5 hour @ $16 = $ 8.00

Product 202   .8 hour @ $16 = $12.80

Schedule II.B provides estimated total outlays for direct labor.

The standard for raw materials is as follows:

Product 101   3 lb @ $1.10 = $3.30

Product 202   4 lb @ $1.30 = $5.20

Management estimates that ending inventory of raw materials should be approximately one month's supply—115,000 lb for product 101 and 123,000 lb for product 202. Schedule II.C summarizes *required purchases of raw material*.

Schedule II.D indicates predicted overhead costs (all assumed) and the resultant *overhead charging rate*. It focuses on anticipated overhead costs at but a single level of activity. Whereas a schedule of this type may be useful in planning overall expenditures and in calculating the overhead charging rate, it is of limited value in controlling expenditures and in evaluating deviations from plans. Unless actual volume is exactly equal to that budgeted, the schedule provides no insight into the amount that overhead costs "should be." To facilitate the control function, a *flexible budget*—one that distinguishes between fixed and variable overhead costs (to be described in Chapter 22)—is required.

SCHEDULE II.A

Number of Units to Be Produced

	Product 101	Product 202
Unit sales (per sales budget)	480,000	360,000
Add: Required ending inventory (per discussion)	40,000	30,000
Total requirements	520,000	390,000
Less: Beginning inventory (per January 1, 1994, balance sheet)	60,000	20,000
Number of units to be produced	460,000	370,000

SCHEDULE II.B

Direct Labor Cost

	Product 101	Product 202	Total
Units to be produced (per Schedule II.A)	460,000	370,000	
Hours per unit (per discussion)	× .5	× .8	
Required hours	230,000	296,000	526,000
Cost per hour	× $16.00	× $16.00	× $16.00
Direct labor cost	$3,680,000	$4,736,000	$8,416,000

SCHEDULE II.C

Raw Material Required to Be Used and Purchased

	Product 101		Product 202		
	Units	Dollars @ $1.10 per lb	Units	Dollars @ $1.30 per lb	Total Dollars
Units to be produced	460,000	—	370,000	—	—
Pounds per unit (per discussion)	× 3	—	× 4	—	—
Manufacturing requirements	1,380,000	$1,518,000	1,480,000	$1,924,000	$3,442,000
Add: Required ending inventory (per discussion)	115,000	126,500	123,000	159,900	286,400
Total requirements	1,495,000	$1,644,500	1,603,000	$2,083,900	$3,728,400
Less: Beginning inventory (per January 1, 1994 balance sheet)	97,000	106,700	101,000	131,300	238,000
Required purchases	1,398,000	$1,537,800	1,502,000	$1,952,600	$3,490,400

SCHEDULE II.D

Overhead Costs and Charging Rate

Supplies	$ 200,000
Indirect labor	1,500,000
Depreciation	1,100,000
Insurance and local taxes	150,000
Building occupancy costs	180,000
Other costs	26,000
Total overhead costs	$3,156,000
Number of direct labor hours (per Schedule II.B)	÷ 526,000
Overhead charging rate	$ 6.00

SCHEDULE II.E

Unit Cost of Goods Manufactured

	Product 101	Product 202
Direct labor		
.5 hour @ $16	$ 8.00	
.8 hour @ $16		$12.80
Direct materials		
3 lb @ $1.10	3.30	
4 lb @ $1.30		5.20
Overhead ($6.00 per direct labor hour as indicated in Schedule II.D)		
.5 hour @ $6.00	3.00	
.8 hour @ $6.00		4.80
Unit cost of goods manufactured	$14.30	$22.80

Schedule II.E combines the direct labor, direct materials, and overhead costs to arrive at the unit cost of *goods manufactured*.

Cost of Goods Sold

Once manufacturing costs as well as beginning and ending inventory levels have been projected, then cost of goods sold can be calculated. Schedule III illustrates the computation of cost of goods sold and indicates the value to be assigned to ending inventory on the end-of-year balance sheet.

SCHEDULE III

Cost of Goods Sold and Ending Inventory

	Product 101	Product 202	Total
Finished goods beginning inventory (Exhibit 21-1)			
January 1, 1994 per balance sheet			
60,000 units @ $13	$ 780,000		
20,000 units @ $21		$ 420,000	$ 1,200,000
Add: Cost of goods manufactured (Schedules II.A and II.E)			
460,000 @ $14.30	6,578,000		
370,000 @ $22.80		8,436,000	15,014,000
Goods available for sale	$7,358,000	$8,856,000	$16,214,000
Less: Finished goods inventory, December 31, 1994			
(per discussion of production budget)			
(Schedules II.A and II.E)			
40,000 @ $14.30	$ 572,000		
30,000 @ 22.80		$ 684,000	$ 1,256,000
Cost of goods sold	$6,786,000	$8,172,000	$14,958,000

Selling and Administrative Budget

Schedule IV summarizes selling and administrative expenses. In a comprehensive system of budgeting, each of the expenditures would be supported by subsidiary budgets.

SCHEDULE IV

Selling and Administrative Budget

Selling expenditures, including sales commissions	$1,300,000
Executive salaries	800,000
Clerical costs	950,000
Audit and legal costs	85,000
Other costs	670,000
Total selling and administrative costs	$3,805,000

Projected Income

Given the projections of revenue and the major categories of expenses, a forecast of income before taxes, tax expense, and income after taxes is straightforward. Schedule V represents a *pro forma* statement of income for the year ending December 31, 1994. The tax rate (including state and local taxes) is assumed to be 40 percent.

SCHEDULE V

Pro Forma Statement of Budgeted or Projected Income for the Year Ending December 31, 1994

Sales revenue (per Schedule I)	$20,640,000
Less: Cost of goods sold (per Schedule III)	14,958,000
Gross margin	$ 5,682,000
Less: Selling and administrative expenses (per Schedule IV)	$ 3,805,000
Income before taxes	$ 1,877,000
Less: Income taxes @ 40%	750,800
Net income	$ 1,126,200

Cash Budget

A budget of cash receipts and disbursements permits management to evaluate the adequacy of its cash resources. It enables the firm to make arrangements to borrow any additional funds that might be necessary if it is to satisfy its obligations as they mature and to invest or distribute to shareholders any excess cash.

Schedule VI.A indicates projected cash receipts as well as the year-end balance in accounts receivable. It is premised on the assumption that 2 percent of the beginning-of-year balance in accounts receivable and 10 percent of the 1994 sales will be uncollected and carried over as accounts receivable to 1995. The remaining amounts will have been received as cash during 1994.

Schedule VI.B projects cash disbursements and the December 31, 1994, balance in accounts payable. It assumes that the entire opening balance in accounts payable will be liquidated during the year. All manufacturing, selling, and administrative expenses are recorded as accounts payable prior to payment. Of these manufacturing, selling, and administrative costs incurred during 1994, only 95 percent will be paid during the year; the remaining 5 percent will be reported as accounts payable at year end.

SCHEDULE VI.A

Cash Receipts and December 31, 1994 Balance in Accounts Receivable

Accounts receivable, January 1, 1994		
(per January 1 balance sheet)		$ 1,800,000
Add: 1994 projected sales (per Schedule I)		20,640,000
Total available for collection		$22,440,000
Less: Projected accounts receivable, December 31, 1994		
2% of January 1 balance in accounts		
receivable ($1,800,000)	$ 36,000	
10% of 1994 projected sales	2,064,000	$ 2,100,000
Projected cash receipts, 1994		$20,340,000

SCHEDULE VI.B

Cash Disbursements and Projected December 31, 1994 Balance in Accounts Payable

Accounts payable, January 1, 1994			
(per January 1 balance sheet)			$ 1,400,000
Add: Manufacturing, selling, and			
administrative obligations, 1994			
Purchases (per Schedule II.C)		$3,490,400	
Direct labor (per Schedule II.B)		8,416,000	
Overhead (per Schedule II.D)	$3,156,000		
Less: Depreciation	(1,100,000)	2,056,000	
Selling and administrative costs			
(per Schedule IV)		3,805,000	$17,767,400
Beginning balance and obligations			
credited to accounts payable			$19,167,400
Less: Projected December 31, 1994, balance			
in accounts payable (5% of $17,767,400			
in obligations incurred during 1994)			(888,370)
Disbursements for manufacturing,			
selling, and administrative costs			$18,279,030
Add: disbursement for acquisition of			
plant and equipment (per discussion)		$2,000,000	
Disbursement for income taxes (per Schedule V)		750,800	$ 2,750,800
Total projected cash disbursements			$21,029,830

The schedule has been prepared on the additional assumption that the firm has projected its purchases of plant and equipment to be $2,000,000. This amount as well as the obligation for taxes owing to 1994 earnings will be paid in full during the year.

Of special note in the schedule is that the disbursement for overhead costs excludes depreciation. Depreciation, of course, is a noncash expense.

Schedule VI.C summarizes expected activity in the cash account during 1994.

Projected Balance Sheet

The schedules that have been prepared to this point indicate the year-end balances in several of the balance sheet accounts. The remaining balances can be obtained by analyzing the fixed asset and retained earnings accounts.

SCHEDULE VI.C

Projected Balance in Cash Account
December 31, 1994

Balance, January 1, 1994 (per January 1 balance sheet)	$ 2,450,000
Add: Cash receipts (per Schedule VI.A)	20,340,000
Sum of beginning balance and cash receipts	$22,790,000
Less: Cash disbursements (per Schedule VI.B)	(21,029,830)
Projected balance, December 31, 1994	$ 1,760,170

Schedule VII.A describes the activity in the fixed asset account. As indicated previously, the firm plans to acquire $2,000,000 in plant and equipment.

Schedule VII.B summarizes the activity in retained earnings. No dividends are expected to be declared during the year.

Schedule VII.C, a projected balance sheet for December 31, 1994, ties together each of the other schedules.

THE BUDGET AS A MOTIVATOR

Through the budgeting process, the organization establishes overall goals as well as specific targets for subunits. Managers are made aware of what is expected of them and hopefully will, as a consequence, be motivated to achieve the budgeted results.

Organizational goals and the incentives to achieve them involve complex phenomena and, in fact, may be chimerical. An organization's goals are now thought to represent a variety of objectives held by dominant coalitions of persons within the organization. In other words, organizational goals may not be as important as are the goals held by the people within the organization. As a starting point for the budgeting process, the management accountant must

SCHEDULE VII.A

Projected Balance in Plant and Equipment
Accounts, December 31, 1994

	Plant and Equipment	Accumulated Depreciation
Balance, January 1, 1994 (per January 1 balance sheet)	$10,000,000	$4,000,000
Expected purchases, 1994 (per discussion)	2,000,000	
Depreciation, 1994 (per Schedule II.D)		1,100,000
Projected balance, December 31, 1994	$12,000,000	$5,100,000

SCHEDULE VII.B

Projected Balance in Retained Earnings,
December 31, 1994

Balance, January 1, 1994 (per January 1 balance sheet)	$5,288,000
Income, 1994 (per Schedule V)	1,126,200
Projected balance, December 31, 1994	$6,414,200

SCHEDULE VII.C

Pro Forma Statement of Position, December 31, 1994

Assets		
Cash (Schedule VI.C)		$ 1,760,170
Accounts receivable (Schedule VI.A)		2,100,000
Inventory—raw materials (Schedule II.C)		286,400
Inventory—finished goods (Schedule III)		1,256,000
Plant and equipment (Schedule VII.A)	$12,000,000	
Less: Accumulated depreciation (Schedule VII.A)	5,100,000	6,900,000
Total assets		$12,302,570
Liabilities and owners' equity		
Accounts payable (Schedule VI.B)		$ 888,370
Owners' equity		
Common stock (January 1, 1994, balance sheet)	$ 5,000,000	
Retained earnings (Schedule VII.B)	6,414,200	11,414,200
Total liabilities and owners' equity		$12,302,570

identify and understand perceptions of the real goals of dominant coalitions and attempt to incorporate them in the budgeting process. Failure to reflect these underlying and very real goals may frustrate and subvert the budgeting process and the resultant budget documents.

Employees' motives are often viewed as functions of both the types of rewards that are likely to be realized if organizational goals are achieved and the probability or expectancy that the goals will be achieved. The reward for achieving identified goals may be the intrinsic satisfaction of successfully doing one's job or of being part of a prestigious organization. Other obvious benefits associated with goal achievement are more tangible (or extrinsic), such as pay, bonuses, promotions, or a larger office. Most important about motives for the budgeting process is that it is the perceptions of the participants that matter, not the "official" goals or even the reward structure publicized in the personnel manual.

Moreover, perceptions of the probability of achieving those rewards will have more impact on the successful functioning of the budgeting process than will more high-powered staff, impressive computer systems, or elaborate budget manuals. Management accountants must not assume that people are lazy or that they will only succumb to pressure and fear. Such attitudes will only lead to an ineffective or failed budgeting process. The resultant budget will fail to achieve its purpose and may represent little more than management's "delusions of budget grandeur" or other "budget dementia."

There is no doubt that budgets can have a powerful influence on the managers and employees whose performance is covered by them. But the nature and direction of that influence is an open question. The "behavioral" aspects of accounting—the effect of budgets as well as other forms of accounting information on decisions and performance—is an area about which there is as yet little understanding. Researchers have demonstrated the significance of behavioral issues; they have yet to resolve them.[3]

The manner in which budgets are prepared and administered may color an individual's attitudes toward the organization as a whole. Evidence suggests that hostility toward budgets is associated with diminished job satisfaction, less

[3]See Ahmed Belkaoui, *Behavioral Accounting: The Research and Practical Issues* (New York: Quorum Books, 1989) for a review of literature in this area.

commitment to the organization, and greater willingness to leave the firm. Other possible consequences include antagonism, resistance, non-compliance, less reliable budget inputs, need for more supervision, and higher administrative costs associated with budget preparation. These negative attitudes are likely, in turn, to reduce productivity.

Owing to past experience with budgets, or popular misconceptions about them, employee feelings of enmity toward them are common. These attitudes may be difficult for an organization to overcome. Nevertheless, the experience of many companies, as well as a number of academic research projects, indicates that it is possible at least to ameliorate them.

Importance of Participation

The nature and extent of participation in the budget process is a key factor that affects employee attitudes toward budgets. It is widely recognized today that employees should be closely involved in establishing the goals which they are expected to achieve. Regardless of whether the supervisor or the subordinate makes the initial budget estimates, there must be communication between the two as to whether they are realistic. Communication must be accompanied by a willingness on the part of the supervisor to take into account the views of the subordinate. Furthermore, participation must be accompanied by an open and uncritical sharing of information about budget priorities and constraints. Participants must not be "put down" or chastised over their inputs to the budgeting process.

Research has shown that participation can have positive effects on the budgeting process and on achievement levels within the organization (1) when there are frequent individual and group meetings, (2) when results are used as part of the performance evaluation process, but not as single indicators of performance, (3) when there are allowable margins for error or tolerance for unexpected events (in both positive and negative directions), and (4) when the use of "ratchets" are eschewed.[4] *Ratcheting* in budgeting occurs when the next period's budget is always set at a lower or tighter level than the preceding period. Budget antagonism and reduction of participation almost always accompany the use of budget ratchets.

Attaining meaningful participation in the budgetary process is not easy. Subordinates may consider it in their interest to negotiate targets that are as modest as possible. By exceeding the readily attainable objectives, they will be credited with favorable budgetary variances and they may believe that their performance will be evaluated positively. Mindful of this, supervisors may tend to press initially for unrealistically demanding goals. Token or sham participation, however, will not do, and if it is intended to deceive employees into thinking that they have had a say in budget estimates, it is worse than no participation at all.

A classic description of *pseudo participation* was provided long ago by Chris Argyris:

> We bring them in, we tell them that we want their frank opinion, but most of them just sit there and nod their heads. We know they're not coming out

---

[4]See Frank Collins, Paul Munter, and Don W. Finn, "The Budgeting Games People Play," *The Accounting Review* (June 1987), pp. 29–49.

with exactly how they feel. I guess budgets scare them; some of them don't have too much education. . . . Then we request the line supervisor to sign the new budget so he can't tell us he didn't accept it. We've found a signature helps an awful lot. If anything goes wrong, they can't come to us, as they often do, and complain. We just show them their signature and remind them they were shown exactly what the budget was made up of. . . .[5]

Reducing Budget Slack

Another adverse consequence of participation is the potential for increased *budget slack*. Slack represents overestimates of expenditures or underestimates of revenues. To the company, it is a net cost beyond what is necessary for efficient operations. Managers bargain for slack (often as a contingency allowance, a miscellaneous expenditure, or a rounding adjustment) because it provides a buffer against uncertainties and a means of stabilizing period-to-period fluctuations.

Companies may minimize slack by more carefully monitoring their unit managers and employees. This can be accomplished by closer supervision, more effective management information systems, improved auditing, and more open and effective communication. However, enhanced monitoring, if taken by employees as evidence that management does not fully trust their budget projections, may undermine policies of increased employee participation in the budgetary process. Hence, as with most progressive concepts, management must balance competing objectives and recognize that there are few managerial prescriptions that come free of deleterious side-effects.

Effective Communication

Also important are the ways budget variances are communicated, interpreted, and reacted to. Reports, for example, should be issued with sufficient frequency to facilitate adjustments to off-target operations. Open discussion between superior and subordinate should take place so that the reasons for the variances are understood by both parties. If a subordinate is to receive a negative evaluation as a consequence of unfavorable deviations from budget estimates, it should be only for those failures over which it was possible to exercise control.

Research into the influence of budgets on individual behavior suggests that the reasonableness of budgeted amounts has a direct impact on results achieved. If budgeted amounts are set at levels which are perceived as being unreachable, participants are likely to reject them as being too extreme. No effort will be made to meet the established goals. If they are set so low that they can be reached without effort, they will discourage maximum performance. If, in contrast, they are set at a level within the aspirations of the individual, within a range considered attainable, then they are likely to inspire peak output.

Individuals react to financial information in unpredictable ways. Budgeting, therefore, is not merely a mechanical exercise that can be left to technicians. Budgets will affect employee behavior. The psychological ramifications of budgeting, although unclear at this time, are too important to be overlooked by either managers or accountants.

[5]Chris Argyris, "Human Problems with Budgets," *Harvard Business Review* (January-February 1953), pp. 97–110.

Periodically, new budgetary "systems" are developed that are intended to add a measure of "rationality" to the budgetary process. One such system is *program budgeting*, which was a predecessor of *zero-base budgeting*. Zero-base budgeting is an example of a budgeting process with several desirable features.

New budgetary systems inevitably fail to fulfill all of the promises made for them by their proponents. But they are of interest to managers and accountants for a number of reasons. First, they formalize the budgeting process. Many of their elements may be integral to sound management. To organizations that are already well managed, they contribute little but at the same time demand little. To those that are not, they provide a framework for improvement. Second, they have been applied with great success in a number of organizations. Where circumstances are favorable, they can have an exceedingly positive effect on organizational performance. Third, as new systems or variations on these systems are proposed, managers and accountants must be able to evaluate them in the context of experience with similar systems. New budgeting systems are often fads. Executives rush to adopt them, accepting without question the enthusiastic claims made in journal articles and management seminars. Managers must have the perspective to distinguish substance from fluff.

Zero-base budgeting, although identified most closely with nonprofit organizations, was in fact first reported as being used at Texas Instruments, a manufacturer of calculators and other electronic devices, to allocate nonmanufacturing costs.[6] It has several noteworthy characteristics.

Program Structure

Zero-base budgeting requires that the activities of an organization be grouped into programs. Programs are collections of activities that have similar goals and are targeted toward similar constituencies. Within a state government, examples of programs dealing with the environment are air quality control, water quality control, wildlife preservation, and chemical disposal.

Decision Packages

For each activity that an organizational unit carries out and for which it requests support, the unit must prepare a decision package, which includes the following:

a. A statement of purpose, in which the objectives of the activity are set forth.

b. An indication of the benefits, in quantifiable terms, that would accrue to the organization or the constituency that it serves assuming various levels of funding. Most organizations that have adopted zero-base budgeting require that the lowest level of funding be one that is considerably below that at which the activity is presently operating. In fact, assessment of alternative levels of funding is one of the primary benefits of zero-base budgeting.

---

[6]Peter A. Pyhrr, "Zero-Base Budgeting," *Harvard Business Review*, 48 (November-December 1970), pp. 111–121; and Bruce R. Neumann and James D. Suver, "Zero-Base Budgeting," *Hospital and Health Services Administration* (spring 1979), pp. 41–62.

The specific amounts that a unit requests must take into account the relationships between costs and benefits, with specific attention directed to the incremental costs to be incurred throughout the "relevant range." If substantive benefits can be achieved only by the addition of a complete package of resources, such as an additional training center or research laboratory, it makes little sense to appropriate to the unit sufficient funds for only one-half of a package. Such funds would be wasted; they would not enable the unit to increase output. This feature recognizes the "lumpiness" of many costs. Implicit in zero-base budgeting is the abandonment of practices whereby the appropriation to a unit is increased by a fixed, "across the board" percentage over what it was in a previous year without due regard for the "steps" in its cost function. This "radical" change can often benefit every budget process.

c. An indication of alternative means by which the objective might be accomplished. This requirement is intended to assure that the unit managers have given thought to other, perhaps more effective ways of accomplishing their mission.

Ranking

Each increment of funding within a decision package must be ranked in order of priority with similar increments of decision packages for other activities within the same program. The title "zero-base budgeting" is derived from the requirement that all activities for which funds are requested—not only new activities—be incorporated into the rankings and thereby be subject to review. Justification of funds should start from base zero. If an agency wants to be assured of receiving funding for a new activity, it would ordinarily have to rank it higher than at least some increments of existing activities. It thereby runs the risk that a new activity will be funded only at the expense of an existing one. It is expected that existing activities will be reviewed each budgetary cycle and those that are no longer as effective as proposed new ones will be ranked low and thus receive either little or no funding.

The Contribution of Zero-Base Budgeting

While zero-base budgeting is no longer required by the federal government, it is effectively used by many state and local governmental units and human service agencies. Empirical studies have provided no evidence that zero-base budgeting has had a significant effect on the allocation of available resources. This is to be expected. Budgeting in organizations, be they government or business, reflects the relative desires and powers of various constituents. In jurisdictions in which the constituents have diverse and often conflicting interests and views of what the objectives of the organization ought to be, there is no single "rational" or optimum allocation scheme. Irrespective of how persuasive the budgetary justifications may be, they are unlikely to change underlying beliefs and values.

The primary contribution of program budgeting or zero-base budgeting is that it institutionalizes practices that should be followed in any budgeting system. It requires organizations to establish goals, express benefits in quantifiable terms, analyze costs, consider alternatives, and establish priorities. Many organizations need this structure to develop effective managerial processes. To such organizations, the improvements caused by these budgeting processes can be dramatic.

COMPUTER SPREADSHEETS

Budgets are the quintessential spreadsheet application. Spreadsheets permit multiple-column worksheets to be prepared with elaborate linkages among their various elements. Because dependent variables can be recalculated rapidly and automatically, they facilitate ''what if'' analysis, thereby enabling managers to test the impact of alternative assumptions and courses of action.

Computer spreadsheets, however, can impair as well as promote sound budgeting. They can easily surround budgets with an aura of accuracy and reliability that is undeserved. Spreadsheet budgets are, of course, no more dependable than the underlying projections and assumptions and are subject to computational flaws caused by human errors in data and formula entry.

The more serious shortcoming of spreadsheets is that they take considerable time to develop. Ironically, therefore, they may encourage rigidity rather than flexibility. Once managers have invested time in a particular budgetary format, they may be reluctant to change it.

Further, spreadsheet budgets may give an unjustified illusion of comparability among departments. Different departments can readily prepare budgets that are in the same form. However, their underlying equations and projections—not necessarily visible on the printed page or computer screen—may not be identical.

Summary

Budgeting is not merely a technical activity in which an organization and its components must periodically engage; it represents the essence of management. The budgeting process enables an organization to determine its objectives, develop strategies and plans, allocate resources, and establish the basis for measuring performance.

Budgets can take many forms. None is inherently preferable to others. The superiority of one form over another depends ultimately on the extent to which it provides the information necessary to carry out the functions of management. The manner in which budgets are prepared and executed can, however, have a significant impact on the attitudes and performance of those affected by them. The ''behavioral'' effects of budgets may not yet be well understood. Nevertheless, managers and accountants must be sensitive to their potential dysfunctional consequences for the organization and do what they can to ameliorate them.

Exercise for Review and Self-Testing

Robertson Lighting Fixtures, Inc., has established as an objective for 1994 a 10 percent increase in gross margin (defined as sales revenue minus cost of goods sold). The company estimates that each of the factors which enters into production of its lighting fixtures will increase by 6 percent over what it was in 1993. At the same time, the company believes that it will be able to increase the selling prices of its fixtures by 6 percent.

In 1993 the cost of producing each fixture, based on a volume of 60,000 units, was $17, comprising the following elements:

Variable costs		
Direct labor	$6.00	
Raw materials	6.00	
Variable overhead	2.00	$14.00
Fixed costs		
Depreciation	$1.00	
Other fixed costs	2.00	3.00
Total cost per unit		$17.00

Inasmuch as the firm does not intend to acquire new assets in 1994, the charge for depreciation can be expected to remain the same as it was in 1993.

The selling price of the lighting fixtures was $20 per unit in 1993. In 1993 the firm sold as many units as it produced; it expects to do the same in 1994. Operating profit in 1993 was $180,000.

1. How many units must the firm produce and sell in 1994 if it is to meet its objective of a 10 percent increase in gross margin?
2. The firm allows its customers 30 days from date of sale to make payment. Under the assumptions that sales are spread evenly throughout the year and that the firm meets the sales target determined in part 1, how much can the company expect to collect in cash in 1994?
3. How much cash should the company budget to meet production requirements, assuming that all production costs (excluding depreciation, of course) are paid for in the year incurred?
4. The firm is taxed at an effective rate of 40 percent. The fixed assets on which depreciation is charged were acquired in January 1993 at a cost of $360,000. Useful life is expected to be six years with no salvage value. The firm charges depreciation for general-purpose reporting on the straight-line basis, but uses the sum-of-the-years' digits method for tax computations.
   a. How much cash should the firm allocate for the payment of 1994 taxes?
   b. What would be the amount of the tax expense to be reported on its 1994 financial statement? (Assume that the firm incurs no costs other than those indicated.)

Questions for Review and Discussion

1. Why is it difficult, if not impossible, to prepare a budget without taking into account organizational goals? Why is it also difficult to establish objectives without due regard for the organizational budget?
2. What is meant by "operational" objectives? Why is it particularly important that not-for-profit organizations develop operational objectives?
3. Why may maximization of profits be an objective of limited utility for many units of a corporation?
4. What are three broad categories of techniques that can be used to forecast sales?
5. Why is a budget a "political" document, in *both* nonbusiness and business organizations?

6. Why might it be said that the budget is a much more significant document in government organizations than it is in business firms?
7. What is a "master" budget?
8. What are the essential elements of *zero-base* budgeting? What is the significance of the term *zero base*?
9. Why may budgets result in diminished rather than enhanced performance?
10. In what ways can hostility toward budgets be ameliorated?

Problems

1. *Principles of cost behavior are as fundamental to budgeting in the public sector as in the private sector.*

   The Eyes for the Needy Center, an agency of a State Department of Welfare, provides eyeglasses for children of parents who are receiving government financial assistance. Children are referred to the center after receiving preliminary eye examinations by either school teachers or social workers.

   In 1993, its second year of operation, the center served 21,000 children. It gave each child an eye examination and issued 21,000 pairs of eyeglasses. The total cost of operating the center was $2,142,000—approximately $102 per client served—broken down as follows:

Director	$ 72,000
Ophthalmologist	120,000
Optometrists (7 @ $69,000)	483,000
Technician	30,000
Secretaries (2 @ $30,000)	60,000
Nurses (7 @ $39,000)	273,000
Maintenance worker	24,000
Department of Welfare charge for overhead (fixed cost)	306,000
Glasses (21,000 @ $30)	630,000
Other supplies (21,000 @ $3)	63,000
Other operating costs ($18,000 + 21,000 @ $3)	81,000
Total operating costs	$2,142,000

   The director of the center recently submitted a budget request for 1994 for $2,573,613. This represents a 20 percent ($428,400) increase in costs over the budget for 1993. According to the budget officer, such an increase would allow for the expansion of the program so that 20 percent (4,200) additional children might be served.

   Within the range relevant to this problem all costs behave as implied by the data. To the extent that additional employees must be hired, they must be employed full time.

   a. Assume that you are a budget officer of the Department of Welfare and you accept the need for a 20% increase in services provided. How much of an increase in expenditures (both in dollars and percent) would you be willing to approve?

   b. Suppose that for the following year, 1995, the director believes it necessary to serve an additional 1,800 clients. What is the dollar amount of a budget increase that you as a budget officer would be willing to approve? Compare the percent increases in services and in costs with those budgeted for 1994.

   c. The director of the center has established a policy that one month's supply of glasses should be on hand at all times. The director has estimated that as of

December 31, 1993, only 1,400 pairs of glasses will be on hand. All will be paid for in January 1994. The December 31, 1994, inventory will be based on number of glasses to be dispensed in 1994 (i.e., 25,200).

Glasses must ordinarily be paid for within 30 days after they are received. Glasses ordered in 1994 will be received uniformly throughout the year.

How much cash will have to be disbursed to pay for eyeglasses in 1994? Do you think that the budgeted amount for eyeglasses should be based on cost of eyeglasses (1) received, (2) dispensed, or (3) paid for? Explain.

2. *Cash disbursements depend on timing of production, purchases, and payments.*

LHG Industries assembles electronic devices. It purchases required components in sets.

The firm orders the components twice per month, on the 4th and 19th days of the month. Orders are filled in 10 days. Terms are 2/10, n/30. A 2 percent discount is granted for payment within 10 days; payment is due within 30 days. Invoices are received along with the goods (on the 14th and 29th of the month) and payment is made eight days later (on the 22nd and 7th of the month).

It is the policy of the firm to order a sufficient quantity of components so that it will have on hand on the 1st and 16th of the month, 140 percent of the number of sets to satisfy the requirements of the next 15 days. The 40 percent above the actual requirements represents a safety stock in the event of a delay in the receipt of an order.

The firm forecast that the number of devices to be assembled in December 1993 and the first four months of 1994 will be as follows.

December 1993	9,000 units
January 1994	6,000 units
February	5,000 units
March	7,000 units
April	8,000 units

Assembly takes place uniformly throughout the month.

Cost per set of components is $3 after taking into account the cash discount of 2 percent.

a. Compute the number of sets of components that the firm must order each 15-day period in the first three months of 1994.

b. Determine the amount of each cash payment the firm must make during the first three months of 1994. Summarize by month the expected cash disbursements.

3. *Budgeted cost of goods sold may differ substantially from budgeted production costs.*

Aranya, Inc., forecasts that sales for 1994 and first quarter 1995 will be (by quarter and in units):

Quarter	Units
1994	
I	26,000
II	34,000
III	40,000
IV	80,000
Total, 1994	180,000
1995	
I	26,000

Sales price per unit is $100. Manufacturing costs are expected to be as follows:

Variable costs per unit	$ 63
Fixed costs, total	$2,514,400

Selling and administrative costs are anticipated to be $4,000,000 per year.

The firm has established a policy of maintaining an inventory at the end of each quarter of approximately 10 percent of estimated sales for the coming quarter. However, ending inventory as of December 31, 1993 is expected to be 3,000 units.

Fixed manufacturing costs as well as selling and administrative costs are incurred evenly throughout the year.

a. Prepare a schedule in which you indicate the number of units that should be produced, by quarter, in 1994.

b. Prepare a schedule in which you indicate, by quarter, forecasted cash flow for 1994. Assume that collections on sales are made in the quarter in which the sales are made and that all manufacturing, selling, and administrative costs are paid in cash in the quarter in which they are incurred.

c. Prepare a schedule in which you indicate estimated earnings by quarter for 1994. Assume that fixed manufacturing costs are assigned to units produced via an overhead charging rate based on estimated annual production (as determined in part a) and costs. The per unit cost of goods held in inventory on December 31, 1993 is the same as that of the goods to be produced in 1994.

4. *Careful cash budgeting facilitates tight controls over the amounts in interest-free accounts and enables calculation of the opportunity cost associated with average balance requirements.*

Barlev Industries has a weekly payroll of $280,000. It issues checks to its employees each Wednesday. The following schedule indicates the company's estimate, based on past experience, of the percentage of checks that will clear its bank on the days subsequent to that on which they were issued.

Thursday	20%
Friday	30%
Monday	20%
Tuesday	10%
Wednesday	5%
Thursday	5%
Friday	5%
Monday	5%

The company maintains a separate bank account for its payroll transactions. Because its bank does not pay interest on commercial checking accounts, the company maintains no more than the minimum required balance. That minimum, as determined by the company, is the dollar amount of the checks expected to clear on any given day plus a safety stock of $10,000. Each afternoon, just prior to the close of business, the company transfers the funds necessary to satisfy the checks that will clear the following day from an interest-bearing account to the payroll account. The deposit required to meet the checks that will clear on Monday is made on Friday afternoon.

The company is considering accepting a line of credit from the bank. Under the terms of the credit agreement, it will be required to maintain an average daily balance in a checking account (the payroll account is acceptable) of $100,000. Average daily balance is based on the amount on deposit at the close of each day.

The company earns interest at the rate of 12 percent per annum on funds on deposit in its interest-bearing account.

a. Prepare a schedule in which you indicate the dollar amount of checks that will clear each day over any period of seven days. Determine the balance required at the start of business on each of the days taking into account the safety stock.

b. Compute the *average* balance that the firm would have to maintain over the period of seven days.

c. Calculate the effective incremental cost to the company of maintaining the balance that would be required under the terms of the line of credit agreement.

5. *A cash receipts budget must take into account the timing of collections on sales.*

The Paskow Co. sells on terms 2/10, n/30. A 2 percent discount is granted for payment within 10 days; payment is due within 30 days.

Experience indicates the following pattern of collections:

Within the 10-day discount period	60%
Within 1 month of sale	18%
Within 2 months of sale	15%
Within 3 months of sale	5%
Uncollectible	2%
	100%

Sales are made uniformly throughout the month, and collections tend to occur at the end of the month or within the discount period—whichever comes sooner. (Thus, for sales on December 1 that will be collected within the discount period, 60 percent will be collected before December 10 and another 18 percent will be collected by the end of December. For sales on December 21–31, 60 percent will be collected by the end of December and another 18 percent by the end of January.)

Sales for the month of December were $300,000.

Prepare a schedule in which you indicate the amount of December sales that will be collected in December, January, February, and March. For convenience, assume that each month has 30 days.

6. *Cash receipts and disbursements can be ''modeled'' by a series of algebraic equations.*

Times Square Industries intends to develop a computer program that will project monthly cash requirements. In order to facilitate the programming, budget analysts must first develop a cash flow ''model'' that expresses in the form of algebraic equations the influences on cash receipts, cash disbursements, and ending cash balances.

The analysts have identified the following relationships:

Of the sales in a particular month, 75 percent are collected in the month of sale and 25 percent are collected in the following month.

The firm requires an inventory of finished goods equal to 15 percent of the expected sales of the following month. Production each month is equal, therefore, to 85 percent of current sales plus 15 percent of the next month's anticipated sales.

The firm requires an inventory of raw materials equal to 10 percent of the expected production of the following month. Raw materials purchases are equal, therefore, to 90 percent of current production plus 10 percent of next month's anticipated production. Eighty percent of raw materials are paid for in the month of purchase; the remaining 20 percent are paid for in the following month. Three pounds of raw materials are required for each unit of production.

Seventy-five percent of labor costs are paid in the month in which the employees provide their services; the remaining 25 percent are paid for in the following month. Each unit of product requires 0.1 hours of direct labor. Fixed labor costs are $20,000 per month.

Administrative costs are $50,000 per month.

Sales commissions are 3 percent of sales; they are paid on sales of the previous month.

The analysts have agreed on the following notation:

$$
\begin{aligned}
B &= \text{cash balance, end of month} \\
R &= \text{cash receipts in a month} \\
O &= \text{total cash outlays in a month} \\
D &= \text{disbursements for raw materials} \\
L &= \text{disbursements for labor costs} \\
A &= \text{disbursements for administrative costs} \\
C &= \text{disbursements for sales commissions} \\
P &= \text{production in units} \\
M &= \text{purchases of raw materials (in dollars)} \\
S &= \text{sales in units} \\
Pr &= \text{selling price per unit} \\
H &= \text{labor rate per hour} \\
U &= \text{raw materials price per pound}
\end{aligned}
$$

Amounts of a previous or subsequent month are to be indicated by the subscript $n - 1$ or $n + 1$. Thus if sales in units for the current month are indicated by S, sales for the past month would be denoted by S_{n-1} and those of the next month by S_{n+1}.

a. Develop a model, consisting of a series of related equations, which can be used to determine the cash balance at the end of a month. If possible, enter these equations into a spreadsheet budget model.

b. Applying the equations on the spreadsheet model, determine the cash balance that can be anticipated at the end of February 1994. Sales for the first four months of 1994 are expected to be as follows:

January	40,000 units
February	30,000 units
March	50,000 units
April	50,000 units

Other variables are expected to be:

Selling price per unit (Pr)	$10.00
Labor rate per hour (H)	$16.00
Raw materials price per pound (U)	$2.00
January production in units (P_{n-1})	38,500 units
January purchases of raw materials (M_{n-1})	$227,700
Cash balance, January 31, (B_{n-1})	$8,000

7. *A master budget links together a number of related schedules.*

Vitality Cosmetics, Inc., produces two products, a cologne for men and a cologne for women. Management of the firm forecasts that the balance sheet for the year ending December 31, 1993, will be (in condensed form) as follows:

Statement of Position
(December 31, 1993)

Assets

Cash		$1,500,000
Accounts receivable		1,280,000
Raw materials inventory		200,000
Finished goods inventory		160,000
Plant and equipment	$1,800,000	
Less: Accumulated depreciation	600,000	1,200,000
Total assets		$4,340,000

Liabilities and Owners' Equity

Accounts payable		$ 950,000
Owners' equity		
Common stock	$3,000,000	
Retained earnings	390,000	3,390,000
Total liabilities and owners' equity		$4,340,000

Management has decided that preparation of the 1994 budget will be governed by the following assumptions:

Sales of men's cologne will be 420,000 bottles at $12 per bottle; sales of women's cologne will be 360,000 bottles at $15 per bottle.

Inventory of finished goods at December 31, 1994 should be at a level equal to production of one month (i.e., 35,000 bottles of men's cologne; 30,000 bottles of women's cologne).

Inventory of raw materials at December 31, 1994 should be at a level equal to 10 percent of the production for the year.

The inventory of finished goods at December 31, 1993 comprises 20,000 bottles of men's cologne produced at a cost of $2.70 per bottle and 40,000 bottles of women's cologne produced at a cost of $2.65 per bottle.

Direct labor costs will be $.50 per bottle for both the men's and the women's cologne.

Direct materials costs will be $2 per bottle for the men's cologne and $2.10 per bottle for the women's cologne.

Manufacturing overhead, which is applied to products via an overhead charging rate based on direct labor dollars, will be:

Supplies	$ 40,000
Indirect labor	80,000
Building occupancy costs	34,750
Depreciation	120,000
Total	$274,750

Selling and advertising costs for the year will be $3,200,000. Administration costs will be $1,480,000.

The ending balance in accounts receivable will be equal to 12 percent of dollar sales for the year.

Income taxes are paid at a rate of 40 percent.

The ending balance in accounts payable will be equal to 10 percent of obligations incurred during the year, including those for purchases of raw materials, direct labor, overhead (excluding depreciation), selling and advertising, administration, and income taxes.

Prepare a budget comprising the following schedules:
1. Sales
2. Units to be produced
3. Direct labor costs
4. Direct materials costs
5. Purchases (dollars)
6. Manufacturing overhead
7. Per unit cost of goods manufactured
8. Cost of goods sold
9. Statement of income
10. Cash receipts
11. Cash disbursements
12. Summary of changes in cash balance
13. Statement of Position, December 31, 1994

8. *Subjective probabilities can be used in forecasting cash flows and assessing the need for a line of credit. (This problem requires knowledge of "subjective probabilities," a topic often dealt with in courses in statistics. An introduction to subjective probabilities was provided in this text in Chapter 20.)*

Quality Brands, Inc., has assigned the following subjective probabilities to sales in 1994 (in millions):

Sales	Probability
$400	.2
500	.5
600	.3

Variable costs are approximately 60 percent of sales revenue. Fixed costs are $180 million per year. In the course of 1994 the firm will have to retire $30 million in long-term debt. It may be assumed that all revenues will be received and all costs will be paid in cash.

The firm expects to have zero cash on hand at the start of 1994.
a. Determine the anticipated cash balance (or deficit) at year end 1994 for each level of sales as well as the *expected* value of the cash balance (or deficit).
b. Insofar as the firm has a cash deficit at year end 1994 it would be required to borrow funds in the amount of the shortage. The period of the loan would be for one year. It is anticipated that interest rates will increase substantially during 1994. The firm has the opportunity to obtain a line of credit from a bank at the start of 1994. The line of credit would allow the firm to borrow the required funds up to an agreed-upon limit at an interest rate of 10 percent regardless of subsequent increases in prevailing rates. The cost of the line of credit would be 1 percent of the funds that are available to the firm for borrowing (i.e., the credit limit less the amount that has already been borrowed). Economists forecast that by the end of 1994 prevailing rates of interest will increase to 16 percent.

Management of Quality Brands is considering whether it should establish a line of credit with a limit equal to the maximum amount that it might have to borrow. If, for example, the maximum cash shortage (as determined in part a) were $100 million, then the cost of establishing the line of credit at the start of 1994 would be $1 million (1 percent of $100 million). In return for this amount, the firm would have the right to borrow up to $100 million at the end of 1994 at the rate of 10 percent. If it did not establish the line of credit, the rate of interest on amounts to be borrowed would be 16 percent.

Should the firm establish a line of credit equal in amount to the *maximum* cash shortage that might exist as of the end of 1994? Explain.

9. *Can academic accountants apply the theories that they espouse?*

The recently appointed chairman of the Department of Accounting of a large midwestern state university gave a presentation on budgeting for nonprofit organizations. He concluded his remarks with the following comment:

> In summary, let me emphasize that the budget must relate to organizational objectives. The budgetary materials must include a statement of *operational* objectives. Such objectives must be specific and quantifiable. If additional funds are requested in the budget, then supporting documents should indicate the resultant benefits to the constituents served by the organization. Such benefits should, of course, be tied directly to the objectives and should, if at all possible, be quantified. At the conclusion of the period covered by the budget it should be possible to measure the extent to which the anticipated benefits were, in fact, realized and the organizational goals achieved.

The mission of an academic department of accounting is, in general terms, threefold:

(1) To educate students
(2) To conduct research
(3) To serve the university, the accounting profession, and the academic community at large

The faculty and the chairman of the department of accounting agree that budgetary allocations from the university administration need to be increased. Additional funds are required to increase faculty salaries, to provide funds so that faculty members can travel to professional conferences, to raise the level of secretarial services, to provide summer research grants for faculty and graduate students, to purchase instructional equipment and materials, to support development of new courses, and to increase the amount of computer time available to students.

The Department of Accounting is in direct competition for funds with other academic departments throughout the University.

a. Prepare the rudiments of a budget request in which you set forth operational goals, specify the benefits to be derived from an increase in the funds allocated to the Department of Accounting, and indicate the criteria by which departmental performance can be measured. Draw on your own general knowledge of the goals of an academic department and the activities in which it engages.

b. Comment on the extent to which the objectives you set forth are truly the goals of the Department of Accounting rather than merely factors that can conveniently be quantified. Will it be possible to measure objectively the extent to which the objectives have been realized?

10. *Zero-base budget decision packages highlight the dangers of across-the-board budget reductions.*

As a consequence of an unprofitable year, the chief executive officer of Beauty-Wax, Inc., ordered a minimum 20 percent across-the-board cut in all nonmanufacturing costs for 1994. The budget of Unit A of the firm's research department for 1993 is as follows:

Senior chemist	$ 65,000
Staff chemists (2 @ $45,000)	90,000
Laboratory technician	25,000
Supplies	15,000
Total	$195,000

Unit A is working on the development of a new household wax. Each chemist is researching a different phase of the project. Each phase can be performed concurrently, and it is estimated that the project can be completed by the end of 1994 at the present rate of progress. If, however, any one member of the team is eliminated, then that phase will have to be delayed until the other chemists can turn their attention to it upon completion of their other work. Even if two chemists were to work on any one phase, however, the phase could not be completed more rapidly than if a single chemist were to work on it.

If one chemist were eliminated, supply costs could be reduced by $4,000. The work could not be carried out satisfactorily without a laboratory technician.

It is expected that the new product will provide earnings of $500,000 per year.

a. Prepare a zero-base budget decision package (containing the type of information described in the text) for 1994 which includes data for two levels of funding: the current level and a level that would put the unit in compliance with the order of the chief executive officer (i.e., a reduction in costs of at least 20 percent). Be sure to indicate the consequences of the reduction in funds. Omit consideration of specific work load performance measures and alternative means of carrying out the project.

b. Comment on the dangers of across-the-board budget cuts.

11. *Budgets, even if only in summary form, must be designed to provide information that is useful to those who will use them.*

Exhibit 21-2 is the complete budget summary of the Department of Public Welfare of a large southwestern state. It is an actual budget, not merely a textbook illustration.

The budget item "Assistance payments" represents direct grants to various groups of needy, including families with dependent children, the aged, the blind, and the disabled. "Medical assistance programs" include medical services in nursing homes and state institutions for the mentally retarded, diagnostic medical exams, dental services, drugs, and hearing aids. "Social services programs" comprise protective and support services (e.g., counseling) for children, the aged, the blind, and the disabled. "Contract services" are services which the Department contracts out to private parties, such as nursing homes.

A member of the state legislature has many retired persons in his district and, as a consequence, is especially concerned with the commitment of the state to provide services for the aged. He requests that you review the budget summary in order to learn how much the Department of Public Welfare intends to spend on services and direct financial aid to the aged.

a. Review carefully the budget summary. Can you determine how much the Department of Public Welfare intends to spend on services and direct financial aid to the aged?

b. In contrast, can you determine how much the Department of Public Welfare intends to spend on "gas, oil, and grease" or "transportation of things"?

c. Which of the two questions is likely to be of greater significance to members of the legislature or citizens of the state?

d. Suppose that you were able to examine the detailed budget, not merely the summary. Why is it likely that you would still be unable to obtain the information requested by the legislator?

e. Based on information contained in the budget, as well as on your general knowledge of the activities carried out by a state department of public welfare, indicate how the budget could be recast in order to provide information that would be of greater utility to members of the legislature and citizens of the state.

EXHIBIT 21-2

State Department of Public Welfare
Operating Budget—Statewide Budget Summary

Administration			Rentals	
Personal services			Office and warehouse space	$ 2,277,315
Board members' per diem	$ 3,600		Equipment—data processing	1,929,840
Exempt positions	1,127,500		Other	175,210
Salaries of classified positions	72,848,166		Employees' insurance premiums	1,366,603
Seasonal help	41,590		Merit system expenses	226,489
Planned future program adjustments due to changing	1,948,590		Allocation of federal funds to counties (operating expense fund)	666,025
Planned food stamp adjustment	1,681,474		Commodity emergency (rider appropriation)	30,000
Professional educational stipends	225,985		Professional educational services to graduate schools of social work	500,000
Professional fees and services	1,499,998		Other operating expenses	5,916,641
Examining and professional fees—medical	831,010		Subtotal, operating expenses	$ 18,283,552
Supplemental income (matching)	4,352,439			
Employees' retirement matching	4,621,329		Capital outlay	
Subtotal: Personal services	$89,191,681		Equipment and furniture	$ 789,666
Less: Estimated salary lapse	(3,051,603)		Land purchased	0
			Land improvements	0
Total, personal srvices	$86,130,078		Buildings	0
			Subtotal, capital outlay	$ 789,666
Travel expense	$ 5,258,427		Total, administration	$110,461,712
			Assistance payments	235,218,794
Operating expense			Medical assistance programs	506,448,957
Printing and office supplies	$ 964,002		Social services programs	35,024,375
Gas, oil, grease, etc.	24,960		Contract services	9,041,235
Other supplies and materials	776,127		Grand total, Department of Public Welfare	$896,195,073
Postage	1,790,591			
Utilities, telephone, and telegraph	1,438,751			
Transportation of things	83,998			
Other repairs	117,000			

12. *A university budget cannot necessarily be relied on to reveal the extent to which the football team is subsidized.*

The following is an excerpt of a letter to the editor of *The Wall Street Journal* (published February 18, 1981) from the President of The University of Texas:

> In your Jan. 29 front page article, "Colleges Spend Millions to Modify Buildings for Disabled Students," you quoted a federal bureaucrat as saying, "The University of Texas subsidizes its football team heavily." Not true. The Department of Intercollegiate Athletics for Men, which includes the football team, earns its own way from gate receipts, television income and private benefactions. We do subsidize Women's Intercollegiate Athletics.

a. Suppose that you were the federal bureaucrat referred to in the letter. You are asked to support your assertion that the University of Texas subsidizes its football team heavily. You examine the budget of the Department of Intercollegiate Athletics for men and find that, as the President indicated, the Department receives no University revenues.

Assuming that you have access to the budget of the entire University, how might you go about defending your position? What questions would you want to resolve?

b. Suppose that your investigation reveals that The University of Texas does, in fact, "subsidize" intercollegiate athletics when *all* benefits provided are taken into account. What deficiencies or limitations does this suggest with respect to University budgeting practices? Are there any changes that you would recommend?

13. *Effective budgeting requires that costs be related to objectives. Nevertheless, budgeting remains, to a great extent, a political process.*

Case: Halfway House Program

A southwestern state operates a program of "halfway houses" for teenagers who have run away from home or have been delinquent (primarily those who have been arrested for minor drug violations). The halfway houses are located throughout the state, and teenagers are assigned to a house that is located within or near their county of residence. The centers provide food and lodging for the teenagers. While they are residing at the houses, the teenagers are encouraged to meet, both individually and in groups, with trained counselors, who help them work out their problems and pave the way for a return to their homes and schools. In addition, the program provides that each teenager receives a thorough physical exam and medical counseling to help control any physical problems (such as weight) that might contribute to his or her emotional problems.

To date the program has been generally successful. A recent survey indicated that over 75 percent of the teenagers who spent time at the halfway houses returned to their homes, improved their grades at school, abandoned the use of drugs, and did not subsequently run away.

Each center serves approximately 40 teenagers at a time. The average stay is two months; hence each house serves approximately 240 teenagers per year.

There are currently 20 halfway houses in operation throughout the state. Since the program began, each of the centers has always been filled to its prescribed capacity of 40. Indeed, there is a considerable waiting list for admission to each of the houses. As a consequence, the administrators of the program see a need to expand the number of teenagers served. They prefer to increase the number of halfway houses, but as an alternative they would increase the prescribed enrollment at each house from 40 to maximum practical capacity of 50. An increase in the number served at existing houses may, of course, decrease the level of service, but the administrators believe that an increase in stated capacity of each house will better serve the people of the state than the existing limitations on the number of teenagers served.

The administrators also believe that the program would be considerably more effective if the ratio of counselors to teenagers improved. At present, a ratio of one counselor for each ten teenagers is maintained. The administrators would like to increase that ratio to one counselor for each eight teenagers.

The cost of operating the entire program is $10,480,000 per year; that of operating each of the 20 centers is $524,000. The cost of maintaining a teenager at the center is, on average, $13,100 per year (or $2,184 for a two-month stay). The breakdown of costs is presented in Exhibit 21-3.

a. Specify the costs and benefits of increasing capacity of each of the existing 20 centers by 10 teenagers (a total of 1,200, assuming that each teenager stays at a center for one-sixth of a year).

EXHIBIT 21-3

Annual Cost of Operating a Halfway House
(Based on Capacity of 40)

Rent	$24,000
Director	56,000
Counselors (4 @ $40,000)	160,000
Kitchen and maintenance employee	32,000
Furniture and fixtures[a]	12,000
Food ($4,000 per teenager per year)	160,000
Supplies and miscellaneous costs ($600 per teenager per year)	24,000
Utilities	6,000
Medical and drugs ($800 per teenager per year)	32,000
Central office costs[b]	18,000
Total costs per center	$524,000

Total cost of program: $524,000 × 20 centers = $10,480,000

[a]Total cost of furniture and fixtures is $48,000; useful life is four years.
[b]Central office costs are $360,000. They are divided equally among the 20 centers. Of the central office costs, approximately $240,000 are fixed; the remainder vary with the number of centers.

b. Specify the costs and benefits of serving the additional 200 teenagers (1,200 per year) at five *new* centers, each with 40 teenagers. The centers would be located in areas not presently served by the program.

c. Which of the alternatives described in parts a and b would you recommend? Explain.

d. Specify the costs and benefits of increasing the ratio of counselors to teenagers at each of the existing 20 centers from 1:10 to 1:8.

e. Suppose that the state was forced to reduce the scope of the program. The administrator of the program was informed that his budget would be reduced by 15 percent ($1,572,000). How would you recommend that the cuts be effected? Indicate the reductions in costs and benefits that would result.

Solutions to Exercise for Review and Self-Testing

1. Required number of units to be produced and sold to meet objective of 10 percent increase in gross margin.

a. Required margin: 110% of 1993 margin of $180,000; thus, $198,000.

b. Anticipated selling price: 106% of $20.00; thus, $21.20.

c. Anticipated variable costs: 106% of $14.00; thus, $14.84 per unit.

d. Anticipated depreciation: no change; $1.00 per unit times
1993 production volume of 60,000 units .... $ 60,000
Anticipated other fixed costs:
106% of $2.00 per unit times
1993 production volume of 60,000 units 127,200
Total anticipated fixed costs $187,200

e. Revenue − Fixed costs − Variable costs = Required margin
Let x = number of units required to be produced and sold
$$\$21.20x - \$187,200 - \$14.84x = \$198,000$$
$$\$6.36x = \$385,200$$
$$x = 60,566 \text{ units}$$

2. Anticipated cash collections in 1994
   a. Units sold per month in 1993:
      60,000 ÷ 12 = 5,000
      Units to be sold per month in 1994:
      60,566 ÷ 12 = 5,047
   b. Collections from sales of 1993
      (1 month; 5,000 units @ $20.00) $ 100,000
      Collections from sales of 1994
      (11 months; 5,047 units @ $21.20
      times 11)   1,176,960
          Total cash collections $1,276,960

3. Anticipated cash disbursements to meet 1994 production requirements
   Anticipated fixed costs, excluding
      depreciation (per part 1.d.) $ 127,200
   Anticipated variable costs: $14.84 per unit
   (per part 1.c.) times anticipated production
   of 60,566 units (per part 1.e.)   898,799
       Total cash disbursements to meet 1994
       production requirements $1,025,999

4. a. Required tax payment. Depreciation for tax purposes using sum-of-the-years'
      digits method (sum of digits for useful life of 6 years = 21; in 1994, assets have
      5 years of useful life remaining): 5/21 × 360,000 = 85,714.

Sales revenue		
(60,566 units @ 21.20)		$1,283,999
Less: Cost of goods produced and sold		
Variable costs (60,566 @ $14.84)	$898,799	
Depreciation	85,714	
Other fixed costs	127,200	1,111,713
Taxable income		$ 172,286
Tax rate		× .40
Required tax payment		$ 68,914

   b. Reported tax expense. Depreciation for reporting purposes is computed using
      the straight-line method and is, as indicated in part 1.d, $60,000 per year. The
      reported tax expense would be based on reported income.

Sales revenue		$1,283,999
Less: Cost of goods produced and sold		
Variable costs		
(60,566 @ $14.84)	$898,799	
Depreciation	60,000	
Other fixed costs	127,200	1,085,999
Income before taxes		$ 198,000
Tax rate		× .40
Tax expense		$ 79,200

22

Reporting On and Controlling Performance

Management accounting focuses primarily on costs. As emphasized throughout this text, cost information must be tailored to the managerial objectives it is intended to help achieve:

- In Chapter 17, we investigated various cost concepts and showed how cost control can be facilitated by distinguishing between fixed and variable costs.
- In Chapter 18, we discussed how costs can be applied to particular products.
- In Chapter 19, we investigated how costs can be presented to expedite *ad hoc* decisions, such as at what price a product should be sold, and whether to continue or discontinue a product line, make or buy goods or services, and sell products now or process them further.
- In Chapter 20, we considered how costs should be fashioned for long-range plans, such as those involving capital acquisitions.
- In Chapter 21, we examined short-run budgeting and control.

In this chapter, we explore the performance assessments and control techniques that are an integral part of a comprehensive management system. Management must continuously evaluate its plans as events unfold, and if the plans are not being met must either change them or take appropriate corrective measures. We start with an overview of performance assessment and then turn our attention to means of identifying and controlling specific variances from plans and standards.

INTERNAL PERFORMANCE ASSESSMENTS

A reporting system within an organization must provide the information that will enable the employees and members of that organization to carry out efficiently and effectively the activities for which they are responsible. The reporting system should be designed to facilitate not only routine decisions, but unusual, strategic decisions as well. A reporting system encompasses the entire accounting system of an organization—the procedures designed to accumulate, record, and summarize data relating to the goods or services that it provides or sells. Because reports intended to facilitate *strategic* decisions must be unique to the question at hand, this section shall focus only on *performance* reports. Performance reports are those designed to facilitate *management control* and, as the name implies, to evaluate the accomplishments of managers and the activities for which they are accountable. They compare actual results with those that were planned and, to the extent possible, explain any differences. They serve as the basis for correcting off-target operations and for developing plans for the future.

Performance reports are primarily a means of communicating to responsible parties the results of operations. But they are much more than that. They are implicit expressions of the objectives of the units being reported on and the criteria by which their performance will be evaluated. They indicate which of the activities engaged in by the units are sufficiently important to measure and inform managers about.

Significance of Form as Well as Substance of Information Presented

The significance of decisions as to what specific information should be included in reports cannot be minimized. Managers have neither the time nor the mental capacity to accumulate and process *all* data that might be pertinent to their responsibilities. In evaluating possible courses of action, they establish a limited number of criteria and focus on a subset of the facts that bear upon those criteria. As long as the reports available to them contain a satisfactory amount of relevant information, they are unlikely to seek out additional data. To a considerable extent, therefore, the information provided in the reports may determine the decisions made.

The *form* in which information is presented is also important and may have a direct bearing upon the messages that are conveyed by a report. As pointed out in earlier chapters, account balances by themselves have little meaning. Only when associated with other data by way of ratios and trends over time do they become of consequence. A report which indicates sales on one page and costs of goods sold on another may contain the same basic raw data as one which, in a single table, relates sales to fixed costs and variable costs. But the signals conveyed by the latter may be much more forceful than those by the former.

The perceptions of managers, like those of all human beings, are affected by subtle, subliminal factors of which they may not be aware. A graphic presentation, for example, may bring forth relationships that would go undetected if the same data were set forth in tabular form. Moreover, a graph in which a scale is compressed may lead to different inferences than one in which it is expanded. Even the use of one color as opposed to another on a graph or table may alter the perceptions of the reader.

Worthwhile Characteristics of Performance Reporting Systems

Systems of reporting are likely to continue to undergo radical changes in the next decade as they have in the past decade as the use of real-time computer systems accelerates. The concept of *periodic* reports may give way to that of continually updated, always available information. In many companies, managers at all levels already have at their desks networked computers which they can use to summon data on any aspect of operations within their control.

The discussion that follows sets forth several characteristics that a system of performance reporting should possess. They are general in nature and are applicable to online as well as to periodic reports.

Should Be Tailored to Organizational Structure

A reporting system must be designed to serve the needs of a specific organization and should be reflective of its organization chart. Information should be accumulated and reported for each *responsibility center*. A responsibility center is a segment of an organization responsible for specific activities which must be planned for, controlled, reported on, and evaluated.

A reporting system should be integrated. The total of costs and revenues of one unit should tie into the report of the unit by which it is supervised. Exhibit 22-1 illustrates the organizational chart of a manufacturing concern. Exhibit 22-2 illustrates the framework of a cost reporting system tailored to the specific hierarchy of responsibility centers. The costs flow upward from the lowest responsibility center to the highest (the office of the president).

Should Be Tailored to Individual Recipients

Reports should be tailored to individual recipients. Internal reports need not be bound by the same constraints as those intended for outsiders. Firms are free to base them on any accounting principles and present them in any form that their managers find useful.

Reports should be simple and understandable. They should contain information that is relevant to the responsibilities of the parties that will use them. They should be uncluttered by extraneous data.

If reports are to be used by more than one individual, it is obviously not feasible to design statements that satisfy completely each party's needs. Compromises must be made. The capability of computers in permitting reporting flexibility is increasing rapidly, and there is no reason for managers to be wedded to existing types of reports. They must constantly be looking for new ways to reduce the gap between information that they would like and that which is available to them.

For some individuals, data displayed graphically are more understandable than those presented in table form. Until recently, the cost of translating more than a very few numerical tables into graphs was prohibitive for most companies. Accountants, after all, are not artists and their time cannot justifiably

EXHIBIT 22-1
Excerpts from an Organization Chart

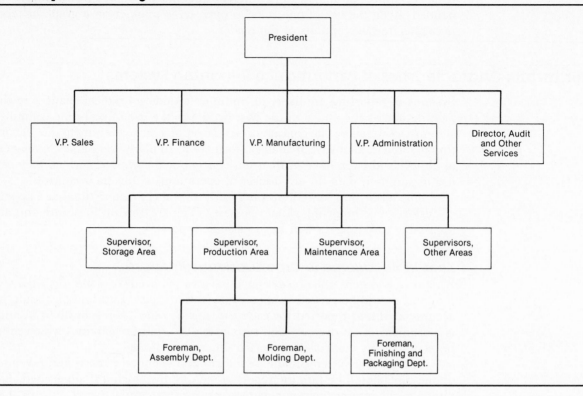

be expended on the preparation of pictures. Today, however, software packages are available which enable information to be depicted as economically in graphic as in tabular form.

Should Provide Timely Information

Reports should be prepared as often as is cost justified. The length of a reporting cycle depends on the activity being reported upon. Some processes, especially those in industrial plants, can be monitored on an ongoing basis, and any corrective action can have an instantaneous effect. The benefits to be derived from frequent reports—several per day or even per hour—may outweigh their costs. Obviously, such reports would not be comprehensive; they would focus exclusively on specific phases of a process, such as the number of gallons flowing through a particular line. Other operations—those of an accounting department, for example—cannot be controlled with such precision. The operating cycle of an accounting department may be monthly or quarterly. Control reports at more frequent intervals might provide little or no information that can be acted upon effectively.

Irrespective of how frequently reports are compiled, they should be made available to responsible officials as soon after the end of the period covered as possible. The longer the delay, the longer an aberrant condition will be permitted to exist. The contribution of the computer with regard to timely reporting is that it reduces the cost of report preparation and allows reports to be prepared more frequently as well as more rapidly.

EXHIBIT 22-2

Illustration of Hierarchical Cost Relationships

	Monthly Costs		Variance: Unfavorable (Favorable)
	Actual	Budgeted	
Report to the President			
Selling	$ 453,710	$ 430,600	$23,110
Finance	42,900	42,300	600
Manufacturing	910,576	928,600	(18,024)
Administration	108,100	106,000	2,100
Other	132,856	130,500	2,356
Total	$1,648,142	$1,638,000	$10,142
Report to the Vice-President of Manufacturing			
Production	$ 781,890	$ 803,100	($21,210)
Storage	20,710	21,000	(290)
Maintenance	92,856	90,000	2,856
Other	15,120	14,500	620
Total	$ 910,576	$ 928,600	($18,024)
Report to the Production Supervisor			
Molding Department	$ 250,124	$ 250,000	$ 124
Assembly Department	350,890	358,100	(7,210)
Finishing and Packaging Department	180,876	195,000	(14,124)
Total	$ 781,890	$ 803,100	($21,210)
Report to the Assembly Department Foreman			
Direct labor	$ 125,230	$ 123,000	$ 2,230
Direct materials	137,890	148,000	(10,110)
Total direct costs	$ 263,120	$ 271,000	($ 7,880)
Controllable overhead			
Supervision	$ 40,600	$ 40,600	$ -0-
Setup time	6,240	6,000	240
Employee benefits	25,111	24,500	$ 611
Maintenance	15,819	16,000	($ 181)
Total controllable overhead	$ 87,770	$ 87,100	$ 670
Total	$ 350,890	$ 358,100	($ 7,210)

Should Highlight Variances from Budget and Reasons for These

Performance reports should highlight deviations from budgets and standards. They should facilitate the practice of "management by exception." The emphasis of this chapter is on the interpretation of differences between plans and results. Performance reports should not only indicate the differences between budgeted and actual amounts but should explain them by way of variance analysis. Budgeted amounts should be derived from flexible rather than fixed budgets. Flexible budgets, not fixed budgets, allow for the decomposition of deviations into their elements: budget or spending variance; efficiency variance; price and volume variances.

A common type of performance report is that illustrated previously in Exhibit 22-2. It compares actual and budgeted costs and indicates the variances from budget. Often it contains three additional columns—for year-to-date amounts. This type of report is satisfactory as a means of summarizing total discrepancies. But if not used with discretion, it can do as much to mislead as to elucidate. Because costs are presented as budgeted for the *anticipated* volume of production, the report provides no indication of what they should have been at the *actual* volume. The simple magnitude of the budget variances shown are inappropriate measures of performance. We consider the *price and volume components* of variances in some detail later in this chapter.

Should Focus on Control

Finally, reports on the performance of a unit should focus on costs over which the unit has control. As indicated in this as well as previous chapters, a unit seldom has control over all costs for which it is charged. In order to determine the "full" costs of a product—costs which must be incorporated into external financial reports—overhead, such as factory rent and heat, must be allocated to the various production departments. They may be apportioned on the basis of factors, such as amount of floor space, over which the production departments have no control and, therefore, for which they should not be held accountable. To be sure, it may be desirable to include such costs on unit cost summaries in order to make the managers aware that costs are being incurred on behalf of their departments. But noncontrollable costs should be clearly segregated from those that are controllable; the emphasis of the reports should be on the controllable costs.

ANALYSIS OF VARIANCES AND CONTROL

In this chapter, we are concerned primarily with systems of reporting and control intended to facilitate the fulfillment of *operational* or *routine* plans and budgets—those which relate to the regular day-to-day, month-to-month, or quarter-to-quarter activities of a firm. We addressed the information needed for solving nonroutine, *ad hoc* decisions in Chapters 19 and 20.

Central to a sound system of internal performance assessment and control are accounting and reporting procedures that yield useful information as to deviations from plans. The data should allow for inferences as to the reasons for the deviations and, insofar as possible, should affix responsibility for them. A report that the manufacturing cost of a product was $4.00 instead of the planned $3.50 may serve as a warning that something may be amiss. But by itself it is neither illuminating as to the cause of the variance nor suggestive of what corrective actions, if any, should be taken.

Using Standard Costs for Budgeting and Evaluation

The concept of *standard cost* is at the core of many managerial control systems. *Standard cost systems* will be discussed in the sections that follow in the context of a manufacturing firm, because that is their traditional setting. However, as shall be demonstrated in a subsequent example, they are equally applicable to organizations of all types, including health-care and nonprofit enterprises.

Definition and Advantage of Standard Costs

A *standard* cost is a planned or allowable cost. The standard cost of a particular unit, be it a unit of input such as direct labor or materials, or a unit of output, such as a product manufactured, can be viewed as the amount budgeted for that unit. A *standard cost system* is one in which units are recorded at *predetermined standard* costs as opposed to actual costs incurred.

The introduction of standard costs enriches a management planning and control system in at least three ways:

1. Budgeting and planning are facilitated in that a planner can readily determine the number of units of input that should be required to produce a specific number of units of output. The costs of production can then be estimated.
2. The accounting system can be designed so that deviations from standards are automatically calculated and reported to responsible managers.
3. The recording process can be simplified because transfers from one account to another can be made on the basis of fixed, predetermined amounts rather than actual costs, which, of course, are subject to continual change.

In Chapter 18 pertaining to characteristics of costs, the advantages of applying overhead by means of a predetermined—or standard—rate were demonstrated. In this section, the additional benefits to be derived from applying direct labor and direct materials at standard costs will be discussed.

Types of Standards

At least four types of standards may be identified.

First, standards may represent an ideal level of performance—one which could be attained only under the most favorable of circumstances. Often, ideal standards are engineered standards, and once they have been established they remain set at that level until there is a change in product, manufacturing process, materials prices, or labor rates. Ideal standards generally do not take into account the frailties and imperfections of either humans or machines.

Second, standards may represent reasonably attainable goals. These standards may be less demanding than ideal standards, and they are set at a level intended to bring forth the best efforts on the part of those whose performance will be measured against them. They are *motivational* in purpose. They will not be so rigorous as to discourage attainment, but at the same time will not be so lax as to be met without maximum effort.

Third, standards may indicate what is anticipated over an extended period of time, usually a year or longer. These standards are referred to as *normal* standards. They are established with reference to past experience. They indicate what is *expected*, not necessarily what is desired. They are attainable over the period that they are designed to cover, but within shorter time spans there likely will be both favorable and unfavorable deviations.

Fourth, standards may be based on what is expected within the *immediate future*. These standards take into account current operating conditions and are revised with frequency. It is expected that they will be attained. Therefore, they represent short-term expectations.

Analysis of Variances in Direct Costs

There are two primary reasons why direct costs in manufacturing may differ from what was planned (i.e., from standard costs). First, the *price* paid for materials or direct labor may have been higher or lower than standard; second, the *quantity* of materials or direct labor used may have been greater or less than standard. Each of these reasons suggests a type of variance about which it is critical for management to be informed on a timely basis. The difference between actual and standard price forms the basis of a *price* or *rate variance*; that between actual and standard quantity forms the basis of a *quantity* or *usage (efficiency) variance*. Both of these variances in direct costs can be calculated and recorded as materials or direct labor are purchased and used.

Direct Materials Variances: Price versus Quantity

Suppose that a firm has adopted the following standards and achieved during a month the following results:

Standard amount of raw material for *one* unit of product	100 lb.
Standard cost per lb of raw materials	$1.00
Actual results for month	
Units produced	2,000 units
Raw materials purchased and used	240,000 lb
Cost of raw materials ($1.05 per lb)	$252,000

The standard materials cost of producing 2,000 units would be $200,000 (200,000 lb @ $1.00). The *total materials variance* is, therefore, $52,000 (unfavorable):

Actual materials cost of producing 2,000 units (240,000 lb @ $1.05)	$252,000
Standard materials cost of producing 2,000 units ($2,000 × 100 lb @ $1.00	200,000
Total materials variance	$ 52,000 U

In our variance formulas, when actual costs exceed standard costs (an *unfavorable* outcome), the variance will be *positive*. When standard costs exceed actual costs (a *favorable* outcome), the variance will be *negative*. Hence positive variances are additional costs; negative variances are cost savings.

Algebraically the variances can be expressed as follows (with Q and P representing *quantity* and *price*, respectively, and the subscripts A and S denoting *actual* and *standard*):

$$Q_A \times P_A - Q_S \times P_S$$

$$240,000 \times \$1.05 - 200,000 \times \$1.00$$

$$\$252,000 - \$200,000$$

Price Variance

This total variance can now be disaggregated into separate variances for price and quantity. The price variance can be determined by comparing the actual cost of the materials *acquired* with the expected *standard cost*:

Materials price variance = Actual cost of materials acquired

– Standard cost of materials acquired

or

Materials price variance = (Actual price – Standard price)

× Actual number of units of material acquired

In this example, the materials price variance is $12,000 (unfavorable):

(Actual price – Standard price) × Actual number of units acquired

($1.05 – $1.00) × 240,000 lb = $12,000

One means of recording the acquisition of materials so that the price variation is isolated immediately is to enter the raw materials inventory at standard prices and charge the amount paid in excess of standard to a special variance account. Thus,

(a)

```
Raw materials (240,000 lbs @ $1.00) .........................$240,000
Materials price variance (240,000 lb @ $.05) ...................   12,000
        Accounts payable (240,000 lb @ $1.05) .......................$252,000
        To record the acquisition of raw materials
```

In many companies, raw materials are charged initially at actual rather than standard prices. When used, they are added to work in process at standard cost, and the price variance is recorded at that time. The advantage of isolating the variance at the time the goods are acquired (the procedure illustrated) instead of when they are used is that management is made aware of the deviation at an earlier date and can take corrective action more promptly. With regard to the purchase of some types of raw material, there is little that management can do to eliminate an unfavorable price variance. Prices may be established in a competitive market and the company can do no more than pay the price at which items are offered. The prices paid for other types of raw materials, however, may be more susceptible to negotiation or careful buying practices.

Quantity Variance

The materials quantity variance can be expressed as the difference between the amount of materials *actually* used and the *standard* amount that should have been used, both amounts being valued at *standard prices*. Thus,

Materials quantity variance

= Standard value of actual amount of materials used

– Standard value of standard amount of materials

or

$$\text{Materials quantity variance} = (\text{Actual units of materials}$$
$$- \text{Standard units of materials})$$
$$\times \text{Standard price per unit of materials}$$

In the case at hand, the materials quantity variance is \$40,000 (unfavorable):

$$(\text{Actual units of materials} - \text{Standard units of materials})$$
$$\times \text{Standard price per unit of materials}$$
$$(240,000 \text{ lb} - 200,000 \text{ lb}) \times \$1.00 = \$40,000$$

The materials quantity variance can be identified and recorded at the time the materials are put into process by charging work in process with only the standard number of units required for the actual output. Any extra materials used would be charged to a quantity variance account:

(b)

Work in process (2,000 units × 100 lb @ $1) $200,000
Materials quantity variance (40,000 extra lb @ $1) 40,000
    Raw materials (240,000 lb @ $1) $240,000
To record the use of 240,000 pounds of material to manufacture 2,000 units of product. The 2,000 units of product should have required the use of only 200,000 pounds of raw materials

Alternatively, under some systems, actual amounts of raw materials are recorded in work in process. The variance is then computed and recorded when completed goods are transferred to finished goods inventory. The advantage of the procedure illustrated, as with the price variance, is earlier recognition of the variance and, as a consequence, the opportunity for more prompt action to rectify unfavorable deviations.

The two variances can be expressed algebraically as

$$Q_A(P_A - P_S) + P_S(Q_A - Q_S)$$
$$240,000(\$1.05 - \$1.00) + \$1.00(240,000 - 200,000)$$
$$\$12,000 + \$40,000$$

(Price variance)   (Quantity variance)

Since $-Q_A P_S$ and $+Q_A P_S$ cancel, the combined variance is $Q_A P_A - Q_S P_S$—actual costs minus standard costs.

Exhibit 22-3 depicts the variances diagrammatically. The unshaded inside area represents the total standard costs. The total area signifies the total actual costs. The shaded area at the top denotes the price variance, while that to the right is the quantity variance.[1] The two variances are *unfavorable* since each enlarges the standard cost area.

---

[1]The upper right corner, in which the two variances intersect, can be assigned to either variance, but obviously not to both. We have assigned it to the *price* variance, since the price variance was determined by multiplying the excess price by the *actual* quantity and the quantity variance was calculated by multiplying the excess quantity by the *standard price*. Alternatively, it could have been assigned to the quantity variance by computing the price variance as $Q_A(P_A - P_S)$ and the quantity variance as $P_S(Q_A - Q_S)$. The corner represents the excess price ($.05) times the excess quantity ($40,000 lb)—a total of $2,000.

EXHIBIT 22-3
Material Variances: Price and Quantity

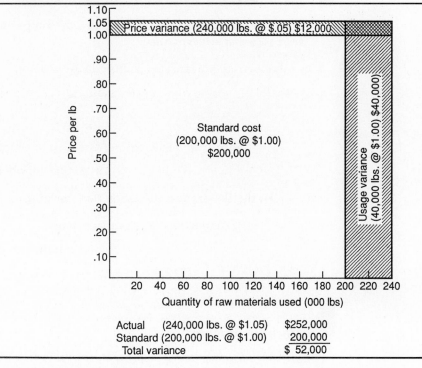

Actual	(240,000 lbs. @ $1.05)	$252,000
Standard	(200,000 lbs. @ $1.00)	200,000
Total variance		$ 52,000

Direct Labor Variance

Labor costs can be accounted for in a way that closely corresponds to material costs. As with materials, there are two fundamental reasons why actual labor costs may vary from standard: The rate (the price) actually paid may be different from the standard rate; or the efficiency with which labor was used (the quantity) may be different from standard. These price and quantity effects are analogous to the price and quantity variances associated with materials.

Assume the following standards and actual results:

Standard amount of direct labor for *one* unit of product	5 hours
Standard labor rate per hour	$12.00
Actual results for month	
Units produced	2,000 units
Direct labor hours used	9,750 hours
Cost of direct labor ($12.40 per hour)	$120,900

The *total labor variance* is, therefore, $900 (unfavorable):

Actual labor cost of producing 2,000 units (9,750 hours @ $12.40)	$120,900
Standard labor cost of producing 2,000 units (2,000 units × 5 hours @ $12)	120,000
Total labor variance	$ 900 U

This total variance may also be disaggregated into two parts.

Rate Variance

The *labor rate variance* may be calculated by comparing *actual labor costs* with *actual hours valued at standard rates*:

Labor rate variance = Actual labor costs

– Standard cost of labor hours actually used

or

Labor rate variance = (Actual rate – Standard rate)

× Actual number of hours worked

In the illustration the labor rate variance is $3,900 (unfavorable):

(Actual rate – Standard rate)

× Actual number of hours worked

($12.40 – $12.00) × 9,750 = $3,900

Efficiency Variance

The *labor efficiency variance* represents the difference between the number of hours *actually* used and the *standard number of hours* that should have been used, both numbers of hours being stated at *standard* rates. The labor efficiency variance is a function of the number of hours that should have been used to produce the actual outputs. This quantity is often referred to as the *standard hours allowed*. Thus,

Labor efficiency variance = Standard cost of actual number of hours used

– Standard cost of standard hours allowed

or

Labor efficiency variance = (Actual hours – Standard hours)

× Standard rate

In the case at hand, the variance (this time favorable) is $3,000:

(Actual hours – Standard hours) × Standard rate

(9,750 – 10,000) × $12.00 = ($3,000)

Inasmuch as direct labor, unlike materials, is added to work in process as it is "acquired," the entries to record the variances may be made concurrently. First, direct labor is charged with number of hours actually used, valued at standard rates, and a liability account is credited with the amount actually to be paid to the employees. The difference is charged (or credited) to a variance account:

(c)

Direct labor (9,750 hours @ $12.00) $117,000
Labor rate variance (9,750 hours @ $.40)   3,900
      Payroll liability (9,750 hours @ $12.40) $120,900
To record payroll liability

Then, the standard number of direct labor hours, valued at standard rates, is added to work in process. The difference between that amount and the amount initially charged to direct labor is recognized as the labor efficiency variance:

(d)

Work in process (10,000 hours @ $12) $120,000
    Direct labor (9,750 hours @ $12) $117,000
    Labor efficiency variance (250 hours @ $12)   3,000
To record the use of 9,750 direct labor hours to manufacture 2,000 units of product.
The 2,000 units of product should have required the use of 10,000 direct labor hours

As with materials, under some systems the number of labor hours actually used is added to work in process and the efficiency variance is recorded when the completed units are transferred to finished goods inventory. The entries illustrated provide for *more timely* recognition of the variances.

The two labor variances can be expressed algebraically in a form comparable to the two materials variances. Thus (with H and W representing *number of hours* and *wage rate*, respectively, and the subscripts A and S denoting *actual* and *standard*),

$$H_A(W_A - W_S) + W_S(H_A - H_S)$$

$$9{,}750(\$12.40 - \$12.00) + \$12(9{,}750 - 10{,}000)$$

$$\$3{,}900 + (\$3{,}000)$$

$$\text{(Rate variance)} \qquad \text{(Price variance)}$$

Exhibit 22-4 shows the variances in diagrammatic form. Exhibit 22-5 summarizes the price and quantity variances for both materials and labor.

Analysis of Overhead Variances

Characteristics of Overhead Costs

The definition and interpretation of overhead variances is more complex than that of the direct labor and materials variances because of the characteristics of overhead and the way in which it is absorbed into a product.

First, some components of overhead can be controlled in the short term, while others only over the long term. Variable costs are dependent upon the level of activity and can be controlled in the short term. Fixed costs, however, particularly those affecting the capacity of the plant, are not immediately dependent upon the level of activity and can be controlled only over the long term. Therefore, the *standard* or "ideal" costs for a specified level of output may only be obtainable in the long term.

Second, overhead costs may be influenced by factors beyond the control of the department responsible for providing the overhead services. For example,

EXHIBIT 22-4
Direct Labor Variances: Rate (Price) and Efficiency (Quantity)

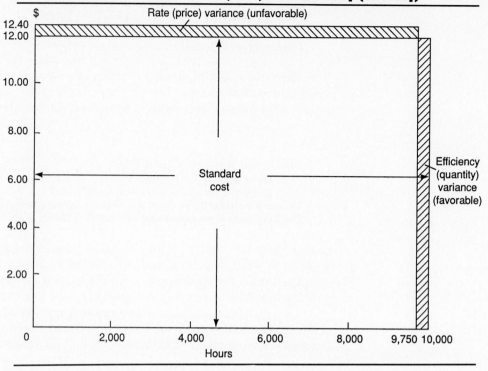

EXHIBIT 22-5

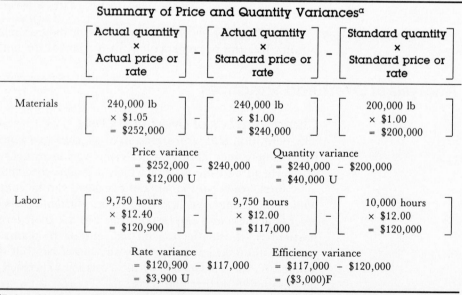

Summary of Price and Quantity Variances[a]

	Actual quantity × Actual price or rate		Actual quantity × Standard price or rate		Standard quantity × Standard price or rate
Materials	240,000 lb × $1.05 = $252,000	−	240,000 lb × $1.00 = $240,000	−	200,000 lb × $1.00 = $200,000

Price variance = $252,000 − $240,000 = $12,000 U

Quantity variance = $240,000 − $200,000 = $40,000 U

	Actual quantity × Actual price or rate		Actual quantity × Standard price or rate		Standard quantity × Standard price or rate
Labor	9,750 hours × $12.40 = $120,900	−	9,750 hours × $12.00 = $117,000	−	10,000 hours × $12.00 = $120,000

Rate variance = $120,900 − $117,000 = $3,900 U

Efficiency variance = $117,000 − $120,000 = ($3,000)F

[a]F, favorable variance; U, unfavorable variance.

if the variable portion of maintenance (an overhead cost) varies in relation to direct machine hours, then total overhead will be affected by both the department responsible for machine usage and the department in charge of machine maintenance.

Third, overhead costs are *absorbed* into a product by means of an *overhead charging rate*, preferably one that is predetermined. The overhead charging rate is calculated by dividing budgeted or expected overhead costs by expected units of activity. Thus,

$$\text{Overhead charged rate } = \frac{\text{Budgeted overhead}}{\text{Expected activity level}}$$

The amount of overhead absorbed is determined by multiplying the overhead charging rate by units of activity. If a company maintains a standard cost system, then the units of activity are typically expressed as the *standard* or *allowed* units of activity rather than the actual units of activity. That is,

$$\text{Overhead absorbed } = \text{(Overhead charging rate)}$$
$$\times \text{ (\textit{Standard} units of activity for the actual output)}$$

Once the predetermined overhead charging rate and the direct labor and materials standards have been established, the amount of overhead absorbed is driven *entirely* by the number of units produced.

Three Reasons for Overhead Variances

There are three reasons why actual overhead may differ from the amount absorbed. First, production volume may be greater or less than normal. If it were greater—and the company were making more effective use of its facilities than anticipated—then (other factors held constant) overhead would be over absorbed. If it were less and the company were not getting the full benefit of its capacity, then overhead would be underabsorbed. The overhead variance suggested by this difference is known as the *volume* of *capacity* variance.

Second, the amount of direct labor or materials—or whatever production factor drives the variable portion of overhead—may be greater or less than standard. Any inefficiency in this production factor will require additional *variable* overhead costs. The overhead variance attributable to deviations in this production factor is known as the *efficiency* variance.

Third, the services represented by the overhead costs may have been performed at greater or less cost than anticipated, even after taking into account unanticipated changes in volume or variances in direct labor or materials. For example, the maintenance department may have used more labor hours or paid higher wages than necessary to perform routine maintenance. Or, owing to unusually cold weather, heating costs may have been greater than planned. The overhead variance that can be attributed to greater or less than standard overhead costs *after* taking into account the factors which explain the other two variances is known as a *budget* or *spending variance*.

Each of these three variances may be illustrated by expanding upon our previous example.

The following data pertain to operations of a particular month:

Number of units produced	2,000 units
Standard direct labor hours for 2,000 units (5 per unit)	10,000 hours
Actual number of direct labor hours used	9,750 hours
Normal production volume per *month* (26,400 per *year*)	2,200 units

Overhead costs for a month are budgeted on the basis of the following estimates:

Fixed portion of overhead	
Depreciation	$ 4,000
Supervision	20,000
Maintenance employee wages	35,000
Allocations from other cost centers	7,000
Total fixed overhead	$66,000

Variable portion of overhead (per direct labor hour)	
Fringe benefits and other payroll costs	$3.20
Rework and inspection	.80
Supplies and miscellaneous	1.00
Allocations from other cost centers	2.00
Total variable overhead	$7.00

Actual overhead costs incurred during the month were

Fixed overhead	$ 68,000
Variable overhead	71,000
Total overhead costs	$139,000

Flexible Budgets

Central to the analysis—and therefore the control—of overhead costs is the concept of a *flexible budget*. The total of variable overhead costs incurred by a firm may be influenced by factors beyond the control of the departments responsible for providing the overhead services. Therefore, the performance of those departments cannot be measured by simply comparing actual costs with those budgeted for a predetermined level of output. In this example, for instance, overhead costs are affected by the number of direct labor hours used. The efficiency with which overhead services were rendered cannot be provided until the number of direct labor hours actually used is known.

A flexible budget indicates the expected overhead costs that should be incurred at various levels of activity. It explicitly distinguishes between the fixed and variable portions of overhead. A flexible budget based on fixed costs of $66,000 and variable costs of $7.00 per direct labor hour is presented in Exhibit 22-6. To highlight the relationship between the overhead charging rate and the flexible budget, the calculation of the overhead charging rate is shown as an addendum to the budget. The budget itself is shown in condensed form since the component elements of both fixed and variable costs are each summarized in a single amount. The normal level of activity is the 11,000 direct labor hours needed to produce the normal output of 2,200 units.

EXHIBIT 22-6

Flexible Budget for Overhead

Level of Activity in Direct Labor Hours

	9,750	10,000	Normal 11,000	12,000	13,000
Fixed overhead costs	$ 66,000	$ 66,000	$ 66,000	$ 66,000	$ 66,000
Variable overhead costs @ $7 per direct labor hour	68,250	70,000	77,000	84,000	91,000
Total overhead costs	$134,250	$136,000	$143,000	$150,000	$157,000
Normal level of activity (direct labor hours)			÷ 11,000		
Overhead charging rate			$ 13[a]		

[a]The overhead charging rate is conventionally based on annual rather than monthly estimates of costs and activity. It is assumed in this example that normal monthly costs and activity are $1/12$ of the estimated annual amounts.

The overhead charging rate comprises two elements:

A fixed element ($66,000 divided by the 11,000 direct labor hours)	$ 6
A variable element (the budgeted variable costs per direct labor hour)	7
Overhead charging rate	$13

At the normal level of activity—and only at that level—the overhead charging rate times the number of direct labor hours is equal exactly to the total budgeted overhead costs. At that level also, the amount of costs absorbed into a product would be equal to costs that were budgeted. At activity levels less than normal, budgeted costs would exceed amounts absorbed; at activity levels greater than normal, amounts absorbed would exceed budgeted costs.

Budget or Spending Variance

The budget or spending variance compares actual overhead costs with those budgeted for the actual level of activity. It focuses on variances from budget *after* taking into account deviations from normal in both the number of units produced and the amount of input (such as direct labor hours) required to produce that output. Actual total overhead costs per the data provided were $139,000. Yet the overhead that would have been budgeted (per the flexible budget) for the *actual* number of direct labor hours used (9,750, per data provided) was only $134,250. The difference of $4,750 between the two amounts represents the *budget* or *spending* variance. A spending variance indicates the difference between actual overhead costs and those budgeted per the flexible budget for the inputs *actually* used.

Since either fixed costs or variable costs can vary from the standard provided by the flexible budget, the budget variance has both a fixed and a variable element. As shown in Exhibit 22-7, both are *unfavorable*.

The budget variance is solely the *responsibility* of the departments in charge of providing the overhead services. An unfavorable variance may of course signify inadequate control over costs. In the example, the variance in fixed costs may represent overtime paid to maintenance employees for work that could have been performed during regular working hours had job assignments been properly

EXHIBIT 22-7

	Summary of Overhead Variances[a]		
	Fixed Element	Variable Element	Total
Actual overhead costs	$68,000	$71,000	$139,000
Overhead budgeted, per flexible budget, for actual input (9,750 direct labor hours)	66,000	68,250	134,250
Budget variance	$ 2,000 U	$ 2,750 U	$ 4,750 U
Overhead, per flexible budget, for actual input (9,750 direct labor hours)	$66,000	$68,250	$134,250
Overhead budgeted for standard input (10,000 direct labor hours) required to produce actual output (2,000 units)	66,000	70,000	136,000
Efficiency variance	$ -0- *	($ 1,750)F	($ 1,750)F
Overhead budgeted for standard input (10,000 direct labor hours) required to produce actual output (2,000 units)	$66,000	$70,000	$136,000
Overhead absorbed at standard input (10,000 direct labor hours) required to produce actual output (2,000 units)	60,000	70,000	130,000
Volume variance	$ 6,000 U	$ -0- *	$ 6,000 U
Total variance	$ 8,000 U	$ 1,000 U	$ 9,000 U

[a]F, favorable variance; U, unfavorable variance; *, always zero.

scheduled. At the same time, however, an unfavorable variance may be the consequence of factors beyond the control of the department with which it is associated. The overtime wages paid to the maintenance employees may have been necessitated by a power outage which prevented them from performing required services in the course of their normal working hours. The purpose of the budget variance, as well as *all* variances, is *not to affix blame*. Rather, it is *to assign responsibility* for explanation.

Efficiency Variance

As indicated by the data, the firm was efficient in its use of direct labor. The standard for the actual output of 2,000 units is 10,000 direct labor hours. The firm used only 9,750 hours. The saving to the firm was greater than merely the wages for 250 hours, however. Variable overhead costs are directly affected by the number of direct labor hours used. The greater the use of labor, the higher the costs for fringe benefits, rework, inspection, and supplies. Indeed, because as each hour of direct labor results in $7 of overhead costs, the 250 direct labor hours saved caused a reduction in *variable* overhead costs of $1,750. In contrast, the efficient use of direct labor had no impact on fixed overhead costs. Fixed costs are unaffected by changes in level of activity. As shown in Exhibit 22-7, the overhead efficiency variance indicates the difference between the overhead that is budgeted for the actual number of direct labor hours used and the overhead that would be budgeted for the *standard* number of direct labor hours required to produce the actual output.

The efficiency variance is solely the responsibility of the department accountable for direct labor. It measures the cost to the firm in variable overhead attributable to the inefficient use of direct labor.

Volume or Capacity Variance

Per the information presented, the firm produced at a volume less than normal—2,000 units were produced instead of the expected 2,200. As a consequence, the firm did not fully utilize its capacity. An indication of the cost of the wasted capacity may be obtained by comparing the budgeted overhead costs for the actual output with the costs that were absorbed into the product. The purpose of the volume variance is to focus attention on the cost attributable to the reduced production volume. Therefore, the amounts that are both budgeted and absorbed are based on *standard* number of direct labor hours for the actual output. Production inefficiencies thereby have no impact on the variance. The volume variance pertains only to *fixed* costs. At any specified level of output, the budgeted variable costs (e.g., $7 per direct labor hour) will always equal the variable costs absorbed (also $7 per direct labor hour). As illustrated in Exhibit 22-7, the volume variance, in this example, indicates the "cost" of operating at a volume of 2,000 units (10,000 direct labor hours) when there is capacity for 2,200 units (11,000 direct labor hours).

The utility of the volume variance in controlling overhead costs is limited. Unlike both the budget and efficiency variances, the volume variance does not indicate an actual out-of-pocket cost incurred by a firm. Instead, it indicates the opportunity cost of not fully utilizing capacity. It signifies a failure to fully absorb fixed costs. The volume variance is generally controllable not by manufacturing departments, but by a sales department. In the main, it is attributable to inadequate production, which is commonly the result of inadequate sales. The performance of sales departments can almost always be more effectively evaluated and controlled from sales reports directly than from manufacturing reports.

The three overhead variances may be summarized in three forms: tabular (Exhibit 22-7), diagrammatic (Exhibit 22-8), and graphic (Exhibit 22-9). The diagram (Exhibit 22-8) does not include the variable overhead volume variance and the fixed overhead efficiency variance. Both of these variances, by the way they are defined, are always zero.

In the graph (Exhibit 22-9), the slope of the overhead budget line is 7—the variable cost per unit. That of the overhead absorption line is 13—the overhead charging rate.

The overhead variances are shown as follows:

- The budget variance of $4,750 by line *DE*—the actual overhead costs of $139,000 less the budgeted costs (per the flexible budget) of $134,250
- The efficiency variance of $1,750 by line *AC* (which is the same *vertical* distance as point *A* to point *D*)—the budgeted costs of $134,250 less the $136,000 that would have been budgeted for the standard number of hours required to produce the actual output
- The volume variance of $6,000 by line *AB*—the $136,000 that would have been budgeted for the standard number of hours required to produce the actual output less the $130,000 that was absorbed at the standard number of hours required to produce the actual output

EXHIBIT 22-8
Summary of Overhead Variances

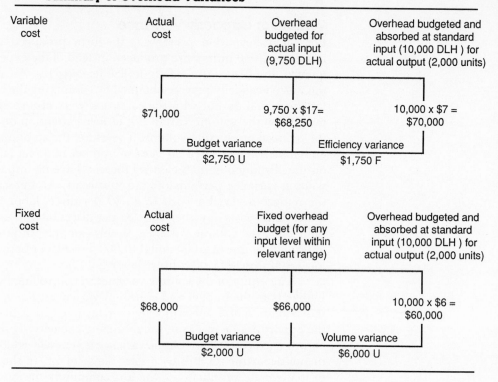

In journal entry form, the overhead costs can be added to work in process and the variances recorded, as follows:

(e)

Overhead control	....	$139,000
Various overhead accounts (depreciation,		
supervision, maintenance, etc.)	....	$139,000

To summarize overhead costs in the overhead control account

(f)

Work in process	....	$130,000
Budget variance	....	4,750
Volume variance	....	6,000
Efficiency variance	....	$ 1,750
Overhead control	....	139,000

To transfer overhead costs to work in process and record overhead variances

When the goods are completed, they would be transferred from work in process to finished goods at their standard cost. Standard cost, including labor, materials, and overhead, in this example is $450,000. Thus,

(g)

Finished goods inventory	....	$450,000
Work in process	....	$450,000

To transfer completed goods to finished goods inventory at standard cost

EXHIBIT 22-9
A Graphical Representation of Overhead Variance Analysis

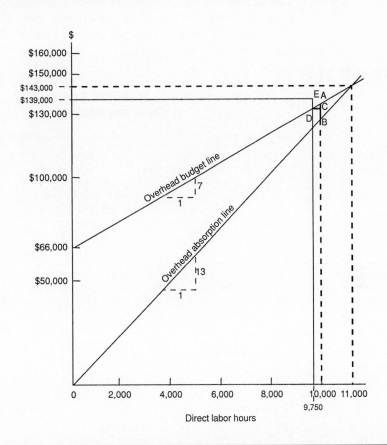

The actual cost of producing 2,000 units was $511,900; the standard cost was $450,000. The following table summarizes the reason for the $61,900 discrepancy:

				Dollars			
	Actual	Standard	Price variance	Quantity variance	Volume variance	Efficiency variance	Budget variance
Materials	252,000	200,000	12,000	40,000			
Direct labor	120,900	120,000	3,900	(3,000)			
Overhead							
Fixed	68,000	60,000			6,000		2,000
Variable	71,000	70,000				(1,750)	2,750
Totals	511,900	450,000	15,900	37,000	6,000	(1,750)	4,750

61,900   61,900

Exhibit 22-10 indicates the impact of the recording process on the general ledger accounts. Each of the seven variances is recorded in a separate account. Note that the balances in the seven variance accounts and the finished goods inventory account sum to the total actual costs, $511,900 (the $252,000 in materials, the $120,900 in direct labor, and the $139,000 in overhead).

EXHIBIT 22-10

Summary of Ledger Accounts
(in thousands)

Raw Materials Inventory

(a) Purchases at standard	240	**(b)** To goods in process	240

Work in Process Inventory

(b) Raw materials at standard	200	**(g)** To finished goods	450
(d) Direct labor at standard	120		
(f) Overhead at standard	130		

Direct Labor

(c) Incurred at standard	117	**(d)** To goods in process	117

Finished Goods Inventory

(g) From goods in process inventory	450		

Overhead Control

(e) Incurred at actual	139	**(f)** To goods in process	139

Various Overhead Accounts

		(e) Incurred at actual	139

Materials Price Variance

(a) 12	

Materials Quantity Variance

(b) 40	

Direct Labor Rate Variance

(c) 3.9	

Direct Labor Efficiency Variance

	(d) 3

Overhead Budget Variance

(f) 4.75	

Overhead Volume Variance

(f) 6	

Overhead Efficiency Variance

	(f) 1.75

Accounts Payable

	(a) 252

Payroll Liability

	(c) 120.9

It stands to reason that *all* reported variances should be reviewed by management. Otherwise, there would be no point in calculating and reporting them. But whether corrective action should be taken or whether even a comprehensive investigation into the cause of the variance should be made depends on a number of considerations. Among them are the following:

1. *The appropriateness of the standards.* When standards are so rigorous that it is expected that they will not be met, unfavorable variances may indicate performance short of perfection, but nevertheless adequate and not in need of management intervention. Standards that exceed expectations may well serve to motivate, but their utility as a means of control is limited. Management can circumvent the deficiencies of unduly rigorous standards by establishing a variance threshold such that variances will be investigated only when they exceed a permissible level. The practical effect of establishing a variance threshold would be to create a dual set of standards, one for motivation, the other for control.

2. *The probability that the variance is significant.* Virtually all production processes are subject to random fluctuations. Standards are point estimates. Most processes, however, can be properly described only by probability distributions. A standard may require that an operation be completed in 30 minutes. But regardless of how efficient the employees, very rarely will the operation be done in exactly 30 minutes. Sometimes it will be done in 29 minutes; sometimes in 32 minutes. A series of several jobs could be characterized by unfavorable labor efficiency variances. Both the process, as well as the workers, could nevertheless be operating efficiently. The deviations could be nothing more than random fluctuations from the mean (average) expected operating time. Statistical tests can be applied to determine the probability that a sample of variances represents a true operating inefficiency or merely a normal operating fluctuation. These tests are described in many standard texts on production quality control.

3. *The materiality of the variance.* The larger a variance, the less the probability that it is a mere statistical aberration and the greater the probability that it warrants investigation and corrective action. As a substitute for elaborate statistical quality control guidelines, many organizations use materiality guidelines—whenever a variance is greater than a fixed percentage of standard the variance must be investigated and appropriate corrective measures taken.

4. *The cost to investigate and, if necessary, correct.* In some productive processes, the cost to investigate and, if necessary, correct variances may be substantial. Production lines may have to be shut down, experts may have to be called in, chemical tests may have to be performed. It is in the interest of management to incur the investigative and corrective outlays only when it is probable that they will be less than any resultant savings in operating costs. The literature of both cost accounting and quality control contains descriptions of statistical models that can facilitate a determination as to when investigation and correction is worthwhile.

5. *The interrelationship among variances.* A single unfavorable variable, even if statistically significant, is not necessarily a sign of inefficiency. A firm can make trade-offs among the four factors (the prices and quantities of both labor and materials) which are described by the variances illustrated. Suppose, for example, that in determining labor standards, it was assumed that the work would be performed by employees with a particular degree of skill and experience. In a particular period the firm may be required, or may have the opportunity, to substitute employees with less skill or less experience who are in a lower pay classification. The consequence of the substitution may be an unfavorable labor efficiency variance, offset by a favorable labor rate variance. Similarly, a firm may elect to substitute a lower quality material for that on which the standard is based. This material may cause a greater number of units than standard to be rejected. The result may be a favorable materials price variance but unfavorable quantity variances for materials as well as for labor.

The seven basic variances illustrated in this chapter may be further refined to account for changes in the mix of the factors of production. The refinements serve to formalize and quantify a necessary element in the interpretation of variances—the analysis of the variances in combination with, rather than in isolation of, one another.

6. *The controllability of variances.* Although the operations of a firm may be at variance with standard, there may be little that management can do by way of corrective action—at least in the short run. Materials price variances, for example, may be beyond the ability of management to eliminate, particularly if the firm acquires the materials in a competitive market and can make no substitutions. This is not to suggest that variances which are not subject to immediate correction should be of no concern to management. Given sufficient time, management can adjust all factors of production, and variances serve to put management on notice that certain costs may be getting out of line.

LEARNING CURVES

In establishing prices, in bidding on contracts, and in setting standards, it is necessary for management to estimate the labor time necessary to complete each phase of a production process. When new products or processes are being introduced, however, it may be difficult to make the required estimate because the labor time demands are in a state of change. The literature of production management provides descriptions of a number of estimation techniques. One, based on *learning curves*, is widely used and, as a consequence, both accountants and managers who may be involved in the process of making, interpreting, or using cost estimates should be familiar with it.

Learning curves give quantitative or graphic expression to an intuitively obvious phenomenon: As workers gain production experience, their productivity increases—at least up to a point. Each batch of units produced will take less time to complete than previous batches. Per the theory on which learning curves are based, whenever the *cumulative* production output is *doubled*, the *average* time to produce each unit of *cumulative* production will be a certain per-

EXHIBIT 22-11
Eighty Percent Learning Curve

Number of Units in Batch	Cumulative Production (units)	Cumulative Average Time per Unit (minutes)	Total Time Accumulated (minutes)	Average Time per Unit in Particular Batch[a] (minutes)	Number of Units Produced per Hour[b]
1,000	1,000	10.00	10,000	10.00	6.00
1,000	2,000	8.00	16,000	6.00	10.00
2,000	4,000	6.40	25,600	4.80	12.50
4,000	8,000	5.12	49,060	3.84	15.63
8,000	16,000	4.10	65,600	3.08	19.48
16,000	32,000	3.28	104,960	2.46	24.39
32,000	64,000	2.62	167,680	1.96	30.61

[a]Difference in total time accumulated between a particular batch and the previous batch divided by number of units in the batch [e.g., for the second batch, (16,000 − 10,000) ÷ 1,000 = 6.00 minutes].
[b]60 minutes divided by average time per unit.

centage of the time required to produce the units up to that point. The particular percentage will vary from process to process, but usually it is between 60 and 90 percent.

Suppose, for example, that it requires 10,000 minutes to produce the first 1,000 units of product—an average of 10 minutes per unit. If an 80 percent learning curve is appropriate, then it would take 16,000 minutes, an average of 8 minutes per unit (80 percent of 10 minutes) to produce a *cumulative* total of 2,000 units (double 1,000 units) and 25,600 minutes, an average of 6.4 minutes per unit (80 percent of 8 minutes) to produce a cumulative total of 4,000 units (double 2,000 units). Exhibit 22-11 provides a more detailed illustration of an 80 percent learning curve given the assumptions regarding the time required to produce the initial batch.

Exhibit 22-12 displays graphically the effect of learning on the average cumulative times needed for production. The curve makes clear that the improvements to be expected as a consequence of experience are great at first, but they are quickly reduced as the production process achieves a "steady state."

The phenomenon of the learning curve must be taken into account in establishing standards and in making related forecasts of expenditures. Management must recognize that standards based on experiences represented by the rapidly declining section of the curve will prove to be unnecessarily lax as operations move toward a steady state. Correspondingly, those based on expectations of operations at a steady state will be unduly rigorous when the learning process has just begun.

STANDARD COSTS, VARIANCE ANALYSIS, AND EXTERNAL FINANCIAL REPORTS

Generally accepted accounting principles require that financial reports intended for parties external to the organization incorporate *actual* as opposed to estimated costs. Standards and predetermined charging rates necessarily reflect management estimates rather than actual costs. As a consequence, when the

EXHIBIT 22-12
Eighty Percent Learning Curve

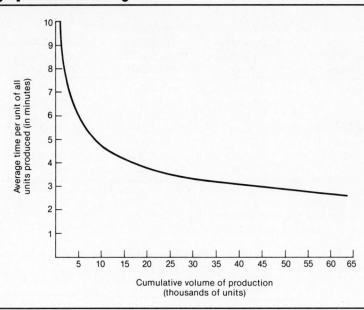

accounting procedures described in this and other chapters are applied, both cost of goods sold and ending inventory accounts (raw materials, work in process, and finished goods) must be translated from estimated or standard amounts to actual. Although most record-keeping processes do not provide sufficient information for the firm to adjust the accounts item by item or job by job, they do permit it to do so by the account representing cost of goods sold and the major groupings of inventory. Seldom is there need for greater detail.

In standard cost systems, the differences between actual costs and standard costs are accumulated in variance accounts. In systems in which direct labor and materials are applied in actual amounts but overhead is charged using an overhead charging rate, the difference between actual overhead and that which has been applied remains at year end in the overhead control account. The transformation of the records so that they indicate actual rather than estimated costs can be accomplished by *prorating the balances* in the variance or overhead control accounts on the basis of the production factor out of which the discrepancy arose. Materials and labor variances would be distributed in proportion to the amounts of raw materials or labor costs incurred. Overhead variances (or under- or overabsorbed overhead) would be distributed in proportion to the production factor on which the initial application of overhead was made.

The following two tables, using the data from the examples in this chapter, are illustrative of the calculations required. It will be assumed that of the 2,000 units produced during the period 1,500 (75 percent) were sold and 500 (25 percent) remain in finished goods inventory.

The first table indicates the percentages of the materials- and labor-related variances that will be allocated to the appropriate accounts:

Factor of Production	Costs Applied During Period (at Standard)					
		Portion Charged to (or Remaining in Accounts)				
		Finished Goods Inventory		Cost of Goods Sold		
	Total	Amount	%	Amount	%	
Materials	$200,000	$ 50,000	25	$150,000	75	
Labor	$120,000	$ 30,000	25	$ 90,000	75	
Overhead	$130,000	$325,000	25	$ 97,500	75	
Total	$450,000	$112,500	25	$347,500	75	

The proration in this instance is relatively simple because all of the raw materials purchased were used and all of the goods started were completed. As a result, the allocation percentages are the same for both labor and materials. If this were not the case, it would be necessary to prorate the variances among raw materials inventory and work in process as well as finished goods inventory and cost of goods sold. Different allocation percentages would then have to be applied.

The second table indicates the allocation of the variances based on the percentages shown in the first table:

Variance	Basis of Proration	Amount of Unfavorable (Favorable) Variance	Proration	
			Finished Goods Inventory (25%)	Cost of Goods Sold (75%)
Materials price	Materials	$12,000	$ 3,000	$ 9,000
Materials quantity	Materials	40,000	10,000	30,000
Labor rate	Labor	3,900	975	2,925
Labor efficiency	Labor	(3,000)	(750)	(2,250)
Overhead volume	Labor	6,000	1,500	4,500
Overhead budget	Labor	4,750	1,187	3,563
Overhead efficiency	Labor	(1,750)	(437)	(1,313)
Total variances		$61,900	$15,475	$46,425

The journal entry to effect the proration would be as follows:

Finished goods inventory	$15,475	
Cost of goods sold	46,425	
Labor efficiency variance	3,000	
Overhead efficiency variance	1,750	
Materials price variance		$12,000
Materials quantity variance		40,000
Labor rate variance		3,900
Overhead volume variance		6,000
Overhead budget variance		4,750

The data in this illustration were for a month. Generally, however, variances are closed out only annually. In practice, many firms do not prorate either variances or under- or overabsorbed overhead. Instead, they charge or credit the entire amount to cost of goods sold or some other expense account. This approach fails to make a complete transformation from estimated to actual costs; at best, it may be overlooked when the amounts involved are not material.

INDUSTRY EXAMPLE: NONPROFIT HEALTH CARE

Variance analysis is as applicable to service and nonprofit organizations as to private-sector manufacturing firms. It is particularly relevant to health-care organizations, which in recent years have become exceedingly cost conscious and thus concerned with identifying out-of-line conditions. In fact, because both private insurers and the federal government now reimburse for services only at preestablished rates, irrespective of the actual cost of patient care, many health-care providers have instituted standard cost systems that are remarkably similar to those in manufacturing plants.

Exhibit 22-13 illustrates how one health-care organization presents information on cost variances. Our objective in presenting this example is twofold:

1. To emphasize that variance analysis should be an essential element of cost control in all organizations, not just manufacturing firms
2. To point out that the variances described in this chapter are merely examples of the ways in which differences between actual and budgeted costs can be analyzed. The specific variances that an organization calculates should depend on the information that it can most effectively use to control costs and enhance efficiency and effectiveness. Therefore, the variances that are calculated should focus on factors that are within the ability of the firm to control and that, when properly controlled, can have a material impact on costs.

Exhibit 22-13, Part I, summarizes the variances of a radiology department by its several cost centers, while Part II presents the details of one of these cost centers, diagnostic X-ray.

The radiology department disaggregates its total variances into four components:

Volume/mix variance. This variance indicates the combined effects of changes in the number of units of output (e.g., patients served, tests performed, or treatments rendered) and changes in the mix of the volume from what was planned. The mix portion of the variance measures the cost of providing different proportions of outputs than was budgeted. For example, the organization may have treated a greater percentage of cases categorized as complex than intended. Many organizations separate volume from mix variances, because combining the two (particularly if they are of offsetting signs) can mask both their magnitude and cause.

Efficiency. This variance represents the difference between actual resources (such as labor hours or units of materials) used and those allowed per preestablished standards, with both stated at standards prices.

Rate. This reveals the difference between actual wages or prices for the actual numbers of hours or units of material used.

Nonproductive planning and other. These variances, which have been tailored to the particular organization, denote the differences between actual and planned costs of "nonproductive" activities, such as planning, education, training, and various administrative functions.

EXHIBIT 22-13
Variance Analysis by a Health-Care Organization

Part I. Department Variance Summary by Cost Center

Department: 2000 Radiology

Cost center	Planned	Actual	Volume/mix[a]	Period-to-date variances				Total
				Efficiency	Rate	Nonproductive planning	Other	
1400 X-ray therapy								
Current period	$ 46,133	$ 45,000	$ 2,500	$ (596)	$ (300)	$ 150	$ (621)	$ 1,133
Period-to-date	138,399	136,379	4,920	3,025	(1,000)	(587)	(4,338)	2,020
1500 Diagnostic X-ray								
Current period	209,526	205,218	56,786	(35,915)	(9,750)	2,052	(8,865)	4,308
Period-to-date	598,725	580,735	120,496	(82,815)	(25,700)	9,929	(3,920)	17,990
1600 Nuclear medicine								
Current period	23,645	22,500	1,000	500	(400)	(290)	335	1,145
Period-to-date	70,935	51,890	12,906	7,287	(2,832)	(1,611)	3,295	19,045
1700 Ultra sound								
Current period	12,636	12,000	1,000	350	(300)	240	(654)	636
Period-to-date	37,908	23,273	4,917	2,799	(3,013)	4,158	5,774	14,635
Department totals								
Current period	$291,940	$284,718	$ 61,286	$(35,661)	$(10,750)	$ 2,152	$(9,805)	$ 7,222
Period-to-date	$845,967	$792,277	$143,239	$(69,704)	$(32,545)	$11,889	$ 811	$53,690

[a]Below planned/(above planned)—all others favorable/(unfavorable).

EXHIBIT 22-13 Continued

Part II: Cost Center Variance Summary by Ledger Detail

Cost center: 1500—Diagnostic X-ray

| Sub-account | Account description | Planned | Actual | Current period variances | | | | | |
				Volume/mix[a]	Efficiency	Rate	Nonproductive planning	Other	Total
10	Department manager	$ 4,100	$ 4,100	$ 1,200	$ (1,000)	$ 0	$ (200)	$ 0	$ 0
20	Chief technician	6,466	6,500	1,500	(1,700)	0	166	0	(34)
30	Special procedures technician	15,748	14,000	5,500	(3,987)	300	(65)	0	1,748
40	Registered technician	49,885	47,600	23,450	(19,293)	(2,950)	1,078	0	2,285
50	Aide/orderly	14,518	12,000	9,000	(6,535)	(900)	953	0	2,518
60	Clerical/administrative	5,605	5,800	1,200	(371)	(400)	(624)	0	(195)
	Total salary and wages	$ 96,322	$ 90,000	$41,850	$(32,886)	$(3,950)	$1,308	$ 0	$ 6,322
100	FICA	$ 6,745	$ 6,200	$ 1,200	$ (399)	$ (300)	$ 44	$ 0	$ 545
120	Pension	4,340	4,200	200	(100)	(50)	90	0	140
140	Health insurance	2,010	1,000	2,000	(1,500)	(500)	610	400	1,010
	Total benefits	$ 13,095	$ 11,400	$ 3,400	$ (1,999)	$ (850)	$ 744	$ 400	$1,695
215	Film	$ 20,616	$ 21,000	$ 7,100	$ (530)	$(4,950)	$ 0	$(2,004)	$ (384)
295	General supplies	18,160	21,087	3,000	(500)	0	0	(5,427)	(2,927)
340	Purchased services	3,000	1,564	1,436	0	0	0	0	1,436
	Total supply/other	$ 41,776	$ 43,651	$11,536	$ (1,030)	$(4,950)	$ 0	$(7,431)	$(1,875)
300	Repairs and maintenance	$ 20,000	$ 22,343	$ 0	$ 0	$ 0	$ 0	$(2,343)	$(2,343)
325	Rent/lease	14,000	13,824	0	0	0	0	176	176
335	Movable equipment	24,333	24,000	0	0	0	0	333	333
	Total capital	$ 58,333	$ 60,167	$ 0	$ 0	$ 0	$ 0	$(1,834)	$(1,834)
	Cost center totals	$209,526	$205,218	$56,786	$(35,915)	$(9,750)	$2,052	$(8,865)	$ 4,308

[a]Below planned/(above planned)—all others favorable/(unfavorable).

EXHIBIT 22-13 Continued

Part III: Cost Center Labor Efficiency Variance by Skill Level

Cost center: 1500—Diagnostic X-ray

Sub-account	Account description	Current period				Period to date			
		Earned FTEs[a]	Actual FTEs	Variance amount	Efficiency percentage	Earned FTEs	Actual FTEs	Variance amount	Efficiency percentage
10	Department manager	.6	.8	(.2)	75%	.7	.8	(.1)	88%
20	Chief technician	1.3	1.8	(.5)	72%	1.4	1.8	(.4)	78%
30	Special procedures technician	4.2	6.0	(1.8)	70%	4.4	5.2	(.8)	85%
40	Registered technician	11.8	22.0	(10.2)	54%	16.4	21.6	(5.2)	76%
50	Aide/orderly	4.8	11.8	(7.0)	41%	8.4	12.6	(4.2)	67%
60	Clerical/administrative	5.5	6.1	(.6)	90%	6.3	6.6	(.3)	95%
	Cost center totals	28.2	48.5	(20.3)	58%	37.6	48.6	(11.0)	77%
	Favorable (unfavorable)								

[a]FTE stands for full-time equivalents.

Source: George M. Kis and George Bodenger, "Cost Management Improves Financial Performance," *Healthcare Financial Management* (May 1989), pp. 36–48.

Part III of Exhibit 22-13 provides additional details on staffing for the diagnostic X-ray cost center. It compares the standard or "earned" full-time equivalent (FTE) number of employees with the actual number.

MANAGERIAL ACCOUNTING IMPLICATIONS OF DECENTRALIZATION

Although organizational structure is a topic typically considered in courses in management and organizational behavior, form of organization is directly tied to issues of accounting. As discussed earlier in this chapter, organizational structure influences the goals of a firm's subunits, and these, in turn, dictate performance measures and reports. Thus, performance measures and reports of *profit centers* will differ significantly from those of both *cost* and *revenue centers*. A *profit center* is an organizational unit which is responsible for both revenues and costs. For example, a corporate division which both manufactures and sells a particular product would typically be a profit center. In contrast, a *cost center* has responsibility only for costs, not revenues; a *revenue center* has responsibility only for revenues, but not costs. Therefore, a manufacturing department that must transfer its output to other corporate departments and that controls neither product demand nor price would be a cost center. A sales unit, which is unable to influence production costs, would be a revenue center.

Equally important, seemingly technical accounting practices, such as establishing the prices at which goods or services are transferred from one corporate unit to another, can either support or undermine an otherwise sound organizational structure. In this section, we summarize the virtues and shortcomings of a *decentralized* organizational structure. We then show how the issue of transfer pricing is closely tied to that of decentralization.

In its extreme form, a decentralized organization is one in which the various divisions are profit centers. Hence, the most fundamental strategic and operating decisions are delegated to divisional or local managers rather than being limited to top management. In terms of managerial authority, each division is, in effect, an independent business. Few companies, however, permit their divisions to have autonomy over all factors that enter into the determination of profit. For example, most companies raise capital at the corporate level, so that divisions have little or no influence over the cost of capital. Indeed, even in firms that are highly decentralized, divisions must obtain headquarters' approval for projects requiring an investment above a stated amount.

There are numerous advantages to decentralization. First, decisions can ordinarily be made much faster by divisional, as opposed to corporate, management. This is mainly because fewer parties are involved and less documentation is required.

Second, the decisions can be made by managers who are "closer to the action." They have more direct contact with the organization's employees, suppliers, and customers. Thus, they may have greater insight into the consequences of the decisions.

Third, decentralization can stimulate managers and other employees to be more innovative and creative. It may encourage managers to respond to local conditions. A national grocery chain, for example, was highly centralized. Regional, but not store, managers had the responsibility of selecting the mix of products to be sold. Thus, all stores within a region carried identical items. No recognition was given to differences in the ethnic or economic make-up of stores' customers. As a consequence, the chain lost business to its decentralized competitors, which were able to cater to the unique characteristics of the neighborhoods that they served. Eventually the chain was sold, reduced in size, and reorganized.

Decentralization, however, is not without its shortcomings. First, it can easily lead to dysfunctional decisions. A dysfunctional decision as used in this discussion is one in which the benefits to the particular unit outweigh the costs to the entire organization—that is, when the decision may be in the best interests of the unit, but not of the organization. For example, if a company such as Gillette were divided into independent razor and blade divisions, the razor division might establish razor prices at a level that maximizes its profits and therefore is in its best interests. A lower price, however, might stimulate razor sales and correspondingly lead to both higher sales and profits for the blade division. The pricing decision would be dysfunctional if it led to higher profits for the razor division but lower profits for the company as a whole.

Second, decentralization may encourage employees to misdirect their loyalties from the organization at large to their specific units. At the extreme, it may push divisional managers to enhance performance data, falsify records, and withhold information from corporate managers.

Third, decentralization may lead to duplication of efforts and consequently to increased costs. For example, decentralized companies may carry out controllership and personnel functions at both divisional and headquarters levels.

Fourth, decentralization may result in a transfer of decision authority from more to less knowledgeable, skilled, and experienced managers. Quality of management is not a factor that can be easily measured. Nevertheless, in many corporations, the standard career path is from divisions to headquarters, not from headquarters to divisions. Thus managerial sophistication *may* (certainly not always) be higher at the headquarters than at the divisional level.

Our main concern with decentralization stems mainly from the unique accounting problems that are created when divisions are generally autonomous but nevertheless do not have unlimited authority to buy from or sell to outsiders. In the next section, therefore, we shall address one of those problems—*transfer pricing*.

TRANSFER PRICING

Management decisions as to where, and at what price, a corporate unit may buy and sell its products and services are referred to as *sourcing* decisions. In the purest form of decentralization, local managers face virtually no restrictions on available sourcing options. They have no obligation to give preferences to other corporate units and are thereby free to trade with outsiders and insiders on equal terms. Most companies, however, impose restrictions on sourcing opportunities. They may insist, for example, that corporate units acquire goods or services from within the firm, as long as the corporate units have the capacity to meet their requirements and the price is reasonable.

The internal price—the *transfer price*—at which the goods or services exchanged within the organization are recorded establishes the expenses of the acquiring unit and the revenues of the providing unit. Therefore, it has a direct—in some circumstances, critical—impact on the apparent fiscal performance of each unit.

In addition, however, the transfer price may influence substantive decisions made by the organizational units. If organizational units are permitted to buy and sell outside, the internal price will obviously affect the extent to which corporate resources are derived from, and diverted to, outsiders. Furthermore, even if units are required to trade within the organization, the internal price will affect directly the quantity of goods or services bought and sold. Therefore, it will affect indirectly virtually all economic parameters of both the supplier and seller, including production volume, sales prices to outsiders, and long-term capacity.

Objectives of a Transfer Pricing Policy

Because transfer prices are so important, they are often a source of conflict and dissension. Three objectives, however, must be paramount in establishing a corporate policy as to transfer prices:

- Transfer prices should motivate decisions that are in the best interests of individual divisions as well as the entire firm. Thus, they should assure *goal congruence*.
- They should contribute to the evaluation of divisional performance in a way that is both reliable and accurate.
- They should contribute to, and enhance, the aims of a decentralized organizational structure.

Transfer pricing policies have received considerable attention in the literature. However, owing in large part to the extensive variety of circumstances faced by different firms, it has proven difficult to reduce what is a complex area to a few simple generalizations.

An example, set in the context of a municipal government, can be used to highlight the key issues.

Example

A city's vehicle repair department provides services to all other city departments and charges them for labor based on the number of hours of employee time actually devoted to their repairs. The department's fixed costs are $80,000 per month; its variable costs are $40 per hour. On average it provides 4,000 hours of service per month. The vehicle repair department is not permitted to offer its services to outsiders; the other departments may not use outside repair shops as long as the internal department is capable of making the repairs. What should be the rate per hour at which the vehicle repair department bills the other city units to which it provides service?

Among the options are (1) full cost; (2) market price; (3) incremental cost; and (4) hybrid prices.

To better assess several alternative transfer pricing policies, assume further that the police department determines that repairs to a particular car are economically justifiable if they can be done for $3,000 or less. Otherwise, the car should be replaced. The repair service estimates that the job will take 60 hours.

1. Full Cost

If the city bases the transfer price on full cost, then the cost per hour would be the variable costs ($40) plus a proportionate share of estimated overhead costs ($80,000 divided by the 4,000 hours of expected service). Thus,

Variable costs		$40
Fixed costs	$80,000	
Divided by estimated hours of service per month	÷4,000	20
Cost per hour		$60

The billing rate per hour would be $60. For the repair job requiring 60 hours, the police department would be billed $3,600. Therefore, it would elect not to have the job done, since the estimated cost would exceed its limit of $3,000.

As long as the repair department had the available capacity, the decision of the police department would be dysfunctional. It would be in its best interest, but not that of the city at large. The incremental cost to the city of repairing the vehicle would have been only $2,400—that is, 60 hours at $40 variable cost per hour. Thus, the job would have been economically justifiable.

Full-cost pricing assures that each receiving unit pays its "fair share" of the provider's cost and that when the provider's estimated costs are equal to its actual cost, its revenues cover its costs. But it is unlikely to motivate decisions that are in the best interest of the organization as a whole.

2. Market Price

Use of a market price to measure the transfer assures that both parties to the transaction are held accountable for the values of services received or provided as determined by the marketplace. In that regard, market price is consistent with the goals of decentralization. Moreover, the transfer price is objective; it is based on independent transactions between outside parties. It is likely to result in the least amount of friction among divisions. Nonetheless, a market-based price suffers from the same deficiencies as the full-cost price—it may lead to dysfunctional decisions. Suppose, for example, that the market price for repairs were $55 per hour—$3,300 for the

60-hour job. The police department would reject the bid since it exceeds the $3,000 limit. As with the full-cost transfer price, the incremental cost to the city would have been only $2,400.

3. Incremental Cost

Use of incremental cost as a transfer price equates the short-run cost to acquire goods or services with the cost of providing them. Nevertheless, it permits the acquiring unit to escape all charges for the fixed costs. In organizations in which the fixed costs are a substantial share of total costs, the goods or services will be measured at fire-sale rates, thereby limiting the usefulness of profit as a measure of performance.

4. Hybrid Prices

To compensate for the inherent deficiencies in cost- as well as market-based prices, many companies have adopted hybrid policies that are a compromise of the advantages and disadvantages of their component policies. Under one policy, units are charged a specified ''capacity'' fee each period irrespective of the quantity of goods or services that they take. The capacity fee represents the unit's share of the provider's fixed costs and may be determined by the proportion of the provider's output the recipient unit took in the past or was expected to take in the future. Thus, the police department may be charged $20,000 per month plus $40 per hour of repair service consumed. With this approach, the provider is compensated for its fixed and variable costs. The recipient is charged for capacity that is maintained on its behalf but thereafter pays only the standard cost of the goods or services that it consumes.

Other firms require the providing and receiving units to negotiate prices. Typically, the ''floor'' price is the provider's incremental cost; the ceiling is the market price. Still others, in an effort to assure that each unit is properly motivated to make decisions in the best interest of the firm at large, may calculate the provider's revenues based on one rate and the recipient's expenses based on another. The company then eliminates the disparities with journal entries at headquarters.

International Issues

Transfer pricing policies are especially important to multinational firms because of their influence on income taxes and trade regulations. International tax laws are diverse, confusing, and inconsistent. Transfer prices are a means of allocating earnings among company divisions, which may be located in different countries and thereby subject to different tax rates and regulations. Suppose, for example, that a company manufactures components in one country, assembles them in a second, and sells the finished goods in a third. By establishing artificially high or low transfer prices, the company can shift income from the high- to the low-tax country. Obviously, taxing authorities in all countries are aware of these opportunities for income shifting and have established regulations to reduce them. For example, the U.S. Internal Revenue Code (Section 482) provides that the Internal Revenue Service may itself distribute costs and revenues among organizations if necessary "to prevent evasion of taxes or clearly to reflect the income" of the component businesses.

The customs regulations of the United States (as well as other countries) give trade concessions to foreign-owned companies that manufacture their products in U.S. plants. Thus, for example, Honda is exempt from certain automobile import restrictions because its vehicles are assembled in the United States and thereby satisfy specified "domestic content" requirements. Nevertheless, Honda as well as other companies with U.S. plants has been accused of transferring parts imported from Japan at artificially low prices to understate the proportionate share of vehicles made overseas.[2]

Because of the subjectivity in determining what is a reasonable transfer price, as well as the complexities of international business and tax laws, transfer price policies remain a significant variable that corporations can control in their efforts to minimize taxes and circumvent import restrictions. But transfer pricing remains an imprecise art, with few definitive available guidelines or models as to how companies can simultaneously fulfill all of their internal as well as external objectives.

BEYOND TRADITIONAL MEASURES OF PERFORMANCE

This text has focused almost exclusively upon financial measures of performance. No matter how well they are formulated, however, financial measures alone cannot capture all dimensions of effort and accomplishment. Some aspects of an organization's inputs and outputs cannot meaningfully be expressed in monetary terms.

In a manufacturing setting, nonfinancial measures could include percentage of items that are below specified standards of quality, percentage of machine downtime, number of orders on backlog, percent of scheduled shipments made on time, and outputs to inputs (yield ratios). In service organizations as well as manufacturing firms, they could include staff ratios, number of jobs created, percentage of minorities hired or promoted, number of new patents or products, and number of customer complaints.

Government and other nonprofit organizations are especially concerned with nonfinancial measures because their overall objective is to provide service, not to maximize profit. Therefore, "profit" is not a meaningful indicator of performance. In government and other nonprofit organizations, measures of performance, including both financial and nonfinancial measures, are often referred as to indicators of *service efforts and accomplishments*.

A recent research report by the Governmental Accounting Standards Board (GASB), the governmental accounting equivalent of the Financial Accounting

[2]*Business Week*, "Honda, Is It an American Car," November 18, 1991, pp. 105–112.

Standards Board, set forth four categories of nonfinancial measures of performance:[3]

- *Input indicators.* These show the level of resources applied to a service and include financial resources (money) and other resources, such as employee hours, square feet of building, and capacity of landfills.
- *Output indicators.* These are designed to report the quantity or units of service or product that are being provided to the target population. Examples are number of student days, number of persons screened, number of passenger trips provided by public transit vehicles, and tons of waste processed.
- *Outcome indicators.* These show the results being received from the service. Examples include student scores on achievement tests, crime rates and crime ''clearance'' rates, police response times, and quality of water treatment.
- *Efficiency indicators.* These compare inputs to either outputs or outcomes. Examples are cost per gallon of water treated, costs per student day, cost of road repair, and cost of public transit trip-mile.

The GASB report also provided examples of specific indicators for 12 government functions, including universities, hospitals, police, fire, and mass transit. It is directly applicable to the private sector inasmuch as many government agencies and departments have corporate counterparts in the private sector. Moreover, many of the activities carried out by corporations have characteristics of programs undertaken in government and other nonprofit organizations. Like those in the nonprofit sector, they cannot be meaningfully assessed by conventional financial measures alone. They are often accounted for in cost, rather than profit, centers because their contribution to corporate profits is remote and cannot easily be assessed. Suppose, for example, that a company operates a training facility for its employees. As with any educational institution, its goals are elusive and difficult to quantify—especially in the short term. Fiscal criteria, such as return on investment, are clearly inappropriate. Consequently, performance measures of the type proposed by the GASB may be more salient than those associated with the typical manufacturing or even service organization.

As continually stressed throughout this text, technological developments are forcing a dramatic transformation of business and economic practices. These, in turn, necessitate equally extraordinary changes in performance measurement and other aspects of accounting. Therefore, the practices described in this text must be seen as solutions to the problems only of yesterday and perhaps today, but certainly not of tomorrow. At best, they are the foundation upon which the systems of the future will be constructed.

---

[3]*Service Efforts and Accomplishments Reporting: Its Time Has Come* (Norwalk, CT: Governmental Accounting Standards Board), 1990.

This chapter has been concerned with performance reports and control techniques that contribute to a comprehensive management system. We emphasized that, above all, the reports prepared for managers must be useful. They must relate to each organization's own specified objectives. Further, they must provide the information required for managers to assess the extent to which each organizational subunit is meeting its expectations and to take timely measures to correct any deficiencies. Because each organization has unique characteristics and goals, its reporting system must be custom tailored to assure a proper fit.

Much of this chapter has focused on the control of costs in manufacturing operations. Its purpose, however, was not to present technical material of interest only to cost accounting specialists in industrial plants. Instead, it provides a perspective on control that would be of value to managers regardless of industry. Indeed, the approach to control that we set forth can be applied to virtually all organizations, both business and nonprofit.

A central theme of this chapter was that deviations from plans must be evaluated in terms of the variables that explain them. A mere comparison between planned and actual results may prove deceptive as to the character as well as the cause of a deviation. Seemingly unfavorable overhead variances, for example, may actually be favorable when the volume of production is taken into account. The ultimate cause of a discrepancy between actual and planned overhead costs may be the excessive use of direct labor or materials—factors beyond the control of the departments responsible for controlling overhead costs.

Variance analysis can seldom, by itself, affix blame for deviations from plans. It can, however, point to a need for explanations and identify the parties who should be called upon to make them. It is but a preliminary, though nevertheless essential, step in the process of determining whether the deviations warrant corrective action.

Decentralized organizations present special problems of performance measurement and control. This is mainly because organizational subunits may take actions that are in their own best interests, but do not necessarily enhance the well-being of the organization as a whole. In this chapter, we summarized the advantages and disadvantages of decentralization. We then addressed one aspect of the decentralization dilemma that is of special concern to accountants—that of establishing the prices at which goods or services are transferred between subunits.

Exercise for Review and Self-Testing

The property department of a corporation is responsible for processing documents pertaining to real estate owned by the company. According to standards established by the firm, each document should take two hours to complete. Clerical employees who work on the documents are called documentation specialists and are of classification Specialist III. They receive wages of $16 per hour. In a typical month the department processes 250 documents.

Each document processed requires, in addition to the direct labor of the documentation specialists, services provided by a service pool. These services include word processing, computer input, copying, and verification. Monthly fixed costs of the service pool are $2,000. Variable costs of the service pool have been found to be closely associated with the number of hours worked by the documentation specialist. They approximated $3.00 for each hour worked by the documentation specialists.

The costs of the service pool are charged to the property department by a predetermined overhead charging rate. The rate is related to number of hours worked by the documentation specialists. It is based on estimates of fixed costs of $2,000 per month, of variable costs of $3.00 per hour of labor performed by the documentation specialists, and of volume of 250 documents (500 hours of documentation specialist labor) per month.

In June, owing to filing delays on the part of corporate regional offices, the property department was required to process only 220 documents. Instead of assigning employees of Specialist III classification to the processing work, the department assigned employees of Specialist IV classification. The wage rate of Specialist IV employees is only $14 per hour. Owing to their inexperience, the Specialist IV took an average of 2.4 hours to process each of the 220 documents; they worked a total of 528 hours and were paid a total of $7,392.

The service pool incurred total costs of $3,480. Of these, $2,200 were fixed and $1,280 were variable.

1. Evaluate the efficiency of the property department in using the "direct labor" of the documentation specialists.
   a. Determine the amount saved by compensating each hour of labor at a wage rate lower than standard (i.e., the *labor rate variance*).
   b. Determine the value, at standard rates, of the additional hours of labor that were required (i.e., the *labor efficiency variance*).
   c. Determine the total direct labor variance.
2. Analyze the costs incurred by the service pool.
   a. Determine the "opportunity costs" (i.e., the *volume variance*) of employing service pool capacity to process 220 documents instead of the usual 250 documents.
      (1) Calculate the fixed portion of the overhead charging rate based on the standard number of direct labor hours required to process 250 documents.
      (2) Indicate the fixed overhead that should be budgeted to support a volume of 250 documents.
      (3) Calculate the fixed overhead that would be absorbed, assuming that only 220 documents were processed with standard efficiency.
      (4) Determine the difference between items 2 and 3.
   b. Determine the additional costs incurred by the service pool owing to the inefficiency in the use of the direct clerical labor (i.e., the overhead *efficiency* variance).
      (1) Compute the amount of variable overhead that the service pool should budget for the *actual* number of direct labor hours used to process 220 documents.
      (2) Compute the amount of variable overhead that the service pool should budget for the *standard* number of direct labor hours required to process 220 documents.
      (3) Calculate the difference between items 1 and 2.
   c. Determine the deviation from planned costs incurred by the service pool attributable to its own apparent efficiency or inefficiency (i.e., the *budget* or *spending* variance).
      (1) Indicate the costs that were actually incurred.
      (2) Indicate the amounts of fixed and variable overhead (previously computed) that the service pool should budget for the actual number of direct labor hours for which support was provided.

(3) Compute the differences between items 1 and 2 for fixed and variable overhead.

Questions for Review and Discussion

1. What are standard costs? How do they facilitate control?
2. Why is it important that variances be analyzed in conjunction with one another rather than independently?
3. Under one record-keeping system, efficiency variances are identified and recorded at the time resources are added to work in process. Under another they are identified and recorded as goods are transferred from work in process to finished goods. What is the advantage of the former system?
4. "Standards should represent an ideal level of performance, one that employees should strive to attain but should seldom be able to do so." Do you agree? Explain.
5. "An unfavorable variance indicates the need for corrective action on the part of management." Do you agree? Explain.
6. Explain why there is likely to be a direct connection between either a direct labor or materials variance and the overhead efficiency variance.
7. What is the key advantage of a *flexible* over a *fixed* budget in controlling overhead costs?
8. What does the volume variance represent and why is it of limited usefulness in controlling overhead costs?
9. Why does the overhead budget or spending variance contain both fixed and variable elements whereas the efficiency variance contains only a variable element?
10. What is a *learning curve*, and how can it contribute to improved control over labor costs?
11. Why can't standard costs be incorporated into general-purpose reports intended for external users? What adjustments must be made to standard cost accounts so that they can be used in general-purpose reports?

Problems

1. *Variances can be isolated through the normal recording process.*

Hall Office Equipment manufactures desk trays at a standard cost of $8.40 per set determined as follows:

Materials (3 feet of sheet metal @ $2)	$6.00
Labor (.4 hour @ $6)	2.40
Total cost per unit	$8.40

In a particular period, the company purchased 600 feet of sheet metal for $1,260 ($2.10 per foot). It produced 180 sets of trays using 520 feet of sheet metal and 75 direct labor hours. The labor hours were compensated at a total cost of $465 ($6.20 per hour).

The company records manufacturing variances as soon as they are identified. That is, price or rate variances are recorded at the time goods or services are acquired; quantity or efficiency variances at the time goods or services are added to work in process.

Prepare journal entries to record the purchase of the raw materials and the manufacture of 180 sets of desk trays.

2. *Actual and standard costs can be derived from entries to selected manufacturing accounts.*

The Strauss Corp. manufactures refrigeration systems. In one department, plastic tubing is shaped into required configurations.

The operations of the department are accounted for by a standard cost system. Both direct labor and materials (measured in feet of tubing) are added to work in process in standard quantities valued at standard prices. Assume, for simplicity, that no overhead is added.

Total debits and credits (not balances) to selected manufacturing accounts for the month of April were as follows:

	Debits	Credits
Materials (plastic tubing)	$12,600	$ 9,240
Accounts payable (for materials only)	5,000	?
Materials price variance	600	
Materials quantity variance	840	
Direct labor	5,850	5,850
Wages payable	5,500	?
Labor rate variance	156	
Labor efficiency variance		150
Work in process { Labor	6,000	
Materials	8,400	14,400
"Finished" goods (units completed and available for transfer to other departments)	14,400	14,400

During the month, the department started and completed 500 units. There were no beginning-of-month inventories of materials. The department purchased (but did not necessarily use) 3,000 feet of tubing, and it used 780 hours of direct labor.

Determine the *actual* and *standard* cost (divided into direct labor and materials) of completing each unit of product. You might find it helpful to reconstruct, in summary form, each of the journal entries that was made during the month.

3. *A flexible budget forms the basis for analysis of overhead variances.*

Lamar Tool Corp. has found that manufacturing overhead is most closely associated with *direct labor dollars.* Monthly fixed overhead is $18,000; variable overhead is $.12 per direct labor dollar.

Manufacturing standards indicate that standard *direct* labor cost is $20 per unit. Normal monthly output is 3,000 units ($60,000 in direct labor costs).

a. Prepare a flexible overhead budget for each of the following levels of activity, as expressed in direct labor dollars: $50,000; $55,000; $60,000; $65,000; $70,000.

b. Determine the overhead charging rate based on normal monthly activity of $60,000 direct labor hours.

c. Determine the amount of overhead that would be *absorbed* into work in process at each level of activity indicated in the flexible budget (i.e., $50,000, $55,000, etc.).

d. Assuming that direct labor costs incurred during a month conformed to standard, which overhead variance would be indicated by the difference, at each level of activity, between the overhead budgeted and the overhead absorbed?

e. Suppose that direct labor costs of $57,000 were incurred to produce 2,750 units of output. Determine the *volume* variance.

f. Assume that the firm incurred (as per standard) direct labor costs of $70,000 to produce 3,500 units of product. It also incurred fixed overhead costs of $19,000 and variable overhead costs of $8,600. Determine the *budget* or *spending* variance. Determine also the *volume* variance.

g. Assume that the firm incurred direct labor costs of $65,000.
  (1) Indicate the amount of *overhead* that the firm must incur for there to be zero overhead *efficiency* variance.
  (2) Indicate the number of *units* that the firm must produce for there to be zero overhead *efficiency* variance.
  (3) Indicate the number of *units* that the firm must produce for there to be zero *volume* variance.

4. *Data on manufacturing costs can be derived from income statement and variance accounts.*

The following income statement represents the operations of Hauquitz Company for July. Variable manufacturing costs at standard are 50 percent of total standard manufacturing cost. Standard fixed cost per unit is based on normal activity of 30,000 units per month.

<table><tr><td colspan="3" align="center">**Hauquitz Company**
Income Statement for July</td></tr><tr><td>Sales (20,000 units)</td><td></td><td>$200,000</td></tr><tr><td>Cost of goods sold (at standard)</td><td></td><td>120,000</td></tr><tr><td>Gross profit (at standard)</td><td></td><td>80,000</td></tr><tr><td>Manufacturing variances:</td><td></td><td></td></tr><tr><td>Materials</td><td>$2,000 U</td><td></td></tr><tr><td>Direct labor</td><td>1,000 F</td><td></td></tr><tr><td>Overhead budget</td><td>1,000 U</td><td>2,000 U</td></tr><tr><td></td><td></td><td>78,000</td></tr><tr><td>Volume variance</td><td></td><td>24,000 U</td></tr><tr><td>Gross profit, actual</td><td></td><td>54,000</td></tr><tr><td>Selling, general, and administrative costs</td><td></td><td>48,000</td></tr><tr><td>Net income before taxes</td><td></td><td>$ 6,000</td></tr></table>

U = unfavorable; F = favorable.

a. What are fixed and variable standard costs per unit?
b. What are monthly fixed manufacturing costs?
c. How many units were produced in June?
d. If beginning inventory of finished goods was $60,000 at standard cost, what is the ending finished goods inventory at standard cost?
e. What other reports would managers use to evaluate monthly performance? Describe the kinds of information you would prefer to see in such reports. Explain why such information would be desirable.

5. *Variable analysis may help to explain deviations from standards.*

The Ann Arbor Company manufactures Product Z in standard batches of 100 units. A variable standard cost system is used. The standard costs for one batch of Z are:

Raw materials (60 pounds @ $.45)	$ 27.00	
Direct labor (36 hours @ $4.00)	$144.00	
Variable overhead (36 hours @ $2.75)	$ 99.00	
Total standard cost per unit	$270.00	

The overhead rate was based on normal volume of 240 batches. The flexible budget for overhead is:

Budgeted overhead per month = $15,120 + $2.75 per direct labor hour

Production for May amounted to 210 batches. There were no beginning or ending inventories. Actual data for May were:

Raw materials used	13,000 pounds
Cost of raw materials used	$ 6,110
Direct labor cost	$31,600
Actual overhead (of which $14,544 is fixed)	$35,344
Average actual variable overhead rate per hour	$ 2.60

Prepare a schedule that contains a detailed explanation of the variances between actual costs and standard costs. Identify possible causes of each variance, and write a short explanation of each significant variance.

6. *Overhead application rates are based on a choice of activity levels.*

   The managers of Rolla Shield Shutter Company have been trying to select the budgeted overhead application rate for next year. Most managers agree that total manufacturing overhead should be budgeted at $1,200,000 plus $1.50 times direct labor hours, but they are not sure how many direct labor hours should be budgeted. One manager argues that 300,000 hours is as good an estimate as any; another that 360,000 hours are required.

   a. Compute the predetermined overhead rate using (1) 300,000 hours and (2) 360,000 hours.
   b. Suppose that the firm actually works 320,000 direct labor hours and incurs total manufacturing overhead costs of $1,710,000.
      (1) What would the budget variance and volume variance be if the firm had selected 300,000 hours to set the predetermined rate?
      (2) What would the same two variances be if the firm has used 360,000 hours to set the rate?

7. *Standard costs and income statement data are related.*

   An income statement for Cycle Company is as follows:

Sales (200,000 units)		$2,000,000
Cost of sales:		
Materials	$300,000	
Direct labor	400,000	
Overhead	600,000	$1,300,000
Standard gross profit		700,000
Manufacturing variances:		
Materials	$12,000 U	
Direct labor	18,000 F	
Variable overhead spending	4,000 U	
Variable overhead efficiency	8,000 F	
Fixed overhead budget	7,000 F	
Underabsorbed overhead	20,000 U	3,000 U
Actual gross profit		697,000
Selling and administrative expenses		600,000
Net income before taxes		$ 97,000

U = unfavorable; F = favorable.

In addition, you learn the following:
 (1) There were no beginning inventories.
 (2) Fixed overhead absorbed per unit is $2, based on budgeted production of 250,000 units and budgeted fixed costs of $500,000.
 (3) The standard direct labor rate is $4 per hour.
 (4) Variable overhead standard cost is based on a rate of $2 per direct labor hour.
 (5) The firm used 116,000 direct labor hours.
 (6) The standard price for materials is $0.50 per pound.
 (7) Material purchases were 800,000 pounds at a total of $3,000 over standard price.

Calculate the following:
 a. Standard cost per unit, including standard prices and quantities for each cost element
 b. Standard variable cost per unit
 c. Production quantity for the year
 d. Ending inventory at standard cost
 e. Fixed overhead costs incurred
 f. Cost of materials purchased
 g. Material use variance
 h. Pounds of material used in production
 i. Direct labor efficiency variance
 j. Direct labor rate variance
 k. Direct labor costs incurred
 l. Variable overhead costs incurred
 m. Amount by which income would have increased if 100 more units had been sold (assuming no additional production)

8. *Relationships between volume variances, production levels, and standard costs can affect net income.*

 Ayres Rock Inc. began the year with 13,000 units of product on hand. During the year, 90,000 units were sold, and 15,000 units were in inventory at year end. Standard fixed cost per unit is $5 based on budgeted fixed overhead of $500,000 for the year.
 a. Compute the volume variance for the year.
 b. Determine what would have happened to Ayres Rock's total income if production had increased by 1,000 units but sales had remained the same.

9. *Standard cost data may be derived from incomplete data.*

 The Cunningham Co. drew the following data from its standard cost system:

Total overhead incurred	$134,000
Flexible budget for overhead	$90,000 + $.60 per DLH
Total overhead rate (fixed and variable)	$2.10
Spending variance	$8,000 U
Volume variance	$7,500 F

U = unfavorable; F = favorable; DLH = direct labor hours.

Using the preceding data, calculate:
 a. The normal or expected volume used to calculate the overhead rate
 b. The actual labor hours used
 c. The standard hours allowed for the actual production
 d. The overhead efficiency variance

10. *The purpose of variance analysis is to assign responsibility, not to affix blame.*

Luxury Leathers, Inc., has established the following standards for the manufacture of belts:

Materials (.5 lb of leather @ $6)	$3.00
Direct labor (.25 hour @ $8)	2.00
Overhead ($1 per unit)	1.00
Total	$6.00

Overhead is applied on the basis of a predetermined charging rate of $4 per direct labor hour based on normal monthly volume of 1,000 units (250 direct labor hours). Fixed overhead per month is estimated at $600; variable overhead at $1.60 per direct labor hour.

In September the company produced 1,100 belts. Actual costs were:

Materials purchased and used (580 lb of leather @ $6.20)		$3,596
Direct labor (290 hours @ $8.30)		2,407
Overhead		
Fixed	$700	
Variable	435	1,135
Total costs incurred		$7,138

Fixed overhead comprises primarily depreciation of equipment, repair and maintenance costs, and building occupancy costs. Variable overhead is mostly payroll-related costs.

a. To the extent that the data permit, explain the differences between actual and standard costs in terms of materials, labor, and overhead variances.

b. Indicate in a general way the departments which should most likely be held responsible for explaining each of the variances.

11. *The volume variance has only a fixed element; the efficiency variance only a variable element; the budget variance both a fixed and variable element.*

Housewares, Inc., estimates that its annual fixed overhead costs are $720,000 ($60,000 per month). Variable overhead costs are $1 per direct labor hour. Estimated production volume is 120,000 units per year (10,000 per month). Per company standards, each unit requires two hours of direct labor.

In June actual overhead costs were $80,000—$61,200 fixed and $18,800 variable. The firm used 18,000 direct labor hours in producing 8,800 units.

The firm applies overhead to the product by means of a predetermined charging rate.

a. Determine the overhead charging rate. Distinguish between the fixed and variable portions.

b. Compare actual overhead costs incurred with those that the firm would have budgeted for the month had it known that it would operate at an activity level of 18,000 direct labor hours. Compare separately the fixed and variable elements of the costs. Comment briefly on why the *budget* or *spending* variance that you calculated can have both fixed and variable elements even if "fixed" costs are truly fixed.

c. Compare the overhead costs expected at an activity level of 18,000 direct labor hours with those that should be budgeted to produce 8,800 units using the standard number of direct labor hours. Compare separately the fixed and variable portions of the costs, and comment briefly on why the *efficiency* variance that you calculated has only a variable element.

d. Compare the overhead costs that the firm would have budgeted to produce 8,800 units based on the standard number of direct labor hours (and the fixed overhead budget) with the amount of overhead that would be *absorbed* at a volume of 8,800 units (using the standard number of direct labor hours). In addition, compare the fixed overhead that would be *absorbed* at the normal volume of 10,000 units with that which would be *absorbed* at the actual volume of 8,800 units. Comment briefly on why the *volume* variance that you calculated has only a fixed element, and comment on when the volume variance will be zero.

12. *Overhead variances can be depicted graphically.*

   The Stern Company estimates that fixed overhead is $9,000 per month and variable overhead is $5 per direct labor hour. Per the company's standards, one direct labor hour is required for each unit of product. Normal monthly volume is 3,000 units of product (also 3,000 direct labor hours).

   In a particular month, the firm incurred actual overhead costs of $25,000. It used 2,000 direct labor hours to produce 1,600 units of output.
   a. Determine the overhead charging rate, based on 3,000 direct labor hours per month.
   b. Prepare a graph in which the horizontal axis represents level of activity expressed in terms of direct labor hours (0 to 5,000) and the vertical axis represents overhead costs ($0 to $35,000). Draw two lines: the first representing the amount of overhead that would be *absorbed* (based on the overhead charging rate) at various levels of activity; the second indicating the amount of overhead that should be budgeted for the various levels of activity.
   c. Show by a point the actual overhead costs incurred. Indicate the amount of overhead that would be budgeted for actual number of direct labor hours used (2,000). Denote the budget or spending variance.
   d. Indicate the amount of overhead that would be budgeted for the *standard* number of direct labor hours that should have been used to produce the actual output of 1,600 units. Indicate also the amount of overhead that would have been absorbed at that level of activity. Denote the *volume* variance.
   e. Compare the amount of overhead that would be budgeted for the actual number of direct labor hours used with the amount that would be budgeted for the standard number of direct labor hours required to produce the actual output of 1,600 units. Denote the overhead efficiency variance.

13. *The volume variance differs in concept from both the budget and efficiency variances.*

   The Davies Corp. estimates that fixed overhead per month is $40,000 and variable overhead is $3 per direct labor hour. In a normal month, the firm produces 1,000 units of output, each of which requires, per standard, four hours of direct labor. The company charges overhead to work in process using a predetermined charging rate of $13 per direct labor hour. The charging rate was calculated on the assumption that in a typical month the firm would use 4,000 direct labor hours and incur $40,000 of fixed overhead costs and $12,000 of variable overhead costs.

   In July the firm produced only 900 units of output. It used 3,780 hours of direct labor and incurred total overhead costs of $53,000. All costs were paid as incurred.
   a. Determine the overhead budget variance. Indicate the *incremental cash per unit* that the firm was required to expend as a consequence of incurring greater overhead costs than were budgeted for the actual number of direct labor hours used.
   b. Determine the overhead efficiency variance. Indicate the *incremental cash per unit* that the firm was required to expand as a consequence of using a greater number of labor hours than is standard for the actual number of units produced.

c. Determine the overhead volume variance. Indicate the *incremental cash per unit* of additional cash that the firm was required to expend as a consequence of producing at a volume different than planned.

d. Comment on the utility of the volume variance in controlling overhead costs. To which department in an organization can responsibility for the volume variance ordinarily be attributed? Why does the volume variance provide information that is of limited usefulness to management?

14. *Estimates of volume can affect reported product cost.*

Industrial Products has determined that the fixed portion of its overhead costs is $720,000 and the variable portion is $4 per direct labor hour. One direct labor hour is required for each unit of product.

The firm bases its predetermined overhead charging rate on estimated annual volume of 240,000 units.

a. Determine the overhead charging rate.

b. Suppose that actual volume was only 200,000 units. Indicate the per unit amount of overhead that would be applied to the product, and calculate the total amount that would be applied.

c. Suppose alternatively that the firm was better able to forecast volume and based its overhead charging rate on estimated volume of 200,000 units.
   (1) Determine the overhead charging rate.
   (2) Indicate the per unit amount of overhead that would be applied to the product, and calculate the total amount that would be applied.

d. The impact of arbitrary estimates on amounts reported in external financial reports must be minimized. Assume that actual volume was 200,000 units but that the overhead charging rate was based on 240,000 units. Of the 200,000 units produced, 160,000 were sold; the other 40,000 remained in inventory. Prepare a journal entry so that the accounts will reflect actual overhead costs rather than those which were applied on the basis of an arbitrary estimate of volume.

15. *The issue of how to account for variances in interim reports points to conceptual differences between the volume variance and other variances.*

Adult Games, Inc., a manufacturer of electronic games, engages in operations that are highly seasonal. Production volume in the first quarter of a year can be expected to be considerably less than in other quarters. Anticipated volume for a year is 12,000 units.

Budgeted fixed overhead for the year is $96,000; per quarter it is $24,000. Variable overhead is $1 per direct labor hour. Standard overhead per unit is $11.

Standard labor cost is $21 (3 hours @ $7) and standard materials cost is $30. Total standard cost per unit is $62.

In the first quarter of the year, the firm produced and sold 1,500 electronic games. Actual labor costs were $32,200 (4,600 hours @ $7). Actual materials costs were $45,000. Actual overhead costs were $29,000.

At the end of the first quarter, the accounts of the firm revealed the variances that follow; there were no other variances:

Labor efficiency	$ 700
Overhead spending	400
Overhead efficiency	100
Overhead volume	12,000

a. Show how each of the variances was determined.

b. The firm is required to prepare interim financial reports to stockholders and regulatory authorities after the first quarter. What amount do you think should be reported as cost of goods sold?

c. Do you think that the volume variance (which represents underabsorbed overhead) should be accounted for differently than the other variances in determining interim cost of goods sold? Explain, directing specific attention to any conceptual differences between the volume variance and other variances. Can the volume variance be expected to be eliminated by year end?

16. *Employees may be entitled to a cost-saving bonus despite unfavorable variances.*

Industrial Generators, Inc., contracted with employees of selected production departments to provide them a bonus equal in amount to 20 percent of any savings in costs that are within their control. The amount of the savings will be determined by comparing actual costs with standard costs.

The standard cost of overhauling a Type I generator is $126;

Direct labor (4 hours @ $10)	$ 40
Parts (1.1 sets @ $60)	66
Overhead ($5 per direct labor hour; 4 hours @ $5)	20
Standard cost per unit	$126

In fact, only one set of parts is required for each generator. The standard of 1.1 sets takes into account normal waste and breakage.

The overhead charging rate of $5 per direct labor hour assumes a volume of 4,500 generators (18,000 direct labor hours) and was determined as follows:

Fixed overhead costs	$54,000
Variable overhead costs ($2 per direct labor hour;	
4,500 units × 4 direct labor hours × $2)	36,000
Anticipated overhead costs	$90,000
Anticipated activity (direct labor hours)	÷ 18,000
Charging rate per direct labor hour	$ 5

At the end of the first year of the bonus plan, the following data were compiled and presented to the employees responsible for overhauling Type I generators.

Actual number of units overhauled		4,200 units
Direct labor hours (an average of 3.7 per unit)		15,540 hours
Direct labor cost ($10 per hour)		$155,400
Number of sets of parts purchased and used		
(an average of 1.05 per generator)		4,410 sets
Cost of parts (an average of $70 per set)		$308,700
Overhead		
Fixed	$56,000	
Variable (an average of $2.10 per direct labor hour)	32,634	$ 88,634
Total manufacturing costs (an average of		
$131.60 per unit)		$552,734

Inasmuch as the standard cost of overhauling 4,200 units is, at $126 per unit, only $529,200, management informed the employees that they would receive no bonus for the year.

The number of units overhauled is determined by management, not the employees eligible for the bonus. Manufacturing overhead is also beyond the control of the employees, except insofar as it is influenced by number of direct labor hours. All acquisitions of parts are made by a corporate purchasing department.

Contrary to the determination of management, the employees believe that they are entitled to a bonus. Assume that they have engaged you to represent them in negotiations with management.

a. Prepare an analysis in which you account, as far as permitted by the data available, for the unfavorable variance of $23,535 between actual costs ($552,734) and standard costs ($529,200) for output of 42,000 units.

b. Determine the amount of the bonus to which the employees should be entitled if it is truly to be based on savings in costs over which they have control. Justify your analysis.

17. *Dollars saved may not be dollars earned.*

A purchasing agent recently entered into a contract for which he believes he deserves commendation from corporate management. The agent was able to acquire electronic components from a new supplier at a price of $.80 less than that which the company pays to its usual supplier.

The components are used in the manufacture of electronic test equipment.

Because the equipment has to be constructed with precision, a considerable number of units are usually rejected after they have been completed. In fact, production standards have been set that allow for the production of 105 units for every 100 that are able to pass final inspection.

Each unit of equipment produced requires one set of components and .5 hours of labor. The standard labor rate is $8 per hour.

Budgeted fixed overhead is $18,000 per month. Variable overhead is $1.90 per direct labor hour. In a normal month, production employees work 3,150 direct labor hours. This is the number of hours that are required to produce a total of 6,300 units, of which 6,000 (6,300 × 100/105) should be sufficiently free of defects so that they can be shipped.

The purchasing agent was able to obtain the components from the new supplier at a price of $5.20 per unit rather than the standard $6.00. He recognized that the components were not of the same quality as those obtained from the usual supplier, but he believed that the substantial saving in price would more than offset the cost of any additional units that would have to be rejected. He estimated— an estimate that proved to be accurate—that using the components from the new supplier, 115 units of equipment would have to be manufactured in order to produce 100 units that passed inspection. As a consequence, to satisfy the monthly demand for 6,000 units suitable for shipment, he purchased 6,900 (6,000 × 115/100) components.

Based on the information provided, did the purchasing agent enter into a contract that could be justified economically? Assume that in the month that the substandard components are used, production will be "at standard," except insofar as the inferior components cause the standards to be violated. Assume also that the completed units that are rejected have no value.

a. Calculate the standard cost of producing 6,000 acceptable units and compare it with cost that would be incurred using the substandard components.

b. Analyze the difference between actual and standard costs in terms of the following variances:
   (1) Materials price
   (2) Materials quantity
   (3) Labor quantity
   (4) Volume (based on number of *acceptable* units)
   (5) Overhead efficiency

c. Comment on whether the contract entered into by the purchasing agent merits a commendation.

18. *Reports which compare actual and standard costs should explain, as far as possible, the reasons for any variances.*

Queens Shirts, Inc., has established the following standards for each shirt manufactured:

Material: 2 yards @ $6	$12
Labor: .3 hour @ $9	3
Total	$15

In March the company produced and shipped 4,000 shirts. In addition, it was forced to reject and discard a batch of 300 shirts in midproduction upon discovering an error in a pattern. The company had applied 450 yards of material and 55 hours of labor to the defective units.

In March the company purchased and used 9,000 yards of material at a cost of $5.85 per yard. It applied to production 1,300 hours of labor at a cost of $12,408.

The labor standards do not take into account a wage increase of $.40 per hour, effective March 1. To make up for the loss in production owing to the defective pattern, the firm was required to schedule 40 hours of overtime (included in the 1,300 hours of labor), which were compensated at time and a half.

Prepare a report in which you explain, to the extent the data permit, the difference between actual costs and standard costs for a volume of 4,000 shirts. Be sure to indicate the portions of the variance attributable to the defective pattern and the wage increase.

19. *Standard costs are inappropriate for external financial reports.*

The Hall Corporation maintains the accounts for its manufacturing operations on a standard cost system. Both labor and materials are recorded in work in process at standard quantities valued at standard prices. Raw materials are stated at actual quantities valued at standard prices.

As of December 31, the firm's trial balance reflected the following amounts (all debits):

Raw materials inventory	$ 40,000
Work in process inventory	97,200
Finished goods inventory	48,600
Cost of goods sold	972,000
Raw materials price variance	30,704
Raw materials quantity variance	22,080
Labor rate variance	21,390
Labor efficiency variance	18,860

The standard cost of each unit of product is $48.60;

Labor (3 hours @ $8.20)	$24.60
Materials (6 lb @ $4)	24.00
Total standard cost	$48.60

For convenience, it may be assumed that overhead is applied as a percentage of direct labor and that the labor rate of $8.20 includes an element of overhead. For purposes of this problem, there is no need to deal with overhead independently of labor.

As of the start of the year, there were zero balances in all of the accounts indicated.

Work in process represents goods that are one-half complete with respect to both labor and materials; thus for purposes of determining productivity for the year, it contains a number of units equivalent to one-half the number actually in process.

The company needs to adjust the inventory and cost-of-goods-sold balances indicated in the trial balance so that actual costs can be reflected in the financial statements to be included in the firm's annual report.

a. Determine the number of units of output represented by the balances in cost of goods sold, finished goods, and work in process. Determine also the number of pounds of raw materials held in inventory.
b. Using the variances indicated in parentheses, derive the following actual amounts:
   (1) Pounds of materials used (materials quantity)
   (2) Price of materials purchased (materials price, based on number of pounds purchased rather than used)
   (3) Number of hours of direct labor (labor efficiency)
   (4) Hourly labor rate (labor rate)
c. Determine the actual materials and labor cost per unit.
d. Determine the amounts that should be reported in the raw materials, work in process, finished goods, and cost of goods sold accounts in the financial statements. Prepare a journal entry to adjust the amounts indicated in the trial balance and to assign the variances to these accounts.

20. *Year-end proration of under- or overabsorbed overhead correct for "errors" in the predetermined overhead charging rate.*

Sherwood Company uses a job order costing system. Overhead is applied by means of a predetermined rate based on direct labor dollars. Records for the year indicate the following:

Budgeted factory overhead	$400,000
Actual factory overhead	369,000
Budgeted direct labor dollars	800,000
Actual direct labor dollars	820,000

All jobs that were worked on during the year, with the exception of two, were completed and sold. Job 68 has been completed but has not yet been sold; job 69 is still in process. At year end, there were no other jobs in process or in inventory. Direct labor and materials costs applicable to these two jobs were:

	Direct Labor	Direct Materials
Job 68 (in finished goods inventory)	$60,000	$50,000
Job 69 (in work in process inventory)	40,000	20,000

a. Determine the cost of job 68 prior to any reallocation of under- or overabsorbed overhead.
b. At year end, the firm prorates under- or overabsorbed overhead to work in process, finished goods inventory, and cost of goods sold based on the direct labor dollars included in each of the accounts. Determine the balance in finished goods inventory (job 68) after the proration of under- or overabsorbed overhead.

c. Suppose that the company had perfect foresight and was able, at the start of the year, to accurately predict both factory overhead and direct labor cost. Determine, first, what the overhead charging rate would have been and, second, what the total charges to job 68, including direct labor, direct materials, and overhead, would have been. Compare the total amount that would have been charged to job 68 with that charged per part b.

21. *Standards must reflect reductions in time owing to experience.*

Electronic Controls, Inc., is about to begin production of a new control device. It is attempting to develop labor cost standards that can be incorporated into a standard cost accounting system.

The firm's engineers have estimated that the first batch of 200 control devices will require 2,000 direct labor hours—an average of 10 hours per unit. Thereafter, the time required to complete subsequent units will reflect an 80 percent learning curve.

The standard hourly wage rate paid by the firm is $8. The combined standard work-month for all employees assigned to production of the control device is a total of 2,000 labor hours.

a. Prepare a table in which you indicate the average number of direct labor hours required to manufacture various "batches" of control devices, up to a cumulative total of 12,800 units.

b. Suppose that the firm adjusts its standards each month.
   (1) What should be the standard labor cost of producing a single unit during the first month?
   (2) What should be the standard labor cost of producing a single unit during the fourth month? (In this and subsequent parts of this problem, you need not interpolate between points on the learning curve. For convenience, where a range of production is between two points on the curve, use the point representing the lesser amount of time.)

c. Suppose that the firm adjusts its standards quarterly. What should be the standard labor cost of producing a single unit during the first quarter (the first 8,000 hours)?

d. Suppose that the firm adjusts its standards annually. What should be the standard labor cost of producing a single unit during the first year (the first 24,000 hours)?

22. *Market-based transfer prices may not be appropriate in the absence of genuine decentralization.*

A plastic manufacturer has a molding division and an assembly division. The molding division produces parts exclusively for the assembly division, and the assembly division must purchase all its parts from the molding division. Consequently, the assembly division dictates the molding division's production volume.

The molding division's estimated costs for a year are:

Fixed costs	$100 million
Variable	$40 per unit

Its expected volume is 2 million parts, and at that volume cost per unit would be $90:

Fixed costs	$100 million
Variable costs (2 million @ $40)	80 million
Total costs	$180 million
No. of units	÷ 2 million
Total cost per unit	$ 90 per unit

If the assembly division had to contract with outside molders to supply its parts, it would have had to pay $120 per unit. The company uses this "market price" as its transfer price for the molded parts. The manager of the molding division is given an annual bonus equal to 0.1 percent of the division's profits.

Assume that in one year, the assembly division requests 2.5 million parts; in the next, however, it requests only 1.0 million parts.

a. Determine the bonus of the molding division manager for each of the two years. What objections might the manager raise to the market-based transfer price? Comment on the extent to which this company is genuinely decentralized.

b. Assume instead that the assembly division is permitted to purchase its parts requirements from outside suppliers as well as from the molding division. Correspondingly, the molding division is permitted to sell its parts to outsiders. Would the objections of the molding division manager to the market-based transfer price still be legitimate? Could a stronger case be made for the market-based transfer price? Explain.

23. *Transfer prices may have to serve competing objectives.*

An international equipment manufacturer has two subsidiaries. Its European subsidiary manufactures the basic components of a machine, while its U.S. subsidiary assembles the components and sells the completed product.

The per unit manufacturing costs of the European subsidiary are as follows, assuming a normal volume of 1,000 units per month (in thousands):

Fixed costs per month	$4,000,000	
No. of units per month	÷ 1,000	$ 4,000
Variable costs per unit		7,000
Total costs per unit		$11,000

Those of the U.S. subsidiary are (in thousands):

Fixed costs per month	$2,000,000	
No. of units per month	÷ 1,000	$ 2,000
Variable costs per unit		3,000
Total costs per unit		$ 5,000

The company estimates that the components needed to manufacture the machine could be obtained in the United States from independent suppliers for $16,000 per unit.

The selling price of the completed machine is $26,000 per unit.

The company is considering two prices to charge the U.S. subsidiary for the components shipped from Europe:

(1) The actual cost of producing the equipment plus a markup of 20 percent. Thus, at normal volume of 1,000 units per month the transfer price would be $13,200 ($11,000 plus $2,200).

(2) The market-based price of $16,000.

a. Suppose that the company wishes to minimize its overall income tax liability. The European subsidiary faces an overall tax rate of 50 percent; the U.S. subsidiary of 30 percent. Determine the total tax under each of the alternative transfer prices.

(1) Assume first that the company produces and sells the normal volume of 1,000 per month.

(2) Assume instead that volume falls to 500 units per month.

Which of the transfer price policies would better accomplish this objective?

b. Suppose further that the company faces severe U.S. tariffs and other import restrictions unless it can demonstrate that the equipment contains more than a specified percentage of "domestic content." Domestic content would be measured by the U.S. subsidiary's ratio of total assembly costs incurred in the United States to its total cost of goods sold. Which pricing policy would better enable the company to meet this requirement, assuming each of the two alternative production and sales volumes?

Solutions to Exercise for Review and Self-Testing

1. a. Actual direct labor hours at actual rate
   (528 hours @ $14) $7,392

   Actual direct labor hours at standard rate
   (528 hours @ $16)   8,448

   Labor rate variance (favorable)   ($1,056)

   b. Actual direct labor hours at standard rate
   (528 hours @ $16)   8,448

   Standard direct labor hours at standard rate
   (440 hours @ $16)   7,040

   Labor efficiency variance $1,408

   c. Total direct labor variance $ 352

2. a. 1. Fixed portion of overhead charging rate

   $$= \frac{\text{Fixed costs}}{\text{Number of hours required to process 250 documents}} = \frac{\$2,000}{500}$$

   = $4 per direct labor hour

   2. Fixed costs budgeted for 250 (or any number of) documents would be $2,000.

   3. Overhead absorbed at production volume of 220 documents at standard efficiency
   (i.e., 440 direct labor hours)

   Standard number of hours   440

   Fixed portion of overhead charging rate   ×4.00

   Overhead absorbed $1,760

   4. Budgeted fixed costs [per (2)] $2,000

   Less: Fixed costs absorbed at
   standard number of hours to process
   actual number of documents [per (3)]   1,760

   Volume variance $ 240

   b. 1. Variable overhead budget for *actual*
   (528) hours used to process 220 documents
   (528 hours @ $3.00)   1,584

   2. Variable overhead budget for *standard*
   (440) hours to process 220 documents
   (440 hours @ $3.00) $1,320

   3. Variable overhead efficiency variance $ 264

---

c.

	Fixed Element	Variable Element	Total
1. Actual costs	$2,200	1,280	$3,480
2. Budget for actual number of direct labor hours (per b.1 for variable element)	$2,000	$1,584	$3,584
3. Budget or spending variance (favorable)	$ 200	($ 304)	($ 104)

Appendix

TABLE 1

Future value (a) after n periods from investing a single sum (x)
(= $1) at time 0 with interest i:

$$a_{\overline{n}|i} = x(1 + i)^n$$

No. of periods	2%	3%	4%	5%	6%	7%	8%
1	1.0200	1.0300	1.0400	1.0500	1.0600	1.0700	1.0800
2	1.0404	1.0609	1.0816	1.1025	1.1236	1.1449	1.1664
3	1.0612	1.0927	1.1249	1.1576	1.1910	1.2250	1.2597
4	1.0824	1.1255	1.1699	1.2155	1.2625	1.3108	1.3605
5	1.1041	1.1593	1.2167	1.2763	1.3382	1.4026	1.4693
6	1.1262	1.1941	1.2653	1.3401	1.4185	1.5007	1.5869
7	1.1487	1.2299	1.3159	1.4071	1.5036	1.6058	1.7138
8	1.1717	1.2668	1.3686	1.4775	1.5938	1.7182	1.8509
9	1.1951	1.3048	1.4233	1.5513	1.6895	1.8365	1.9990
10	1.2190	1.3439	1.4802	1.6289	1.7908	1.9672	2.1589
11	1.2434	1.3842	1.5395	1.7103	1.8983	2.1049	2.3316
12	1.2682	1.4258	1.6010	1.7959	2.0122	2.2522	2.5182
13	1.2936	1.4685	1.6651	1.8856	2.1329	2.4098	2.7196
14	1.3195	1.5126	1.7317	1.9799	2.2609	2.5785	2.9372
15	1.3459	1.5580	1.8009	2.0789	2.3966	2.7590	3.1722
16	1.3728	1.6047	1.8730	2.1829	2.5404	2.9522	3.4259
17	1.4002	1.6528	1.9479	2.2920	2.6928	3.1588	3.7000
18	1.4282	1.7024	2.0258	2.4066	2.8543	3.3799	3.9960
19	1.4568	1.7535	2.1068	2.5270	3.0256	3.6165	4.3157
20	1.4859	1.8061	2.1911	2.6533	3.2071	3.8697	4.6610
21	1.5157	1.8603	2.2788	2.7860	3.3996	4.1406	5.0338
22	1.5460	1.9161	2.3699	2.9253	3.6035	4.4304	5.4365
23	1.5769	1.9736	2.4647	3.0715	3.8197	4.7405	5.8715
24	1.6084	2.0328	2.5633	3.2251	4.0489	5.0724	6.3412
25	1.6406	2.0938	2.6658	3.3864	4.2919	5.4274	6.8485
26	1.6734	2.1566	2.7725	3.5557	4.4594	5.8074	7.3964
27	1.7069	2.2213	2.8834	3.7335	4.8223	6.2139	7.9881
28	1.7410	2.2879	2.9987	3.9201	5.1117	6.6488	8.6271
29	1.7758	2.3566	3.1187	4.1161	5.4184	7.1143	9.3173
30	1.8114	2.4273	3.2434	4.3219	5.7435	7.6123	10.0627
31	1.8476	2.5001	3.3731	4.5380	6.0881	8.1451	10.8677
32	1.8845	2.5751	3.5081	4.7649	6.4534	8.7153	11.7371
33	1.9222	2.6523	3.6484	5.0032	6.8406	9.3253	12.6760
34	1.9607	2.7319	3.7943	5.2533	7.2510	9.9781	13.6901
35	1.9999	2.8139	3.9461	5.5160	7.6861	10.6766	14.7853
36	2.0399	2.8983	4.1039	5.7918	8.1473	11.4239	15.9682
37	2.0807	2.9852	4.2681	6.0814	8.6361	12.2236	17.2456
38	2.1223	3.0748	4.4388	6.3855	9.1543	13.0793	18.6253
39	2.1647	3.1670	4.6164	6.7048	9.7035	13.9948	20.1153
40	2.2080	3.2620	4.8010	7.0400	10.2857	14.9745	21.7245
41	2.2522	3.3599	4.9931	7.3920	10.9029	16.0227	23.4625
42	2.2972	3.4607	5.1928	7.7616	11.5570	17.1443	25.3395
43	2.3432	3.5645	5.4005	8.1497	12.2505	18.3444	27.3666
44	2.3901	3.6715	5.6165	8.5572	12.9855	19.6285	29.5560
45	2.4379	3.7816	5.8412	8.9850	13.7646	21.0025	31.9204
46	2.4866	3.8950	6.0748	9.4343	14.5905	22.4726	34.4741
47	2.5363	4.0119	6.3178	9.9060	15.4659	24.0457	37.2320
48	2.5871	4.1323	6.5705	10.4013	16.3939	25.7289	40.2106
49	2.6388	4.2562	6.8333	10.9213	17.3775	27.5299	43.4274
50	2.6916	4.3839	7.1067	11.4674	18.4202	29.4570	46.9016

TABLE 1 Continued
Future value (a) after n periods from investing a single sum (x)
(= \$1) at time 0 with interest i:

$$a_{\overline{n}|i} = x(1 + i)^n$$

9%	10%	11%	12%	13%	14%	15%
1.0900	1.1000	1.1100	1.1200	1.1300	1.1400	1.1500
1.1881	1.2100	1.2321	1.2544	1.2769	1.2996	1.3225
1.2950	1.3310	1.3676	1.4049	1.4429	1.4815	1.5209
1.4116	1.4641	1.5181	1.5735	1.6305	1.6890	1.7490
1.5386	1.6105	1.6851	1.7623	1.8424	1.9254	2.0114
1.6771	1.7716	1.8704	1.9738	2.0820	2.1950	2.3131
1.8280	1.9487	2.0762	2.2107	2.3526	2.5023	2.6600
1.9926	2.1436	2.3045	2.4760	2.6584	2.8526	3.0590
2.1719	2.3579	2.5580	2.7731	3.0040	3.2519	3.5179
2.3674	2.5937	2.8394	3.1058	3.3946	3.7072	4.0456
2.5804	2.8531	3.1518	3.4785	3.8359	4.2262	4.6524
2.8127	3.1384	3.4985	3.8960	4.3345	4.8179	5.3503
3.0658	3.4523	3.8833	4.3635	4.8980	5.4924	6.1528
3.3417	3.7975	4.3104	4.8871	5.5348	6.2613	7.0757
3.6425	4.1772	4.7846	5.4736	6.2543	7.1379	8.1371
3.9703	4.5950	5.3109	6.1304	7.0673	8.1372	9.3576
4.3276	5.0545	5.8951	6.8660	7.9861	9.2765	10.7613
4.7171	5.5599	6.5436	7.6900	9.0243	10.5752	12.3755
5.1417	6.1159	7.2633	8.6128	10.1974	12.0557	14.2318
5.6044	6.7275	8.0623	9.6463	11.5231	13.7435	16.3665
6.1088	7.4002	8.9492	10.8038	13.0211	15.6676	18.8215
6.6586	8.1403	9.9336	12.1003	14.7138	17.8610	21.6447
7.2579	8.9543	11.0263	13.5523	16.6266	20.3616	24.8915
7.9111	9.8497	12.2392	15.1786	18.7881	23.2122	28.6252
8.6231	10.8347	13.5855	17.0001	21.2305	26.4619	32.9190
9.3992	11.9182	15.0799	19.0401	23.9905	30.1666	37.8568
10.2451	13.1100	16.7386	21.3249	27.1093	34.3899	43.5353
11.1671	14.4210	18.5799	23.8839	30.6335	39.2045	50.0656
12.1722	15.8631	20.6237	26.7499	34.6158	44.6931	57.5755
13.2677	17.4494	22.8923	29.9599	39.1159	50.9502	66.2118
14.4618	19.1943	25.4104	33.5551	44.2010	58.0832	76.1435
15.7633	21.1138	28.2056	37.5817	49.9471	66.2148	87.5651
17.1820	23.2252	31.3082	42.0915	56.4402	75.4849	100.6998
18.7284	25.5477	34.7521	47.1425	63.7774	86.0528	115.8048
20.4140	28.1024	38.5749	52.7996	72.0685	98.1002	133.1755
22.2512	30.9127	42.8181	59.1356	81.4374	111.8342	153.1519
24.2538	34.0039	47.5281	66.2318	92.0243	127.4910	176.1246
26.4367	37.4043	52.7562	74.1797	103.9874	145.3397	202.5433
28.8160	41.1448	58.5593	83.0812	117.5058	165.6873	232.9248
31.4094	45.2593	65.0009	93.0510	132.7816	188.8835	267.8635
34.2363	49.7852	72.1510	104.2171	150.0432	215.3272	308.0431
37.3175	54.7637	80.0876	116.7231	169.5488	245.4730	354.2495
40.6761	60.2401	88.8972	130.7299	191.5901	279.8392	407.3870
44.3370	66.2641	98.6759	146.4175	216.4968	319.0167	468.4950
48.3273	72.8905	109.5302	163.9876	244.6414	363.6791	538.7693
52.6767	80.1795	121.5786	183.6661	276.4448	414.5941	619.5847
57.4176	88.1975	134.9522	205.7061	312.3826	472.6373	712.5224
62.5852	97.0172	149.7970	230.3908	352.9923	538.8065	819.4007
68.2179	106.7190	166.2746	258.0377	398.8813	614.2395	942.3108
74.3575	117.3909	184.5648	289.0022	450.7359	700.2330	1083.6574

TABLE 2

Present value (p) at time 0 of a single sum (x) (= \$1) to be paid or received after n periods in the future with interest i:

$$p_{\overline{n}|i} = x/(1 + i)^n$$

No. of periods	2%	3%	4%	5%	6%	7%	8%
1	.9804	.9709	.9615	.9524	.9434	.9346	.9259
2	.9612	.9426	.9246	.9070	.8900	.8734	.8573
3	.9423	.9151	.8890	.8638	.8396	.8163	.7938
4	.9238	.8885	.8548	.8227	.7921	.7629	.7350
5	.9057	.8626	.8219	.7835	.7473	.7130	.6806
6	.8880	.8375	.7903	.7462	.7050	.6663	.6302
7	.8706	.8131	.7599	.7107	.6651	.6227	.5835
8	.8535	.7894	.7307	.6768	.6274	.5820	.5403
9	.8368	.7664	.7026	.6446	.5919	.5439	.5002
10	.8203	.7441	.6756	.6139	.5584	.5083	.4632
11	.8043	.7224	.6496	.5847	.5268	.4751	.4289
12	.7885	.7014	.6246	.5568	.4970	.4440	.3971
13	.7730	.6810	.6006	.5303	.4688	.4150	.3677
14	.7579	.6611	.5775	.5051	.4423	.3878	.3405
15	.7430	.6419	.5553	.4810	.4173	.3624	.3152
16	.7284	.6232	.5339	.4581	.3936	.3387	.2919
17	.7142	.6050	.5134	.4363	.3714	.3166	.2703
18	.7002	.5874	.4936	.4155	.3503	.2959	.2502
19	.6864	.5703	.4746	.3957	.3305	.2765	.2317
20	.6730	.5537	.4564	.3769	.3118	.2584	.2145
21	.6598	.5375	.4388	.3589	.2942	.2415	.1987
22	.6468	.5219	.4220	.3418	.2775	.2257	.1839
23	.6342	.5067	.4057	.3256	.2618	.2109	.1703
24	.6217	.4919	.3901	.3101	.2470	.1971	.1577
25	.6095	.4776	.3751	.2953	.2330	.1842	.1460
26	.5976	.4637	.3607	.2812	.2198	.1722	.1352
27	.5859	.4502	.3468	.2678	.2074	.1609	.1252
28	.5744	.4371	.3335	.2551	.1956	.1504	.1159
29	.5631	.4243	.3207	.2429	.1846	.1406	.1073
30	.5521	.4120	.3083	.2314	.1741	.1314	.0994
31	.5412	.4000	.2965	.2204	.1643	.1228	.0920
32	.5306	.3883	.2851	.2099	.1550	.1147	.0852
33	.5202	.3770	.2741	.1999	.1462	.1072	.0789
34	.5100	.3660	.2636	.1904	.1379	.1002	.0730
35	.5000	.3554	.2534	.1813	.1301	.0937	.0676
36	.4902	.3450	.2437	.1727	.1227	.0875	.0626
37	.4806	.3350	.2343	.1644	.1158	.0818	.0580
38	.4712	.3252	.2253	.1566	.1092	.0765	.0537
39	.4619	.3158	.2166	.1491	.1031	.0715	.0497
40	.4529	.3066	.2083	.1420	.0972	.0668	.0460
41	.4440	.2976	.2003	.1353	.0917	.0624	.0426
42	.4353	.2890	.1926	.1288	.0865	.0583	.0395
43	.4268	.2805	.1852	.1227	.0816	.0545	.0365
44	.4184	.2724	.1780	.1169	.0770	.0509	.0338
45	.4102	.2644	.1712	.1113	.0727	.0476	.0313
46	.4022	.2567	.1646	.1060	.0685	.0445	.0290
47	.3943	.2493	.1583	.1009	.0647	.0416	.0269
48	.3865	.2420	.1522	.0961	.0610	.0389	.0249
49	.3790	.2350	.1463	.0916	.0575	.0363	.0230
50	.3715	.2281	.1407	.0872	.0543	.0339	.0213

TABLE 2 Continued
Present value (*p*) at time 0 of a single sum (*x*) (= $1) to be paid
or received after *n* periods in the future with interest *i*:

$$P_{\overline{n}|i} = x/(1 + i)^n$$

9%	10%	11%	12%	13%	14%	15%
.9174	.9091	.9009	.8929	.8850	.8772	.8696
.8417	.8264	.8116	.7972	.7831	.7695	.7561
.7722	.7513	.7312	.7118	.6931	.6750	.6575
.7084	.6830	.6587	.6355	.6133	.5921	.5718
.6499	.6209	.5935	.5674	.5428	.5194	.4972
.5963	.5645	.5346	.5066	.4803	.4556	.4323
.5470	.5132	.4817	.4523	.4251	.3996	.3759
.5019	.4665	.4339	.4039	.3762	.3506	.3269
.4604	.4241	.3909	.3606	.3329	.3075	.2843
.4224	.3855	.3522	.3220	.2946	.2697	.2472
.3875	.3505	.3173	.2875	.2607	.2366	.2149
.3555	.3186	.2858	.2567	.2307	.2076	.1869
.3262	.2897	.2575	.2292	.2042	.1821	.1625
.2992	.2633	.2320	.2046	.1807	.1597	.1413
.2745	.2394	.2090	.1827	.1599	.1401	.1229
.2519	.2176	.1883	.1631	.1415	.1229	.1069
.2311	.1978	.1696	.1456	.1252	.1078	.0929
.2120	.1799	.1528	.1300	.1108	.0946	.0808
.1945	.1635	.1377	.1161	.0981	.0829	.0703
.1784	.1486	.1240	.1037	.0868	.0728	.0611
.1637	.1351	.1117	.0926	.0768	.0638	.0531
.1502	.1228	.1007	.0826	.0680	.0560	.0462
.1378	.1117	.0907	.0738	.0601	.0491	.0402
.1264	.1015	.0817	.0659	.0532	.0431	.0349
.1160	.0923	.0736	.0588	.0471	.0378	.0304
.1064	.0839	.0663	.0525	.0417	.0331	.0264
.0976	.0763	.0597	.0469	.0369	.0291	.0230
.0895	.0693	.0538	.0419	.0326	.0255	.0200
.0822	.0630	.0485	.0374	.0289	.0224	.0714
.0754	.0573	.0437	.0334	.0256	.0196	.0151
.0691	.0521	.0394	.0298	.0226	.0172	.0131
.0634	.0474	.0355	.0266	.0200	.0151	.0114
.0582	.0431	.0319	.0238	.0177	.0132	.0099
.0534	.0391	.0288	.0212	.0157	.0116	.0086
.0490	.0356	.0259	.0189	.0139	.0102	.0075
.0449	.0323	.0234	.0169	.0123	.0089	.0065
.0412	.0294	.0210	.0151	.0109	.0078	.0057
.0378	.0267	.0190	.0135	.0096	.0069	.0049
.0347	.0243	.0171	.0120	.0085	.0060	.0043
.0318	.0221	.0154	.0107	.0075	.0053	.0037
.0292	.0201	.0139	.0096	.0067	.0046	.0032
.0268	.0183	.0125	.0086	.0059	.0041	.0028
.0246	.0166	.0112	.0076	.0052	.0036	.0025
.0226	.0151	.0101	.0068	.0046	.0031	.0021
.0207	.0137	.0091	.0061	.0041	.0027	.0019
.0190	.0125	.0082	.0054	.0036	.0024	.0016
.0174	.0113	.0074	.0049	.0032	.0021	.0014
.0160	.0103	.0067	.0043	.0028	.0019	.0012
.0147	.0094	.0060	.0039	.0025	.0016	.0011
.0134	.0085	.0054	.0035	.0022	.0014	.0009

TABLE 3

Future value (A) of an annuity (X) (= $1) paid or received at the end of every period for n periods

$$A_{\overline{n}|i} = X \cdot \frac{(1 + i)^n - 1}{i}$$

No. of periods	2%	3%	4%	5%	6%	7%	8%
1	1.0000	1.0000	1.0000	1.0000	1.0000	1.0000	1.0000
2	2.0200	2.0300	2.0400	2.0500	2.0600	2.0700	2.0800
3	3.0604	3.0909	3.1216	3.1525	3.1836	3.2149	3.2464
4	4.1216	4.1836	4.2465	4.3101	4.3746	4.4399	4.5061
5	5.2040	5.3091	5.4163	5.5256	5.6371	5.7507	5.8666
6	6.3081	6.4684	6.6330	6.8019	6.9753	7.1533	7.3359
7	7.4343	7.6625	7.8983	8.1420	8.3938	8.6540	8.9228
8	8.5830	8.8923	9.2142	9.5491	9.8975	10.2598	10.6366
9	9.7546	10.1591	10.5828	11.0266	11.4913	11.9780	12.4876
10	10.9497	11.4639	12.0061	12.5779	13.1808	13.8164	14.4866
11	12.1687	12.8078	13.4864	14.2068	14.9716	15.7836	16.6455
12	13.4121	14.1920	15.0258	15.9171	16.8699	17.8885	18.9771
13	14.6803	15.6178	16.6268	17.7130	18.8821	20.1406	21.4953
14	15.9739	17.0863	18.2919	19.5986	21.0151	22.5505	24.2149
15	17.2934	18.5989	20.0236	21.5786	23.2760	25.1290	27.1521
16	18.6393	20.1569	21.8245	23.6575	25.6725	27.8881	30.3243
17	20.0121	21.7616	23.6975	25.8404	28.2129	30.8402	33.7502
18	21.4123	23.4144	25.6454	28.1324	30.9057	33.9990	37.4502
19	22.8406	25.1169	27.6712	30.5390	33.7600	37.3790	41.4463
20	24.2974	26.8704	29.7781	33.0660	36.7856	40.9955	45.7620
21	25.7833	28.6765	31.9692	35.7193	39.9927	44.8652	50.4229
22	27.2990	30.5368	34.2480	38.5052	43.3923	49.0057	55.4568
23	28.8450	32.4529	36.6179	41.4305	46.9958	53.4361	60.8933
24	30.4219	34.4265	39.0826	44.5020	50.8156	58.1767	66.7648
25	32.0303	36.4593	41.6459	47.7271	54.8645	63.2490	73.1059
26	33.6709	38.5530	44.3117	51.1135	59.1564	68.6765	79.9544
27	35.3443	40.7096	47.0842	54.6691	63.7058	74.4838	87.3508
28	37.0512	42.9309	49.9676	58.4026	68.5281	80.6977	95.3388
29	38.7922	45.2189	52.9663	62.3227	73.6398	87.3465	103.9659
30	40.5681	47.5754	56.0849	66.4388	79.0582	94.4608	113.2832
31	42.3794	50.0027	59.3283	70.7608	84.8017	102.0730	123.3459
32	44.2270	52.5028	62.7015	75.2988	90.8898	110.2182	134.2135
33	46.1116	55.0778	66.2095	80.0638	97.3432	118.9334	145.9506
34	48.0338	57.7302	69.8579	85.0670	104.1838	128.2588	158.6267
35	49.9945	60.4621	73.6522	90.3203	111.4348	138.2369	172.3168
36	51.9944	63.2759	77.5983	95.8363	119.1209	148.9135	187.1021
37	54.0343	66.1742	81.7022	101.6281	127.2681	160.3374	203.0703
38	56.1149	69.1594	85.9703	107.7095	135.9042	172.5610	220.3159
39	58.2372	72.2342	90.4091	114.0950	145.0585	185.6403	238.9412
40	60.4020	75.4013	95.0255	120.7998	154.7620	199.6351	259.0565
41	62.6100	78.6633	99.8265	127.8398	165.0477	214.6096	280.7810
42	64.8622	82.0232	104.8196	135.2318	175.9505	230.6322	304.2435
43	67.1595	85.4839	110.0124	142.9933	187.5076	247.7765	329.5830
44	69.5027	89.0484	115.4129	151.1430	199.7580	266.1209	356.9496
45	71.8927	92.7199	121.0294	159.7002	212.7435	285.7493	386.5056
46	74.3306	96.5015	126.8706	168.6852	226.5081	306.7518	418.4261
47	76.8172	100.3965	132.9454	178.1194	241.0986	329.2244	452.9002
48	79.3535	104.4084	139.2632	188.0254	256.5645	353.2701	490.1322
49	81.9406	108.5406	145.8337	198.4267	272.9584	378.9990	530.3427
50	84.5794	112.7969	152.6671	209.3480	290.3359	406.5289	573.7702

TABLE 3 Continued

Future value (A) of an annuity (X) $(= \$1)$ paid or received at the end of every period for n periods

$$A_{\overline{n}|t} = X \cdot \frac{(1 + t)^n - 1}{t}$$

9%	10%	11%	12%	13%	14%	15%
1.0000	1.0000	1.0000	1.0000	1.0000	1.0000	1.0000
2.0900	2.1000	2.1100	2.1200	2.1300	2.1400	2.1500
3.2781	3.3100	3.3421	3.3744	3.4069	3.4396	3.4725
4.5731	4.6410	4.7097	4.7793	4.8498	4.9211	4.9934
5.9847	6.1051	6.2278	6.3528	6.4803	6.6101	6.7424
7.5233	7.7156	7.9129	8.1152	8.3227	8.5355	8.7537
9.2004	9.4872	9.7833	10.0890	10.4047	10.7305	11.0668
11.0285	11.4359	11.8594	12.2997	12.7573	13.2328	13.7268
13.0210	13.5795	14.1640	14.7757	15.4157	16.0853	16.7858
15.1929	15.9374	16.7220	17.5487	18.4197	19.3373	20.3037
17.5603	18.5312	19.5614	20.6546	21.8143	23.0445	24.3493
20.1407	21.3843	22.7132	24.1331	25.6502	27.2707	29.0017
22.9534	24.5227	26.2116	28.0291	29.9847	32.0887	34.3519
26.0192	27.9750	30.0949	32.3926	34.8827	37.5811	40.5047
29.3609	31.7725	34.4054	37.2797	40.4175	43.8424	47.5804
33.0034	35.9497	39.1899	42.7533	46.6717	50.9804	55.7175
36.9737	40.5447	44.5008	48.8837	53.7391	59.1176	65.0751
41.3013	45.5992	50.3959	55.7497	61.7251	68.3941	75.8364
46.0185	51.1591	56.9395	63.4397	70.7494	78.9692	88.2118
51.1601	57.2750	64.2028	72.0524	80.9468	91.0249	102.4436
56.7645	64.0025	72.2651	81.6987	92.4699	104.7684	118.8101
62.8733	71.4027	81.2143	92.5026	105.4910	120.4360	137.6316
69.5319	79.5430	91.1479	104.6029	120.2048	138.2970	159.2764
76.7898	88.4973	102.1742	118.1552	136.8315	158.6586	184.1678
84.7009	98.3471	114.4133	133.3339	155.6196	181.8708	212.7930
93.3240	109.1818	127.9988	150.3339	176.8501	208.3327	245.7120
102.7231	121.0999	143.0786	169.3740	200.8406	238.4993	283.5688
112.9682	134.2099	159.8173	190.6989	227.9499	272.8892	327.1041
124.1354	148.6309	178.3972	214.5828	258.5834	312.0937	377.1697
136.3075	164.4940	199.0209	241.3327	293.1992	356.7868	434.7451
149.5752	181.9434	221.9132	271.2926	332.3151	407.7370	500.9569
164.0370	201.1378	247.3236	304.8477	376.5161	465.8202	577.1005
179.8003	222.2515	275.5292	342.4294	426.4632	532.0350	664.6655
196.9823	245.4767	306.8374	384.5210	482.9034	607.5199	765.3654
215.7108	271.0244	341.5896	431.6635	546.6808	693.5727	881.1702
236.1247	299.1268	380.1644	484.4631	618.7493	791.6729	1014.3457
258.3759	330.0395	422.9825	543.5987	700.1867	903.5071	1167.4975
282.6298	364.0434	470.5106	609.8305	792.2110	1030.9981	1343.6222
309.0665	401.4478	523.2667	684.0102	896.1984	1176.3378	1546.1655
337.8824	442.5926	581.8261	767.0914	1013.7042	1342.0251	1779.0903
369.2919	487.8518	646.8269	860.1424	1146.4858	1530.9086	2046.9539
403.5281	537.6370	718.9779	964.3595	1296.5289	1746.2358	2354.9969
440.8457	592.4007	799.0655	1081.0826	1466.0777	1991.7088	2709.2465
481.5218	652.6408	887.9627	1211.8125	1657.6678	2271.5481	3116.6334
525.8587	718.9048	986.6386	1358.2300	1874.1646	2590.5648	3585.1285
574.1860	791.7953	1096.1688	1522.2176	2118.8060	2954.2439	4123.8977
626.8628	871.9749	1217.7474	1705.8838	2395.2508	3368.8380	4743.4824
684.2804	960.1723	1352.6996	1911.5898	2707.6334	3841.4753	5456.0047
746.8656	1057.1896	1502.4965	2141.9806	3060.6258	4380.2819	6275.4055
815.0836	1163.9085	1668.7712	2400.0182	3459.5071	4994.5213	7217.7163

TABLE 4 Continued

Present value (P) of an annuity (X) (= \$1) paid or received at the end of every period for n periods

$$P_{\overline{n}|i} = X \cdot \frac{1 - 1/(1 + i)^n}{i}$$

9%	10%	11%	12%	13%	14%	15%
.9174	.9091	.9009	.8929	.8850	.8772	.8696
1.7591	1.7355	1.7125	1.6901	1.6681	1.6467	1.6257
2.5313	2.4869	2.4437	2.4018	2.3612	2.3216	2.2832
3.2397	3.1699	3.1024	3.0373	2.9745	2.9137	2.8550
3.8897	3.7908	3.6959	3.6048	3.5172	3.4331	3.3522
4.4859	4.3553	4.2305	4.1114	3.9975	3.8887	3.7845
5.0330	4.8684	4.7122	4.5638	4.4226	4.2883	4.1604
5.5348	5.3349	5.1461	4.9676	4.7988	4.6389	4.4873
5.9952	5.7590	5.5370	5.3282	5.1317	4.9464	4.7716
6.4177	6.1446	5.8892	5.6502	5.4262	5.2161	5.0188
6.8052	6.4951	6.2065	5.9377	5.6869	5.4527	5.2337
7.1607	6.8137	6.4924	6.1944	5.9176	5.6603	5.4206
7.4869	7.1034	6.7499	6.4235	6.1218	5.8424	5.5831
7.7862	7.3667	6.9819	6.6282	6.3025	6.0021	5.7245
8.0607	7.6061	7.1909	6.8109	6.4624	6.1422	5.8474
8.3126	7.8237	7.3792	6.9740	6.6039	6.2651	5.9542
8.5436	8.0216	7.5488	7.1196	6.7291	6.3729	6.0472
8.7556	8.2014	7.7016	7.2497	6.8399	6.4674	6.1280
8.9501	8.3649	7.8393	7.3658	6.9380	6.5504	6.1982
9.1285	8.5136	7.9633	7.4694	7.0248	6.6231	6.2593
9.2922	8.6487	8.0751	7.5620	7.1016	6.6870	6.3125
9.4424	8.7715	8.1757	7.6446	7.1695	6.7429	6.3587
9.5802	8.8832	8.2664	7.7184	7.2297	6.7921	6.3988
9.7066	8.9847	8.3481	7.7843	7.2829	6.8351	6.4338
9.8226	9.0770	8.4217	7.8431	7.3300	6.8729	6.4641
9.9290	9.1609	8.4881	7.8957	7.3717	6.9061	6.4906
10.0266	9.2372	8.5478	7.9426	7.4086	6.9352	6.5135
10.1161	9.3066	8.6016	7.9844	7.4412	6.9607	6.5335
10.1983	9.3696	8.6501	8.0218	7.4701	6.9830	6.5509
10.2737	9.4269	8.6938	8.0552	7.4957	7.0027	6.5660
10.3428	9.4790	8.7331	8.0850	7.5183	7.0199	6.5791
10.4062	9.5264	8.7686	8.1116	7.5383	7.0350	6.5905
10.4644	9.5694	8.8005	8.1354	7.5560	7.0482	6.6005
10.5178	9.6086	8.8293	8.1566	7.5717	7.0599	6.6091
10.5668	9.6442	8.8552	8.1755	7.5856	7.0700	6.6166
10.6118	9.6765	8.8786	8.1924	7.5979	7.0790	6.6231
10.6530	9.7059	8.8996	8.2075	7.6087	7.0868	6.6288
10.6908	9.7327	8.9186	8.2210	7.6183	7.0937	6.6338
10.7255	9.7570	8.9357	8.2330	7.6268	7.0997	6.6380
10.7574	9.7791	8.9511	8.2438	7.6344	7.1050	6.6418
10.7866	9.7991	8.9649	8.2534	7.6410	7.1097	6.6450
10.8134	9.8174	8.9774	8.2619	7.6469	7.1138	6.6478
10.8380	9.8340	8.9886	8.2696	7.6522	7.1173	6.6503
10.8605	9.8491	8.9988	8.2764	7.6568	7.1205	6.6524
10.8812	9.8628	9.0079	8.2825	7.6609	7.1232	6.6543
10.9002	9.8753	9.0161	8.2880	7.6645	7.1256	6.6559
10.9176	9.8866	9.0235	8.2928	7.6677	7.1277	6.6573
10.9336	9.8969	9.0302	8.2972	7.6705	7.1296	6.6585
10.9482	9.9063	9.0362	8.3010	7.6730	7.1312	6.6596
10.9617	9.9148	9.0417	8.3045	7.6752	7.1327	6.6605

TABLE 4

Present value (P) of an annuity (X) (= $1) paid or received at the end of every period for n periods

$$P_{\overline{n}|i} = X \cdot \frac{1 - 1/(1 + i)^n}{i}$$

No. of periods	2%	3%	4%	5%	6%	7%	8%
1	.9804	.9709	.9615	.9524	.9434	.9346	.9259
2	1.9416	1.9135	1.8861	1.8594	1.8334	1.8080	1.7833
3	2.8839	2.8286	2.7751	2.7232	2.6730	2.6243	2.5771
4	3.8077	3.7171	3.6299	3.5460	3.4651	3.3872	3.3121
5	4.7135	4.5797	4.4518	4.3295	4.2124	4.1002	3.9927
6	5.6014	5.4172	5.2421	5.0757	4.9173	4.7665	4.6229
7	6.4720	6.2303	6.0021	5.7864	5.5824	5.3893	5.2064
8	7.3255	7.0197	6.7327	6.4632	6.2098	5.9713	5.7466
9	8.1622	7.7861	7.4353	7.1078	6.8017	6.5152	6.2469
10	8.9826	8.5302	8.1109	7.7217	7.3601	7.0236	6.7101
11	9.7868	9.2526	8.7605	8.3064	7.8869	7.4987	7.1390
12	10.5753	9.9540	9.3851	8.8633	8.3838	7.9427	7.5361
13	11.3484	10.6350	9.9856	9.3936	8.8527	8.3577	7.9038
14	12.1062	11.2961	10.5631	9.8986	9.2950	8.7455	8.2442
15	12.8493	11.9379	11.1184	10.3797	9.7122	9.1079	8.5595
16	13.5777	12.5611	11.6523	10.8378	10.1059	9.4466	8.8514
17	14.2919	13.1661	12.1657	11.2741	10.4773	9.7632	9.1216
18	14.9920	13.7535	12.6593	11.6896	10.8276	10.0591	9.3719
19	15.6785	14.3238	13.1339	12.0853	11.1581	10.3356	9.6036
20	16.3514	14.8775	13.5903	12.4622	11.4699	10.5940	9.8181
21	17.0112	15.4150	14.0292	12.8212	11.7641	10.8355	10.0168
22	17.6580	15.9369	14.4511	13.1630	12.0416	11.0612	10.2007
23	18.2922	16.4436	14.8568	13.4886	12.3034	11.2722	10.3711
24	18.9139	16.9355	15.2470	13.7986	12.5504	11.4693	10.5288
25	19.5235	17.4131	15.6221	14.0939	12.7834	11.6536	10.6748
26	20.1210	17.8768	15.9828	14.3752	13.0032	11.8258	10.8100
27	20.7069	18.3270	16.3296	14.6430	13.2105	11.9867	10.9352
28	21.2813	18.7641	16.6631	14.8981	13.4062	12.1371	11.0511
29	21.8444	19.1885	16.9837	15.1411	13.5907	12.2777	11.1584
30	22.3965	19.6004	17.2920	15.3725	13.7648	12.4090	11.2578
31	22.9377	20.0004	17.5885	15.5928	13.9291	12.5318	11.3498
32	23.4683	20.3888	17.8736	15.8027	14.0840	12.6466	11.4350
33	23.9886	20.7658	18.1476	16.0025	14.2302	12.7538	11.5139
34	24.4986	21.1318	18.4112	16.1929	14.3681	12.8540	11.5869
35	24.9986	21.4872	18.6646	16.3742	14.4982	12.9477	11.6546
36	25.4888	21.8323	18.9083	16.5469	14.6210	13.0352	11.7172
37	25.9695	22.1672	19.1426	16.7113	14.7368	13.1170	11.7752
38	26.4406	22.4925	19.3679	16.8679	14.8460	13.1935	11.8289
39	26.9026	22.8082	19.5845	17.0170	14.9491	13.2649	11.8786
40	27.3555	23.1148	19.7928	17.1591	15.0463	13.3317	11.9246
41	27.7995	23.4124	19.9931	17.2944	15.1380	13.3941	11.9672
42	28.2348	23.7014	20.1856	17.4232	15.2245	13.4524	12.0067
43	28.6616	23.9819	20.3708	17.5459	15.3062	13.5070	12.0432
44	29.0800	24.2543	20.5488	17.6628	15.3832	13.5579	12.0771
45	29.4902	24.5187	20.7200	17.7741	15.4558	13.6055	12.1084
46	29.8923	24.7754	20.8847	17.8801	15.5244	13.6500	12.1374
47	30.2866	25.0247	21.0429	17.9810	15.5890	13.6916	12.1643
48	30.6731	25.2667	21.1951	18.0772	15.6500	13.7305	12.1891
49	31.0521	25.5017	21.3415	18.1687	15.7076	13.7668	12.2122
50	31.4236	25.7298	21.4822	18.2559	15.7619	13.8007	12.2335

Glossary

Absorption costing A method of assigning manufacturing costs to units produced by which both fixed and variable costs are treated as product costs. Required under Generally Accepted Accounting Principles (GAAP). It may be contrasted with *direct* or *variable costing* and may also be called *full costing* or *full absorption costing*.

Accelerated Cost Recovery System (ACRS) A depreciation method required by the U.S. tax code, whereby most types of property are divided into main classes reflecting the number of years over which depreciation may be charged—for example, 3, 5, 10, or 15 years.

Accountability The responsibility of individual managers for the resources generated and used in their departments and for reporting the results of their activities to managers at a higher level in the organization.

Accountant's report The report issued by an independent certified public accountant in which the firm expresses an opinion on whether the financial statements audited are in conformity with generally accepted accounting principles.

Accounting Principles Board (APB) The standard-setting authority of the accounting profession from 1959 to 1973; the predecessor of the *Financial Accounting Standards Board*.

Accounts payable   Amounts owed to suppliers for services, supplies, and raw materials purchased.

Accounts receivable   Claims against debtors, usually resulting from the sale of goods, performance of services, or lending of funds.

Accrual basis of accounting   A means of accounting whereby revenues are realized when there is evidence that a firm is economically better off because of its production and sales activities and costs are charged as expenses in the same periods as the revenues to which they relate are recognized; distinguished from *cash basis*.

Accumulated benefit obligation (pensions)   The actuarial present value of all benefits that have been earned (not taking into account estimated future increases in wages and salaries).

Accumulated depreciation   An allowance (contra account to a related asset) to reflect the ''consumption'' of an asset over time by wear and tear as well as by technological obsolescence; equal to the sum of the depreciation charges over time on the related asset.

Activity-based costing (ABC)   A method of assigning manufacturing and non-manufacturing overhead to products or services based on the activities necessary to produce those products or services. The activities are the cost drivers used to allocate or assign the overhead costs.

Activity ratio   A ratio which measures the effectiveness of management in utilizing specific resources under its command; also referred to as *turnover ratio*.

Actuarial cost method (pensions)   A technique used by actuaries to determine the required contributions to a pension fund or amounts to be charged as pension expense.

Additional paid-in capital   Amounts that a company receives when it issues stock in excess of the stock's par or face value.

Adjusting entries   Entries, especially those at the end of an accounting period, to bring the accounts up to date and to correct known errors.

Aging of accounts receivable   A means of classifying accounts receivable by the number of days they are past due; for example: current, up to 30 days, up to 60 days, etc.

AICPA   See *American Institute of Certified Public Accountants*.

Allocation   The process of assigning or distributing overhead or other common costs to departments, products, or services. Also called *spreading* costs or *distributing* costs.

Allocation base   The cost driver or measure of activity that is used to assign or allocate costs to departments, products, or services. Common allocation bases include direct labor hours, direct labor dollars, or machine hours.

Allowance for bad debts   See *Allowance for doubtful accounts*.

Allowance for depreciation   See *Accumulated depreciation*.

Allowance for doubtful accounts   An estimate of the amounts owed to a company that will be uncollectible; usually reported ''contra'' to accounts receivable.

Allowance for uncollectible accounts   See *Allowance for doubtful accounts*.

Allowance method (uncollectible accounts)   A method of accounting for uncollectible accounts whereby a bad-debt expense is charged in the same period as the sales to which it relates; correspondingly, accounts receivable is reduced by adding to a contra account, ''Allowance for uncollectibles.''

American Accounting Association (AAA) The leading association of accountants directed primarily to the interests of academic accountants.

American Institute of Certified Public Accountants (AICPA) The professional society of certified public accountants.

Amortization The process of allocating (amortizing) the cost of assets (usually intangible or natural resources) or a deferred charge over the accounting periods that it will benefit; a generic term for *depreciation*.

Annuity A series of equal payments at fixed intervals.

Annuity due An annuity in which the payments are made or received at the beginning of each period.

Annuity in arrears An annuity in which the payments are made or received at the end of each period.

Application The process of assigning manufacturing overhead to departments, work-in-process accounts, or other product costing categories.

Applied overhead Overhead assigned to a job or product or service using a predetermined or budgeted overhead rate.

Arm's-length transaction A transaction in which the buyer and seller are unrelated and independent, with both parties seeking to advance their own economic interests.

Assets Resources or rights incontestably controlled by an entity at the accounting date that are expected to yield future economic benefits to the entity.

Audit An examination of financial statements to determine whether they are presented fairly in accordance with generally accepted accounting principles; any systematic investigation or procedure to determine conformity with prescribed standards or guidelines.

Authorized stock The maximum number of shares, per its corporate charter, that a company is permitted to issue.

Average cost Total cost divided by total quantity where quantity may be expressed in either units of input or output.

Bad debt An uncollectible receivable.

Balance sheet See *Statement of financial position*.

Betterments Costs incurred to enhance an asset's service potential from what was anticipated when it was first purchased; distinguished from *repairs*.

Bond A certificate of indebtedness in which the issuer promises to make one or more payments both in repayment of the amount borrowed and in interest.

Breakeven The volume of sales or sales revenue where total revenues equals total costs. Also called *breakeven point*. May be expressed in units of output or in dollars of revenue.

Budget A financial plan to control and evaluate the results of future operations. A budget indicates the resources necessary during a specific time period to accomplish the organization's goals. See also *Capital budget*; *Cash budget*.

Budget slack Budget surpluses or allowances that are created by manipulating budgetary estimates. Slack may be created by underestimating revenues, prices, and sales volumes or by overestimating costs, by deferring maintenance activities, by not filling authorized positions, and by delaying process improvements.

Budget variance   Variance or difference between actual costs and budgeted costs. May also refer to difference between actual fixed costs and budgeted fixed costs at the expected level of activity. May also be called *spending variance*.

Burden   Another term for overhead or overhead costs. The term connotes the onerous nature of overhead costs and the negative view that many managers hold toward overhead costs.

Burden rate   Another term for *overhead rate*. A burden rate if calculated by dividing the estimated or budgeted overhead costs by the estimated units of activity for any cost driver.

Call premium (bonds)   An amount, in addition to the face value of a bond, that must be paid to the lender when a bond is redeemed (called) prior to its maturity.

Call provision (bonds)   A provision in a bond agreement which gives the borrower a right to redeem the bond prior to its maturity.

Capacity variance   See *Volume variance*.

Capital budget   A budget that is restricted to long-term projects; contrasted with an operating budget which is for a current time period.

Capital in excess of par   See *Additional paid-in capital*.

Capital lease   A lease which in economic substance involves the purchase and sale of an asset in exchange for a promise to make a series of payments in the future; a lease which is recorded on the books of both the lessee and the lessor as if it were a purchase/borrow transaction.

Capital stock   The ownership shares of a corporation; see also *Common stock*, *Preferred stock*.

Capitalize   To record the debit side of an expenditure as an asset and thereby defer its recognition as an expense until a later period.

Cash   Currency and demand deposits in banks.

Cash basis of accounting   A means of accounting whereby revenues and expenses are recognized if, and only if, there is a receipt or disbursement of cash; distinguished from *accrual basis of accounting*.

Cash budget   A budget based on cash flows, showing anticipated cash receipts and disbursements.

Centralization   An organizational structure where key decisions, or most decisions, are made by a few high-ranking managers.

Certified public accountant   The professional designation conferred by each of the states upon accountants who have satisfied specified educational and experience requirements and who have passed a uniform examination administered by the American Institute of Certified Public Accountants.

Close (accounts or books)   To transfer the balances in each revenue and expense account to retained earnings or a comparable owners' equity account.

Closely held corporation   A corporation owned by a comparatively few stockholders.

Common stock   Certificates of corporate ownership which typically give the holder the right to vote for members of the corporation's board of directors, as well as on numerous other corporate matters, and the rights to share in corporate profits whenever dividends are declared by the board of directors.

Common stock equivalents   Securities which, for purposes of earnings per share computations, are treated as if they were common stock. They are generally convertible into common stock. Examples are options, warrants, convertible bonds, and preferred stock that satisfy stipulated criteria.

Compound interest   Interest resulting from applying a specified rate of interest to the sum of the original principal of an investment or loan plus any interest that has been earned on that principal from previous periods that has not yet been paid; interest accumulating on an investment of principal over a number of periods at a specified rate of interest.

Comprehensive income   The excess of revenues and other gains over and above expenses and losses of any entity. This difference represents the change in the entity's net assets (excluding the effect of transactions between the entity and its owners involving dividends and contributions of capital).

Comptroller   See *Controller*.

Computer-Integrated Manufacturing (CIM)   Computer-controlled or numerically controlled manufacturing processes, often governed by robots or other mechanized means. Also called *factory automation* or *flexible manufacturing*.

Conservatism   The accounting convention that it is generally preferable that any possible errors in measurement be in the direction of understatement rather than overstatement of net income and net assets; that in the absence of certainty, recognition of gains should be delayed, but that of losses should be accelerated.

Consolidated financial statements   Statements that report the financial positions and earnings of two or more corporations as if they were a single economic entity.

Constant dollars   Dollars of different dates adjusted so that they represent monetary units of equivalent purchasing power.

Constraints   Any set of limiting resources or boundary conditions. Equations incorporated into a linear programming or other optimization model.

Consumer Price Index (CPI)   An index which expresses prices of various years as percentages of prices of a selected base year.

Contingencies   Gains or losses that are uncertain as to both occurrence and amount.

Contingent liability   A potential liability, one that would have to be recognized only if a specific event (e.g., loss of a lawsuit) occurred.

Contra account   An offset account in which the balance is always opposite, and reported directly beneath, that of the account with which it is associated (e.g., accumulated depreciation, allowance for bad debts, and bond discount).

Contribution margin   Revenues minus *variable* expenses. An income statement can be arranged to emphasize and report contribution margins rather than gross margins.

Contribution margin per unit   Price per unit minus *variable* expenses per unit. Also may be computed by dividing contribution margin by number of units.

Contribution margin ratio   Contribution margin divided by sales revenues. Also may be computed by dividing contribution margin per unit by price per unit. The contribution margin ratio and variable cost ratio are complementary and must total 100%.

Control   Managerial actions to monitor activities, evaluate performance, and eliminate or minimize undesirable outcomes.

Control account   A general ledger account, the balance of which is equal to the sum of the individual balances in a subsidiary ledger. For example, a fixed asset control account is equal to the total of the individual fixed assets recorded in the fixed asset subsidiary ledger.

Controllable costs   Costs that can be affected, changed, or influenced by managers in the short-run. In the long-run, all costs are controllable; i.e., all costs may be changed in the long-run.

Controllable variance   A variance that should be investigated because the underlying costs are controllable in the short-run and an unfavorable variance may be reduced in the future by taking immediate corrective action.

Controller   The chief accountant of a company or other type of organization.

Conversion costs   The sum of direct labor and manufacturing overhead costs. Conversion costs are prominent in computer-integrated manufacturing (CIM) processes as the proportion of labor is often lower and the proportion of overhead is often higher in contrast to traditional manufacturing processes.

Convertible securities   Securities, usually bonds or preferred stock, that can be exchanged for shares of common stock.

Copyright   An exclusive right, granted by law, to publish, sell, reproduce, or otherwise control a literary, musical, or artistic work.

Corporation   A legal entity, separate and distinct from its stockholder-owners, that is authorized to operate by the federal or a state government.

Cost behavior   The extent to which costs vary with changes in volume or other cost drivers.

Cost–benefit analysis   A comparison of the costs of a proposal or activity with its benefits. For example, in accounting, this criterion is used to weigh the advantages of obtaining additional accounting information. In government, cost–benefit criteria are used to assess public policy options.

Cost center   An organizational unit or sub-unit in which managers are responsible or accountable for the costs in the unit.

Cost driver   The volume of services, output, inputs, or any other factor that affects the magnitude of costs. A cost driver should have a high predictive (ideally a causal) relationship with the resultant costs. Common cost drivers are direct labor hours, machine hours, and number of transactions.

Cost method (intercorporate investments)   A method whereby a company records its investment in the stock of another company at the amount paid to acquire the stock and recognizes revenue from its investment only when the subsidiary declares dividends; distinguished from *equity method*.

Cost method (treasury stock)   A method whereby treasury shares acquired by the entity are reported in a separate account, which is shown on the balance sheet contra to the other equity accounts, in an amount equal to the cost to acquire the shares; distinguished from *par value method*.

Cost of goods sold   An expense representing the cost to acquire or produce goods that have been sold.

Cost or market   See *Lower of cost or market rule*.

Cost savings   See *Holding gain*.

Cost–volume–profit (CVP) Analysis of the relationships between costs, volume, and profits. Incorporates cost behavior patterns into graphical or equation-based analysis showing alternative profits at different levels of volume.

Coupon rate (of interest on bonds) The rate of interest specified in a bond indenture (agreement) that will be paid each period; distinguished from *yield rate*.

CPA *Certified public accountant.*

Credits Entries in accounts (in the United States, to the right-hand side of ledger accounts) that signify increases in liabilities and owners' equity (e.g., revenues) or decreases in assets; distinguished from *debits*.

Current assets Assets that will either be transformed into cash or will be sold or consumed within one year (or sometimes within the normal operating cycle of the business if longer than one year); assets which are cash, are likely to be turned into cash within one year, or will obviate the need for cash in the coming year (e.g., prepaid expenses). Also included are marketable securities, accounts receivable, and inventory.

Current cost The amount that would have to be paid to purchase an asset today (an *input* or *entry* value or purchase price); see also *Replacement cost*.

Current liabilities Liabilities expected to be satisfied out of current assets (or through the creation of other current liabilities) within one year (or sometimes the normal operating cycle of the business if longer than one year); include wages payable, accounts payable, interest, taxes payable, and deferred credits.

Current operating income Revenue at current prices less expenses at current prices; the income computation that might be considered a long-run sustainable amount if present conditions do not change in the future.

Current ratio A liquidity ratio that compares current assets to current liabilities.

Date of record (corporate stock) The date as of which the list of stockholders and their holdings is established so as to determine dividend distributions.

Debentures Unsecured bonds.

Debits Entries in accounts (in the United States, to the left-hand side of ledger accounts) that signify increases in assets or decreases in liabilities and owners' equity (e.g., expenses); distinguished from *credits*.

Debt-to-equity ratio A financing ratio that compares claims of creditors (liabilities) with the equity of stockholders (stockholders' equity).

Declining balance (depreciation) A method of computing depreciation whereby a greater proportion of asset cost (less salvage value) is allocated to the earlier periods of use than the later periods.

Deferred charge A cost not recognized as an expense of the period in which incurred, but carried forward as an asset to be written off in future periods.

Deferred credits Deferred revenue; increases in net assets not recognized as revenue in one period, but carried forward to be recognized in future periods.

Deferred income taxes The excess of income taxes recognized for reporting purposes over that recognized for tax purposes when such excess is attributable to timing differences. Deferred income taxes are reported as liabilities which will be written off as the underlying timing difference is reversed.

Defined benefit plan (pensions)   A plan which requires an employer to provide employees with specified benefits upon their retirement; distinguished from a *defined contribution plan*, in which the contributions rather than the benefits are specified.

Defined contribution plan (pensions)   A plan which requires the employer to make specified contributions to a pension plan; distinguished from a *defined benefit plan*, in which the benefits rather than the required contributions are specified.

Depletion   The process of allocating the cost of natural resources over an anticipated recovery period.

Depreciation   The process of allocating the cost of plant and equipment over an anticipated useful life.

Deprival value   The lesser of *current* (replacement) *cost* of an asset and its recoverable amount, where recoverable amount is the higher of *present value* and *net realizable value*.

Differential cost   Differential costs are equivalent to incremental costs and represent costs that will be incurred or saved as a result of a specific action or decision. Contrast with *sunk costs*, which will not be incurred or saved no matter what decision is made.

Direct costs   Direct costs can be traced directly to a product, service, responsibility center, or other organizational unit. Direct costs can be readily attributed to a product or service. Contrast with *indirect costs* or *overhead*, which cannot be easily traced.

Direct write-off method (uncollectible accounts receivable)   A method whereby an account receivable is written off and bad-debt expense is charged only when it is known to be uncollectible; distinguished from *allowance method*.

Discount (bonds)   The excess of the face value of a bond over its issue price or other recorded value. Usually this difference results when the interest rate prevailing at a time when a bond is issued or sold is greater than the coupon rate.

Discount note   A note in which face value may include not only the amount originally borrowed but also the applicable interest charges.

Discounted cash flow   The amount which if invested today at a specified rate of return would be the equivalent of a series of cash payments to be received at various times in the future.

Distress price   A distress price represents a selling price in an abnormal or unusual market. Distress prices will be obtained at "fire sales" or liquidation or bankruptcy sales.

Dividends   Distributions of the net assets of an enterprise to its owners; see also *Stock dividend*.

Double-entry record-keeping system   A method whereby each transaction is recorded in two or more accounts so as to affect the basic accounting equation, assets = liabilities + owners' equity.

Earned surplus   See *Retained earnings*.

Earnings   See *Income*.

Earnings per share   Net income less preferred stock dividends divided by the average number of common shares outstanding during a period.

Entry value   The amount that would have to be paid to replace an asset; see also *Current cost*.

Equities The claims against an enterprise, including liabilities and owners' equity.

Equity method (intercorporate investments) A method by which a company records its investment in another company at cost, but periodically adjusts the carrying value of the investment to take into account its share of the investee's earnings subsequent to the date the investment was acquired; distinguished from *cost method*.

Executory contract An agreement contingent upon the mutual performance of the two sides to the contract.

Exit value The amount for which an asset can be sold; see also *Net realizable value*.

Expenses Outflows or other consumption of assets or incurrences of liabilities (or a combination of both) from delivering or producing goods, rendering services, or carrying out other activities that constitute an entity's ongoing major or central operations.

Extraordinary items Gains and losses that are exceptional in nature and unlikely to recur, including fires, natural disasters, and expropriations of property by foreign governments.

Fair market value A value based on arm's-length transactions between buyers and sellers.

FASB See *Financial Accounting Standards Board*.

FICA (Federal Insurance Contribution Act) The federal law that established the social security system.

FIFO (first in, first out) A method of accounting for inventory in which the items acquired first are assumed to be sold or used first.

Financial accounting The branch of accounting that is concerned with reporting to parties, such as investors and creditors, external to the organization; distinguished from *management* accounting.

Financial Accounting Standards Board The authoritative body which is the generally accepted standard-setting organization for private-sector financial accounting and reporting.

Financing lease See *Capital lease*.

Fixed assets Tangible assets held for the services they provide, such as land, plant, equipment, furniture, and fixtures.

Fixed cost A cost that does not vary with changes in volume, at least in the short-run. Fixed costs are usually fixed only within some relevant range and will vary at other levels of volume.

Flexible budget A budget that incorporates alternative levels of volume.

Foreign currency A currency other than the *functional* currency of an entity.

Full costing The allocation of both fixed and variable manufacturing costs of products or services. Also called *absorption costing* or *full absorption costing*.

Full-cost method (oil drilling costs) A method by which costs associated with unsuccessful prospects (dry holes) are capitalized rather than expensed as incurred; distinguished from *successful-efforts method*.

Functional currency The currency of the primary economic environment in which an entity, especially a foreign unit, operates.

Funds Variously defined as (1) cash; (2) cash plus selected current assets (such as cash, marketable securities, and accounts receivable) less current liabilities; (3) working capital (all current assets less all current liabilities).

Future value of an annuity   The amount to which a series of equal payments at fixed intervals will accumulate at a specified interest rate and in a specified number of periods.

GAAP   See *Generally accepted accounting principles*.

Gains   Increases in net assets resulting from transactions that are not typical of a firm's day-to-day operations.

GAO   See *General Accounting Office*.

GASB   See *Governmental Accounting Standards Board*.

General Accounting Office (GAO)   The congressional audit office responsible for examining and evaluating federal agencies and programs.

General ledger   A ledger in which all balance sheet and income statement accounts are maintained.

Generally accepted accounting principles (GAAP)   Accounting practices that are either specifically mandated by authoritative rule-making organizations or are considered acceptable because of widespread use, convention, or tradition.

Going-concern concept   The assumption that the enterprise being reported upon will continue operating indefinitely into the future so that the firm will realize the benefits of all its assets and have to satisfy all its liabilities.

Goodwill   The excess of an amount paid to acquire a company over the fair market value of the company's net assets; an asset that arises exclusively out of the process of consolidation and can be thought to represent the value of certain intangible assets, such as reputation, location, and trademarks that cannot normally be specifically identified.

Governmental Accounting Standards Board   The authoritative body which is the generally accepted standard-setting organization for state and local government financial accounting and reporting.

Gross margin   Sales revenue minus cost of goods sold.

High–low method   A method of estimating costs based on two observed levels of costs and volumes—a high-volume point and a low point.

Historical cost   The amount paid to acquire an asset, adjusted for subsequent amortization or depreciation.

Holding gain   A gain attributable to an increase in price since an asset was acquired; distinguished from *trading gain*.

Imprest basis   A means of accounting for petty cash whereby the general ledger account for petty cash will always indicate a specified balance. The actual petty cash on hand, plus receipts for payments made with petty cash; should always equal that balance.

Imputed interest   Interest, at a rate approximately equal to prevailing rates, applied to a borrowing transaction to reflect economic substance, when the actual rate charged is considerably less than the prevailing rate.

Income   The excess of revenues over expenses; in general, the change in equity (net assets) of an entity during a period from transactions (other than those with the entity's owners) and selected other events; see also *Comprehensive income*.

Income statement   A report that summarizes the revenues (and other gains) and expenses (and any losses) of a period.

Incremental costs   Differential costs; represents costs that will be saved or incurred as a result of a specific action or decision. Contrasted with *sunk costs*, which cannot be avoided no matter what decision is made.

Indirect costs   Costs that cannot be easily traced or attributed to specific products, services, or activities. Indirect costs are usually allocated to specific products, services, responsibility centers, or other organizational activities or units on the basis of direct labor, machine hours, or other cost drivers. Distinguished from *direct costs*.

Inflation   An increase in the number of monetary units required to acquire a basket of typical goods and services.

Input value   The amount required to replace an asset by purchase, manufacture, or construction; see *Replacement cost*.

Installment basis (revenue recognition)   A means of recognizing revenue based on cash collections.

Intangible asset   An asset that lacks physical existence but is instead characterized by rights or other benefits. Examples include patents, trademarks, research and development costs, and goodwill.

Interest   A service charge for the use of money, usually expressed as an annual percent of outstanding principal.

Interim financial report   A report that covers less than a full year, usually a quarter or half year.

Internal auditor   An auditor who carries out his or her activities within a single organization and is employed by that organization.

Inventory   Goods held for sale to customers as well as raw materials, supplies, and parts to be used in the production or other activities of the entity.

Inventory turnover   A ratio that measures the number of times the annual cost of sales exceeds average inventory.

Investment center   A responsibility center with control over revenues, expenses, profits, and capital resources such as assets and liabilities. Contrasted with *revenue centers*, *cost centers*, and *profit centers*, which have more limited control.

Investments   Property acquired to yield a return, such as the stock or bonds of another firm.

Invoice   A document showing the terms of sale, including quantity, price, and discounts; a bill.

Institute of Management Accountants (IMA)   The leading professional association of industrial accountants.

Job-order costing   A cost accounting system whereby manufacturing costs are accumulated for a specific product or batch, known as a job, as it is produced. These costs are accumulated on a job-cost sheet or other job-related record (which may be a computer file). Contrasted with *process costing*.

Journal   A book of original entry to record transactions. Transactions of similar types may be recorded in specialized journals, while the remainder are recorded in a general journal.

Journal entry   The written notation of a transaction in a journal, consisting of both debits and credits equal in amount.

Just-in-time (JIT)   System of managing inventories such that the materials or supplies are acquired or delivered to production departments just prior to the time they are required. JIT inventory management enables a firm to minimize inventory stocks, thereby reducing or even eliminating carrying costs. However, it increases the risk of shortages and stockouts and necessitates frequent deliveries or internal transfers of materials and supplies.

KANBAN   A term used in flexible manufacturing systems to denote a series of integrated production activities, usually involving robots or other numerically controlled equipment, and characterized by a uniform or continuous flow of products between work stations. KANBAN systems usually incorporate visual or verbal indicators of stock shortages, system breakdowns, or quality slippage.

Learning curve   A graph or mathematical function that indicates the effects on labor costs of the workers becoming more efficient as new tasks or processes are learned and become more familiar.

Lease   A contract providing the right to use land, buildings, equipment, or other property for a specified period of time in return for rent or other compensation.

Ledger   A book which contains accounts; see *General ledger, Subsidiary ledger.*

Legal capital   That part of paid-in capital which is the equivalent of par or stated value.

Lessee   The party which leases property *from* another.

Lessor   The party which owns property and leases it *to* another.

Leverage   The issuance of debt or other securities having a fixed interest or dividend rate, rather than common stock, to finance asset acquisitions. This is done in the expectation that relatively small increases in net income will result in disproportionately large increases in return to existing common stockholders.

Liabilities   Obligations of an entity at the accounting date to make future transfers of assets or services (sometimes uncertain as to timing and amount) to other entities.

LIFO (last in, first out)   A method of accounting for inventory in which the items acquired most recently are assumed to be those sold or used first.

Linear programming   A mathematical technique for optimizing production or other activities, expressed in terms of a linear objective function and a series of linear constraints.

Liquidation value   The amount that could be realized if the firm were to be dissolved and its assets put up for sale.

Liquidity   The ability of a firm to convert its noncash assets to cash so as to satisfy its obligations as they mature.

Liquidity ratios   The ratios which show a company's ability to meet its short-term obligations; include current ratio and quick ratio.

Losses   Decreases in net assets resulting from transactions that are not typical of a firm's day-to-day operations.

Lower of cost or market rule   The principle of valuation which requires assets to be written down to market value whenever such value is less than historical cost.

Make or buy decision A decision whether to produce goods or provide services internally or to purchase them externally.

Management (managerial) accounting Concerned with accounting and reporting information to managers within an organization. Includes information for decision making, planning and control, and performance evaluation. Distinguished from *financial accounting*.

Management advisory services The branch of the public accounting profession which provides consulting services to the management of corporations or other types of organizations.

Market value The price at which an asset could be bought or sold.

Marketable securities Securities, such as bonds, stock, and treasury bills, which are held by the reporting entity as short-term investments.

Master budget A comprehensive budget, or the entire set of budgets used for an organization for a year or other time period. All of the budgets within a master budget are related and will include data that are derived from other budgets.

Matching principle The principle which holds that costs should be recognized in the same accounting period as the revenues that they generate.

Matrix responsibility center A responsibility center that is not hierarchical according to the organization chart. A matrix structure may be viewed as a task force or project team comprising individuals from various departments, divisions, or other organizational units.

Mixed costs A combination of fixed and variable costs. May also be called *semi-fixed costs or semi-variable costs*. May be expressed as a linear equation $y = a + bx$, where a denotes the fixed costs and b denotes the variable costs per unit, and x is the number of units, such that bx represents total variable costs.

Mix variance A variance attributed to a change in the proportions of inputs to a production process. Also may refer to variances in proportions of products or services sold.

Monetary items Assets and liabilities which are contractually fixed or which are convertible into a fixed number of dollars, regardless of changes in price.

Net realizable value The amount for which an asset can be sold, less any costs that would normally be incurred to bring it to a salable condition; a current exit value or sale price, as contrasted to current cost, which is an entry value or purchase price.

Neutrality The concept that economic activity should be reported as objectively as possible in a way not subject to any bias intended to influence users to a predetermined conclusion or in a particular direction.

Nominal dollars Dollars that are not adjusted to take into account differences in purchasing power.

Noncurrent assets Assets that cannot be expected to be sold or transformed into cash within one year (or sometimes the normal operating cycle of the business if longer than one year); include land, plant, and equipment; natural resources; and intangibles.

Noncurrent liabilities Liabilities not expected to be liquidated within one year (or sometimes the normal operating cycle of the business if longer than one year); include bonds and other long-term obligations.

Normal operating cycle The time it takes a business to purchase, provide, or manufacture goods or services, sell them to a customer, and collect the proceeds.

Note receivable A written promise enabling its holder to collect a specified amount.

NSF (nonsufficient funds) check A check returned by a bank to a depositor because the party which wrote the check had insufficient funds in its account to cover the check.

Number of days' sales in accounts receivable Accounts receivable as of a particular date, divided by average sales per day.

Objective function The function or goal statement in a linear programming function that is to be maximized or minimized.

Objectivity The characteristic of accounting information suggesting that it faithfully describes what it purports to represent and is verifiable and free from bias.

Operating budget A budget that covers a month or year or other limited time period; usually pertains to the normal production or service activities of the organization.

Operating cycle See *Normal operating cycle*.

Operating lease A contract that provides for the right to use property for a limited time in exchange for periodic rent payments; distinguished from *capital lease*.

Opportunity cost The value of the sacrificed opportunity to employ an asset in its next-best use. Represents the lost cost or benefit of an alternative course of action. May refer to the benefit foregone by rejecting one alternative in favor of another. May also refer to amounts that might be received by selling an asset and using the proceeds in the next-best alternative manner.

Organization costs The costs incurred to organize a corporation. These include the legal fees required to draw up the documents of incorporation, filing fees, and clerical costs.

Other postemployment benefits Benefits provided to retired employees in addition to pensions, the most common of which are life insurance and paid health care.

Output value The amount for which an asset could be sold or exchanged.

Overhead Any cost not directly associated with production, sale, or provision of services. Also called *burden* or *indirect costs*. In Britain and Australia, overhead costs are called ''on costs.'' May refer to manufacturing overhead, which represents all manufacturing costs other than raw materials and direct labor.

Overhead rate A predetermined rate that is used to apply manufacturing overhead to products or to services. Usually computed by dividing budgeted annual overhead costs by the estimated activities or units of the cost driver expected during the same year.

Owners' equity The residual interest in the assets of an entity that remains after deducting its liabilities; the interests of the owners in a business enterprise.

Par value An arbitrary value, having some legal but little economic significance, which is assigned to a share of stock; similar to *stated value*; the minimum capital (i.e., net assets) that must be retained in an entity and thereby cannot be distributed to shareholders.

Par value method (treasury stock)   The method of accounting for treasury stock whereby the shares acquired are treated as if they were retired; distinguished from *cost method*.

Parent company   A company that owns an interest in, and controls, another company (known as a subsidiary). Control is typically indicated by ownership of at least 50 percent of the subsidiary's common stock.

Participating preferred stock   Preferred stock that entitles the holders to share in distributions in excess of the stipulated minimum dividend.

Partnership   A firm owned by two or more parties.

Patent   An exclusive right, granted by the federal government, to an inventor to produce and sell an invention.

Payable   A liability; see also *Accounts payable*.

Pension   A sum of money paid to a retired or disabled employee owing to his or her years of employment.

Percentage of completion method   A means of recognizing revenue, generally on long-term construction projects, whereby the amount of revenue recognized in each period is based on the percentage of the project completed in that period. The percentage completed in a period is determined by the ratio of costs incurred in that period to total anticipated costs.

Period costs   Costs that are recognized as expenses based strictly on time and assigned to particular periods irrespective of productive output in that period; distinguished from *product costs*.

Periodic method   A means of accounting for inventory or other assets and liabilities, and their related revenues or expenses, whereby accounts are adjusted at the end of each period to bring them up to date. The adjustment is usually made on the basis of a physical count, or a comparable measure, of the actual assets or liabilities. During the period, the account is debited or credited only for selected transactions and therefore may not be current. For example, when the periodic method is used to account for inventory, the inventory account may be debited during the period only for goods purchased. At year end a physical count of goods on hand is taken, and both the inventory balance and cost of goods sold are adjusted to reflect this count; distinguished from *perpetual method*.

Perpetual method   A means of accounting for inventory or other assets and liabilities, and their related revenue or expenses, whereby the accounts are continually updated during a period as each transaction takes place; distinguished from *periodic method*.

Physical inventory   A count to determine the actual amount of inventory on hand.

Planning   The process of developing a set of budgets and activities to achieve the organization's goals. Planning may be short-term, for weeks or months, or it may be long-term, for a year or longer.

Planning variance   A planning variance is due to a difference between the original planning premises and the subsequent reality. Planning variances are not usually controllable by any individual manager or department. Large planning variances indicate a need to use different, and presumably more effective, planning processes and procedures. Similar to a *volume variance*.

Pooling of interests (intercorporate investments) A method of consolidation whereby, for accounting purposes, two companies are joined together, with neither acquiring the other. The assets and liabilities from the books of each of the companies are normally recorded at historical cost and carried over to the consolidated statement without adjustment; distinguished from *purchase*.

Preemptive rights Rights granted by a corporation to existing stockholders to acquire newly issued shares of stock and thereby to preserve their proportionate interests in the company.

Preferred stock A class of stock with specified preferences and priorities, as well as limitations, as compared with common stock; often does not grant voting rights. The most common preference is a stipulated minimum dividend.

Premium (bonds or preferred stock) The amount in excess of par or face value received by a corporation on bonds or capital stock. This additional payment is ordinarily made to equate the stipulated interest or dividend rate with lower prevailing market rates.

Preopening costs Costs incurred prior to the commencement of a business's operations.

Prepaid expense An expenditure for benefits to be received or recognized in the future; see also *Deferred charge*.

Present value The value today of one or more future cash flows when these cash flows are discounted at a specified rate of interest.

Present value of an annuity The dollar equivalent today of a series of equal payments at fixed intervals, discounted at a specified interest rate and over a specified number of periods.

Price/earnings (P/E) ratio The ratio of the market price of a firm's common stock to its earnings per share for the year.

Price-level adjustments Adjustments to take account of the changing value of the monetary unit.

Price variance Difference between actual costs and budget costs per a flexible budget based on actual quantities and standard prices. Variance is due to a difference between actual prices or rates and standard prices or rates.

Prime costs The costs of raw materials and direct labor. Prime costs exclude overhead costs.

Principal The amount of a loan; distinguished from *interest*.

Prior-service cost (pensions) A component of pension expense arising from an employee's service in prior years.

Process cost A cost accounting system used to measure product costs in assembly line or continuous manufacturing settings. Production costs are summarized for a period of time and then allocated to the units produced during that time period. Contrasted with *job-order costing*.

Product costs The costs, such as labor, materials, and overhead, that are assigned to a product; distinguished from *period costs*.

Profit See *Income*.

Profit center A responsibility center in which managers are held responsible and accountable for revenues, costs, and the resultant profits.

Pro forma statements   Hypothetical or forecast statements. Also synonymous with ''what if'' analyses conducted using spreadsheet software. *Pro forma* statements indicate what could happen under a certain set of circumstances.

Projected benefit obligation (pensions)   The actuarial present value of all benefits that have been earned (taking into account estimated future increases in wages and salaries).

Promissory note   See *Note receivable*.

Proprietorship   A firm owned by a single individual.

Provision for bad debts   See *Allowance for doubtful accounts*.

Pseudo participation   A behavioral style that is a sham or that is manipulated to give the appearance of recognizing and valuing the inputs provided by subordinates or peers.

Purchase (intercorporate investments)   A method of consolidation whereby the acquisition price of an investment is allocated to assets of the acquired company based on fair market value; distinguished from *pooling of interests*.

Purchasing power gains or losses   The gain or loss attributed to holding monetary assets and liabilities during a period in which the value of the monetary unit changes.

Quantity variance   A variance due to differences between actual quantities and standard quantities allowed. May also be called an *efficiency variance*.

Quick ratio   A liquidity ratio that compares cash, marketable securities, and accounts receivable to current monetary liabilities; a more rigorous test of ability to satisfy short-term obligations than the current ratio.

Realizable gain or loss (current cost accounting)   The total gain or loss on assets and liabilities that is earned during a period involving both resources and obligations that remain on hand at the end of a period and resources and obligations that were sold or consumed during the period.

Realize   To recognize a gain or loss upon the receipt of cash, receivables, or corresponding assets owing to the sale or exchange of goods or services.

Receivable   A claim, usually stated in terms of a fixed number of dollars, arising from sale of goods, performance of services, lending of funds, or from some other type of transaction which establishes a relationship whereby one party is indebted to another.

Reciprocal method   A method of allocating or distributing service department costs to producing departments. Requires the simultaneous solution of a set of linear equations, usually by means of matrix algebra.

Regression analysis   Data analysis and cost analysis performed to establish a mathematical relationship between two variables in the form of a curve or equation. The method allows for the computation of various summary statistics to measure the predictive ability or ''goodness of fit'' of that relationship.

Relevance   A characteristic of information indicating that it will meet the needs of the manager or other party to whom it is communicated and will influence the decision it is intended to facilitate.

Relevant range   A range of activity within which an observed cost pattern will be relatively stable. A fixed cost will be unchanged within the relevant range. A variable cost will change in a linear or proportionate amount within the relevant range. Outside of the relevant range, these cost patterns may change.

Repairs   Costs incurred to restore an asset's service potential to what was anticipated when it was acquired; distinguished from *betterments*.

Replacement cost   The amount that would be required to purchase, manufacture, or construct a comparable asset (adjusted for age and use) at today's prevailing market prices; see also *Current cost*.

Reserve recognition accounting   A means of accounting for natural resources that requires that proven reserves be reported at the present value of the net cash flows that they are likely to generate.

Residual income   Net income (excluding any actual interest costs) less an imputed cost of capital.

Residual value   See *Salvage value*.

Responsibility center   An organizational segment or unit within which managers are held responsible for its performance. Cost centers, profit centers, and investment centers are typical examples of responsibility centers.

Retained earnings   The sum of the earnings of the accounting periods that the company has been in existence less the amounts paid as dividends to stockholders.

Return on assets (ROA)   A performance ratio calculated by dividing net income by total assets.

Return on equity (ROE)   A performance ratio calculated by dividing net income by stockholder's equity. See also *Return on investment (ROI)*.

Return on investment (ROI)   A generic term used to indicate a variety of profit-based performance ratios. May refer to return on stockholders' equity, return on all owners' equity, or return on assets.

Revenue center   An organizational segment or unit in which the manager is held responsible only for the revenues or sales achieved by the unit.

Revenues   Inflows or other enhancements of assets of an entity or settlements of its liabilities (or a combination of both) from delivering or producing goods, rendering services, or from other activities that constitute the entity's ongoing major or central operations.

Rolling budget   A budget that is updated monthly or quarterly by selecting the expired time period and adding another time period into the future. For example, a 12-month rolling budget will always contain budget estimates for 12 months. As January is eliminated, the following January is added. As February is eliminated, the next February is added.

Sale   A business transaction involving the delivery of property or services in exchange for cash or other consideration.

Salvage value   The amount for which a fixed asset can be sold at the conclusion of its useful economic life as anticipated by its owner.

SEC   See *Securities and Exchange Commission*.

Securities and Exchange Act of 1934   The act that granted the Securities and Exchange Commission (SEC) the statutory authority to control practices of financial reporting.

Securities and Exchange Commission (SEC)   The federal regulatory agency created by the U.S. Congress in 1934 to administer the federal securities acts; powers include oversight of accounting procedures employed by all public corporations.

Sinking fund Cash or other assets set aside to repay debt, redeem stock, or achieve a similar objective.

Slack See *Budget slack*.

Sole proprietorship A firm owned by a single individual.

Sourcing decision A decision by an organizational unit as to the source of its supplies or raw materials. May also refer to a decision about whether to sell or transfer products or services to other segments of the same organization. Usually used in conjunction with *transfer pricing*.

Spinoff A corporation's distribution to its own shareholders of its stock in a subsidiary as part of a plan to divest itself of the subsidiary.

Standard cost A predetermined cost or a measure of what a cost should be. An anticipated cost of producing or selling a product or service.

Start-up costs Costs incurred prior to the point at which a venture is fully operational.

Stated capital The amount for which capital stock was actually issued or an amount designated (similar to par value) by the issuer which generally establishes a floor on the payment of dividends (i.e., a company cannot pay dividends that will reduce its owners' equity to less than its stated capital).

Stated value See *Par value*.

Statement of cash flows A report that reconciles cash at the beginning of the year with that at the end, the objective being to provide information about an enterprise's cash receipts and disbursements; one of the three primary financial statements, along with the income statement and balance sheet.

Statement of changes in financial position A report which indicates the flow of *funds* into and out of the firm.

Statement of changes in retained earnings A report that reconciles beginning- and end-of-year retained earnings; links the income statement and balance sheet, since beginning retained earnings plus income less dividends equals ending retained earnings.

Statement of financial position A report indicating the financial position of an entity as of a specific point in time in terms of the entity's assets, liabilities, and owners' equity; commonly known as a *balance sheet*.

Stock dividend A distribution by a corporation to its shareholders of additional shares of its own stock; a form of a stock split, but typically involving the issuance of a smaller number of new shares.

Stock option A right granted by a corporation to purchase shares of its own stock at a specified price.

Stock rights See *Preemptive rights*.

Stock split A distribution by a corporation to its shareholders of additional shares of its own stock in proportion to number of shares already owned; a form of stock dividend, but typically involving the distribution of a larger number of new shares.

Straight-line method (depreciation) A method of computing depreciation whereby the cost of the asset (less anticipated salvage value) is allocated to the periods of asset service in equal amounts.

Subsidiary company A company owned or controlled by a parent corporation.

Subsidiary ledger   A supporting ledger which contains the individual accounts that compose a control account. For example, an accounts receivable subsidiary ledger would contain the individual customer accounts that support the accounts receivable control account.

Successful-efforts method (oil drilling costs)   A method by which the costs associated with unsuccessful prospects (dry holes) are expensed as incurred rather than capitalized; distinguished from *full-cost method*.

Sum-of-the-year's digits (depreciation)   A method of depreciation whereby a varying fraction of asset cost (less salvage value) is allocated to each period of asset use. The denominator of the fraction, which remains constant over the life of the asset, is a sum of numbers starting with 1 and continuing to the total estimated useful life of the asset. The numerator, which changes from year to year, is the number of years remaining in the asset's useful life at the beginning of the year in question.

T account   A representation of a ledger account in the form of a T, with debits on the left side of the vertical line and credits on the right; used to demonstrate the effect of transactions on the accounts.

Tangible assets   Assets having physical form, such as land, buildings, equipment, vehicles, and furniture and fixtures.

Times-interest-earned ratio   A ratio that indicates the relationship between interest on the one hand and income before deducting both interest and income taxes on the other.

Time value of money   The concept that money received earlier is worth more than money received later since the cost of waiting involves interest and foregone opportunities.

Trading gain   A gain arising out of the normal purchasing, manufacturing, and sales activities of a firm; distinguished from *holding gain*.

Transfer pricing   The prices that are charged for products or services transferred between organizational segments.

Treasurer   A senior fiscal officer of a company who is concerned primarily with the acquisition of capital, stockholder and bondholder relations, managing the firm's investments, and administration of insurance.

Treasury stock   Stock that is acquired and retained by the issuing corporation.

Trial balance   A listing of all accounts in a ledger, the purpose of which is to verify that the total debits equal the total credits.

Turnover   The number of times that specified resources, such as inventory, accounts receivable, and plant and equipment, are replaced during a period.

Turnover ratio   A measure of asset efficiency calculated by dividing sales (or cost of goods sold) by the balance in an asset account; also known as *activity ratio*.

Uncontrollable cost   A cost that cannot change within a specific time period. Most costs are not controllable in a very short time period, e.g., a day or hour. However, many costs are capable of being reduced or eliminated in a week or a month.

Unrealized gain or loss   An increase in net assets that has not yet been incorporated into income.

Value   An assigned or calculated numerical quantity; the worth of something sold or exchanged; the worth of a thing in money or goods at a certain time; its fair market price; worth in usefulness or importance to its possessor; utility or merit.

Variable cost   A cost that changes proportionately with changes in volume or activity. For example, if volume changes by 10%, then costs that are variable on the basis of volume will also change by 10%.

Variable cost ratio   A ratio of variable costs to revenues. Also the ratio of variable cost per unit to price per unit. The variable cost ratio plus the contribution margin ratio must sum to 100%.

Variances   The deviation between actual costs and standard costs. Represents the difference between actual and expected performance, e.g.,

    Budget variance;   see *Budget variance*

    Capacity variance;   see *Volume variance*

    Efficiency variance;   see *Quantity variance*

    Mix variance;   see *Mix variance*

    Planning variance;   see *Planning variance*

    Price rate;   see *Price variance*

    Quantity variance;   see *Quantity variance*

Volume variance   The amount of overhead variance resulting from operating at an activity level different from the budgeted activity level. It represents the difference between applied overhead and budgeted overhead for the anticipated level of output.

Voucher   An internal document authorizing a disbursement.

Warrants   Certificates, usually issued in association with notes, bonds, or stock, that entitle the holder to purchase shares of stock at a specified price.

Warranty   The promise of a seller to repair or compensate a buyer for any defects in the product sold.

Weighted-average method (inventory)   The method of accounting for inventory whereby the costs assigned to each item that has either been sold or remains in inventory is the weighted average of the costs of all inventory items available for sale during a particular period.

Window dressing   The practice of taking deliberate steps to inflate the current and quick ratios.

Working capital   The excess of current assets over current liabilities.

Worksheet   A columnar collection of accounting data organized in a fashion that may help the user move through the accounting process from trial balance to completed statements.

Yield rate (of interest on bonds)   The actual rate of interest to be paid on a bond, based on the coupon payments, the actual price for which the bond was issued, and the number of periods to maturity; distinguished from *coupon rate*.

Zero–base budget   A budget requiring the preparer to justify each activity and cost on its own merits each time a new budget is created. Contrasted with incremental budgets in which only new expenditures need be justified.

Index

Taxes, income, recognition issues, 397
Time horizon, 805
Timely information, 914
Time series, 744
Time value of money, 222–235, 719
   tables, 717–725
   See also Future value; Present value
Transaction costing, 776–777
Transaction versus economic event, 38–39,
   80–81
Transfer pricing, 943–947
Treasury stock, transactions in, 467–470
   cost method, 467–469
   par value method, 469–470
Trends, 744
Trial balance:
   adjusted, 89
   post-closing, 89, 92–93
   pre-closing, 89, 90
   unadjusted, 89

U

Unavoidable costs, 805
Uncertainty, 719, 855–858
Uncollectibles; *See* Accounts receivable
Usage variance, 918–920
Usefulness of accounting information, 4, 218, 219
Users of accounting information, 2, 3
   See also Creditors; Employees; Investors;
      Managers
Utility, 860
Utility analysis, 861
Utils, 860

V

Value in accounting, 217–218

See also Accounts receivable; Assets; Current
   cost or entry value; Historical cost; Intangible assets; Liabilities; Market
   values; Marketable securities; Net
   realizable assets payable and receivable
   price or exit value; Notes payable and
   receivable; Present value; Property,
   plant and equipment
Value of the dollar, 861–862
Variable costing, 781–785
Variable costs, 720–726, 734–739, 741–747,
   765–766, 809, 883
Variance correction, 933–934
Variance investigation, 933–934
Variances, 915–933
Volume variance, 925, 929–931

W

Warranty obligations, 186–187
   recognition issues, 397, 685
Weighted average cost of capital, 843
Weighted average method, 780
Window dressing, 286
Working capital:
   defined, 604
   statement of:
      and fundamental equation, 604
      as substitute for cash flow statement, 603–606
Worksheet for balance sheet and income state-
   ment, 132–136

Y

Yield ratio, 947

Z

Zero-base budgeting (ZBB), 894–896